Let's Go

CALIFORNIA

is the best book for anyone traveling on a budget. Here's why:

▨ No other guidebook has as many budget listings.

In California we list over 5,000 budget travel bargains. We tell you the cheapest way to get around, and where to get an inexpensive and satisfying meal once you've arrived. We give hundreds of money-saving tips that anyone can use, plus invaluable advice on discounts and deals for students, children, families, and senior travelers.

▨ Let's Go researchers have to make it on their own.

Our Harvard-Radcliffe researcher-writers travel on budgets as tight as your own—no expense accounts, no free hotel rooms.

▨ Let's Go is completely revised each year.

We don't just update the prices, we go back to the place. If a charming café has become an overpriced tourist trap, we'll replace the listing with a new and better one.

▨ No other guidebook includes all this:

Honest, engaging coverage of both the cities and the countryside; up-to-the-minute prices, directions, addresses, phone numbers, and opening hours; in-depth essays on local culture, history, and politics; comprehensive listings on transportation between and within regions and cities; straight advice on work and study, budget accommodations, sights, nightlife, and food; detailed city and regional maps; and much more.

▨ Let's Go is for anyone who wants to see California on a budget.

Books by Let's Go, Inc.

EUROPE

Let's Go: Europe

Let's Go: Austria & Switzerland

Let's Go: Britain & Ireland

Let's Go: Eastern Europe

Let's Go: France

Let's Go: Germany

Let's Go: Greece & Turkey

Let's Go: Ireland

Let's Go: Italy

Let's Go: London

Let's Go: Paris

Let's Go: Rome

Let's Go: Spain & Portugal

NORTH & CENTRAL AMERICA

Let's Go: USA & Canada

Let's Go: Alaska & The Pacific Northwest

Let's Go: California

Let's Go: New York City

Let's Go: Washington, D.C.

Let's Go: Mexico

MIDDLE EAST & ASIA

Let's Go: Israel & Egypt

Let's Go: Thailand

Let's Go

The Budget Guide to

CALIFORNIA

1995

Brooke A. Rogers
Editor

Mary T. Sadanaga
Associate Editor

Written by
Let's Go, Inc.
A subsidiary of
Harvard Student Agencies, Inc.

St. Martin's Press ■ **New York**

MACMILLAN

HELPING LET'S GO

If you have suggestions or corrections, or just want to share your discoveries, drop us a line. We read every piece of correspondence, whether a 10-page e-mail letter, a velveteen Elvis postcard, or, as in one case, a collage. All suggestions are passed along to our researcher-writers. Please note that mail received after May 5, 1995 will probably be too late for the 1996 book, but will be retained for the following edition.

Address mail to:

**Let's Go: California
Let's Go, Inc.
1 Story Street
Cambridge, MA 02138
USA**

Or send e-mail to:

letsgo@delphi.com

In addition to the invaluable travel advice our readers share with us, many are kind enough to offer their services as researchers or editors. Unfortunately, the charter of Let's Go, Inc. and Harvard Student Agencies, Inc. enables us to employ only currently enrolled Harvard-Radcliffe students.

About Let's Go

Back in 1960, a few students at Harvard University got together to produce a 20-page pamphlet offering a collection of tips on budget travel in Europe. For three years, Harvard Student Agencies, a student-run nonprofit corporation, had been doing a brisk business booking charter flights to Europe; this modest, mimeographed packet was offered to passengers as an extra. The following year, students traveling to Europe researched the first full-fledged edition of *Let's Go: Europe*, a pocket-sized book featuring advice on shoestring travel, irreverent write-ups of sights, and a decidedly youthful slant.

Throughout the 60s, the guides reflected the times: one section of the 1968 *Let's Go: Europe* talked about "Street Singing in Europe on No Dollars a Day." During the 70s, *Let's Go* gradually became a large-scale operation, adding regional European guides and expanding coverage into North Africa and Asia. The 80s saw the arrival of *Let's Go: USA & Canada* and *Let's Go: Mexico*, as well as regional North American guides; in the 90s we introduced five in-depth city guides to Paris, London, Rome, New York City, and Washington, DC. And as the budget travel world expands, so do we; the first edition of *Let's Go: Thailand* hit the shelves last year, and this year's edition adds coverage of Malaysia, Singapore, Tokyo, and Hong Kong.

This year we're proud to announce the birth of *Let's Go: Eastern Europe*—the most comprehensive guide to this renascent region, with more practical information and insider tips than any other. *Let's Go: Eastern Europe* brings our total number of titles, with their spirit of adventure and reputation for honesty, accuracy, and editorial integrity, to 21.

We've seen a lot in 35 years. *Let's Go: Europe* is now the world's #1 best selling international guide, translated into seven languages. And our guides are still researched, written, and produced entirely by students who know first-hand how to see the world on the cheap.

Every spring, we recruit over 100 researchers and 50 editors to write our books anew. Come summertime, after several months of training, researchers hit the road for seven weeks of exploration, from Bangkok to Budapest, Anchorage to Ankara. With pen and notebook in hand, a few changes of underwear stuffed in our backpacks, and a budget as tight as yours, we visit every *pensione*, *palapa*, pizzeria, café, club, campground, or castle we can find to make sure you'll get the most out of *your* trip.

We've put the best of our discoveries into the book you're now holding. A brand-new edition of each guide hits the shelves every year, only months after it is researched, so you know you're getting the most reliable, up-to-date, and comprehensive information available. The budget travel world is constantly changing, and where other guides quickly become obsolete, our annual research keeps you abreast of the very latest travel insights. And even as you read this, work on next year's editions is well underway.

At *Let's Go*, we think of budget travel not only as a means of cutting down on costs, but as a way of breaking down a few walls as well. Living cheap and simple on the road brings you closer to the real people and places you've been saving up to visit. This book will ease your anxieties and answer your questions about the basics—to help *you* get off the beaten track and explore. We encourage you to put *Let's Go* away now and then and strike out on your own. As any seasoned traveler will tell you, the best discoveries are often those you make yourself. If you find something worth sharing, drop us a line. We're at Let's Go, Inc., 1 Story Street, Cambridge, MA, 02138, USA (e-mail: letsgo@delphi.com).

Happy travels!

Contents

Maps

■ Acknowledgments

First and foremost I have to thank Mary, a California native and Hawaii expert who was my friend and salvation. Next, my thanks goes to Alexandra, Amara, Dave, Carrie and Ericka—you were fantastic. Not a day passed that I did not thank my lucky stars for my Researcher-Writers. I saw the competition and I know I got the best. Thanks to Alexis and Liz, the computer gurus, for bailing me out countless times, and to Jahan, our stoic M.E. Shana, thank you for being my friend and confidant, it was nice to have someone to come home to (even if there never was anything in the refrigerator). Thanks Mom, Dad and Heather for being my family. And the best for last, thanks to Steve, our pool-side LA consultant who gave me the inside scoop on a mind-boggling city and moral support from the *very* beginning. **BAR**

Brooke—we made it! (Although we did end up spending an all-nighter at the office.) Thank you for being a wonderful editor, and a better friend. Thanks also to the Domestic Room, especially Amy, with whom I learned the AE ropes. We domestics had a powerful A/C and great people—what more could I want? Jahan deserves much credit for good-naturedly editing batch after batch and for taking care of the "Doggies." Alexis and Liz, you are incredible. Amelia, you were a great MAC partner. I never thought I could work so hard and still enjoy myself. B&J, footie, the Vineyard, Long Island, the 24th, popcorn...some things won't be forgotten. To my roommates, Annabel and Renee, thanks for putting up with me. Wasn't that Jell-o beautiful? And finally, thanks to my mom, dad, and brother—just because. **MTS**

STAFF

Editor	Brooke A. Rogers
Associate Editor	Mary T. Sadanaga
Managing Editor	Jahan Sagafi-nejad
Publishing Director	Pete Keith
Production Manager	Alexis G. Averbuck
Production Assistant	Elizabeth J. Stein
Financial Manager	Matt Heid
Assistant General Manager	Anne E. Chisholm
Sales Group Manager	Sherice R. Guillory
Sales Department Coordinator	Andrea N. Taylor
Sales Group Representatives	Eli K. Aheto
	Timur Okay Harry Hiçyılmaz
	Arzhang Kamerei
	Hollister Jane Leopold
	David L. Yuan
President	Lucienne D. Lester
General Manager	Richard M. Olken

Researcher-Writers

Amara Balthrop-Lewis   *San Francisco, Bay Area, Wine Country, Santa Cruz, Monterey, Carmel, Salinas*

Invariably, we'd start reading Amara's incredible restaurant reviews before lunch. She did so much more than we asked, working herself ragged in the process. Nonetheless, she always sent back cheerful copy batches decorated with smiley-faced marginalia. Her sense of enthusiasm and positive energy were boundless. Whether befriending locals or championing the cause of the San Mateo Coast, she did it whole-heartedly. Amara danced through her very long itinerary with good spirits and then went home for some much-deserved relaxation on the beaches of Florida.

Carrie Busch   *Hawaii*

Last year Carrie researched the Rocky Mountains by bus, more than earning the most coveted itinerary at *Let's Go* for this summer. There could've been a hurricane on Hawaii and Carrie still would've completed her coverage without blinking an eye (well, maybe at the wind-blown sand). She dealt with paths leading for miles to nowhere and with lizard and insect infested motel rooms, so you wouldn't have to. While tirelessly searching for secret beach spots, she managed to enjoy the touristy ones too. We owe Carrie many shave ices (and mailstops). Mahalo.

Alexandra Jacobs   *Los Angeles, San Diego, Orange County, Santa Barbara, Cambria, San Simeon, Big Sur, San Luis Obispo*

Sending Alexandra, a New Yorker, to cover our Southern Cal beach itinerary might have seemed odd. Yet she had visited L.A. before (for the Emmy Awards, no less) and was excited about returning. She attacked the city like an urban Margaret Mead, studying the institutions and behavior of the natives with an anthropologist's care and scrutiny. Her copy had a freshness and sense of perspective (even on the O.J. mess) that only an outsider could provide. Alexandra was not immune to the city's attractions; she did indulge in the perfect margarita and developed an attachment to the mystical "Vanilla Ice Blended." We doubt Alexandra did much surfing, but she reorganized and rewrote, bringing logic to the chaos and sprawl that is Los Angeles.

Ericka Kostka   *The Desert, Sierra Nevada, South Coastal Ranges, Fresno, Julian*

Ericka, our fearless desert fox and high country explorer, braved the harshest climates and toughest roads that California has to offer. If a place was scorchingly hot and dry, Ericka went there. And despite flat tires and 116°F weather, she sent us thorough, carefully researched copy. A steady diet of rice and beans got her through it all. If you go to the Sierras or the Desert to bike, hike, rock-climb, or ski, thank Ericka for her comprehensive recreational activities coverage and perseverance.

David Rogers   *Sacramento Valley and Cascades, Gold Country, Lake Tahoe, Northern Coast, Stockton, Reno*

Dave, an avid outdoorsman and an offensive tackle, is at least 6'5'' and 250 pounds. Northern California—big trees, big cliffs, big mountains, big omelettes, big burgers, a big lake, and big expanses of ocean—was perfect for him. Dave explored and relished all of it in an old VW van. He was a natural RW and a master of marginalia. His only regrets were an unmarked "short cut" (and that counted as an adventure), Stockton ("stay inside and lock the door"), and not having enough time for his beloved fly fishing. Dave's credo: "Walk softly and a carry a five weight fly rod."

Michael Shapiro   *Tijuana, Ensenada*

Despite nine-hour bus rides, scorching heat, and relentless persecution by border-town weirdos, Mike, a thoughtful, witty writer and incredibly conscientious researcher, rarely changed his clothes and never lost his quirky sense of humor.

Michael M. Stockman   *Las Vegas, Grand Canyon*

Michael brought a unique perspective to the gaping crevasse of the Grand Canyon, and, for the sake of research, willingly immersed himself in the Las Vegas culture.

How To Use This Book

Don't just bring *Let's Go: California* with you on your journey, use it to acquaint yourself with your chosen destination before you leave. A little advanced planning will give you more time to enjoy yourself once you arrive.

The **Essentials** section begins the book with vital tips on packing, security, money, transportation, and other necessary information that you should know before you embark on your travels. It will save you time-consuming research and help you avoid many problems that plague travelers.

The main body of the guide is divided into regional sections. The **California** section begins with Los Angeles and covers the southern part of the state before heading up the coast to San Francisco, the Bay Area, and the Wine Country. After covering the Northern Coast, it turns inland to the Sacramento Valley and Gold Country and ends with the Sierra Nevada and the San Joaquin Valley. The next four sections of the book are **Nevada** (Las Vegas and Reno), the **Grand Canyon, Baja California** (Tijuana and Ensenada), and, finally, **Hawaii** (Oahu, Maui, the Big Island, Kauai, Molokai, and Lanai). Each section includes practical information and orientation, accommodations and food listings, and descriptions of sights, entertainment, and activities in the area.

The key word on the cover of this book is "guide." Our purpose is not to tell you where to go or what to do, but instead to give you the information necessary to make the right decision for yourself. This is why we list so many options. We have located everything we think would interest a budget traveler, from nude sunbathing to local libraries, and described it so you know what to expect when you find it.

If you are interested in further travel in North America, consult *Let's Go: USA & Canada, Let's Go: Alaska & the Pacific Northwest,* and *Let's Go: Mexico.*

A NOTE TO OUR READERS

The information for this book is gathered by *Let's Go*'s researchers during the late spring and summer months. Each listing is derived from the assigned researcher's opinion based upon his or her visit at a particular time. The opinions are expressed in a candid and forthright manner. Other travelers might disagree. Those traveling at a different time may have different experiences since prices, dates, hours, and conditions are always subject to change. You are urged to check beforehand to avoid inconvenience and surprises. Travel always involves a certain degree of risk, especially in low-cost areas. When traveling, especially on a budget, you should always take particular care to ensure your safety.

ESSENTIALS

PLANNING YOUR TRIP

Every traveler must set priorities. If you're on a shoestring budget, recognize your situation before you leave. When you're planning a hectic, whirlwind tour, make sure to verify travel arrangements in advance. And if you're taking a leisurely, well-financed journey, do the background reading and planning that will enable you to fully appreciate the places you visit. Whatever your choice, every trip requires heavy preparation.

This Essentials section and our Practical Information listings in state and city introductions provide addresses and phone numbers of services that can provide preliminary information. Write or call these organizations ahead of time.

■■■ WHEN TO GO

Whether it's for snorkeling, snowshoeing, or just lying around in the sun, visitors flock to California and Hawaii year-round. Between December and April, in particular, the warmer shores of these two states are packed with cold-weather refugees.

Many seasonal attractions in California have lower rates and smaller crowds during the off-season, but some facilities close when the flow of tourists tapers to a trickle. The weather (winter rains in the north, summer heat farther south) can also be uncooperative. May and September lie midway between the established "seasons" in most tourist destinations and often bring lower prices, fewer tourists, and beautiful weather. In Hawaii, the weather is more uniformly dazzling and tourist attractions remain open year-round. As a consequence, more visitors from less hospitable climates travel to Hawaii during the winter.

Official holidays may mean extended hours at some tourist attractions, but many banks and offices will close for the day. U.S. national holidays for 1995 are: **New Year's Day,** Sun. Jan. 1; **Martin Luther King, Jr.'s Birthday,** Mon. Jan. 16 (observed); **Presidents Day,** Mon. Feb. 20 (observed); **Good Friday,** Fri. April 14; **Easter,** Sun. April 16; **Memorial Day,** Mon. May 29 (observed); **Independence Day,** Tues. July 4; **Labor Day,** Mon. Sept. 4; **Columbus Day,** Mon. Oct. 9 (observed); **Veterans Day,** Fri. Nov. 11; **Thanksgiving,** Thurs. Nov. 23; **Christmas Day,** Mon. Dec. 25.

■■■ USEFUL ORGANIZATIONS AND PUBLICATIONS

When planning your trip, the organizations and publications listed below may be a helpful starting point of inquiry. These listings do not cover all resources available; additional sources appear throughout the book.

■ TOURIST BUREAUS AND OFFICES

Contact the tourist bureau (sometimes called the "Visitors Information Center") in any city you plan to visit for more than a few days. Ask them anything. They can provide invaluable last-minute advice about special deals on accommodations, tours, or newly opened establishments. Some might even make reservations for you. Do not hesitate—you aren't the first tourist they've met. Contact addresses for local tourist offices throughout California and Hawaii can be found in the Practical Information section for each town or region. Before your trip, it is best to call the U.S. **consulate** nearest you, as they handle all the promotional tourism needs outside the United

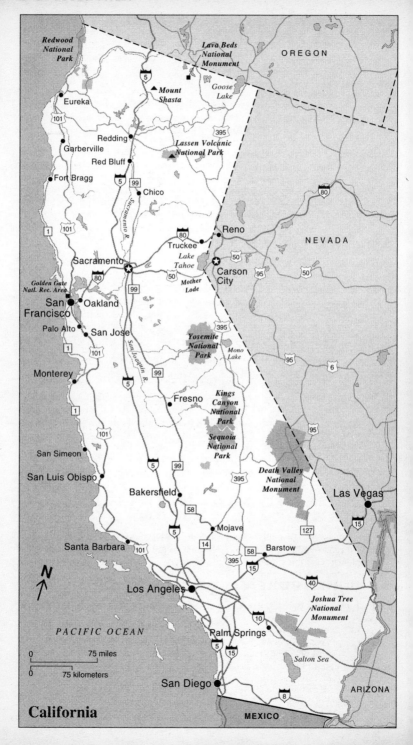

California

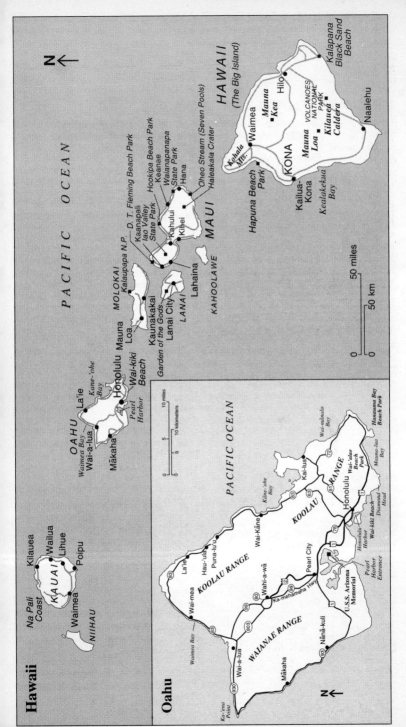

Hawaii

PACIFIC OCEAN

N

KAUAI
Na Pali Coast
Kilauea
Wailua
Lihue
Waimea
Poipu

NIIHAU

OAHU
La'ie
Kāne-'ohe Bay
Waimea Bay
Wai-a-lua
Mākaha
Honolulu
Wai-kiki Beach
Pearl Harbor
Mauna Loa

MOLOKAI
Kalaupapa N.P.
Kaunakakai
Garden of the Gods
Lanai City
LANAI

D. T. Fleming Beach Park
Hookipa Beach Park
Keanae
Kaanapali
Iao Valley State Park
Waianapanapa State Park
Hana
Kahului
Kihei
Oheo Stream (Seven Pools)
Haleakala Crater
MAUI
Lahaina

KAHOOLAWE

HAWAII
(The Big Island)
Kalapana Black Sand Beach
Mauna Kea
Hilo
VOLCANOES NATIONAL PARK
Mauna Loa
Kilauea Caldera
Waimea
Kohala Mts.
KONA
Naalehu
Kailua-Kona
Hapuna Beach Park
Kealakekua Bay

50 miles
50 km

Oahu

PACIFIC OCEAN

N

Ka-ena Point
Waimea Bay
Wai-a-lua
Mākaha
Nānā-kuli
WAIANAE RANGE
Wai-mea
Hau-'ula
La'ie
Puna-lu'u
KOOLAU RANGE
Wai-kāne
Kāne-'ohe Bay
Kai-lua
Wai-mānalo Bay
Hanauma Bay Beach Park
Maunu-lua Bay
Wai-'alae Beach Park
KOOLAU RANGE
Honolulu
Wahi-a-wā
Pearl City
Ka-mehameha Hwy.
U.S. Arizona Memorial
Pearl Harbor Entrance
Pearl Harbor Memorial
Honolulu Harbor
Wai-kiki Beach
Diamond Head

10 miles
10 kilometers

States. General information for foreigners planning to travel to the U.S. is provided by the **United States Travel and Tourism Administration** (Department of Commerce, 14th St. and Constitution Ave. NW, Washington, DC 20230, 202-482-4003 or 202-482-3811). The USTTA has branches in Australia, Belgium, Canada, France, Germany, Japan, Mexico, and the United Kingdom; contact the Washington office for information about the branch in your country.

■ BUDGET TRAVEL SERVICES

Council on International Educational Exchange (CIEE), 205 East 42nd St., New York, NY 10017 (212-661-1414). A private, not-for-profit organization, CIEE administers work, volunteer, academic and professional programs around the world. They also offer identity cards, (including the ISIC and the GO 25) and a range of publications, among them the useful magazine *Student Travels* (free, postage $1), and *Going Places: The High School Student's Guide to Study, Travel and Adventure Abroad* ($13.95, postage $1.50). Call or write for further info.

Council Charter, 205 East 42nd St., New York, NY 10017 (212-661-0311 or 800-800-8222). A subsidiary of CIEE, Council Charter offers a combination of inexpensive charter and scheduled airfares from a variety of U.S. gateways to most major European destinations. One-way fares and open jaws (fly into one city and out of another) are available.

Council Travel, a subsidiary of CIEE, is an agency specializing in student and budget travel. They sell charter flight tickets, guidebooks, ISIC, ITIC, and GO 25 cards, hostel cards, and travel gear. Forty-one U.S. offices, including: 729 Boylston St., Suite 201, **Boston,** MA 02116 (617-266-1926); 1153 N. Dearborn St., 2nd floor, **Chicago,** IL 60610 (312-951-0585); 6715 Hillcrest, **Dallas,** TX 75205 (214-363-9941); 1093 Broxton Ave., Suite 220, **Los Angeles,** CA 90024 (310-208-3551); 205 E. 42nd St., **New York,** NY 10017 (212-661-1450); 715 S.W. Morrison, Suite 600, **San Francisco,** CA 94108 (415-421-3473); 1314 N.E. 43rd St., Suite 210, **Seattle,** WA 98105 (206-632-2448). Council Travel also has offices in Europe, including: 28A Poland St. (Oxford Circus), **London** WIV 3DB, England ((0171) 437 77 67); 22, Rue des Pyramides, 75001 **Paris**, France ((1) 44 55 55 44); and 18 Graf-Adolf-Strasse, 4000 Dusseldorf 1, **Germany** ((211) 32 90 88).

American Automobile Association (AAA) Travel Related Services, 1000 AAA Dr. (mail stop 100), Heathrow, FL 32746-5080 (407-444-7883). Provides road maps and travel guides free to members. Provides full travel services to general public. Contact your local AAA office for more information. Also see By Car, page 37.

Campus Travel, 52 Grosvenor Gardens, London SW1W 0AG ((0171) 730 88 32; fax 730 57 39). 37 branches in the UK. Puts out booklets including travel suggestions, average prices, and other general information for British travelers in Europe and North America. Offers bookings service via telephone: from London/Europe (730 34 02), from North America (730 21 01), worldwide (730 81 11).

Educational Travel Centre (ETC), 438 North Frances St., Madison, WI 53703 (800-747-5551; fax 608-256-2042). Flight information, HI-AYH cards, Eurail and regional rail passes. Write for their free pamphlet *Taking Off*.

Federation of International Youth Travel Organisations (FIYTO). For information on the office closest to you, write to FIYTO Secretariat, Bredgade 25H, DK 1260 Copenhagen K, Denmark (45 33 33 96 00; fax 45 33 93 96 76). This organization of youth and student travel services suppliers sponsors the GO 25 Card, which offers various discounts and benefits worldwide.

International Student Exchange Flights (ISE), 5010 East Shea Blvd., #A104, Scottsdale, AZ 85254 (602-951-1177). Budget student flights, International Student Exchange Identity Card, and travel guides. Free catalog.

International Student Travel Confederation (ISTC), Store Kongensgade 40H, 1264 Copenhagen K, Denmark (45 33 93 93 03). Affiliated with travel agencies throughout the world. Offers the ISIC card.

Let's Go Travel, Harvard Student Agencies, 53-A Church St., Cambridge, MA 02138 (800-5-LETS GO, 5-5387-46) or 617-495-9649). Let's Go Travel is operated by the same students who publish this book. Let's Go offers railpasses, HI-AYH memberships, ISICs, International Teacher ID cards, FIYTO cards, guidebooks (including every *Let's Go* at a substantial discount), maps, bargain flights, and a complete line of budget travel gear. All items available by mail; call or write for a catalog (or see catalog in center of this publication).

STA Travel, 5900 Wilshire Blvd., Suite 2110, Los Angeles, CA 90036 (800-777-0112 nationwide). A student and youth travel organization with over 100 offices around the world offering discount airfares (for travelers under 26 and full-time students under 32), railpasses, accommodations, tours, insurance, and ISICs. Eleven offices in the U.S., including: 297 Newbury Street, **Boston,** MA 02116 (617-266-6014); 48 E. 11th St., **New York,** NY 10003 (212-477-7166); 2401 Pennsylvania Ave., **Washington, DC** 20037 (202-887-0912); 51 Grant Ave., **San Francisco,** CA 94108 (415-391-8407). In the UK, 86 Old Brompton Rd., **London** SW7 3LQ and 117 Euston Rd., **London** NW1 2SX ((0171) 937 99 71 for North American travel). In New Zealand, 10 High St., **Auckland** ((09) 398 99 95). In Australia, 222 Faraday St., **Melbourne** VIC 3050 ((03) 349 24 11).

Travel CUTS, 187 College St., Toronto, Ontario M5T 1P7 (416-798-CUTS, -2887; fax 416-979-8167). Canada's national student travel bureau and equivalent of CIEE, with 40 offices across Canada. Also in the UK: 295-A Regent St., London W1R 7YA ((0171) 637 31 61).

Travel Management International (TMI), 39 JFK St., 3rd Floor, Cambridge, MA 02138 (617-661-8187 or 800-245-3672). Diligent, prompt, and very helpful travel service offering student fares and discounts.

University and Student Travel (USTN). A national association of university travel agencies who specialize in student travel. They sell ISICs, GO 25 cards, youth hostel cards, STA and CIEE student tickets, etc. 23 member agencies across the country, including ASUCLA Travel Service, Ackerman Union, 308 Westwood Plaza, **Los Angeles,** CA 90024 (310-825-9131; fax 206-3212); Berkeley Northside Travel, 1824 Euclid Ave., **Berkeley,** CA 94709 (510-843-1000; fax 843-7537).

■ USEFUL PUBLICATIONS

Bon Voyage!, 2069 W. Bullard Ave., Fresno, CA 93711-1200 (800-995-9716, from abroad 209-447-8441). Annual mail order catalog offers an amazing range of products. Books, travel accessories, luggage, electrical converters, maps, etc.

Forsyth Travel Library, P.O. Box 2975, Shawnee Mission, KS 66201 (800-367-7984; fax 913-384-3553). Call or write for catalog of maps, guidebooks, railpasses and timetables. They also have a separate catalog of travel gear.

Hippocrene Books, Inc., 171 Madison Ave., New York NY 10016 (212-685-4371; orders 718-454-2360; fax 718-454-1391). Free catalog. Publishes travel reference books, travel guides, maps, and foreign language dictionaries and learning guides.

Hunter Publishing, 300 Raritan Center Parkway, Edison, NJ 08818 (908-225-1900; fax 908-417-0482). Offers an extensive catalog of useful travel books, guides, and maps, mostly country or region-specific.

Michelin Travel Publications, Michelin Tire Corporation, P.O. Box 19001, Greenville, SC 29602-9001 (800-423-0485; fax 803-458-5665). Michelin publishes Green Guides, for sight-seeing, maps, and driving itineraries; Red Guides, for hotel and restaurant ratings; and detailed, reliable road maps and atlases.

Rand McNally, 150 S. Wacker Dr., Chicago, IL 60606 (800-333-0136) publishes one of the most comprehensive road atlases of the U.S. and Canada, available in most bookstores for $8. Phone orders are also available.

Specialty Travel Index, 305 San Anselmo Avenue, San Anselmo, CA 94960 (415-459-4900; fax 415-459-4974). Published twice yearly, this is an extensive listing of "off the beaten track" and specialty travel opportunities. Write for copies or subscriptions.

Superintendent of Documents, U.S. Government Printing Office, P.O. Box 371954, Pittsburgh, PA 15250-7954 (202-783-3238; fax 202-275-2529). Publishes a series of region-specific pamphlets, Tips for Travelers, as well as more general information on travel abroad. Call or write for a list of regions covered or to order a particular pamphlet (most for $1).

Travelling Books, P.O. Box 521491, Salt Lake City, UT 84152 (801-461-3345). Mail-order service specializes in travel guides, books, and accessories. Call or write for a free catalog.

Wide World Books and Maps, 1911 N. 45th St., Seattle, WA 98103 (206-634-3453; fax 206-634-0558). A good selection of travel guides, travel accessories, and hard-to-find maps. Phone, fax, and mail orders welcome.

■■■ DOCUMENTS AND FORMALITIES

In preparing for a trip to California or Hawaii from another country, be sure to file all applications several weeks or months in advance of your planned departure date. Most offices suggest you apply in the off-season (Aug.-Dec.) for speedier service.

When you travel, *always carry on your person two or more forms of identification, including at least one photo ID*. A passport combined with a driver's license or birth certificate usually serves as adequate proof of your identity and citizenship. Most establishments require several IDs before cashing traveler's checks. Never carry your passport, travel ticket, identification documents, money, traveler's checks, insurance, and credit cards all together, or you risk being left entirely without ID or funds in case of theft or loss. It is wise to carry a half dozen extra passport-size photos that you can use for the sundry IDs you will eventually acquire.

If you plan an extended stay, you might want to register your passport with the nearest embassy or consulate.

■ ENTRANCE REQUIREMENTS

U.S. or Canadian citizens who are adults may cross the U.S.-Canadian border with proof of citizenship (passport, birth certificate, or voter registration card). U.S. citizens under 18 need the written consent of a parent or guardian; Canadian citizens under 16 need notarized permission from both parents. Travelers who are not citizens of either country will need a visa to cross the border. **Mexican citizens** may cross into the U.S. with an I-186 form. Non-immigrant visas prohibit citizens from staying more than 72 hours in the U.S. or traveling more than 25 miles from the border. All other foreign visitors to the United States are required to have a **passport, visitors visa,** and **proof of intent to leave** (an exiting plane ticket, for example). To work or study in the United States, you must obtain special documents (see Work and Study, page 21).

■ PASSPORTS

As a precaution in case your passport is lost or stolen, photocopy the page of your passport that contains your photograph and identifying information including your passport number. Carry this photocopy in a safe place apart from your passport and leave another copy at home. Better yet, carry a photocopy of all the pages of the passport, including all visa stamps, apart from your actual passport, and leave a duplicate copy with a relative or friend. These measures will help prove your citizenship and facilitate the issuing of a new passport in case of loss. Consulates also recommend that you carry an expired passport or an official copy of your birth certificate (not necessarily the one issued at birth) in a part of your baggage separate from other documents.

If your passport is lost or stolen, immediately notify the local police and the nearest embassy or consulate of your home government. Some consulates can issue new passports within two days if you give them proof of citizenship. In an emergency, ask for immediate temporary traveling papers that will permit you to return to your home country. Your passport is a public document that belongs to your nation's government. You may have to surrender it to a foreign government official; if you don't get it back in a reasonable time, inform the nearest mission of your home country.

Applying for a passport is complicated, so make sure your questions are answered in advance.

British citizens can obtain a **full passport** valid for 10 years (5 yrs. if under 16) for £18. Apply in person or by mail to the passport offices in Liverpool, Newport, Peterborough, Glasgow, or Belfast; applications can also be picked up at post offices. The London office offers same-day, walk-in service; arrive early. Along with a completed application, you must submit: a birth certificate; a marriage certificate (if applicable); and two identical, recent photos signed by a guarantor.

Irish citizens can apply for a 10-year passport for £45; citizens younger than 18 or older than 65 can order a 3-year passport for £10. Apply by mail to the Department of Foreign Affairs, Passport Office, Setanta Centre, Molesworth St., Dublin 2. Applications can also be obtained from local Garda stations. First-time applicants should send birth certificate and two identical photographs. To renew, send only the old passport (after photocopying it) and two photos.

Australian citizens must apply for a passport in person at a local post office, a passport office, an embassy or consulate, an Australian diplomatic mission overseas, or one of the passport offices in Adelaide, Brisbane, Canberra, Darwin, Hobart, Melbourne, Newcastle, Perth, and Sydney. Along with application, submit the following: proof of citizenship (an expired passport, birth certificate, or citizens certificate from the immigration service); proof of present name; two identical, signed photographs (45mm x 35mm) less than six months old; other forms of ID (such as a driver's license, credit card, rate notice, etc.).

New Zealanders can obtain passports good for up to ten years. Obtain an application form from your local Link Centre, travel agent, or New Zealand Representative; Mail completed applications to the New Zealand Passport Office, Documents of National Identity Division, Department of Internal Affairs, Box 10-526, Wellington ((914) 474 81 00). Also submit: proof of citizenship; proof of identity; and two certified photos. The fee is NZ$80, if under age 16, NZ$40.

South African citizens can apply for a passport at any Home Affairs Office. Submit: two photos; a birth certificate or an identity book; the R38 fee; a completed application. For further information contact the nearest Home Affairs office.

■ VISAS

Almost all foreign visitors to the U.S. are required to have a passport, a visitor's visa (issued by the visitor's country of origin and valid for 6 months beyond the planned length of stay), and proof of intent to leave (usually a return ticket). (See Entrance Requirements, above.) To obtain a U.S. visa, contact the nearest U.S. Embassy or Consulate.

Most visitors obtain a **B-2**, or "pleasure tourist," visa, usually valid for six months. If you lose your I-94 form (arrival/departure certificate attached to your visa upon arrival), replace it at the nearest **U.S. Immigration and Naturalization Service** office. (If you lose your passport in the U.S., you must replace it through your country's embassy.) **Extensions** for visas (max. 6 months) require form I-539 as well as a $70 fee and are also granted by the INS. For a list of offices, write the INS Central Office, 425 I St. NW #5044, Washington, DC 20536 (202-514-4316). The **Center for International Business and Travel (CIBT),** 25 W. 43rd St., Suite 1420, New York, NY 10036 (800-925-2428), secures travel visas to and from all possible countries (service charge varies).

Travelers from certain nations may enter the U.S. without a visa through the **Visa Waiver Pilot Program.** Visitors qualify as long as they are traveling for business or pleasure, are staying for 90 days or less, have proof of intent to leave and a completed I-94W, and enter aboard particular air or sea carriers. Participating countries are Andorra, Austria, Belgium, Brunei, Denmark, Finland, Germany, Iceland, Italy, Japan, Liechtenstein, Luxembourg, Monaco, the Netherlands, New Zealand, Norway, San Marino, Spain, Sweden, Switzerland, and the UK. Contact the nearest U.S. consulate for more information.

■ CUSTOMS

Unless you plan to import a BMW or a barnyard beast, you will probably pass right over the customs barrier with minimal ado. The U.S. restricts the importation of fire-arms, explosives, ammunition, fireworks, controlled drugs, most plants and animals, lottery tickets, obscene literature and films, and articles made from the skins and furs of certain animals. To avoid problems when you transport prescription drugs, ensure that the bottles are clearly marked, and carry a copy of the prescription to show the customs officer.

You may bring the following into the U.S. duty free: 200 cigarettes, 50 cigars, or 2 kilograms of smoking tobacco; $100 in gifts (this may include 100 cigars); personal belongings such as clothing and jewelry. Travelers ages 21 and over may also bring up to 1L alcohol, although state laws may further restrict the amount of alcohol you can carry. Articles imported in excess of your exemption will be subject to varying duty rates to be paid upon arrival.

You can bring any amount of currency, but if you carry over $10,000, you'll need to report it. The pamphlet *Know Before You Go* may be helpful. It is available from the State Department, 2201 C St. NW, Washington, DC (202-647-6047).

■ RETURNING HOME

Upon returning home, you must declare all articles acquired in the U.S. and must pay a duty on the value of those articles that exceeds the allowance established by your country's customs service. Holding onto receipts for purchases made in the U.S. will help establish values when you return. It is wise to make a list, including serial numbers, of any valuables (not that you would travel with any!) that you carry with you from home; if you register this list with customs before your departure and have an official stamp it, you will avoid import duty charges and ensure an easy pas-sage upon your return.

Canadian citizens who remain abroad for at least one week may bring back up to CDN$300 worth of goods duty-free once every calendar year. Citizens over the legal age (which varies by province) may import in-person (not through the mail) up to 200 cigarettes, 50 cigars, 400g tobacco, 1.14L wine or alcohol, and 355ml beer; the value of these products is included in the CDN$300 allowance. For more informa-tion, call Canada Customs (613-957-0275).

British citizens are allowed an exemption of up to £36 of goods purchased out-side the EC, including not more than 200 cigarettes, 100 cigarillos, 50 cigars, or 250kg of tobacco; and no more than 2L still table wine plus 1L alcohol over 22% by volume. You must be over 17 to import liquor or tobacco. For more information, contact Her Majesty's Customs and Excise, Customs House, Heathrow Airport North, Hounslow, Middlesex, TW6 2LA ((0181) 750 15 49).

Irish citizens may return home with the equivalent of IR£34 goods purchased out-side the EC, including: 200 cigarettes, 100 cigarillos, 50 cigars, or 250g tobacco; 1L liquor or 2L wine; 2L still wine; 50g perfume; 250ml toilet water. For more informa-tion, contact The Revenue Commissioners, Dublin Castle ((01) 679 27 77; fax (01) 671 20 21).

Australian citizens may import AUS$400 of goods duty-free, including 250 ciga-rettes, 250g tobacco, and 1L alcohol. For more information, contact the Australian Customs Service, 5 Constitution Ave., Canberra, ACT 2601.

New Zealand citizens may bring home up to NZ$700 worth of goods duty-free if they are intended for personal use or as unsolicited gifts. You may also bring in 400 cigarettes, 250g tobacco, 50 cigars, or a combination of all three not to exceed 250g; 4.5L beer or wine; 1.125L liquor; 250ml toilet water; 50ml perfume. For more information, consult the *New Zealand Customs Guide for Travelers*, available from customs houses, or contact New Zealand Customs, 50 Anzac Avenue, Box 29, Auckland ((09) 377 35 20; fax 309 29 78).

South African citizens can return home with 400 cigarettes, 50 cigars, 250G tobacco, 2L wine, 1L spirits, 250ml toilet water, 50ml perfume, and other items up to a value of R500. Address customs inquiries to The Commissioner for Customs and Excise, Private Bag X47, Pretoria, 0001. This agency distributes the pamphlet *South African Customs Information,* for visitors and residents who travel abroad.

For more information, including the helpful pamphlet *U.S. Customs Hints for Visitors (Nonresidents)*, contact the nearest U.S. Embassy or write the U.S. Customs Service, P.O. Box 7404, Washington, DC 20004 (202-927-2095).

■ HOSTEL MEMBERSHIP

Hostelling International (HI) is the new and universal trademark name adopted by the International Youth Hostel Federation (IYHF). The 6,000 official youth hostels worldwide will normally display the new HI logo (a blue triangle) alongside the symbol of one of the 70 national hostel associations.

A one-year Hostelling International (HI) membership permits you to stay at youth hostels all over California and Hawaii. Despite the name, you need not be a youth; travelers over 25 pay only a slight surcharge for a bed. You can save yourself potential trouble by procuring a membership card before you leave home. For more details on youth hostels, see In California and Hawaii: Accommodations, page 43.

One-year hostel membership cards are available from some travel agencies (see Useful Organizations, page 1), and from HI organizations, which can be contacted for hostel reservations and information.

Hostelling International (trademark name of the International Youth Hostel Federation), Headquarters, 9 Guessens Rd., Welwyn Garden City, Herts AL8 6QW, England ((44) 0707 33 24 87). An umbrella organization for more than 200 hostels in the U.S. and more than 6000 worldwide.

American Youth Hostels (HI-AYH), 733 15th St. NW, Suite 840, Washington, DC, 20005 (202-783-6161; fax 202-783-6171). Also dozens of regional offices across the U.S.1-year membership fee $24, under 18 $10, over 54 $15.

Hostelling International—Canada (HI-C), 400-205 Catherine St., Ontario, Canada K2P 1C3 (613-237-7884; fax 613-237-7868). 1-year membership fee CDN$26.75, under 18 CDN$12.84, 2-year CDN$37.45. Life membership is also available.

Youth Hostels Association of England and Wales (YHA), Treveylan House, 8 St. Stephens Hill, St. Albans, Herts AL1 2DY ((44) 727 85 52 15). Fee £9, under 17 £3.

An Oíge (Irish Youth Hostel Association), 61 Mountjoy Sq., Dublin 7, Ireland ((01)353 304 555; fax 353 1 305 808). Fee £9, under 18 £3.

Australian Youth Hostels Association (AYHA), Level 3, 10 Mallet St., Camperdown, New South Wales, 2050 Australia ((61) 25 65 16 99; fax 565 12 35). Fee AUS$40, renewal AUS$24; under 18 AUS$12.

Youth Hostels Association of New Zealand, P.O. Box 436, 173 Gloucester St., Christchurch 1, New Zealand ((64) 33 79 99 70; fax (03) 365 44 76). Fee NZ$24.

The International Booking Network (IBN) is a computerized booking network service available to Hostelling International members. With a local phone call to any Hostelling International regional office or booking center, travelers can book overnight accommodations in over 120 hostels around the world. Reservations can be made up to six months prior to departure. For more information call your local HI office or hostel.

Reservations can also be made through the mail by sending a letter or postcard to the hostels with the date and estimated time of your arrival, the number of nights you plan to stay, and the number of beds you will need. Also send a check for the first night and a SASE in order to receive confirmation of the reservation.

■ YOUTH AND STUDENT IDENTIFICATION

In the world of budget travel, youth has its privileges. Two main forms of student and youth identification are accepted worldwide; they are extremely useful, especially for the insurance packages that accompany them.

The **International Student Identity Card (ISIC)** is the most widely accepted form of student identification. It can garner you discounts for sights, theaters, museums, accommodations, train, ferry, and airplane travel, and other services throughout California and Hawaii. It also provides accident insurance of up to US$3,000 as well as US$100 per day of in-hospital care for up to 60 days. Cardholders have access to a toll-free, multilingual Traveler's Assistance hotline. Many student travel offices issue ISICs (see above). When you apply for the card, procure a copy of the *International Student Identity Card Handbook*, which lists some of the available discounts. You can also write to CIEE for a copy (see addresses above).

To apply, supply in person or by mail: (1) current, dated proof of your degree-seeking student status (a letter on school stationery signed and sealed by the registrar, a photocopied grade report, or a Bursar's receipt with school seal that indicates full payment for fall 1994, spring 1995, or summer 1995 sessions); (2) a 1½" x 2" photo (vending machine-size) with your name printed and signed on the back; (3) proof of your birthdate and nationality; (4) the name, address, and phone number of a beneficiary. Applicants must be at least 12 years old and must be a student at a secondary or post-secondary school. The 1995 card is valid from Sept. 1994 through Dec. 1995. The fee is $16.

Because of the proliferation of phony and improperly issued ISIC cards, many airlines and some other services now require double proof of student identity; carry your school ID card. In some cases, establishments will also honor an ordinary student ID from your college or university for student discounts.

The new, **International Teacher Identity Card (ITIC)** offers identical discounts to the ISIC, in theory, but because of its recent introduction many establishments may be reluctant to honor it. The application process is the same, except teachers need to present an official document from their department chair or another school official. The fee is $17.

The **GO 25 Card** is issued by the **Federation of International Youth Travel Organizations (FIYTO)** for travelers who are not students but are under 26 and offers many of the same benefits as the ISIC. Most organizations that sell ISIC also sell GO 25. A brochure that lists discounts is free when you purchase the card. To apply, bring: (1) proof of birthdate (copy of birth certificate or passport or a valid driver's license); (2) a passport-sized photo (with your name printed on the back). The fee is US$16, CDN$12, and £10. For more information, contact FIYTO at Bredgade 25H, DK-1260, Copenhagen K, Denmark ((45) 33 33 96 00; fax 33 93 96 76).

■ INTERNATIONAL DRIVER'S PERMIT

If you plan to drive during your visit, be sure to obtain an **International Driver's Permit (IDP)** from your national automobile association before leaving (you can't get one here), and make sure you have proper insurance (required by law). The IDP does not replace a visitor's valid driver's license from the home country; it does help visitors from non-English speaking nations whose driver's licenses might confuse American authorities. You will need a green card or International Insurance Certificate to prove that you have liability insurance. Application forms are available at any AAA office or car rental agency. Some foreign driver's licenses will be valid in the U.S. for up to one year (check before you leave).

Don't forget to write.

Now that you've said, "Let's go," it's time to say "Let's get American Express® Travelers Cheques." If they are lost or stolen, you can get a fast and full refund virtually anywhere you travel. So before you leave be sure and write.

■■■ MONEY

Money will cause you continual anxiety—even if you have it. No matter how low your budget, if you plan to travel for more than a couple of days, you will need to keep handy a much larger amount of cash than usual.

■ CURRENCY AND EXCHANGE

CDN$1 = US$0.7283	US$1 = CDN$1.3730
UK£1 = US$1.5375	US$1 = UK£0.6504
IR£1 = US$1.5208	US$1 = IR£0.6575
AUS$1 = US$0.7440	US$1 = AUS$1.3441
NZ$1 = US$0.6001	US$1 = NZ$1.6664

U.S. currency uses a decimal system based on the **dollar ($).** Paper money ("bills") comes in six denominations, all the same size, shape, and dull green color. The bills now issued are $1, $5, $10, $20, $50, and $100. You may occasionally see denominations of $2 and $500, which are no longer printed but are still acceptable as currency. Some restaurants and retail stores may not accept bills of $50 and higher. The dollar divides into 100 cents (¢); fractions such as 35 cents can be represented as 35¢ or $0.35. The penny (1¢), the nickel (5¢), the dime (10¢), and the quarter (25¢) are the most common coins. The half-dollar (50¢) and the one-dollar coins (which come in two sizes) are rare but valid currency.

It is nearly impossible to use foreign currency in California and Hawaii. In some areas you may even have trouble **exchanging your currency** for U.S. dollars. Convert your currency infrequently and in large amounts to minimize fees.You should acquire some dollars before you leave home. Bring at least enough U.S. currency to last for the first 24-72 hours of a trip. Also buy U.S. **traveler's checks,** which can be used in lieu of cash. **Personal checks** can be very difficult to cash in the U.S.; most banks require that you have an account with them to cash one. You may want to bring a U.S.-affiliated credit card such as Interbank (MasterCard), Barclay Card (Visa), or American Express. See also **Banking and Credit Cards,** below.

■ TRAVELER'S CHECKS

Widely accepted, traveler's checks are the safest way to carry large sums of money. They are refundable if lost or stolen, and many issuing agencies offer additional services such as refund hotlines, message relaying, travel insurance, and emergency assistance. Most tourist establishments will accept traveler's checks and almost any bank will cash them. Buying checks in small denominations ($20 as opposed to $50 or higher) is safer and more convenient. Be prepared to convert at least US$100 of traveler's checks; most places will not exchange less than that. Call any of the toll-free numbers below to find out the advantages of a particular type of check and the name of an agency near you that sells them.

American Express: (800-221-7282 in the U.S. and Canada; (0800) 52 13 13 in the U.K.; (008) 25 19 02 in Australia; (0800) 44 10 68 in New Zealand) for questions or to report lost or stolen cheques. AmEx travelers cheques are the most widely recognized worldwide and easiest to replace if lost or stolen; call the information number or the AmEx Travel office nearest you. The small fee for purchasing cheques is waived for U.S. Platinum Card members and AAA members. Cheques can be purchased at AmEx Travel Services offices, banks, and AAA offices. Members can also purchase checks at AmEx Dispensers and by ordering them via phone (800-ORDER-TC, -67337-82). AmEx offices cash their own cheques commission-free (except where prohibited by national government) and sell cheques which can be signed by either of two people traveling together ("Cheque for Two"). A host of other travel-related benefits come with purchasing AmEx cheques and/or being a cardmember. AmEx offers a Global Assist Hotline. From overseas, call collect 202-783-7474; in the U.S. call 800-554-2639 for emergency medical, legal, and financial services and advice. AmEx also offers a mail-holding service, assistance with lost travel documents, and reservation assistance. Travel services and offices are described in the very useful *American Express Traveler's Companion.*

Barclay's Bank sells Visa traveler's checks. A 1-3% commission is charged depending on the bank where the checks are purchased. For lost or stolen checks in the U.S. call Visa at 800-227-6811.

Citicorp sells both Citicorp and Citicorp Visa traveler's checks. For information and to report lost checks call 800-645-6556 in the U.S. Commission (about 1-2%) varies from bank to bank. Check-holders are automatically enrolled for 45 days in Citicorp's Travel Assist Hotline (800-523-1199), which provides English-speaking doctor, lawyer, and interpreter referrals as well as check refund assistance.

Mastercard International: 800-223-9920 in the U.S. and Canada, from abroad call collect 609-987-7300. Commission varies from 1-2% for purchases depending on the bank. Issued in US dollars only.

Thomas Cook Thomas Cook and Mastercard International have formed a "global alliance" by which Thomas Cook distributes traveler's checks with both the Mastercard and Thomas Cook logos. Call 800-223-7373 for refunds in U.S., 800-223-4030 for orders. Commissions range from 0-2%.

Visa: 800-227-6811 in the US and Canada; from abroad, call New York collect 212-858-8500 or London (0171) 937-8091.

Always keep your traveler's check receipts, a list of their serial numbers, and a record of which ones you've cashed separate from the checks themselves; this speeds up replacement if they are lost or stolen. Never countersign checks until you're prepared to cash them. Be sure to keep some cash on hand in less touristy regions as smaller establishments may not accept traveler's checks. Also, be certain to bring your passport with you any time you plan to use traveler's checks.

■ CREDIT CARDS

Credit cards can prove invaluable in a financial emergency. Visa and Mastercard are the most common, followed by American Express and Diner's Club. You can often reduce conversion fees by charging a purchase instead of changing traveler's checks. With credit cards such as **American Express, Visa,** and **Mastercard,** associated banks will give you an instant cash advance in the local currency as large as your remaining credit line. Unfortunately, in most cases you will pay mortifying rates of interest for such an advance.

If you're a student and your income level is low, you may have difficulty acquiring a recognized credit card. American Express, as well as some of the larger, national banks have credit card offers geared especially towards students. Otherwise, you may have to find someone older and more established (such as a parent) to co-sign your application. If someone in your family already has a card, they can usually ask for another card in your name (this encourages travel economy, as they will see the bill before you do). When using most credit cards, beware the hefty interest rate if you do not pay your balance each month.

Budget travelers should also be aware of credit card limitations; many small, cheap establishments won't accept them.

American Express (800-528-4800) has a hefty annual fee ($55) but offers a number of services to cardholders. AmEx cardholders can cash personal checks at AmEx offices abroad (up to US$1000, with Goldcard $US5000). **Global Assist,** a 24-hr. hotline offering information and legal assistance in emergencies, is available to cardholders (800-554-2639 in U.S.) Card holders can take advantage of the American Express Travel Service. There's a Purchase Protection Plan for cardholders that will refund or replace deficient products you buy with the card (certain restrictions apply). **Mastercard** (800-999-0454) and **Visa** (800-336-8472) credit cards are sold by individual banks. Ask bankers about the travel benefits card ownership affords when purchasing. **Working Assets** (800-522-7759), offers a Visa card through which a portion of money from all Visa purchases will go to different non-profit organizations.

■ ELECTRONIC BANKING

Automatic Teller Machines (frequently abbreviated "ATMs"; operated by bank cards) offer 24-hour service in banks, groceries, gas stations, and even in telephone booths across the U.S. Most banks are connected to an international money network, usually **PLUS** (800-843-7587) or **CIRRUS** (800-424-7787). ATM machines employ the wholesale exchange rate which is generally 5% better than the retail rate most banks use. Four-digit PINs (Personal Identification Numbers) are standard in California and Hawaii. Contact your bank or credit card company if you do not have a PIN so you can be assigned one before leaving.

American Express is planning to begin disbursing traveler's cheques from ATM machines. Inquire about this service before departing.

■ SENDING MONEY

If you run out of money on the road, you can have more mailed to you in the form of **traveler's checks** bought in your name, a **certified check,** or through **postal money orders,** available at post offices (orders under $25, 75¢ fee; $700 limit per order; cash only). Certified checks are redeemable at any bank, while postal money orders can be cashed at post offices upon display of two IDs (1 of which must have a photo). Keep receipts since money orders are refundable if lost.

Money can be **wired** directly from bank to bank for about $30 for amounts less than $1000, plus the commission charged by your home bank. Once you've found a bank that will accept a wire, write or telegram your home bank with your account number, the name and address of the bank to receive the wire, and a routing number. Also notify the bank of the form of ID that the second bank should accept before paying the money. **Bank drafts or international money orders** are cheaper than wiring but slower. You pay a commission of $15-20 on the draft, plus the cost of sending it registered air mail. As a last, last resort, **consulates** will wire home for you and deduct the cost from the money you receive. But they will not be very happy about it.

Another alternative is **cabling money.** Through **Bank of America** (800-346-7963), money can be sent to any affiliated bank. Have someone bring cash, a credit card, or a cashier's check to the sending bank—you need not have an account. You can pick up the money one to three working days later with ID, and it will be paid out to you in U.S. currency. There is a $37 flat fee for receiving incoming funds and an additional $8.50 flat fee if you are a Bank of America member. If you are not a member, you will pay any charges requested by the sending bank (at least $15). **American Express's Moneygram** service (800-543-4080) will cable money to the U.S. Fees depend on amount of money being sent and the speed of service requested.

To use **Western Union** (800-325-6000), you or someone else can phone in a credit card number, or else someone can bring cash to a Western Union office. As always, you need ID to pick up your money. Their charge is, by credit card, $50 for $500, $60 for $1000. Charges are $10 less by cash. Service takes only minutes.

■ SALES TAX AND TIPPING

Sales tax is the U.S. equivalent of the Value Added Tax. The sales tax in California varies slightly from region to region, but is usually around 7 or 8%. In Hawaii, the tax is a uniform 4.167%; in Nevada, 7%. Some areas charge a hotel tax; ask in advance. In addition, a **tip** of 15 to 20% is expected by restaurant servers and taxi drivers, although restaurants occasionally include this service charge in the bill. Tip hairdressers 10%, and bellhops $1 per bag. It is also customary to tip bartenders 25¢ to $1 for a drink and 50¢ to $2 for a pitcher.

HEALTH

■■■ HEALTH

For **medical emergencies** in California and Hawaii, dial **911.**

■ BEFORE YOU GO

Common sense is the simplest prescription for good health while you travel: eat well, drink enough, get enough sleep, and don't overexert yourself. While it is rather difficult to lead a normal life while living out of a backpack, several tips will make preventative care easier. If you're going to be doing a lot of walking, take along some quick-energy foods to keep your strength up. You will need plenty of protein (for sustained energy) and fluids (to prevent dehydration and constipation, two of the most common health problems for travelers). Carry a canteen or water bottle and make sure to drink frequently.

For minor health problems on the road, a compact **first-aid kit** should suffice. Some hardware stores carry ready-made kits, but it's easy to assemble your own. Include bandages, aspirin, acetaminophen or ibuprofen, antiseptic soap or antibiotic cream, a thermometer in a sturdy case, a Swiss Army knife with tweezers, moleskin, a decongestant, a motion sickness remedy, medicine for diarrhea and stomach problems, sunscreen, insect repellent, burn ointment, and an elastic bandage.

Always go prepared with any **medication** you may need while away as well as a copy of the prescription and/or a statement from your doctor, especially if you will be bringing insulin, syringes, or any narcotics into the United States. Travelers with chronic medical conditions should consult with their physicians before leaving. Be aware that matching prescriptions with foreign equivalents may be difficult. If you wear **glasses or contact lenses,** take an extra prescription with you and make arrangements with someone at home to send you a replacement pair if necessary in an emergency.

Any traveler with a medical condition that cannot be easily recognized (i.e. diabetes, epilepsy, heart conditions, allergies to antibiotics) may want to obtain a **Medic Alert Identification Tag.** In an emergency, the internationally recognized tag indicates the nature of the bearer's problem and provides the number of Medic Alert's 24-hr. hotline. Attending medical personnel can call this number to obtain information about the member's medical history. Lifetime membership (tag, annually-updated wallet card, and 24-hr. hotline access) begins at US$35. Contact Medic Alert Foundation, P.O. Box 1009, Turlock, CA 95381-1009. (800-432-5378). The **American Diabetes Association,** 1660 Duke St., Alexandria, VA 22314 (800-232-3472), provides copies of an article "Travel and Diabetes" and diabetic ID cards which carry messages in 18 languages on the carriers diabetic status. Contact your local ADA office for information. Another resource is **Diabetic Travel Services, Inc.,** which provides worldwide information on diabetic treatment and physicians (39 East 52nd St., New York, NY 10022).

All travelers should be concerned about **Acquired Immune Deficiency Syndrome (AIDS),** transmitted through the exchange of body fluids with an infected individual (HIV-positive). Remember that there is no assurance that someone is not infected: HIV tests only show antibodies after a six-month lapse. Do not have sex without using a latex condom and do not share intravenous needles with anyone. Lambskin condoms provide no protection from the HIV virus. Those travelers who are HIV-positive or have AIDS should thoroughly check on possible immigration restrictions in the United States. The Center for Disease Control's **AIDS Hotline** provides information on AIDS in the U.S. (800-342-2437, 24 hrs.; Spanish 800-344-7432, daily 8am-2am; TTD 800-243-7889, Mon.-Fri. 10am-10pm).

Reliable **contraception** may be difficult to come by while traveling. Women on the pill should bring enough to allow for possible loss or extended stays. In California and Hawaii, as in most of the U.S., **condoms** can be purchased from nearly all drugstores and pharmacies, usually straight off the shelf.

Abortion is currently legal in the United States, and highly accessible in metropolitan areas. The **National Abortion Federation's hotline** (800-772-9100, Mon.-Fri. 9:30am-5:30pm) refers callers to U.S. clinics that perform abortions.

For additional information before you go, you may wish to contact the **International Association for Medical Assistance to Travelers (IAMAT).** IAMAT provides several brochures on health for travelers, an ID card, a chart detailing advisable immunizations for 200 countries and territories, and a worldwide directory of English-speaking physicians who have had medical training in Europe or North America. Membership is free (although donations are welcome) and doctors are on call 24 hrs. a day for IAMAT members. Contact chapters in the **U.S.,** 417 Center St., Lewiston, NY, 14092, (716-754-4883); in **Canada,** 40 Regal Rd. Guelph, Ont., N1K 1B5, ((519) 836-0102), and 1287 St. Clair Ave. West, Toronto, Ont., M6E 1B8 ((416) 652-0137); in **New Zealand,** P.O. Box 5049, 438 Pananui Rd., Christchurch 5 ((03) 352-9053; fax (03) 352-4630).

■ FIRST AID

While you travel, pay attention to the signals of pain and discomfort that your body may send you. The following paragraphs list some health problems you may encounter but should not be your only information source on these common ailments. Check with the publications and organizations listed above for more complete information or send for the **American Red Cross's** *First-Aid and Safety Handbook* ($15), purchasable by writing to your local office or to American Red Cross, 61 Medford St., Somerville, MA 02143 (617-623-0033). If you are interested in taking one of the many first-aid and CPR courses that the American Red Cross offers before leaving on your trip, contact your local office.

When traveling in the summer, protect yourself against the dangers of the sun and heat, especially the dangers of **heatstroke.** This term is often misapplied to all forms of heat exhaustion, but it actually refers to a specific ailment that can cause death within a few hours if it is not treated. Heatstroke can begin without direct exposure to the sun; it results from continuous heat stress, lack of fitness, or overactivity following heat exhaustion. In the early stages of heatstroke, sweating stops, body temperature rises, and an intense headache develops, soon followed by mental confusion. To treat heatstroke, cool the victim off immediately with a drink of fruit juice or salted water, wet towels, and shade, then rush him or her to the hospital. Wear a hat and sunglasses and a lightweight longsleeve shirt to avoid heatstroke.Less debilitating, but still hazardous, are sunburn and its cohort, the suntan. If you're prone to sunburn, carry sunscreen with you and apply it liberally and often.

Extreme cold is no less dangerous—it brings risks of hypothermia and frostbite. **Hypothermia** is a result of exposure to cold and can occur even in the middle of the summer, especially in rainy or windy conditions. Body temperature drops rapidly, resulting in the failure to produce body heat. Other possible symptoms are uncontrollable shivering, poor coordination, and exhaustion followed by slurred speech, sleepiness, hallucinations, and amnesia. Experts recommend keeping victims awake if they are in advanced stages—if they lose consciousness, they might die. To avoid hypothermia, always keep dry and stay out of the wind; wind carries heat away from the body. **Wearing wool,** is also recommended *especially* in soggy weather— it retains its insulating properties even when wet. Dress in layers, and remember that most loss of body heat is through your head, so always carry a wool hat with you. **Frostbite** occurs in freezing temperatures. The affected skin will turn white, then waxy and cold. To help counteract the problem, the victim should drink warm beverages, stay or get dry, and gently and slowly warm the frostbitten area in dry fabric or with steady body contact. NEVER rub frostbite—the skin is easily damaged. Take serious cases to a doctor or medic as soon as possible.

Travelers in **high altitudes** should allow their body a couple of days to adjust to the lower atmospheric oxygen levels before engaging in any strenuous activity. This particularly applies to those intent on setting out on long alpine hikes. Those new to high-altitude areas may feel drowsy, and one alcoholic beverage may have the same effect as three at a lower altitude.

If you plan to romp in the **forest**, try to learn of any regional hazards. Know that any three-leaved plant might be poison ivy, poison oak, or poison sumac—itchy, pernicious plants. (As Marge Simpson tells Bart and Lisa before they leave for camp, "Leaves of three, let it be.") Look before you leap into any wilderness area, even if it is simply the side of the highway; many areas have their own local snakes, spiders, insects, and creepy-crawlies. Consider wearing long pants and long-sleeved shirts to protect against ticks, which can carry **Lyme disease,** a bacterial infection caused by the bite of certain small, infected ticks. Along with a circular rash often come flu-like symptoms. There is no vaccine; however, Lyme can be treated effectively with antibiotics if caught early on. While in wooded areas, periodically check to brush ticks off. If you find a tick attached to your skin, grasp the tick's head with tweezers as close to your skin as possible and apply slow, steady traction. If you touch poison oak or other varieties, wash your skin as soon as possible in cold water and soap. Calamine lotion, cortisones, or aloe vera gel may stop insect bites from itching.

One of the most common symptoms associated with eating and drinking while traveling is **diarrhea.** Known variously as *turista* and *Montezuma's revenge,* diarrhea has unmistakable symptoms but also, thankfully, some means of relief. Many people take over-the-counter remedies (such as Pepto-Bismol). Since dehydration is the most common side effect of diarrhea, those suffering should drink plenty of fruit juice and pure water. The simplest anti-dehydration formula is still one of the most effective: 8 oz. of water with a ½ tsp. of sugar or honey and a pinch of salt.

Parasites (tapeworms, etc.) also hide themselves in unsafe water and food and some are additionally transmitted by insects. *Giardia,* for example, is one serious parasitic disease you can get by drinking untreated water from streams or lakes. General symptoms of parasitic infection include swollen glands or lymph nodes, fever, rashes or itchiness, digestive problems, eye problems, and anemia. Don't let these nasty creatures ruin your vacation. Boil your water, wear shoes, avoid bugs, and eat well-cooked food.

Women traveling in unsanitary conditions are vulnerable to **bladder infections,** common and severely uncomfortable bacterial diseases which cause a burning sensation and painful and sometimes frequent urination. A strong antibiotic (often available without prescription) usually gets rid of the symptoms within a couple of days. Other recommendations are to drink enormous amounts of vitamin C-rich juice and plenty of water. Treat an infection the best you can while on the road; if it persists, take time out to see a doctor.

A number of health-oriented publications may prove useful to the traveler. The pamphlets *How to Adjust to the Heat, How to Adapt to Altitude,* and the perennial favorite, *How to Avoid Traveller's Diarrhea,* can be ordered from the **IAMAT.**

■ ■ ■ INSURANCE

Beware of unnecessary coverage—your current policies might well extend to many travel-related accidents. **Medical insurance** (especially university policies) often cover costs incurred abroad. Canadians are protected by their home province's health insurance plan: check with the provincial Ministry of Health or Health Plan Headquarters. Your **homeowners' insurance** (or your family's coverage) often covers theft during travel.

Buying an **ISIC,** International Teacher ID, or Student Card in the U.S. provides $3000 worth of accident and illness insurance and $100 per day up to 60 days of hospitalization while the card is valid. **CIEE** offers the inexpensive Trip-Safe plan with options covering medical treatment and hospitalization, accidents, baggage loss, and even charter flights missed due to illness; **STA** offers a more expensive, more comprehensive plan. **American Express** cardholders receive automatic car-rental and flight insurance on purchases made with the card. (For addresses for CIEE and STA, see Useful Organizations: Budget Travel Services, page 4.)

Insurance companies usually require a copy of the police report for thefts, or evidence of having paid medical expenses (doctor's statements, receipts) before they will honor a claim and may have time limits on filing for reimbursement. Some of the plans listed below offer cash advances or guaranteed bills. Check with each insurance carrier for specific restrictions. If your coverage doesn't include on-the-spot payments or cash transferals, budget for emergencies.

Access America, Inc., 6600 West Broad St., P.O. Box 11188, Richmond, VA, 23230 (800-284-8300). Covers trip cancellation/interruption, on-the-spot hospital admittance costs, emergency medical evacuation. 24-hr. hotline.

ARM Coverage, Inc./Carefree Travel Insurance, 100 Garden City Plaza, P.O. Box 9366, Garden City, NY 11530-9366 (800-323-3149 or 516-294-0220; fax 516-294-1821). Offers 2 comprehensive packages including coverage for trip delay, accident and sickness, medical, baggage loss, bag delay, accidental death and dismemberment, travel supplier insolvency. Trip cancellation/interruption may be purchased separately at a rate of $5.50 per $100 of coverage. 24-hr. hotline.

Globalcare Travel Insurance, 220 Broadway, Lynnfield, MA, 01940 (800-821-2488; fax 617-592-7720). Medical, legal, emergency, and travel-related services. On-the-spot payments and special student programs.

Travel Guard International, 1145 Clark St., Stevens Point, WI 54481 (800-826-1300 or 715-345-0505; fax 715-345-0525). Offers "Travel Guard Gold" packages: Basic ($19) Deluxe ($39) and comprehensive (9% of total trip cost) for medical expenses, baggage and travel documents, travel delay, baggage delay, emergency assistance and trip cancellation/interruption. 24-hr. emergency hotline.

Travel Insured International, Inc., 52-S Oakland Ave., P.O. Box 280568, East Hartford, CT 06128-0568 (800-243-3174; fax 203-528-8005). Insurance against accident, baggage loss, sickness, trip cancellation/interruption, and company default. Covers emergency medical evacuation.

Wallach & Company, Inc., 107 West Federal St., P.O. Box 480, Middleburg, VA 22117-0480 (800-237-6615; fax 703-687-3172). Comprehensive medical insurance including direct payment of claims to providers of services. Other optional coverages available. 24-hr. toll free international assistance.

Worldwide Assistance Services, Inc., Member of the Europe Assistance Group, 1133 15th St. NW, Washington, DC 20005 (800-821-2828; fax 202-331-1530). Provides on-the-spot medical coverage ranging from US$15,000 to US$90,000 and unlimited medical evacuation insurance, 24-hr. emergency multilingual assistance hotline and worldwide local presence. Optional coverages are also offered. Short-term, and long-term plans available.

■■■ STAYING SAFE

Tourists are particularly vulnerable to crime for two reasons: they often carry large amounts of cash and they are not as savvy as locals. To avoid such unwanted attention, the best tactic is therefore to blend in as much as possible: the gawking camera-toter is much easier prey than the casual local look-alike. This is often harder than it sounds—chances are you will not be able to fully hide the fact that you're a tourist. Even so, time spent learning local style will be well worth it. If you do feel nervous, walking purposefully into a cafe or shop and checking your map there is better than checking it on a street corner. Walking with nervous, over-the-shoulder glances can be a tip that you have something valuable to protect. Never carry money in a back pocket. Women should sling purses over the shoulder and under the opposite arm. Carry your valuables (including your passport, railpass, traveler's checks, and airline ticket) in a **money belt** or a **neckpouch** stashed securely inside your clothing. The best combination of convenience and invulnerability is the nylon, zippered pouch with belt that should sit inside the waist of your pants or skirt. Making **photocopies** of important documents will allow you to recover them if they are lost or filched. Carry one copy separate from the documents and leave another at home. Keep some money separate from the rest, to use in an emergency

STAYING SAFE

or in case of theft. Label every piece of luggage both inside and out. If possible, use an address where there will be someone to accept returned baggage; on your valuables, like cameras, write "call collect" and a trusted phone number at home.

When exploring a new **city,** extra vigilance may be wise, but no city should force you to turn precautions into panic. If you'll be spending some time there, find out about unsafe areas from tourist information, from the manager of your hotel or hostel, or from a local. You may feel safer sleeping in places with a curfew or a night attendant. Both men and women may want to carry a small whistle to scare off attackers or attract attention, and it's not a bad idea to jot down the number of the police. When walking during the day, common sense will almost always be a good guide. Avoid passing too close to dark alleyways or doorways and stay in the light. If a place looks seedy or spooky, don't enter, and don't let yourself be forced into speaking to those with whom you'd rather not speak. When walking at night, turn day-time precautions into mandates. In particular, stay near crowded and well-lit areas and do not attempt to cross through parks, parking lots, or any other large, deserted areas.

Among the more colorful aspects of many large cities are the **con artists.** Be aware of certain classics: sob stories that require money, rolls of bills "found" on the street, mustard spilled (or saliva spit) onto your shoulder distracting you for enough time to snatch your bag. Hustlers often work in groups, and children, unfortunately, are among the most effective at the game. A firm "no" should communicate that you are no dupe.

If you are traveling by **car,** particularly in Tijuana, avoid being taken in by city **window-washers** who harass cars stopped at traffic lights by beginning to wash without permission and then demanding payment for their unsolicited services. If you're approached, shake your head emphatically and make it clear that they won't be paid. Most will hold off; if not, drive away when the light changes.

If you choose to sleep in the car, be aware that this is one of the most dangerous ways to get your rest—when you lock other people out, you also lock yourself in; it is thus advisable to park in a well-lit area as close to a police station or 24-hr. service station as possible. Camping is recommended only in official, supervised, campsites or in wilderness lands.

Wearing a **seatbelt** is law in California. Children under 40 lbs. should ride only in a specially-designed **carseat,** which can be obtained for a small fee from most car rental agencies. Remember, the convenience or comfort of riding unbelted will count for little if you or someone you care about is injured or killed in an accident.

There is no sure-fire set of precautions that will protect you from all situations you might encounter when you travel. A good self-defense course will give you more concrete ways to react to different types of aggression, but it might cost you more money than your trip. **Model Mugging** (East Coast 617-232-7900; Midwest 312-338-4545; West Coast 415-592-7300), teaches a very effective, comprehensive course on self-defense (course prices vary from $400 to 500). Community colleges frequently offer self-defense courses at more affordable prices. More complete information on safety while traveling may be found in *Travel Safety: Security and Safeguards at Home and Abroad,* from **Hippocrene Books, Inc.,** 171 Madison Ave., New York, NY 10016 (212-685-4371, orders 718-454-2360; fax 718-454-1391).

■DRUGS AND ALCOHOL

In California and Hawaii, as in the rest of the United States, the drinking age is a strictly enforced 21 years of age. Be prepared to show a photo ID (preferably some government document—driver's license or passport) if you look under 30. Have a copy of the prescription for all **prescription drugs** you carry with you. Traveling with **illicit drugs** is a remarkably bad idea. In California and Hawaii, possession of marijuana can result in a citation and fine; being found in possession of cocaine, heroine, or large quantities of marijuana constitutes a felony offense, punishable by imprisonment. The United States takes **drunk driving** very seriously. If your driving suggests possible intoxication to a police officer, you will be pulled over and asked to take the **field sobriety test**. Your ability to perform simple motor functions such as walking toe-to-heel in a straight line will determine whether your blood-alcohol level (the percentage, by weight, of alcohol in your blood) will need to be tested. In California, the legal **blood-alcohol limit** for drivers is 0.08%. If you are found to exceed this limit, criminal charges will be pressed against you. You will face a $1000 fine and will have to appear in court. In Hawaii, exceeding the legal limit of 0.10% will result in the suspension of your drivers license, enrollment in an alcohol rehabilitation program, and a possible 48 hours in jail.

■■■ WORK AND STUDY

■ WORKING

Finding a job far from home is often a matter of luck and timing. Your best leads in the job hunt often come from local residents, hostels, employment offices, and Chambers of Commerce. Temporary agencies often hire for non-secretarial placement as well as for standard typing assignments. Marketable skills, i.e. touch-typing, dictation, computer knowledge, and experience with children will prove very helpful (even necessary) in your search for a temporary job. Consult local newspapers and bulletin boards on local college campuses.

Volunteer jobs are readily available throughout California and Hawaii. Some jobs provide room and board in exchange for labor. Write to **CIEE** (see Useful Organizations, page 1) for *Volunteer! The Comprehensive Guide to Voluntary Service in the U.S. and Abroad* ($8.95, postage $1.50). CIEE also administers the **International Voluntary Service Program,** an international workcamp program which places young people interested in short-term voluntary service with organizations conducting projects worldwide, including the United States. Room and board are provided. For more information, write to CIEE. If you're into fresh air and sublime scenery, consider working for the **National Park Service.** U.S. citizens ages 18 and over can apply for positions as aids, rangers, and technicians at national parks or monuments. For more information on positions with the National Park Service or the U.S. Forest Service, contact the USDA Forest Service, Human Resource Program Office, P.O. Box 96090, Washington D.C., 20090-6090 (703-235-8832; fax 703-235-1597).

Many student travel organizations arrange work-exchange programs. **CIEE** runs a summer travel-work program designed to provide students with the opportunity to spend their summers working in the U.S. University students studying in Australia, Canada, Costa Rica, the Dominican Republic, France, Germany, Ireland, Jamaica, New Zealand, Spain, and the United Kingdom are eligible and should contact CIEE offices in their respective countries. In some areas you may be able to work a desk job at an AYH Hostel in exchange for a bed. Check at hostels in the area in which you are interested for openings. Foreign university-level students can get on-the-job technical training in fields such as engineering, computer science, agriculture, and natural and physical sciences from the **Association for International Practical Training,** the U.S. member of the **International Association for the Exchange of Students for Technical Experience (IAESTE).** You must apply through the IAESTE office in your home country; application deadlines vary. For more informational, contact the local IAESTE committee—try universities or colleges in your area—or write to IAESTE, c/o AIPT, 10 Corporate Center, Suite 250, 10400 Little Patuxent Pkwy., Columbia, MD (410-997-2200).

■ STUDYING

If you would like to study in the U.S., there are a number of different paths you can take. The **American Field Service** provides summer, semester, and year-long homestay exchange programs for high school students. Short-term adult programs are also offered. Write to American Field Service Intercultural Programs, 220 E. 42nd St., 3rd Floor, New York, NY 10017 or call 800-237-4636 or 212-949-4242.

In order to live the life of a real American college student, you might want to consider a visiting student program lasting either a semester or a full year. Many colleges and universities in California and Hawaii welcome visiting students. Contact colleges and universities in your home country to see what kind of exchanges they administer. A more complicated option is to enroll full-time in an American institution. California is home to a number of outstanding private institutions, such as Stanford, Cal Tech, and Pomona. At the same time, the three-tiered state system is among the finest in the country: the **University of California** has nine campuses, **California State University** has 14, and there are innumerable community colleges. From UCLA to Humboldt State to San Francisco City College, there is an astounding array of course offerings (try Aeronautical Engineering, or, alternately, Underwater Basketweaving—the choices are endless). Unfortunately for non-Californians, these state schools can have rather high out-of-state tuition and are extremely popular with residents, who receive priority consideration. At the larger UC schools, plan to apply as much as a year in advance (some have rolling admissions). The free booklet *Introducing the University of California* gives a quick rundown of the system and individual UC campuses. To order, write to Communication Services, University of California, Office of the President, 300 Lakeside Drive, 17th Floor, Oakland, CA 94612-3550 (415-987-9716). For information about California State University, write the California State University Chancellor's Office, 400 Golden Shore, AAAR #318, Long Beach, CA 90802-4275 (310-985-2500).

Specializing in earth and marine sciences, tropical agriculture and Pacific Asian studies, the **University of Hawaii at Manoa** is the principal campus in Hawaii's ten-campus state university system. Write University of Hawaii, Office of Admissions, 2530 Dole St. #C-200, Honolulu, HI 96822 (808-956-8975).

Youth for Understanding International Exchange (YFU), 3501 Newark St., Washington, DC 20016 (800-833-6243 or 202-966-6800; fax 202-895-1104) offers a Community College program in which international students from 18-29 years of age spend one year with an American family and attend a community college.

If you want more information on schools in California and Hawaii, check out your local bookstore for college guides. The *Insider's Guide to Colleges* ($16), published by St. Martin's Press, offers a student's perspective on many public and private institutions. Also useful are the *Fiske Guide to Colleges*, by Edward Fiske (N.Y. Times Books, $16), and *Barron's Profiles of American Colleges* ($19).

If English is not your native language, you will generally be required to pass the **Test of English as a Foreign Language and Test of Spoken English (TOEFL/TSE)**, administered in many countries. You may also need to take the **Test of Spoken English (TSE).** For more information, contact the TOEFL/TSE Publications, P.O. Box 6154, Princeton, NJ 08541-6154 (609-771-7760).

One excellent source of information on studying in the U.S. and abroad is the **Institute of International Education (IIE),** which administers many exchange programs in the US and abroad. IIE publishes *Academic Year Abroad,* which describes over 2,100 semester and academic-year programs offered in the US and abroad ($43 plus $4 shipping), *Vacation Study Abroad*, with information on 1,500 short term programs in the US and abroad ($37, shipping $4), and *English Language and Orientation Programs*, detailing language and cultural programs, (1993/4 edition $43, plus $4 shipping). Contact IIE Books, Institute for International Education, 809 United Nations Plaza, New York, NY 10017-3580 (212-883-8200). IIE Books also operates the International Education Center; open Tues.-Fri. 11am-4pm.

■ VISA REQUIREMENTS

If you want to work or study in the United States, you need to obtain the appropriate visas and other documentation.

If you are not a citizen of the U.S. and hope to **work** in this country, there are a few rules of which you must be aware. This alphabet soup may seem complex, but it is very important. Working or studying in the U.S. with only a B-2 visa is grounds for deportation. Before an appropriate visa can be issued to you, you must—depending on the visa category you are seeking—join a USIA-authorized Exchange Visitor Program (J-1 visa) or locate an employer who will sponsor you (usually an H-2B visa) and file the necessary paperwork with the Immigration and Naturalization Service (INS) in the United States on your behalf. In order to apply to the U.S. Embassy or Consulate for a J-1 visa you must obtain an IAP-66 eligibility form, issued by a U.S. academic institution or a private organization involved in U.S. exchanges. The H-2 visa is more difficult to obtain, as your employer must prove that there are no other American or foreign permanent residents already residing in the U.S. with your job skills. For more specific information on visa categories and requirements, contact your nearest U.S. Embassy or Consulate and the Educational Advisory Service of the Fulbright Commission (a U.S. embassy-affiliated organization).

Foreign students who wish to study in the United States must apply for either a J-1 visa (for exchange students) or an F-1 visa (for full-time students enrolled in an academic or language program). To obtain a J-1, you must fill out an IAP-66 eligibility form, issued by the program in which you will enroll. Both are valid for the duration of stay, which includes the length of your particular program and a brief grace period thereafter. In order to extend a student visa, submit an I-538 form 15-60 days before the original departure date.

If you are studying in the U.S., you can take any on-campus job to help pay the bills once you have applied for a social security number and have completed an Employment Eligibility Form (I-9). If you are studying full-time in the U.S. on an F-1 visa, you can take any on-campus job provided you do not displace a U.S. resident. On-campus employment is limited to 20 hours per week while school is in session, but you may work full-time during vacation if you plan to return to school. For further information, contact the international students office at the institution you will be attending.

■ ■ ■ PACKING

Pack light. Set out everything you think you need, then pack only half of it. And leave space for gifts. The less you carry, the less you will be treated like a tourist and the less you will get exhausted. If you're unsure about cutting things out, take a short walk while carrying all of your luggage. You'll get a preview of just how inconvenient transporting too much stuff can be.

You might consider a light suitcase or duffel bag if you'll be staying in one city for a long time. Large shoulder bags that close securely are easy to stuff into lockers and crowded baggage compartments and ideal for all-purpose lugging. Bus riders and hikers who cover a lot of ground on foot will find sturdy backpacks the most convenient option (see below). Whatever your choice, an additional, small daypack is useful for carrying on plane flights and for short sight-seeing trips. Carry essentials, but never place valuables in outside pockets, an easy target for pickpockets.

Backpacks come with either an internal frame or an external frame. Internal frame models are less bulky and cumbersome, and less easily damaged by baggage handlers. Because they mold to the back and have a lower center of gravity, internal frame packs may be better-suited for hikers, who must carry them over uneven terrain. On the other hand, external frames offer added support and lift the pack off your back for greater ventilation, which makes them more comfortable for long-distance walking over level ground. Don't buy a cheap pack; besides mauling your shoulders, the straps will rip or fray under the strain of hard traveling. Unfortunately, a good pack costs at least $150. Go to a reputable camping store and try out several models. The size of a backpack is measured in cubic inches. Any serious backpacking requires at least 3300 of them, while longer trips require around 4000. Add an additional 500 cubic inches for internal-frame packs, since you'll have to pack your sleeping bag inside, rather than strap it on the outside as you do with an external-frame pack. A front-loading (rather than top-loading) pack saves you from having to dig to the bottom and grope for your last pair of clean underwear. Place heavy items up against the inside wall of the pack so you can more easily maintain your balance.

Pack sturdy, comfortable, inconspicuous clothes in colors that won't show wear and tear. To shorten time spent in laundromats, take wrinkle-free clothing that can be washed and dried outdoors or in a motel bathroom overnight. Those heading to sunstruck California and Hawaii should know that natural fibers or cotton blends are best-suited to warm weather. Unfortunately, natural fibers wrinkle more easily than synthetics. For cooler weather, stick to the "layer concept." Start with polypropylene thermal underwear, and layer on more clothing as necessary. Avoid wearing cotton in foul weather—when it gets wet, it's worse than wearing nothing at all. Wool is a good choice for cold-weather dressing. The sunshine of California and Hawaii can take its toll on your eyes—sunglasses and a sunhat will serve you well.

Shoes are another crucial item on your packing list, whether you hike seriously or not. It's best to break them in before you leave. Don't forget to bring comfortable, absorbent socks to keep your feet happy and dry. Dust your feet with talcum powder to prevent sores and to keep feet fresh, but bring some moleskin in case you do get blisters. Bring some kind of waterproof footwear, especially if you're traveling during the rainy season.

Bottled volcano ashes, "Clint Eastwood for President" t-shirts, artichoke bread, and many other things you've never dreamed of are awaiting you in California and Hawaii. You may, however, want to bring along a few items from home. A travel alarm, sewing kit, rain gear, bath towel, plastic water bottle, padlock, pocketknife (with gizmos), sleeping bag, sleep sack (required at many hostels), tweezers, and plastic bags to keep items dry in the rain are among the most useful. Mild, biosafe liquid soap (Dr. Bonner's and Mountain Suds are two popular brands) kept in a small plastic bottle is useful for laundry and bathing. A budget laundry kit can be made by supplementing the soap with a clothesline and a rubber squash ball to block drains.

Campers should bring a first-aid kit, insect repellant, waterproof matches, and a battery operated lantern or flashlight as well.

In the United States, **electricity** is 110 volts AC. Visit a hardware store for an adapter (which changes the shape of the plug) and a converter (which changes the voltage). Do not make the mistake of using only an adapter, or you'll likely damage a valued appliance and have a hair-raising experience.

■ CAMERAS AND FILM

Keep in mind that photographic equipment is valuable, fragile, and often heavy. The more you leave behind, the less you'll worry and the better your back will feel. Make sure your camera is in good repair before you leave, and bring along a supply of film or pick it up in larger cities as you travel. If you are purchasing equipment before you leave, look into credit card purchase protection plans which insure your purchase from loss, theft, or damage.

Disposable cameras, which are self-contained film and camera units —you turn in the entire contraption for processing—are widely available in California and Hawaii and will eliminate the stress of traveling with an expensive camera

The sensitivity of film to light is measured by the ASA/ISO number: 100 is good for normal outdoor or indoor flash photography, 400 or (usually) higher is necessary for night photography. Consult a photo store for advice about the right film for special types of photography. Sun or extreme heat can damage exposed film; if you need to open your camera while it is loaded with film, do so in relative darkness. Despite disclaimers to the contrary, airport X-ray equipment can sometimes fog high-speed film (rarely under ASA1000); ask the security personnel to hand-check your equipment. Serious photographers should purchase a lead-lined pouch for film.

Consider shooting slides instead of prints—slides are cheaper to process, too—or at least opt for larger prints (4 x 6 in.). Process your film after you return home; you will save money, and it's much simpler to carry rolls of film as you travel, rather than easily damaged boxes of slides or packages of prints and negatives.

■ ■ ■ SPECIFIC CONCERNS

■ WOMEN AND TRAVEL

Women exploring any area on their own inevitably face additional **safety concerns**. In all situations it is best to trust your instincts: if you'd feel better somewhere else, don't hesitate to move on. You may want to consider staying in hostels which offer single rooms which lock from the inside or religious organizations which offer rooms for women only. Stick to centrally located accommodations and avoid late-night treks or metro rides. Remember that hitching is *never* safe for lone women, or even for two women traveling together. Choose train compartments occupied by other women or couples. To escape unwanted attention, follow the example of local women; the less you look like a tourist, the better off you'll be. In general, dress conservatively, especially in more rural areas. If you spend time in cities, you may be harassed no matter how you're dressed. Look as if you know where you're going (even when you don't) and ask women or couples for directions if you're lost or if you feel uncomfortable. Your best answer to verbal harassment is no answer at all. In crowds, you may be pinched or squeezed by oversexed slimeballs; wearing a conspicuous wedding band may help prevent such incidents. Don't hesitate to seek out a police officer or a passerby if you are being harassed. Memorize the emergency numbers in the countries you visit, and always carry change for the phone and enough extra money for a bus or taxi. Carry a whistle or an airhorn on your key-chain, and don't hesitate to use it in an emergency.

A **Model Mugging** course (see Staying Safe, page 19) will not only prepare you for a potential mugging, but will also raise your level of awareness of your surroundings as well as your confidence. All of these warnings and suggestions should not discourage women from traveling alone. Don't take unnecessary risks, but don't lose your spirit of adventure either.

National Organization for Women, with branches across the country, can refer women travelers to rape crisis centers, counseling services, and provide lists of feminist events in the area. Main offices include 22 W. 21st, 7th floor, New York, NY 10010, (212-807-0721) and 3543 18th St., San Francisco, CA 94110 (415-861-8880).

For helpful **tips and suggestions,** consult *The Handbook for Women Travelers* (£8) by Maggie and Gemma Moss, published by Piatkus Books, 5 Windmill St., London W1P 1HF England ((44) 0171 631 07 10). *Places of Interest to Women*, Ferrari Publications, P.O. Box 35575, Phoenix, AZ (602-863-2408) is an annual guide for women traveling in the U.S., Canada, the Caribbean, and Mexico ($8). *A Journey of One's Own*, by Thalia Zepatos, (Eighth Mountain Press $15), offers interesting and good advice, plus a specific and manageable bibliography of resources. Also consult *Women Going Places* ($14), a new women's travel and resource guide emphasizing women-owned enterprises. The guide is geared towards lesbians, but offers advice appropriate for all women. Available from Inland Book Company, P.O. Box 120261, East Haven, CT 06512 (203-467-4257).

A series of recent **travelogues** by women outline their sojourns; check a good library or bookstore for these and other books: *Nothing to Declare: Memoirs of a Woman Traveling Alone* (Penguin Books; $9) by Mary Morris; *One Dry Season* (Knopf) by Caroline Alexander; *Tracks* (Pantheon) by Robin Davidson; and anything by Isak Dinesen, especially *Out of Africa* (Random House).

■ BISEXUAL, GAY, AND LESBIAN TRAVELERS

Unfortunately, prejudice against gays and lesbians still exists in many areas of California and Hawaii. In recent years, law enforcement authorities in California have become more aggressive in arresting and prosecuting those who physically assault and otherwise harass gays and lesbians. San Francisco and Los Angeles have large, political, and active gay and lesbian communities. Wherever possible, *Let's Go* lists local gay and lesbian information lines and community centers.

Damron, P.O. Box 422458, San Francisco, CA 94142 (800-462-6654 or 415-255-0404), publishes the *Damron Address Book* ($14) which lists over 800 bars, restaurants, guest houses, and services catering to the gay male. Covers the U.S., Canada, and Mexico. The *Damron Road Atlas* ($13) contains color maps of 56 major U.S. and Canadian cities and gay and lesbian resorts, and listings of bars and accommodations. *The Women's Traveler* ($10) includes maps of 50 major U.S. cities, lists bars, restaurants, accommodations, bookstores, and services catering to lesbians. Mail order available, add $4 shipping.

Ferrari Publications, P.O. Box 37887, Phoenix, AZ 85069 (602-863-2408). Publishes *Ferrari's Places of Interest* ($16), *Ferrari's Places for Men* ($15), *Ferrari's Places for Women* ($13), and *Inn Places: USA and Worldwide Gay Accommodations* ($15). Available in bookstores, or by mail order (postage $3.50 for the first item, 50¢ each additional item.)

Gay's the Word, 66 Marchmont St., London WC1N 1AB, England (0171 278 76 54). Open Mon.-Fri. 11am-7pm, Sat. 10am-6pm, Sun. and holidays 2-6pm. Information for gay and lesbian travelers. Mail order service available.

Gayellow Pages (U.S./Canada edition $12) is an annually updated listing of accommodations, resorts, hotlines, and other items of interest to the gay traveler. Available from Renaissance House (see listing below).

Giovanni's Room, 345 S. 12th St., Philadelphia, PA 19107 (215-923-2960; fax 215-923-0813). International feminist, lesbian and gay bookstore with mail-order service. Call or write for free catalog.

Renaissance House, P.O. Box 533, Village Station, New York, NY 10014 (212-674-0120; fax 212-420-1126). A comprehensive gay bookstore which carries many of the titles listed in this section. Send a SASE for a free mail order catalog.

Spartacus International Gay Guide, published by Bruno Gmunder, Postfach 301345, D-1000 Berlin 30, Germany ((30) 25 49 82 00). Lists of bars, restaurants, hotels, and bookstores around the world catering to gay men. Also lists hotlines for gay men in various countries. Available in the U.S. from Giovanni's Room and from Renaissance House ($30).

■ OLDER TRAVELERS AND SENIOR CITIZENS

Senior citizens are eligible for a wide range of discounts on transportation, museums, movies, theater, concerts, restaurants, and accommodations. Proof of age is usually required.

Hostelling International (HI) sells membership cards at a discount to those over 54 ($15). To explore the outdoors, seniors 62 and over can obtain a **Golden Age Passport** ($10) allowing free entry into all national parks and a 50% discount on recreational activities. See Camping and the Outdoors: Parks and Forests, page 49, for more information. Also consult the following organizations for information on discounts and special services:

AARP (American Association of Retired Persons), 601 E St. NW, Washington, DC 20049 (202-434-2277). U.S. residents over 50 and their spouses receive benefits including the AARP Travel Experience from American Express (800-927-0111), the AARP Motoring Plan from AMOCO (800-334-3300), and discounts on lodging, car and RV rental, air arrangements and sight-seeing. $8 annual fee.

Elderhostel, 75 Federal St., 3rd floor, Boston, MA 02110. You must be 60 or over, and may bring a spouse who is over 50. Educational programs at colleges and universities in over 40 countries focus on varied subjects and generally last one week.

Contemporary Books publishes *Unbelievably Good Deals and Great Adventures That You Absolutely Can't Get Unless You're Over 50* ($8) by Joan Rattner Heilman.

Gateway Books, 2023 Clemens Road, Oakland, CA 94602 (510-530-0299; fax 510-530-0497). Publishes *Get Up and Go: A Guide for the Mature Traveler* ($11) and *Adventures Abroad* ($13) which offer general hints for the budget-conscious senior considering a long stay or even retiring abroad. For credit card orders, call 800-669-0773.

National Council of Senior Citizens, 1331 F St. NW, Washington, DC 20004 (202-347-8800). For $12 a year or $150 for a lifetime, an individual or couple of any age can receive hotel and auto rental discounts, a senior citizen newspaper, use of a discount travel agency, and supplemental Medicare insurance (if you're over 65).

Pilot Books, 103 Cooper St., Babylon, NY 11702 (516-422-2225). *The International Health Guide for Senior Citizens* ($5, postage $1) and *The Senior Citizens' Guide to Budget Travel in the United States and Canada* ($6, postage $1).

■ TRAVELERS WITH DISABILITIES

Planning a trip presents extra challenges to individuals with disabilities, but the difficulties are by no means insurmountable. As a general rule, inform airlines and hotels of your disability when making travel arrangements; some time may be needed to prepare special accommodations. Hotels and motels have become more and more accessible to people with disabilities, and exploring the outdoors is often feasible. If you research areas ahead of time, your trip will go more smoothly.

Arrange transportation well in advance. **Hertz, Avis,** and **National** have hand-controlled vehicles at some locations (see Getting There and Getting Around: By Car, page 37). **Amtrak** and all **airlines** can better serve passengers with disabilities if notified in advance; tell the ticket agent when making reservations which services you'll need. Both **Greyhound** and Canada's **VIA Rail** allow a person who is disabled and a companion to ride for the price of a single fare with a doctor's statement confirming that a companion is necessary. Wheelchairs, seeing-eye dogs, and oxygen tanks are not counted against your luggage allowance. If you are without a fellow traveler, call Greyhound (800-231-2222) at least 48 hours before you plan to travel so that they can make arrangements to assist you.

If you're planning to visit a national park, get a **Golden Access Passport** (free) at the park entrance or at federal park offices. This exempts travelers who are disabled and their families from the entrance fee and allows a 50% discount on recreational activity fees.

The following organizations provide information or helpful publications:

American Foundation for the Blind, 15 W. 16th St., New York, NY 10011 (212-620-2147). ID cards ($10); write for an application, or call the Product Center (800-829-0500). Also call this number to order AFB catalogs in braille, print, or on cassette or disk. Open Mon.-Fri. 9am-2pm.

Facts on File, 460 Park Ave. S, New York, NY 10016 (800-829-0500, 212-683-2244 in Hawaii). Publishes *Access to the World* ($17), a guide to accessible accommodations and sights. Available in bookstores or by mail order.

Mobility International, USA (MIUSA), P.O. Box 10767, Eugene, OR 97440 (503-343-1284 voice and TDD; fax 503-343-6812). International headquarters in Britain, 228 Borough High St., London SE1 1JX (+44 (071) 403 56 88). Contacts in 30 countries. Information on travel programs, international work camps, accommodations, access guides, and organized tours. Membership costs $20 per year, newsletter $10. Sells *A World of Options: A Guide to International Educational Exchange, Community Service, and Travel for Persons with Disabilities* ($14 for members, $16 for nonmembers, ppd.).

Moss Rehabilitation Hospital Travel Information Service,1200 W. Tabor Rd., Philadelphia, PA 19141 (215-456-9603). Information on international travel accessibility and other travel-related concerns.

Society for the Advancement of Travel for the Handicapped, 347 5th Ave., Suite 610, New York, NY 10016 (212-447-7284; fax 212-725-8253). Publishes quarterly travel newsletter *SATH News* and information booklets (free for members, $3 each for nonmembers). Advice on trip planning for people with disabilities. Annual membership is $45, students and seniors $25.

Twin Peaks Press, P.O. Box 129, Vancouver, WA 98666 (206-694-2462, orders only 800-637-2256). *Travel for the Disabled* lists tips and resources for disabled travelers ($20). Also available are the *Directory for Travel Agencies of the Disabled* ($20) and *Wheelchair Vagabond* ($15).

The following organizations organize tours or make other travel arrangements for those with disabilities:

Directions Unlimited, 720 North Bedford Rd., Bedford Hills, NY 10507 (800-533-5343 or 914-241-1700). Arranges individual and group vacations, tours, and cruises for those with disabilities.

The Guided Tour, Inc., Elkins Park House, Suite 114B, 7900 Old York Road, Elkins Park, PA 19117-2339 (215-635-2637 or 800-738-5841). Organizes year-round travel programs, domestic and international, for persons with developmental and physical challenges as well as those geared to the needs of persons requiring renal dialysis. Call or write for free brochure.

■ TRAVELERS WITH CHILDREN

If you're planning a family vacation with the kids, you'll need to adapt your travel pace to their needs. California and Hawaii offer activities, both educational and entertaining, that are sure to delight children. Consult local newspapers or travel bureaus to find out about events that might be of special interest for young children. Most national parks offer **Junior Ranger** programs, which introduce kids ages 8-12 to nature in half- or full-day trips (see Camping and the Outdoors: Parks and Forests, page 49). Remember that children are often eligible for discounts on food, admission prices, and transportation.

Children require additional health and safety considerations while on the road. If you're renting a car, be sure that the company supplies a child safety seat for children under five years old. When outside, avoid areas with extreme climatic conditions since children are more vulnerable to frostbite, hypothermia and heatstroke (see Health, page 16). Have children carry some sort of ID in case of emergency or if they get lost.

Consider picking up one of the following publications:

Lonely Planet Publications, Embarcadero West, 155 Philbert St., Suite 251, Oakland, CA 94607 (510-893-8555 or 800-275-8555; fax 510-893-8563); also P.O. Box 617, Hawthorn, Victoria 3122, Australia. Publishes Maureen Wheeler's *Travel with Children* ($11, postage $1.50 in the U.S.).

John Muir Publications, P.O. Box 613, Santa Fe, NM 87504 (800-285-4078). The *Kidding Around* series ($10-13 each; $4.25 shipping) are illustrated books intended for children, depicting mostly U.S. destinations.

Wilderness Press, 2440 Bancroft Way, Berkeley, CA 94704-1676 (800-443-7227 or 510-543-8080). Publishes *Backpacking with Babies and Small Children* ($11).

■ TRAVELING ALONE

The freedom to come and go at will, to backtrack or deviate from a schedule or route, is the solitary traveler's special prerogative. Traveling alone has its downside, though. Single accommodations are usually much more costly per person than doubles. In addition, if you do travel alone, you should be extremely careful about where you sleep: outdoor locations make the lone traveler an easy target.

Even if you're alone, chances are you won't be hurting for company along the way. If you carry your copy of *Let's Go*, you might be noticed by others doing the same. Another trick for finding people with whom you may have some connection is to wear a baseball cap or t-shirt from your home state or college. Striking up acquaintances in this fashion might lead you to visit somewhere you hadn't considered, or to pool your resources and rent a car, or to get a free ride.

■ VEGETARIAN AND KOSHER TRAVELERS

Vegetarians should have no problem finding nourishing and delicious meals in California and Hawaii. *Let's Go* attempts to list restaurants with meatless options throughout California and Hawaii. Vegans, people who use and eat no animal products, will find fewer hassles traveling in California than elsewhere. Services in many college towns cater to vegans, offering meat- and dairy-free entrees in restaurants as well as "cruelty-free" products in retail stores. Vegetarian travelers can contact the **North American Vegetarian Society,** P.O. Box 72, Dolgeville, NY 13329 (518-568-7970) for a free catalog of several travel-related titles. To order the **Vegetarian Times,** call 800-435-9610.

Travelers who follow **kosher** laws should contact synagogues in the larger cities for information on kosher restaurants there; your own synagogue or college Hillel should have access to lists of Jewish institutions across the nation. *The Jewish Travel Guide* ($12 plus $1.75 shipping), from **Sepher-Hermon Press,** 1265 46th St., Brooklyn, NY 11219 (718-972-9010) or Jewish Chronicle Publications, 25 Furnival St., London EC4A 1JT England ((0171) 405 92 52; fax 831 51 88), lists Jewish institutions, synagogues, and kosher restaurants in over 80 countries.

■ MINORITY TRAVELERS

In certain parts of California and Hawaii, tourists of color or members of certain religious groups may feel unwelcomed by local residents. Furthermore, either historical or newly developed discrimination against established minority residents may surface against travelers who are members of those minority groups. It is, however, illegal in the United States for any business to discriminate against someone based on race, ethnicity, or religion.

In terms of safety, there are few easy answers. Traveling in groups and taking a taxi whenever you are uncomfortable are always good ideas; your personal safety should always be your first priority. The best answer to xenophobic comments and other verbal harassment is no answer. Keep in mind that your own ethnicity or religion will not necessarily be problematic; you very well may find your vacation trouble-free and your hosts open-minded.

GETTING THERE AND GETTING AROUND

■■■ BY AIR

■ COMMERCIAL AIRLINES

When dealing with any commercial airline, buying in advance is almost always the best bet. The commercial carriers' lowest regular offer is the **APEX** (Advanced Purchase Excursion Fare); specials advertised in newspapers may be cheaper, but have correspondingly more restrictions and fewer available seats. APEX fares provide you with confirmed reservations and often allow "open-jaw" tickets (landing and returning from different cities). APEX tickets must usually be purchased two to three weeks ahead of the departure date. Since it's impossible to predict exactly how far in advance a given ticket will need to be purchased, it's best to call for information as soon as you have even a rough idea of when you'll be traveling. Be sure to inquire about any restrictions on length of stay.

To obtain the cheapest fare, buy a round-trip ticket and stay over at least one Saturday; traveling on off-peak days (Mon.-Thurs. morning) is usually $30-40 cheaper than traveling on the weekends. You will need to pay for the ticket within 24 hours of booking the flight, and tickets are entirely non-refundable. Any change in plans incurs a fee of between $25 (for some domestic flights) and $150 (for many international flights), even if only to change the date of departure or return. Since travel peaks between June and August and around holidays, reserve a seat several months in advance for these times. When inquiring about fares, get advance purchase as well as length of stay requirements, or else you may not be able to buy your ticket in time, or be forced to return home sooner than expected.

In the last few years the major U.S. carriers have taken to waging price wars in the spring and early summer months. Because there is no way to tell when (if at all) such sales will occur, advance purchase may not always guarantee the lowest fare. It will guarantee a seat, though, which has its advantages.

Last-minute travelers should also ask about "red-eye" (all-night) flights which are common on popular business routes. It is not wise to buy "free" tickets (i.e. **"frequent-flyer" coupons** given by airlines allowing the passenger named on them to fly a stated number of miles) from others—it is standard policy on most commercial airlines to check a photo ID, and you could find yourself paying for a new, full-fare ticket. Whenever and however you fly, call the airline the day before your departure to reconfirm your flight reservation, and get to the airport early to ensure you have a seat; airlines often overbook. (On the other hand, being "bumped" from a flight does not spell doom if your travel plans are flexible—you will probably leave on the next flight and receive either a free ticket or a cash bonus. You might even want to bump yourself when the airline asks for volunteers.) Chances of receiving discount fares increase on competitive routes. Flying smaller airlines instead of the national giants can also save money. Most airlines allow children under two to fly free (on the lap of an adult), but discounts for older children and seniors are more rare.

Be sure to check with your travel agent for system-wide air passes and excursion fares, especially since these generally have fewer advance-purchase requirements than standard tickets. Consider **discount travel agencies** such as **Travel Avenue,** 10 S. Riverside Plaza, Chicago, IL 60606 (800-333-3335), which rebates 4-7% on the price of all airline tickets minus a $15 ticketing fee. Student-oriented agencies such as **CIEE, Travel CUTS,** and **STA Travel** (see Useful Organizations, page 1) sometimes have special deals that regular travel agents can't offer. The weekend travel sections of major newspapers (especially *The New York Times*) are good places to seek out bargain fares from a variety of carriers. If you're looking to bypass travel agents altogether, consult the *Official Airline Guide* (*OAG*), 2000 Clearwater Dr., Oakbrook IL 60521 (800-323-3537), which publishes both North American (bimonthly) and worldwide (monthly) editions. The *OAG* lists every flight and every connection on nearly every carrier; the guide also lists toll-free phone numbers for all the airlines which allow you to call in your reservations directly. Since schedules change frequently and the guides are updated twice monthly, a far better idea than purchasing the guides is to look at copies in a library reference room.

A total **smoking** ban is in effect on all scheduled service flights within and between the all 50 U.S. states, except on flights to and from Hawaii and Alaska of 6 hours or more. Flights touching a point outside the U.S. are not affected. The Canadian policy is still more stringent: a total smoking ban is in effect on all aircraft registered in Canada. This includes service within and between points in Canada as well as all international service (except flights to and from Japan).

WITHIN NORTH AMERICA

International travelers should realize that given the long distances between points within the United States and Canada, North Americans rely on buses and trains for travel much less than everyone else in the world. You may use these forms of transportation less than you would at home. The major carriers serving California and Hawaii are listed below, together with the lowest fares for a round-trip ticket purchased in summer 1994.

American Airlines, P.O. Box 619616, Dallas/Ft. Worth Airport, Dallas, TX 75261-9616 (800-433-7300). NYC to LA $388. LA to Honolulu $400.

Air Canada, P.O. Box 14000, St. Laurent, Quebec H4Y 1H4 (800-776-3000). Toronto to LA $424.

America West, 4000 E. Sky Harbor Blvd., Phoenix, AZ 85034 (800-235-9292). NYC to LA $388. This is primarily a West Coast airline: call for relevant fares.

Continental, 2929 Allen Parkway, Houston, TX 77210 (800-525-0280). NYC to LA $516. LA to Honolulu $427.

Delta Airlines, Sales Office, #2 Airport Service Rd., Logan International Airport, Boston, MA 02128 (800-241-4141; fax 617-567-3026). NYC to LA $388. LA to Honolulu $399.

Northwest, 5101 Northwest Dr., Customer Relations M.S. SC 5270, St. Paul, MN 55111 (800-225-2525). NYC to LA $464. LA to Honolulu $439.

Southwest, P.O. Box 36611, Dallas, TX 74235-1611 (800-435-9792). Baltimore to LA $458.

TWA, S. Bedford Rd., Mt. Kisco, NY 10549 (800-221-2000). NYC to LA $325. LA to Honolulu $439.

United Airlines, P.O. Box 66100, Chicago, IL 60666 (800-241-6522). NYC to LA $458. LA to Honolulu $359.

USAir, Crystal Park Four Dr., Arlington, VA 22227 (800-428-4322). NYC to LA $350.

Many major U.S. airlines offer special **"Visit USA"** air passes and fares to **international travelers.** This involves buying a book of coupons in Europe or Asia when you buy your normal ticket. Once in the US, these coupons may be used for domestic flights at reduced fares. The maximum stay restriction is often waived for students. Mexican residents who live more than 100 mi. from the border may be eligible for "Visit USA" discount flight passes on some carriers. Otherwise, because flying in the U.S. is expensive, it may be cheaper to fly on a Mexican airline to one of the border towns, and then to travel by train or bus from there. Contact **AeroMexico** (800-237-6639) for more information.

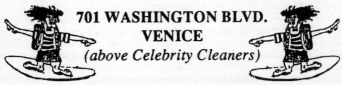

In recent years **American Express** has run promotions whereby students are offered a pre-approved green card along with vouchers for inexpensive domestic flights. Be sure to read the fine print about black-out dates and other restrictions.

FROM EUROPE

Travelers from Europe will experience the least competition for inexpensive seats during the off-season; but "off-season" need not mean the dead of winter. Peak-season rates generally take effect on either May 15 or June 1 and run until about September 15. You can take advantage of cheap off-season flights within Europe to reach an advantageous point of departure for North America. (London is a major connecting point for budget flights to the U.S.; New York City is often the destination.) Once in the States, you can catch a coast-to-coast flight to make your way out West; see Within North America, above for details.

If you decide to fly with a commercial airline rather than through a charter agency or ticket consolidator (see below), you'll be purchasing greater reliability, security, and flexibility. Many major airlines offer reduced-fare options, such as three-day advance purchase fares: these tickets can only be purchased within 72 hours of the time of the departure, and are restricted to youths under a certain age (often 24). Check with a travel agent for availability. Seat availability is known only a few days before the flight, although airlines will sometimes issue predictions. The worst crunch leaving Europe takes place from mid-June to early July, while August is uniformly tight for returning flights; at no time can you count on getting a seat right away.

Another reduced-fare option is the **APEX**, described at the beginning of the Commercial Airlines section. For summer travel, book APEX fares early; by June you may have difficulty getting the departure date you want.

The lowest fares for a round trip ticket from Europe on major airlines in July 1994 were as follows: **British Airways** (London to NYC $630), **Continental** (London to Newark, NJ $745), **Northwest** (London to NYC $774), **TWA** (London to NYC $781), **United** (London to NYC $745), **USAir** (London to NYC $740). Smaller, budget airlines often undercut major carriers by offering bargain fares on regularly scheduled flights. Competition for seats on these smaller carriers during peak season is fierce—book early. Discount trans-Atlantic airlines include **Virgin Atlantic Airways** (London to NYC $630; 800-862-8621) and **IcelandAir** (London to NYC $616; 800-223-5500).

FROM AUSTRALIA, ASIA, AND AFRICA

Whereas European travelers may choose from a variety of regular reduced fares, their counterparts in Asia, Australia, and Africa must rely on APEX. A good place to start searching for tickets is the local branch of one of the budget travel agencies listed above. **STA Travel** is probably the largest international agency you will find: they have offices in Sydney, Melbourne, and in Auckland. For more information on STA, see Useful Organizations, page 1.

Qantas (800-227-4500), **United,** and **Northwest** fly between Australia or New Zealand and the United States. Prices are roughly equivalent among the carriers; typical fare from Sydney to Los Angeles ranges $1250-1400 peak-season, and $1000-1200 off-season. Advance purchase fares from Australia have extremely tough restrictions. If you are uncertain about your plans, pay extra for an advance purchase ticket that has only a 50% penalty for cancellation. Many travelers from Australia and New Zealand reportedly take Singapore Air or other Far East-based carriers during the initial leg of their trip.

From Japan, **Delta Airlines** (800-241-4141) and **Japan Airlines** (800-525-3663) usually offer lower rates than **Northwest** (800-225-2525) and **United Airlines** (800-538-2929). In July 1994, round trip fares from Tokyo to LA ranged from $1050 (Delta) to $2571 (Northwest). From Hong Kong, fares on these airlines generally run $300-400 less than from Tokyo for round-trip tickets.

South African Airways (800-722-9675), **American** (800-433-7300), and **Northwest** (800-225-2525) all connect South Africa with North America. Round-trip fares for the 16½-hour flight between Johannesberg and New York City ranged between $1152 (American) and $1684 (Northwest) in July 1994.

■ CHARTER FLIGHTS AND TICKET CONSOLIDATORS

Those wishing to bypass the larger commercial airlines should consider booking through a charter company or through a ticket consolidator. **Charter flights** are roughly equivalent to flying a commercial airline: your reservation guarantees you a seat on the plane, and you can be certain that if you don't get on the flight someone (other than you) is to blame. You must choose your departure and return dates when you book, and you will lose all or most of your money if you cancel your ticket. Charter companies themselves reserve the right to change the dates of your flight or even cancel the flight a mere 48 hours in advance. To be safe, get your ticket as early as possible, and arrive at the airport several hours before departure time. Many of the smaller charter companies work by contracting service with commercial airlines, and the length of your stay is often limited by the length of the company's contract. Prices and destinations can change (sometimes markedly) from season to season, so be sure to contact as many organizations as possible in order to get the best deal.

Ticket consolidators are companies which sell unbooked commercial and charter airline seats. Companies work on a space-available basis which does not guarantee a seat. For more information, contact the charter companies and travel consolidators listed below:

Air-Tech, Ltd., 584 Broadway #1007, New York, NY 10012, 212-219-7000; fax 219-0066).

1-800-FLY-ASAP, P.O. Box 9808, Scottsdale, AZ 85252-3808 (800-FLY-ASAP, -359-2727; fax 602-956-6414).

Council Travel (a subsidiary of CIEE) sells charter flight tickets and other budget travel necessities. (For more information, see Useful Organizations, page 1.)

DER Tours, 9501 W. Devon Ave., Suite 400, Rosemont, IL 60018 (800-782-2424; fax 800-282-7474).

Last Minute Travel, 800-527-8646; fax 617-424-1943.

Travac, 989 6th Ave., New York, NY 10016 (800-872-8800; fax 212-563-3631).

Travel Charter International, 1301 W. Long Lake, Suite 270, Troy, MI 48098 (800-521-5267; fax 800-329-3888).

■ FLYING AS A COURIER

Another alternative to buying tickets directly from airlines is **courier** travel. Flying as a courier involves contacting a courier company delivering something to where you want to go. Consult the *Courier Air Travel Handbook* published by Thunderbird Press, 5930-10 W. Greenway Blvd. #112H, Glendale, AZ 85306 (800-345-0096; fax 602-978-7836).

Also try the following companies:

Now Voyager, 74 Varick St. #307, New York, NY 10013 (212-431-1616).

Halbart Express, 147-05 176th St., Jamaica, NY 11434 (718-656-8189; international flights only).

■■■ BY TRAIN

Locomotion is still one of the cheapest and most comfortable ways to tour California. It is essential to travel light; not all stations will check your baggage and not all trains carry large amounts (though most long-distance ones do).

Amtrak, 60 Massachusetts Ave. N.E., Washington D.C. 20002 (800-872-7245), offers a discount **All-Aboard America** fare which divides the Continental U.S. into three regions—Eastern, Central, and Western. Amtrak charges the same rate for both one-way and round-trip travel, with three stopovers permitted and a maximum trip duration of 45 days. During the summer and around Christmas, rates are $198 if you travel within one region, $278 within and between two regions, and $338 among three. Your itinerary, including both cities and dates, must be set at the time the passes are purchased; the route may not be changed once travel has begun, although times and dates may be changed at no cost. All-Aboard fares are subject to availability, and Amtrak recommends reserving two to three months in advance for summer travel.

Another discount option, available only to those who aren't citizens of North America, is the **USA Rail Pass** which allows unlimited travel and unlimited stops over a period of either 15 or 30 days. The cost of this pass depends on the number of regions within which you wish to travel. The pass allowing 30 days of travel nationwide sells for $399 peak season, and $319 off-season; the 15-day nationwide pass sells for $318/218. The 30-day pass which limits travel to the western region only (as far east as Denver) sells for $239/219; the 15-day pass for the western region sells for $188/168.

Full fares vary according to time, day, and destination. One-way fares usually don't vary with the season, but round-trip tickets can be significantly cheaper if traveling between late August and late May, excepting during Christmas. Several routes, such as the *Coast Starlight* between Seattle and L.A., cross stunning countryside; round-trip tickets sell for $128 peak season, and $108 off-season.

Amtrak offers several **discounts** off its full fares: children under 15 accompanied by a parent (half-fare); children under age two (free); senior citizens (15% off for travel Mon.-Thurs.) and travelers with disabilities (25% off); current members of the U.S. armed forces and active-duty veterans (25% discount) and their dependents (12.5% discount). Circle trips and special holiday packages can save you money as well. Keep in mind that discounted air travel, particularly for longer distances, may be cheaper than train travel. For up-to-date information and reservations, contact your local Amtrak office or call 800-872-7245 (use a touch-tone phone).

A final discount option on Amtrak is the **Air-Rail Travel Plan,** offered in conjunction with United Airlines, which allows you to travel in one direction by train and then fly home, or to fly to a distant point and then return home by train. The train-portion of the journey allows up to three stopovers, and you have 180 days to complete your travel. The transcontinental plan, which allows coast-to-coast travel originating in either coast, sells for $550 peak season and for $463 off-season. The West Coast plan, which allows travel roughly as far east as Tucson, AZ, sells for $370/320. A multitude of variations on this plan are available as well; call for details.

■■■ BY BUS

Riding the bus is often the most sensible way to reach an out-of-the-way town without a car. For up-to-date information, check local offices. Call twice to verify information, and be aggressive; your whole trip might depend on an obscure detail. Your biggest challenge when you travel by bus is scheduling. *Russell's Official National Motor Coach Guide* ($12.80 for a single copy, $88.70 for a yearly subscription, postage included) is an indispensable tool for constructing an itinerary. Updated each month, *Russell's Guide* contains schedules of literally every bus route (except Greyhound) between any two towns in the United States and Canada. Russell's also publishes a semiannual *Supplement,* which includes a Directory of Bus Lines, Bus Stations, and Route Maps ($5 each). To order any of the above, write Russell's Guides, Inc., P.O. Box 278, Cedar Rapids, IA 52406 (319-364-6138; fax 364-4853).

Greyhound, P.O. Box 660362, Dallas TX 75266-0362 (800-231-2222 in the U.S.), operates the largest number of routes in both the U.S. and Canada. Regrettably, Greyhound does not operate in Hawaii. Greyhound allows passengers to carry two pieces of luggage (up to 45 lbs. total) and to check two pieces of luggage (up to 100 lbs.). Whatever you stow in compartments underneath the bus should be clearly marked; be sure to get a claim check for it.

If you plan to tour a great deal by bus within the U.S., you may save money with the **Ameripass,** which entitles you to unlimited travel for seven days ($250), 15 days ($350), or 30 days ($450); extensions for the seven- and 15-day passes cost $15 per day. The pass takes effect the first day used, so make sure you have a pretty good idea of your itinerary before you start. Before you purchase an Ameripass, total up the separate bus fares between towns to make sure that the pass is indeed more economical, or at least worth the unlimited flexibility it provides.

A number of **discounts** are available on Greyhound's standard-fare tickets (restrictions apply): senior citizens ride 15% off; children ages two to 11 ride 50% off; children under age two travel free (if they'll sit on your lap). A traveler with a physical disability may bring along a companion for free.

Greyhound **schedule information** can be obtained from any Greyhound terminal, or from the reservation center at the new toll-free number (800-231-2222). Greyhound is implementing a reservation system much like the airlines, which will allow you to call and reserve a seat or purchase a ticket by mail. If you call seven days or more in advance and want to purchase your ticket with a credit card, reservations can be made and the ticket mailed to you. Otherwise, you may make a reservation up to 24 hours in advance. You can also buy your ticket at the terminal, but arrive early. If you are boarding at a remote "flag stop," be sure you know exactly where the bus stops. It's a good idea to call the nearest agency and let them know you'll be waiting at the flag-stop for the bus and at what time. Catch the driver's attention by standing on the side of the road and flailing your arms wildly—better to be embarrassed than stranded. If the bus speeds on by (usually because of over-crowding), the next less-crowded bus should stop.

Greyhound is a useful organization for the budget traveler; its fares are cheap, and its tendrils poke into virtually every corner of America. Be sure, however, to allow plenty of time for connections, and be prepared for possibly unsavory traveling companions. By all means avoid spending the night in a bus station. Bus stations can be hangouts for dangerous or at least frightening characters. Try to arrange your arrivals for reasonable day or evening times. This will also make it easier for you to find transportation out of the station and accommodations for the night.

For a more unusual and social trip, consider **Green Tortoise,** 494 Broadway, San Francisco, CA 94133 (800-227-4766 or 415-956-7500, 800-867-8647 in Canada; fax 956-4900). Hop aboard one of these lime-green "hostels on wheels," equipped with bunks and communal kitchens, but no toilets. Green Tortoise can take you coast-to-coast, one-way, for $279-349 plus $71-81 for the group "Food Fund." Stops might include a hike in the Grand Tetons, and night on the town in Chicago, a midnight dip in Lake Michigan, or a mass "mud yoga" session. Green Tortoise's Pacific Coast "Alternative Commuter" route connects Los Angeles with Seattle and all points in between—hop on at any stop.

Green Tortoise also operates a slew of round-trip tours, most beginning in San Francisco. Trips include a 16-day loop via train around Baja's beaches and a 6-day swing through northern California redwoods and national parks. Prices range from $59-1750. Reservations two months in advance are recommended; however, some trips may have last-minute space available. A deposit of $50-400 is required in advance. Schedules and fares may be flexible up to a few months before the trip, and exact itineraries are never set, so be prepared to just go with the flow.

In most areas **mass public transport** remains limited; local buses, while often cheap (fares 25¢-$1.35), are sparse. Call city transit information numbers and track down a public transport map with schedules. *Let's Go* helps you find this information wherever possible.

■■■ BY CAR

■ GETTING REVVED UP

If you'll be relying heavily on car travel, you might do well to join an automobile club. For an annual fee, clubs offer a variety of services ranging from roadside assistance to trip planning to car-rental discounts.

American Automobile Association (AAA), 1050 Hingham St., Rocklin, MA 02370 (800-AAA-HELP, 222-4537) offers emergency road service anywhere in the U.S., 3 mi. of free towing, free trip-planning services, road maps and guidebooks, the International Driver's License, and commission-free American Express traveler's cheques. Your membership card doubles as a $5000 bail bond or a $1000 arrest bond certificate (usable in lieu of being arrested for any motor vehicle offense except drunk driving, driving without a valid license, or failure to appear in court for prior motor vehicle arrest). Annual membership $54 per year for first year, $40 per year for renewal. AAA Plus membership for $76 per year offers 100 miles of free towing and $100 locksmith reimbursement. Members of national automobile associations affiliated with the American Automobile Association can receive services from the AAA while they're in the U.S. Automobile associations in 19 countries have full reciprocity agreements with the AAA. Check your country's club for details.

AMOCO Motor Club, P.O. Box 9041, Des Moines, IA 50368 (800-334-3300) provides emergency road-side service, 5 free mi. of towing, trip-planning service, travel information, and hotel and car-rental discounts for $50 per year. Premier membership ($75 per year) includes 50 miles of free towing and a trip guarantee of up to $500 reimbursement for lodging, meals, and transportation.

Mobil Auto Club, 200 N. Martingale Rd., Schaumburg, IL 60714 (800-621-5581). 10 mi. free towing, $60 locksmith reimbursement, $5000 accidental death and dismemberment coverage, trip planning, free traveler's checks, discounts on hotels and car-rental, emergency travel expense reimbursement. $52 per year.

Montgomery Ward Auto Club, 200 N. Martingale Rd., Schaumburg, IL 60713-2096 (800-621-5151). Emergency roadside assistance, up to $80 towing reimbursement, $5000 accidental death and dismemberment coverage. $52 per year.

If you'll be driving during your trip, make sure that your insurance is up-to-date and that you are completely covered. Car rental companies often offer additional insurance coverage, as does American Express if you use them to rent the car.

■ RENTING

Although the cost of renting a car for long distances is often prohibitive, renting for local trips may be reasonable. **Auto rental agencies** fall into two categories: national companies with thousands of branches and local agencies that serve only one city or region.

National companies usually allow cars to be picked up in one city and dropped off in another, for a price. They also provide toll-free numbers that let you reserve a car anywhere in the country. On the other hand, they tend to have steep prices and high minimum ages for rentals (usually 25). Locally-owned licensee locations of national companies may be more flexible in their policies. Younger drivers, who are able to rent a car should expect to pay an additional charge of $15-20 per day.

Try **Alamo** (800-327-9633), **Avis** (800-331-1212), **Budget** (800-527-0700), **Dollar** (800-800-000), **Hertz** (800-654-3131), **National** (800-328-4567), and **Thrifty** (800-367-2277). Alamo and Dollar allow drivers ages 21-24 with a major credit card to rent for a $15 per day additional fee. Some Budget, National, and Thrifty branches may do the same. **Rent-A-Wreck** (800-421-7253) supplies cars that are past their prime, but they run and they're cheap.

Local companies are often more flexible and cheaper than major companies, but you'll generally have to return the car to its point of origin. Some local companies may accept a cash deposit in lieu of a credit card.

When dealing with any car rental company make sure the price includes insurance against theft and collision. This may be an additional charge, known as the collision and damage waiver (CDW), which usually comes to $12-15 per day. If you use American Express to rent a car, AmEx will automatically insure the car and you will not need to pay the CDW. American Express coverage for cars and minivans includes collision, fire, theft, and damage for up to 31 days if the car is rented on a weekly or daily rate. To extend coverage, the rental contract must be renewed.

Basic rental charges for the bare-bones compact car run $17-45 per day, $85-250 per week, but most companies offer specials. Standard shift cars are usually a few dollars cheaper than automatics. Most packages allow you a certain number of "free" miles before the usual charge of 30-40¢ per mile takes effect. If you'll be doing a lot of long-distance driving, look into an unlimited mileage package. For rentals longer than a week, automobile leasing, which can cost less than renting over long periods, is another option. Make sure, however, that the car is covered by a service plan to avoid the risk of outrageous repair bills.

■ AUTO TRANSPORT COMPANIES

Automobile transport companies match drivers with car owners who need cars moved from one city to another. Would-be travelers give the company their desired destination; the company finds the car. The only expenses are gas, food, tolls, and lodging. The company's insurance covers breakdowns or damage. You must be at least 21, have a valid license (U.S. or international), and agree to drive about 400 mi. per day on a fairly direct route—a typical time allowance is six days from Chicago to California. Companies regularly inspect current and past job references, take your fingerprints, and require a cash bond. Cars are available between most points, although it's easiest to find cars for traveling from coast to coast; New York and Los Angeles are popular transfer points.

If offered a car, look it over first. With the company's approval, you may be able to share the cost with several companions. For more information, contact **Auto Driveaway**, 310 S. Michigan Ave., Chicago, IL 60604 (800-346-2277), **A Anthony's Driveaway**, P.O. Box 502, 62 Railroad Ave., East Rutherford, NJ 07073 (201-935-8030; fax 201-935-2567), or **Across America Driveaway**, 312-889-7737 (from Chicago) 310-798-3377 (from LA).

■ ON THE ROAD

Learn a bit about minor automobile maintenance and repair before you leave, and pack an easy-to-read manual—it may at the very least help you keep your car alive long enough to reach a reputable garage. If you've never done it before, practice changing your tire once or twice without help, learn how to change the oil, and spend an afternoon discovering what's under the hood. Your trunk should contain a spare tire and jack, jumper cables, extra oil, flares, blankets, extra water, food, a flashlight, and first-aid supplies. Always have plenty of gas and check road conditions ahead of time when possible, particularly during the winter. (*Let's Go* provides road condition hotline numbers where available.) Carry a good map with you at all times. **Rand McNally** publishes the most comprehensive road atlas of the U.S., available in bookstores for around $8. Also carry enough cash for tolls and gasoline emergencies. Quarters can be handy for toll booths and pay phones.

Gas is generally cheaper in towns than at interstate service stops. Oil company credit cards are handy, but many stations offer a discount of 3-5¢ per gallon if you pay with cash. MasterCard and Visa are not always accepted, and those stations that do accept them are often more expensive. The enormous travel distances of California and Hawaii will require you to spend more on gas than you might expect. You'll get much better mileage out of your car if it's in good shape—check tire alignment and air pressure, oil level, internal engine fluid levels, avoid over-packing, and don't run the air conditioner more than you have to. Don't use a roof luggage rack if possible; it will increase air drag and is a great sign that you've overpacked. You can split gas bills and get more for your dollar by taking passengers. Check ride boards on college campuses, bulletin boards, and the classified ads to find traveling companions willing to split gasoline costs.

If you take a car into a major city, protect it so that you will be able to take it out again. Try not to leave valuable **possessions**—such as radios or luggage—in it while you're away. Radios are especially tempting; if your tape deck or radio is removable, put it in the trunk or take it with you. If it isn't detachable, at least conceal it under some junk. Similarly, hide baggage in the trunk—although some savvy thieves can tell if a car is heavily loaded by the way it is settled on its tires. (Solution: travel light; see Packing, page 23.) Park your vehicle in a garage or a well-traveled, well-lit area. Sleeping in a car or van parked in the city is extremely dangerous and is not worth the money you might save.

In general, the **speed limit** in the U.S. is 55mph, but rural sections of major interstates are often 65mph (when posted). It is illegal to drive with open containers of alcohol (that includes empties) in the car.

Believe it or not, there is actually an easily comprehensible, consistent system for numbering **interstates.** Even-numbered interstates run east-west and odd ones run north-south, decreasing in number the further north or west they are. If the interstate has a three-digit number, it is a branch of another interstate (i.e. I-285 is a branch of I-85), often a bypass skirting around a large city. An *even* digit in the *hundred's* place means the branch will eventually return to the main interstate; an *odd* digit means it won't. *Let's Go* lists U.S. highways in this format: "I" (as in "I-95") refers to Interstate highways, "U.S." (as in "U.S. 1") to United States Highways, and "Rte." (as in "Rte. 7") to state and local highways.

The greatest difficulty posed by interstates is not the state troopers, the other drivers, or even bad road conditions (although these can be imposing)—it's the sheer **boredom.** For a normally active brain, license plate games only stave off the monotony for so long. Do everything you can to **stay awake and alert.** To prevent "frozen vision," don't keep your eyes glued to the road. If you feel drowsy, pull off the road and take a break, even if there are no official rest areas in the vicinity. Driving in the early morning through to the afternoon may help you avoid over-exhaustion (this way, you'll also have more time to find accommodations). When driving with companions, insist that one of them is awake at all times, and keep talking. If you absolutely can't pull over, try listening to an aggravating radio talk show (music can be as lulling as silence) and open a window to let in cool air. A thermos of coffee or snacks to munch on are also helpful.

Don't drive drunk. And don't drive if you have taken any potentially impairing substance—check medicine labels carefully for side effects. A cold shower and coffee will not help you sober up. The only "remedy" is time. Be especially careful when driving during weekend nights and on holidays. You may not be driving under the influence, but those around you could be.

■ DRIVING IN CALIFORNIA

The automobile and the interstate highway are two ubiquitous aspects of life on the West Coast. If you're planning a comprehensive tour of California, get used to white lane markings and green road signs—at least some of your trip will be by car.

A number of major interstates and highways crisscross California. Travelers moving north-south have the choice of three major routes. If you're looking for speed, hop on **I-5**, which runs north-south from the Mexican border through San Diego, Los Angeles, the San Joaquin Valley, and Sacramento on its way to the Oregon border. I-5 is quick and direct and the fastest route from L.A. to San Francisco (8 hours), but it's also deadly boring. The best scenery that it offers is agricultural flatlands and cow pastures. **U.S. 101** winds north-south from Los Angeles, closer to the coast than I-5, through Santa Barbara, San Luis Obispo, Salinas, San Francisco, Santa Rosa, Ukiah, and Eureka. It's slower than I-5 but considerably more scenic and pleasant a drive. The third option is **Rte. 1**, the **Pacific Coast Highway**, which follows the California coast. PCH is very slow driving but the scenery is some of the most spectacular in the West, particularly on the breath-taking, cliff-hanging turns of Big Sur.

There are also several major east-west highways. **I-10**, the Christopher Columbus Transcontinental Highway, originates at the pier in Santa Monica, near Los Angeles and crosses the Mojave Desert on its way to Arizona and Phoenix. **I-15** runs north-northeast from the Los Angeles area and is the most direct route from Southern California to Las Vegas. Finally, **I-80** originates in the Bay Area and takes travelers to the High Sierras—Lake Tahoe, the ski resorts and Reno—before continuing on to Salt Lake City and the Rocky Mountains.

■ ■ ■ BY MOTORCYCLE

It's cheaper than driving a car, but the physical and emotional wear and tear of motorcycling may negate any financial gain. Fatigue and the small gas tank force the motorcyclist to stop more often on long trips. Lack of luggage space is another limitation. If you must carry a load, keep it low and forward where it won't distort the cycle's center of gravity. Fasten it either to the seat or over the rear axle in saddle or tank bags.

Annoyances, though, are secondary to risks. Motorcycles are incredibly vulnerable to crosswinds, drunk drivers, and the blind spots of cars and trucks. *Always ride defensively.* The dangers skyrocket at night; travel only in the daytime. Understand that serious mishaps are remarkably common and often fatal. If you must ride, wear the best helmet you can get your head into; helmets are required by law in California. For information on motorcycle emergencies, ask your State Department of Motor Vehicles for a motorcycle operator's manual.

■■■ BY BICYCLE

Travel by bicycle is about the cheapest way to go. You move much more slowly for much more effort, but that doesn't mean you'll be ill-rewarded. The leisurely pace gives you a chance to take in the view.

Get in touch with a local biking club if you don't know a great deal about bicycle equipment and repair. When you shop around, compare knowledgeable local retailers to mail-order firms. Make your first investment in an issue of *Bicycling* magazine (published by Rodale Press; see below), which advertises low sale prices. **Bike Nashbar**, 4111 Simon Rd., Youngstown, OH 44512 (800-627-4227 for a catalog, 216-788-6464 for questions about repair and maintenance), is the leading mail-order catalog for cycling equipment and accessories. They will beat any nationally-advertised price by 5 cents. Their own line of products is the best value. Another exceptional mail-order firm which specializes in mountain bikes and full suspension cycles is **Supergo Bikes**, 1660 9th St., Santa Monica, CA 90404 (800-326-2453 or 310-450-2224).

Safe and secure cycling requires a quality helmet and lock. A **Bell** or **Tourlite** helmet costs about $40—much cheaper than critical head surgery. U-shaped **Kryptonite** or **Citadel** locks start at around $30, with insurance against theft for one or two years if your bike is registered with the police.

Long-distance cyclists should contact **Adventure Cycling Association,** P.O. Box 8308-P, Missoula, MT 59807 (406-721-1776; fax 721-8754), a national, non-profit organization that researches and maps long-distance routes and organizes bike tours for members. Their 4450-mi. TransAmerican Trail has become the core of a 19,000-mi. route network of cycling-specific North American maps. Membership ($25 in the U.S., $35 in Canada and Mexico, $45 overseas) entitles you to the *Cyclists' Yellow Pages* sourcebook, a subscription to *Bike Report,* their touring magazine, catalogs listing equipment and reading materials, discounts on cycling maps, and information on their extensive organized tour program. **American Youth Hostels**, 733 15th St., NW, Suite 840, Washington, DC 20005 (202-783-6161) also offers group biking tours.

Bicycling the Pacific Coast: A Complete Route Guide, Canada to Mexico ($15) is available from **The Mountaineers Books,** 1011 S.W. Klickitat Way #107, Seattle, WA 98134, 800-553-4453. There are also a number of good books about bicycle touring and repair in general. **Rodale Press,** 33 E. Minor St., Emmaus, PA 18908 (610-967-8447) publishes *Mountain Biking Skills, Bicycle Touring in the 90's,* and *Basic Maintenance and Repair* ($6.95 apiece). *Bicycle Gearing: A Practical Guide* ($9, from **The Mountaineers Books**) discusses in lay terms how bicycle gears work, covering everything you need to know in order to shift properly and get the maximum propulsion from the minimum exertion. *The Bike Bag Book* ($5 plus $3.50 shipping), available from **10-Speed Press,** Box 7123, Berkeley, CA 94707 (800-841-2665 or 415-845-8414; fax 510-524-1052), is a bite-sized manual with broad utility.

■■■ BY THUMB

Let's Go urges you to consider the large risks and disadvantages of hitchhiking before thumbing it. Hitching means entrusting your life to a randomly selected person who happens to stop beside you on the road. While this may be comparatively safe in some areas of Europe and Australia, it is generally *not* so in the United States. We do NOT recommend it. We strongly urge you to find other means of transportation. Do not put yourself in a situation where hitching is the only option.

If you feel you have no other alternative, if you *insist* on ignoring our warnings, and decide to hitchhike anyway, there are many precautions that must be taken. First, assess the risks and your chances of getting a ride. Women traveling alone should never, ever, *ever* hitch in the United States. Never. It's too big of a risk. Don't believe assurances to the contrary. For single men, it is slightly less dangerous, but also much more difficult to get a ride. A woman and a man is perhaps the best compromise between safety and utility. Two men will have a hard time getting rides and three men won't be picked up.

Next, don't take any chances with drivers. Choosy beggars might not get where they're going the fastest, but at least they'll get there alive. Don't get in the car if you don't know where the driver is going. Don't put yourself in a position where you can't exit the car quickly. Never get into the back seat of a two-door car, or into a car whose passenger door doesn't open from the inside. Beware of cars with driver-controlled electric door locks which can keep you in against your will. Women especially should turn down a ride when the driver opens the door quickly and offers to drive anywhere. Never let your belongings out of your reach, and *never* hesitate to refuse a ride if you will feel at all uncomfortable alone with the driver.

Experienced hitchers talk with the driver—even idle chatter informs hitchers about their driver—but never divulge any information that they would not want a stranger to know. They also won't stay in the car if the driver starts making sexual innuendoes. If at all threatened or intimidated, experienced hitchers ask to be let out no matter how uncompromising the road looks, and they know *in advance* where to go if stranded and what to do in emergencies.

Near metropolises like San Francisco and Los Angeles, hitching is tantamount to suicide. In rural areas, hitching is reportedly less unsafe. All states prohibit hitchhiking while standing on the roadway itself or behind a posted freeway entrance sign; hitchers more commonly find rides on stretches near major intersections where many cars converge.

Hitchhiking in the United States is a BAD idea. Don't compromise your safety.

IN CALIFORNIA AND HAWAII

■■■ ACCOMMODATIONS

California and Hawaii have a pleasant variety of inexpensive alternatives to hotels and motels. Before you set out, try to locate places to stay along your route and make reservations, especially if you plan to travel during peak tourist seasons. Even if you find yourself in dire straits, don't spend the night under the stars; it's often uncomfortable, unsafe, and sometimes illegal, even in national parks and forest areas. If you don't have the money for lodgings, the local crisis center hotline may have a list of persons or groups who will house you in such an emergency.

■ YOUTH HOSTELS

Youth hostels offer unbeatable deals on indoor lodging, and they are great places to meet traveling companions from all over the world; many hostels even have ride boards to help you hook up with other hostelers going your way. As a rule, hostels are dorm-style accommodations where the sexes sleep apart, often in large rooms with bunk beds. (Some hostels allow families and couples to have private rooms.) You must bring or rent your own sleep sack (two sheets sewn together); sleeping bags are often not allowed. Hostels often have kitchens and utensils for your use, and some have storage areas and laundry facilities. Many also require you to perform a communal chore, usually lasting no more than 15 minutes.

Hostelling International-American Youth Hostels (HI-AYH) maintains over 300 hostels in the U.S. and Canada. For information on hostelling in Canada, see the introduction to Let's Go Canada. Basic HI-AYH rules (with some local variation): check-in between 5 and 8pm, check-out by 9:30am, maximum stay three days, no pets or alcohol allowed on the premises. All ages are welcome. Fees range from $7

ACCOMMODATIONS

to $14 per night. Hostels are graded according to the number of facilities they offer and their overall level of quality—consult *Let's Go* evaluations for each town. Reservations may be necessary or advisable at some hostels, so check ahead of time. HI-AYH membership is annual: $25, $15 for ages over 54, $10 for ages under 18, $35 for a family. Nonmembers who wish to stay at an HI-AYH hostel usually pay $3 extra, which can be applied toward membership. The **International Youth Hostel Federation (IYHF)** recently changed its name to **Hostelling International (HI)**. HI memberships (and IYHF memberships that have not yet expired) are valid at all HI-AYH hostels. For more information, contact HI-AYH, 425 Divisadero St. #301, San Francisco, CA 94117 (415-863-9939); the AYH Handbook is free with membership, and lists and describes all hostels. HI recently established an international booking network (IBN) for advance reservations. Contact any participating hostel for more information.

■ HOTELS AND MOTELS

If you are addicted to Hiltons and Hyatts beyond your means, consider joining **Discount Travel International**, 114 Forrest Ave. #203, Narberth, PA 19072 (215-668-7184; fax 668-9182). For an annual $45 membership, your household is privy to a wealth of discounts on organized trips, cruises, airline tickets, car rentals (National, Alamo, and Hertz) and unsold hotel rooms, which can save you as much as 50%.

Many budget motels preserve single digits in their names (e.g. Motel 6), but the cellar-level price of a single has matured to just under $30. Chains usually adhere more consistently to a level of cleanliness and comfort than locally operated budget competitors; some budget motels even feature heated pools and cable TV. In bigger cities, budget motels are just off the highway, often inconveniently far from the downtown area. Contact these chains for free directories:

Motel 6, 3391 S. Blvd., Rio Rancho, NM 87124 (505-891-6161).
Super 8 Motels, Inc., 1910 8th Ave. NE, P.O. Box 4090, Aberdeen, SD 57402-4090 (800-800-8000 or 605-229-8708; fax 605-229-8900).

Choice Hotels International, 10750 Columbia Pike, Silver Springs, MD 20901-4494 (800-453-4511).

Best Western, 6201 N. 24th Parkway, Phoenix, AZ 85016-2023 (602-957-5751; fax 602-957-5505).

You may also want to consult an omnibus directory, like the *State by State Guide to Budget Motels* ($11) from **Marlor Press, Inc.,** 4304 Brigadoon Drive, St. Paul, MN 55126 (800-669-4908 or 612-484-4600; fax 612-490-1182), or the *National Directory of Budget Motels* ($7, shipping included), from **Pilot Books**, 103 Cooper St., Babylon, NY 11702 (516-422-2225 or 422-2227).

■ BED AND BREAKFASTS (B&BS)

As alternatives to impersonal hotel rooms, bed and breakfasts (private homes with spare rooms available to travelers) range from the acceptable to the sublime. B&Bs may provide an excellent way to explore an area with the help of a host who knows it well, and some go out of their way to be accommodating by accepting travelers with pets or giving personalized tours. The best part of your stay will often be a home-cooked breakfast (and occasionally dinner). However, many B&Bs do not provide phones, TVs, or private showers with your room.

Prices vary widely. B&Bs in major cities are usually more expensive than those in out-of-the-way places. Doubles can cost anywhere from $20 to $300 per night. Most are in the $30 to $50 range. Some homes give special discounts to families or senior citizens. Reservations are almost always necessary, although in the off-season (if the B&B is open), you can frequently find a room on short notice.

For information on B&Bs, contact **Bed and Breakfast International,** P.O. Box 282910, San Francisco, CA 94128-2910 (800-872-4500 or 415-696-1690, fax 415-696-1699), or CIEE's (212-661-1108) *Where to Stay USA* ($15) which includes listings for hostels, YMCAs, and dorms, along with B&Bs with singles under $30 and doubles under $35. Two useful guidebooks on the subject are *Bed & Breakfast, USA,* ($14) by Betty R. Rundback and Nancy Kramer, available in bookstores or through Tourist House Associates, Inc., RD 2, Box 355-A, Greentown, PA 18426 (717-676-3222), and *The Complete Guide to Bed and Breakfasts, Inns and Guesthouses in the U.S. and Canada,* by Pamela Lanier, from Ten Speed Press, available in book stores or direct from **Lanier Press,** P.O. Box 20467, Oakland, CA 94620 (510-644-8018; fax 510-644-2651). In addition, check local phone books, visitors' bureaus, and information at bus and train stations.

■ YMCAS AND YWCAS

Not all Young Men's Christian Associations (YMCAs) offer lodging; those that do are often located in urban downtowns, which can be convenient though a little gritty. Rates in YMCAs are usually lower than a hotel but higher than the local hostel and include use of the showers (often communal), libraries, pools, and other facilities. Many YMCAs accept women and families, but some will not accept ages under 18 without parental permission. Reservations (strongly recommended) are $3 in the US and Canada, except Hawaii ($5), and key deposits are $5. Payment for reservations must be made in advance, with a traveler's check (signed top and bottom), US money order, certified check, Visa, or Mastercard; personal checks are not accepted. For information and reservations, write the Y's Way to Travel, 224 E. 47th St., New York, NY 10017 (212-308-2899). Send a self-addressed envelope with a 65¢ stamp for a free catalogue.

Most Young Women's Christian Associations (YWCAs) accommodate only women. Nonmembers are usually required to join when lodging. Write **YWCA of the USA,** 726 Broadway, New York, NY 10003 (212-614-2700), for more info.

Marina Hostel
2915 Yale Avenue
Marina Del Rey, CA
90292
310-301-3983

Only 1 mile from Venice Beach
No curfew - open 24 hours
$12.00 a night
6 miles from LAX • Cable T.V.
Kitchen and laundry facilities • Lockers

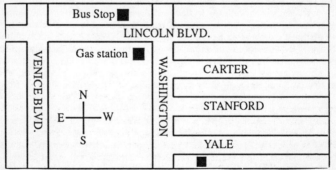

From LAX take Santa Monica Blue Bus #3, going north. Get off at Washington Blvd. Walk 3 blocks to Yale Avenue.

From downtown Greyhound take RTD Bus #33 on Spring St. Get off at Venice Blvd. Cross Venice and walk south on Lincoln until Washington Blvd. Turn right on Washington Blvd. and walk 3 blocks to Yale Avenue.

■ ALTERNATIVE ACCOMMODATIONS

Many **colleges** and **universities** open their residence halls to travelers when school is not in session—some do so even during term-time. No general policy covers all of these institutions, but rates tend to be low, and many schools require that you express at least a vague interest in attending their institution. You should call or write ahead for reservations (See Work and Study, page 21, for names and addresses of colleges and universities in California and Hawaii).

Students traveling through a college or university town while school is in session might try introducing themselves to friendly looking local students. In general, college campuses are some of the best sources for information on things to do, places to stay, and possible rides out of town. In addition, dining halls often serve reasonably priced, reasonably edible all-you-can-stomach meals.

Another alternative is **Servas,** an international cooperative system devoted to promoting peace and understanding by providing opportunities for more personal contacts among people of diverse cultures. Travelers are invited to share life in host's homes in over 100 countries. You are asked to contact hosts in advance, and you must be willing to fit into the household routine. Homestays are two nights. Prospective travelers must submit an application with references, have an interview, and pay a membership fee of $55, plus a $25 deposit for up to five host lists which provide a short description of each host member. Write to U.S. Servas Committee, 11 John St. #407, New York, NY 10038 (212-267-0252).

World Learning's Homestay/USA, formerly The Experiment in International Living, conducts programs for international visitors of all ages to stay from several days to several months in urban, suburban, and rural areas, in volunteer hosts' homes. For more information, contact Homestay/USA at 25 Bay State Rd., Boston, MA 02215 (800-327-4678 or 617-247-0350).

For a different type of homestay experience, **International Home Rentals,** P.O. Box 329, Middleburg, VA 22117 (800-221-9001 or 703-687-3161; fax 703-687-3352), has home rentals in several states including California.

■ WHEN IN DIRE STRAITS

Every year, enterprising travelers sleep in locations ranging from cemeteries to sewage treatment plants in order to save money on accommodations. While it is undeniably cheap, sacking out is often uncomfortable, unsafe, and illegal. Always know when and where it's safe before you crash. In the city, ask locals about areas to avoid. In the country, ask before you sleep on someone's lawn or in a barn or shed. Otherwise, you may get mauled by the family dog or arrested (or shot) for trespassing. In California's San Joaquin Valley, avoid large farms where tension between migrant workers and their employers sometimes runs high. In Hawaii and Northern California, stick to established paths in wooded areas: growers afraid that you might stumble upon hidden fields of marijuana or magic mushrooms boobytrap and guard their fields zealously. Even national forest properties aren't necessarily safe; stray from roads and trails only in the high country, where marijuana won't grow. Never take advantage of the availability of crops in the fields—small farmers and agribusinesses alike get annoyed with freeloaders.

In addition, exercise the same caution against crime in national parks that you would elsewhere.

■■■ CAMPING AND THE OUTDOORS

From craggy mountains to shady woods to sandy beaches, California and Hawaii present a variety of camping alternatives, ranging from privately run campsites that include swimming pools and other amenities to a grassy clearing by the side of the road. Few areas in the world are as accessible to the traveler or as majestic.

CAMPING AND THE OUTDOOORS

■USEFUL PUBLICATIONS

For information about camping, hiking, and biking, write or call the publishers listed below to receive a free catalog.

Sierra Club Bookstore, 730 Polk St., San Francisco, CA 94109 (415-923-5500). Books on many national parks, as well as *The Best About Backpacking* ($11), *Cooking for Camp and Trail* ($12), *Learning to Rock Climb* ($14), and *Wildwater* ($12). Shipping $3.

The Mountaineers Books, 1011 Klickitat Way, Suite 107, Seattle, WA 98134 (800-553-4453) or (206-223-6303). Numerous titles on hiking (the *100 Hikes* series), biking, mountaineering, natural history, and environmental conservation.

Wilderness Press, 2440 Bancroft Way, Berkeley, CA 94704-1676 (800-443-7227 or 510-843-8080; fax 548-1355). Specializes in hiking guides and maps for the Western U.S. Also publishes *Backpacking Basics* ($11, including postage) and *Backpacking with Babies and Small Children* ($11).

REI, P.O. Box 1700, Sumner, WA 98352–0001 (800-426-4840), publishes *The Great Outdoor Getaways* ($17) and *The U.S. Outdoor Atlas* ($17).

Woodall Publishing Company, P.O. Box 5000, 28167 N. Keith Dr., Lake Forest, IL 60045-5000 (800-323-9076 or 708-362-6700; fax 362-8776). Covering the U.S., Mexico, and Canada, Woodall publishes the ever-popular and annually updated *Woodall's Campground Directory* (Western and Eastern editions, $12) and *Woodall's Plan-it, Pack-it, Go!: Great Places to Tent, Fun Things To Do* (North American, $13) which are generally available in American bookstores.

Go Camping America Committee, P.O. Box 2669, Reston, VA 22090-0669 (703-620-6003). Send a SASE for a free catalog that lists RV camping publications and state campground associations.

For topographical maps, write the U.S. Geological Survey, Map Distribution, Box 25286, Denver, CO, 80225 (303-236-7477).

■ PARKS AND FORESTS

At the turn of the century it may have seemed unnecessary to set aside parts of the vast American wilderness for conservation, but today that act is recognized as a stroke of genius. National parks protect some of the most spectacular scenery in California and Hawaii. Though their primary purpose is preservation, the parks also make room for recreational activities such as ranger talks, guided hikes, skiing, and snowshoe expeditions. Most national parks have backcountry with developed tent camping; others welcome RVs, and a few offer opulent living in grand lodges. Internal road systems allow you to reach the interior and major sights even if you are not a long-distance hiker. For information on camping, accommodations, and regulations write the National Park Service, Office of Public Inquiries, P.O. Box 37127, Washington, DC 20013-7127.

Entry fees vary from park to park. The larger and more popular national parks charge a $5-10 entry fee for vehicles and sometimes a nominal one for pedestrians and cyclists. Most national parks sell the annual **Golden Eagle Passport** ($25), which allows the bearer and family free entry into all parks. U.S. citizens ages 62 and over qualify for the **Golden Age Passport** ($10) entitling them to free entry and a 50% discount on recreational fees; travelers with disabilities enjoy the same privileges with the **Golden Access Passport.** These passports are also valid at national monuments.

Many states have parks of their own, which are smaller than the national parks but offer some of the best camping around—handsome surroundings, elaborate facilities, and plenty of space. In contrast to national parks, the primary function of **state parks** is recreation. Prices for camping at public sites are almost always better than those at private campgrounds. Seniors should note that they will receive a $2 discount at most state parks. Write the California Department of Parks and Recreation, Attn.: Publications, P.O. Box 942896, Sacramento, CA 94296-0001 (916-653-4000). They offer state parks brochures and the *Guide to California State Parks* ($2 for a map, $17 for detailed book). For Hawaii, write the Department of Land and Natural Resources, Division of State Parks, P.O. Box 621, Honolulu, HI 96809 for reservations and information, including the pamphlet *Guide to Hawaii's State Parks* (808-587-0300, fax 808-587-0311).

Don't let swarming visitors dissuade you from seeing the large parks—these places are huge, and even at their most crowded (summer is peak tourist season) they offer many chances for quiet and solitude. At the more popular parks in California and Hawaii, reservations are absolutely essential; make them through **MISTIX** (800-365-2267 for national parks, 800-444-7275 for state parks, 619-452-8787 when calling from outside the U.S.). Lodges and indoor accommodations should be reserved months in advance. However, most campgrounds are strictly first-come, first-camped. Arrive early: many campgrounds, public and private, fill up by late morning. Some limit your stay and/or the number of people in a group.

If the national parks are too developed for your tastes, **national forests** provide a more pure alternative. Most have recreation facilities, though a few are equipped only for primitive camping. Fees range from $10-20. Forests are well-marked and accessible, but can often get crowded, especially in the summertime. Backpackers can take advantage of specially designated **wilderness areas** (sometimes accessible through the campgrounds), which have regulations barring all vehicles. **Wilderness permits,** required for backcountry hiking, can generally be obtained (usually free, sometimes $3-4) at parks. They can also be ordered by mail in advance; check ahead to be sure they aren't booked, especially in summer. Adventurers who plan to explore some real wilderness should always check in at a U.S. Forest Service field office before heading out. Write ahead to order detailed accurate maps ($3-6). Always try the **Pacific Southwest Region,** U.S. Forest Service, 630 Sansome St., San Francisco, CA 94111 (415-705-2874), as they are more helpful and less busy than the central office.

Believe it or not, the U.S. Department of the Interior does more than grant public lands to oil companies for exploitive development. Its **Bureau of Land Management (BLM)** offers a wide variety of outdoor recreation opportunities—including camping, hiking, mountain biking, rock-climbing, river rafting, and wildlife viewing—on the 270 million acres it oversees in ten Western states and Alaska. These lands also contain hundreds of archaeological artifacts, such as ancient Indian cliff dwellings and rock art, and historic sites like ghost towns. For more information, write or call BLM Public Affairs, Room 5600, 1849 C St. NW, Washington D.C., 20240 (202-208-5717).

■ TENT CAMPING AND HIKING

EQUIPMENT

Whether buying or renting, finding sturdy yet inexpensive equipment is a must. Spend some time examining catalogs and talking to knowledgeable sales people. There are many reputable mail-order firms with cheap rates. Order from them if you can't do as well locally. In the fall especially, look for last year's equipment; prices can come down by as much as 50%.

At the core of your equipment is the **sleeping bag.** What kind you buy should depend on the climate in which you will be camping. Sleeping bags are rated according to the lowest outdoor temperature at which they will still keep you warm. If a bag's rating is not a temperature but a seasonal description, keep in mind that "summer" translates to a rating of 30-40°F, "three-season" means 20°F, and "winter" means below 0°F. Bags are made either of down (warmer and lighter) or of synthetic material (cheaper, heavier, more durable, and warmer when wet). Lowest prices for good sleeping bags are: $65-80 for a summer synthetic, $135-180 for a three-season synthetic, $170-225 for a three-season down bag, and upwards of $270-550 for a down sleeping bag you can use in the winter. **Sleeping bag pads** range from $15-30, while **air mattresses** go for about $25-50. The best pad is the **Therm-**

A-Rest, which is part foam and part air-mattress and inflates to full padding when you unroll it (from $50-80).

When you select a **tent,** your major considerations should be shape and size. The best tents are free-standing, with their own frames and suspension systems. They set up quickly and require no staking (though staking will keep your tent from blowing away). Low profile dome tents are the best all-around. When they are pitched, their internal space is almost entirely usable; this means little unnecessary bulk. Be sure your tent has a rain fly. Good two-person tents start at about $135; $200 fetches a four-person. Backpackers and cyclists prefer especially small, lightweight models ($145 and up). **Sierra Design,** 2039 4th St., Berkeley, CA 94710, sells excellent tents, including the 2-person "Clip Flashlight" ($160) that weighs less than 4 lbs.

If you intend to do a lot of hiking or biking, you should have a **frame backpack** ($200-300). Buy a backpack with an internal frame if you'll be hiking on difficult trails that require a lot of bending and maneuvering—internal frame packs have enough flexibility to follow you through your contortions. An excellent choice is a conversion pack, an internal frame pack which converts easily to a suitcase. Regular packs don't travel as well; bring a duffle bag to protect yours in baggage compartments. Make sure your pack has a strong, padded hip belt, which transfers much of the pack's weight from delicate shoulders to sturdier legs. Backpacks with many compartments generally turn a large space into many unusable small spaces; use separate stuff-sacks instead. See Packing, page 23, for more hints.

Other necessities include a **battery-operated lantern** (*never* gas) and a **plastic groundcloth** to protect the tent floor. When camping in autumn, winter, or spring, bring along a "space blanket," a technological wonder that helps you retain your body heat ($3.50-13; doubles as a groundcloth). Large, collapsible **water sacks** will significantly improve your lot in primitive campgrounds and weigh practically nothing when empty, though they can get bulky. **Campstoves** come in all sizes, weights, and fuel types, but none are truly cheap ($30-85). Beware: stove gas can be heavy and bulky if you bring too much.

Shop around your area for the best deals on camping equipment. If you can, buy from a local retailer who can give you advice about using your equipment. Several mail-order firms offer lower prices, and they can also help you determine which item is the one you need. Call or write for a free catalog:

Recreational Equipment, Inc. (REI), P.O. Box 700, Sumner, WA 98352-0001 (800-426-4840). Stocks a wide range of the latest in camping gear and holds great seasonal sales. Many items guaranteed for life (excluding normal wear and tear).

L.L. Bean, Freeport, ME 04033-0001 (800-341-4341). Open 24 hrs., 365 days a year. Supplies its own equipment and national-brand merchandise. 100% satisfaction guaranteed on all purchases: if it doesn't meet your expectations, they'll replace or refund it.

Cabela's, Inc. 812 13th Ave., Sidney, NE 69160 (800-237-4444). Offers great prices on quality outdoor equipment.

Campmor, P.O. Box 700, Saddle River, NJ 07458-0700 (800-526-4784). Has a monstrous selection of equipment at low prices. One year guarantee for unused or defective merchandise.

Eastern Mountain Sports, One Vose Farm Rd., Peterborough, NH 03458 (603-924-7231). EMS has stores from Colorado to Virginia to Maine. Though slightly higher-priced, they provide excellent service and guaranteed customer satisfaction (i.e. a full refund if you're unhappy) on all items sold.

Sierra Design, 2039 4th St., Berkeley, CA 94710 (510-843-0923) has a wide array (all seasons and types) of especially small and lightweight tent models. You can often find last year's version for half the price.

Cheaper equipment can also be obtained on the used market, but only by those who know what they're buying. Consult publications like the want-ads and student bulletin boards, and take someone along who is knowledgeable, or you might be

Pensione International
Hotel
B&B
875 POST ST.
San Francisco, CA. 94109
415 775 3344
CIVIC CTR.
POLK ST.
UNION SQ.

taken. Spending a little more money up front may save money later because you won't have to replace equipment.

A good initial source of information on **recreational vehicles (RVs)** is the **Recreational Vehicle Industry Association,** P.O. Box 2999, 1896 Preston White Dr., Reston, VA 22090-0999 (703-620-6003). For information regarding RV camping publications and state campground associations, send a SASE to the **Go Camping America Committee,** P.O. Box 2669, Reston, VA 22090-0669.

WILDERNESS CONCERNS

The first thing to preserve in the wilderness is you—health, safety, and food should be your primary concerns when you camp. See Health for information about basic medical concerns and first-aid. A comprehensive guide to outdoor survival is *How to Stay Alive in the Woods,* by Bradford Angier (Macmillan, $8). Many rivers, streams, and lakes are contaminated with bacteria and parasites such as giardia, which causes gas, cramps, loss of appetite, and violent diarrhea. To protect yourself, always boil your water vigorously for at least five minutes before drinking it, our use an iodine solution made for purification. *Never go camping or hiking by yourself for any significant time or distance.* If you're going into an area that is not well-traveled or well-marked, let someone (perhaps the ranger) know where you're hiking and how long you intend to be out. If you fail to return on schedule or if you need to be reached for some reason, searchers will know where to look for you.

The second thing to protect while you are outdoors is the wilderness. The thousands of outdoor enthusiasts that pour into the parks every year threaten to trample the land to death. Because firewood is scarce in popular parks, campers are asked to make small fires using only dead branches or brush; using a campstove is the more cautious way to cook. Check ahead to see if the park prohibits campfires altogether. To avoid digging a rain trench for your tent, pitch it on high, dry ground. Don't cut vegetation, and don't clear campsites. If there are no toilet facilities, bury human waste at least four inches deep and 100 feet or more from any water supplies and campsites. Always pack up your trash in a plastic bag and carry it with you until you reach the next trash can; burning and burying pollute the environment. Remember, if you carry it in, carry it out.

BEAR NECESSITIES

No matter how tame a bear appears, don't be fooled—they're wild and dangerous animals. If you're close enough for a bear to be observing you, you're too close. To avoid a grizzly experience, never feed a bear or tempt it with such delectables as open trash cans. They will come back to demand seconds as a right. Keep your camp clean. Do not cook near where you sleep. Do not leave trash or food lying around camp.

When you sleep, don't even think about leaving food or other scented items (trash, toiletries) near your tent. The best way to keep your toothpaste from becoming a condiment is to **bear-bag**. This amounts to hanging your delectables from a tree, out of reach of hungry paws. Ask a salesperson at a wilderness store to show you how. Food and waste should be sealed in airtight plastic bags, all of which should be placed in duffel bags and hung in a tree ten feet from the ground and five feet from the trunk. Park rangers can tell you how to identify bear trails (don't camp on them!). Bears are attracted to perfume smells; do without cologne, scented soap, and hairspray while camping. Also avoid indulging in greasy foods, especially bacon and ham. Leave your packs empty and open on the ground so that a bear can nose through them without ripping them to shreds.

If you see a bear at a distance, calmly walk (don't run) in the other direction. If it seems interested, some suggest waving your arms or a long stick above your head and talking loudly; the general flailing creates the impression in the bear's eyes that you're much taller than a person, and it may decide that you are the menacing High Lord of the Forest. Always shine a flashlight when walking at night: the bears will clear out before you arrive, given sufficient warning. If you stumble upon a sweet-looking bear cub, leave immediately, lest its over-protective mother stumble upon you. If you are attacked by a bear, experts recommend getting in the fetal position to protect yourself, putting your arms over the back of your neck, and playing dead The aggressiveness of bears varies from region to region; always ask local rangers for details.

ORGANIZED ADVENTURE

If you're a novice at roughing it, don't lose heart—many organized adventure tours are designed especially for amateurs. Before you sign up for any organized trip, make sure to do a substantial amount of bargain shopping. Begin by consulting tourism bureaus, which can suggest parks, trails, outfitters, and answer general questions. *Outside Magazine*, 400 Market St., Santa Fe, NM (505-989-710), publishes an Expedition Services Directory in each issue. The **Sierra Club,** 730 Polk St., San Francisco, CA 94109 (415-776-2211), plans a variety of outings. So does **Trekamerica,** P.O. Box 470, Blairstown, NJ 07825 (800-221-0596); call or write for more information. If exploring California and Hawaii by bus appeals to you, **Green Tortoise** offers a variety of tours at excellent prices (see By Bus, page 35).

HIKING

Hiking can be the only way to reach some of the most beautiful areas in California and Hawaii. *Let's Go* describes many daytrips; ask fellow travelers, locals, travel offices, park ranger stations, and outdoor equipment shops for other potential treks. Before setting off, it's a good idea to take a mile-long, pre-trip practice hike to test your shoes and pack weight. When heading into the wilderness, let park officials know your route and expected return time. If you get lost, your chances for emerging safely will increase if you conserve your energy. Don't wander around until you're exhausted. Wait for others to find you.

Bring sturdy, comfortable shoes, and a complete map and compass. For information on heatstroke, hypothermia, and other hiking concerns, see Health.

The **Pacific Crest Trail,** stretching from the Mexican border into Canada, is particularly attractive for one- or two-week hiking trips along shorter segments. The San Bernardino National Forest, in the San Gorgonio Wilderness Area, has a beautiful stretch of trail in southern California. In central California, Desolation Wilderness and Mt. Whitney, in the John Muir Wilderness, are particularly scenic. Although all of the trail's scenery in northern California is awe-inspiring, the Trinity Alps, Castle Crags, and Russian Wilderness (in the Shasta Trinity National Forest), as well as the Lassen National Forest—a volcanic park—come especially highly recommended. For the USDA Forest Service's information packet on the trail write them at the address listed above under Parks and Forests, page 49.

When hiking always be wary of unstable rock formations, ledges, and cliffs. Also, clean your boots before moving on to another island to prevent the spread of plant diseases.

■■■ KEEPING IN TOUCH

■ MAIL

Individual offices of the U.S. Postal Service are usually open Monday to Friday from 9am to 5pm and sometimes on Saturday until about noon; branches in many larger cities open earlier and close later. All are closed on national holidays. The Postal Service has requested price increases. As of this book's press date, the increases had not yet been approved. The prices listed below are from July 1994. **Postcards** mailed within the U.S. cost 19¢ and **letters** cost 29¢ for the first ounce and 23¢ for each additional ounce. To Canada, it costs 30¢ to mail a postcard, and 40¢ to mail a letter for the first ounce and 23¢ for each additional ounce. It costs 30¢ to mail a postcard to Mexico; a letter is 35¢ for a half-ounce, 45¢ for an ounce, and 10¢ for each additional ounce up to two pounds. Postcards mailed overseas from the U.S. cost 40¢, and letters are 50¢ for a half-ounce, 95¢ for an ounce, and 39¢ for each additional half-ounce up to 64 ounces. Within the U.S., up to two pounds of material can be sent **Priority Mail** (2-3 days to domestic locations) at a cost of $2.90. **Aerogrammes,** printed sheets that fold into envelopes and travel via air mail, are available at post offices for 45¢. Domestic mail takes from two to three days to reach its destination. Mail to northern Europe, Canada, and Mexico takes a week to 10 days; to southern Europe, North Africa, and the Middle East, two weeks; and to South America or Asia, a week to 10 days. Of course, all of the above estimated times of arrival are dependent on the particular foreign country's mail service as well. Be sure to write "Air Mail" on the front of the envelope for the speediest delivery. Large cities' post offices offer an **International Express Mail** service, which is the fastest way to send an item overseas (guaranteed delivery to a major city overseas in 48-72 hrs.; often takes but a day). A package under eight ounces can be sent to most foreign destinations for cost between $11.50 and $14.

The U.S. is divided into postal zones, each with a five-digit ZIP code particular to a region, city, or part of a city. Some addresses have nine-digit ZIP codes, used primarily for business mailings to speed up delivery. Writing a ZIP code on letters is essential for delivery. The normal form of address is as follows:

Roger D. Tuazon (name)
American Footie Club (name of organization, optional)
524 General Armstrong St., Suite 96 (address, apartment number)
Brueggersville, ID 64131 (city, state abbreviation, ZIP)
USA (country, if mailing internationally)

If in the U.S. and ordering books and materials from abroad, always include with your request an **International Reply Coupon**—a method of "pre-paying" in the U.S. for postage on letters to be mailed from foreign countries that belong to the Universal Postal Union (95¢). IRCs should be available from your home post office. Be sure that your coupon has adequate postage to cover the cost of delivery.

Depending on how neurotic your family is, consider making arrangements for them to get in touch with you. Mail can be sent **General Delivery** to a city's main branch of the post office. Once a letter arrives it will be held for about 30 days; it can be held for longer at the discretion of the Postmaster if such a request is clearly indicated on the envelope.

Family and friends can send letters to you labeled like this:

Ms. Anne M. <u>INDIGO</u> (underline last name for accurate filing)
c/o General Delivery
Main Post Office
Brine Bright Building
4800 Los Feliz Blvd.
Domus City, TN 20870

American Express does not automatically offer a Poste Restante service, but offices throughout the U.S. will act as a mail service for cardholders if you contact them in advance. Under this free "Client Letter Service," they will hold mail for 30 days, forward upon request, and accept telegrams. If you wish mail to be held for more than 30 days, indicate the requested length on the envelope. For a complete list of offices and instructions on how to use the service, call 800-528-4800 and request the "Traveler's Companion."

■ TELEPHONES

Most of the information you will need about telephone usage—including area codes for the U.S., foreign country codes, and rates—is in the front of the local **white pages** telephone directory. The **yellow pages,** published at the end of the white pages or in a separate book, is used to look up the phone numbers of businesses and other services. Federal, state, and local government listings are provided in the **blue pages.** To obtain local phone numbers or area codes of other cities, call **directory assistance** at 411. Calling "0" will get you the **operator,** who can assist you in reaching a phone number and provide you with general information. For long-distance directory assistance, dial 1-(area code)-555-1212. The operator will help you with rates or other information and give assistance in an emergency. You can reach directory assistance and the operator free from any pay phone.

In order to place a call, you must first hear the dial tone, a steady tone indicating that the line is clear. After dialing, you usually will hear an intermittent purring sound indicating that the call has gone through. Or you might hear a "busy signal," a rapid beeping tone signifying that the number you have called is in use.

Telephone numbers in the U.S. consist of a three-digit area code, a three-digit exchange, and a four-digit number, written as 123-456-7890. Only the last seven digits are used in a **local call. Non-local calls** *within* the area code from which you are dialing require a "1" before the last seven digits, while **long-distance calls** *outside* the area code from which you are dialing require a "1" and the area code. For example, to call Harvard University in Cambridge, MA from Las Vegas, NV, you would dial 1-617-495-5000. Canada and much of Mexico share the same system. Generally, phone services give **discount rates** (Sun.-Fri. 5-11pm) and even cheaper **economy rates** (daily 11pm-8am, plus Sat. all day and Sun. until 5pm).

You can place **international calls** from any telephone. To call direct, dial the universal international access code (011) followed by the country code, the city code, and the local number. Country codes and city codes may sometimes be listed with a zero in front (e.g. 033), but when using 011, drop succeeding zeros (e.g., 011-33). In some areas you will have to give the operator the number and he or she will place the call. Rates are cheapest on calls to the United Kingdom and Ireland between 6pm and 7am (Eastern Time); to Australia between 3am and 2pm; to New Zealand between 11pm and 10am; and to South Africa between 5pm and 6am.

Travelers with British Telecom, Telecom Eireann, New Zealand Telecom, Telkom South Africa, or Telecom Australia accounts at home may wish to use special **access numbers** to place calls from the U.S. through their home systems. All companies except Telkom South Africa have different access numbers depending on whether their cooperative partner in the U.S. is AT&T, MCI, or Sprint. Access numbers are: British Telecom (800-445-5667 AT&T, 800-444-2162 MCI, 800-800-0008 Sprint); Telecom Eireann (800-562-6262 AT&T, 800-283-0353 MCI, 800-473-0353 Sprint); New Zealand Telecom (800-248-0064 AT&T, 800-666-5494 MCI, 800-949-7027 Sprint); Telecom Australia (800-682-2878 AT&T, 800-937-6822 MCI, 800-676-0061 Sprint); Telkom South Africa (800-949-7027).

Many large companies operate **toll-free numbers** to provide information to their customers at no charge. These consist of "1" plus "800" plus a seven-digit number. To obtain specific toll-free numbers, call 1-800-555-1212. Be careful—the age of technology has recently given birth to the **"900" number.** Its area code is deceptively similar to the toll-free code, but "900" calls are staggeringly expensive. Average charges range from $2-5 for the first minute, with a smaller charge for each additional minute. You can have phone sex, make donations to political candidates, or hear about the Teenage Mutant Ninja Turtles, but it'll cost you.

Pay phones are plentiful, most often stationed on street corners and in public areas. Put your coins (10-25¢ for a local call, depending on the region) into the slot and listen for a dial tone before dialing. If there is no answer or if you get a busy signal, you will get your money back after hanging up; connecting with answering machines will prevent this. To make a **long-distance direct call,** dial the number. An operator will tell you the cost for the first three minutes; deposit that amount in the coin slot. The operator or a recording will cut in when you must deposit more money. A second, rarer variety of pay phone can be found in some large train stations and charges 25¢ for a one-minute call to any place in the continental U.S.

If you are at an ordinary telephone and don't have barrels of change, you may want to make a **collect call** (i.e., charge the call to the recipient). First dial "0" and then the area code and number you wish to reach. When the operator answers, say you want to place a collect call, and give your name. Anyone who answers may accept or refuse the call. If you tell the operator you are placing a **person-to-person collect call** (more expensive than a regular, station-to-station collect call), you must give both your name and the receiving person's name; the benefit is that a charge appears only if the person with whom you wish to speak is there (and accepts the charges, of course). One method of reversing the charges is MCI's new 1-800-COL-LECT service: just dial 1-800-COLLECT, tell the operator what number you want to engage (it can be anywhere in the world), and receive a 20% to 44% discount off normal rates). Finally, if you'd like to call someone who is as poor as you, simply bill to a third party, also by dialing "0," the area code, and then the number; the operator will call the third party for approval. Note that in some areas, particularly rural ones, you may have to dial "0" alone for any operator-assisted call.

In addition to coin-operated pay phones, AT&T and its competitors operate a **coinless** version. Not only can collect and third-party calls be made on this kind of phone, but you can also use a **telephone credit card;** begin dialing all calls with "0." Generally, these phones are operated by passing the card through a slot before dialing, although you can always just punch in your calling-card number on the key-pad—a desirable alternative if you happen to be traveling in an area where carrying around credit cards is unwise. Many of these phones—especially of those located in airports, hotels, and truckstops—accept Visa, Mastercard, and American Express as well. The cheapest way to call long-distance from a pay phone is by using a calling card or credit card. For information on obtaining an AT&T calling card, call 800-874-4000 or 800-331-1140 within the U.S. Overseas, callers should dial the access code for the country they are in and ask for AT&T customer service. Information on MCI calling cards is available from 800-444-3333.

Overseas Access is a verbal message service offered by **EurAide,** P.O. Box 2375, Naperville, IL 60567 (708-420-2343). Between May 2 and Octoberfest, travelers can have phone messages collected for them in Munich. They can then call and retrieve their messages at any time. The cost is $15 per week or $40 per month, plus a $15 registration fee. For $20, EurAide will forward mail sent to Munich to any address.

■ TELEGRAMS

Sometimes cabling may be the only way to contact someone quickly (usually by the next day). Western Union (800-325-6000) delivers telegrams overseas and within the U.S. Foreign telegrams are more expensive and are usually priced on a per word basis. The minimum cost for a domestic, same day, hand-delivered telegram is $30.90 for 15 words. "Mailgrams" ($18.95 for 50 words) will arrive on the next mail day.

■ ELECTRONIC MAIL

Electronic mail (e-mail) is a phenomenally popular and inexpensive, often free method to stay in touch with other e-mail users. Unfortunately, few travelers will hit the road with portable computers and modems. Those who wish to gain access to their e-mail accounts while away from home should seek out university computer centers. Although many computer centers are officially restricted to use by registered students, some students may not be averse to helping a friendly visitor log in.

CALIFORNIA

California is the most populous state in the U.S., and in terms of diversity, wealth, and size, is practically a nation unto itself. Californians have an understated pride which comes across as the quiet confidence of a people who firmly believe that they have found the best, or at least the most interesting, living space on the planet. However, few Californians will stop to debate such a claim—in their eyes the conclusion is too obvious to warrant discussion.

They should know; aspiring Californians travel from all corners of the globe in search of the California Dream. People are attracted to the state by more than its natural beauty, seemingly limitless opportunity, and toleration of different lifestyles. The spirit of California is a potent mixture of these qualities infused with a streak of narcissism—California's relentless celebration of individuality almost demands this from its residents. Only here could self-realization be an industry.

California inspires a great loyalty in its citizens. Surprisingly, especially in a state known for its tolerance, a defiant "love it or leave it" sentiment lurks in the hearts of many of the state's otherwise placid residents.

One final note, don't come to the Golden State looking for America. You won't find it. You will, however, find cultures and lifestyles that are peculiarly Californian. Even as they share the collective identity of Californians, the residents of the Golden State are as distinctive as the metropoli and hamlets they call home. In California, you will find sprawling Los Angeles and compact San Francisco, sweltering deserts and cool alpine mountains, towering redwoods and drifting sands. And in the end, you will perhaps understand how Californians can still exhibit vestiges of provincialism in the age of the global village—with a whole world right in their backyard, why would they look any further?

■■■ PRACTICAL INFORMATION

Postal Abbreviation: CA.
Capital: Sacramento.
Nickname: The Golden State.
Motto: Eureka (I have found it).
State Song: *I Love You, California.*
State Animal: Grizzly Bear.
State Tree: Redwood.
Time Zone: Pacific (1 hr. behind Mountain, 2 hrs. behind Central, 3 hrs. behind Eastern, 3 hrs. ahead of Hawaii).
Visitors Information: California Office of Tourism, 801 K St. #1600, Sacramento 95814 (call 800-862-2543, ext. A1003 to have a package of tourism materials sent to you).
National Park Information: 415-556-0560.

■■■ LIFE IN CALIFORNIA

■ HISTORY

The Spanish *conquistadores* named the region *California* after a mythical land full of gold, jewels, and tall, bronze-colored Amazons. While they did not happen upon these legendary "California girls," they did find a number of Native American communities that had been living in the area for thousands of years. California was not vigorously colonized until the coming of the Franciscan *padres* from Mexico in 1769. Mission communities established by Father Junípero Serra and his Spanish cohorts housed thousands of Native American "converts." In 1821 restless Mexico

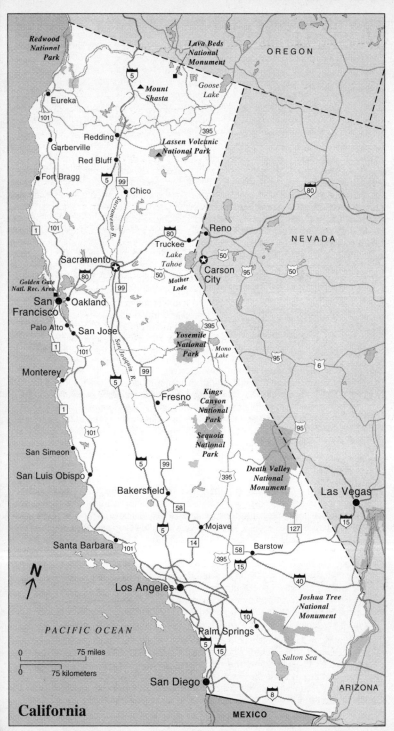

California

achieved independence from Spain and made California a colony. By 1833 the mission system dissolved. The subsequent distribution of Franciscan land among private citizens resulted in a new class of aristocratic cattle raisers, the *rancheros*. These men, presiding over vast *ranchos*, soon dominated the West.

U.S. settlers began migrating overland in the 1800s to set up farms in California's fertile inland valleys. In 1845, settlers staged a revolt against the Mexican government and proclaimed California's independence. Soon after, U.S. soldiers seized control of the newly formed Bear Flag Republic and Mexico was forced to cede California and the Southwest. For the U.S., the timing was golden; almost immediately after the cession became official, James Marshall discovered the precious metal at Sutter's Mill in Sacramento, and the rush was on.

The gold rush era spawned a handful of priceless nuggets, a host of frontier towns, and a mother lode of tall tales. A motley torrent of American, Asian, Mexican, English, and French fortune seekers—known collectively as the '49ers—deluged the region, and the population proliferated sixfold within four years. The miners' demands for food and supplies created an economic boom, galvanizing San Francisco's development into an international port. A savvy retailer named Levi-Strauss capitalized on the miners' demand for sturdy pants by making denim jeans the clothing of choice for miners (and generations since).

Desert temperatures aside, California in 1849 was a hot item. The steamy political and social climate among the settlers sparked robberies, murders, and raids of Native American villages, to which a few self-righteous settlers reacted with vigilantism. Cooler minds called for a constitutional convention, and Californians established their own constitution and inaugurated their first governor a full year before they were granted statehood by the federal Congress.

In the latter part of the 19th century, the continuing influx of eastern settlers, along with wars, massacres, new diseases, and famine, decimated the Native American population. The completion of the transcontinental railroad in 1869 encouraged even more settlers to head west. Rapid growth continued into the 20th century as the state's population doubled between the two World Wars. The area around Los Angeles grew in tandem with the automobile, and innovations such as center dividing lines on highways and automatic traffic signals got their start in LA. By 1939, agricultural products such as the Valencia and navel oranges made California the leading agricultural state in the nation. In addition, the grape industry grew a bunch following the repeal of Prohibition. By 1940 California supplied 90% of the nation's wine, table grapes, and raisins.

After the war production boom of the '40s, post-war projects such as the irrigation canals and freeways of Southern California promoted still swifter expansion. In 1964, California redefined the power centers of America by overtaking New York as the nation's most populous state. During the '60s, nationwide waves of upheaval began in the college campuses and ghettoes of California, and in 1967, San Francisco's Haight-Ashbury neighborhood declared a Summer of Love, when the craze was for the psychedelic and the thing to do was LSD. Many young people voiced their disgust with the Establishment by—in Timothy Leary's words—"turning on, tuning in, and dropping out." But even as this carefree radicalism flourished, California managed to thrust Richard Nixon and Ronald Reagan into the political limelight.

In the '70s, water and fuel shortages and the unbearable L.A. smog forced Californians to alter their once inviolable ways of life. Proposition 13, a popular initiative limiting state taxes, captured nationwide attention. The enthusiasm died out, however, when state services were stripped to the bone, and Californians found out that "you get what you pay for." New problems arrived in the 1980s. Pollution, the need for public transportation, and gross industrialization continued to cloud the state's utopian vision. The AIDS epidemic began, striking California's gay community first and then the general population. These same problems persist in the '90s, and every so often, Northern Californian politicians introduce a bill to secede from the rest of the state. In 1992, the Los Angeles riots signalled that the U.S. has yet to solve what W.E.B. DuBois prophetically called "the problem of the 20th century"—the issue of race. As California rushes headlong into the 21st century, its tradition of tolerance and acceptance clashes with its thinly veiled history of racial prejudice and class division—whether the state can learn from its past and become a model of racial harmony for the rest of the nation remains to be seen.

■ LITERATURE

For over a hundred years, West Coast writers have found inspiration in California. Early chroniclers of the frontier spirit include Bret Harte and Mark Twain. In the 1930s John Steinbeck followed in Frank Norris's footsteps, capturing the needs and desires of the underprivileged. Nathanael West, F. Scott Fitzgerald, and Evelyn Waugh satirized the darker side of the California dream. In Carmel and Big Sur, Robinson Jeffers and Henry Miller penned epic poems and sprawling prose reminiscences. During the '50s, Allen Ginsberg and Jack Kerouac combined candid autobiography with visionary rapture to become the gurus of the Beat Generation. Joan Didion and Thomas Pynchon explored the mystical mundane of southern California in the '60s and '70s. More recently, writers such as Maxine Hong Kingston, Maya Angelou, and Amy Tan have used California as a setting for the exploration of the anxieties and excitements of an increasingly multicultural nation.

Check libraries and bookstores for these Western-oriented titles: Maya Angelou, *I Know Why the Caged Bird Sings;* James M. Cain, *Double Indemnity;* Raymond Chandler, *Farewell, My Lovely;* Joan Didion, *Play It as It Lays;* F. Scott Fitzgerald, *The Last Tycoon;* Allen Ginsberg, *Howl, and Other Poems;* Dashiell Hammett, *The Maltese Falcon;* Aldous Huxley, *After Many a Summer Dies the Swan;* Robinson Jeffers, *Selected Poetry;* Jack Kerouac, *On the Road;* Maxine Hong Kingston, *Tripmaster Monkey* and *Woman Warrior;* Jack London, *Martin Eden;* Henry Miller, *Big Sur and the Oranges of Hieronymus Bosch;* John Muir, *Wilderness Essays;* Frank Norris, *McTeague* and *The Octopus;* Thomas Pynchon, *The Crying of Lot 49;* Tom Robbins, *Even Cowgirls Get the Blues;* John Steinbeck, *Cannery Row* and *The Grapes of Wrath;* Amy Tan, *The Joy Luck Club;* Hunter S. Thompson, *Hell's Angels;* Mark Twain, *The Celebrated Jumping Frog of Calaveras County and Other Stories* and *Roughing It;* Evelyn Waugh, *The Loved One;* Nathanael West, *The Day of the Locust;* Tom Wolfe, *The Electric Kool-Aid Acid Test.*

■ ART AND ARCHITECTURE

Despite New York's presumed aesthetic dictatorship, West Coast artists have played an important role in the history of American art. Painters have found many subjects, along with the favorites of sunsets and surf; Clyfford Still's jagged abstract Expressionist canvases and Richard Diebenkorn's landscapes of the Santa Monica seashore (the *Ocean Park* series) are found in many California museums. In the '60s, Minimalist Robert Irwin stripped away color, texture and volume. Wayne Thiebaud captured San Francisco in the '70s with hyperbolic perspective and strikingly rich color, while two of the city's native sons, sculptors Mark Di Suvero and Richard Serra, helped redefine the human relationship to large metal objects. The brilliant hues and geometrical perspectives of David Hockney's paintings of California people and places attracted attention during the '80s, and western artist has since explored new media, embracing photography and stage design. Frank Ruscha's "word silhouettes" are ironic commentary on the power of language in modern life.

Photographers have also found inspiration in California. In the '30s, Dorothea Lange's photos of the working and living conditions of migrant workers helped to convince the federal government to build public housing projects. Her 1936 photo *Migrant Mother* became a national symbol of the suffering caused by The Great Depression. In a different vein, Ansel Adams's photographs of Yosemite National Park and the Sierras have become among the most recognized and loved photos in the U.S.

Much of the best work of Californian artists remains in the region's museums. The Oakland Museum only exhibits works of the state's residents. The Fine Arts

Museum, the Palace of the Legion of Honor, the de Young Museum, the Asian Art Museum, and the San Francisco Museum of Modern Art in the Bay Area have broad collections. The County Museum of Art, the Museum of Contemporary Art, and the J. Paul Getty Museum are important museums in the Los Angeles area.

Until the late 19th century, the architecture of California generally consisted of simple, practical structures or emulations of the eastern Victorian and Queen Anne styles. However, the architecture of the west eventually took on a flavor of its own. The "missionary revival" architecture of the 1890s, inspired by the Mexican ranch-style, first incorporated native materials and local design traditions. In the 1910s and '20s, architects like Charles Sumner Greene and Henry Mather Greene developed the shingle-style of California's redwood bungalows. In the '30s, Julia Morgan designed over 600 homes, among them the famous Hearst castle. Frank Lloyd Wright, one of the 20th century's most experimental architects, designed 25 buildings in the state, including the Barnsdale House in Hollywood and the Marin Civic Center. In recent years, Frank Gehry has attracted attention by building houses with angular surfaces and unorthodox materials, such as sheet-metal and raw plywood. The California jumble of materials and methods was evident as early as 1930, when Nathanael West noted that L.A.'s canyons were lined with "Mexican ranch houses, Samoan huts, Mediterranean villas, Egyptian and Japanese temples, Swiss chalets, Tudor cottages, and every possible combination of these styles."

■ FOOD AND DRINK

California's gastronomic libido is satisfied by its sumptuous produce and innovative cuisine. Kitchens across the state turn out mouth-watering concoctions running the gamut from local favorites such as sourdough bread and dungeness crab to Basque and Chinese specialties. California leads the country in agricultural production, with fruits, vegetables, and nuts pouring forth in a 365-days-per-year growing season. This agricultural bounty helped give the state the apt nickname "Land of Fruits and Nuts." The state was also the inventor of a number of national food fads, including the 1950s-revival diner and drive-thru fast food.

The California wine industry has successfully overcome obstacles from Prohibition to pesticides and today, four out of every five bottles sold in the U.S. are corked in the West. Many California wines have earned a reputation for quality, and the best California wines rival the finest of France. Other innovations in Wine Country include canned wine (cringe) and wine coolers. Visitors can also keep their taste buds hopping with local beers at the dozens of excellent microbreweries across the state.

Health-conscious but gastronomically snobbish Californians pioneered creative vegetarian cuisine to prove that carnivores weren't having all the fun. But there is now a new twist in meat-free diets: veganism. Vegans add a dash of the political to the nutritional by forsaking all animal products. Not only do they bypass meat and dairy products, but their clothing and cosmetics are animal-free as well. Of course, other Californians are content with their organic produce and free-range chickens, grilled or sauteed in white wine. And nearly everyone enjoys granola.

■ MOVIES

Detroit mass produces cars. Pittsburgh manufactures steel. Hollywood makes movie stars. Shirley Temple, Clark Gable, Grace Kelly, John Wayne, Mickey Mouse—these are the products of California's dream machine.

Hollywood has no counterpart. It is a strictly West Coast phenomenon, sometimes evoking disdain from its Eastern counterparts as nothing more than a glitzy, overblown fake for "the legitimate theater." As the English actor Sir Cedric Hardwicke once said, ""I believe that God felt sorry for actors so he created Hollywood to give them a place in the sun and a swimming pool."

Hollywood's selection as movie capital of the U.S., however, was born from more than this desire for "a place in the sun." Before 1910, independent New York filmmakers were being continually harassed by a movie trust who sought to drive out competition. The independents moved west and set up shop in the sunny sheep-raising town of Hollywood. From there, a quick dash across the Mexican border could foil attempts to confiscate cameras and film. Moreover, they could take advantage of California's sun to light shots; artificial lighting had not yet been perfected.

As the balance of power shifted west, the Hollywood studios instituted a "star system." For the first time actors themselves were advertised and used to attract adoring fans to movie after movie. Florence Lawrence became the first star. She was soon joined by Mary Pickford ("America's Sweetheart"), Charlie Chaplin, Buster Keaton, Douglas Fairbanks, and that lover of lovers, Rudolph Valentino.

The 1920s witnessed two major developments: sound and scandal. "Talkies," the first films with sound, were introduced with Al Jolson's *The Jazz Singer* in 1927. Scandals were ushered in with Fatty Arbuckle's trial for the death of starlet Virginia Rappe. Several other notorious incidents convinced movie moguls of the need for censorship. As a result, Postmaster General Will Hays was appointed "movie czar." According to critics, Hays's puritanical edicts established a model "such as would have suited the strictest of convent nuns."

Gone With the Wind swept away more conservative notions of film in the late '30s, pioneering exorbitant budgets, flamboyant costumes, and casts of thousands. (The city burning as Scarlett fights flames to leave Atlanta is the Emerald City set from the *Wizard of Oz.*) Movies like *Bringing Up Baby* and *The Awful Truth* were characterized by wit and sophistication, while other films displayed an endearing optimism. During the war-ravaged '40s, films like *Citizen Kane* and *The Maltese Falcon* infused a measure of cynicism into the American Dream.

The '50s brought the rapid spread of television; California studios involved in movie production decided to try their hands at the small screen. Programming matured in the '60s with *The Twilight Zone, Bonanza,* and *Star Trek.* Television in the '70s became more aware of social concerns in series such as *All in the Family* and *M*A*S*H*,* but also fell to new depths of banality in *Three's Company* and *The Love Boat.* The '80s and '90s have seen American television go global, with *Dallas, The Cosby Show* and *Baywatch* becoming favorites around the world. The latest craze is tabloid TV, with *Hard Copy* and *Inside Edition* leading the way.

Along with television, the motion picture industry continued to thrive. Beautifully choreographed musicals in the '50s packed 'em in with *Singing in the Rain* and *Funny Face,* while such films as *On the Waterfront* and *Rebel Without a Cause* raised troubling social issues. The '60s encompassed a variety of styles and themes ranging from Robert Wise's *The Sound of Music* to more offbeat works like *The Graduate.* This trend continued into the '70s, when box-office successes included gritty films like *The Godfather* as well as escapist movies like *Superman* and *Star Wars.* The '80s saw Hollywood celebrate excess and self-absorption. Currently, the '90s continue to surprise.

■ RECREATION

Creative Californians entertain themselves with every conceivable combination of wheels, wings, sails, and skis. For an overview of the sporting scene, you might try a hike through the Sierra Nevada or a Napa Valley hot air balloon ride. If you get tired of the heights, you can always snorkel in the depths of the Pacific.

For inland entertainment, California offers countless ways to get wet, including canoeing, kayaking, and river rafting. The River Travel Center, Box 6, Pt. Arena, CA 95468 (800-882-7238) serves as a liaison between would-be rafters and outfitters. They can place you in one of over 1000 white-water rafting trips ranging in length from 2 to 21 days. Mountain schools at Yosemite offer instruction in rock-climbing and spelunking. When the weather grows cold (yes, it *does* happen), the Sierra Nevada features a number of large ski resorts. The Sierra Club, 730 Polk St., San Francisco, CA 94109 (415-776-2211), has information on year-round outings.

SPECTATOR SPORTS

California is home to more professional sport teams than any other state in the Union. Five major league baseball teams, four NFL football teams, four NBA basketball teams, and, even in the land of surf and sun, three NHL ice hockey teams. After thriving in the '80s with multiple championships in several sports, California's professional teams have encountered tougher times in the '90s. The college sports scene includes USC, UCLA, Stanford, and U.C. Berkeley; all boast powerhouse NCAA Division I sports programs. The New Year's Day Rose Bowl football game in Pasadena is known as "the granddaddy of them all."

California also makes room for more offbeat sports. There's beach volleyball, surfing tournaments, and, yes indeed, the world's first long-distance rollerblade race.

SAND AND SURF

California, more than anywhere else, has developed a distinct beach subculture. Bronze, bewhistled lifeguards survey Vuarnet-sporting surfers, middle-aged, book-toting sunbathers, and sand-sculpting children alike. Radios still blast the tunes of those California icons, the Beach Boys, recalling the days of Annette and Frankie and *Gidget Goes Hawaiian.*

Dedicated tanners (like *Doonesbury*'s Zonker Harris, for whom a California beach is actually named) devote their beach hours to oil and prostration, but you can indulge in a number of more active—and less carcinogenic—beach activities, including bodysurfing, snorkeling, scuba diving, and windsurfing. On the quiet and more visually spectacular northern coast, beachcombing, clamming, and fishing are all popular.

Although illegal in some areas, nude sunbathing flourishes. There are often clothed people at nude beaches, and, occasionally, the reverse is true. *Let's Go* lists nude beaches whenever possible.

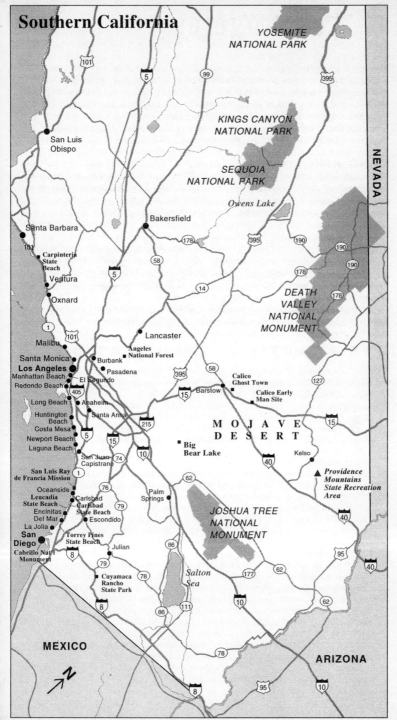

SOUTHERN CALIFORNIA

Los Angeles

Though it defies the very notion of "urban," Los Angeles paradoxically remains the most American of cities. It embodies much of what many find wrong with the U.S., yet millions of people would never live anywhere else. Since L.A.'s most celebrated industry is the production and dissemination of images, it is not surprising that Angelenos are often accused of confusing perception with reality. Increasingly, however, they have been forced to look beyond the glitter of Universal Studios, the mammoth billboards of the Sunset Strip, and the opulence of Rodeo Drive, and acknowledge a growing range of social and environmental problems.

In the past few years, L.A. has had to contend not only with its perennial woes (overcrowded freeways, smog, and drought), but also with the fires in Malibu, the looting and arson in the wake of the acquittal of the police officers implicated in the beating of Rodney King, and an earthquake measuring 6.6 on the Richter scale. But Angelenos have proved themselves a resilient bunch, facing each fresh tragedy with renewed affirmation of the philosophy that made their city famous: it is here that the most extravagant dreams can be realized.

However battered, this credo persists; for some becoming a reality and for others a cruel reminder of their plight. Through it all, L.A. keeps growing. A drive into the far reaches of the L.A. Basin, to Simi Valley, to San Bernardino, and even up Rte. 14 toward Lancaster and Palmdale and the Mojave Desert reveals the wooden skeletons of new tract houses and the creeping tendrils of outer suburbia. Even Bakersfield, over 100 mi. to the northwest, plans to build a light-rail connection to L.A. anticipating the day when it forms just another of the proverbial "suburbs in search of a city."

■■■ PRACTICAL INFORMATION

Basic Orientation: Los Angeles is enormous; it is wise to acquaint yourself with its layout before you arrive. L.A. is best understood as a set of five distinctive regions: **Downtown, Hollywood,** the **Westside** (including West Hollywood, Westwood, Century City, and—unofficially—Beverly Hills), **Coast** (including Malibu, Santa Monica, Venice, and the southern beaches), and the **Valley region** (including the San Fernando Valley, San Gabriel and Pasadena.) The information given below is by no means a comprehensive listing for these regions. For further details, refer to each individual region.

Visitors Information:

Los Angeles Convention and Visitors Bureau, 685 S. Figueroa St. 90017 (213-689-8822), between Wilshire and 7th St. Downtown, in the Financial District. Hundreds of brochures. Staff speaks Spanish, Filipino, Japanese, French, and German. Good maps for downtown streets, sights, and buses. Publishes *Destination Los Angeles,* a free booklet including tourist information, a lodgings guide, and a shopping directory. Open Mon.-Fri. 8am-5pm, Sat. 8:30am-5pm. In **Hollywood** at 6541 Hollywood Blvd. (213-461-4213). Open Mon.-Sat. 9am-5pm.

National Park Service, 30401 Agoura Rd., Agoura Hills, in the San Conejo Valley (818-597-9192 for local parks Info Center; 800-533-7275 for other parks). Info. on the Santa Monica Mountains and other parks. Open Mon.-Sat. 8am-5pm.

Los Angeles County Parks and Recreation, 433 S. Vermont (213-738-2961). Complete directions to and information about parks, services, and sports. Helpful specifics for cyclists. Open Mon.-Thurs. 7am-5:30pm.

Sierra Club, 3345 Wilshire Blvd. #508 (213-387-4287). Hiking, biking, and backpacking information. Ask about group outings. Open Mon.-Fri. 10am-6pm.

Budget Travel: Council Travel, 1093 Broxton Ave. Suite 220, Westwood Village (310-208-3551), above the Wherehouse record store. Cheap flights, HI-AYH memberships, ISICs. Open Mon.-Fri. 9am-5pm, Sat. 10am-2pm. **STA Travel,** 7202 Melrose Ave. (213-934-8722). Similar services; open Mon.-Fri. 10am-6pm.

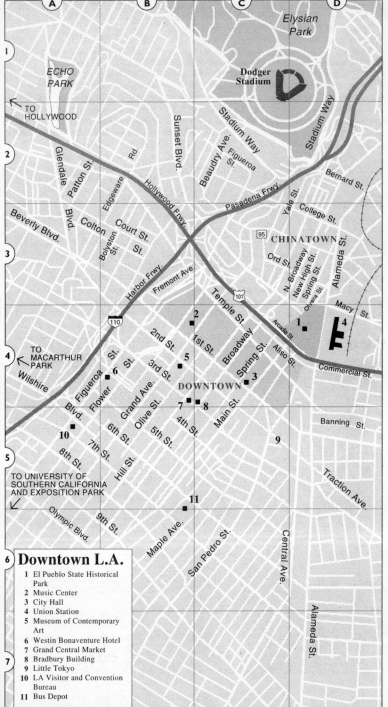

Downtown L.A.

1 El Pueblo State Historical Park
2 Music Center
3 City Hall
4 Union Station
5 Museum of Contemporary Art
6 Westin Bonaventure Hotel
7 Grand Central Market
8 Bradbury Building
9 Little Tokyo
10 LA Visitor and Convention Bureau
11 Bus Depot

Los Angeles Council AYH: 1434 2nd St., Santa Monica (310-393-3413). Information and supplies for travelers. Guidebooks, backpacks, low-cost flights, rail passes, and ISICs. Open Mon.-Fri. noon-7pm, Sat. 10am-5pm.

Consulates: U.K., 1766 Wilshire Blvd. (310-477-3322). Open 9am-5pm for calls, 9am-1pm for visas. **Japan,** California Plaza II, 350 South Grand Ave., 17th floor (213-624-8305). Open Mon.-Fri. 9:30-11:30am and 1-4pm for calls. **Australia,** 611 N. Larchmont Blvd. (213-469-4300). Open Mon.-Fri. 8:45am-5pm. **South Africa,** 50 N. La Cienega Blvd. (310-657-9200). Open Mon.-Fri. 9am-5pm.

Currency Exchange: at most LAX terminals (see Getting There, page 72), and most banks.

American Express: 901 W. 7th St. (213-627-4800), downtown. Open Mon.-Fri. 8am-6pm. Also in **Beverly Hills** across from the Beverly Center at 8493 W. 3rd St. (310-659-1682; open Mon.-Fri. 9am-7pm, Sat. 10am-6pm). More locations in **Pasadena, Torrance,** and **Costa Mesa.**

Los Angeles International Airport: see Getting There, page 72.

Greyhound-Trailways Information Center: 716 E. 7th St. (800-231-2222), at Alameda, downtown. Call for fares, schedules, and local ticket information. See neighborhood listings for other stations. See Getting There, page 72, for information on the main downtown terminal.

MTA Bus Information Line: 213-626-4455. Customer Service Center at 5301 Wilshire Blvd. Open Mon.-Fri. 8:30am-5pm.

Taxi: Checker Cab (213-482-3456), **Independent** (213-385-8294), **United Independent** (213-653-5050), **Celebrity Red Top** (213-934-6700). If you need a cab, it's best to call. Approximate fare from LAX to downtown is $27.

Car/Bicycle Rentals: see Getting Around, page 73.

Automobile Club of Southern California: 2601 S. Figueroa St. (213-741-3111), at Adams. Lots of maps and information free to AAA members. Their *Westways* magazine is a good source for daytrips or vacations. Open Mon.-Fri. 9am-5pm. Numerous other offices in the Greater L.A. area. Call for locations.

Central Public Library: 433 S. Spring St. (213-612-3200). A Los Angeles address is required to check out books, but reading rooms are open to all. Open Mon.-Sat. 10am-5:30pm. Another location at 630 W. 5th St. between Grand and Flower. Open Mon., Thurs.-Sat. 10am-5:30pm, Tues.-Wed. 2-8pm, Sun. 1-5pm.

Gay and Lesbian Community Services Center: 1625 N. Hudson Ave., Hollywood (213-993-7400), 1 block from Hollywood Blvd. Youth and senior groups, counseling, employment, housing, educational, legal and medical services. Building open Mon.-Sat. 9am-10pm, but most offices close around 5pm.

Japanese-American Cultural and Community Center: 244 S. San Pedro St., Room 506 (213-628-2725). Offers the Doizaki Gallery, Franklin G. Murphy Library, and a movie theater. Administration offices open Mon.-Fri. 9am-6pm.

Jewish Community Center: 5870 W. Olympic Ave. (213-938-2531). Recreational facilities, senior citizens' services, day care, health club. Pool and gym open until about 9pm, other facilities 9am-3pm. 1-day guest pass $10.

Senior Citizens Information: Department of Aging, 2404 Wilshire Blvd., Suite 400 (213-368-4000). Open Mon.-Fri. 8am-5pm.

Los Angeles County Commission on Disabilities: 500 W. Temple St. (213-974-1053). Information on transportation and recreational facilities for people with disabilities. Open Mon.-Fri. 8:30am-5pm.

California Relay Service for the Hearing Impaired: 800-735-2929 (TTD/TTY). 24-hr. assistance.

Ticketmaster: 213-480-3232.

Beach Information: 310-457-9701, recording for Malibu, Santa Monica, and South Bay. Most FM radio stations have a surf report at noon.

Weather: 213-554-1212. An excruciatingly detailed region-by-region report.

Highway Conditions: 213-626-7231. May help you stave off an afternoon stuck on the freeway. AM radio stations offer frequent reports.

Hotlines: AIDS Hotline, 800-922-2437. For recorded information, call 976-4700. There is a small charge for this service. **Rape Crisis,** 310-392-8381. 24-hr. hotline. **Crisis Response** service, 310-855-3506. **Police,** 213-626-5273. **Fire,** 213-483-6721.

TO
GRIFFITH
PARK

Vermont Ave.

Franklin Ave.

Hollywood Frwy.

HOLLYWOOD

Western Ave.

Santa Monica Blvd.

3rd St.

Olympic Blvd.

Crenshaw Blvd

Highland Ave.

La Brea Blvd.

WEST
HOLLYWOOD

Sunset Blvd.

Hollywood Blvd.

Franklin Ave.

Melrose Ave.

Beverly Blvd.

Fairfax Ave.

Kings Rd.

San Vincente Blvd.

Pico Blvd.

Venice Blvd.

La Cienega

3rd St.

Blvd.

BEVERLY
HILLS

Sunset
Blvd.

Wilshire Blvd.

Olympic Blvd.

Santa Monica Frwy.

Rodeo Dr.

WESTWOOD

Westwood Blvd.

N ←

University
of California
Los Angeles

WESTWOOD
VILLAGE

BEL AIR

Sunset Blvd.

San Diego Frwy.

TO
SANTA MONICA
AND VENICE

TO
SANTA MONICA
AIRPORT

L.A. Westside

1 Armand Hammer Museum of
  Art and Cultural Center
2 Century City
3 Beverly Hills Hotel
4 Pacific Design Center
5 Schindler House
6 Beverly Center
7 Farmer's Market
8 Los Angeles County Museum
  of Art

9 La Brea Tar Pits
10 Max Factor Museum
11 Mann's Chinese Theater
12 Hollywood Wax Museum
13 Frederick's of Hollywood
14 Barnsdall Park
15 I. Magnin BW Wilshire

Medical Services (see local listings below for more hospitals):
Ambulance: Los Angeles City Ambulance Emergency Service, 213-483-6721. **MedExpress Services,** 213-461-8704, a private ambulance company.
Hospitals: Good Samaritan, 616 S. Witmer St. (213-977-2121). **Cedars-Sinai Medical Center,** 8700 Beverly Blvd. (310-855-5000, emergency 310-855-6517).
Planned Parenthood: 1057 Kingston St. (213-226-0800), near downtown. Call for other locations. Birth control, pre-natal care, treatment of STDs, abortions, and counseling. Call 1 week ahead for appointment. Sliding scale for fees. Open Mon.-Fri. 8am-6pm.
Hollywood-Sunset Free Clinic: 3324 W. Sunset Blvd. (213-660-2400). Open daily 10am-10pm.
Valley Free Clinic: 5648 Vineland, Hollywood (818-763-8836). Women's health, birth control, optometry, medical and legal counseling, and drug "diversion" services. Hours vary; appointments required by phone Mon.-Fri. 10am-4pm.
Physicians Referral Service: 150 N. Robertson Blvd. (310-657-6494).
24-Hour Pharmacy: Sav-On, 3010 S. Sepulveda Blvd. (310-478-9821), near downtown in West L.A. Call 800-627-2866 for other 24-hr. locations.
Post Office: Most convenient branch at 900 N. Alameda, at 9th St. (310-431-6546). Open Mon.-Fri. 9am-5pm, Sat. 9am-noon. **ZIP Code information:** 213-586-1737. **General Delivery ZIP Code:** 90086.
Area Codes: Downtown Los Angeles, Hollywood, Huntington Park, Vernon, and Montebello **213.** Malibu, Pacific Coast Highway, Westside, southern and eastern Los Angeles County **310.** Northern Los Angeles County, San Fernando Valley, and Pasadena **818.** Orange County **714.** San Diego County **619.** Ventura County **805.**

HOLLYWOOD

Visitors Information: The Janes House, 6541 Hollywood Blvd. (213-624-7300), in Janes House Sq. Provides L.A. visitor guides. Open Mon.-Sat. 9am-5pm. **Hollywood Chamber of Commerce,** 7000 Hollywood Blvd., Suite 1 (213-469-8311). Open Mon.-Fri. 9am-5pm.
MTA Customer Service Center: 6249 Hollywood Blvd. (213-972-6000). Free information, maps, timetables. Open Mon.-Fri. 10am-6pm. **Important buses:** #1 along Hollywood Blvd., #2 and 3 along Sunset Blvd., #4 along Santa Monica Blvd., #10 along Melrose. Fare $1.10, transfers 25¢. 1-month pass $42, ½-month $23.
Greyhound: 1409 N. Vine St. (213-466-6381), 1 block south of Sunset Blvd. To: Santa Barbara (9 per day, $14, $26 round-trip); San Diego (13 per day, $20, $38 round-trip); San Francisco (10 per day, $29). Terminal open daily 6:30am-11pm. Locker storage available.
Hospital: Queen of Angels Hollywood Presbyterian Medical Center, 1300 N. Vermont Ave. (213-413-3000). 24-hr. emergency room.
Police: 1358 N. Wilcox Ave. (213-485-4302).
Post Office: 1615 Wilcox Ave. (213-464-2194). Open Mon.-Fri. 8am-5pm, Sat. 8am-1pm. **General Delivery ZIP Code:** 90028
Area Code: 213.

SANTA MONICA

Visitors Information: 1400 Ocean Ave. (310-393-7593), in Palisades Park. Sparse selection of local maps and brochures, but the helpful staff can provide information on attractions and events. Open daily 10am-5pm; winter 10am-4pm.
American Express: 1250 4th St. (395-9588).
Greyhound: 1433 5th St. (310-394-1648), between Broadway and Santa Monica Blvd. Open Mon.-Sat. 9:30am-5pm. To: Santa Barbara (2 per day, 2½hr., $13); San Diego (4 per day, 3½hr., $21); San Francisco (3 per day, 11hr., $29). No lockers.
Santa Monica Municipal (Big Blue) Bus Lines: 1660 7th St. (310-451-5444), at Olympic. Open Mon.-Fri. 8am-5pm. Faster and cheaper than the MTA. Fare 50¢ for most routes, and 25¢ transfer tickets for MTA buses. Transfers to other Big Blue buses are free. **Important buses:** #1 and #2 connect Santa Monica and Venice. Bus #10 provides express service from downtown Santa Monica (at 7th and Grand) to downtown L.A.

The Tide Shuttle: A free service connecting Santa Monica Place to Barnard Way and Main St. Runs every 15 min. daily from noon-9pm.

Parking: 3 hrs. free in municipal structures 7 and 8 on 2nd St. All other city parking is metered (25¢ per hr.). All-day beachside parking $5.

Library: Main Branch at 6th and Santa Monica Blvd. (310-458-8600).

Laundromat: Easywash Laundromat, 1306 Wilshire Blvd. (310-451-0046). Many hostels also have laundries; check accommodations listings.

Hospital: St. John's, 1328 22nd St. (310-829-5511), at Arizona St.

Police: 1685 Main St. (310-395-9931).

Post Office: 5th and Arizona (310-576-2626). Open Mon.-Fri. 9am-6pm, Sat. 9am-1pm. **General Delivery ZIP Code:** 90406.

Area Code: 310.

■ PUBLICATIONS

The free *L.A. Weekly* (213-468-9909) is the definitive source of entertainment listings. *Weeklys* come out on Thursday. You can pick up a copy at record stores, restaurants, coffee houses, liquor stores, and newsstands all over L.A. *The Reader* is the *Weekly's* smaller competitor. L.A., of course, has a number of "industry" (e.g. movie) papers, with the best-known being *Variety. The Hollywood Reporter* is the next best.

The *Los Angeles Times* (newsstand 35¢) defeats all rival **dailies** with top reporting and a wonderful crossword. The *Times's* "Calendar" section is a good source of accurate and up-to-date dope about what's going on where.

Most areas in L.A. have smaller papers describing local news and events. *The Goodlife* is a small throw-away serving Marina del Rey. The daily *Santa Monica Evening Outlook* serves the westside and beach areas. The *San Gabriel Valley Tribune* is a daily serving (you guessed it) the San Gabriel Valley. Beverly Hills is graced with a number of gossipy throw-aways (*213, The Courier, The Independent). The Los Angeles Sentinel* is L.A.'s largest **African-American** paper. *The Daily Bruin* is **UCLA**'s student paper, published during the school year. The two most popular **gay** newspapers are *The Frontiers* and *Edge.*

A multinational city, L.A. also has numerous foreign language publications. The **Spanish** *La Opinión* is the largest, but two **Korean** papers (*The Korean Central Daily,* and *The Korean Times)* are also among L.A.'s 10 largest periodicals. The *International Daily News* serves the **Chinese**-speaking community.

■ WEATHER

L.A.'s near-perpetual sunshine and mild temperatures, combined with its majestic geography are among its biggest attractions. However, this appealing combination, and the millions it has attracted, has resulted in poor air quality as the surrounding mountains trap lingering pollutants within the Los Angeles basin and inland valleys. The severity of the problem has been recognized and steps are being taken to improve air quality, but the smog lingers. On especially smoggy days, ozone readings are often two and a half times higher than federal standards. The smog is worst in industrial areas and in the inland valleys; the coastal areas are clearer. While the smog is noticeable to visitors and unhealthy for all, most residents have grown used to it. One perverse side effect of the smog is the eerily beautiful Southern California sunsets. If you catch this city on a clear day, take a moment to appreciate its breathtaking vistas of snow-capped peaks on one side and the ocean on the other. (**Weather information:** 213-554-1212. **Air quality information:** 800-242-4666.)

■■■ ORIENTATION

GETTING THERE

Los Angeles sprawls along the coast of Southern California, 127 mi. north of San Diego and 403 mi. south of San Francisco. You can still be "in" L.A. even if you're 50 mi. from downtown. Greater L.A. encompasses the urbanized areas of Orange, Riverside, San Bernardino, and Ventura counties.

By Car

General approaches to Greater L.A. are **I-5** from the south, **Rte. 1, U.S. 101,** or **I-5** from the north, and **I-10** or **I-15** from the east. The city itself is crisscrossed by over a dozen freeways. Driving into L.A. can be unnerving if you've never before run the gauntlet of ramps, exits, four-story directional signs, and confident, speedy natives.

By Train and Bus

Amtrak rolls into Union Station, 800 N. Alameda (213-624-0171), at the northwestern edge of the heart of downtown Los Angeles. Buses travel out of the station to Pasadena and Long Beach; get information upon arrival. Trains run to San Francisco (1 per day, 12hr., $75) and San Diego (9 per day, 3hr., $24).

Visitors arriving by **Greyhound** disembark at 716 E. 7th St. (800-231-2222), downtown, in a rough neighborhood. Greyhound also stops in Hollywood, Santa Monica, Pasadena, and other parts of the metropolitan area (see Practical Information, above). Continuing to other area stations is far safer than disembarking downtown, especially after dark. It is possible, though not recommended, to reach area stations by MTA's public buses. Exercise caution when seeking out 7th and Alameda St., one block southwest of the downtown station. Here, you can catch MTA buses #320 and #20 traveling westward along Wilshire Blvd. Bus #1 stops at 5th and Broadway, four blocks to the west and one block north, and travels westward along Hollywood Blvd. Greyhound buses go to: San Diego (68 per day, 2-3hr., $12); Tijuana (39 per day, 3-4hr., $17.50, $26 round-trip); Santa Barbara (27 per day, 2-3½hr., $11.50); San Francisco (38 per day, 8-10hr., $29). Lockers are $1 per day.

Green Tortoise (310-392-1990), has northbound "hostels on wheels" leaving L.A. every Sunday night with stops in Venice, Hollywood, and downtown. Call for reservations and exact departure location and times. (See Essentials: By Bus, page 35, for more information.)

By Plane

Los Angeles International Airport (LAX) is located in **Westchester,** about 15 mi. southwest of downtown, 10 mi. southeast of Santa Monica, and 1 mi. east of the coast. The airport complex is divided into two levels, the upper serving departures and the lower, arrivals. Terminal 2 serves international carriers. LAX can be a confusing airport, but there are plenty of help stations and electronic information kiosks inside. **LAX information** is 310-646-5252. **Travelers Aid,** an information and referral service for people in transit having major emergencies, is available in all terminals (open daily 7am-10pm). **Currency Exchange** is available at **L.A. Currency Agencies** (310-417-0366) in terminals 2 and 5, and in the international terminal (7am-11pm). 24-hr. **airport security** can be contacted at 310-646-4268.

Do *not* accept an offer of free transportation to an unknown hostel from the airport—chances are good you'll end up being charged $30 a night to stay in someone's garage. Airport solicitation is illegal and is a good indicator that a potential hostel is operating illegally as well. Do not compromise your safety in exchange for a ready ride and an empty promise. *Let's Go* lists a number of established hostels, many of which *will* provide transportation assistance if you call from the airport or bus stations. See Accommodations, page 80.

Aside from renting a car, there are several **transit** options from the airport:

Metropolitan Transit Authority (MTA) service stops at the **transfer terminal** at Sepulveda and 96th St. To: **downtown,** bus #439 (Mon.-Fri. rush hr. only) or #42 (from LAX daily 5:30am-11:15pm; from downtown daily 5:30am-12:10am); **Westwood/UCLA,** express #560; **Long Beach,** #232; **West Hollywood** and **Beverly Hills,** #220; **Hollywood,** from West Hollywood, bus #1 (along Holly-wood Blvd.), #2 (along Sunset Blvd.), or #4 (along Santa Monica Blvd.). For spe-cific information regarding MTA buses, cabs, and shuttles, ask at the **information kiosks** located on the sidewalks directly in front of the terminals, or look for a **courtesy phone.** Savvy travelers will also use the courtesy phones to call several shuttle companies or car-rental companies and compare prices.

Metered cabs (see Practical Information, page 68) are costly; fare to downtown is about $27; Hollywood $30; Disneyland a goofy $80.

Shuttle vans offer door-to-door service from the terminal to different parts of L.A. for a flat rate. Compare rates at the information booth; prices vary widely. Typical rates are $15 downtown, $16 to Santa Monica, $35 to San Fernando Valley. A bar-gain to San Fernando is $6 round-trip on **FlyAway** (818-994-5554).

Before hopping into any of the above vehicles, check with the hostel or hotel at which you plan to stay; many of them offer complimentary transportation from the airport.

GETTING AROUND

Before you even think about navigating Los Angeles's 6500 mi. of streets and 40,000 intersections, get yourself a good **map**—Los Angeles defies all human comprehen-sion otherwise. A sound investment is the *Thomas Guide; Los Angeles County Street Guide and Directory* ($15). Travelers should also purchase regional maps for the neighborhoods in which they plan to stay.

L.A. is a city of distinctive boulevards; its shopping areas and business centers are distributed along these broad arteries. Streets throughout L.A. are designated east, west, north, and south from First and Main St. at the center of downtown.

Once the sun sets, those on foot anywhere, especially outside West L.A. and off well-lit main drags, should exercise caution. It is unwise to walk in many areas alone after dark. Be aware of the character of the neighborhood you are traveling in and be extra cautious when necessary. In L.A. there are also neighborhoods that are bet-ter avoided altogether. When exploring, plan your route carefully, and remember-— it is worth a detour to avoid passing through particularly crime-ridden areas.

A legitimate **downtown** Los Angeles does exist, but it won't help orient you toward the rest of the city. Streets running east-to-west in downtown are numbered for the most part and are crossed by streets such as Figueroa, Flower, Broadway, and Main. The heart of downtown, where most of *Let's Go's* listed downtown lodgings are found, is reasonably safe on weekdays. Park your car in a paid lot or a secure motel lot rather than on the street, not only for safety reasons, but because a quarter will buy a mere 7½ minutes of parking time on the street. The generously dispensed parking violations are some of L.A.'s less beloved souvenirs. Avoid walking around downtown after the workday ends or on weekends.

The predominately Latino section of L.A., begins east of downtown's Western Ave., with the districts of **Boyle Heights, Montebello,** and **El Monte.** South of down-town are the **University of Southern California (USC), Exposition Park,** and the districts of **Watts** and **Compton,** home to a large concentration of African Ameri-cans. The area south of downtown, known as **South Central,** suffered the brunt of the fires and looting that erupted in 1992 following the acquittal of four white police officers videotaped beating African-American Rodney King. These primarily residential districts east and south of downtown, known as South Central and **East LA,** are considered crime-ridden and have little to attract tourists. If you decide you must visit, go during the day and if you park, don't leave anything valuable in the car.

Northwest of downtown is **Hollywood,** whose most significant east-west thor-oughfares (from south to north) are Beverly, Melrose Ave., Sunset, and Hollywood.

Sunset Boulevard, which runs from the ocean to downtown, presents a cross-section of virtually everything L.A. has to offer: beach communities, lavish wealth, famous nightclubs along "the strip," sleazy motels, the old elegance of Silver Lake, and Chicano murals. Hollywood Boulevard runs just beneath the Hollywood Hills, where split-level buildings perched precariously on hillsides are home to screenwriters, actors, and producers.

The next major region, known informally as the **Westside,** encompasses West Hollywood, Westwood, Century City, Culver City, Crenshaw, Bel Air, Brentwood and (for our purposes) the independent city of **Beverly Hills.** Containing some of L.A.'s most affluent communities, the Westside also is home to the University of California at Los Angeles (UCLA, in Westwood Village), and the trendy, off-beat Melrose Avenue hangouts. The area west of downtown is known as the **Wilshire District** after its main boulevard. **Hancock Park,** a green and affluent residential area, covers the northeast portion of the district—the 5900 area—and harbors the Los Angeles County Museum of Art and the George C. Page Fossil Museum.

The **Valley Region** spreads north of the Hollywood Hills and the Santa Monica Mountains. For most people, *the* valley is the **San Fernando Valley,** where more than a million people live in the suburbs of a basin bounded in the north and west by the Santa Susanna Mountains and the Simi Freeway, in the south by the Ventura Freeway, and to the east by the Golden State Freeway. The valleys also contain the suburbs of **San Gabriel** and **Pasadena.**

Eighty mi. of beach line L.A.'s **Coastal Region. Zuma** is northernmost, followed by **Malibu,** which lies 15 mi. up the coast from **Santa Monica.** Just a bit farther south is the funky and famous beach community of **Venice.** The beach towns south of Santa Monica, comprising the area called the **South Bay,** are Marina del Rey, El Segundo, and Manhattan, Hermosa, and Redondo Beaches. South across the **Palos Verdes Peninsula** is **Long Beach,** a port city of a half-million people. Finally, farthest south are the **Orange County** beach cities: Seal Beach, Sunset Beach, Huntington Beach, Newport Beach, and Laguna Beach. Confused yet? Invest in good maps.

Public Transportation

Nowhere in America is the great god of Automobile held in greater reverence than in L.A. In the 1930s and '40s, General Motors, Firestone, and Standard Oil colluded to buy up the street car companies and run them into the ground, later ripping up the rails. This increased dependence on buses and, after they were largely phased out, on cars. In 1949 G.M. was convicted in federal court of criminal conspiracy—but it didn't bring back the trolleys or make public transportation any easier.

Most Angelenos insist that it's impossible to live in or visit Los Angeles without a car, but the **Metropolitan Transit Authority (MTA)** does work—sort of. The MTA was formerly known as the RTD (Rapid Transit District) and some older buses may still be labeled as such. With over 200 routes and several independent municipal transit systems complementing the MTA, you may need an extra day just to study timetables. Using the MTA to sightsee in L.A. can be frustrating simply because attractions tend to be spread out. Those determined to see *everything* in L.A. should get behind the wheel of a car. If this is not possible, base yourself in downtown or in Hollywood (where there are plenty of bus connections), make daytrips, and have plenty of change for the bus. Bus service is dismal in the outer reaches of the city, and two-hour journeys are not unusual. The buses themselves are speedy (although not as fast as in *Speed* and you probably won't spot Keanu on them), but transferring often involves interminable waits, and the omnipresent L.A. traffic congestion is enough to make you cry.

To familiarize yourself with the MTA write for a **Riders Kit,** MTA, Los Angeles 90001 (this address is sufficient), or stop by one of the 10 **customer service centers.** There are three **downtown:** ARCO Plaza, 505 S. Flower St., Level C (open Mon.-Fri. 7:30am-3:30pm); 419 S. Main St. (open Mon.-Fri. 8am-4:30pm); and 1016 S. Main St. (open Tues.-Sat. 10am-6pm, Sat. 10am-6pm). The MTA prints **route maps** for the different sections of the city: Downtown, West L.A., Burbank/Glendale/Pasadena,

South Central L.A., South Bay, and the San Fernando Valley. Also available are a list of customer service centers and a brochure called *MTA Self-Guided Tours,* which details how to reach the most important sights from downtown. If you don't have time to map your route in advance, call 800-2-LA-RIDE, -2-52-7433, (TDD 800-252-9040; daily 5:30am-11:30pm) for transit information and schedules. Ninety percent of MTA's lines offer **wheelchair-accessible buses** (call 1 hr. in advance, 800-621-7828 daily 6am-10pm). All bus stops with accessible service are marked with the international symbol of access.

Bus service is best downtown and along the major thoroughfares west of downtown. (There is 24-hr. service, for instance, on Wilshire Blvd.) The downtown **DASH shuttle** is only 25¢ and serves Chinatown, Union Station (use DASH to get downtown from Union Station), Olvera Street, City Hall, Little Tokyo, the Music Center, ARCO Plaza, and more. DASH also operates a shuttle on Sunset Blvd. in Hollywood, as well as shuttles in Pacific Palisades, Fairfax (running from Farmer's Market to 3rd and La Brea), Venice Beach, and Watts. (Downtown DASH operates Mon.-Fri. 6:30am-6:30pm, Sat. 10am-5pm; the Pacific Palisades shuttles do not run on Sat. Schedule information, 800-2LA-RIDE, -252-7433.) MTA's **basic fare** is $1.10, passengers with disabilities 45¢; transfers 25¢, 10¢ for seniors and disabled; exact change, bills accepted. (60 DASH coupons $15.) Transfers operate from one MTA line to another or to another transit authority, such as Santa Monica Municipal Bus Lines, Culver City Municipal Bus Lines, or Long Beach Transit. **All route numbers given are MTA unless otherwise designated.**

Gray Line Tours, 6541 Hollywood Blvd., Hollywood (213-856-5900), is a more expensive but easier way to reach distant attractions. Costs include transportation and admission: Disneyland $62 for the day, $65 for day and evening; Magic Mountain $62; Universal Studios $50; San Diego Zoo $57; Sea World $60. Prices listed are for adults; children's prices are $10-15 less. Tours leave from the Gray Line office for 200 different locations in summertime.

Some youth hostels offer bus trips to area beaches and attractions for reasonable fees or free. Call or inquire upon checking in.

In a desperate, expensive, last-ditch effort to alleviate the congestion that threatens to choke the city, LA has finally started building a **subway.** The first leg of L.A.'s 300-mi. Metro Rail Plan, the Blue Line, presently runs from 7th St. in Downtown to Long Beach (call 213-626-4455 for information). The Red Line currently runs from MacArthur Park Station in Westlake to Union Station downtown (5 stops, 7 min.).

Freeways

The freeway is perhaps the most enduring of L.A.'s images. When uncongested, these well-marked, 10- and 12-lane concrete roadways offer speed and convenience; the trip from downtown to Santa Monica can take as little as 20 minutes. A nighttime cruise along the Harbor Hwy. past downtown—whizzing through the tangle of interchanges and on- and off-ramps, with the lights of L.A.'s skyscrapers providing a dramatic, futuristic backdrop—can be exhilarating.

The most frustrating aspect of driving is the sheer unpredictability of L.A. traffic. It goes without saying that rush hours, both morning and evening, are always a mess and well worth avoiding, but with construction performed at random hours there can be problems anytime. The solution? Patience. A little reminder: no matter how crowded the freeway is, it's almost always quicker and safer than taking surface streets to your destination.

Californians refer to their highways by names rather than by numbers. These names are little more than hints of a freeway's route, at best harmless, at worst misleading. For freeway information, call **CalTrans** (213-897-3693).

I-405, the **San Diego Freeway.** At times, roughly parallel to the Pacific Coast Highway (Rte. 1), but approximately 10 mi. inland, it links the San Fernando Valley with Westwood, Beverly Hills, LAX, and Long Beach. (Connects with I-10 in West-

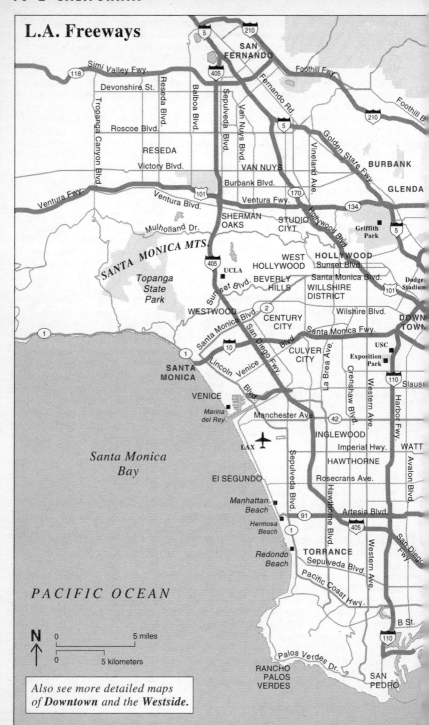

L.A. Freeways

*Also see more detailed maps of **Downtown** and the **Westside**.*

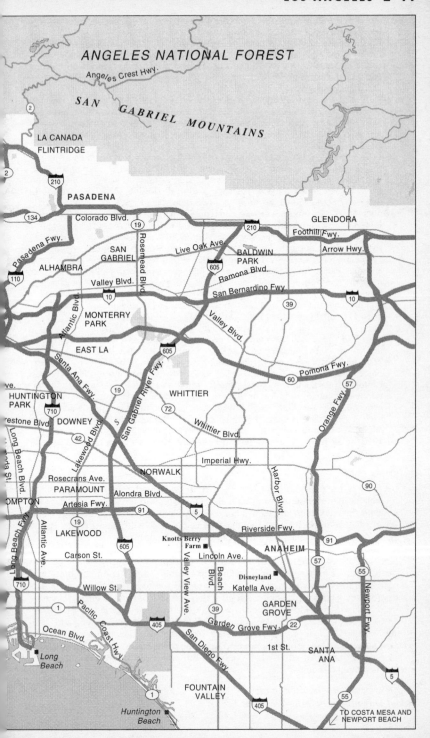

wood, U.S. 101 in Van Nuys, I-5 in the northern reaches of the San Fernando Valley, I-110 in San Pedro at the southern end of the city.)

I-10, the **Santa Monica Freeway,** west of downtown. The main commuter link to the western portions of the city: Century City, Westwood, and Santa Monica. Called the **San Bernardino Freeway** east of downtown. (Connects with Rte. 1 in Santa Monica, I-405 in Westwood, I-110 in downtown, Rte. 60 in East L.A., I-210 in Pomona.)

I-5, the **Golden State Freeway,** pierces the heart of central California parallel to I-405 and Rte. 1. It comes to within 50 mi. of the coast as it moves through the San Fernando Valley. Called the **Santa Ana Freeway** south of downtown, it serves Anaheim and Orange County. (Connects with I-110 just north of downtown, U.S. 101 in Glendale.)

I-110, called the **Pasadena Freeway** north of downtown (it starts in Pasadena) or the **Harbor Freeway** south of downtown where it runs by USC, Exposition Park, and Watts on its way to San Pedro, is the nation's first freeway. (Connects with Rte. 1 in San Pedro, I-405 in Torrance, I-10 in downtown L.A., U.S. 101 also in downtown L.A., and I-5 just north of downtown.)

Route 60, the **Pomona Freeway,** runs roughly parallel to I-10 east of downtown. It is sometimes less crowded. (Connects with I-10 in East Los Angeles.)

U.S. 101, the **Ventura Freeway** from Ventura to North Hollywood, runs inland from Ventura along the outer rim of the Santa Monica Mountains in the San Fernando Valley, serving Thousand Oaks, Woodland Hills, Encino, Van Nuys, Sherman Oaks, Studio City, and North Hollywood. In North Hollywood it veers over the Santa Monica Mountains toward Hollywood, Silver Lake, and downtown—becoming the **Hollywood Freeway.** (Connects with Rte. 1 in Ventura, I-405 in Sherman Oaks, Rte. 134 in Studio City, and I-110 downtown.

Route 118, the **Simi Valley Freeway,** runs east-west linking such increasingly far-flung bedroom communities as Simi Valley with I-5 in San Fernando.

Route 134, also called the **Ventura Freeway,** continues east from U.S. 101 in Studio City through Glendale and Pasadena. (Connects with Rte. 210 in Pasadena.)

I-210, the **Foothill Freeway,** runs at the base of the San Gabriel Mountains at the outer edge of the San Fernando Valley. Less crowded than most, it links La Crescenta, Pasadena, and Pomona. (Connects with Rte. 134 in Pasadena, I-10 at its terminus in Pomona, and I-5 at its other end in northern San Fernando Valley.)

Route 605, the **San Gabriel Freeway,** runs north-south from Long Beach to the San Gabriel Valley. (Connects with I-405 in Long Beach, I-5 in Downey, Rte. 60 in Whittier, I-10 in El Monte, Rte. 210 in the San Gabriel Valley.)

I-105, the $2 billion **Glen Anderson Freeway,** runs east from LAX and the San Diego Fwy. to the San Gabriel Riverbed, which parallels Rte. 605.

Cars

L.A. may be the most difficult city in the U.S. to get around in without a car. Unfortunately, it may also be the most difficult city in which to rent a car, especially for younger travelers. Most places will not rent to people under 21, and the ones that do are likely to impose a surcharge that may nearly double the standard rate. Rental agencies impose a smaller fine on anyone between 21 and 25.

Nationally known agencies are reputed to have more dependable cars, but the demand for rental cars assures that even small local companies can survive, and many have far lower rates or be willing to bargain. Comparison shopping and searching for weekly rates will help you save. Be warned, local rental companies may quote a very low daily rate, but once they are sure of your business, they may more than make up the difference by adding extra fees when you return the car. Be sure to read the fine print and ask questions. Remember that the Collision and Damage Waiver (CDW) is optional, but be sure that you have sufficient insurance coverage. And again, shop around before you rent. The prices quoted below are intended to give you a rough idea of what to expect, but prices can vary widely. Ask about airline-related discounts.

Avon Rent-A-Car, 8459 Sunset Blvd. (213-654-5533; fax 654-4979). Rent econ-
omy-size cars for as low as $15 per day with 100 free mi.; 20¢ per mi. thereafter.
$90 per week. CDW $9 per day. Drivers 18-20 pay $15 per day surcharge, $5 per
day for 21-24. Open Mon.-Fri. 7:30am-8pm, Sat.-Sun. 9:30am-4pm.

Thrifty Car Rental (800-367-2277), at LAX. As low as $26 per day, unlimited mile-
age within the U.S. $140 per week. CDW $9 per day. Must be 21 with credit card,
under 25 pay $15 per day surcharge. Open 24 hrs.

Alamo Rentals (800-327-9633), at LAX. Prices vary with availability, $21 per day,
$120 per week, unlimited mileage. CDW $9 per day. Must be over 21 with major
credit card. Under 25 pay $15 per day surcharge. Open 24 hrs.

Capri Rent-A-Car, 8620 Airport Blvd. (310-641-2323). Offers free transportation
to and from LAX. $23 per day with 150 free mi. Must be 25 with a major credit
card. Open daily 8am-8pm.

Penny Rent-A-Car, 12425 Victory Blvd., N. Hollywood (818-786-1733). $25 per
day with 75 free mi., 15¢ per additional mi. $150 per week with 500 free mi.
CDW $9 per day. Must be at least 18. Open Mon.-Fri. 8am-6pm, Sat. 8am-2pm,
Sun. 10am-noon.

The city's most comprehensive **rideboard** is at UCLA's Ackerman Union, Level A.
Ackerman is the center of campus, two blocks north of the Westwood Blvd. terminus. Also check the classified section of papers such as *The Chronicle.* Hostels frequently post ride boards and may have contacts to auto transport companies.

Bicycles

Unless you're in Tour de France form, a bicycle in L.A. is useful only for recreational
purposes. Traffic is heavy, distances are long, and drivers aren't used to looking out
for cyclists. Try Sunday morning, when traffic is light. Always wear a helmet.

The best bike routes are along beaches, where bikers are increasingly joined by a
parade of in-line skaters. The most popular route is the **South Bay Bicycle Path.** It
runs from Santa Monica to Torrance (19 mi.), winding over the sandy beaches of the
South Bay past sunbathers, boardwalks, and in-line skaters. (Even the police ride
bikes here.) The path continues all the way to San Diego. Other bike paths include
San Gabriel River Trail, 37 mi. along the river with views of the San Gabriel Valley;
Upper Rio Hondo and **Lario Trails,** 9 and 22 mi., both free from traffic; **Kenneth
Newell Bikeway,** 10 mi. through residential Pasadena; **Sepulveda Basin Bikeway,** 7
mi. around the Sepulveda Dam Recreation Area, a large loop of some major San
Fernando Valley streets; **Griffith Park Bikeway,** 4½ mi. past the L.A. Zoo and Travel
Town train park; **Bolsa Chica Bike Path,** 10 mi. along Huntington Beach; **Santa
Ana River Bike Trail,** 22 mi. along the Santa Ana River; and the **Santa Ana Canyon
Bikeway,** 7 mi. of both street and canyon terrain. Recently, there has been some vio-
lence and gang-related activity on bike trails (South Bay Bicycle Path, San Gabriel
River Trail, Lario Trails, Santa Ana River Bike Trail), and several shootings. Never ride
alone, and if you see anything suspicious, turn around.

Most rental shops stand near the piers of the various beaches, with an especially
high concentration on Washington Blvd. near the beach in Venice/Marina del Rey.
Specific shops for these areas are listed individually under Sights (page 82, page 100,
page 101).

Walking and Hitchhiking

The band Missing Persons was right-on when it sang "Nobody walks in L.A." L.A.
pedestrians are a lonely breed. The largely deserted streets of commercial centers
will seem eerie to the first-time visitor. Unless you're running in the L.A. Marathon,
moving from one part of the city to another on foot is a ludicrous idea—distances
are just too great. Nevertheless, some colorful areas such as Melrose, Westwood,
The Santa Monica Promenade and Hollywood are best explored by foot. For lovers
of coastal culture, Venice Beach is one of the most enjoyable places to walk. Here,
you'll be in the company of thousands of other Venetian beach-goers (even more on
weekends), and Venice's sights and shopping areas are all relatively close to one

another. You may also wish to call **Walking Tours of Los Angeles** for tours of El Pueblo de Los Angeles State Historic Park (213-628-1274), City Hall (213-485-4423), or the Music Center (213-972-7483). The **Los Angeles Conservancy** (213-623-2489) offers ten different tours of the downtown area. Tours cost $5 and advance reservations are required. Call 818-753-4600 for information on Sunday walking tours of **Coldwater Canyon Park.**

Do not hitchhike. In Los Angeles, it is tantamount to suicide. It is also illegal on freeways and many streets.

■■■ ACCOMMODATIONS

As in any large city, cheap accommodations in Los Angeles are often unsafe ones as well. It can be difficult to gauge from the exterior whether a potential hotel is a dream bargain or a nightmare. Be suspicious of unusually low posted rates, they are rarely the bargains they seem. Ask to see a room before you commit. Hotels in L.A. should cost at least $35 or they're probably not the kind of hotels most travelers would feel secure in. For those willing to share a room and a bathroom, hostels (more info. below) are a saving grace. Americans should be aware that some hostels accept international travelers only. These hostels require an international passport. (One explanation for this policy is that hostels are often cheaper than paying rent, and owners fear locals will use them as permanent residences.)

Tolerable budget lodgings fall roughly into four categories: hostels, run-down but relatively safe hotels, residential hotels offering weekly rates (these can save you a bundle), and budget motels located well off the beaten track but reasonably close by car. It never hurts to ask for off-season or student discounts, and occasionally managers will lower prices to snare a prospective, but hesitating customer.

In choosing where to stay, the first consideration should be how much access you have to a car. If you don't have wheels, you would be wise to decide what element of L.A. appeals to you the most. Those visiting for the beaches would do well to choose lodgings in Venice or Santa Monica. Avid sightseers will probably be better off in Hollywood or the slightly more expensive (but cleaner and nicer) Westside. Downtown has numerous public transportation connections but an eerie lack of nightlife. Even those with a car should weigh whether they care more for the seaside or the studio tours, and choose accommodations accordingly.

Listed prices do not include L.A.'s 14% hotel tax.

DOWNTOWN

Though busy and relatively safe by day, the downtown area empties and becomes dangerous when the workday ends and on weekends. Both men and women should travel in groups after dark, especially in the area between Broadway and Main. Again, don't be afraid to haggle, especially during the off-season. Ask about weekly rates, which can be significantly cheaper.

Royal Host Olympic Motel, 901 W. Olympic Blvd. (213-626-6255; fax 488-3481). A ritzy budget hotel—beautiful rooms with bathtubs, telephone, radio, and cable TV. Singles $30, doubles $35, with kitchenettes $45. Students can sometimes get a double room for as low as $25. Discounts for stays longer than 3 days.

Hotel Stillwell, 838 S. Grand Ave. (800-553-4774 or 213-627-1151). Recently refurbished, this ultra-clean hotel is one of the most sensible downtown options. Rooms are bright and pleasantly decorated. Indian restaurant and American grill in hotel, Mexican restaurant next door. A/C, color TV. Singles $35, $175 per week. Doubles $45, $225 per week.

Milner Hotel, 813 S. Flower St. (213-627-6981 or 800-827-0411; fax 623-4751), Central location and good upkeep compensate for the slightly shabby decor. Pub, grill, and pleasant lounge area in lobby. A/C, color TV. Singles $35. Doubles $45.

Orchid Hotel, 819 S. Flower St. (213-624-5855; fax 624-8740). Next door to the Milner, the Orchid has small, but clean rooms with private baths. A/C, color TV.

Singles $30, $137 per week. Doubles $35, $162 per week. Reservations recommended.

Park Plaza Hotel, 607 S. Park View St. (213-384-5281; fax 488-3481), on the west corner of 6th St. across from sometimes noisy MacArthur Park. Built in 1927, this grandiose Art Deco giant has a 3-story marble-floored lobby and a monumental staircase. The lobby deserves a visit for its sake alone—it's a reminder of an earlier era. Was the doorman wearing a watch fob? The Plaza once entertained Bing Crosby and Eleanor Roosevelt, but now caters mainly to semi-permanent residents, especially students from the Otis Art Institute next door. A/C (in some rooms) and color TV in the clean but small and newly renovated rooms. Olympic pool. Singles from $50. Doubles $55.

City Center Motel, 1135 W. 7th St. (213-628-7141; fax 629-1064), 2 blocks west of the Hilton. Pleasant and clean. A/C, color TV, pool. Single $35, $210 per week. Double $40, $240 per week. Parking in courtyard.

Motel de Ville, 1123 W. 7th St. (213-624-8474; fax 624-7652), next door to the City Center Motel. Pool, clean rooms with free HBO. Singles $35. Doubles $43.

HOLLYWOOD

Epitomizing L.A. for many, Hollywood combines convenience and excitement for tourists; it is well-connected to other areas of the city and contains the most famous sights, restaurants, and night spots. Exercise caution if scouting out one of the many budget hotels on Hollywood or Sunset Blvds.—especially east of the main strips, the area can be frightening, particularly at night. The hostels below are often filled with plucky international travelers of all ages.

Banana Bungalow Hollywood, 2775 Cahuenga Blvd. (213-851-1129 or 800-4-HOSTEL, -467735; fax 851-1569), in Hollywood, just past the Hollywood Bowl on Highland Ave. Opened in 1992, this hostel offers a bounty of attractions, an efficient, no-nonsense staff, and a rambunctious backpacker clientele—not for quiet, shy types. The atmosphere is relentlessly fun-loving and a bit goofy, with a restaurant/party area and lots of amenities that encourage lively socializing. The hostel runs free shuttle service from the airport, as well as to area beaches and attractions (including Disneyland, Magic Mountain, and Universal Studios). Free nightly movies, arcade, and frequent parties with bouncy people bopping around. Pool, basketball court, weight room, and "snack-shack" on premises. Full restaurant serving breakfast ($1-3), lunch ($2), and dinner ($3-5) daily.24-hr. check-in. Check-out 10:30am. Standard bunks in rooms for 6, with bathroom and color TV. Rooms are mostly mixed-sex, although some are women-only. Linen included. $15 per night. Doubles $45.

Hollywood International Guest House and Hostel, 6561 Franklin Ave. (213-850-6287, 800-750-6561 in CA only), located 2 blocks north of Hollywood Blvd., corner of Whitley. A beautiful and cozy house, somewhat hidden by trees and a high fence (look for a street number, not a sign). Extremely close to Hollywood attractions. Shuttle service to LAX, beaches, tourist attractions. Home-style amenities include full kitchen, living room with books, and free coffee. Shared rooms for 2-4 people are decorated with colorful carpets and partitions. Linen included. Check-in 9am-8pm. No curfew. $12 per night. Make reservations early.

Hollywood Wilshire YMCA International Hostel, 1553 N. Hudson Ave. (213-467-4161). Located 1½ blocks south of Hollywood Blvd., the dorm-style rooms are clean and light. Common room with cable TV, full kitchen, pool table, laundry facilities, and storage lockers. Slightly cheaper than its competitors, this hostel's draw lies partly in the friendly staff and convenient location, but primarily in the complimentary use of the adjacent Y facilities: two pools, aerobic classes, high-tech weights and exercise machines, and other services. Must be over 18 and out of state. No curfew. Single sex rooms $11 per night, plus refundable $4 deposit. Free linen and breakfast. Reservations recommended 2 weeks ahead.

Hollywood International Hostel, 7038½ Hollywood Blvd. (213-463-0797 or 800-750-6561 in CA only), across the street from the Hollywood Galaxy Shopping Center. A small, low-key, 2nd-floor hostel in the heart of Hollywood Blvd. Shuttle service to beach, LAX, and amusement parks.Clean and new, though facilities limited. Slightly more urbane clientele. Small common room with 2 TVs and a microwave. Single $12 per night in room for 3-4 people, $75 per week. Double $30.

Hollywood Hills Hostel, 1921 Highland Ave. (213-850-7733; fax 310-301-2537), immediately to the left of the Hollywood Terrace Hotel and 3 blocks from the middle of Hollywood Blvd. Free pickup from airport, Greyhound, and Amtrak. Free linen and free transportation to area attractions. Large common room with TV. Laundry facilities and game room. 24-hr. check-in, 11am check-out. No curfew. Complimentary breakfast and coffee. Dinner around $5.4-6 per room; some single-sex rooms, $15.50. Double $45.

Hollywood Downtowner Motel, 5601 Hollywood Blvd. (213-464-7191). Somewhat grungy neighborhood. Pleasant, clean rooms. Swimming pool. A/C, telephone, TV. Full kitchen units $2-3 extra (min. 4-night stay for kitchenette rooms). Singles $38. Doubles $40-46. Cheaper rates in winter. Free parking.

WESTSIDE: BEVERLY HILLS, WESTWOOD, WILSHIRE DISTRICT

The Westside is an attractive and safer part of town, but for the most part, room rates are out of sight. Call the **UCLA Off-Campus Housing Office** (310-825-4491; 100 Sproul Hall; open Mon.-Fri. 8am-5pm) and see if they can put you in touch with students who have a spare room through their "roommate share board."

Century City-Westwood Motel, 10604 Santa Monica Blvd. (310-475-4422; fax 475-3236), on the southern part of the boulevard, on "Little Santa Monica," the smaller road that parallels the divided boulevard. Spanking-clean rooms have elegantly tiled bathrooms, refrigerators, color TVs, A/C, and the occasional futon for extra guests. Bathrooms *sparkle*—more than you usually get at this price. Singles $35-50, each additional person $5, up to 5 in a room. Weekly rates negotiable.

Hotel Del Flores, 409 N. Crescent Dr., Beverly Hills (310-274-5115), only 3 blocks east of chic Rodeo Dr. and 1 block south of Santa Monica Blvd. It's hard to believe that you can stay in Beverly Hills this cheaply. Communal microwaves and refrigerators. Some rooms with color TV and ceiling fans. Singles $42, with private bath $45. Doubles $55.

Crest Motel, 7701 Beverly Blvd. (213-931-8108; fax 805-371-8868), near Hollywood and Beverly Hills. An agreeable place with peachy-pink exterior. Pool, color TV, and A/C. Singles $36. Doubles $38. Lower rates in winter. $5 key deposit.

Bevonshire Lodge Motel, 7575 Beverly Blvd. (213-936-6154; fax 934-6640). Near Farmers Market and Beverly Center. Clean, attractive motel with quiet, enclosed pool area. A/C, color TV, telephones. Singles $38.50. Doubles $42.50. Kitchen in room $48.50.

Westwood Inn Motel, 10820 Wilshire Blvd. (310-474-3118), down the street from the AVCO Cinema. Marilyn Monroe is buried next door. Helpful management and special car-rental rates for guests. Parking, A/C, and TV. Spacious, reasonably clean rooms. Singles have 2 double beds, $45; $3 per additional person.

Wilshire Orange Hotel, 6060 W. 8th St. (213-931-9533), in West L.A. near Wilshire Blvd. and Fairfax Ave. Buses #20, 21, and 22 serve Wilshire Blvd. from downtown. One of L.A.'s best-located budget accommodations, but not the cheapest. Near many major sights, in a residential neighborhood. Most rooms have refrigerators, color TV; all but 2 have their own bath or share a bath with one other room. Weekly housekeeping. Many semi-permanent residents. Singles $45. Doubles $54. Reservations recommended 2 weeks in advance, especially in summer.

COASTAL: SANTA MONICA AND VENICE

The hostels at Venice Beach are havens for the young, sociable budget traveler whose highest priority is to meet other people and have an overtly "good time." You may miss the Sunset Strip (and L.A. traffic), but in return you'll find well-populated beaches, kinky architecture, and a mellow and unpretentious community devoted to worshiping the sun and cultivating its own eccentricities. If you do decide to venture into L.A.'s depths, the city center connects to Santa Monica's Big

Blue Bus or the MTA. The hostels are a popular destination for foreign students, who are lured by Venice's lively blend of indulgent beach culture (beaches *are not* safe at night) and relentless nightlife, centered around the 3rd St. Promenade. In fact, the foreign presence is so dominant that some hostels cater exclusively to foreigners. These hostels require a passport and Americans might find themselves turned away even when there are available rooms. Try to call in advance to avoid this inconvenience.

Santa Monica International HI-AYH Hostel, 1436 2nd St., (310-393-9913; fax 393 1769), Santa Monica. Not the best of neighborhoods. Only hostel guests with receipts are allowed in and the desk is always staffed. Tighter security than most hostels in the area. Take MTA bus #33 from downtown to 2nd and Broadway, or take Blue Bus #3 from airport to 4th and Broadway, Blue Bus #10 from downtown. 2 blocks from beach. Colossal kitchen, laundry facilities, and weekend BBQs. TV room, movies every night, storage room, and lockers. Sunny, spacious, attractive courtyard. $2 linen rental. 2-week max. stay. Bunk in a dorm-style room $16 per night, double $43; nonmembers $19, $46. IBN reservations available.

Venice Marina Hostel, 2915 Yale Ave. (310-301-3983), Marina del Rey. Located at the end of a quiet residential street, this homey hostel offers a respite from the manic pace closer to the shore. Free shuttle from LAX, Amtrak, etc. Low-key atmosphere calls to mind *Dazed and Confused.* TV room, laundry, and Brady Bunch-like kitchen. No curfew. 24-hr. check-in. Flexible check-out. Includes linen, breakfast, and local phone calls. $13 per night, $84 per week gets you a bed, but be prepared to share the room with 3-8 others. Reservations helpful.

Venice Beach Hostel, 1515 Pacific Ave. (310-452-3052; fax 821-3469), Venice, on the corner of Windward Ave. Not to be confused with the Venice Beach Hostel on Washington Blvd. (see below; no affiliation). Take the #1 or #2 Big Blue Bus or MTA #3. Recipient of the Venice Historical Society's Annual Award in 1994 for its renovations, this hostel used to be the Trolley Hotel building. Game room with pool, darts, video poker, cable TV. Kitchen. Sauna in the works. Free coffee and breakfast. Occasional free dinner and beer. Linen provided. Laundry facilities. 24-hr. check-in. Check-out 10am. No curfew. 4-person dorm rooms; $10-11 per person. Doubles $30-35.

Cadillac Hotel, 401 Ocean Front Walk (310-399-8876), Venice. A beautiful art-deco landmark directly on the beachfront. Call for airport shuttle service. Limited parking. The boardwalk and beach are just outside. Sundeck and gym. Max. stay 1 week. Check-out 11am. No curfew. Free linen and lockers. Shared accommodations $18 per night. Private ocean-view rooms $55 and up. Reservations for groups of 4 only. Wheelchair accessible.

Stardust Motor Hotel, 3202 Wilshire Blvd., (310-828-4584), Santa Monica. Well-kept accommodations with cable TV, telephone, A/C, and a tiny pool. Singles from $36. Doubles $45. Room with kitchen $45-50.

Jim's at The Beach, 17 Brooks Ave., Venice (310-399-4018; fax 399-4216). Outstanding location ½ block off the boardwalk. **International Passport required.** No more than 6 beds per room. The rooms are clean and sunny. Kitchen. No curfew. Linen included. Free breakfast, and BBQs on weekends. $15 per night, $90 per week.

Venice Beach Cotel, 25 Windward Ave., Venice (310-399-7649; fax 399-1930), on the boardwalk, between Zephyr Court and 17th Ave. Located 1½ blocks from the beach. Caters to an international crowd, **international passport required.** Don't ask about the name. Shuttle from LAX ($5). A lively hostel full of young international travelers. No food allowed. Bar and social area (no T.V.) loud and animated 7pm-1am. Check-out 11am. No curfew. 3-6 people share each of the tidy, functional rooms. $13 per night, with bath $15. Private rooms with and without ocean view $30-44.

Venice Beach Hostel, 701 Washington Blvd. (508-306-5180), near a somewhat noisy street. Not to be confused with the Venice Beach Hostel on Pacific Ave. (see above; no affiliation). **International passport required.** Free shuttle bus from airport. Relaxed atmosphere and large common room. Rooftop deck is popular with sun-lovers. Full kitchen. Keg parties Thurs. night. Lockers available. No curfew or lock-out. Reception open 24 hrs. $12 per night, $70 per week. One room for couples available at $30 per night.

Airport Interclub Hostel, 2221 Lincoln Blvd., Venice (310-305-0250; fax 305-8590), near Venice Blvd. Take MTA #3 from the airport or #33 from downtown. **International passport required.** Festive after-hours common-room atmosphere in which many nationalities bump elbows. Free airport pick-up, bike and skate rental, pool table, and TV. Psychedelic decor. Mixed- or single-sex accommodations. Kitchen with stove and fridge. Linen. Laundry room. Check-out 10:30am. Rooms sleep 6, or you can sleep in the prison-like 25-bed dorm for the same price. $14 per person, $84 for a week. Doubles $32, $200 per week. $5 deposit.

INGLEWOOD

This hostel and the hotel that contains it are located in this residential community southeast of Venice and Santa Monica. Inglewood is far from most major attractions.

Backpackers Paradise, 4200 W. Century Blvd., Inglewood, CA 90304 (310-419-0999; fax 412-9100). Located in the California Trade Winds Hotel (see below). Free shuttle transportation from airport to hostel and Venice Beach is useful—you don't want to walk in this neighborhood. Semi-private rooms with TV. Continental breakfast, nightly champagne party, and movies included. Laundry facilities, lockers. Pool, jacuzzi, game room. No curfew. $16 per night.

California Trade Winds Hotel, 4200 W. Century Blvd. (310-419-0999). Also houses Backpacker's Paradise (above). Amazing prices, free shuttle service, pool, jacuzzi, free continental breakfast, and free champagne party are an effort to compensate for the less than ideal location. 2-room suite $35, 3-room suite $55.

CAMPING

Los Angeles has no **campgrounds** convenient to public transport. Even motorists face at least a 40-minute commute from the nearest campsites to downtown. A relatively pleasant place to camp in L.A. County that is vaguely nearby is **Leo Carrillo State Beach** (310-457-1324), on PCH (Rte. 1), 20 mi. north of Malibu at the Ventura County line, at Thornhill Broome (80 primitive sites. $16 per night. Hike/bike sites $3. Chemical toilets but no showers.) Inland, at **Point MUGU** near Sycamore Canyon, there are developed sites with flush toilets and coin showers for $16 per night. Call 800-444-7275 to make reservations (mandatory in summer) for either site. A bit removed from L.A. proper (so you'll be able to relax after the 40-min. drive from Hollywood), the **LA/San Fernando Valley KOA** has tent sites for $14 per night, RV sites for $22.

A number of RV sites do exist in the L.A. area, near Long Beach, Malibu, and the Valley. The **Malibu Beach RV Park,** 25801 Pacific Coast Hwy., Malibu Beach (310-456-6052) affords ocean views from a bluff overlooking the beach. Sites with electric hookup $30; sites on the oceanfront $35. For other campgrounds, see Santa Monica National Recreation Area (page 105) or call the L.A. Visitors Bureau (213-689-8822) or California Travel Parks Association in Auburn (916-885-1624).

■■■ FOOD

The range of culinary options in L.A. is directly proportional to the city's ethnic diversity—keep in mind that Angelenos speak 116 different languages. Certain types of food are concentrated in specific areas. Jewish and Eastern European food is most prevalent in the **Fairfax** area; Mexican in **East L.A.;** Japanese, Chinese, Vietnamese, and Thai around **Little Tokyo** and **Chinatown,** and seafood along the coast. There are Hawaiian, Indian, and Ethiopian restaurants scattered throughout the city. In L.A. there are restaurants where the main objective is being seen, and the food is secondary, as well as those where the food itself seems too beautiful to be eaten—it was here, after all, that '80s nouvelle cuisine reached its height.

Fortunately for the budget traveler, Los Angeles elevates fast-food and chain restaurants to heights virtually unknown in the rest of the country. The city's car-centered population has nurtured many high-quality chains (most with take-out), each of which offers something special, cheap, and standardized in the most positive sense of the word. Chains are a way of life in L.A., and an attempt to localize a culture that is as diffuse as they come.

For the optimal burger-and-fries experience, try **In 'n' Out Burger** (various locations, call 818-287-4377 for the one nearest you), a family-operated chain that has steadfastly refused to expand beyond the L.A. area. In 'n' Out also sells popular t-shirts. **Johnny Rocket's** returns you to the lost era of American diners. **California Pizza Kitchen,** (CPK) spawned the now-national interest in wood-fired, well-decorated pizza. (Their pastas, salads, and desserts are also excellent.) The restaurant at 121 N. La Cienega Blvd. (213-854-6555), is a good place to start, but new locations keep popping up.

L.A. restaurants tend to shut down early. Angelenos eat out between 7 and 10pm, and restaurants are closed by 11pm. Even fast-food chains are rarely open past midnight. For restaurant listings, see the different neighborhoods of Los Angeles below. To find listings on **late-night** restaurants and cafés see Entertainment, page 85. Recently, Los Angeles became the first city in the U.S. to ban smoking in all restaurants, excluding bars and clubs.

MARKETS

L.A.'s proximity to the San Joaquin Valley, the state's major agricultural region, assures a plentiful supply of fresh fruits and vegetables. To sample California's freshest, find a health-food store or cooperative market that sells organic and small-farm produce. An impressively large and airy example is **Ereution,** 7660-A Beverly Blvd. (310-937-0777). You may also want to check out the **Venice Ocean Park Food Co-op,** 839 Lincoln Blvd. (310-399-5623). Stands selling just one or two items are scattered throughout the San Fernando Valley and along the way to Ventura. Prices are lower than those in stores, and the quality superior.

Visit one of the enormous public markets to appreciate the variety and volume of foodstuffs. The **Farmer's Market,** 6333 W. 3rd St. (213-933-9211), at Fairfax in the Wilshire District, has over 160 produce stalls including a phenomenal juice bar. There's delectable produce; however, because the market has become a tourist attraction, bargains are becoming increasingly rare. (Open Mon.-Sat. 9am-7pm, Sun. 10am-6pm; Oct.-May Mon.-Sat. 9am-6:30pm, Sun. 10am-5pm.) A less touristy and less expensive source of produce is the **Grand Central Public Market,** 317 S. Broadway (213-624-2378), a large baby-blue building downtown, between 3rd and 4th. The main market in the Hispanic shopping district, Grand Central has more than 50 stands selling not only produce, but also clothing, housewares, costume jewelry, vitamins, and fast food. This vast space is always riotously busy and entertaining. The chaos is interrupted by a formica oasis—a lunch counter where shoppers, oblivious to the melee, enjoy *taquitos* and *carnitas*. (Open Mon.-Sat. 9am-6pm, Sunday 10am-5pm.) All other food listings for L.A. are in the following Food and Sights section.

■■■ FOOD AND SIGHTS IN AND AROUND LOS ANGELES

DOWNTOWN L.A.

The downtown area provides a theoretical, if not geographical, centerpoint for Los Angeles's dispersed neighborhoods. Residents of virtually all of L.A.'s different communities can be found downtown. Financiers who flee to valley domiciles every evening and a substantial street population that retires and rises on the street, coexist here. An uneasy truce prevails, but visitors should be cautious; the area is especially unsafe after business hours and on weekends. Don't bring valuables with you and leave nothing costly in your car. Park in a secure lot, rather than on the streets.

Food

Lunch specials are easy to find in the financial district as restaurants contend for the businessperson's lunchtime dollar. However, finding a reasonably priced dinner that won't send you rushing to the Department of Health can be a challenge. Nearby, **Chinatown** has restaurants with standard specials as well as generally inexpensive delis; **Weller Court** by the New Ofani Hotel and Garden surrounds several Japanese restaurants, a few of which are in budget range.

The Pantry, 877 S. Figueroa St. (213-972-9279). Open since the '20s, and it's easy to see why—the Pantry defies culinary trendiness. You may have to share a table with a complete stranger, and the waiter is as likely to insult you as to talk your ear off, but the patrons like it that way. The restaurant seats only 84 yet serves 2500-3000 meals a day. The owners recently opened a deli/bakery next door (roast beef sandwich $4.25). Be prepared to wait for the enormous breakfast specials ($6), especially on weekends. Sun. brunch at the Pantry is an L.A. tradition. Open 24 hrs.

Philippe's, The Original, 1001 N. Alameda (213-628-3781), 2 blocks north of Union Station. The sheer variety of food combined with sizable portions and low, low prices make this a great place for lunch. Philippe's claims to have originated the French-dipped sandwich; varieties include beef, pork, ham, turkey, or lamb ($3-4). Brace yourself for their hot mustard and *don't* ask for ketchup. Macaroni salad 70¢, iced tea 40¢. Top it off with a large slice of pie ($1.90) and a 10¢ cup of coffee, and you've got a colossal lunch at this L.A. institution. Open daily 6am-10pm.

La Luz Del Día, 1 W. Olvera St. (213-628-7495). This authentic and inexpensive Mexican restaurant is hidden amidst the many tourist-trap Mexican joints along historic Olvera St. Tortillas are handmade on the premises, and the salsa is sharp. Combination plates $4-5. Open Tues.-Sun. 11am-10pm.

Country Life Vegetarian Buffet, 888 S. Figueroa St. (213-489-4118), across the street from the Pantry. An interesting L.A. phenomenon: located next to a health club in a sunless basement, this New Age restaurant features all-you-can-eat soups with breads and spreads ($4) and a weigh-and-pay selection of "wheat" meats and healthy whole-food options. Even carnivores may enjoy the tasty vegetarian hot dogs. Open Mon.-Thurs. 11am-3:30pm, Fri. 11am-2:30pm.

Café China, 1123 W. 7th St. (213-689-9898). Filling combination plates, like spicy shrimp and almond chicken, served with soup, egg roll, and rice ($4.50). Get take-out, or eat in the standard red-boothed interior. American breakfasts. Open Mon.-Fri. 8am-7pm. Sat 9am-2am.

Mon Kee Restaurant, 679 N. Spring St. (213-628-6717), in Chinatown. Expensive, but widely acclaimed as one of L.A.'s best restaurants. Dinner $10 and up. The decor here is light and tasteful, especially for Chinatown. The menu is vast; the seafood is excellent. Entrees around $8. Open Sun.-Thurs. 11:30am-9:45pm, Fri.-Sat. 11:30am-10:15pm.

Mandarin Deli, 356 E. 2nd St. (213-617-0231), in Little Tokyo. Generous portions of the very best in this neighborhood: assorted noodle soups (around $4-5), boiled fish, and plates of pan-fried dumplings. Not really a deli, in the traditional sense—has quite comfortable booths, though skimps on the ambience. Open daily 11:30am-9:30pm.

Thank Vi, 422 Ord St. (213-687-3522). A favorite spot among Chinatown denizens for Vietnamese cuisine and justifiably so; the clean, light setting matches the eats. Everything under $7.75; most items under $5. Open Thurs.-Tues. 7:30am-6:30pm.

Sights

The Los Angeles downtown area alone is larger than most cities. The **financial district** is a typical urban conglomeration of glass and steel, where the gigantic offices of such companies as ARCO, the Bank of America, Wells Fargo, and AT&T crowd the busy downtown center (an area bounded roughly by 3rd and 6th St., Figueroa St., and Grand Ave.). The I.M. Pei-designed **First Interstate World Center,** 633 W. 5th St., perched atop Bunker Hill, dominates the skyline; at 73 stories and 1017 ft., it's the tallest building west of the Mississippi River.

The financial district's skyline was made familiar by the TV show *L.A. Law,* and includes some of L.A.'s most magnificent buildings. The **Oviatt Building** at 617 S. Olive St. is the downtown area's Art Deco masterpiece. The top two floors were originally used as an apartment by Mr. Oviatt. With the exception of its 1970s addition, the **Times-Mirror Building** at 220 W. 1st is a classic example of Cal Moderne and the area's most impressive building. The **Westin Bonaventure Hotel,** 4045 Figueroa St., with its five cylindrical fingers, is worth a visit to relive the climactic battle between John Malkovich and Clint Eastwood in *In the Line of Fire.*

To the north of the financial district is L.A.'s **Music Center,** 135 N. Grand Ave. (213-972-7211), comprised of the **Dorothy Chandler Pavillion** (site of the Oscars), the **Mark Taper Forum,** and the **Ahmanson Theatre.** The center is home to the Los Angeles Philharmonic Orchestra and the Joffrey Ballet. Local music-lovers hit Chinatown or Little Tokyo for dinner before a night at the opera.

The **Civic Center,** a solid wall of bureaucratic architecture bounded by the Hollywood Fwy. (U.S. 101), Grand, 1st, and San Pedro St., runs east from the Music Center. It ends at **City Hall,** 200 N. Spring St. Another of the best-known buildings in the Southland, the hall was cast as the home of the *Daily Planet* in the *Superman* TV series. The building has an **observation deck** on the 27th floor.

Farther north lies the historic birthplace of Los Angeles, bounded by Spring St., Arcadia St., and Macy St. In the place where the original city center once stood, **El Pueblo de Los Angeles State Historic Park** (213-680-2525; open daily 10am-3pm) preserves a number of historically important buildings from the Spanish and Mexican eras. Start out at the **Visitors Center,** 622 N. Main, in the Sepulveda House (213-628-1274). The center offers free walking tours (Tues.-Sat. hourly 10am-noon; call to check).

The **Old Plaza,** with its century-old Moreton Bay fig trees and huge bandstand, is at the center of the pueblo. Tours start here and wind their way past the **Avila Adobe,** 10 E. Olvera St., the oldest house in the city (the original adobe has been replaced with concrete in order to meet earthquake regulations), followed by **Pico House,** 500 N. Main St., once L.A.'s most luxurious hotel. Farther down, at 535 N. Main St., the **Plaza Church,** established in 1818, has an incongruously soft, rose adobe façade. Most tours also include the **catacombs** that formerly held gambling and opium dens. The **visitors center** screens the film *Pueblo of Promise,* an 18-minute history of Los Angeles. **Olvera Street,** one of L.A.'s original roads, is now called Tijuana North by the locals. The street is packed with touristy little stands selling Mexican handicrafts. Olvera St. is the sight of the Cinco de Mayo celebrations of L.A.'s Chicano population. (See Seasonal Events, page 116). Across Alameda St. from El Pueblo is the grand old **Union Station.** The station is being renovated through L.A. Conservancy efforts, but is ready to be opened to the public.

Chinatown lies north of this area, roughly bordered by Yale, Spring, Ord, and Bernard St. From downtown, take the DASH shuttle (see Getting Around, page 73). Roman Polanski's *Chinatown,* staring Mr. L.A. himself, Jack Nicholson was filmed in this once vice-ridden neighborhood. **Little Tokyo** is centered on 2nd and San Pedro St. on the eastern edge of downtown. The **New Otani Hotel,** 120 S. Los Angeles St., 1 block south of the Civic Center between 1st and 2nd, rents lavish Meiji-style rooms for up to $700 per night. For slightly less, you can have a drink in the elegant rooftop garden. The **Japanese Village Plaza** (213-620-8861), in the 300 block of E. 2nd St., is the center of the district and is a florid fusion of American shopping mall and Japanese design. The **Japanese-American Cultural and Community Center** (see page 68) was designed by Buckminster Fuller and Isamu Noguchi, who crafted a monumental sculpture for the courtyard. (Administrative offices open Mon.-Fri. 9am-5pm.)

Broadway south of 1st St. is predominantly Mexican. All billboards and store signs are in Spanish, and the **Grand Central Public Market** (see Food, page 84) takes a center seat. Inspect the stars in the sidewalk out front, each bearing the name of a Chicano celebrity—a *rambla de fama* to complement Hollywood's. Across the street, the **Bradbury Building,** 304 S. Broadway, stands as a relic of L.A.'s Victorian past. Uninspiring from the street, this 1893 office building is mostly lobby. Its ornate staircases and elevators (wrought in iron, wood, and marble) are often bathed in sunlight, which pours in through the glass roof. Crews film period scenes here with some regularity (open Mon.-Fri. 9am-5pm, Sat. 9am-4pm).

The most striking (and chic) museum in the area is the **Museum of Contemporary Art (MOCA),** showcasing art from 1940 to the present. The main museum is located at California Plaza, 250 S. Grand Ave. (213-626-6222), and is a sleek and geometric architectural marvel. Its collection focuses on abstract expressionism, and includes works by Pollock, Calder, Miró, and Giacometti. Its interior is spacious and illuminated by pyramidal skylights. The second MOCA facility is the **Temporary Contemporary,** 152 N. Central Ave., in Little Tokyo. Originally intended to house exhibits only while the main museum was under construction, ironically, this building has since become a permanent part of the MOCA package. This location has been closed until 1995 to accommodate construction. (Main MOCA hrs. are Tues.-Wed. and Fri.-Sun. 11am-5pm, Thurs. 11am-8pm. $6, seniors and students with ID $4; under 12 free. Free Thurs. 5-8pm. Wheelchair accessible.)

Across from City Hall East, between the Santa Ana Fwy. and Temple in the L.A. Mall, is the **L.A. Children's Museum,** 310 N. Main St. (213-687-8800), where nothing is behind glass and everything can be handled. There is always an exhibit on an L.A. ethnic group. Children are invited to overcome the confusion of a hyper-technological society by participating in demonstrations of scientific principles, and to create MOCA pieces of their own. (Open Tues.-Fri. 11:30am-5pm, in winter also Sat.-Sun. 10am-5pm. $5.)

Los Angeles's **Museum of African-American Art,** 4005 Crenshaw Blvd., 3rd floor (213-294-7071), the first of its kind in the American West, thoughtfully contextualizes pieces within their proper historical framework (open Wed.-Sat. 11am-6pm, Sun. noon-5pm; free).

Near Downtown: Exposition Park

At the turn of the century, this area was an upscale suburb of downtown; it deteriorated in the '20s but was renewed when the Olympiad first came to town in 1932. This neighborhood was revitalized yet again by the 1984 Olympics, and today it is one of the few parts of L.A. where a number of important attractions are clustered together. Observers may note that decaying areas could use another Olympic-class revitalization. Museums are generally safe and well-visited, and keep early hours—visitors should take the hint. The park is southwest of downtown, just off the Harbor Fwy., and is bounded by Exposition Blvd., Figueroa St., Vermont Ave., and Santa Barbara Ave. From downtown, take bus #40 or 42 (from Broadway between 5th and 6th St.) to the park's southern edge. From Hollywood, take #204 down Vermont. From Santa Monica, take bus #20, 22, 320, or 322 on Wilshire, and transfer to #204 at Vermont.

The park is dominated by several major museums, including the **California Museum of Science and Industry,** 700 State Dr. (213-744-7400). Enter at the corner of Figueroa and Exposition next to the United DC-8 parked out front. Many of the exhibits are either corporate or governmental propaganda. IBM and Bell Telephone sponsor mathematics and communications, while McDonald's sponsors a display on nutrition. The **Aerospace Building,** as big as a hangar, exhibits $8 million worth of aircraft, including the Gemini 11 space capsule. (Museum open daily 10am-5pm. Free. Parking $3; bring quarters.)

Lovers and lovers of roses should enjoy the expansive, formal **rose garden** in the courtyard in front of the Museum of Science and Industry. More than 16,000 specimens of 190 varieties of roses surround walking paths, green lawns, and gazebos.

In the same complex, but separate from the MSI is the **California Afro-American Museum,** 600 State Dr. (213-744-7432), with a permanent sculpture collection, a research library, and exhibits focused on African-American contributions to science, humanities, and athletics. (Open Tues.-Fri 10am-5pm. Free. Research library open by appointment only.)

Another of the parks attractions is the **Los Angeles County Natural History Museum,** 900 Exposition Blvd. (213-744-3466). The museum has exhibits about pre-Columbian cultures, North American and African mammals, American history from 1472 to 1914, and dinosaurs. The **Hands On Discovery Center** allows visitors to pet dead and stuffed wild animals. Just think what you've been missing! (Open Tues.-Sun. 10am-5pm. $5, seniors and students $2.50, ages 5-12 $1, under 5 free.)

Exposition Park also includes the **Los Angeles Memorial Coliseum,** 2601 S. Figueroa St., home of the **Los Angeles Raiders** and the **USC Trojan** football teams, and the **Sports Arena,** home of the **Los Angeles Clippers** basketball team and a common venue for rock concerts. The colossal Coliseum, which seats over 100,000, was a main venue during the 1932 and 1984 Summer Olympic Games.

The **University of Southern California (USC)** campus sits opposite Exposition Park on Exposition Blvd. The campus is beautiful and generally safe, although caution should be exercised after dark. (213-740-2300; walking tours of the campus are available on the hr., Mon.-Fri. 10am-2pm.) The **Fisher Gallery,** 823 Exposition Blvd. (213-740-4561), includes portions of the Armand Hammer collection of 18th- and 19th-century Dutch paintings and will feature special exhibits of Baroque masters from the Dutch and Flemish schools until April 1995. (Open early Sept. to summer Tues.-Fri. noon-5pm, Sat. 11am-3pm. Free.)

Seven or eight mi. southeast of the USC campus lies **Watts,** a neighborhood made notorious by riots in 1965. This is an area where meandering tourists will probably feel unwelcome or unsafe. The only tourist attraction per se is the **Watts Towers,** 1765 E. 107th St. (213-569-8181), which is a reasonably safe destination if you remain aware and responsible. These remarkable pieces of folk art were built single-handedly over a period of 33 years by Watts resident Simon Rodia. The towers of glistening fretwork, decorated with mosaics of broken glass, ceramic tile, and sea shells, are a testament to one man's extraordinary vision and dedication. After completing the towers in 1954, Rodia retired to Martinez, California and deeded the land occupied by the towers to a neighbor. Since then, the City of Los Angeles has undertaken the care and preservation of the sculptures. (On-the-spot tours $1, children free if accompanied by adult; open Sat.-Sun. 10am-4pm.) During the week the towers undergo restoration, and appointments must be made in advance.

Next door, at 1727 E. 107th St. is the **Watts Tower Arts Center** (213-847-4646), which houses a permanent exhibit of folk instruments, as well as a changing gallery (open Tues.-Sun. 10am-4pm). The Towers and Arts Center are a good 7-mi. drive from the nearest tourist attractions at Exposition Park. The safest parking is in the Arts Center lot. To reach the center by bus, take MTA #56 downtown to Wilmington and 108th St. Walk one block west on 108th to Graham, then one block north. Or, from downtown take the Metro Blue Line and get off at 103 St. Station. Walk on 104th east to Beach, and then south to the corner of 106th and 107th. As always, pedestrians will feel and remain safer in groups and during the day.

Also south of Exposition Park, but to the west, is the city of **Inglewood.** Considered by many a rough neighborhood, Inglewood is not without points of interest. At the corner of Manchester and Prairie Ave. is the **Great Western Forum** (310-673-1300), home of the **Los Angeles Kings** hockey team (and "The Great One," Wayne Gretzky), as well as the **Los Angeles Lakers** basketball team. For Lakers and Kings tickets (and for tickets for other Forum events) call the **Forum Box Office** (310-419-3182; open daily 10am-6pm) or **Ticketmaster** (213-480-3232). Tickets range in price from $11 to $110.

WILSHIRE DISTRICT AND HANCOCK PARK

The cosmopolitan Wilshire District contains a wide variety of attractions from art museums to a baseball stadium. Most of the action centers around sprawling Wilshire Boulevard which connects downtown Los Angeles with Santa Monica.

Food

Although inexpensive, quality food can be difficult to find in the Wilshire District, La Brea Ave. and Pico Blvd. are good streets to explore. Both offer an assortment of restaurants.

The Apple Pan, 10801 W. Pico Blvd. (310-475-3585), in West L.A. between Westwood and Overland. From downtown, take bus #431. This nondescript little building is easily overshadowed by the mammoth Westside Pavilion shopping center across the street, but it's been open since 1927 and continues to draw crowds for large, juicy hamburgers ($3.60) and sandwiches ($3-5) with huge slices of apple pie for dessert ($2.50). Almost legendary status. Much of the clientele is a colorful bunch of locals. Open Sun. and Tues.-Thurs. 11am-midnight, Fri.-Sat. 11am-1am. Closed the first 2 weeks in July.

El Nopal, 10426 National Blvd. (310-559-4732), in West L.A., between Motor and Overland, just south of the Santa Monica Fwy. Known as the "home of the pregnant burrito." The famed burrito *embarrasado* ($6.25), stuffed with chicken and avocado, lives up to its name. Smaller burritos $2-4. Tasty tacos and tangy salsa ($2). Take-out available. Open Sun.-Thurs. 11am-9pm, Fri.-Sat. 11am-10pm.

Cassell's Hamburgers, 3266 W. 6th St. (213-480-8668), in the Wilshire District. Some say these burgers are the absolute finest in the city. They're juicy, enormous, and come with lots of free sides like cottage cheese and potato salad. Cassell's has been around for over 30 years. Basic burger $4.75. Open Mon.-Sat. 10:30am-4pm.

Sights

Wilshire Boulevard, especially the "Miracle Mile" between Highland and Fairfax Ave., played a starring role in Los Angeles's westward suburban expansion. On what was then the end of the boulevard, the Bullocks Corporation gambled on attracting shoppers from downtown and in 1929 erected one of L.A.'s few architecturally significant buildings, the massive, bronze-colored **Bullocks Wilshire** at 3050 Wilshire Blvd., near Vermont Ave., now called the **I. Magnin BW Wilshire.** The nearby residential neighborhoods and their 1920s architecture are also worth touring by car. The streets south of Wilshire opposite Hancock Park are lined with Spanish-style bungalows and the occasional modernist manse. The **Los Angeles Conservancy** (213-623-2489) offers Saturday tours of downtown Art Deco sights for $5 (make reservations 1 week in advance).

A few mi. farther down Wilshire, in **Hancock Park,** the acrid smell of tar pervades the vicinity of the **La Brea Tar Pits,** one of the most popular hangouts in the world for fossilized early mammals. Many of the beasts who came, thousands of years ago, to drink from the pools here found themselves stuck in the tar that lurks below a thin film of water. Most of the one million bones recovered from the pits between 1913 and 1915 have found a new home in the **George C. Page Museum of La Brea Discoveries,** 5801 Wilshire Blvd., at Curson and Wilshire (recording 213-936-2230, operator 213-857-6311). Wilshire buses stop right in front of the museum. The museum includes reconstructed Ice Age animals and murals of L.A. Ice Age life, a laboratory where paleontologists work behind plate-glass windows, and a display that shows what it's like to stick around in the tar. Archaeological digging continues in **Pit 91** behind the adjacent county art museum. (Open daily 10am-5pm. $5, seniors and students $3.50, ages 5-10 $2, under 5 free. Free admission 1st Tues. of month. Parking $4. Museum tours Wed.-Sun. 2pm. Tours of grounds 1pm.)

The **Los Angeles County Museum of Art (LACMA),** 5905 Wilshire Blvd. (213-857-6000), at the west end of Hancock Park, has a distinguished, comprehensive collection that should rebut those who argue that L.A.'s only culture is in its yogurt.

Opened in 1965, the LACMA is the largest museum in the West. Five major buildings cluster around the **Times-Mirror Central Court:** a Japanese pavilion, the Ahmanson Building (the museum's original building and home to most of its non-modern permanent collection), the Hammer Building, the Bing Center, and the Robert O. Anderson Building, a spectacular 1986 addition to the museum. The museum offers a variety of tours and free talks daily. For schedules, check with the information desk in the Central Court (ticket office 857-6010) or contact the Docent Council at 857-6108. (Open Mon. and Wed. 10am-5pm, Fri. 10am-9pm, Sat.-Sun. 11am-6pm. $6, seniors and students $4, ages 6-17 $1. Free 2nd Wed. of each month.)

About 3 mi. northeast of downtown is **Elysian Park;** with 525 acres of greenery, the park is ideal for picnicking. The park curves around the northern portion of Chavez Ravine, home of the well-designed and sparkling-clean **Dodger Stadium** (213-224-1400) and the **Los Angeles Dodgers** baseball team. Tickets, which cost for $6 to $11 (all seats have good views of the field), are a hot commodity when the Dodgers are playing well; purchase in advance, if possible. Scalpers sell them illegally and at a substantial mark up outside.

HOLLYWOOD

For decades, this tiny chunk of a massive city has defined glamour for the world. Countless numbers of young people have crossed land and oceans for a chance to share in the glitz and fame associated with this capital of the movie industry. For years, Hollywood has symbolized the American desire to "make it"—to forget one's past and fabricate an instant persona of sophistication and wealth. For years, it succeeded, generating the image and style associated with California, and in large part, with America itself.

Hollywood today has lost much of its sparkle. To catch a fleeting glimpse of the orange groves and farm lands that first lured movie men, travel into the Hollywood Hills north of the more urban and grittier world of central Hollywood. Here, in neighborhoods like Beachwood, Laurel Canyons, and Nichols, beautiful homes, palm trees, and swimming pools are still abundant. The rest of Hollywood feels overworked and run-down. The major studios have moved over the mountains into the roomier San Fernando Valley and blockbusters are increasingly shot "on location" elsewhere in the U.S. or overseas. As a result, the Golden Road has its share of figurative potholes. Hollywood Boulevard and other thoroughfares, once glittering and glamorous, are now rated X. Hollywood is still a fascinating place, but a far cry from the Emerald City it was once thought to be. At 108, Hollywood is tired; yet its glorious past assures that it will remain larger than life for decades to come.

Food in Hollywood and West Hollywood

Forget those rumors about outrageously priced celebrity hangouts—they're here, but you can ignore them. Most of Hollywood and West Hollywood's residents are young, single, hungry, and near broke after paying the rent on their bungalows. As a result, Hollywood has the best budget dining in L.A. Hollywood and Sunset Boulevards offer an range of excellent and diverse cuisines, while Fairfax (the traditionally Jewish area of town) has Mediterranean-style restaurants and delis. Melrose is full of chic cafés and eateries; many with outdoor seating perfect for watching winningly frivolous and stylized Melrosians. The geographical closeness of Hollywood and West Hollywood causes the two areas to blend together around the edges. It can be difficult to tell where the district (Hollywood) ends and the city (West Hollywood) begins. Their relative proximity makes it convenient for visitors in search of good food to consider restaurants in both areas. For West Hollywood Sights, see page 94.

Lucy's El Adobe Café, 5536 Melrose Ave. (213-462-9421), 1 block east of Gower St., in Hollywood. This family-run restaurant is a favorite among downtown politicians and Paramount executives from across the street. Ignore the glitzier joints on the avenue and indulge in some of the best Mexican food in town. Former California governor/Presidential candidate Edmund "Jerry" Brown and Linda Ronstadt allegedly met here. As you munch on your tostada ($7), glance at the celebrity photos or the commendation from the City Council adorning the walls. Full dinners $10-11. Open Mon.-Sat. 11:30am-11pm.

Duke's, 8909 Sunset Blvd. (310-652-3100), at San Vicente, in West Hollywood. Hangout for L.A.'s music industry bigwigs; its walls are a kaleidoscope of posters and autographed album covers. Perfect for brunch—carry a copy of *Spin* to pass the time while you wait for a table. Try the "Revenge"—eggs scrambled with avocado, sour cream, onions, tomatoes, and peppers. Entrees $4-7. Open Mon.-Fri. 7:30am-9pm, Sat.-Sun. 8am-4pm.

Chin Chin, 8618 Sunset Blvd. (310-652-1818), in West Hollywood. Other locations in Brentwood, Studio City, and Woodland Hills. Immensely popular with the lunchtime set for its handmade "dim sum and then sum" (averages $5). This combination of Chinese and American dining is undeniably a happy one. The shredded chicken salad ($6) is a perfect example of California-ized Chinese cuisine. Outdoor seating and take out. Open Sun.-Thurs. 11am-11pm, Fri.-Sat. 11am-midnight.

El Chavo, 4441 Sunset Blvd. (213-664-0871), in Hollywood. The fact that this slightly out-of-the-way spot is so crowded is testimony to the quality of its divinely frothy, huge margaritas ($3.75). (They were the best our researcher has ever had and she's had quite a few.) Dimly lit; you'll have to rely on your sense of taste (no problem with any of these entrees, which range from $5.50-9.75). Try the *tostada con chorizo* ($7.75). Open daily 11:30am-11pm. No credit cards accepted.

Toi on Sunset, 7505½ Sunset Blvd. (213-850-9220), in Hollywood. Serves hearty, reasonably priced Thai food amid psychedelic op-art and decor. Popular with young stars and starlets living in the Hollywood area. The attitude you'll encounter here may be what you came to L.A. expecting to find. *Pad thai* or vegetable curry $6.25.

Pink's Famous Chili Dogs, 711 N. La Brea Ave. (213-931-4223), in Hollywood. The chili dogs are good and cheap ($2.10) and that's why this friendly stand has been around since 1939. They're a better bargain now, if you factor in inflation and the shrinking dollar. Open Sun.-Thurs. 8am-2am, Fri.-Sat. 8am-3am.

The Nature Club Café, 7174 Melrose Ave. (213-931-8994), in Hollywood. Next door to an herb shop, this cool, green restaurant has an expansive vegetarian and vegan menu. The large plants will encourage you to take advantage of the salad buffet ($6), which includes a choice of *farfaille,* herbed potato, spicy sesame, and several others. Open daily 11:30am-10pm. Wheelchair accessible.

Atch-Kotch, 1253 N. Vine (213-467-5537), in Hollywood. Inexpensive Japanese food in a spare, modern setting. Ramen goes from $4, with add-on toppings. Also has sushi and *dim sum.* Broiled mackerel $5. Open Mon.-Sat. 11:30am-9pm.

The Old Spaghetti Factory, 5939 W. Sunset Blvd. (213-469-7149), in Hollywood. Now a chain, this restaurant claims to be "a reminder of the color and charm of early Hollywood." With purple wallpaper and a trolley car in the middle of the dining room, some people would call it tacky. The food, however, is cheap and plentiful. A full dinner (including bread, salad, and ice cream) runs $4.25-8. Open Mon.-Thurs. 11:30am-2pm and 5-10pm, Fri.-Sat. 11:30am-2pm and 5-11pm, Sun. noon-10pm.

Sights

The **Hollywood sign**—those 50-ft.-high, slightly erratic letters perched on Mt. Cahuenga north of Hollywood—stands with New York's Statue of Liberty and Paris's Eiffel Tower as a universally recognized symbol of its city. The original 1923 sign, which read HOLLYWOODLAND, was an advertisement for a new subdivision in the Hollywood Hills (a caretaker lived behind one of the "L"s). Over the years, people came to think of it as a civic monument, and the city, which by 1978 had acquired the sign, reconstructed the crumbling letters, leaving off the last syllable. The sign has been a target of pranksters (USC frat boys and Cal Tech hackers) who have made it read everything from "Hollyweed" to "Ollywood," after the infamous Lt. Col. Oliver North. For a closer look at the site, follow Beachwood Dr. up into the hills (bus #208; off Franklin Ave. between Vine St. and Western Ave.). Drive along the narrow, twisting streets of the Hollywood Hills for glimpses of the multi-colored homes and lifestyles of the Rich and Famous. **Hollywood Boulevard** itself, lined with souvenir shops, clubs, and theaters, is busy day and night. Most sights in this area now focus around the intersection of Highland Ave. and Hollywood Blvd., and then west down Hollywood. To the east, things turn seedier. The façade of **Mann's Chinese Theater** (formerly Grauman's), 6925 Hollywood Blvd. (213-464-8111), between Highland and La Brea, is a garish rendition of a Chinese temple. There's always a crowd of tourists in the courtyard, worshiping impressions made by movie stars in the cement outside the theater. The impressions are of parts of the stars' anatomy or trademark possessions. (Al Jolson's knees, Trigger's hooves, R2D2's wheels, Jimmy Durante's nose, George Burns's cigar, etc.) Passersby can sometimes get free passes to sit in the audience of live TV shows from studio workers standing outside the theater. Just across the street from Mann's is the newly-renovated **El Capitan Theatre,** 6838 Hollywood Blvd. (213-467-9545). This restored cinema house held the 1941 Hollywood premier of *Citizen Kane*, and now shows only Disney films.

If you want to stroll among the stars, have a look at the **Walk of Fame** along Hollywood Blvd. and Vine St. More than 2500 bronze-inlaid stars are embedded in the sidewalk, inscribed with the names of the famous. Film, television, and radio celebrities are commemorated, but many names will be meaningless to the under-40 generation. To catch a glimpse of today's (or yesterday's) stars in person, call the Hollywood Chamber of Commerce (213-469-8311) for the times and locations of upcoming star-unveiling ceremonies. Across the street and two blocks east from the El Capitan is another unique theater, the **UA Egyptian,** 6712 Hollywood Blvd. (213-467-6167), inspired in 1922 by the newly discovered tomb of King Tut. The theater is currently closed for renovation.

Also two blocks east of Mann's is the **Hollywood Wax Museum,** 6767 Hollywood Blvd. (213-462-5991), where you'll meet 200 figures, from Jesus to Elvis. (Open Sun.-Thurs. 10am-midnight, Fri.-Sat. 10am-2am. $9, children $7.) Across the street from the Wax Museum you'll find two touristy "Odd-itoriums," **Frederick's of Hollywood** (including the museum of lingerie with classic ads extorting you to "put your breasts on a shelf"), and the **Max Factor Museum,** which features dozens of glamourous photos paying tribute to the most celebrated make-up artist of all time, and some dramatic "before" and "after" photos proving that beauty is—or can be— a process. Free admission makes it worth traipsing through these shrines (open Mon.-Sat. 10am-4pm).

Down the street, **Larry Edmund's Cinema and Theater Bookshop,** 6644 Hollywood Blvd. (213-463-3273), sells Ken Schessler's *This Is Hollywood: Guide to Hollywood Murders, Suicides, Graves, Etc.,* a guide to nondescript places made famous by the fact that stars courted, married, fooled around, were discovered, made movies, or committed suicide there (open Mon.-Sat.10am-6pm). **Hollywood Fantasy Tours,** 6731 Hollywood Blvd. (213-469-8184), offers two-hour tours of Tinseltown in double-decker buses with knowledgeable but corny tour guides. (Hollywood tour $14, tour of Beverly Hills $25. Open daily 9am-6pm.)

Two blocks west of the Chinese Theater, the **Hollywood Galaxy Cineplex** shopping center, at 7021 Hollywood Blvd., holds a food court, bar, six movie theaters (957-9687), and some unusual stores in a large, neon-lit courtyard.

The **Hollywood Studio Museum,** 2100 N. Highland Ave. (213-874-2276), across from the Hollywood Bowl, provides a refreshing look at the history of early Hollywood film-making. Back in 1913, when it was a barn, famed director Cecil B. DeMille rented this building as a studio and shot Hollywood's first feature film, *The Squaw Man,* there. Antique cameras, costumes, props, vintage film clips, and other memorabilia clutter the museum. (Open Sat. and Sun. 10am-4pm. $4, seniors and students $3, ages 6-12 $2. Tours for $3 per person. Ample free parking.)

Music is another industry that, like film, finds a center in Los Angeles. The pre-eminent monument of the modern record industry is the 1954 **Capitol Records Tower,** 1750 Vine St., just north of Hollywood Blvd. The building, which was designed to look like a stack of records, is cylindrical with fins sticking out at each floor (the "records") and a needle on top.

If you're still not sated, visit the **Hollywood Cemetery,** 6000 Santa Monica Blvd. (213-469-1181), between Vine St. and Western Ave., which has the remains of Rudolph Valentino, Douglas Fairbanks, Sr., and other Hollywood legends (open daily 8am-5pm; mausoleums close at 4:30pm).

Barnsdall Park, 4800 Hollywood Blvd., relatively small and discreet, contains the **Municipal Art Gallery,** 4804 Hollywood Blvd. (213-485-4581), a modern building that displays the works of Southern California artists in a low-key setting. (Open Tues.-Sun. 12:30-5pm. $1, under 13 free.) Adjacent to the museum, on top of the hill, the **Hollyhock House,** 4808 Hollywood Blvd. (213-662-7272), commands a 360° view of Los Angeles and the mountains. Completed in 1922 for eccentric oil heiress Aline Barnsdall, the house remains one of Frank Lloyd Wright's most important works. It is the first building by this American architect to reflect the influence of pre-Columbian Mayan temples. The name of the house derives from Barnsdall's favorite flower, which she had Wright reproduce (grudgingly) in abstract all over the house. (Tours Tues.-Sun. on the hour from noon-3pm. $1.50, seniors $1, under 12 free. Buy tickets at the Municipal Art Gallery. 213-485-4581.)

WEST HOLLYWOOD

Once considered a no-man's land between Beverly Hills and Hollywood, West Hollywood was incorporated in 1985 and was one of the first cities in the country to be governed by openly gay officials. Although the famed thoroughfares of Melrose Ave. and Sunset Blvd. (and their respective attractions) pass through both the city of West Hollywood and the neighboring Hollywood district, West Hollywood and Hollywood are distinct communities in every other sense. Even if the average visitor remains largely ignorant of their geographical boundary, he or she is bound to notice their distinct characters. A list of weekly events in West Hollywood can be found in the *L.A. Weekly* (see Publications, page 71).

In the years before incorporation, lax zoning and other liberal laws gave rise to today's **Sunset Strip.** Long the nightlife center of L.A., the Strip was originally lined with posh nightclubs frequented by stars.Today the strip plays host to several rock clubs (see Nightlife: Clubs, page 115). The area's music scene is among the country's most fertile, and many world-famous bands from The Doors to Guns 'n Roses got their start here. These days, most of the music on this stretch is heavy metal and hard rock, and weekend nights draw tremendous crowds and traffic jams. Restaurants and comedy clubs flourish here as well. The **billboards** on the Strip are vividly hand-painted, many heralding the latest motion pictures.

Melrose Avenue, running through the southern portion of West Hollywood, is lined with swish restaurants, ultra-trendy boutiques, and art galleries. Punk clothing pits like **Retail Slut** and functional novelty shops like **Condom Mania** outfit clubbies for the evening. The choicest stretch is between La Brea and Fairfax, but the entire 3-mi. stretch between Highland and Doheny is a fertile stumping ground for the stylized.

The massive **Beverly Center,** 8500 Beverly (310-854-0070), an expensive shopping complex, is found at the corner of Beverly and La Cienega. Escalators snake up the building's exterior, encased in glass tubing. Glossy shops, high-priced restaurants, and the **Beverly Cineplex** (13 theaters) occupy the plate-glass decorated interior. At the corner of Beverly and San Vicente Blvd. is the Los Angeles **Hard Rock Café** (310-276-7605), a restaurant whose popularity may seem inexplicable to some. A pistachio-green '57 Chevy juts out of the roof. Indiana Jones's leather jacket, one of Pete Townsend's guitars, a 6-ft.-tall martini glass, license plates, and college banners adorn the interior. Expect to wait for a table most nights—over an hour on weekends. The line to buy t-shirts is formidable as well. (Open Sun.-Thurs. 11:30am-11:30pm, Fri.-Sat. 11:30am-midnight.)

North of the Beverly Center, at Melrose and San Vicente, is the **Pacific Design Center,** 8687 Melrose Ave. (310-657-0800), a huge, blue-and-green glass complex with a wave-like profile (nicknamed the **Blue Whale**). The building, completed in 1976, is no doubt destined for immortality in architectural history texts. In addition to some design showrooms, the PDC houses a public plaza with a 350-seat amphitheater, used to stage free summer concerts on Sundays. Call or inquire at the information desk in the entryway for details about such events. West Hollywood's **Gay Pride Weekend Celebration** (in late June) is usually held at the PDC plaza.

Free from the regulations imposed by the City of Los Angeles's landmark protection legislation, many of West Hollywood's more famous homes have been torn down. Still, a few remain and deserve a visit. The **Schindler House,** 833 N. Kings Rd. (213-651-1510), built in 1922, is a classic craftsman-style home with both Latino and Japanese influences (open Sat.-Sun. 1-4pm; free). Frank Lloyd Wright's **Storer House,** 8161 Hollywood Blvd., stands overlooking Hollywood Blvd. (no public access). The **Garden Apartments,** between Sunset and Fountain Ave., are some of the most beautiful homes in the area. The **Andalusia** at 1475 Havenhurst Dr. is a Spanish Classical Revival building whose grandeur is surpassed only by the **Villa d'Este** at 1355 Laurel Ave.

GRIFFITH PARK

The L.A. Zoo, the Greek Theater, Griffith Observatory and Planetarium, Travel Town, a bird sanctuary, tennis courts, two golf courses, campgrounds, and various hiking trails decorate the dry hills and mountains of Griffith Park (open daily 5:30am-10pm). This formidable recreational region stretches from the hills above North Hollywood to the intersection of the Ventura and Golden State Freeways. Pick up a map at any of the entrance points. Several of the mountain roads through the park, especially Vista Del Valle Dr., offer panoramic (though often smog-obscured) views of Los Angeles, looking south over downtown, Hollywood, and the Westside. For information, stop by the **Visitors Center and Ranger Headquarters,** 4730 Crystal Spring Dr. (213-665-5188; open 24 hrs.).

The white stucco and copper domes of the Art Deco **Observatory and Planetarium** (213-664-1181, for a recording 664-1191) structure are visible from around the park. You might remember the planetarium from the climactic last scene of the James Dean film *Rebel Without a Cause*. Even if you don't, the planetarium is a must-see. One of its most interesting exhibits is a seismograph that runs continually. If you're there when the Big One comes, you'll be among the first to know just how big it is. A telescope with a 12-in. lens is open to the public every clear night (dusk-9:45pm; winter Tues.-Sun. 7-10pm; sky report and information 213-663-8171). The planetarium also presents popular **Laserium** light shows (818-997-3624), psychedelic symphonies of lasers and music. (Observatory open daily 12:30pm-10pm; winter Tues.-Sun. 2-10pm. Planetarium show Mon.-Fri. at 3 and 7:30pm, Sat.-Sun. also at 4:30pm; in winter Tues.-Fri. 3 and 7:30pm, Sat.-Sun. also at 4:30 pm. $4, seniors $3, under 12 $2, under 5 not admitted. Laser shows Sun. and Tues.-Sat. 6 and 8:30pm, summer also Fri.-Sat 9:45pm. $6.50, children $5.50.)

A large **bird sanctuary** at the bottom of the observatory hill serves its function well, but if you crave a wider assortment of animal life, you might prefer the **L.A. Zoo,** 5332 Western Heritage Way, at the park's northern end (213-666-4090). The zoo's 113 acres accommodate 2000 animals; the facility is consistently ranked among the nation's best. (Open daily 10am-5pm. $8, seniors $5, ages 2-12 $3.) **Travel Town** (213-662-5874), is an outdoor museum showcasing period vehicles, trains, and even horses. (Open Mon.-Fri. 10am-5pm, Sat.-Sun. and holidays 10am-6pm. In winter they close 1 hr. earlier. Free.)

On the southern side of the park, below the observatory, the 4500-seat **Greek Theater** (213-665-5857) hosts a number of concerts in its outdoor amphitheater year-round. Check the *Sunday Times* "Calendar" section for coming attractions.

Those with a hankerin' to relive those wild days of yore will enjoy the recently opened **Gene Autry Western Heritage Museum,** 4700 Zoo Dr. (213-667-2000), also located within Griffith Park at the junction of Golden State (I-5) and Ventura Fwy. (Rte.134). The museum's collection covers both fact and fiction of the Old

West, with exhibits on pioneer life and on the history of Westerns, including costumes donated by Robert Redford, Gary Cooper, and Clint Eastwood. (Open Tues.-Sun. 10am-5pm. $7, seniors and students $5, children $3.)

To get to the Observatory and Greek Theater, take bus #203 from Hollywood. To reach the Zoo and Travel Town, take bus #97 from downtown. There is no bus service between the northern and southern parts of Griffith Park.

Forest Lawn Cemetery, 1712 Glendale Ave., Glendale (818-241-4151), was analyzed by Jessica Mitford as the showy emblem of the "American Way of Death." Its grounds include reproductions of many of Michelangelo's works, the "largest religious painting on earth" (the famous 195-ft. version of the *Crucifixion*), a stained-glass *Last Supper,* and innumerable other works of art. Stop at the entrance for a map of the cemetery's sights and pick up a guide to the paintings and sculpture at the administration building nearby. (Grounds open daily 8am-6pm, mausoleum until 4:30.) From downtown, take bus #90 or 91 and disembark just after the bus leaves San Fernando Rd. to turn onto Glendale Ave. Forest Lawn is easily approached via the Golden State Fwy. or Glendale Fwy. (Rte. 2).

BEVERLY HILLS

Located in the north of Greater Los Angeles, about two-thirds of the way between downtown L.A. and the coast, Beverly Hills remains a steadfast enclave of wealth. Beverly Hills seceded from L.A. in 1914 and has remained distinct (physically and ideologically) ever since. This is especially apparent along Robertson Ave., at the eastern edge of the city, where only the western side of the street (the Beverly Hills side) is lined with luxuriously shady trees. Similarly, driving west from the Sunset Strip, the sleaziness of Hollywood stops cold at the Beverly border.

You may consider hopping on a stargazing tour bus. Be forewarned: the only people visible on the streets are gardeners, and many of them don't even know whom they're working for. It is even difficult to get a good view of the homes of the rich and famous; almost all are surrounded by high walls. Celebrity-hungry visitors should have plenty of time and pride to spare before buying a street corner *Star Map.* Hawkers do their best to convince you that every map besides theirs is fraudulent. Believe all of them. The truly determined stargazer might want to frequent Studio City, where entertainment's luminaries work and dine (page 106), and the star-unveiling ceremonies on Hollywood's Walk of Fame (page 93).

Food

Beverly Hills is home to some of the best (and most expensive) restaurants in America. Don't expect too many bargains.

The Cheesecake Factory, 364 N. Beverly Dr. (310-278-7270), also in Brentwood (310-826-7111). Very, very popular—expect to stand in line. Once you get in, you'll be treated to ridiculously huge portions. The menu looks like a spiral notebook and contains a dizzying number of appealing options. A smart option is the half-sandwich with soup or salad ($6). The dessert could be the main event. The cheesecakes come in dozens of flavors and the strawberry shortcake is heavenly ($4.50-5.25). Like so many L.A. restaurants, the Cheesecake Factory has nationwide locations, including one in Washington D.C. Open Sun. 10:30am-11pm, Mon.-Thurs. 11am-11:30pm, Fri.-Sat. 11am-12:30am.

Ed Debevic's, 134 N. La Cienega Blvd. (310-659-1952), in Beverly Hills. Far and away the most mirthful of the phony '50s diners ("famous since 1984"). Always crowded. All dishes under $7—and served by dancing waitpeople on weekend nights. Full bar. Open Sun.-Thurs. 11:30am-11pm, Fri.-Sat. 11:30am-1am.

La Salsa: Tacos al Carbon, 9631 Santa Monica Blvd. (310-276-2373), in Beverly Hills. Actually on "Little" Santa Monica, 1 short block south of the big boulevard, between Camden and Bedford on the north side. The prettiest taco stand you'll ever see. Fast-food Mexican cuisine prepared with an eye toward low cholesterol and low price. $4 should set you up. (Stay away from the hot salad unless you have *la sangre de la raza!*) Mon.-Sat. 11am-9pm, Sun. noon-8pm.

Dragon Garden, 2625 S. Robertson (310-837-3626). Not the best Chinese food in L.A., but you can't beat the $1.20-per-item lunch special (11:30am-4:30pm).

J.P. Throckmorton Grille, 255 S. Beverly Dr. (310-550-7111). This grill features a good-sized burger for $3 and a variety of hot and cold sandwiches at around $4. Thick milkshakes ($2.25). Open Mon.-Sat. 11:30am-8:30pm, Sun. noon-5pm.

Sights

There is nothing understated about this city's riches. Walk along Rodeo Dr. for 15 minutes, and count how many BMWs, Porsches, and Rolls purr past you; the Beverly Hills Post Office (on Beverly Dr.) must be the only one in the country with valet parking. The heart of the city is in the **Golden Triangle,** a wedge formed by Wilshire and Santa Monica Blvd. centering on **Rodeo Drive,** known for its many opulent clothing boutiques and jewelry shops. Don't let the snooty attitudes dissuade you from window-shopping—or, if you're feeling particularly indulgent, splurging like Julia Roberts in *Pretty Woman.* Beverly Hills's European aspirations consume the Golden Triangle, where signs proudly proclaim Cannes as the sister-city of Beverly Hills. One particularly outlandish attempt to make customers believe they have strayed into Europe is the cobblestoned street of **Via Rodeo.** Faking antiquity, the entire street, hill, lampposts and all, was constructed in the last decade. Across the way is the venerable **Beverly Wilshire Hotel** (310-275-5200), whose old and new wings are connected by **El Camino Real,** a cobbled street with Louis XIV gates. Inside, hall mirrors reflect the glitter of crystal chandeliers and marble floors.

The new **Beverly Hills City Hall** (310-285-1000), stands, looking a bit out of place, on Crescent Dr. just below Santa Monica Blvd. This Spanish Renaissance building was erected during the heart of the Great Depression, and is now engulfed in Beverly Hills's new **Civic Center.** Completed in September 1990, the Civic Center, which includes the Beverly Hills Fire Department, Police Station, and library, took nine years to build and cost $120 million. The **Beverly Hills Library,** 444 N. Rexford Dr. (213-228-2220), is a case study in the city's overriding concerns—the interior is adorned with marble imported from Thailand, but contains a paltry collection of books. As always, though, Beverly Hills coordinates well: the library's tiling matches the colors on City Hall's dome. Moving farther north, the **Beverly Hills Hotel,** 9641 Sunset Blvd. (310-276-2251), is a pink, palm-treed collection of poolside cottages. The jungle-bungalow atmosphere mixes California cool, tropical paradise lushness, and Beverly Hills luxury. (This is where Howard Hughes established his infamous germ-free apartment.)

The **"Greystone Mansion"** (or Doheny House), 905 Loma Vista Dr. (310-550-4654), just off Doheny Rd., is a modern-day Versailles. Built by oil mogul Doheny for his son, the Tudor and Jacobean house includes the main building, two gatehouses, glorious gardens, and a stunning view of Los Angeles (open daily 10am-6pm; gardens free). The **Virginia Robinson Gardens** (310-276-5367) nearby are open to the public by reservation only. (Tours of gardens and 1911 Beaux Arts house Tues.-Fri. 10am and 1pm. $3; seniors, students, and children $2.25.)

Fans of *Beverly Hills 90210* will be disappointed to find that West Beverly High, alas, is only a television construct. They can, however, cruise **Beverly Hills High** (located on Moreno, between Olympic and Spalding). Beverly Hills High must be the only high school in the country with its own **oil well.** The **indoor swimming pool** is open for public use in summer (310-550-4796; open Mon.-Thurs. 1pm-5pm, Fri. 2-4pm), and has a sliding floor cover that converts the pool into a basketball court. This is where Jimmy Stewart and Donna Reed danced the aquatic Charleston in *It's a Wonderful Life.*

Just west of Beverly Hills High is **Century City,** whose broad awe-inspiring avenues frame the ABC Entertainment Center and the Century City Shopping Center and Market Place. Action movie buffs may recognize **Fox Plaza** on the Avenue of the Stars from the explosive Bruce Willis thriller *Die Hard.*

Just outside of Beverly Hills, the **Beit HaShoa Museum of Tolerance,** 9786 W. Pico Blvd. (310-553-9036), corner of Roxbury, opened in April of 1992. Previously known as the **Simon Wiesenthal Center,** the museum received $5 million from former Governor Deukmejian to build a new, larger, structure on the condition that the museum include displays on the Armenian and Native American genocides, as well as the Jewish Holocaust. The new museum holds high-tech wizardry designed to help visitors explore their own prejudices, and offers displays on the Holocaust, anti-Semitism, prejudice in the U.S., and the U.S. civil rights movement. One room features unseen voices that hurl insults at visitors. (Mandatory tours leave at 10-min. intervals and last 2½ hrs. Tickets cannot be reserved and often sell out on Fri. and Sun. Last tours leave 2½ hrs. before closing. Open Mon.-Wed. 10am-5pm, Thurs. 10am-8pm, Fri. 10am-3pm, Sun. 10:30am-5pm. $7.50, seniors $5.50, students $4.50, ages 3-12 $2.50.)

WESTWOOD AND UCLA

The university has left a clear impact on this region of Los Angeles. Many of the activities in the area are directed at the energetic student body. However, enclaves of more reserved attractions persist in the halls of Armand Hammer's museum and the tree-lined streets of Bel Air.

Food

Mongols B-B-Q, 1064 Gayley Ave. (310-824-3377). Follow the lunchtime crowd as they stream into this colorful little joint. In the center of it all, a glass-enclosed chef sizzles up various specialties. Full of people slurping up big bowls of noodles and looking pretty happy. Buffet-style lunch (Mongolian BBQ, $5.45). Come early to beat the line. Open Sun.-Thurs. 11:30am-10pm, Fri.-Sat. 11:30am-11pm.

Sphinx, 1779 A Westwood Blvd. (310-477-2358), ½ block north of Santa Monica Blvd. A bit out of the way from Westwood proper, but the Arabic-speaking clientele is evidence it's worth the trip. Excellent Middle Eastern cuisine. The falafel ($2.75) is tasty, and the BBQ chicken kebab ($3.50) is delectable. Open Mon.-Fri. 10am-10pm, Sat. 11am-10pm.

Sak's Teriyaki, 1121 Glendon Ave. (310-208-2002), in Westwood. Excellent, low-priced Japanese plates including chicken and beef teriyaki ($3.70-5). Popular with students. Happy hour special from 3-6pm ($2.75). Open Mon.-Wed. 10am-10pm, Thurs.-Fri. 10am-11pm, Sat. 11am-11pm, Sun. 11am-10pm.

Tacos Tacos, 1084 Glendon Ave. (310-208-2038), Westwood Village. Trendy "Southwestern Café" with blue corn chicken tacos ($2). Try the *horchata* (cinnamon-flavored rice water, $1.25). Open Mon.-Sat. 11am-10:30pm, Sun. 11am-9pm.

Sights

The gargantuan **University of California at Los Angeles** campus (it covers over 400 acres in the foothills of the Santa Monica Mountains, bounded by Sunset, Hilgard, Le Conte, and Gayley) and the dearth of parking spaces make it virtually impossible to park. UCLA, described in *Let's Go: USA 1969* as where "most of Playboy's pin-up beauties ripen," is not the uni-dimensional, hedonistic colony of blond, deep-tanned party animals it was once thought to be. On the contrary, it is one of the top research universities in the world. Among California's extensive and highly regarded public universities, UCLA is second in reputation for academic quality only to U.C. Berkeley.

The school is directly north of Westwood Village and west of Beverly Hills. To reach the campus by car, take the San Diego Fwy. (I-405) north to the Wilshire Blvd./Westwood exit, heading east into Westwood. Take Westwood Blvd. north off Wilshire, heading straight through the center of the village and directly into the campus. By bus, take MTA routes #20, 21 (the best, since it goes directly to the campus), 22, 320, or 322 along Wilshire Blvd. to Westwood. Exit at Wilshire and Gayley and walk north to Gayley and Weyburn Ave., where you can pick up a free UCLA Campus Express shuttle. Drivers can find free parking behind the Federal Building. Campus information stands sell a $4 day permit to park in student garages.

The best place to start a tour of UCLA is at the **Visitors Center,** 10945 Le Conte Ave., #147 (310-206-8147), located in the Ueberroth Olympic Office Building. An

18-minute film called *UCLA: The Future is Now* shown here upon request. Free 90-minute walking tours of the campus also depart from the visitors center (Mon.-Fri. 10:30am and 1:30pm or by appointment; call 310-206-8147). Campus maps are also available at the information kiosks.

At the northernmost reach of the campus, the **Dickson Art Center** (310-825-1462) houses the Wight Art Gallery, home to the Grunwald Center for the Graphic Arts, as well as internationally recognized exhibitions, many of which are being moved to the Armand Hammer building (call 310-443-7097 for the details). (Open Sept.-June Tues. 11am-8pm, Wed.-Fri. 11am-5pm, Sat.-Sun. 1-5pm. Free.) The **Murphy Sculpture Garden,** containing over 70 pieces scattered through five acres, lies directly in front of the Art Center. The collection includes works by such major artists as Rodin, Matisse, and Miró. Opposite the sculpture garden is **MacGowen Hall,** which contains the **Tower of Masks.** UCLA's **Inverted Fountain** is located between Knudsen Hall and Schoenberg Hall, directly south of Dickson Plaza. An innovation in the field of fountain design, the fountain spouts water spouts from its perimeter that rushes down into the gaping hole in the middle.

The **Fowler Museum of Cultural History** in Haines Hall (310-825-4361), displays artifacts from contemporary, historic, and prehistoric cultures of Africa, Asia, Oceania, and the Americas. (Basically, it covers all of time and everywhere except Europe and Antartica; open Wed. and Fri.-Sun. noon-5pm, Thurs. noon-8pm.) The museum is presently the source of controversy since Native American bones are stored here for their archaeological value, despite laws which provide for Native Americans' rights to sacred burial. The **Botanical Gardens** (310-825-3620), in the southeast corner of the campus, encompass the Zen Buddhist-inspired Japanese Garden, which can be viewed only by appointment. (Open Tues. 10am-1pm, Wed. noon-3pm. Call 310-825-4574 two weeks in advance to arrange for a tour.) The garden also includes a subtropical canyon where redwoods and venerable palms mingle brook-side (open Mon.-Fri. 8am-5pm, Sat.-Sun. 8am-4pm).

Ackerman Union, 308 Westwood Plaza (310-825-7711), stands southwest of the Quadrangle, at the bottom of the hill. Ackerman is the campus information bank. A calendar lists the lengthy line-up of movies (first-runs often free), lectures, and campus activities. The Expo Center, on level B, has travel information and a complete **rideboard** (see Getting Around, page 79). The ground floor is swallowed by the huge **Associated Students' Store,** the perfect spot to buy UCLA insignia items, including t-shirts, pens, and notebooks (310-825-0611; open Mon.-Thurs. 7:30am-7:30pm, Fri. 7:30am-6pm, Sat. 8:30am-7:30pm, Sun. 8:30am-6:30pm).

Westwood Village, just south of the campus, with its myriad of movie theaters, trendy boutiques, and upscale bistros, is geared more toward the residents of L.A.'s Westside than UCLA students. Like most college neighborhoods, however, Westwood is humming on Friday and Saturday nights. For the most part, Westwood is safe, and generally overrun by the high school and college crowd. Off the main drag at 1218 Glendon Ave. is the **Westwood Memorial Cemetery.** Flowers, teddy bears, and even sprouted Chia Pets are left by family and fans who make pilgrimages to the graves of Marilyn Monroe and Natalie Wood.

Westwood's theaters are among the oldest in the city and are a reasonable alternative to the tourist-trap atmosphere of Hollywood. Of particular note is the **Village Theatre,** 961 Broxton Ave. (310-208-5576), a movie theater with a high tower, large auditorium (complete with a balcony for crowded shows), and an impressive sound system. Celebs make quiet appearances here ($7.50, students with ID $5; daily matinees $4.50).

The **Armand Hammer Museum of Art and Cultural Center,** 10899 Wilshire Blvd. (310-443-7000), was opened to the public in November 1990. Hammer purportedly wanted to donate his collections to the L.A. County Museum of Art but demanded that the works be exhibited together in a separate wing. The museum refused, telling Hammer to build his own place—and he did just that. Impressive from the outside and light, airy, and clad in marble on the inside, Edwards Larrabee Barnes's tribute to Hammer's wealth is a welcome addition to the Westwood scene.

The museum houses a large collection of European and American works from the 16th to the 20th century. The museum's gem is Van Gogh's *Hospital at Saint-Rémy,* a startling, flame-like image of the private hospital in which Van Gogh died just a year after the painting's completion. The museum also holds the world's largest collection of works by French lithographer Honoré Daumier, Leonardo da Vinci's 18-page codex containing his ideas on hydraulics and engineering (not particularly interesting unless you can read 16th-century Italian written backwards in second grade penmanship), and various traveling exhibitions. (Parking in Westwood $2.75; open Tues.-Sat. 11am-7pm, Sun. 11am-6pm; tours Sun. and Thurs. at 1pm. $4.50, students and seniors $3, under 17 free.)

Directly across from UCLA is the opulent community of **Bel Air,** where Ronald Reagan has retired. Farther west on Sunset Blvd. (the setting for the car race in *Against All Odds*), are the neighborhoods of **Brentwood** (former neighborhood of Nicole and O.J. Simpson) and beautiful **Pacific Palisades.** The cliffs give way to the ocean at the popular **Will Rogers State Beach,** on the 16000 block of Pacific Coast Highway.

At 14523 Sunset, hike around **Will Rogers State Historical Park** (310-454-8212) and take in the panoramic views of the city and the distant Pacific. You can visit the famous humorist's home and eat a picnic brunch while watching a Saturday afternoon polo match. (Matches Sat. 2-5pm and Sun. 10am-noon.) Follow Chatauqua Blvd. inland from PCH to Sunset Blvd., or take bus #2 which runs along Sunset. (Park open daily 8am-7pm; Rogers's house open daily 10am-5pm.)

SANTA MONICA

Santa Monica, the Bay City of Raymond Chandler's novels, was once known as the "Gold Coast" because of the fabulously wealthy stars who called it home. With a little imagination, you may be able to relive the past glory days by strolling down the famous pier. It takes about half an hour (with no traffic) on express bus #10 or on the Santa Monica Fwy. (I-10) from downtown to reach Santa Monica.

Food

Unfortunately, many of Santa Monica's eateries are quite expensive. The new **EATZ Café** in Santa Monica Place (at the end of the 3rd St. Promenade on Broadway) offers 17 different types of mall food to choose from, a number of which are tasty and reasonably priced.

Ye Olde King's Head, 116 Santa Monica Blvd. (310-451-1402), in Santa Monica. An authentic British pub owned by a Manchester expatriate. Fish and chips for $7.50, a variety of other English entrees are $7-9. The King's Head also features a broad assortment of English beers and ales. They're expensive, but not many publicans in Santa Monica know the difference between Whitbread and Bud. Open Mon.-Thurs. 11am-11pm, Fri.-Sat. 11am-midnight, Sun. noon-11:30pm.

Skorpio's, 109 Santa Monica Blvd. (310-393-9020), ½ block from Ocean Ave. Standard and solid Greek fare for under $6. Giant gyro sandwiches ($3.50) and great spanakopitas ($5.50). Beer, wine, and cappuccino. Open daily 11am-11pm.

Benita's Frites, 1437 3rd St. Promenade (310-458-2889), in Santa Monica. French fries are the sole option on this menu. They're served the Belgian way, in a paper cone with any of the 20 hot and cold sauces—try the garlic-lemon-mayonnaise. Small order with one sauce $2, each additional sauce 50¢. Open Sun. noon-8pm, Mon. 11:30am-4pm., Tues.-Thurs. 11:30am-10pm, Fri.-Sat. 11:30am-10:30pm.

Sights

Santa Monica's beach is the closest to Los Angeles proper and is thus crowded and dirty. Still, the lure of sun, surf, and sand causes nightmarish summer traffic jams on I-10 and I-405. There are much prettier and cleaner beaches to visit to the north and south, but at least Santa Monica Beach has public bathrooms. Santa Monica Beach may not be good for swimming, but a paved path stretching along the beach all the way to Venice is perfect for walking, in-line skating, and bicycling. (Rental shops are plentiful.) The colorful **Santa Monica Pier** is a nostalgic and popular, if a bit sleazy, spot. The gem of the pier is the turn-of-the-century carousel, which was featured in *The Sting*. The nearby beach made a more recent entertainment appearance on *Beverly Hills 90210* as the site of the beach club where the gang spent their summer. The beach club used on the television show is located a short walk north of the Santa Monica Pier. The main walk of the pier offers the familiar aroma of popcorn, a few pizza joints, several arcades, and tons of tacky souvenirs. **Palisades Park,** on the bluff overlooking the pier, offers a magnificent view of the ocean, especially at sunset.

With the creation of the **Third Street Promenade** in 1989, and the recent remodeling of **Santa Monica Place,** Santa Monica has become one of L.A.'s major walking, movie-seeing, and yuppie-gathering areas. The Third Street Promenade sports some cool cafés, a couple of L.A.'s better bookshops, popular bars and restaurants, and a variety of street artists (not to mention some water-spouting, ivy-lined, mesh dinosaur sculptures). Main Street attracts notice for its vintage collectible and apparel shops and browser-friendly galleries. There are also two small museums: the **Santa Monica Museum of Art,** 2437 Main St. (310-399-0433), and the **Santa Monica Heritage Museum,** 2612 Main St. (310-392-8537).

Military, aerial, and military-aerial enthusiasts will enjoy Santa Monica's **Museum of Flying,** Santa Monica Airport, 2772 Donald Douglas Loop North (310-392-8822; open Tues.-Sun. 10am-5pm; $5, seniors $3, and children $2). The museum's changing exhibits include the 1924 Douglas World Cruiser "New Orleans" (the first plane to go around the world), authentic B-51s, and a replica of the Voyager spacecraft. There are also several films shown daily.

VENICE

Venice is Los Angeles to the max—it perpetuates the image that evokes L.A. for so many people. A perennial favorite among foreigners, Venice is wacky on weekdays and wild on weekends. A typical Sunday includes trapeze artists, spontaneous Rollerblade dancing competitions, clowns, jugglers, comedians, glass-eaters, hemp advocates, bikini-clad skaters, fortune tellers, as well as people with acts that are nearly impossible to describe (for example, picture a man standing on his head while playing the guitar, balancing books on his feet and doing several other things at the same time), and finally, nonchalant Angelenos cruising the boardwalk and taking it all in stride.

In recent months, police have been added to the mix; both to regulate the flow of traffic and to intimidate the gangs that sometimes show up here. Don't let yourself be distracted by the excitement to the point of forgetting about personal safety, although, for the most part, you should have no reason to worry. Also remember that all the crazy acts taking place are attempts to generate income, if you stop to watch, you will be asked and perhaps *strongly* encouraged to make a donation.

Venice's story begins just after the turn of the century, when Abbot Kinney dug a series of canals throughout the town and filled them with water, intending to bring the romance and refinement of Venice, Italy, to Southern California. But Kinney's vision wasn't realized; the water of the canals became dirty and oily and Venice became home to gamblers, bootleggers, and other rogues. Eventually, most of the canals were filled in and forgotten. Skateboarders use some of the others.

For a sense of the Venice that Kinney envisioned, head for the traffic circle at Main St. and Windward Ave., three blocks inland from the beach pavilion. This was once a circular canal, the hub of the whole network. The post office's mural sums up Venice's cluttered history in an appropriately jumbled way—with oil derricks seemingly perched on Kinney's shoulders. One of the sole surviving canals is at Strong's Dr., off Washington St. Ducks are its lively inhabitants.

To get to Venice from downtown L.A., take bus #33 or 333 (or 436 during rush hour). From downtown Santa Monica, take Santa Monica bus #1 or 2. Drivers can avoid hourly meter-feedings by parking in the $5 per day lot at Pacific and Venice.

Food

Venice runs the gamut from greasy to health-conscious, as befits its beachy-hippie population.

Windward Farms Restaurant, 1512 Pacific Ave. (310-399-8505), across the street from the Venice Beach Hostel. Offering "healthy, home-style cooking," this clean spot is well-stocked with simple, hearty items, try the thick, satisfying beef stew ($3.65). Vegetarians should have no problem assembling a meal (black bean soup $2.25). Open Mon.-Fri. 8am-7pm, Sat.-Sun. 8am-6pm. Breakfast 'til 11am on weekdays, noon on weekends—lots of specials.

Tito's Tacos, 11222 Washington Place (310-391-5780), a bit out of the way in Culver City at Sepulveda, 1 block north of Washington Blvd., virtually *beneath* the San Diego Fwy. The name should have been Tito's Burritos, since the burrito, with its huge hunks of shredded beef, is the star attraction (at $2.10, it's also the most expensive thing on the menu). Tostadas and enchiladas $1.25, tacos 95¢. Plenty of parking. Open daily 9am-11:30pm.

Sights

Ocean Front Walk, Venice's main beachfront drag, is a dramatic demographic departure from Santa Monica's promenade. Street people converge on shaded clusters of benches, yelping evangelists drown out off-color comedians, and bodybuilders of both sexes pump iron in skimpy spandex outfits at the original **Muscle Beach** (1800 Ocean Front Walk, closest to 18th and Pacific Ave.). This is where the roller-skating craze began. Fire-juggling cyclists, joggers, groovy elders (such as the "skateboard grandma"), and bards in Birkenstocks make up the balance of this playground population. Vendors of jewelry, snacks, and beach paraphernalia overwhelm the boardwalk. Collect your wits and people-watch at one of the cafés or juice bars. The **Sidewalk Café,** 1401 Ocean Front Walk (310-399-5547), with free live music most evenings, is nearly always packed (open daily 7am-11pm). If your feet don't move you through the crowds fast enough, rent skates or a bike. **Skatey's Sports,** 102 Washington (310-823-7971), rents in-line skates ($5 per hr., $10 per day) and bikes ($7.50 per hr., $15 per day; open Mon.-Fri. 9am-7pm, Sat.-Sun. 9am-6pm).

Venice's **street murals** are another free show. Don't miss the brilliant, graffiti-disfigured homage to Botticelli's *Birth of Venus* on the beach pavilion at the end of Windward Ave.: a woman of ostensibly divine beauty, wearing short shorts, a Bandaid top, and roller skates, boogies out of her seashell. The side wall of a Japanese restaurant on Windward is covered with a perfect imitation of a Japanese Hokusai print of a turbulent sea. To look at paintings indoors, you might want to stop by **L.A. Louver,** 77 Market St. and 55 N. Venice Blvd. (310-822-4955), a gallery showing the work of some hip L.A. artists (open Tues.-Sat. noon-5pm).

MARINA DEL REY

Venice's immediate neighbor to the south, Marina del Rey, is older, more expensive, and considerably more sedate. The **Marina del Rey Chamber of Commerce,** 14014 Tahiti Way (821-0555), can provide travelers with a decent map, but not much else. (Open Mon.-Fri. 9am-noon and 1-5pm.)

Food

Aunt Kizzy's Back Porch, 4325 Glencoe Ave., C-9 (578-1005). Voted best soul food by L.A. Magazine and frequented by Magic Johnson, this place deserves a better location than a SoCal strip mall. Daily lunch specials like chicken and dumplings or smothered pork chops crowd the plate with cornbread, rice, gravy, and 2 scoops of veggies ($7). Open Sun.-Thurs. 11am-10pm, Fri.-Sat. 11am-11pm. Sun. buffet brunch.

Moose McGillacutty's, 13535 Mindinao Way (574-3932), just west of Lincoln Blvd. Dancing nightly to top-40 tunes. Full menu ranging from $3-4 for bar food to $8.50 for chicken fettuccine. Outdoor patio with views of the marina. College nights (Thurs.) offers $1 drafts and no cover for anyone with a college ID or sweatshirt. Cover starts at 8pm and averages $5. Open Mon.-Sat. 11:30am-2am, Sun. 10am-2am.

Sights

Built in 1965 as a yacht harbor, Marina del Rey is the largest man-made **marina** in the world, home to 6,000 private yachts and 3,000 boats in dry storage; it has wide, uncrowded, sandy beaches, no doubt because of the minimal wind and waves. Watch seacraft parade through the main channel from the breezy North Jetty at Pacific Ave. Fisherman's Village (823-5411), at 13763 Fiji Way, is the marina's picturesque shopping and strolling area. The marina offers sail- and motor-boat rentals, as well as a harbor cruise ($7, call Horns's 310-301-6000). The marina village becomes a singles' scene at night, when swingers come out of the woodwork. It's also home to some excellent, albeit overpriced, seafood restaurants. (The ridiculously expensive **Warehouse Restaurant** is allegedly one of the best in the world.)

The next patch of sand, **Dockweiler State Beach,** provides a welcome break from the built-up environment paralleling the Bay's immensely popular **bike path,** but lies a mere ½ mi. from the runways of LAX (earplugs or a Walkman may help). The small community of **El Segundo** is the site of the second Standard Oil refinery in California. The stench expelled by the refinery cannot, unfortunately, be avoided. The bike path here follows the coastal road and can be a little harrowing in heavy traffic.

ROUTE 1: THE PACIFIC COAST HIGHWAY

Originating among the surfer beaches south of L.A., Rte. 1—or the Pacific Coast Highway (PCH)—sweeps grandly along the California coast. Never straying more than a few miles from the sea, the highway ends in the magnificent wave-splattered redwood groves near Garberville, more than 200 mi. north of San Francisco. Along the way, its two lanes of blacktop offer a taste of the Californian experience. Across rolling hills filled with extravagant mansions, through cow pastures and fruit orchards, and past hip urban centers, the Pacific Coast Hwy. traverses a cross-section of the state's landscape. Hang gliders, farmers, lumberjacks, and campers mix with seekers of the quaint, the sophisticated, or the grandiosely picturesque. The Pacific Coast Highway may not be all of California, but it's an admirable sampling.

Begun in 1920, the highway required $10 million and 17 years for completion. Many of the numerous bridges on the route were architectural wonders in their day; and some—such as the Bixby Creek Bridge, one of the longest single-span bridges in the world—still are. Some segments of the highway have been rebuilt more than once; earthquake damage forced a stretch of Rte. 1 in Marin County to close for nearly a year. But too much of California's identity is tied to this highway for locals to give it up.

Although the loopy length of PCH makes it perhaps impractical for a complete journey up the California coast, no traveler with access to a car should bypass the opportunity to experience at least sections of this legendary highway. There is more information about Route One in the chapters titled Central Coast (page 192), San Francisco Bay Area (page 305), and Northern Coast (page 324). PCH should not be missed. *Nothing can compare to a drive on the One.*

From Santa Monica, where it temporarily merges with I-10, PCH runs northward along the coast. Several of L.A. County's best beaches line this stretch of PCH between Santa Monica and the Ventura County line.

Heading north from Santa Monica, the first major attraction is the **J. Paul Getty Museum,** 17985 PCH (310-458-2003), set back on a cliff above the ocean. Getty, an oil magnate, built this mansion as a re-creation of the first-century Villa dei Papiri in Herculaneum, with a beautiful main peristyle garden, a reflecting pool, and bush-lined paths. Appropriately, the collection of Greek and Roman sculpture is given center stage—it includes a bronze athlete that is the only surviving work of Lysippos, a sculptor contemporaneous with Alexander the Great. Although Getty himself collected 13th- to early 20th-century European paintings (with an emphasis on the

Renaissance and Baroque periods), the museum owns an incredible variety of artwork, including decorative arts and illuminated manuscripts. Unfortunately, only a small selection is displayed at any one time. The museum has also recently added an excellent collection of 19th- and 20th-century photography, as well as one of Van Gogh's Iris paintings. With a $2.9 billion endowment (New York's Metropolitan Museum of Art has "only" $350 million), the trustees can afford to keep their purse strings loose. Because of the museum's operating agreement with its residential neighbors, access to the museum is tricky. The parking lot is small and reservations are needed at least a day in advance, and weeks in advance in summer. You are not permitted to park outside the museum unless you do so at the county lot. Bicyclists and motorcyclists are admitted without reservations. To avoid the parking hassle, take MTA #434 (which you can board at Sunset and PCH in Malibu or Ocean and Colorado in Santa Monica) to the museum. Mind that you ask for a free **museum pass** from the bus driver or you will not be admitted. The museum gate is a ½ mi. from the bus stop, so be prepared to walk (open Tues.-Sun. 10am-5pm; free).

There is an attractive garden **tea room** at the museum which serves light food and desserts (open 9:30am-4:30pm). But you may want to save your appetite and, on your way back, stop at the popular **Gladstone's-4-Fish,** at 17300 PCH (310-454-3474). The food is a bit expensive and the restaurant is often extremely crowded. However it is worth the wait to enjoy the tasty fresh seafood served right on the water's edge. In keeping with the oceanside theme, the floor of the restaurant is covered with sand. Watch the sun set and savor one of Gladstone's enormous desserts—the mile-high chocolate cake ($7) is enough for four people. (Open Sun.-Thurs. 7am-11pm, Fri.-Sat. 7am-midnight.)

Just north of the museum is **Topanga State Beach,** 18500 PCH, a quiet surfing beach (a bit rocky for sunbathing) with lifeguards and restaurants but no concessions stands. The out-of-the-way community of **Topanga,** where granola and macrame are serious business and the New Age is now, is 4 mi. up Topanga Canyon Rd.

The celebrity colony of **Malibu** stretches along the low 20000 blocks of PCH. With their multi-million-dollar homes and famous neighbors, Malibu residents can afford to be hostile to outsiders. If you have a car, you might enjoy a drive up one of the curving, narrow roads toward the mountains. Look at the homes and dare to dream. A public beach lies along the 23200 block of the PCH. You can walk onto the beach via the **Zonker Harris** access way at 22700 PCH, named after the quintessential Californian of Garry Trudeau's comic strip *Doonesbury.* One reasonably priced eatery in the area is the **Reel Inn,** 18661 PCH (310-456-8221). The patio in the back is especially pleasant at night, with flaming lanterns. Get your food inside, then eat it outside in the low-key atmosphere. (Brunch about $4-8. Hot shrimp pasta $10. Open daily 11am-10:30pm.) **Natural Progression Surfboards,** 22935½ W. Pacific Hwy. (310-456-6302), in Malibu, rents surfboards ($20 per day, plus $5 insurance) and wetsuits ($8). Windsurfer rental is $30 per day, plus $5 insurance. (Open daily 9am-6pm.)

If you're a fan of the TV show *Baywatch,* you have plenty of company—with more than 1 billion viewers, it's the most-watched show in the world. Rumor has it that *Baywatch* is filmed on a state beach somewhere between Malibu and Santa Monica. Those eager to witness all the gorgeous *Baywatch* bodies in action may want to scan beachside highways for television crew vans.

Corral State Beach, an uncrowded, windsurfing, swimming, and scuba-diving beach, lies on the 26000 block of PCH, followed by **Point Dume State Beach,** which is small and generally uncrowded. North of Point Dume, along the 30000 block of PCH, lies **Zuma,** L.A. County's northernmost, largest, and most popular county-owned sandbox, with lifeguards, restrooms, and a $5 parking fee. The beach is frequented by a wide variety of visitors. Stations 8 to 12 belong to solitude seekers. Valley high-schoolers have staked out 6 and 7, which are the most crowded and lively parts. Zuma 3, 4, and 5 are frequented by families who keep things slightly more sedate. If you don't want to bring food, pick something up at **Trancas Market** (PCH and Trancas Canyon, around Station 12). There are fewer footprints at **West-**

ward Beach, just southeast of Zuma. Cliffs shelter the beach from the highway and provide a vantage point for watching the boogie-boarders and surfers who frequent the beach.

Visitors with cars should not miss **Mulholland Drive,** nature's answer to the roller coaster. Twisting and turning for 15 spectacular miles along the crest of the Santa Monica Mountains, Mulholland stretches from PCH, near the Ventura County line, east to the Hollywood Fwy. and the San Fernando Valley. Whoever's driving will have a hard time concentrating—numerous points along the way, especially between Coldwater Canyon and the San Diego Fwy., have compelling views of the entire Los Angeles basin.

SANTA MONICA NATIONAL RECREATION AREA

It is difficult to pin down exactly what the above term describes; the range of topographies comprised by the area is vast. Because of the extreme population crush of Los Angeles, the National Recreation Area represents less an enclave of wilderness than an ongoing cooperation among private landowners, public agencies, and concerned volunteers. As such, it is fairly decentralized. The best place for the nature-lover to gather information is at the **National Park Service headquarters,** 30401 Agoura Rd. (818-597-9192), in Agoura Hills. For general information on individual parks within the mountains, call the **Mountain Parks Information Line** (800-533-7275).

The national park service itself administers only one set of campgrounds: the **Circle X Site Campgrounds.** Two are first-come, first-camped. The **Happy Hollow Family Walk-in** costs $6 per night, while the **Backcountry Hike-in** requires only a free backcountry permit, available from the Circle X or Rancho Sierra Vista Site Ranger Stations. However, the latter site has been closed due to fire damage; call the above information number for updates. For group camping reservations, call 310-457-6408; the fee is $2 per person per night. To reach Circle X Ranch, take the PCH to Yerba Buena Rd., then go north approximately 5 mi. The **ranger station** will be on your right. All sites are for tent camping only; vehicles must be parked in a designated area (flush toilets; no wood fires permitted).

The **Rancho Sierra Vista/Satwina Site** is a daytime facility which includes hiking trails, a Native American Culture Center, and Moorpark College's Equine Training and Management Program. There are also picnic areas. To reach the site, take U.S. 101 to Thousand Oaks/Newbury Park. Then take the Wendy exit, follow Wendy Rd. until it ends, then make a right on Potrero Rd. Turn left at the stop sign; a left at Pinehill Rd. will take you to the entrance.

Another place of interest administered by the National Park Service is the **Paramount Ranch Site.** In 1927, Paramount pictures bought 2700 acres of what used to be Rancho Las Virgenes, in the Agoura Hills area. The site included a mountain that bore some resemblance to the company's logo. It served as a location for a number of films until it was sold to private individuals during the '40s and '50s. The Hertz family bought the southeast portion of the ranch, converting it into the backdrop for numerous television westerns. The **Western Town** remains available for use by independent production companies, and is open to visitors during filming. Three hiking trails are accessible as well. To reach the ranch, take U.S. 101 to Agoura Hills. Exit at Kanan Rd., travel south ¾ mi., turn left on Cornell Rd.; continue 2½ mi. to the entrance on the right.

SAN FERNANDO VALLEY

When city engineer William Mulholland brought water to what is now the San Fernando Valley in 1913, he stood on a hillside overlooking the basin, watched the first torrents pour out of the Aqueduct, and proclaimed "There it is! Take it!" The city rushed to obey.

Now the end of the Ventura Freeway marks the spiritual center of American suburbia—a long series of communities with tree-lined streets, cookie-cutter homes, lawns, and shopping malls. A third of L.A.'s population resides here. The portion of the valley incorporated into the City of Los Angeles alone covers 140 million acres.

Food

Ventura Blvd. is filled with restaurants. Eating lunch near the studios in **Studio City** is your best stargazing opportunity. The famous are willing to dine outside the studios because of Studio City's unwritten law—you can stare all you want, but don't bother them, *and don't ask for autographs.*

Dalt's Grill, 3500 W. Olive Ave. (818-953-7752) in Burbank at the corner of Olive and Riverside. Swank grill next door to Warner Studios. Healthy chicken fajita Caesar salad $6.59. Burgers and sandwiches $4-5. Stocked lacquered oak bar. Open Mon.-Thurs. 11am-midnight, Fri.-Sat. 11am-1am, Sun. 10am-midnight.

Poquito Más, 3701 Cahuenga Blvd. (818-760-8226). Wildly popular Mexican spot known for its fish tacos. Skimps on atmosphere, but a fabulous *carnita* is only $1.75. Open Sun.-Thurs. 10am-midnight, Fri.-Sat. 10am-1am.

Brasilia, 12186 Ventura Blvd. (818-761-0213). A sunny semi-trattoria, blond in its decor and clientele—the latter at least *look* as though they star in soap operas. Good cappuccino. Breads from 85¢; salads $5-6. Open Mon.-Thurs. 7am-10pm, Fri.-Sat. 7am-midnight, Sun. 8am-10pm.

Versailles, 17410 Ventura Blvd. (818-906-0756), in Encino. Despite the name, the restaurant serves Cuban food (this is the *other* Versailles—the one in Cuba where the owner was born). Try the roasted chicken dinner ($6.50), served with Mojo Sauce, black bean soup, rice, and fried banana, and you'll understand why locals flock here. $4 lunch special. Open Sun.-Thurs. 11am-10pm, Fri.-Sat. 11am-11pm.

Sights

Ventura Boulevard, the main commercial thoroughfare, today combines business and recreation with its office buildings, restaurants, and shops. The sprawling valley viewed from the foothills at night, particularly from Mulholland Drive, is spectacular. It's a nice place to live, but you wouldn't want to visit. Aside from the major attractions of Magic Mountain and tours of nearby movie studios (both listed under Entertainment, page 109), the valley is best known as the land of the infamous and stereotypical valley girls and dudes.

Once you've finished searching Ventura Blvd. for the ultimate valley hangout (try a Denny's on a weekend night between 2 and 4am), you may want to check out the **Museum of Neon Art,** 1000 Universal Dr. (818-761-MONA, -6662), at the City Walk in Universal City. Exhibits range from neon artwork to other types of electric and kinetic sculpture. While you're there, pick up a MONA T-shirt, depicting a neon sculpture of the Mona Lisa. (Open daily 11am-11pm. Free.) **Universal City** also boasts a number of restaurants, theaters, and clubs to waylay the traveler in search of a good time (and who isn't?).

Another sight of interest is the **Mission San Fernando Ray De España** (818-361-0186). The mission was founded in 1797 by Padre Fermin Lasuen, but unfortunately, no structures remain from this period. The old **Iglesia** was destroyed by the 1971 earthquake, and the **Convento** has been covered with stucco, making the cemetery and the park across the street the most intriguing part of the mission (open daily 9am-5pm). West of the mission, at 10940 Sepulveda, sits the **Adres Pico Adobe,** the former home of Pico, who started the first wave of construction in the valley in 1845 when he built up his own copious tracts of land.

After about an hour's drive along the San Fernando Freeway you'll reach **Simi Valley,** home to the **Ronald Reagan Presidential Library,** 40 Presidential Dr. (805-522-8444). (Open Mon.-Sat. 10am-5pm, Sun. noon-5pm. $4, seniors $2, under 15 free.) A new exhibit is the "Madame President" display, which celebrates 200 years of First Ladies. Don't worry, all gowns have been paid for in full.

PASADENA

Pasadena, a city-sized suburb about 10 mi. northeast of downtown Los Angeles, offers some respite from the frenetic pace of Greater L.A., although things pick up during major sporting events (the 1994 World Cup finals were held here). Pasadena, with tree-lined streets and outstanding cultural facilities, is usually placid. The **Pasadena Fwy.** (Rte. 110 N.), built as a WPA project between 1934 and 1941, is one of the nation's oldest. The WPA engineers did not anticipate the needs of the modern motorist; 50 years later, drivers at a dead stop are required to merge almost instantaneously with 55+ mph traffic. (Almost no one in L.A. drives 55, unless they are stuck in heavy traffic. *Let's Go* does not recommend speeding.) A good first stop in Pasadena is the **Convention and Visitors Bureau,** 171 S. Los Robles Ave. (818-795-9311; fax 795-7656), which has numerous promotional materials and guides to the arts.

Food

There are lots of good restaurants in Pasadena, including the popular hangouts below. Fair Oaks Ave. and Colorado Blvd., in the Old Town section of Pasadena, are both filled with cafés and Mexican restaurants.

Mijares Mexican Restaurant, 145 Palmetto Dr. (818-792-2763), entrance on Pasadena Ave. Vast and very popular, with a festive atmosphere and bar. Combination dinners $6-8. Open Mon.-Thurs. 11am-9pm, Fri.-Sat. 11am-10pm, Sun. 10am-9pm.
Pie 'n' Burger, 913 E. California Blvd. (818-795-1123), near Lake Ave. The name says it all. The decor is drab, with a long counter and a handful of tables, but the pies (about $2 per slice) and burgers ($4-5) are sublime. Serves breakfast too. Open Mon.-Fri. 6am-10pm, Sat. 7am-10pm, Sun. 7am-9pm.

Sights

In the gorge that forms the city's western boundary stands Pasadena's most famous landmark, the **Rose Bowl,** 991 Rosemont Blvd. (818-577-3106). Home to the "granddaddy" of the college-football bowl games, the annual confrontation between the champions of the Big Ten and Pac 10 conferences, the Rose Bowl is also regular-season home to the **UCLA Bruins** football team.

Over the hill and east of the stadium lies the **Gamble House,** 4 Westmoreland Pl. (818-793-3334). Designed in 1907 by brothers Charles and Henry Greene for the heirs to the Proctor and Gamble fortune, David and Mary Gamble, this bungalow-style masterpiece has become part of USC's School of Architecture. Everything down to the trim, paneling, and carpets was designed by the Greene brothers, much of it actually crafted in their Pasadena workshop (1-hr. tours Thurs.-Sun. noon-3pm. $4, seniors and students $3, children free). A map and a pamphlet detailing other renowned neighborhood buildings are available in the **Gamble House Bookstore** for $1. One nearby stop is the **Fenyes Estate,** just a couple of blocks east off Orange Grove, at 470 W. Walnut St. (818-577-1660). The mansion is the residence of the **Pasadena Historical Society and Museum** and has a collection of turn-of-the-century furnishings and art. Much of the decor is in a schlock-Mediterranean style, and the presence of mannequins in faded "period" costumes does little to improve matters ($4, students and seniors $3; tours of museum Thurs.-Sun. 1-4pm; closed Aug.).

South of this neighborhood, at the western end of the downtown area (also called Old Pasadena), lies Pasadena's answer to LACMA and the Getty Museum, the **Norton Simon Museum of Art,** 411 W. Colorado Blvd. (213-681-2484), at Orange Grove Blvd. Sleek and modern, it contrasts with the classic design of the Getty. There are numerous Rodin and Brancusi bronzes, and the paintings include pieces by Rembrandt, Raphael, and Picasso. There is also an impressive Impressionist and Post-Impressionist hall. The collection of art from ancient Southeast Asia is one of the world's best, and the presentation is flawless. Simon's eclectic, slightly idiosyncratic taste, as well as the well-written descriptions of the works, make this museum more interesting than similar assemblages elsewhere. Don't miss the sculpture garden. (Open Thurs.-Sun. noon-6pm. $4, seniors and students $2, under 12 free. Wheelchair accessible.) From downtown L.A. take bus #483 from Olive St.; anywhere between Venice Blvd. and 1st St., to Colorado Blvd. and Fair Oaks Ave. in Pasadena. Then take #180 or 181. The museum is four blocks west.

Continuing east into downtown, the area around Fair Oaks Ave. and Colorado Blvd., once home to thrift shops, shows signs of gentrification. The **Pasadena Civic Center,** 300 E. Green (818-449-7360), north of Colorado Blvd., is the centerpiece of the city's Spanish-influenced architectural heritage. The City Hall is built in the Spanish style and bordered by a beautiful open courtyard, complete with gardens and a fountain. This is where the red carpet is rolled out each year for television's Emmy Awards. Just east of the Civic Center is the **Pacific Asia Museum,** 46 N. Los Robles Ave. (818-449-2742), between Colorado Ave. and Union St. This museum displays a collection of Asian paintings, drawings, and jade sculpture. (Open Wed.-Sun. noon-5pm. $3, seniors and students $1.50. Tours Sun. 2pm.) The **Pasadena Playhouse,** 39 S. El Molino Ave. (818-356-7529), between Colorado and Green, was founded in 1917 and has nurtured the careers of William Holden and Gene Hackman, among others. Restored and reopened in 1986, it currently offers some of the finest theater in L.A. (call 818-356-7529 for ticket info and see Theater, page 112).

Some of the world's greatest scientific minds do their work at the **California Institute of Technology (Cal Tech),** 1201 E. California Blvd. (818-356-6811), about 2½ mi. southeast of downtown. The buildings of the lush campus incorporate a mishmash of Spanish, Italian Renaissance, and modern styles. Cal Tech, founded in 1891 as Throop University, has amassed a faculty that includes several Nobel laureates (Albert Einstein once taught here) and a student body that prides itself both on its collectively staggering I.Q. and its elaborate and ingenious practical jokes. These range from the mundane (unscrewing all the chairs in a lecture hall and bolting them in backwards) to the ingenious (altering the Rose Bowl scoreboard during the game with the aid of computers).

Near Pasadena

A ½-mi. south of Cal Tech lies the **Huntington Library, Art Gallery,** and **Botanical Gardens,** 1151 Oxford Rd., San Marino 91108 (818-405-2100, ticket information 818-405-2273). The complex was built in 1910 as the home of businessman Henry Huntington, "the Carnegie of the West," who made his money in railroads and Southern California real estate. The stunning botanical gardens are home to 207 acres of plants, many of them rare. (No picnicking or sunbathing allowed.) The library houses one of the world's most important collections of rare books and English and American manuscripts, including a Gutenberg Bible, Benjamin Franklin's handwritten autobiography, and a 1410 manuscript of Chaucer's *Canterbury Tales.* The art gallery is known for its 18th- and 19th-century British paintings. Sentimental favorites on exhibit include Thomas Gainsborough's *Blue Boy* and Sir Thomas Lawrence's *Pinkie.* American art is on view in the **Virginia Steele Scott Gallery.** The Annabella Huntington Memorial Collection features Renaissance paintings and 18th-century French decorative arts. (Open Tues.-Fri. 1-4:30pm, Sat.-Sun. 10:30am-4:30pm; $4.) The Huntington museum sits between Huntington Dr. and California Blvd. in San Marino, south of Pasadena. From downtown L.A., bus #79 leaves from Union Station and takes you straight to the library (40- to 45-min. trip).

Recent remodeling and a spate of innovative exhibits may earn the **Southwest Museum,** 234 Museum Dr. (213-221-2163), the attention it deserves. The museum's collection of artifacts includes contemporary Native American art. Founded in 1912 by Westophile Charles Lummis, the museum is housed in a palatial Hispano-Moorish home on a hill fairly close to the east side of downtown. Take bus #83 along Broadway to Museum Dr. and trek up the hill. Drivers should take the Pasadena Fwy. (Rte. 110) to Ave. 43 and follow the signs. (Open Tues.-Sun. 11am-5pm. $5, seniors and students $3, ages 7-18 $2. Library open Wed.-Sat. 11am-5pm.)

Forest Lawn Cemetery and Griffith Park are also located nearby. (See Griffith Park: Sights, page 95.)

■■■ ENTERTAINMENT

AMUSEMENT PARKS

Those not sated by Disneyland can drive 40 minutes north of L.A. to Valencia and give **Six Flags Magic Mountain** a shot (818-367-5965). Not for novices, Magic Mountain has the hairiest roller coasters in Southern California. Highlights of the park are The Revolution, a smooth metal coaster with a vertical 360°; Colossus, the world's largest wooden roller coaster; the Viper, which is said to approach the limits of what coaster builders can do without *really* hurting people; and the park's newest coaster, Batman (remember, he flies upside down standing up). For roller-coaster-o-phobes, there's a crafts fair area and a children's playland with a Bugs Bunny theme. However, the truth is that few people over 48 in. tall come to Magic Mountain for the love of Bugs. (Open Sun.-Thurs. 10am-10pm, Fri.-Sat. 10am-midnight; mid-Sept. to Memorial Day Sat.-Sun. only, save Christmas and Easter holiday weeks which follow summer hours. $29, seniors $18, under 3 free. Parking $6).

The only sight of note in Bill and Ted's home town of San Dimas is the **Raging Waters Park,** 111 Raging Waters Dr. (909-592-6453 for recorded message and directions). Beat the heat with 44 acres and five million gallons of slides, pools, whitewater rafts, inner tubes, fake waves, and a fake island (don't fret, they recycle)—a cool but costly alternative to the beach. Hurl yourself over the seven-story waterslide "Drop Out"(if you dare), or slide through a tropical rain forest. (Open Mon.-Fri. 10am-9pm, Sat.-Sun. 9am-10pm until early Sept. During winter open daily 9am-9pm. $20, 42- to 48-in. $12, under 42" free. Senior and evening discounts.) "San Dimas High School Football Rules!"

For information on **Disneyland** and **Knott's Berry Farm,** see Orange County, page 127.

FILM AND TELEVISION STUDIOS

All of the major TV studios offer free tickets to shows' tapings. Some are available on a first-come, first-serve basis from the **Visitors Information Center** of the Greater L.A. Visitor and Convention Bureau or by mail. Most networks won't send tickets to out-of-state addresses but will send a guest card or letter that can be redeemed for tickets. Be sure to enclose a self-addressed, stamped envelope. Write: Tickets, Capital City/**ABC** Inc., 4151 Prospect, Hollywood 90027 (213-557-7777); **CBS** Tickets, 7800 Beverly Blvd., Los Angeles 90036 (310-852-2624); **NBC**-TV Tickets, 3000 W. Alameda Ave., Burbank 91523 (818-840-3537); or **FOX** Tickets, through Audiences Unlimited at 100 Universal City Plaza, Bldg. 153, Universal City 91608 (818-506-0067). Tickets are also available to shows produced by **Paramount Television,** 860 N. Gower St., Hollywood 90038 (213-956-5575). Tickets don't guarantee admittance; arrive a couple of hours early, as seating is also first-come, first-served. The minimum age for many tapings is 16. The **L.A. City Film and Video Permit Office,** 6922 Hollywood Blvd. Suite 602 (213-485-5324), has lists of shooting locations for films being made around Los Angeles (open Mon.-Fri. 9am-5pm).

Universal Studios, Universal City (818-508-9600). Hollywood Fwy. to Lankershim. Take bus #424 to Lankershim Blvd. For a hefty fee, the studio will take you for a ride; visit the Bates Hotel from *Psycho* and other sets, watch Conan the Barbarian flex his pecs, be attacked by Jaws, get caught in a flash flood, experience an 8.3 earthquake, and witness a variety of special effects and other demonstrations of movie-making-magic from films such as *Backdraft* and *The Flintstones.* Reservations not accepted; it's best to arrive early to secure a ticket—despite the price, the tour is quite popular. Allow 2½ hrs. for the tour and at least 1 hr. to wander around afterward. Tours in Spanish daily. Open summer and holidays daily 8am-8pm (last tram leaves at 5pm); Sept.-June 9am-6:30pm. $31, ages 3-11 and over 60 $25. Parking $5.

NBC Television Studios Tour, 3000 W. Alameda Ave. (818-840-3572), at Olive Ave. in Burbank, 2 mi. from Universal. Hollywood Fwy. north, exit east on Barham Blvd., which becomes Olive Ave. Take bus #96 or 97 on Olive going north-bound. Open Mon.-Fri. 9am-3pm, Sat. 10am-2pm. $6, ages 6-12 $3.75.

Paramount Studios Inc., 860 N. Gower St. (213-956-5000) in Hollywood. Guided 2-hr. historical walking tour. Mon.-Fri. 9am-2pm every hr. on the hr. $15. Under 10 yrs. not admitted.

Warner Bros. VIP Tour, 4000 Warner Blvd., Burbank (818-954-1744). Personalized, unstaged tours (max. 12 people) through the Warner Bros. studios. These are technical, 2-hr. treks which chronicle the detailed reality of the movie-making craft. No children under 10. Tours every ½-hr. Mon.-Fri. 9am-4:30pm, additional tours in summer. Reservations recommended in advance. $27 per person.

KCET Public Television, 4401 Sunset Blvd. (213-666-6500). Like the Warner Bros. Tour, but free. 1½ hrs. Under 10 not admitted. Tours given Tues. and Thurs. at 10am. Reservations required.

CONCERTS AND CLASSICAL MUSIC

L.A.'s concert venues range from small to massive. The **Wiltern Theater** (213-380-5005) has presented artists such as Suzanne Vega and The Church. The **Hollywood Palladium** (213-962-7600) is of comparable size with 3500 seats. Mid-size acts head for the **Universal Amphitheater** (818-777-3931) and the **Greek Theater** (213-665-1927). Huge indoor sports arenas, such as the **Sports Arena** (213-748-6131) or the **Forum** (310-419-3182), double as concert halls for large shows. Few dare to play at the 100,000+-seat **L.A. Coliseum.** Only U2, Bruce Springsteen, the Rolling Stones, and Guns 'n Roses have filled the stands in recent years.

The famous Hollywood Bowl and the Music Center are popular sites for classical music, ballet, and opera performances.

Hollywood Bowl, 2301 N. Highland Ave. (213-850-2000), in Hollywood. Perfect for a summer evening, the bowl hosts a summer festival, which runs from early July to mid-Sept. Although sitting in the back of this outdoor, 18,000-seat amphitheater makes even the L.A. Philharmonic sound like AM radio, the bargain tickets and the sweeping view of L.A. from the bowl's south rim make it worthwhile. Even more of a bargain are free open-house rehearsals by the Philharmonic and visiting orchestras. Call to inquire about sessions, Tues., Thurs., and Fri. Bring a picnic. Going to the bowl by car is a major production; parking is complicated and expensive ($9). If you're willing to hike, park away from the bowl and walk up Highland. It's easier to use MTA's Park 'n' Ride service. Bus #150 takes you to the bowl from the valley, and bus #420 runs from downtown.

Music Center, 135 N. Grand Ave., (213-972-7211), downtown at the corner of 1st in the heart of the city. Includes the **Mark Taper Forum** and the **Dorothy Chandler Pavilion,** and the **Ahmanson Theatre.** Performance spaces host the Los Angeles Opera, Broadway and experimental theater, and ballet. Some performances have $10 rush tickets 10 min. prior to the show. Call in advance and arrive 1 hr. early.

CINEMA

In the technicolor heaven of Los Angeles, you'd expect to find as many movie theaters as stars on the Walk of Fame. You won't be disappointed. Numerous theaters show films the way they were meant to be seen: in a big space, on a big screen, and with high-quality sound. L.A. locals are often amazed at the "primitive" theaters they find in the rest of the country. Admission to a first-run film in greater L.A. has paused for the moment at $7.50.

Watching a movie at one of the **Universal City** or **Century City** theaters is an amazing experience. The theaters in **Westwood Village** near UCLA are also incredibly popular, especially on weekends. You *will* wait in line at all the best theaters, especially for new releases, but the lively crowds, state-of-the-art sound systems, and large screens more than justify the wait. In Santa Monica, 22 theaters rest between Santa Monica Place and the Third St. Promenade.

Devotees of second-run, foreign-language, and experimental films are rewarded by the Santa Monica theaters away from the Promenade. Foreign films play consis-

tently at the six **Laemmle Theaters** in Beverly Hills, West L.A., Santa Monica, Pasadena, Encino, and downtown. (Check phone book for numbers.)

Though admission is a challenge without connections, occasional free films are
shown on weekday afternoons during the **Los Angeles International Film Festival.**
Popularly known as **Filmex,** the annual program runs in late June and early July.
Also in late June, Hollywood hosts one of the largest film events in the country with
its **American Film Industry L.A. Film Festival**. Obscure and foreign films are
screened around town for expounders on cinematic theory. Other film festivals
include **Black Talkies on Parade** (late April; 213-737-3292); the **UCLA Festival of
Film Preservation** (Melnitz Theatre, on campus; $5, students $3; 310-206-3456);
the **L.A. Film Fest** (late April; 213-876-77070); **International Gay and Lesbian Film
Festival** (early July; 7920 Sunset Blvd. at the Director's Guild of America; 213-466-
1767); the **Native American Film Festival** (Sept. and Jan.; Southwest Museum; free
with admission; 213-221-2164); the **Women in Film Festival** (late Oct.; 213-463-
6060); and the **¡Viva! Mexican American Images in Hollywood Summer Film
Series** (Griffith Park; 213-667-2000).

For film-screening information, dial 213-777-FILM (213-777-3456). Tickets at all
theaters listed below are $7.50, seniors and children $4, discounts where noted.

Cineplex Odeon Universal City Cinemas (818-508-0588), atop the hill at Universal Studios. Take the Universal Center Dr. exit off the Hollywood Fwy. (U.S.
101). Opened in 1987 as the world's largest cinema complex. The 18 wide-screen
theaters, 2 *Parisienne*-style cafés, and opulent decoration put all other cinema
complexes to shame. Hooray for Hollywood! ¼-price before 6pm. Ask for $5
parking refund.

Pacific Cinerama Dome, 6360 Sunset Blvd. (213-466-3401), near Vine. The
screen stretches nearly 180° around the theater. You can't miss this illuminated
geodesic dome, also known as "The Hollywood Boil."

Mann's Chinese, 6925 Hollywood Blvd. (213-464-8111). Hollywood hype to the
hilt. For more details, see Hollywood Sights, page 91. Students with ID $5; seniors
$4.50.

Beverly Cineplex (310-652-7760), atop the impressive Beverly Center, on Beverly
Dr. at La Cienega. Unlike most first-run cinemas, the Cineplex screens movies in
auditoriums hardly bigger than your living room. But it shows 14 of them every
night, a combination of recent artsy discoveries. Matinees $4.

Village Theatre, 961 Broxton (310-208-5576), in Westwood. No multiplex non-
sense here. One auditorium, one big screen, one great THX sound system, a balcony, and Art Deco design. Watch the back rows and balcony for late-arriving
celebrities. Students $5, matinees $4.50.

The following theaters screen **classic and cult films:**

Nuart Theatre, 11272 Santa Monica Blvd. (310-478-6379), in West L.A. at the San
Diego Fwy. Perhaps the best-known. The playbill changes nightly; ask for a copy
of the monthly guide. Classics, documentaries, and modern films. $7.50, seniors
and children $4.

Silent Movie, 611 N. Fairfax Ave. (213-653-2389), in L.A. near 3rd St. 250 seats
creak to the live musical accompaniment to these silent film screenings. Largest
private collection of pre-talkie gems. 8pm. $6, children $3.

Monica 4-Plex Laemmle Theater, 1332 2nd St. (310-394-9741). Restoration
showcase features Hollywood classics, foreign films, and weekend matinee film
festivals. Catch special-interest films on Shakespeare, psychology, and opera. $7,
children and seniors $4. Parking 50¢.

UCLA's Melnitz Theater (310-206-8365), on the northeastern corner of campus
near Sunset and Hilgard. An eclectic range of film festivals. Catch student films
free at the end of each school quarter, international films from school archives, or
sneak previews of Universal films. $5.

THEATER

Los Angeles is blessed with one of the most active theater circuits on the West Coast. One hundred and fifteen "equity waiver theaters" (under 100 seats) offer a dizzying choice for theater-goers, who can also take in small productions in museums, art galleries, universities, parks, and even garages. During the summer hiatus, TV stars frequently take parts in "legitimate theater" to hone their skills. The *L.A. Weekly* has comprehensive listings of L.A. theaters both big and small.

Pasadena Playhouse, 39 S. El Molino Ave. (818-356-PLAY, -7529), in Pasadena. California's premier theater and historical landmark has spawned Broadway careers and productions. Call for rush tickets. Sat. and Sun. matinee.

Shubert Theatre, 2020 Ave. of the Stars, Century City (800-233-3123). Big Broadway shows.

Pantages, 6233 Hollywood Blvd. (213-480-3232). L.A.'s other place for big Broadway spectacles.

Santa Monica Playhouse, 1211 4th St. (394-9779). Non-profit theater. Hors d'oeuvres or buffet suppers precede drama and children's matinees.

Bob Baker Marionette Theater, 1345 W. 1st St. (213-250-9995). The longest-running marionette theater in the U.S. 250-seat theater filled mostly with kids and their parents. Daily shows. Bob's marionettes have been used in a number of films (*Close Encounters, Escape to Witch Mountain, Bedknobs and Broomsticks*).

■■■ NIGHTLIFE

LATE-NIGHT RESTAURANTS

Few and far between, but we found them for you. Also check the Food section of your desired location for hours of other places that stay open late.

Canter's, 419 N. Fairfax (213-651-2030). An L.A. institution, this delicatessen is the heart and soul of the Fairfax community. The matzoh ball soup served here will change the way you look at the world. Giant sandwiches $4-6. The bakery offers everything it should and more. A young crowd invades the Kibbitz Room every night to hear live music including rock, blues, jazz, and cabaret-pop stylists (from 9:30pm). Open 24 hrs.

Tommy's Original Hamburgers, 2575 W. Beverly Blvd. (213-389-9060), Wilshire District. Ignore the multitude of Tommy's knock-offs and head to the winner of the sloppiest chili dog contest—the paper towel dispensers every 2 ft. along the counters aren't there just for looks. Tommy's burgers win rave reviews too. Chili dog $1.50, chili burgers $1.40, double cheeseburger (for those with galvanized stomachs) $2.20. Open 24 hrs.

Larry Parker's, 206 S. Beverly Dr. (310-274-5655), in Beverly Hills. Yup, another L.A. '50s diner. Neon lights, disco balls, and risque videos light up the vintage booths, jukeboxes, telephones, and corny '50s signs. Gigantic portions, but expensive. The chicken fajita plate ($12) with rice and beans is the best deal on the menu. Open 24 hrs.

Original Pantry Café, 877 S. Figueroa St. (213-972-9279), downtown. Valets may take care of your car, but inside is casual. Fresh sandwiches from $5. Open 24 hrs.

Barney's Beanery, 8447 Santa Monica (213-654-2287). Is it a pool hall or a diner? Billiards $1 a game. Strange mixture of international crowd and local pool sharks. Wide variety of omelettes $4-7. Over 200 kinds of beer. Open daily 6am-2am.

Jerry's Deli, 12655 Ventura Blvd. (818-980-4245), in Studio City. The Valley's coolest restaurant, according to its clientele. Magic Johnson and KROQ DJs eat here. Monstrous sandwiches $7-10. Mario, Chilo, and Doug ensure your satisfaction. Locations also in Encino and Westwood Village. Open 24 hrs.

Won Kok, 210 Alpine St. (213-613-0700), in Chinatown. *Dim sum* and seafood entrees around $7. Open daily 11am-3am.

COFFEEHOUSES

Espresso bars are the latest, largest fad in L.A. nightlife, and for good reason: they offer a cheap, quiet alternative to L.A.'s buzzing club scene, often with entertainment gratis. They range from the obscure to the franchised. One popular chain is the **Coffee Bean and Tea Leaf.** There are locations in Santa Monica, Westwood (near UCLA), and Beverly Hills. Buy ten beverages and get another free—you might scoff at this deal, but wait 'til you taste their Vanilla Ice Blended, the most delicious drink in the entire world ($2.75). It won't take you long to down ten. Call 800-TEA-LEAF, -832-5323, to find a location near you.

Insomnia Café, 7286 Beverly Blvd. (213-931-4943). Popular espresso bar featuring grandiose velvet couches and peculiar artwork. People bring their laptops here and pretend to be working on scripts. Open Sun.-Thurs. 9:30am-2am, Fri.-Sat. 9:30am-3am.

Bourgeois Pig, 5931 Franklin Ave. (213-962-6366). Perhaps the most dramatically gothic of the cafés, Bourgeois Pig has a gloomy yet glamorous atmosphere—black walls, red felt pool table, and mind-numbing espresso ($1.65). Open Mon.-Fri. noon-2am, Sat.-Sun. 8am-2am.

The Living Room, 110 S. La Brea (213-933-2933). This small café, with its fairly hoity-toity atmosphere and comfortable sofas, is favored by the late-night crowd. No bands or reading—the entertainment is in the assortment of pretentious decorations: melting candles and Dalí-esque clocks. Good espresso, cappuccino, and cheesecake. Open Sun.-Thurs. 9am-midnight, Fri.-Sat. 9am-2:30am.

Nova Express, 426 N. Fairfax Ave. (213-658-7533). Entering this sci-fi café is like walking into the bar scene in Star Wars. The wacky space-art was created by the owner. Sci-fi books and comics adorn the bookshelves, for reading and sale. Espresso around $2, sandwiches $2.50-5. Live rock music on Fri., acoustic on Sat. Open daily 5pm-4am.

Big and Tall, 7311 Beverly Blvd. (213-939-1403), across the street from the Insomnia café. This late-nighter doubles as a bookstore and video rental. You'll find everything from Dr. Seuss to volumes on the occult. Occasional poetry readings. Salad with mushrooms $5.25. Breakfast served all day, $8-9. Open Mon.-Thurs. 8am-1am, Fri.-Sat. 8am-2am, Sun. 10am-1am.

The Espresso Bar, 34 S. Raymond (818-356-9095), Pasadena, in an alley to the left of the building marked 32 S. Raymond St. Just when you thought Pasadena had no hip cafés in which to ponder Kafka, this bare, ratty little place rides to the rescue. Bagel with brie $3.15, steamed milk $1.25. And, of course, espresso ($1.50). Mon. is jazz night, Tues. is open mike for local bands. Wed. is open poetry night, and Fri. night has a booked band. Open Sun.-Thurs. noon-1am, Fri.-Sat. noon-4am.

Highland Grounds, 742 N. Highland Ave. (213-466-1507), in Hollywood. Features live entertainment every night from 8pm and poetry readings on Tues. Outdoor patio with continuously burning fire pit. Ah, ambience. Full menu. Open Sun.-Thurs. 9am-12:30am, Fri-Sat. 9am-1am.

Anastasia's Asylum, 1028 Wilshire Blvd. (310-394-7113), in Santa Monica. Narrow, with two levels of comfortably worn furniture, board games, and a full vegetarian menu. Entertainment nightly, starting between 8 and 9pm. Hours vary; call first.

BARS

The bar scene in L.A. is ever-growing. Bars on Santa Monica Promenade are currently some of the most popular in L.A.

Chiller's, 1446 3rd St. (310-394-1993), on the Santa Monica Promenade. This popular chain specializes in imaginative frozen drinks. The Suicide (151 rum, light rum, dark rum, triple sec, vodka, and 5 fruit juices) will knock you out. The Purple Orgasm lives up to its name. Nightspot of choice for college crowd and young professionals. Wed. night drinks are $1. DJ some nights. Open Sun.-Thurs. 11am-1am, Fri.-Sat. 11am-2am. Cover varies.

Molly Malone's, 575 S. Fairfax (213-935-1579). Not your typical Irish pub—showcases some of L.A.'s big up-and-coming bands. Cover varies. Open 10am-2am.

Al's Bar, 305 S. Hewitt St. (213-625-9703), in downtown. One of L.A. nightlife's best-hidden secrets. Wide range of nightly entertainment: traditional rock 'n' roll, poetry, experimental bands, performance art and more. Open daily 6pm-2am.

Yankee Doodle's, 1410 3rd St. (310-394-4632), on the Santa Monica Promenade. Lively bi-level sports bar has 32 (count 'em) pool tables and the de rigeur big screen TV. Outdoor seating (for when the action gets too intense). Open daily 11am-2am.

Stratton's, 1037 Broxton Ave. (310-208-0488). Hot spot with UCLA students (though they all look like Santa Monica yuppie barhoppers in training). Open daily 11am-2am.

Atlas Bar and Grill, 3760 Wilshire Blvd. (213-380-8400), in the Wilshire District. A glamorous nightspot with retro decor. Offers jazz and cabaret. Open Mon.-Thurs. 11:30am-1am, Sat.-Sun. 11:30am-2am.

The Snake Pit, 7529 Melrose Ave. (213-852-9390), in W. Hollywood. Unpretentious little hole amid many poseur bars. Crowded with young, affable jetset. Open Sun.-Thurs. 4:30pm-2am, Sat.-Sun. 11:30am-2am.

Burgundy Room, 1621½ N. Cahuenga Blvd. (213-465-7530). Frequented by a very Hollywood set—think "industry" and you should get the picture. Features a well-stocked jukebox and a bar that's been transported from locale to locale—it now loosens up a busy scene. Open daily 8pm-2am.

COMEDY CLUBS

The talent may be imported from New York and other parts of the country, but that doesn't change the fact that L.A.'s comedy clubs are the best in the world (unless you happen to chance upon an amateur night, which is generally a painful, painful experience). Quality makes prices steep, of course, but it's worth the setback to catch the newest and wackiest stand-up comedians, chuckle as famous veterans hone new material, or preside at the latest development in stand-up—comedy competitions. Call ahead to check age restrictions. Cover charges are cheaper during the week; the clubs are less crowded, but just as much fun.

Comedy Store, 8433 Sunset Blvd. (213-656-6225), in West Hollywood. The shopping mall of comedy clubs, with 3 different rooms, each featuring a different type of comedy. (Each room charges its own cover.) Go to the Main Room for the big-name stuff and the most expensive cover charges ($10-12). The Original Room features mid-range comics for $7-10. The Belly Room has the real grab-bag material, with cover of $0-3. 21 and over only; 2-drink min. Reservations taken all week.

The Improvisation, 8162 Melrose Ave. (213-651-2583), in West Hollywood. Offers L.A.'s best talent, including, on occasion, Robin Williams and Robert Klein. Restaurant serves Italian fare (entrees $6 and up). Open nightly; check *L.A. Weekly* for times. Cover $8-10, 2-drink min. Reservations recommended.

Groundling Theater, 7307 Melrose Ave. (213-934-9700), in Hollywood. Conventional wisdom says that this is the best improv "forum" in town. Alums include Jon Lovitz, PeeWee Herman, and Elvira. Polished skits and light refreshments. Cover $10-20.

The Comedy Act Theater, 3339 W. 43rd St. (310-677-4101). A comedy club targeted at a black audience, often featuring such nationally known comedians as Robert Townsend and Marsha Warfield. Opens at 8:30pm Thurs.-Sat. Cover $10.

Igby's Comedy Cabaret, 11637 Tennessee Pl. (310-477-3553), in West L.A. Nationally known comedians. Restaurant and bar. West L.A.'s best comedy club, although parking can drive you crazy. Must be over 16. Cover $5-10, 2-drink min. Reservations required.

The Ice House, 24 N. Mentor Ave. (818-577-1894), in Pasadena. This is the 30-year-old granddaddy of clubs, and its famous graduates occasionally pop in to surprise patrons. Showroom seats 200; restaurant and bar. Cover $7.50-11.50. 2-drink min. Dinner and show package Tues.-Thurs. $8.50.

CLUBS

L.A.'s nightlife is famous for its club scene. With the highest number of bands per capita in the world, most clubs are able to book top-notch acts night after night. The distinction between music clubs and dance clubs is a bit sketchy in L.A.—most music clubs have DJs a couple times a week, and most dance clubs have bands a couple times a week. Many clubs are simply host spaces for managements that change every night. These clubs can be the hottest thing in L.A. one month, and disappear the next. Underground clubs are generally cheaper, more fun, and more elite (of course, you'll have to find these roving parties yourself by making friends with knowledgeable clubgoers). If you see a lot of long-haired, scantily clad people walking into an unmarked building late at night, they could be on their way to a fabulous party—but you shouldn't go searching for parties alone—bring a friend or two. Back on the strip, Sunset has been and continues to be the property of L.A.'s enormous heavy metal scene—many Angelenos don't know that anything else exists.

Clubs are often expensive, but many are still feasible for budgeters. Coupons in *L.A. Weekly* (see Publications, page 71) can save you a bundle, and many are also handed out in bushels inside the clubs. To enter the club scene it's best to be at least 21—the next-best option is to look it. (Now's the chance to grow that beard.) Nevertheless, if you're over 18, you can still find a space to dance, but it may mean a hefty cover charge.

Whisky A Go-Go, 8901 Sunset Blvd. (310-652-4205), in W. Hollywood. A venerable spot on the Strip, part of L.A.'s music history. The Whisky played host to many progressive bands in the late '70s and early '80s, and was a major part of the punk explosion. Hard rock to alternative. Full bar; cover varies. No age restrictions.

Roxy, 9009 Sunset Blvd. (310-276-2222). Also known as the "Sizzling Showcase," one of the best-known of L.A.'s Sunset Strip clubs, the Roxy is filled with record-company types and rockers waiting to be discovered. Many big and popular acts play here. Cover varies. No age restrictions.

The Palace, 1435 N. Vine St. (213-462-3000), in Hollywood. A legendary Hollywood nightclub—has featured both Rudy Vallee and the Rolling Stones. Has a main room with dance floor, patio and VIP lounge, and balcony with seating. Palace Café has full bar and menu. Cover varies, but around $10. Ages 16 and over (usually). Open from 9pm. Lots of discounts.

Anti-Club, 4658 Melrose Ave. (213-661-3913), in East Hollywood. Appropriately named. To understand the difference between clubs and Anti-Club: the graffiti on the walls here wasn't coordinated by the management; more tattoos per person than any other place in L.A. David Lynch would love it. Underground "avant-core." Has presented the Red Hot Chili Peppers, Soundgarden, and many more. Full bar; cover varies. No age restrictions.

Coconut Teaszer, 8117 Sunset Blvd. (213-654-4773). Dingy, grungy, loud, and popular. Peace and green decor provide odd background for live bands (Sun.), DJ with dancing (Fri.-Sat.), and excellent drink specials. Full bar. No cover. *Official* policy is 21 and over, especially on Mon.-Tues.

Club Lingerie, 6507 Sunset Blvd., Hollywood (213-466-8557). Enormously varied bookings: lots of indie rock. Come early. 2 full bars. Open Mon.-Sat. 9pm-2am. 21 and over.

Kingston 12, 814 Broadway (310-451-4423), Santa Monica. L.A.'s only full-time reggae club presents both local and foreign acts. Dredlocks flow freely. Jamaican food, dance floor, 2 bars. Open Thurs.-Sun. 8:30pm-2am. Cover varies. 21 and over.

Florentine Gardens, 5951 Hollywood Blvd. (213-464-0706). Hollywood's giant dance club for an 18-and-over crowd. Features a light show and free buffet. Dressy attire. Open Fri.-Sat. 8pm-4am. $8 cover before 10:30pm, and higher afterwards.

Dragonfly, 6506 Santa Monica Blvd. (213-466-6111), in Hollywood. Drink specials offered frequently at this multivaried venue: three different rooms, an outdoor patio, and a "trance garden." Intense dancing Fri.-Sat. with funk, groove, lots of DJs. Cover varies. 21 and over.

Roxbury, 8225 W. Sunset (213-656-1750), in Hollywood. L.A. pretense at its fullest. One of the most hotsy-totsy places in the city (you probably won't get in, but it might be fun trying). Jazz room downstairs, huge bar and dancing upstairs. VIP room admits only the wealthy, famous, or startlingly beautiful. Open Tues.-Sat. 7pm-2am.

Shark Club, 1024 S. Grand Ave. (213-747-0999), downtown. Popular dance club for L.A. young and trendy. Huge dance floor, laser lighting, monstrous bar, and a 40,000-watt sound system. Latin American music Thurs. night, House/techno/pop Fri.-Sat. Restaurant takes reservations. Open Thurs.-Sun. 9pm-2am.

GAY AND LESBIAN CLUBS

Many clubs have special gay nights. Check the *L.A. Weekly* for additional listings or contact the Gay and Lesbian Community Services Center (see Practical Information, page 68).

The Palms, 8572 Santa Monica Blvd. (310-652-6188), West Hollywood's oldest women's bar. Pool room. Top-40 dancing every night. Full bar. Low cover, if any. 21 and over.

7969, 7969 Santa Monica Blvd. (213-654-0280), in West Hollywood. Sometimes it is a strip club, sometimes it features top alternative acts. Dancing nightly. Mainly gay. 18 and over.

Rage, 8911 Santa Monica Blvd., West Hollywood (310-652-7055). Dance and R&B sounds for a gay male crowd. Full bar. Cover varies. 21 and over.

Jewel's (Catch One), 4067 W. Pico Blvd. (213-734-8849), east of Crenshaw. Underground, after-hours hangout for gay and straight crowd—welcoming "to all persuasions." Two floors of dancing, live music Sat. Thurs. is lesbian night. Cover varies. Open Sun.-Thurs. 9pm-3am, Fri.-Sat. 9pm-4am.

Cosmos, 1608 Cosmo St. (213-466-7800). Laid-back, cozy place with pool table. Thurs. night features house and other dance music in the Men's Room. Fri.-Sat. dancing and drink specials. Cover varies. Must be 21 and up.

■■■ SEASONAL EVENTS

Tournament of Roses Parade and Rose Bowl (818-449-4100), Jan. 1. New Year's Day is always a perfect day in Southern California. Snowed-in Midwesterners and Easterners eat their collective heart out watching the parade and the football game on TV. Making a slumber party out of New Year's Eve at the parade is a SoCal tradition, and most Angelenos have done it at least once. Some of the wildest New Year's Eve parties happen along Colorado Blvd., the parade route. If you miss the parade, you can still see the floats up close on display on January 2 (call Pasadena's tourist office).

World Frisbee Tournament, during the Rose Bowl. Champions compete in individual freestyle, Ultimate Frisbee, and other events.

Chinese New Year (213-617-0396), late Feb., Chinatown. Fireworks and dragon processions.

Whale-watching, a favorite of Southern Californian ocean worshipers, is best Dec.-March. Boats depart from Long Beach and San Pedro Harbors to witness the migration of giant whales from the north Pacific to the waters off Baja California. Call any of the state beaches.

Grunion runs occur throughout spring and summer. This late-night pastime appeals to those who want to watch slippery, silver fish squirm onto the beaches (especially San Pedro) to mate. The fish can be caught by hand, but a license is required for those over 16. Obtain licenses from the Fish and Game Department (310-590-5132) for $10.50; they're valid until Dec. 31 each year. 1-day license $5.50. Fishing prohibited April-May. Free programs on the Grunion run given at the Cabrillo Marine Museum in San Pedro (310-548-7562).

Renaissance Pleasure Faire (415-892-0937), from the daffodil's first blossom to the days of shortest night (weekends, late April to mid-June). Friends, Romans, and countrymen hasten to the city of Devore. From the haven of the angels (L.A.), gallop apace on fiery-footed steeds (drive) from Phoebus' lodging (east) along I-10 to I-15 north and look for signs as you draw near the site of happy reveling. Garbed in their best Elizabethan finery, San Bernardino teenagers are versed in the phrases of the bard before working at the Faire. Eat, drinke, and be merrye! Open 9am-6pm. $15, over 62 $11.50, children $8.

Cinco de Mayo (213-680-2821), May 5, especially downtown at Olvera St. Huge celebrations mark Mexican Independence Day.

UCLA Mardi Gras (310-825-8001), mid-May, at the athletic field. Billed as the world's largest collegiate activity (a terrifying thought). Proceeds benefit charity.

UCLA Jazz and Reggae Festival (310-825-6564), late May, at the intramural field. Free concerts of these musical genres, as well as a cultural marketplace, crafts, and food.

Summer Nights at the California Plaza (213-687-2195), weekend nights through the summer, California Plaza in downtown L.A. Concert festival features dance, music, theatre, circuses, and more. Free admission. Parking $4.40.

Playboy Jazz Festival (310-449-4070), mid-June, Hollywood Bowl. 2 days of entertainment by top-name jazz musicians of all varieties, from traditional to fusion.

Gay Pride Week (213-656-6553), late June. The lesbian and gay community of L.A. celebrates in full force. Art, politics, dances, and a big parade all center on the Pacific Design Center, 8687 Melrose Ave., Hollywood. Tickets $16.

Shakespeare Festival/LA (213-489-1121), July-Aug. This theater company aims to make the Shakespeare tradition accessible to all. Canned food donation accepted in lieu of admission at most performances. Locations include Hollywood, downtown, Palos Verdes.

America Fest (213-684-2560), 4th of July, in the Rose Bowl in Pasadena. This evening of pageantry by Universal stunt artists, concerts, and fireworks costs $10 for general bench seating.

L.A. Poetry Festival (213-660-4306), late Oct. Showcases the region's poetry with readings and discussions throughout the city.

Los Posados (213-625-5045), Dec. 16-24. This celebration including a candlelight procession and the breaking of a piñata takes place here along Olvera St.

NEAR LOS ANGELES

■■■ SOUTH BAY

Several beachside communities cluster along the southern curve of Santa Monica Bay, in the area known as South Bay: **Manhattan Beach, Hermosa Beach,** and **Redondo Beach.** Though these areas certainly have their share of surfers, volleyball players, and sunbathers, their sun-glazed coasts also give way to a surprisingly diverse mixture of pleasure-seekers. If you investigate, you will find trendy coffeehouses, unusually stocked bookstores, and museums that merit your temporary withdrawal from the undeniably compelling sand and surf. Convenient to the Los Angeles International Airport (LAX), the region also encompasses the lovely, affluent **Palos Verdes** and the calm **San Pedro.**

PRACTICAL INFORMATION

Visitors Information: Hermosa Beach Chamber of Commerce and Visitor's Information Center, 323 Pier Ave. (310-376-0951). Open Mon.-Fri. 9am-5pm. **Redondo Beach Chamber of Commerce,** 200 N. Pacific Hwy. (310-376-6911). Open Mon.-Fri. 8:30am-5pm. **San Pedro Peninsula Chamber of Commerce,** 390 W. 7th St. (310-832-7272). Open Mon.-Fri. 9am-5pm.

MTA: 800-252-7433. Bus #40 from downtown joins the coast road at El Segundo and serves Manhattan, Hermosa, and Redondo Beaches. Hermosa Beach has a free shuttle bus. Buses #225 and 226 cross the Palos Verdes area.

Car Rental: Robin Hood Rent-A-Car, 116 8th St. (310-318-9955), in Manhattan Beach. Promises to beat other rental companies by 15%.

AAA Offices: Manhattan Beach, 700 S. Aviation Blvd. (376-0521). **San Pedro,** 852 N. Western Ave.

Bicycle Rentals: Each community generally has at least a couple; just scan the blocks close to the beach. In-line skates are also widely available.

Horse Rentals: Palos Verdes Stables, 4057 Via Apolla (378-3527). $13 first hr., $11 per additional hr. License required to ride.

Laundromat: 509 Pier Ave. (374-9543), in Hermosa.

Surfing and Weather Conditions Hotline: 379-8471.

Pharmacy: Sav-On-Drugs (310-546-3481), in Manhattan Beach Village (a really good mall) off Sepulveda Blvd. Open Mon.-Fri. 7am-11pm, Sat.-Sun. 10am-10pm.

Harbor Free Clinic: 599 9th St. at the corner of 9th and Grand (547-0202), in San Pedro. Call Mon.-Thurs. 10am-5pm for appointments.

Hospital: San Pedro Peninsula Hospital, 1300 W. 7th St. (832-3311), in San Pedro.

Emergency: 911.

Police: San Pedro Police Department, 2175 Gibson Blvd.

Post Office: 545 Pier Ave. in **Hermosa. General Delivery ZIP Code:** 90254. 1201 N. Catalina Ave. (310-376-2472), in **Redondo Beach.** Open Mon.-Fri. 8:30am-5pm, Sat. 8:30am-12:30pm. **General Delivery ZIP Code:** 90277. Also at 839 S. Beacon St. (310-831-3246), in **San Pedro.** Open Mon.-Fri. 8:30am-5pm, Sat. 9am-12:30pm. **General Delivery ZIP Code:** 90731.

Area Code: 310.

ACCOMMODATIONS

Motels along these beaches fall well above the budget price range. Inexpensive to mid-priced motels lie near the airport and along the Pacific Coast Highway (PCH). There are no campsites convenient to this area.

Los Angeles International Youth Hostel (HI-AYH), 3601 S. Gaffey St., Bldg. #613, San Pedro 90731 (831-8109; fax 831-4635), at Angels Gate Park (entrance by 34th St.), is a good option for those with a car. Public transportation, however, suffices. Bus #446 runs from here to downtown and Union Station during rush hours. From the LAX transfer terminal take bus #232, get off at Avalon and Anaheim, where you can catch #446. These ormer army barracks are adjacent to Angels Gate Park. The park's spectacular Korean Friendship Bell dominates the nighttime sky and lends an almost mystic feel to the place. Clean, spacious, and homey: nametags on the bunkbeds, a reading room with a paperback library, a clean and orderly kitchen, and an especially friendly staff. Bus schedules, travel books, some food available at desk. Laundry, TV room, volleyball courts, free parking. Mixed, slightly older clientele. No sleeping bags allowed, linens available for $2. 3-day max. stay. Reception open Mon.-Sat. 7am-midnight, Sun. 7am-noon and 5pm-midnight; winter daily 7-11am and 4pm-midnight. Private rooms $27, semi-private (2 people) $12.50 per person, dorms (3-6 beds) $10.50. Nonmembers add $3.

FOOD AND NIGHTLIFE

Several cheap eateries cluster around Pier Ave. on the Strand in Hermosa Beach. Nightlife revolves around combination bar/restaurants. There has been a recent spate of coffeehouses, many less pretentious and with better entertainment and/or beerage than what L.A. proper tends to offer. Establishments are listed by community, going from north to south.

La Villa, 1141 Manhattan Ave. (310-546-4163), in Manhattan Beach. Modest setting for delicious, inexpensive Mexican food. Combos with sides of rice and beans or tortillas and home fries from $4-5.75. Tacos and enchiladas start at $1.55. Huge, fresh tostadas are piled high; salsa adds kick. Wash it all down with a cold Corona ($1.50). Open Sun.-Thurs. 11am-11pm, Fri.-Sat. 11am-midnight.

Islands, 3200 Sepulveda Blvd. (546-4456), in Manhattan Beach at the Rosecrans Ave. end of the mall. Exotically named sandwiches with familiar ingredients. The Pelican ($6) features BBQ chicken with Swiss. The Makaha ($4.55) is a chili cheeseburger. The famous cheese fries are fabulous. Popular with families. Open Mon.-Thurs. 11am-11pm, Fri.-Sat. 11am-11:30pm, Sun. 11am-10pm.

The Hungry Mind, 916 Manhattan Ave. (310-318-9029), in Manhattan Beach. This combination bookstore and coffeehouse offers many delicious, dessert-like caffeinated beverages as well as simpler fare. Try a big, frothy bowl of mocha ($2) with a "Horton Hears a Who" sandwich ($2.50). Scrumptious cheesecake $3.75. Lots of books and magazines, poetry readings, diverse crowd in the evenings. Open Mon.-Thurs. 6am-11pm, Fri. 6am-midnight, Sat. 7am-1am, Sun. 7am-11pm.

Good Stuff, 13th St. and the Strand (374-2334), in Hermosa Beach. Truth in advertising—they actually *do* serve excellent health food. "Best Surfer Breakfast in Hermosa Beach," served throughout the bay. Avocado and sprouts rolls, soy burgers, and other sandwiches $4.50-6. Dinner specials about $6. Open daily 7am-9pm.

Eco Café, 1320 Hermosa Ave., 2 blocks away from Hermosa Beach (310-376-8326). A spacious, cool respite from the beach mayhem by the Strand. Doggedly vegetarian and environmentally conscious, this spot manages to be quietly elegant as well, with its high ceilings and large open front. Sandwiches $4.50-6.50, entrees slightly more. Tues. is jazz night, Wed. features acoustic music.

Lighthouse Café, 30 Pier Ave. (372-6111), in Hermosa Beach. Way cool dance-music club/bar frequented by local volleyball players. Reasonably priced munchies. Pizza $1.50, chicken sandwich $5. Fri. night drink specials ($1.50 from 4-9pm.) Cheap food specials at the beginning of the night (2 mini-burgers $1). Opens Mon.-Thurs. at 5pm, Fri. at 4pm, Sat. at 11am, and Sun. at 9am. Doors close nightly around 2am.

Captain Kidd's Fish Market, 209 N. Harbor Dr. (372-7703), in the Redondo Beach Marina. Buy a piece of fresh fish from their market (around $5), and for $3 extra, they will cook it for you according to your bidding and throw in 2 side dishes (i.e. french fries, rice, or clam chowder) to make a complete meal. Not the most intimate setting in the world, but they have great pictures on the wall of the devastating sea storms of the 1980s. Open Sun.-Thurs. 9am-9pm, Fri.-Sat. 9am-10pm.

Toe's Tavern, 732 N. Catalina Ave. (818-577-6675), in Redondo Beach. Surfer hangout with pong, pool, even shuffleboard (yes, it can be cool). Live rock on weekends. Cover free-$5. Open 7pm-1am.

Sacred Grounds Coffee House and Art Gallery, 399 6th St. (514-0800), in San Pedro. Low-key, spacious joint pays tribute to famous, recently deceased resident Charles Bukowski (poet and novelist). Excellent coffee; bands and poetry readings on weekends ($3 cover). Open Mon.-Thurs. 8am-11:30pm, Fri.-Sat. 8am-midnight, Sun. 11am-9pm.

SIGHTS

The **Pacific Coast Highway** (Rte. 1) swings by the sand at **Manhattan Beach** and continues through **Hermosa Beach,** which together are the most pleasant urban beach environments in L.A. County. The sort of community spirit found in Venice prevails, though in a more upscale style. Along the central pier of Manhattan Beach, you'll find cheap fish and chips, a small museum, and several amateur and professional fisherpeople (if you bring your own pole, be forewarned that no overhead casting is allowed). In addition, Manhattan is the place for serious **beach volleyball.** The sandy courts at **Marine Avenue,** along with those at the **State Beach** in Pacific Palisades, are the elite training grounds for young players. The **Manhattan Beach Open** in early July is the oldest professional beach volleyball tournament, while the **Hermosa Beach Open** (around July 4) awards the most prize money. Both tourneys are part of the Association of Volleyball Professionals (AVP) tour, which makes stops at several Southland beaches. If the tour is in town, don't miss it; muscled and sun-darkened Adonises and Athenas play an energetic and physical game, fearlessly diving into the sand for exciting digs (plus, most are free). Call the Torrance Chamber of Commerce (818-386-2486; open Mon.-Fri. 8:30am-5pm) for schedule information. Numerous public courts line Hermosa Beach and surfing takes place just about anywhere there's water. (A rental shop is standard at most beaches.) The **International Surf Festival,** another beachside spectator spectacular, takes place each year in early August at Manhattan Beach (540-5858).

The **Strand** is a sidewalk/bike path that runs along Manhattan south through Hermosa. This stretch of L.A. County's most popular trail is a blur of bikers and skaters. (Pedestrians would be well advised to watch from the sidelines.) If approaching Hermosa by car from the San Diego Fwy. and Artesia Blvd., stop at the booth at Gould Ave. (the continuation of Artesia) and Valley Dr. for a map of the route and then find a parking space. Parking near the ocean is metered 24 hrs. and closely monitored (25¢ per 15 min.). Instead, buy the $2 day permit for any municipal lot.

Redondo Beach is the next town down the coast, and its main attractions are the pier, boardwalk, and marina complex. The Redondo Beach Marina and adjacent **King Harbor** shelter thousands of pleasure boats from the ocean's fury and host some excellent sport fishing. The **Redondo Fun Factory** contains hundreds of quarter-munching games and rides. (Open Sun.-Thurs. 2-10pm, Fri.-Sat. 2pm-midnight.) The **Monstad Pier** supports bars, restaurants, and assorted nightlife joints. While the view from the pier is picturesque at night, be aware that it is best not seen alone.

The lovely **Palos Verdes Peninsula** juts out of the coast, south of Redondo Beach, forming the southern edge of Santa Monica Bay. This is a wealthy area: Spanish-Mediterranean homes climb to the cliffs overlooking the ocean, while farther inland, residents ride horses along Palos Verdes Dr. Beaches are inaccessible here, due to the steep cliffs and exclusivity of the residences. You can legally peek at the red-tiled roofs from the cliffs of Palos Verdes Dr. The nearby **Ports o' Call Village** at Berth 77 is modeled on a New England seaport with cobblestone streets and lots o' open-air fisheries. Whale-watch here from December 31 to March 31. Also deserving examination is **Malaga Cove Plaza,** located on Palos Verdes Dr. between Via Corta and Via Chico. The only one of four plazas planned by the city in the '20s that was ever actually built, the building is a triumph of the Mediterranean Revival style.

For a concentrated dose of the floral paradise of Southern California, head to the **South Coast Botanic Gardens,** 26300 Crenshaw Blvd. (544-6815), in Rancho Palos Verdes. This former county disposal site (i.e. dump) has been splendidly metamorphosed into an 87-acre garden. (Open Mon.-Fri. 9am-5pm, Sat.-Sun. 9am-3pm. $3, seniors and students $1.50, ages 5-12 75¢.)

Lining the peninsula's major thoroughfare, **Wayfarer's Chapel,** at 5755 Palos Verdes Dr. (377-1650), a gorgeous all-glass church overlooking the ocean, is Frank Lloyd Wright's most famous creation in Southern California. Exhibits and a 12-minute film on Wright are shown inside. (Chapel open daily 10am-4pm. Grounds open 10am-7pm.) Two popular coves lurk behind the shrubbery across the road from the chapel: **Smugglers Cove,** a nudist beach frequented by gay men, and **Abalone Cove.** Parking is limited and the Abalone Cove lot charges $5. The path to Abalone Cove begins at the far end of the parking lot. To get to Smugglers Cove, leave the parking lot and walk 1 mi. east on Palos Verdes Dr. At the sign for Peppertree Dr., look for a path down to the cove.

The still water and tide pools draw many families to **Cabrillo Beach** farther south in **San Pedro.** The beach itself is small and a bit lacking in the sparkling sands department—not the place to swim or sunbathe. The **Cabrillo Marine Museum,** 3720 Stephen White Dr., presents sea-life and marine history exhibits (open Tues.-Fri. noon-5pm, Sat.-Sun. 10am-5pm). Call 548-7562 for information on such exhibits as the Tide Pool Touch Tank, as well as evening **grunion runs** ($1 per person) in the early summer. Programs are geared toward children but are educational for all. The museum is free but parking is $5.50 at the beach. To avoid the charge, park in the surrounding neighborhood. To explore above-water sea critters, visit the **Los Angeles Maritime Museum** (213-832-6537), at the foot of 6th St. The museum houses large-scale models of the Queen Mary and ill-fated Titanic as well as exhibits on Pacific maritime history. (Open Tues.-Sun. 10am-5pm. Donation $1.)

The City of San Pedro holds a number of festivals throughout the year. Downtown San Pedro is the site for September's **Street Fair,** and the October **Fisherman's Fiesta.** Call the Chamber of Commerce for more information. (see Practical Information, page 117).

■■■ LONG BEACH

Long Beach, the nation's leading fishing and canning port, owes its success to a man named Phineas Banning. In 1898, Banning, who owned large amounts of property in Long Beach along the San Pedro Bay, greased a few palms and replaced the "Get Off and Push Railroad" (actually a wooden horse-car line) with a real one. The new locomotive railroad connected Long Beach to downtown Los Angeles and thereby enabled his town to overcome Santa Monica in the race to become Los Angeles's primary port. Nicknamed **Worldport L.A.,** with a population of 400,000, Long Beach is the world's largest point of entry for goods imported from the Pacific Rim.

With the flashy, mercantile prosperity of its waterfront, grubby but lively neighborhoods, and suburbanite-thronged shopping centers, Long Beach is mostly indifferent to tourists. Nonetheless, the city's hopping nightlife and 11 mi. of wide beaches make it a worthwhile stopover.

PRACTICAL INFORMATION AND ORIENTATION

Visitors Information: Long Beach Convention and Visitors Council, One World Trade Center #300, at Ocean Blvd. and the Long Beach Fwy. (436-3645 or 800-234-3645). Tons of free brochures (like *101 Things to Do in the Long Beach Area*). The **Chamber of Commerce,** just down the hall, has an excellent map of the area. Visitors might find more personal help here. Open Mon.-Fri. 8:30am-5pm.

Long Beach Airport: 4100 Donald Douglas Dr. (421-8293), northeast of downtown.

Greyhound: 464 W. 3rd St. (603-0141). Open Mon.-Sat. 7am-7pm, Sun. 7am-6pm. Another location at 6601 N. Atlantic Ave. 24-hrs. As always, call 800-231-2222 for bus info.

Long Beach Transit: 1300 Gardena Ave. (591-2301). Open Mon.-Fri. 7am-7pm, Sat.-Sun. 8am-5pm. Call for a free transit guide, or stop by the information center at 1st and Long Beach Blvd. Open Mon.-Fri. 7:30am-4:30pm, Sat. 10am-2pm. Most buses stop at the Transit Mall downtown on 1st St. between Pacific Ave. and Long Beach Blvd. High-tech bus shelters have route maps and video screens that announce the next bus. Fare 75¢, students 50¢, transfers 5-25¢.

Long Beach Runabout: 591-2301. A separate division of the LBT, this shuttle service cruises downtown Mon.-Fri. 7am-6pm, Sat.-Sun. 10am-5pm. A 3rd route offers service to the Queen Mary. Look for the cute little flags with the seagulls on top. Free.

MetroRail Blue Line (213-620-7245). This sleek light rail system hits 22 stops between downtown L.A. and Long Beach. Daily 5am-9pm. One-way pass $1.10.

Car Rental: FLAT RATE Rent-A-Car, 6285 E. PCH (433-7283). A fantastic deal assuming you're not going very far—Toyotas for $16 a day but only 75 free mi. (must be 23 with credit card). Open Mon.-Fri. 8am-5pm, Sat.-Sun. 9am-4pm. Otherwise, **Budget Rent-A-Car** has branches both at the Long Beach Airport (421-0143) and at 727 Long Beach Blvd. (495-0407). Rentals start at $20 with unlimited mileage. Ages 18-20 need proof of insurance. Drivers under 25 subject to $10 surcharge per day and need credit card. Open Mon.-Fri. 7:30am-6pm, Sat.-Sun. 8am-4pm.

AAA: 4800 Airport Plaza Dr. (498-6611). Open Mon.-Fri. 9am-5pm.

Laundromat: Speed Wash, 235 4th St. (432-2866).

Weather Conditions: 714-675-0503. **Beach/Surf Conditions:** 451-8761.

Emergency: 911. Main **police** station is at 400 W. Broadway.

Post Office: 300 Long Beach Blvd. (983-3056). Open Mon.-Fri. 8:30am-5pm, Sat. 9am-2pm. **General Delivery ZIP Code:** 90801.
Area Code: 310.

Long Beach is located 24 mi. south of downtown L.A. and just down the coast from South Bay. To reach Long Beach from downtown L.A. by public transit, take the MetroRail Blue Line or take MTA bus #456, the "Freeway Express." Bus #232 runs from LAX to Long Beach, about a 20-mi. trip ($4.50). By car from downtown, take the Harbor Fwy. (Rte. 110) south to the San Diego Fwy. (I-405). Exit the San Diego Fwy. at the Long Beach Fwy. (Rte. 710), which runs south, directly into downtown Long Beach. From West L.A. take the San Diego Fwy. to the Long Beach Fwy.

ACCOMMODATIONS

The Blue Line light rail makes daytrips to Long Beach cheap and easy, but there is enough to do and see that an overnight stay may be desirable. For cheaper accommodations check the Bixby Knolls neighborhood of Long Beach, north of downtown. The **Shoreline RV Park,** 200 W. Shoreline Dr. (310-435-4960), next to the Marina, provides 70 sites ($20 per site, $23 with full hookup) and views of the Queen Mary. You might also try **Brooks College** (597-6611), which rents out dorm space during the summer months.

Friendship Inn, 50 Atlantic Ave. (800-453-4511 or 435-8369; fax 932-3799), 1 block east of Ocean Blvd. Clean, beautiful rooms with refrigerators and coffeemakers, TVs with HBO. Breakfast $3. Singles $39, doubles $41. In summer reserve 4 weeks in advance.

Belmont Shore Inn, 3946 E. Ocean Blvd. (434-6236). A great deal. $35 gets you a clean single within walking distance of the beach, but the real steal is the room with large kitchenette for only $5 more. Weekly rates $175. Reservations recommended.

Surf Motel, 2010 E. Ocean Blvd. (437-0771). Immaculate rooms in sea-blue shades directly on the water. Singles $39, $245 per week. Doubles $45. Rooms with ocean view and kitchenette $55. Reservations recommended.

FOOD

The downtown area has a number of inexpensive restaurants. Many of the intriguing eateries lining Pine St. between 1st and 3rd aren't as expensive as the valets out front might lead you to believe. Buy cheap produce at the **open air market** (Fri. 10am-4pm) on Promenade St.

Alegria, 115 Pine Ave. (436-3388). *Tapas* bar with bakery next door. Decor is a colorful if somewhat uneasy mix between a café with pretensions and a storefront diner: loud TV, paintings on the walls, rainbow-colored mosaic tile. Full bar. Trout fillet with mint sauce $2.25, *sopa de ajo* $1.95. Open daily 11am-2am.

Cocoreno's Taco Stand, 3400 E. Broadway (438-4590). Mexican dishes at a small, pretty storefront restaurant with mock-adobe inner walls painted with stylized saguaro cacti. Same management as the **Reno Room** next door, which supplies the margaritas. 2 tacos $3. Open Mon.-Thurs. 11am-midnight, Fri. 11am-1am, Sat. 10am-1am, Sun. 10am-midnight.

The Omelette Inn, 108 W. 3rd St. (437-5625). Small, friendly breakfast and lunch place. Serves a huge omelette with toast and home fries ($4-5.50). Open daily 7am-2:30pm.

Williamsburg Restaurant, 355 E. 1st St. (590-0220). A budget buffet. Very traditional fare (beef, turkey, ham, etc.) in a kitschy, fast-food-like dining room. Lunches from $5.29, dinners start at $6.29. Vegetarian plate $5.29. Breakfast special $3. Affiliated bakery next door. Open Mon.-Sat. 6am-6pm, Sun. 11am-6pm.

Bonadonna's Shorehouse Café, 5271 E. 2nd St. (433-2266). Large selection of sandwiches and Tex-Mex dishes in comfortable setting. Bar too. Spinach and avocado sandwich with choice of side dish $6. Open 24 hrs.

SIGHTS

Long Beach's central preoccupation is shipping; tourism is clearly an afterthought. To get a hold on the city's cargo, walk along the waterfront or drive along Ocean Blvd. west across the ship yards. Crossing the majestic **Vincent Thomas Bridge** to central San Pedro costs 50¢, but it's worth it for the gripping view of the vast shipping terminals. (Incidentally, it's free from the other direction.)

If you're absolutely determined to do the tourist thing, head over to the **Queen Mary,** a boat parked at the end of the Long Beach Fwy. (I-710). The *Queen Mary,* an 81,000-ton 1934 luxury liner is now a hotel. (Open 10am-5pm. Entrance fee $7, children $4. Parking $5. Tours $7, children $4.) The next waterfront marvel is the **Convention and Entertainment Center** (310-436-3695), where the Long Beach Grand Opera, the Civic Light Opera (310-436-3645), and the Symphony perform.

Shoreline Village (590-8427), along Shoreline Dr. and Pine Ave., is a cheaper, though no less mobbed, tourist spot along the waterfront. Several thousand visitors per day mill through its pseudo-vintage shops. A spin on the authentic 1906 carousel is $1. (Shops open daily 10am-9pm, summer 10am-10pm.) Escape the crowds by visiting **El Dorado East Regional Park,** 7550 E. Spring St. (421-9431). These 80 acres of semi-wilderness shelter picnickers, cyclists, hikers, and fisherfolk. (Open daily 7am-dusk. $3 per vehicle Mon.-Fri., $5 Sat.-Sun.)

Downtown Long Beach is home to several historical buildings, such as **Villa Riviera Apartment Building.** Built in 1929, the Gothic-Tudor design calls to mind a 16-story French chateau. The downtown area around Long Beach Blvd. is also home to a number of thrift shops, while Broadway Blvd., east of downtown, is the site of boutiques and dance clubs.

North of the Convention Center in Long Beach Plaza is the **Long Beach Children's Museum,** 945 Long Beach Blvd. (495-1163), with cultural and educational hands-on displays for children. (Open Thurs.-Sat. 11am-4pm, Sun. noon-4pm. $4.) East of the Convention Center, along the waterfront, is the **Long Beach Museum of Art,** 2300 Ocean Ave. (310-439-2119). Famed Pasadena architects Greene and Greene designed the museum's turn-of-the-century home, which displays the pagoda-like lines and woodwork of the California arts and crafts style. (Open Sat.-Mon. 10am-5pm, Fri. 10am-8pm. $2, students and seniors $1, free on Fri. 5-8pm.) The view from the museum's lovely outdoor sculpture gardens grants a breathtaking panorama of the Pacific. Concerts are held in the gardens Wednesdays 7 to 9pm in summer. Next door, **Café Chatz,** 2300 E. Ocean Ave. (434-5077; open Thurs.-Tues. 7am-5pm, Wed. 7am-9pm), serves truly innovative, yummy coffees (Caffé Borgia with orange and chocolate, $2.25).

Belmont Shores, Long Beach's upscale, uptown neighborhood, lies east of downtown and contains Long Beach's best public beach facilities and most popular parks. The beaches closer to downtown are less desirable. You can park by the eastern side of the beach near the intersection of Ocean Blvd. and La Verne for 25¢ per hr. This is a quiet, family-oriented beach that seems far too unglamorous to be in California. It's pretty, but when you gaze into the distance you see the shipyards. **Second Street** (between Santa Ana and Park) in Belmont Shores is Long Beach's prime walking and people-watching area.

Just past Belmont Shores is **Naples Island,** which, like Venice Beach, was planned around a series of canals. Unlike Venice Beach, the canals here still exist, and the Rivo Alto canal even has **gondoliers.** (Call 433-9595 for information on a moonlight voyage; 1-hr. cruise $55 for 2.)

North of downtown Long Beach, past Signal Hall, **Rancho Los Cerritos,** 4600 Virginia Rd. (424-9423) off San Antonio Dr., offers a romantic glimpse of what the early Spanish ranches looked like before they were subdivided and sold. This *rancho* was used for cattle-ranching until the 1860s. The ranch house itself dates back to 1844. (Tours Wed.-Sun. 1-5pm. Free.) Cerritos's sister ranch, **Rancho Los Alamitos,** 6400 Bixley Hill Rd. (431-3541), is filled with early 20th-century furnishings, as well as garden farms and a blacksmith shop (open Wed.-Sun. 1-5pm; free).

The **Long Beach Yacht Club,** 6201 Appian Way (310-598-9401), hold races throughout the year. During the summer a number of music festivals take place in downtown Long Beach, the most prominent of which are the **Jazz Fest** in mid-August and the **Blues Extravaganza** about a month later. For more on seasonal events, contact the Long Beach Area Convention and Visitors Council (see Practical Information, page 121).

NIGHTLIFE

The many slightly touristy bars along 2nd St. attract a regular crowd from the greater L.A. area. Visitors seeking a less restrained, less predictable nightlife might try the eastern part of Broadway.

Bayshore, 5335 E. 2nd St. (433-9150), is one of the liveliest of 2nd St.'s many night spots. Home of "shoot-the-root"—invented here in 1986, this drink contains a shot of root beer schnapps in a cup of beer ($3.25). Open Mon.-Tues. and Thurs. 3pm-2am, Wed. and Fri.-Sun. 1pm-2am.

Club 740, 740 E. Broadway (437-7705), features a variety of DJs and music ranging from Latin to top-40. Call for the latest information on cover charges. Open Wed.-Sun. Mexican food is available at **La Ventana** (435-6564) in the same building. Restaurant open Thurs.-Sun. 6-11pm.

The Library, 3418 E. Broadway (433-2393). This simultaneously imposing and comfortable coffeehouse offers everything you could ever want: enormous couches, fabulously rich cheesecake, a wide selection of used books, artsy clientele, and a damn good cup of coffee ($1.25, with refills). The truly divine Vanilla Goddess and other special drinks cost $2-3. Jazz on Sun., Wed., and Fri. nights. Open Mon.-Thurs. 7am-midnight, Fri. 7am-1am, Sat. 8am-1am, Sun. 8am-midnight.

The Reno Room, 3400 E. Broadway (438-4590), has the same management as Cocoreno's Taco Stand. A dim, smoky bar with dusty pink walls to inspire thoughts of faded California glamour. Appealingly nostalgic Elvis- and Sinatra-heavy jukebox. Free pool. Beer $2. Bar open daily until 2am. Happy hours daily 6-11am, 4-7pm.

■■■ CATALINA ISLAND

One of the most striking features of Catalina Island is the relative scarcity of automobiles; due to strict environmental and residential regulations, almost all who enter here are forced to abandon their cars and submit to the more slow-paced pursuits of boating, hiking, or bicycling. Separated from the mainland by twenty-two miles of open ocean, Catalina devotes itself to the carefully calibrated promotion of its wildlife (marine and terrestrial) so that tourists can enjoy, but not destroy, this small island's remarkably clear waters and undeveloped expanses. The island's proximity to L.A. a makes it a popular destination for a wide variety of travelers, from the enormously wealthy to the amateur budget-conscious hedonist.

Because it is difficult to stay cheaply in Catalina (though not impossible; see Camping page 125), visiting the island makes a good daytrip if you leave early and plan ahead. **Avalon,** the island's only city and tourist center, is helpful in orienting oneself and gathering necessary equipment, but the most interesting sights in Catalina lie outside the city's boundaries.

PRACTICAL INFORMATION

Visitors Information: Chamber of Commerce, P.O. Box 217 (310-510-7520; fax 510-7606). Located on the left side of Catalina's "pleasure pier," the chamber will send a brochure if you write in advance. Open Mon. and Wed.-Sat. 8am-5pm, Tues. 8am-4:30pm, Sun. 9am-4pm. **Tourist Information Center,** P.O. Box 747 (310-510-2000, ext. 272). Located just off the pleasure pier to the right facing inland. Answers basic questions, provides information on tours. The **Los Angeles County Parks and Recreation,** 213 Catalina Ave. (510-0688), issues free **camp-**

ing permits which are required by island law, and a good selection of maps. Open daily 8:30am-1pm and 2-4pm.

ATM: Don't worry about being isolated from quick cash in Avalon. The most convenient ATM is at the **Bank of Southern California** branch at 303 Crescent St.

Bicycle Rental: Renting a bike in Catalina can be frustrating and costly because biking outside Avalon requires a $50 permit. **Brown's Bikes,** 120 yds. from the boat dock (510-0986), rents cycles and sells permits. 1-5-speed bikes $5-6 per hour, $12-15 per day. Tandems $10-12 per hr., $25-30 per day. 18-speed mountain bike $9 per hr., $25 per day.

Market: Von's, 121 Metropole St. (510-0280). Open Mon.-Thurs. 8am-9pm, Fri.-Sat. 8am-10pm.

Laundromat: Catalina's Coinwash is next door to Von's. Open summer daily 7am-10pm, winter 7am-8pm.

Public Showers: on Main St. across from the Tuna Club. 50¢ token required to enter, 50¢ for 1st 2min. and each additional min. Open Sun.-Thurs. 7am-5pm, Fri.-Sat. 7am-7pm.

Pharmacy: Leo's Drug Store, 401 Crescent Ave. (510-0189), at the corner of Crescent and Sumner. Open daily 9am-6pm.

Emergency: 911.

Post Office: in the Arcade Building between Sumner and Metropole. **General Delivery ZIP Code:** 90704.

Area Code: 310.

GETTING THERE

If you don't have your own yacht, the best (and cheapest) way to get to Catalina is on **Catalina Cruises** (410-1062 or 800-CATALINA, -22825462), which departs from Long Beach, San Pedro, and Redondo (round-trip $21, ages 2-11 $19). The trip takes two hrs.; departure times change seasonally. A faster, more expensive way is the sleek **Catalina Express** ($35, seniors $32, ages 2-11 $26, under 2 $2; up to 22 departures daily). Call 310-519-1212 or 800-464-4228 for more information. The trip can be as short as 55 min. Bring along Dramamine if you're prone to sea-sickness—the ride to the island can be at once exhilarating and nauseating.

CAMPING AND ACCOMMODATIONS

Camping is the least expensive option at $10 per night. There are five sites of varying primitiveness and distance from Avalon; contact the L.A. County Parks and Recreation (see Practical Information, page 124) for the necessary information and to make required reservations.

The only hotel on Catalina that approaches budget prices is the **Hermosa Hotel & Catalina Cottages** (510-1070 or 800-666-3383), which offers pleasant, modest rooms close to (though not on) the waterfront. Rates start at $35 for a double with washbasin only, and can sink to $20 in winter.

FOOD, SIGHTS, AND ENTERTAINMENT

Inexpensive hamburger joints and breakfast places are to be found all along Crescent Ave., the island's main drag. **Shipwreck Joey's** (510-2755) has a prime location (on a deck parallel to the **casino** that commands your attention when you land at Catalina) and good prices. "Spinnaker Spuds"—potatoes with gobs of melted cheese and green onions are $3, and a grilled cheese sandwich is only $2. Sit and watch the anchored boats sway in the breeze as you eat your ice-cream cone ($1). There are moderately priced, more adventuresome restaurants and bars just a little bit inland; check menus before you enter as the priciest places are juxtaposed with the cheapest. If you're **hiking** or **picnicking, Von's** supermarket on Metropole is large and well-stocked.

There aren't many shopping bargains along the streets of Avalon; probably the smartest move is to strap on mask and snorkel or hop on a tour boat to take advantage of the extraordinary clarity of the waters. Diving gear from the elementary to the most sophisticated is available at **Catalina Divers Supply,** Box 126 (510-0330), on the left-hand side of the "pleasure pier" facing the water. (Wetsuits $11, mask/snorkel $6. Rates are for 24-hr. rental; deposit required, certification required for regulators and tanks.) You can propel yourself around with paddleboards ($5 per hr.), pedalboats ($10 per hr.), or rowboats ($10 per hr., $30 per ½-day, $50 for 8 hrs.); motorboats will likely cost you at least $30 per hr. The less athletic have numerous **tour** options. Combined packages will get you the most for your precious dollar; ask around for the best deals. Two of the most popular tours are the **Glass Bottom Boat Trip** (40min.; $7.50, seniors $6.50, ages 2-11 $3.75), which is even more striking at night ($8, seniors $7, ages 2-11 $4), and the **Flying Fish Boat Trip** (55min.; $8.50, seniors $7, 2-11 $4.25). Both are run by **Discovery Tours**, P.O. Box 737 (510-2500).

Those who prefer to stay on solid ground can visit the **Casino Building**, a grandiose, rotund structure parallel to the "pleasure pier." Its lower part conceals the **Catalina Island Museum** (510-2414), which has exhibitions on island history, prehistory, and natural history (open daily 10:30am-4pm). The **Wrigley Memorial Garden** (510-2288) pays tribute to Catalina's developer and his family; it's a 1½-mi. trek southwest of Avalon. If you're determined to see Avalon's wildlife and sites but don't want to hike, Discovery has land tours as well; the most comprehensive is the **Inland Motor Tour** (departs daily 9am; 3¾hr.; $24.50, seniors $22, children $13).

All in all, Catalina is most rewarding when explored without the constraints of tours and schedules. Keep the scripting of your day to a minimum and take advantage of the possibility for seclusion by finding a quiet beach and relaxing.

Orange County

Orange County, Los Angeles's neighbor to the south, was part of Los Angeles County until 1861, when "O.C." seceded over a tax dispute. Since then, it has managed to organize itself quite efficiently into a region that contrasts sharply with L.A.'s heterogeneous sprawl.

Orange County has a higher per capita income and a less ethnically diverse population than Los Angeles. Many of O.C.'s residents live in "planned communities," neighborhoods designed by strict codes governing where schools and shopping centers must be placed, as well as what houses must look like. Though it is more diverse than in the past, Orange County still exemplifies impenetrable suburbia. Still, millions of visitors flock to the Anaheim area each year to catch California Angels and L.A. Rams games or, most of all, to visit the perpetually happy Disneyland.

If suburbia isn't to your taste, you can always head for the coast, where Orange County's fine surf and string of clean, uncrowded beaches have produced a true approximation of stereotypical Southern California beach life, complete with a fun-oriented population of deeply tanned, full-time surfers and beach bums.

PRACTICAL INFORMATION

Visitors Information: Anaheim Area Visitors and Convention Bureau, 800 W. Katella Ave., Anaheim 92802 (999-8999), in the Anaheim Convention Center. Free brochures. Open Mon.-Fri. 8:30am-5pm. **Huntington Beach Conference and Visitors Bureau,** 2100 Main St., Suite 190, Huntington Beach 92648 (969-3492 or 800-SAY-OCEAN, -729-62326). Open Mon.-Fri. 8:30am-noon and 1-5pm.

Airport: John Wayne Orange County, Campus Dr. (general info. 252-5006). Flights to and from many major U.S. cities.

Amtrak: (800-872-7245 for reservations). 5 stops: 120 E. Santa Fe Ave. (992-0530), in Fullerton, at Harbor Blvd.; 1000 E. Santa Ana (547-8389), in Santa Ana; Santa Fe Depot (240-2972), in San Juan Capistrano; 2150 E. Katella (385-1448), in Anaheim by the stadium; unattended stop in San Clemente, off I-5 by the municipal pier.

Greyhound: 2080 S. Harbor (999-1256), in Anaheim, 3 blocks south of Disneyland (open daily 6:30am-8pm); 1000 E. Santa Ana Blvd. (542-2215), Santa Ana (open daily 7am-8pm); and 510 Avenida de la Estrella (492-1187), San Clemente (open Mon.-Thurs. 7:45am-6:30pm, Fri. 7:45am-8pm).

Orange County Transit District (OCTD): 11222 Acacia Parkway (636-7433), in Garden Grove. Thorough service, useful for getting from Santa Ana and Fullerton Amtrak stations to Disneyland, or for beach-hopping along the coast. Long Beach, in L.A. County, serves as the terminus for several OCTD lines. Bus #1 travels the coast from Long Beach down to San Clemente, with service once per hr. early morning-8pm. Fare $1, transfers 5¢. Most buses accept dollar bills. Information center open Mon.-Fri. 6am-7pm, Sat.-Sun. 8am-5pm.

Local RTD Information: 800-2-LA-RIDE, -2-52-7433. Lines open daily 4:55am-10:45pm. RTD buses run from L.A. to Disneyland and Knott's Berry Farm.

AAA Service: Huntington Beach (641-0833); Anaheim (921-2850). Open Mon.-Fri. 9am-5pm, Sat. 9am-1pm.

Surf and Weather Reports: 536-9303.

Poison Control Center: 24 hrs., 800-777-6476.

Rape Crisis Hotline: 957-2737. 24-hr. service of the O.C. Sexual Assault Network.

Gay-Lesbian Community Center: 14131 Yorba (731-5445 or 534-0862). Open Mon.-Thurs. 11am-1pm and 3-8:30pm, Fri. 11am-3pm. Bookstore and counselling.

Hospital: Pacifica Hospital (842-0611). 24 hrs.

Free Clinic of Orange County: 1215 E. Chapman (633-4600). Call to find out when applications are accepted.

Police: Anaheim, 425 S. Harbor Blvd. (254-1900). **Huntington Beach,** 960-8811.

Emergency: 911.

Post Office: 701 N. Loara (520-2600), Anaheim, 1 block north of Anaheim Plaza. Open Mon.-Fri. 8:30am-5pm, Sat. 8:30am-2pm. **General Delivery ZIP Code:** 92803.

Area Code: 714; 310 in Seal Beach.

■■■ ANAHEIM

ACCOMMODATIONS AND CAMPING

It's easy to stay in **Anaheim** cheaply, as a plethora of motels compete for the Disney-goer's dollar. Driving down Harbor Blvd. or Katella Ave. you'll be confronted with long strings of economy motels, many with special rates for families including kids stay free specials. However, because it's fairly remote from the area's other sights, there is no reason to stay here unless you plan to linger in the Magic Kingdom. Start with the Anaheim Visitors Center, a travel industry dating service, which matches people with rooms they can afford.

Fullerton Hacienda Hostel (HI/AYH), 1700 N. Harbor Blvd. (738-3721), in Fullerton, 15-min. drive north of Disneyland. Shuttle from LAX $18. OCTD bus #43 runs up and down Harbor Blvd. to Disneyland, and the hostel managers can arrange car rentals for groups. Wonderfully refurbished hostel with an international clientele. This big, Spanish-style house complete with porch swing is set back from the road on a quiet hill. Their "magic book" is full of ideas and information on the area; the charming and enthusiastic staff invites questions but frowns on drinking. Modern kitchen, clean communal bathrooms, and spiffy single- and mixed-sex accommodations. 5-day max. stay. No curfew. Registration daily 7:30-10:30am and 5-11pm. $14, $17 for non-members. Reservations accepted.

Motel 6, 4 Anaheim locations, and 2 more in adjacent suburbs at 921 S. Beach Blvd. (220-2866), and 7450 Katella Ave. (891-0717), both within a 10-min. drive of Disneyland. The excitement of the nearby amusement park permeates these motels; both have pools and are filled with couples and their rambunctious, Mickey Mouska-eared children. Most rooms have HBO. All offer A/C and free local calls. The S. Beach Blvd. location is the best deal for groups ($32 for 1-4 persons). The Katella Ave. motel is in better shape and a steal: Singles $25. Doubles $29.

Skyview Motel, 1126 W. Katella Ave. (533-4505) at the southwest corner of Disneyland—a terrific location for Disneygoers. Big, clean rooms with HBO and A/C. Balconies offer a good view of Disney's nightly fireworks. Small pool, affable management. Singles $24, $4 per additional person. Up to 4 per room.

FOOD

Cheap food is easy to find in Anaheim; there are countless fast-food restaurants to choose from and many hotels offer all-you-can-eat buffets as part of Disneyland packages. For a break from the standard fare, try one of the various inexpensive ethnic restaurants tucked into the strip malls that line Anaheim's streets. Many specialize in take-out—a true Southern California phenomenon—or will deliver chow right to your motel room. Anaheim's budget eateries are not remarkable but the following are worth a visit if you're in town and hungry.

Kong Paro, 1851 W. Katella (535-0902), has low-priced lunch specials ($3.45-4.50). Delicious 3-flavored sizzling rice soup will serve 2 ($6.50). Open Mon. and Wed.-Sat. 11:30am-3pm and 4:30-9:30pm, Sun. 4:30-9:30pm. Free delivery 3 mi.

Anand Food, 2755 W. Lincoln Blvd. (761-3494). A variety of unusual, well-spiced and vegetarian Indian dishes. A full dinner costs under $10. Open daily 10am-9pm.

Normandy's Café, 1788 Euclid Blvd. (533-8205). Anaheim's mall answer to the café explosion. A good selection of magazines (to read, not buy). Coffee and biscotti for under $3. A destination of choice for young hipster Republicans. Open daily 7:30am-10pm.

SIGHTS

Disneyland

The stunningly animated, well-received *The Lion King* and the controversial proposed American history "theme park" in West Virginia are but two examples of Disney's influence over American popular culture. In spite of Disney's growth, the spiritual heart of Michael Eisner's ever-growing empire is still found, however, where Walt wanted it, in the former orange groves of Anaheim. "The Happiest Place on Earth" has delighted hundreds of millions of visitors over the last 39 years. Soviet premier Nikita Khrushchev was livid when Walt barred him from the park at the height of the Cold War.

The attractions are inspired testaments to the charm and wit of child-like creativity, but the crowds of 75,000 young-at-heart per day jamming into the park can be a little unnerving, even though most of the rides themselves are fairly tame. The **Unlimited Use Passport** (1 day $31, ages 3-11 $25) grants admission and use of all rides. There are obscured costs, however, at every corner, thanks to a constant barrage of souvenirs, arcades, and food. (Park open Sun.-Fri. 9am-midnight, Sat. 8am-1am. Hours subject to change, call 999-4565 for information.)

Getting There

The park is located at 1313 Harbor Blvd., in Anaheim in Orange County, bounded by Katella Ave., Harbor Blvd., Ball Rd., and West St. From L.A. take bus #460 from 6th and Flower St. downtown, about 1½ hours to the Disneyland Hotel. (Service to the hotel begins at 4:53am, service back to L.A. until 1:20am.) From the hotel take the free shuttle to Disneyland's portals (or go in style via the Disneyland monorail). The park is also served by Airport Service, OCTD, Long Beach Transit, and Gray Line (see Practical Information). If you're driving, take the Santa Ana Fwy. (I-5) to the Katella Ave. exit. Be forewarned that while parking in the morning should be painless, leaving in the evening often will not be. It costs $6 to use Disney parking; to avoid the charge and the line to leave, park in the adjacent neighborhood and head to Disneyland on foot. When the park closes early, Disneygoers must contend with the tail-end of L.A. and Orange County's maddening rush-hour traffic.

In the Park

Visitors enter the Magic Kingdom by way of **Main Street, USA,** a collection of shops, arcades, and even a movie theater, designed to look like the towns of Walt's turn-of-the-century childhood memories. The broad avenue leads to a replica of Sleeping Beauty's castle at the center of the park. There's also a bank (closes at 1pm), an information booth, lockers, and a first aid station. Pick up a free map of the park at the information booth—it's essential! Strollers and wheelchairs are available for rent at $6 per day as you enter the park.

The **Disneyland Railroad** arrives every five to ten minutes and takes its passengers on a ride that circles the park with limited stops. Though it provides a decent overview of the park, the long line for seats should encourage you to explore on foot. Disneyland is more compact than the grandiose rhetoric would lead you to believe; remember it is designed for little feet.

It is at night that Disneyland comes closest to meeting the fantastic expectations it raises. During the day, the park can be hot and crowded, but at night the **Main Street Electrical Parade** transforms the masses into an excited, unified whole. Each summer night at 8:50pm and 10:25pm (the earlier parade is followed by fireworks) floats and humans, adorned with thousands of multicolored lights, generate a thrilling nighttime display. This is one of Disneyland's most popular events and people begin lining the sidewalks on Main Street by 7pm for a front-row view. The **Fantasmic!** laser show projects fiery villains and whirling heroes onto the night sky. (Nightly performances in summer.)

To the right of Main St. lies **Tomorrowland**—futuristic home to two of Disney's premier attractions. **Space Mountain** is arguably the park's most thrilling ride. A high-tech looking roller coaster whizzes through almost total darkness inside the "mountain." Disney is not particularly big on letting people request seats, but this is the one ride where groveling for the front is justified. Less frightening, but more high-tech is the George Lucas-produced **Star Tours,** where the masterfully engineered line is almost as entertaining as the ride itself. Long lines are a fact of life at Disneyland. For the shortest wait, go to the park early or stay late. Either way, avoid the **Submarine Voyage,** which purports to take you to the North Pole and back but is really just a dull ride full of fake starfish and papier-mâché mermaids.

On the other side of the railroad tracks is the community of **Mickey's Toontown,** where the youngest of Disney's visitors will probably have the most fun. A new ride, **Roger Rabbit's Car Toon Spin,** is gentle enough for those too small to relish the more thrilling rides. It is in the various Houses of Toontown that you are most likely to encounter "live" Disney characters.

Recrossing the tracks and moving counter-clockwise around the park, **Fantasyland** sports numerous fairy tale-inspired kids' rides. The most dominating feature is the **Matterhorn Mountain,** through and around which winds a high-speed bobsled. Sadly, the Matterhorn offers little in the way of thrills—this "average roller coaster with scenery" is probably the least impressive of the major rides. Nearby is the ever popular **It's a Small World** cruise (a hint: unless you want the cute, but annoying theme song running through your head for the rest of the day, you may want to save this one for last).

Next stop on the counter-clockwise tour is **Frontierland,** featuring the **Thunder Mountain Railroad** coaster and **Tom Sawyer Island.** While not exactly death-defying, Thunder Mountain is far more entertaining than the Matterhorn, its Fantasyland counterpart. Tucked in behind Tom's Island are **Critter Country** and **New Orleans Square. Splash Mountain,** the newest of the super-rides, climaxes with a wet, five-story drop, but the rest of the water-bound cruise is relatively tame. The closer to the front you sit the wetter you will be. Be aware that you'll be photographed as you start that final descent and arrange your expression accordingly (a copy of the photo will set you back $6-10). **Pirates of the Caribbean,** another floating adventure, showcases Disney magic at its finest. The amazingly elaborate and realistic journey puts the nearby **Haunted Mansion** to shame (although this ghoulish abode is still well worth seeing). Rounding out the trip (both physically and metaphorically) is **Adventureland,** with the **Jungle Cruise** and the **Swiss Family Robinson Treehouse.**

Food services in the park ranges from sit-down establishments to fast-food eateries such as the Lunching Pad in Tommorowland. You can save time and money by packing a picnic lunch and eating a big breakfast before you leave home. (Disney officially forbids bringing food and drink into the park, but there is a picnic area conveniently located just to the left of the main exit.) Food in the park is mediocre and generally overpriced. No alcohol is served in the Magic Kingdom.

For further tips, consult *The Unofficial Guide to Disneyland* ($13, ISBN #0671503065), available from MacMillan Publishing, Attn.: Sales Publishing, 201 W. 103rd St., Indianapolis, IN 46290 (800-428-5331). The authors have earned their mouska-ears by cramming the book with time-saving hints. The guide evaluates every attraction in the park and suggests several specific itineraries.

Other Sights

Another amusement park, **Knott's Berry Farm,** 8039 Beach Blvd. (714-220-5200 for a recording), is at La Palma Ave. in Buena Park just 5 mi. northeast of Disneyland. (Take the Santa Ana Fwy. south, exit west on La Palma Ave. Bus #460 stops here on its way to Disneyland.) A berry farm in its early days, Knott's now cultivates a country fair atmosphere with a re-created ghost town, Fiesta Village, Roaring Twenties Park, a variety of rides, and a replica of Independence Hall. Thrill-seekers may find Knott's roller coasters substantially more suited to their needs than those in the Magic Kingdom. (Open Mon.-Fri. 10am-11pm, Sat. 9am-midnight, Sun. 9am-11pm. $27, over 60 $18, ages 3-11 $16.)

If you still have not had enough of amusement parks, take in **Wild Rivers Water-park,** I-405 south to 8600 Irvine Center Dr., Laguna Hills (714-768-9453). Cool off with over 40 waterslide rides and two wave pools. (Call for hours. $17, ages 3-9 $13.)

For another sign of Disney's widespread influence, check out the **Pond,** 2695 E. Katella Ave. (7(′ .2400), one block east of Rte. 57. This arena serves as the home of the NHL's **Mighty Ducks,** who hope to share the success of their Disney movie counterparts.

Crystal Cathedral, 12141 Lewis St., Garden Grove (971-4000), was completed in 1980 by Phillip Johnson and John Burgee. Opinions are split on this shining all-glass structure' some find it inspiring, others call it garish. Dr. Robert H. Schuller preaches his weekly TV show, *Hour of Power,* from the pulpit of this church. With 7,000 people moving in and out every Sunday, the Cathedral is a model of effi-ciency. (Tours Mon.-Sat. 9am-3:30pm. Free.)

Farther inland you'll find a well-outfitted, highly uncritical monument to Tricky Dick—**The Richard Nixon Library and Birthplace.** Listen to taped excerpts from the Watergate hearings, or satisfy twin obsessions and see the pistols Elvis gave to Nixon. You may have to tolerate hordes of junior high school students. Recover from the excitement in Pat Nixon's peaceful rose garden. (18001 Yorba Linda Blvd., Yorba Linda (993-3393). $5, seniors $3. Open Mon.-Sat. 10am-5pm, Sun. 11am-5pm.)

From early April to early October, you can catch the **California Angels** at home in Anaheim for as little as $4 (general admission; 800-6-ANGELS, -6-264357). Flea market fans should stop by the **Anaheim Market Place,** 1440 S. Anaheim Blvd. (999-0888), the largest of SoCal's swap meets. There are over 250 variety shops under one roof. (Open Wed.-Mon. 10am-7pm.)

■■■ COASTAL AREAS

ACCOMMODATIONS AND CAMPING

The county's coastline is very appealing, but visitors may have trouble finding bar-gain rates, especially in the wealthier residential areas. A good place to look for a bargain room is along the Pacific Coast or Newport Blvd. in Newport Beach. You might also try basing yourself inland and making daytrips to the coast.

Huntington Beach Colonial Inn Youth Hostel, 421 8th St. (536-3315), in Hun-tington Beach, 4 blocks inland at Pecan. Staff fosters a sense of family at this large yellow wooden house shaded by huge palm trees. Common showers, bathroom, large kitchen. Reading/TV room. Both the large deck and the surfboard shed out back are frequently used by the hostel's tan, young guests. Check-in 7am-11pm. No lockout. After 11pm, entry requires late-night key, free with $20 deposit. Multi-person dorms $12 per person. Doubles $14. Must have picture ID. Call 2 days in advance for summer weekends.

Mesa Motel, N. Newport Blvd. (646-3893). ½ mi. to the beach. Attractive location near many more expensive establishments. Small swimming pool, TV, and typical motel rooms. Singles $35. Doubles $40.

There are state beaches in Orange County with campgrounds, listed below from north to south. All will probably fall well short of your beach camping fantasies, but this doesn't prevent them from being *extremely* popular. Reservations are required for all sites except the Echo Arch Area in San Onofre, which is first-come, first-camped. Reservations can be made through MISTIX (800-444-7275) a maximum of 8 weeks in advance, and should be made as soon as possible in the summer. (Note: There is a $6.75 *non-refundable* fee for every reservation made. If you want a spot, though, it's $6.75 well spent.)

Doheny (496-6172), Rte. 1 at the south end of Dana Point. Beachside location turns this place into a zoo. TVs, lounge furniture, play pens, aquariums, and more. Offers the only sites in the area with real beach sand (and yes, they go very fast!) Beachfront sites $21, others $16. Off-season, beachfront sites $19, others $14.

Bolsa Chica (848-1566), Rte. 1, 3 mi. west of Huntington Beach. Self-contained RVs only. No hookups. 7-day max. stay. $14 per vehicle, $13 for seniors.

San Clemente (492-3156), I-5, get off on Avenida del Presidente and follow the state beach signs (there are no signs for the campground itself). Heavy on sites (a total of 157, 85 with hookups) and RVs, short on trees. Great vistas of ocean, and, unfortunately, of the adjacent neighborhoods as well. Sites $16.

San Onofre (492-0802), I-5, 3 mi. south of San Clemente. 221 campsites along an abandoned stretch of Pacific Coast Hwy.; about 90 are suitable for tents, others are for RVs only. The waves of highway traffic drown out those of the distant surf. Camp on a 10-ft. strip of dirt crammed between the parking area and the nearby bluff. Six ¼-mi. trails provide access to a lovely beach. The **Echo Arch Area** has 34 more primitive hike-in sites between the bluffs and the beach. Sites $16.

San Mateo (492-0802), I-5, 2 mi. south of San Clemente. Technically a part of the San Onofre Beach, this ground is even farther from the ocean than its companions. (A 1-mi. trail leads to the famous "Trestles" surfing area.) Location is blessed with more peace and privacy than any other spot in the area. Sites $16.

FOOD

Numerous casual restaurants and cafés along the coast offer tasty and filling meals.

Café Zinc, 350 Ocean Ave. (494-6302), in Laguna Beach. Somewhat pricey but varied menu of quality vegetarian specialties. "Pizettes" with pesto or goat cheese $5.75. Rosemary biscuits 85¢. Open Mon.-Sat. 7am-5:30pm, Sun. 7am-5pm.

Sugar Shack, 213½ Main St. (536-0355), in Huntington Beach. A friendly hangout with outdoor seating and lots of tan surfer-types selecting multiple toppings for their egg burritos ($4.50, includes lots of fixings). Popular with the locals. Open Sun.-Thurs. 7am-3:30pm, Fri.-Sat. 6:30am-9pm.

Sea Breeze Café, 1640 El Camino Real (498-4771), in San Clemente. Friendly waitresses rattle off a list of 10 specials, all under $5. Fantastically filling breakfast burrito ($4.65) and popular banana and blueberry pancakes ($4). Open Mon.-Sat. 6am-2pm, Sun. 7am-2pm.

Studio Café, 100 Main St. (675-7760), on the Balboa Peninsula. Blue-green and airy, this spot serves up good burgers for around $6. Lots of live music. R&B, with jazz on Wednesday and occasional rock bands. Never a cover. Open Mon.-Fri. 11:30am-2am, Sat.-Sun. 10am-2am.

Coffeehouses are the center of Orange County nightlife and where the best live music is found. During the day the cafés are empty and peaceful since almost everyone is at the beach, but at night you may have to fight for a table. Good spots for nightlife are **Midnight Espresso,** 201D Main St. (960-5858), in Huntington Beach and in Costa Mesa **Rock 'n' Java,** 1749 Newport Blvd. (650-4430), and **Diedrich's Coffee House,** 474 E. 17th St.(646-0323), located next to a Wendy's.

Laguna Beach is home to two popular **gay bars.** The **Boom-Boom Room,** at the Coast Inn, 1401 S. Coast Hwy. (494-7588), has bartenders in Calvin Klein underwear and bow ties every Fri. (cover $5 on Fri.-Sat.; open daily 11:30am-2am). **Little Shrimp,** 1305 S. Coast Hwy. (494-4111), has an older, marine, and preppy crowd. The food is expensive. (Bar open Mon.-Fri. 10am-1am, Sat.-Sun. 11am-1am.)

SIGHTS

Despite the inland amusement parks, recreation for residents and visitors of all ages frequently revolves around the ocean. The **beaches** are generally cleaner, less crowded, and more charming than those in L.A. County. Visitors should not be lulled off-guard by the swishing coastal waters and magical inland attractions. All the Disney magic in the world could not vanquish the smog, traffic, and crime problems that plague Orange County and Los Angeles. Pedestrians should take extreme care in the cities. After dusk, situate yourself in a taxi or among a good-sized group of traveling companions. It is unsafe and illegal to spend the night on the beach unless you are in an official campsite.

Huntington Beach

Huntington Beach served as a port of entry for the surfing craze, which transformed the California coast life after being imported from Hawaii in the early 1900s. Riding or shredding the waves remains the activity of choice and the newly remodeled pier provides a perfect vantage point for oglers. Nightlife here is scant, and most locals head to 2nd Street in Long Beach for after-hours fun.

Newport Beach and the Balboa Peninsula

Newport Beach and the surrounding inland cities are the jewels of Orange County. Stunning multimillion dollar homes line **Newport Harbor,** the largest leisure craft harbor in the world. The beach itself displays few signs of ostentatious wealth; it is crowded with young, frequently rowdy hedonists in neon-colored bikinis and trunks. In the shadow of a giant Ferris wheel, the area around Newport Pier is a haven for families; the streets from 30th to 56th give way to students. To appreciate the shoreline from the water, you can rent a **party pontoon boat** for $30 per hour. Each holds up to six adults. Contact Anchors Away Boat Rentals at 673-3372.

The sands of Newport Beach run south onto the **Balboa Peninsula,** separated from the mainland by Newport Bay. The peninsula itself is only two to four blocks wide and can be reached from Pacific Coast Hwy. (PCH) by Balboa Blvd. The ornate **Balboa Pavilion** at the end of Main St., once a sounding ground for Big Band great Benny Goodman, is now a hub for harbor tours and winter whale-watching. The bi-level *Pavilion Queen* and smaller *Pavilion Paddy* offer six 45-minute cruises per day. (Fare $6, children $1.) Close to this landmark, the **Ocean Front Walk** extends the length of the peninsula and provides excellent views of the ocean and numerous waterfront homes. At the end of the peninsula, **The Wedge,** seasonally pounded by storm-generated waves up to 20 ft. tall, is a **bodysurfing** mecca. Advanced surfers risk life and limb for a monster ride.

Melt into the crowd on Newport Beach or the Balboa Peninsula by hopping on a bicycle or strapping on a pair of in-line skates. Rental shops cluster around the Newport Beach pier and at the end of the peninsula. (Bike rentals run $5 per hr., $15 per day. Skates $3-6 per hr., $15 per day. Boogie-boards $5-6 per day.)

Once you have reached the end of the peninsula, from the harbor side you can see **Balboa Island,** largest of the three islands sheltered by the peninsula. The island is expensive and covered with chic eateries, boutiques, and bikini shops. A vintage **ferryboat** (673-1070) will take you there from the peninsula. (Ferry runs every 3-5 min., Sun.-Thurs. 6:30am-midnight, Fri.-Sat. 6:30am-2am. Car and driver $1, additional passengers 35¢, children 15¢.) Balboa Island can also be reached from PCH by a bridge on Jamboree Rd.

Costa Mesa

North of Newport Beach is **Costa Mesa,** home of the new and dazzling **Orange County Performing Arts Center,** 600 Town Center Dr. (556-2121), on Bristol St. off I-405. The opulent, 3000-seat structure was constructed in 1986 at a cost of $70 million and has hosted the American Ballet Theatre and the Kirov Ballet, among others. The several square blocks around the Performing Arts Center hold various modern sculptures and outdoor set installations, including Isamu Noguchi's *California Scenario.* This massive and dramatic sculpture garden is located in the bank complex framed by Anton Blvd., Ave. of the Arts, and I-405. Get a map and guide describing the various sculptures at the information booth inside the **South Coast Plaza Mall,** off I-405, across from the Performing Arts Center.

Laguna Beach

Back along the coast, **Laguna Beach,** 4 mi. south of Newport is nestled between canyons. Back in the old days, Laguna was a Bohemian artists' colony, but no properly starving artists can afford to live here now. The surviving galleries and art supply stores nevertheless add a unique twist to the standard SoCal beach culture that thrives on Laguna's sands. Punctuated by rocky cliffs, coves, and lush hillside vegetation, the town is decidedly Mediterranean in character. South of Laguna Beach, the California coastline takes on a dry, dusty appearance—there's a significant change in the landscape. **Main Beach** and the shops nearby are the prime parading areas, though there are other, less crowded spots as well. One accessible beach (with a sizable gay crowd) is **Westry Beach,** which spreads out south of Laguna just below **Aliso Beach Park.** Park on Pacific Coast Hwy. or residential streets to the east and look for "Public Access" signs between private properties.

Laguna Beach's artwork is displayed at the **Laguna Beach Museum of Art,** 307 Cliff Dr. (494-8971), which houses recent works by important Californian artists including an excellent collection of early 20th-century Impressionist works. (Open Tues.-Fri. 11am-5pm, Sat. 11am-9pm, Sun. 10am-7pm. $4, seniors and students $3, under 12 free. Tours Tues.-Wed. and Sun. 2pm.)

Mission San Juan Capistrano and San Onofre State Beach

More tourists than swallows return every year to **Mission San Juan Capistrano** (248-2048), a half-hour south of Anaheim on I-5 (take Ortega Hwy. to Camino Capistrano). Established in 1776 as one of California's 21 Catholic missions, it is somewhat run-down due to an 1812 earthquake. Father Junípero Serra, the mission's founder, officiated from inside the beautiful **Serra Chapel,** which at 215 years is the oldest building in the state. The dark chapel is warmed by the 17th-century Spanish cherrywood altar and the Native American designs painted on walls and ceiling. It's still used by the Catholic Church, so enter quietly. (Open daily 8:30am-5pm. Admission $4, seniors and ages 3-12 $3.)

The mission is best known as a home to the thousands of swallows who return here from their winter migration each year to nest in mid-March. According to legend they return to Capistrano on St. Joseph's Day, March 19. They usually leave in mid-October. The best time to see the birds is when they feed on flying insects in the early morning or early evening.

The marine base of **Camp Pendleton** stands at attention next door, asserting a measure of stern decorum in this part of the coast. Nevertheless, **San Onofre State Beach** is a prime surfing zone (particularly the world famous "Trestles" area). The southern end of the beach is frequented by nudists (drive down as far as you can go, and walk left on the trail for ¼-½ mi.; beach contains both a gay and a straight area). Nude bathing is illegal, and you'll be fined if you're caught with your pants down.

■ SEASONAL EVENTS

Strawberry Festival (638-7950), Memorial Day weekend in downtown Garden Grove on the village green. Garden Grove is the U.S.'s leading producer of strawberries, and the festival includes some arduous strawberry pie-eating contests.

OP Pro Surfing Championships (580-1888), late June at Huntington Beach.

Festival of Arts and the **Pageant of the Masters** (494-1145, for tickets 497-6582), July-Aug., take place in the Irvine Bowl, 650 Laguna Canyon Rd. in Laguna Beach. Life literally imitates art in the pageant as residents who have rehearsed for months don the makeup and costumes of figures in famous paintings and then pose for 90-second tableaux, astonishingly similar to the original artwork. $2, seniors $1, under 12 free. Art show open daily 10am-4pm. Tickets $12-30. Both the pageant and the festival run from the second week of July to the last week of August. To reserve a place contact the Festival of Arts, P.O. Box 1659, Laguna Beach, CA 92652.

Newport SeaFest Week (644-8211), late Sept. in Newport Harbor.

Christmas Boat Parade of Lights (644-8211), the week before Christmas, in Newport Harbor. Includes over 200 boats.

South Coastal Ranges

Southern California residents are blessed with proximity not only to the Pacific Ocean, but also to the pine forests of the **Coastal Ranges.** A two-hour drive transports the traveler from the crowded, smoggy streets of Los Angeles to the solitude and clean air of the **San Gabriel Mountains** and the **San Bernardino Mountains**.

In these mountains, outdoor activities flourish year-round, but winter is definitely the high season. While the Sierra Nevada resorts that cluster around Lake Tahoe and Mammoth Lake are the destination of choice for serious Californian skiers, daytrips to the mountain resorts of San Bernardino have become increasingly popular. Temperatures typically allow ski resorts to operate between November and April. Always call ahead to check conditions.

When ski conditions are favorable, many resorts sell out lift tickets with astonishing rapidity. **Tickets** for the resorts listed below may be purchased over the phone with Visa or MasterCard through Ticket-Master (213-480-3232 or 714-740-2000). All resorts rent equipment and offer lessons and special package rates, but it is advisable to rent equipment before venturing up the hill to avoid lines and high prices at the resort. Many ski shops in the mountain towns just outside of the ski areas also rent equipment with prices rising proportionately with proximity to the slopes. Lift tickets are usually around $32 for a full day; most resorts have half-day rates and some others have discounted nighttime skiing.

When the snow melts, the coastal mountains become an ideal summer and fall getaway for city dwellers. The **Angeles** and **San Bernardino National Forests** have many campgrounds, hiking trails, and mountain villages to visit.

■■■ ANGELES NATIONAL FOREST

The San Gabriel Mountains encompass thick timberwoods, barren peaks, and green meadows. Their highest peak of **Mount San Antonio,** or "Old Baldy," measures in at 10,064 ft. This area is popular year-round and attracts, in season, skiers, mountain bikers, anglers, and hikers.

National Forest land covers 693,000 acres, about a quarter of the area of Los Angeles County, and offers over 110 campgrounds ($5-12 per night, payment by the honor system). Choose a district of the forest and then contact the appropriate ranger office for information. Campsites are first-come, first-camped (14-day max. stay). With 526 mi. of hiking trails and three lakes with boating and swimming areas, the Angeles National Forest is an excellent place to get away from the frantic pace of L.A. without trekking all the way to the Sierras.

Mt. Wilson Skyline Park is in Arroyo Seco (see below), with its world-famous 100-in. telescope and observatory (310-333-3478; open Sat.-Sun. 10am-4pm).

RANGER STATIONS

All the ranger stations listed are open Mon.-Fri. 8am-4:30pm unless closed on Wednesday as noted below. For emergencies, contact the Angeles National Forest Dispatcher at (818) 447-8991 or dial 911.

Angeles National Forest Headquarters, Supervisor's Office, 701 N. Santa Anita Ave., Arcadia 91006 (818-574-5200). Comprehensive map of the forest available here ($2), as well as a wide selection of other literature about the area.

Arroyo Seco Ranger District, Oak Grove Park, Flintridge 91011 (818-790-1151). This is the south-central area of the forest, just north of Pasadena. Part of the **Pacific Crest Trail** passes through here, as well as numerous short self-guided nature trails. There are 17 campgrounds in the district.

Mt. Baldy Ranger District, 110 N. Wabash Ave., Glendora 91740 (818-335-1251). The southeastern district of the forest includes several 8000 ft. peaks, hiking trails, the cascading San Antonio Falls, and scenic Glendora Ridge Road.

Saugus Ranger District, 30800 Bouquet Canyon Rd., Saugus 91350 (805-296-9710). A separate district to the northwest of the main body of the forest; Pyramid, Elizabeth, and Castaic Lakes have boating and fishing facilities. A wide variety of campgrounds is available.

Tujunga Ranger District, 12371 N. Little Tujunga Canyon Rd., San Fernando 91342 (818-899-1900). Tujunga covers the western end of the San Gabriel Mountains. It features a myriad of hiking and horseback riding trails and 5 overnight campgrounds. The spectacular Angeles Crest Hwy. (Rte. 2) starts its waterfall-ridden course through the forest from this district. Closed Wed.

Valyermo Ranger District, P.O. Box 15, 29835 Valyermo Rd., Valyermo 93563 (805-944-2187). This district sprawls across the northeastern sector of the San Gabriels. Many campgrounds are along the Big Pines Hwy., which runs southeast out of Pear Blossom and Valyermo into the northeast corner of the forest. The town of Big Pines marks the start of the earthquake fault tour, a self-guided route showcasing the lifts, sags, and scars left behind by major tremors. Closed Wed.

SKI AREAS

Keep in mind that this is by no means the best skiing in California. The only thing that keeps most of these places in business is their proximity to L.A. The best time to ski is on weekdays, within two or three days after a major snowfall.

Mt. Baldy (818-982-0800), 45 min. from downtown L.A. Take I-10 east, exit Mountain Ave., and drive north for 16 mi. 4 double-chair lifts, 26 runs. Lift tickets $35, students on weekdays $27, 65 and over $18, under 13 $21.

Ski Sunrise (619-249-6150), 5 mi. west of Wrightwood, north of Rte. 2, 1½ hr. from L.A. Follow Rte. 2 to Big Pines; go 1 mi. on Table Mt. Rd. and follow signs. Family atmosphere set in inviting piney hills. Popular ski school and separate beginner areas. 1 quad lift, 3 surface lifts, 80- to 800-ft. drops, artificial-snow equipment. Lift tickets $25, students and ages 7-12 $14, under 7 free. Equipment rental $14, under 13 $10. Snowboards $20. Beginner's package (lesson, rental, and lift) $35.

Mountain High (619-249-5821), 3 mi. west of Wrightwood on Rte. 2, is 80 min. from downtown L.A. From L.A., take San Bernardino Fwy. (I-10) to I-15 north, then U.S. 138 to Wrightwood. From the San Fernando Valley, take I-5 north to Antelope Valley Fwy. (Rte. 14), then the Pear Blossom turn-off (U.S. 138) to Wrightwood. 13 lifts, 30 runs, 80- to 1600-ft. vertical drops, night-skiing, and snowmakers. Lift tickets $38.75, students on weekdays $29.75, under 12 $15.

Two smaller resorts, **Mt. Waterman** (818-790-2002) and **Kratka Ridge** (818-440-9749), are located just 45 minutes from downtown L.A., along Rte. 2 in La Cañada. Snow patches suitable for snowball fights persist into June, but skiing ends in April.

SUMMER RECREATION

In summer, ski trails are often open for **mountain biking. Mountain High** operates lifts to its alpine bike park, Saturday and Sunday 9am to 4:30pm for $7 one way or $15 all day. Helmets are required and can be rented for $6.50. Bike rentals (including helmet) are available for $8.50 per hour or $24 for a half-day. Bikers are also welcome at **Mt. Waterman** and **Kratka Ridge,** although lifts do not operate in the summer. Off-road cyclists can find challenging terrain throughout the forest. Biking along the Pacific Crest Trail and in designated wilderness areas is prohibited.

Miles of trail allow **hikers** to wander through the forest, skirt waterfalls, and spot elusive fauna like the bighorn sheep. Portions of the **Pacific Crest Trail** can be reached from the **Buckhorn** to **Little Creek** traverse. Forested sites at **Cooper Canyon** along the way are free and provide tables and restrooms. Follow the **Vincent Gap** trailhead to **Mt. Baden-Powell,** up 2800 ft., for an impressive and popular view of towering **Mt. Baldy,** the highest peak of the San Gabriel Mountains (10,064 ft.). Check at a ranger station for directions, maps, and local conditions.

Creeks and lakes in every district of the park are stocked with fish regularly by the Department of Fish and Game. Rangers will direct interested **anglers** to catch-and-keep or catch-and-release areas.

Close by the Angeles National Forest in La Cañada is **Descanso Gardens,** 4118 Descanso Dr. (818-952-4400), near the intersection of Rtes. 2 and 210. This lovely 165-acre retreat is similar to the L.A. Arboretum. The garden includes the world's largest camellia forest, a historic rose collection, and man-made waterfalls ($5, students and ages 62 and above $3, ages 5-12 $1; open daily 9am-4:30pm).

■■■ BIG BEAR

Hibernating in the **San Bernardino Mountains,** the town of **Big Bear Lake** entertains visitors with winter skiing and summer boating. The consistent winds make the lake one of the best for sailing in the state. The **Big Bear Chamber of Commerce,** 630 Bartlett Rd. (mailing address: P.O. Box 2860), Big Bear Lake 92315 (909-866-4607), dispenses glossy ski brochures and arranges accommodations/ski packages (open Mon.-Fri. 9am-5pm, Sat.-Sun. 10am-5pm). Call the **Big Bear Hotline** (866-7000) for recorded lodging and events information. Midweek chalet rates are not out of budget's reach, especially for groups of six or more. The **Big Bear Ranger Station,** Rte. 38 (909-866-3437), 3 mi. east of Fawnskin, on the opposite side of the lake, has camping and trail information (open Mon.-Sat. 8am-4:30pm).

To reach Big Bear Lake, take **I-10** to Junction 30/330. Follow **Rte. 30** to **Rte. 330,** also known as Mountain Rd., and continue to **Rte. 18.** About halfway up the mountain, Rte. 18 becomes Big Bear Blvd., the main route encircling the lake. An alternative route via the **San Bernardino Fwy.** (I-10) to Redlands and then **Rte. 38** to Big Bear Lake, is frequently less congested. Driving time from L.A. is about 2½ hours, assuming you manage to avoid serious traffic (Fri. nights, Sat. mornings, and Sun. tend to be worst). The loneliest route to Big Bear Lake curls across the High Desert along Rte. 18 through the Lucerne Valley. Day skiers might want to linger on the mountain and avoid the 4pm mad rush from the slopes and the resulting traffic problems on the weekends by waiting until after 6pm to head home.

Public transportation to Big Bear Lake is in development, but currently unavailable. **Big Bear Shuttle** (866-9493 or 585-7427) schedules service from the mountain communities to San Bernardino and desert areas. (Round-trip to Yucca Valley $29. Door-to-door service around Big Bear $1 per mile.) **Rim of the World Transit Bus** (866-4444; 60¢) connects Big Bear with Running Springs, Snow Valley, and Lake Arrowhead. The **Big Bear Valley Transit** trolley (866-4444) covers stops around Big Bear (75¢) and provides **Dial-A-Ride** service for seniors and the disabled ($1). **Enterprise Rent-a-Car,** 41725 Big Bear Blvd. (866-1156), rents to drivers over 21 with a credit card.

ACCOMMODATIONS

Big Bear has few budget accommodations, especially in the winter. Big Bear Blvd., the main drag on the lake's South Shore, is lined with lodging possibilities but finding bargains is a challenge. Groups can find the best deals by sharing a cabin. Things fill up quickly, especially on winter weekends; call ahead and make reservations.

Hillcrest Lodge, 40241 Big Bear Blvd. (909-866-7330). Pine paneling lends these cozy rooms an expensive feel at a budget price. The smallest of rooms cost $32 in summer, Suite #1 goes for $56 and comes equipped with fireplace and kitchen. In winter, the lowest rental rate is $39 midweek and a 4-person unit rents for $64. Amenities include outdoor jacuzzi and free local calls.

Motel 6, 1200 Big Bear Blvd. (909-585-6666). One of the cheaper options for single travelers or groups of 2, especially in winter. Simple rooms are within budget reach for those who can't split the cost of cozier lodging. Pool, A/C. Singles $37, winter $41. Doubles $41, winter $46.

The Cozy Hollow Lodge, 40409 Big Bear Blvd. (909-866-9694 or in Southern California 800-882-4480). Rooms have attractive wood paneling, country-style quilts, coffee pots, refrigerators, color TVs, private baths, and fireplaces. Two-person cabins, with one queen-sized bed, start at $49 midweek in summer, $62 on weekends. In winter, rates rise to $55 midweek, $69 weekends.

Smoke Tree Lodge, 40210 Big Bear Blvd. (866-2415). Cheapest rooms are tucked in the main lodge building. Queen or king beds, wood-burning fireplaces, TV, private baths. Complimentary breakfast. Mon.-Thurs. $59. Fri.-Sun. $69. Rates rise $10 in winter.

CAMPING AND FOOD

Camping is permitted at U.S. Forest Service sites throughout the area. Several of the grounds listed below accept reservations (through 800-280-2267). Most are open from May to November.

Pineknot (7000 ft.). From Big Bear go south on Summit Blvd. to end, then left ¼ mi. to sites. Surprisingly isolated. 48 heavily wooded spots, half of which accept reservations. Wheelchair accessible, flush toilets, water. Sites $11.

Hanna Flat (7000 ft.), on Forest Rd. 3N14, 2½ mi. northwest of Fawnskin. 88 roomy sites surrounded by lush vegetation. Hiking, water, flush toilets, and hot showers. Sites $12.

Serrano (6800 ft.), 2 mi. east of Fawnskin off Rte. 38. This campground is one of the most popular around owing to its hot showers. Remarkably commercial and within sight of the road, this is city-slicker camping. Reservations accepted. 132 sites. Tents $12. RVs with hookups $20.

Big Pine Flat (6800 ft.), on Forest Rd. 3N14, 7 mi. northwest of Fawnskin. Dry with a slight desert atmosphere. Popular with dirt-bikers and other off-roaders, because there is an off-roading area just west of the campsite. 17 sites.

Holcomb Valley (7400 ft.), 4 mi. north on Forest Rd. 2N09 to 3N16, east for ¾ mi. Located near Pacific Coast Trail. 19 sites, pit toilets. No water. Free.

Horse Springs (5800 ft.), 14 mi. northwest of Fawnskin on FS Rd. 3N14, east on 3N17. Dry and desert-like, in the middle of nowhere. Remote and peaceful. 17 sites. No water. Free.

Tent campers can avoid crowds and fees by camping outside of designated campgrounds on U.S. Forest Service land. Sites must be at least 200 ft. from streams and lakes. Obtain maps and free permits from the Big Bear Ranger Station.

Food is pricey in the mountains. Cook your own if you have a kitchen. Groceries are available at **Slater Bros.,** 42171 Big Bear Blvd. (866-5211; open 7am-10pm daily). **Red Baron Pizza** (866-4744) next door is inexpensive and filling. A large cheese pizza goes for $8.75. (Open Sun.-Thurs. 11am-9pm, Fri.-Sat. 11am-10pm.)

SUMMER RECREATION

Mountain biking is a popular activity in Big Bear when the snow melts. Both **Big Bear Mountain** and **Snow Mountain** operate lifts in summer so thrill-seeking bikers can plummet downhill without the grueling uphill ride. The chair lift costs $7 per ride or $16 for a day pass (helmet required). Save money and get a great workout by biking up the hill yourself; trails are open and free to all riders. Beautiful national forest land to the east and west of ski country invites exploration. **Team Big Bear** (909-866-4565) sponsors several organized bike races each season for men, women, and youths. (April-Oct. daily 9am-5pm.) For more information contact Team Big Bear, Box 2932, Big Bear Lake 92315. Bikes can be rented from **Big Bear Bikes,** 41810 Big Bear Blvd. (866-2224) for $6 per hour or $21 per half-day.

Magic Mountain Recreation Area operates an **alpine slide** and **water park** for summer visitors. A single ride on the alpine slide is $3, $12 for unlimited rides. A waterslide ride is $1, $10 for unlimited rides. (Open Sun.-Fri. 10am-6pm, Sat. 10am-9pm.)

Fishing, boating, and **horseback riding** are also popular Big Bear summer activities. No license is required at **Alpine Trout Lake** (866-4532) ¼ mi. off Big Bear Lake Blvd. Fishing boats can be rented at **Gray's Landing** (866-2443) on North Shore Dr., for $12 per hour or $25 per half-day. Call Big Bear Lake's **Fishing Association** (866-6260) for answers to your fishing questions. Inexpensive horseback tours are available in the evening from **Big Bear Riding Stable** (585-1260) in Big Bear City (tours $10 per hr. on weekdays, $12 weekends).

WINTER RECREATION

Skiers and snowboarders pack area slopes during the winter. Driving the crowded mountain roads to destinations of choice can challenge both vehicle and driver. Gas up completely before heading onto the mountain routes as stations are scarce. Use tire chains when they are required by posted signs. Call 800-427-7623 for information on road conditions and closures.

Bear Mountain Ski (and Golf) Resort (909-585-2517). 1½ mi. southeast of downtown Big Bear Lake. 11 lifts, 250 acres of terrain, 100- to 1300-ft. vertical drops, snowmaking. More expert runs than other area slopes. Lift tickets $38, 65 and over $21. Midweek student discount (13-23) $28. Equipment rental $16 for skis, $27 for boots and snowboards. New skier packages include a group lesson, lift ticket and equipment rental for $29 on weekdays and $39 on weekends.

Snow Summit (909-866-5766). About 4 mi. south of Big Bear Lake. 11 lifts including 3 high-speed quads, over 40 runs, with a well-rounded assortment of beginner runs, snowmaking, and night skiing. Lift tickets $38.75, students midweek $29.75, ages 13-18 midweek $21.75. Snowboards rent for $28, skis for $16. Deposit required. Ticket prices may vary. For reservations call 909-851-4900.

Snow Valley (714-867-2751; snow report 714-867-5151). Near Running Springs. 13 lifts, 800 to 5000 ft. runs, snowmaking, and night skiing. The most family-oriented of the resorts, with a children's obstacle course and beginner trails. Lift ticket $37 (1-9pm $28), under 13 $22 (1-9pm $16). Equipment rental $14, children $10.

You can save money by renting equipment off the mountain at **Goldsmith's Ski Rental and Board House,** 42071 Big Bear Blvd. (866-2728), for $5-10 less than on the slopes. Skiing and lodging packages may also shave dollars. **Mountain Lodging Unlimited** (800-487-3168) can arrange lodging and lift packages from $46 per person midweek. An alternative and less expensive winter attraction is the **Magic Mountain Recreation Area** (714-866-4626), which offers inner tube sledding daily in winter. ($10 per day, includes rope tow and tube rental. Open daily 10am-4pm.)

■ NEAR BIG BEAR: SAN BERNARDINO

San Bernardino is the anchor city for California's mega-county by the same name. While not a likely vacation destination in itself, San Bernardino may be a convenient stopping point for wilderness-bound travelers heading to the mountains and forests.

Practical Information The **San Bernardino Convention and Visitors Bureau** is located at 440 W. Court St. Suite 108, San Bernardino 92401 (889-3980). Follow the signs off Rte. 215. (Open Mon.-Fri. 8am-5pm.) The **Chamber of Commerce** is at 5462 6th St. (885-7515; open Mon.-Fri. 9am-4:30pm). Both agencies provide listings of local events and other helpful information. The **Greyhound** station at 596 N. G St. (889-5596) is convenient to downtown motels. Buses go to: San Diego ($19); L.A. ($10); San Francisco ($52). (Open daily 7am-11pm.) The **Metrolink** (800-371-LINK, -5465) connects L.A. and San Bernardino with 75 trains on five routes. (One way $7.50. Call Mon.-Fri. 4:30am-10:30pm, Sat.-Sun. 9am-9pm.) **Omnitrans** (889-0811) is a local bus system with 75¢ fare. For **Checker Cab** call 884-1111. **Ugly Duckling,** 200 W. Base Ln. (885-4433) rents economy cars from $22 per day or $120 per week. Drivers must be 21 with major credit card. (Open Mon.-Fri. 8am-5:30pm, Sat. 8am-2pm.) **Above and Beyond Sports,** 3545 E. Highland Ave. (425-0877), rents mountain bikes for $25 per day. Important phone numbers include: **highway conditions** (800-427-7245); **rape crisis** (626-4357); **AIDS Project L.A.** (800-922-2437). **San Bernardino Community Hospital** provides 24-hr. emergency care at 1805 Medical Ctr. Drive (887-6333). Call 911 in an **emergency.** The **police** can be reached at 384-5742. The **post office** is at 390 W. 5th St. (884-3626) in downtown San Bernardino. (Open Mon.-Fri. 9am-5pm.) The **area code** is 909.

Accommodations and Food San Bernardino has a wide variety of hotels; check amenities carefully before trading cash for a key in this city. North San Bernardino is near California State University's San Bernardino campus and is generally more appealing than the southern section of the city. **Highland Inn Motel,** 1386 E. Highland (881-1702), is close to Rte. 30 in north San Bernardino, with easy access to Big Bear and Arrowhead Lakes. Newly redecorated rooms have refrigerators, A/C, and HBO. (Singles $30.80. Doubles $35.20. $10 refundable key deposit.) **Motel 6,** 1960 Ostrems Way (887-8191), at the University Parkway exit off Rte. 215 is close to the university. (Singles $28. Doubles $32.) **Villa Bernardino Motel,** 685 W. 6th St. (888-5775), is directly across from the Greyhound station; a good location for bus travelers. The bleak exterior masks clean rooms with large beds. (Singles $28. Doubles $30.)

For cheap, hearty Mexican food, stop at **Pacos Tacos,** 1689 W. Kendl Dr. (880-2755), in University Plaza. The friendly family cooks up combination plates with rice and beans for $4. (Open Mon.-Sat. 10:30am-9pm, Sun. 11:30am-7pm.) **China Palace,** 2035 E. Highland (862-5311), off Rte. 215 offers a daily all-you-can-eat lunch buffet for $4.25 from 11am to 3pm. (Open 11am-9pm daily.) Vegetarians may want to head to **SOUPLANTATION,** 228 W. Hospitality Ln. (381-4772) off Rte. 215 at the Waterman exit. The daily lunch buffet includes salads and soups for $5.59. (Open Sun.-Thurs. 11am-9pm, Fri.-Sat. 11am-10pm.)

Shopping and Sights San Bernardino lies a quick 45-min. downhill drive from Big Bear Lake and other mountain attractions. Stopover visitors should prepare for high elevation escape by stocking up at **Vons,** 2028 E. Highland Ave. (862-4660; open daily 6am-midnight). Camping and outdoor equipment is cheapest at **J & T Military Surplus,** 1298 North E St. (888-9651; open Mon.-Fri. 10am-6pm, Sat. 9am-5pm). A convenient clump of retail stores can be found at the **Carousel Mall,** 295 Carousel Mall Rd. (open daily 10am-9pm).

Nearby **San Bernardino Forest** (see Idyllwild, below) spans the San Bernardino and San Jacinto mountain ranges and is open for all-season recreation. Phone the district ranger for more information on your destination. (Arrowhead, 337-2444; Big Bear, 866-3437; Cajon, 887-2576; San Gorgonio, 794-1123; San Jacinto, 656-2117.)

■■■ IDYLLWILD AND NEARBY MOUNTAINS

Idyllwild, if not idyllic, comes close. Vanilla-scented Jeffrey pine forests and lush alpine meadows offer a respite from the smog and unbearable summer heat of its lower-altitude city neighbors, Banning and Beaumont. Northern transplants to the Southland, bereft of the four seasons, come here to be reminded of turning leaves and frozen ponds.

The San Jacinto and Santa Rosa Mountains, two contiguous mountain ranges running north-south, are scarcely known to out-of-state visitors. However, to Southern Californians this territory is a godsend. The mountains often top 10,000 ft., and the alpine scenery brings to mind the Sierra Nevada. Although hemmed in by desert to the south and east and by the Los Angeles smog channel to the north, Idyllwild itself (at 5400 ft.) enjoys cool evenings, even when summer scorches the valley below.

PRACTICAL INFORMATION AND ORIENTATION

Visitors Information: Idyllwild Chamber of Commerce, 54225 N. Circle (659-8525), in "the fort." Look for the signs downstairs in this prominent wooden complex. Open Mon. and Thurs.-Sun. 10am-5pm. When the chamber is closed, visitors should go to **Uniquies Melting Pot,** 54200 North Circle (659-6310), across the street in the Village Lane Shops. The boutique owner has maps, guides, and the answers to tourists' questions. Open daily 10am-6pm; winter 11am-5pm.

U.S. Forest Service: San Jacinto Ranger District, 54270 Pine Crest, P.O. Box 518, Idyllwild 92549 (659-2117, recorded info. during non-office hours). Maps of hiking trails and camping spots in and out of the wilderness. Issues special-use permits for USFS land; get these before the weekend. Also has information on all Riverside County Parks. Open daily 8am-4:30pm; winter Mon.-Sat. 8am-4:30pm. Call first as hours may change.

Mt. San Jacinto State Park and Wilderness Headquarters: 25905 Rte. 243, P.O. Box 308, Idyllwild 92549 (659-2607), follow the signs just north of downtown on Rte. 243. Offers knowledgeable advice on the area's camping and hiking resources without the crowds of the national forest station. Day hiking permits (mandatory on almost all trails) also available here. **Long Valley Ranger Station** is located ½ mi. from the Palm Springs Aerial Tramway station (off Rte. 111) and provides topographic maps, and hiking and camping information. Open daily 8am-5pm.

Idyllwild County Park Nature Center, Rte.243, P.O. Box 341, Idyllwild 92549 (659-3850), 0.8 mi. northwest of Idyllwild. Often neglected by tourists, the center provides rich information on the local and natural histories of the area. Talks and tours for astronomers, bird-watchers, and other outdoor hobbyists. Open Thurs.-Fri. 9am-5pm, Sat.-Sun. 9am-6pm; winter daily 10am-4pm.

Idyllwild's Mountain Line, 659-3259. 24-hr. recording disseminates info. on lodging, activities, weather, and road conditions. **Hiking Information:** 659-2607.

Ski Conditions and Tram Information: 619-325-1391. Tram from Palm Springs to Mt. San Jacinto. Round-trip tram fare $16, seniors $12, under 12 $10. Open Mon.-Fri. 10:45am-9pm, Sat.-Sun. 8am-9pm. In winter, it closes 1 hr. earlier.

Riverside Mountain Rescue Unit, Inc., P.O. Box 5444, Riverside, CA 92817 (654-6200). Search and rescue missions for injured climbers and lost hikers in the San Jacinto mountains.

Emergency: 911.

Sheriffs: Riverside County (800-950-2444) and **Banning** (849-6744) are closest. 24 hrs.

Post Office: 54391 Village Center Dr., Idyllwild 92549 (659-2349) in the Strawberry Creek shopping center. 24-hr. lobby. Counter open Mon.-Fri. 9am-5pm.

Area Codes: 909; 619 when noted (Mt. San Jacinto marks the dividing line).

From L.A., the swiftest approach is via I-10, then south from Banning on Rte. 243 (nighttime rides provide sparkling views of the cities below). From San Diego and the desert south of the mountains, all the routes are via state highways. The trip is long but scenic. Palm Springs, at the northeastern foot of Mt. San Jacinto, is the most appealing base city. From there, you can drive Rte. 111 east to Rte. 74, also known as the Palms-to-Pines Highway, which climbs up to Idyllwild. You can also take the Palm Springs Aerial Tramway, the only public transportation into the mountains, to a station on Mt. San Jacinto; from there hike or ski to the town of Idyllwild. (See Practical Information, above and Palm Springs: Sights and Activities, page 173 for more information on the tramway.)

ACCOMMODATIONS

Hiking and camping enthusiasts could stay for weeks; those who would rather relax on the porch of a cabin will find steep prices unless they're traveling in a group of four or more. Some inexpensive lodging for single travelers and couples can be found in the mountains but reasonable rooms are more plentiful in lowland (and low appeal) cities such as Hemet, Beaumont, or Banning.

Your best bet is probably **Knotty Pine Cabins,** 54340 Pine Crest Dr., P.O. Box 477, Idyllwild 92549 (659-2933). There is a marked entrance off Rte. 243 north of town. The eight cabins are clean with wood-panelled interiors in an alpine setting; one sleeps up to eight people, the rest six. The best deal is the "security lodge," in which six can enjoy a living room with fireplace, kitchen, dining room, and porch for $120 a day ($8 per additional person in any cabin up to a max. of 10). If you're not traveling en masse, stay in one of the pine cabins for $47-70 (cabins sleep at least 2 each). Linen, dishes, cooking utensils, and cable TV are included. Stay more than one night during the week and they'll knock $5 per night off the bill.

A cheaper option for solo travelers or smaller groups is the **Singing Wood Motel-Lodge,** 25525 Idyllwild-Banning Rd. (659-2201), about 1 mi. from Idyllwild center along Rte. 243. Piney interiors and woodsy surroundings are pleasant. Doubles run $32, with oven $35; $37 and $40 on weekends. The **Bluebird Hill Lodge,** 26905, Rte. 243 (659-2696), offers motel rooms and cabins named for different winged fauna. Motel rates for one or two people are $38, $45 on weekends. Cabin size and amenities vary, as does price. Budget-minded readers should know that unpublished bargains abound during the week when Idyllwild's weekend tourists head home. Some on-the-spot rate reductions may be offered to savvy travelers and gentle bargaining may profit the tactful.

Many of Idyllwild's 1500 residents are here for only part of the year and rent their places while they're gone. **Idyllwild Property Management,** 54085 S. Circle Dr., P.O. Box 222, Idyllwild 92349 (659-5015), rents cabins and homes in the area. Call well in advance especially for summer and holidays. **Associated Idyllwild Rentals (AIR),** P.O. Box 43, Idyllwild 92549 (659-5520), also has information on available lodging in the vicinity.

CAMPING

Campsites in the area are operated by the **San Bernardino National Forest, Mt. San Jacinto State Park, San Bernardino County,** and private entrepreneurs. Note that most U.S. Forest Service (USFS) campsites are closed for the winter months, and camping on state park lands requires greater expertise; there are fewer amenities in general and almost none in winter. Also bear in mind, in Idyllwild, the national campgrounds are superior to the state and local ones in almost every respect.

USFS accepts reservations for several popular campsites in the San Jacinto Ranger District. (See Practical Information, above, for more info.) Dispersed camping is allowed anywhere on USFS land, but a free permit and registration are required so that the Forest Service can monitor backcountry movement. The application is available at any ranger station from a box on the front porch and can be filled out and dropped in the receptacle (see Practical Information, above).

It is also possible to make reservations at all state park campsites. Two developed campgrounds, **Idyllwild** (on the edge of town) and **Stone Creek,** can be reserved through MISTIX (800-444-7275) from Memorial Day to Labor Day (both tend to fill up quickly, though somewhat undeservedly). Reservations for the wilderness sites are handled by the state park itself. Since dispersed camping is prohibited on state park land and the campgrounds are relatively small, you should reserve well in advance (as early as 8 weeks) for summer. Limited walk-in sites may be available on some summer weekends. Write the Idyllwild ranger station (see Practical Information, above) for an application.

San Bernardino National Forest

This area contains many developed campsites, most accessible by vehicle. **Dark Canyon,** 6 mi. north of town on Rte. 243, is by far the best campsite in Idyllwild. With water, vault toilets, hiking, fishing, and a congenial set of hosts, the 22 sites fill up fast—call well in advance on summer weekends (sites $9; 800-280-2267 for reservations). The other campgrounds in the area, **Fern Basin** and **Marion Mountain,** are worthy backups (sites $9). Fifteen mi. north of Idyllwild along Rte. 243 is the turnoff for **Boulder Basin** campsite, high on the Black Mountain. The 34 sites offer vault toilets, water, and splendid views of Marion Mountain and surrounding valleys, but the dirt road is difficult in spots and not recommended for RVs (sites $9). **Pinyon Flat,** on Rte. 74 east of Garner Valley, has the only sites that are wheelchair accessible. At only 4000 ft., it has much warmer temperatures than the other campsites in the area. All campgrounds in San Bernardino National Forest, except Pinyon Flat, are closed from approximately October to April. The **U.S. Forest Ranger Station** (659-2117) distributes maps, directions, and more complete listings of the many other campsites in the area. For wilderness sites, bring sufficient water. **Apple Canyon** on the east end of Garner Valley is close to great fishing.

Mt. San Jacinto State Park

San Jacinto State Park Headquarters can be reached at 909-659-2607. The park's two developed campgrounds, **Idyllwild** (5400 ft.; 33 sites) and **Stone Creek** (6100 ft.; 50 sites) are accessible via Rte. 243. Idyllwild ($14) is well-equipped with flush toilets, drinkable water, showers, grills, tables, and food lockers but is located close to the road. Stone Creek ($9) is more primitive, with vault toilets, tables, drinkable water, and wooded sites. Both campgrounds are $2 less from Labor Day to Memorial Day. For reservations call 800-444-7275. The four wilderness camps do not have drinkable water (you must treat the available water or bring your own) and require a free wilderness permit (available through park headquarters). No applications are accepted earlier than eight weeks in advance; book weekends early. Visitors arriving from the east on the Tramway may find **Tamarack Valley** and **Round Valley** convenient. Hikers from western trails often stop at **Strawberry Jct.** or **Little Round Valley.** All Mt. San Jacinto sites are open year-round (except for parts of Stone Creek, which are closed in winter months).

County Parks

Idyllwild County Park Campground (659-2656), lies off Rte. 243, south of the state park campground of almost the same name. Ask for directions as you pass into town from the north; follow the signs to Idyllwild Park when arriving from the south. Open year-round, the 96 sites of this campground provide water, showers, restrooms, stoves, and tables for $12 per vehicle. **Hurkey Creek Campground,** (659-2050), on Rte. 74 across from Lake Hemet, has 100 sites in a grassy, park-like area open year-round. Amenities include stoves, restrooms, showers, and proximity to great fishing and hiking trails. Reservations are required for group camping. Call 800-464-6316 for reservations up to three months in advance. Some sites are available on a first-come, first-camped basis.

FOOD

Restaurants and cafés are generally overpriced in Idyllwild. Supermarkets are the cheapest option. Although supplies are best purchased in lowland cities (food prices rise with the altitude), **Fairway Supermarket,** in the Strawberry Creek Square off Village Center Dr. (659-2737), offers well-stocked shelves and reasonable prices (open Mon.-Sat. 9am-9pm, Sun. 9am-7pm). The **Squirrel's Nest** (659-3993) on the corner of Rte. 243 and Pinecrest Ave. provides a site for rapid calorie consumption. Simplified service and limited menu (basic burger $1) draw casual crowds. Daily specials and vegetarian sandwiches are also available (open Sun.-Thurs. 10am-9pm, Fri.-Sat. 10am-10pm; closes 1 hr. earlier in winter). If it's pancakes you're craving, head to **Jan's Red Kettle,** 54220 N. Circle Dr. (659-4063), for crinkly pancakes ($4 and up) and soup and sandwich lunch specials for $4.50 (open daily 7am-3pm). Excellent soups and sandwiches (such as the $5.50 avocado sandwich) are for sale at **Pastries by Kathi,** 54360 N. Circle Dr. (659-4359), above the Rustic Theater (open Thurs.-Mon. 8am-5pm).

SIGHTS

Idyllwild's natural setting, with impressive granite monoliths arching above the forest, offers the visitor far more than the town itself. The mountains' faces challenge

IDYLLWILD

rock-climbers and hundreds of miles of trails lead hikers through the forests. Summer comes slowly; it is customary for over 10 ft. of snow to blanket the mountain peaks above the town in May and even June. From meadows, you can catch an occasional glimpse of the hot desert below. The view is amazing, especially where the **Santa Rosa/San Jacinto** mountain ranges come to a screeching halt and plummet 9000 ft. in under 6 mi.

To experience the transition from desert to mountain by car, follow the Palms-to-Pines Highway, coincident with Rte. 74. The highway runs between Mountain Center (south of Idyllwild at the junction of Rtes. 74 and 243) and Palm Desert near Palm Springs. This 36-mi. drive will take you past pine trees, meadows, and 10-ft. ocotillo plants with brilliant red blossoms.

In order to enjoy this region to the fullest, leave your vehicle, hike away from the shops and ice cream parlors of Idyllwild proper, and camp in the wilderness (see Camping, above). The **Ernie Maxwell Scenic Trail** (2.6 mi.) makes a gentle loop through the forest for day hikers. More serious backpackers can travel a section of the 2600-mi. **Pacific Crest Trail**. Pick up the trail at Rte. 74 1 mi. east of Rte. 371 or to the north at Black Mountain's scenic **Fuller Ridge Trail.** Rangers can direct visitors to many other trails including desert and high mountain routes. Some of the most rewarding and exhausting hikes begin in the canyons owned by Native Americans on the southwest fringe of Palm Springs and climb slowly into the foothills. Routes along the **Devil's Slide Trail** are excellent, but the limited number of permits for this area are given out by the ranger station within 20 minutes of its opening on summer weekends. The **Deer Spring Trail** to Suicide Rock (3.3 mi.) is a popular and moderate day hike.

Idyllwild also abounds with angling opportunities. The Department of Fish and Game regularly stocks two lakes and several streams in the area. **Lake Hemet** (659-2680), a large reservoir located 7 mi. southeast of Idyllwild off Rte. 74, has a free day-use area for trout, catfish, and bass fishing, ($7 park entrance fee). No swimming is allowed because the lake is a domestic water supply, but you can rent a motorboat for $25 per day or a rowboat for $12. (Prices include a $5 deposit. Rentals available daily 6am-7pm.) **Lake Fulmor** is a small, easily accessible picnic and fishing area 10 mi. north of town along Rte. 243. **Dark Canyon Creek,** located near the campsite of the same name, **Strawberry Creek,** which runs through Idyllwild just south of the village center, and **Fuller Mill Creek** are all regularly stocked in the spring and summer. Licenses are required in each of these areas, and there is a daily bag limit of five trout. Out-of-state residents can purchase one-day licenses for $8.50 at the Lake Hemet Market on Rte. 74.

Festivals and cultural events in Idyllwild provide alternatives to outdoor recreation. Many community events fill the calendar, from June's annual **Timber Festival** to October's **Halloween Street Fair. Idyllwild School of Music and the Arts (ISOMATA),** on Toll Gate Rd. off Rte. 243 (659-2171) gives frequent performances ($5-7.50), exhibitions, and workshops. Summer classes in music, drama, dance, creative writing, Native American arts, ceramics, photography, and more are offered. Contact the school or see the *Town Crier* community newspaper for scheduling information.

Although Idyllwild during the off-season (Oct.-April) has many charms, surprisingly few Southern Californians choose to leave their eternal summer during the "winter" months. Besides encountering lower prices for accommodations and food, off-season visitors can enjoy autumn colors that roll slowly down the mountainsides, snowy winter nights, and the wild streams of spring. The **Palm Springs Aerial Tramway** is a popular winter approach for the relatively few people who take advantage of the exhilarating cross-country skiing and snow camping available in the state park. For a description of facilities and activities in the immediate vicinity of the tram's top, see Palm Springs: Sights and Activities, page 173.

San Diego

As tourists and relocating Northeasterners join the flood of documented and undocumented immigrants from Mexico in the rush to San Diego, the question is not why so many, but why not more? San Diego manages to maintain clean air and beaches, a sense of culture and history, and lush greenery, while faced with rapid growth and water shortages. A solid Navy presence cushions the economy; local architecture is pleasant, not gaudy. Rain and cold weather are virtually unknown.

San Diego has ample tourist attractions—a world-famous zoo, Sea World, and Old Town—but the most enjoyable destination might simply be a patch of sand at one of the area's superb beaches. There is also much to see outside the city proper. Explore the nearby mountains and deserts and the surrounding communities such as Hillcrest, La Jolla, and Ocean Beach, or head for Mexico, right next door.

■■■ PRACTICAL INFORMATION

Old Town and State Park Information: 4002 Wallace Ave. (220-5422), in Old Town Square next to Rancho El Nopal restaurant. Take the Taylor St. exit off I-8, or bus #5. Brochures on Old Town $2. Also, information on Cuyamaca Rancho, Palomar Mountain, and Anza Borrego Desert State Parks. Open daily 10am-5pm.

International Visitors Information Center: 11 Horton Plaza (236-1212), downtown at 1st Ave. and F St. Like an old-fashioned hardware store, they don't display much, but they have whatever you need under the counter. Multilingual staff. Open Mon.-Sat. 8:30am-5pm. Also Sun. 11am-5pm in summer.

National Parks Information: 226-6311. Recorded information and directory assistance for Yosemite, Kings Canyon, Sequoia National Parks, and Grand Canyon.

San Diego Council of American Youth Hostels: 335 W. Beech St. (239-2644). Great source of student travel information. Bike accessories, travel gear, and guides for sale. Ride schedule published in *The Hostel Bulletin*. Sponsors domestic and European trips. Open Tues.-Fri. 10:30am-5:30pm, Sat. 9:30am-4:30pm.

The Transit Store: at 5th and Broadway (234-1060). Tickets, passes, and timetables for all transit vehicles. Open Mon.-Fri. 8:30am-6:30pm.

American Express: 1640 Camino Del Rio North (297-8101). Other locations are 258 Broadway (234-4455) and in La Jolla, 1020 Prospect (459-4161).

Airport: San Diego International Airport (Lindbergh Field) lies at the northwestern edge of downtown, across from Harbor Island. San Diego Transit bus #2 ("30th and Adams") goes downtown ($1.50); transfer to other routes. #2 buses run Mon.-Fri. 4:30am-1:10am, Sat.-Sun. 4:45am-1:05am. Cab fare downtown $7.

Travelers Aid: Airport, 231-7361. One station in each terminal. Directions for lost travelers. Open daily 7am-11pm. **Downtown office,** 1765 4th Ave., Suite #100, at Elm St. (232-7991). Open Mon.-Fri. 8:30am-noon and 2-4pm.

Amtrak, Santa Fe Depot, 1050 Kettner Blvd. (239-9021, for schedules and information 800-872-7245), at Broadway. To: L.A. (Mon.-Fri. 8 per day 5:05am-9pm; one way $24, round-trip $32). Information on bus, trolley, car, and boat transportation available at the station. Ticket office open 4:45am-9:15pm.

Bus: Greyhound, 120 W. Broadway (239-8082), at 1st Ave. To L.A. (every 45 min. 2:30am-11:45pm; one way $12, round-trip $24). Terminal open for ticket sales 2am-midnight.

AAA: 815 Date (233-1000, after 5pm and on weekends and holidays 668-0991).

Public Library: Main branch, 820 E St. (236-5800), downtown. Open Mon.-Thurs. 10am-9pm, Fri.-Sat. 9:30am-5:30pm, Sun. 1pm-5pm. Local branches include **La Jolla** (552-1657), **Pacific Beach** (581-9933), **Chula Vista** (691-5069), and **Point Loma** (531-1539). Branches open Mon. and Wed. noon-8pm, Tues. and Thurs.-Sat. 9:30am-5:30pm, Sun. 1pm-5pm.

Lesbian and Gay Men's Center: 3916 Normal St. (692-2077), provides info. about happenings and counseling. Open daily 9am-10pm. **Crisis Line:** 692-4297, Mon.-

Sat. 6am-10pm. For people under 24, the **Gay Youth Alliance** (233-9309), is a support and social group. For a listing of all gay events and establishments check the *Update* (299-0500), available at virtually all gay businesses, bookstores, and bars. The *Gay and Lesbian Times,* published Thurs., lists events, bars, clubs, etc.

Senior Citizen's Services: 202 C St. (236-6905), in the City Hall Bldg. Provides ID cards with which seniors can take advantage of senior discounts. Plans daytrips and sponsors "nutrition sites" (meals) at 8 locations. Open Mon.-Fri. 8am-5pm.

The Access Center: 1295 University Ave. #10 (293-3500, TDD 489-8313), Hillcrest. Attendant referral, wheelchair repair and sales, emergency housing, motel/hotel accessibility referral. Open Mon.-Fri. 9am-5pm. **Accessible San Diego,** 2466 Bartel St. (279-0704), also has information.

Women's Center: 2467 E St. (233-8984). Open Mon.-Fri. 8:30am-4:30pm.

Ticketmaster: Concert Hotline (268-8526); tickets (220-8497).

Laundromat: Pacific Services, 500 W. Broadway (239-9820), in the YMCA building. Wash $1, dry 25¢ for 10 min. Open Mon.-Fri. 7am-7pm, Sat. 8am-7pm.

Events: 560-4094. Recorded calendar of events.

Beach and Weather Report: 221-8884. Updated daily.

Rape Crisis Hotline: 233-3088. 24 hrs.

Crime Victims Help Line: 236-0101. 24 hrs.

Pharmacy: Thrifty Drugs, 535 Robinson Ave. (291-3705). Open 24 hrs.

Mission Bay Hospital, 3030 Bunker Hill St. (274-7721). 24-hr. emergency care, physician referral service, and geriatric care.

Emergency: 911.

Police: 531-2000.

Post Office: Main Branch, 2535 Midway Dr. (627-0915), between downtown and Mission Beach. Bus #6, 9, or 35. Open Mon.-Fri. 7am-1am, Sat. 8am-4pm. **General Delivery ZIP Code:** 92138. **Downtown Post Office,** 51 Horton Plaza (232-9253). Open Mon.-Fri. 8am-6pm, Sat. 9am-5pm.

Area Code: 619.

■ ■ ■ GETTING AROUND

San Diego rests in the extreme southwestern corner of California, 127 mi. south of L.A. and only 15 mi. north of the Mexican border. **Interstate 5** runs south from Los Angeles and skirts the eastern edge of downtown. **Interstate 15** runs northeast to Nevada. **Interstate 8** runs east-west along downtown's northern boundary, connecting the desert to the east with Ocean Beach in the west. The major downtown thoroughfare, **Broadway,** also runs east-west. **Bus** and **train** stations sit on the western end of Broadway in reasonably safe areas. Most downtown hotels listed are in safer areas east and north of these stations, but as always, exercise caution; sometimes the downtown area is frequented by aggressive panhandlers.

A group of skyscrapers in the blocks between Broadway and I-5 defines **downtown** San Diego. On the northeastern corner of downtown lies **Balboa Park.** To the north and east of Balboa Park are the main residential areas. **Hillcrest,** San Diego's most cosmopolitan district and a center for the gay community, lies at the park's northwestern corner. **University Heights** and **North Park** sit along University Ave., El Cajon Blvd., and Adams Ave.

West of downtown is the bay, 17 mi. long and formed by the Coronado Peninsula (jutting northward from Imperial Beach) and Point Loma (dangling down from Ocean Beach). North of Ocean Beach are Mission Beach, Pacific Beach, and La Jolla.

Public Transportation

A car is extremely helpful in San Diego, but it is possible to reach most areas of the city by bus. The **regional transit systems** (San Diego Transit, North County Transit, DART, FAST, and Dial-A-Ride) cover the area from Oceanside in the north to Tijuana in Mexico, and inland to Escondido, Julian, and other towns. Call for **public transit information** (233-3004; Mon.-Fri. 5:30am-8:25pm, Sat.-Sun. 8am-5pm) or stop by the **Transit Store** (see Practical Information, above), offering the *Transit Rider's*

GETTING AROUND

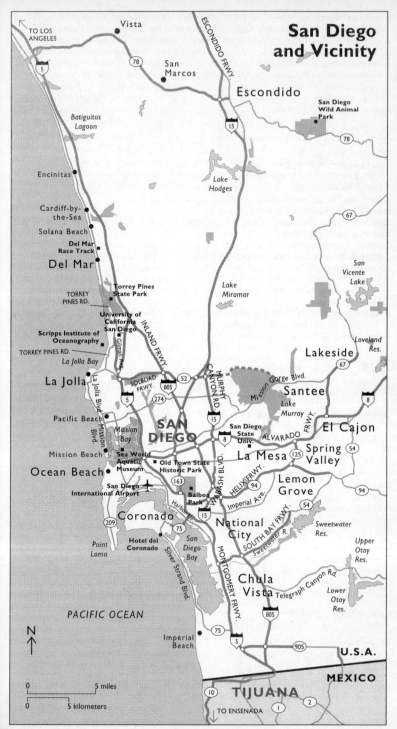

San Diego and Vicinity

TO LOS ANGELES

Vista

San Marcos

78

Escondido

San Diego Wild Animal Park

78

ESCONDIDO FRWY.

15

Batiguitos Lagoon

Encinitas

Lake Hodges

67

Cardiff-by-the-Sea

Solana Beach

Del Mar Race Track

Del Mar

San Vicente Lake

Lake Miramar

Torrey Pines State Park

TORREY PINES RD.

University of California San Diego

Scripps Institute of Oceanography

TORREY PINES RD.

La Jolla Bay

La Jolla

INLAND FRWY.

Loveland Res.

Lakeside

67

Mission Gorge Blvd.

SOLEDAD FRWY.

52

MURPHY CANYON RD.

805

274

Santee

Lake Murray

8

La Jolla Blvd.

Gilman Ave.

5

Pacific Beach

Mission Blvd.

Mission Bay

SAN DIEGO

15

San Diego State Univ.

8

ALVARADO

El Cajon

125

Spring Valley

54

HELIX FRWY.

Mission Beach

Sea World Aquatic Museum

Old Town State Historic Park

La Mesa

Ocean Beach

163

Lemon Grove

94

San Diego International Airport

Balboa Park

Imperial Ave.

54

Harbor Dr.

15

94

Coronado

209

75

National City

SOUTH BAY FRWY.

Sweetwater R.

Sweetwater Res.

Upper Otay Res.

Point Loma

Hotel del Coronado

San Diego Bay

Silver Strand Blvd.

MONTGOMERY FRWY.

Chula Vista

Telegraph Canyon Rd.

Lower Otay Res.

805

PACIFIC OCEAN

N

Imperial Beach

75

5

905

U.S.A.

MEXICO

0 ——— 5 miles

0 ——— 5 kilometers

10

TIJUANA

TO ENSENADA

1

2

MARSH BLVD.

Guide. (Fare $1.05 for North County and local routes, $1.75-2 for express routes, and $2-3 for commuter routes. One transfer free in San Diego. Exact change; many accept dollar bills. 60% of buses are wheelchair accessible.) Buses on some routes, especially those to the beaches, have bike racks. **Day Tripper passes** allow unlimited travel on buses, trolleys, and even the Bay Ferry ($4 for 1 day, $15 for 4 days).

The **San Diego Trolley** runs two lines from a starting point near the Santa Fe Depot on C St., at Kettner. (To: El Cajon, daily 4:45am-1:15am; San Ysidro "the Tijuana Trolley," 5am-1am. Wheelchair accessible. Fare $1-1.75.) From the border, cabs to the **Tijuana** Cultural Center or shopping district are $3-5, but it is also an easy walk (see Tijuana, page 428). Purchase a ticket from machines at stations and board the trolley. There are no turnstiles or ticket takers, but inspectors frequently check for tickets. **Lost and found** for the trolley is located at the Transit Store.

Various tour buses and trolley-shaped vans carry tourists around San Diego. **Old Town Trolley Tours** (298-8687) allows travelers to stop and sightsee before reboarding trolleys (daily every 30 min. 9am-5pm; fare $16, ages 6-12 $7).

Cars

Southern California is land of the auto; renting a car will make your life easier and your trip more enjoyable.

Rent-A-Wreck, 1904 Hotel Circle N. (224-8235 or 800-228-8235). $20-40 per day, $130-170 per week, 150 free mi. per day, 19¢ per additional mi. 150-mi. radius restriction (in California only). Under 25 pay $5 per day or $20 per week surcharge. Must be 21 with credit card or $250 deposit. Open Mon.-Fri. 8am-6pm, Sat.-Sun. 9am-3pm.

Aztec Rent-A-Car, 2401 Pacific Hwy. (232-6117 or 800-231-0400). $22-50 per day with unlimited mi. (in California only). Must be 21 with major credit card. With purchase of Mexican insurance ($16.23 per day), cars may venture as far as Ensenada, Mexico (80 mi.). Open Mon.-Fri. 6am-8pm, Sat.-Sun. 8am-5pm.

Dollar Rent-A-Car, 2499 Pacific Hwy. (234-3388). $22-31 per day with unlimited mileage, though rates vary with availability. Must be 21 with major credit card. Can travel as far as Ensenada with $16 Mexican insurance. Under 25 pay $10 per day surcharge. Open daily 5:30am-midnight.

Bicycles

A bicycle is useful in the summer, especially around the beaches, where traffic can be heavy. The satisfaction of cruising by sweltering motorists will compensate for fatigue. Buses equipped with bike carriers make it possible to cart two-wheelers even farther (call 233-3004 to find out which routes have carriers). Bikes on the San Diego Trolley require a $3 permit (239-2644).

San Diego has an extensive system of bike routes meandering through level terrain perfect for cycling. Bike routes are sometimes separate from the road, sometimes specially marked outer lanes, and sometimes non-existent. The flat, occasionally crowded route along Mission Beach and Pacific Beach toward La Jolla affords amazing ocean views and soothing sea breezes. The **San Diego Council of AYH** hosts at least one ride a day (see Practical Information, page 145).

For bike information, contact **Caltrans,** 4040 Taylor St., San Diego 92110 (231-2453), in Old Town. They will send you maps and pamphlets, including the *San Diego County Bike Route Map.* Caltrans also handles storage lockers. (Open Mon.-Fri. 8am-5pm). For more information, call the City Bicycle Co-ordinator (533-3110).

See Downtown (page 152), Coronado (page 157), and Mission Beach and Pacific Beach (page 158) for specific bike rental shops.

Walking

Downtown, Balboa Park, and Old Town easily handled on foot. Beaches, however, are not as accessible. **Walkabout International,** 835 5th Ave. #407 (231-7463), sponsors several free walks each week, including architectural walks downtown and 20-mi. treks to La Jolla and back (open Mon.-Fri. 9:30am-2:30pm; expect an answering machine). Those accustomed to muscling their way across a street against the light will be amused by the San Diegan habit of waiting for the walk signal, no matter how empty the street. Jaywalking is illegal (tickets are given out occasionally) and frowned upon by natives.

■■■ ACCOMMODATIONS

Although San Diego attracts visitors throughout the year, both lodging rates and the number of tourists skyrocket in summer, particularly on weekends. Reservations can save you disappointment. Many hostels and residential hotels offer weekly rates. The latter are numerous, especially downtown, and some are quite appealing. If you have a car, consider camping outside of San Diego (see Camping, below). If not, downtown hotels are near bus routes that will take you most places you want to go.

DOWNTOWN

Downtown Hotel at Baltic Inn, 521 6th Ave. (237-0387). Well-equipped, clean rooms (each has toilet, sink, microwave, mini-fridge, table TV, closets). Clean communal showers. No curfew, 24-hr. security. Laundry facilities. Great location for downtown connections. Singles $15. Doubles $20. Weekly rates from $80.

Hostel on Broadway (HI/AYH), 500 W. Broadway (232-1133), in the core of downtown, close to train and bus stations, as well as Horton Plaza and the Gaslamp District. Communal bathrooms, common room with TV. Laundry and game room (with pool table) downstairs. Panhandlers sometimes cluster outside but security cameras and guards monitor the hostel. Desk open 8am-11pm. No curfew. $12, nonmembers $15. Doubles (with bunk) $13 per person, regular doubles $14. Storage fee $1. Use of YMCA facilities $5. IBN reservations available.

Jim's San Diego, 1425 C St. (235-0234), south of the park, 2 blocks from "City College" trolley. Spruce, hostel-type rooms for 4 with wooden bunks and free linen. Kitchen, sun deck, common room, laundry. Homey atmosphere and backpacker clientele. Check-out noon. $13 per night, $11 in winter, $77-80 per week. Breakfast and Sunday BBQ included. No reservations.

The Inn at YMCA, (234-5252; fax 234-5272) just downstairs from the **Hostel on Broadway.** Singles, doubles or family rooms, each with color TV and cable. Communal bathroom, free towel and linen. Singles $20, $89 per week. Doubles or family rooms (1 double bed, 1 single bed) $33, $125 per week. $25 deposit for 1-week stay. Front desk open 24 hrs.

Downtown Inn Hotel, 660 G St. (238-4100), just east of the Gaslamp District. Comfortable, tastefully furnished rooms with microwave or toaster oven, refrigerator, TV, and ceiling fan. Convenient to buses. Laundry facilities. Check-out 1pm. Singles $27, weekly $99. Doubles $27, weekly $117.

La Pacifica, 1546 2nd Ave. (236-9292), downtown. Close to I-5. New European-style building with pretty courtyard. Sharp rooms with phone, microwave, and big refrigerator. Remote cable TV and ceiling fan make lounging irresistible. Common room and laundry room open to guests. Singles $40-50, weekly $140-180. Doubles $50-55, weekly $150-200.

Corinthian Suites Hotel, 1840 4th Ave., at Elm St. (236-1600; fax 231-4734), 2 blocks from zoo and park. Brand new hotel surrounds a courtyard garden and fountain. Every room equipped with refrigerator, bar, sink, and microwave. Building provides laundry and cable TV. Singles $35, weekly $140. Doubles $40, weekly $145. Security deposit $15, weekly $25.

The Maryland Hotel, 630 F St. (239-9243; fax 235-8968). Well-located and affordable, this hotel's clean rooms and dapper staff make up for some absent amenities. Lots of long-term residents. Laundry facilities, cable TV available. Singles $17, $22 with half bath, $25 with full bath, second guest $8. Weekly rates $85, with half bath $95, with full bath $115, second guest $40.

OLD TOWN AND HILLCREST

Hillcrest Inn, 3754 5th Ave., Hillcrest (293-7078). Sunny garden, jacuzzi, and spiffy rooms. Each room has a kitchenette with microwave, bar, sink, and fridge.

Updates on local entertainment, and staff is trained to direct tourists around San Diego's attractions and nightlife. Young clientele. Ask for handy map of Hillcrest. Singles $49-55. No official weekly rates.

Old Town Budget Inn, 4444 Pacific Hwy. (260-8024; for reservations 800-225-9610), near Old Town. Simple and reasonable. Ask for rooms in the old building. Check-out 11am. Singles $30-45. Doubles $38-48. Inquire about weekly rates.

EL CAJON BOULEVARD

There are many inexpensive, bland motels along this large commercial strip devoted primarily to selling cars, but there are also a few pleasant surprises. Bus #15 runs along El Cajon Blvd.

Lamplighter Inn, 6474 El Cajon Blvd. (582-3088; for reservations 800-545-0778; fax 582-6873). Trim rooms, cable TV with HBO, A/C, pleasant grounds with palmtrees, laundry facilities, and a sparkling pool. Check-out 11am. Singles $40. Doubles $43. Single rooms with kitchen $44.

Aztec Budget Inn, 6050 El Cajon Blvd. (582-1414; for reservations 800-225-9610). Pleasant garden patio. High-ceilinged rooms include A/C and cable TV. Check-out 11am. Singles from $35. Doubles from $36.

Campus Hitching Post Motel, 6235 El Cajon Blvd. (583-1456). Clean rooms with HBO and A/C. Swimming pool. Singles from $35, weekly $152. Doubles from $40, weekly $162.

THE COAST

Banana Bungalow, 707 Reed Ave. (237-1440 or 800-5-HOSTEL, -467835), just off of Mission Blvd., on Mission Beach. Take Bus #34 to Mission Blvd. and Reed Ave. Opened in July of 1993, the Bungalow has become the most popular hostel in the city. Offers a long list of amenities: great location, (directly on a beautiful beach) friendly staff, free breakfast, cheap keg parties ($3 all-you-can-drink), and bonfires and BBQs on the beach. Also bike, boogie-board, and rollerblade rental. Located near bars and restaurants. No curfew. Check-out 10:15am. Dorm $11-15, private double $45. Common room with cable TV and porch overlooking the beach. Linen included. Blankets and overnight key require $10 deposit. Call in advance.

Elliot-Point Loma Hostel (HI/AYH), 3790 Udall St., Point Loma (223-4778). Take bus #35 from downtown; get off at the first stop on Voltaire and walk across the street. If driving a car, take I-5 to Sea World exit, then left to Sunset Cliffs Blvd. Take left on Voltaire, right on Warden and look for hostel sign painted on a remodeled church. The airy 2-story building is 1½ mi. from Ocean Beach. Wooden bunks for 60, common room, large kitchen, and patio. Check-out 10am. Office open 8-10am and 4:30-10pm. Lockout 10:30am-4:30pm. No curfew. 3-night max. stay; reserve 48 hrs. in advance. Members $12, nonmembers $15.

Western Shore Motel, 4345 Mission Bay Drive (273-1121; fax 273-2944), just off I-5, opposite Grand Ave. Take bus #30. 2 mi. from the beach, ½ mi. from the bay. High-ceilinged rooms with A/C and TV. Helpful staff. Singles $29. Doubles from $34. Stay 6 nights and 7th is free if you pay up front. Reservations recommended.

Loma Lodge, 3202 Rosecrans St. (222-0511; fax 222-1087; reservations 800-266-0511). Fairly luxurious, distinctive decor in comfortable rooms with HBO and ESPN. Swimming pool and laundry rooms for guests. 5 min. from beaches. Singles from $40. Doubles from $50.

■■■ CAMPING

All **state** campgrounds are open to bikers for $3 per night. State law requires that no cyclist be turned away no matter how crowded the site. Only **Campland on the Bay** is within city limits. For information on state park camping, call the enthusiastic people at San Elijo Beach (753-5091). Camping reservations are handled by MISTIX (800-444-7275) as well as by individual campgrounds. Most parks are completely full in summer, and it's common to make weekend reservations eight weeks in advance. A complete list of county campgrounds is available at the visitors center.

Campland on the Bay, 2211 Pacific Beach Dr. (581-4212). Take I-5 to Grand Ave. exit and follow the signs, or take bus #30 and get off on Grand at the campground sign on the left. Expensive and crowded because it's the only central place to pitch a tent or plug in an RV. The cheapest sites are in a "dirt area" with nothing to block the wind coming off the water. Scheduled family activities. Some wooded areas, a pool, and a boat launch. Market, laundry, and game room on grounds. Sites $22-52; in winter $19-37.

South Carlsbad Beach State Park (431-3143), Rte. 21 near Leucadia, in north San Diego County. 215 sites, half for tents. On cliffs over the sea. Showers, laundry facilities. No hiking trails. Sites $16-21. Reservations necessary in summer.

San Elijo Beach State Park (753-5091), Rte. 21 south of Cardiff-by-the-Sea. 271 sites (150 for tents) in a setting similar to that at South Carlsbad to the north. Strategic landscaping gives a secluded feel. Hiker/biker campsites too. Laundry and showers, but no hiking or biking trails. Make reservations for summer through MISTIX (800-444-7275). Oceanfront sites $21, inland $16.

San Diego Metropolitan KOA, 111 N. 2nd Ave. (427-3601), Chula Vista. Pool and jacuzzi. Check-out noon. Tent sites $26. RV sites $32. Rates lower in winter. One-room cabins $34, two-room cabins $42. Reserve before holidays.

■■■ CENTRAL SAN DIEGO

The inland neighborhoods of San Diego form a tangible record of the city's history. **Old Town** is home to many early 19th-century Spanish-style adobe buildings. Extending south from Broadway is the **Gaslamp Quarter,** home to pre-1910 commercial buildings now being resurrected as upscale shops and restaurants. Downtown San Diego bears witness to the city's naval background with the Embarcadero. Sprawling **Balboa Park** encloses museums and the San Diego Zoo while holding the lion's share of cultural attractions in the city. When planning museum visits, be aware that San Diego has a "free Tuesdays" program—lots of museums offer discounts or free admission on certain Tuesdays. Call your destination for information.

DOWNTOWN

The skyscrapers of San Diego's central business district coexist with the ships and museums that line the waterfront. Farther inland, the restored Gaslamp Quarter is home to historic buildings and pricey shops.

Food

The lunchtime business crowd has nurtured a multitude of restaurants specializing in well-made, inexpensive meals. Nearly 100 restaurants located in this part of town cater to the throngs of executives. Unfortunately, many of the places close around 3pm, making dinner a challenge. The food court on the top floor of the **Horton Plaza** offers more variety than the standard 31 flavors of junk food. Wandering down C St., Broadway, and the Gaslamp Quarter is also an option.

If you have access to a kitchen or barbecue pit, stop at **Anthony's Fish Mart,** 555 Harbor Ln. (232-6624). You can sauté, broil, or fry the very dishes for which others shell out big money at the swank restaurants bearing the same name. Several of the more popular (and expensive) Gaslamp Quarter restaurants are better known as popular bars and nightclubs. See Nightlife (page 161) for more information on these establishments.

Machos, 1125 6th Ave. (231-1969). Some of the best, cheapest, and most authentic Mexican food you'll find in the neighborhood. Simple decorations, cheerful pink tablecloths, endless chips and salsa if you eat in. Daily specials. Two beef enchiladas $2.85. Freshly made iced tea. Open Mon.-Fri. 7am-7pm, Sat.-Sun. 8am-5pm.

Anthony's Fishette, 555 Harbor Ln. (232-2933), at the foot of Market St. on the bay. A downscale version of **Anthony's** posh restaurants. A catch, with bay view and a bar. Dinners $5-10. Open Sun.-Thurs. 11am-8pm, Fri.-Sat. 11am-8:30pm.

D O W N T O W N

Old Spaghetti Factory, 275 5th Ave. (233-4323). A Gaslamp Quarter favorite that offers salad, fresh spaghetti (despite the name), authentic sauces, loaves of warm sourdough bread, and ice cream for $4-6. Very filling. Open Mon.-Thurs. 5-10pm, Fri.-Sat. 5-11pm, Sun. 4-10pm. Open for lunch Mon.-Fri. 11:30am-2pm.

Caffe Italia, 1704 India St. (234-6767) in the heart of Little Italy. This glossy Euro-style café has excellent coffee and sells foreign and domestic periodicals and dailies. *Formaggi* sandwich $4, Caesar salad $4.25. Open Mon.-Thurs. 7am-10pm, Fri. 7am-11pm, Sat. 8am-11pm, Sun. 8am-10pm.

Sights

Moored windjammers, cruise ships, and the occasional naval destroyer face the boardwalk shops and museums along the **Embarcadero,** the Spanish name for a dock. The vessels on the Embarcadero, along with North Island's seaplanes, Point Loma's submarine base, and South Bay's mothball fleet, are reminders of San Diego's number-one industry as well as of the city's role as a major West Coast naval installation (tours of naval craft are free on afternoons when they are in port). The magnificently restored 1863 sailing vessel, *Star of India,* is docked in front of the touristy **Maritime Museum,** 1306 N. Harbor Dr. (234-9153). Alongside are anchored both the 1904 British steam yacht *Medea* and the 1898 ferryboat *Berkeley,* a bay ferry that slunk away from its mooring after the 1906 earthquake. (Open daily 9am-9pm. $6, ages 13-17 and over 55 $4, 6-12 $2, families $12.). South along the harbor, tacky and touristy **Seaport Village** (235-4014) houses shingled boutiques and ice cream shops (open daily 10am-10pm). Take a ride on the village's **Broadway Flying Horses Carousel,** built a century ago (open daily 10am-10pm; $1).

From Harbor Drive, the **Coronado Bridge** stretches westward from Barrio Logan to the Coronado Peninsula. High enough to allow the Navy's biggest ships to pass underneath, the sleek, sky-blue arc rests upon spindly piers and executes a graceful, swooping turn over the waters of San Diego Bay before touching down in Coronado. From the bridge, one can see San Diego's skyline to the north and the main naval base to the south. (Toll $1. Bus #901 and other routes also cross.) When the bridge was built in 1969, its eastern end cut a swath through San Diego's largest Chicano community. In response, the community created **Chicano Park,** obtaining the land beneath the bridge and painting splendid murals on the bridge's piers. The murals, best appreciated by a walk around the park, are heroic in scale and theme, drawing on Hispanic-American, Spanish, Mayan, and Aztec imagery. Take bus #11 or the San Ysidro trolley to Barrio Logan station.

South of Broadway, between 4th and 5th Ave., lie 16 blocks of antique stores, Victorian buildings, and trendy restaurants that comprise the historic **Gaslamp Quarter.** Formerly the city's red-light district and home to the original **Pappy's, Inc.** adult bookstore, the area is now a battleground for restorationists fighting the forces of vacancy and budget crunches. Gentrification has brought a number of new bars and bistros to the Quarter and the area is now well-frequented by upscale after-hours revelers. The area is a National Historic District, with several 19th-century landmarks worth a visit. The **Gaslamp Quarter Foundation** (233-4692) shares the William Heath Davis House, 410 Island Ave., with the **Horton Grand Hotel** (reputedly occupied by supernatural guests). The Foundation offers walking tours of the Quarter (Sat. 11am. 90-min. tours $5; seniors, students, ages 12-18 $3; under 12 free).

The centerpiece of San Diego's redevelopment is **Horton Plaza,** at Broadway and 4th Ave. This pastel-colored confection of glass and steel is an open-air, multi-leveled shopping center encompassing seven city blocks. A noteworthy example of local architecture is the domed **Santa Fe Depot,** on Kettner Blvd., a Mission Revival building whose grand arches welcomed visitors to the 1915 Exposition. Standing just three blocks west of Horton Plaza, the building is now the Amtrak depot. On weekdays, Broadway moves with professionals and panhandlers. At night and on weekends, the latter remain.

Rent-A-Bike, at 1st and Harbor Dr. (232-4700), in downtown, offers a bike, helmet, and lock for $8 per hour, $28 per day or $75 per week. (Open Mon.-Fri. 8am-6pm, Sat.-Sun. 7am-6pm.)

BALBOA PARK

Balboa Park was the creation of pioneering horticulturists whose plantings transformed a once-treeless pueblo tract into a botanical montage. Planting began in 1889, when San Diego's population was only about 3000. Today, primitive Cycad and Coast Redwood trees tower above climbing roses and water lilies, and the city's population is over one million. Close to that number are drawn each year to Balboa Park for its concerts, cultural events, Spanish architecture, lush vegetation, and of course, its zoo. Balboa Park is accessible by bus #7, or by driving east from downtown on Laurel St. Parking is free at museums and zoo lots; posted signs warn parkgoers against scam artists who attempt to wheedle lot fees from the unsuspecting.

Food

For the best food near Balboa Park, head north and west to nearby Hillcrest, Mission Hills, and University Heights. This is definitely prime budget cuisine territory. The restaurants and coffeehouses along and around University Ave. offer discounts and freebies on Tuesday nights.

The Golden Dragon, 414 University Ave., Hillcrest (296-4119; delivery 275-7500). Staggeringly varied menu offers over a hundred dishes and a special vegetarian menu. Almost all under $8. Perfect for late-night dining. Open daily 3pm-3am.

Corvette Diner Bar & Grill, 3946 5th Ave. (542-1001). '50s decor includes a real Corvette and booming oldies. Old-fashioned shake $3. Open Sun.-Thurs. 11am-11pm, Fri.-Sat. 11am-midnight.

Monsoon, 3975 5th Ave., Suite 100 (298-3155), across the street from the Corvette. Airy, contemporary decor. Vegetarian dishes like mixed vegetable curry $4.75. Abundance of juices, fruits, and smoothies. Open daily 10am-10pm.

Pasta Al Dente, 420 A Robinson Ave. (295-2727). Fresh pastas and pizzas prepared to go, or served at outdoor tables. Enjoy your Spaghetti Bolognese ($6.25) or Primavera Pizza ($8) to unobtrusive Vivaldi. Open Mon.-Fri. 11am-10:30pm, Sat. noon-midnight, Sun noon-10:30pm.

Por Favor, 530 University Ave. (291-11717). A clean, friendly restaurant. Margaritas come in 3 sizes, all generous. Order draft beer by the foot or ½ yd. in amusingly long vessels. Lunch specials $4.45. Steak picado, sauteed in vegetable sauce $7. Open Mon.-Thurs. 11am-11pm, Fri.-Sat. 11am-midnight.

Hamburger Mary's, 308 University Place (491-0400). Enjoy creative burgers under any one of the shaded options: flowered trellises, tables with umbrellas, or palm trees. Vegetarian sandwiches $4.75. 7pm brings a country DJ and dance lessons. Open Sun.-Thurs. 10am-10pm, Fri.-Sat. 10am-11pm.

Sights

With over 100 acres of exquisite fenceless habitats, the **San Diego Zoo** (234-3153) deserves its reputation as one of the finest in the world. It even attracts more than animal lovers; its flora is as exotic as its fauna. The zoo recently moved to a system of "bioclimatic" areas, in which animals and plants are grouped together by habitat, rather than by taxonomy. Joining the stunning **Tiger River** and **Sun Bear Forest** is the **Gorilla Tropics** enclosure, housing lowland gorillas and plant species imported from Africa. In addition to the usual elephants and zebras, the zoo houses such unusual creatures as Malay tapirs and everybody's favorite, koalas. The **Wings of Australasia Aviaries,** completed in 1993, is another popular exhibit.

The most efficient way to tour the zoo is to arrive as early as possible and take the 40-minute open-air **double-decker bus tour,** which covers 70% of the park. ($3, ages 3-11 $2.50. Sit on the left, given a choice.) Young *homo sapiens* can watch the hatching and feeding of other animal kingdom toddlers in the **children's petting zoo.** The **Skyfari Aerial Tramway** rises 170 feet above the park. (Both free with admission.) Most of the zoo is wheelchair accessible (wheelchairs can be rented), but steep hills make assistance necessary. (Main entrance open Mon.-Wed. 9am-5pm, exit by 9pm; Thurs.-Sun. 9am-9pm, exit by 10pm; Labor Day-Memorial Day open daily 9am-4pm, exit by 6pm. $13, ages 3-11 $6, military in uniform free. Group rates available. Free on Founder's Day, Oct. 1.) Look for discount coupons for zoo entrance in guidebooks.

In addition to the zoo, Balboa Park has the greatest concentration of museums in the U.S. outside of Washington, DC. **El Prado,** a street running west to east through the **Plaza de Panama,** is lined with resplendent Spanish colonial architecture, designed by Bertram Goodhue for the Panama California Exposition of 1915-16 and for the California Pacific International Exposition of 1935-36. Constructed in the florid Spanish colonial style, many of the buildings now housing museum collections were intended to be temporary structures, but their elaborate ornamentation and colorfully tiled roofs were deemed too beautiful to demolish.

Before exploring El Prado on your own, you might want to stop by the **House of Hospitality** at 1549 El Prado St., which contains the park **information center** (239-0512). The center sells simple maps of the park for a well-spent 65¢, and the **Passport to Balboa Park,** which contains nine coupons for a week's worth of entry to all of the park's museums ($13). (Passports are also available at participating museums. Open daily 9:30am-4pm.) Exhibits and shows rotate often.

The star of the western axis of the Plaza de Panama is Goodhue's California State Building, now the **Museum of Man** (239-2001). The much-photographed tower and dome are covered with gleaming tiles in a Spanish design. Inside, human evolution is traced through permanent exhibits on primates and early man. Several displays focus on the Maya and Hopi cultures, and other Native American societies. Half the museum is allotted to innovative temporary exhibits. (Open daily 10am-4:30pm. $4 or 2 coupons, ages 13-18 $2, 6-12 $1.)

Behind the Museum of Man is the **Old Globe Theater** (239-2255), the oldest professional theater in California. Classical and contemporary plays are performed nightly (Tues.-Sun.), with weekend matinees. The **Lowell Davies Outdoor Theatre** across the street also draws top name performers. Ticket prices for both performance spaces range from $18-36. Planes flying overhead cause the actors to occasionally freeze in mid-performance and wait for the engine roar to die down before resuming. The **Spreckels Organ Pavillion** at the south end of the Plaza de Panama, opposite the Museum of Art, boasts the world's largest outdoor musical instrument. The resonance of the organ's 4400 pipes can be heard across 2 mi. (226-0819; free performances Sun. 2pm, Mon. 8pm; winter, Sun. 2pm).

Across the Plaza de Panama is the **San Diego Museum of Art** (232-7931), which maintains a comprehensive collection, ranging from ancient Asian to contemporary Californian. In addition to permanent masterpieces by El Greco, Matisse, Dalí, and O'Keefe, San Diego's largest museum hosts intriguing temporary exhibits. (Open Tues.-Sun. 10am-4:30pm. $7, seniors $6, military with ID $5, ages 6-18 and students with ID $2, under 6 free. Free 3rd Tues. of each month.) Nearby is the outdoor **Sculpture Garden and Court** (236-1725), with a sensuous Henry Moore piece presiding over other large abstract blocks. The **Sculpture Garden Café** (236-1725), on a terrace over looking the garden, serves typical and over priced museum food. (open Tues.-Sun. 10am-3pm; sandwiches around $4.75. Garden open until 5pm).

Next door is the **Timken Art Gallery,** 1500 El Prado (239-5548). The small, choice collection features several superb portraits by David, Hals, Rubens, and others. An excellent collection of large, prematurely abstract Russian church icons also fills this gallery. (Open Oct.-Aug. Tues.-Sat. 10am-4:30pm, Sun 1:30-4:30pm; free).

Farther east along the plaza stands the Botanical Building (236-5717), a wooden Quonset structure accented by tall palms threatening to burst through the roof. The scent of jasmine and the splash of fountains make this an authentic oasis (open Sat.-Thurs. 10am-4:30pm; free). The same botanists run the **Desert and Rose Gardens** one block east at 2200 Park Blvd. (236-5717; free). Cacti and stunted desert vegetation in one building provide a striking contrast to the abundant roses next door.

The **Casa de Balboa,** a recent reconstruction of the 1915 Electricity Building, contains four museums. The **Museum of Photographic Arts** (239-5262) presents controversial exhibits that rotate every six to eight weeks. (Open Fri.-Wed. 10am-5pm, Thurs. 10am-7pm. $3, under 13 free. Free 2nd Tues. of every month.) The **San**

Diego Hall of Champions (234-2544) is a slick sports museum with astroturf carpet and the square footage of a baseball diamond. Perhaps overplaying civic pride, it enshrines representatives of over 40 sports who made it big in San Diego. Only a glass pane (thankfully olfactory-proof) will separate you from the jerseys and shoes worn by Ted Williams and Bill Walton. (Open Mon.-Sat. 10am-4:30pm, Sun. noon-5pm. $3, seniors and military with ID $2, ages 6-17 $1, under 6 free.) The San Diego Historical Society operates both the **Research Archives** and the **Museum of San Diego History** (232-6203). The museum is showing temporary exhibits while a permanent collection is being gathered. (Open Wed.-Sun. 10am-4:30pm. $3, 13 and under free.) Downstairs, hobbyists preside over four giant model railroads and to-scale countrysides in the **San Diego Model Railroad Museum** (696-0199; open Wed.-Fri. 11am-4pm, Sat.-Sun. 11am-5pm. $3, under 15 free.)

From the end of El Prado St. (which is closed to cars), a left onto Village Place St. will take you to **Spanish Village,** a colony of 250 artists at work in 39 studios. As you leave the Village, notice the most popular of all of Balboa's arboreal delights, the Moreton Bay fig tree, towering 63 feet from its gnarled roots. At the east end of El Prado lies the **Natural History Museum** (232-3821). Life-size robotic dinosaurs enhance the standard fossils and a recreated mine houses gem displays. (Open Fri.-Wed.9:30am-5:30pm, Thurs. 9:30am-6:30pm. Admission $6, seniors and military with ID $5, ages 6-17 $2. Free 1st Tues. of month. Half-price Thurs. 4:30-6:30pm.) Across the street (El Prado) from the Natural History Museum is the **Reuben H. Fleet Space Theater and Science Center** (238-1233), with two Omnimax projectors, 153 speakers, and a hemispheric planetarium. The impressive Omnimax screens seem to "swallow up" the audience—transforming a movie into a thrilling experience. (10-14 per day; Sat. 10 and 11am shows are subtitled in Spanish. $6, senior citizens $4.50, ages 5-15 $3.50, military and students with ID $4.80. Call 232-6860 for advance tickets.) The **Laserium** features the rhythms of Pink Floyd's "Dark Side of the Moon" (9 and 11pm; $6, seniors $4.50, children $3.50, under 5 not admitted). Tickets to the space theater include admittance to the Science Center, where visitors can play with a cloud chamber, telegraph, light-mixing booth, and other gadgets. (Open Sun.-Tues. 9:30am-9:30pm, Sat. 9:30am-10:30pm. Science Center admission alone $2.50, ages 5-15 $1.25.)

The other main area of Balboa Park, the **Pan American Plaza,** was developed for the California-Pacific International Exposition of 1935-36. The buildings here are less unified, their styles drawing on Central and South American motifs, the Moderne movement, and Native American architecture. The **Aero-Space Museum and Hall of Fame** (234-8291), in the drum-shaped Ford Pavilion, exhibits early-model planes (mostly replicas) and gadgets from aviation history. See the working replica of Lindbergh's *Spirit of St. Louis,* and Imperial Japan's fighter planes. (Open daily 9am-5pm. $4, ages 6-17 $1, under 6 and military with ID free.) The **Automotive Museum,** 28 Pan American Plaza (231-2886), is a shrine to California's unofficial state deity (open daily 10am-4:30pm; $5, seniors and military with I.D. $4, ages 6-17 $2). Singing puppets grace the **Marie Hitchcock Puppet Theatre,** where the city's puppet guild performs on summer and holiday weekends ($1.50, children $1).

For a focused overview of Balboa's gardens, architecture, or history, catch one of the free one-hour walking tours that meet on Saturdays, in front of the Botanical Building. Call the Park Department for specifics (235-1121).

OLD TOWN

To find San Diego's roots, look in **Old Town** and nearby **Presidio Park,** northwest from downtown on I-5 or bus #5.

Food

There are many festive Mexican restaurants and *cantinas* in the Old Town vicinity, as well as several inexpensive places clustered nearby along I-5. Although fast food dominates the San Diegan cuisine scene, many of these establishments prove that fast food is not always bad news. In the land of the speedy burrito, some restaurants have perfected the art of Mexican fast food. One of the best is **Roberto's Taco Shop** (at 3202 Mission Blvd. and other locations).

El Indio, 3695 India St. (299-0333), in India St. Colony. El Indio opened its doors in 1940. A half-century later, folks are still lining up for the delicious food. Counter-style service is speedy and quality remains high. Sizable portions; combination plates around $3-5.50, a la carte tacos and burritos from $2. Open daily 7am-9pm.

Casa de Bandini, 2660 Calhoun St. (297-8211), next to Bazaar del Mundo. Eat in the lush and festive courtyard, the first floor of which is an original 1829 adobe mansion, complete with rose trellises, *mariachis,* and fountains. Enormous chicken and avocado salad, around $7. Mexican corn soup $2.65. Monstrous margaritas. Open Mon.-Sat. 11am-9:30pm, Sun. 10am-9:30pm.

Conora's, 3715 India St. (291-5938), in India St. Colony. Sandwich shop extraordinaire. Over 60 varieties, almost all $3.50-4.50. Call ahead if you're in a hurry, and Conora's will have your order ready. Open Mon.-Sat. 8am-6pm, Sun. 11am-4pm.

Gelato Vero, 3753 India St. (295-9269), in India St. colony. Simply divine dark chocolate gelato. 11 other flavors ($1.65-4.25), plus pastries and coffees. Open Mon.-Thurs. 7am-midnight, Fri. 6am-1am, Sat. 7:30am-1am, Sun. 7am-midnight.

Boll Weevil, 9330 Clairemont Mesa Blvd. (571-6225). Dark, ski-lodge-like atmosphere filled with people trying to finish what they'll later take home in doggie bags. Friendly service. Home of the famous "½-pound steerburger" ($3). Open Sun.-Wed. 11am-midnight, Thurs.-Sat. 10am-midnight.

Sights

The Spanish **Presidio,** or military post, was established in 1769 at a site chosen because the hill to the east—now Presidio Park—provided defense, and the San Diego River, now a mere trickle, coursed just to the north. Southern California's first Europeans settled here in the late 1700. Later, Old Town was the site of the county courthouse, the town gallows, and a busy commercial district. The district blends restored historical buildings with less authentic (though not insultingly so) retail areas. The state park people (237-6770) offer free daily walking tours, starting from their office at San Diego Ave. and Wallace St. at 2pm. To appreciate Old Town's buildings on your own, the visitors center's walking tour/history book ($2) is indispensable. Most of the buildings, such as the Presidio commander's **Casa de Estudillo** (1827), are furnished adobes central to San Diego's early history. Less ancient is the **Bazaar del Mundo,** a motel designed by Richard Requa in the 1930s to blend in with its aged neighbors. This re-creation of a colonial Mexican market features entertainment from costumed performers and handicrafts from native artisans. **La Panaderia** serves coffee and Mexican pastries (75¢).

In **Presidio Park,** next to and north of Old Town, the **Serra Museum** (297-3258), built in 1929, is styled after the original San Diego mission on the site. The collection includes antique Spanish furniture and Native American artifacts. The park itself ranges over a hill the Spaniards used for sighting enemy approaches; now you can see and hear only the freeways that surround the bluff. Lower down, shady paths allow secluded strolling. (Open Tues.-Sat. 10am-4:30pm, Sun. noon-4:30pm; museum admission $3, under 12 free; park admission free.)

Mission Basilica San Diego de Alcalá (281-8449) was moved 6 mi. in 1774 to its present location in the hills north of the Presidio. Take I-8 east to Mission Gorge Rd. and follow the signs, or take bus #43. Still an active parish church where mass is held (daily 7am and 5:30pm), Mission San Diego has a chapel, a garden courtyard, a small museum of artifacts, and a reconstruction of the living quarters of mission-builder extraordinaire Junípero Serra.

West of the mission is Jack Murphy Stadium, home of the **San Diego Chargers** football team and baseball's **San Diego Padres.** For Padres tickets, call 525-8282. If you'd rather witness gridiron glory, call 280-2121 for Chargers tickets.

■■■ COASTAL SAN DIEGO

There are 70 mi. of beaches in this city, each with a subtly different character, all with enticing sands and clear waters despite the large number of sunbathers and surfers. The most appealing aspect of San Diego's beaches is the views they offer of the curving coastline—the varied topography has made the area a point of interest for oceanographers as well as athletes, families, and the ubiquitous sun-worshippers. It is interesting, also, to wander inland and examine the corresponding differences among the beach communities. Though the primary attractions of this region remain Sea World and sun, sand, and surf—of which you will encounter ample supplies—there is plenty to explore away from the shore.

CORONADO

The graceful Coronado Bridge, built in 1969, guides cars from I-5 (toll $1) or bus #901 from downtown to Coronado. The **Bay Ferry** shuttles passengers ($2, every hour 9am-10pm, return on the ½-hr. 9:30am-10:30pm). Tickets are available at **San Diego Harbor Excursion,** 1050 N. Harbor Dr. (234-4111). Once across, the **Coronado Shuttle** carries passengers from the ferry landing to the Hotel Del Coronado and back for 50¢.

Coronado's most famed sight is its Victorian-style **Hotel del Coronado,** Orange Ave. (435-6611). The long, white verandas and the red, circular towers of the "Del" were built in 1898 as a resort getaway. One of the world's great hotels, it has hosted twelve presidents and was featured in the 1959 classic *Some Like It Hot.* Wander onto the white, seaweed-free beach in back, one of the prettiest in San Diego. Its uncrowded shore invites shell-gathering and shoes-in-hand strolling. On the other side of the island you can explore the **Old Ferry Landing,** where harborside restaurants tantalize those just arrived by ferry. For two-wheeled exploration, **Bikes and Beyond** (435-7180; open daily 8:30am-dusk), at the ferry landing on 1st St., rents bikes (cruisers $5 per hr., mountain bikes $6 per hr., tandems $10 per hr., quadro-cycles $15 per hr.) and in-line skates ($5 per hr.). **Bike Coronado,** 131 Orange Ave., in Coronado (437-4888; open daily 10am-dusk), rents cruisers and tandems ($4 per hr., $16 per day) and supplies child seats, carriers, and small bikes for children.

POINT LOMA

Point Loma walks a fine line between residential community and naval outpost. The government owns the outer two-thirds of the peninsula but keeps most of it open to visitors. The Navy presence is concentrated near the base of the point. Point Loma residents range from Ocean Beach hippies to sedate, monied residents.

Food

There's a **natural food market** at 4765 Voltaire St. (224-1387). If you're in the mood for Mexican, check out **Margarita's,** 4955 Newport Ave. (224-7454), which has a pleasant, relaxed atmosphere and inexpensive a la carte and combination meals. There are lots of vegetarian plates ("Bean-LT sandwich $4") and a delicious variant on the margarita—the "wine margarita," which comes in pink or pale green ($1.50).

Sights

The **Cabrillo National Monument** (557-5450), at the tip of Point Loma, is dedicated to Portuguese explorer João Rodriguez Cabrillo (the first European to land in California), but it is known for the views of San Diego and the herds of migrating whales that pass beyond the offshore kelp beds. **Whale-watching** season is mid-December to February and the Monument is prime seating. (Whale information in winter 236-1212.) From downtown, take I-5 to Rosecrans Blvd. and follow signs for Rte. 209 to the entrance, or take bus #6A. The 2-mi. **Bayside Trail** winds through the brush along the coast on the harbor side; the trail exhibits describe the native vegetation and historic military installations. When the tide is low, there are tide pools on the ocean side of Point Loma. At the highest point of the peninsula sits **Old Point Loma**

Lighthouse, now a museum. (Open daily 9am-sunset; winter 9am-5:15pm. Lighthouse closes 15 min. earlier. Parking is $4 per car, walk-ins and bikers $2.) No restaurants, so pack lunch. If you have access to cooking facilities, you might want to take home some shellfish from **Point Loma Seafoods,** 2805 Emerson (223-1109 or 223-6553), off Rosecrans.

Ocean Beach (O.B.) caters to a surfing crowd that is slightly less upscale (and more low-key) than farther up the coast. Although the waves here are considered miserable by hot-dog surfers, they are suited for beginners. To fish yourself or just people watch, join the anglers on the longest fishing pier in the Western Hemisphere. Ocean beach has been renovating its image over the past few years (it was once the hang-out of choice for drug addicts and dealers). New businesses have improved the area and contribute to an unpretentious, pleasant beach scene.

At **Sunset Cliffs** on Ocean Beach, timing can mean the difference between an afternoon of noisy children and a tranquil sojourn in the sun. Come at sunset. Newport Ave., the main drag of Ocean Beach, has many inexpensive shops and hosts occasional festivals.

MISSION BEACH AND PACIFIC BEACH

These strands are more respectable wave-wise than O.B. and consequently draw a younger, more surf oriented crowd. (Learning when to say "O.B." and "P.B." and when to say Ocean Beach and Pacific Beach is an art.)

Food

There are tons of bar and grills along these shores (see Nightlife, page 161). Most are crowded and noisy, i.e. very popular. **Kono's Surf Club,** 704 Garnet Ave. (483-1669) is a surfer's shrine that serves breakfast all day ($2-3). Wake up with the Egg Burrito #3 (includes bacon, cheese, potatoes, pica-sauce) for $2.75. Kono's is located across from the Crystal Pier. Nearby is **Smokey Mountain,** 712 Garnet Ave. (274-7427), a small restaurant with red-checked tables that serves a range of ribs and wings, all meticulously smoked by the amiable staff. They'll package your food for the beach and picnics (a party bucket, which feeds 3-4, runs around $16; open Wed.-Mon. 3-9pm). **Rubio's,** 910 Grand Ave. (270-4800), in Pacific Beach, offers the legendary Fish Taco, a favorite with beachgoers. Try the Fish Taco Especial (with guacamole, jack/cheddar, and onion and lettuce) for $1.85.

Sights

Ocean Front Walk is packed with joggers, walkers, bicyclists, and the usual beachfront shops. The three blocks between the sea and Mission Blvd. are quintessentially suburban. Low cottages inhabited by the rich or lucky line alleys that bear the names of famous resort cities from around the world. The neighborhoods near Mission Beach are the most densely populated in San Diego. P.B., though less crowded, also offers an active shore scene and good surfing waters.

Although both beaches accommodate those who limit their physical activity to shifting on their towels to keep their tans even, active beaching is trés chic. Swimming, surfing and the usual assortment of beach side sports are everywhere and the sidewalks swarm with bicycles, joggers, and in-line skaters. Outnumbered pedestrians have begun to voice complaints in local newspapers about the proliferation of skaters. Make sure to wear protective gear if you're biking or blading, and don't swim near surfers. You can rent surfboards ($4 per hr., $17 per day) and boogieboards ($2.50 per hr., $10 per day) at **Star Surfing Co.,** 4655 Mission Blvd. (273-7827), in P.B. north of Garnet Ave. Driver's license or credit card is required (open daily 10am-6pm). **Mike's Bikes 'n' Blades,** 756 Ventura Pl. (488-1444; open daily 8am-9pm), in Mission Beach., rents bikes ($5 per hr. with 2nd hr. half-price, $10 per day) and skates. **Crown Point Motor Sports,** 1710 W. Mission Bay Dr. (226-8611) rents sailboats large enough for three ($15 per hr., $50 per ½-day).

MISSION BAY

Although the prices and number of gift shops at **Sea World** (226-3901) won't let you forget that it's a commercial venture, the Mission Park attraction is far more educational than your average amusement park. To get there, take I-5 or W. Mission Bay Dr. to Sea World Dr. (Bus #9 runs right to the entrance, but stops running in the early evening, making it impossible to see the night show or fireworks in summer without a car.) Aside from the dolphin-shaped hand-puppets for sale, Sea World offers 20 major attractions, as well as numerous daytime and nighttime shows. There are several indoor **aquariums,** whose fine lighting and state-of-the-art acrylic cases give astonishingly clear views of all types of marine life. The **penguin** encounter moves visitors through an enclosed Antarctic environment where penguins feed and play on simulated glaciers. The **open pools** allow visitors to approach sea turtles, starfish, and bat rays. Alaskan sea otters can be seen in their new coastal habitat exhibit, **Rocky Point Reserve.** You can even purchase fish ($1 a basket) to feed to the dolphins and sea lions. Finally, the **animal shows** parade the abilities of both marine mammals and their trainers. It's not every day that you get to see five-ton killer whales breach high above the water. (This and other shows can be a bit messy, so sit more than 10 rows back or prepare to be drenched in whale wake and walrus wash.) Unfortunates relegated to the back can enjoy the high-technology Sham Cam as they view Baby Shamu on Shamuvision. While some of the shows seem a tad exploitative, Sea World strives to inform as well as entertain—detailed captions, a knowledgeable staff, and guided tours ($5, children $4) give you a notion of the creatures' lives in the wild. Sea World's landmark **Skytower** ride (approx. 10 min.) offers spectacular views of San Diego County and the sea ($2). The most recent and high-tech addition to the park is **Mission Bermuda Triangle,** a virtual reality underwater adventure video. (Open Sun.-Thurs. 9am-10pm, Fri.-Sat. 9am-11pm, ticket sales end 1½ hr. before closing. $28, ages 3-11 $20. Shorter hours off-season. Parking $5 for cars, $7 RVs.)

■■■ LA JOLLA

La Jolla means "the jewel" and this gilded city fulfills all the expectations its name inspires. Situated on a small rocky promontory, La Jolla (pronounced la HOY-a) in the 1930s and 40s was a hideaway for wealthy Easterners who built luxurious houses and gardens atop the bluffs over the ocean. The pink exterior and Spanish mosaics of the **La Valencia Hotel,** 1132 Prospect St. (451-0772), still glow with the wealth of moneyed tenants. But newer money and a younger population have moved in. To reach La Jolla, turn from I-5 and take a left at the Ardath exit or take buses #30 or 34 from downtown.

Food

There are plenty of upscale eateries along and near Grand Ave.; if you look hard you'll be able to find some fairly inexpensive ones.

La Terraza, 8008 Grand Ave. (459-9750). Blessed with an ocean view and nightly flamenco music, this pleasantly cool spot specializes in *cucina Tuscana,* featuring such delicacies as pasta with eggplant and smoked mozzarella. Pizzas are $7-9. From 10pm-midnight beer, sangria, and pizza are each $2. Open daily 11am-4:30pm and 5-11pm.

José's Courtroom, 1037 Prospect St. (454-7655). Popular with just about everyone. Munch on chips and salsa and spicy carrots as you perch on stools which flank a generous bar. José's specialties are the cheapest items on the menu: a beef *torta* is $4.25 and a vegetarian tostada is $3.75. Combo plates are more expensive. Generous portions. Try the thick, hearty *albondigas* soup: meatballs and vegetables, with rice and tortillas ($3.75). Open daily 11am-10pm.

Pannikin, 7467 Girard Ave. (454-5453). Chic eatery with a sunny patio and attractively tiled tables. You can always get what you want from a full range of teas and coffees, including the Keith Richards mocha espresso ($3.50). Chicken curry $5.25. Popular with students from nearby UCSD. Open Mon.-Thurs. 6am-10pm, Fri. 6am-midnight, Sat.-Sun. 7am-midnight.

John's Waffle Shop, 7906 Girard Ave. (454-7371). $2.95 for the basic golden waffle, up to $5.60 for whole grain banana nut waffles. Breakfast and sandwiches about $5. Open Mon.-Sat. 7am-3pm, Sun. 8am-3pm.

Porkyland, 1030 Torrey Pines Rd. (459-1708). Don't let the name scare you away. Quick, inexpensive Mexican food. Pork may be their speciality, but the soft, guacamole-laced beef tacos excel as well: our researcher Alexandra said it was the best taco she had in San Diego, and she had a *lot* of tacos. Everything under $3.50. Open Mon.-Thurs. 11am-8pm, Fri.-Sat. 11am-9pm, Sun. 11am-7pm.

Five Star Thai Cuisine, 7863 Grand Ave., Suite 103 (456-1353), across the Atheneum library at Wall St. Bright, cheery, unpretentious restaurant with reasonably priced Thai specialties. The *pad thai* ($7) was recommended by CBS-TV. Lunch menu is a good deal. Open daily 11am-9:30pm.

Sights

The **San Diego Museum of Contemporary Art,** 700 Prospect St. (454-3541), houses an impressive collection of pop, minimalist, conceptualist, and Californian artwork in galleries overlooking the Pacific. Unfortunately, the museum is closed for renovation and won't reopen until 1996. Meanwhile, their galleries remain open at 1007 Ketner Blvd. in downtown La Jolla. Several commercial **art galleries** welcome browsers on Prospect St. The **Tasende Gallery** (454-3691), two doors down from the museum, features contemporary sculpture and painting. For those interested, the **Animation Celection** gallery, 1002 Prospect St. (459-4278), features hand-painted acetate originals of everything from Bugs Bunny to Pinocchio.

The **Scripps Aquarium-Museum,** 2300 Expedition Way (534-FISH, -3474), at the Scripps Institute of Oceanography (a UCSD graduate school), is home to sharks, moray eels, a big, fat octopus named Humphrey, and various exhibits on oceanographic research. (Open daily 9am-5pm. Feeding time varies. $6.50, seniors $5.50, ages 13-17 $4.50, ages 4-12 $3.50.)

Location is perhaps the most interesting aspect of the **Mingei International Museum of World Folk Art,** 4405 La Jolla Village Dr. (453-5300), in University Towne Centre, a major bus terminus and transfer point. The idea was to make *mingei,* the "art of the people," accessible to the American people, and what better place to find people than in a shopping mall? The small museum features several exhibits each year—one at a time—on everything from weather-vanes to the art of Lappland. (Open Tues.-Sat. 11am-5pm, Sun. 2-5pm. $3, students $1.)

Beaches

In addition to these attractions, La Jolla claims some of the finest beaches in the city. The **La Jolla Cove** is popular with scuba divers, snorkelers and brilliantly colored Garhibaldi Goldfish. Surfers are especially fond of the waves at **Tourmaline Beach** and **Windansea Beach.** The waves at these beaches can be too much for non-surfers. **La Jolla Shores,** has gentler waves ideal for bodysurfers, boogie-boarders, and swimmers. This beach, next to Scripps/UCSD, is exceptionally clean. Popular with families, this beach is everything an all-purpose beach should be. The few surfers who visit stay near the pier, where the waves are bigger. (Sand volleyball , fire pits, bathrooms and in the summer, lifeguards.) **Black's Beach,** a public beach, is not *officially* a nude beach, but you wouldn't know it from the sun-kissed hue of most beachcombers' buns. The northern part of the beach generally attracts gay patrons.

Torrey Pines Glider Port is where hang gliders leap into the breeze and the young and unafraid cliff dive into the high tide. *Let's Go* does not recommend cliff diving. To reach the Glider Port, take I-5 to Genesee Ave., go west and turn left on N. Torrey Pines Rd. To reach the beach, take the steep staircase just south of the Glider port down to the ocean. A rather treacherous (do not let the locals scurrying down at full speed fool you) cliff-side trail lies at the far end of the long parking lot to the north of the Glider Port.

The **University of California at San Diego** (UCSD) rests above La Jolla. Despite the thousands of eucalyptus trees and varied architecture, the campus is bland. Buses #30 and 34 take you to campus, but once there a car or bike is invaluable for trekking from one of the five colleges to the next. See the information pavilions on Gilman Dr. and Northview Dr. for helpful maps (534-2208; open daily 7am-9pm).

The **La Jolla Playhouse** presents productions at the Mandell Weiss Theatre on the UCSD campus. Ticket prices vary, call 550-1070 for details.

■■■ NIGHTLIFE

Although San Diego's nightlife is not centered around a particular strip or avenue, definitive pockets of action are scattered throughout the city. The Gaslamp Quarter is home to numerous upscale restaurants and bars that feature live music nightly. Hillcrest draws a young, largely gay crowd to its clubs and restaurants once the sun has set. The beach areas (especially Garnet Ave. at Pacific Beach) are host to dozens of dance clubs, bars, and inexpensive eateries, which attract college-age revelers in masses. *Around San Diego* previews nightlife, galleries, and performing arts, and is available at street vendors throughout the city. *E Ticket* is a weekly rundown of movies, concerts, and dinner theaters, *San Diego Arts Monthly* details gallery and art events, and includes street maps. Both are free in restaurants and shops. **Arts Tix,** 121 Broadway (238-3810), at 1st Ave., offers cheap same-day tickets.

RESTAURANT-CLUBS

Although the restaurants below offer complete meals, they are better-known as nightspots—bars, music clubs, or dance clubs—and are therefore listed below.

Pacific Beach Grill and Club Tremors, 860 Garnet Ave., in Pacific Beach (2-PB-PARTY, 2-72-72779). A flight of steps connects the club and the restaurant. Attracting the young and unattached en masse with a nightly DJ, Club Tremors is open nightly 8:30pm-2am. Cover varies $1-5. The upstairs bar is quieter and has an ever-changing menu of cheap food (open 11am-2am, kitchen 'til 11pm).

Dick's Last Resort, 345 4th Ave. (231-9100), in the Gaslamp Quarter. Visitors and natives alike turn out in droves for buckets o' Southern chow and a wildly irreverent atmosphere. Dick's stocks beers from around the globe, from Africa to Trinidad, on top of native brews like Dixieland Blackened Voodoo Lager and Pete's Wicked Ale. No cover for the nightly rock or blues, but you'd better be buyin'! Burgers under $4, other dinners $10-15. Open daily 11am-1:30am.

Kansas City Barbeque, 610 W. Market St. (231-9680), south of Broadway near the bay in downtown. Enjoy decent barbeque in the self-proclaimed sleaziest bar in San Diego, where scenes from *Top Gun* were shot. Dinners with 2 side orders, for around $8. Open daily 11am-2am; food served until 1am.

Cafe Lu Lu, 419 F. St. (238-0114), in the Gaslamp Quarter. This vegetarian coffee house was designed by local artists. Funky. Progressive music. See and be seen as you have dinner for under $5 and sip a raspberry-mocha espresso ($3.50). Standing room only after midnight. Open Sun.-Thurs. 10am-2am, Fri.-Sat. 10am-4am.

Barefoot Bar and Grill, 1404 W. Vacation Rd. (274-4630), across the bay from Mission Beach. Ocean view and nightly entertainment ranging from rock to blues. Grill items and sandwiches from $2-8. Open daily 11am-1:30am.

CLUBS AND BARS

The Comedy Store, 916 Pearl St., La Jolla (454-9176). Drinks around $3. Potluck night Mon. 8pm, in which local comics air their schtick. (Call and sign up after 3pm.) Well-known comedians featured other evenings. Shows Thurs. at 8pm ($7), Fri.-Sat. at 8 and 10:30pm ($10). Wed.-Thurs. 2-for-1 admission with any college ID. 2-drink minimum enhances performances. Must be 21.

Velvet, 2812 Kettner Blvd. (692-1080), near Old Town. Live and loud, the Velvet hosts San Diego's rock 'n' roll up-and-comers, as well as more established bands. Alternative rock 6 nights a week. $3-10 cover charge (Wed.-Sat.). Pool table. Must be 21. Open daily 4pm-2am.

Java Joe's, 4994 Newport Ave. (523-0356). Formerly the Rumors Café, this coffee-house has a genuinely cozy, church-basement atmosphere with a few pool tables. Bigger venue for live music than most coffeehouses. Open Mon.-Fri 7am-midnight and Sat.-Sun 8am-midnight.

Croce's Top Hat Bar and Grille and Croce's Jazz Bar, 802 Fifth Ave., at F St. in Gaslamp District (233-6945). Ingrid Croce, wife of late singer Jim Croce, created a rock/blues bar and a classy jazz bar side by side in the 1st floor of the historic Keating building. Live music nightly, up to $5 cover. Open daily 7:30am-2am.

Chillers, 3105 Ocean Front Walk, Mission Beach (488-2077). Like an adults-only "7-11," this club offers intoxicating "slurpees." Behind the neon-lit bar are 30 frozen drink machines. Choose from an assortment of brightly-colored slushes. Every-thing from the mundane "Strawberry Daiquiri" and "Long Island Ice Tea" to the "Attitude Adjustment" (grain alcohol, vodka, pineapple juice, lemonade, and grenadine). Be sure to sample your slush in a free taste cup before you invest the $4 (small) or $6 (large). Full bar, live bands often. Open 11am-2am daily.

Society, 1051 Garnet Ave. at Pacific Beach (272-7665). Amid the black interior of this slick pool hall you'll find 15 pool tables on 2 floors. Don't be fooled by the wanna-be Fast Eddie types, there are plenty of beginners around. And we thought places like this only existed in New York. Appetizers, wine, gourmet coffees, and 46 beers. No cover. Open daily 11am-2am.

Some of the more popular **lesbian** and **gay clubs** include: **The Flame** (3780 Park Blvd. in Hillcrest, 295-4163), a lesbian dance club; **West Coast Production Company** (2028 Hancock St. in Middletown, 295-3724), a gay club offering dancing, bil-liards, videos, and a patio; **Bourbon Street** (4612 Park Blvd. in University Heights, 291-0173), a piano bar with a gay following; and **The Brass Rail** (3796 5th Ave. in Hillcrest, 298-2233), with dancing and female impersonators on weekends.

■■■ SEASONAL EVENTS

Gorgeous weather and strong community spirit make San Diego and surrounding towns an ideal place for local festivals. The visitors bureau (see Practical Informa-tion, page 145) publishes a thorough yearly events brochure, available for $5. Also check local papers—the beach community weeklies are often your best source for San Diegan happenings.

Penguin Day Ski Fest (276-0830), New Year's Day, De Anza Cove on Mission Bay. The object is to water-ski or lie on a block of ice without a wet suit; those who do are honored with a "penguin patch." Those who fail come away with a "chicken patch." Festivities 8am-1pm.

Ocean Beach Kite Festival (531-1527), 1st Saturday in March, 4741 Santa Monica Ave. in Ocean Beach. A kites-and-kids event. Kite-making materials provided free. Judging at 1pm followed by a parade to the beach for the kite flying competition.

San Diego Crew Classic (480-0700), April 9-10, 1995, in Mission Bay. Collegiate crew heaven. Teams from both coasts compete in this regatta. Best viewing from the west side of Mission Bay by the Bahia Hotel or from Santa Clara Point.

Summer Stargazing (594-1413), Fri.-Sat. nights from June 1-Labor Day, at San Diego State University's Mount Laguna Observatory. Open to the public with free tickets available through the U.S. Forest Service on Fri. 2-6pm, Sat. 9am-5pm.

Ocean Beach Street Fair and Chili Cook-Off (224-4906), last weekend in June in Ocean Beach. Thousands attend this 2-day festival, when Newport Street is closed off and arts and crafts booths line the pavement.

Surf, Sand, and Sandcastle Days (424-6663), mid-July in Pacific Beach, by the pier at 9:30am. In conjunction with the **U.S. Open Sandcastle Competition.** "Castles of the Mind" and "Creatures of the Sea." Spectacular entries that kick sand in the face of childhood bucket-and-shovel creations. Parade and fireworks.

La Jolla Chamber Music Society (459-3728), mid-Aug. 2-week chamber music festival with eleven concerts and other events.

San Diego Rodeo (298-4708), mid-Sept. Sponsored by the Golden State Gay Rodeo Association.

La Jolla Rough Water Swim (456-2100), early Sept. Start and finish at the La Jolla cove. Largest annual rough water swim in the U.S.

Annual Great American Dixieland Jazz Festival (297-5277), late Nov. Features Dixieland bands from throughout the U.S. Also sponsors monthly Sunday jazz concerts throughout the summer.

SAN DIEGO'S NORTH COUNTY

Exploring the various points strung along the Pacific Coast Highway (Rte. 21) can be an appealing alternative to tanning. A **bike route** with a number of manageable hills follows Rte. 21 all the way to Camp Pendleton north of Oceanside, with spurs inland at many points. North County Transit District (NCTD) bus #301 from University Towne Centre in La Jolla also goes all the way to Oceanside ($1, free transfers; every ½-hr. daily 6am-10pm). You can transfer to bus #301 from downtown buses #30 or 34 at the VA Hospital or N. Torrey Pines Rd. in La Jolla. For North County information, call 743-6283 or 722-6283.

DEL MAR

Just north of La Jolla lies the affluent suburb of **Del Mar,** home to famed fairgrounds and thoroughbred racing. The Del Mar **Amtrak** station (481-0114), the first stop on the run from San Diego to Los Angeles, is on the beach (8 per day). Take a left onto 15th St., off Camino Del Mar.

Food Intruding among the real estate offices along Rte. 21 (here called Camino del Mar), **Del Mar Danish Pastry and Coffee,** 1140 Camino del Mar (481-8622), offers delicious danishes for under $1 and free refills on coffee (open daily 6am-5pm). For standard deli fare, try **Board and Brew,** 1212 Camino del Mar (481-1021), a block down. Specialty sandwiches are $3.50-5 (open Mon.-Sat. 10am-7pm, Sun. 10am-6pm). Both merit a visit for their pleasant porches alone. **Fidel's,** 607 Valley Ave. (755-5292; open daily 11am-9:30pm weekdays, 11am-10:30pm weekends), cooks up some of the best Mexican food in North County. Revel in the patio atmosphere and scarf all the chips you want for free. The $5.55 lunch special usually means enchilada, quesadilla, or tostada with a beer or margarita included. The Early Bird Special (Mon.-Fri. 5-6:30pm) offers any combo dinner for $7. Just down the street, **Tony's Jacal,** 621 Valley (755-2274), a family-run establishment serving up hot and zesty burritos ($2.75), is a North County staple. (Open Mon. and Wed.-Thurs. 11am-2pm and 5-9:30pm, Fri.-Sat. 11am-2pm and 5-10pm, Sun. 3-9:30pm.)

Sights and Entertainment Racing season at the **Del Mar Racetrack** (755-1141) is a celeb-fest (late July to mid-Sept. Wed.-Mon.) Take I-5 to Via de la Valle, then head west to Jimmy Durante Blvd. Gates open at noon weekdays, 11:30am weekends, first post time at 2pm. (Admission $3 for grandstand, $6 for clubhouse. Parking $2.) This is one of the most beautiful racetrack settings in the world and has long been popular with the entertainment world; Bing Crosby and Pat O'Brien founded it in 1937.

Torrey Pines State Park, 2680 Carlsbad Blvd. (755-2063), on the coast 4 mi. south of Del Mar, is one of only two native Torrey Pine groves on earth. (The other is on the Channel Islands off Ventura.) Unless you're an expert, however, the Torrey pine trees are just plain ol' pine trees. The **lodge** provides information on hiking trails and park activities (open daily 9am-6pm). The park trails are wonderful for runners, cyclists, and those who enjoy rules—no picnicking, no food, no smoking, no dogs (even if kept in cars), and no straying off the established trails. The 6 mi. of slightly rocky beach are popular with hang gliders (park open 9am-sunset).

More earthy than neighboring Del Mar, **Solana Beach** is also more hospitable to tourists who'd like to relax rather than spend. Or follow rules. From the **Solana Beach City Park** parking lot (755-1569), you can climb a steep staircase to a promontory commanding a spectacular view of the ocean below. Bring your pet and a picnic lunch. The **Belly Up Tavern,** 143 S. Cedros Ave. (481-9022), near Fidel's and Tony's Jacal, once a warehouse near the train tracks, now belts blues, rockabilly, reggae, and swing jazz. Patrons can shoot pool or go bottoms up at the long bar. "Big Mama" Thornton, The Smithereens, John Lee Hooker, and Taj Mahal have all played here. (Open daily 11am-1:30am; live music daily at 9pm with occasional afternoon shows. Cover varies with artist.)

The town entertains and employs its young every summer at one of the largest county fairs in the country, the **Southern California Exposition** (755-1161). Held from late June to early July at the Del Mar Fairgrounds, the expo features traditional livestock shows, rides, and barbecues, as well as musicians and artists ($7, seniors $4, ages 6-12 $2).

Cardiff-by-the-Sea is enhanced by **San Elijo Beach State Park** (753-5091) and **Cardiff State Beach** just to the south. For camping information, see San Diego: Camping, page 150. If you have a car, this is a beautiful place to stay near San Diego.

ENCINITAS, LEUCADIA, AND CARLSBAD

Shaded by eucalyptus trees, Rte. 21 passes next through the towns of Encinitas and Leucadia, which still betray traces of their hippie-mecca past. Farther up the coast, the lagoon hideaway of Carlsbad is decidedly charming. Wild rose bushes twine around low stone and shingled homes, emphasizing the old resort town feel. Romance emanates from Carlsbad's antique shops and lagoon shores. You may even find secluded coastline.

Accommodations, Camping, and Food The cheapest indoor lodging near Carlsbad is **Motel 6,** 6117 Paseo del Norte (438-1242; fax 931-7948). From I-5, take the Palomar Airport Rd. exit, go east on Palomar to Paseo del Norte, and turn right. (Singles $28. Doubles $34.) Other locations are in downtown Carlsbad (434-7135) and further south at Raintree Dr. (431-0745).

You can camp on the beach at **South Carlsbad State Park** (438-3143), although you probably won't be able to obtain one of the 226 sites in summer without a reservation. Call MISTIX (800-365-2267; sites $21 off the ocean, $16 inland).

In Encinitas, but close to Carlsbad, **Alberto's Mexican Food,** 476 1st St. (944-6836), serves up *carne asada* burritos (beef and guacamole) for $2.75 (open 24 hrs.). **Roxy Restaurant,** 517 1st St. (436-5001), in Encinitas, is a pleasingly non-doctrinaire vegetarian place with full bar and ice cream in an upscale diner atmosphere. Try the "Avotaco," stuffed with avocado, cheese, olives, onions, tomatoes, and sprouts, for $3.25 (open Mon.-Sat. 11am-10pm, Sun. 11am-9pm).

Sights The state has taken over the beaches here, so they're still available for sunning and surfing. The stone steps at **Leucadia State Beach** descend from the cliffs at South El Portal St. to just over 1 mi. of public sands. **Moonlight State Beach** is a long family beach. **Carlsbad State Beach** is 3 mi. long and attractive; the view is only spoiled by the mammoth Encinitas Power Plant, occupying the coast to the south. You can rent a board at **Offshore Surf Boards,** 3179 Carlsbad Blvd. (729-4934), on Rte. 21. (Boogie-boards $3 per hr., $10 per day. $100 deposit or credit card. Open daily 8am-8pm.) **Bicycles** are available for rent at the **Carlsbad Cyclery,** 2796 Carlsbad Blvd. (434-6681). Bikes or in-line skates are $10 for two hours, $15 per day. Boogie-boards go for $2 per hour, $8 per day. Fins or beach chair rent for $5 per day. A major credit card is required. There is no additional charge for protective gear. (Open Mon.-Sat. 10am-6pm, Sun. 10am-5pm.)

The understated oasis of **Rancho Santa Fe** is east of Encinitas. The Santa Fe Railroad bought the land here years ago and planted thousands of eucalyptus trees in hopes of using the wood for railroad ties, later abandoning the trees to such stellar ex-residents as Mary Pickford, Douglas Fairbanks, and Bing Crosby. To this day, the community remains an exclusive retreat from the encroaching threat of suburbia, and the town's streets are lined with stately red-tile buildings. Continue north to find the **Self-Realization Fellowship Temple,** a shoreline Taj Mahal established by the guru Paramahansa Yogananda.

OCEANSIDE

Oceanside is the largest and, accordingly, the most varied of the beach towns north of San Diego. Nowadays it's the only place near San Diego where real estate is still "almost" affordable. In the past couple of years Oceanside has also been afflicted with increasing gang violence. The community remained unscathed, however, by the 1992 L.A. riots, and gang tensions are unlikely to be part of a visitor's experience. The beach at **Oceanside Harbor** (I-5 and Oceanside Harbor Dr.) is touted as one of the world's greatest surfing beaches. The 6th Avenue pier attracts serious surfers year-round, especially during the annual West Coast Pro-Am Surf Contest (June), PSSA Championships (mid-June), World Body Surfing Championships (mid-Aug.), and Longboard Championships (late Aug.). Beaches are patrolled by life-guards and there are designated areas for surfers.

If you're interested in seeing a well-preserved Spanish mission, make a pilgrimage to **Mission San Luis Rey de Francia** (757-3651), built to "save" the Luiseño Natives. Follow Missions Ave. (Rte. 76) east from Hill St. (Rte. 21) for 5 mi., or take NCTD bus #303 at Hill and Mission. The mission was founded in 1798, but the only original building still standing is the 1807 church. The museum exhibits artifacts of monastery life. (Museum and church open Mon.-Sat. 10am-4:30pm, Sun. noon-4:30pm. $3, ages 8-14 $1.)

Amtrak (722-4622) and **Greyhound** (722-1587) share the **Oceanside Transit Center,** 205 and 225 Tremont St. The center's towering signs make it easy to spot from any point in town.

ESCONDIDO

Thirty mi. northeast of San Diego, Escondido counts among its diverse denizens both rich celebrities and masses of undocumented laborers looking for agricultural work. Eager for tourism, Escondido merits the short drive from the coast or San Diego as a daytrip or en route to somewhere else.

Practical Information The **Escondido Chamber of Commerce,** 720 N. Broadway (745-2125), dispenses information. (Open Mon.-Fri. 8am-5pm; 24-hr. hotline 800-848-3336.) **Greyhound** stops in Escondido at 700 W. Valley Parkway (745-6522). The **North Country Transit Department** can be reached at 743-6283.

Accommodations, Camping, and Food A Motel 6, 509 W. Washington Blvd. (743-6669), by the City Center Parkway, is everybody's favorite. And yes, it has a pool, TV, HBO, and A/C. (Singles $25. Doubles $32.) The **Palms Inn,** 2650 S. Escondido Blvd. (800-727-8932), has a pool, jacuzzi, lounge, and laundry. Rooms start at $34. **Dixon Lake,** 1700 La Honda Dr. (741-3328), north of town, has 45 campsites in attractive, hilly country overlooking the reservoir. (Sites $10, with hookup $14; reservation fee $5 per site.) Follow Broadway north to El Norte Parkway, turn right, then left onto La Honda. Reserve in summer at least 18 days in advance. The lake is stocked with trout and catfish; swimming is prohibited. Fishing permits are sold at the camp. Rent motorboats and rowboats for reasonable prices. Park open for day use Sun.-Tues. 6am-8pm, Wed.-Sat. 6am-11pm, with permit for night fishing. There's a **Farmers' Market** (745-8877) with handmade crafts and organic produce every Tuesday on Grand Ave. near Broadway.

Sights Visitors can poke through the late "wunnerful, wunnerful" champagne music conductor Lawrence Welk's memorabilia at the **Lawrence Welk Museum,** 8860 Lawrence Welk Dr. (800-932-WELK, -9355; open Sun.-Mon., and Wed. 10am-

5pm, Tues. and Thurs.-Sat. 10am-1pm; free). Like its cousin, the San Diego Zoo, the **San Diego Wild Animal Park** (234-6541) strives to do right by both its animals and its human visitors. The park is specifically dedicated to the preservation and display of endangered species. The park's 700 acres of developed land (another 1100 acres remain untouched) give the animals much more room than an ordinary zoo. Animals pad about freely in recreations of their native habitat. Take Rte. 15 north to Via Rancho Parkway and follow the signs. From downtown Escondido, take NCTD bus #307 from Valley Parkway and Escondido Blvd. The open-air **Wgasa Bush Line Monorail** takes visitors on a 50-minute tour through a variety of habitats. (Tours 9:30am-6pm, Sept.-mid-June 9:30am-4pm. Included in admission; sit on the right if possible.) Renting binoculars ($2.50) at the camera hut before boarding the monorail may enhance the tour. Besides the monorail, the Wild Animal Park offers the 1¼-mi. Kilimanjaro Hiking Trail, botanical exhibits, dusk-time screen shows, and animal shows. But while its large enclosures and successful breeding program are a boon to our furry friends, the park really can't compete with the San Diego Zoo in terms of accessibility and variety. Most of the park, including the monorail, is wheelchair accessible, but steep hills may require detours or assistance. Ask for a map to help avoid hills. (Admission including 50-min. Wgasa Bush Line tour and animal shows $17.50, seniors $15.50, ages 3-11 $10.50. Parking $3. Open Mon.-Wed. 9am-7pm, Thurs.-Sun 9am-10pm.)

North of Escondido

Although the Hale telescope at **Palomar Observatory** (742-2119) on Palomar Mountain is over 40 years old, it remains one of the world's largest and greatest astronomical tools. Take San Diego County Rte. S6, the "Highway to the Stars." The drive up through avocado orchards and dense woods offers lovely views of the valleys below, though the cities ensconced in these vales increasingly threaten Palomar's heavenly research with light and air pollution. Inside the observatory, a museum displays photographs of awesome celestial objects taken through Hale's 200-in. aperture. A photo gallery and videotaped account of the observatory's activities are the only other concessions made to the tourist trade. A smug notice points out that research, not education, is the observatory's mission, and touring is consequently limited to gazing at the telescope from behind plate glass. The more curious are referred to L.A.'s Griffith Planetarium, three hours away (see Griffith Park, page 95). (Palomar open daily 9am-4pm. Free.)

The observatory and several campgrounds are contained within **Cleveland National Forest**. Rte. S6 will rocket you past federally run **Fry Creek** and **Observatory Campgrounds,** and a left onto Rte. S7 at the mountaintop will touch you down at **Palomar Mountain State Park** (742-3462). Camping is permitted at the park's state-run **Doane Valley Campground** (742-3462). Sites are over 5000 ft. above sea level, so bring your longjohns. Showers, hiking trails, and fishing are available, but no swimming is allowed. (Sites $14. Hiker/biker communal site $3 per night.)

West of Mt. Palomar, halfway to Oceanside on Rte. 76, is one of the few remaining operating missions in California, **Mission Asistencia San Antonio de Pala** (742-3300), on the Pala Indian Reservation. The mission was founded as an outpost of Oceanside's Mission San Luis Rey in 1816 and converted thousands of Native Americans to Christianity before secularization in 1846. The buildings are restorations of the facilities that decayed during the last half of the 19th century. In 1903, the mission was revived when the Cupeño Natives were booted from their ancient village of Cupa to make way for Warner Hot Springs. San Antonio still ministers to Native Americans. The walls of the long, low chapel are painted with Native motifs, and the rough-hewn timbers and undulating brick floors reflect rustic origins. In the cemetery, hundreds of Native Americans are buried in unmarked graves or beneath crudely lettered crosses graced by humble offerings of flowers in rusted coffee cans.

■■■ CUYAMACA RANCHO STATE PARK

Cuyamaca is a Spanish corruption of Ah-ha Kwe-ah-mac, the native Kumeya'ay name for the area that means "the place where it rains"—something of an oddity in Southern California, where miles of deserts prevail and greenery survives only where water has been artificially introduced. Cuyamaca Rancho State Park is indeed an oddity; with acres of mountainous deciduous forest, it encompasses more than 26,000 acres of willows, sycamores, and enormous live canyon oak. In the northeast corner of the park is Cuyamaca Lake and a transitional desert zone between Cuyamaca Rancho and Anza-Borrego Desert State Parks. The **park headquarters** are on Rte. 79 in the center of the park (765-0755). The mailing address is Cuyamaca Rancho State Park, 12551 Rte. 79, Descanso 91916. (Open Mon.-Fri. 8am-5pm.)

Be sure to see the **Indian Museum** (open daily 8:30am-4:30pm) at park headquarters. The exhibits explore the park's mining past and the history of its native peoples. The Kumeya'ay resisted European and American influences well into the 19th century until they were forced onto a reservation in the 1870s. An interpretive trail near the museum describes how the Kumeya'ay lived off this land.

The **Stonewall Mine Ruins** on Cuyamaca Lake consist of building foundations and old mining equipment left to rust and weather. A town once stood here, when the mine coughed up over $2 million of gold from 1872 to 1892. (There is a $5 day-use fee for the campground/picnic area.)

Over 160 mi. of hiking trails and 50 mi. of mountain bike trails crisscross the park. One of the best is the **Cuyamaca Peak Trail** (actually a paved fire road) which traverses Paso Picacho (3½ mi.) and Green Valley (8 mi.) up through the pine and fir trees, passing mountain springs on the way to the 6512-ft. summit, from which the Pacific Ocean, Mexico, and the Salton Sea are visible. An excellent hiking trail ascends **Stonewall Peak** (5730 ft.), 2 mi. from Paso Picacho. The park also offers guided walks and campfire programs. Check with park headquarters for details.

Campgrounds abound here; stick to the official sites. All except Arroyo Seco and Granite Springs are developed sites with tables, fireplaces, water, and showers. Call 765-0755 for information. **Reservations** at all sites (advisable in summer and necessary on weekends) can be made through MISTIX (800-444-7275). The primitive camps, to which you must bring your own water and utensils, are on hiking trails. Arroyo Seco and Granite Springs each accommodate up to 40 people. Sites, here listed from north to south, are $14 from May 1 to October 31 ($12 in off-season).

Los Caballos Horse Camp (4750 ft.). 16 sites with corrals just south of Cuyamaca Lake. You must have your own set of hooves to get here.

Paso Picacho (4780 ft.). 40 tent sites, 45 RV sites with access to scenic trails, as well as 4 environmental sites.

Green Valley (3957 ft.). 40 tent sites, 41 RV sites on the Sweetwater River— known as the Sweetwater Trickle during the droughts of recent years.

Arroyo Seco (4290 ft.). 1½ mi. west of Green Valley by foot.

Granite Springs. 4½ mi. east of Green Valley by foot.

Cuyamaca Rancho is a little more than an hour inland from San Diego along I-8, then north on Rte. 79. The easiest way to reach Cuyamaca is via the **Northeast Rural System** (765-0145), which also serves the mountain and desert towns of Julian, Santa Ysabel, Warner Springs, Borrego Springs, and Ocotillo Wells Tuesday through Saturday and El Cajon daily. (Office open Mon.-Sat. 7am-noon and 2-5pm.) Buses depart from Parkway Plaza in El Cajon and make four stops in town (take San Diego Transit bus #115 from downtown San Diego or the trolley to El Cajon). While the system is the lifeline for the rural folk, it is generally not designed for tourists who want to come and go the same day. The buses can be flagged down anywhere along the way and will even make pick-ups slightly off their designated route if you call 24hrs. ahead. (One trip daily per route; fares from $1-3.50.) Route #878 (Wed. and the 2nd and 4th Thurs. of each month) grazes the top of Cuyamaca Rancho State Park.

JULIAN

■■■ JULIAN

Visitors from San Diego and surrounding communities find Julian's range of seasons and small-town charm major attractions. Julian is like a pocket of New England in California; leaves turn, rain falls, snow drifts, and pies cool. When approached from Rte. 78, through the Anza-Borrego Desert State Park, Julian is part of a miraculous transition from desert terrain to orchard country in just ten highway miles.

Most San Diegans agree that Julian's apple pie and home-town atmosphere make the less-than-booming Gold Rush town worth the trek. Orchards and mines collide in this relic of the Old West where the population has hovered at a mere 1500 for years. Julian and the other small towns of the region—Santa Ysabel and Warner Springs—are excellent respites when traveling across Southern California. This cozy, but pricey hamlet is a good place to refuel, recharge, and rest before heading into less hospitable territory.

Practical Information and Orientation Visitor's information can be found at the **Chamber of Commerce** (765-1857) in the Town Hall (open Fri.-Mon. 10am-4pm in this "weekend town"). Call the **Julian Information Center** (765-0707) for details on the art shows and music festivals hosted by Julian throughout the year.

The **Northeast Rural Bus System** (765-0145) provides transportation joining Julian with its neighbors in the San Diego backcountry. Fares vary with destination. Call the dispatcher (Mon.-Sat. 7am-noon and 2-5pm) for rate inquiries, reservations, and wheelchair pick-up. Free public **restrooms** are at the Julian Pioneer Museum (corner of 4th and Washington). Coin-operated restrooms are located behind Town Hall on Main St.

Sights, Accommodations, and Food Julian's history as a mining town is recalled in a one to two-hour presentation at **Eagle High Peak Mines** (765-0036; take Main St. to C St. and follow Old Miners Trail). Visitors examine machinery and minerals from the heyday of the 1870 when $15 million worth of gold was mined from the hills. Some 1000 ft. of tunnel are open to the public (tours daily 9am-3pm; $7, children $3, under 5 $1).

The centerpiece of this quintessential town is, predictably, **Main Street.** Around the #2000 blocks of this drag, the aroma of baked apple pie drags crowds into restaurants and bakeries against their will. San Diegans fill up on pie and cider, then pack their cars with Julian's honey, preserves, olives, dried fruit, and candy as defense against urban life. The **Apple Festival** in October includes dramatic arts and farmers markets.

There are a few inns and bed and breakfasts, but most are not for the budget traveler. Some "bargains" may be secured in person on weekdays when swankier lodges cut their prices, but campgrounds are the best option for those on a budget. The **William Heise County Park** (694-3049; 7 mi. from town on Pine Hills Rd.) has 103 campsites ($11; $1 day use) equipped with running water and fire rings. Call for reservations up to eight weeks in advance. Beautiful camping sites are also available at the **Cuyamaca Rancho State Park** 9 mi. from town (see Cuyamaca Rancho State Park, above). If camping is not for you, the **Mt. Laguna Lodge** (445-2342) is 12 mi. away in Mt. Laguna, and reasonably priced. (Doubles with fireplace, microwave, and refrigerator $32, $41 on weekends and holidays.) For a full register of inexpensive, out-of-town lodgings, secure a pamphlet or map from the Town Hall.

Julian's cheapest eats can be had at one of the markets or bakeries on Main St. For a snack, try a delicious slice ($1.75) from one of **Mom's Pies, Etc.,** 2119 Main St. (765-2472; open Mon.-Fri. 8:30am-5:30pm, Sat.-Sun. 8:30am-6pm), or make a sandwich at the **Julian Market & Deli,** 2202 Main St. (765-2606; open Mon.-Sat. 8am-8pm, Sun. 8am-7pm). Meals in most of the nearby restaurants are expensive. Farther out of town in Ramona, **Daniel's Market,** 1326 Main St. (789-1155; open 6am-11pm daily), stocks fresh produce and breads at better prices than those in Julian.

The Desert

Mystics and misanthropes have long been fascinated by the desert—its vast spaces, austere scenery, and brutal heat. Native Americans, pioneering fortune hunters, the young Jim Morrison, and modern city slickers disenchanted with smoggy L.A. have all felt the power of this region. In the winter the desert is a pleasantly warm refuge, in the spring a technicolored floral landscape, and then in the summer a blistering wasteland. A barren place of overwhelming simplicity, the desert's beauty lies not so much in what it contains, but in what it lacks—congestion, pollution, and throngs of visitors craning to see the same sights.

ORIENTATION

Southern California's desert lies at the fringe of the North American Desert, a 500,000-square-mi. territory stretching east into Arizona and New Mexico, northeast into Nevada and Utah, and south into Mexico. Despite receiving only six in. of rain each year, the desert supports an astonishing array of plant and animal life. The desert also serves as host to a substantial human population: settlements range from the posh destination resorts of Palm Springs to bland highway pit-stops serving those speeding to points beyond.

California's desert divides roughly into two zones. The **Sonoran,** or **Low Desert,** occupies southeastern California from the Mexican border north to Needles and west to the Borrego Desert; the **Mojave,** or **High Desert** spans the south central part of the state, bounded by the Sonoran Desert to the south, San Bernardino and the San Joaquin Valleys to the west, the Sierra Nevada to the north, and Death Valley to the east. As their names imply, the Low and High Deserts lie at different elevations, resulting in two different climates. The Low Desert, home of the **Anza-Borrego Desert State Park,** and the **Salton Sea,** is flat, dry, and barren. The oases in this area are essential to the existence of human, animal, and plant life, with the largest of them supporting the super-resort of Palm Springs. Despite the arid climate, much of this region has become agriculturally important as water from the Colorado River irrigates the Imperial Valley and the Coachella Valley.

In contrast, the High Desert consists of foothills and plains nestled within mountain ranges approaching 5000 ft. Consequently, it is cooler (by about 10°F in summer) and wetter. Though few resorts have been developed, **Joshua Tree National Park** is a popular destination for campers. **Barstow** is the central city of the High Desert and an important rest station on the way from L.A. to Las Vegas or the Sierras. **Death Valley** represents the eastern boundary of the Mojave but could be considered a region unto itself, since it has both high and low desert areas. Major highways cross the desert east-west: I-8 hugs the California-Mexico border, I-10 goes through Blythe and Indio on its way to Los Angeles, and I-40 crosses Needles to Barstow, where it joins I-15, running from Las Vegas and other points west to L.A.

DESERT SURVIVAL

Here, water, not bread, is the staff of life. The body loses at least a gallon of liquid per day in the desert (two gallons during strenuous activity such as hiking), so keep drinking even when you're not thirsty. Always have a container of water at your side. While driving, keep back-up containers in a cooler in the trunk, pulling them out as you need them. If you're drinking sweet beverages, dilute them with water to avoid an over-reaction to high sugar content—even orange juice and Gatorade should be diluted by at least 50%. Avoid alcohol and coffee because they cause dehydration. For long-term stays, a high-quality beverage with potassium compounds and glucose, such as ERG (an industrial-strength Gatorade available from wilderness outfits and camping suppliers), will help keep your strength up. Thirst is the first sign of dehydration, which comes on rapidly. Drinking enormous quantities of water after the fact is not effective—in fact, it's dangerous to do so in high temperatures. Take preventive measures and stay hydrated. Whether you are driving or hiking, tote *two gallons of water per person per day*. Try to designate at least one large container as a supply to be used in the case of an emergency.

Allow yourself a couple of days to adjust to the heat, especially if you're planning a hike or other strenuous activity. Make sure to carry sunglasses with 100% UV protection, sunscreen, and a hat. A bandanna or towel dipped in water and wrapped around the head will give added protection and relief, as will a t-shirt covering the back of your neck. Keep clothing on (light colors reflect heat), not off; a sweaty shirt, though uncomfortable, will prevent dehydration more effectively than removing it. Thick-soled shoes and two pairs of socks can help to keep feet comfortable on a hike during the summer as the sand can register a scorching 150-200°F.

The desert is home to a variety of extremes. Heat is not the only concern for desert-trekkers. At high elevations, temperatures during winter nights can be well below freezing, even with afternoon temperatures in the 60s or 70s. You should take along at least a sweater, even in the summer. In the fall and spring, the desert is infamous for flash floods. Avoid camping in dry gulches, which can turn into raging rivers with astonishing speed. Even if it's not raining where you are, water can come down from rain-drenched higher elevations and wreak Biblical devastation.

Hiking expeditions should be attempted only when the temperature is under 90°F, and *never* alone. Almost all parks require hikers to register with the park office before setting out. If you're on private or unmanaged public land, *always* notify someone of your itinerary. The National Park Service recommends that a support vehicle follow all hikers.

Hitchhiking is risky year-round and suicidal in the summer.

Driving in the Desert

Before **driving** in the desert, make sure that your car has been recently serviced and is in good running condition. Carry water for drinking and for the radiator, as well as a spare tire and necessary tools. Five gallons of water are recommended for each vehicle. Also bring extra coolant and a couple quarts of oil; check your car owner's manual for the recommended weight of oil, which can vary with temperature. A board and shovel are useful in case your car gets stuck in sand. If you plan to leave paved roads, an off-road vehicle with 4-wheel-drive is recommended.

Although settlements are sometimes sparse, enough traffic usually passes on major roads to help you if you have car trouble. The isolated areas of the parks pose a threat, especially in summer, when few tourists visit. *Stay with your vehicle if it breaks down;* it is easier to spot than a person and provides crucial shade.

Use air conditioning with extreme restraint. If you see the temperature gauge climbing, turn it off. Air from open windows should be sufficiently comfortable at highway speeds. If an overheating warning light comes on, pull over to the side of the road. Turn the heater on full force to cool the engine. If radiator fluid is steaming or bubbling over, turn off the car for about half an hour; if not, put it in neutral and run it at about 1500rpms for a few minutes. The coolant in your car will continue to circulate, ideally bringing the temperature down. Never pour water over the engine to cool it. Never try to lift a searing hood; wait for your engine to cool first.

Drivers can purchase a desert water bag for about $5 to $10 at a hardware or automotive store. This large canvas bag is strapped onto the front of the car and filled with water; the wind causes evaporation and prevents overheating. Driving in the evening, night, and early morning is preferable to searing mid-day trips.

■■■ PALM SPRINGS

For years, the singularly lackadaisical brand of decadence offered by Palm Springs has attracted people from all walks of life. Many year-round residents are retirees. However, Palm Springs is also a popular spring break destination for students and a winter destination for middle-aged, monied golfers and hip, young scene-seekers from coastal communities. Memorial Day weekend is a crowded time, then things thin out for the slow summer months, when temperatures are consistently in the 100s. On Labor Day weekend the town is busy again and prepared for the winter rush of visitors. Reliably warm and smoldering with hot springs, the desert city draws those seeking a sunny respite from their everyday lives.

PRACTICAL INFORMATION AND ORIENTATION

Visitors Information: Chamber of Commerce, 190 W. Amado (325-1577). Friendly advice and a map for $1. Acquire *The Desert Guide,* a free monthly magazine outlining attractions and entertainment. Open Mon.-Fri. 8:30am-4:30pm. **Palm Springs Visitors Center,** 2781 N. Palm Canyon Dr. (800-34-SPRINGS (34-777-4647) or 748-8418). Highlights local arts and entertainment events. Open Mon.-Sat. 9am-5pm, Sun. 8am-4pm.

Airport: Palm Springs Regional Airport, 3400 S. Tahquitz-Canyon Rd. (323-8161). Intrastate, as well as limited national service.

Buses: Greyhound, 311 N. Indian Canyon (800-231-2222). An easy walk from downtown. 7 buses per day to and from L.A. ($17, $32.30 round-trip; 3-day advance purchase $13.60, $25.85 round-trip). Call to check restrictions. **Desert Stage Lines:** 251-6162. Service to Twentynine Palms and Joshua Tree National Park (Friday, pay $8.80 fare directly to driver). In Palm Springs, stop at the Greyhound terminal.

Sun Bus: 343-3451. The local bus system connects all Coachella Valley cities daily 6am-6pm. 75¢ to ride (exact change). Seniors and people with disabilities ride for 25¢ during the week, free on weekends. Bus #20 stays on a straight course along Palm Canyon Dr. and from there along Rte. 111 to Palm Desert (1 bus every ½ hr.). Bus #2 covers the downtown area. A *Riders Guide,* available at any info. center and in most hotel lobbies, includes schedules and a system map.

People with Disabilities Transportation Information: 343-3451. *Sun-Dial* transports people with disabilities from their doorstops to their destinations. Fare $1.50. 3-day notice required.

Taxi: Desert Cab, 325-2868. **Valley Cabousine,** 340-5845. Both 24 hrs.

Car Rental: Rates fluctuate seasonally (higher in the winter and lower in the summer). **Rent-A-Wreck,** 67555 E. Palm Canyon (324-1766). Must be 21 with major credit card. **Budget Car,** Palm Springs Regional Airport (327-1404) will rent to drivers 18-21 with proof of full-coverage insurance for a $10 surcharge per day. Ages 21-25 need only pay surcharge.

Automobile Club of Southern California (AAA): 800-400-4222.

Bicycle Rental: Canyon Bicycle Rentals, 305 E. Arenas (327-7688). Mountain bikes $4 per hour, $20 for ½-day, $25 for 24 hrs. Open winter daily 9am-5pm; summer Thurs.-Tues. 9am-2pm.

Library: Welwood-Murray Library, 100 S. Palm Canyon Dr. (323-8296) also stocks tourist information. Open Tues.-Sat. 9am-1pm.

Laundromat: Arenas Coin-Op, 220 E. Arenas Rd. (322-7717), ½ block east of Indian Canyon. Wash $1; dry 25¢ for 10 min. Open daily 5am-9pm.

Road and Weather Conditions: 345-2767 (recording), 345-3711 (updated).

Hotlines: Rape Crisis Hotline, 568-9071; **Regional Poison Control Center,** 800-544-4404; **AIDS Hotline of Southern California,** 800-922-2437 or 800-400-7432 (Spanish).

Hospital: 1150 N. Indian Canyon (323-6511). For 24-hr. emergency care, call 323-6251.

Emergency: 911.

Post Office: 333 E. Amado Rd. (325-9631). Open Mon.-Fri. 8am-5pm, Sat. 9am-1pm. **General Delivery ZIP Code:** 92263-9999.

Area Code: 619.

Approaching the city from **I-10** East, take **Rte. 111** to the Palm Springs exit. The visitors center is located one block beyond Tramway Rd. on the right side. Approaching from the north on I-15, take Rte. 215 east to Rte. 60 east to 10 east. Then take Rte. 111 to the Palm Springs exit. To orient yourself within the town, find **Indian Canyon Drive** and **East Palm Canyon Drive,** the city's two main drags. East Palm

Canyon winds west-northwest through town before subtly turning due north and turning into Indian Canyon. In addition to these north-south roads, there are two major east-west boulevards. **Tahquitz-Canyon Rd.** runs east to the airport, while **Ramon Rd.**, four blocks to the south, provides access to I-10. Take the scenic **Palms-to-Pines Hwy.** (Rte. 74) back to L.A., watching as the sparse desert cactus and sagebrush dramatically give way to lush pines.

ACCOMMODATIONS

Palm Springs may challenge the budget traveler, but affordable lodging is available. Motels slash their prices by 20-30% in the summer; call ahead to check prices and don't be shy about bargaining. If possible, plan to visit during the week, when weekend visitors return to their homes and room rates fall. Be aware that room tax in the county is 10% and all prices quoted below do not include tax.

Budget Host Inn, 1277 S. Palm Canyon Dr. (800-829-8099 or 325-5575) has large, clean rooms with refrigerators, phones and pool access. In-room movies and continental breakfast included. Laundry room. Rooms $29 for 1-4 persons on weekdays, $39 on summer weekends.

Motel 6, three locations: 660 S. Palm Canyon Dr. (327-4200), 149 units conveniently located south of city center; 595 E. Palm Canyon Dr. (325-6129), 125 units; 63950 20th Ave. (251-1425), 90 units near the I-10 off-ramp. The cheapest rates in town (*especially* during winter). Each has a pool and A/C, and is usually booked up. Reservations are accepted up to one year in advance. Some on-the-spot rooms are available and no-shows are frequent. At all locations: singles $32, doubles $36.

Travelodge, 333 E. Palm Canyon Dr. (327-1211 or 800-255-3050). Resort with private balconies and patios. All rooms equipped with coffee makers, A/C, and color TV. Pool and jacuzzi. Summer rooms for 1 or 2 people, $35 during the week, $39 on weekends. Winter rates $65 during week, $85 on weekend. Also offers a fall rate about halfway in between winter and summer prices.

Westward Ho, 701 E. Palm Canyon Dr. (800-854-4345 or 320-0777). Attached to a Denny's Restaurant, this motel emphasizes convenience over charm. Clean comfortable rooms with TV, phones, A/C. Pool. Doubles $33.90, $41.90 in winter.

FOOD

Las Casuelas—The Original, 368 N. Palm Canyon Dr. (325-3213). The remarkable success of this Mexican restaurant has inevitably led to expansion, but locals still insist that The Original is where it's at. Best Mexican rice ever. Combos start at $7. Open Sun.-Thurs. 10am-10pm, Fri.-Sat. 10:30am-11pm.

Thai Smile, 651 N. Palm Canyon Dr. (320-5503), between Tamarisk and Alejo. Tasty options for vegetarians. Vegetable soups from $2.50, tempura $5.25. Spicy *pad thai* chicken for $6.25. Open Sun.-Thurs. 11am-10pm, Fri.-Sat. 11am-11pm.

Carlo's Italian Delicatessen, 119 S. Indian Canyon (325-5571). Palm Springs' finest deli for the money. Overgrown sandwiches in the $5 range. Local personalities portrayed on the wall. Open Tues.-Sun. 10am-7pm; closed Wed. in winter.

Hamburger Hamlet, 105 N. Palm Canyon Dr. (325-2321). Only in Southern California—a gourmet burger grill with a Shakespearean motif (the walls are adorned with playbills from various performances of *Hamlet*). ½-lb. guacamole burger $7.25. Entrees $5-10. Open Mon.-Thurs. 11am-10pm, Sat.-Sun. 9am-11pm.

Jenson's, 102 S. Sunrise (325-8282). Specialty grocery store with an excellent deli. Ask them to make you a sandwich to go ($3-4). Open daily 7am-9pm.

Vons Stores, 4733 E. Palm Canyon Dr. (800-283-8667). Sells drinking water, fresh produce, and other desert essentials. Open daily 6am-midnight.

Evenings are the perfect time to do a little people-watching and enjoy the cooler night air and Palm Springs nightlife. Bars offer nightly drink specials to lure revelers. **La Taqueria,** 125 E. Tahquitz Way (778-5391), attracts customers by spritzing its lovely tile patio with mist and serving Moonlight Margaritas for $2.25. Another option is **Chillers,** 262 S. Palm Canyon Dr. (325-3215). Order a vodka and pink lemonade from the spinning wall of frozen drinks. Both bars book live music nightly. **Zelda's,** on 169 North Indian (325-2375), has dancing and drinks daily from 8pm-2am. (Mon.-Thurs. cover charge $5, Fri. $6, with music provided by two DJs, on Sun. cover charge $10 for a live band.)

SIGHTS AND ACTIVITIES

Rising nearly 6000 ft., the **Palm Springs Aerial Tramway** (325-1391) climbs up the side of Mt. San Jacinto to an observation deck that affords excellent views. Hiking trails are accessible year-round and cross-country skiing is available in the winter. The tramway station is located on Tramway Dr., which intersects Rte. 111 just north of Palm Springs. (Trams runs at least every ½ hr. Mon.-Fri. starting at 10am, Sat.-Sun. starting at 8am. Last car leaves at 9pm; Nov.-April at 8pm. Round-trip fare $16, seniors $12, under 12 $10.)

A touch of true natural beauty has been marketed at the remarkable **Desert Museum,** 101 Museum Dr. (325-0189). The museum offers an impressive collection of Native American art, talking desert dioramas, and live animals. The museum also sponsors the performing arts in the 450-seat **Annenberg Theatre** as well as curator-led field trips ($3) into the canyons. Accessible by Sun Bus #111. (Museum open late Sept.-early June Tues.-Fri. 10am-4pm, Sat.-Sun. 10am-5pm. $4, seniors $3, students and under 17 $2, under 6 free. Free first Tues. of each month.) The **Living Desert Reserve** in Palm Desert, located 1½ mi. south of Rte. 111 at 47900 Portola Ave. (346-5694), houses Arabian oryces, iguani, desert unicorns, and Grevy's zebras alongside indigenous flora in the **Botanical Gardens.** The twilight reptile exhibit is a must-see. (Open daily Sept.-mid-June 9am-5pm. $7, seniors $6, under 15 $3.50. Wheelchair access.) Less polished and more bizarre, **Moorten's Desertland Botanical Gardens,** 1701 S. Palm Canyon Dr. (327-6555), is advertised as the world's first "cactarium." (Open Mon.-Sat. 9am-4:30pm, Sun. 10am-4pm; closed Wed. in summer. $2, ages 5-16 75¢).

The **Indian Canyons** (325-5673), once home to the Agua Caliente Cahuilla Indians, are oases that contain a wide variety of desert life and remnants of the human communities they once supported. All four canyons can be accessed at the end of S. Palm Canyon Dr., 5 mi. from the center of town. (Open daily Sept. 5-July 4, 8am-6pm. $5, students $2.50, seniors $2, ages 6-12 $1.)

Coachella Valley is the self-proclaimed "Date Capital of the World." **Oasis Date Gardens** (399-5665) in Thermal is an easy drive from Palm Springs along Rte. 111. Tours, date shakes, and an educational film titled "The Sex Life of the Date" will bring you closer to your favorite fruit.

For those travelers who saw more than enough desert simply getting to Palm Springs, a tour of **celebrity homes** offers an alternative view. The budget method for this sight-seeing tour is to buy a map downtown and guide oneself; rented bikes offer a somewhat less conspicuous way of getting around. Be forewarned that these celebrities came to the desert for seclusion and your closest brush with greatness might be seeing Bob Hope's gardener working outside of Bob's high adobe wall.

The most idiosyncratic sight in the region is **Cabot's Old Indian Pueblo,** 67616 E. Desert View Ave. (329-7610), 1 mi. east of Palm Dr. in **Desert Hot Springs.** Take bus #19 from downtown Palm Springs to Desert View Ave. The 35 rooms in the Hopi-style pueblo were built from materials found in the desert from 1941 to 1964. (Open 10am-4pm daily. $2.50, seniors $2, ages 5-16 $1.)

Palm Springs has a number of public **tennis** and **golf** facilities. There are eight courts at **Ruth Hardy Park,** 700 Tamarisk Dr., at Avenida Caballeros. **The Palm Springs Municipal Golf Course,** 1885 Golf Club Dr. (328-1005; open dawn-dusk), claims to be one of the nation's top municipal golf courses. Try the links for $18 during the week, or shell out $28 on the weekend. For complete information about facilities, call the city's **Leisure Center** at 323-8272. To hear the incongruous roar of surf (and screaming children) among the sagebrush, visit **Oasis Water Park** (325-SURF, -7873), off I-10 South on Gene Autry Trail between Ramon Rd. and E.

Palm Canyon Dr. (Open daily 11am-7pm. $17, seniors and ages 4-11 $11.50, under 4 free. Boogie-boards and surfboards extra.)

Village Fest (320-3781) closes Palm Canyon Dr. in the downtown area every Thursday night from 6 to 10pm. Vendors from surrounding communities market jewelry and local crafts at spectacular bargains, while townsfolk enjoy live music and other entertainment.

A trip to Palm Springs would not be complete without a visit to the town's namesakes. The naturally hot mineral pools at the **Desert Hot Springs Spa**, 10805 Palm Dr. (329-6495), feature pools of different temperatures, saunas, and professional masseurs. (Open daily 8am-10pm. Mon.-Fri. $5, after 3pm $3; Sat.-Sun. $6, after 3pm $3. Refundable $4 lock deposit; $4 towel deposit, plus $1 rental.) The best deal in Palm Springs may be the free **weekend hikes** arranged by the Sierra Club (346-0798; a home phone number, so be considerate and call 9am-10pm). Or, plan your own hike through the **Thousand Palm Oasis** or the mesas in **Coachella Valley Preserve.** If you visit in spring, don't miss the **desert wildflowers.**

SEASONAL EVENTS

Attempting to fulfill his campaign promise to heighten Palm Springs' glamour quotient, Mayor Bono instituted the **Palm Springs International Film Festival** (322-2930), held each year during the second week of January. If you happen upon the city during the second or third week in February (18-27), don't miss the 48th annual **National Date Festival,** fashioned along the lines of a eupeptic Arabian fantasy. Call Date Festival Fairgrounds (342-8247), Rte. 111 in Indio, for more information. Palm Springs is also infamous for its professional golf and tennis tournaments like the **Bob Hope Chrysler Classic** (341-2299) in February.

■■■ ANZA-BORREGO DESERT STATE PARK

This huge state park claims a wedge of Southern California's Lower Desert that is layered with natural and human history. Anza-Borrego is the home of many cacti and plant species found nowhere else in California. Barbed cholla, bruise-blossomed indigo bush, and thirsty tamarisk all draw life from earth that is covetous of water but generous with sunlight. Adventurous travelers who brave the desert's searing heat will discover a barren area still marked by the Native Americans, Spanish explorers, and gold-hungry settlers who struggled for existence on this forbidding landscape. Visit in the winter months when the park temperatures are livable. In the words of one ranger, "It is just plain stupid" to visit this area during the scorching summer months when much of the park is closed and the temperature makes exploring unpleasant and dangerous.

PRACTICAL INFORMATION AND ORIENTATION

Visitors Information: Anza-Borrego Desert State Park Visitors Center, 200 Palm Canyon Dr. (767-4205) in Borrego Springs. Topographical maps, books, and slideshows available to visitors. Rangers offer lifesaving backcountry and safety information. Stop here before hiking or camping in the park. Open Sept.-May daily 8am-5pm, June-Aug. Sat.-Sun. 9am-5pm. For more information during summer months, call **Anza Park Headquarters** at 767-4205 Mon.-Fri. 8am-5pm.

Buses: Northeast Rural Bus System services the San Diego backcountry. Call 765-0145 Mon.-Sat. 7am-noon, 2-5pm for information on routes.

AAA: 800-458-5972. Provides emergency roadside service.

Weather: 289-1212.

Desert Wildflower Hotline: 767-4684.

Hospital: Borrego Medical Center, 4343 Yaqui Pass Rd. on Rams Hill (767-5051) in Borrego Springs. Clinic open Mon.-Fri. 8am-noon, 1:30-5pm, Sat. 8am-noon.

Emergency: 911.

Area Code: 619.

The park can be reached on **Rte. 78,** which runs directly through it. From the west, Rte. 79 from I-8 will connect to 78 in Julian. From the east, Rte. 86 runs south from I-10 to 78. Follow the signs on County Rte. 53 to Borrego Springs.

ACCOMMODATIONS AND CAMPING

The small community of **Borrego Springs** provides a wide range of accommodations from hotels by shimmering pools to campsites by chemical toilets. **Whispering Sands Motel,** 2376 Borrego Springs Rd. (767-3322) lies one block north of town off Christmas Circle. Eight units share a pool and outdoor cooking facilities. Singles and doubles with A/C cost $35, $45 in winter. **Hacienda del Sol,** 610 Palm Canyon Dr. (767-5442), offers comfortable rooms. (Singles $34. Doubles $37. $10 more in winter.) **Camping** may be an option for hard-core desertphiles, but is not feasible in the summer. Temperatures in the 100s will spoil food, hasten dehydration, and turn tents into solar-powered ovens. Backpackers in any season should carry sufficient water (2 gal. per person per day) and register their itinerary with park officials.

Anza-Borrego permits free open camping anywhere in the park. The most hospitable of the primitive locations is along County Rte. S-3 in **Culp Valley.** At 3400 ft., it is the highest and coolest camp in the park. For better amenities than Culp Valley's pit toilets, the **Borrego Palm Canyon Campground** three mi. from town on County Rte. S-3 features flush toilets, showers, and food lockers. (Sites $8 and up.) **Agua Caliente Springs Park** on Rte. S-2 south of Vallecito Stage Station has restrooms, laundry facilities, a wading pool, and several natural hot springs. The nearby store and gas station make it a convenient base for day hikes (sites $10-15). Call MISTIX (800-444-7275), for reservations and information for developed campgrounds.

FOOD

Groceries and supplies can be purchased at **Center Market,** 590 Palm Canyon (767-5513), in Borrego Springs. (Open Mon.-Sat. 8:30am-6:30pm, Sun. 8:30am-5pm.) Next door at **George's Little Italy** (767-3938), hikers can carbo-load on hefty pasta dishes (open Mon. 5-9pm, Tues.-Sat. 11am-2pm and 5-9pm).

SIGHTS

The most popular areas of exploration in Anza-Borrego are **Coyote Canyon Creek** and its network of tributaries. These canyon-forming creeks water the lands around them, giving life to plants unable to survive elsewhere in the park. Wildlife are also drawn to these waters, including the magnificent **bighorn sheep.** The canyon is closed from mid-June to mid-September to protect the sheep and their habitat. Approaching Coyote Canyon from the south from Borrego Springs affords the easiest and most attractive access, four-wheel-drive is a must for travel off paved roads.

■ THE SALTON SEA

This man-made "wonder" was formed in 1905-1907 when the aqueduct from the Colorado River broke and flooded the Coachella Valley. The accident resulted in a stagnant 35 mi. by 15 mi. lake covering a patch of desert. In the 1960s an attempt to market the sea as a tourist attraction was made. Fresh and saltwater fish were stocked in the sea, and marinas were built in anticipation of a thriving resort and vacation industry. Unfortunately, decaying vegetation in the still water produced a foul odor and high salt content killed all but a few hardy species of fish. The sea is now ringed by abandoned buildings and **Salton City** is a defunct resort town that never had a chance. The Salton Sea lies northeast of Anza-Borrego State Park. Salton City is located at the intersection of Rte. 86 and County Rte. S-22.

Sport fishing remains somewhat popular around the Salton Sea. Contact the **West Shores Chamber of Commerce,** P.O. Box 5185, Salton City, CA 922705 (394-4112) for more information. Travelers in Southern California won't miss much if they skip the Salton Sea and head north to more appealing destinations.

■■■ JOSHUA TREE NATIONAL PARK

When the Mormons crossed this desert area in the 1800s, they named the enigmatic desert tree they encountered after the Biblical prophet Joshua. The tree's crooked limbs reminded them of the Hebrew leader, who with his arms upraised, beckoned the weary traveler to the promised land. After crossing the more arid Arizona desert, finding the slightly cooler and wetter Mojave must have been like arriving in God's country. The Joshua trees of the Mojave desert meet the wildflowers of the Sonoran desert at this spectacular preserve. Joshua Tree National Park contains a full spectrum of high and low desert landscapes and life forms.

Piles of quartz monzonite boulders, some over 100 ft. high, punctuate the desert terrain. The campsites throughout the area center around these formations because they provide shade and create rain-catching gullies, resulting in denser vegetation. The boulders were formed by subterranean lava flows seeping up through soft sandstone layers. A billion years of erosion carried away the sand and left the boulders exposed to the elements. Desert winds and floods have created textures and shapes majestic to the viewer and irresistible to the climber. Vestiges of past human occupation: ancient rock petroglyphs, dams built in the 19th century to catch the meager rainfall for livestock, and the ruins of gold mines, still dot the park.

Five oases speckle the park, providing a contrast to the desolate rock piles. Twentynine Palms, Fortynine Palms, Cottonwood Spring, Lost Palms, and Monson Canyon all grow out of springs of water rising through faults in the earth. Though not as luxurious as the oases of Arabian tales, they do support remarkable numbers of plant and animal life, ranging from California tree frogs to bighorn sheep.

Native desert flora and fauna can be as dangerous and as beautiful as their surroundings. Cacti flourish during the short spring, making that time the park's most crowded season. The *cholla* (CHO-ya) cactus is one to admire at a safe distance. The slightest brush against it will detach a spiny friend who will never leave your side (without the persuasion of pliers). If you relish the thought of sleeping under the crystalline skies of the high desert, invest in a cot. Otherwise, rattlesnakes and scorpions may be uninvited bedfellows. And remember, a coyote could add your unleashed pet to his diet. Leashes are mandated throughout the park and pets are restricted to roads, campgrounds, and picnic areas.

Most campgrounds do not have water; bring your own. Be sure to stop by the visitor center. The rangers are friendly and will help orient you. The heat and expanse of the park make an automobile a necessity. For desert safety, refer to Desert Survival, page 169.

PRACTICAL INFORMATION AND ORIENTATION

Visitors Information: Headquarters and Oasis Visitor Center, 74485 National Monument Dr., Twentynine Palms 92277 (367-7511), ¼ mi. off Rte. 62. Displays, guidebooks, maps. Open daily 8am-4:30pm. **Cottonwood Visitor Center,** at the southern gateway, located approximately 7 mi. north of I-10; exit 4 mi. west of the town of Chiriaco Summit, 25 mi. east of Indio. Open daily 8am-3:30pm, but hours are sometimes irregular. **Indian Cove Ranger Station** is on the road to Indian Cove campground. Open Oct.-May daily 8am-4pm; summer hours vary. **West Entrance Information Kiosk,** Park Blvd., 5 mi. southeast of the town of Joshua Tree. Those impatient to get into the park may want to enter here rather than drive on to Twentynine Palms.

Park entrance fee: $3 per person on foot, bicycle or motorcycle; $5 per vehicle.

Buses: Desert Stage Lines, (251-6162), based in Palm Springs. Stops in Twentynine Palms. Fare from the Palm Springs Greyhound Station to Twentynine Palms is $8.80, with 1 trip per week departing Palm Springs on Fri. 3:30pm. The bus returns to Palm Springs, departing from Twentynine Palms Fri. at 5:45pm.

Auto Rental: Tropical Car Rental, 6136 Adobe Rd. (361-8000), in Twentynine Palms. From $130 per week. Must be 21 with major credit card.

Twentynine Palms Chamber of Commerce: 367-3445, can provide updated information on transportation options.
Weather: Summer highs 95-115°F; winter highs 60-70°F. Warmer in the eastern area. 4-5 in. rain per year. The most comfortable places in summer are above 4000 ft.; in winter, stick to the lower elevations.
Hi-Desert Medical Center, 6601 White Feather Rd. (366-3711) in Joshua Tree. 24-hr. emergency care.
Emergency: 911. Call 367-3523 for a ranger. For the 24-hr. dispatch center, call 714-383-5651 collect.
Post Office: 73839 Gorgonio Dr. (367-3501), in Twentynine Palms. Open Mon.-Fri. 9am-5pm. **General Delivery ZIP Code:** 92277.
Area Code: 619.

Joshua Tree National Park covers 558,000 acres northeast of Palm Springs, about 160 mi. (3-3½ hr. by car) east of L.A. It is ringed by three highways: **I-10** to the south, **Rte. 62** (Twentynine Palms Hwy.) to the west and north, and **Rte. 177** to the east. From I-10, the best approaches are via Rte. 62 from the west, leading to the towns of **Joshua Tree** and **Twentynine Palms** on the northern side of the park, or from the south entrance at Cottonwood Springs, via an unnamed street that exits the interstate about 25 mi. east of Indio.

CAMPING

Most campgrounds in the park operate on a first-come, first-camped basis and accept no reservations. Exceptions are the group sites at Cottonwood, Sheep Pass, and Indian Cove and family sites at Black Rock Canyon. Call MISTIX (800-365-2267). Otherwise, to secure a decent site for the weekend, arrive in the early afternoon hours on Friday, and earlier on holiday weekends (rangers recommend staking your claim before noon during the busiest periods). Many spring weekends find all campsites full. Black Rock Canyon is usually the last to fill. No overflow camping is permitted at the designated campgrounds, but the backcountry is open for unlimited camping.

All campsites have tables, fireplaces, and pit toilets, and are free unless otherwise noted. Water (hence flush toilets) is available only at Black Rock Canyon and Cottonwood campgrounds. The visitors center and Indian Cove Ranger Station have water if you run out, but these facilities might be a half-hour drive from your site. There are no RV hookups or showers. BYOF (bring your own firewood), because burning anything you find in the park is a major offense. Fires are only permitted in the campsite pits. Bring a camping stove for cooking in the backcountry. Tents in the backcountry must be pitched at least 500 ft. from a trail and 1 mi. from a road. Your camping stay is limited to 14 days between October and May and to 30 days in the summer. Be sure to register first at a backcountry board found along the park's main roads so park staff knows where you are. Otherwise, your car will not be in the parking lot to greet you upon your return.

Hidden Valley (4200 ft.). In the center of the park off of Quail Springs Rd. With secluded alcoves in which to pitch a tent, and shade provided by enormous boulders, this is far and away the best and most wooded of the campsites. 39 sites in the Wonderland of Rocks. A haven for rock-climbers. Near Barker Dam Trail.
Jumbo Rocks (4400 ft.). Located near Skull Rock Trail on the eastern edge of Queen Valley. Take Quail Springs Rd. 15 mi. south of the visitors center. 125 well-spaced sites (65 in summer) surrounding (you guessed it) jumbo rocks. Front spots have best shade and protection. Wheelchair accessible.
Indian Cove (3200 ft.). 120 sites (45 in summer) on the northern edge of the Wonderland of Rocks (see Sights and Activities). Waterfalls after rain. Enter from north of park. 13 group sites, most are $15, and the two largest are $30.
Ryan (4300 ft.). 29 sites. With not as many rocks, and therefore, not as much privacy or shade, as nearby Hidden Valley. 3-mi., round-trip trail leads up 5470-ft.

Ryan Mountain. Horses allowed. Right down the road from Key's View (see Sights and Activities, below), if you're inspired to try and catch the spectacular sunrise.

White Tank (3800 ft.). 15 sites. Excellent for RVs, except for the slightly bumpy road going in. Give it credit for having a small, cozy feel in middle of the desert.

Black Rock Canyon (4000 ft.). 100 sites in a woodland environment. Take Joshua Lane off of Rte. 62, 2 mi. north of Yucca Valley. Horses permitted. Flush toilets, running water. Sites $10. Reservations accepted. Wheelchair accessible.

Cottonwood (3000 ft.). 62 sites (30 in summer) in the midst of arid, open desert. No shade. Located in the Colorado Desert portion of the park. Trail to Cottonwood Spring Oasis. Flush toilets, running water. Sites $8; 3 group sites for 10-70 people, featuring covered tables, $15. Wheelchair accessible.

Sheep Pass (4500 ft.). 6 group sites, each $10. Located in center of park near Ryan Mtn. trail. Call up to 3 months in advance for reservations.

Belle (3800 ft.). 17 sites within view of the Pinto Mountains. Accessible from north entrance by a rough 4-wheel-drive only road. Closed in summer.

ACCOMMODATIONS AND FOOD

Those who are neither equipped nor eager for desert camping, but who want to spend more than a day at the park, can find inexpensive motels next door in **Twentynine Palms.** There are some very cheap options, but don't press your luck—some of the local establishments have been known to feature more fauna than the park itself. **Motel 6,** 72562 Twentynine Palms Hwy. (367-2833) is reliably clean and well-equipped with A/C, color TV, and a pool. ($30 per person plus $4 per additional person.) **Best Western Gardens Motel,** 71487 Twentynine Palms Hwy. (367-9141), is a Spanish-style oasis with heated pool and spa (doubles from $62). This option is more affordable for travelers sharing the cost of a double.

There are no food facilities in the park, but Twentynine Palms suffices for groceries and grub. The **Circle K,** 73943 Twentynine Palms Hwy. (367-7319; open 24-hrs.), 2 mi. from the visitors center, is a convenient place to buy water and other essentials. For serious grocery shopping, however, the **Stater Bros.** market, 71727 Twentynine Palms Hwy. (367-6535), will save you a bundle and offers a better selection (open Mon.-Sat. 8am-9pm, Sun. 9am-8pm). **Rocky's New York Style Pizzeria,** 73729 Twentynine Palms Hwy. (367-9525; open Sun.-Thurs. 11am-11pm, Fri.-Sat. 11am-midnight), has pizza, pasta, $1.25 mugs of Michelob, and locals. Try **El Ranchito,** 73741 Twentynine Palms Hwy. (367-2424; open 11am-10pm daily), for impressive Mexican food.

SIGHTS AND ACTIVITIES

Over 80% of the park (mostly the southern and eastern areas) has been designated by Congress as a wilderness area—meaning trails but no roads, toilets, or campfires. For those seeking backcountry desert hiking and camping, Joshua Tree offers fantastic opportunities to explore truly remote territory. There is no water in the wilderness except when a flash flood comes roaring down a wash (beware your choice of campsite), and even then, it doesn't stay long. The most temperate weather is in late fall (Oct.-Dec.) and early spring (March-April). Temperatures in other months often span uncomfortable extremes.

Joshua Tree draws thousands of climbers each year and is one of the most popular destinations in the world for **rock-climbing.** The visitors center can provide information on established top rope routes and will identify wilderness areas where placement of new bolts is restricted. Ground-bound visitors may enjoy watching the grace and technique of experts at the **Wonderland of Rocks** and **Hidden Valley.** For instruction and equipment rentals contact **Ultimate Adventures,** Box 2072, Joshua Tree (366-4758) or **Wilderness Connection,** Box 29, Joshua Tree (366-4745).

A self-paced driving tour is an easy way to explore the magic of Joshua Tree without specialized equipment (although 4-wheel-drive wouldn't hurt). Paved roads branch through the park's varied sights, and roadside signs indicate points of interest scattered throughout the park. A 34-mi. stretch crosses the center of the park from Twentynine Palms to the town of Joshua Tree. The longer drive through the park, between Twentynine Palms and I-10, traverses a sampling of both high and low desert landscapes. Some of the most outstanding scenic points can be reached by the side roads. One sight that must not be missed is **Key's View** (5185 ft.), 5 mi. off the park road just west of Ryan Campground. On a clear day, you can see forever—or at least to Palm Springs and the Salton Sea, also a fabulous spot to watch the sun rise. The **Palm Oases** (Twentynine Palms, Fortynine Palms, Cottonwood Spring, Lost Palms, and Monson Canyon) also merit a visit, as does the **Cholla Cactus Garden,** off Pinto Basin Rd. Four-wheel-drive-vehicles can access dirt roads, such as Geology Tour Road. This 18-mi. road climbs through fascinating rock formations and ends in the Little San Bernardino Mountains. Unpaved mountain biking trails provide bikers with a safer option than the tortuous paved roads. Biking is allowed only on designated roads and paths.

Hiking through the park's trails is perhaps the best way to experience Joshua Tree. Hikers can tread through sand, scramble over boulders, and walk among the hardy Joshua trees. Visitors will probably find the **Barker Dam Trail** packed with tourists. Painted petroglyphs and a tranquility that rises above the crowd make the reservoir worth a trip. Get an early start and you should miss the masses. The **Lost Horse Mine** is reached by a 1½-mi. trail and evokes the region's gold prospecting days. Rusted machinery and abandoned mineshafts eerily clutter the landscape. Wildflowers, cooler temperatures, and the indelible picture of the encircling valleys reward the hardy hiker who climbs the 3 mi. to the summit of **Ryan Mountain** (5461 ft.). Bring plenty of water for this strenuous, unshaded climb. Information on many other hikes, ranging from a 15-minute stroll to the **Oasis of Mara** (wheelchair accessible) to a three-day trek through the park's 35 mi. of the **California Riding and Hiking Trail,** is available at the park center. Ask about ranger-led weekend programs, hikes, and special events on spring and fall weekends. Count on slow progress even on short walks; the heat is often oppressive, and shade is a rare luxury. Pack extra water on all hikes.

Even if you view Joshua Tree merely as a break from the interstate's monotony, do get out of your car once in a while to take a closer look at things. Note the adaptations that plants have made in order to survive the severe climate and admire their delicate blooms. More animals can be seen at dawn and dusk than at high noon, but watch for kangaroo rats and lizards at all times. Look for the cactus wren in the branches of **Pinto Basin's** *cholla*. You may meet an enormous swarm of ladybugs near the oases; and be aware that enormous swarms of bees are equally common. Golden eagles and bighorn sheep also draw life from the oases. Coyote and bobcats stalk their prey at night. If you come equipped with time, patience, and a sharp set of eyes, the desert's beauty will gradually reveal itself.

Wildflower season (mid-March-mid-May) is an especially colorful season in the park. Thousands journey to see the floor of the desert exploding with yucca, verbena, cottonwood, mesquite, and dozens of other wildflowers. To avoid the stigma of floral ignorance and to insure that there will be flowers in the first place (dry years result in very drab springs), call the **Wildflower Hotline** (818-768-3533).

Many areas throughout California are said to be most spectacular at **sunrise** and **sunset**; this is true of nowhere more than Joshua Tree. Visitors miss out terribly when they head for dinner at 6pm. Seeing the trees' contorted silhouettes against the deep oranges of the setting sun may well be the highlight of your trip.

■ NEAR JOSHUA TREE

The **Yucca Valley,** northwest of the park, is graced with a couple of tourist attractions and a genuinely helpful **Chamber of Commerce,** 56020 Santa Fe Trail, #B, 92284 (365-6323; open Mon.-Fri. 8:30am-5pm). The **Hi-Desert Nature Museum,** 57117 Twentynine Palms Hwy. (228-5452), has gemstones, captive scorpions and snakes, and chunks of bristlecone pine, including a cone from the world's oldest living tree. In wildflower season, dozens of cut flowers collected by museum staff-members rest in vases along the tops of the display cases. If you wish to see the wildflowers growing wild, take one of the two trails that start from the museum. The **South Park Nature Trail** (1.3 mi.) overlooks the Joshua Tree National Park. The **North Park Nature Trail** (over 2 mi.) offers breathtaking views of the entire Morongo Basin area (museum open Wed.-Sun. 1-5pm; free).

Yucca Valley's other attraction is a series of bizarre hillside tableaux of 10- to 15-ft. concrete figures depicting biblical stories. **Desert Christ Park,** 57090 Twentynine Palms Hwy. (mail only; no phone), is located at the end of Mohawk Trail; turn north off Twentynine Palms Hwy. (open dawn-dusk; free).

■■■ MOJAVE DESERT

Scorching, silent, and barren, the Mojave is a picture of desolation. John Steinbeck called it a "terrestrial hell," and, in the summer months, only the most sun-crazed desert rats would disagree with this description. Today, the empty spaces and scattered trailer towns of the area serve as a bleak backdrop for a rootless subculture of military itinerants. Travelers usually hurry through, anxious to reach gentler climes.

It's hard to argue with such instincts. But the desert offers an opportunity to banish the confusion of civilization. The Mojave leaves a mark on undaunted adventurers patient and brave enough to explore it. Genuine attractions are rare and the summer heat would wither many mortals. However, winter temperatures are pleasant, even chilly. Hike across dizzying sand dunes; poke around the colorful gulches rife with fossils, obsidian, and Native American petroglyphs; inspect ghost towns. Notice the temperature gradation as webs of heat rise from the blistering desert floor, their minuscule strands lashing at your bare legs. The desert montage will leave its pattern on your spirit.

BARSTOW

Barstow is the place to prepare for forays into the desert. But do not expect to revel in this town—the commercial hub of the Mojave—or in Baker, a roadside settlement that comes in a distant second (which says a lot). This desert oasis (pop. 60,000) thrives on business from local military bases, tourists, and truckers. Barstow is midway between Los Angeles and Las Vegas on I-15; it is the western terminus of I-40.

Practical Information and Orientation
The **California Desert Information Center,** 831 Barstow Rd., Barstow 92311 (256-8313), off I-15 has the best tourist information on the area, including local off-road vehicle areas. (Open daily 9am-5pm.) An eerily silent and chilly **Amtrak** station lies at 7685 N. 1st St. (800-872-7245), well past Main St., over the bridge that crosses the railroad tracks. Buy tickets on board or at a travel agency. Trains go to: L.A. (2 per day, $34); San Diego ($54); Las Vegas ($45). The **Greyhound,** 681 N. 1st St. (256-8757), has buses to L.A. (11 per day, $21.50) and Las Vegas (10 per day, $32). It's removed from motels and other conveniences, so prepare for a trek or call a cab. (Open daily 8am-2pm, 3:30-6pm, and 8-11:30pm.) **Yellow Cab,** 831 W. Main (256-6868), doesn't have very competitive rates ($2 per mi.), but then again, there's no competition. **Dial-A-Ride** (256-0311) is Barstow's limited bus service with routes throughout the city. (Mon.-Sat. 7am-5pm. Sun. service for seniors and people with disabilities only. Service is a bit unpredictable. 75¢.) **Enterprise Car Rental,** 620 W. Main St. (256-0761), offers economy cars for $130 per week with 1050 free mi. Drivers must be 21 with credit card. **Barstow Laundromat,** 1300 E. Main St. (256-5312), charges $1 for a wash, 25¢ for a 12-min. dry (open 6:30am-9pm). Laundromats come as a standard feature at most of the area's strip malls. In an **emergency** call 911. Other useful numbers are: **police** (256-2211), **sheriff** (256-1796), **fire** (256-2251), and **highway patrol** (256-1617). The **post office** is at 425 S. 2nd Ave. (256-8494; open Mon.-Fri. 9am-5pm, Sat. 10am-noon.) **General Delivery ZIP Code** is 92312. The **area code** is 619.

If you're going to
SAN FRANCISCO

Forget wearing flowers in your hair!! (This is the 90's.)

Just bring the incredible coupon on the other side of this page!

Accommodations What Barstow lacks in charm it makes up for by its abundant inexpensive motels and eateries. (For campgrounds outside of Barstow, see Near Barstow and Eastern Mojave Desert, below.) **Motel 6,** 150 N. Yucca Ave. (256-1752), is relatively close to Greyhound and Amtrak stations, and only a block from a 24-hr. grocery and drugstore. Standard, clean rooms have cable TV. (Singles $22. Doubles $26.) **Motel Calico,** 35556 Yermo Rd. (254-2419), at I-15 and Ghost Town Rd. in Yermo, 8 mi. east of Barstow offers seven attractive rooms decorated with desert photographs taken by the owner. (Singles $24. Doubles $30.) **Economy Motels of America,** 1590 Coolwater Lane (256-1737), lies off E. Main near I-40. (Singles $22. Doubles $29. Quads $33.) **Barstow/Calico KOA** (254-2311), 7 mi. northeast of Barstow on north side of Outer Rte. 15, between Ft. Irwin Rd. and Ghost Town Rd. exits caters to corporate campers with a pool, showers, and snack bar. It can get uncomfortably crowded. (Tent sites for 2 $17, additional person $2.50. RVs $20, with electric and water hookup. Sewer hookup $2 extra.)

Food and Sights Every restaurant chain west of the Mississippi has a representative on Main St. You'll find a more inviting variety on E. Main St. than along W. Main St. The **Barstow Station McDonald's,** 1611 E. Main St. (256-8023), made from old locomotive cars, is the busiest Mickey D's in the U.S., and is complete with a kid's playground, gift shop, and liquor store (open Sun.-Thurs. 5am-10pm, Fri.-Sat. 5:30am-midnight). You may wish to drop by **Vons,** 1270 E. Main St. (256-8105), where you can purchase a variety of supermarket specialties (open daily 6am-midnight). **Carlo's and Toto's,** 901 W. Main. St. (256-7513) is a favorite local diner that offers huge platters of delicious Mexican cuisine (entrees $4-7). (Open Sun.-Thurs. 11am-10pm, Fri.-Sat. 11am-11pm.) The best bet for breakfast is probably the **IHOP** at 1441 E. Main (256-1020), which serves up a filling stack of pancakes for $3.75. Barstow is studded with rough and rowdy bars, such as **Katz,** 1st and Main (256-3275; open 6am-2am).

Barstow is also home to the **Factory Merchants Outlet Plaza,** 2837 Lenwood Rd. (253-7342), just south of town off I-15. Over 50 shops sell the surplus of such designers as Ralph Lauren, Bass, Nautica, and Anne Klein at prices 20-70% below retail in this fashion oasis (open daily 9am-8pm). Dial-A-Ride operates hourly service to the plaza daily from 7am to 5pm.

Near Barstow

What happens when Walter Knott of Knott's Berry Farm gets his hands on a piece of California's history? **Calico Ghost Town,** Ghost Town Rd. (254-2122), 10 mi. northeast of Barstow via I-15, is the answer. Set high in multi-colored hills (hence the name), Calico died in 1907 after having produced $86 million in silver and $9 million in borax. At its height, the city supported about 4000 people and eight saloons. Circumvent the admission package (tram, mine tour, train ride, "mystery shack" and vaudeville show $5, under 13 $3) by climbing the staircase at the tram/tour entrance and walking around for free. This Old West town and amusement park is a restored, commercialized version of the old mining community. For extended visits, there are 110 campsites in a shady canyon (sites $15, RV hookups $19; camping fee includes admission to the town). Call 254-2122 for reservations. ("Town" open daily 7am-dusk, shops 9am-5pm.)

For a less artificial look at a much older period (Pleistocene), visit the **Calico Early Man Site** (256-3591), farther east along I-15 at the Minneola Rd. off-ramp. This is the only New World site "Lucy" discoverer Louis Leakey ever bothered to excavate. The 20,000-year-old stone tools unearthed here make Calico the oldest find in the Western Hemisphere. On display are artifacts from the excavations and photographs of the dig. (Open Thurs.-Sun. 8:30am-4:30pm. Free tours run every 2 hrs. 9:30am-3:30pm.)

Twelve mi. north of Barstow along Barstow Rd. is **Owl Canyon,** colored with jasper, agate, and turquoise. Note that rockhounding (taking rocks) is illegal, and bears a steep penalty. Nearby, **Rainbow Basin** offers an exceptional vantage for stargazing, with almost no light pollution. Bureau of Land Management camping facilities at Owl Canyon are equipped with fireplaces, drinking water, and toilets cost $4.

EASTERN MOJAVE DESERT

The land between I-15 and I-40 east of Barstow is among the most isolated in California. The list of human settlements begins and ends with Barstow and Baker. Visitors who make only these pitstops, however, bypass Mojave's stunning natural attractions. Dramatic geological formations rise from the seemingly infinite landscape and hardy creatures crawl along the scorched terrain. Serene as the emptiness may be, it is still empty, and most drivers press onward, praying that their cars remain faithful.

Afton Canyon Natural Area (256-3591) lies 38 mi. northeast of Barstow on the way to Las Vegas. Follow I-15 to Afton Rd. The flowing water you see in this "Grand Canyon of the Mojave" is no play of sunlight on the sands; here, the Mojave River makes a rare above-ground appearance. Canyon walls tower 300 ft. above the rushing water and its willow-lined shores. Golden eagle, bighorn sheep, and desert tortoise reside around the canyon. Hikers may enjoy exploring the **caves** and side canyons tucked along unmarked trails. Bring a flashlight. Visitors can stay in 22 developed sites ($4) with water, fire pits, tables, restrooms, and equestrian facilities. Riders bring their own horses, as there are no rental facilities in the area. No troughs or guzzlers are maintained in the canyon away from the campsites, so riders must pack sufficient water for themselves and their horses. **Equestrian Trails, Inc.,** P.O. Box 1641 (619-247-6911), in Apple Valley organizes several canyon rides each year.

Near **Kelso** is the most spectacular system of dunes in California. Four mi. long and reaching heights of 700 ft., the dunes are off-limits to off-road vehicles. Hiking in the dunes is permitted and can be a toe-curling barefoot (in winter) experience. From the top, you can hear the dunes sing—the cascading sand mimics the vibration of cello strings. Kelso is about 30 mi. southeast of Baker via Kelbaker Rd. from Barstow; either take I-40 to the Kelbaker Rd. exit 80 mi. to the east or I-15 to Baker.

Providence Mountains State Recreation Area, P.O. Box 1, Essex 92332 (389-2281), a popular, high-altitude (4000-5000-ft.) region, is 10 mi. east of Kelso as the vulture flies. You can camp there in six primitive campsites for $6. But unless you have four-wheel-drive, the direct route will be too much for your vehicle to handle. Instead, you'll have to backtrack from Kelso northward along Kelso Rd. toward Cima, then make a U-turn onto Black Canyon Rd. south to Essex Rd. and into the park. Or, backtrack southward to I-40 via Kelbaker Rd. and find the northbound Essex Rd. exit, 20 mi. farther east along the freeway. Inviting trails for hiking and horseback riding weave through lowland sage and juniper trees, flanked by toothy crags. **Mitchell Caverns Natural Preserve,** located in this area, is a pleasant 65°F respite from desert heat. Tours are offered through stalactite-cluttered limestone chambers (1½-hr. tours Sept. 16-June 15 Mon.-Fri. at 1:30pm, Sat.-Sun. at 10am, 1:30pm, and 3pm; tours $3, ages 6-17 $1). The preserve is closed to all but campers in summer. Gas and supplies are available 23 mi. away in Essex.

The BLM maintains 48 primitive, but beautiful sites ($4) at the **Mid Hill** and the **Hole-in-Wall** campgrounds in the East Mojave National Scenic Area. From Essex Rd., follow Black Canyon Rd. to Mid Hill or Wild Horse Canyon Rd. to Hole-in-Wall. Both sites provide restrooms, tables, and fire rings, and, occasionally, water. Mid Hill is pleasantly cool in the summer at 5600 ft. and rests in a forest. Hole-in-Wall (4200 ft.) is embellished with rock formations and draws climbers in the spring and fall.

Dune buggies and **Jeeps** are still permitted free rein at the **DuMont Dunes,** about 25 mi. north of Baker, just off Rte. 127. Ask a local to show you on a map exactly where they are—there is no sign. Be aware that tracks persist in the desert sands for 20 to 30 years. Striations from World War II training exercises are still visible in parts of the Mojave. Consider what legacy you want to leave behind before plunging into the dunes.

The **Bun Boy Restaurant** in Baker is a good place to stop for coffee and information. If you tried, you couldn't miss Baker's claim to fame: the world's tallest working thermometer.

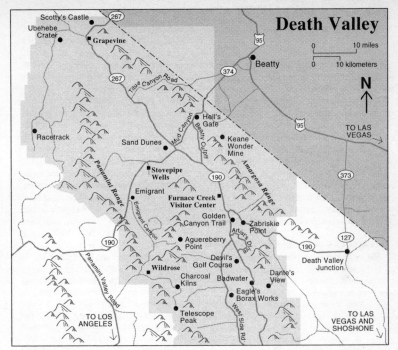

■■■ DEATH VALLEY NATIONAL PARK

Dante and Milton could have found inspiration for further visions of hell in Death Valley. No place in the Old World approaches the searing temperatures that are the summer norm here. Much of the landscape resembles photographs of the surface of Mars, with its stark, desolate reddish crags and canyons. The highest temperature ever recorded in the Western Hemisphere (134°F in the shade) was measured at the Valley's Furnace Creek Ranch on July 10, 1913. Of that day, the ranch caretaker Oscar Denton said, "I thought the world was going to come to an end. Swallows in full flight fell to the ground dead, and when I went out to read the thermometer with a wet Turkish towel on my head, it was dry before I returned."

Fortunately, the fatal threshold of 130°F is rarely crossed, and the region sustains a surprisingly intricate web of life. The elevation ranges from Telescope Peak at 11,049 ft. down to Badwater at 282 ft. below sea level. There are pure white salt flats on the valley floor, impassable mountain slopes, and enormous, shifting sand dunes. Nature focuses all of its extremes and varieties here at a single location, resulting in a landscape that is at once harshly majestic and improbably delicate.

In 1849, a group of immigrants looking for a shortcut to California's gold country stumbled into the valley. After weeks of searching for a western pass through the Panamint Range, the group found a way out of the valley. Looking back at the scene of misery, one member exclaimed, "Good-bye, death valley!", thus naming the area for posterity. After this tragedy, few were anxious to return until 1883, when borax was discovered. The mining of this salt provided fortunes for a few and a livelihood for many in towns like Rhyolite and Skidoo. However, the rapid depletion of the borax mines transformed boom towns into ghost towns, which have been preserved by the area's low humidity. With no promise of new industry, most folks have forsaken the valley itself, leaving it a largely untouched desert wilderness.

WHEN TO VISIT

Few venture to the valley floor during the summer and it is foolish to do so; the average high temperature in July is 116°F, with a nighttime low of 88°F. Ground temperatures hover near an egg-frying 200°F. When traveling through or visiting Death Valley in any season, follow the information given in the Desert Survival section, page 169, with care. In addition, check at the visitors center for the free pamphlet, *Hot Weather Hints*. To enjoy the park, visit in winter, *not* summer.

Late November through February are the coolest months (40-70°F in the valley, freezing temperatures and snow in the mountains) and also the wettest, with infrequent but violent rainstorms that can flood canyons and obliterate roads; know which areas, if any, are washed out before exploring the park. Desert wildflowers bloom in March and April, accompanied by moderate temperatures and tempestuous winds that whip sand and dust into an obscuring curtain for hours or even days. Over 50,000 people crowd into Death Valley's facilities during the **49ers Encampment** festival, held the last week of October and the first two weeks of November. Traffic jams, congested trails and campsites, hour-long lines for gasoline, and four-hour waits at Scotty's Castle also plague the area on three-day winter weekends, Thanksgiving, Christmas through New Year's, and Easter.

PRACTICAL INFORMATION

Visitors Information: Furnace Creek Visitor Center (786-2331), on Rte. 190 in the east-central section of the valley. For information by mail, write the Superintendent, Death Valley National Park, Death Valley 92328. A simple and informative **museum** dispels some myths (such as the claim that all the original settlers perished here) and houses an impressive contour model of the valley. Slide show every ½-hr. and a nightly lecture during the winter. Purchase guides and topographic maps (the park service map/guide is "free" with payment of the entrance fee), get a schedule of activities and guided ranger hikes, check the latest weather forecast, and have a cool drink from the water fountain (one of the few cold ones in the park). Open summer daily 8am-4pm, winter 8am-7pm.

Fee: The $5 per vehicle entrance fee is collected only at the visitors center in the middle of the park. Resist the temptation not to pay; the Park Service needs all the money it can get (besides, it's a nice map). Year-long pass, $15.

TTY Information: For the hearing impaired (786-2471), daily 8am-5pm.

Ranger Stations: Grapevine, junction of Rte. 190 and 267 near Scotty's Castle; **Stovepipe Wells,** on Rte. 190; **Wildrose,** Rte. 178, 20 mi. south of Emigrant via Emigrant Canyon Dr.; and **Shoshone,** outside the southeast border of the valley at the junction of Rtes. 178 and 127. Also **Beatty,** on Rte. 374 in Beatty, NV. Weather report, weekly naturalist program, and park information posted at each station. Also provides emergency help. All closed during most of the summer.

Gasoline: Tank up outside Death Valley at Olancha, Shoshone, or Beatty, NV. Otherwise, you'll pay about 20¢ per gallon more at the stations across from the Furnace Creek Visitors Center, in Stove Pipe Wells Village, and at Scotty's Castle Don't play chicken with the fuel gauge; fill up when you can. **AAA towing service, propane gas,** and **diesel fuel** are available at the Furnace Creek Chevron; **white gas** at the Furnace Creek Ranch and Stove Pipe Wells Village stores.

Death Valley Hikers' Association: write for information c/o Darrell Tomer, P.O. Box 123, Arcata 95521. Ask for a copy of the *Dustdevil*.

Car Rental: Nothing nearby. Check Las Vegas or Barstow.

Horseback Riding: Furnace Creek Ranch (786-2345). One-hr. guided tours $15 per person. Trail rides offered Oct.-May. Minimum age 6 years; ages 6-11 must be accompanied by adult. Closed in summer.

Laundromat: at Furnace Creek Ranch on Roadrunner Ave. Open 24 hrs.

Groceries and Supplies: Furnace Creek Ranch Store, is well-stocked and expensive. Open daily 7am-9pm. **Stove Pipe Wells Village Store,** is smaller and in the same price range. Treat yourself to a can of real venison, hotter-'n-hell chili for $3.50. Open daily 7am-8pm. Both stores sell charcoal, firewood and ice.

Swimming Pools and Showers: $2 fee covers both shower and swimming for non-guests at Stove Pipe Wells Village (daily 9am-9pm); swimming $2, showers $1 for non-guests at Furnace Creek Ranch (daily 9am-10pm; showers 9am-9pm).
Emergency: 911 or 786-2330 for 24-hr. ranger dispatch.
Police: 786-2330.
Post Office: Furnace Creek Ranch (786-2223). Open Mon.-Fri. 8:30am-5pm, June-Sept. Mon.-Fri. 8:30am-3pm. **General Delivery ZIP Code:** 92328.
Area Code: 619.

ORIENTATION

Death Valley spans over two million isolated acres northeast of Mojave in Inyo County. However, visitors from the south will find it only a small detour on the road to the Sierra Nevada's eastern slope, and those from the north will find it convenient to Las Vegas. The park lies about 300 mi. from Los Angeles, 500 mi. from San Francisco, and 140 mi. from Las Vegas.

There is no regularly scheduled public transportation into Death Valley. Bus tours are monopolized by **Fred Harvey's Death Valley Tours.** They begin at Furnace Creek Ranch, which also handles reservations (786-2345, ext. 222), and are offered from early October to late May. A two-hour tour of the lower valley costs $20 (children $12) and leaves at 9am, stopping briefly at Zabriskie Point, Mushroom Rock, Devil's Golf Course, Badwater, and Artists' Drive. A five-hour tour to the north begins at 8:15am and explores Scotty's Castle, Ubehebe Crater, Sand Dunes, and Stovepipe Wells ($27, seniors $24, children $18). The best tour is the five-hour excursion into Titus Canyon (leaves 9am). This region is accessible by four-wheel-drive-vehicle only, making it a side of the park few casual tourists ever see. ($30, children $20. Reservations must be made a day in advance.)

The best way to get into and around Death Valley is by car. With a couple of pals to share gas expenses, renting a car can prove cheaper and far more flexible than any bus tour. The nearest agencies are in Las Vegas (page 414), Barstow(page 180), and Bishop (page 389). Although a four-wheel-drive-vehicle will give you access to narrow roads that lead to some of Death Valley's most spectacular scenery, it is important to remember that these roads are intended for drivers with backcountry experience; these paths are dangerous no matter what you're driving.

Of the 13 **park entrances,** most visitors choose Rte. 190 from the east. The road is well-maintained, the pass is less steep, and you arrive more quickly at the visitors center, located about midway along the 130-mi. north-south route through the valley. But since most of the major sights adjoin not Rte. 190 but the north-south road, the daytripping visitor with a trusty vehicle will be able to see more of the park by entering from the southeast (Rte. 178 west from Rte. 127 at Shoshone) or the north (direct to Scotty's Castle via NV Rte. 267 from U.S. 95). Unskilled mountain drivers should not attempt to enter via the smaller Titus Canyon or Emigrant Canyon Drive roads; neither has guard rails to prevent your car from sliding over the canyon's precipitous cliffs.

Eighteen-wheelers have replaced 18-mule teams, but driving in Death Valley still takes stubborn determination. Read Driving in the Desert (page 170) before venturing in. Overheating is a common problem, especially on trips from the hot valley floor up into the mountains. **Radiator water** (*not* for drinking) is available at critical points on Rte. 178 and 190 and NV Rte. 374, but not on any unpaved roads. There are only three service stations in the park (see Gasoline listings, page 184), and the extreme heat, rapid increases in altitude, and air conditioning will drain your tank rapidly; keep your tank as full as possible at all times.

Believe the signs that say "Four-Wheel-Drive Only." Those who do bound along the backcountry trails by four-wheel-drive should carry chains, extra tires, gas, oil, water (both to drink and for the radiator), and spare parts. Know how to make minor repairs, bring along appropriate topographic maps, leave an itinerary with the visitors center, and bring a CB radio. Get information and suggestions at the visitors center (see Practical Information, page 184). Check ahead for road closings—especially in summer. Do not drive on wet backcountry roads.

Hitchhike and die. It's that simple.

Death Valley has **hiking** trails to challenge the mountain lover, the desert daredevil, the backcountry camper, and the fair-weather day hiker. Ask a ranger for advice, and see Sights and Activities (page 178). Backpackers and day hikers alike should inform the visitors center of their trip, and take along the appropriate topographic maps. During the summer, the National Park Service recommends that valley floor hikers plan a route along roads where assistance is readily available, and outfit a hiking party of at least two people with another person following in a vehicle to monitor the hikers' progress. Carrying salve to treat feet parched by the nearly 200°F earth is also wise (do not wear sandals or lightweight footwear). Better yet, reschedule your trip for a cooler time of year. Check the weather forecast before setting out—roads and trails can disappear during a winter rainstorm. Canyon and valley floors are transformed into deadly torrents during heavy rains.

ACCOMMODATIONS AND FOOD

In Death Valley, enclosed beds and fine meals within a budget traveler's reach are as elusive as the desert bighorn sheep. Cheaper options in surrounding towns draw many visitors outside the park at nightfall. During the winter months, camping out with a stock of groceries is a good way to save both money and driving time. **Fred Harvey's Amfac Consortium** offers golf, tennis, and bingo (Wed. 8:30pm) at the **Furnace Creek Ranch** complex (786-2345, for reservations 800-528-6367), a former terminus that once housed and fed the people working the Death Valley borax mines. This "true refuge" is deluged with video arcades, tour bus refugees, and hundreds of palm trees. The spring-fed pool maintains itself at a constant 85°F and feels refreshing when summer air temperatures shatter 120°F. Older cabins with A/C and two double beds will set you back $76. Remodeled motel-style accommodations start at $98 for a double.

Furnace Creek has a **cafeteria** (open daily 5:30-9am and 11am-8:30pm) and a **coffee shop** (open 7-9pm). Breakfasts average $4, and dinners $8. Last call at the adjacent bar, the **Corkscrew Saloon,** sounds at 12:45am. The ranch comes equipped with a **general store, post office,** and nearby **Chevron station.** Book sight-seeing tours and horseback rides (see Practical Information, page 184) at the front desk, but be aware that Furnace Creek's only truly budget options are the commodious **free public toilets** and inexpensive **shower/pool** day-use fees.

Stove Pipe Wells Village (786-2387), comes complete with pseudo-ranch houses, a large, heated **mineral pool,** and a beauty salon. The hotel charges $58 per night for one or two people, each additional person $10. The pool stays open until midnight in the hot summer months; it's open to the public for $2 per person. The hotel office is open October to May; in other months inquire at the **general store.** Stove Pipe Wells also operates an **RV park** ($10 per night, inclusive of pool use), not to be confused with the nearby park service sites. Across from the hotel are a general store and a **service station** (both open year-round daily 7am-9pm). The resort's **restaurant** offers an expensive breakfast and dinner buffet in the summer and a full menu for breakfast, lunch, and dinner in the winter (open Nov.-May daily 7-10am, 11:30am-2pm, and 5:30-8:30pm), and a gift shop. During the off-months grilled food is served in the **saloon** (open 11am-1am).

CAMPING

The National Park Service maintains nine campgrounds, only one of which accepts reservations (Furnace Creek takes them from Oct.-April). The visitors center (see Practical Information, page 184) keeps tabs on how crowded the sites are. Call ahead to check availability and be prepared to battle for a space if you come during peak periods (see When to Visit, page 184). All campsites have toilets. Water availability is not completely reliable, supplies can at times be unsafe or unavailable. Always pack your own. Where open fires are prohibited bring a stove and fuel. Collecting wood, be it alive or dead, is forbidden everywhere in the park; carry in your own firewood. Roadside camping is not permitted, but **backcountry camping** is free and legal, provided you check in at the visitors center and pitch tents at least 1 mi. from main roads and 5 mi. from any established campsite. The campgrounds listed below are in geographic order from north to south. Stays at all sites are limited to 30 days, except for the 14-day limit at Furnace Creek.

Wildrose (4100 ft.), on the road to the Charcoal Kilns in Wildrose Canyon, 40 mi. north of Trona, 21 mi. south of Emigrant campground. The most secluded location that is still easily accessible for cars and RVs. 30 sites. Convenient base for trips to Skidoo ghost town, Aguereberry Point, and Telescope Peak. Pleasant in summer, chilly to frigid in winter. No water. Tables provided and open fires permitted. Free.

Texas Springs (sea level), in the hills above the Furnace Creek Inn, 200 yd. beyond the Sunset campground on the same road. Best place for tents near the Furnace Creek center activities. Some of the 93 sites are shaded. For wind protection stick close to the base of the hills. Generators prohibited. Water and tables provided. Open fires permitted. Sites $5. Open Nov.-April.

Mesquite Springs (1800 ft.), near Scotty's Castle, 2 mi. south of the Grapevine Ranger Station. 50 sites all without shade. Overlooks Death Valley Wash and alluvial fans. Listen for coyote and owls. Ideal for tents. Tables provided and open fires permitted. Sites $5.

Emigrant (2100 ft.), off Rte. 190, 9 mi. west of Stove Pipe Wells Village across from the ranger station, on the way down from Towne Pass through the Panamint Range. The 10 sites are comfortable in summer. No fires. Free. Open April-Oct.

Thorndike (7500 ft.) and **Mahogany Flat** (8200 ft.), 10 mi. east of Wildrose and over ½ mi. higher, just beyond the Charcoal Kilns in Wildrose Canyon. Depending on conditions, a sturdy car with an able driver may make it to either site, although a 4-wheel-drive-vehicle is preferable for the road to Mahogany Flat. No trailers. Gets cold and dark early; the sun sets quickly in the canyon. Can be snowy even in April and Oct. Tables provided. No water. Free. Open March-Nov.

Furnace Creek (196 ft. below sea level), north of the visitors center. Convenient to Furnace Creek Ranch facilities—pool, showers, laundry. A few of the 168 sites are shaded. HOT in summer. Packed with trailers, first to get crowded. Sites $8. (Don't confuse with $14 sites offered by the Furnace Creek Ranch.) Open year-round. Reservations available Oct.-April through MISTIX (800-365-CAMP, -2267).

Stove Pipe Wells (sea level). Near an airstrip, Jeep trails, and sand dunes. Reminiscent of a drive-in-movie lot. Tenters will have to compete with clumps of RVs for one of 200 gravel sites. Try for a spot close to the trees for protection from spring sandstorms. Short walk to all the hotel and general store amenities. No fires. Sites $4. Open Nov.-April. (Don't confuse with the Fred Harvey-operated trailer park.)

Sunset (190 ft. below sea level), across from the visitors center. An RV city of 1000 sites. No fires. Sites $4. Pool at nearby Furnace Creek. Open Nov.-April.

SIGHTS AND ACTIVITIES

It pays to figure out ahead of time the optimal approach to Death Valley. See Orientation (page 185), for a discussion of the various entrances. If you're doing the Valley in a day, you should adopt a north-south or south-north route, rather than heading directly to the Furnace Creek visitors center via Rte. 190, which connects east with west.

South of the Visitor Center

The **Visitor Center and Museum** (see Practical Information, page 184) is the place to expand your knowledge of tours and hikes. No programs are available in the summer, but many popular programs (such as the **car caravan tours** and **stargazing talks**) are available in the winter. If you're interested in astronomy, speak to one of the rangers; some set up telescopes at Zabriskie Point and offer free-lance stargazing shows. In **wildflower season** (Feb.-mid-April), there are tours of the choicest bloom-sites. **Hell's Gate** and **Jubilee Pass** are beautiful, and **Hidden Valley** even more so, though it is accessible only by a difficult, 7-mi. four-wheel-drive only route from **Teakettle Junction** (25 mi. south of Ubehebe Crater).

The **Harmony Borax Works** and the **Borax Museum** are a short drive from the visitors center. The first successful borax operation in Death Valley, the Harmony plant is not terribly scenic, although the free museum (originally the company's bunkhouse, kitchen, and office) merits investigation. There's a stunning mineral display, plenty of mining implements, Native American artifacts, and historical trinkets and trivia. Alongside the entrance to the ranch are the remains of a 20-mule-team wagon which put in appearances at the 1904 St. Louis World's Fair and at President Wilson's inauguration. Old Dinah, the "Iron Mule" replacement for the real thing, languishes nearby.

Artist's Drive is a one-way loop off Rte. 178, beginning 10 mi. south of the visitors center. The road twists and winds its way through rock and dirt canyons on the way to **Artist's Palette,** a rainbow of green, yellow, and red mineral deposits in the hillside. The effect is most intense in the late afternoon as the colors change rapidly with the setting sun. The dizzying 9-mi. drive turns back upon itself again and again, ending up on the main road 4 mi. north of the drive's entrance. About 5 mi. south of this exit, you'll reach **Devil's Golf Course.** There's no green here. The true green is next to the golf course—witness the miracle of irrigation. The "Golf Course" is a plane of spiny salt crust made up of the precipitate left from the evaporation of ancient Lake Manly, the virile 90-mi.-long pond that once filled the lower Valley.

Three mi. south of Devil's Golf Course lies **Badwater,** an aptly named briny pool four times saltier than the ocean. Magnitudinous in the winter, it contracts to a large puddle a few inches deep in the summertime. The trek across the surrounding salt flat dips to the lowest point in the Western Hemisphere—282 ft. below sea level. This shining pool forms the habitat for the threatened Badwater snails (*Assiminea infirma Berry),* whose bodies are routinely crushed by the trampling feet of wading tourists.

Immortalized by Antonioni's film of the same name, **Zabriskie Point** is a marvelous place from which to view Death Valley's corrugated badlands. The view is particularly stunning when the setting sun fills the dried lake beds with burnt light. Later on, scamper 2 mi. (and 900 ft.) down Gower Gulch to colorful **Golden Canyon** (3 mi. south of Furnace Creek). Just before Zabriskie Point is the turn-off for four-wheel-drive **Echo Canyon,** and beyond is the turn-off for the two-wheel-drive **Twenty Mule Team Canyon Road,** which twists 3 mi. past abandoned borax prospects, exiting onto Rte. 190.

Perhaps the most spectacular sight in the entire park is the vista at **Dante's View,** reached by a 15-mi. paved road from Rte. 190. Just as the Italian poet stood with Virgil looking down on the damned, so the modern observer gazes upon a vast inferno punctuated only by the virgin-white expanse of the salt flats. At 5475 ft. you can see Badwater, Furnace Creek Ranch, the Panamint Range, and, on a clear day, the Sierra Nevada. On a really clear day, you can see the highest point in the continental United States (Mt. Whitney, 14,494 ft.) and the lowest (Badwater, 282 ft. below sea level). It can be snowy here in mid-winter and cold anytime but mid-summer. Behind lie the Panamint Mountains and the 14-mi. trail up to **Telescope Peak** (11,049 ft.). If you are prepared to hike in Death Valley, climb up the peak in the cool early morning to watch the light play upon the diminutive landscape below.

North of the Visitor Center

For an entertaining one-day excursion, take **Beatty Road** (turn-off 12 mi. north of the visitors center) east toward the Nevada border. Five mi. along you'll reach the turn-off to the **Keane Wonder Mine and Mill,** a site that died fast, but not before yielding sacks of gold. You'll need a four-wheel-drive to reach the mine, and take care when poking around the mill's ramshackle wooden trams. Continuing along Beatty Rd., cross Hell's Gate before traversing Daylight Pass, the apex of which marks the California-Nevada border. Ten mi. downhill will bring you to **Rhyolite** and then to **Beatty, Nevada.** The return trip to Death Valley via **Titus Canyon**

Road (open Oct.-April) shows off the gorge's jagged cliffs and startling vistas. The 26-mi. trek down this rough, narrow way, full of dips and switchbacks, is recommended for four-wheel-drive-vehicles only. Make sure you have gas, water, and a non-flooded canyon. En route you will pass **Leadfield,** a mining boomtown that survived less than a year, and a grotesquely twisted stand of faulted rock monoliths.

About 10 mi. farther along is the turn-off to Death Valley's tallest **sand dunes.** (The dunes were favorites of Ansel Adams. If you try to emulate the master, know that sand will fool your light meter; increase exposure one F-stop to catch such details as footprints and ripples.) The largest behemoths are hundreds of feet high. Although barefoot galumphing on the dunes (especially on winter nights) can be sensuous when the sands are cool, be wary of tumbleweeds and mesquite spines. The most accessible dunes for day hikers lie 2.2 mi. east of Stove Pipe Wells Village. Park in the Sand Dunes Parking area and follow the 2-mi. trail to upswept pompadours of sand. Visit in the late afternoon, when the dunes glow with a golden cast.

Scotty's Castle (from Rte. 190, look for sign near mi. marker 93 and take road junction to Park Rte. 5; follow Rte. 5 for 33 mi. to castle) seems remarkably out of place in the desert, and therein lies its interest. Chicago insurance millionaire Albert Johnson became enamored of the infamous flim-flam man Walter Scott (a.k.a. "Scotty"). When Johnson fell ill, Scotty convinced him to come to the desert and build this palatial hacienda. Johnson and Scotty lived here until they expired in 1945 and 1954, respectively. The waterfall in the living room has been switched off, but you can still see the remote-controlled piano and organ. This $2.5 million pseudo-Moorish folly is complete with minaret and Arabian-style colored tiles. The real fascination of the castle is its imaginative exterior, which can be enjoyed for free, but the interior provides welcome relief from the heat. Park service tours (1 hr.) depart hourly from October to April, less frequently in the off-season. Call 786-2392 for schedule information. You can purchase tickets until one hour before closing, but there are often massive lines to get in. (Open daily 9am-5pm. Tours $8, seniors and ages 6-11 $4.)

Ubehebe Crater, 5 mi. west of Grapevine Ranger Station, just south of Scotty's Castle, is a blackened volcanic blast site nearly 1 mi. wide and 462 ft. deep. The view from the vantage point is spectacular, but steady yourself for the gale-force winds that assault the edges of this giant hole. The windy gravel trail leading to the floor of the crater increases your respect for the hole's dimensions, but not nearly as much as the grueling climb back out. An unpaved road continues for 20 mi. south of the crater to the vast and muddy **Racetrack,** a dried-up lake basin providing access to four-wheel-drive routes into Hidden Valley and up White Top Mountain.

Mosaic Canyon is a ½-mi. long narrows of collaged, polished marble, which can be viewed by a 2½-mi. walk, horseback ride, or drive up an alluvial fan from a turn-off 1 mi. west of Stove Pipe Wells. Winding **Emigrant Canyon Road** leads from the Emigrant Campground to Wildrose Canyon Drive. On the way, you'll pass the turn-off for the four-wheel-drive skedaddle to the ruins of **Skidoo,** yet another ghost town 5700 ft. up in the Panamint Range. A few mi. farther is the turn-off for the unpaved road up to **Aguereberry Point,** known for its fine morning views.

A right turn at Wildrose Canyon Drive followed by a 10-mi. drive will bring you to the 10 conical furnaces known as the **Charcoal Kilns,** which are 25 ft. high, 30 ft. in diameter, and which once held 45 cords of wood. Fire up the barbecue!

Animal life persists in the Valley, despite the desolate environment. Fragile pupfish inhabit tiny pools. Rare desert bighorn sheep step among the rocks at higher elevation. The infamous Death Valley **burros**—beasts of burden transported from their native Middle East in the 1850s and freed when the automobile made them obsolete—unwittingly decimated the park's bighorn sheep population by wolfing down edible shrubs and by fouling the water. Several years ago the park service authorized a three-year burro banishment plan to get their asses out of there with helicopters (they were sold as pets). Over 6000 have been removed, and few remain. Remaining burros may be adopted for $75. Contact the California Federal Building, 2800 Cottage Way #E-2841, Sacramento, CA 95825 (916-978-4725).

■ NEAR DEATH VALLEY: WEST

Only ghost towns like **Darwin** and a few slightly more populated communities remain on U.S. 395 near the Rte. 190 turn-off. In **Olancha**, the **Ranch Motel** (764-2387) on U.S. 395 provides spruce, attractive rooms in cottage-type buildings. (Singles $40. Doubles $45. 4-day "Getaway Special" Mon.-Thurs. for $95.) The motel fills up fast so call ahead. The truckers' rigs outside signal that the finest place to eat in town is the **Ranch House Cafe** (764-2363). The Ranch House's bacon and eggs breakfast ($4.10) will stick with you far into Death Valley (open 24 hrs.). Nearby **A&P Market** sells groceries (open daily 6am-midnight).

The **Rustic Motel** (764-2209) rests 3 mi. south of the Rte. 190 turn-off. A yappy dog protects the lodgings. (Singles $32. Doubles $36. Rooms have A/C and TV.) A wee bit farther north than the Rustic is the **Wagon-Wheel Camper-Tel** (764-2222). There's no greenery in sight (except for the off-green sagebrush) so pitch tents on the gravel. Tent and trailer sites are $10 per night, hookups $12. Hot showers, a pool, and impromptu Navy jet shows are included. The wise traveler tanks up at the **Texaco station** across from the Ranch Cafe (open daily 7am-9pm).

■ NEAR DEATH VALLEY: SOUTHEAST

Amid the natural splendor of this region, you can meet a human wonder at **Death Valley Junction** (junction of Rte. 127 and 190, 29 mi. from Furnace Creek) in the person of mime and ballet dancer Marta Becket. With the exception of Wayne Newton concerts in Vegas, Becket's **Amargosa Opera House** (852-4441) is the sole outpost of desert high culture. Becket fell in love with the tiny, decaying town when her car died here in 1968. She and her husband revitalized the old movie theater that had entertained employees of the Pacific Coast Borax Company during the early 20s. Marta commissioned the painting of a continuous wall and ceiling mural depicting a fanciful audience of cupids, kings, angels, monks, and nuns. In her one-woman shows, Becket incorporates classical ballet, modern dance, and pantomime for frequently packed houses. (Performances given Nov.-April Mon. and Fri.-Sat.; May and Oct. Sat.; Doors open at 7:45pm, shows begin at 8:15pm. $8, under 12 $5.) **Death Valley Tours** (see Orientation, page 185) will take you from Furnace Creek to the Opera House (tours $22, under 12 $12).

The town of **Shoshone** stands at the junction of Rte. 127 and 178, 56 mi. southeast of Furnace Creek. It serves as an automotive gateway to the Valley. The **Charles Brown General Store and Service Station** (852-4224) is open daily 8am-8pm. The **Shoshone Inn** (852-4335) next door has a natural spring swimming pool. (Singles $36. Doubles $44.) The **Red Buggy Cafe and Crowbar** (852-9988) serves generous meals (open daily 7am-9:30pm). The **Shoshone RV and Trailer Park** (852-4367) is ready for tired travelers (sites $15).

Legend says that Paiute Chief Tecopa ceded the lands and springs now comprising **Tecopa** and **Tecopa Hot Springs** (towns 1 mi. east off Rte. 127, 5 mi. south of Shoshone) to the government on the condition that they would not be privately developed. Either the legend is false or the chief was taken for a ride, because today the baths and their accompanying resorts and RV parks are choked with visitors.

■ NEAR DEATH VALLEY: NORTHEAST

When approaching Death Valley from the north, consider kicking back for a brief spell in the town of **Beatty, Nevada.** Located about 90 mi. northwest of Las Vegas on Rte. 95, Beatty offers the weary traveler relaxation and air conditioning, as well as ample gambling facilities, before the desolation of the valley.

According to one resident, the favorite pastimes in this town, which has the feel of a hick's Las Vegas, are "drinkin' an' gamblin'." Compared to those in Reno and Las Vegas, Beatty's several casinos are homespun. Wager as little as $1 at blackjack and jaw with the dealers, folk who play slow and seem genuinely sorry to take your money. (But take it they do; some things are universal.) All casinos are theoretically open 24 hrs., but by 2am the dealers start eyeing the clock. Prostitution is the other great vice of Beatty. In fact, Beatty is a scheduled stop on the Hell's Angels' annual "Whorehouse Run."

Information about the town can be collected at the **Beatty Visitor Information Center** (702-553-2424) on Main and 4th St. (open daily 8am-4pm). The **Beatty Ranger Station** (553-2200) is staffed daily from 8am to 4pm and is well-stocked with books, maps, and safety information for desert-bound drivers. Sleep in peace at the **Stagecoach Hotel** (533-2419 or 800-4-BIG WIN, 4-244-946), ½ mi. north of town on Rte. 95. Singles and doubles start at $35 and are remarkably quiet. Amenities include a pool, jacuzzi, casino and bar. The **Burro Inn** (553-2225), at Rte. 95 and 3rd St., serves up standard lunch counter fare. Don't pass over the gas and water at the service station before heading out of town.

Just outside of town, heading toward Death Valley on Rte. 374, lurks **Rhyolite,** a ghost town. Rhyolite exploded around prospector Shorty Harris' 1904 discovery of gold in the area. For several heady years, the town pitched ahead on a frenetic rush of prospecting, building, and saloon-hopping. Townsfolk fled when a 1911 financial panic struck. The most infamous relic of its heyday is the "Bottle House" constructed from 51,000 liquor and beer bottles by miner Tom Kelly.

Central Coast

The Central Coast offers tangible, palpable proof of what many fail to find in Los Angeles. Here, as one winds along the coast, the smog lifts, the freeways narrow, and the traffic jams loosen, bringing into stark relief the California that has inspired New Agers, surfers, good and bad poets, and lovers of the sublime. The Central Coast is your most picturesque postcards come to life, with the most dramatic scenery *and* relaxed cosmopolitanism the state has to offer.

ROUTE 1: THE PACIFIC COAST HIGHWAY

After skirting the coastal communities of Los Angeles, slowly and spectacularly, the Pacific Coast Hwy. (Rte. 1) curves north from Ventura and Oxnard to genteel Santa Barbara. The PCH winds by vineyards, fields of wildflowers, and miles of beach on the journey northward to San Luis Obispo. William Randolf Hearst's San Simeon, north of San Luis Obispo, anchors the southern end of Big Sur, the legendary 90-mi. strip of sparsely inhabited coastline. Climbing in and out of Big Sur's mountains, Rte. 1 inches motorists to the edge of jutting cliffs hanging precipitously over the surf. On the Monterey Peninsula, Carmel and Monterey cater to waves of tourists intent on seeing rural Carmel and Steinbeck's Cannery Row, neither of which really exists any longer. Just above Monterey, and 79 mi. south of San Francisco, Santa Cruz breeds a youthful surfer and university culture with San Francisco's off-beat quirkiness, resulting in a uniquely conscious beach community. From Ventura to Santa Cruz, state parks and national forests offer peaceful campgrounds and daring recreation. See text below for information on Santa Barbara through Santa Cruz. See Los Angeles (page 103), San Francisco Bay Area (page 305), and Northern Coast (page 324) for more on PCH's route.

■■■ VENTURA

There's not much here other than fairly clean, uncrowded sands to waylay you on your trip along the coast, but for the tired motorist, this beachside suburb might be a logical stop. **Oxnard,** nearby, has similar attractions. However, Ventura has more to offer the traveler. Ventura and Oxnard lie near the confluence of PCH and U.S. 101; PCH resumes an independent route 26 mi. north of Santa Barbara.

Practical Information and Accommodations Ventura Visitors **Bureau,** 89-L S. California St. (648-2150), has a good selection of maps and brochures (open Mon.-Fri. 8:30am-5pm, Sat.-Sun. 10am-4pm). Those interested in visiting the wildlife preserve of the **Channel Islands** should seek out the **National Park Headquarters** at 1901 Spinnaker Dr. (658-5730). The **area code** for Ventura is 805.

The unusually ritzy **Motel 6,** 3075 Johnson Dr. (650-0080; fax 339-0926), off U.S. 101, offers singles for $35, doubles for $39. Beachside lodgings tend to be expensive or of questionable reputation, but one safe, cheap option is the **Pacific Inn Motel,** 350 El Thompson (653-0877 or 800-4-SLEEP-1, -75337-1). It's close to the action, has been recently renovated, and has affable management. Rooms come with TV—refrigerators and microwaves, too, for a bit extra. (Singles $38. Doubles $41-43.)

Food and Entertainment You'll find inexpensive food and lots of civic pride along Main St. in Ventura's downtown. **Franky's,** 456 E. Main St. (648-6282), is an attractive café that serves bowls of vegetarian or non-veggie soup with croissant for $2.75; pita sandwiches are about $6. (Open Mon.-Thurs. 7am-3pm, Sat.-Sun. 7am-7pm.) **Nicholby's Coffee House,** 404 E. Main St., (653-2320), at the corner of Oak, makes a mean Café Vienna ($1.25) and is the locus for a lot of what's cool in Ventura. (Open Mon.-Thurs. 7:30am-midnight, Fri. 7:30am-1am, Sat. 9am-1am, Sun.

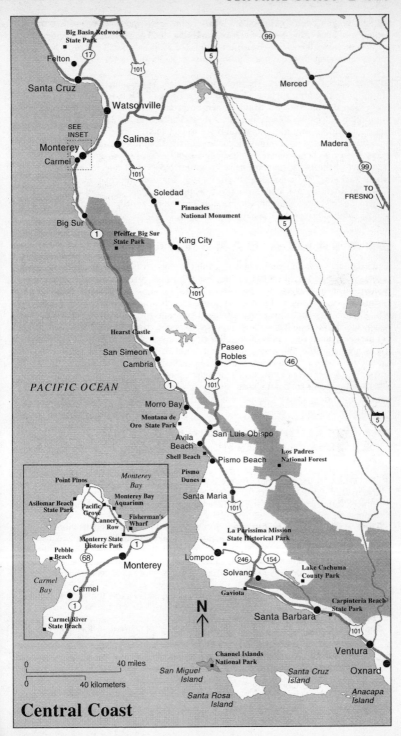

Central Coast

9am-midnight.) The hip **Nicholby's Upstairs** has a bar, pool table, and live music (open from 6pm daily; cover $5). **Flavor of India,** 1795 S. Victoria #106 (650-8825), has a delicious all-you-can-eat buffet lunch for $6 (Mon.-Sat. 11:30am-3pm) and serves reasonably priced dinners (Sun.-Thurs. 5:30-10pm, Fri.-Sat. 5:30-10:30pm).

Sights and Activities The state beaches near Ventura are clean, uncrowded, and offer respectable surfing. **Oxnard State Beach Park** is serene and peaceful, while **San Buena Ventura State Beach** entertains a family-oriented crowd. For equipment, check out **Beach Rentals,** 901 San Pedro (641-1932), which rents everything for outdoor fun from mountain bikes to wetsuits.

Ventura serves as the point of departure for the **Channel Islands,** home to many, many brown pelicans as well as the ruins of a Paleolithic village. Unfortunately, transport to the islands is expensive (round-trip $37, $20 for children). Contact **Island Packers,** 1867 Spinnaker Dr. (642-1393), for more information.

Within town, there's a fair amount of shopping on Main St. Other than that, the only real tourist attractions are the **Mission San Buena Ventura** on 225 Main St. and the adjacent **Albinger Archaeological Museum,** 113 Main St. (648-5823).

■■■ SANTA BARBARA

Santa Barbara's first human inhabitants, the Chumash tribe, thrived on the region's serene waters and fertile soil. In 1782, Spanish missionaries, with an unerring eye for natural beauty, chose the site for a mission. In subsequent years many of the Chumash were converted and many more died from diseases the friars brought with them. Over the ruins of the extinct Chumash, the Spanish, followed by the Americans, built Santa Barbara into a prosperous port town. In the 1920s, Santa Barbarans discovered an oil deposit and the city boomed even louder. After a devastating earthquake in 1925, residents rebuilt Santa Barbara in Spanish colonial style. Today, the city's alluring display of red tile and white stucco dominates the landscape. The resort getaway of choice for many wealthy Los Angelenos, Santa Barbara will not disappoint fans of the soap opera—it's crowded with beautiful people. The climate and unaggressive lifestyle also attract the homeless, European tourists, and students of all ages.

PRACTICAL INFORMATION AND ORIENTATION

Visitors Information: Chamber of Commerce, 504 State St. (965-3021). Mailing address: Santa Barbara Conference and Visitors Bureau, 510A State St., Santa Barbara 93101. Open Mon.-Fri. 9am-5pm. **Second branch** at 1 Santa Barbara St. (965-5334), at Cabrillo Blvd. right by the beach. Open Mon.-Sat. 9am-6pm, Sun. 10am-6pm; Oct.-April Mon.-Sat. 9am-4pm, Sun. 10am-5pm. Maps, brochures, pamphlets. Info. also available at **The City Store,** 106 State St. Open Mon.-Sat. 10am-6pm, Sun. noon-5pm.

Airport: Santa Barbara Aviation, 500 Fowler Rd., Goleta (683-4011). Intrastate as well as limited national service, including **American** and **United.**

Amtrak: 209 State St. (963-1015; for schedule and fares, 800-872-7245), downtown. Be careful after dark. Open daily 7am-1:45pm, 2:30-6:30pm, 7-11pm. Tickets sold until 9:30pm. To L.A. ($20) and San Francisco ($67; reserve in advance for this one).

Greyhound: 34 W. Carrillo St. (966-3962), at Chapala. Lockers for luggage storage (for ticketed passengers only). To L.A. (11 per day, $10.50) and San Francisco (7 per day, $43.75). Open daily 5:45am-11:30pm.

Green Tortoise: 800-227-4766 or 415-956-7500. Call for more information about their "Alternative Commuter" route which links Los Angeles and Seattle and all points in between.

Santa Barbara Metropolitan Transit District: Transit Center, 1020 Chapala St. (683-3702), at Cabrillo, behind the Greyhound station.

Taxi: Yellow Cab Company, (965-5111). 24 hrs.

Car Rental: U-Save Auto Rental, 510 Anacapa (963-3499). $20 per day with 100 free mi., $109 per week with 700 free mi.; 15¢ per additional mi. Must be 21 with major credit card. Open Mon.-Fri. 8am-5:30pm, Sat.-Sun. 9am-1pm.

Bike Rental: Cycles-4-Rent, 101 State St. (966-3804), 1 block from the beach. Rent a 1-speed beach cruiser for $4 per hr., $17 per day. 21-speed $7 per hr., $30 per day. Open Mon.-Fri. 9am-6:30pm, Sat.-Sun. 8:30am-7:30pm.

In-line Skates Rental: Ocean Wear Sports, 22 State St. (966-6733). $5 for 1st hr.; $3 per additional hr. Helmet, knee pads, wrist guards included. Open daily 8am-8pm.

Kayak Rental: Paddle Sports of Santa Barbara, 100 State St., (899-4925). $20 for 2 hrs.; $40 per day. Rentals Sat.-Sun. 9am-5pm (call for weekday rental info.).

Public Library: 40 E. Anapamu (962-7653), across from the courthouse. Open Mon.-Thurs. 10am-9pm, Fri.-Sat. 10am-5:30pm, Sun. 1-5pm.

Laundromat: Economy Laundromat, 500 N. Milpas (936-9169). $1.50 per load (7am-10pm), or let them do it for you for 90¢ per lb. (8am-5pm).

Gay and Lesbian Resource Center: 126 E. Haley, #A-17 (963-3636), on the downtown side of the freeway. Counseling for alcohol and drug abuse. AIDS hotline, testing, and social services. Open Mon.-Fri. 10am-6pm.

Crisis Hotline: 569-2255. 24 hrs.

Pharmacy: Samson Clinic Pharmacy, 317 W. Pueblo (682-6507). Open 24 hrs.

Hospital: St. Francis Hospital, 601 E. Micheltorena St. (962-7661), 6 blocks north of State St.

Emergency: 911.

Police: 215 E. Figueroa (897-2300). **Fire:** 121 W. Cabrillo (965-5254).

Post Office: 836 Anacapa St. (564-2266), 1 block east of State St. Open Mon.-Fri. 8am-5:30pm. Package pick-up Sat. 10am-5pm. **General Delivery ZIP Code:** 93102.

Area Code: 805.

Santa Barbara is 96 mi. northwest of Los Angeles and 27 mi. past Ventura on **U.S. 101.** Because the town is built along an east-west traverse of shoreline, its grid pattern is slightly skewed. The beach lies at the southern end of the city, and **State Street,** the main street in Santa Barbara, runs northwest from the waterfront. All streets are designated east and west from State St. The major east-west arteries by the ocean are U.S. 101 and Cabrillo Blvd.

Pick up **bus** route maps and schedules from the visitors center or the transit center behind the Greyhound station on Chapala, which serves as the transfer point for most routes. Several lines have evening and weekend service. One out of three buses on each route is wheelchair accessible. (Fare 75¢, disabled and over 61 30¢, under 5 free. Free transfers.)

A 25¢ **downtown/waterfront shuttle** runs along State St. (Sun.-Thurs. 10:10am-5:40pm, Fri.-Sat. 10:10am-8:40pm; every 10min. 11am-5:40pm, otherwise every 30min.). Stops designated by circular blue signs include route maps.

Biking is a breeze, as most streets are equipped with special lanes. The **Cabrillo Bikeway** runs east-west along the beach from the Bird Refuge to the City College campus. Driving in Santa Barbara can be bewildering; dead-ends and one-way streets abound. **Parking** is easier; many downtown lots offer 90 minutes of free parking, but keep track of the time—you can be sure ticketers will.

ACCOMMODATIONS

If you have a car, a 10-minute drive north or south on U.S. 101 will reward you with cheaper, though perhaps more bland lodgings than those in Santa Barbara proper. As always, **Motel 6** is an option. There are five in the area, to be exact.

The Schooner Inn, 533 State St. (965-4572; fax 962-2412), central downtown. Sizable hotel in a beautiful building. Plush lobby has piano and wicker chairs. Singles and doubles $40, with bath $50-65. For weekend stays, make reservations at least a week in advance.

Santa Barbara International Backpackers Hostel, 409 State St. (963-0154), 5-min. walk from beach and 2 blocks from Amtrak terminal. Relatively safe and clean, located in one of the most happening parts of town. International clientele; **passport required.** $14 per night covers a bed, a hot shower, and an optional afternoon activity which usually involves alcohol and the outdoors. Fringe benefits include MTV in the lounge and a surfboard you can rent for $7 per day.

Hotel State Street, 121 State St. (966-6586; fax 962-8459), just off the beach. Cable TV. Continental breakfast included. European travelers comprise 80% of the clientele. Occupants share hallway bathrooms, but have private bedrooms which are small yet spruce. $45 for one double bed, $55 for two. A room with two twin beds is $45. In winter, rooms are $5 less. Reservations recommended.

Hope Ranch Motel, 4111 State St. (967-2901), off the San Marcos Pass. Take bus #6 or 11. This blue and white building has been around since the 40s, but you wouldn't know it from the well-maintained rooms with cable TV. Friendly. Singles from $34. Doubles from $39 (weekends and kitchenettes higher).

Californian Hotel, 35 State St. (966-7153), near beach. One of S.B.'s older hotels. TV, phone, private bath, good location. Singles $35-50. Doubles $45-70. $10 per person after 2.

New Faulding Hotel, 15 E. Haley St. (963-9191; fax 963-3467), central downtown. Friendly management. Many semi-permanent residents. Hotel guests must sign in. Singles and doubles start at $27.50, weekly $130. Cable TV. No reservations.

CAMPING

The *Santa Barbara Campsite Directory* lists prices, directions to sites, and reservation numbers for all campsites in the area. It's free and available at the visitors center. State campsites can be reserved through MISTIX (800-444-7275). **Carpinteria Beach State Park** (684-2811), 12 mi. southeast of Santa Barbara along U.S. 101, has 262 developed tent sites with hot showers. (Sites $16, $20-25 with hookups.) There are three state beaches under 30 mi. west of Santa Barbara (sites at all three $16), but none are served by buses. **El Capitan** (968-3294), the closest, has 200 well-kept sites with hot showers; some have dramatic views of the Channel Islands. **Gaviota** (968-3294), with 56 sites, and **Refugio** (968-1350), with 85 sites, are farther away and not as well-kept. Gaviota may be closed for construction. Refugio is especially popular among snorkelers. If all of these are full, you may want to try the **private campground** next door to El Capitan (also called El Capitan), which has a swimming pool (685-3887; sites $16-19, hookups $3, extra vehicle $6). Be warned, however, that sites are dusty and close-packed.

North of Santa Barbara are more than 100 sites in the **Los Padres National Forest.** The nearest of these are almost 20 mi. from downtown, but many are free and the others are inexpensive ($8). Get a map for $2 at the Supervisor's Office, U.S. Forest Service, 6144 Calle Réal, Goleta 93117 (683-6711; open Mon.-Fri. 8am-4:30pm). Direct specific questions to the **Los Prietos Ranger Station,** U.S. Forest Service, Santa Barbara Ranger District, Star Route, Santa Barbara, CA 93105 (967-3481; open Mon.-Fri. 8am-5pm, Sat. 8am-noon and 1-5pm). Reservations are not accepted. Unlikely to be full, **Lake Cachuma County Park** (688-4658) has 435 campsites ($12, $16 with hookup), on a first-come, first-camped basis.

FOOD

Santa Barbara's sunny meteorological and socioeconomic climate causes sidewalk cafés to burgeon like hothouse flowers. Try one of the many *taquerías*.

Restaurants cluster on State St., Milpas St., and E. Canon Perdido St.; State St. tends to be a little more upscale. Ice cream aficionados should head to award-winning **McConnel's** (1213 State St.; 965-5400). There's a **farmer's market** on old town State St. (Tues. 4-7:30pm), and another at Santa Barbara St., downtown (Sat. 8:30am-noon). **Trader Joe's** (29 S. Milpas; 564-7878) and **Tri-County Produce** (335 S. Milpas; 965-4558) sell luscious fruit and prepared foods.

Flavor of India, 3026 State St. (682-6561). Even better than its sister restaurant in Ventura, this clean, friendly establishment is the place to go for astoundingly good tandoor and vegetarian dishes. You'll wish you had a bigger stomach during the all-you-can-eat lunch buffet ($6). Curry dishes are about $8. Buffet Mon.-Sat. 11:30am-3pm. Open for dinner Sun.-Thurs. 5:30-10pm, Fri.-Sat. 5:30-10:30pm.

Esau's Coffee Shop, 403 State St. (965-4416), near the hostel. "The best breakfast in town!" exclaim visitors and locals. Friendliest staff around. Blueberry wheat-germ pancakes ($5 for a big stack of 5) are the house specialty. Early birds (Mon.-Fri. 6-9am) get 2 pancakes, 2 eggs, and 2 strips of bacon for a mere $3.25. Open Mon.-Fri. 6am-1pm, Sat.-Sun. 7am-1pm.

La Super-rica Taquería, 622 N. Milpas (963-4940). Julia Child's favorite Mexican restaurant. Popular place to chat. Dishes $1.30-5.10. Open Sun.-Thurs. 11am-9:30pm, Fri.-Sat. 11am-10pm.

The Natural Café, 508 State St. (962-9494). Both vegetarians and carnivores can approve of the plants and oak interior. Healthy, attractive clientele dines on healthy, attractive food. Smoothies ($3) and sandwiches ($3.50-5). Veggie Grill ($5). Open daily 11am-11pm.

R.G.'s Giant Hamburgers, 922 State St. (963-1654). Voted best burgers in S.B. 6 years running. Basic burger ($3.11). Be adventurous and spring for an excellent guacamole burger or a chili cheeseburger ($4). Expect a 10-min. wait—they're cooked to order. Open Mon.-Sat. 7am-10pm, Sun. 7am-9pm.

Italian/Greek Market, 636 State St. (962-6815). The best deli in town. The name says it all: hot and cold sandwiches $3-5, gyros $4, Greek salad $3.25, spaghetti and meatballs $4.50. Packed at lunch. Open Mon.-Sat. 8am-6pm, Sun. noon-5pm.

Piranha, 714 State St. (965-2980). This primarily sushi-serving hook caters to a range of tastes. Vegetarians might try the enoki mushrooms ($3.75), while *maki*-lovers could enjoy the Pink Padillac (sea eel, crab, avocado, and cucumber rolled in soybean paper; $5.25 for 6 rolls). Open Tues.-Fri. 11:30am-2pm and 5:30-10:30pm, Sat. 12:30-2:30pm, Sun. 5:30-10:30pm.

SIGHTS

State Street is Santa Barbara's monument to city planning. Everything that doesn't move—mailboxes, telephones, the restrooms at the public library—has been encased in Spanish tile. To get the full impact of the city's architectural homogeneity, climb to the observation deck of the **Santa Barbara County Courthouse** at 1100 Anacapa St. (962-6464). The courthouse itself is one of the West's great public buildings. Built by William Mooser in 1929, its highlights include a sculpted fountain, sunken gardens, historical murals, wrought-iron chandeliers, and hand-painted ceilings. Compared to the more prosaic Mission Revival buildings found elsewhere in California, the courthouse is a work of genius. (Building open Mon.-Fri. 8am-5pm, Sat.-Sun. 9am-5pm. Tower closes at 4:45pm. Free.) Pick up "Santa Barbara's Red Tile Tour," a map and walking tour guide, at the Chamber of Commerce.

The **Public Library** and the **Santa Barbara Museum of Art** also blend different styles of architecture into an eye-pleasing ensemble. The library, 40E Anapamu St. (962-7653), and the museum, 1130 State St. (963-4364), are linked by a pedestrian plaza. Inside the library, the **Faulkner Gallery** usually displays works for sale by local artists; get 'em while they're young. (Open Mon.-Thurs. 10am-9pm, Fri.-Sat. 10am-5:30pm, Sun. 1-5pm. Free.) Built as a post office in 1914, the art museum owns an impressive collection of classical Greek, Roman, Asian, and European art, but prides itself on its American art and the portraits in the Preston Morton Gallery. (Open Tues.-Wed. and Fri.-Sat. 11am-5pm, Thurs. 11am-9pm, Sun. noon-5pm. Tours Tues.-Sun. 1pm. $3, seniors $2.50, ages 6-16 $1.50. Free Thurs.)

The **Arlington Center for Performing Arts,** 1317 State St. (box office 963-4408), is one of that rarest of movie theater species—a uniplex. Call the box office for information on upcoming events, or to catch the artsy films (*not* movies) on the silver screen. The murals over the entrance of the Spanish-Moorish building depict scenes from California's Hispano-Mexican era. Its tower is one of the few structures in this low stucco town to rival the palm trees in height.

At the center of Montecito and Chapala Streets stands the famed **Moreton Bay Fig Tree.** Brought from Australia by a sailor in 1877, the tree's writhing branches now span 160 ft., and can provide shade for upwards of 1,000 people.

The beach west of State St. is called **West Beach;** the longer stretch in the other direction, **East Beach.** The latter is preferable because **Chase Palm Park** acts as a buffer between it and Cabrillo Blvd. The park threads nearly 2 mi. of bike and foot paths through green lawns and tall palms. A short detour to the east will lead you to the widely acclaimed **Music Academy of the West,** 1070 Fairway Rd. (969-4726), founded in 1947, whose main building (Miraflores), is surrounded by 10 acres of gardens overlooking the Pacific (see Seasonal Events, page 199). The outdoor **art show and sale** along Palm Park celebrates creativity (Sun. 10am-sunset). At the far end are the **Andree Clark Bird Refuge** and the **Santa Barbara Zoo,** 500 Niños Dr. (962-6310), off Cabrillo Blvd. From U.S. 101, take either Milpas St. or Cabrillo Blvd. exits to Cabrillo Blvd., then turn toward the mountains at Niños Dr. The zoo is also served by bus #21 and the downtown waterfront shuttle. The delightfully leafy zoo has low fences and such an open feel that the animals seem kept in captivity only through sheer laziness. Many of the animals are too injured to survive outside captivity, and others are endangered. Attractions include a miniaturized African *veldt,* where giraffes stroll, lazily silhouetted against the Pacific. A miniature train provides a tour of the park. (Open daily 10am-5pm; Labor Day-June daily 9am-6pm. $5, seniors and ages 2-12 $3, under 2 free. Free parking.)

If the zoo doesn't sate your appetite for wildlife, check out the **Sea Center** (962-0885) on **Stearns Wharf** (the oldest operating wharf on the Pacific), for aquatic mammals and more. A model of a gray whale hangs over video exhibits. Sea-life dioramas, an aquarium which often features hatching fish, and an excellent touchtank are other attractions at this small aquatic museum. (Open daily 10am-5pm. $2, seniors $1.50, ages 3-17 $1.)

At the end of Laguna St. on the northern side of town is **Mission Santa Barbara** (682-4713). (Take bus #22.) Praised as the "Queen of Missions" when built in 1786, the mission assumed its present majestic incarnation in 1820. Towers containing splayed Moorish windows stand on either side of a Greco-Roman façade, and a Moorish fountain splashes in front of the church. The museum contains period rooms and a sampling of items from the mission archives. The lush inner courtyard is cordoned off, but you're free to wander the cemetery, where friars and 4000 Native Americans are buried. (Open daily 9am-5pm. Museum $2, under 16 free.)

Two blocks north of the mission is the **Santa Barbara Museum of Natural History,** 2559 Puesta del Sol Rd. (682-4711); follow the signs. Ecologically aware and educational, this outstanding museum's noteworthy features include a collection of original lithographs by Audubon and other naturalists, the largest collection of Chumash artifacts in the West, an extensive archive on the Channel Islands, and the only **planetarium** between San Francisco and L.A. (Open Mon.-Sat. 9am-5pm, Sun. 10am-5pm. Planetarium shows summer; observatory 682-3224. $5, seniors and ages 13-17 $4, under 12 $3; off-season $1 less.) **Rocky Nook Park,** across the street, is rocky, wooded, and perfect for a picnic.

Nearby is the **Santa Barbara Botanical Garden,** 1212 Mission Canyon Rd. (682-4726). Unfortunately, the garden is not served by bus and is a trek without a car. Three mi. of hiking trails wind through 65 acres of trees, wildflowers, and cacti. The garden's water system built by the Chumash is one of the last vestiges of the region's Native American heritage. (Open Mon.-Fri. 9am-5pm, Sat.-Sun. 9am-6pm. Tours daily 2pm; Thurs., Sat., and Sun. 10:30am and 2pm. $3; students, seniors, and teens $2; ages 5-15 $1; under 5 free.) Also see the ruins of a pottery shack just across the street from the mission and a small cave painting in the hills (off Camino Cielo; locals refer to it as "the painted cave"). The hills around Santa Barbara are filled with **hiking trails.** Two popular ones are **Seven Falls,** at the top of Tunnel St., near the Botanic Garden, and **Cold Springs,** off Mountain Drive.

The **University of California at Santa Barbara (UCSB)** is in Goleta, a shapeless mass (and mess) of suburban homes, gas stations, and coffee shops that surrounds the university. Take U.S. 101 or bus #11 to the university and visit the school's excellent **art museum** (893-2951), which houses the Sedgwick Collection of 20 15th- to 17th-century European paintings (including a Bellini *Madonna and Child*) and hosts innovative contemporary exhibits. (Open Tues.-Sat. 10am-4pm, Sun. 1-5pm. Free.) University Arts and Lectures manages a program of over 150 events centered around the academic year. Call 893-3535 for current offerings. For other entertainment options connected with the university, contact the Music Department (893-3261) and the Associated Students Union (893-2064).

For a lovely view of the city and its harbor, follow the "Scenic Drive" signs to **Alameda Padre Serra,** a road along the hillside bordering the town on the northeast. This part of town is known as the **American Riviera,** and if money could talk this would be a vocal neighborhood indeed.

The beach situation in Santa Barbara is satisfying, although shores can get chilly. **East Beach** in Santa Barbara, with volleyball and biking trails, is universally popular. The beach at **Summerland,** east of Montecito (bus #20), is frequented by the gay and hippie communities. **Rincon Beach,** 3 mi. southeast of Carpinteria, has the best surfing in the county. **Gaviota State Beach,** 29 mi. west of Santa Barbara, offers good surf, and the western end is a (sometimes) clothing-optional beach. Keep in mind, however, that nude sunbathing is illegal in Santa Barbara. **Whale-watching** takes place from late November to early April, as the grays migrate.

ENTERTAINMENT AND NIGHTLIFE

It seems as if no one in Santa Barbara works (or is perpetually on vacation); hundreds spend their afternoons in bars and cafés on State St. drinking espressos, sipping margaritas, or just people-watching. Most clubs and bars are located in the square formed by State, Ortega, Cota, and Haley Streets. The clubs change names frequently, but the location, decor, and theme stay pretty much the same. For the scoop, pick up a free copy of *The Independent* or *The Metro,* available at the Chamber of Commerce, in restaurants, or in boxes on the street.

Santa Barbara Theater Group, Garvin Theater (965-5935), at Santa Barbara City College. Serious theater of uneven quality. Box office open Mon.-Fri.10am-5pm, Sat. noon-5pm; also open 1 hr. prior to each performance.

Green Dragon Art Studio and Espresso Bar, 22 W. Mission (687-1902). A coffeehouse inside an old church. The walls display the patrons' artwork. Entertainment from poetry to music. Open Sun.-Thurs. 7am-11pm, Fri.-Sat. 7am-1am.

Joseppi's, 434 State St. (962-5516). Jazz and blues nightly in a tiny club (the oldest jazz club in Santa Barbara) that occasionally spills into the street. Shows begin at 8pm. Cover $2-3. Open whenever Joe, the owner, feels like it. Smoke-free.

Alex's Cantina, 633 State St. (966-0032), downtown. Also at 5918 Hollister Ave. (683-2577), in Goleta between downtown and UCSB. The Happiest Hour in town, 3:30-8pm daily with drink specials. Drafts $1.25, margaritas and well drinks $1.50. Dancing nightly 9pm-2am. Live bands 6 nights per week, alternative music Sat. Cover varies, usually less than $5. Hollister location has comedy and sports Fri.-Sat.; also has more DJ time.

Calypso, 514 State St. (966-1388). Tropical theme. Crowded with local frat-types. Live performances every night: blues, jazz, rock, reggae. 14-oz. Coors Light 50¢ every night 7-10pm. Open daily 11am-2am.

The Gold Coast, 30 W. Cotu St. (965-6701). Polished and popular, this bar attracts a diverse gay crowd. Noisy at night. Full bar. "Beer bust" Sun. 4-7pm. No cover. Open daily 4pm-2am.

SEASONAL EVENTS

A free and extensive list of annual events is available at the visitors center.

Hang Gliding Festival (965-3733), early Jan.

Santa Barbara International Film Festival (963-0023), March. Sponsored by the Arlington Theater (see Sights, page 197). Premieres of U.S. and foreign films.

Italian Street Painting Festival, Memorial Day weekend. Chalk paintings both professional and amateur decorate the Old Mission Courtyard.

Sandcastle and Sculpting Contest, during the lowest tide of the year at East Beach.

Summer Solstice Parade and Fair (965-3396), on the Saturday nearest the summer solstice (June 21). Pre-Bacchanal fun. Come as an 18-ft. dinosaur or a tidal wave and you'll fit right in.

Old Spanish Days (966-9222), early Aug. Spirited fiesta with rodeos, carnivals, and flamenco guitar.

Music Academy of the West, 1070 Fairway Rd., (969-4726), holds a series of inexpensive concerts throughout the summer. Stop by for a brochure.

Santa Barbara International Jazz Festival (310-452-5056), early Oct.

■ NEAR SANTA BARBARA

The vast **Los Padres National Forest** (683-6711) stretches north of Santa Barbara, into San Luis Obispo County and beyond. The area includes four mountain ranges. Its climatic zones range from semiarid desert to coniferous forests. The **San Rafael Wilderness** alone contains 125 mi. of trails and a sanctuary for the nearly extinct California condor. (See Santa Barbara: Camping.)

To the northwest of Santa Barbara, **Lake Cachuma County Park** (688-4658) offers picnic grounds and camping. The lake is accessible by Rte. 154, a wonderfully scenic drive across the Santa Ynez Mountains down to the Santa Ynez Valley. (Sites with tables, fire pits, water, and restrooms $12 per night, $16 with hookup).

Although one usually associates California wines with Sonoma or Napa Valley, Santa Barbara County cultivates 11,000 acres of vineyards. One of the prettiest is the **Gainey Vineyard,** 3950 E. Rte. 246 (688-0558), just where Rte. 246 intersects with Rte. 154. (tours daily 10:30am-3:30pm every hr. on the ½-hr.). Stop in for a tasting ($2.50 for 4 wines, $3.50 for 7 wines; you keep the glass), offered during tours.

Solvang Village, an overpriced Disneyesque Danish-land, is a stone's throw away down Rte. 246. Look out for the big windmill. Solvang is crammed with excellent *konditoris* (bakeries), shops selling Scandinaviana, and tourists. Solvang is also home to **Mission Santa Ines,** one of the last missions founded in Spanish California. (Tours daily 9am-7pm in the summer, 9am-6pm at any other time. Donation $2.)

Farther to the northwest, at the juncture of Rte. 1 and 246, is the city of **Lompoc,** home of the **Lompoc Flower Fields,** the nation's largest producers of flower seed. The acres upon acres of blooms, which peak near the end of June, are both a visual and an olfactory treat. Purple sweet elysium and crimson sweet pea are only a few of the blossoms. Lompoc holds a **flower festival** at the season's peak.

Also in Lompoc is **La Purissima Mission State Historic Park,** site of **Mission La Purissima Concepción** (733-3713). This 1787 mission was almost completely restored by the Civilian Conservation Corps during the '30s, and now offers a fascinating but disturbing glimpse of life on a Spanish mission. The mission gardens have also been restored, and while only 986 of the mission's original 300,000 acres remain, beautiful trails frequented by Great Horned Owls wind through the hills nearby. At Christmas, hundreds of *luminarias* (candles in paper bags) line the paths, and a concert is held in the chapel. (Open daily 9am-6pm. $5 per vehicle.)

■■■ SAN LUIS OBISPO

Although San Luis Obispo (pronounced in a flat monotone, without Spanish inflection) is a town in geographical limbo, situated halfway between the cultural and physical extremes of San Francisco and Los Angeles, it has a distinctive personality all its own. Surrounded by undeveloped areas, SLO combines small-town friendliness with most of the characteristics found in hip parts of your average city, making it a fine example of a college town that smoothly integrates students and community life, without allowing one to dominate the other.

PRACTICAL INFORMATION AND ORIENTATION

Visitors Information: Visitors Center for the Chamber of Commerce, 1039 Chorro St., San Luis Obispo 94301 (781-2777). Watch for signs on U.S. 101. Open Tues.-Fri. 8am-5pm., Sat.-Sun. 10am-noon and 2-5pm, Mon. 9am-5pm.

State Parks Information: State Parks, 5220 South Itiguera St. #311 (549-3312). Open Mon.-Fri. 8am-4:30pm.

Amtrak: (541-0505; for schedules, fares, and reservations 800-USA-RAIL, -872-7245), at foot of Santa Rosa St. 7 blocks south of Higuera. 1 per day to: L.A. ($31); San Francisco ($58); Salinas ($30). Open daily 8:30am-7pm. Reservations necessary.

Greyhound: 150 South St. (543-2121), ½ mi. from downtown. To get to downtown, walk west on South St. to Higuera St., north on Higuera. To: L.A. (5-6hrs., 9 per day, $31). San Francisco (5-6hrs., 6 per day, $33). Pismo Beach ($3.50). Station has luggage lockers (for ticketed passengers only). Open daily 5:45am-1:30am.

Car Rental: Cheap Wheels, 169 Granada Dr. (543-3792). From $17 per day. 100 free mi. per day, 15¢ per additional mi. Must be 21. **Thrifty Car Rental,** 2750 Broad St. (544-3777). Cars start at $27 per day with unlimited mileage. Must be $21. $4 per day additional surcharge if under 25. Open daily 9am-9pm.

Equipment Rental: Pismo Bike Rental and Beach Supply, 500 Cypress (733-0355). Bikes $5 per hr., $15 per ½-day. Boogie-boards $2 per hr., $6 per ½-day. **Luv 'm Skates and Blades,** 670 Cypress (773-8317), in Pismo Beach. Open Wed.-Mon. 11am-7pm.

Public Library: 995 Palm St. (781-5991). Open Mon.-Wed. 10am-8pm, Thurs. and Sat. 10am-5pm, Fri. 11am-5pm.

Laundromat: Broad St. Laundromat, 2161 Broad (541-2612). Wash 75¢, 12-min. dry 25¢. Open daily 7am-11pm.

Weather: 541-6666, ext. 25. **Road Conditions:** 800-427-ROAD, -7623.

Crisis Hotline: 549-8989. 24 hrs.

Pharmacy: Thrifty, 271 Madonna Rd. (544-1255). Open daily 10am-7pm.

Emergency: 911.

Police: 1042 Walnut St. (781-7310).

Hospital: SLO General Hospital, 2180 Johnson Ave. (781-4800).

Post Office: 893 Marsh St. (543-1881). Open Mon.-Fri. 8:30am-5:30pm, Sat. 10am-5pm. **General Delivery ZIP Code:** 93406.

Area Code: 805.

San Luis Obispo is in the heart of the Central Coast, but it is not *on* the coast. It sits inland on **U.S. 101,** burrowed among ranch-laden mountains halfway between Los Angeles and San Francisco (3-4 hrs. by car). This small town is flanked by Morro Bay, 12 mi. north on Rte. 1, and Avila, Shell, and Pismo Beaches, about 12 mi. south on Rte. 1.

SLO Transit (541-BUSS, -2877; for schedule, 541-2228), would be a funnier acronym if the description weren't so accurate. Buses operate from 6:25am to 6:51pm, with extended night hours only for Routes 1, 4, and 5, and hardly any service on weekends. (Fare 50¢, under 5 free; transfers free.) Weekday service to Morro Bay ($1) and Los Osos ($1.25) is provided by Regional Transit on Rte. #7, which departs from City Hall at Osos and Palm St.

Downtown San Luis Obispo centers on **Higuera St.,** running north to south, with other shopping avenues crossing the spine east to west. Walking about downtown is easy, and bicycle lanes are abundant, but the long grades are not for the weak.

ACCOMMODATIONS

Asked for their rates, proprietors in San Luis Obispo frequently respond, "That depends"—on the weather, the season, the number of travelers that day, even, one suspects, on the position of the earth in relation to the moon; motel prices rise and fall faster than the nearby waves. There is a little less fluctuation in nearby Pismo Beach or Morro Bay, but the average prices are the same. If you can find a $40 room in downtown SLO, grab it. And definitely reserve *well* in advance if you plan to be here in mid-June, when Cal Poly seniors graduate.

Economy Motel, 652 Morro (543-7024). Bungalow-type accommodations. A bargain: cable TV, refrigerators and stoves. Singles $27. Doubles $32. However, most rooms are rented on a weekly basis, so call at least 2 days in advance.

Los Padres Motel, 1575 Monterey St. (543-5017 or 800-543-5090). Your friendly hosts Harry and Nina have renovated their pretty Monterey Street motel and offer color TV and delicious complimentary breakfast. Rooms $38-45.

Adobe Inn, 1473 Monterey St. (549-0321, general information; 800-676-1588, reservations). Bed and breakfast with wonderful management. Personable rooms, each named after a species of cacti. Phone, color TV, cable. Some rooms have coffee machines and refrigerators. Singles $35-60. Doubles $49-65. Cheaper rates are for off-season and do not include breakfast. Reservations recommended.

Budget Motel, 345 Marsh St. (543-6443). What you'd expect from a place called "Budget Motel." Rooms are furnished, comfortable, but nothing spectacular. Color TV, cable, phone, continental breakfast. Singles $36-44. Doubles $44-48.

Motel 6, 1433 Calle Joaquin (549-9595), 2½ mi. out of town. A ½-mi. walk from the nearest bus stop. Check-out noon. Singles $32. Doubles $38. Reserve at least 1 month in advance in summer. 3 additional locations: in Atascadero (466-6701), Morro Bay (772-5641), and Pismo Beach (773-2665).

CAMPING

All state park sites can be reserved through MISTIX (800-444-7275) from two days to eight weeks in advance. In summer, you need reservations at beach parks.

Pismo Beach State Park (489-2684), on Rte. 1 south of Pismo Beach. 2 campgrounds. **North Beach** has 103 tent sites ($16) and restrooms. **Oceano** has 42 tent sites ($16) as well as 42 sites with water and electrical hookups ($20). Oceano also has showers, but North Beach sites are larger and closer to the beach. Call for reservations.

Oceano County Park (489-7354), across Pier Ave. from the Oceano campground. 24 sites with full hookups ($18). No reservations accepted.

Montana de Oro State Park, Pecho Rd. (528-0513), south of Los Osos, 12 mi. from SLO via Los Osos Valley Rd. 50 primitive sites in a gorgeous, secluded park (see page 204). Outhouses, cold running water (but bring your own drinking water). Sites $9, winter $7. Reserve between Memorial Day and Labor Day.

Morro Bay State Park, Rte. 1 (772-2560), 12 mi. west of SLO. 135 developed sites, 20 with hookups. Popular park (see page 204). Hot showers and running water. More accessible than Montana de Oro but also more likely to be full. Sites $16, winter $14; with hookups $20, winter $18. Reserve for visits between Memorial Day and Labor Day.

FOOD

Higuera and the streets running across it are lined with eateries and cafés. The area below the mission by the creek is a popular place with lunchtime crowds. **Cisco's** (on the creek) has live music, inexpensive sandwiches and salads, and many outdoor tables. Every Thursday night, fresh fruits and vegetables overflow at the **Farmers Market.** From 6 to 9pm, Higuera St. is closed to all but vendors' stalls and browsing shoppers. Pick up a copy of the *Bounty of the County: Food & Wine Tour* pamphlet at the visitors center for comprehensive information.

Woodstock's Pizza Parlour, 1000 Higuera St. (541-4420). Popular Tommy's-style hangout deservedly sweeps annual best-pizza awards. Young crowd, lively even late at night. 12-in. cheese pizza $8, 16-in. $10.45. A mini 8-in. ($3.75) is ideal for lunch. Beer by the pitcher. Open Sun.-Thurs. 11am-1am, Fri.-Sat. 11am-2am.

Rhythm Café, 1040 Broad St. (541-4048). Sunday brunch (9:30am-2:30pm) allows 2 people to share a never-ending supply of English scones, orange poppy seed muffins, and coffee cakes for under $10. They're all made fresh on the premises and served with scrumptious praline butter. While you eat, you can watch ducks and children drift by in the San Luis Creek below the balcony. Open Mon.-Sat. 7am-10pm, Sun. 9:30am-2:30pm and 4:30-8:30pm.

Tio Alberto's, 1131 Broad St. (546-9466) or 295 Santa Rosa (542-9321). Huge burritos run $2.50-4, fajitas $4. Large portions in a simple setting. The food more than makes up for the unassuming ambience. Open daily 7am-midnight.

Blazing Blenders, 1108 Broad St. (546-8122). A hole-in-the-wall with incredible shakes ($2-3), bizarre juices (ever tried wheat grass juice?), and frozen yogurt (generous small $1.45). The bee pollen topping will leave you buzzing. Open Mon.-Wed. 7:30am-7pm, Sat.-Sun. 8:30am-7pm.

Golden China, 675 Higuera St. (543-7345). All-you-can-eat buffet from 11:30am-2:30pm: 15 Chinese food, complimentary soup, fresh fruit, and jello. Lunch $5, dinner $7. The restaurant next door offers Chinese take-out for $3.25 per lb. Open Sun.-Wed. 11:30am-2:30pm and 5-9pm, Thurs.-Sat. 11:30am-2:30pm and 5-9:30pm.

Linn's (546-8444), at the corner of Charro and Marsh. A varied menu that has something for everyone. Interesting breakfasts (sliced polenta cakes, $3.75), snappy cappuccino ($2.25), and lots of sandwiches and salads. Meat pies $5.25. Open Sun.-Thurs. 8am-10pm, Fri.-Sat. 8am-midnight.

Debbie's Ice Cream Factory and Deli, 1023 Monterey St. (541-5520). Half-sandwiches for $1.95; full ones $4.25. Thurs. night special is a rocky road drumstick. Try the vanilla butterfinger (cone $1.65). Open Mon.-Thurs. 11am-10pm, Fri. 11am-11pm, Sat. noon-11pm, Sun. noon-10pm.

SIGHTS AND ACTIVITIES

San Luis Obispo grew up around **Mission San Luis Obispo de Tolosa** (543-6850; smack in the center of town). Founded in 1772, the mission was at one time covered in white clapboards and crowned with a steeple in emulation of a New England church. In the late 1800s, however, the town made a concerted effort to revive the mission's Spanish origins; by the 1930s, it was fully restored and still serves as the Catholic parish church for SLO. (Church, museum, and gift shop open daily 9am-5pm. Donation $1.) The Chamber of Commerce brochure, *Heritage Walks,* describes four walking tours of 38 architecturally impressive homes. All the tours begin in Mission Plaza. Most of the houses are in the Queen Anne or Victorian style, built by New England merchants who went west during the gold rush, but there are also examples of the craftsman style (simple buildings of wood and stone on an intimate scale), a Frank Lloyd Wright, and a few 20s Mission Revival homes.

California Polytechnic State University (information desk 2792), roughly one mi. north of the town center, a right turn off U.S. 101 (Grand Ave.) in Highland, could inspire you to "go back to the land." The facilities include a Beef Pavilion, Crops Unit, Poultry Unit, and Swine Unit. The school boasts one of California's most-respected engineering and architecture programs. The **Shakespeare Press Museum,** in the Graphic Arts Building, owns a collection of 19th-century printing presses (museum open by appointment; call Mon.-Fri. 8am-4pm, 756-1108). Campus tours (756-5734) depart Monday, Wednesday, and Friday at 10am and 2pm from the second floor lobby of the Union. To reach the campus, take SLO Transit or the PolyShuttle from City Hall (routes #1 and 2).

The **Madonna Inn,** 100 Madonna Rd. (543-3000), off U.S. 101 on the southern end of town, is probably the only hotel in the world that sells postcards of each room. (Take the Madonna Rd. off-ramp.) Alex S. Madonna, the building contractor behind the construction of much of U.S. 101 and I-5, decided in 1958 to build a Queen Anne-style hotel of 12 rooms, and he put his wife, Phyllis, in charge of the design. By 1969, the vision had grown into a hot pink colossus of 110 rooms on 2200 acres of land. There's a Flintstonesque gas station; the men's room features a giant waterfall. Every room has a theme—the Caveman Room, the Daisy Mae Room, and a room with a working waterwheel serving as a headboard. (Rooms $82-180. Seven to nine people in the 3-bedroom Harvard Square suite is actually a bargain at $180.) Even non-guests can enjoy coffee and a Danish ($2-3.50), baked in the Madonna's own bakery. At night, there's often swing music to keep things lively.

NIGHTLIFE AND SEASONAL EVENTS

Somewhat sheltered from California's recreational extremes, SLO's amusements have the ambience of a local bar combined with a block party. Various festivals bring practically the entire community into the downtown, and Thursday nights virtually everyone, including the shopkeepers, stays up late. A favorite festival is the **Mozart Festival,** in the end of July, which will celebrate its 25th anniversary in 1995. Concerts play at the California Polytechnic State University (Cal Poly), the mission, and local churches. Tickets (from $8) go on sale in May, but some are available until the night of the concert. To order, write P.O. Box 311, San Luis Obispo 93406 (756-1421). The **Shakespeare Festival** (543-7635) is also widely acclaimed. **Mission Plaza,** a delightful public space below the mission, is the scene of **La Fiesta de San Luis** in May, with arts, crafts, and concerts. The mission also hosts an **American Indian Art Festival** (498-623-2379), in mid-July, which feature dancers, art, and native food. For information about other local happenings, consult the weekly *New Times,* a free paper available at most downtown stores. Smoking is not allowed in public areas in SLO, including bars. Most of the bars have a youthful Cal Poly atmosphere. Just head to Higuera St.

> **Tortilla Flats,** 1051 Nipomo St. (544-7575), specializes in Californian and Mexican food. Happy hours (4-6pm, 4-7pm on Fri.) feature $1 margaritas. Tortilla Flats is also the dance capital of SLO with top-40 and club music blasting nightly. Big pick-up scene. Open daily 11am-9pm for food. Dancing 9pm-2am.
>
> **Café Linnaeus,** 1110 Garden St. (541-5888). A popular evening hangout, especially with the artsy set. Displays local artists' works on the wall and features occasional folk and blues. Breakfast and lunch, homemade cookies at night. Open daily 7:30am-midnight. Rarely a cover; "pass the hat" for live performers instead.
>
> **SLO Brewing Company,** 1119 Garden St. (543-1843). Some food, but mostly drink, in an upstairs bar/micro-brewery. Popular among locals. Amazingly good porter (pints $2.50). Happy hour Mon.-Fri. 4-5:30pm features half-price pitchers and pints. Live entertainment Thurs.-Sat. 9:30pm-1:30am. Open Mon.-Wed. 11:30am-10pm, Thurs.-Sat. 11:30am-1:30am, Sun. 11:30am-6pm.
>
> **Spike's,** 570 Higuera St. (544-7157). Beer lovers come for Spike's globe-spanning selection of brews. Casual dining of the potato skins genre (most selections around $5). Open daily 11am-11:30pm.

■ NEAR SAN LUIS OBISPO

San Luis Obispo County was once a hotbed of volcanic activity. Today the remnants of the lava which once flowed here make for dramatic shorelines and vistas.

 Montana de Oro State Park (528-0513), 20 minutes west of SLO on Los Osos Valley Rd., remains relatively secluded. Here herons, owls, deer, and other wildlife run amuck in the hills and forests that surround the miles of hiking trails, beaches, and campsites. **Bluff Trail** leads you on a dramatic walk around thundering surf and sheer cliffs. The nearest bus service is to **Los Osos,** 6 mi. away, but you can bike to the park (along Los Osos Valley Rd.) from San Luis Obispo.

 Morro Bay State Park is more developed but still attractive. The **Museum of Natural History** (772-2694) trains its curatorial cannon on the aquatic environment and the wildlife of the coastal headlands, including hands-on exhibits. A bulletin board at the entrance lists a variety of free nature walks led by park rangers in summer. (Open daily 10am-5pm. $2, ages 6-17 $1, free to state park campers.) The long peninsula that forms Morro Bay also lies within the park boundaries. The dunes on the peninsula house a **bird sanctuary,** sheltering rare herons, among other birds.

 The town of **Morro Bay** is just to the north of its namesake park. Lodgings here are cheaper than in SLO, and you can often find early-bird dinner specials at the seafood restaurants along Embarcadero. Bus #7 serves Morro Bay from SLO. (5 per day. Fare $1.25. For more information call 541-2228.)

If you have a sturdy car and about 45 spare minutes, see **See Canyon Drive** (not a typo, honest). Locals take it for granted, but most tourists don't know about this beautiful 10-mi. stretch (although it *is* crowded in apple season). Part pavement, part gravel, it's a rough road best driven with 4-wheel-drive. See Canyon Drive begins just off U.S. 101 north of Avila Beach (take the See Canyon exit) and ends on Los Osos Valley Rd., which leads back to U.S. 101 and SLO.

Two beaches just southwest of San Luis Obispo enjoy anonymity: no signs announce their existence to the masses. **Pirate's Cove,** well-frequented, has unusually warm water. Take U.S. 101 south from San Luis Obispo, exit at the Avila Rd. off-ramp, head west 2 mi. and turn left on Cave Landing Dr., just before the oil tanks. Park in the dirt lot and take a path to the cove. Rocky **Shell Beach** is 1 mi. down U.S. 101, south of Avila and Pirate's Cove. Take the Shell Beach exit and turn left, then drive until you see little brown "coastal access" signs. Park at the gazebo, and try to climb down to the ocean. Many people bring their bikes down to Pirate's Cove, but the path at Shell Beach is too steep.

Avila and **Pismo Beaches** are both more developed and crowded. Avila presents the typical California beach scene, with a steady stream of cars cruising the boardwalk. It also has the warmest air and water of the entire coastline. Drive as if you're going to Pirate's Cove; Avila beach is on your left after you pass Pirate's. You can also take **South County Transit** to Avila. Bars and fast-food places line the boardwalk; watch the flow of traffic to determine the season's hot spot. Pismo Beach, 1½ mi. south of Shell Beach, is even more developed and congested than Avila and is accessible by **Greyhound** (see Practical Information, page 201). The air at Pismo Beach rings with the bells and buzzers of what looks (and sounds) like the world's largest pinball and video game arcade. Yet, at the end of the day, Pismo can be beautiful. Since the beach faces south, the sun sets behind the hills that jut into the sea, creating a gorgeous sand-on-fire effect at the surf line. Picnics are permitted.

Pismo Dunes, actually south of Pismo Beach in Grover City, is a "State Vehicular Recreation Area," where for a $4 day-use fee you can take your car or ATV down onto the dunes and spin-out to your heart's content. **Camping** here is an option for the serious budget traveler. At $6 ($1 if you walk in) it's the cheapest place to sleep in the SLO area; on the weekends, though, the sounds of squealing tires and revving engines can drown out the surf.

The **wineries,** located north of San Luis Obispo around the town of Paso Robles, are well-respected. The Paso Robles Chamber of Commerce, 1225 Park St. (238-0506), has a list of wineries, including visiting hours, tours, and tastings. In August, all the local wineries (more than 25) come together for the **Central Coast Wine-tasting Festival** (tickets $15, call 238-0506 for info).

Mission San Miguel Archangel (467-3256) is 43 mi. north of San Luis Obispo in San Miguel, a few blocks from U.S. 101. Take the Mission off-ramp. The 1818 complex has colorful frescoes, painted in 1821 by Monterey's Esteban Munras and his team of Native American artists. (Open daily 9:30am-5:30pm. Donation requested.)

■■■ CAMBRIA AND SAN SIMEON

Cradled by a valley 10 mi. south of San Simeon, tiny Cambria has a solid and friendly feel to it, a far cry from the empty, ostentatious splendor of **Hearst Castle.** The western half of the town, as well as the entire village of San Simeon, is prepared for the steady stream of tourists stopping on their way to Hearst Castle, but is refreshingly unexploitive of them. In recent years, Cambria has attracted many art galleries from the Carmel area.

PRACTICAL INFORMATION

Visitors Information: San Simeon Chamber of Commerce, 9255 Hearst Dr. (927-3500 or 800-342-5613), on the west side of Rte. 1, by the Bleschyu Golf

Course—look for the course's orange sign. Open Mon.-Fri. 9am-5pm; winter Mon.-Fri. 10am-2pm. **Cambria Chamber of Commerce,** 767 Main St. (927-3624). Open daily 9am-5pm.

ATM: Bank of America, 2258 Main St., in Cambria. None in San Simeon.

Public Transportation: Central Coast Area Transit (CCAT) connects San Simeon and Cambria to San Luis Obispo, Los Osos, and Morro Bay. You have to flag buses to get them to stop.

Bicycle Rental: Central Coast Adventures, P.O. Box 160 (927-4386), in San Simeon. Mountain bikes $15 per ½-day, $25 per day. Tours $30, under 16 $20.

Supermarket: Soto's Market, 2244 Main St. (927-4411). Open Mon.-Sat. 7am-7pm, Sun. 8am-5pm.

Laundromat: Main Street Laundromat, 1601 Main St. Wash $1.50, 48-min. dry 50¢. Open daily until 10pm.

Emergency: 911.

Post Office: Cambria Post Office, 4100 Bridge (927-3654). Open Mon.-Fri. 9am-5pm. **General Delivery ZIP Code:** 93428. **San Simeon Post Office,** Rte. 1 (927-4156), in the back of Sebastian's General Store (and gas pumps). To get here, take the road opposite the entrance to Hearst Castle. Open Mon.-Fri. 8:30am-noon and 1-5pm. **General Delivery ZIP Code:** 93452.

Area Code: 805.

ACCOMMODATIONS AND CAMPING

There are some very nice hotels in Cambria but rooms are cheaper in San Simeon. Prices skyrocket everywhere during the summer.

Creekside Inn, 2618 Main St. (927-4021 or 800-269-5212), in Cambria. A charming motel just outside of the town's shopping area. Grandparently management. Color TV, VCR in room (rent movies from the office). Check-out 11am. Singles and doubles with nosegays, gingham, and pink walls $45, winter $35.

Motel 6, 9070 Castillo Dr. (927-8691), at the Vista del Mar exit in San Simeon. Rooms with 2 queen beds, color TV, and cable $48 for 1-4 people.

San Simeon Lodge, 9520 Castillo Dr. (927-4601), at the Pico Ave. exit in San Simeon. Spotless. A king bed with color TV, cable, A/C and access to the pool costs a mere $29 for 1-2 people during the winter. Summer: $55 and up. Make reservations 1 month in advance for summer. Restaurant attached.

San Simeon State Beach, just north of Cambria on Rte. 1 (for reservations call MISTIX, 800-365-2267). 2 camping areas, **San Simeon Creek** and **Washburn.** San Simeon Creek has 116 sites near the beach and showers. Washburn sits on a hill overlooking the ocean and provides breathtaking sunsets. Portable toilets and cold running water only. San Simeon facilities are not available for use by Washburn campers. San Simeon sites $16, winter $14. Washburn sites $9, winter $7.

FOOD

Food is generally better in Cambria but there are some worthy spots in San Simeon.

The Tea Cozy, 604 Main St., Suite D (927-8765), in Cambria. Authentic English management. Not as cutesy as it sounds—offers genuine and mouthwatering English cream teas ($5 per person gets you tea, two scones, preserves, and double Devon cream). Also a selection of English sandwiches ($3 and up) and a daily soup. The teapots wear amusing cozies (caps) with pom-poms.

El Chorlito Mexican Eatery, 9155 Hearst Dr. (927-3872), in San Simeon. Fresh, lard-free, zippy Cali-Mex food. Attentive staff. Try the specialty—an unusually spiced green chile and cheese soup ($2.75 for a cup). Open daily noon-10pm.

Creekside Gardens Café, 2114 Main St. (927-8646), in Cambria. A petite restaurant in the Redwood Shopping Center, frequented by locals. Indoor or patio dining for breakfast and lunch. Pancakes with eggs and bacon $4. Desserts ($2-3) made daily. Open Mon.-Sat. 7am-2pm, Sun. 7am-1pm.

Chuckwagon (927-4644), Moonstone Dr., at Cambria's only stoplight. Across the highway from the Shell Station. Draws senior citizens and vacationing families. Home-style cooking of the mashed potatoes variety. Meals include soup, bread, and dessert. Mon.-Fri. breakfast and lunch $5.89, dinner $8.29 (beverages extra). Sat.-Sun. dinner $8.29. Open daily 6:30am-8:30pm; Nov.-March 11am-8pm.

Canozzi's Saloon, 2267 Main St. (927-8941), in Cambria between Burton and Bridge St. A well-known watering hole with mock-saloon decor. Older clientele. Pool tables and occasional live music. Beer $1-2, well drinks $1.75-3. Open daily 10am-2am.

SIGHTS AND ACTIVITIES

Big Sur's dramatic coastline begins here and extends north along Rte. 1. Sea otters, once near extinction, now prosper in the kelp beds of **Moonstone Beach** (Rte. 1 toward San Simeon). Along this stretch of coast surfers are occasionally nudged off their boards by playful seals. (And, more rarely, by not so playful sharks who mistake the surfers for basking seals.) **San Simeon** and **Hearst State Beaches** are ideal for cliff-climbing and beachcombing and offer the best swimming for miles. Be wary of trespassing as you approach the beach; the Hearst Corporation owns much of the land in this area. A single entrance ticket ($3) is good for one day at all state parks, but many people avoid the fee by parking on the road outside the Hearst beach's entrance point and crossing Hearst lands to reach the beach. Look for turn-outs on Rte. 1 between San Simeon and the lighthouse at Piedras Blancas; these and the nearby wooden stairs over Hearst Corporation fences provide the only legal access.

Cambria features its own unique abode, though on a smaller scale than San Simeon's Castle. **Nitt Witt Ridge,** another in the long tradition of eccentric California dream homes, was designated a California Historical Landmark in 1981. The Nitt Witt is a rustic conglomeration of rocks, bones, feathers, tiles, driftwood, and even a broken television set. The creator, Art Beal, popularly known as Captain Nitwit or Dr. Tinkerpaw, began building his dream house in the 1920s, and continued to add to it for six decades. The house is unsafe and no longer inhabited. Trespassing is illegal (there is a caretaker), so you'll have to gawk from the street. To reach the house, head south on Main, turn left on Arlington, right on Cornwall, then left on Hillcrest.

Hearst Castle

Commonly known as Hearst Castle, the **Hearst San Simeon Historic Monument** (927-2010) lies 5 mi. east of Rte. 1 near San Simeon. William Randolph Hearst, infamous magnate *cum* yellow journalist and instigator of the Spanish-American War, began building this Hispano-Moorish indulgence in 1919. For 28 years his devoted and gifted architect, Julia Morgan of San Francisco, took the night train here to work in her tiny office, adapting Hearst's outlandish requests to the physical setting.

To turn the barren hill into a verdant garden, thousands of tons of topsoil were hauled in, and adult trees were planted all the way down to the sea. Hearst, lacking the patience to allow gardens to mature, planted orange trees in a hedge, not caring that they would choke each other within 50 years. He later traveled to Spain and became infatuated with a Mudéjar cathedral. Unable to buy it, he had Morgan blast off the existing towers of his 115-room "ranch house" and build reproductions in their stead. Much of the castle's "art" is fake: concrete statuary, plaster pilasters, artificially aged tiles. Yet genuine treasures remain tucked away: the world's largest private collection of Greek vases lines the library shelves; medieval tapestries grace the halls; and ancient Chinese ceramics perch on the mantelpieces of Gothic fireplaces.

Ultimately, though, Hearst reached beyond his means. Even isolated in his Gothic-style personal suite, the Great Depression hit him hard, and much of the castle was left incomplete. Nearly half of the walls are still exposed concrete, and the cheap building materials require costly, frequent maintenance.

Visitors have a choice of five **tours,** each 1¾-2 hours long. It's possible to take them all in one day, but each costs $14 (ages 6-12 $8; plus a $2.75 service charge if you don't buy the tickets at the Castle). Groups are taken up the hill in buses, shepherded around, then taken back down. You must take a tour to see the castle; wandering around on your own is not allowed. Tour One is an overview, covering the gardens, the swimming pools, a guest house, and the first floor of the main house.

BIG SUR

Tour Five, an evening tour available only in the spring and fall, emphasizes "living history," and features actors in period costume strolling the grounds. This tour is more expensive than the others ($25, ages 6-12 $13; call for details on when it is offered). Tours are offered at least every hour from 8:20am to 3pm. Wheelchair-accessible tours are available; reservations must be made 10 days in advance for these (927-2020). If you want to see the Castle in summer, advance reservations are a must (800-444-4445). The gates to the visitors center open in summer at 6am, in winter at 7am. Tickets go on sale daily at 8am.

■■■ BIG SUR

In 1542 Cabrillo, sailing off the coast of Big Sur, wrote "here there are mountains which seem to reach the heavens, and the sea beats on them." He was a master of understatement. Big Sur is inextricable from its imposing geography; its sheer grandeur is bound to win over even those most oblivious to nature's beauty. The 90-mi. stretch of coast and the cliffs that tower over it, backdropped by fields of wildflowers and mist-laden mountains, is the only sight Big Sur has to offer, probably because very little could compete with it. It isn't even apparent that people live here; while perfectly willing to sell tourists sandwiches and souvenirs, residents hide their houses and themselves in the woods.

PRACTICAL INFORMATION

Visitors Information: Big Sur Chamber of Commerce, P.O. Box 87, Big Sur 93920 (667-2100). Send a self-addressed, stamped envelope for a guide to Big Sur.
Big Sur Station: 667-2315. On Rte. 1, inside **Big Sur State Park**. This is a multi-agency station that includes the **State Park Office,** the **U.S. Forest Service Office,** and the **Cal-Trans Office.** The station can provide info on all area State Parks, U.S. Forest Service campgrounds, and local transit. In addition, the station provides permits and maps, and sponsors ranger-led hikes and campfires. Open daily 8am-5:30pm.
AAA Emergency Road Service: 800-400-4222. **Road Information:** 757-2006.
Post Office: 667-2305. On Rte. 1, next to the Center Deli in Big Sur Center. Open Mon.-Fri. 8:30am-5pm. **General Delivery ZIP Code**: 93920.
Area Code: 408.

Monterey's Spanish settlers simply called the entire region below their town "El Sur Grande"—the Large South. Today, "Big Sur" signifies a more exact coastal region bordered on the south by San Simeon and on the north by Carmel. Big Sur is best enjoyed by car and by camping. The coast is thinly inhabited, dotted with gas stations approximately every 20 mi. and the occasional house at the end of a drive plastered with signs commanding tourists to keep out. The few lodges are all beyond the budget traveler's range. Almost everything—fuel, food, beer, toiletries—is more expensive in Big Sur than in real life. Last-chance stops are the supermarket on Rio Rd. in Carmel, for the budget-minded southbounder, and the market in Morro Bay for the northbounder.

Despite its isolation, Big Sur can be reached by public transit. Monterey-Salinas bus #22 leaves every 3 hours (May-Oct.only) from the Monterey conference center, and runs as far south as Nepenthe, 29 mi. below Carmel, including stops at all points of interest in between. (Fare $2.50, over 64 or under 19 $1. Call 899-2555 for more information.) Hitching in Big Sur can be difficult, especially near the state parks, where competition is fierce. *Let's Go* does not recommend hitchhiking. When the road is crowded with lurching RVs, frustrated speedsters, and oblivious Sunday drivers, walking and bicycling become treacherous, and traffic slows to a crawl.

Spring, when wildflowers bloom and the hills glow with color, is the optimal time to survey Big Sur. Avoid visiting on crowded summer weekends. It is wise to bring both warm and cold weather clothing to this stretch of coast; the proximity of the mountains and the sea leads to a typical day of cool morning with coastal fog, followed by a sunny and pleasant afternoon and a chilly evening.

The Big Sur Chamber of Commerce puts out a helpful guide listing privately owned accommodations, campgrounds, and restaurants. Pick up the guide in San Simeon, or Carmel's Chamber of Commerce, or in the State Park. Locations in Big Sur are generally described in terms of mi. north of the Hearst Castle or south of Carmel, along Rte. 1. The entire length is 91 mi.

ACCOMMODATIONS AND CAMPING

Places to camp are abundant and beautiful. If you neglect to bring equipment, you've made a big mistake. But even if you did, be warned—site prices tend to change quickly. If all sites below are booked, check with the Forest Service Station (see Practical Information). The cheapest way to stay in Big Sur is to camp for free in the Ventana Wilderness (pick up a permit at Big Sur Station). Ventana, at the northern end of Los Padres National Forest, is a backpack-only area—no automobiles.

Big Sur Campgrounds and Cabins (667-2322), 26 mi. south of Carmel, near the Big Sur River. Campsites ($22, with hookup $25); tent cabins in summer ($40). Store, laundry, playground, volleyball courts, and hot showers.

Fernwood Motel (667-2422), Rte. 1, 2 mi. north of the post office. On the Big Sur River in a redwood forest. 2 swimming holes. 60 sites. Registration open 8am-midnight. Check-out noon. Sites $21, with hookup $23. 12 motel rooms from $50. $3 per extra person, max. 5 people. Reserve 1 yr. in advance.

Los Padres National Forest, U.S. Forest Service Campgrounds: **Plaskett Creek** (667-2315), south of Limekiln, near Jade Cove. 43 sites. **Kirk Creek,** about 5 mi. north of Jade Cove. 33 beautiful spots, but they're close to the highway. No showers, only toilets and cold running water. Open 24 hrs. Check-out 2pm. Sites $15, hikers and bikers $3. No reservations.

Pfeiffer Big Sur State Park (667-2315), just south of Fernwood, 26 mi. south of Carmel. An inland park, but no less popular than those on the beach. All 218 developed campsites do fill up at times (no hookups). The Big Sur River flows peacefully alongside the campground. Hot showers. Sites $16. Day-use fee $6. Reservations through MISTIX (800-444-7275).

Andrew Molera State Park (667-2315), 5 mi. north of Pfeiffer Big Sur. No numbered sites, tent camping only. Beach, pit toilets, no showers. A ¼-mi. walk on a level trail to reach campsites. This is where the Big Sur River pours into the ocean. Sites $3 per person, $1 extra for Fido.

FOOD

Grocery stores are located at River Inn, Ripplewood, Fernwood, Big Sur Lodge, Pacific Valley Center, and Gorda, but it's better to arrive prepared; prices are high.

Center Deli (667-2225), right beside the Big Sur Post Office. The most reasonably priced goods in the area, sandwiches ($2.75). Broad selection of groceries. If you're lucky, they'll have fresh local boysenberries available. Open daily 8am-9pm; winter 8am-8pm.

Fernwood Burger Bar (667-2422), Rte. 1, 2 mi. north of post office. Chicken breast San Luis sausage $2.75. Hamburgers from $4. There's a homey bar too, as well as a grocery store. Fill up your tank here: gas is slightly less expensive than elsewhere in Big Sur. Open daily 11:30am-10pm.

Nepenthe Restaurant, (667-2345), Rte. 1. A local favorite. The hamburger—excuse us—the *ground steak sandwich* is $10 (yes, $10). Holly's quiche (spinach and mushrooms) is $9.25. Fire pit at night. Outdoor seating provides a spectacular view of water, mountains, and mist. Feel free to wander around and take pictures; most people do. Open daily 11:30am-4:30pm and 5-10pm.

Café Kevah (667-2344), on Rte. 1 next to Nepenthe. Less stuffy and less shady than Nepenthe, with an outdoor patio that stretches to the edge of a strategically scenic cliff. Homemade granola with yogurt $5.75. Open daily 9am-3pm.

Big Sur River Inn, (667-2700), on Rte. 1 24 mi. south of Carmel. Eat breakfast on the deck under the redwoods by a stream (3 pancakes with 2 eggs $5.25), or try the specialty of the house at any time—pan-fried trout ($14). Open 8am-10pm, with live music (usually jazz) Sat. night and Sun. 11am-5pm. Poetry readings Tues.

SIGHTS AND ACTIVITIES

The **state parks** and **wilderness areas** are exquisite settings for dozens of outdoor activities. **Hiking** on Big Sur is fantastic: the state parks and **Los Padres National Forest** all have trails that penetrate redwood forests and cross low chaparral, offering even grander views of Big Sur than those available from Rte. 1. The northern end of Los Padres National Forest has been designated the **Ventana Wilderness** and contains the popular **Pine Ridge Trail.** Grab a map and a required permit at the USFS ranger station (see Practical Information, above).

Within **Pfeiffer Big Sur State Park** are eight trails of varying lengths (50¢ map available at park entrance). Try the **Valley View Trail,** a short, steep path overlooking the valley below. **Buzzard's Roost Trail** is a rugged two-hour hike up tortuous switchbacks; if you can make it to the top, you'll be treated to a panorama of the Santa Lucia Mountains, the Big Sur Valley, and the Pacific Ocean.

Roughly at the midway point of Big Sur lies quiet **Julia Pfeiffer Burns Park** (day use only, $6), which features picnic tables among the redwoods and a chance to sea otter-watch in McWay Cove. These parks are local favorites; come midweek to avoid the throng. Big Sur's most jealously guarded treasure is USFS-operated **Pfeiffer Beach,** 1 mi. south of Pfeiffer State Park. Turn off Rte. 1 at the stop sign and the "Narrow Road not suitable for trailers" sign. Follow the road 2 mi. to the parking area; take the footpath to the beach. The small cove, partially protected from the Pacific by an offshore rock formation, is replete with sea caves and sea gulls. There are no lifeguards; riptides make swimming dangerous. North of this, the 1889 **Lighthouse Station** (625-4419) perches atop Point Sur. (Tours Sat.-Sun., weather permitting. $5, ages 13-17 $3, ages 5-12 $2. Arrive 1 hr. early; be prepared for a steep hike.)

Big Sur is not *all* nature and no civilization, however. The **Coast Gallery** (667-2301), on Rte. 1 just north of the Julia Pfeiffer Burns State Park, has long been a showcase for works by local artists (open daily 9am-6pm, winter 9am-5pm). It also houses paintings and lithographs by the author of *Tropic of Cancer* and title character in the film *Henry and June,* Henry Miller, who lived near here for 17 years. Miller's casual reminiscences and prophetic ecstasies made hundreds of readers aware of Big Sur. His more explicit works drew many to Big Sur seeking the sex cult he purportedly led (he didn't). The writer's fans may want to stop by the **Henry Miller Memorial Library** (667-2574), 4 mi. north of the gallery and 1 mi. south of Nepenthe. (Open Tues.-Sun. 11am-5pm, but call ahead.)

■■■ CARMEL

Upper-class Californians migrate to Carmel to live out their fantasies of rural life, and the town responds remarkably well to their wishes. Carmel possesses one of Northern California's most beautiful beaches, a gloriously restored Spanish mission, and a main street lined with stores that sell jewelry, silk dresses, and fine art. The town works hard to maintain its image. Local ordinances forbid parking meters (though police chalk tires to keep careful track of how long you have parked), normal-sized street signs, address numbers, billboards, home mail delivery, and, at one time, eating ice-cream cones outside—all considered undesirable symbols of urbanization. All of the houses have names, and franchise stores are forbidden in the city proper. Carmel has a long history of preventive legislation. In 1916, because rapid development caused flooding when steep hills were denuded, the town passed a law making it a felony to cut down any tree. As a result, pines and cypresses grow everywhere—in the middle of streets, sidewalks, and houses.

Budget travelers may find Carmel unwelcoming. This side of paradise is largely private property. Police patrol the streets on bicycle, on the alert for ragtag travelers and wandering indigents, and there are few inexpensive places to eat or sleep.

Carmel was adopted by San Francisco intellectuals as a temporary home after their urban haunts were destroyed by the 1906 earthquake. Traces of the resulting artist colony (frequented by Upton Sinclair and Robinson Jeffers) still linger. Much of the artwork offered for sale in Carmel galleries is locally produced. The quality of the paintings (mostly land and seascapes) varies from museum to motel-room quality. A few of the town's 43 galleries, such as "Golf Arts and Imports," stretch the boundaries of aesthetics. Nevertheless, residents (such as former mayor Clint Eastwood) can easily invest in such quality kitsch.

PRACTICAL INFORMATION AND ORIENTATION

Visitors Information: Carmel-by-the-Sea Business Association (624-2522), San Carlos between 5th and 6th, in the Eastwood Building, upstairs (next door to the Hog's Breath Inn). Free city maps. Open Mon.-Thurs. 9am-5pm, Fri. 9am-6pm, Sat. 11am-5pm, Sun. noon-4pm (summer only).

Monterey-Salinas Transit (MST): 899-2555 or 424-7695. Buses #4, 5, 22 or 24 will take you to Carmel. Bus #4 runs between the Monterey Transit Plaza and 6th and Mission in Carmel; Mon.-Sat. 7:15am-5:15pm, Sun. 10:15am-5:15pm. Bus #5 runs closer to the beach, stopping at Carmelo St. and Santa Lucía Ave.; 1 per hr. Mon.-Sat. 7:30am-11:30pm, Sun. 8am-6pm. Bus #22 stops at 6th and Mission on its way to Big Sur; departs from Monterey Conference Center May-Oct. 1 per hr. daily 10am-2pm. Bus #24 to Carmel Valley also stops at Mission St.; daily 6:15am-10:15pm. Fare $1.25, over 64 and under 19 50¢, under 5 free.

Bicycle Rental: Bay Bikes II (625-BIKE, -2453), on Lincoln between 5th and 6th. $6 first hr., $4 per additional hr. $18 1st day, $12 per additional day or $60 per week. Includes helmet and bike locks. Open daily 9am-6pm.

Post Office, 5th St., between San Carlos and Dolores St. (624-1525). Open Mon.-Fri. 9am-4:30pm. **General Delivery ZIP Code:** 93921.

Area Code: 408.

Carmel lies at the southern base of the Monterey Peninsula off **Rte. 1.** The city is contained within a giant square: Rte. 1 to the east, the beach on the west, **Ocean Ave.** (the town's main street) on the north, and Rio Rd. and Santa Lucía Ave. on the south. The shopping district, however, is much larger. Obtain a free street map of the town, produced by the Carmel Innkeepers Hosting Service, at any hotel.

The free weekly *Monterey Peninsula Review* (624-0162) carries detailed theater, music, dance, art, and restaurant listings. It is available at the information center in Monterey and in restaurants, bookstores, and cafés in Carmel. The *Pine Cone* is another publication that lists local events.

ACCOMMODATIONS AND CAMPING

Most motels in Carmel offer only double-occupancy rooms that never dip below $60 per night. The rates at Carmel's B&Bs and inns are high by *Let's Go* standards, but usually do include full breakfasts (information available at visitors center, see above). A 15-minute bus ride north to Monterey will bring more reasonable prices. Camping is illegal within the city limits, and there are no nearby state parks. There are, however, a few private campgrounds. The cheapest camping in Carmel Valley is 4½ mi. east of the city at **Saddle Mountain Ranch** (624-1617), a resort on Schulte Rd. Fifty sites with showers are available ($17, with hookup and dump $28).

FOOD

Although many of Carmel's restaurants, like the town itself, are a bit pretentious, it is still possible to dine well without blowing your budget.

Em Lee's (625-6780), Dolores between 5th and 6th St. Comfortable breakfast and lunch joint with brick-tiled floors and plants. Many breakfast specials, including plate-sized blueberry waffles ($5). Famous and unique French toast in a wide assortment of shapes, served with fresh peaches ($8). Open daily 6:30am-3pm.

Le Bistro (624-6545), San Carlos between Ocean and 7th. Charming and relaxed, complete with fireplace. While the BistroBurger ($4.50) is their specialty, the chef also knows what to do with fresh fish. Try the Monterey Bay Snapper with salad and garlic bread ($6.50). Open Mon.-Fri. 7am-4pm and 5-9pm, Sat.-Sun. 8am-4pm and 5-9pm. In winter, Mon.-Thurs. 7am-4pm, Fri.-Sun. 8am-4pm and 5-9pm.

The Hogs Breath Inn, San Carlos St. (625-1044), between 5th and 6th Ave. Court-yard filled with benches, fire pits, heavy wooden tables, and comfortable chairs. This place gets a bit touristy, with patrons eagerly hoping to catch a glimpse of half-owner Clint Eastwood. Make your day with the Dirty Harry dinner ($9.75). Tiny bar has free hors d'oeuvres Mon.-Fri. 4-6pm. Lunch Mon.-Sat. 11:30am-3pm; Sun. brunch 11am-3pm; dinner daily 5-10pm. Bar open daily 11am-2am.

Monterey Baking Company (625-3998), at Lincoln and Ocean. A café and patis-serie, with other branches in Monterey and Santa Cruz. Sandwiches $4-5. Good kosher pickles. Open daily 8am-6pm.

Paolina's (624-5599), San Carlos between Ocean and 7th, in the "Doud Arcade." Place orders at the counter. Hearty pastas with a variety of toppings $7.25. Pizzas from $6.25. Open daily 8am-9pm.

China Gourmet (624-3941), on 5th between San Carlos and Dolores. Bright orange vinyl booths. Delicious Cantonese and Szechuan food, most dishes $6.50-10.50. Lunch specials $4.50-5.50. Open Tues.-Sun. 11am-9:30pm.

SIGHTS

Carmel City Beach, at the end of Ocean Ave., is where the northern Big Sur coast truly begins. No signs mark the exact spot, but it's unmistakable: a crescent of white sand frames a cove of clear, chilly aquamarine waters. The beach ends abruptly at the base of distant red cliffs. Cypress-covered hills wreathed in clouds surround the whole area. The west-facing beach makes a fine grandstand for sunsets.

Less crowded and more remote, the **Carmel River State Beach** lies around the southern point at the end of City Beach. This beach, windier and colder than the city's, but blessed with better surf, can be reached by walking about 1 mi. along Sce-nic Rd. or by driving to the end of Carmelo St. off Santa Lucía Ave. The parking lot closes at dusk and no fires are allowed on the beach.

To glimpse Carmel as it might have been in the '20s and '30s, take the short walk from the river beach to **Tor House** (624-1813) at Ocean View Ave. and Scenic Rd. Inspired by the Big Sur coast, poet Robinson Jeffers built this house in 1919, using boulders from the beach. (Tours Fri.-Sat. 10am-3pm. Reservations required. $5, col-lege students $3.50, high school students $1.50, under 12 not admitted.) The **Cen-ter for Photographic Art** (625-5181; San Carlos between 8th and 9th) is housed in the Sunset Center offices once occupied by Ansel Adams. Exhibits include work by local and internationally known artists. (Open Tues.-Sun. 1-5pm. Free.) Art buffs may enjoy wandering through Carmel's countless galleries (free).

Mission Basilica San Carlos Borromeo del Rio Carmelo, 3080 Rio Rd. (624-3600), off Rte. 1, is a mouthful to say but a marvel to see. Founded in 1770 at Monterey and transported to Carmel in 1771, the mission "converted" 4000 Native Americans before it was abandoned in 1845. Sir Harry Downie supervised its resto-ration in 1931, fastidiously following the original construction methods and replant-ing the luscious gardens. A Mudéjar tower supporting bells and swallows' nests crowns the popular church. Father Junípero Serra, founder of the California mission system and eponymous to the omnipresent California juniper bush, is buried in the sanctuary. Over 2300 Native Americans are also buried in the cemetery. The three **museums** at Carmel Mission are extensive, displaying the original silver altar fur-nishings, handsome vestments, a library, and much more from the mission's early days. (Open Mon.-Sat. 9:30am-4:30pm, Sun. 10:30am-4:30pm. $1.)

The extraordinary **Point Lobos Reserve** (624-4909), 4 mi. south of Carmel on Rte. 1, is a state-run wildlife sanctuary popular with skindivers and day hikers. Otters, sea lions, seals, brown pelicans, and gulls are visible from footpaths along the cliffs;

bring a windbreaker and binoculars. Point Lobos encompasses tide pools and has marvelous vantage points for watching the winter whale migration. Don't neglect the interior trails through cypress forests, but watch out for poison oak. Free guided tours are offered daily. Park outside the toll booth and walk or bike in for free. There is frequently a line of cars waiting to get in by 8am on weekends. (Open daily 9am-7pm; in winter 9am-5pm. $6 per car plus 50¢ for a map; over 61 $5 per car. No pets allowed.) To reach Point Lobos, take MST bus #22 ("Big Sur") from Monterey.

ENTERTAINMENT

Carmel's bars are often overpriced and overdone. Watering holes are full of tourists, many of whom are either on their honeymoon or revisiting the scene of their first love. But bars are not the only places to hang out. For a touch of the fabled California beach life, try walking down the **Carmel City Beach** or **River Beach** (see Sights, above) shortly after sunset to find young people gathered around communal beach fires, listening to music, and drinking assorted refreshments. Congregations around conflagrations are officially illegal. People determined to participate must walk beyond sight of the main road for a chance to glimpse the twinkle of firelight.

California's first outdoor theater, the **Forest Theatre** (626-1681), at Mountain View Ave. and Santa Rita St., about 2 blocks east of the northern end of Ocean Ave., was founded in 1910. The theatre provides light drama (8pm), weekend musical entertainment, and free Sunday afternoon concerts in July and August (2pm; call 624-3996 for info). During the winter, the Staff Players perform classics in the Indoor Theatre (624-1531). Tickets, available at the Carmel Business Association office (San Carlos between 5th and 6th), vary in price.

Catch the annual **Bach Festival** (624-1521) if you happen to be in Carmel July 15 to August 6, 1995. Tickets ($10-45) can be purchased in advance from the Carmel Bach Festival, P.O. Box 575, Carmel 93921 (fax 624-2788) or, close to the concert date, at the Festival Office, 11 Sunset Center, San Carlos at 9th St. (Open Mon.-Sat 9am-3pm.) The festival includes a number of free events: lectures, symposia, master classes, and outdoor brass concerts.

■■■ MONTEREY

In the 1940s, Monterey was a coastal town geared toward sardine fishing and canning. But the sardines disappeared in the early '50s, and when John Steinbeck revisited his beloved Cannery Row around 1960, he wrote scornfully of how the district had become a tourist trap. Today, few traces of the Monterey described in *Cannery Row* remain; along the famous Row and Fisherman's Wharf, packing plants have been converted to multiplex souvenir malls, and the old bars where sailors used to drink and fight now feature wax recreations.

Monterey was explored by the Spanish as early as 1602, but didn't take off until 1770, when Father Serra passed through on his journey up the coast. After being invaded and claimed by the U.S. in 1846, the city lost its bureaucratic prestige and was eclipsed as a port by San Francisco. But the growth of the whaling and sardine industries kept Monterey alive. While the sardine era is remembered most through junky souvenirs, public buildings and adobe houses recall the days before the Gold Rush. Along with the ineradicable beauty of the coastline, the seafood, and a world-class aquarium, these remnants of an earlier era justify a journey to Monterey.

PRACTICAL INFORMATION AND ORIENTATION

Visitors Information: Monterey Peninsula Chamber of Commerce, 380 Alvarado St., P.O. Box 1770, Monterey 93942 (649-1770), downtown. Free pamphlets and an eager staff. 112-page Visitor's Guide ($3) has restaurant, accommodation, and tourist info. Open Mon.-Fri. 8:30am-5pm. Additional **Visitors Center:** 401 Camino El Estero. Open Mon.-Sat. 9am-6pm, Sun. 10am-5pm. **Sierra Club,** Ocean Ave. between Dolores and San Carlos (624-8032). Above the Village Shoe Tree, in Carmel. Information on sights. Open Mon.-Sat. 12:30-4:30pm.

Greyhound: No office, but a stop at 351 Del Monte Ave., site of the old office with a schedule posted on the door. Tickets may be purchased from the driver or at another station (like Salinas or Santa Cruz). For more info., call 800-231-2222.

Monterey-Salinas Transit (MST): One Ryan Ranch Rd. (899-2555 or 424-7695, TTY available). MST serves the region from Watsonville in the north to Salinas in the south, and inland to Pacific Grove. Many buses stop at **Transit Plaza** downtown, where Munras, Tyler, Pearl, Alvarado, and Polk St. converge. Fare per zone $1.25; ages 5-18, over 64, and people with disabilities 50¢ (each zone encompasses 1 or 2 towns, 4 zones total); exact change; transfers free. 2 ride for the price of 1 on weekends. A **Day Pass** ($3.75) is valid for unlimited rides for 1 day within a single zone. The free Rider's Guide to Monterey-Salinas Transit (MST) service contains complete schedules and route information (available on buses, at motels, and the library). Bus #22 runs between Monterey and the Nepenthe restaurant near Big Sur (4-5 per day April-Sept., $2.50). Drivers may balk at backpacks, so be charmingly persuasive and dress decently. Phone lines open Mon.-Fri. 7:45am-5:15pm, Sat. 10am-4pm.

Taxi: Yellow Cab (646-1234), $1.50 plus $1.75 per mi.

Bicycle Rental: Free-wheeling Cycles, 188 Webster St. (373-3855), on the northern fringe of downtown. 10-speeds $10 per day, $35 per week, $20 deposit. Mountain bikes $15 per day, $50 per week. Open Mon.-Fri. 9am-6pm, Sat.-Sun. 9am-5pm; Dec.-April daily 9am-5pm. **Bay Bikes,** 640 Wave St. (646-9090), on Cannery Row. Bikes $6 for first hr., $4 each additional hr., $18 per day. Includes lock and helmet. Open daily 9am-6pm.

Moped Rental: Monterey Moped Adventures, 1250 Del Monte Ave. (373-2696). Mopeds $10 per hour, $40 per day. 2-hr. min. Must be 18 with drivers license.

Public Library: 625 Pacific (646-3930). Pleasant courtyard for reading. Open Mon.-Thurs. 9am-9pm, Fri. 9am-6pm, Sat. 9am-5pm, Sun. 1-5pm.

Laundromat: Surf and Suds, 1101 Del Monte Ave. (375-0874). Washers $1.25, 10-min. dry 25¢. Open daily 7am-9pm.

Rape Crisis Line: 375-4357. Open 24 hrs.

Emergency: 911.

Post Office: 565 Hartnell (372-5803). Open Mon.-Fri. 8:45am-5:10pm. **General Delivery ZIP Code:** 93940.

Area Code: 408.

The Monterey Peninsula, 115 mi. south of San Francisco, contains Monterey, Pacific Grove, a residential community, and Pebble Beach, an exclusive nest of mansions. Carmel, southwest of Monterey, stands where the peninsula ends on its southern side. Motorists can approach Monterey from **U.S. 101** (Munras Ave. exit), which runs north-south slightly inland from the peninsula, or **Rte. 1,** the coastal highway.

There are several free guides to activities in Monterey and surrounding areas. *Coasting* (625-5656), published weekly, includes articles about the arts and is available from the visitors center, stores, and hotels. The *Review* is a free dining and entertainment guide that also lists happy hours. The free *Coast Weekly* (625-5656), found at local stores, contains food and events listings and excursions ideas.

Monterey's main street, **Alvarado,** runs north-south. At its northern end stand luxury hotels and the magnitudinous Conference Center; beyond the brick plaza are a large parking lot, the marina, and Fisherman's Wharf. Most sights of interest lie within a few blocks of Alvarado, in a tangle of streets toward its southern end. Cannery Row and the aquarium are 1½ to 2 mi. northwest of downtown Monterey.

The relative isolation of Monterey does little to insulate the city from prodigious traffic jams. The Monterey Traffic Department's earnest attempts to correct the congestion with abundant one-way signs and complicated traffic signals seem only to make matters worse. If you drive, park at the 12-hour meters near Cannery Row (25¢ per 30 min.) and explore the city by foot.

Bicycling is a splendid way to see the peninsula provided you exercise caution on the narrow, twisting roads. There are few bike paths per se, but the Monterey Peninsula Recreation Trail follows the coast from Fisherman's Wharf in Monterey through Pacific Grove, Pebble Beach and Carmel, then back up Rte. 1, where a bike lane begins. The circuit takes four hours at a leisurely pace, all day for those who like to make frequent stops to admire the scenery.

Monterey experiences the benefits of coastal weather, with sunny summer highs in 70-80°F as the norm. However, early mornings and evenings are often chilly and foggy, so be prepared.

ACCOMMODATIONS AND CAMPING

Finding cheap lodging in Monterey requires diligent searching. Prices often vary by day, month, and proximity to a popular event, such as the Jazz Festival. Reasonably priced hotels are often found in the 2000 block of Fremont St. in Monterey (bus #9 or 10) and Lighthouse Ave. in Pacific Grove (bus #2 or some #1 buses). Other motels cluster along Munras Ave. between downtown and Rte. 1. The cheapest hotels in the area, however, are in the less appealing town of Marina, just north of Monterey.

Monterey Peninsula Youth Hostel (HI-AYH) (649-0375). Theoretically, the location is not fixed, but the hostel has been in the Monterey High School for the past few summers. To reach the high school, take Pacific away from the water, turn right on Madison and left on Larkin St. Mattresses are put on the floor along the gymnasium walls. Staff tries to make up for the lack of amenities by providing lots of info. and inexpensive food. Ample parking. Lockout 9:30am-6pm. Curfew 11pm. $6, nonmembers $9. Under 18 50% off. Open daily mid-June to mid-Aug.

Del Monte Beach Inn, 1110 Del Monte (649-4410). Close to downtown, across the street from the beach, this Victorian-style inn offers pleasant rooms (shared bath) and a hearty breakfast for $45-60. Mention that you're a grizzled *Let's Go* budget traveler and you'll save 10% on weekdays.

Paramount Motel, 3298 Del Monte Blvd. (384-8674), in Marina, 8 mi. north of Monterey. This tidy motel (and its decor) dates from the '50s. Check-out 11am. Singles $25. Doubles $30. No reservations; arrive at noon to get a room.

Motel 6, 2124 N. Fremont (646-8585), near the county fairgrounds. One of the few motels whose rates stay relatively constant. Singles and doubles $46 in summer, $6 for one more person, $3 for a fourth person. If the additional person is under 18 he/she stays free. Rates are lower in winter. Reserve in advance year round.

Veterans Memorial Park Campground (646-3865), Via Del Rey (1½ mi. from the town center). Take Skyline Dr. off the section of Rte. 68 called W.R. Holman Hwy. From downtown, take Pacific St. south, turn right on Jefferson, and follow the signs, or take bus #3. Perched on a hill with a view of the bay. 40 sites, hot showers. First-come, first-camped. Arrive before 3pm in summer and on weekends in winter. Sites $15, hikers $3.

Laguna Seca Recreational Area (422-6138), Rte. 68 10 mi. east of Monterey, near the racetrack. 178 campsites, of which 103 are equipped with hookups. Showers, restrooms, barbecue pits, tables, and a dump station. Sites $15, with hookup $20. A park with oak-strewn verdant hills overlooking valleys

FOOD

The sardines may be gone, but the unpolluted Monterey Bay teems with squid, crab, rock cod, sand dab, red snapper, and salmon. You can enjoy your seafood as Sicilian marinated octopus, English fish & chips, Thai sweet-and-sour snapper, or artfully wrapped sushi. Although seafood is bountiful, it is often expensive—try eating an early bird special (4-6:30pm or so) to save money. Or head to **Fisherman's Wharf,** where the smoked salmon sandwiches ($5.50) are a wonderful way to sample a local delicacy. Don't despair if you loathe seafare; you can still dine well in this land of artichokes and strawberries. The **Monterey Farmer's Market** takes place on Alvarado St. every Tuesday from 4 to 8pm.

Casa de Gutiérrez, 590 Calle Principal (375-0095), at the south end of the street. Mother Gutiérrez raised 15 kids in this 1841 adobe house. The patio delights, with weathered wooden tables and Mexican wrought-iron chairs. Huge portions of traditional fare. A taco (2 really) $2.75. Combination plate $6-10. Good vegetarian dishes. Open Mon.-Thurs. 11am-9pm, Fri.-Sun. 10am-10pm.

Tutto Buono Gastronomic Specialties, 469 Alvarado (372-1880). Large, very Californian, with track lighting and black and white tile. Large Caesar salad with organic romaine hearts ($3.95). Homemade pastas and sauce. Fresh brick-oven pizzas (from $6), hearty pastas ($8-10), and seafood specials. Open Mon.-Sat. 11am-3pm, for lunch. Dinner served daily starting at 5pm.

London Bridge Pub, Wharf II (625-2879), under Tony Roma's. English pub overlooking the marina. Outstanding pub food includes delicious fish and chips ($8) and an English breakfast of bacon, sausage, eggs, grilled tomato, and fried bread ($6). Large beer selection. Open daily 11:30am-2am, food served until 10pm.

Red's Donuts, 433 Alvarado (372-9761). Locals have flocked to Red's since 1950 for fresh donuts and coffee. Attracts businessmen, fishermen, policemen, and more. Also serves sandwiches ($3). Smoking allowed. Open 6am-2:30pm.

Amarin Thai Cuisine, 807 Cannery Row (373-8811), near the Aquarium. Hidden behind ice cream and fudge shops. Many entrees (numerous fresh seafood dishes) for $7-10. Open daily 11am-10pm.

Jillie Gort's, 111 Central Ave. (373-0335), in nearby Pacific Grove. Mostly vegetarian restaurant with local art decorating the walls. All-in-one-plate (brown rice, black beans, veggies with *tahini, tamari,* or salsa, and pita bread) is $6.50. Open Mon.-Fri. 11:30am-10:30pm, Sat.-Sun. 8am-10:30pm.

Del Monte Produce, 2400 Del Monte Ave. (373-5800). Incredibly low prices for fruit, nuts, and veggies. Open daily 8am-6pm.

Troia's Market & Deli, 350 Pacific St. (375-9819), at Pacific and Del Monte Ave. Inexpensive picnic fixings. Open Sun.-Thurs., Sat. 8am-9pm, Fri. 8am-10pm.

SIGHTS

At the northwest end of Cannery Row, the renowned **Monterey Bay Aquarium,** 866 Cannery Row (648-4800), stands all but open to the bay. Taking advantage of the bay's ocean-swept purity, valves continually pump in raw, unfiltered seawater. This not only guarantees a genuine ocean environment in the tanks, it also lets in eggs and larvae which eventually grow to join the exhibits. The result is that the environment inside the aquarium is almost exactly like that in the bay, right down to the algae and the simulated waves. In addition to such standards as over-sized octopi and static starfish, the aquarium contains 30-ft.-tall strands of kelp, diving birds, and a clever exhibit that allows otters to be viewed from above and below. Other attractions are the touch tanks and tidal pools, which allows visitors to touch starfish, rays, and other animals. Upstairs, galleries house special rotating exhibits. A new exhibit dealing with dangerous and/or poisonous marine animals and their conservation will open March 17, 1995. The aquarium is packed on holidays and can be crowded in the mornings, but after 3pm things usually calm down. (Open daily 9:30am-6pm. $11.25; students, active military, and over 65 $8.25; ages 3-12 $5.)

Cannery Row lies along the waterfront south of the aquarium. Once a depressed street of languishing sardine packing plants, this ¾-mi. row has been converted into glitzy mini-malls, bars, and discos. All that remains of the earthiness and gruff camaraderie celebrated by John Steinbeck in *Cannery Row* and *Sweet Thursday* are a few building façades: 835 Cannery Row once was the Wing Chong Market, the bright yellow building next door is where *Sweet Thursday* took place, and Doc Rickett's lab at 800 Cannery Row is now owned by a private men's club.

For a stylized look at Steinbeck's Cannery Row, take a peek at the **Great Cannery Row Mural,** which stretches 400 ft. along the "700" blocks of Cannery Row. Fifty panels by local artists depict Monterey in the '30s—the sum effect is impressive.

Built in 1846 by prisoners, military deserters, and a "volunteer" crew of Native Americans, **Fisherman's Wharf** was for decades the center of one of the largest fishing and whaling industries in the West. Since WWII, however, fishermen have followed the fish to Moss Landing, south of Monterey Bay. Fisherman's Wharf is currently awash with tourists, junk-food stalls, and cheap shops selling seashells and Steinbeck novels.

Several companies on the wharf offer **sight-seeing boat trips** around Monterey Bay. **Monterey Sport Fishing,** 96 Fisherman's Wharf (372-2203), provides 25-minute tours every half-hour ($7, under 12 $5). You can frequently spot sea lions, seals, and sea otters on the trips. **Sea-Life** tours (372-7150) offers a 25-minute glass-bottom boat ride ($5, under 12 $4). Tours leave every half-hour. During the California gray whale migration from mid-December through March **whale-watching** trips are available from the same companies. The cruises, lasting nearly two hours, leave every day ($12-15, ages 7-12 $8-10). Pregnant women and children under six are not allowed on the cruises.

Located at the base of Fisherman's Wharf in the Historic Customs House Plaza is the new **Stanton Center's Maritime Museum of Monterey** (373-2469). Ship models, photographs, navigational instruments, logs, and other paraphernalia sketch the history of Monterey from its inception as a stop on Juan Cabrillo's 16th-century journey to its emergence as the "Sardine Capital of the World." The center-piece of the museum is the original Fresnel Lens of Point Sur Lighthouse, a two-story structure of gear-works and cut glass that was replaced by the modern electrical lighthouse. The museum also provides workshops, lectures, and a 4,000-volume library. Visitors need not pay admission to see the 15-minute film on Monterey. (Open daily 10am-5pm. $5, seniors and disabled $4, ages 13-18 $3, ages 6-12 $2.)

Making the rounds of the historic buildings in central Monterey will give you a sense of the region's history. Monterey's early days spawned a unique architectural trend, influenced by East Coast seafarers. The typical house features South Carolina details, such as wrap-around porches, balconies, and pane windows, as well as Mexican adobe characteristics such as yard-thick walls and exterior staircases. Most of the town's historical buildings downtown now belong to the **Monterey State Historic Park.** Each house is clearly marked by a sign and can provide information and free maps of walking tours. If you plan to visit more than one of the houses which charge admission, you'll want to purchase a $5 pass which allows you to enter all historic park buildings and participate in any or all of the walking tours. Buy your ticket at the **Visitors Center** (649-7118) inside the Park Headquarters in the Customs House Plaza (open daily 10am-5pm, in winter 10am-4pm). The center sells the *Path of History* walking tour book ($2), and offers the Monterey Historic Park **House and Garden Tour** for history fans (daily 10:30am, 12:30, and 2:30pm). The 1½-hour tour features 10 historic buildings and five gardens ($2, under 18 $1.50).

One historic adobe is the **Stevenson House,** 530 Houston St., with Robert Louis Stevenson memorabilia. (Tours Fri.-Sun., Tues., Thurs. 2, 3, and 4pm.)

Other historical sights include **Colton Hall** and its museum on Pacific St. between Jefferson and Madison St. The hall was completed in the spring of 1849 and had its 15 minutes of fame that autumn, when the California State Constitution was written and signed between its walls. The building has since been dedicated to the memory of the convention. (Open Mon.-Fri. 10am-5pm, Sat.-Sun. 10am-noon and 1-5pm. Closes at 4pm in winter. Free.) The **Old Whaling Station,** near the Customs House, is packed with mementos of Monterey's pre-sardine days. The sidewalk in front, made from whale bones, is enough making even Ahab sad. (Open Fri. 10am-2pm.)

You can find the **Monterey Peninsula Museum of Art,** 559 Pacific St. (372-7591), in the same neighborhood as the historic adobes. Currently undergoing expansion, the museum exhibits etchings, woodcuts, and paintings from the 17th through the 20th centuries, as well as displays of international folk arts. The Ralph K. Davies Collection of Western Art includes many of Charlie Russell's well-known bronze statues of bronco-busters. (Open Tues.-Sat. 10am-4pm, Sun. 1-4pm. $2.)

Monterey's beach lacks the drama and surf of its neighbors; head west and north for the most impressive shoreside scenery. Around the northern end of the peninsula, the beach runs uninterrupted for 3 to 4 mi., first as **Pacific Grove Municipal Beach,** then as **Asilomar State Beach.** (Bus #2 goes to within 4 blocks of the ocean in Pacific Grove. You can also bike the 2 mi. from downtown.) There are numerous tidepools here, and the rocky shore is a curious place to explore.

Sunset Drive is, appropriately, the best place for watching the sun go down. People arrive a full two hours before sunset in order to secure front row seats along the road (also known as Ocean Blvd.). You might consider walking westward to Point Pinos before the sun does its thing. At the western tip stands **Point Pinos Lighthouse,** a New England-style structure that is the oldest California beacon still in use. Inside are exhibits on Coast Guard history. (Open Sat.-Sun. 1-4pm. Free.)

Pacific Grove took root over a 100 years ago as a Methodist enclave, and many of the Victorian houses are extant and shipshape. This unpretentious middle-class town (even the mail carriers wear Bermuda shirts and straw hats) has a beautiful coastline, numerous lunch counters, and lots of funky shops. In addition, Pacific Grove houses thousands of **monarch butterflies** which annually flee Canada to winter in its cypress groves from October to March. Look, but don't touch; harming butterflies is a $1000 offense. Even if it's not the time of year for monarchs, you can visit the **Pacific Grove Museum of Natural History,** Forest and Central Ave. (648-3116, 648-3119 for recorded info.), one block north of Lighthouse Ave. Mounted specimens of the regal insects and local wildlife fill the first floor. On the balcony, watercolors of wildflowers hang next to pressed specimens of seaweed. (Open Tues.-Sun. 10am-5pm. Free.) Across the street from the museum is the **Pacific Grove Chamber of Commerce** (373-3304). It has information on local attractions and accommodations, maps, and videos. (Open Mon.-Fri. 9am-5pm, Sat. 11am-3pm.)

17-Mile Drive meanders along the coast from Pacific Grove through **Pebble Beach** and the forests around Carmel. Once owned by Del Monte, Pebble Beach has become the playground of the fabulously well-to-do. Its enormous, manicured golf courses creep up almost to the shore's edge, providing a strange contrast with the dramatically jagged cliffs and turbulent surf. The Drive is rolling, looping, and often spectacular, though sometimes plagued by heavy tourist traffic and an outrageous $6.50 entrance fee. Save your money and bike it; bicyclists and pedestrians are allowed in at no cost. To come and go as you please in one day, present your receipt to the guard and make sure he or she records your license plate number. One point of interest along the drive is The **Lone Cypress**—an old, gnarled tree growing on a rock promontory. To some, especially when viewed in the forgiving dimness of twilight, the tree is a silent testimony to perseverance and solitary strength; to others the extensive trusses that support the tree make it appear pathetic.

NIGHTLIFE

Monterey's nightly entertainment centers around the same areas that click with cameras by day; bars downtown attract fewer tourists. If you are fresh from San Francisco or L.A., Monterey's nightlife will seem insipid. One option is to tire yourself biking, hiking, or kayaking in the beautiful peninsula and go to bed early.

Planet Gemini, 625 Cannery Row (373-1449), on the 3rd floor. Comedy and dance club that features rock on Tues., country/western on Wed., and comedy Thurs.-Sat. Doors open at 8pm, shows start at 9pm. Dancing Thurs.-Sat. 10:30pm-2am. Cover varies.

Viva Monterey, 414 Alvarado St. (646-1415). Modern video-bar showing music and sports videos. Also has live rock bands occasionally. Serves lunch and dinner and offers a pub menu. Pizzas from $7.50. Jumbo drafts $3.50. Pool tables. Open daily 2pm-2am. Food served 5pm-1am. Must be 21.

Doc Ricketts Lab, 95 Prescott St. (649-4241), on Cannery Row. Not exactly the oceanographer's laboratory described by John Steinbeck. Happy hour Mon.-Fri. 8-10pm. A local crowd dances to live rock and blues nightly 9pm-1:30am. 2 pool tables. Occasional D.J. Cover varies with act. Open daily 8pm-2am.

SEASONAL EVENTS

Monterey Bay's Theatrefest, late June-early Aug., between the Customs House and the Pacific House. Free afternoon theatre Sat.-Sun. 11am-6pm. Evening performances $10, students and seniors $8.

Monterey Jazz Festival (373-3366), third week of Sept. The great names of jazz (closer to Buddy Rich than Alex Ross for the most part).

Monterey County Fair, mid-Aug. at the Monterey County Fairgrounds and Exhibition Park. Features a variety of exhibits and performers.

Laguna Seca Raceway, late May-early Oct., off Rte. 68 east of Monterey. Highlights of the season include the Monterey Sports Car Grand Prix (late July), the Historic Automobile Races (late Aug.), and the Monterey Grand Prix PPG Indy Car World Series (early Oct.). Call 800-327-SECA, -7322 for ticket information.

■■■ SALINAS

Salinas lies 25 mi. inland from Monterey, and is the heart of John Steinbeck Country. The renowned author (the only American to win both the Pulitzer and Nobel Prizes) lived here until he was 17. This is where *East of Eden* and *The Red Pony* are set, where many of Steinbeck's characters come from, and where his ashes are buried.

Two hours south of San Francisco, Salinas is bordered by the Monterey Peninsula to the west and vast farmlands to the south. Other than a wealth of information and exhibits on Steinbeck and a highly acclaimed rodeo, Salinas has little to offer travelers. The more scenic route and destinations along the coast may be more enjoyable.

Practical Information The **Salinas Chamber of Commerce,** 119 E. Alisal (424-7611), has city maps ($2; open Mon.-Fri. 8:30am-noon, 1-5pm). The **Amtrak** station is at 40 Railroad Ave. (422-7458). Trains leave for San Francisco ($19), Los Angeles ($67), and all points between. (Open daily 10am-1:30pm and 3-6pm. Call 800-872-7245 for ticket info.) Public transportation is coordinated by the **Monterey-Salinas Transit (MST),** 110 Salinas St. (899-2555 or 424-7695), at Central Ave. Fare per zone is $1.25, under 19 and over 64 50¢ (free transfers). Bus #20 or 21 will take you to Monterey. **Greyhound** (424-4418), at Salinas and Gabilan, 1 block from the MST center, sends out 6 northbound and 5 southbound buses per day to San Francisco ($18), Los Angeles ($38), Santa Cruz ($11). (Open daily 6am-11:30pm.) Wash your dirty duds at **Salinas Wash & Dry,** 509 E. Alisal St. (Wash $1, 10-min. dry 25¢. Open Mon.-Fri. 8am-9pm, Sat.-Sun. 6am-9pm.) The **post office** is located at 100 W. Alisal (758-3823), at Lincoln Ave. (Open Mon.-Fri. 8:30am-5pm.) The **General Delivery ZIP Code** is 93907. The **area code** is 408.

Accommodations and Camping Salinas's position on U.S. 101 just 20 mi. east of the Monterey Peninsula allows it to support a large number of hotels. Clusters of lodgings are found throughout the city; on N. Main St. near the Rodeo Grande, S. Main at John St., and E. Alisal near the highway. Few are impressive, but events in Santa Cruz or Carmel can fill the rooms here.

Motel 6, 1010 Fairview Ave. (758-2122), near the airport, has standard rooms, but the best rates in town—singles $28, doubles $34, winter singles $26, doubles $32. A slightly more expensive second location, 1257 De La Torre Blvd. (757-3077), is just a few blocks away.

Food A number of very good, very cheap, very authentic Mexican restaurants call Salinas home. It is difficult to determine which are the best. Those looking to stock up on fresh fruits and vegetables should check out the **Old Town Salinas Farmers' Market** on Main St. (Wed. 3-8pm).

Mi Tierra, 18 E. Gabilan (422-4631), offers huge portions, low prices, and a family-run feel. This friendly establishment is a premium choice for great Mexican food. (Bean burrito $2. 3 enchiladas with rice and beans $6.50. Open Sun.-Thurs. 7am-9pm, Fri.-Sat. 7am-10pm.) For that *tsunami*-size appetite, try the all-you-can-eat sushi for $22 at **Shogun Japanese Restaurant,** 216 S. Main St. (757-6105). Dinners with salad and rice cost $8-14 at this popular local restaurant. (Open Mon.-Fri. 11:30am-2pm and 5-9:30pm, Sat. 5pm-9:30pm.) Take out pints or quarts of Mexican fare from **El Águila Bakery and Deli,** 42 W. Market (422-3629). Spanish rice sells for

$1.10 per pint, $1.70 per quart. Two enchiladas (beef, chicken, or cheese) with rice and beans will cost you $2.59. (Open Mon.-Sat. 7:30am-6pm, Sun. 8am-8pm.) **La Plaza Bakery,** 20-A N. Sanborn Rd. (422-0578), at E. Alisal, far north of downtown, but close to U.S. 101, offers a full line of authentic Mexican pastries (30¢-$1; open daily 5am-9pm.) Satisfy a craving for American food and Coca-Cola-inspired decor at **The Recipe Box,** 35 W. Gabilan (424-0188; open Mon.-Fri. 10am-3pm.)

Sights and Entertainment The house where Steinbeck grew up (appropriately called The Steinbeck House), is located at 132 Central Ave., and is presently a restaurant. A scrumptious lunch ($6.50) is served family-style with two sittings. (Mon.-Fri. 11:45am and 1:15pm; dessert $2.50, coffee and tea $1, menu changes daily. Call 424-2735 for reservations.) The **Steinbeck Library,** 350 Lincoln Ave. (758-7311), is for the most part a normal municipal library, but does contain a room of Steinbeck memorabilia, and information on Steinbeck sights in the area. (Open Mon.-Wed. 10am-9pm, Thurs.-Sat. 10am-6pm.) Photographs, manuscripts, and personal letters can be found on display at the **Steinbeck Center Foundation,** 371 Main St. (753-6411). The center also offers tours and information on Steinbeck Country. (Open Mon.-Fri. 8am-5pm, June-Aug. also Sat. 10am-3pm.)

Salinas's other significant tourist sight, the **Boronda History Center** (757-8085), is home to the Boronda Adobe, built in 1848. Also located on the grounds are a one-room schoolhouse and a genealogical archive. (Open Mon.-Fri. 9am-3pm. Free.)

After seeing the sights, the **Penny Farthing Tavern,** 9 E. San Luis St. (424-5652), is a good place to unwind. This authentic British pub seems extremely out of place in Salinas. It offers the local population Spicy Scottish meatloaf ($7), fish and chips ($6), cottage pie ($6.50), and 10 British beers on tap. Open daily 11am-10pm.)

Salinas's biggest nonliterary tourist pull is the **California Rodeo Salinas and Intertribal Indian Village.** This, the fourth largest rodeo in the world, attracts ropers, wrestlers, riders, cows, bulls, and horses from across the West in late July. The Indian village showcases the culture of several different tribes. While the rodeo officially lasts for only one weekend, related events—including cowboy poetry readings—take place throughout the last three weeks of July. (Tickets $6-15, $52 for all 4 days. Call 757-2951 or 424-7355 or write P.O. Box 1648, Salinas, CA 93902 for more information.) Salinas's other noteworthy annual event is the **Steinbeck Festival,** held in early August. The festival features bus and walking tours of the area, films, and talks. For information, contact the Salinas Chamber of Commerce (see Practical Information, above) or call the Steinbeck Foundation (753-6411).

Thirty mi. north of Salinas on U.S. 101, the town of **Gilroy** hosts the **Garlic Festival** (842-1625), a celebration of the pungent bulb's multifarious applications, in the last full weekend of July.

■■■ SALINAS VALLEY AND PINNACLES NATIONAL MONUMENT

South of Salinas, U.S. 101 stretches out toward far-away San Luis Obispo, running through the wide and green Salinas Valley. Self-styled as the "salad bowl of the nation," the valley lives up to its name. Acres upon acres of tomatoes, lettuce, grapes, and garlic thrive here. The few small towns that are to be found stick close to the highway and do little to spoil the rural flavor of the area. But if the Salinas Valley is a salad bowl of greens, then the stunning, mysterious peaks of Pinnacles National Monument are the bacon bits. They make a visit to this land of produce worth your while.

Practical Information and Orientation For the usual info., check out the **King City Chamber of Commerce and Agriculture,** 203 Broadway, King City, CA 93930 (385-3814; open Mon.-Fri. 10am-noon, 1-4pm), or the **Greenfield Cham-**

ber of Commerce, P.O. Box 333, Greenfield, CA 93927 (674-3222; open Mon.-Fri. 8:30am-5pm). If you run into trouble, call the **Sheriff's Department: 385-8311** in King City; 755-5111 in other areas. There is a **post office** in King City, 125 S. 3rd St. (385-3339), at Bassett St. (Open Mon.-Thurs. 8:30am-4:45pm, Fri. 8am-5pm.) The **General Delivery ZIP Code** is 93930. The **area code** for the Salinas Valley is 408.

Gonzales, Soledad, Greenfield, and King City are the four towns in the Salinas Valley. While each is accessible by Greyhound bus service four or five times per day (from north or south), none of the nearby sights can be accessed without a car. If you're intent on coming here by bus, call the terminal in King City (385-3121) for the latest information; fares and rates change seasonally.

Accommodations, Camping, and Food As a general rule, the farther south from Salinas you go, the lower prices will be. Motels charge about $38 in Gonzales, and drop down to an average of $25 in King City. **Motel 6** in King City, 3 Broadway Circle (385-5000), is the best of the bunch. (Pool, cable TV, and vibrating beds $24 per night. Doubles $30.) The **Overniter Lodge**, 22 4th St. in Greenfield (674-5995), offers rooms for one or two at $20. **Camping** is to be found only at **Pinnacles National Monument** (389-4485). The campground is walk-in, but some of the sites are just 50 yds. from the parking lot. Reservations are not accepted, and with only 23 sites, it's best to show up early on weekends. The campground has fire pits, restrooms, and picnic tables, so you'll also have to fight off daytripping picnickers. (Sites $10.) East of Pinnacles is **Pinnacles Campground Inc.** (389-4462), a privately owned campground with pool, flush toilets, and hot showers ($6 per person per night up to $24 maximum; electrical hookups $2 extra). Be warned—there is no direct access by road from the east side of the park to the west side.

Food, like lodgings, is cheaper to the south. On the whole, fast food reigns supreme in these small towns, but try **Moody's Pizza,** 721 Broadway (385-3213), in King City, for great prices and service that's right on the mark. Get two (yes, two) 10-inch pizzas for $9, or a generous slice of pepperoni with a 20-oz. drink for $2.50. (Open Mon.-Sat. 11am-9:30pm, Sun. 11am-8pm.)

Outdoors, Sights, and Entertainment Towering dramatically over the chaparral east of Soledad, **Pinnacles National Monument** contains the spectacular remnants of an ancient volcano. Set aside as a national park by Teddy Roosevelt in 1908, the park preserves the erratic and unique spires and crags that millions of years of weathering carved out of prehistoric lava flows. Thirty mi. of hiking trails wind through the park's low chaparral, boulder-strewn caves, and pinnacles of rock. The **High Peaks Trail** runs a strenuous 5.3 mi. across the park between the east and west entrances, and offers amazing views of the surrounding rock formations. For a less exhausting trek, try the **Balconies Trail,** a 1½-mi. promenade from the park's west entrance up to the Balconies Caves. If you visit on a weekday, you will have the park nearly to yourself. Wildflowers bloom in the spring, and Pinnacles offers excellent bird-watching all year long. Pinnacles also has the widest range of wildlife of any park in California, including a number of rare predators: mountain lions, bobcats, coyotes, golden eagles, and peregrine falcons (park admission $4). The park headquarters is located at the East side entrance (Rte. 25 to Rte. 146; 389-4485), but there is also a ranger station on the west side (U.S. 101 to Rte. 146).

The **Mission Nuestra Señora de la Soledad** (678-2586) rests in Soledad, just west of Pinnacles. Constructed in 1791 and aptly named "Our Lady of Solitude," the mission is a quiet place in the middle of a lush valley. Floods destroyed the mission several times, but it was restored in the 1950s, and today a small museum exhibits various artifacts. (Open Wed.-Mon. 9am-4pm.)

If you still haven't had enough of Salad Bowl Country, stick around for the **Salinas Valley Fair,** held in mid-May in King City (385-3243 for information). Or head down to the **Greenfield Broccoli Festival** (674-5240) in early September.

■■■ SANTA CRUZ

Santa Cruz sports the kind of uncalculated hipness of which other coastal towns can only dream. The city was born as one of Father Junípero Serra's missions in 1791 (the name means "holy cross"), but today, Santa Cruz is nothing if not liberal. One of the few places where the old 60s catch-phrase "do your own thing" still applies, it simultaneously embraces macho surfers and a large lesbian community. In Santa Cruz, the spirit of the 60s has not died or been slicked up, remade, and crassly exploited. The city continues to go its own way in the 90s, with its own style.

Santa Cruz is the epitome of California cool; its prime location is crucial to its identity: without a beach, it would be Berkeley; with a better one, it would be Ft. Lauderdale. Along the beach and the boardwalk, tourism and surfer culture reign supreme. On the other side of Front St., the University of California at Santa Cruz takes over. Restaurants offer avocado sandwiches and industrial coffee; merchants hawk UCSC paraphernalia alongside the flyers for summer courses in ethics which query—"Should you kill your superego?"

While the earthquake of October 17, 1989 is infamous for the damage it did in Oakland and San Francisco, its epicenter was only 10 mi. from Santa Cruz. The city was by no means reduced to a pile of rubble, but it did lose a bridge, the popular Pacific Garden Mall, and several retail other shops. A statewide tax increase sped the restoration efforts, and the city has recovered almost entirely.

PRACTICAL INFORMATION

Visitors Information: Santa Cruz Conference and Visitor's Council, 701 Front St. (425-1234 or 800-833-3494). Extremely helpful staff. Publishes the excellent *Visitors Guide, Dining Guide,* and *Accommodations Guide* (all free). Open Mon.-Sat. 9am-5pm, Sun. 10am-4pm. Two information kiosks, one on Ocean St. in front of the County Building and the other at the top of Rte. 17 next to the Summit Inn Restaurant, are open Memorial Day-Labor Day Mon.-Fri. 10am-4pm, Sat.-Sun. 10am-6pm. The Summit Inn kiosk maintains the hours year-round.

Parks and Recreation Department: 307 Church St. (429-3663). Call for directions to the city's many parks. Open Mon.-Fri. 9am-6pm.

Greyhound/Peerless Stages: 425 Front St. (423-1800 or 800-231-2222). To San Francisco (3 per day, $10). To L.A. via Salinas (4 per day, $47). Luggage lockers. Open Mon.-Fri. 7:45am-11am, 2-7:45pm., Sat.-Sun. 7-11am, 3-4pm, 6-7:45pm.

Santa Cruz Metropolitan District Transit (SCMDT): 920 Pacific Ave. (425-8600 or 688-8600), at the Metro Center in the middle of the Pacific Garden Mall. Pick up a free copy of *Headways* for route info. Bus fare is $1 (no bills accepted), but day passes obtained at the Metro Center are $3 (those over 61 40¢, day pass $1.10; under 5 free). A shuttle from Metro Center to the beach runs Sat.-Sun. Memorial Day-Labor Day. Listen to AM 1610 for details. Open Mon.-Fri. 8am-5pm.

Taxi: Yellow Cab, 423-1234. 24 hrs. $1.75 plus $1.75 per mi.

Bicycle Rental: The Bicycle Rental Center, 415 Pacific Ave. (426-8687), at Front St. Mountain bikes and cruisers. 1st hour $6, $4 per additional hr. $25 per day, $50 per weekend, $75 per week. Helmets and locks provided. Summer open daily 10am-6pm. Winter open daily 10am-5pm.

Public Library: 224 Church St. (429-3526). Open Tues.-Thurs. 10am-8pm, Fri.-Sat. 10am-5pm.

Laundromat: Ultramat, 501 Laurel (426-9274). Wash $1.25, 10-min. dry 25¢, soap 25¢, and since this is Santa Cruz, espresso $1.15, cappuccino $1.50, and scones $1.25. Open daily 7:30am-midnight. Last load 10:30pm.

Weather: 415-364-7974=a long-distance call=70¢=don't bother—it's sunny today.

Lesbian, Gay, and Bisexual Community Center: 1332 Commerce Lane, 95060 (425-5422). The *Lavender Reader* is the excellent quarterly journal of the county's gay and lesbian community. The center is usually open in late afternoon and evening. Call before visiting.

Women's Crisis Line: 429-1478. 24 hrs.

Hospital: Santa Cruz Dominican: 1555 Soquel Dr. (462-7700 or Telmed 462-7736). Take bus #71 on Soquel Ave. from the Metro Center. 24 hrs.

Police: 809 Center St. (non-emergency 429-3711). 24 hrs.
Emergency: 911
Post Office: 850 Front St. (426-5200). Open Mon.-Fri. 8:30am-5pm. Sat. 9am-4pm.
  General Delivery ZIP Code: 95060.
Area Code: 408

ORIENTATION

Santa Cruz is about one hour south of San Francisco on the northern lip of Monterey Bay. Take **U.S. 101** or **Rte. 1** from S.F. The Santa Cruz beach and its boardwalk run roughly east-west, with Monterey Bay to the south. The narrow San Lorenzo River runs mainly north-south, bisecting the city and infesting it with mosquitoes. Chestnut, Front, and Ocean St. run roughly parallel with the river while Laurel-Broadway, Lincoln-Soquel, and Water cross it. Pacific Ave. lies to the west of Front St.

The gorgeous **University of California at Santa Cruz (UCSC)** is about 5 mi. up Bay St., in the redwood-covered foothills of the Santa Cruz Mountains (see Sights).

Downtown parking is relatively easy at one of the many two-hour lots or meters, but there is a $30 fine if you overstay your welcome. Do not be discouraged by a seeming dearth of beachfront parking or swayed by rip-off artists attempting to flag you into $5 all-day parking lots. The streets just behind the row of beach motels are a mere two minutes from the action and relatively empty.

Santa Cruz averages 300 sunshine-filled days per year. Temperatures hover around 80°F on sunnier days and drop into the high 50s at night.

ACCOMMODATIONS

Like many a beach town, Santa Cruz gets crowded during the summer and on weekends and doubly crowded on summer weekends. At these times, room rates skyrocket and availability plummets. Midweek, motels may be willing to bargain, but they are still going to cost you. Fortunately, a number of hotels on the winding San Lorenzo-East Cliff-Murray Dr. offer a few unreservable rooms for about $30. Show up around noon to get one of these rooms. Sleeping on the city beaches is prohibited and can result in hefty vagrancy fines.

Carmelita Cottage (HI-AYH), 321 Main St. (429-8541), 4 blocks from Greyhound and 2 blocks from the beach. Offers 24 beds, although planned additions may increase capacity. Kitchen, common room. 3-day max. stay. Curfew 11pm. Lock-out 9am-5pm. Office hours 5-10pm. $12, nonmembers $15. Reservations by mail only to P.O. Box 1241, Santa Cruz, CA 95061.

Harbor Inn, 645 7th Ave. (479-9731), near the harbor and a few blocks north of Eaton St. A small and beautiful hotel well off the main drag. 1 queen bed per room (1 or 2 people). Check-out 11am. Rooms $30, with bath $45. Weekends $45, with bath $70. In the winter, rooms even come with coupons for a free breakfast at the **Yacht Harbor Cafe,** 2 blocks south on 7th St. 9 RV sites with full hookup in back for $25, $95 per week. Reservations important on summer weekends.

Salt Air, 510 Leibrant (423-6020). 2 blocks from the beach, the boardwalk, and the wharf. Swimming pool. Singles and doubles $40-50. During promotions $28.

Santa Cruz Inn, 2950 Soquel Ave. (475-6322), located just off Rte. 1. 20 clean and comfortable rooms and amiable management. Coffee and pastries for guests. Check-out 11am. Singles $35-59. Doubles $45-69. Prices may vary, call for details.

INNCAL, 370 Ocean St. (458-9220), at Broadway, a 10-min. walk north of the Boardwalk. Cross bridge east from Boardwalk, take Edge Cliff Dr. north until it intersects Ocean St., and take Ocean north. A touch more tasteful than the average budget motel. A/C, TV, coin-op laundry. Room rates vary widely. Rooms with double beds: Sun.-Thurs. $30.75, Fri.-Sat. $55, $5.50 per additional person. Other rooms available for about $15 higher.

West Wind Motel, 204 2nd St. (426-7878). Across the parking lot from the Santa Cruz Boardwalk; you can hear the thunderous roller coasters in the rooms. Recently refurbished, but nothing fancy. Office open 9am-11pm Check-out 11am. Singles $30, on weekends $60. Doubles $60, on weekends $80.

CAMPING

Reservations for all state campgrounds can be made through MISTIX (800-283-2267). Two weeks is generally sufficient advance notice, except for holidays. Sites below are listed in geographical order, starting south of Santa Cruz. Lack of a car should not deter campers from staying at New Brighton State Beach or Big Basin Redwoods State Park, the most scenic spots in the area. Both are accessible by public transportation.

Manresa Uplands State Beach Park (761-1795), 12 mi. south of Santa Cruz. Take Rte. 1 and exit Larkin Valley. Veer right and follow San Andreas Rd. for 4 mi. then turn right on Sand Dollar. 64 campsites, tents only. $16, winter $14.

New Brighton State Beach (475-4850 or 444-7275), 4 mi. south of Santa Cruz off Rte. 1. Take SCMDT bus #54 "Aptos". Fall asleep to the murmur of the breakers in one of 112 campsites on a bluff overlooking the beach. Tall pines and shrubs maintain privacy between sites. Showers get crowded 7-9am. 1-week max. stay. No hookups. Check-out noon. Sites $16, winter $14. Reservations required.

Sunset State Beach (724-1266). South of Santa Cruz on Rte. 1 to Mar Monte exit. Take San Andreas Rd. to Sunset Beach Rd., or take SCMDT bus #54B. 90 campsites near the beach. Not as nice as New Brighton, but far superior to RV-choked **Seacliff State Beach.** Sites $16, winter $14. Reservations required in summer.

Henry Cowell Redwoods State Park (335-4598), off Rte. 9, 3 mi. south of Felton. Take Graham Hill Rd. or SCMDT bus #34, 35, or 30. 113 campsites in summer, 35 in winter. Not surprisingly, known for its giant redwoods. Hot showers and not-so-hot restaurants. 1-week max. stay. Sites $16, winter $14.

Big Basin Redwoods State Park (338-6132), north of Boulder Creek. Take Rte. 9 north to Rte. 236 North. On Sat.-Sun. at 6pm there is direct service from downtown, as bus #35 runs to Big Basin. This spectacular park was the first in the California State Park system. The best camping south of Point Reyes and north of Big Sur. Mountain air and dark red trees, some more than 2000 years old. 188 campsites with showers, 36 recently added tent cabins. 80 mi. of trails, including the 2-day Skyline-to-the-Sea Trail. Mountain bikes for rent (338-7313) and horseback tours available. 15-day max. stay. Sites $14, tent cabins $36. Backpackers $7 at backcountry sites. Parking $5 per night. Reservations required in summer.

FOOD

Santa Cruz sports an astounding number of restaurants in budget range. There's the normal spread of chain burger joints, but better food (served just as fast) is available at the Pacific Mall's **Food Pavilion** at Lincoln and Cedar (open daily 8am-9pm). Fine local produce sells at the **Farmer's Market,** at Pacific and Cathcart Ave. (Open May-Sept. Wed. 3-7pm, Oct.-April Wed. 2-6pm. If it's a sit-down meal you crave, you have many mouth-watering options:

Zachary's, 819 Pacific Ave. (427-0646). Bustling and happy, with hot coffee. In the morning locals crowd in for Mike's Mess: 3 scrambled eggs with bacon, mushrooms, and home fries topped with cheese, sour cream, tomatoes, and green onions served on toast ($5.50). The sourdough pancakes are also popular. Diverse crowd of business people, families, teenagers, young, and old. Open Tues.-Sun. 7am-2:30pm. Come before 9am on weekends to avoid long waits.

Royal Taj, 270 Soquel Ave. (427-2400). Exquisite and exotic Northern Indian dishes in a comfortable, batik-filled setting. Freshly baked *roti* $1.50-2. Choose from 14 vegetarian specialties. Lunch buffet 11:30am-2:30pm for $6.50 offers all-you-can-eat from 25 items! The *Saag lamb* (lamb curried with spiced cream spinach) is delicious ($6.95). Open daily 11:30am-2:30pm and 5:30-10pm.

Saturn Café, 1230 Mission St. (429-8505). A few blocks from downtown, but you're rewarded with vegetarian meals at their Santa Cruz best (generally under $4). Wheat germ is right-wing at this busy mixed hangout. Women's music Wed. 6:30-8:30pm. Open Mon.-Fri. 11:30am-midnight, Sat.-Sun. noon-midnight.

Zoccoli's Pasta House, 2017 N. Pacific Ave. (423-1717). Hearty and zesty helpings of pasta—you choose what sauce goes with which noodles. Most entrees $8-13, including baskets of fresh sourdough and soup or salad. You'll leave stuffed. Open Tues.-Sun. 11:30am-2pm, Tues.-Thurs. and Sun. 5-9pm, Fri.-Sat. 5-10pm.

Zoccoli's Delicatessen, 1534 Pacific Ave. (423-1711). Great food, great prices. Lunch special of lasagna, salad, garlic bread, salami and cheese slices, and Italian cookie $4.65. Sandwiches $3-5. Open Mon.-Sat. 9am-6pm, Sun. 11am-4:30pm.

The Crêpe Place, 1134 Soquel (429-6994), between Ocean St. and Seabright St. A casual but classy restaurant with a lovely outdoor setting. Feast on hearty dinner *crêpes* or enjoy the lighter fruit-filled confections ($5.75-7.55). Try "The Whole Thing": chocolate, bananas, walnuts, and ice cream in a *crêpe* ($5.50). Also serves local brews from the Front St. Pub. Open Mon.-Thurs. 11am-midnight, Fri. 11am-1am, Sat. 10am-1am, Sun. 10am-midnight.

The Whole Earth, Redwood Tower Building, UCSC (426-8255). Good vegetarian and vegan food by any standard, but simply amazing for a university food service ($4.75 buys a full meal and a view of the stunning redwoods). Casual atmosphere. Open Mon.-Fri. 7:30am-4pm; mid-Sept.-mid-June Mon.-Fri. 7:30am-7:30pm, Sat. 9am-5pm, Sun. 11am-5pm.

Staff of Life, 1305 Water St. (423-8041), about 1 block off Soquel. A natural foods market with organic whole grain bakery, produce, and vegetarian deli. Salads $4-5.50 per lb. Also carries grilled items, sandwiches, and organic California wines. Open daily 9am-9pm, deli open 9am-8pm, grill open 11:30am-2:30pm and 5-8pm.

SIGHTS AND ACTIVITIES

The **Boardwalk** (426-7433), a three-block arcade of caramel apples, ice-cream, and taco joints dominates the Santa Cruz beach area and provided the setting for teen vampire flick *The Lost Boys.* Video games, pinball, shooting galleries, and Bing-o-Reno complement miniature golf and amusement-park rides. The classiest rides are two veterans, both national historic landmarks: the **Giant Dipper** and the **Looff Carousel.** The 1924 Giant Dipper roller coaster, one of the largest surviving wooden coasters in the country, has miraculously weathered numerous quakes undamaged. A three-minute ride is $3. The 1911 Looff Carousel, also in good condition, is accompanied by an 1894 band organ ($1.50). The more modern rides are just variations on these classics, only you go round and round a good deal faster. The last week in August is "1907 Week"—rides, sodas, hot dogs, cotton candy, and red candied apples are all 50¢. (Tickets for unlimited rides $17. Discounts often available. Open Memorial Day-Labor Day daily; weekends and some holidays the rest of the year.)

The **Santa Cruz Beach** (officially named Cowell Beach) itself is broad and sandy, and generally packed with students. If you're seeking solitude, try the banks of the San Lorenzo River immediately east of the boardwalk. If you are craving nude sunbathing head for the **Red White and Blue Beach.** Take Rte. 1 north to just south of Davenport and look for the line of cars to your right ($7 per car). Do not venture here unaccompanied. If you don't feel like paying for the privilege of an all-over tan, try the **Bonny Doon Beach,** at Bonny Doon Rd. off Rte. 1, 11 mi. north of Santa Cruz. This surfer favorite is free and somewhat untamed. 18 other local beaches are listed in the Santa Cruz *Visitor's Guide* pamphlet, available at the visitors center (see Practical Information). To try your hand at riding the waves, contact the **Richard Schmidt Surf School** (423-0928; 1-hr. private lesson $50).

The Boardwalk is flanked on both sides by more studious areas. To the east lies the **Santa Cruz City Museum,** 1305 E. Cliff Dr. (429-3773), by Pilkington Ave. Scheduled to undergo expansion in the next few years, this small natural history museum includes exhibits on local geography, geology, and biology. As a break from gawking at UCSC beach volleyball stars, you can gawk at a 10,000-year-old Columbian Mammoth tooth found in nearby Watsonville, or climb on the realistic whale sculpture outside (open Tues.-Fri. 10am-5pm, Sat.-Sun. 1-4pm; free).

A pleasant 10-minute walk along the beach toward the southwest will take you to two unusual Santa Cruz museums, both worth short visits. The first is the **Shroud of Turin Museum,** 1902 Ocean St. Extension (426-1601), at St. Joseph's shrine. Science and faith clash over whether this famous piece of linen bearing the image of a man was used to bury Jesus. (Open Mon.-Sat. 1-4pm. Donation requested. Call ahead before visiting.) Just south of this museum lies Lighthouse Point, home to the **Santa Cruz Surfing Museum** (429-3429). Opened in 1986, the museum was the first of its kind. The main room of the lighthouse displays vintage wooden boards, early wetsuits, and surfing videos, while the tower contains the ashes of Mark Abbott, a local surfer who drowned in 1965 and to whom the museum is dedicated. (Open Wed.-Mon. noon-5pm, winter Thurs.-Mon. noon-4pm; $1.) The beach east of the point is **Steamer Lane,** a famous and popular spot for surfers since Hawaiian Duke Nakahuraka founded California's surfing aristocracy here 100 years ago.

Misión de Exaltación de la Santa Cruz, 126 High St. (turn north onto Emmet St. off Mission St.), was one of the later Christian outposts in California. Consecrated in 1791, the mission prospered until 1857, when an earthquake severely damaged the buildings. In the late 1920s, however, a local movement to restore the mission culminated in the reconstruction of the original church and the dedication of a park to mark the site of the original buildings. The peaceful, fragrant church allows some contemplative quiet (open daily 9am-5pm; donation requested).

The 2000-acre **University of California at Santa Cruz (UCSC)** campus lies 5 mi. northwest of downtown. The campus is accessible by public bus, auto, and bicycle. (From the Metro Center, bus #1 leaves every 15 to 30 minutes on Mon.-Fri. 6:30am-12:45am, Sat.-Sun. 7:30am-12:45am). Then-governor Ronald Reagan's plan to make UCSC a "riot-proof campus" (i.e., without a central point where radicals could inflame a crowd), when it was built in the late '60s, resulted instead in a stunning, sprawling campus. University buildings appear intermittently amid spectacular rolling hills and redwood groves. Santa Cruz is famous (or infamous) for extracurricular leftist politics supplemented by a curriculum offering such unique programs as "The History of Consciousness." UCSC was once the "safety school" of the UC system, but now it regularly turns away large numbers of aspiring Slugs (the school mascot is the banana slug). Guided tours start from the **visitors center** at the base of campus. If you drive on weekdays, make sure you have a parking permit. Trails behind the campus are perfect for day hikes, but it is not safe to go alone. (Parking permits and maps available at the police station, 429-2231.) The UCSC arboretum is one of the finest in the state (open daily 9am-5pm; free).

Directly south of UCSC is the **Natural Bridges State Park** (423-4609), at the end of W. Cliff Drive. While its lone natural bridge has collapsed, the park nevertheless offers a beach, tidepools, and tours twice a day during Monarch butterfly season from October to March. The best time to go is in November or December, when thousands of the stunning lepidoptera swarm along the beach. (Open daily sunrise-sunset; parking $6 per day.)

You can rent ocean-going **kayaks** at the Santa Cruz Wharf. One outfitter is **Kayak Connection,** 413 Lake Ave. (479-1121) A single rents for $32 per day, a double for $45. Rentals include paddle, life jacket, and skirt. Lessons ($35) are also available. (Open Tues.-Fri. 10am-5pm, Sat.-Sun. 8:30am-5pm.)

ENTERTAINMENT AND NIGHTLIFE

As in most university towns, carding at local bars is stringent. The restored ballroom at the **Boardwalk** makes a lovely spot for a drink in the evening, and the Boardwalk bandstand offers free Friday night concerts. *Good Times* and UCSC's *City on a Hill* are particularly informative free weeklies. The Santa Cruz Parks and Recreation Department publishes a free *Summer Activity Guide* useful for long-range planning; pick one up at their office (see Practical Information, above).

Kuumbwa Jazz Center, 320-2 Cedar St. (427-2227). Great jazz, renowned throughout the region. Under 21s are welcome in this simple, enthusiastic setting. The big names play here on Mon. ($12-17); Fri. is the locals' turn (about $5). Rarely sold out. Most shows around 8pm.

Louden Nelson Community Center, 301 Center St. (429-3504), at Laurel St. Another home for local repertory groups and dance classes. Offerings include poetry readings and summer concerts. Prices vary, call for info.

The Catalyst, 1011 Pacific Ave. (423-1336). This 700-seat concert hall draws second-string national acts, college favorites, and local bands. Big, boisterous, beachy bar and dance club. Pizza by the slice ($1.75), sandwiches ($2-5). Cover for local bands $1 until 9pm, $2 after. Must be 21. Shows at 9:30pm. Open daily 9am-2am.

Front St. Pub, 516 Front St. (429-8838). Hip brewery. Three-glass sampler of excellent beer $2.50. Bar food runs $5-7. Happy hour Mon.-Fri. 3-6pm offers $2 pints, $6.50 pitchers. Open daily 11:30am-midnight (later if it's really packed).

Blue Lagoon, 923 Pacific Ave. (423-7117). Relaxed gay bar. Giant aquarium in the back of the room contributes a pleasantly flickering light. Sun.-Wed. videos, dancing; no cover. Thurs.-Sat. DJ, $1 cover. Drinks about $1.50. Open daily 4pm-2am.

SEASONAL EVENTS

Whale-watching season (425-1234), Jan.-April. Boats depart from the Santa Cruz Municipal Wharf.

13th Annual Clam Chowder Cook-Off (423-5590), late Feb.

Longboard International surfing tournament (684-1551), late May.

Mr./Ms. Santa Cruz Bodybuilding Classic (335-7946), late May. Held in the civic auditorium.

Roaring Camp Civil War Encampment (335-4400), Memorial Day Weekend. Held at the Roaring Camp and Big Trees Narrow Gauge Railroad.

Santa Cruz County Vintner's Festival (458-5030), June. Buy an empty glass in Santa Cruz, then follow the provided map and have a designated driver take you through the county as you visit vineyards and imbibe free wine.

National Nude Weekend (353-2250), mid-July. Celebrated at the Lupin Naturalist Club in the Santa Cruz Mountains. Enjoy bands (playing in the buff) or come paint the posing models (on canvas). Free, but reservations are required.

Jose Cuervo Professional Volleyball Tournament (429-3665), early Aug.

Cabrillo Music Festival (426-6966), first 2 weeks in August. Held in the civic auditorium, the festival brings contemporary and classical music to the Central Coast. It's hard to get tickets ($16-25), so reserve well in advance.

Santa Cruz County Fair (724-5671), at the fairgrounds in mid-Sept.

Shout for Sprouts Festival, Oct. Honors the oft-neglected brussels sprout with sprout ice cream, sprout-chip cookies, and other sprout delicacies.

Santa Cruz Christmas Craft and Gift Festival (423-5590), late Nov. Held at the Santa Cruz Coconut Grove.

■ NEAR SANTA CRUZ

Santa Cruz is surrounded by gently sloping hills that make hiking a delight; the paths are only mildly strenuous and the scenery is magnificent. To the north, **Big Basin Redwoods State Park** offers trails that novices should be able to enjoy (see Camping). Farther to the south, the gorgeous **Henry Cowell Redwoods State Park** has trails suitable for daytrips in the redwoods (see Camping, page 224). Beware of the highly touted **Felton Covered Bridge,** located about a half hour north of Santa Cruz. Although it is the "tallest covered bridge of its kind in the United States," it's ramshackle, not really picturesque, and not worth going out of your way to see.

The **Roaring Camp and Big Trees Narrow Gauge Railroad,** Graham Rd., Felton (335-4484), runs an old steam-powered passenger train on a spectacularly scenic route from Felton through the redwoods to Bear Mountain. (Round-trip fare $14, ages 3-17 $8.95, under 3 free.) To reach Felton take scenic Rte. 9, which passes through Henry Cowell Redwoods State Park. In Felton take Graham Hill Rd. southeast, and turn south for Roaring Camp as indicated by road signs.

The **Mystery Spot** (423-8897), 3 mi. northeast of Santa Cruz at Branciforte Dr., is an indescribable tourist attraction where gravity, perspective, and velocity seem to run amok. While it's clear that the area is a source of magnetic disturbance, the true interest of the Mystery Spot lies in its owner's unintentionally hilarious efforts to augment the spectacle through optical illusions—would you believe trees respond to magnetism? (Open daily 9:30am-4:30pm. $3, ages 5-11 $1.50.)

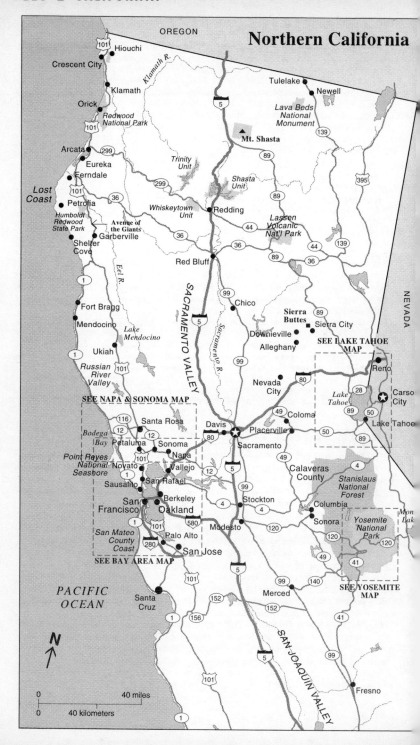

Northern California

San Francisco

Occupying only 47 square miles at one end of an enormous urban horseshoe, San Francisco proper appears small and separate. Yet there is a great city of nearly three-quarter million people on this plot of land and its magical name cannot help but conjure some image—of gold, cable cars, LSD, or gay liberation—in the mind of anyone familiar with America.

Originally inhabited by the Miwok nation, the Bay Area remained quiet until 1776, when Father Junípero Serra arrived and planted another in his long string of missions, naming it after *San Francisco de Asis* (St. Francis of Assisi). The area remained sparsely populated until 1848, when gold was discovered in the Sierra Nevada's foothills. San Francisco's 800 or so residents realized that in addition to living a short river trip from the gold fields, they were also sitting on one of the greatest natural ports in the world. That year 10,000 people passed through San Francisco to get to the gold and a city was born.

The city's growth was neither smooth nor stable. It soon had its share of murders, fires, and earthquakes. But these misfortunes paled in comparison to the 8.3 temblor that rocked the city on April 18, 1906, leaving San Francisco to three days of fire and looting. Unfazed, residents rebuilt their city within three years. The 1936 and '37 openings of the Golden Gate and Bay Bridges ended the city's isolation from the rest of the Bay Area, and San Francisco soon took advantage of the economic boom brought about by World War II.

Always responsive to the unorthodox, the city served as home to the Beat Generation in the 1950s; the '60s saw Haight-Ashbury become the hippie capital of the cosmos; and in the '70s, the gay population emerged as one of the city's most visible groups. This community continues to be a powerful influence. In addition to promoting gay rights, it leads a creative battle against the AIDS epidemic, working to comfort victims and increase public awareness of the disease.

San Francisco's latest trial came on October 17, 1989, when the biggest quake since 1906 killed 62 people, knocked out the Bay Bridge, and interrupted the World Series game between the San Francisco Giants and the Oakland A's. Some of the hardest-hit sections of the city, including the wealthy Marina District, have since been almost completely rebuilt.

To understand San Francisco one must get to know its neighborhoods; most San Franciscans think of their city in segments. These neighborhoods pack an amazing level of diversity into a small area, lending San Francisco a cosmopolitan character unknown outside of world capitals. A few blocks will take you from affluent Pacific Heights to the impoverished Western Addition; the Italian community of North Beach borders the largest concentration of Chinese people outside of China. Today, San Francisco's community spirit continues to rest on mutual tolerance and appreciation of differences between the groups of people who call the city home.

■■■ PRACTICAL INFORMATION

Visitors Information and Consulates

Visitor Information Center, Hallidie Plaza (391-2000), Market at Powell St., beneath street level in Benjamin Swig Pavillion. A great many pamphlets on display, but even more hidden from view behind counter. Ask staff for specific information. Especially helpful are the free street map with sights key and the quarterly and annual events calendars. Among staff members are speakers of Italian, English, French, German, Japanese, and Spanish. Open Mon.-Fri. 9am-5:30pm, Sat. 9am-3pm, Sun. 10am-2pm. Event and information recordings in English (391-2001), French (391-2003), German (391-2004), Japanese (391-2101), Italian (391-2010), and Spanish (391-2122). **Travelers' Aid Society,** at the airport (877-0118) and at 1049 Market St. between 6th and 7th (255-2252),

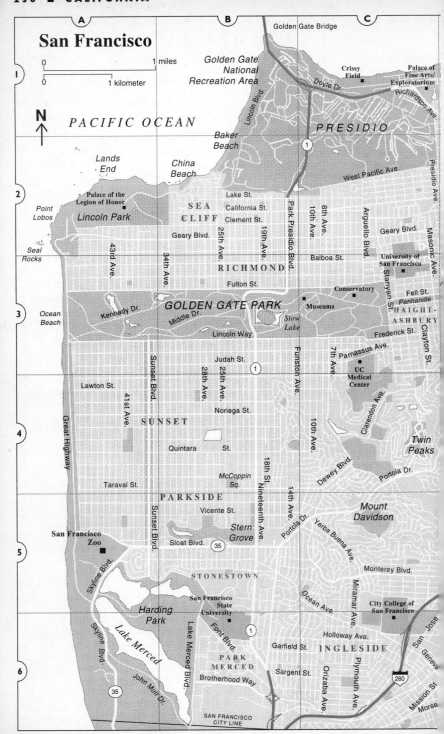

San Francisco

0 _____ 1 miles
0 _____ 1 kilometer

N

PACIFIC OCEAN

Golden Gate Bridge

Golden Gate National Recreation Area

Crissy Field

Palace of Fine Arts/ Exploratorium

Doyle Dr.

Richardson Ave.

PRESIDIO

Baker Beach

Lands End

China Beach

West Pacific Ave.

Presidio Ave.

Point Lobos

Palace of the Legion of Honor

Lincoln Park

SEA CLIFF

Lake St.

California St.

Clement St.

Geary Blvd.

8th Ave.

10th Ave.

Arguello Blvd.

Geary Blvd.

Masonic Ave.

Seal Rocks

43rd Ave.

34th Ave.

25th Ave.

19th Ave.

Park Presidio Blvd.

Balboa St.

RICHMOND

University of San Francisco

Stanyan St.

Fulton St.

Ocean Beach

Kennedy Dr.

GOLDEN GATE PARK

Middle Dr.

Stow Lake

Museums

Conservatory

Fell St.

Panhandle

HAIGHT-ASHBURY

Clayton St.

Lincoln Way

Frederick St.

Judah St.

Funston Ave.

7th Ave.

Parnassus Ave.

UC Medical Center

Clarendon Ave.

Lawton St.

Sunset Blvd.

28th Ave.

25th Ave.

Twin Peaks

41st Ave.

SUNSET

Noriega St.

10th Ave.

Great Highway

Quintara   St.

McCoppin Sq.

18th St.

Nineteenth Ave.

14th Ave.

Dewey Blvd.

Portola Dr.

Taraval St.

PARKSIDE

Vicente St.

Mount Davidson

San Francisco Zoo

Sunset Blvd.

Stern Grove

Sloat Blvd.

35

Portola Dr.

Yerba Buena Ave.

Skyline Blvd.

STONESTOWN

Monterey Blvd.

San Francisco State University

Miramar Ave.

City College of San Francisco

Harding Park

Lake Merced

Lake Merced Blvd.

Font Blvd.

Ocean Ave.

Holloway Ave.

1

Garfield St.

INGLESIDE

Plymouth Ave.

San Jose

San Geneva

Skyline Blvd.

PARK MERCED

Brotherhood Way

Sargent St.

Orizaba Ave.

280

Mission St.

Morse

35

John Muir Dr.

SAN FRANCISCO CITY LINE

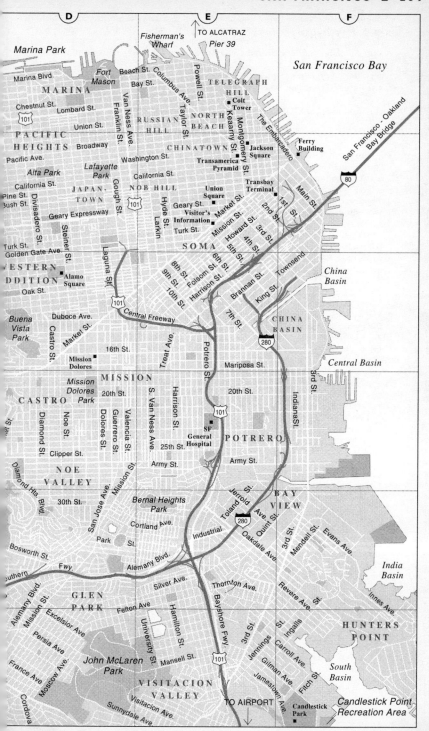

can provide meals and limited funds for travelers who have been robbed. **Redwood Empire Association,** 785 Market St., 15th floor (543-8334), at 4th St. by Union Sq. Maps and brochures on the area from San Francisco to Oregon. Open Mon.-Fri. 9am-5pm. The **Sierra Club Bookstore** has maps, books, and helpful staff (see page 248). **Wine Institute,** 425 Market St. #1000 (512-0151), between 1st and Fremont. Free wine country maps. Open Mon.-Fri. 9am-5pm.

Consulates: Canadian, 50 Fremont St. (687-7412). **British,** 1 Sansome St. #850 at Sutter (981-3030). Open Mon.-Fri. 9am-1pm and 2-4pm. **Australian,** 1 Bush St., 7th floor (362-6160). Open Mon.-Fri. 8:45am-5pm. **French,** 540 Bush St. at Stockton (397-4330). Open 9am-12:30pm. **German,** 1960 Jackson St. (775-1061). Open Mon.-Thurs. 8am-1pm and 2-4:30pm, Fri. 8am-3pm. **Japanese,** 50 Fremont at Mission (777-3533). Open Mon.-Fri. 9:30-11:30am, 1:30-4:30pm.

Passport and Visa Office: 525 Market St., Suite 200 (744-4444), at 1st St., near Montgomery St. BART/MUNI station. Open Mon.-Fri. 9am-4pm.

Currency Exchange: Thomas Cook, Pier 39 in Fisherman's Wharf (362-6271; open daily 10am-7pm); also at 75 Geary (362-3452; open Mon.-Fri. 9am-5pm).

Transportation: the **MUNI** system is by far the cheapest and most efficient way to travel within the city. See Getting Around, page 235 for more information.

Bay Tours and Ferries: see Fisherman's Wharf, page 260.

Taxi: Yellow Cab, 626-2345. **Luxor Cabs,** 282-4141. **DeSoto Cab,** 673-1414. For each, $1.70 plus $1.80 per additional mi. Open 24 hrs.

Car Rental: Budget (415-875-6850) has several conveniently located branches, including Pier 39 and 321 Mason St. in Union Sq. Compacts are about $25 per day, $150 per week. Unlimited mi. $15 per day surcharge for drivers under 25.**Bob Leech's Auto Rental,** 435 S. Airport Blvd. (583-3844 or 800-635-1240), South San Francisco. '91-'93 Toyota Camry $30 per day; Corolla $20 per day. 150 free mi., 10¢ per additional mi. Must be 23 with major credit card. Travelers flying into SFO can ask for pickup. Open Mon.-Fri. 8am-9pm, Sat.-Sun. 9am-5pm.

AAA: 150 Van Ness St. at Hayes St. in the Civic Center (565-2012). Open Mon.-Fri. 8:30am-5pm. Most services for AAA members only.

Public Library: Civic Center Library Building (557-4400; MUNI bus #5 goes right past the library's main entrance) at Larkin and McAllister. Open Mon., Wed.-Thurs., and Sat. 10am-6pm, Tues. noon-9pm, Fri. noon-6pm. California residents can sign out books freely; visitors can pay $25 for 3-month borrowing privileges.

Cultural, Community, and Religious Centers:

Booker T. Washington Community Center (African-American), 800 Presidio at Sutter St. (928-0398). Educational and recreational programs. Open daily 9am-5pm.

Chinese Culture Center, 750 Kearny St., 3rd floor of Holiday Inn (986-1822), at Washington St. Information on Chinatown and Chinese community events. Educational and cultural programs and walking tours (see Chinatown, page 266). Open Tues.-Sat. 9am-5:30pm.

Gay Switchboard and Counseling Services, 2712 Telegraph Ave. (510-841-6224), in Berkeley. Information on gay community events, local clubs, etc., as well as counseling. *Extremely* helpful staff. Suggested fee for some services. Open Mon.-Fri. 10am-9pm, Sat. noon-4pm, Sun. 6:30-10pm.

Japanese Cultural & Community Center of Northern California, 1840 Sutter between Buchanan and Webster (567-5505). Cheerful and informative staff. Open daily 9am-10pm.

Jewish Community Information and Referral, 777-4545. Open Mon.-Thurs. 10am-1pm. Emergency, call the Jewish Family and Children Service (567-8860) until 5pm, and Board of Rabbis Crisis Line (788-3630) after 5pm.

Mission Cultural Center (Hispanic-American), 2868 Mission (821-1155), between 24th and 25th; MUNI bus #14 runs past the center. Information, art, and cultural exhibits (see Mission District, page 248). Gallery open Wed.-Fri. 10am-6pm, Sat.-Sun. 11am-4pm.

San Francisco Ticket Box Office Service (STBS): 251 Stockton St. between Post and Geary (433-7827). Tickets to concerts, clubs, plays, and sports. ½-price tickets often available on day of show (inquire in person). BASS tickets. **Concert Information:** 397-5635. Open Tues.-Thurs. 11am-6pm, Fri.-Sat. 11am-7pm.

Laundromat: Brainwash, 1122 Folsom St. (861-3663; MUNI bus #12 runs along Folsom between 7th and 8th St. in South-of-Market. Laid-back locals sip cappuccino ($1.50) and eat pasta specials ($7) or "Wash-day Blues," Brian Wash's blueberry pancakes ($4.75) for brunch. Oh yeah, and wash ($1.50) and dry (25¢) your clothes yourself, or pay 75¢ per lb. (10 lb. min.) and have the friendly staff do it for you. Open daily 7:30am-11pm.

Road Conditions: 557-3755. 24-hr. driving information for the state (by CalTrans). Touch-tone phone required.

Weather: 936-0100. 24-hr. recording.

24-Hour Emergency Hotlines: Poison Control, 800-523-2222. **Drug Crisis Line,** 752-3400. **Rape Crisis Center,** 647-RAPE, -7273, operated by San Francisco Women Against Rape. **United Helpline,** 772-HELP, -4357. **SF AIDS Foundation Hotline** 800-367-2437, tri-lingual.

AIDS/HIV Nightline: 668-2437 or 800-273-2437. Trained staff provides support and information for those concerned about AIDS. Open daily 5pm-5am.

Haight-Ashbury Switchboard: 487-5632. Referrals for housing, rides, and legal and medical help. Call for recording.

Health Services:

San Francisco General Hospital, 1001 Portrero Ave. (206-8000; MUNI bus #9 runs along Portrero past the hospital), between 22nd and 23rd St. 24-hr. emergency room with walk-in service.

Health Care: Haight-Ashbury Free Medical Clinic, 558 Clayton St. (487-5632). Open for appointments only, call Mon.-Thurs. 1-8pm, Fri. 1-5pm. **University of California Dental Clinic,** UCSF Medical Center, 707 Parnassus (476-1891; 476-5814 for emergencies). Complete dental exam $10. By appointment only. Open Mon.-Fri. 8am-5pm. **Gay and Lesbian Medical and Dental Referral Service,** 565-4400. Program of Bay Area Physicians for Human Rights. May be expensive; inquire carefully about prices. **Health Center,** 1490 Mason St. (705-8610), near Broadway. Contraceptives and counseling (English or Chinese) about birth control and STDs. Fees set on a sliding scale. By appointment only. Open Mon.-Fri. 8am-5pm.

Information Highway: SF NET (695-9824), places coin-op computer terminals in public places so that travelers can have access to the Internet. Locations include cafés and clubs at 1409 Haight St., 1122 Folsom St., and 1398 9th St.

Post Office: 101 Hyde St., at Golden Gate Ave. Open Mon.-Fri. 7am-5:30pm, Sat. 7am-3pm. **General Delivery ZIP Code:** 94142. General Delivery open Mon.-Sat. 10am-2pm. **Bell Bazaar Station,** 3030 16th St., at Mission St. Open Mon.-Fri. 9am-5pm.

Area Code: 415.

■■■ ORIENTATION

San Francisco, the "City by the Bay," and the fourth-largest city in California (pop. 726,700), is 403 mi. north of Los Angeles and 390 mi. south of the Oregon border. The city proper lies at the northern tip of a peninsula that sets off San Francisco Bay from the Pacific Ocean. For information on the cities that surround the bay, see San Francisco Bay Area, page 273.

San Francisco's numerous neighborhoods are organized along a few central arteries. Each neighborhood is compact enough to explore comfortably on foot.

Referring to the city map will make the following orientation information clearer. San Francisco radiates outward from its docks, on the northeast edge of the peninsula just inside the lip of the bay. Most visitors' attention still gravitates to this area. Many of San Francisco's shining attractions are found within a wedge formed by **Van Ness Avenue** running north-south, **Market Street** running northeast-southwest, and the **Embarcadero** (waterfront road) curving along the coast. Market Street takes a diagonal course and interrupts the regular grid of streets.

At the top of this wedge lies **Fisherman's Wharf** and slightly below, around **Columbus Avenue,** is **North Beach,** a district shared by Italian-Americans, artists, and professionals. The focal point of North Beach is **Telegraph Hill,** topped by Coit

Tower. Across Columbus Ave. begin the **Nob Hill** and **Russian Hill** areas, home of the city's old money. This fan-shaped oasis is confined by Columbus along its northeast side, Van Ness along the west, and (roughly) Geary and Bush Streets on the south. Below Nob Hill and North Beach, and north of Market, **Chinatown** covers around 24 square blocks between Broadway in the north, Bush St. in the south, Powell St. in the west, and Kearny St. in the east. The heavily developed **Financial District** lies between Washington St. in the north and Market in the south, east of Chinatown and south of North Beach, and is home to the skyscrapers which define the city's skyline. Down Market from the Financial District, toward the bottom of the wedge, you pass through the core downtown area centered on **Union Square** and then, beyond Jones St., the **Civic Center,** an impressive collection of municipal buildings including City Hall, the Opera House, and Symphony Hall. The Civic Center occupies the base of the wedge and spills out over Van Ness to Gough St., 2 blocks west. Also within this wedge is the **Tenderloin,** where drugs and homelessness prevail among the sprouting high-rises both day and night. The Tenderloin is roughly bounded by Larkin St. to the west and to the east by Taylor St. extending from Market St. north to Geary, and encroaches upon the South-of-Market-Area from 6th St. to 9th St.

Below Market St. lies the **South-of-Market-Area (SoMa),** largely deserted during the day but home to much of the city's nightlife. Here, the best of San Francisco's nightclubs are scattered among darkened office buildings and warehouses. Decide beforehand exactly where you're going and share a cab with friends on the way there and back; the relative security of a cab is reassuring. South-of-Market extends inland from the bay to 10th St., at which point the Latino **Mission District** begins and spreads south. The **Castro,** center of the gay community, adjoins the Mission District at 17th and also extends south, radiating from Castro St.

On the north end of the peninsula, Van Ness Ave. leads to the commercially developed **Marina,** which includes a yacht harbor and **Fort Mason. Fisherman's Wharf** lies immediately to the east of the Marina and to the west lie the **Presidio** and **The Golden Gate Bridge**. Inland from the Marina rise the wealthy hills of **Pacific Heights.** South of Pacific Heights and west of Van Ness is the **Western Addition,** extending west to Masonic Ave. This district is the site of many of the city's public housing projects and can be dangerous, especially near Hayes St. Other than **Japantown,** there is little to interest tourists in the Western Addition. Farther west is the rectangular **Golden Gate Park,** which extends to the Pacific and is bounded by Fulton Street to the north and Lincoln Street to the south. At its eastern end juts a skinny panhandle bordered by the **Haight-Ashbury** district. North of **Golden Gate Park** is the **Richmond District,** with a large Asian-American population. South of the park is the **Sunset District,** home to the UCSF Medical Center.

GETTING THERE

By Airplane

San Francisco International Airport (SFO) (general information 761-0800) is located on a small peninsula in San Francisco Bay about 15 mi. south of the city center via U.S. 101. SFO has luggage lockers ($1 first day, $2 per additional day).

There are two ways to commute from SFO to the city by public transportation. First, **San Mateo County Transit,** or **samTrans** (800-660-4287), runs two buses from SFO to downtown San Francisco. The express allows only carry-on luggage, although some backpackers have been successful negotiators. (#7F; 35min.; runs 6-9am and 4-6pm every 30-60 min., 9am-4pm less frequently; $1.75, off-peak 85¢, under 18 85¢, over 64 60¢.) Bus #7B takes longer, but you can carry all the luggage you want (55min.; same frequency; 85¢, under 18 35¢, over 64 25¢). An **Airporter** bus (495-8404) runs a shuttle route between all three terminals and a downtown terminal at 301 Ellis St. and major downtown hotels (to the airport 5:20am-10:35pm, to the hotels 6am-11pm every 10 min.; $8, round-trip $14). If Oakland is your destination, take bus #3B to Daly City (5:45am-6:20pm every 30 min.), and from there catch a **BART train** to Oakland. **Taxi rides** to downtown San Francisco from SFO cost about $25 (for details, see Practical Information, page 232).

   Lorrie's Travel and Tour (334-9000), on the upper level at the west of all three terminals, provides door-to-door van service to and from the airport. Reserve at least one hour in advance for service to the airport. No reservations are needed for travel from the airport (vans run 6:30am-12:30am; $10, ages 2-12 $6). **Franciscus Adventures** (821-0903) operates a small bus between San Francisco and SFO ($8, $7 per person for groups of 3 or more). Call ahead from 4:30am-11:30pm to arrange a time.

By Train or Bus

Greyhound (800-231-2222) serves the **Transbay Terminal,** 425 Mission St. (495-1551), between Fremont and 1st St. downtown (open 5am-12:35am; to L.A. $39). The terminal is a regional transportation hub; buses from **Golden Gate Transit** (Marin County), **AC Transit** (East Bay), and **samTrans** (San Mateo County) all stop here. An information center on the second floor has maps, displays, and free phone lines for each of these systems. Downstairs, free buses shuttle passengers to **Amtrak** (800-872-7245) on 16th in Oakland where the real train station lies. (Amtrak open daily 6:45am-10:45pm; to L.A. $75.) Amtrak also has a desk at Transbay Terminal. First St. and Natoma is the pickup point for **Green Tortoise** (285-2441), the half-transportation company, half-commune located at 494 Broadway in North Beach. Green Tortoise runs trips down the coast to L.A. every Fri. night ($30) and to Seattle on Mon., Fri., and Sat. ($49). (Reservations required at least 1 week in advance. Open daily 8am-8pm.) **CalTrain** (800-660-4287 for voice or TDD) is a regional commuter train that runs south to Palo Alto ($3.25, seniors and disabled $1.50) and San Jose ($4.50, seniors and disabled $2.25), with service to Santa Cruz. The depot at 4th and Townsend St. is served by **MUNI** buses #15, 30, 32, and 42.

By Car

From the south, the city can be reached by car via U.S. 101, via I-5 to I-580, or via Rte. 1. If approaching from the east on I-580 or I-80, go directly over the Bay Bridge into downtown. From the north, U.S. 101 leads directly into the city over the Golden Gate Bridge (toll $3).

   I-5 is certainly the fastest way to traverse north-south distances to San Francisco. The speed limit is 65mph and you can make it from L.A. in 6 hours if you hustle. Rte. 1 takes twice as long, but is one of the most beautiful roads in the country. U.S. 101 is just the right blend of scenery, route through major cities, and speed. If you run into trouble, you can call the **California State Automobile Association** (565-2012; AAA members only).

   If you're a driver who needs a passenger or a passenger who needs a driver, call the **Berkeley Ride Board** (510-642-5259) for free, 24-hr. listings. **San Francisco International Hostel** (771-7277) at Fort Mason in the Marina and **San Francisco State University** (469-1842, in the student union; open Mon.-Fri. 7am-10pm, Sat. 10am-4pm) also have ride boards. **KALX Radio** (642-5259), on the Berkeley campus, broadcasts a ride list (Mon.-Sat. 10am and 10pm). Call them to put your name and number on the air for free.

GETTING AROUND

Buses and Subways

Buses, many of them quiet, clean, electrical models, run promptly and frequently, and the routes blanket the city. Despite its location in a state of automobile worshippers, San Francisco has not neglected rail transportation; the Bay Area is the easiest area in the West Coast to explore without a car. Connections to neighboring cities are well-coordinated and speedy via Bay Area Rapid Transit (BART). See San Francisco Bay Area for regional transportation information. The *Comprehensive Regional Transit Guide* ($4) covers all regional bus and subway services.

   San Francisco Municipal Railway (MUNI) (673-6864) operates buses, cable cars, and a combined subway/trolley system. Fares for both buses and trolleys are

$1, seniors and ages 5-17 35¢. Ask for a free transfer, valid in any direction for several hours, when boarding. (MUNI PASSPORTS valid on all MUNI vehicles: 1 day, $6; 3 days, $10; 7 days, $15; 1 calendar month, $35.)

MUNI buses run quite frequently throughout the city. In addition, **MUNI Metro** runs streetcars through subway tunnels along Market St. and above ground along five lines serving points south and west of downtown. The Metro and bus lines along a few major streets run all night. Most other buses run daily from 6am to midnight. Wheelchair accessibility is variable—some bus routes are completely equipped with lifts while others have none at all, and while all subway stations are accessible, the Metro is not accessible at all of its above-ground sites.

Even if you're only going to be in the city for a short time, purchase the *San Francisco Street and Transit Map* ($2), which contains information on frequency, wheelchair accessibility, and late-night service, as well as a complete street index allowing it to double as a general street map. Copies of this map are posted in bus shelters, but they are generally faded to illegibility or obscured by graffiti.

Cable cars have been transporting San Franciscans since 1873. (They were named a national historic landmark in 1964.) The cars are noisy, slow (9.5mph, to be precise), and so often full as to be a totally unreliable method of getting from point A to point B. You won't be the first person to think of taking one to Fisherman's Wharf. In fact, the Union Square cable car stop, en route to the wharf, is nicknamed "Fantasy Island" because the car is almost always full by the time it arrives—you're dreaming if you think you'll be able to board. Still, there is something undeniably charming about these relics, and you'll probably want to try them, especially if you have a MUNI pass. The strategy to avoid the mobs is to get up early and climb the hills with the sunrise. Of the three lines, the California (C) line is by far the least crowded; it runs from the Financial District up Nob Hill. The Powell-Hyde (PH) line, however, might be the most fun, for it has the steepest hills and the sharpest turns. (Runs daily 7am-1am. $2, seniors $1 9pm-7am. 3-hr. unlimited transfers.)

Bay Area Rapid Transit (BART) (778-2278) does not (alas) serve the entire Bay Area, but it does operate modern and carpeted trains along four lines connecting San Francisco with the East Bay, including Oakland, Berkeley, Concord, and Fremont. However, BART is not a local transportation system within the city of San Francisco; use the MUNI system for that. (BART trains run Mon.-Sat. 6am-1:30am, Sun. 8am-1:30am. One way 80¢ to $3.) Maps and schedules are available at all stations. All stations and trains are wheelchair accessible.

The **Gray Line** (558-9400) offers 3½-hour bus tours of the city ($25, ages 5-11 $12), plus a variety of other tours. Day tours leave from Transbay terminal and night tours from Union Square. Reservations required. Tours are available in a variety of languages; call for details.

Cars, Bicycles, and Feet

A car here is not the necessity it is in Los Angeles, thanks to the efficient MUNI system. Furthermore, parking in the city is *hell* and very expensive. In San Francisco, contending with the treacherous hills is the first task; if you've arrived in a standard transmission vehicle, you'll need to develop a fast clutch foot, since all hills have stop signs at the crests. If you're renting, get an automatic. And remember: in San Francisco, cable cars have the right of way.

The street signs admonishing you to "PREVENT RUNAWAYS" refer not to wayward youths but to cars poorly parked on hills. When parking facing uphill, turn the wheels toward the center of the street and leave the car in first gear (if you're driving a standard—we hope you're not). If your car starts to roll, it will stop (God willing) when the tires hit the curb. When facing downhill, turn the wheels toward the curb and leave the car in reverse (in a standard). *Always* set the emergency brake.

Think twice about attempting to use a bike to climb up and down the hills of San Francisco. Even the proudest year-round bike couriers have been spotted walking their bikes up the especially steep grades. Narrow roads and traffic are additional hazards. Golden Gate Park is a more sensible location for biking.

Even walking in this city is an exciting exertion—some of the sidewalks are so steep they have steps cut into them. Nevertheless walking is worthwhile and unavoidable. There are many **walking tours** of the city. Some even promise "no steep hills." Call **City Guides** (332-9601) for info on their free summer tours, or stop by the visitors center for info on the many commercial tours (hotline 332-9611).

■■■ PUBLICATIONS

Several free tourist magazines are available from sidewalk boxes in the heavily trafficked Fisherman's Wharf and Union Square areas as well as at the Visitor Information Center in Hallidie Plaza. Especially-for-tourists, listings-filled publications include the *San Francisco Tourist Guide*, the unusually glossy *Where* (546-6101), and the article-less *Key* (202-1900). The *San Francisco Guide* (775-2212) and the *Bay City Guide* (929-7722) are geared more toward the affluent shopper than the budget traveler, but they have up-to-date information on galleries and clubs.

Locals look up events in free weekly newspapers, including the *Bay Guardian* (255-3100). Crammed with reviews, news, and a weekly jazz calendar, the *Guardian* lives by Wilbur Storey's statement: "It is a newspaper's duty to print the news and raise hell." *Downtown* has entertainment listings for downtown San Francisco.

The *San Francisco Weekly* (541-0700) has city-wide listings. For gatherings of the visual and performing arts, try the *Arts Monthly* (543-6110), a downtown neighborhood newspaper. The *Bay Area Music Magazine* (BAM) is available at the more rocking cafés and restaurants in town. The *American Music Press,* also free, has a comprehensive "SF Club and Gig Guide." *club,* the urban scene magazine, is free.

Herb Caen's weekday column in the *San Francisco Chronicle* (777-1111, 50¢), the largest Bay Area **daily,** is a San Francisco institution not to be missed. Although non-locals won't recognize many of the names in his "who's who"-style column, Caen nabs the best stories in the city. The pink "Datebook" section of the Sunday edition ($1.50) is also a worthwhile entertainment resource. The *San Francisco Examiner* (777-7800), started by yellow journalist William Randolf Hearst (of *Citizen Kane* fame), has lunchtime and evening editions. The Sunday edition is put out jointly with the *Chronicle.*

A **gay and lesbian paper,** the *Bay Times* (626-8121), appears monthly. It boasts a thorough entertainment section and scintillating articles and letters. The *Bay Area Reporter,* also a newspaper for gays and lesbians, contains articles on gay pride as well as a highly varied "Arts & Entertainment" section. *The Sentinel* (281-3745) offers information on gay community events. *ODYSSEY Magazine* (621-6514) lists bars, cafés, and current events. These publications can be found easily in the gay neighborhoods around Castro and Polk St.

If it's **services** you're after, consult the quarterly *Open Exchange* (510-526-7190), which starts with astrology lessons and ends with yoga instruction. For a comprehensive collection of classified ads, check *The San Francisco Advertiser* (863-3151). Travelers enthusiastic about **leftist political agitation** in Northern California should consult the bimonthly *Radiation: An Alternative Bulletin* (861-0592).

Sports publications include the *California Bicyclist* (546-7291; available at most bike shops), a monthly chronicle of bicycle races and other events. The *Northern California Schedule* (free; available at sporting goods stores) has comprehensive listings of cycling, running, and multi-sport events (and cool running shoe ads).

■■■ ACCOMMODATIONS

There are a tremendous number of reasonably priced and conveniently located places to stay in San Francisco. Hostels and many cheap hotels dot the city. Many of the hotels and hostels listed here are in areas where extra caution is advisable, particularly at night. The Tenderloin and the Mission District can be particularly unsafe. Never hesitate to go elsewhere if uncomfortable about a neighborhood or establishment: even if prices are steeper—a cent of prevention is worth many dollars of cure.

HOSTELS

For those who don't mind sharing a room with between two and seven strangers (or in some cases, none at all), San Francisco's hostels definitely outdo its budget hotels. The better hostels are cleaner and safer than most budget hotels, have friendlier and more helpful staffs, and cost considerably less. Hostels also provide ample opportunity to meet fellow travelers. Making friends through hostels is not uncommon, and the experience can make your days (and nights) in San Francisco all the more fun and entertaining.

Pacific Tradewinds Guest House, 680 Sacramento St. (433-7970), in the **Financial District** between Montgomery and Kearny. From Transbay Terminal, take MUNI bus #38. At Market and Kearny, transfer to bus #15 northbound. Get off at Kearny and Sacramento. Tucked among the high-rises of the financial district, Pacific Tradewinds is one of the best around. With just 29 beds, an extremely cheerful and helpful staff, and Dr. Seuss readings, this cozy place has a communal atmosphere. No TV. Laundry ($4, they do it), kitchen, free tea and coffee.Clean and environmentally conscious. No smoking. Check-in 8am-midnight. Check-out 10:30am. No curfew. $14 per night with 14-day max. stay.

San Francisco International Hostel (HI-AYH), Bldg. 240, Fort Mason (771-7277), in the **Marina** west of Fisherman's Wharf. Entrance at Bay and Franklin St., 1 block west of Van Ness Ave. From Greyhound at Transbay Terminal, take MUNI bus #42 from Mission and Fremont St. northbound, then walk up the hill to Bay St.; follow signs to hostel. Conveniently close to buses. In the middle of Fort Mason, with gorgeous views of both the Bay and the Golden Gate Bridge, this hostel is in an incredibly beautiful location. The wooden buildings, free-standing fireplace, and sturdy bunks make it feel more like a campground than a city hostel. Free movies, walking tours, fully equipped kitchens, dining room, laundry. No smoking. $13 per night. Registration 7am-2pm and 3pm-midnight daily. Lines start at 6am. Visa, MasterCard, and JCB accepted. IBN reservations available.

Green Tortoise Guest House, 1116 Kearny St. at Broadway (834-9060) in the colorful place where **North Beach** and **Chinatown** meet. San Francisco's newest hostel-type accommodation provides clean, nicely finished rooms in an old Victorian building. Charming touches include chandeliers and brass swan bathroom fixtures. Wonderfully friendly atmosphere. Lockers under each bed, bring your own lock. Sauna, laundry room ($1.25 wash, 75¢ dry), kitchen. 25-day max. stay. $12 per bed in shared room. Singles $19.50. Doubles $30-35. $20 key deposit. Reserve and pay for rooms in advance.

Hostel at Union Square (HI-AYH), 312 Mason St. (788-5604), 1 block from **Union Square**. From Transbay Terminal, take MUNI bus #14 to Mission and 5th. Then take #27 north to Mason and Ellis. With 220 beds, this is the 3rd largest hostel in the country. Acceptable neighborhood, located between the expensive Union Square hotels and the unappealing Tenderloin. The management is very safety conscious. Big, clean common areas, TV room, vending machines. $14 per night, nonmembers $17. $5 key deposit. 20% of rooms can be reserved by phone with credit card. Show up at noon for the rest. IBN reservations available.

Globetrotter's Inn, 225 Ellis St. (346-5786), **Downtown** at Mason St. For bus directions, see Hostel at Union Square, above. On the border of a dangerous neighborhood; caution is advised. However, the Globetrotter itself is comfortingly small and intimate. Large kitchen adjoins common room with piano and TV. Check-in summer 8am-11pm; winter 8am-1pm and 5-11pm. Check-out 11am. No curfew. $12 per night; $75 per week. Call to reserve a bed and confirm 2 days ahead.

San Francisco International Student Center, 1188 Folsom St. (255-8800), in **South-of-Market.** Almost across the street from the Globe (see above for bus information). Newly opened in the summer of 1993. With bay windows, brick walls, and a big comfy couch, this place prides itself on cleanness, coziness, and conversation. Only 17 rooms. Great massage showerheads in the hall bathrooms. Free coffee and tea. 2 week max. stay in summer. Registration 9am-11pm. No curfew. $12 per night. $10 key deposit. Pre-paid reservations required.

San Francisco International Guest House, 2976 23rd St. (641-1411), at Harrison in the **Mission District.** From the Transbay Terminal, take bus #7B to Portrero and 24th. Walk to 23rd, then turn left. **International passport required.** A genuinely warm atmosphere in a beautiful Victorian house. Hardwood floors, wall tapestries, and houseplants make this hostel feel like a home. Be prepared for longish journeys to and from San Francisco's major attractions. Amazingly huge private rooms for couples. Free sheets and coffee. Two large kitchens, one of which is the only smoke-free area in the place. 5-day min. stay. All beds $13 per night; $11 per night after 10 days.

Interclub Globe Hostel, 10 Hallam Place (431-0540), in **SoMa** off Folsom St. between 7th and 8th. From Transbay Terminal (weekday daytime) take MUNI bus #12 to Folsom and 8th; any other time take MUNI bus #42 to corner of Harrison and 8th, walk up to Folsom, and turn left. **International passport required.** Catering to an "adventurous crowd," the lobby blares international music. The common room is home to a pool table, some fairly wild parties, and the Globe Cafe, which serves breakfast and dinner. Free sheets, blankets and pillows. $15 per night. A $10 deposit is required for a reservation.

HOTELS

An important hotel-related fact to consider is that accommodations costing more than $20 (i.e., all of the hotels and none of the hostels) must charge a 12% bed tax which is not included in the prices listed below. Even more important, many budget-range hotels in San Francisco are in unsafe areas, and in terms of cleanliness and helpfulness, you often get what you pay for. All hotels are busy during the summer months. Although lucky walk-ins sometimes get rooms, it's best to call several weeks in advance to reserve a spot. Hostels generally offer a better package, but there are also several budget hotels with great deals.

Downtown

Adelaide Inn, #5 Isadora Duncan (441-2261; fax 441-0161), at the end of a little alley off Taylor near Post St., 2 blocks west of Union Square. With its warm hosts and jumbled paintings, this is perhaps the most charming of San Francisco's many "European-style" hotels. Steep stairs, no elevator. All rooms with large windows. Kitchenette with microwave and fridge. Continental breakfast included. Doors close at 11pm, adding to the feeling of security. Office hours Tues.-Fri. 9am-1pm, 4-9pm, Sat.-Mon. flexible. 18 rooms. Hall baths. Singles $38. Twin beds or doubles $48. Reservations encouraged.

Golden Gate Hotel, 775 Bush St. (392-3702), between Powell and Mason St., 2 blocks north (uphill) of Union Square. A warm, charming, and well-situated 1913 hotel with tasteful antiques and bay windows. The perfect place to treat yourself without going broke. An iron cage elevator carries you to the comfy, beautiful rooms with white wicker furniture and color TV. Spotless hall toilets and bath. Friendly, multi-lingual staff. Check-out noon. Rooms $59, with bath $89. Continental breakfast included. Garage parking $14 per 24 hrs. 2-week advance reservations advisable June-Sept.

Sheehan Hotel, 620 Sutter St. (775-6500 or 800-848-1529), at Mason St. near Union Sq. Excellent location with nearby access to cable cars, buses, and BART. Across the street from trendy art galleries. The elegant lobby—complete with tea room serving wine and tea—is busy and something of a scene on warm summer evenings. International students galore. 68 rooms, cable TV, phone. Indoor swimming pool. Exercise room. Continental breakfast of freshly-baked scones and muffins included. Singles $45, with bath $60. Doubles $55, with bath $75. $10 per additional person. Children under 12 free with parents. 15% discount with European Countdown card.

The Amsterdam, 749 Taylor St. (673-3277 or 800-637-3444; fax 673-0453), between Bush and Sutter St., 2 blocks from Nob Hill, 3½ blocks from Union Sq. Beautiful rooms in a very central location. Built in 1909, the hotel has a charming lobby complete with chandeliers and several sets of encyclopedias. Check-out 11am. Continental breakfast included. Singles $45, with bath $60. Doubles $50, with bath $69.

Allison Hotel, 417 Stockton St. (986-8737, outside CA 800-628-6456, within CA 800-344-6030), just south of the Stockton St. tunnel, 2 blocks north of Union Sq.—a prime location. Recently renovated, the lobby features crystal chandeliers, plants in brass pots, and shiny white paint. Pleasant rooms with cable TV, phones. Check-out 11am. Singles and doubles $50, with bath $59. Triples $65. Quads $75. Reserve ahead in summer.

Grant Hotel, 753 Bush St. (421-7540; fax 989-7719), between Mason and Powell St., 2 blocks north (uphill) of Union Sq. Wholesome, though not exactly elegant. Lounge with fireplace downstairs. 76 rooms with bath, telephone, and color TV. Check-out noon. Singles $45. Doubles $49.

Pensione International, 875 Post St. (775-3344), east of Hyde St., 4½ blocks west of Union Square. Attractive building filled with international art and helpful staff. Comfortable, clean, though erratically decorated rooms. Continental breakfast included. Singles $30, with bath $55. Doubles $50, with bath $75.

Olympic Hotel, 140 Mason St. (982-5010), at Ellis St., a few blocks from Union Sq., snuggled up against the snazzy Parc Fifty-Five Hotel. Caters mostly to Japanese students and Europeans. Clean and comfortable. Small laundry room (wash $1.25, dry 75¢). Singles $30. Singles and doubles with bath $45.

Pacific Bay Inn, 520 Jones St. at Geary St. (673-0234, outside the Bay Area 800-445-2631). 3 blocks west of Union Square. Neighborhood feels unsafe. Modern, clean and simple rooms with TV, phone, and bath. Singles $45. Doubles $65-75, $249 per week.

Herbert Hotel, 161 Powell St. (362-1600), at O'Farrell St, very close to Union Sq. Near cable car turnaround. Prime location. Singles $25, per week $90, with bath $125 per week. Doubles with bath $40, per week $150.

Chinatown

YMCA Chinatown, 855 Sacramento St. (982-4412), between Stockton St. and Grant Ave. Convenient location for those wanting to be near the center of the city in general and Chinatown in particular. *Men over 18 only.* Friendly young staff, pool, and gym. Rooms are not exactly fancy. Registration Mon.-Fri. 6:30am-10pm, Sat. 9am-5pm, Sun. 9am-1pm. Check-out 1pm. No curfew. Singles $27.70, with bath $37.84. Doubles $36.04. 7th day free. No reservations.

Gum Moon Women's Residence, 940 Washington (421-8827), at Stockton in Chinatown's center. *Women only.* Bright, spacious rooms with shared bath in a truly beautiful house. Kitchen and laundry facilities (50¢ wash, 35¢ dry). Primarily a boarding house; call ahead to make sure there are rooms available. Registration 9am-6pm. Check-out noon. Singles $24, per week $100. Doubles $20 per bed, per week $81.50.

Grant Plaza, 465 Grant Ave. (434-3883 or 800-472-6899, within CA 800-472-6805), at Pine St. 1 block from the Chinatown gate. Excellent location. Renovated to look like a chain motel, but more colorful. Clean, bright rooms with bath, phones, and color TV. Parking available for $8.50 per day. Check-in after 2:30pm. Check-out noon. Singles $42. Doubles $52. Reservations advised 3 weeks in advance.

Obrero Hotel, 1208 Stockton (989-3960), between Pacific Ave. and Broadway in Chinatown. 12 comfortable, cheerful rooms with fluffy comforters on the beds. Full breakfast included. No smoking. Check-out 11am. Singles $38, with bath $45. Doubles $45, with bath $52. Triples $57. Quads $60. Reservations required at least 2 weeks ahead.

Financial District

Temple Hotel, 469 Pine St. (781-2565), between Montgomery and Kearny St. Across from the new Bank of America building. A decent, well-maintained hotel close to the Transbay Terminal. Room decor recalls the '60. All rooms have dead-bolt locks and TVs. The hotel feels secure, but the surrounding area has little charm. Helpful staff. Check-in 8am-10pm. Check-out noon. Singles $30, with bath $40. Doubles $35 per person, with bath $45 per person. Discounts for stays longer than 2 nights.

Haight-Ashbury

The Red Victorian Bed and Breakfast Inn, 1665 Haight St. (864-1978), 3 blocks west of Masonic Ave., 2 blocks east of Golden Gate Park in Haight-Ashbury. 3 mi. from downtown, but close to buses and the MUNI Metro "N" trolley. Barely describable, the Red Vic is more a state of mind than a hotel. 18 individually and lovingly decorated rooms honor butterflies, the nearby Golden Gate Park, and the less proximate (except in the Haight) 1960s, among other subjects. Even the 4 hall baths, shared by some of the rooms, have their own names and motifs. The aquarium bathroom has a fish tank which encloses the normal toilet mechanisms on top of the tank. When you flush, you can see it in action! If the canopied and teddy-bear-festooned bed in the Teddy Bear room isn't enough to soothe your mind, try the meditation room, with its transformational art, or a tête-à-tête with the hotel cat, Charlotte. Downstairs, a newly opened global family network center promotes planetary consciousness and a café and market are scheduled to open soon. The Red Victorian offers a non-smoking, angst-free living environment that you won't want to miss if your pocketbook is up for the experience. Even if it isn't, at least stop by for a tour. You don't want to forego a visit to this fabulous place "Where the Summer of Love and Today's World meet." Among the owners and staff members are speakers of Korean, Portuguese, Spanish, German, Italian, French, and English. Check-in 3-6pm. Check-out 11am. Fresh breakfast included. Complimentary tea, coffee, popcorn, and cheese in the afternoons. 2-night stay usually required on weekends. Discounts on stays longer than 3 days. Doubles $76-200, with discount $64-134. Reserve well in advance for summer.

Near the Civic Center

Harcourt Residence Club, 1105 Larkin (673-7720). One of the city's most popular residence clubs offers rooms by the week or by the month. Price includes maid service, TV room, 2 meals a day, and Sunday brunch. Filled by a younger set of traveling students and local residents. Occasional barbecues. Office hours 9am-5pm. Weekly rates $130-200 per person, depending on size of room and private or hall bath.

YMCA Hotel, 220 Golden Gate Ave. (885-0460), at Leavenworth St., 2 blocks north of Market St. on the edge of the infamous Tenderloin. Men and women allowed. One of the largest hotels in the city (with 110 rooms), but the rooms don't quite measure up to the impressive postmodern façade. Nonetheless, they provide a refreshing, reassuring refuge from the dangerous surrounding neighborhood. Double locks on all doors and policy requiring visitors to stay in the lobby enhance security. Pool, gym, and racquetball court. Breakfast included. Laundry $1 wash, 50¢ dry. Register 24 hrs. No curfew. Singles $28, with bath $37.50. Doubles $38. Triples $60. Hostel beds $15 for HI-AYH members only. $5 key deposit. No reservations for hostel beds allowed. For room reservations, send money order for first night's stay.

Hotel Essex, 684 Ellis St. (474-4664; within CA 800-44-ESSEX, -37739; outside CA 800-45-ESSEX), at Larkin, north of Civic Center. Just renovated, the Essex is one of the best budget hotels around. Popular with German tourists in summer. Free coffee and tea. Clean and charming rooms with color TVs and phones. Surprisingly elegant lobby. Person at front desk 24 hrs. Check-out noon. Singles $39, with bath $49. Doubles $44, with bath $59. Weekly rates: singles $175, with bath $225, doubles $225, with bath $250.

■■■ SAN FRANCISCO'S NEIGHBORHOODS

Mark Twain called San Francisco "the liveliest, heartiest community on our continent." Any resident will tell you that this city is not made of landmarks or "sights," but of neighborhoods. If you blindly rush from the Golden Gate Bridge to Coit Tower to Mission Dolores, you'll be missing the point—the city itself. Whether defined by ethnicity, tax brackets, topography, or a shared spirit, these neighborhoods present the visitor with constant contrasts. Off-beat bookstores, Chinatown *dim sum,* Pacific Heights architecture, SoMa's nightlife, Japantown folk festivals, Golden Gate Park's Strawberry Hill, North Beach's Club Fugazi, and Haight-Ashbury simply for being itself…these are San Francisco.

DOWNTOWN AND UNION SQUARE

Union Square is the center of San Francisco. Now an established shopping area, the square has a rich and somewhat checkered history. During the Civil War, a large public meeting was held here to decide whether San Francisco should secede. The square became the rallying ground of the Unionists, who bore placards reading "The Union, the whole Union, and nothing but the Union"—hence its name.

The sounds of Union Square today are far removed from politics. The clanging of the cable cars mixes with the contented cooing of overfed pigeons. Large palm trees and bushes enclose the center of the square and create a calm refuge in the middle of the storm of shoppers, tourists, and business people.

When the Barbary Coast (now the Financial District) was down and dirty, Union Square's Morton Alley was dirtier. At the turn of the century, murders on the alley averaged one per week, and prostitutes waved to their favorite customers from second-story windows. After the 1906 earthquake and fire destroyed most of the flophouses, a group of merchants moved in and renamed the area **Maiden Lane** in hopes of changing the street's image. Surprisingly enough, the switch worked. Today Maiden Lane—extending 2 blocks from Union Square's eastern side—is home to smart shops and ritzy boutiques.

Food

Union Square restaurants are remarkably insipid. Department store cafeteria food can be surprisingly tasty but is consistently overpriced. There is a legion of coffee shops, but good hot food is hard to find. There are corner markets in the blocks surrounding the square itself. Have a piece of fresh fruit (usually 50¢) or a large baked muffin ($1.25) to tide you over until you have a chance to explore nearby Chinatown or North Beach and enjoy a much tastier meal. (For food listings in North Beach and Chinatown see page 263 and page 266.) The following restaurants are the best options in the area.

Lori's Diner, 500 Sutter St. at Powell (981-1950) across the street from the Circle Gallery of Animation (see Sights, below). Uptown diner with '50s music, pinball machines, juke box, neon signs, shiny red booths, and Marilyn Monroe posters. Standard burger ($5) and roast turkey dinner with "all the fixin's" ($9) are sure to please. Still hungry? Have a hot fudge sundae ($4) or a thick malted banana shake ($3.50). Open 6am-midnight. Another smaller location, on 336 Mason between Geary and O'Farrell, is open 24 hrs. (392-8646).

Sears Fine Food, 439 Powell St. (986-1160). An old-fashioned breakfast joint popular with old-timers. Sears' is known for its cornucopic bowls of fresh fruit ($3.50 and up), sourdough french toast ($5.40), and fluffy pancakes ($4.50). Open Wed.-Sun. 6:30am-3:30pm.

San Francisco Health Food Store, 333 Sutter St. (392-8477), between Stockton St. and Grant Ave. Crunchy and healthy is the name of the game. Extensive selection of nuts and dried fruits. Shakes ($3) with wheat germ or yeast. Granola with yogurt and banana $1.75. Open Mon.-Fri. 9:15am-5:45pm, Sat. 9:15am-5:30pm.

The Cellar, Macy's West, enter from Geary St. on the south side of the square. The Cellar contains a bakery, a pizza stand, and a frozen yogurt place. You can also buy fresh salads ($4-6), sandwiches ($5-5.75), packaged crackers, jams, and cheese at the deli and make a picnic to eat in the square.

Café de la Presse, 352 Grant Ave. at Bush (398-2650) across from the Chinatown gate. This busy, centrally located café serves American and international food and sells publications from around the world. Join the throngs of European tourists who eat nicoise salad ($8.75) and homemade cured prosciutto and melon ($6.75) while reading French magazines. Open Mon.-Sat. 7am-11pm, Sun. 7am-10pm.

Sights

One of the Maiden Lane's main attractions is the **Circle Gallery,** 140 Maiden Lane. The only Frank Lloyd Wright building in San Francisco, the gallery sells some of the city's most expensive art. Walk up the unusual circular ramp and admire both the art and the architecture (open Mon.-Sat. 10am-6pm, Sun. noon-5pm; free).

The best free ride in town is on the outside elevators of the **Westin St. Francis Hotel** on Powell at Geary. As you glide up the building, the entire Bay Area stretches out before you. The "elevator tours" offer an unparalleled view of Coit Tower and the Golden Gate Bridge. For another ride with an excellent view, take the Powell St. cable cars. To relax and enjoy a potable, go to the 30th floor of the **Holiday Inn,** 480 Sutter St. (398-8900; take MUNI bus #2, 3, or 4), where the **Sherlock Holmes Esquire Public House** has been meticulously decorated to the specifications of 221B Baker St.

The **Circle Gallery of Animation and Cartoon Art,** 501 Sutter St. at Powell is America's oldest, largest, and most experienced gallery specializing in the arts of animation and cartooning. The sign at the door beckons "Come in. Look. Ask questions. And above all, enjoy." Even if you can't afford to buy anything, obey the sign. (Open Sun.-Thurs. 10am-6pm, Fri.-Sat. 10am-10pm. Extended hours in summer.)

Fans of bookstores should not miss **McDonald's,** 48 Turk (673-2235). This self-described "dirty, poorly-lit place for books" presents a deceivingly small face to the street. The inside is packed and stacked with facts and tracts (open Mon.-Tues. and Thurs. 10am-6pm, Wed. and Fri.-Sat. 10:30am-6:45pm).

FINANCIAL DISTRICT

North of Market and east of Kearny, snug against the bay, beats the West's financial heart, or at least one of its ventricles. Montgomery Street, the Wall Street of the West, is of only passing interest to the visitor and is best seen before the workday ends. After 7:30pm, the heart stops, only to be resuscitated the next morning.

Parking is next to impossible during business hours. If you must drive, park your car South-of-Market (SoMa) and walk from there. Public Transportation is a better option; take any MUNI Metro line (J, K, L, M, or N) or BART to the Montgomery or Embarcadero station or hop on MUNI bus #1, 2, 3, 4, 6, 7, 9, 12, 15, 30, 41, 42, or 45. The California St. cable car is another way to reach the district.

Food

The Financial District can be a tricky place to eat cheaply, especially for dinner. Many places close early, when the bankers and brokers go home. Watch out for expense-account establishments that may look better than they taste. For more options nearby and after-5pm dining see South-of-Market: Food, page 245.

The Fruit Gallery, 301 Kearny St. (362-2216), at Bush. This smallish restaurant is packed between noon and 1pm. Terra cotta tile floors, wooden tables, and vibrant Chinese paintings give it a pleasant, fresh feel. Large salads (around $6) are sure to fill you up. Try the strawberry mango spinach salad with grilled chicken and honey-mustard vinaigrette. Heavenly Dutch apple pie $3. Open Mon.-Thurs. 7am-3pm and 5-9pm, Fri. 7am-3pm.

Levy's Bagels and Co., 21 Drumm St. (362-5580), between California and Sacramento. This upscale bagel joint serves great bagels (try the wonderful cranberry version, 50¢), great sandwiches ($4-7), delicious New York knishes ($2.75), and more. Open Mon.-Fri. 6am-5pm, Sat. 7:30am-4pm, Sun. 7:30am-1pm.

Tadich Grill, 240 California St. (391-1849), between Front and Battery, in the very heart of the Financial District. The oldest restaurant in California and the "original cold day restaurant"—it's a San Francisco tradition. It isn't cheap, but it is possible to eat inexpensively and take in the abundant atmosphere. Entrees range from $10-17, but you can order from the side order menu provided you meet the $7.50 min. charge per seat. A bowl of delicious clam chowder ($4) complements the tangy sourdough bread. Open Mon.-Fri. 11am-9pm, Sat. 11:30am-9pm.

Franciscan Croissant, 301 Sutter St. at Grant Ave. is a tiny food bar with huge croissants. Cinnamon raisin $1.65. Also serves up delicious sandwiches like smoked turkey ($4) and hot mushroom florentine ($3.75). Cappuccino $1.75. Open 7:30am-6:30pm.

Café Claude, 7 Claude Ln. (392-3505), off Bush, between Grant and Kearny. Tucked back in one of the Financial District's many alleyways. Trendy and popular. A large French clientele and suave French waiters. And what do you know? The menu is French too. *Salade chévre chaud* (salad with baked goat cheese) $5.50. Live jazz Tues.-Wed. 6:30-9:30pm, Thurs.-Fri. 7-10pm, Sat. 8-11pm. Restaurant open Mon.-Thurs. 8am-10pm, Fri. 8am-11pm, Sat. 10am-11pm.

Belden Park Taqueria, 56 Belden St. (989-9750), on a small alley between Kearny and Montgomery. Enjoyable patio dining at a budget price. Try the lunch special: an enchilada, tostada, or taco with Spanish rice, refried beans, and salad for $4. Open Mon.-Fri. 11am-3pm.

Oh La La!, 485 Pine St. at Belden St. (981-7378) This conveniently located café serves standard breakfast and lunch fare. Pasta salad $3, large scones $1.35. After 1pm, all pastries are ½-price. A generously sized "small" frozen yogurt costs $1.50. Open Mon.-Fri. 6am-4pm.

Sights

Note the commemorative plaques nailed to skyscrapers' flanks, they help tell the story of the district's past. Modern architecture enthusiasts may have a field day in this glass-box wonderland.

In the east end of the district, at the foot of Sacramento St., stands **Embarcadero Center** (772-0500), a three-level complex housing over a hundred expensive and mostly trivial shops. It is worth a visit just to admire the scale of development and the dozens of outdoor sculptures. At the foot of Market St. is **Justin Herman Plaza** and its famous geodesic **Vallaincourt Fountain.** You can walk through the fountain and remain dry while the water flows overtop. The area is often rented out by bands or for rallies during lunch from noon to 1:30pm. One such free lunchtime concert, performed by U2 in the fall of 1987, resulted in lead singer Bono's arrest for spray painting "Stop the Traffic—Rock and Roll" on the fountain. Connected to the $300-million complex is the **Hyatt Regency** hotel (788-1234). Its 17-story atrium, dominated by a four-story geometric sculpture, is worth a peak. The glass elevator up the building's side leads to the 20th floor and the **Equinox Revolving Rooftop Restaurant and Lounge.** There is a lovely view of the bay from this fabulous revolving cocktail lounge every 45 minutes, and a decent view of nearby office buildings the rest of the time. Slightly spiffed up, you can usually bluff your way to a window table, but the view is spectacular from just about anywhere. Buy a drink and ample dawdling time for $3 and up (open Mon.-Thurs. 4pm-midnight, Fri. 4pm-1:15am, Sat. noon-1:15am, Sun. noon-midnight).

San Francisco's tallest and most distinctive structure, the defining element of the city's skyline, is the **Transamerica Pyramid** at Montgomery St. between Clay and Washington St. (take MUNI bus #15). The Montgomery Block, a four-story brick building, once stood in its place. The Montgomery's in-house bar lured the likes of Mark Twain, Robert Louis Stevenson, Bret Harte, and Jack London. These gruff storytellers wrote and got drunk on the bar's renowned Pisco Punch. In the basement a man named Tom Sawyer operated sauna baths that Twain frequented, and in 1856, the victim of one of the city's most notorious murders—newspaper editor James King of William—was shot on the building's doorstep over one of his controversial editorials. The Chinese revolutionary Sun Yat-Sen plotted the overthrow of the Manchu Dynasty and wrote the 1911 Chinese constitution in an apartment here. Today, the Transamerica Pyramid covers the one time locale of the Montgomery Block, and you can be sure Twain would not recognize his old hangout. The pyramid was designed by William Pereira and Associates as a show of architectural virtuosity and was never actually meant to be built. But built it was. The building's pyramidal shape and subterranean concrete "anchor" base make it one of the city's most stable, earthquake-resistant buildings. All new buildings in San Francisco are now required to be "earthquake-proof," a measure which saved many lives in the '89 quake. The observation deck is a disappointment because it is only half way up and only faces north. It does provides a nice view of the Golden Gate, the Bay, Marin, and the North Beach area (open Mon.-Fri. 9am-4pm; free). Free jazz concerts are held Fridays at noon during June and July in the Pyramid's Redwood Park.

The Transamerica Pyramid, at 853 ft., is the tallest of San Francisco's buildings. The next four in height are all Financial District neighbors of the pyramid. They are the Bank of America building at 778 ft., the California Center (345 California St.) at 724 ft., Five Fremont Center (50 Fremont St.) at 600 ft. and, with honors for being smallest of the tall, 101 California St. at 410 ft. The Bank of America building is the only one of the four with an observation deck open to the public. The **Bank of America** building (555 California St. at Kearny), also houses the Carnelian Room (433-7500). This cocktail lounge and restaurant offers more sweeping views (open for cocktails after 3pm Mon.-Fri., for dinner Mon.-Sun. 5-10pm). The most impressive views of the pyramid itself are caught from up the hill on Columbus Ave.

Diagonally across from the pyramid is the **Old Transamerica Building,** 701 Montgomery St., at Washington St., the opulent showpiece of the corporation and a gem of older commercial architecture. The elaborate entryway is fenced with wrought iron and laced in gilt.

The Financial District also offers some interesting free museums, most of them sponsored by the public relations departments of large banks. The **Wells Fargo History Museum,** 420 Montgomery St. (396-2619), between California St. and Sacramento St., contains an impressive display of Gold Rush exhibits, including gold nuggets, maps, a 19th-century stagecoach and information sheets in different languages. (open Mon.-Fri. 9am-5pm). Another Gold Rush exhibit is the Bank of California's **Museum of Money of the American West,** 400 California St. (765-2402), at Sansome, which has 19th-century coins, nuggets, and devices to detect counterfeit money. (Open Mon.-Thurs. 10am-4pm, Fri. 10am-5pm). For a bigger exhibit on money, go to the Old Mint (see SoMa, page 246).

The **Pacific Stock Exchange,** located at 301 Pine St. is a much smaller and more relaxed version of its counterpart in New York (free 45-min. tours by appointment; call 393-4133).

The **Golden Gate Ferries** (332-6600) sends boats to Larkspur and Sausalito (see Marin County). Ferries depart frequently from the Ferry Building at the terminus of market St. on the Embarcadero across the street from Justin Herman Plaza. Although primarily for commuters, the ferries offer a pleasing view of San Francisco's skyline and bay. (Fare to Sausalito $4, ages 6-12 $3; to Larkspur $2.50, ages 6-12 $1.90. Seniors and people with disabilities travel ½-price. On weekends, children 11 and under ride free with parent.) Ferries also travel to Alameda, Oakland, Tiburon, Vallejo, and Harbor Bay.

SOUTH-OF-MARKET (SOMA)

The area south of Market St. to about 10th St. is now home to the city's hottest nightlife: yesterday's leather bars are today's stylish nightclubs. During the day the area fills with workers from the encroaching Financial District. At night, SoMa is the place for hip young professionals to dine at chic restaurants before hitting the club scene. (See Entertainment, page 268.)

South-of-Market, with its many self-park lots, is one of the easiest areas of the city in which to park your car, but lock it securely, and don't leave valuables inside. To reach the center of the area on public transportation take samTrans bus #1A or 1L (weekends and holidays) or #1C, 22D, 10L, or 10T (8-10am and 4-6pm only). Or take MUNI bus #9x, 12, 14, 15, 26, 27, 30, 45, or 71.

Food

South-of-Market has many trendy places to eat, to see, and to be seen. These are just a few.

LuLu, 816 Folsom at 4th (495-5775). This large, Mediterranean restaurant is the place to go for a nice night out. Take a shower, don't wear a t-shirt, and enjoy delicious food that's worth paying a bit more for. Unique pizzas ($8.00), succulent chicken ($9.95), and huge plates of family-style fire-roasted vegetables. Tasty appetizers, such as roasted white corn with red pepper and basil butter ($2.75), can make a meal in themselves. Chic bar frequented by a young, happy crowd. Reservations are essential at this popular place. Open Mon.-Thurs. 11:30am-10:30pm, Fri.-Sat. 11:30am-11:30pm, Sun. 5-10:30pm.

Hamburger Mary's, 1582 Folsom St. (626-5767), at 12th St. Biker joint turned hip. A sign of the times. You'll find every kind of person here; it's like a mini-San Francisco (and it's renowned through the life-sized S.F.). Tofu Mary (the original Tofu-Veggie burger) $6, Mary Burger with bacon $7. Open Tues.-Thurs. 11am-12:15am, Fri.-Sat. 11am-1:15am.

Max's Diner (536-MAXS, -6279) on 3rd St. at Folsom in St. Francis Place. Proudly proclaims "This is a bad place for a diet" on the front door. Resist the temptation to order the delicious onion rings, you won't need an appetizer. Max's award-winning sandwiches are gargantuan! BLT on sourdough toast with potato salad, cole slaw, and pickle $7. Vegetarian club $7. The strawberry shortcake ($5) would feed a family of four. Free refills on soda. Open Mon.-Thurs. 11am-11pm, Fri. 11am-midnight, Sat. 11:30am-midnight, Sun. 11:30am-10pm.

Cadillac Bar and Restaurant, One Holland Ct. off Howard St. between 4th and 5th (543-TACO, -8226). This noisy, festive, converted warehouse serves the beautiful people who flock to SoMa to gobble the famous mesquite-grilled fajitas ($10) and delicious margaritas ($3.50). Special dishes available upon request, "We'll give you whatever you want," says owner Leon Morales. Open Mon.-Thurs. 11am-11pm, Fri. 11am-midnight, Sat. noon-midnight, Sun. noon-10pm.

Sights

The **Old Mint** (744-6830), on 5th St. at Mission St., is worth a peek. In one room, a lone, placid guard watches over a stack of gold bullion, coins, and raw gold worth more than $150,000. The other rooms house assorted historical artifacts, including a collection of ornate and imaginative gramophones downstairs. (Tours on the hr., 10am-3pm. Informative films shown on the ½-hr., 10:30am-3:30pm. Mint open Mon.-Fri. 10am-4pm. Free.)

The **San Francisco Museum of Modern Art,** 151 3rd St. between Mission and Howard displays an impressive collection of both European and American 20th-century works. The museum's new site in the Yerba Buena Gardens was one of the largest building projects ever undertaken by an American museum. It is hoped that the $60 million complex will become the premier facility for collecting, displaying, and preserving modern contemporary art. (Open Tues.-Wed. and Fri.-Sun. 11am-6pm, Thurs. 11am-9pm. $7, over 61 and students $3.50, under 13 free. Thurs. 5-9pm half price. 1st Tues. of month free. Hours scheduled to take effect Jan. 31, 1995.) The **Ansel Adams Center,** 250 4th St. (495-7000), at Howard and Folsom, houses a permanent collection of the master's photographs, as well as temporary shows by other photographers ($4, students $3, over 64 and ages 13-17 $2, under 13 free; open Tues.-Sun. 11am-6pm). The **San Francisco Chronicle building** is at 901 Mission St. The *Chronicle,* the newspaper with the largest paid circulation west of the Mississippi, has been printed here since construction on the building finished in 1924. The paper's credo is "We propose to publish a bold, bright, fearless, and truly independent newspaper."

THE TENDERLOIN

There is little to attract the tourist to the Tenderloin—if you must visit come in a large group during the day or take a drive-thru tour. The Tenderloin is south of Market St. between Geary and Golden Gate Ave. on the north and south and between Taylor St. and Larkin St. on the east and west. Long considered one of San Francisco's worst areas, the Tenderloin is showing signs of change. New businesses are opening and hotels and offices are pushing at the edges of the neighborhood. The newest facelift to the area is the vast indoor shopping metropolis, the **San Francisco Centre,** at 5th and Market St (open Mon.-Sat. 9:30am-8pm, Sun. 11am-6pm). The shopping center is decidedly ritzy with an elegant Nordstrom's and six curved escalators (the only of their kind in the world) sweeping shoppers through the nine-story atrium. The day the center opened, it set retail records by doing nearly a million dollars in business.

If you are in town on a Sunday, visit the **Gilde Memorial United Methodist Church** at 330 Ellis St. at the corner of Ellis and Taylor (771-6300). The Reverend Cecil Williams, a major civil rights activist in the '60s, delivers stirring sermons. (Services on Sundays 9am and 11am.)

CIVIC CENTER

The vast Civic Center is a collection of massive buildings arranged around two expansive plazas. Street people and itinerant travelers used to camp out on the lawns surrounding the plazas, but the city has worked to move them out of the area and, when necessary, into shelters. Parking is relatively easy on streets around the Civic Center. To get there by public transportation, take MUNI Metro to the Civic Center/City Hall stop or MUNI bus #5, 16X, 19, 21, 26, 42, 47, or 49. You can also take the J, K, L, M, or N lines to Van Ness station or Golden Gate Transit bus #10, 20, 50, or 70.

Food

Petite restaurants are plentiful throughout the entire Civic Center area and **Hayes Street** offers an extensive selection of cafés. In the summer, load up on produce at the **Farmers Market** in the U.N. Plaza (every Wed. and Sun.). Use caution in this area at night.

Pendragon Bakery, 450 Hayes St. (552-7017), at Gough St. Natural ingredients go into the excellent, handmade, and imaginative pastries, soups, and vegetarian dishes. The fluffy blueberry scones ($1.85) are a real treat. A large chicken London roll ($4.50) will leave you with little room left for the fresh berry trifle ($2). Open Mon. and Thurs. 6:30am-5pm, Tues.-Wed., Fri. 7am-4pm, Sat. 8am-4pm, Sun. 8am-3pm.

Nyala Ethiopian Restaurant, 39A Grove St. (861-0788), east of Larkin St. Nyala's combination of Ethiopian and Italian cuisine is excellent. Newcomers should try *doro wet,* a traditional Ethiopian dish of slowly simmered chicken in a rich garlic and ginger sauce ($6 at lunch). Or try the vegetarian all-you-can-eat buffet, which features two types of lentils, spicy mushrooms, cabbage, and other saucy vegetables to ladle onto rice or to scoop up with spongy *injera* bread. Buffet Mon.-Sat. 11am-3pm ($5) and 4pm-closing ($7). Open Mon.-Sat. 11am-10pm.

Miss Pearl Jam's, 601 Eddy St. at Larkin (775-5267). Reggae + jerk-chicken + steel-drums + swimming pool = superb brunch ($5-11). Mellow and loud twisted into one on live music nights (when it's open later, cover $5). Check the papers for Sun. pool parties. Located in the Phoenix hotel. Open Tues. 6-10pm, Wed. 11:30am-2:30pm and 6-10pm, Thurs.-Sat. 11:30am-2:30pm and 6-11pm, Sun. 11am-2:30pm and 5:30-10pm. Bar open and live entertainment Tues.-Sun. 5:30pm-1:30am. Reggae shows Wed.-Sat. 9:30pm-1:30am with $5 cover.

Tommy's Joynt, 1101 Geary Blvd. (775-4216), at Van Ness Ave. Outrageously painted San Francisco landmark with a stunning selection of beers brewed everywhere from Finland to Peru. A carnivore's delight—try the famous buffalo stew sandwich ($4.65) or the oxtail sauté with buttered noodles ($4.65). Thick pastrami sandwich $3.64. With two types of mustard and horseradish on every table, Tommy's clearly knows what it's doing. Open daily 10am-1:50am.

Stars Café, 500 Van Ness at McAllister (861-4344). The menu changes daily at this discount outlet for the famous Stars Restaurant next door. Unusual wood oven fired pizzas ($7.50) are a cheap and delicious way to sample super-chef Jeremiah Tower's creations. Entrees at lunch ($8-12), dinner ($7.50-16). Open Tues.-Thurs. 11:30am-11pm, Fri.-Sat 11:30am-midnight.

Sights

The largest gathering of *Beaux Arts* architecture in the U.S. is centered on the palatial **San Francisco City Hall,** which was modeled after St. Peter's Cathedral. *(Beaux Arts* is a style of Neoclassical architecture taught at the Ecole de Beaux Arts in Paris in the late 1800s.) The city hall was the site of the tragic 1978 double murder of Mayor George Moscone and City Supervisor Harvey Milk, the first openly gay politician to be elected to public office in the United States. At the eastern end is the United Nations Plaza and public library, at the western end the Opera House and Museum of Modern Art.

In the evenings, the **Louise M. Davies Symphony Hall,** 201 Van Ness Ave. (431-5400; see Entertainment, page 268 for ticket info.), at Grove St., rings with the sounds of the San Francisco Symphony. The seating in this glass-and-brass $33-million hall was intended to appeal not only aurally but visually, giving most audience members a close-up view of performers. But while the building may be a visual success, its acoustics are poor, and 10 years after its opening, baffled engineers still tinker with seating arrangements and baffles. On the other hand, the orchestra itself has improved greatly, perhaps to compensate for its new hall. Next door, the **War Memorial Opera House,** 301 Van Ness Ave. (864-3330), between Grove and McAllister, hosts the well-regarded **San Francisco Opera Company** (864-3330) and the **San Francisco Ballet** (621-3838 for info.). See Entertainment Section, page 268, for ticket information for the opera and the ballet. Also in the block of Van Ness between Grove and McAllister is the **Veterans Building** (252-4000). Within you'll find the **Herbst Theatre** (392-4400) which hosts string quartets, solo singers, ensembles, and lecture series. Between the Opera House and the Veterans Building lies **Opera Plaza,** a beautifully maintained grassy lawn planted with rows of trees and encased by gilded gates with hanging lamps. (Tours of the Davies Symphony Hall, the War Memorial Opera House, and Herbst Auditorium leave every ½ hr. from the Grove St. entrance to Davies Hall Mon. 10am-2pm. Tours of Davies Hall are only offered on Wed. 1:30-2:30pm, Sat. 12:30-1:30pm. $3, seniors and students $2. For more information, call 552-8338.)

On a smaller scale, the Civic Center area has a number of one- or two-room galleries. You don't have to buy that $30,000 Expressionist cityscape in the corner to enjoy browsing in these white-walled boutiques of contemporary art. The **San Francisco Women Artists Gallery,** 370 Hayes St. (552-7392), between Franklin and Gough, exhibits women's photographs, paintings, prints, and crafts (open Tues.-Wed. and Fri.-Sat. 11am-6pm, Thurs. 11am-8pm).

Quality examples of the other half of "literature and art" can be found at the excellent bookstores near the Civic Center. The **Sierra Club Bookstore,** 730 Polk St. (923-5600) between Ellis and Eddy St. has the best collection of trail guidebooks in the country as well as a friendly and helpful staff. (Open Mon.-Sat. 10am-5:30pm.) Next door to the Sierra Club is **Acorn Books,** 740 Polk St. (563-1736), which has an enormous collection of primarily used books. Couches invite weary shoppers to sit and read in the store. (Open Mon.-Sat. 10:30am-8pm, Sun. noon-7pm.)

MISSION DISTRICT

The colorful **murals** along 24th St. in the Mission District reflect the rich cultural influence of Latin America. The Germans and Scandinavians who inhabited the Mission District in the 1800s have been largely replaced by Latinos, Filipinos, and Southeast Asians. The district, which lies south of the Civic Center area, is roughly bordered by 16th St. to the north, Noe St. to the west, Army St. to the south, and U.S. 101 to the east. The Mission District is laced with MUNI bus routes, including #9, 12, 22, 26, 27, 33, and 53.

Food

The Mission is the one of the best places in the city to find excellent, satisfying, cheap food. The only frustrating thing is choosing between all the inexpensive taquerías and other internationally flavored eateries. Once you've discovered the

Mission district, you won't be able to enjoy Mexican food anywhere else. It also boasts the city's best and cheapest produce. Even the most substantial appetites will be satisfied by the Mexican, Salvadoran, and other Latin American restaurants located on 24th St. (east of Mission St.). After a burrito or some raw cuttlefish, nearby Castro Street (see page 250) is a great place for an evening coffee or drink.

La Cumbre, 515 Valencia St. (863-8205) between 16th and 17th St. As you stand in line, your mouth-watering, raw steak is brought in from the back kitchen, dripping in marinade. It is then grilled to perfection, quickly chopped, combined with rice and beans, and deftly folded into a flour tortilla to make a superlative burrito. ($2.50 for a regular, which is ample; $4 for a "super," sure to fill any *gordito*). Vegetarian burritos contain rice and beans. A standout among *taquerías,* La Cumbre has a much deserved local following. Open Mon.-Sat. 11am-midnight, Sun. noon-midnight.

New Dawn Café, 3174 16th St. (553-8888), at Guerrero. An intense sensory experience. Absolutely anything is considered "art" at this hip restaurant, from the doll body parts and eggbeaters hanging on the walls to the music blasting through the restaurant. The menu, consisting mainly of breakfast food and burgers, is written around the room on mirrors. Enormous servings prepared with care by a 56-year-old drag queen. New Dawn has won the Best of San Francisco for "cheap gluttony" award two years in a row. Vegetable home fries $5.25, vegetarian chili $3.50, burgers $4.25. Open Wed.-Thurs., Sun. 8:30am-8:30pm, Fri.-Sat. 8:30am-9pm. No reservations. There may be a 45-min. wait on weekend mornings, but don't worry, they often serve coffee to patrons standing in line.

Café Macondo, 3159 16th St. (863-6517), between Guerrero and Valencia. Appetizing Central American food and coffee in an eccentrically decorated café that seems more a museum than a restaurant. A display case in one of the old refrigerators exhibits anti-war posters and art. Oriental rugs adorn the hardwood floors. Wicker furniture, couches, and an assortment of lamps complete the cafe's straight-out-of-the-attic look. Chessboard awaits eager players. Bring a book or read one of theirs as you sip cappuccino ($1.50). Chicken tamale $3.50, pita bread sandwich $3.25. Open Mon.-Thurs. 11am-10pm, Fri.-Sun. 11am-11pm.

Manora, 3226 Mission (550-0856). This attractive Thai restaurant serves delicious cuisine at reasonable prices. Manora prepares sauces with a refreshingly light hand, so the food isn't smothered in peanut. The red beef curry garners high praise from locals ($5.75). Most dishes under $10. Open Tues.-Sun. 5-10pm.

Taquería San José, 2830 Mission St. (282-0203), at 24th. Don't be put off by the fast-food-style menu; loving care goes into the cooking. Soft tacos with your choice of meat, from magnificent spicy pork to brains or tongue ($1.70), 5 for $3.50. Free chips and guacamole. Open daily 8am-3am.

Sights

Celebrating its 202nd birthday this year, **Mission Dolores,** at 16th and Dolores St. in the old heart of San Francisco, is considered the oldest building in the city. The mission was founded in 1776 by Father Junípero Serra and, like San Francisco itself, was named in honor of St. Francis of Assisi. The mission, however, sat close to a marsh known as *Laguna de Nuestra Señora de los Dolores* (Laguna of Our Lady of Sorrows) and despite Serra's wishes, gradually became known as *Misión de los Dolores.* Exotic bougainvillea, poppies, and birds-of-paradise bloom in the cemetery, which was featured in Hitchcock's *Vertigo* (open daily 9am-4:30pm, Nov.-April 9am-4pm; $1).

The Mission is best seen by strolling during the day. Take BART to the 16th or 24th St. stops and walk south down Mission St. You'll pass a few scattered **murals** (some of the best are around 21st), marking the city as the ideological and artistic center of the Chicano movement of the late '60s and early '70s. The **Mission Cultural Center,** 2868 Mission St. (821-1155), between 24th and 25th St., includes a graphics workshop, a theater, and often-stunning art exhibitions, as well as other cultural events throughout the year. (Gallery open Tues.-Fri. noon-6pm, Sat. 10am-4pm. Free. Box office 695-6970.)

For spiritual and physical rejuvenation, women might enjoy a plunge into the waters at **Osento,** 955 Valencia St. (282-6333), between 20th and 21st St. Osento is a women's bathhouse in the Mission with wet and dry sauna, jacuzzi, and pool. (Sliding entrance fee $7-11, unlimited time. $1 towel rental. $1 refundable locker deposit. Open daily 1pm-1am.)

The **Liberia Pathfinder Bookstore,** 3284 23rd St. (282-6255), is a small but full-fledged communist bookstore (open Mon.-Fri. 3-7pm, Sat. 10am-6pm). Those interested in "women's visions and books" should drop by **Old Wives' Tales,** 1009 Valencia St. (821-4675). This bookstore contains sections ranging from politics to lesbian issues to women's fiction (open Mon.-Sat. 11am-7pm, Sun. 11am-6pm). The **Womanscraft West** gallery next door (648-2020; open Tues.-Wed. and Fri.-Sun. 11am-6pm, Thurs. 11am-8pm), showcases and sells the works of hundreds of women.

A few blocks' walk east down 24th Street will give you the best sights, sounds, and tastes of the Mission district. **La Galeria de la Raza,** 2857 24th St. (826-8009) at Bryant, is small but shows excellent exhibitions of Chicano and Latino art by local and international artists. The gift shop next door sells impressive pieces of folk art from Mexico and Latin America. (Gallery free. Open Tues.-Sat. noon-6pm.)

CASTRO

Castro and the Mission District enjoy the city's best weather, often while fog blankets nearby Twin Peaks. Residents proudly say "The sun always shines in the Castro." Much of San Francisco's gay community calls the area home. As AIDS has taken its toll, the scene has mellowed considerably from the wild days of the '70s, but Castro Street remains a proud and assertive emblem of gay liberation. Most of the action takes place along Castro St. to the south of Market Street, although the neighborhood itself extends south from Market to Noe Valley and west from the Mission to Portola Drive and Twin Peaks.

Food

Café Pazole, 2337 Market (626-2666) between Castro and Noe. Known in the Castro for its good-looking waiters, this festive and colorful restaurant serves healthy seafood and vegetarian Mexican plates. The Burrito Californiano ($5.50) is stuffed with tender cactus, peppers, tomato, garlic, and black beans. Wash it down with an icy Corona or a Sangria ($3). Open Mon.-Fri. 2-11pm, Fri.-Sat. noon-midnight, Sun. noon-11pm.

Harvest Ranch Market, 2825 Market St. (626-0805), at 16th and Noe. Founded by the Zen Center of San Francisco, this specialty health food store sells a huge variety of organic breads and produce. They specialize in California and European products, including organic California wine. The salad bar is outstanding, and should be at $4.29 per lb. Cup of soup $2.75. Look for free samples. Open Sun.-Thurs. 9am-11pm, Fri.-Sat. 9am-midnight.

Sparkey's Diner and Pizzeria, 242 Church St. (626-8666), at Market. This 24-hr. diner attracts two main crowds—the weekend brunchers who come for the stacks of fluffy pancakes ($3.65) and the late-night bar- and club-hoppers who crave the juicy burgers named after former employees. Veronica's Baby Burger ($4.50) is perfect for the 3am munchies. Veggie options include pesto fettuccini, $6. Open 24 hrs.

Sights

The best way to see Castro Street is through the district's shops and bars. Two popular hangouts are **Café Flore,** 2298 Market St. (621-8579), and **The Café,** 2367 Market St. (861-3846). The Café Flore serves wine, beer, coffee, and buttery croissants ($1.45) in an unhurried atmosphere. As the name suggests, flowers and plants are abundant. Many customers bring newspapers to read on the patio; if you don't have one, you can pick up a free weekly. (Open daily 8am-5pm.) The Café is two stories with pool tables, a New-Age glass bar, and a popular outside deck. (Open Sun.-Thurs. 2pm-2am, Fri.-Sat. noon-2am.) While traditionally a lesbian bar, it is frequented by men and women of all sexual orientations. See Nightlife, page 271, for additional listings.

Down the street, **The Names Project,** 2362 Market St. (863-1966), sounds a more somber note. This is the headquarters of an organization that has accumulated over 12,000 3 ft. x 6 ft. panels for the **AIDS Memorial Quilt,** including ones from 30 other countries. Each panel is a memorial to a person who has died of AIDS. In addition to housing the project's administration, the building contains a workshop where victims' friends and relatives create panels. Several panels are always on display. (Open Mon. noon-6:30pm, Tues.-Wed. and Fri. noon-7pm, Sat.-Sun. noon-5pm. Quilting bee Wed. 7-10pm is open to the public.) **Cruisin' Castro** gives **walking tours** of Castro St. (daily 10am). Guide Trevor Hailey, a member of Castro's gay community since 1972, was named one of San Francisco's top tour guides in 1992. (Tours are $30, including brunch at the famed Elephant Walk Restaurant. Call Trevor at 550-8110 for reservations.) MUNI bus #24 runs along Castro St. from 14th to 26th.

West of Castro, the peninsula swells with several large hills. On rare fogless nights, you can get a breathtaking view of the city from **Twin Peaks,** between Portola Dr., Market St., and Clarendon Ave. The three-masted radio tower can be seen from all around town. The Spanish called Twin Peaks "Mission Peaks" or *"Los Pechos de la Choca"* (the Breasts of the Indian Maiden). South of the peaks on Portola Dr. is **Mount Davidson,** the highest spot in San Francisco (938 ft.). In 1923, a wooden cross was erected on the summit, but fires later destroyed both this cross and its replacement. The builders of the third cross didn't take any chances; in 1934 they constructed a still-standing 103-ft. concrete cross. West of the Mt. Davidson, south of Golden Gate Park, and on the edge of the peninsula, is the **San Francisco Zoo** (753-7061), on Sloat Blvd. at the Pacific Ocean. The zoo is especially strong on the closest relatives of *Homo sapiens*. However, with so many uniquely San Franciscan sights to see, only the most die-hard primate fans should make the journey to the otherwise distant and unremarkable zoo. (Open daily 10am-5pm. $6.50, seniors and ages 12-16 $3, under 12 free.)

HAIGHT-ASHBURY

The '60s live in Haight-Ashbury. The Haight, located at the eastern edge of Golden Gate Park and surrounding its panhandle, willfully preserves an era that many seek to experience, others desire to forget, and some can't quite remember. Originally a quiet lower-middle-class neighborhood, the Haight's large Victorian houses—perfect for communal living—and the district's proximity to the University of California in San Francisco (UCSF) drew a massive hippie population in the mid and late 1960s. LSD—possession of which was not yet a felony—pervaded the neighborhood. The hippie voyage reached its apogee in 1966-67 when Janis Joplin, the Grateful Dead, and the Jefferson Airplane all lived and made music in the neighborhood. During 1967's "Summer of Love," young people from across the country converged on the grassy panhandle for the celebrated "be-ins." To some, the Haight seemed the very center of human consciousness. To others, it was just a dirty street of runaways and bad drugs. Despite recent gentrification, the past lives on in Haight-Ashbury. Many of the bars and restaurants are remnants of yesteryear, with faded auras and live-in regulars. The Haight is great for browsing; bookstores are everywhere, as are vintage clothing stores and inexpensive cafés. MUNI buses #6, 7, 16x, 43, 66, 71, and 73 all serve the area, while Metro line N runs along Carl St., four blocks south.

Food

The Haight boasts a terrific selection of **bakeries,** from **Holey Bagel** on Masonic at Haight to the **Black Muslim Bakery Outlet** off Haight on Cole (try the cinnamon rolls). There are also some great ethnic restaurants with reasonable prices. Select your restaurant carefully—quality varies greatly between establishments.

Cha Cha Cha, 1801 Haight St. (386-5758). Love-children fighting against the stream of capitalist society join hands with upwardly mobile professionals and line up for a chance to eat at this trendy Latin restaurant, thought to be the best in the Haight. Try the *tapas* ($4.50-7). Fried bananas in black bean sauce are a specialty ($4.50). Entrees $6.50-12.50. Open Mon.-Thurs. 11:30am-3pm and 5-11:30pm, Fri. 11:30am-3pm and 5:30-11:30pm, Sat. 9am-3pm and 5:30-11:30pm, Sun. 9am-3pm and 5-11pm. Be prepared to wait up to 2 hrs., no reservations.

Ganges, 775 Frederick St. (661-7290), not exactly in the Haight, but close enough. Delicious vegetarian Indian food draws health-conscious locals to this warm and intimate restaurant. Between 11 and 15 curries prepared every day. The unusual Indian vegetables are grown in the Bay Area. Traditional, low Indian seating in back. Try the mashed banana *pakoda*, the stuffed baby potato in spinach and coconut sauce, and don't miss the delicious raisin-tamarind chutney. Dinners $8.50-12.50. Live music Fri.-Sat. starting at 7:15pm. Open Tues.-Sat. 5-10pm. Reservations a good idea.

Tassajara Bread Bakery, 1000 Cole St. (664-8947), at Parnassus, a bit of a trek from Haight but well worth it. Tassajara is one of the city's best bakeries. There's also a branch at Fort Mason (771-6331). Great bread, muffins, scones, pastries, cakes, and pies in a homey atmosphere. The orange pecan muffins ($1) and the scrumptious foccacia with pesto, artichoke hearts, feta, and garlic ($2.50) should not be missed. Sandwiches $3.50. Day-old pastries 30-50% off. Open Mon.-Sat. 7am-11pm, Sun. 8am-11pm.

Real Foods Company, 1023 Stanyan St. (564-2800), at Carl, 1 block from the southeast corner of the Golden Gate Park and only 4 blocks from Haight St. This organic grocery sells beautiful produce and tasty organic breads. Terrific selection of dried fruit and picnic supplies. Open daily 9am-8pm.

Real Food Deli (564-1117) sits next door to the grocery, also on Stanyan St. Pastries, breads, soups, sandwiches, salads, and coffee drinks at reasonable prices. Large bowl of vegetarian chili $3. The apple-cinnamon smiles ($1.65) are so good they'll put one on your face. Open Mon.-Fri. 7:30am-80m, Sat.-Sun. 9am-8pm.

Holey Bagel, 1206 Masonic (626-9111). Holey takes a successful bite out of the Big Apple. 15 varieties of bagels 50¢, with one of 10 "shmeers" $1.25. Day-old bagels are $1 for a bag of four. Fri. 6-7pm: buy 6 bagels, get 6 more free! Open Mon.-Sat. 6am-7pm, Sun. 6am-6pm.

Haight Street Natural Foods, 1621 Haight St. between Cole and Clayton (863-5336) offers a wide selection of healthy victuals in a clean, friendly store. Recently opened, they have over 200 items in bulk. Also sells homeopathic medicines and animal-friendly cosmetics. Open daily 9am-8pm.

Sights

The **Love 'n' Haight Tour** takes visitors past the **Psychedelic Shop** and the one-time residence of the Grateful Dead (2½hr.; $20; call to make reservations). Northeast of the Haight, at Hayes and Steiner St., lies **Alamo Square,** the vantage point of a thousand postcards. Climb the gentle, grassy slope and you'll understand why it's a favorite with photographers—a string of lovely Victorian homes (the "Painted Ladies") is presented with the metropolitan skyline as a backdrop. The view seems to capture the essence of the entire city.

An excellent way to explore the Haight is on foot. Walking down Haight St. from the Golden Gate Park and exploring the stores and cafes along the way will acquaint you with the ambience of the neighborhood. With a bit of inspiration, you'll gain an appreciation for the Haight's respectful remembrance of the '60s. If pounding the pavement it is just too slow, **Skates on Haight,** 1818 Haight St. (752-8375), will help you glide through the Haight. (In-line skates and pads $7 per hr. Passport or driver's license and major credit card required. 20% off for San Francisco hostelers with coupon. Open Mon.-Sat. 10am-6:30pm.)

The **Red Victorian Movie House,** 1727 Haight St. (668-3994), between Cole and Shrader, is a collective-owned and operated theater that shows foreign, student, and recently-run Hollywood films. The cheerful owners sell homemade cookies ($1) and freshly popped organic popcorn. The movie house is not affiliated with the

B&B. (See Cinema, page 268 for more info.) The **Global Family Networking Center,** 1665 Haight St. (864-1978), is housed in the **Red Victorian Bed and Breakfast Inn** (see Accommodations, page 241, for more on the inn). The networking center hopes to enhance understanding among peoples of the world by encouraging dialogue in its unique "common meeting place."

Wasteland, 1660 Haight St. (863-3150), is an immense used clothing store, deserving of notice, if only for its wonderful façade and window displays. (Open Mon.-Fri. 11am-6pm, Sat. 11am-7pm, Sun. noon-6pm.) Vintage meets rummage sale at **Buffalo Exchange,** 1555 Haight St. (431-7733; open Mon.-Sat. 11am-7pm, Sun. noon-6pm). **Great Expectations Bookstore,** 1512 Haight St. (863-5515) has a terrific selection of postcards and t-shirts. The current hot seller is a tie-dyed shirt with the famous Haight and Ashbury street signs on the front. (Open 9am-9pm daily in summer; winter 10am-8pm.) Search **Reckless Records,** 1401 Haight St. (431-3434), for some groovy tunes. The extensive collection of used LPs is priced according to the number of scratches and the rarity of the album (open Mon.-Sat. 10am-10pm, Sun. 10am-8pm). **Bound Together Bookstore: An Anarchist Collective,** 1369 Haight St. at Masonic (431-8355), has surprisingly orderly stacks of new and used books. Subject headings include "commie" and "magical arts." (Open daily 11:30am-7:30pm, although they say they're open "whenever probable which is sometimes unlikely, but sometimes we're open, sometimes we're closed, just check it out to find out.")

Resembling a dense green mountain in the middle of the Haight, **Buena Vista Park** has, predictably, a reputation for free-wheeling lawlessness. (Of course it may all be hype.) Enter at your own risk, and once inside, be prepared for those doing their own thing.

GOLDEN GATE PARK

No visit to San Francisco is complete without a visit to Golden Gate Park. Frederick Law Olmsted—designer of New York's Central Park—said it couldn't be done when San Francisco's 19th-century elders asked him to build a park to rival Paris's Bois de Boulogne on their city's western side. But engineer William Hammond Hall and Scottish gardener John McLaren proved him wrong. Hall designed the 1000-acre park—gardens and all—when the land was still just shifting sand dunes, and then constructed a mammoth breakwater along the oceanfront to protect the seedling trees and bushes from the sea's burning spray. McLaren planted more than one million trees in the park during his 55 years as the Golden Gate's godfather, transforming the sand into soil with sea-bent grass, humus, and Aegean truckloads of manure. When the early groundskeepers wanted to preserve the pristine lawns by enforcing a "keep off the grass" rule, McLaren was outraged and threatened to pave over the park if the rule were enforced. A strong-minded character, McLaren disliked statues in "his" park and tried to hide them in bushes. Despite his explicit orders, a statue of McLaren was erected after his death at age 93. However, the best memorial to McLaren is the beautiful park he helped to create.

To get to the park from downtown, hop on bus #5 or 21. Bus #44 passes right by the major attractions and serves 6th Ave. to California Ave. to the north and the MUNI Metro to the south. Most of the park is bounded by Fulton St. to the north, Stanyan St. to the east, Lincoln Way to the south, and the Pacific Ocean to the west. The major north-south route through the park is named **Park Presidio By-Pass Drive** in the north and **Cross Over Drive** in the south. The **Panhandle,** a thin strip of land bordered by Fell and Oak St. on the north and south respectively, is the oldest part of the park. Originally the "carriage entrance," it contains the most elderly trees and extends into the realm of Haight-Ashbury.

Food

The park contains two conveniently located **snack bars.** One sits behind the bandstand between the Academy of Sciences and the Asian Art Museum. The other is located in the Stow Lake boathouse. Both sell basic junk food. Pack a picnic; bringing your own food is a cheaper and usually a tastier and healthier option.

Outside the park it is fairly easy to find good food. Four blocks north, Geary St. runs parallel to the park. The stretch of Geary between 5th and 28th Ave. is filled with grocery stores, pizza places, and other fairly inexpensive restaurants. One block south of the park, Irving St. runs east from the ocean and is the home of produce markets, bakeries, and cafés. Ninth Ave. south of the Golden Gate also has some good restaurants.

Gordos, 1233 9th Ave. (566-6011), ½ block from the park between Lincoln and Irving. Drop by for some of the best burritos in the city. Watch as the friendly guys behind the counter create your very filling Super Burrito (with meat $3.55, vegetarian $3.05). For hot stuff get the jalapenos. Open daily 10am-10pm.

Stoyanof's, 1240 9th Ave. (664-3664), a ½-block from the park, between Lincoln and Irving. Join the crowds at this upscale cafeteria that serves fresh and delicious Mediterranean food. Have a Greek salad ($4) and spinach in filo ($1.60). For dessert nibble a piece of baklava and wander through the park. Open Tues.-Sun. 10am-4:30pm and 5-9:30pm for dinner, Fri.-Sat. 5-10pm, Sun. 4:30-9pm.

Owl and Monkey Café, 1336 9th Ave. (665-4840), 1½ blocks from the park, between Irving and Judah. Fill up on fresh, homemade, healthy food in this neighborhood restaurant. Generous sandwiches ($3.25-4.65). Garden seating available. Open Sun.-Wed. and Fri. 9am-10:30pm, Thurs. and Sat. 9am-11pm.

Sights

Park Headquarters (666-7200), where you can procure information and maps, is in McLaren Lodge at Fell and Stanyan St., on the eastern edge of the park (open Mon.-Fri. 8am-5pm).

There are three magnificent **museums** in the park, all in one large complex on the eastern side south of John F. Kennedy Dr., where 9th Ave. meets the park. On the south side of the complex is the California Academy of Sciences, and facing it are the M. H. de Young Memorial Museum and the Asian Art Museum. The **California Academy of Sciences** (221-5100; 750-7145 for a recording)—one of the nation's largest institutions of its kind—houses several smaller museums that specialize in different bodies of science. To the left of the entrance hall stands the **Stinson African Hall,** to the right the **North American Hall.** They both encase preserved specimens of native animals. To the left of the **Whale Courtyard,** the **Wattis Hall of Man** details the various stages of human evolution. The **Steinhart Aquarium** (home to members of over 14,000 aquatic species) is more lively than the natural history exhibits. Here you can see the dungeness crab before it's been steamed and hear the plaintive song of the croakerfish. The alligator and crocodile pool is engaging but pales in comparison with the unique Fish Roundabout, a tank shaped like a doughnut where the fish swim around you. The aquarium also boasts a display explaining why San Francisco's beaches are particularly prone to great white shark attacks (it's the seals), as well as a second, equally comforting disquisition on the San Andreas fault. (See the seals and dolphins fed Fri.-Wed. 10:30am-4:30pm every 2 hr.; and the penguins, daily 11:30am and 4pm.) Competing with the Universal Studios Tour, the **Space and Earth Hall** shows a video of a simulated earthquake. For a break from so much heavy data, the **"Far Side of Science"** gallery shows over 150 of Gary Larson's zaniest cartoons. (Academy open daily 10am-5pm; Sept. 2-July 3 10am-5pm. $7, $5 with MUNI Fast Pass or transfer, seniors and ages 12-17 $3, 6-11 $1.50. Free 1st Wed. of month until 8:45pm.)

The Academy's **Morrison Planetarium** (750-7141) re-creates the heavens above with an impressive show ($2.50, seniors and students $1.25). The **Laserium** (750-7138) orients its argon laser show to such rocking themes as Pink Floyd's "The Wall" and several U2 albums. ($6, over 65 and 6-12 $4, 5pm matinee $5; call for schedule). The synesthetic spectacle may be too intense for young children.

The **M. H. de Young Memorial Museum** (750-3600) takes visitors through a 21-room survey of American painting, from the colonial period to the early 20th century, including several works by John Singer Sargent, and a gallery of late-19th-century *trompe l'oeil* paintings. Several sculptures and pieces of antique furniture are mixed in with this survey. Also noteworthy is the museum's glass collection, which features ancient, European, Tiffany, and Steuben pieces. The **Asian Art Museum** (668-7855) in the west wing of the building is the largest museum outside Asia dedicated entirely to Asian artwork. The museum's beautiful collection includes rare pieces of jade and porcelain, in addition to works in bronze, which are over 3000 years old. Both museums offer a variety of free (with price of admission) tours, some daily and others once a week. Call for details. (Both museums open Wed.-Sun. 10am-5pm. Admission to both $5; $3 with MUNI Fast Pass or transfer; seniors and ages 12-17 $2; under 12, 1st Wed. of month, and Sat. 11am-noon free).

Despite its sandy past, the soil of Golden Gate Park appears rich enough today to rival the fertile soil of the San Joaquin Valley. Flowers bloom all around, particularly in spring and summer. The **Conservatory of Flowers,** erected in 1879, is the oldest building in the park, allegedly constructed in Ireland and shipped from Dublin via Cape Horn. The delicate and luminescent structure is modeled after Palm House in London's Kew Gardens and houses scintillating displays of tropical plants, including the very rare Masdevallia and Dracula orchids. (752-8080. Open daily 9am-6pm; Nov.-April 9am-5pm. $1.50, seniors and ages 6-12 75¢, under 6 free. Free daily 9:30-10am and 5:30-6pm, 1st Wed. of month and holidays.) The **Strybing Arboretum,** on Lincoln Way at 9th Ave. (661-1316), southwest of the academy, is home to 5000 varieties of plants. The **Garden of Fragrance** is designed especially for the visually impaired; the labels are in Braille and the plants are chosen specifically for their texture and scent. (Open Mon.-Fri. 8am-4:30pm, Sat.-Sun. 10am-5pm. Tours daily 1:30pm, Thurs.-Sun. 10:30am. Free.) Near the Music Concourse on a path off South Dr., the **Shakespeare Garden** contains almost every flower and plant ever mentioned by the herbalist of Stratford-upon-Avon. Plaques with the relevant quotations are hung on the back wall, and there's a map to help you find your favorite hyacinths and cowslips (open daily dawn-dusk; in winter closed Mon.; free). **Rhododendron Dell,** between the Academy of Sciences and John F. Kennedy Dr., honors John McLaren with a splendid profusion of his favorite flower. In the middle of Stow Lake, **Strawberry Hill** is covered with strawberry plants. Rent a boat ($9.50-14.50 per hour), or cross the footbridge and climb the hill for a dazzling view of the San Francisco peninsula. At the intersection of Lincoln Way and South Dr., the **Japanese Cherry Orchard** blooms intoxicatingly during the first week in April; it remains beautiful year-round.

Created for the 1894 Mid-Winter Exposition, the elegant **Japanese Tea Garden** is a serene collection of dark wooden buildings, small pools, graceful footbridges, carefully pruned trees, and plants. Buy tea and cookies for $2 and watch the giant carp circle the central pond. (Open daily 9am-6:30pm; Oct.-Feb. 8:30am-dusk. $2, seniors and ages 6-12 $1, under 6 free. Free 1st and last ½ hr. and on holidays.)

At the extreme northwestern corner of the park, the **Dutch Windmill** turns and turns again. The powerhouse, built in 1905 to pump irrigation water for the emerging park, measures 114 ft. from sail to sail. Rounding out the days of yore is the **carousel** (c. 1912), which is accompanied by a $50,000 Gebruder band organ. (Open daily 10am-5pm; Oct.-May Wed.-Sun. 10am-4pm. $1, ages 6-12 25¢.)

The multinational collection of gardens and museums in Golden Gate Park would not be complete without something distinctly American; what could be more American than a herd of **buffalo?** A dozen of the shaggy beasts roam a spacious paddock at the western end of John F. Kennedy Dr., near 39th Ave.

On Sundays traffic is banned from park roads, and bicycles and in-line skates come out in full force. Bikes are available for rent at Stow Lake ($7 per hour or $28 per day) or from the **Lincoln Cyclery,** 772 Stanyan St. (221-2415), on the east edge of Golden Gate Park. (Mountain bikes $5 per hr., $25 full day. Driver's license or major credit card and $25 deposit required. Open Mon. and Wed.-Sat. 9am-5pm, Sun. 11:30am-5pm.)

RICHMOND

Geary Blvd. is a main thoroughfare through the area which extends east from Point Lobos to the Financial District. Clement St. and California St. run parallel to Geary. The region enclosed by these streets and 28th and 5th Ave. on the west and east is known as the Richmond District, a largely residential neighborhood north of Golden Gate Park. This quiet district contains many ethnic neighborhoods and restaurants for exploration. "Inner Richmond," the area east of Park Presidio Blvd. has a large Chinese population, earning it the nickname "New Chinatown."

Food

Some locals claim that the Chinese restaurants in Richmond are better than the ones in Chinatown. A trip to one of Richmond's popular and authentic Chinese restaurants will prove the feasibility of this claim. In addition, the area contains fine Thai, Burmese, Cambodian, Japanese, Italian, Russian, Korean, and Vietnamese restaurants.

The Red Crane, 1115 Clement St. (751-7226), between Park Presidio Blvd. and 12th Ave., is an award-winning Chinese vegetarian and seafood restaurant. The sweet and sour walnuts ($5.75) and the spicy Szechuan eggplant ($5) are divine. Lunch special Mon.-Fri. 11:30am-2:30pm includes entree with soup and rice for just $3.50. Open daily 11:30am-10pm.

Ernesto's, 2311 Clement St. (386-1446), at 24th Ave. A well-kept San Francisco culinary secret. Dinners at this family-run Italian restaurant are reasonably priced (entrees $8-11.25, pizza $7.75-$15.50) and are as authentic as anything in North Beach, if not Italy. Try the filling linguine with red clam sauce ($8.75). You might encounter a line for dinner, but fear not—the food is worth the wait and wine is often served free to guests waiting outside the door. Open Tues.-Sun. 4-10pm.

The Golden Turtle, 308 5th Ave. (221-5285), at Clement. Prices at this small Vietnamese restaurant are reasonable, and the food is delicious. Vegetarian options abound. Service makes you feel like royalty. Entrees $7-$17. Open daily 11am-3pm and 5-11pm.

Narai Restaurant, 2229 Clement St. (751-6363), between 23rd and 24th Ave. This charming restaurant is known for its excellent Chinese and Thai cuisine. Delicious plates of *pad thai* ($4.25) attract the likes of author Amy Tan, actor Richard Gere, and supermodel Cindy Crawford. Open Tues.-Sun. 11am-10pm.

Little Café, 914 Clement St. (668-3829), between 10th and 11th Ave. This charming French and Italian restaurant caters to the gourmet with European ambience and delicious entrees ($7-15). Dinner served daily 5-10pm.

Toy Boat Dessert Café, 401 Clement St. (751-7505), at 5th Ave. Sells San Francisco's famous Double Rainbow ice cream and delicious baked goods as well as puppets, masks, figurines, and other traditional toys. The walls are decorated with flamingo lights, papier-mâché masks, and puppets. Open Mon.-Thurs. 7:30am-11:30pm, Fri. 7:30am-midnight, Sat. 9am-midnight, Sun. 9am-11:30pm.

Sights

Lincoln Park, at the northwest extreme of the San Francisco, is the biggest attraction in the Richmond District. To reach Lincoln Park, follow Clement St. west to 34th Ave., or Geary Blvd. to Point Lobos Ave. (MUNI bus #1 or 38). The grounds around the park also offer a romantic view of the Golden Gate Bridge. Take the **Land's End Path,** running northwest of the cliff edge, for an even better look. The **Palace of the Legion of Honor,** which normally houses San Francisco's best collection of European art, is closed for renovations. The projected opening date is November 1995. Southwest of Lincoln Park sits the precarious **Cliff House,** the third of that name to occupy this picturesque spot (the previous two burned down before the present structure was erected in 1909). The nearby **National Park Service Visitors Center** (556-8642), dispenses information on the whiskered wildlife of the cliffs area, as well as on the history of the present and previous Cliff Houses. (Open 10am-4:30pm daily. Free.)

Turning out to sea from the western cliffs along Point Lobos Ave., you can see **Seal Rocks,** often occupied by the sleek animals. Don't feed the coin-operated binoculars which look out over the seals—simply head into the visitors center and have a free look through its telescope. **Ocean Beach,** the largest and most popular of San Francisco's beaches, begins south of Point Lobos and extends down the northwestern edge of the city's coast line. The undertow along the point is so strong that swimming is prohibited and even wading is dangerous. However, die-hard surfers gladly brave the treacherous undertow and the ice-cold water in order to ride the best waves in San Francisco. Swimming is allowed at **China Beach** at the end of Seacliff Ave. on the eastern edge of Lincoln Park. The water is COLD here too, but the views of the Golden Gate Bridge are stunning (lifeguards on duty April-Oct.).

To the east of the Cliff House are the ruins of Adolph Sutro's 1896 dream baths. Cooled by ocean water, the **Sutro Baths** were capable of squashing in 10,000 occupants at a time, and generations of San Franciscans got to know one another in this steamy spa. Sadly, the baths burned down in 1966. Several paths lead from Point Lobos Ave. down to the ruins, and provide an invigorating half-hour stroll. Use caution when exploring the ruins and nearby cliffs and caves—the signs which warn of ferocious waves washing people from the cliffs are not for shock value.

The **Green Apple Bookstore,** 506 Clement St. (387-2272), lies inland from the baths in the heart of Richmond. This legendary bookstore buys, sells, and trades used books. (Open Mon. and Thurs. 10am-6pm, Tues. and Wed. 10am-8pm, Fri.-Sun. 10am-5pm.) **Temple Emmanuel,** 2 Lake St. at Arguello Ave. (751-2535), is a peaceful and beautiful example of Moorish architecture, designed by the same architect who designed the Civic Center. The **Presidio Bicycle Shop,** 5335 Geary (752-2453), between 17th and 18th Ave., rents bikes for $6 per hour, $25 per day (open Mon.-Sat. 10am-6pm, Sun. 11am-4pm).

THE PRESIDIO AND THE GOLDEN GATE BRIDGE

Established in 1776, the **Presidio,** a sprawling army-owned preserve that extends all the way from the Marina in the east to the wealthy Sea Cliff area in the west, provides endless opportunities for perambulating through the trees or along the beach. The preserve also supports the southern end of San Francisco's world-famous Golden Gate Bridge. (MUNI bus #28, 29, or 76). The 6th Army occupied the park for years, but the U.S. Congress recently ordered it to leave.

Food

When visiting the sights of the Presidio, it is smart to bring a picnic idea as restaurants are in short supply. For good sit-down food, head to the nearby neighborhood of Richmond (page 256).

Sights

At the northern tip of the Presidio (and the peninsula), under the tower of the Golden Gate Bridge, **Fort Point** (556-1693) stands guard over the entrance to San Francisco Bay. The fort was built in 1853 as one of a series of bunker defenses designed to protect San Francisco from invasion by the British during the tense dispute over the Oregon boundary; it now houses a museum and is a perfect place to watch the sea-savaged surfers below and the steady bridge above. It is also the spot where Kim Novak dove into the Bay in Hitchcock's *Vertigo.* Guided tours are given by National Park Rangers. (Museum open Wed.-Sun. 10am-5pm. Free 1-hr. **walks** with presentation 10:30am, 1:30, and 3:30pm with extra 12:30pm walk on weekends. Cannon drill demonstration noon and 2pm. 25-min. movie on Golden Gate Bridge construction 3:30pm. Movie on Fort Point at 10, 11am, 1, 2, and 4pm.) Aficionados of military regalia and Presidio history may want to stop at the **Presidio Army Museum** (556-0856), Lincoln Blvd. at Funston Ave. The collection is heavy on guns, old uniforms, and sepia-toned photographs (open Wed.-Sun. 10am-4pm; free).

The Spanish once called the entrance to the San Francisco Bay *La Boca del Puerto de San Francisco* (the mouth of the Port of San Francisco). Scorning simplicity, indecisive abolitionist and presidential hopeful General John C. Frémont decided to rename it *Chrysopylae* "for the same reason that the harbor of Byzantium was called *Chrysoceras,* or Golden Horn." He failed to explain the connection, but "golden" stuck and today the **Golden Gate Bridge,** the rust-colored symbol of the West's bounding confidence, sways above the entrance to San Francisco Bay. Built in 1937 under the direction of chief engineer Joseph Strauss, the bridge is almost indescribably beautiful from any angle on or around it. Even though you have doubtless seen pictures before, when you see the real bridge for the first time you won't be able to get over its tremendous size, yet extraordinarily graceful and delicate design, especially if it is partially cloaked in the renowned San Francisco fog. The bridge's overall length is 8981 ft., the main span is 4200 ft. long. The stolid towers are 746 ft. high. Built to swing, the bridge was undamaged by the '89 quake. Just across the bridge, **Vista Point** is just that, providing an incredible view of the city.

MARINA, PACIFIC HEIGHTS, AND PRESIDIO HEIGHTS

The Marina, Pacific Heights, and the adjoining Presidio Heights are the most sought-after addresses in San Francisco for young, urban professionals. **Fillmore Street, Union Street,** and **Chestnut St.** are the centers of activity for the upwardly mobile folk who make this area their home. Although the affluence of this area virtually guarantees that most of its chichi boutiques will fall beyond the means of most budget travelers, it does provide the thrifty *Let's Go*-er with a bounty of impressive mansions, well-kept parks, and pristine paths to enjoy at no cost.

Food

Pacific Heights and the Marina abound in high-quality restaurants serving good, fresh food. Some are expensive, but it is fairly easy to find a great meal for under $10. Most of the restaurants in this area lie on the main commercial streets.

Leon's Bar*B*Q, 1911 Fillmore St. (922-2436), between Pine and Bush. At the southern end of yuppified Fillmore, Leon's has been serving up Cajun jambalaya ($5) and the like since 1963. Dinner plates with ribs or seafood and fixin's for $8-15.25. Open daily 11am-9:30pm for table service, until 10pm for take out.

Jackson Fillmore Trattoria, 2506 Fillmore St. (346-5288). Where does the staff from Chez Panisse go on their day off? Jackson Fillmore. Great southern Italian cuisine and a lively atmosphere can always be counted on at this hip *trattoria.* The portions are large and if you're careful you can sneak out for less than $10 per person. The *tiramisu* ($5) is arguably the best in town. Reservations required for more than 3 people; always recommended for 2. After 6:30pm, counter space may still be available. Open Mon. 5:30-10pm, Tues.-Thurs. 5:30-10:30pm, Fri.-Sat. 5:30-11pm, Sun. 5-10pm.

Bepple's Pies, 1934 Union St. (931-6225). These pies are divine creations, combining succulent fruit filling with a miraculous crust that is moist yet flaky, absorbing the flavor of the fruit. Slices of pie are $3-4, another $1.35 for a solid slab of excellent vanilla ice cream and 70¢ for melted cheddar. "A pie without cheese is like a hug without a squeeze." Dinner pies with soup or cole slaw ($5-7). Whole fruit pies to go $14. Open Mon.-Thurs. 7am-midnight, Fri. 7am-1am, Sat. 8am-2am, Sun. 8am-midnight. Another Bepple's is at 2142 Chestnut St. (931-6226).

Sweet Heat, 3324 Steiner St. (474-9191), between Chestnut and Lombard. Inside, the hand-painted slogan says "Eat well, enjoy life, be healthy." This spunky little place serves south-of-the-border food to a health-conscious Marina crowd. Delicious chicken or steak taco ($3), grilled veggie burrito in whole wheat tortilla ($4). Eat in or take out. Open Sun.-Thurs. 11am-midnight, Fri.-Sat. 11am-2am.

Chestnut Street Grill, 2321 Chestnut St. (922-5558), at Scott. Honors its 125 regulars with sandwiches in their names ($4-6). Older male clientele. TVs perpetually turned to sports programing. Full dinners for $8.25-11. Garden seating in the back. Open Mon.-Thurs. 11am-11pm, Fri.-Sat. 11am-midnight, Sun. 10am-10pm.

Pasta Pomodoro, 2027 Chestnut St. (474-3400), at Fillmore. New pasta joint with the slogan "gourmet pasta at fast-food prices." Yuppies in business suits or alma mater sweatshirts fill up on salads ($3-5) and fresh pasta ($3.75-6). Open daily 11am-11pm. Take-out too.

Medioevo, 1809 Union St. (346-7373), between Laguna and Octavia. This medieval-style restaurant serves simple, hearty, family-style Italian food. The staff is in costume, the menu is on a scroll, and you can wear one of their fancy hats if you like. Pastas under $10, salads $4-6.50. Open Tues.-Sun. 5:30-10pm.

Sights

While exploring the Pacific Heights neighborhood on foot, do not neglect to admire the beautiful views of the bay. One truly memorable vista (seen from Fillmore St.) is a panorama of the Golden Gate Bridge and the Marina with the Palace of Fine Arts in the foreground.

Centered about Union and Sacramento St., Pacific Heights boasts the greatest number of **Victorian buildings** in the city. The 1906 earthquake and fire destroyed most of the northeast part of San Francisco, but left the Heights area west of Van Ness Ave. unscathed. The Marina was the hardest hit in 1989, but the Heights area was not as lucky this time around and sustained serious damage. Victorian restoration has become a full-fledged enterprise: consultants are hired to determine the original form of fretwork, friezes, fans, columns, corbels, cartouches, pediments, stained glass, rosettes, and Rococo plaster for even the smallest repairs. The Octagon House and Haas-Lilienthal House are two houses that provide the public with a glimpse inside a Victorian building. The **Octagon House,** 2645 Gough St. (441-7512), at Union St., is currently the headquarters of the National Society of Colonial Dames. The house was built in 1861 with the belief that such architecture would bring good luck to its inhabitants; apparently, they already had the good luck to build it, and the house's survival of the many earthquakes and fires that have swept the city shows more good fortune. (Open 2nd Sun. and 2nd and 4th Thurs. of all months except Jan. noon-3pm; group tours by arrangement available on any weekday.) The **Haas-Lilienthal House,** 2007 Franklin St. (441-3004), is another grand example of Victorian architecture run rampant. (Open Wed. noon-4pm, Sun. 11am-4pm. $5, seniors and under 18 $3.)

If you prefer shopping to architectural studies, **Union Street** is still an excellent place to be. Between Scott and Webster St., Union St. is chock-full of upscale shops, galleries, bars, restaurants, and bakeries. **Sacramento Street** is Union's slightly less expensive, less cosmopolitan cousin.

Down from Pacific Heights toward the bay and past Union is the **Marina** district. Chestnut Street, once a neighborhood lane of small grocers, has recently become the destination of choice for a young crowd of shoppers, diners, and drinkers. The **Marina Safeway,** 15 Marina Blvd. (563-4946), is known throughout the city as a pick-up market for singles. By the water, **Marina Green** seethes with joggers and walkers and is famous for spectacularly flown two-line kites. Wear a college sweatshirt for camouflage. To the east of Marina Green at Laguna and Marina lies **Fort Mason.** The army's former embarkation facility has been converted into a center for non-profit organizations (many of a decidedly anti-military bent) and is also a place for young people to meet. The center is part of the Golden Gate National Recreation Area, but is operated by the Fort Mason Foundation (441-5706). The Fort Mason Center houses many small museums with adjoining gift shops. The **San Francisco Museum of Modern Art Rental Gallery** (441-4777), Building A, provides prospective collectors with the opportunity to view art and then rent it on a monthly (or trial) basis. Works of all different media by several hundred artists are on display (open Tues.-Sat. 11:30am-5:30pm; closed Aug.). The **San Francisco Craft and Folk Art Museum** (775-0990), Building A, is smart and self-explanatory. (Open Tues.-Fri. and Sun. 11am-5pm, Sat. 10am-5pm. $1.) The **African-American Historical and**

Cultural Society Museum (441-0640), Building C, Room 165, focuses on contemporary African arts and crafts (open Wed.-Sun. noon-5pm; donation requested). **Museo Italo Americano** (673-2200), Building C #100, displays work created by artists with Italian heritage (open Wed.-Sun. noon-5pm; $2, students and seniors $1). The **Mexican Museum** (441-0404), Building D, offers free tours, exhibits, and educational workshops. (Open Wed.-Sun. noon-5pm; $4, seniors and students $2, under 10 free.) The **Magic Theater** (441-8822), Building D, founded in 1967 by John Lion, is renowned for hosting Sam Shepard as its playwright-in-residence from 1975 to 1985. Commissioned by the Magic Theater to write, write, write, Shepard produced such works as *Fool for Love* and *Angel City* and went on to receive ten Obie awards and an Academy Award nomination for *The Right Stuff*. The Magic Theater continues to stage contemporary American plays (Oct.-July Wed.-Sun.).

A walk eastward over the hill of Fort Mason takes you to Ghirardelli Square and Fisherman's Wharf. To the west lies the **Palace of Fine Arts,** on Baker St. between Jefferson and Bay St. The beautiful domed structure and the two curving colonnades are reconstructed remnants of the 1915 Panama Pacific Exposition, which commemorated the opening of the Panama Canal and signalled San Francisco's recovery from the great earthquake. The palace was designed by Bernard Maybeck and constructed out of staff (a plaster and fiber substance that resembles marble but decays rapidly). In 1959, a wealthy citizen was dismayed by the erosion and paid to have it rebuilt in stone. The grounds of the Palace of Art, complete with swans and an artificial lake, are some of the best picnic spots in the city. On summer days performances of Shakespeare are sometimes given in the colonnade section.

Next to the domed building is the **Exploratorium,** 3601 Lyon St. (561-0360). Here, expansive exhibits expounding the wonders of science range from giant bubble makers to shadow machines. Hundreds of interactive exhibits may teach even poets a thing or two about the sciences. (Open Sun.-Tues. and Thurs.-Sat. 10am-6pm, Wed. 10am-9:30pm. $8.50, students and seniors $6.50, ages 6-17 $4.50. Free on the first Wed. of every month.) Within the Exploratorium dwells the **Tactile Dome** (561-0362), a pitch-dark maze of tunnels, slides, nooks, and crannies designed to help refine your sense of touch. Claustrophobes and those afraid of the dark should stay away (open Mon.-Fri. 10am-5pm; $10; call to reserve). The **Wave Organ** is a short walk along the bay from the Exploratorium's main entrance. The organ, designed by local artists Peter Richards and George Gonzales, is activated by the motion of waves and is an inviting place to sit or even meditate to the water's natural *om*.

FISHERMAN'S WHARF AND GHIRARDELLI SQUARE

Traveling eastward, along the waterfront, one arrives at the most popular tourist destination in San Francisco. Stretching from Pier 39 in the east to Ghirardelli Square in the west is "Fisherman's Wharf," home to ¾ mi. of porcelain figurines, gifts for lefties, and enough t-shirts to have kept Washington's army snug at Valley Forge. This area can be very crowded and expensive, but don't let that keep you away from this prime people-watching place. Enjoy the street performances, the (window) shopping opportunities, meet fellow tourists, and don't be too offended by the occasional crude bumper sticker. Conventional attractions aside, the best way to appreciate the wharf is to wake up at 4am, put on a warm sweater, and go down to the piers to see why it's called Fisherman's Wharf. You can take in the loading and outfitting of small ships, the animated conversation, the blanket of the morning mist, and the incredible views—without the rapacious scene and crowds. (Then go home and crawl back into bed.)

Food

Although many restaurants along the wharf and the waterfront are expensive, it is possible to sample some great seafood at the many stands that line the sidewalks. An especially good spot for delicious and affordable cuisine is the 2800 block of Taylor St. at Jefferson. A row of family-run stands sell filling clam chowder in sourdough bread bowls ($3.50), fish and chips ($4.75), and shrimp cocktails ($3). Or indulge in a whole Dungeness crab for $10-15 each. (Most stands stay open Sun.-Thurs. 6am-10:30pm, Fri.-Sat. 6am-11:30pm.)

Boudin Sourdough Bakery, 156 Jefferson (928-8249), between Taylor and Mason. This San Francisco chain of bakeries serves some of the best, most famous sourdough bread in the city. Bread is baked fresh daily on the premises. Buy a ½-lb. baguette ($1.65) or have a more filling meal of spicy Western beef chili in a sourdough bread bowl ($4.85). Open daily 7:30am-9pm; winter Sun.-Thurs. 7:30am-8pm, Fri.-Sat. 7:30am-9pm.

Buena Vista, 2765 Hyde St. (474-5044), at Beach St. Famous for introducing Irish coffee to the U.S., this noisy bar and restaurant is almost always packed. At night it fills to the gills with people interested in quaffing that creamy, alcoholic beverage. Friendly waitresses with coiffed '60s hairstyles serve Reuben sandwiches ($6), seafood chowders ($3.60), and filling dinners of prawns, fries, veggies, salad, and bread ($10). Open Mon.-Fri. 9am-2am, Sat.-Sun. 8am-2am.

Ricos, 943 Columbus Ave. (928-5404), near Lombard. Located between Fisherman's Wharf and North Beach, but it's well worth the walk. Monstrous burritos. Exceptional enchiladas. No fuss. ISIC discounts. Open daily 10am-10pm.

Sights

Pier 39 (981-7437), built on pilings that extend several hundred yards into the harbor, was designed to recall old San Francisco. Unfortunately, it looks more like a Dodge City scene from a Ronald Reagan Western (shops open daily 10:30am-8:30pm). Toward the end of the pier is **Center Stage,** where mimes, jugglers, and magicians do their thing. Also situated on Pier 39 are several colorful food stands that will make your mouth water. As an alternative to chocolate and shrimp, **Vlaho's Fruit Orchard** sells primo California produce (juicy cherries $4 per lb., peaches $2 per lb., luscious strawberries $6 per lb.) and provides a sink in which to rinse it (open daily May-Sept. 9am-8:30pm).

Tour boats and ferries dock just west of Pier 39. The two main tour fleets, the Blue and Gold Fleet and the Red and White Fleet, were named after the colors of UC Berkeley and Stanford University to symbolize the long-running rivalry between the two Bay Area schools. The **Blue and Gold Fleet** (781-7877) offers 1¼-hour tours on 400-passenger sight-seeing boats. The tours cruise under both the Golden Gate and Bay Bridges, past Angel Island, Alcatraz, and Treasure Islands, and provide sweeping views of the San Francisco skyline (tours begin at 10am, last boat 5:30pm; $15, seniors, ages 5-18, and military $8). The **Red and White Fleet** (546-2700 for reservations, 546-2628 for recorded information within CA; also 800-BAY-CRUISE, -229-278473, or 800-229-2784) at Pier 41 offers both tours and ferry rides. The 45-minute Bay Cruise leaves from Piers 41 and 43½ and goes under the Golden Gate Bridge and past Alcatraz and Angel Islands. ($15, over 62 and ages 12-18 $12, ages 5-11 $8; ask about the multi-lingual narratives.) Red and White boats also ferry passengers to Alcatraz (see below). Both bay cruises are fully narrated. For a really pleasant escape, try one of the **sailboat charters** that line the wharf. The *Ruby* (861-2165) provides tours. Reservations are required for sailboat charters. Bring a heavy sweater in summer and a jacket in winter. Tours and prices vary, call for more information.

Easily visible from boats and the waterfront is **Alcatraz Island.** Named in 1775 for the *alcatraces* (pelicans) that flocked to it, this former federal prison looms over the San Francisco Bay, 1½ mi. from Fisherman's Wharf. During World War I, conscientious objectors were held on the island along with men convicted of violent crimes while in the service. In 1934, Alcatraz was brought under federal purview and used to hold those who had wreaked too much havoc in other prisons. Of the 23 men who attempted to escape, all were recaptured or killed, except for five who were "presumed drowned" although their bodies were never found. The story of the most probable escape is related in the film *Escape from Alcatraz*. Robert Stroud, "The Birdman of Alcatraz," spent 17 years in solitary confinement—no escape for him. Although sentenced to death for killing a prison guard, he was spared by President Wilson and went on to write two books on bird diseases. In 1962, Attorney General Robert Kennedy closed the prison, and the island's existence was uneventful until 1969, when about 80 Native Americans occupied it as a symbolic gesture, claiming the rock as their property under the terms of a broken 19th-century treaty. Alcatraz is currently a part of the **Golden Gate National Recreation Area,** the largest park in an urban area in the United States, administered by the National Park Service. The **Red and White Fleet** (546-2896) runs boats to Alcatraz from Pier 41. Once on Alcatraz, you can wander by yourself or take a two-hour audiotape-guided tour, full of clanging chains and the ghosts of prisoners past. (Boats depart every ½ hr. from Pier 41; summer 9:15am-4:15pm, winter 9:45am-2:45pm. Fare $5.75, seniors $4.75, ages 5-11 $3.25; tours cost $3.25 extra, ages 5-11 $1.25 extra. Passengers can remain on the island until the final 6:30pm ferry departs.) Reserve tickets in advance through Ticketron (392-7469) for $1 extra or confront long lines and risk missing the boat.

At Pier 45, past the ferry docks, you'll see the *U.S.S. Pampanito,* a World War II submarine. (Open daily 9am-9pm; winter Sun.-Thurs. 9am-6pm, Fri.-Sat. 9am-8pm. $4, over 62 and ages 12-18 $2, ages 6-11 $1, under 6 free.) Pier 45 also provides one of the best views of Alcatraz Island from land.

As you continue along the waterfront and pass the shops and restaurants on Jefferson Street, don't neglect to veer from the tourist-ridden sidewalks and explore the docks and old fish houses. The **Maritime National Historic Park** (929-0202), at the Hyde Street Pier where Hyde meets Jefferson, displays the *Balclutha,* a swift trading vessel that plied the Cape Horn route in the 1880s and '90s and was featured in the first Hollywood version of *Mutiny on the Bounty.* The vessel was recently restored with donated union labor. (Open daily 9am-6pm, last ticket sold at 5:30pm. $3, ages 12-17 $1, over 61 and under 12 free.)

Aquatic Park is the area of the bay enclosed by the Hyde Street Pier and the curving Municipal Pier (see below). As you walk past the park, you are likely to see, believe it or not, swimmers. Members of the Dolphin Swimming and Boating Club, 502 Jefferson St. (441-9329), swim laps in the chilly 57°F water. The Dolphin and the neighboring South End Club invite courageous members of the public to join them in the water. For just $6.50 you too can swim in the San Francisco Bay, and perhaps more important, you can enjoy the warmth of the club's showers and sauna after your aquatic excursion. The two clubs take turns in sponsoring swims. (Open Tues.-Sat. 11am-6pm; winter 10am-5pm. Call for more info.)

A stroll along Aquatic Park will bring you to **Municipal Pier,** which juts into the bay and is said to be the inspiration for the song "(Sittin') On the Dock of the Bay." Don't miss the chance to wander around this windy pier where you'll see people fishing, lots of seagulls, and best of all, stunning views of the Golden Gate Bridge and Alcatraz.

The grassy hill south of Aquatic Park is **Victorian Park.** Watch the cable cars of the Hyde-Powell line get turned around manually at the end of the day. Street performers entertain the masses of tourists who wait here to board the cars during the day. The park also has benches and pleasant spots to enjoy a picnic or just rest.

The **Maritime Museum,** north of Beach St., at the head of Polk St., displays related memorabilia. The views from the terrace overlooking the bay are worth a visit even though the museum itself is best suited for those with a deep thirst for seafaring trivia. (Open daily 10am-5pm. Free.)

Ghirardelli Square (GEAR-ah-deh-lee), 900 N. Point St. (information booth 775-5500; open daily 10am-9pm) is the most famous of the shopping malls in the area around Fisherman's Wharf and rightfully so—it houses some of the best chocolate in the world. Today, the only remains of the machinery from Ghirardelli's original **chocolate factory** (transformed from a uniform factory in the 1890s by Domingo Ghirardelli's family) are in the rear of the **Ghirardelli Chocolate Manufactory,** an old-fashioned ice-cream parlor. Here the original machinery demonstrates the Ghirardelli chocolate-making process. Follow the numbered signs to gargantuan vat after vat of rich, liquid chocolate. Suddenly craving chocolate? The nearby Soda

Fountain serves up loads of its world-famous hot fudge sauce on huge sundaes ($5.50). For a dessert extravaganza, try the Earthquake Sundae (with several ravenous friends)—eight flavors of ice cream, eight toppings, bananas, whipped cream, nuts, and cherries for a symbolic $19.06. (Get it?) If your appetite outpaces your financial resources, look for the free chocolate samples inside the Ghirardelli store (771-4903; open daily 10am-midnight). The old Ghirardelli factory buildings were going to be destroyed until William Rorth, a financier with an aesthetic conscience, saved them and made a killing in the process. The square is now a popular and scenic destination, with acclaimed restaurants and an elegant mermaid fountain. Pricey boutiques fill the rest of the old factory's brick buildings, and local musicians and magicians entertain the masses. (Stores open Mon.-Sat. 10am-9pm, Sun. 10am-6pm.)

NORTH BEACH

As one walks north along Stockton St. or Columbus Ave., there is a gradual transition from supermarkets displaying ginseng to those selling provolone, and from restaurants luring customers with roast ducks in the window to those using *biscotti*. Lying north of Broadway and east of Columbus is the Italian neighborhood of North Beach. In the '50s, this area was split between the Bohemian Beats (Allen Ginsberg, Jack Kerouac, Lawrence Ferlinghetti, and others) who made it their home and the residents of the once traditional Italian neighborhood. More than one poet still tinkers with the language of Blake and Whitman, but the Beats are gone. North Beach today is an old Italian neighborhood filled with restaurateurs, shoe repairers, bakers, and cappuccino makers. It maintains a sense of serenity while being an entertaining, energetic, and popular place for San Franciscans and tourists both day and night. The blending of old times and the North Beach of the '90s is elegant and graceful.

Food

North Beach is home to oodles of noodles served in a wide variety of ways in traditional (and not so traditional) pasta restaurants. Meals are virtually guaranteed to be filling, but you'll want to save room for homemade *cannoli* and cappuccino at one of the many cafés. North Beach restaurants can be pricey; choose wisely.

Tommaso's, 1042 Kearny St. (398-9696), between Pacific and Broadway, just below Van Ness Ave. Try some of the best traditional Italian pizza anywhere. The super deluxe, piled high with mushrooms, peppers, ham, and Italian sausage is enough for two ($18.50). The *pizza Neapolitan* is simple and fulfilling. Francis Ford Coppola tosses pizza dough once in a while in front of Tommaso's wood burning ovens. Open Tues.-Sat. 5-10:45pm, Sun. 4-9:45pm.

U.S. Restaurant, 431 Columbus Ave. (362-6251), at Stockton St. Once a hangout for Kerouac and buddies, now popular with young San Franciscans. Long wait at dinner. Titanic, tasty portions. Calamari ($9, ½-portion $7), served Fri., is their most popular dish. Most dishes under $10. Open Tues.-Sat. 6:30am-9:30pm. Closed for 2-3 weeks in June or July (vacation time).

North Beach Pizza, 1310 Grant St. (433-2444). A fine specimen of the New York thin-crust school. Very popular. Small pie $6.79, extra-large $11.71. Try the Verdi's Special ($12.27) with spinach, pesto, onions, and feta. Open Mon.-Thurs. 11am-1am, Fri.-Sat. 11am-3am, Sun. noon-1am.

The Stinking Rose, 325 Columbus Ave. (781-ROSE, -7673). "We season our garlic with food" is their motto. Behind all the garlic paraphernalia is excellent, *very* aromatic cuisine. Indulge in garlic chowder, salads, pastas, and pizettes. The "vampire fare" lasagna is delicious, and doesn't contain garlic. Open Sun.-Thurs. 11am-11pm, Fri.-Sat. 11am-midnight. Reservations recommended.

Basta Pasta, 1268 Grant Ave. (434-2248). A favorite for late-night dining. Known for fresh pasta and wood-fired pizzas. Open daily 11:30am-2am.

Sodini's Green Valley Restaurant, 510 Green St. (291-0499), at Grand Ave. In the true heart of North Beach, one of the area's oldest family restaurants, established in 1906. Try the *Ravioli alla Casa* ($7.95). Open Mon-Thurs. 5pm-11pm, Fri.-Sat. noon-midnight.

Italian French Baking Co., 1501 Grant Ave.(421-3796), at Union St. Locals love the *Bastoni,* sour French loaves, $1.25. This corner bakery sells all kinds of bread, biscotti, and sweets. Read a newspaper at the small bar. Open daily 7am-6pm.

Sights

Lying between Stockton and Powell is **Washington Square** (North Beach's *piazza* and the wedding site of Joe DiMaggio and Marilyn Monroe), a lush lawn edged by trees and watched over by a statue of Benjamin Franklin. In the early morning the park fills with men and women practicing *Tai Chi.* Across Filbert, to the north of the square is the **Church of St. Peter and St. Paul** (421-0809), beckoning tired sight-seers to take refuge in its dark, wooden nave. The fathers present mass in Italian, English, and Cantonese. In the square itself is the **Volunteer Firemen Memorial,** donated by Mrs. Lillie Hitchcock Coit, who was rescued from a fire in childhood. Coit's most famous gift to the city is **Coit Tower** (often called "the candle"), which stands a few blocks east. The tower sits on **Telegraph Hill,** the steep mount from which a semaphore signalled the arrival of ships in Gold Rush days. (Rumor has it that the tower was built to resemble a fire nozzle.) Coit Tower's spectacular 360° view makes it one of the most romantic spots in the city. An elevator will take you to the top. (362-0808; open daily 10am-7pm; Oct.-May 9am-4pm. Elevator fare $3, over 64 $2, ages 6-12 $1, under 6 free. Last ticket sold ½-hr. before closing.) There is very limited parking, so leave your car on Washington St. and walk up the **Filbert Steps** which rise from the Embarcadero to the eastern base of the tower. The walk is short, allows excellent views, and passes by many attractive Art Deco buildings. At night, watch the city light up from the tower's base.

North Beach Bohemianism flourished when the artists and brawlers nicknamed the Beats first moved in. Drawn to the area by low rents and cheap bars, the group came to national attention when Ferlinghetti's **City Lights Bookstore,** 261 Columbus Ave. (362-8193), published Allen Ginsberg's anguished and ecstatic dream poem *Howl.* Banned in 1956, the book was found "not obscene" after an extended trial, but the resultant publicity turned North Beach into a must-see for curious tourists. City Lights has expanded since its Beat days, and continues to publish under its own imprint the works of poets new and old. A comfortable poetry room contains self-published works, including lots of Beats. Browse through the thought-provoking selection or relax in one of the store's chairs and read a magazine (open daily 10am-midnight).

The **Tattoo Art Museum,** 841 Columbus (775-4991; open Mon.-Sat. noon-1pm, Sun. noon-8pm), displays a fantastic collection of tattoo memorabilia, including hundreds of designs and exhibits on different tattoo techniques. Unfortunately, there is not enough space to display the entire collection, the largest one of its kind. Instead, works are exhibited on a rotating basis. In the same room, a modern, clean tattoo studio is run by the eminent professional Lyle Tuttle, himself covered in tattoos from head to foot. $50 will buy a quick, glowing rose on the hip, larger tattoos are $100 an hour. *Let's Go* recommends that you carefully evaluate the durability of your current relationship before getting that "X and X Forever" tattoo.

The **North Beach Museum,** 1435 Stockton at Columbus (391-6210), depicts the North Beach of yesteryear in a series of vintage photographs. Artists and filmmakers should scale the incline elevating the **San Francisco Art Institute** (800 Chestnut St.; 771-7020). Although the view from the school's large balcony (with adjoining café) lacks the surreal tempo said to have inspired alumnus Stanley Brakhage, it is cinematic nonetheless. Student work is usually on display.

NOB HILL AND RUSSIAN HILL

Before the earthquake and fire of 1906, Nob Hill was home to the mansions of the great railroad magnates. Today, Nob Hill remains one of the nation's most prestigious addresses. The streets are lined with many fine buildings, and the aura is that of idle and settled wealth. Sitting atop a hill and peering down upon the *hoi polloi* can be a pleasant afternoon diversion.

Food

It can be a challenge to find inexpensive restaurants at the tops of Nob and Russian Hills. However, if you descend the slopes and travel several blocks east or west, good, affordable eats are readily available. To the east you'll reach Chinatown; to the west you'll encounter Polk St., which is lined with great neighborhood dining spots, sip coffee, or drink pints of brew. The following restaurants are west of Nob Hill. See the Chinatown food section (page 266) for more listings.

Swan Oyster Depot, 1517 Polk St. (673-1101), near the California St. cable car at the western base of Nob Hill. Avoid the elbow-to-elbow lunch-time squeeze by coming during an off hour for some of the best and freshest seafood in the city. Pull up a stool to the marble counter (they don't have tables) and consume what most agree is the city's finest chowder ($3.50). The combination seafood salads ($11.25) change everyday and are a favorite among regulars. Try the clam cocktail with Swan's zesty red sauce for $5. Open Mon.-Fri. 8am-5:30pm.

U-Lee, 1468 Hyde St. (771-9774), at Jackson. This tiny Chinese restaurant is famous for its lemon chicken ($6.85) and giant potstickers (6 for $3.85). Many fresh vegetable dishes too. Entrees $3-6. Open daily 11am-10:30pm.

Ristorante Milano, 1448 Pacific Ave. (673-2961), between Larkin and Hyde. Although not entirely cheap, this extremely popular neighborhood *trattoria* serves entirely pleasurable food. The family-run kitchen puts out delicious *al dente* pastas ($10). You'll walk away well-fed without being weighted down. Open Tues.-Sat. 5:30-10:30pm, Sun. 5-10pm.

Swensen's (775-6818), Hyde St. at Union. This tiny, take-away ice cream parlor engendered a national chain. Earl Swensen has owned this store since 1948. Scoop $1.35. Open daily 11:30am-10pm.

Sights

After the steep journey up Nob Hill you will understand what inspired the development of the vehicles celebrated at the **Cable Car Powerhouse and Museum,** 1201 Mason St. (474-1887), at Washington. The building is the working center of the cable-car system. You can look down on the operation from a gallery or view displays to learn more about the picturesque cars, some of which date back to 1873 (open daily 10am-6pm; Nov.-March 10am-5pm; free).

Grace Cathedral, 1051 Taylor St. (776-6611), the most immense Gothic edifice west of the Mississippi, crowns Nob Hill. The castings for its portals are such exact imitations of Ghiberti's on the Baptistry in Florence that they were used to restore the originals. Inside, modern murals mix San Franciscan and national historical events with scenes from the lives of the saints. Visitors should respect the fact that the Cathedral is still used as a house of worship.

Once the site of the enormous and majestic mansions of the four mining and railroad magnates who "settled" Nob (Charles Crocker, Mark Hopkins, Leland Stanford, and Collis Huntington), the hilltop is now home to upscale hotels and bars. Two bars—the **Top of the Mark,** One Nob Hill (392-3434), in the Mark Hopkins Hotel at Mason and Pine St. (MUNI buses #2, 3, and 4 cross Mason on Sutter, 2 blocks south of Pine), and the **Fairmont Crown** at the Fairmont Hotel, 950 Mason St. (772-5131)—vie fiercely for the title of Bar with the Best View. The Top of the Mark offers a 360° view of the city, while the Crown is the highest public observation point in San Francisco. Both are superb, but the Mark is bigger and has a better bar. Drinks at both cost about $7. (Cocktails served at the Crown: Sun.-Thurs. 11am-12:30am, Fri.-Sat. 11am-1:30am; at the Mark: Sun.-Thurs. 4pm-12:30am, Fri.-Sat. 4pm-1:30am. The Mark also has live music Wed.-Sat. and dancing Fri.-Sat.)

Nearby Russian Hill is named after Russian sailors who died during an expedition in the early 1800s and were buried on the southeast crest. At the top of Russian Hill, the notorious **Lombard Street curves,** on Lombard (the crookedest street in the world) between Hyde and Leavenworth St. afford a fantastic view of the city and harbor—that is, if you dare to allow your eyes to stray from the road down this plunge. The switchbacks which test your driving prowess were installed in the

1920s to allow horse-drawn carriages to negotiate the extremely steep hill. The street was designed by Italians homesick for Genoa, where such curves originated.

NIHONMACHI (JAPANTOWN)

Nihonmachi encompasses an area three blocks long by three blocks wide. This small neighborhood 1.1 mi. from downtown San Francisco is bounded on its east side by Fillmore St., on its west side by Laguna St., by Bush St. to the north, and by the Geary Expressway to the south. Take MUNI buses #2, 3, and 4.

Food

Despite the number of restaurants in Japantown, it's fairly difficult to find inexpensive, quality food. Your best bets are lunch specials and filling bowls of noodle soup; or spending more to indulge in carefully sculpted sushi.

Akasaka, 1723 Buchanan Mall between Webster and Laguna in the Peace Plaza 921-5360). This small, friendly restaurant offers a dinner special of *tempura, teriyaki, gyoza* (fried potstickers), California rolls, rice, *miso* soup, salad, *tsu kemono* (pickled veggies), and tea for $9. No meal here would be complete without the green tea ice cream $1.25. Open Mon.-Thurs. 8am-2:30pm and 4-9:30pm, Sun. 8am-noon, Fri.-Sat. 8am-2:30pm and 5-10pm.

Sanppo, 1702 Post St. at the Peace Plaza (346-3486). Unpretentious restaurant with good food at inexpensive prices. Vegetable *tempura* $7.50. Open Tues.-Sat. 11:45am-10pm, Sun. 3pm-10pm.

Ino Sushi, 1620 Webster St. (922-3121), between Post and Sutter, is the place to go. Prices are average (for sushi); sushi quality is excellent. Two fresh salmon rolls $3.50. Try the *kappa maki* (delicious cucumber rolls; 6 for $3). The sushi bar has a $9 minimum. Open Mon.-Sat. 5-10:30pm.

Super Koyama, 1790 Sutter St. at Buchanan (921-6529) sells a wide variety of Japanese products, ranging from candies to soy paste and seafood. Worth a trip just to see the exotic products. Staff is happy to answer any questions. Open Mon.-Sat. 9am-7pm, Sun. 10am-6pm.

Sights

Nihonmachi is centered around the aptly named **Japanese Cultural and Trade Center** at the corner of Post and Buchanan. Similar to the Tokyo Ginza, the five-acre center includes Japanese *udon* houses, sushi bars, and a massage center and bathhouse. Japan gave as a gift to the 12,000 Japanese-Americans of San Francisco the **Peace Pagoda,** a magnificent 100-ft. tall, five-tiered structure which graces the heart of Japantown. The **Kabuki Complex** (931-9800) at Post St. and Fillmore shows current films, and during early May it is the main site of the San Francisco International Film Festival (see page 271).

The weary traveler with some money to spend might want to invest in a rejuvenating *Shiatsu* massage at **Fuji Shiatsu,** 1721 Buchanan Mall. Call 346-4484 for an appointment (open Mon.-Fri. 9am-8pm, Sat. 9am-7pm, Sun. 10am-6pm; $30 per hr. in morning, $33 per hr. in afternoon).

CHINATOWN

The largest Chinese community outside of Asia (over 100,000 people), Chinatown is also the most densely populated of San Francisco's neighborhoods. Chinatown was founded in the 1880s when, after the gold had been dug and the tracks laid, bigotry fueled by unemployment engendered a racist outbreak against what was then termed the "Yellow Peril." In response, Chinese-Americans banded together to protect themselves in a small section of the downtown area. As the city grew, speculators tried to take over the increasingly valuable land, especially after the area was leveled by the 1906 earthquake, but the Chinese were not to be expelled, and Chinatown, which has gradually expanded, remains almost exclusively Chinese. Most visitors come to Chinatown for the food, but there are plenty of other attractions.

Food

Chinatown abounds with downright cheap restaurants; in fact, their multitude and incredible similarity can make a choice nearly impossible.

House of Nanking, 919 Kearny St. between Columbus and Jackson (421-1429). Outstanding Chinese food in a crowded, but pleasant, atmosphere. This small restaurant which prepares its food within the dining area always has lines out the door, consisting partially of people who have walked all the way from the Financial District on their lunch breaks. *Mu-shu* vegetables $5, onion cakes $1.75. Tsing Tao beer sauce is essential. Open Mon.-Sat. 11am-10pm, Sun. 4-10pm.

Sam Wo, 813 Washington at Grant (982-0596). The late hours and BYOB policy, not to mention the exceptionally cheap prices, make this restaurant a favorite among students from all over the Bay Area. To get to the restaurant, customers must pass by the chefs as they prepare the food in the kitchen. If you want to hang with the really rowdy crowd, ask to be seated on the 3rd floor. Most dishes $2-5. Shrimp noodle soup $2.75, chicken chow mein $3.60. Open Mon.-Sat. 11am-3am; summer Mon.-Sat. 11am-3am, Sun. 12:30-9:30pm.

Brandy Ho's, 217 Columbus Ave. (788-7527). The paintings of hot peppers are a warning to the unsuspecting customer: the food is SPICY! Order everything mild or extra mild if you're feeling timid. Large interior. Very service-oriented. Entrees a la carte $6-10. *Gon pou* shrimp $9. Open daily 11:30am-midnight.

DPD, 901 Kearny at Jackson (982-0471). Friendly corner restaurant with a crowd of devoted regulars. $3.25 special features entree with rice, soup, and tea. Try the prawns with cashew nuts. Open Mon.-Thurs. 11am-10pm, Fri. 11am-10:30pm, Sat. 11:30am-10:30pm, Sun. 11:30am-10pm.

Yuet Lee, 1300 Stockton (982-6020), at Broadway. Not much for atmosphere, but the seafood makes up for that. Steamed fresh oysters in black bean sauce $8.50. Many exotic seasonal specialties for adventurous diners, such as sauteed pork stomach with boneless duck feet. Open Mon. and Wed.-Sun. 11am-3am.

Dol Ho, 808 Pacific Ave. at Stockton St. (392-2828). A relaxing atmosphere perfect for afternoon tea and *dim sum,* traditionally served as brunch. 4 steamed shrimp dumplings, sweet doughy sesame balls, or pork buns $1.60. Open daily 8am-5pm.

Sights

Grant Avenue is the most picturesque part of Chinatown. The street is a sea of Chinese banners, signs, and architecture. The avenue is lined with shops doing brisk business selling Asian-made tourist wares. Chinatown, once you step off Grant Ave., is a real community, not a tourist fabrication like Fisherman's Wharf. The less famous streets, such as Jackson, Stockton, and Pacific, are a more accurate representation of the neighborhood and the stores there are often less expensive. Pharmacies stock both Western and Eastern remedies for common ailments; produce markets are stacked with inexpensive vegetables; and Chinese newspapers are sold by vendors who eat their morning noodles out of thermoses.

Watch fortune cookies being shaped by hand in the **Golden Gate Cookie Company,** 56 Ross Alley (781-3956; huge bag of cookies $2), between Washington and Jackson St., just west of Grant Ave. This famous alleyway, which has preserved the atmosphere of old Chinatown, has been a filming site for many well-known movies including *Big Trouble in Little China, Karate Kid II,* and *Indiana Jones and the Temple of Doom.* Nearby **Portsmouth Square,** at Kearny and Washington St., made history in 1848 when Sam Brennan first announced the discovery of gold at Sutter's Mill from the square. Now the square is filled with Chinese men playing lively card games. A stone bridge leads from this square to the **Chinese Culture Center,** 750 Kearny St., 3rd floor of the Holiday Inn (986-1822), which houses exhibits of Chinese-American art and sponsors two **walking tours** of Chinatown. The Heritage Walk surveys the history of Chinatown (Sat. 2pm; $15, under 18 $5). The Culinary Walk discusses the preparation of Chinese food. (Sat. 10:30am; $25, under 12 $10. Price includes a *dim sum* lunch at Four Seas of Grant Ave.) Both walks require advance reservations. The **Chinese Historical Society,** 650 Commercial St. (391-1188), between Kearny and Montgomery, relates the tale of the Chinese who came to California through richly informative texts and some remarkable artifacts, including a 1909 parade dragon head (open Tues.-Sat. noon-4pm; donation).

At Grant and Bush stands the ornate, dragon-crested **Gateway to Chinatown,** given as a gift by the Republic of China in 1969. The dragon motif is continued on the lamp posts that line Chinatown's streets. Some of Chinatown's noteworthy buildings include **Buddha's Universal Church** (720 Washington), the **Kong Chow Temple** (855 Stockton), and **Old St. Mary's,** (660 California St. at Grant), built in 1854 of granite cut in China, which was San Francisco's only cathedral for almost four decades.

East Wind Books, 1435 Stockton (772-5899), at Columbus Ave., stocks a large selection of books on Chinese-American subjects, including cooking and healing. (Open Mon.-Sat. 10am-6pm, Sun. noon-5pm.)

■■■ ENTERTAINMENT

Relaxed bars, wild clubs, serious cinema houses, and provocative bookstores assertively satisfy the wide range of San Francisco's entertainment needs.

Sports enthusiasts should check the San Francisco Giants and **49ers** schedules for home games at notoriously windy **Candlestick Park** (467-8000), located 8 mi. south of the city via the Bayshore Freeway (U.S. 101). For **San Francisco Symphony** tickets, contact the box office at the Davies Symphony Hall (431-5400; open 9:30am-5:30pm). The Opera House is the site of box offices for the **San Francisco Opera** and the **San Francisco Ballet.** The opera box office (864-333) is open Monday through Friday from 10am to 6pm. Call 621-3838 for information on the ballet. Tickets can be charged by phone (762-2277) or obtained directly from the box office (open Mon.-Sat. noon-6pm). Any standing-room-only tickets available will go on sale two hours before performance.

The Sights sections above also discusses many entertainment opportunities. See Publications (page 237) for a rundown of magazines and newspapers with ongoing **theater** and other entertainment listings. Or call the **Entertainment Hotline** at 391-2001 or 391-2002. The *Bay Guardian* and *SF Weekly* always have a thorough listing of dance clubs and live music.

CINEMA

Gateway, 215 Jackson St. (421-3353), at Battery. Independent and foreign films $7. Matinee $4, over 61 and under 13 $4. 5 shows for $22. (Deal is good at any Landmark theaters, including Gateway, Clay, and Bridge.)

Clay, 2261 Fillmore (346-1123), at Clay in Pacific Heights. Mainstream foreign films, with the occasional obscure import. $7; over 64, under 13, and first show of the day $4. 5 shows for $22.

Bridge, 3010 Geary Blvd. (751-3212), at Blake 3 blocks west of Masonic. Independent and overlooked films. $7; over 61, under 13, and matinees $4. 5 shows for $22. (Gateway, Clay, and Bridge are all Landmark Theaters.)

Roxie, 3117 16th St. (863-1087), near Valencia. Razor-sharp and fashionably foolish punk and new wave movies. San Francisco's trendiest movie house; partly responsible for the *Eraserhead* cult. $6, seniors and under 12 $3.

Red Victorian Movie House, 1727 Haight St. (668-3994). Munch on organic popcorn while watching art films and revivals from couch-like benches. $5.50; $4.50 on Wed., Sat., and Sun. at 2pm, seniors and children $3.

Castro Theatre, 429 Castro St. (621-6120), near Market St. Beautifully refinished 1920s movie palace. Live organ music between showings. Wide selection of films, week-long festivals, and clever double-features, including Hollywood classics of the '30s and '40s. $7; seniors, under 12, and special matinees $5.

North Point Theater, 2290 Powell St. (989-6061), at Bay St. in North Beach. Average first-run movies, but the super screen and superb sound make even *True Lies* feel like a classic. $7; seniors and children $4. Matinees $4.

The Lumière, 1572 California (885-3200), at Polk St. Independent and smart films. Occasional double features. $7, seniors, children, and matinee $4.

Cinemateque, 800 Chestnut St. (558-8129), between Jones and Leavenworth St. Avant-garde and non-commercial movies in the auditorium of the San Francisco Art Institute. $6, seniors $3. Closed during summer.

BOOKSTORES

San Francisco bookstores can truly be considered part of the entertainment scene. The city's countless paperback palaces hold materials on subjects ranging from Aristotle and anarchy to Zen and zoology. The Haight concentrates more bookstores per block than any other area, but the selection is skewed towards the Bukowski/ *Strange Films*/Jim Morrison bio genre. The legendary **City Lights** in North Beach has the most intriguing selection. Clement Street, Downtown, and the Mission have their share as well. See individual neighborhood sections for more information on this important part of San Francisco life.

■■■ NIGHTLIFE

BARS AND CAFÉS

There are innumerable excellent bars and cafés scattered through the city, each with its own personality and clientele. Much to our chagrin, it's simply impossible to list them all. But here is a good sampling.

Café du Nord (861-5016), on Market St. between Church and Sanchez. Painfully hip. Expansive bar. Dinner served Wed.-Sat. Pool tables 75¢. Live music nightly, jazz and world music. Beers $3.25 each. Cover $1 on the weekends. Open 4pm-2am. Must be 21.

Café Istanbul, 525 Valencia (863-8854), between 16th and 17th, in the Mission. Traditional Middle Eastern music, coffees, teas, food, and low seating under the blue drapery ceiling. Sip *chai* ($1.50) or a rose syrup latté ($2). Fat Chance Bellydance performs Wed. at 8:30 and 9:30pm. Firsan, one of San Francisco's top male bellydancers, performs Tues. 8:30 and 9:30pm. Tues. are smoke-free. Open Fri.-Sat. 11am-4am, Sun.-Thurs. 11am-11pm. Make it a complete evening by dining on distinctive pan-Arabic cuisine at **Amira** (621-6213), across the street. Kebabs or Moroccan *couscous* with your choice of meat or vegetables $8-11. Open Sun.-Thurs. 5-10pm, Fri.-Sat. 5-11pm.

Perry's, 1944 Union St. (922-9022), at Laguna, in Pacific Heights. San Francisco's most famous pick-up junction is a comfortable, vaguely old-fashioned place: lackadaisical by day, hopping at night. Ten beers on tap, large draft beer $3.25. Food until midnight. One of the best-known places on Union St.—popular among the youngest of urban professionals. Open daily 7:30am-1am.

The Elbo Room, 647 Valencia St. (552-7788), near 17th in the Mission. Cover (usually $3) for the music and dancing upstairs only. This place is becoming less and less roomy while getting more and more popular. Open daily 5pm-2am.

The Savoy-Tivoli, 1434 Grant Ave. (362-7023), in North Beach. Sit yourself outside and watch the passersby or enter and play pool. The Savoy goes through phases—it's currently popular with visiting Europeans and local yuppies. Wear your black. Reggae. Daiquiris ($3.75), cappuccino ($3). Crowded, so don't expect speedy service. Open Tues.-Wed. 5pm-2am, Thurs.-Sun. 3pm-2am.

Vesuvio Café, 255 Columbus Ave. (362-3370), in North Beach. Watch poets and chess players from the balcony of this quintessential beat bar, or hide from them in the dark and subdued bar. Drinks average $3.25-6. Open daily 6am-2am.

Caffè Trieste, 609 Vallejo St. (392-6739), at Grant in North Beach. Only a few Beatniks now, but sip coffee and recall the groovy years when Ginsberg and Ferlinghetti hung out here. Loud live music Sat. noon-5pm. Otherwise settle for a tune from the jukebox—sometimes opera, sometimes country, always schmaltzy. Coffees $1-2.75. Open Sun.-Thurs. 7am-11:30pm, Fri.-Sat. 6:30am-12:30am.

Café Babar, 994 Guerrero St. (282-6789), in the Mission. Beverages, hot and cold. Varied musical entertainment. Guerilla poetry readings Thurs. 8pm; sign up. 8 beers on tap. Open Mon.-Sat. 4pm-2am.

Muddy Waters, 521 Valencia St. (863-8005), in the Mission. Slurp down coffee and gobble up *biscotti* while examining the local art that covers the walls. Cappuccino $1.50, mocha $2. Open Mon.-Fri. 6:30am-midnight, Sat.-Sun. 7:30am-midnight.

CABARET

The Club Fugazi, 678 Green St. (421-4222), between Powell St. and Columbus Ave. in North Beach. Presents *Beach Blanket Babylon,* a cabaret-style revue and San Francisco cult classic. Box office open Mon.-Sat. 10am-7:30pm, Sun. noon-7:30pm. $18-22, Sun. matinee $13-21. Under 21 admitted to matinee only.

COMEDY CLUBS

Call ahead to find out who is performing and at what price. Drink purchases are often required. (But they also tend to enhance performances.)

Cobb's Comedy Club, 2801 Leavenworth St. (928-4320). Big and small names at this San Francisco standard. 18 and over. 2-drink min. Purchase tickets through BASS or at the club.

Josie's Cabaret and Juice Joint, 3583 16th St., (861-7933). Shows about "the whole queer scene," male and female. Every Mon. is gay comedy open mike night ($5). Cover ranges from $5-15.

The Punchline, 444 Battery (397-4337). Mon. nights in July, comedians audition here for the San Francisco International Comedy Competition. 2-drink min.

Coffee Cantata Deli, 1980 Union St. (563-7274). Alternative improv. and special shows.

CLUBS

The San Francisco club scene is a lively and active one. Unfortunately for underage would-be clubbers, most establishments are tough carders. Many cafés have a night scene that under-21s can enjoy.

The Paradise Lounge, 1501 Folsom St. (861-6906), at 11th St., in SoMa. With 3 stages, 2 floors, 5 bars, and up to 5 different bands a night, this club is one of those unique places where you feel equally comfortable in spike heels or Birkenstocks. Pool tables upstairs. Open daily 3pm-2am. Must be 21.

Club DV8, 540 Howard St. (957-1730), in SoMa. 3 floors of sheer dance mania. One of those "in places to be." For the best dancing, stick to the 3rd floor "osmosis." 18 and over on Tues.-Wed. Disco flashbacks on Thurs. Cover ranges from free to $10. Open Tues.-Sun. 8pm-4am.

CRASH Palace, 628 Divisadero (931-1914). This hot new club features lots of jazz. Worldbeat on Sun., speakeasy on Tues. Live music nightly. No cover Mon.-Tues., $5-10 otherwise. Open daily 5pm-2am.

Slims, 333 11th St. (621-3330), between Folsom and Harrison, in SoMa. Blues and jazz. Legendary house for American Roots Music. Open nightly. Must be 21.

El Río, 3158 Mission St. (282-3325), in SoMa. The feature entertainment here is the Latin music every Sun. night, but rock bands play regularly as well. World Beat on Fri. Cover $5-7 when there's live music. Open Tues.-Sat. 3pm-2am, Sun.-Mon. 3pm-midnight. Food served Sun. from 4-8pm. Must be 21.

DNA Lounge, 375 11th St. (626-1409), at Harrison, in SoMa. Both live music and dancing. The best night for dancing is Wed. Funk, house, and soul. Cover varies but usually doesn't exceed $10. Open daily until 4am. Must be 21.

The Holy Cow, 1531 Folsom (621-6087), between 11th and 12th St, in SoMa. A life-size plastic cow marks the spot. This bar/dance club tends to attract the trendy mainstream with music to match. Crowded, energetic bar. No cover. Tough carding. Open Wed.-Sun. 9am-2am.

The Mad Dog in the Fog, 530 Haight St. (626-7279). Very relaxed in spite of the name. Guinness served. Bands (mostly acoustic) on Sun. Open mike on Tues. Dancing (with DJ) to soul and funk on Wed. No cover. Open daily 11:30am-2am.

The Top, 424 Haight St. (864-7386). Closer to the housing projects; go with lots of friends. Small, dark, and trendy. Independent music. Adorned with art by local artists. Sat. is gay night, $3 cover. Open daily 8pm-2am.

Covered Wagon Saloon, 917 Folsom St. (974-1585), at 5th St., in SoMa. Theme nights abound. Wed. night 8pm-2am is Hillbilly Honkytonk. Fri. night 9:30pm-2am is "80s loose groove." Sat. night 9pm-2am do the time warp with '80s and '90s old school. Other nights vary; call for info. Happy hour Mon.-Fri. 4:30-7pm features $1 Buds. Open daily 3pm-2am. Must be 21.

3D's (Don's Different Ducks), 669 Haight St. (431-4724), at Pierce. Dance to reggae, funk, jazz, and hip-hop. Popular with African-Americans. Must be 21. No cover. Open 9pm-2am.

Nickie's Barbeque, 460 Haight (621-6508). DJ every night with different themes. A real dive, but that's part of the fun. Great dancing. Music ranges from world music to '70s funk. Open 9pm-2am daily. No cover before 10pm, $1-5 after.

650 Howard, 650 Howard St. (896-1950), in SoMa. An after-hours dance club. Fri. is "Deja vu" night with '70s and '80s funk. Cover $5 on Thurs., $10 on Fri. and Sat. Open daily 9am-2am. Must be 21.

GAY AND LESBIAN CLUBS

Gay nightlife in San Francisco flourishes. Most of the popular bars can be found in the city's two traditionally gay areas—the Castro (around the intersection of Castro St. and Market St., see Sights) and Polk St. (several blocks north of Geary St.). Most "straight" dance clubs in San Francisco feature at least one gay night a week. Also consult the *San Francisco Bay Guardian* or friendly staffers at the **Gay Switchboard** (510-841-6224).

The I-Beam, 1748 Haight St. (668-6006). Tea Dance every Sun. 6pm. Every Fri. is "Club Boneyard" industrial alternative. Happy hour 6-8pm. Cover $5-7. Open daily 8pm-2am.

The Café, 2367 Market St. (861-3846), the Castro. San Francisco's most popular bar for women ("and a few good men"), the Café is the only daily bar for women. 2 levels with pinball, pool tables, and sundeck. DJs lay down fierce music. No cover. Open daily noon-2am.

End Up, 401 6th St. (543-7700), at Harrison. San Francisco's original Tea Dance 6am-9pm, $3. Fri. night is men's night. Sat. night is women's night. Cover $4 (except for Tea Dance). Open daily 9pm-2am, sometimes 3:30am.

The Stud, 399 9th St. (863-6623). A classic gay club with great dance music. Mon. night is funk night. Wed. night is oldies night featuring cheap beer. Thurs. is women's night. Cover $2-4. Open daily 5pm-2am, Fri.-Sat. after hours.

The Phoenix, 482 Castro St. (552-6827), at Market St. International Gay Dance Bar. Non-stop dancing. DJ Michael and DJ Bobby Keith play disco tunes and house music. Friendly to women. No cover. Open daily 1pm-2am. Must be 21.

Kimo's, 1351 Polk St. (885-4535). Remodeled. A cabaret atmosphere with live comedy on weekends at 9pm. Women's night every Thurs. upstairs. Cover $0-10. Open daily 8am-2am.

Club Townsend, 177 Townsend (974-6020), in SoMa. To find the Pleasure Dome, Frankie went to Hollywood, but you can find it right here in San Francisco. The Pleasure Dome, at Club Townsend every Sun. night 8pm-dawn, is San Francisco's largest gay dance club. Fri. and Sat. nights are gay nights as well. The rest of the week is mixed. Cover $7. Open daily 10pm-6am.

■■■ SEASONAL EVENTS

These events are listed chronologically. The Visitors Center has a recording of current events (391-2001). Call to find out what is going on during your stay

Chinese New Year Celebration (982-3000), late Feb. in Chinatown. North America's largest Chinese community celebrates the Year of the Pig (4693 on the lunar calendar) with cultural festivities, a parade, lots of fireworks, and the crowning of Miss Chinatown USA.

Cherry Blossom Festival, 2 weekends in April. Japantown, with fascinating demonstrations of martial arts, *taiko* drumming, and calligraphy.

San Francisco International Film Festival (931-3456), mid-April-mid-May. The oldest film festival in North America. More than 100 films of all genres from around the world are shown. Previous premieres at the festival include *She's Gotta Have It* and Academy Award-winner *The Thin Blue Line.*

Cinco de Mayo Parade and Celebration, early May, starting at 24th and Harrison, in the Mission District. Fiesta, fiesta, fiesta.

San Francisco Examiner Bay to Breakers, mid-May. The largest road race (7.1 mi.) in the United States, done in inimitable San Francisco style. Runners win not only on their times but on their costumes as well. Special centipede category. Over 100,000 participants.

Haight Street Fair (661-8025), early June. 18th annual. Bands, vendors, and masses of people crowd the streets between Masonic and Stanyan.

Stern Grove San Francisco Midsummer Music Festival (252-6252), all summer. Ten free Sundays of opera, ballet, jazz, symphony, and *a cappella* in beautiful Stern Grove. Bring a picnic for the ultimate summer afternoon experience. Arrive early for best seating. Performances 2pm, pre-performance talks 11am.

North Beach Fair (383-9378), mid-June. Little Italy explodes into an extravaganza of fabulous things to see, eat, and drink. There's even Venetian mask painting! Grant Ave. from Columbus to Fillmore and Washington Square Park.

18th San Francisco International Lesbian & Gay Film Festival (703-8650), mid- to late June. The world's largest presentation of lesbian and gay media. Roxie Cinema (16th St. at Valencia), Castro Theatre (Castro St. at Market).

San Francisco Music Day (361-0309), mid-June. Jazz, rock, opera, and more on 20 stages found along Market St., from the Ferry Building to Van Ness.

Ethnic Dance Festival (392-4400), mid- to late June. Music and dance from Russia, Japan, Kenya, Bali, Ireland, Mexico, Peru, etc. Palace of Fine Arts theatre.

Lesbian-Gay Freedom Parade (864-3733), late June. People come from all over the country to join this party. The celebration culminates in a tremendous parade starting at Castro and ending at Market.

Chronicle Fourth of July Celebration (556-1643). Free fireworks (by the legendary Souzas) and free live entertainment. Crissy Field, The Presidio.

Summerfest '94 (853-9834), early July-early Aug. A veritable dance-o-rama. Multiple performances at the New Performance Gallery.

Midsummer Mozart Festival, mid-July. Herbst Theatre, 401 Van Ness Ave. (box office information 392-4400).

Comedy Celebration Day, late July. A day-long festival of comedy. Local and national comics play five-minute acts at the Polo Fields in Golden Gate Park.

18th Annual Bay Area Playwrights Festival (441-8822), late July to mid-August. A whirlwind of plays by area playwrights at the Magic Theatre.

14th Annual San Francisco Fair (703-2729), early Sept. Multiculturalism applied to food and entertainment. Civic Center Plaza, Polk St. and McAllister St.

San Francisco Shakespeare Festival, early Sept.-early Oct. Shakespeare in Golden Gate Park.

San Francisco Jazz Festival (864-5449), late Oct.-early Nov. Includes shows throughout the city, tributes to masters, and the Jazz Film Fest.

Halloween Celebration in the Castro. Some people say that the Castro has become less wild with age. Those people have not been there on Oct. 31.

San Francisco Bay Area

■■■ BERKELEY

Almost 30 years ago, Mario Savio climbed on top of a police car and launched Berkeley's free speech movement. Today, Berkeley is still a national symbol of political activism and social iconoclasm, and Telegraph Avenue—the Champs Elysées of the '60s—remains the home of street-corner soothsayers, funky bookstores, aging hippies, countless cafés, and itinerant street musicians. Despite the diversity of its residents, Berkeley somehow manages to preserve a neighborly sense of unity, maintained by a unique mixture of idealism, tolerance, and activism.

The site of the country's most renowned public university, Berkeley is as famous for its street people and chefs as for its political cadres and academics. Chez Panisse, the restaurant owned by Alice Waters, is believed to have originated the elusive concept of California cuisine. Northwest of campus, the shopping area around Chez Panisse has been termed the "Gourmet Ghetto" because of the abundance of ingredients hawked there. The rest of the city is blanketed by stylish clothing boutiques and specialty stores. Amazingly, Berkeley is able to revel in these bourgeois accoutrements while maintaining its idealistic spirit.

PRACTICAL INFORMATION

Visitors Information: Berkeley Convention and Visitors Bureau, 1834 University Ave. (549-7040), at Martin Luther King, Jr. Way. Open Mon.-Fri. 9am-noon and 1-4pm. 24-hr. Visitor Hotline 549-8710. **U.C. Berkeley Visitor Center,** 101 University Hall, 2200 University Ave. (642-5215). Campus Calendar 642-2294. Open Mon.-Fri. 8am-5pm.

Greyhound: Information 800-231-2222. Closest station is in Oakland.

Amtrak: Information 800-USA-RAIL, -872-7245. Closest station is in Oakland.

Bay Area Rapid Transit (BART): 465-2278. The Berkeley station is at Shattuck Ave. and Center St., close to the western edge of the university, about 7 blocks from the Student Union. $1.80 to downtown San Francisco.

Alameda County Transit (AC Transit): 800-559-4636 or 839-2882. Buses #14, 40, 43, and 51 all run from the Berkeley BART stop to downtown Oakland, via M.L. King Jr. Way, Telegraph Ave., Shattuck Ave., and College Ave., respectively. City bus fare $1.10, seniors, ages 5-12, and disabled 55¢, under 5 free. Transfers 25¢, valid for 1 hr. See Orientation, page 275, for information on taking bus #F to San Francisco.

Transportation Information: Berkeley TRiP, 2033 Center St. (643-7665). Information on public transport, biking, and carpooling. Mostly local transportation. Open Mon.-Wed. and Fri. 8:30am-5:30pm, Thurs. 9am-6pm.

Taxi: Yellow A I Cab, 843-1111. Open 24 hrs.

Car Rental: Budget (524-7237), Gilman St. and 2nd. Compact car $40 per day with unlimited mi. Must be 21, under 25 pay additional $15. (Cheaper options available in San Francisco.) Open Mon.-Thurs. 8am-4:30pm, Fri. 8am-5:30pm, Sat. 8:30am-2:30pm, Sun. 9am-1pm.

Ride Boards: Berkeley Ride Board, 1st level of student store, in student union.

Parking and Transit Operations on the Berkeley campus, 2535 Channing Way. General information, 642-4283. Open Mon.-Fri. 7:30am-noon and 1-5pm.

Tickets: Bass Tix, 762-2277. Open 8:30am-9pm. **Tower Records,** 2510 Durant St. (841-0101). Open 9am-midnight. **Leopold's,** 2514 Durant St. (848-2015). Open Sun.-Mon. and Wed.-Thurs. 10am-10pm, Tues. 9am-10pm, Fri.-Sat. 10am-midnight. **CAL Athletics,** 800-GO-BEARS, -46-23277.

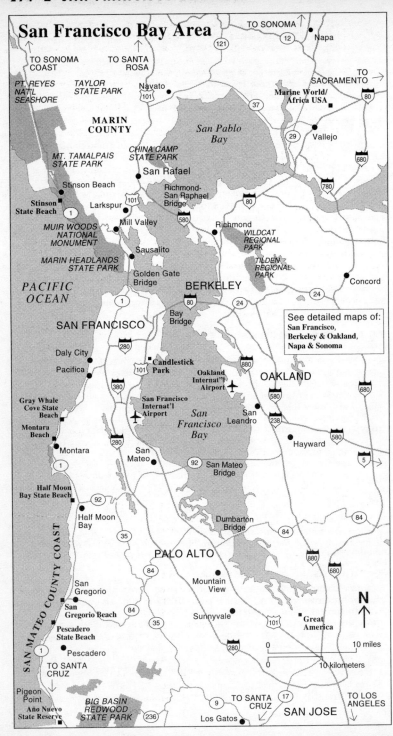

San Francisco Bay Area

TO SONOMA

TO SONOMA
COAST

TO SANTA
ROSA

Napa

121

12

TO
SACRAMENTO

PT. REYES
NAT'L
SEASHORE

TAYLOR
STATE PARK

Navato

Marine World/
Africa USA

80

101

37

MARIN
COUNTY

San Pablo
Bay

29

Vallejo

CHINA CAMP
STATE PARK

680

MT. TAMALPAIS
STATE PARK

San Rafael

780

Stinson Beach

Richmond-
San Raphael
Bridge

Stinson
State Beach

Larkspur

101

80

1

Mill Valley

580

Richmond

WILDCAT
REGIONAL
PARK

MUIR WOODS
NATIONAL
MONUMENT

Sausalito

MARIN HEADLANDS
STATE PARK

PACIFIC
OCEAN

Golden Gate
Bridge

BERKELEY

TILDEN
REGIONAL
PARK

Concord

1

80

24

24

Bay
Bridge

See detailed maps of:
**San Francisco,
Berkeley & Oakland,
Napa & Sonoma**

SAN FRANCISCO

280

Daly City

Candlestick
Park

880

OAKLAND

Pacifica

101

Oakland
Internat'l
Airport

580

680

380

San Francisco
Internat'l
Airport

San
Francisco
Bay

San
Leandro

238

Gray Whale
Cove State
Beach

Montara
Beach

Hayward

580

5

Montara

280

San
Mateo

1

92

San Mateo
Bridge

Half Moon
Bay State Beach

92

84

Half Moon
Bay

Dumbarton
Bridge

84

880

35

PALO ALTO

680

84

Mountain
View

N

San
Gregorio

Sunnyvale

Great
America

San
Gregorio Beach

84

101

Pescadero
State Beach

35

280

0   10 miles

Pescadero

0   10 kilometers

1

TO SANTA
CRUZ

Pigeon
Point

Año Nuevo
State Reserve

BIG BASIN
REDWOOD
STATE PARK

9

TO SANTA
CRUZ

17

TO LOS
ANGELES

236

Los Gatos

SAN JOSE

SAN MATEO COUNTY COAST

Laundromat: Milt's Coin-Op, 3055 Telegraph Ave. (549-3305), near Ashby. Over 100 very clean washers and dryers. "Designer plastic" laundry bags "in exotic colors." $1.25 wash. 25¢ dry. Open 24 hrs.

U.C. Berkeley Switchboard: 1901 8th St. (642-6000). Information on everything from community events to drug counseling. Open daily 8am-5pm.

Rape Hotline: 845-RAPE, -7273. 24 hrs.

Poison Control Center: 800-523-2222. 24 hrs.

U.C. Berkeley Multicultural Bisexual Lesbian Gay Alliance: 642-6942 during the academic year.

Berkeley Free Clinic: 2339 Durant Ave. (548-2570), 2 blocks west of Telegraph. Medical help and referrals to homeless-shelter resources in the area. Open Mon.-Fri. 9:30-11:30am. The clinic is also open Mon.-Fri. in the late afternoon and evening, usually 5:30-7pm, but times vary.

City of Berkeley Department of Health and Human Services, 830 University Ave. at 6th St. (644-8571). Medical help on a sliding payment scale. Open Sun.-Wed. and Fri. 8am-noon and 1-5pm, Thurs. 8am-noon and 1-7pm, Sat. 10am-4pm.

Berkeley Women's Health Center, 2908 Ellsworth Ave. (843-6194), 1 block west of Telegraph. Open Mon. and Fri. 8am-5pm, Tues.-Wed. 10am-7pm, Thurs. 9am-6pm; by appointment only.

South Berkeley Women's Community Health Center, 1802 Fairview St. (601-8282). Anonymous, free HIV tests. Drop in Thurs. 1-3:30pm.

Campus Emergency: 9-911 from campus phone. 642-3333 otherwise. 24 hrs.

Emergency: 911.

Campus Police: 2 Sproul Hall Basement (642-6760). 24 hrs.

Post Office: 2000 Allston Way (649-3100). Open Mon.-Fri. 8:30am-6pm, Sat. 10am-2pm. **General Delivery ZIP Code:** 94704.

Area Code: 510.

ORIENTATION

Berkeley lies across the bay northeast of San Francisco, just north of Oakland. There are two efficient ways to reach the city: by BART from downtown San Francisco or by car (**I-80** or **Rte. 24**).

Berkeley is sandwiched between a series of rolling hills to the east and San Francisco Bay to the west. The **University of California** campus stretches into the hills, but most of the university's buildings are in the westernmost section of campus, near BART. Lined with bookstores and cafés, **Telegraph Avenue,** which runs south from the Student Union, is the spiritual center of town. Undergraduates tend to hang out on Telegraph and other streets on the south side of campus, while the north side is dominated by graduate students. The **downtown** area, around the BART station, contains several businesses as well as the public library and central post office. The **Gourmet Ghetto** encompasses the area along Shattuck Ave. and Walnut St. between Virginia and Rose St. The **Fourth Street Center,** west of campus and by the bay, is home to great eating and window shopping. Northwest of campus, **Solano Ave.** offers countless ethnic restaurants (the best Chinese food in the city is found here), bookstores, and movie theaters, as well as more places to shop. Visitors would be wise to avoid walking alone on Berkeley's streets at night.

Getting There and Getting Around

Constant construction and congestion on the freeway combine to make driving in the Bay Area frustrating. Crossing the bay by **BART** ($1.80-2) is quick and easy, and both the university and Telegraph Ave. are short walks from the station. Alternatively, the university **Perimeter Shuttle** (642-5149) connects the BART station with the university campus (Sept.-June Mon.-Fri. 7am-7pm every 8 min., except on university holidays; 25¢). BART also stops at Virginia and Sacramento St. (in northern Berkeley) and at Ashby St. (west of the university).

Buses reach Berkeley even faster than BART. **Alameda County Transit (AC Transit)** buses ($2.20; over 64, disabled, and ages 5-12 $1.10; under 5 free) leave from the Transbay Terminal for Berkeley (5:50am-midnight every 30 min.). In town,

AC Transit **city buses** run approximately every 20 minutes. Ask a bus driver for schedules, or call AC Transit (839-2882 or 800-559-4636).

Drivers fortunate enough to reach Berkeley despite Bay Area traffic will face new problems within the city itself. In addition to the expected congestion, numerous one-way streets and concrete planters designed to control traffic in residential neighborhoods may thwart those who are less familiar with Berkeley. If most of your chosen destinations lie in the same area, you may want to park in one of the nearby garages and explore on foot.

PUBLICATIONS

Berkeley is awash with free publications. *The Monthly* (658-9811), with dining listings and detailed critiques of local productions is the most reliable and interesting. Pick it up in local coffee shops and restaurants. For more up-to-date news on university happenings, look for the *Daily Californian*, (548-8080). The *Daily Cal* is published on Tues. and Thurs. in the summer and daily during the school year (available in Sproul Plaza.) *Summer in Berkeley,* available end of June, features in-depth write-ups about Berkeley's cafés, pubs, eateries, and outlets. *Resource* is the information guide given to students new to Berkeley. If you can find a recent edition (try the Visitor Information Center at 101 University Hall), grab it.

The weekly *East Bay Express* (540-7400) spills over with entertainment listings, including Berkeley theater and Oakland jazz, available in at bookstores and in bins around campus. Check area record stores and cafes for more local publications. Many of San Francisco's newspapers (see S.F. publications, page 237), most notably the *Chronicle's Datebook* (the Sunday pink pages), include listings for Berkeley.

ACCOMMODATIONS

It is surprisingly difficult to sleep cheaply in Berkeley. There is only one hostel, and clean, budget motels are disconcertingly lacking. You might try renting a fraternity room for the night. Check the classified ads in the *Daily Californian* (see Publications, above) for possibilities. The **Bed and Breakfast Network** (540-5123) coordinates 20 B&Bs in the East Bay, some of which offer reasonable rates. Remember that you can stay in San Francisco and make day trips to Berkeley.

YMCA International Youth Hostel, 2001 Allston Way (848-9622), at Milvia St. New hostel offers a clean, cheap, secure place to stay. Rooms have one bunk bed. TV room, hall baths. Registration 6:30pm. Lockout 9am-6pm. Bring linens. Men and women ages 18-30 only. $12.60 per night, $10.60 for AYH members.

YMCA, 2001 Allston Way (848-6800), at Milvia St. Clean, adequate rooms are available in this hotel-portion of the YMCA. Men and women on different floors. Registration daily 8am-9:30pm. Check-out noon. No curfew. Prices include tax and use of pool and basic fitness facilities. 14-day max. stay. Singles $25, rooms for couples $30. All share hall baths.

Travel Inn, 1461 University Ave. (848-3840), 2 blocks from the North Berkeley BART station, 7 blocks west of campus. Newly redone rooms are clean and comfortable. All have color TV and phones. Singles $32-35, doubles $42-50 depending on season and number of people. Key deposit $1-5.

Golden Bear Motel, 1620 San Pablo Ave. at Cedar (525-6770). Located further away from campus but with recently painted bedrooms and clean white bedspreads. Check-out noon. Room with queen-size bed (for 1 or 2) $41, room with 2 beds $46, room with 2 queen-size beds $49.

University Conference Services, 2601 Warring St. (642-4444; fax 642-2888; after June 1 call 442-5925). Spacious, clean dorm rooms in Stern Hall with large windows and phones available in summer to "university visitors" (i.e. everybody). Arrangements must be made through Conference Services, open Mon.-Fri. 10am-5:30pm. Singles $34. Doubles $44.

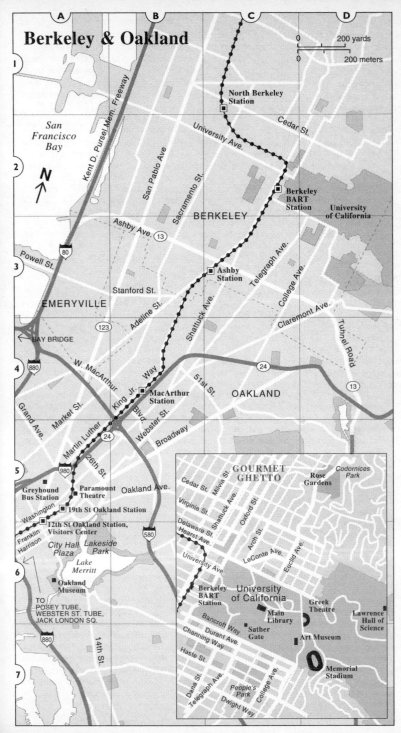

Berkeley & Oakland

FOOD

Berkeley is a relatively small area with a wide range of excellent budget eateries. To help you make your selections we have divided our listings by type of food offered. For information about local culinary delights, consult *Bayfood* (652-6115; available free in Berkeley's cafés and restaurants). **Telegraph Avenue** has more than its share of places to munch pizza, sip coffee, and slurp frozen yogurt. The espresso here is excellent, and several of the restaurants are too, but for the best food in Berkeley head downtown to **Shattuck Avenue** or north to **Solano Avenue.**

Breakfast

Anne's Soup Kitchen, 2498 Telegraph (548-8885), at Dwight. *The* place for breakfast in Berkeley and a favorite with students. Towering portions more than compensate for crowded dining. Weekday special includes 2 whole wheat pancakes with bacon and eggs ($3) or with homefries ($2.75). Open daily 8am-7pm.

Brick Hut, 3222 Adeline (658-5555), near the Ashby BART. This great breakfast place is owned and operated by women; both sexes can enjoy the gigantic omelettes $4.40-6.55. Open Mon.-Fri. 7:30am-2pm, Sat.-Sun. 8:30am-3pm.

Smokey Joe's, 1620 Shattuck Ave. (548-4616), at Cedar. "Where the elite meet to eat no meat"—cozy vegetarian diner noted for its breakfasts. The Swedish Folk breakfast includes oatmeal, toast, seasonal fruit, and raisins ($4.35). Open Mon.-Thurs. 8am-3pm, Fri.-Sat. 8am-3pm and 6-9pm, Sun. 11:30am-9pm.

Sandwich places

Café Fanny, 1603 San Pablo Ave. (524-5447). Alice Water's most recent venture, this tiny café offers limited seating, lots of standing room, and benches under pleasant outdoor trellis. Great sandwiches ($5.25-6.25), muffins ($1.50), and poached eggs with excellent toast. Famous for giant bowls (yes, bowls) of *café au lait* ($2.08). Open Mon.-Fri. 7am-3pm, Sat. 8am-4pm, Sun. 9am-3pm.

Café Intermezzo (849-4592), Telegraph at Haste. The ENORMOUS helpings of salad served with fresh bread distinguish this café from the multitude of others along Telegraph. A combination sandwich and salad ($4.39) will fuel you for the rest of day. Sandwiches $4.15. Open Mon.-Fri. 10:30am-9pm.

Panini, 2115 Allston Way (849-0405), in the Trumpet Vine Court. The best gourmet bargain around. Their *panini* (gourmet sandwiches with fresh vegetables and/or meat on newly baked bread) change daily. Some are hot, at least one is vegetarian, and all are delicious ($4-6). Simmering soup $2.25 (small) or $2.75 (large). Open Mon.-Fri. 7:30am-4pm, Sat. 10am-4pm.

Noah's New York Bagels, 3170 College Ave. (654-0944) and 1883 Solano Ave. (525-4447). Reputedly the best bagels for miles around. Choose from a selection of bagels with flavored cream cheeses ("schmears"). Plain bagels 50¢, with cream cheese $1.35. Open Mon.-Fri. 7am-6:30pm, Sat. 7:30am-6pm, Sun. 7:30am-5pm.

Saul's, 1475 Shattuck Ave. (848-3354). An honorable deli. Saul's flies in its smoked fish from New York, has a special weekend brunch menu, and serves Noah's bagels. Sandwiches $4-7.50; plain bagels 50¢. Open daily 8am-9:30pm.

Asian Food

Plearn, 2050 University Ave. at Shattuck (841-2148), 1 block west of campus. Constant winner of best Thai in the Bay Area, this simple restaurant "rivals Bangkok's best." Very hot, very good curries ($7). Plentiful vegetarian options. Have a *Thai Song Kran,* "the perfect brew for Thai food," to ease the heat of the spices. Lunch specials 11:30am-3:30pm for $4.25. Open daily 11:30am-10pm.

Long Life Vegi House, 2129 University Ave. (845-6072). Tasty and innovative Chinese cooking, generous portions. No red meat. Daily lunch special 11:30am-3pm features entree, egg roll, and soup $3.65. Open daily 11:30am-9:30pm.

Shin Shin, 1715 Solano Ave. (526-4970). Noteworthy for cheap and varied lunch specials. You can get a small bowl of peppery hot and sour soup, 2 flaky fried wontons, and rice with your choice of 34 different entrees, from Hunan smoked pork to black bean sauce prawns—all for $3 (daily 11:30am-3:30pm). Open Sun.-Thurs. 11:30am-9:30pm, Fri.-Sat. 11:30am-10pm.

American Food

Mel's Diner, 2936 Shattuck Ave. (387-2244). Mel says, "Mel's serves the food America is famous for." Burgers, dogs, and shakes in all their splendor. $5-8 for a full meal. Open Mon.-Thurs. 8am-11pm, Fri.-Sat. 8am-12:30am, Sun. 9am-11pm.

Brennan's, 720 University Ave. at 4th St. (841-0960). Established in 1959, Brennan's is truly a Berkeley institution. Locals from all walks of life flock here for huge plates of roasted meat with veggies, mashed potatoes, stuffing, and gravy ($3.25-6). Side dishes ($1) are a great value. The bar serves great Irish coffee ($3) to frat-brothers, yuppies, plumbers, and bikers alike. Restaurant open 11am-9:30pm. Bar open Sun.-Thurs. 11am-11:30pm, Fri.-Sat. 11am-1:30am.

Bette's Oceanview Diner, 1807a 4th St. (548-9494), in the Waterfront District. The food is as colorful as the paint. A popular choice among Bay Area residents for weekend brunch—prepare to wait! Apple Brandy Souffle Pancakes ($7.75) are divine. Sandwiches $4.25-7.50. If you can't stand the wait, stop in at **Bette's To Go** next door. Open Mon.-Sat. 11am-6pm, Sun. 10am-6pm.

Pizza

Zachary's, 1853 Solano Ave. (525-5950). "The 'za is better at Zachary's" Chicago-style pizza. A small stuffed Mediterranean pizza costs $13.25, but serves 2-3 people. Open Sun.-Thurs. 11am-9:30pm, Fri.-Sat. 11am-10:30pm. **Another location** is in Oakland at 5801 College Ave. (655-6385).

Blondie's Pizza, 2340 Telegraph Ave. (548-1129). You must visit this Berkeley landmark and popular student hangout. Employees wear "Make Pizza, Not War" t-shirts. Consume Dagwood-sized slices of greasy pizza for only $1.50. Open Mon.-Thurs. 10:30am-1am, Fri.-Sat. 10:30am-2am, Sun. noon-midnight.

Others

Ethiopian-The Blue Nile, 2525 Telegraph Ave. (540-6777). Winner of Best African food in *SF Focus* magazine, 1993. Authentic Ethiopian food in a rich setting. Beaded curtains separate the different booths. Waitresses wear traditional gowns, and customers eat with their hands. Wide variety of vegetarian dishes. Lunch around $5, dinner $6-7.50. Open Mon.-Sat. 11:30am-10pm, Sun. 4-10pm.

Indian-Vik's Chaat Corner in Vik Distributors, 726 Allston Way (a little out of the way, but worth it). $2.50 per wonderful plate of Papa's *bhel puri* or *aloo tikki cholle.* Open Tues.-Sun. 11am-7pm.

Create-Your-Own Gourmet Picnic

Acme Bread Company, 1601 San Pablo Ave. (524-1327), at Cedar. West of campus but well worth the trek. Crusty, chewy, flavorful bread baked on the premises. Most loaves $2-3. Open Mon. 8am-noon, Tues.-Fri. 8am-5pm, Sat. 9am-5pm. Arrive before 1pm for the best selection.

The Cheese Board Collective, 1504 Shattuck Ave. (549-3183). A pillar of the Gourmet Ghetto. Fantastic selection of a few hundred different cheeses; add a few to the excellent French bread for a great picnic. Very generous about giving samples. Open Tues.-Fri. 10am-6pm, Sat. 10am-5pm.

Berkeley Bowl, 2777 Shattuck Ave. (843-6929). Once a bowling alley by the same name, now it's a fabulous grocery store that sells fresh organic produce for great prices. Fresh meat, fish, cheese, wine, and specialty ethnic foods also available. Open Mon.-Fri. 9:30am-7pm, Sat. 9am-6pm. The **Bakery Café at The Bowl** next door sells fresh California cuisine with a Mexican twist.

Andronico's Park & Shop, 2655 Telegraph Ave. (845-1062). Huge supermarket for the hard-to-please palate. Open daily 9am-11pm. Another location at 1550 Shattuck Ave. at Cedar.

Safeway, 1444 Shattuck Pl. and 1500 Solano. Always an option. Open 24 hrs.

SIGHTS

In 1868, the privately run College of California and the publicly run Agricultural, Mining, and Mechanical Arts College coupled to give birth to the **University of California.** Because Berkeley was the first of the nine University of California campuses, it is permitted the nickname "Cal." The school has an enrollment of over 30,000 students and more than 1000 full professors. Berkeley also boasts more Nobel laureates per capita than any other city. Berkeley's uniqueness has made it home to a student body of unparalleled diversity.

Pass through **Sather Gate** (one of the sites of celebrated student sit-ins) into **Sproul Plaza** (another such site) and enter the university's world of open minds, relaxed atmosphere, and intellectual pursuits. The Berkeley campus encompasses 160 acres, bounded on the south by Bancroft Way, on the west by Oxford St., on the north by Hearst Ave., and on the east by a vast parkland.

The staff at the **Visitor Information Center,** 101 University Hall, 2200 University Ave. (642-5215; open Mon.-Fri. 8am-5pm), happily provides free maps and information booklets. (Campus tours last 1½ hrs. Mon., Wed., Fri. 10am and 1pm.)

The most dramatic campus attraction is **Sather Tower** (much better known as the **Campanile,** Italian for "bell tower"), a 1914 monument to Berkeley benefactor Jane Krom Sather. It was created by campus architect John Galen Howard who designed it after the clock tower in Venice's St. Mark's Square. The 500-ton steel frame was designed to withstand powerful earthquakes; in fact, it's the second-most-earthquake-proof structure at Berkeley, after Sproul Hall. You can ride to the observation level of the 307-ft.-tall tower (the tallest building on campus) for a stupendous view (50¢). The tower's 61-bell carillon is played most weekdays, often by University Carillonist Ronald Barnes, at 7:50am, noon, and 6pm.

The **University Art Museum (UAM),** 2626 Bancroft Way at College (642-0808), holds a diverse and enticing permanent collection and hosts different exhibits yearly. Within the museum, the **Pacific Film Archives (PFA)** (642-1124), with one of the nation's largest film libraries, is a uniquely rich museum of cinematic art. Reels range from the obscure to the classic. (Museum open Wed. and Fri.-Sun. 11am-5pm, Thurs. 11am-9pm. $6; students, over 64 and ages 6-17 $4. Free Thurs. 11am-noon and 5-9pm. PFA shows films in the evening; see Entertainment: Cinema, page 282.)

The **Lawrence Hall of Science** (642-5132), a concrete octagon standing above the northeast corner of campus, shares honors with San Francisco's Exploratorium as the finest science museum in the Bay Area. Exhibits stress learning science through the hands-on use of everyday objects. The courtyard offers a spectacular view of the Bay, a DNA molecule, a whale for children to climb on, and stargazing workshops on clear Saturday evenings. Take bus #8 from the Berkeley BART station. (Open Mon.-Fri. 10am-4:30pm, Sat.-Sun. 10am-5pm. $5; seniors, students, and ages 7-18 $4, ages 3-6 $2.)

Back in the campus center, the excellent **Phoebe Hearst Museum of Anthropology** (642-3681) displays selections from its 500,000 catalogued items in Kroeber Hall. Unfortunately, the museum's limited size means that the bulk of the impressive collection is rarely, if ever, seen. (Open Mon.-Fri. 10am-4:30pm, Sat.-Sun. noon-4:30pm, extended hours Thurs. $2, seniors $1, under 16 50¢.) Also in Kroeber Hall is the **Worth Ryder Art Gallery** (642-2582), in Room 116. The gallery displays contemporary works of wildly disparate quality by students and local artists (open Sept.-June Tues.-Thurs. 11am-4pm; free). The **Heller Gallery** in the Martin Luther King, Jr. Student Union (642-3065), like the Worth Ryder, exhibits the art of students and other community members.

The **Earth Sciences Building** off Hearst Ave. houses the **Museum of Paleontology** (642-1821), the **Museum of Geology,** and the **Berkeley Seismographic Station.** The paleontology division displays hundreds of fossils and dozens of skeletons. The geology museum devotes its galleries to maps detailing the sedimentary structure of California and states nearby. (Earth Sciences Bldg. open Mon.-Fri. 8am-5pm, Sat.-Sun. 1-5pm. Free.) On weekdays in 106 Wurster Hall and in Ramona's Café, the **College of Environmental Design** (642-2942) displays blue prints and photographs. **Bancroft Library,** in the center of campus across from the *Campanile,* is an international center for scholars. Exhibits change frequently and range from California history to folio editions of Shakespeare's plays. A gold nugget purported to be the first one plucked from Sutter's Mill is on display. The immense stacks (7 million volumes) are open to the public. (Open Mon.-Fri. 9am-5pm, Sat. 1-5pm. Free.)

During the school year, **Berkeley's Department of Music** presents concerts. **Noon Concerts** present 45 minutes of music by Berkeley's best performers, including students and faculty members. (Hertz Hall, Wed. 12:15pm. Free.) The **Evening Concerts,** also in Hertz Hall, are performances by such groups as the African Music Ensemble, the Berkeley Contemporary Chamber Players, the Javanese Gamelan, and the 1991 Grammy nominee University Chamber Chorus. (Specific dates and times are available from the Dept. of Music, 104 Morrison Hall, 642-2678.) Finally, **Friday Afternoon Concerts,** in which only undergraduates perform, is the most informal of the three series, in 125 Morrison Hall.

Two buildings of interest were bequeathed to the university by newspaper tycoon, William Randolf Hearst and his wife Phoebe Apperson Hearst. The first is the **Greek Theatre** (642-5550), in the north-central part of the campus, a glorious marble structure modeled after the classical amphitheater in Epidaurus, Greece. The site is currently used for university ceremonies and rock concerts. The locally grown and internationally known Grateful Dead usually play a couple of concerts here each year. The second building is the **Hearst Mining Building** in the northeast part of campus, housing displays on mining and metallurgy (open Mon.-Fri. 8am-4:45pm; free). This building was designed by a pioneer in her field, architect Julia Morgan, who also designed the Hearst Gym on the south side of the campus.

The **Botanical Gardens** (642-3343) in Strawberry Canyon contain over 10,000 varieties of plant life. Berkeley's Mediterranean climate, moderated by coastal fog, provides an outstanding setting for this 33 acre garden. Agatha Christie is said to have come here to examine a rare poisonous plant whose deadly powers she wished to utilize in one of her mystery novels (open daily 9am-4:30pm; free, parking permit $1 for 2 hrs.). The **Berkeley Rose Garden** on Euclid Ave. at Eunice St., north of campus contains a lovely collection of roses. Built by the WPA during the Depression, the garden spills from one terrace to another in a vast semicircular amphitheater. The view of Marin County and the Golden Gate Bridge from the far end is spectacular. (Open May-Sept. dawn-dusk.)

Finally, if you want to sit in on **classes,** some that come highly recommended are: Political Science 2, Introduction to Comparative Politics, taught by Professor Jowitt; Sociology 3, Principles of Sociology, taught by Professor Edwards; Women's Studies 30, Literature and the Question of Pornography, taught by Professor Schwartz.

Noteworthy museums and architectural achievements also exist outside of Berkeley's campus. The **Judah Magnes Museum,** 2911 Russell St. (849-2710), displays a leading collection of Judaica (open Sun.-Thurs. 10am-4pm; free). The **Julia Morgan Theater,** 2640 College Ave. (box office 845-8542), is housed in a beautiful former church designed by its namesake and notable for its graceful and unusual mix of materials. The theater is regarded by some as Morgan's *pièce de résistance.*

People's Park, on Haste St., one block off Telegraph Ave., is a kind of unofficial museum. A mural depicts the '60s struggle between the city and local activists over whether to leave the park alone or to develop it commercially. During the conflict, then-governor Ronald Reagan sent in the National Guard, an action which led to the death of a Berkeley student. Three years ago, despite heated protests, the city and the university bulldozed part of the park to build sand volleyball courts, basketball courts, and restrooms. The park is patrolled by police officers 24 hours a day.

Just east of People's Park, on Dwight Way at Bowditch, is the best known work and masterpiece of architect Bernard Maybeck, the **First Church of Christ Scientist** (845-7199). Built in 1910, the church is a conglomeration of many architectural styles: Gothic, Renaissance, Neo-Classical, Classical, Japanese, Mediterranean, and Industrial. (Tours given Sun. 12:15pm.)

Tilden Regional Park, part of the extensive East Bay park system. Hiking, biking, running, and riding trails crisscross the park and provide impressive views of the Bay Area. Swim in **Lake Anza,** in the center of the park, during the summer (10am-dusk.) A 19th-century carousel appeases juvenile thrill-seekers. The park also con-

BERKELEY

tains a botanical garden that teaches about California's plant life. At the north end of the park, the **Environmental Education Center** (525-2233; open Tues.-Sat. 10am-5pm; free) offers exhibits and naturalist-led programs. To reach the park by car or bicycle, take Spruce St. to Grizzly Peak Blvd. Or take AC Transit bus #7 or 8 from the Berkeley BART station to Golf Course Dr. at Grizzly Peak Blvd.

ENTERTAINMENT

The university offers a number of entertainment options. Hang out with procrastinating students in front of or inside the **Student Union** (642-4636). **The Underground** contains a ticket office, an arcade, bowling alleys, foosball tables, and pool tables, all run from a central blue desk (642-3825; open Mon.-Fri. 8am-6pm, Sat. 10am-6pm; winter Mon.-Fri. 8am-10pm, Sat. 10am-6pm). The **Bear's Lair,** a student pub with live music on Thursday and Friday is next door at 2425 Bancroft. It's *the* popular campus hangout on sunny Friday afternoons when quarts of beer are $2.75. (843-0373; open Mon.-Thurs. noon-midnight, Fri. 11am-8pm; hours vary in summer, usually Sat.-Wed. 11am-6pm). The **CAL Performances Ticket Office,** at the north corner of Zellerbach Hall (642-9988; open Mon.-Fri. 10am-5:30pm, Sat. 10am-2pm), is Berkeley's place to get the lowdown on and purchase tickets for concerts, plays, and movies. Ask them about ushering jobs (a good way to see shows for free). Big concerts are held in the **Greek Theatre** (see page 281) and **Zellerbach Hall.**

Cinema

Berkeley has a surfeit of movie houses with a wide selection of theaters showing off-beat films. In addition to those listed below, there are a number of cinemas lining Shattuck Ave., starting a few blocks west of campus. Most show current releases.

U.C. Theater, 2036 University Ave. (843-6267), west of Shattuck Ave. Reruns, *film noir* series, classics, clever double features, and of course, *Rocky Horror* (Sat. midnight). Hong Kong film festivals on Thurs. Schedules available throughout Berkeley. $6; before 6pm, under 13, and seniors $3.50.

Pacific Film Archives, 2621 Durant Ave. (642-1124 or 642-1412), below College Ave. in the University Art Museum. Elements of its filmacopia include alternative visions of the '60s, Greek cinema, and video by youth. $5.50; over 64, under 12, and disabled $3.50. Occasional $1.50 second feature. Reservations sometimes necessary. Closed Mon.-Tues. in summer. Charge-by-phone for tickets (642-5249; 9:30am-9:30pm; Visa and MC; 50¢ fee).

Act I and 2, 2128 Center (548-7200), between Oxford and Shattuck next to Berkeley BART Station. Art films culled from the Academy Award nominee list. $7, children and over 60 $3.75, matinees at or before 3:30pm $3.75.

Northside Theatre, 1828 Euclid Ave. (841-6000), at Hearst, ½ block north of campus. Second-run foreign films. $6, under 12 and over 65 $3.50, 6pm or earlier $4. Call the message for a sample of Berkeley's corny-intellectual humor.

Theater

Dozens of troupes perform in Berkeley, many with progressive messages and political agendas. The **Durham Studio Theatre** (642-9925) features free summertime theatrical events. The University Art Museum/Pacific Film Archive hosts an **Outdoor Summer Performance Series** in its sculpture garden every year, with dance, song, poetry, theater, and video presentations given by artists of all ages. (Almost always free for those under 20; others sometimes pay $5.50. Call 642-0808 for information.) The **Zellerbach Playhouse** (642-9988) is operated by Berkeley's Department of Dramatic Art and hosts performances throughout the year. During the academic year, see university performing arts concerts in dance, theater, and music for $6-10. The Playhouse also presents musicals and romantic comedies during the summertime. Tickets are usually $5, $3 for students and seniors; can be purchased at the door. Call the CAL Performances Ticket office in Zellerbach Hall for more information. (See beginning of Entertainment, page 282, for hours.)

The Bear Stage Theatre presents one musical per year and other shows. It has produced *Hair, Jesus Christ Superstar,* and *Pippin* in the past. For information, call UC Choral Ensembles at 51 Golden Bear Center, 642-3880.

Berkeley Repertory Theater, 2025 Addison St. (845-4700). Best-known theater in the area, with a diverse repertoire of classics and unknowns. Box office open noon-7pm. Tickets $16-32.50.

Theatre of the Blue Rose, 2525 8th St. (540-5037), at Dwight Way. Modern repertory featuring everything from silly comedy to ancient Greek classics. Performances ($5) run 1 week each month, Thurs.-Sat. 8:30pm, Sun. 3pm.

Bookstores

Cody's, 2454 Telegraph Ave. (845-7852), at Haste. The largest, best, and friendliest for new books. Fire-bombed in 1989 for stocking Salman Rushdie's *The Satanic Verses.* Excellent philosophy section. Good children's and scientific books. Weekly readings by authors. Open Mon.-Sat. 10am-10pm, Sun. 10am-9pm.

Moe's, 2476 Telegraph Ave. (849-2087), between Haste St. and Dwight Way. Featured in *The Graduate.* Four well-arranged floors of second-hand knowledge. Everything from Artaud to Zukofsky. Open Sun.-Thurs. 10am-11pm, Fri.-Sat. 10am-midnight. Art and antiquarian section (849-2133) open daily noon-6pm.

University Press Books, 2430 Bancroft (548-0585). This elegant bookshop sells only university press publications—not only Berkeley's, but those of other universities as well. Open Mon.-Fri. 10am-8pm, Sat. 10am-6pm, Sun. noon-5pm.

Shakespeare and Company, 2499 Telegraph Ave. (841-8916), at Dwight Way. Inspired by, but not related to, the famous Paris store. A well-organized collection, strong on art and literary criticism. Open daily 10am-9:45pm.

The Map Center, 2440 Bancroft Way (841-6277), on the southern edge of campus. You can't do better for maps, guides, and hiking information concerning Berkeley, the Bay Area, the world, and elsewhere. Open Mon.-Sat. 10am-6pm.

Black Oak Books, 1491 Shattuck Ave. (486-0698 or 486-0699), in the Gourmet Ghetto. Selective stock of used, new, and out-of-print literature, art classics, and other scholarly works. They invite you to "sit down and read" *and* supply a chair. Numerous authors give lectures; call for schedule. Open daily 10am-10pm.

Pegasus, 1855 Solano Ave. (525-6888). Great selection of close-outs and used books in mint condition. Also some new books and used records. Open Mon.-Thurs. 8am-10pm, Fri.-Sat. 8am-10:45pm, Sun. 10am-10pm.

Half Price Books, 1849 Solano Ave. (526-6080), and a second location at 2525 Telegraph Ave. (843-6412). They really do charge half-price or less for almost everything in stock. Ask them how. Both locations open daily 10am-10pm.

NIGHTLIFE

Coffeehouses

More than half of the undergrads at Berkeley aren't yet 21. While some of them frequent establishments that serve alcohol anyway, many of them are kept away by noble consciences and zealous bouncers. Cafés have become surrogate bars, as well as surrogate libraries.

Café Strada, 2300 College Ave. (843-5282), at Bancroft. The glittering jewel of the culinary-intellectual complex, known to some as "Café Pretentious" or "Café Be Seen." Enjoy the beautiful outdoor terrace. Hegelian atmosphere at night. Cocoa made with white chocolate. Espresso drinks 75¢-$1.15, cappuccino $1, scones 95¢, and fruit tarts $1.50. Open Mon.-Fri. 6:45am-11pm, Sat.-Sun. 7am-11:30pm.

Espresso Roma, 2960 College Ave. (644-3773), at Ashby. The newest and hottest spot in Berkeley for locals, students, and European visitors to sip and study in the morning, and see and be seen in the evenings. Wine, beer, and coffee drinks are served. Cappuccino $1.10. Sandwiches and pizza also offered. Open Mon.-Thurs. 6:30am-11pm, Fri. 6:30am-midnight, Sat. 7:30am-midnight, Sun. 7:30am-11pm.

Café Milano, 2522 Bancroft (644-3100). With its high wood-beam ceilings, 10-ft. windows, and brick walls, Milano is perhaps the hippest contender in the Telegraph café-a-thon. Open daily 7am-midnight.

Mediterraneum Cafe, 2475 Telegraph Ave. near Dwight (549-1128). For a taste of "old Berkeley," visit this unpretentious cafe. Popular with long-time residents. Munch a pecan chewy ($1.40). *Macciato con café* ($1.30). Open daily 7-11.

The Musical Offering, 2430 Bancroft Way (849-0211). Classical music resonates through this café/music shop. Customers can browse through the classical music CDs or enjoy scones and coffee while listening to the music. 10% discount on CDs if you buy them on the composer's birthday. Salads, sandwiches, and lunch specials $4.65-7.50. No smoking. Café open Mon.-Fri. 8am-8pm, Sat. 10am-8pm, Sun. 11:30am-5pm. Store open Mon.-Sat. 10am-9pm, Sun. 11:30am-5pm.

Au Coquelet, 2000 University Ave. (845-0433), at Milvia. Late-night spot for sandwiches ($3.50-4), tarts ($3), and coffee (75¢). Impressive selection of fresh pastries. Open Mon.-Thurs. 6am-1:30am, Fri. 6am-2am, Sat. 8am-2am, Sun. 8am-1am.

Sufficient Grounds, 2431A Durant (841-3969), 1 block from campus. Students come here to study, eat freshly baked scones ($1.25 each), and drink the *café au lait* ($1.15). Open Mon.-Fri. 7am-midnight, Sat. 8am-midnight, Sun. 8am-10pm.

Peet's Coffee Bar, 2124 Vine St. (841-0564), at Walnut, northwest of campus in the Gourmet Ghetto. Where everybody buys beans. Get a cup of brute-strength brew with cream (60-90¢), 10% off if you bring your own mug. Open Mon.-Sat. 7:30am-6pm, Sun 10am-6pm. Also **Peet's Coffee & Tea,** at 1825 Solano. Open Mon.-Sat. 7:30am-7pm, Sun. 8am-6pm.Tastings noon-1pm weekdays and Sun.

Bars

Henry's, 2600 Durant Ave. (845-8981), in the Durant Hotel. Somewhat upscale frat hangout. Beers from New Zealand, Holland, Jamaica, Canada, Italy, and Switzerland ($2.50-3.25). Open daily 11am-2am.

Blakes, 2367 Telegraph Ave. (848-0886), at Durant. Named "best bar in Berkeley" by the *Daily Californian*, Blake's has 3 stories, 2 happy hours (sometimes), and one classic-packed CD jukebox. Happy hour daily 4-6pm and 9-11pm. Dancing on Tues. and Wed. at "The Cartoon Club." Snacks $1.75-4, meals $4-8. Beverages start at $2. Cover $2-5. Must be 21. Open Mon.-Sat. 11:30am-2am, Sun. 4pm-2am.

Jupiter, 2181 Shattuck Ave. (843-8277), across the street from the BART station. Table-bowling, beer garden, and terrific pizza ($6 for a loaded 8-in. pie). International beers on tap including Anchor Porter ($2.75 per pint) and *Hubsch Brau* pilsner ($3.25 per pint). Open Mon.-Thurs. 11:30am-1am, Fri. 11:30am-1:30am, Sat. 1pm-1:30am, Sun. 1-11pm. Live music Fri.-Sun., no cover.

Bison Brewery, 2598 Telegraph Ave. at Parker (841-7734). Your options include an in-house tobacco blend of smooth vanilla and light shag, a soothing tea called "Wiccan's Women's Brew," and much, much more. "Buck-a-beer happy hour special" Mon.-Fri. 4-6pm and 9-11pm. Live music Thurs.-Sat., $1-3 cover. Open daily 11am-11pm.

Spats, 1974 Shattuck Ave. (841-7225), between University and Berkeley. Locals and students enjoy the warmth provided by the staff, the original drinks (e.g. Borneo Fog Cutter), and the eclectic surroundings. Off-beat decorations include stuffed deer, a Roman soldier, an autographed poster of Walt Disney, and velvet furniture. Hors d'oeuvres 2pm-1am. Order (drinks $3.50-5) from the 8-page drink catalog. Food $6-10. Open Mon.-Fri. 11:30am-2am, Sat.-Sun. 4pm-2am.

Starry Plough, 3101 Shattuck Ave. (841-2082). Posters espouse pro-Irish, anti-nuclear, and U.S.-out-of-Nicaragua sentiments. California bands play Thurs.-Sat. ($3-6 cover). Sun. and Mon. Irish dance lessons at 7pm and traditional Irish music 9pm (no cover). Open Mon.-Sat. 11am-2am, Sun. 4pm-2am.

Triple Rock Brewery, 1920 Shattuck Ave. (843-2739). This micro-brewery produces 3 regular beers (pale, amber, dark) and occasional specialties ($2.50-2.75 per pint). Roof garden (open daily 11:30am-8pm). The shuffleboard court in back awaits those sober enough to stand. After 7pm, the bar is so crowded that you can't do anything but stand. After 8pm, no one under 21 admitted. Food served daily 11:30am-midnight, Thurs.-Sat. last call for drinks at 1:30am.

Schmidt's Tobacco and Trading Company, 1492 Solano Ave. at Santa Fe Ave. (525-1900), in Albany. This place started as an antique shop, but has evolved into what locals call "The Pub." Sip Guinness ($3 for a pint) and chew on a cigar in the cozy, home-like environment. 110% smoking. In the afternoon, the regulars gather (one brings his pet snake). Evenings bring out the college crowd. Open Sun.-Wed. noon-11pm, Thurs. noon-midnight, Fri.-Sat. noon-1am.

SEASONAL EVENTS

Berkeley's **farmers market** takes place on Sundays from mid-July through November, from 11am to 3pm on Haste St. between Telegraph and Bowditch. The **Farmers Market Grand Opening and Parade** starts the season on the second Sunday of July. Authors and jazz musicians come together for the **Telegraph Avenue Book Fair** in late July. You can talk to the authors (and their publishers) while listening to the musicians. Call 649-9500 for information about the market or the book fair.

■■■ MARIN COUNTY

Home to Jerry Garcia, Dana Carvey, and 560 acres of spectacular redwood forest, Marin County (mah-RIN) boasts a bizarre blend of outstanding natural beauty, trendiness, liberalism, and wealth. Marinites love their real estate values as much as their open space and organic food. Neighboring communities grumble about Marin's excesses—most notably the $350 million oil stock fund left to the county by the late Mrs. Beryl Buck, for which many say Marin has little use—but Marin residents will tell you there's no hypocrisy in their indulgent and eco-conscious habits. Life is just *better* in Marin. If you can afford to stay, you may never leave.

Much of Marin can be explored in a daytrip from San Francisco. The area can be reached by car, bus, or ferry. Muir Woods National Monument with its coastal redwoods, Marin Headlands, Mt. Tamalpais State Park, and the Point Reyes National Seashore offer trails for mountain bikers and hikers looking for a day's adventure, a two week trek, or anything in between.

PRACTICAL INFORMATION AND ORIENTATION

Visitors Information: Marin County Chamber of Commerce, 30 N. San Pedro Rd. #150 (472-7470). Open Mon.-Fri. 8:30am-4:30pm. **Sausalito Chamber of Commerce,** 333 Caledonia St. (332-7262). Open Mon.-Fri. 9am-5pm. **Marin Headlands Visitors Center** (331-1540), at the Ft. Barry Chapel, Field and Bunker. Information on the Marin Headlands and camping. Open daily 9:30am-4:30pm. **Point Reyes National Seashore Headquarters (Bear Valley Visitors Center)** (663-1092), Bear Valley Rd., ½ mi. west of Olema. Information, wilderness permits, maps, and campsite reservations. Open Mon.-Fri. 9am-5pm, Sat.-Sun. 8am-5pm. **San Rafael Chamber of Commerce,** 818 5th Ave. (454-4163). Open Mon.-Fri. 9am-5pm.

Greyhound, 850 Tamalpais (453-0795), in San Rafael. To San Francisco: 2 buses per day, $5, leaving at 4:45am and 5pm.

Bay Area Transportation: Golden Gate Transit (453-2100; 332-6600 in San Francisco). Daily bus service between San Francisco and Marin County via the Golden Gate Bridge, as well as local service in Marin. Buses #10, 20, 28, 30, and 50 provide service to Marin from San Francisco's Transbay Terminal at 1st and Mission St. Buses #65 and 24 provide service out to Pt. Reyes and Samuel P. Taylor State Park ($2 into Sausalito, $4 to West Marin). The **Golden Gate Ferry** (same phone numbers) provides transportation between Sausalito or Larkspur and San Francisco. Boats depart from the Ferry Bldg. at the end of Market St. for a 25-min. crossing to downtown Sausalito ($4.25) or a 50-min. trip to the Larkspur ferry terminal (Mon.-Fri. $2.50, Sat.-Sun. $4.25). Seniors, youths, and disabled ½-price.

Taxi: Radio Cab (800-464-7234). Serves all of Marin County.

Car Rental: Budget, 20 Bellam Blvd. (457-4282), San Rafael. $30 per day, unlimited mileage. Will rent to ages 21-25 at no extra charge. **Bay Area Rental,** 780 Anderson Dr. (459-2700), San Rafael. $30 per day, must be at least 25 with credit card. 150 free mi.

Bicycle Rental: A Bicycle Odyssey, 1417 Bridgeway (332-3050). Open Mon.-Wed. and Fri.-Sat. 10am-6pm, Thurs. 11am-7pm, Sun. 10am-5pm. $6 per hr., $25 per day. There are other bicycle rental shops closer to sights, see Mt. Tamalpais

MARIN COUNTY

State Park and Point Reyes National Seashore, page 289. Regardless of whether you have a car, you'll want a bike on the shore.

Library: Mill Valley Library, 375 Throckmorton (388-2190). Beautiful A-Frame building backed by a woodsy park. Non-residents can buy used paperbacks (25¢). Open Tues.-Thurs. 10am-9pm, Fri. noon-6pm, Sat. 10am-5pm.

Senior Services: Marin Senior Coordinating Council, 930 Tamalpais (456-9062), in San Rafael. Health care, legal services, and counseling. Open Mon.-Fri. 9am-5pm.

Bisexual, Gay, and Lesbian Information: Spectrum, 1000 Sir Francis Drake Blvd. (457-1115), in San Anselmo. Information, social services. Mon.-Fri. 9am-5pm.

Laundry: Water Works, 105 2nd St. Sausalito. Wash $1.50, 10-min. dry 75¢. Open Mon.-Fri. 7am-9pm, Sat. 8am-9pm, Sun. 9am-9pm.

Auto Safety: 800-424-9393.

Weather: 936-1212.

Crisis Lines: Rape Crisis, 924-2100. 24hrs. **Poison Control,** 800-523-2222. 24hrs.

Medical Services: Marin Community Clinic (461-7400). Open Mon. and Fri. 8:30am-5pm, Wed. 9:30am-5pm, Tues. and Thurs. 8:30am-8:30pm.

Hospital: Marin General, 250 Bon Air Rd. (925-7000), in Greenbrae.

Emergency: 911.

Police: Non-emergency, 485-3000 in San Rafael; 479-2311 in the county.

Post Office: San Rafael Main Office, 40 Bellam Ave. (459-0944). Open Mon.-Fri. 8:30am-5pm, Sat. 10am-1pm. **General Delivery ZIP Code:** 94915.

Area Code: 415.

The Marin peninsula lies at the north end of San Francisco Bay, and is connected to the city by **U.S. 101** via the Golden Gate Bridge. To the north on U.S. 101 lies Santa Rosa and Sonoma County, and **Rte. 1** creeps north along the Pacific to the Sonoma Coast. The Richmond-San Rafael Bridge connects Marin County to the East Bay via **I-580.**

The eastern side of the county cradles the settlements of **Sausalito, Larkspur, San Rafael, Terra Linda, Ignacio,** and **Novato.** These towns line U.S. 101, which runs north-south through Marin. It is around this 101 corridor that most of the population and development is concentrated. West Marin is more rural, with rolling hills and fog-bound coastal valleys. **Rte 1,** easily the nation's most beautiful highway, runs through **Stinson Beach, Bolinas, Olema, Inverness,** and **Pt. Reyes National Seashore** (from south to north). **Sir Francis Drake Boulevard** runs from U.S. 101 in Larkspur west through the San Geronimo Valley. It passes through the towns of Greenbrae, Kentfield, Ross, San Anselmo, Fairfax, Woodacre, and San Geronimo on the way to Pt. Reyes and its rendezvous with Rte. 1. If you're traveling by car, fill up in town before you head out to West Marin, where gasoline can cost 30¢ per gallon more than elsewhere. Drivers should also be warned that many of West Marin's roads are narrow, sharply curved, and perched on the edge of vertigo-inducing bluffs.

Marin is a relatively safe area with the exception of Marin City and parts of Novato. Hiking in the woods alone is more dangerous, though, and should not be done after sunset. Many signs have been uprooted; it's easy to get lost in the dark.

ACCOMMODATIONS AND CAMPING

Hostels

Golden Gate Youth Hostel (HI-AYH) (331-2777). Located in a historic 1907 building in the Marin Headlands, 6 mi. south of Sausalito and 10 mi. from downtown San Francisco—an ideal escape from the city. The fit and car-less can take the public bus (#2, 10, 20) to Alexander Ave., then make the 4½-mi. uphill hike to the hostel. Taking the bus is unrealistic, though, for the average of health and heavy of backpack—it really is uphill. Those with cars coming from the north should take the Sausalito exit off U.S. 101 (the last one before the bridge) and follow the signs into the Golden Gate Recreation Area. From San Francisco, take U.S.

101 to the Alexander Ave. exit. Surrounded by eucalyptus trees, these former soldiers' quarters now contain a game room with pool table, spacious kitchen, common room, and laundry facilities. 24-hr. check-in. Curfew 12:30am. Dormitory and family-style rooms. Linen rental $1. Members and nonmembers $10. Children under 18 with parent $5. Reservations suggested in summer—or show up early.

Point Reyes Hostel (HI-AYH) (663-8811), sits off Limantour Rd. in the Pt. Reyes National Seashore. By car take the Seashore exit west from Rte. 1, then take Bear Valley Rd. to Limantour Rd. and drive 6 mi. in to the park (at which point you'll see a sign for the hostel). For public transportation information, contact Golden Gate Transit (see Practical Information, page 285) or call the hostel during registration hours. Trail Head Rentals (see Sights, page 289), at Bear Valley Rd. and Rte. 1, rents bikes. You're more likely to get a last-minute room here than in the Golden Gate Hostel, although reservations are advised on weekends. Reservations must be made by mail with a deposit (Box 247, Point Reyes Station, CA 94956) or by phone with credit card. Hostel is spread between two cabins on a spectacular site. Hiking, wildlife, bird-watching, and Limantour Beach are all within walking distance. Kitchen. Cozy common room with a wood stove. Registration 4:30-9:30pm. Hostel closed 9:30am-4:30pm. Sleep sheet and towel $1 each. Members and nonmembers $10; chore also expected.

Campgrounds

Marin Headlands, northwest of the Golden Gate Bridge. 15 campsites. Most are primitive with only picnic tables and chemical toilets. Two sites have running water; one site, Kirby Cove, has a cooking area; another site has space for groups of up to 80 people. Reserve as much as 90 days in advance by calling the **visitors center** (331-1540; 9:30am-noon). Permits are required, but sites are free. The Golden Gate Youth Hostel (see above) permits use of showers and kitchen ($2 each). Free cold showers available at Rodeo Beach (located in the Headlands).

Mt. Tamalpais State Park, 801 Rte. 1 (388-2070). 16 family campsites ($14; first-come, first-served), a group camp, and **Steep Ravine,** an "environmental camp" with cabins ($30 for up to 5 people) and tent sites ($9)—these last are situated on a coastal bluff overlooking the ocean. Tent sites with fire pits, no showers. Cabins have wood-burning stoves with no running water or electricity. Make cabin reservations 90 days in advance (MISTIX 800-444-7275). Reservation fee $6.75.

Samuel P. Taylor State Park (488-9897), on Sir Francis Drake Blvd., 15 mi. west of San Rafael (which in turn is 10 mi. north of Sausalito on U.S. 101). Shady sites in a forested setting. Hot showers (50¢ for 5 min.). Family campground, lots of children. Pets $1 extra; dogs must be leashed. Tent sites $14. Hiker/biker sites $3 per person. 7-day max. stay. Reservations through MISTIX (800-444-7275) necessary April-Oct.; at least 24 hrs. in advance.

There are four campgrounds (accessible by foot) on the **Point Reyes National Seashore** in the southern, inner cape portion of Pt. Reyes. All are fairly rough, with pit toilets, fire pits, and tap water, and require permits from Seashore Headquarters. The camps are well-patrolled, and visitors without permits are likely to be fined. Two camps are coastal, and two are inland. All command exquisite views of the ocean and surrounding hills. (Get permits at the Pt. Reyes National Seashore Headquarters; see Practical Information, page 285. Reservations are taken up to 2 months in advance Mon.-Fri. 9am-noon. Max. stay of 4 nights per visit. All sites are free.)

FOOD

Gourmet, health-conscious Marinites take their fruit juices, tofu, and nonfat double-shot cappuccino very seriously; restaurateurs know this, and raise both the alfalfa sprouts and the prices. A fun, more economical option is to raid one of the area's many organic groceries and picnic in one of Marin's countless parks. The **Real Food Company,** 200 Caledonia, in Sausalito, has spring water (on tap!) and Marin's cherished ACME Bread (open daily 9am-9pm). **Woodland Market,** 735 College (457-8160; open daily 8am-8pm), Kentfield, vends organic sausages and fresh pasta. There are also two **farmers markets** in San Rafael—**Marin Civic Center,** off U.S.

101 (open Thurs. and Sun. 8am-1pm); and **downtown** on 4th St. (open Thurs. 5-8:30pm). All restaurants listed below are wheelchair accessible.

Mama's Royal Cafe, 387 Miller Ave. (388-3261), in downtown Mill Valley. Heartily recommended by locals. Looks like grandma's attic after an explosion—a pack-rat's dream. Self-aware slackers serve up unusual but very good dishes from a menu as packed as the restaurant. Try the Enchilada El Syd ($5.75) or the Hippie-Crit, a veggie- and meat-burger. Huge breakfast selection. Brunch with live music Sat. and Sun. Poetry readings Tues. Some outdoor seating. Open for breakfast/lunch Mon.-Fri. 7:30am-2:30pm, Sat.-Sun. 8:30am-3pm. Dinner Tues.-Sat. 6-10pm.

Stuffed Croissant, etc..., 43 Caledonia St. (332-7103), in Sausalito. Way laid-back bakery-style sandwich shop (sandwiches $3-6). An amazing array of goods from the local bakery. Fantastic pecan-raisin-oat scones ($1.75). Sit at counter or take out. Vegetarian options. Open Mon. 6:30am-9pm, Tues.-Sat. 6:30am-10pm, Sun. 7:30am-9pm.

The Town's Deli, 501 Caledonia (331-3311), in Sausalito. Sandwiches $2.50-3.75. Known for their roasted chicken (half-chicken $3). Vegetarian options. Open Mon.-Sat. 8am-7pm, Sun. 8am-6pm.

Phyllis' Giant Burgers, 72 E. Blithedale Ave. (381-5166), 1 block from downtown Mill Valley. Local burger joint—¼-pounders (from $2.75), ½-pounders (from $3.65), veggie burgers ($3.30), and fries served in red baskets ($1.15). Soft drinks with free refills come in cups big enough to swim in ($1). Is this Marin?

Whole Foods, 414 Miller Ave. (381-1200), across the street from Mama's. One of the nicest of this chain, the fruits and veggies are fresh and organic, there are tons of bulk goods, and the deli foods are scrumptious. Try the Thai black rice (rice and pasta salads $4-8). Open daily 9am-8pm.

The Depot Bookstore and Café, 87 Throckmorton Ave. (383-2665), at the center of downtown Mill Valley. One of the best people-watching places around. Marin-ites sip mocha ($2) and munch on tasty vegetarian roll-ups ($3) on the outdoor plaza. The huge Caesar salad ($4.85) is a great deal. Open daily 7am-10pm.

Lucindas, 930 Redwood Hwy. (388-0754), Mill Valley/Strawberry. Take Frontage Rd. to U.S. 101, then take the Tiburon/Belvedere exit. Lucindas offers heap Cali-Mex fare in gargantuan portions (2 lb. burritos from $3). Sit on a stool or take out. Vegetarian-friendly. Open Mon.-Sat. 11am-10pm, Sun. 11am-9pm.

Bongkot Thai Express, 857 4th St. (453-3350), San Rafael. Murals of Thailand cover the walls. Meat curries ($6-7.25), vegetarian curries ($5-6.25). Satisfying portions made spicy on request (and when they say "extra spicy" they mean it). Open Mon.-Sat. 11am-3pm and 5-9pm.

SIGHTS

Marin's attractions range from the excellent hiking trails that crisscross the county's parks and beaches to unique shopping and dining opportunities in the pleasant towns of Tiburon and Sausalito. Marin's proximity to San Francisco makes it an ideal area for daytrips; the efficient visitor can hop from park to park and enjoy several short hikes along the coast and through the redwood forests in the same day.

Sausalito lies at the extreme southeastern tip of Marin. Initially a fishing center, the city traded its sea-dog days for a bevy of retail boutiques. A complicated, bizarre, and somewhat showy houseboat community now occupies the harbor, fostering such personalities as the "Pope of Soap," a man who builds sculptures out of soap bubbles and then puts people inside of them (call 331-4456 if you'd like a demonstration or a bath). A block away from the harbor, Caledonia St. is lined with stores more affordable than those on the waterfront. The street also offers a good view of the huge houses which smile down from the hill in wry, mild bemusement. For beautiful views of San Francisco and a relaxing daytrip, take the ferry (see Practical Information, page 285) from San Francisco to Sausalito.

The undeveloped, fog-shrouded hills just to the west of the Golden Gate Bridge comprise the **Marin Headlands,** which are oddly populated by abandoned machine gun nests, missile sites, and soldiers' quarters, now converted into picnic spots, a hostel (see Golden Gate Youth Hostel, above), and the **Marine Mammal Center**

(289-7325; open daily 10am-4pm; donation requested). The center offers a sobering look at the rehabilitation of beached marine mammals. Nearly all of the headlands are open to hikers—berry picking is permitted but beware the poison oak—and camping is allowed in designated areas. The vista from the headlands back over the bridge to San Francisco is arguably the most spectacular in the Bay Area. The headlands (and the viewpoints) are easily accessible by car: take the Alexander Ave. exit off U.S. 101 from San Francisco, or if coming from the north take the last exit before the Golden Gate Bridge (after the exit directions are obvious). Consider hiking the ¾-mi. trail which leads from the parking area down to the sheltered (and usually deserted) beach at **Kirby Cove.** In the cooler months, migrating hawks and whales can be seen from hill 129.

Muir Woods National Monument, a 560-acre stand of primeval coastal redwoods, is located about 5 mi. west along Rte. 1 off U.S. 101. These centuries-old massive redwoods are shrouded in soft, slanting sunlight, and an eerie silence reigns. Wildlife in the ancient forest is shy, and much of the action occurs in the canopy—hike uphill to see the treetops and the canopy happenings (open daily 8am-sunset). The **visitors center** (388-2595) near the entrance keeps the same hours as the monument. Ask a ranger to help you find a trail suited to your abilities. Nearby are **Muir Beach** and **Muir Beach Lookout** (open sunrise-9pm). From Muir Beach, a five-minute climb on the shore rocks to the left helps you escape the crowds; if you continue further along the beach you may stumble upon nude sunbathers.

Adjacent to Muir Woods is the isolated, largely undiscovered, and utterly beautiful **Mount Tamalpais State Park** (tam-ull-PIE-us). This park is favored by locals, many of whom consider it much more interesting than Muir Woods. The heavily forested park has a number of challenging trails that lead to the top of **Mount Tam,** the highest peak in the county, and to a natural stone amphitheater. **Cataract Trail** leads to a bubbling waterfall. The mountain bike was invented in this park, which has a number of very challenging mountain bike trails—but don't go off the fire roads or you risk incurring the wrath of eco-conscious Marin hikers. Also in the park is **Stinson Beach,** a local favorite for sunbathing. Although the beach is often cold and windy, valiant sunbathers and windsurfers attempt to create a Bay Area version of Malibu. Red Rock Beach, ½-mi. north, is clothing-optional. The park opens a half-hour before sunrise and closes a half-hour after sunset. On weekends, bus #63 runs from Mt. Tam Ranger Station (commonly called Partoll Ranger Station) to Stinson Beach and back. Nearby bicycle rental shops include **Caesar's Cyclery,** 29 San Anselmo Ave. (258-9920), in San Anselmo (mountain bikes $6 per hr., $30 per day; open Tues.-Sat. 10am-6pm, Sun. 11am-5pm), and **Wheel Escapes,** 1000 Magnolia Ave. (332-0218), in Larkspur. (Bikes $5 per hr. or $21+ per day. Open Mon. and Wed.-Fri. 10am-6pm, Sat.-Sun. 10am-7pm.)

Encompassing 100 mi. of coastline along most of the western side of Marin, the **Point Reyes National Seashore** juts into the Pacific from the eastern end of the submerged Pacific Plate. Sir Francis Drake Blvd. runs from San Rafael through Olema, where it crosses Rte. 1, all the way to Pt. Reyes itself. Here the infamous San Andreas Fault comes to an end. The point's remote position brings heavy fog and strong winds in winter. In summer an explosion of colorful wildflowers attracts crowds of gawking tourists, but with hundreds of miles of amazing trails it's possible to escape the crowds and gawk in solitude at the many worthy sights the park has to offer. The visitors center has a map describing where to see various wildflowers.

Limantour Beach, at the end of Limantour Rd., west of the seashore headquarters, is one of the area's nicest beaches. In summer a free shuttle bus runs to Limantour Beach from seashore headquarters. Both Limantour and Point Reyes boast high, grassy dunes and long stretches of sand. Strong ocean currents along the point make swimming very dangerous. To reach the dramatic **Point Reyes Lighthouse** at the very tip of the point, follow Sir Francis Drake Blvd. to its end and head right along the stairway to Sea Lion Overlook. From December to February, migrating gray whales can occasionally be spotted from the overlook. The best way to get around the seashore is by **bicycle. Trail Head Rentals** (663-1958), at Rte. 1 and Bear Valley Rd., Olema, is conveniently located near the Bear Valley Visitors Center. (Bikes Mon.-Fri. $6 per hr., 2-hr. min., $20 per day. Weekends $24 per day. Open daily 9am-5pm.)

San Rafael, the largest city in Marin County, lies along U.S. 101 on the bay. Architecture buffs may want to check out the **Marin Civic Center,** 3501 Civic Center Dr. (499-7407), off U.S. 101. Frank Lloyd Wright designed this highly unusual, but functional open-air building which looms over the highway. An information kiosk in the lobby supplies brochures and pamphlets; phone ahead for a tour (open Mon.-Fri. 9am-5pm). For a rewarding off-beat experience, visit **Guide Dogs for the Blind,** 350 Los Ranchitos Rd. (499-4000). Take the N. San Pedro exit from U.S. 101 heading west, then turn right onto Los Ranchitos. A docent-led tour (Mon.-Fri. 10:30am, 1:30, 2:30pm; call 24 hrs. ahead) will teach you about the training required before the dogs can be eyes for the blind. People in need of a dog come to the center and complete a 28-day training course with their new companion. The monthly graduation for people-dog teams is open to the public.

NIGHTLIFE AND ENTERTAINMENT

Not even the 7-Elevens are open 24 hours, but Marin does provide a variety of evening diversions. The coffee-drinking crowd should head to downtown Mill Valley—the cheapest cup is at **Peet's Coffee,** 88 Throckmorton (301-8227; open Mon.-Sat. 6:30am-7pm, Sun. 7:30am-6pm), which offers espresso (85¢) and cappuccino ($1.40). The *Independent Journal,* Marin's daily, lists garage sales by city, and the bargains are often unbelievable. Collectors and bargain-hunters from all over the world flock to **Village Music,** 9 E. Blithedale Ave. (388-7400), close to Mill Valley's downtown square. The store's biggest customers include B.B. King, Mick Jagger, Mel Tormé, and Bill Cosby. If it's on vinyl, it's here (albums 25¢-$200).

Sweetwater, 153 Throckmorton Ave. (388-2820), in downtown Mill Valley. Casual, mixed crowd frequents this dark, photo-lined bar, which still draws names like Costello and Clemens to perform. Golden Bear lager is a local favorite. Call in advance for a schedule. Cover ranges from $5-15. 2-drink min. during shows. Open daily 12:30pm-1am.

New George's, 842 4th St. (457-8424), in San Rafael, often wins "best nightlife in Marin" awards. Pints $3.50-4. Comedy on Tues.; funk and rock Wed.-Sat. Thurs. is student night, $1 cover or free with student ID. Fri.-Sat. cover $6-15. Open Mon. 11am-7pm, Tues.-Thurs. 11am-12:30am, Fri.-Sat. 11am-2am. Ages 21 and over.

Marin Brewing Company, 1809 Larkspur Landing Circle (461-4677), across from the ferry terminal in Larkspur. Sit across the bar from the source of your suds. Good beer ($2.25-2.75); a crowd of yuppies. Live jazz Sat. and Sun. afternoons. Open Sun.-Thurs. 11:30am-midnight, Fri.-Sat. 11:30am-1am. No minimum age and never a cover.

Silver Peso, 450 Magnolia, in Larkspur. Loud, sunburned, fun-loving locals make it hard to believe you're in Marin. Pool tables, rock jukebox. Leave backpacks and other traveler's trappings behind. The Peso fills up on Thurs. nights with the college crowd. Opens daily at 1pm. Ages 21 and over.

Smitty's Bar, 214 Caledonia (332-2637), in Sausalito. The last of the Sausalito fishing community waters here, and the bartenders knows everything. This is the kind of place that has a bowling team, a pool league (2 tables), and 2 softball teams—and don't miss the shuffleboard tourney Wed. 7-11pm. Jukebox. No credit cards and no cover. Open daily 11am-late. Ages 21 and over.

■■■ OAKLAND

Oakland strives to refute Gertrude Stein's withering observation: "There is no there there." The city's tourist literature wages a veritable war of attrition against her, assuring visitors that City Square is "always *there* for you," and "there is shopping *there*." Roslyn Mazzilli's sculpture in the square's upper plaza is defiantly entitled

O A K L A N D

"There!" One is tempted to pat the city on the shoulder and say, "There, there, Oakland."

Many locals will admit that Stein's statement is apt—the city lacks a sense of place. The City Square's emphatic "there"-ing attempts to restore a center that the city never really had. Oakland residents look instead to their individual neighborhoods, or travel to Berkeley or San Francisco for excitement and identity. The different Oakland neighborhoods jumble together in a patchwork—destitute areas lie adjacent to prosperous ones; suburbs stand out abruptly against the extensive regional parks along the city's eastern border. Meanwhile, the substantial African-American plurality is proud, involved, self-aware, and assertive. Oakland, the unpretentious Bay partner to cosmopolitan San Francisco and cerebral Berkeley, is one of the most ethnically and culturally diverse cities in the United States.

PRACTICAL INFORMATION

Visitors Information: Oakland Convention and Visitors Bureau, 1000 Broadway #200 (800-444-7270 or 839-9000). You will find that Conventions (and not budget travelers), are this city's main visitor-business. But don't hesitate to pick up a free map and Visitor's Guide. Open Mon.-Fri. 8:30am-5pm.

Alameda County Transit: 839-2882 or 800-559-4636. Routes blanket the city. Fare $1.10, ages 5-12 $1, seniors and people with disabilities 55¢, transfers 25¢.

Travelers Aid: 520 16th St. near Telegraph. Open Mon.-Fri. 9am-12:30pm and 1:30-4:30pm. Call in an emergency.

Rape Crisis Center: 845-7273. Operated by Bay Area Women Against Rape. 24hrs.

Central Public Health Center: 470 27th St. (271-4263). Open Mon.-Fri. 8am-5pm.

Emergency: 911.

Post Office: Main Branch, 1675 7th St. at Willow St. (874-8200). Open Mon.Fri. 6am-10pm. **General Delivery ZIP Code:** 94617.

Area Code: 510.

Partly because Oakland has very little in the way of cheap and safe accommodations, and partly because it has a relatively small number of exciting things to see, Oakland is best visited on a daytrip from San Francisco or Berkeley. Car travelers can take I-80 across the bay via the San Francisco-Oakland **Bay Bridge** to Oakland I-580 and connect with Oakland I-980 South. Get off at one of the three downtown exits: 12th St., 14th St., or 19th St.

The car-less (and those who wish to avoid the hassle of Bay Area traffic) can take advantage of **BART (Bay Area Rapid Transit)** from downtown San Francisco to Oakland's MacArthur, 12th St. (Oakland City Center), or 19th St. stations ($1.55-1.65). The **Greyhound Station** is located in a dangerous part of downtown (2103 San Pablo Ave.)—be careful after dark. A trip from Oakland to Santa Cruz costs $11.85 and from Oakland to Los Angeles, $40.50. The **Amtrak Station** is at 1707 Wood St., and the **Oakland International Airport,** at 1 Airport Drive, is the destination of an increasing number of Bay Area-bound flights; a shuttle bus (Air-BART) connects the airport with the Coliseum BART station (every 10 min., $2; 800-545-2700). An alternative is the AC Transit bus #58 which runs to the Coliseum BART Station (frequent trains; 60¢ with transfer; $1.10 from the airport).

ORIENTATION

Oakland's main artery is **Broadway,** running northeast from **Jack London Square** (a waterfront shopping area), passing the **Produce Market** on its east side at 3rd St., and separating **Old Oakland** (to the west) from **Chinatown** (to the east). Just before the City Center, at 13th St. Northeast, downtown is occupied by the massive **Lake Merritt,** with **Lakeside Park** to its north, and the Lake Merritt Channel, leading to the Oakland Estuary, to its south. **East Oakland** is located south of Old Oakland.

To the north of downtown Oakland are nice neighborhoods with shops, grocers, and restaurants lining main streets. **Rockridge** lies at the border between Oakland and Berkeley and is accessible from downtown Oakland via the #51 bus.

OAKLAND

ACCOMMODATIONS

Although Oakland is full of motels, there is an emphatic lack of safe, economical places to stay. If you're looking for a youth hostel, the closest one is the new YMCA hostel in Berkeley; the hostels in San Francisco are also easily accessible. Otherwise, it might be worth the extra money to stay someplace safe. The **Bed and Breakfast Network** (540-5123) includes some Oakland addresses.

FOOD

The *Oakland Book,* Oakland's premiere tourist guide, boasts of a tremendous variety of international treats available at restaurants throughout the city. Unfortunately, many of the choices are upscale and expensive. Nevertheless, it is possible to sample delicious and economical cuisine from around the world if you select carefully. Every Friday, from 8am to 2pm, the **Old Oakland Certified Farmers Market** (452-3276) takes over the corner of Broadway and 9th St. The largest of its kind in Alameda County, the market offers fresh fruits, vegetables, and the wares of some of the best bakers in the Golden State. The **Rockridge Market Hall,** 5655 College Ave., is a gourmet's delight with exquisite specialty shops galore. **Mi Rancho Market,** at 464 7th St. (451-2393; open Mon.-Fri. 8am-6pm, Sat. 8am-5pm), has tortillas made fresh daily and "everything necessary for Mexican-style cooking." Office buildings have spawned a fair number of lunch counters in the downtown area.

Buongiorno Gourmet Express, 1226 Broadway (832-3000), between 12th and 13th St. Stop in for superb service and tasty fresh food. Sandwiches ($3.50-4.50), unusual salads ($2.50-4), and freshly baked muffins, scones, and pastries. Open Mon.-Fri. 6am-5:30pm, Sat. 7am-3:30pm.

Zachary's, 5801 College Ave. at Oak Grove (655-6385), in Rockridge. The original restaurant in this fabulous chain. You'll have to wait a bit, but the prize-winning, stuffed pizza is worth it. Try Zachary's Pride and Joy, a blend of cheese, spinach, mushrooms, and special spices in a perfect crust ($12 small serves 2-3). Open Sun.-Thurs. 11am-10pm, Fri.-Sat. 11am-10:30pm.

Papasan's New Gulf Coast Bar & Grill, 735 Washington St. at 8th (863-3663). Come for lots of authentic Cajun and Creole cookin'. All-you-can-eat lunch buffet for $7 is by far the best deal. Open Wed.-Fri. 11am-2pm, Thurs. and Sun. 5-9pm, Fri.-Sat. 5-11pm, Sun. brunch 11am-4pm. Reservations recommended.

Rockridge Café, 5492 College Ave. at Lawton (653-1567) in Rockridge. Has satisfied a demanding crowd since 1973. Build your own burger. Fresh salads $2.50-6.75. Fresh pies like pear-blueberry are a must ($2.75 per slice). Open Mon.-Thurs. 7:30am-10pm, Fri.-Sat. 7:30am-10:30pm, Sun. 8am-10pm.

Vi's, 724 Webster between 7th and 8th (835-8375). Modest Vietnamese noodle house serves huge bowls of noodle soup ($4-5). Known for *Bùn Gà,* Vietnamese vermicelli with grilled chicken salad $4.50. The doilies on the tables with chopsticks and spoons indicate high turnover. Open Fri.-Wed. 9am-4pm and 5-9pm.

Flint's Barbecue, 6609 Shattuck at 66th St. (653-0593) offers a new definition for "spicy." Its beef or pork ribs ($7.58), the best in town, are burning hot even when ordered with "medium" sauce. There's no place to sit, but that's okay—the chilies will keep you jumping anyway. Open daily 11am-2am.

Jade Villa, 800 Broadway St. (839-1688) in Chinatown. Offers three fresh-from-the-steamer pork buns for $1.89 and serves dim sum (daily 9am-3pm) that rivals San Francisco's best. Open Sun.-Thurs. 9am-9:30pm, Fri.-Sat. 9am-10pm.

Ike's, 3859 Piedmont Ave. This tiny Middle Eastern rotisserie serves good food at cheap prices. Whole rotisserie chicken $7.50. Open daily 11am-9:30pm.

Fenton's Creamery, 4226 Piedmont (658-7000). Stretch your digestive system to the limit with an outrageously misnamed "regular" sundae ($4.35; contains ¾ lb. ice cream with a flood of fudge). Open daily noon-midnight.

SIGHTS

Oakland presents a blend of natural and human-made attractions, from its own salt-water lake to historic buildings and a mix of museums.

Originally connected to the San Francisco Bay, **Lake Merritt** was dammed in 1869 and has since become Oakland's very own watery playground. The lake is the place for lazy, music-filled afternoons, sailing, bird-watching, and strolling. During the day, the paths surrounding the lake swarm with joggers. At night, you may want to avoid the lake entirely, lest a would-be mugger give you a real run for your money. Daytime activity revolves around **Lakeside Park,** which encompasses a band shell, a bird sanctuary, and a Children's Fairyland park. If you are in the mood for **shopping,** the nearby streets of **Lakeshore, Grand,** and **Piedmont** are lined with thrift shops, bookstores, boutiques, and kosher butchers.

The **Festival at the Lake** takes place during the first weekend in June and lasts three days. The fest is a celebration of urban diversity, with an international food fair, art exhibits, and children's attractions. ($5, under 12 free.)

The **Oakland Museum,** 1000 Oak St. (834-2413), at 10th St., on the south side of the lake, is an intriguing and well-designed complex of three museums, contained in a low-lying structure of soot and ivy covered blocks, devoted to the history, art, and natural splendor of California. The top floor houses the **Gallery of California Art,** with a variety of art ranging from traditional 19th-century portraits to contemporary works framed in rabbit-fur. In addition to paintings and sculptures, the gallery has Gold Rush cartoons and photography exhibits. One floor down, the **Cowell Hall of California History,** with an assortment of inspirational quotations hanging from the ceiling, celebrates California's development with artifacts, photographs, and mini-video presentations. Past museum visitors have been sprayed with plaster and added to the large collection of anonymous "California dreamers" at the end of the tour. (Don't worry, it was done with their consent.) On the lowest level, the **Hall of California Ecology** simulates a trek in the Bay Area, with exhibits on the different ecosystems as they existed before people started their romp through the area. To reach the Oakland Museum, take BART to the Lake Merritt Station or AC Transit bus #14. (Open Wed.-Sat. 10am-5pm, Sun. noon-7pm. Tours Wed.-Sat. 2pm. Suggested donation $4, seniors and children $2.)

Also in the Lake Merritt area is the **Holmes Bookstore,** 274 14th St. (893-6860), one of the largest used bookstores in the Bay Area—and it sells new books, too. Holmes was founded in San Francisco in 1894. After being devastated in the 1906 earthquake, it moved to Oakland, where it flourished. Its special feature is a room on the third floor devoted to rare books and California history. (Open Mon.-Fri. 9:30am-8pm, Sat. 9:30am-5:30pm, Sun. 11am-5pm.)

The vast complex of **City Square** stands at City Center, 13th St. and Broadway. Perhaps the most ambitious of the all-purpose emporia that blossomed in the 80s, this three-block wonderland will eventually encompass five million square feet of business and retail. The lighthouse-like central tower makes the City Square complex easy to spot. (12th St.-City Center BART station.)

Oakland's architectural heritage is quite rich. At the west end of City Center (intersection of 13th St. and Martin Luther King, Jr. Way) lies **Preservation Park** (office at 1233 Preservation Park Way; 874-7580; open Mon.-Fri. 10am-3pm). This lane features 16 lovingly restored **Victorian houses** that have been thoroughly renovated and now serve as office "buildings." The park area provides a pleasant place for a picnic, a quiet stroll, or a self-guided historical tour of these architectural gems. The White House Café (832-6000) serves hearty breakfasts and lunches and offers free music (July-Aug. at noon). For more information on tours call 238-3234.

The **Paramount Theater** (circa 1931), 2025 Broadway at 21st St. (465-6400), is perhaps the most exquisite Art Deco movie palace in the country. The theater shows weekly films and houses the **Oakland Symphony** and the **Oakland Ballet.** The mighty Wurlitzer organ accompanies Oakland concerts and movies. (See Entertainment, page 294 for ticket information.) Tours of the theater are given the first and third Saturdays of the month (no reservations; show up at the box office entrance).

The **Oakland Tribune Building** (1923), 13th and Franklin St., is a structure built in the classic *Daily Planet* mode. The '89 quake was both good and bad news for the paper. The temblor debilitated the brick tower (closed to the public), but the photo staff won a Pulitzer Prize for its coverage of the disaster. Pick up copies of the *Tribune* (839-3939; 25¢, $1 Sun.) and other newspapers, magazines, and paperbacks at **DeLaver's Super Newsstand,** 1310 Broadway (451-6157; open 24 hrs.). In the hills overlooking the city and the Bay, the pure white **Mormon Temple,** 4770 Lincoln Ave. (531-1475), looks particularly ethereal at night. No one except the Latter Day Saints elite can enter the temple itself, but the grounds are open to the public (daily 9am-9pm). If you hazard the adjacent **visitors center,** prepare to stave off (or succumb to) conversion attempts on your soul's path through eternity.

Jack London Square, named after the author who lived in and wrote about this area, is now an eight-block commercial district on the waterfront. **Jack London Village,** on Alice St. along the Oakland Estuary, was modeled after a turn-of-the-century wharf. **Jack London's Cabin,** at Jack London Square near Webster St., was brought to Oakland from Alaska, where the author prospected for gold in the 1890s, and is testimony to the excessive lengths Oakland goes in paying homage to its native hero. From here you can ride the **Alameda County Ferry** (522-3300) across the Bay to the Financial District or Pier 39 in San Francisco, and back (one way $3.50, seniors $2.50, ages 5-12 $1.50). The city also offers free **Oakland Harbor Tours** (272-1188; May-Aug. Thurs.; 1½hr.; reservations required).

ENTERTAINMENT AND NIGHTLIFE

The **Oakland Athletics** play baseball in the **Oakland Coliseum,** Nimitz Fwy. and Hegenberger Rd. (take the BART to the Coliseum station). For schedules and group tickets information, call 638-0500; for individual tickets, call 762-2277. The NBA's **Golden State Warriors** play in the adjacent **Coliseum Arena** (638-6300).

The **Oakland Symphony** and the **Oakland Ballet** perform in the Paramount. The theater also shows a special foreign film or an old classic every week. In the 1994-95 season, the symphony will perform four different concert programs and three repertory programs. The **Oakland Ballet** also performs several programs, including a not-so-traditional *Nutcracker Suite.* (Call 465-6400 for more information, ticket office open Tues.-Fri. noon-6pm, Sat. noon-5pm.)

Music-filled night spots in Oakland include **Eli's Mile High Club,** 3629 Martin Luther King, Jr. Way (655-6661), named by a little-known French newspaper "the best blues club in the U.S." (Blues bands and vocalists Wed.-Sun. 9 or 9:30pm. Cover $4 Thurs. and Sun., $7-8 Fri.-Sat. but discounts occur as the night progresses.) **The Omni,** 4799 Shattuck Ave. (547-7655), showcases an eclectic collection of rock bands (Fri.-Sun. 8pm). Call for current shows and ticket information. The multicultural **Caribee Dance Center,** 1408 Webster St. (835-4006), plays reggae, calypso, and African music on weekends ($5-10; open Wed.-Sat 9pm-1am, Sun. 8pm-midnight). Finally, **Yoshi's,** 6030 Claremont Ave., at College (652-9200) is an upscale Japanese/Californian restaurant that moonlights as a jazz club. It features nationally and locally known jazz artists, with occasional samba and Latin bands. Cover ranges from $6-12 for local bands and $12-20 for big names.

■■■ SAN JOSE

Everyone seems to want to live in San Jose. It is the fastest growing city in California, thanks to its many assets: outstanding weather year-round, clean streets, classy modern buildings, a booming high-tech industry, a professional sports team, good public transportation, and an excellent location that makes it easy to reach by plane, train, or automobile. Much of San Jose's wealth is a direct result of its position at the heart of the computer chip factory known as the Silicon Valley. Therein lies San Jose's problem. The economic boom that quadrupled San Jose's population in a mere ten years never allowed the city to acquire cultural refinements to match its size. When compared to San Francisco, San Jose is an upstart adolescent. While it is clear why many, many people want to live in San Jose, what the city has to offer visitors is less clear.

PRACTICAL INFORMATION

Visitors Information: Convention and Visitors Bureau, 333 W. San Carlos St.
#1000 (283-8833). Maps (some free, others $1.50-4) and information. The view
from their board room is one of the best in the city. Open Mon.-Fri. 8am-5:30pm,
Sat.-Sun. 11am-5pm.

San Jose International Airport: 1661 Airport Blvd. (277-4759). Serviced by most
major domestic airlines. Driving from I-880, take Coleman Ave. to Airport Blvd.
and turn right; from U.S. 101, take Guadalupe Pkwy. to Airport Pkwy. and turn
right. Or take Santa Clara County Transit Light Rail to Metro/Airport station and
transfer to the Rte. 10 bus.

Amtrak: 65 Cahill Ave. (287-7462; information, 800-USA-RAIL, -872-7245.) To: Los
Angeles ($67) and San Francisco ($9).

CalTrain: 800-660-4287. Operates between San Jose and San Francisco with stops
at Peninsula cities. Operates Mon.-Fri. 5am-10pm, Sat.-Sun. 6am-10pm.

Greyhound: 70 S. Almaden Ave. at Santa Clara (800-231-2222), 2 blocks from
downtown. The station feels reasonably safe, even at night. To L.A. ($29) and San
Francisco ($6). Luggage lockers available (for ticketed passengers only). Open
daily 5am-midnight.

Santa Clara County Transit System: 321-2300. Ultra-modern and air-conditioned. $1.10, ages 5-17 55¢, seniors and disabled 25¢. Day passes cost double
regular fare. Exact change.

Ride Board: San Jose State Student Union (924-6350). Open Mon.-Thurs. 7am-
10pm, Fri. 7am-5pm, Sat. 10am-5pm; summer Mon.-Fri. 8am-4:30pm.

Crisis Lines: Rape Crisis, 287-3000. **Poison Control,** 299-5112. Both 24 hrs.

Hospital: San Jose Medical Center, 675 E. Santa Clara St. at 14th (998-3212).
Emergency room (977-4444) open 24 hrs.

Emergency: 911.

Post Office: 105 N. 1st St. (452-4300), at St. John St. Open Mon.-Fri. 9am-5:30pm.
General Delivery ZIP Code: 95113.

Area Code: 408.

THE WAY TO SAN JOSE

The city is on the southern end of San Francisco Bay. San Jose is centered around the
plaza and mall area near east-west **San Carlos St.** and north-south **Market St.** For
information on reaching San Jose from San Francisco on **CalTrain,** see page 235.
The **Transit Mall,** the center of San Jose's transit system, runs north-south along 1st
and 2nd St. in the downtown area. **San Jose State University's** grassy grounds cover
several blocks between S. 4th and S. 10th St. downtown. The Student Union Information Center stocks transit info.

CAMPING AND ACCOMMODATIONS

There are also county parks with **campgrounds** outside the city. **Mt. Madonna
County Park** has 117 campsites, occupied on a first-come, first-served basis. **Joseph
D. Grant County Park** offers 40 mi. of horse and hiking trails, as well as 20 camp-
sites. Call 358-3751 for information. **RV parks** nearby include Casa de Fruta, 6680
Pacheco Pass Hwy. (637-0051) in Hollister, and Cotillion Gardens, 300 Old Big Trees
Road (335-7669), in Felton. (Full hookup at either about $25.)

Sanborn Park Hostel (HI-AYH), 15808 Sanborn Rd., Sanborn County Park
(741-0166), in Saratoga, 13 mi. west of San Jose. Tricky to reach by bus, call the
hostel for directions. Situated in a big old log building with 39 beds. Surrounded
by redwoods, peaceful, serene and clean. Piano, kitchen. Usually has vacancies.
Open daily 5-11pm. Check-out 9am. Curfew 11pm. $7.50, nonmembers $9.50.

San Jose State University (924-6180), 375 S. 9th St. at San Salvador, Joe West
Hall. Rooms rented in summer. Call before noon. SJSU affiliation not required, but
guests must have some university affiliation. Singles $29. Doubles $42, $21 for
one bed in a double.

Motel 6, 2560 Fontaine Rd. (270-3131). Tully Rd. exit off U.S. 101. Old, but adequate and feels secure. Fills early. Check-in after 1pm. Singles $34. Doubles $38.

Park View Motel, 1140 S. 2nd St. (297-8455). 41 rooms. Kitchenettes; pool. Generally pretty quiet. Check-in after 11am. Check-out 11am. Singles or doubles $35.

FOOD

A **Farmers Market** at the Pavilion, at S. 1st and San Fernando St. sells Brentwood's peaches and the San Joaquin Valley's sweet corn. (Open Thurs. 10am-2pm.) The food places listed here are all in downtown San Jose. Outside the downtown area, the city consists of miles of sprawling suburbia with few attractions for visitors.

Casa Diaz, 43 Post St. (977-0303). Chow down or have a drink with the locals. Complete with Mexican juke box and folk art, this small bar and restaurant serves filling, tasty meals. Lunch specials $4.50. Dinners $6-8. Great sangria (½ liter for $4.50). Open Mon.-Fri. 9am-10pm, Sat.-Sun. 8:30am-10pm.

Sal and Luigi's Pizzeria, 347 S. 1st St. (297-1136). Sal split for Florida 30 years ago, but students still flock here. Medium pizza $8.50. Gnocchi and ravioli $7. Open Tues.-Thurs. 11am-11pm, Fri. 11am-midnight, Sat. noon-midnight, Sun. 4-10pm.

Flo's Bar-B-Que, 154 Post St. at San Pedro (295-2300) behind the bus station. Flo's is a fun and convenient place to enjoy a plate of BBQ chicken ($7.75), or the soup of the day and cornbread ($3). Open Mon.-Tues. 10am-3pm, Wed.-Fri. 10am-3pm and 6pm-midnight, Sat. 6pm-midnight.

White Lotus, 80 N. Market St. at E. Santa Clara St. (977-0540). One of few vegetarian restaurants in the area. Non-vegetarians will enjoy the food too. Try the stir-fried vegetable combo ($5.50) or the spicy tofu ($4.75). Open Tues.-Fri. 11am-2:30pm and 5:30-9pm, Sat. 11am-10pm, Sun. 11am-9pm.

La Guadalajara, 45 Post St. (292-7352). Since 1955 this lunch counter has been serving delicious Mexican food and pastries. Jumbo burritos ($2.50) and combo plates ($4) are a bargain. Open Mon.-Sat. 8am-7pm, Sun. 8am-5pm.

California Kitchen Downtown Diner, 150 S. 1st St. (688-6297) in the Pavillion. For some all-American food, come here to dine with other burger-craving conventioneers, tourists, and business people. Roast beef sandwich $6. Burgers with seasoned fries ($5-7.25). Open Mon-Sat. 11am-7pm, Sun. noon-4pm.

Pho Xe Lua, 155 E. San Fernando St. (289-8323), at 4th St. This lively Vietnamese restaurant looks dubious from the outside, but one step inside will testify to its authenticity. Noodle soup (huge bowl, $4) is their specialty. Veggie special over noodles with spring roll $4.50. Open Sun.-Thurs. 8am-10:30pm, Fri.-Sat. 8am-2am.

La Taquería, 15 S. 1st St. (287-1542). More inexpensive Mexican food downtown. You can taste the authenticity. Savory burritos $3.25. Flour quesadillas $1.50. Open Mon.-Thurs. 11am-5pm, Fri.-Sun. 11am-7pm.

Peking House Restaurant, 84 S. 2nd St. (293-0717), at E. San Fernando St. Pay by the item at this lunch or dinner buffet with typical Chinese food. Up to 8 items for $6.40. Open Mon.-Sat. 10:30am-8pm, Sun. 11am-8pm.

The Old Spaghetti Factory, 51 N. San Pedro St. (288-7488). Includes a 1930s cable car. Meals include salad, bread, pasta, and ice cream. Lunch $3-5, dinner $4-6, beer $1.50. Open Mon.-Thurs. 11:30am-2pm and 5-10pm, Fri. 11:30am-2pm and 5-11pm, Sat. 4:30-11pm, Sun. 11am-10pm.

SIGHTS

Some of San Jose's main attractions are bizarrely intriguing. The **Rosicrucian Museum,** 1342 Naglee Ave. (947-3636), at Park Ave. west of downtown, was founded by the quasi-Egyptian mystical order. This eerie museum displays a collection of mummies and amulets, and a walk-in replica tomb. (Open daily 9am-5pm. $6, students and seniors $4, ages 7-15 $3.50, under 7 free.) The **Rosicrucian Planetarium** (947-3634) interprets the heavens. (Open Mon.-Fri. 9am-5pm. $4, seniors and children $3. Schedules vary, call ahead.) The **Winchester Mystery House,** 1525 S. Winchester Blvd. (247-2101), at I-880 and I-280, west of town, was the home of Sarah Winchester, heir to the rifle fortune. The Victorian estate is filled with oddities: stairs leading to ceilings, doors opening to walls, and tourist traps. Yet, contained in a story of love, death and fear, there is an explanation. Visit to discover the mysterious motive behind Winchester's order that construction continue on her home without cease. (Hours vary. $12.50; seniors $9.50, ages 6-12 $6.50, under 6 free.)

San Jose's finest conventional museum is undoubtedly the **San Jose Museum of Art,** 110 S. Market St. (294-2787), which features changing exhibits on the "Art of Our Time." (Open Wed. and Fri.-Sun. 10am-5pm, Thurs. 10am-8pm. $4, students and seniors $2, under 12 and Thurs. free.)

Originally called "The Garage" in honor of the humble beginnings of such technological powerhouses as Hewlett-Packard and Apple, the **Tech Museum of Innovation,** 145 W. San Carlos St. (279-7150), must not be missed. This is truly a museum of innovation. Intel takes its clients here to explain how computer chips are made from simple silicon. Other exhibits deal with robotics, DNA engineering, new technological developments, and space exploration, including an opportunity to drive the Mars Rover. (Open Tues.-Sun. 10am-5pm. $6; students with ID, seniors, and ages 6-18 $4; under 6 free.)

Just southeast of downtown, Coyote Creek runs through **Kelley Park,** located east of Senter Rd. and mostly south of I-280. Although the world really needs only one San Jose, this park contains an ambitious re-creation of the early city. The **San Jose Historical Museum,** 1600 Senter Rd. (287-2290), at Keyes St., features a 1927 gas station, soda shop, pioneer homes, and a turn-of-the-century doctor's office. (Open Mon.-Fri. 10:30am-4:30pm, Sat.-Sun. noon-4:30pm. $4, seniors $3, ages 6-17 $2, under 6 free. Tours every ½-hr. Mon.-Fri.) The **Happy Hollow Park and Zoo** (292-8188) inside Kelley Park offers kiddie attractions like a play park, rides, puppet shows, and petting zoo. ($2.50, ages 2-14 $2, under 2 free. Call for current hours.) Kelley Park also provides the city with a network of bike paths and a **Japanese Friendship Tea Garden** (287-2290; open daily 10am-sunset).

The oldest standing structure in San Jose is the **Peralta Adobe,** 154 W. Saint John St. (287-2290), built in 1804 by Luis María Peralta, who had received the land—48,000 acres of it—from the King of Spain as a reward for "meritorious service." The adobe sits in a small park occupied by many transients. (Open daily 9am-sunset. Tours given Thurs.-Sun. 11am-4:30pm. $6, seniors $5, children $3.)

Founded in 1857, **San Jose State University (SJSU),** 1 Washington Square (924-3280), is the oldest public college in all of California. The campus is centered on San Carlos and 7th St., east of downtown. For information on campus events, call the 24-hr. events line (924-6350) or, in summer, pick up a copy of the *Summer Times,* a weekly publication of the *Spartan Daily* (924-3280), the campus newspaper.

ENTERTAINMENT AND SEASONAL EVENTS

For information on things to see and do in San Jose, look for *Metro,* published weekly and available free on street corners downtown. The Student Union (924-6350) at SJSU has an amphitheater which often hosts concerts and dramatic performances. Hockey fans may want to check out the **San Jose Sharks,** the city's own NHL team. Call 287-4275 for ticket information.

Toon's, 52 E. Santa Clara at 2nd (292-7464). The hottest place in town among San Jose students. Cheap drinks and nightly live music. $1 well drinks Fri.-Sat. 8-10pm, 50¢ beers Mon.-Thurs. 8-9pm. Bands start playing at 9:30, usually no cover. Open Mon.-Tues. 7pm-2am, Wed.-Fri. 6pm-2am, Sat.-Sun. 8pm-2am.

Katie Bloom's Irish Pub and Restaurant, 108 W. 1st St. (297-4408). It's clear why "pub" comes before "restaurant" in the name and why "Irish" comes before both. Drink $3.50 imported drafts with locals while Oscar Wilde and James Joyce watch from the walls. Happy hour with free snacks Mon.-Fri. 4-7pm. Bar food Mon.-Fri. 11am-3pm and 6-9pm. Open Mon.-Fri. 11am-2am, Sat.-Sun. 2pm-2am.

Dos Locos, 150 S. 1st St. in the Pavillion (993-9616), is one of the newest bars in San Jose and has already attracted a devoted college student and local following. Famous for 32-oz. schooner margaritas, $6.50. Live music on Sun. 4:30-8pm. Happy hour Mon.-Fri. 4-7pm. Open daily noon-2am.

San Jose Live, 150 S. 1st St. (291-2222), downtown. The largest club in the city. S.J. Live is an adult's Chuck E. Cheese with 4 bars (including a piano bar), pool tables, a basketball area, dartboards, an arcade, a snack bar, and a comedy stage. You get the idea. Happy hours (daily 4-7pm) offer mean drinks and appetizers for $1. Open Mon.-Sat. 11:30am-2am, Sun. 11:30am-midnight.

Gordon Biersch, 33 E. San Fernando St. (294-6785). California cuisine with a twist (goat cheese tamales $8.25) and excellent beers brewed on the premises ($3 for a half-liter) make fighting your way through throngs of yuppies worth it. Live jazz Tues.-Sat. at 9pm, Sun. at 2pm. Open Sun.-Wed. 11am-11pm, Thurs. 11am-midnight, Fri.-Sat. 11am-1am.

The annual **Blues Festival** (924-6261) in May is the site of the largest free blues concert in Northern California.

■ NEAR SAN JOSE: SANTA CLARA

This commercially focused small town is a worthy a visit only as the site of Mission Santa Clara and Paramount Great America theme park. To reach Santa Clara, take U.S. 101 to the De La Cruz exit and follow the signs to the Santa Clara University.

Mission Santa Clara was the first California mission to honor a woman—Clare of Assisi—as its patron saint. Initially located in 1771 on the Guadalupe River, it moved to its present site in 1825. In 1851, **Santa Clara University** was established in the old mission buildings. The beautiful historic structures have been restored several times and are surrounded by a rose garden, trellises, and 200-year-old olive trees. For more information, call 554-4023. (Church offices open Mon.-Fri. 1-5pm.)

Paramount's Great America theme park (988-1800), on U.S. 101, is one of the nation's largest. (Park open Easter week and June-Aug. Sun.-Fri. 10am-9pm, Sat. 10am-11pm.; April-May and Sept. Sat.-Sun. 10am-11pm. $26, over 54 $19, ages 3-6 $13. Parking $4.) **Raging Waters** (270-8000 or 238-9900), 1½ mi. east of U.S. 101 at the Tully Rd. exit, is the area's best collection of waterslides. (Open daily May-Sept. 10am-7pm. $17, under 42 in. $13.)

■■■ PALO ALTO

Palo Alto has almost enough bookstores to be a proper college town, but the profusion of imported cars, dealers in fine tapestries, and Volvo-driving police tell another story. Much of the city's wealth is due to its position as a corporate adjunct of Silicon Valley, home to Hewlett-Packard and other prominent high-tech firms. In spite of the world-wide prominence of Silicon Valley, it is Stanford University that really puts Palo Alto on the map. (Come to think of it, Hewlett-Packard started in the garage of two young Stanford graduates who wanted to settle near their alma mater.) Just as Palo Alto is not your typical college town, Stanford is not your typical university. Stanford is a study of contrasts; often referred to as "the other Ivy," this private, internationally acclaimed university is also nicknamed "The Farm" and its students enjoy year round sun, dressed in shorts and sandals. (Is it any wonder that academics accustomed to the frozen land of New England sometimes have trouble taking Stanford seriously?) Nonetheless, Stanford is graced with a superb faculty, active and bright students, perfectly groomed grounds, a picturesque lake, and a bulging endowment. Yet, somehow Stanford falls just short of its biggest eastern rivals and seems eternally doomed to the title "the Harvard of the West."

PRACTICAL INFORMATION

Stanford University Information Booth: Front of the **Main Quad** (723-2560); open daily 10am-4pm. Student lead tours leave every day at 11am and 3:15pm; times vary on holidays and during exams.

CalTrain: 95 University Ave. at Alma St. (323-6105) in Palo Alto and at Stanford Stadium on Embarcadero Rd. (no phone). Toll-free information, call 800-660-4297. To San Francisco $3.25 and San Jose $4.50. Half-price for seniors and people with disabilities. Operates Mon.-Fri. 5am-11pm, Sat.-Sun. 6am-11pm.

samTrans: 367-1500. Regular service to San Francisco ($1.75), San Francisco International Airport 85¢, and to Hayward BART Station 85¢.

Santa Clara County Transit: 408-321-2300. Operates in Palo Alto and to points south. Fare $1 (50¢ Mon.-Fri. 9am-2:30pm), ages 5-17 50¢, seniors and disabled 25¢.

Marguerite Shuttle: 723-4375. Free bus service around Stanford University. Mon.-Fri. 6am-6pm. Serves the Palo Alto CalTrain during commute hours.

Car Rental: Budget Rent-A-Car, 4230 El Camino Real (493-6000), out-of-town reservations 800-527-0770. Mid-size cars $31 per day and up with unlimited mileage. Credit card required. Open Mon.-Fri. 8am-5pm, Sat.-Sun. 8am-2pm.

AAA Emergency Road Service: 595-3411. 24 hrs. For AAA members only.

Taxi: Century Taxi Service, 579-2552. 24 hrs.

Bike Rental: Campus Bike Shop, 551 Salvatierra (325-2945), in Stanford, across from the Law School. 3-speeds $5 with same-day return. $8 overnight. Mountain bikes $10 same-day, $20 overnight. Helmets $1 per day. Requires a major credit card or $150-300 cash deposit. Open Mon.-Fri. 9am-5pm, Sat. 9am-3pm.

Tickets: Tressider Memorial Union on the Stanford campus, 725-ARTS for events at Stanford University and in the San Francisco Bay Area. For athletic events, Stanford Dept. of Athletics (723-1021). Office staffed 9am-4pm.

Campus Events: Tressider Memorial Union (723-4311). Open Mon.-Fri. 8:30am-10pm, Sat.-Sun. 10am-10pm; summer Mon.-Fri. 10am-4pm. Closed on holidays. 24-hr. hotline (723-0336).

Emergency: 911 (9-911 from Stanford University telephones).

Palo Alto Police: 275 Forest Ave. (329-2406).

Post Office: Main Office, 2085 E. Bayshore Rd. (321-4310). Open Mon.-Fri. 8:30am-5pm. **General Delivery ZIP Code:** 94303. Stanford University branch, White Plaza (322-0059). Open Mon.-Fri. 9am-5pm.

Area Code: 415.

ORIENTATION AND GETTING AROUND

Palo Alto is 35 mi. southeast of San Francisco near the southern shore of San Francisco Bay. From San Francisco take U.S. 101 south to the University Ave. exit and turn left; or split off to I-280 (the Junipero Serra Hwy.) for a slightly longer but much more scenic route. From I-280 get off at Sand Hill Rd. and follow it to Willow Rd. and the northwest corner of Stanford University. Regional and local bus service and CalTrain rail service is consolidated at the Palo Alto **Transit Center** at the southern end of University Ave., across from the Stanford Shopping Center.

By public transportation, take **samTrans** bus #7F from the Transbay Terminal in San Francisco, from Mission St. between 1st and 9th, or from the San Francisco Airport. Get off at the Stanford Shopping Center or any point thereafter. (Fare $1.75, over 65 at off-peak hours 85¢, ages 7-17 85¢, under 7 free with an adult.) The bus runs every hour from 5am-8am and from 7pm-1am, every half hour during the day, and every 10 minutes from 2:30 to 7pm. Or take MUNI bus #15, 30, 42, or 45 to the **Caltrain station** at 4th and Townsend St. in San Francisco. Trains leave every one or two hours. The **Palo Alto train station** (323-6105; open daily 5am-12:30am) is on University Ave. between El Camino Real and Alma St., while the **California Ave. station** (326-3392; open 5:30am-12:30am) is 1¼ mi. south. The Stanford Shopping Center is connected to points south by **San Mateo County buses** and to the Stanford Campus by the free **Marguerite University Shuttle** (723-4375; runs every 10 mi; Mon.-Fri. 6am-6pm).

ACCOMMODATIONS

Motels are plentiful along El Camino Real, but they're a bit steep (average single $40). The hotels' rates vary in inverse proportion to their distance from Stanford. More reasonably priced accommodations can be found farther north, on El Camino Real towards Redwood City. University housing is a cheaper alternative. Residence halls are available from June 25 to September 16 (singles $33, doubles $48; those under 18 must be accompanied by an adult). Call the **Conference Office** (723-3126) for information. (Open Mon.-Fri. 8am-noon and 1-5pm.)

Hidden Villa Ranch Hostel (HI-AYH), 26870 Moody Rd. 94022 (949-8648), about 10 mi. southwest of Palo Alto in Los Altos Hills. Working ranch and farm in a wilderness preserve. The first hostel on the Pacific Coast. 28 beds. Open daily 4:30-9pm Sept.-May (closed in the summer). $8, nonmembers $11.

Motel 6, 4301 El Camino Real (949-0833). Old Reliable has set up shop close to "The Farm." Always full; call far in advance. Singles $40. Doubles $46. In winter, singles $36, doubles $42. **Another branch** at 806 Ahwanee Ave. (408-720-1222), in Sunnyvale, 7 mi. south of Palo Alto. Singles $33. Doubles $39. Both with pools.

Coronet Motel, 2455 El Camino Real (326-1081). Clean and roomy, with big windows. Swimming pool. Check-out 11am. Singles $38. Doubles $42. The beds have "magic finger" massage mattresses (25¢ for 15 min.).

FOOD

If you decide to eat out in Palo Alto, you will most likely end up dining in one of the many establishments that line University Avenue and El Camino Real. A number of these allow you to feast heartily without sacrificing your budget.

Mango Cafe, 483 University Ave. (325-3229). Caribbean cuisine. *Very* spicy Jamaican "jerked joints" ($5.50). Vegetarian options. The vegetable *roti* ($5) is a delicious curried dish from Trinidad. Open daily 11:30am-8:30pm.

Saint Michael's Art Café, 806 Emerson St. (329-1727). During the day, hearty and wholesome food is served in a relaxed atmosphere with art on the walls. Live music or poetry readings add to the ambience at night. Kids are welcome too. Fresh muffins and scones. Sandwiches on freshly baked bread $4-4.75. Pizzas $5.

The Coffee House, Tressider Union (723-3592), at Stanford. Recent renovations have brightened this popular student hangout. Join the crowds who go to the "coho" for some "fro-yo." Sandwiches, burritos, and salad $3-4. Live music every Thurs.-Sat. at 9:30pm, no cover. During the school year, the Fri.-Sat. "study hall" features beer for $1.50 per pint. Happy hour Mon.-Fri. 4-6pm with $1.50 pints. Open Mon.-Fri. 8am-midnight, Sat.-Sun. 10am-midnight. Tressider Union also houses counters selling salads and Chinese and Mexican food.

Peninsula Fountain and Grill, 566 Emerson at Hamilton (323-3131). Since 1923, this Palo Alto diner has delighted devoted customers with burgers ($4.25) and turkey pot pie dinners ($8.25). Peninsula Creamery supplies the ice cream (1 scoop $1.35). The towering homemade apple pie contains 4 lbs. of apples ($3 per slice). Open Mon.-Wed. 7am-10pm, Thurs. 7am-11pm, Fri. 7am-midnight, Sat. 8am-midnight, Sun. 8am-10pm.

Fresh Choice, 180 El Camino Real (322-6995). This reliable chain provides good, fresh food in all-you-can-eat style. Breads, salads, pasta, and more. Lunch $6.09, dinner $7.09. Ages under 13 half-price. Ages over 54 get 10% off.

Andalé Taquería, 209 University Ave. (323-2939). Tacos which require a knife and fork to appreciate fully ($2.25), as well as sangría made fresh daily ($1.50 for a glass, $5 for a pitcher). Taco salad in a tostada shell $5. Rotisserie chicken too. Open Mon.-Sat. 11am-10pm, Sun. 11am-9pm.

Cafe Borrone, 1010 El Camino Real at the Menlo Center in Menlo Park (327-0830). Popular with Palo Alto's yuppies and Stanford students. Indoor and outdoor seating, adjacent to a well-stocked bookstore. Coffees ($1-3) and heavenly frosted mochas ($3.50) are the specialties. Sandwiches and salads from $2.25-8. Open Mon.-Fri. 7am-11pm, Sat. 9am-11pm, Sun. 9am-5pm.

Frankie, Johnny, and Luigi's Too, 939 El Camino Real (967-5384), between Bailey and Castro in Mountain View. Good pizza, favored by Stanford students for 38 years. Medium hand-tossed, New York-style pizza $10. Open Mon.-Thurs. 11am-midnight, Fri.-Sat. 11am-1am, Sun. 1pm-midnight.

The Oasis Beer Garden, 241 El Camino Real (326-8896), in Menlo Park. "Burgahs" the way they were meant to be ($4), plus a huge selection of beer (pints start at $1.50). The classic Stanford hangout. Open daily 11am-1:30am.

Noah's Bagels, 278 University Ave. (473-0751). Bagel sandwiches $1.35-5.75. Open Mon.-Thurs. 7am-7pm, Sat. 7:30am-9pm, Sun. 7:30am-5pm.

Whole Foods Market, 774 Emerson (326-8666) at Homer. The new wave of California supermarkets, with organic produce, a bakery, juice and espresso bar, grill, deli, meat department (no nitrates), and bulk goods. Store open daily 9am-10pm. Bakery open daily 8am-10pm.

SIGHTS

More than anything else, Palo Alto is the home of **Stanford University.** The university was founded in 1885 as a secular, co-educational school by Jane and Leland Stanford in honor of their 16-year-old son Leland Jr., who died of typhoid on a family trip to Italy. The Stanfords' love of Spanish architecture and their collaboration with Frederick Olmsted, designer of New York City's Central Park, combined to create an red-tiled campus of uncompromising beauty. (Bitter Berkeley students sometimes refer to Stanford as "the World's Largest Taco Time.") Classes began at "The Farm" in 1891.

A few years ago, the undergraduates successfully lobbied the administration to abandon a core curriculum centered around "Western Civilization" in favor of something less "Eurocentric". In spite of the change, the Hoover Institution remains a bastion of right-wing thought, and the Law School has produced such conservatives as Chief Justice William Rehnquist. The university has also been an important high-tech center ever since two alumni named Hewlett and Packard decided to set up shop near their alma mater, thus giving birth to Silicon Valley.

The oldest part of the campus is the colonnaded **Main Quadrangle,** the site of most undergraduate classes. Surrounding the open area of the Quadrangle is the beginning of a ring of diamond-shaped, gold-numbered stone tiles. These mark the locations of time capsules put together by each year's graduating class. Over the years, planners have found little occasion to depart from the basic scheme of sandstone walls and red-tile roofs, leaving the campus remarkably unified. Campus **information** is available at the entrance to the quad and in Tressider Union.

Stanford is too big to see on foot. The free **Marguerite Shuttle** connects the far-flung university (Mon.-Fri. 6am-6pm, every 10 min.). However, a better way to see the campus is by bicycle. You can rent a bicycle from **Campus Bike Shop** (325-2945; see Practical Information, page 299). With its flat boulevards, long distances, and path-filled rolling hills, Stanford is a fantastic place to ride a bike. The vast majority of students own them, leading to term-time bicycle traffic jams and accidents, especially at the notorious "corner of death" near the center of campus. Bike theft is a persistent problem; use a lock.

Tours of the campus leave from the Serra St. entrance to the quadrangle daily at 11am and 3:15pm, and last for one hour (free). Groups of ten or more need reservations. The student guides are entertaining and skilled at walking backwards around the campus, and the tour is fairly comprehensive. For information, call 723-2053 or 723-2560. **Memorial Church** (723-1762), in the Central Quad, is a gold shrine with glittering mosaic walls like those of an Eastern Orthodox church (it is, however, non-denominational). The church lost its tower in the 1906 earthquake and was repaired *sans* tower. The fierce 1989 quake damaged the church anew, but it has been completely restored to its original glory. Thankfully, neither quake harmed its elegant stained glass windows. East of the Main Quad is the **Art Gallery** (723-4177), which usually displays temporary exhibits, but is now showing works from the Stanford Museum's permanent collection while that facility is being repaired. (Open Tues.-Fri. 10am-5pm, Sat.-Sun. 1-5pm, closed during portions of Aug. and Sept.; free) Beyond the gallery, the observation deck of the **Hoover Tower** (723-2053 or 723-2560) offers views of the red-roof campus, the east bay, and a distant San Francisco. (Open daily 9am-6:30pm. $1, over 65 and under 13 50¢, families $2.50.)

Hiking trails are located at the point where Campus Drive meets Junipero Serra Blvd. The area is known by the locals as "The Dish," the summit of which affords a spectacular view of Palo Alto, the Peninsula, and the bay. For information call Stanford Campus Information (723-2560). Make an appointment to see the **Stanford Linear Accelerator Center** (926-2204; tours held once or twice a week; call ahead). Graduate students lead the presentation that includes a bus tour of the facilities and a slide show, all geared toward explaining the fearsome mystery of the **quark.**

The **Stanford University Museum of Art** (723-3469), on Museum Way off Palm Ave., halfway between the Main Quad and El Camino Real, has been closed indefinitely for earthquake-related repairs. Normally, its hours are the same as the Art Gallery's (above). The museum is still worth a visit to see the **Rodin Sculpture Garden,** spread across the lawn. The collection contains a stunning bronze cast of the *Gates of Hell,* along with many other larger figures. Only Paris has a finer Rodin collection but with the recent addition of 35 sculptures, Stanford may soon challenge that claim (open year-round; free).

Off-campus, the incredibly kitschy **Barbie Doll Hall of Fame,** 443 Waverley St.(326-5841), 2nd floor, off University Ave., has over 16,000 Barbie and Ken dolls. The dolls date back to 1959 and follow a chronological history of fashion, including Hippie Barbie and Benetton Barbie. (Open Tues.-Fri. 1:30-4:30pm, Sat. 10am-noon and 1:30-4:30pm. $4.)

ENTERTAINMENT

The *Stanford Weekly,* put out by the *Stanford Daily* (723-2554), contains listings of what's going on all over campus. The *Palo Alto Weekly* (362-8210), distributed around town, has similar listings.

Dinkelspiel Auditorium (723-2448), on campus. Silly name, but great concerts year-round. Tickets available at Tressider Ticket Office in the Tressider Union (723-4317). Open Mon.-Fri. 10am-4pm.

Memorial Auditorium, (723-5758) on campus. Movies on Sun. during the term ($1 for students, $3 general public). Mostly recent hits at "Flicks," though the occasional miralor classic makes the slate.

The New Varsity, 456 University Ave. (323-6411 for movies). Set in the colonnaded courtyard of an old hotel reminiscent of the '20s. Theater features superb off-the-beaten-track films, as well as the *Rocky Horror Picture Show* every Sat. at midnight. $6.75, seniors and under 12 $3.75. First matinee $3.75. Reservations recommended.

The Stanford Theatre, 221 University Ave. (324-3700). Dedicated to Hollywood's "Golden Age." Hitchcock and the Marx Brothers are regulars. Double features $6, seniors $4, children $3. Wurlitzer organ plays before and after the 7:30pm show.

The Edge, 260 California Ave. (324-3343), 2 blocks east of El Camino Real. The students' favorite for live rock music (cover and days vary). Shows usually begin at 9:15pm. Cheap tables and chairs; carpet smells of stale beer. Anyone over 18 welcome, but ages 18-20 must pay a higher cover charge. Sunday is "teen night."

British Banker's Club, Menlo Center in Menlo Park (327-8769). Located at the site of the Old City Hall and Public Library, nightlife inside this vintage Edwardian bar is swarming. Stained glass windows, an Egyptian sarcophagus, library books, and portraits adorn the walls which reach up to an impressive 25-ft.-high ceiling. The crowd varies, representing all ages. Open daily 11:30am-2am.

BOOKSTORES AND SHOPPING

Within walking distance of Stanford are two expensive shopping malls: the **Stanford Shopping Center,** where the Marguerite University Shuttle and the San Francisco samTrans bus stop, and the flower-festooned **Stanford Barn,** where Leland, Sr. once kept his horses. The **North Face Factory Outlet,** 217 Alma St. (325-3231), has marked-down prices for camping equipment and clothing. (Open Mon.-Sat. 10am-8pm, Sun. 11am-6pm.)

The Stanford Bookstore (329-1217), on campus, just southeast of the Main Quad. The 2nd largest college bookstore in the country. Impressive selection of textbooks and general books, plus T-shirts and other insignia items. Café upstairs.

Campus outlet open Mon.-Fri. 7:45am-9pm, Sat. 9am-6pm, Sun. 11m-5pm. Branch at 135 University Ave. in town (327-3680) houses medical, technical, and computer sections. Open Mon.-Fri. 9am-9pm, Sat. 10am-6pm, Sun. 11am-6pm.

Chimaera Books and Records, 165 University Ave. (327-1122). Superb selection of new and used poetry books. Used CDs are $10, $2.50 with an exchange. Open Mon. 10am-11pm, Tues.-Sat. 10am-midnight, Sun. 11am-10pm.

Bell's Books, 536 Emerson St. (323-7822). One of the oldest bookstores in town and worthy of the honor—the whole place smells of books. Walls are stacked from floor to ceiling with new and used. Superb horticultural section. The major drawback is that the first floor has very high ceilings, and of the 15 shelves of books, you can see only eight. Open Mon.-Fri. 9:30am-5:30pm, Sat. 9:30am-5pm.

Kepler's Books, Menlo Center (324-4321), in Menlo Park. The mother of all bookstores. Vast, well-organized selection of paperbacks, hardcovers, and magazines from around the world. Open Sun.-Thurs. 9am-11pm, Fri.-Sat. 9am-midnight.

Printers Inc. Bookstore, 310 California Ave. (327-6500). Huge, airy bookstore with an eclectic selection of books and magazines. Large, airy café next door. Variety of gay and lesbian literature, plus a good selection of periodicals, including foreign newspapers. Open daily 9am-11pm.

■■■ THE SAN MATEO COAST

South of San Francisco, cut off from the encroaching Bay Area sprawl by low mountains running along the coast, you'll find the scenic heart of San Mateo County. The geography here is mild; the cliffs are relatively low, and the land is under cultivation. The beaches of the county lie a world away from the clutter of San Francisco, San Jose, and Santa Cruz. Instead of the bustle of large cities, you'll find charming old towns like Half Moon Bay, San Gregorio, and Pescadero complete with country stores and bakeries still run by the same families who began the business years ago.

PRACTICAL INFORMATION AND ORIENTATION

San Mateo County Coast Convention and Visitors Center, Seabreeze Plaza, 111 Anza Blvd., Suite 410 (800-28-VISIT, -84748), in Burlingame by the San Francisco International Airport. Ask for other pamphlets besides those on display. Open Mon.-Fri. 8:30am-5pm. **Half Moon Bay Coastside Chamber of Commerce,** 520 Kelly Ave. (726-8380). Open Mon.-Fri. 10am-4pm.

San Mateo County Transit (samTrans), 945 California Dr. (800-660-4287). Service from Burlingame (adjacent to San Francisco) to Half Moon Bay. Fare 85¢, seniors and disabled 25¢, ages 5-17 35¢. Monthly passes $29, seniors and disabled $10, ages 5-17 $13. Operates daily 6am-7pm.

Car Rental: Bob Leech's Auto Rental, 435 S. Airport Blvd. (583-3844). Sub-compact $20 per day with 150 free mi. 10¢ per additional mi. Must be 23 with credit card. Open Mon.-Fri. 8am-9pm, Sat.-Sun. 9am-4pm.

AAA Emergency Road Service: 595-3411. 24 hrs. For AAA members only.

Bicycle Rental: The Bicyclery, 432 Main St. in Half Moon Bay. Bikes $6 per hr., $24 per day. Open Mon.-Fri. 9:30am-6:30pm, Sat. 10am-5pm, Sun. 11am-5pm.

Public Library: San Mateo County Library Half Moon Bay Branch, 620 Correas (726-2316). Mon.-Wed. 10am-3pm, Thurs. 1-6pm, Fri. 10am-6pm, Sat. 10am-5pm.

Laundromat: Kelly Street Laundry, 650 Kelly St. at Main St. in Half Moon Bay. Wash $1.25, 10-min. dry 25¢. Open daily 7am-9:30pm.

Crisis Line: 368-6655

Hospital: San Mateo County General Hospital, 222 W. 39th Ave. (573-2222).

Emergency: 911.

Sheriff: 401 Marshall (363-4000), in Redwood City.

Post Office: 500 Stone Pine Rd. at Main St. (726-5517). **General Delivery ZIP Code:** 94019. Open Mon.-Fri. 8:30am-5pm, Sat. 8:30am-noon.

Area Code: 415.

On this stretch of the Pacific coast, a car is the best way to go. Stunning ocean views compete with **Rte. 1** (the Pacific Coast Hwy.) for drivers' attention. If you're traveling by sneaker, you'll have a tougher time; **samTrans** services the area only somewhat successfully (see above for fare information). Bus route maps are available at most CalTrain and BART stations. The shore from Pacifica to Half Moon Bay is serviced by buses #1C, 1L, and 90H. The 1L runs from the Daly City BART to Half Moon Bay (Mon.-Fri. 6am-midnight, Sat. 6am-4pm, Sun. 9am-6pm). The 90H runs from San Mateo every hour (Mon.-Fri. 8am-6pm, Sat. 9am-4pm).

ACCOMMODATIONS AND CAMPING

Pigeon Point Lighthouse Hostel (HI-AYH) (879-0633), 6 mi. south of Pescadero on the highway and 20 mi. south of Half Moon Bay, near the lighthouse (the second-tallest on the West Coast). Limited samTrans service is available; call the hostel for information. Biking down the Bikecentennial trail, and driving are practical means of getting there. (Some hostel guests hitchhike but, as we've said before, *Let's Go* does not recommend hitchhiking.) An absolutely breathtaking location. This 50-bed hostel operates a hot tub in the old lightkeeper's quarters. The beds are spread about between four houses; each house has a big, homey common room. Check-in 4:30-9:30pm. Quiet time and doors locked at 11pm. Check-out and chores completed by 9:30am. Hostel closed 9:30am-4:30pm. Dorm-style beds $9-11, nonmembers $12-14. Call ahead for reservations, especially in summer. 3 women's and 3 men's beds are held on first-come, first-served basis.

Point Montara Lighthouse Hostel (HI-AYH) (728-7177). Wholesome 45-bed facility on windswept Lighthouse Point 25 mi. south of San Francisco, 4 mi. north of Half Moon Bay. There's a samTrans stop one block north at 14th St. and Rte. 1 (#1C, 1L, 90H). Two kitchens. Bikes and hot tubs ($5 per hr.) for rent. Laundry, $1 to wash and 25¢ to dry. Check-in 4:30-9:30pm. Curfew and quiet hours 11pm-7am. $9, nonmembers $12. $5 extra for couple's room. Reservations recommended for weekends, group and private rooms.

Francis Beach at **Half Moon Bay State Beach,** 95 Kelly Ave. (726-6238) has beachside camp sites. 56 campsites. Most sites have a fire pit and picnic table. The park is open 24 hrs. Cold showers. Check-out at noon. Tent sites $14 per night, over 61 $12. Hike/bike sites $3. Dogs $1. No reservations.

Butano State Park (879-0173), 5 mi. south of Pescadero. From the north, turn off Rte. 1 and travel east on Pescadero Rd.; turn right on Cloverdale. From the south take Gazos Creek Road off Rte. 1 to Cloverdale. Extensive paths lace through the tall, lush redwood forests of the Santa Cruz Mountains. 20 drive-in and 19 walk-in camping sites. No showers. Check-out noon. Cars $5, sites $14 per night. No reservations available from Memorial Day-Labor Day. Otherwise, make reservations through MISTIX (800-444-7275).

San Mateo County Memorial Park, 9500 Pescadero Rd. (879-0212). 9½ mi. east of Rte. 1 on Pescadero Rd. This thickly wooded camping area has 163 sites, all with picnic tables and fire pits. Popular with car campers. Showers. No pets or hookups. $10 per vehicle.

FOOD

Despite the area's remote feel, there are a surprising number of restaurants catering to hungry travelers. Those looking for a late night snack or planning to picnic along the coast can find a 24-hr. **Safeway** at the junction of Rtes. 1 and 92.

Half Moon Bay

3 Amigos, 200 N. Cabrillo Hwy. (Rte. 1), at Kelly Ave. (726-6080). Nearly everyone in the area wholeheartedly recommends this restaurant and its savory Mexican fare. Casual atmosphere is perfect for a meal after a day beach combing. Quesadillas $1. Jumbo vegetarian burrito $3. Open daily 9am-midnight.

The Flying Fish Grill, 99 San Mateo Road (712-1125), on Rte. 92 close to Rte. 1 at the southwest corner of Main St. An inexpensive, tasty way to sample the delicious seafood of the coast. Fishburger and fries ($4.25) or a pint of clam chowder ($4.25) will satisfy a seafarer's appetite. Open Wed.-Sun. 11am-7pm.

Moss Beach Distillery Restaurant (728-5595), off Rte. 1 at Beachway and Ocean Blvd., 2 mi. north of Half Moon Bay. Bar and restaurant with a fantastic ocean view. Not fancy, but expensive—remember you're paying for the view too. A possibility for a special treat. Seafood, pastas, and steaks. Entrees $10-20. Opens Mon.-Fri. 11:30am, Sat. 11am, Sun. 10am. Closes "whenever."

Healing Moon Natural Foods Market and Café, 523 Main St. (726-7881). Endearing health food store has several tables where you can enjoy organic soups (huge bowl $3.75) and Suzanne's Dynamite Cookies ($1.25). Suzanne offers springtime herb walks through the coastal, canyon, or redwood regions around Half Moon Bay. Call 726-7190 for info. Store hours Mon.-Sat. 10am-6pm, Sun. 11am-5pm. Café hours Mon.-Sat. 11am-4pm.

Cinha's Country Grocery, 448 Main St. (726-4071), at Kelly. Stop by this 75-year-old family grocery store and experience shopping as it was in days long gone. Open daily 8am-8pm.

South of Half Moon Bay

Ketch Joanne Fish Market & Captain's Deck (728-7850), at Pillar Point Harbor. Delicious and affordable grilled seafood. Salmon fillet with salad, rice, veggies, and bread $8.50. Outdoor seating available. The market sells wonderful smoked salmon. The smoked salmon cheeks ($4 per lb.) are a great deal. They'll also smoke what you catch for $2 per lb. Restaurant open Mon.-Thurs. 11am-5pm, Fri.-Sun. 11am-9pm. Market open Mon.-Thurs. 10am-7pm, Fri.-Sun. 10am-8pm.

Arcangeli Grocery Co. and **Norm's Market,** 287 Stage Rd. (879-0147) in Pescadero. Established in 1929 by the present owner's grandfather, this grocery store has a full meat and deli department, wine, and an outstanding bakery. Loaves $1.50-4. Try the garlic herb artichoke bread. Also sells partially baked breads so you can enjoy fresh-from-the-oven bread in your own kitchen. Pastry selection includes heavenly blueberry scones. Open Mon.-Sat. 10am-7pm, Sun. 10am-6pm.

San Gregorio General Store, 7615 Stage Rd. (726-0565), 1 mi. east of Rte. 1 on Rte. 84, 8 mi. south of Half Moon Bay, has served the fishing and farming town of San Gregorio since 1889. This wonderfully unusual store sells hardware, cold drinks, candy, groceries, gourmet coffee, cast iron pots, candles…you name it. Have a beer ($2) at the bar or stop in for a fresh sandwich ($3). When Beth's there, her café serves giant burritos. Open Sat.-Thurs. 9am-6pm, Fri. 9am-7pm.

SIGHTS AND ACTIVITIES

Route 1, the **Pacific Coast Highway** winds along the San Mateo County Coast from San Francisco to the Big Basin Redwoods State Park. This expanse of shore is scattered with beautiful, isolated, sandy beaches. Although most people find it too cold for swimming (even in summer), the sands offer a royal stroll along the water's edge. State beaches charge $4, with admission valid for the entire day at all state parks—keep your receipt. About 2 mi. south of Pacifica (take samTrans bus #1L) is **Gray Whale Cove State Beach,** a privately owned nudist beach off Rte. 1. You must be 18 and pay $5 to join the fun (but where do you keep your ID?).

Continuing south on Rte. 1, stop by **Pillar Point Harbor,** 4 mi. north of Half Moon Bay and absorb some of the local color. Sample smoked salmon, chat with fishermen, or try your hand at reeling in the big ones with **Captain John's Fishing Trips** (726-2913 or 728-3377) at the harbor. Trips leave daily at 7:30am and return at 3pm (tickets $32, seniors and under 13 $27; weekends $34; check-in 6:30am). Special trips go to the **Farallon Islands.** There are also seasonal salmon fishing trips. (1-day fishing license $5.50; rod and reel rental $5; tackle and bait $5.75.) The **Sea Horse Ranch** and the **Friendly Acres Ranch** (726-2362 or 726-9903), 1 mi. north of Half Moon Bay on Rte. 1, have 200 horses and ponies between them to take on trails and on the beach. A one-hour trail ride costs $22 (open 8am-6:30pm).

Half Moon Bay is an old coastal community 29 mi. south of San Francisco. Locals complain that it's becoming too commercialized but visitors won't notice the change. Half Moon Bay still feels like the small, easy-going beach town it is.

The fishing and farming hamlet of **San Gregorio** rests 10 mi. south of Half Moon Bay. **San Gregorio Beach** is a delightful destination; walk to its southern end to find little caves in the shore rocks. A stream runs into the sea, and may prove a comfortable alternative to dipping in the chillier ocean. (Open 8am-sunset. Day use $4, seniors $3.) To find a less frequented beach, visit **Unsigned Turnout, Marker 27.35.** State-owned but undeveloped, this stretch of beach is located between San Gregorio and Pomponio State Beaches, off Rte. 1.

The historic little town of **Pescadero** was established by white settlers in 1856 after being inhabited by the Ohlone Indians. During the Spanish period, the area was named Pescadero ("fisherman's town") due to the abundance of fish in both the oceans and creeks. Wander through the old town or participate in a local sport, **olallieberry gathering.** This popular pastime originated a couple decades ago when the olallieberry (oh-la-la-BEHR-ree) was created by crossing a blackberry, a loganberry, and a youngberry. Get a-pickin' and pay by the pound at **Phipp's Ranch,** 2700 Pescadero Rd. (879-0787) in Pescadero. (Open mid-June-Aug. 1 10am-7pm. Strawberries, blackberries, olallieberries, and boysenberries 85¢ per lb. Organic raspberries $2 per lb.) **Pigeon Point** (879-0852) takes its name from a hapless schooner that crashed into the rocky shore on its inaugural voyage in 1853. The point turns heads with its tidepools, wave-washed rocks at Pebble Beach, and 30-ft. plumes of surf. The **Pescadero Marsh** shelters various migratory birds including the elegant blue heron, often seen poised on its spindly legs searching for luckless, soon to be lifeless, fish.

Año Nuevo State Reserve (379-0595), 7 mi. south of Pigeon Point and 27 mi. south of Half Moon Bay, is the mating place of the 18-ft.-long **elephant seal.** December to April is breeding season, when males compete for beach space next to the more pleasingly hideous females. It is not unusual for 2000 seals to crowd on the beach together. To see this unforgettable show (Dec. 15-Mar. 31), you must make reservations (8 weeks in advance recommended) by calling MISTIX (800-444-7275), since access to the park is limited. Tickets go on sale November 15 and are generally sold out by the end of the month, so plan ahead (2½-hr. guided tours, $2 per person, 8am-sunset). samTrans runs a special bus to the reserve from the Hillsdale Shopping Center in San Mateo from December through March; call 348-7325 for information. From April to November the reserve is open and free (parking $4). You will need a hiking permit from the park ranger, however. Arrive before mid-August to catch the last of the "molters" and the young who've yet to find their sea-legs. Don't get too close—they may be fat but they're fast, and mothers are intolerant of strangers who appear to threaten their young. The beach is cold and windy regardless of season, so dress warmly. (Open daily 8am-6pm; last permits issued 4pm.)

Just across the highway from Año Nuevo is **Coastways Ranch,** 640 Rte. 1 (879-0414), another olallieberry-picking spot in June and July. Select a pumpkin in October and in November and December harvest kiwis and Christmas trees.

SEASONAL EVENTS

Brew-Ha-Ha (726-7416), early June, Half Moon Bay. Allows you to slurp more than 50 different beers.

Coastside County Fair (726-5202), mid-June-mid-July. Crafts, livestock, and a junior rodeo. (*Let's Go* does not recommend that children ride broncos.)

Chili Cook-off/Chowder Challenge (726-9275), late June, also in Half Moon Bay.

Half Moon Bay Bluegrass Festival (726-4460), late Sept. Draws a variety of locally and nationally known outfits.

Half Moon Bay Art and Pumpkin Festival (726-9652), mid-Oct. Arts, crafts, food, a parade, a masquerade ball, and carving contests.

Napa and Sonoma Wine Country

Wine is what brings most visitors to the quiet vineyards of the Napa and Sonoma valleys, and with good reason—the area's wines are regarded highly by connoisseurs both in the U.S. and abroad. Napa is better known; Sonoma is older and less crowded. The crowds will thin and you'll receive the most personal attention as you move into the Russian River Valley. The valleys themselves are beautiful and rural. Green fields of gnarled grape vines stretch in all directions and scenic mountain views tower along the horizon. But, in spite of the area's natural beauty, you will not forget for long that wine is the focus here.

THE LET'S GO WINE TASTING CRASH COURSE

Most wines are recognized by the grape-stock from which they're grown—**white** grapes produce Chardonnay, Riesling, and Sauvignon; **reds** are responsible for Beaujolais, Pinot Noir, Merlot, Zinfandel, and Cabernet Sauvignon. **Blush** or **rose** wines issue from red grapes which have had their skins removed during fermentation in order to leave just a touch of color. White Zinfandel comes from a red grape often made skinless—the wine is therefore pink in color. **Sparkling** wine (if the grapes are from Champagne, France it's champagne, if they're not it's sparkling wine) is made by adding yeast and sugar during fermentation, a process which adds carbon dioxide. Cheaper imitations are made by bubbling carbon dioxide directly through ordinary white wine. **Dessert** wines are made with grapes that have begun to acquire the "noble rot" *(botrytis)* at the end of the picking season, giving them an extra-sweet flavor.

When tasting, start with a white, moving from dry to sweet (dry wines have had a higher percentage of their sugar content fermented into alcohol). Proceed through the reds, which go from lighter to fuller bodied, depending on tannin content, and end with a dessert wine. It is advisable to cleanse your pallet between each wine. Don't hesitate to ask for advice and information from the tasting-room pourer. Tasting should proceed thus: stare, smell, swirl, swallow (first three steps are optional). Key words to help you seem as cultivated as the grapes during tasting sessions are dry, sweet, light, crisp, fruity, balanced, rounded, subtle, rich, woody, and complex. Feel free to banter these terms about indiscriminately; all that matters is that you sound like you know what you're talking about.

■■■ NAPA VALLEY

While not the oldest, the Napa Valley is certainly the best-known of America's wine-growing regions. The gentle hills, fertile soil, ample moisture, and year-round sunshine are ideal for viticulture. Charles King planted vines brought from Europe in the late 1850s, but producers were crippled by Prohibition, when the grapes were supplanted with figs. The region did not begin to reestablish itself until the 1960s. During the '70s attention focused on Napa's rapidly improving offerings as those in the know started recommending an occasional California bottle. In 1976, a bottle of red from Napa's Stag's Leap Vineyard beat a bottle of château Lafitte-Rothschild in a blind taste test at a Paris salon. American wine had come of age, and tourists from across the country started flocking to the California valley. Today, local vineyards continue to reap national and international awards, and a tasting carnival goes on from sunrise to sunset, dominating life in the valley's small towns. Besides **Napa,** the towns of **Calistoga, St. Helena,** and **Yountville** are convenient, though expensive, bases for exploring.

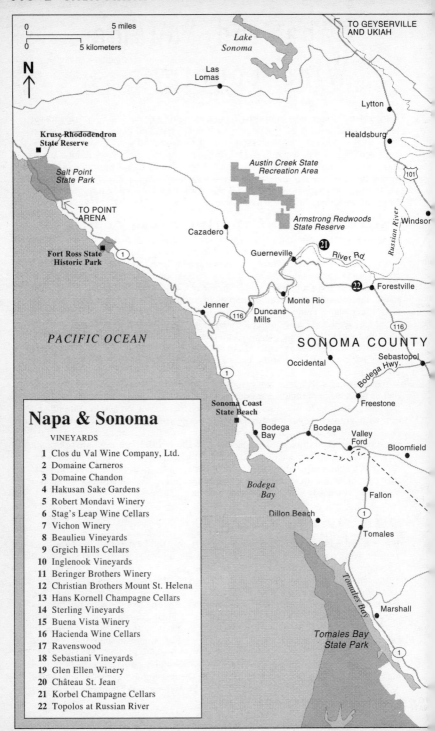

TO GEYSERVILLE
AND UKIAH

0   5 miles
0   5 kilometers

N

Lake
Sonoma

Las
Lomas

Lytton

Healdsburg

Kruse Rhododendron
State Reserve

Austin Creek State
Recreation Area

101

Salt Point
State Park

Armstrong Redwoods
State Reserve

Windsor

TO POINT
ARENA

Cazadero

21

River Rd

Fort Ross State
Historic Park

1

Guerneville

Russian River

22

Forestville

Jenner

116

Monte Rio

Duncans
Mills

116

PACIFIC OCEAN

SONOMA COUNTY

Occidental

Sebastopol

Bodega Hwy.

1

Freestone

Sonoma Coast
State Beach

Bodega
Bay

Bodega

Valley
Ford

Bloomfield

Napa & Sonoma

VINEYARDS

1 Clos du Val Wine Company, Ltd.
2 Domaine Carneros
3 Domaine Chandon
4 Hakusan Sake Gardens
5 Robert Mondavi Winery
6 Stag's Leap Wine Cellars
7 Vichon Winery
8 Beaulieu Vineyards
9 Grgich Hills Cellars
10 Inglenook Vineyards
11 Beringer Brothers Winery
12 Christian Brothers Mount St. Helena
13 Hans Kornell Champagne Cellars
14 Sterling Vineyards
15 Buena Vista Winery
16 Hacienda Wine Cellars
17 Ravenswood
18 Sebastiani Vineyards
19 Glen Ellen Winery
20 Château St. Jean
21 Korbel Champagne Cellars
22 Topolos at Russian River

Bodega
Bay

Dillon Beach

Fallon

1

Tomales

Tomales Bay

Marshall

Tomales Bay
State Park

1

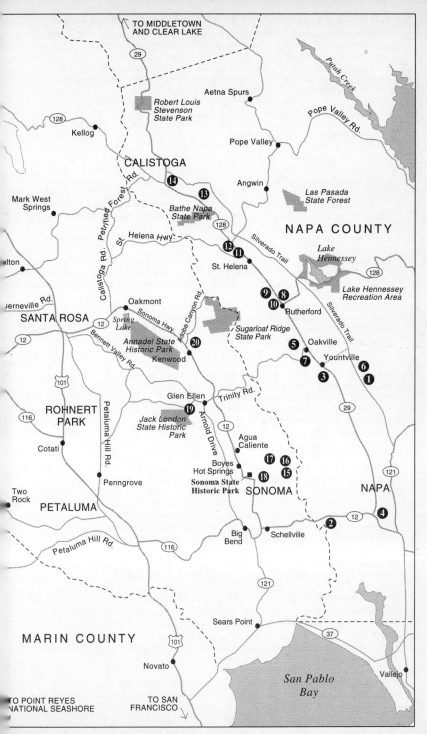

PRACTICAL INFORMATION AND ORIENTATION

Visitors Information: Napa Visitor Center, 1310 Town Center (226-7459), on 1st St. Eager staff and a wide brochure collection. Open Mon.-Fri. 9am-5pm, Sat.-Sun. 9am-3pm. Pick up a copy of *California Visitors Review* (free) for maps, winery listings, and a weekly events guide (also available in many stores). There are additional Chambers of Commerce in **Yountville,** Washington St. (944-0904), **St. Helena,** 1080 Main St. (963-4456; open Mon.-Fri. 10am-noon and 1-4pm, Sat. 10am-4pm), and **Calistoga,** 1458 Lincoln Ave. (942-6333; open daily 10am-5pm).

Amtrak: The nearest Amtrak station is in Martinez and is accessible by bus from the Napa Wine Train Depot, located at 1275 McKinstry St. (253-2111). Reach Amtrak at 800-USA-RAIL, -872-7245.

Greyhound: 2 per day through the valley. It stops in Napa at 9:45am and 6pm in front of Napa State Hospital, 2100 Napa-Vallejo Hwy. Also stops in Yountville, St. Helena, and Calistoga. Closest bus station: Vallejo (643-7661).

Local Transportation: Napa City Bus ("VINE" or Valley Intercity Neighborhood Express—the things people will do to get a cute acronym), 1151 Pearl St. (255-7631). Provides transport throughout the valley and to Vallejo. Buses run Mon.-Sat. 5:30am-7:30pm. Fare varies: Napa to Calistoga $2, to Yountville $1, to Vallejo $1.50. Discounts available for children and seniors.

Car Rental: Budget, 407 Soscol Ave. (224-7845), in Napa. Must be 21 with credit card. $29 per day.

Bicycle Rental: Napa Valley Cyclery, 4080 Byway East (255-3377), in Napa. Bicycles $4 per hr., $20 per day, $70 per week. Tandem bikes $28 per day. Major credit card required for deposit. Open Mon.-Sat. 9am-6pm, Sun. 10am-5pm; in winter Sun. hours are 10am-4pm.

Taxi: Taxi Cabernet (963-2620), in St. Helena. $2 per mi.

Laundromat: Busy Bee, 1132 Imola Ave. 24 hrs.

Crisis: Red Cross, 257-2900. **Emergency Women's Service,** 255-6397. 24 hrs. **Poison Control,** 800-523-2222. **Disabled Crisis,** 800-426-4263.

Pharmacy: Smiths, 1390 Railroad Ave. (926-2794). Open Mon.-Sat. 9am-6pm, Sun. 10am-3pm.

Hospital: Queen of the Valley, 1000 Trancas St. (252-4411).

Emergency: 911.

Police: 1539 First St. (253-4451).

Post Office: 1625 Trancas St. (255-1621). Open Mon.-Fri. 8:30am-5pm. **General Delivery ZIP Code:** 94558.

Area Code: 707.

Rte. 29 runs through the middle of Napa valley from **Napa** at its southern end, to **Calistoga** in the north, passing **St. Helena** and **Yountville** in between. The **Silverado Trail,** parallel to Rte. 29, is a more scenic and less crowded route than the highway. Napa is 25 minutes away from Sonoma on Rte. 12. If you're planning a weekend trip from San Francisco, avoid Saturday mornings and Sunday afternoons, the roads are packed with like minded people and travel is slow. Try to visit the valley on weekdays. It is always a good idea to steer clear of tour buses.

The best way to see Napa is by **bicycle** since the valley is dead level and only 30 mi. long. Rent your own or consider indulging in a bike or bike/canoe tour with **Getaway Bike Tours,** P.O. Box 273, Calistoga (800-499-2453). Half-day trips for $49 include bicycle, helmet, van support, and gourmet picnic lunch.

ACCOMMODATIONS AND CAMPING

Bed and breakfasts, and most hotels, are a budget breaking $55-225 per night. A few resorts have rooms under $40, but they go fast and are inaccessible without a car. If you do have a car, it's better to stay in Santa Rosa, Sonoma, or Petaluma, where budget accommodations are more plentiful. Without a reservation or a car, plan on camping; there are many excellent sites.

Triple S Ranch, 4600 Mountain Home Ranch Rd. (942-6730). Beautiful setting in the mountains above Calistoga. Take Rte. 29 toward Calistoga, and turn left past downtown, onto Petrified Forest Rd. Light, woodsy cabins. The best deal in the valley. Pool, restaurant, and bar. Check-in 3pm. Check-out noon. Singles $37. Doubles $49. $7 per additional person. Call in advance. Open April-Dec. 31.

Silverado Motel, 500 Silverado Trail (253-0892), in Napa near Soscol Ave. Clean, fresh, newly remodeled rooms with kitchenette and cable TV. More personality than a chain-motel. Non-smoking rooms available. Registration noon-6pm. Check-out 11am. Singles $40-45. Doubles $40-48.

Napa Valley Budget Inn, 3380 Solano Ave. (257-6111), in Napa at Redwood Rd. From Rte. 29, take the Redwood Rd. exit and turn left immediately. Crisp and balanced with a subtle edge. (For you beginners, that's wine country talk.) TV, small pool, A/C. Registration after 2pm, usually full by 6pm in summer. Free local calls. Check-out 11am. Singles $36-46. $6 per additional person.

Bothe-Napa Valley State Park, 3601 St. Helena Hwy. (942-4575; for reservations 800-444-7275), north of St. Helena on Rte. 29. Often full, so call ahead to avoid a long, unnecessary drive. Park open 8am-sunset. Hot showers. Sites $14, vehicles $5. Swimming pool $3, under 18 $1. Call for reservations.

Napa County Fairgrounds, 1435 Oak St. (942-5111), in Calistoga. First-come, first-camped. Shaded sites, with showers and electricity. $15 covers 2 adults. Closed June 28-July 5 for county fair. Check-out noon. Open 24 hrs.

FOOD

Sit-down meals are often expensive here, but Napa and its neighboring communities support numerous delis where you can buy inexpensive picnic supplies. Keep an eye out for the many **Safeway** stores.

Villa Corona Panaderia-Tortilleña, 3614 Bel Aire Plaza (257-8685), in Napa. Off of Trancas, behind the Citibank building. Tiny restaurant in an alley, with a piñata-speckled ceiling. Impressive selection of Mexican beers. Large burrito with the works, rice, and beans, $4.35. Pastries 45-95¢. Open Mon.-Sat. 9am-8pm, Sun. 8am-8pm.

Guigni's, 1227 Main St. (963-3421), in St. Helena. An unpretentious, friendly grocery store with sandwiches ($3.55). Lots of locals. Eclectic decorations on the walls. A good place to put a picnic together. If it's raining, sit in the "munch room" at the back. Open Mon.-Fri. 9am-5pm, Sat.-Sun. 9am-5:30pm.

Taylor's Refresher (963-3486), on Rte. 29 across from the Merryvale Winery, near the heart of the wine country. A burger stand with vegetarian and traditional burgers ($2.49), Mexican dishes, and ice-cream cones. Outdoor seating in beautiful picnic area. Open daily 11am-8pm.

Curb Side Café, 1245 1st St. (253-2307), at Randolph St. in downtown Napa. Sandwich place with tasty breakfasts served all day. Pancake special: 4 buttermilk pancakes, 2 eggs, and ham or sausage $5. Sublime sandwiches $5. Open Mon.-Sat. 8am-3pm, Sun. 9:30am-3pm.

Calistoga Natural Foods and Juice Bar, 1426 Lincoln (942-5822), in Calistoga. One of the only natural foods stores around. Also has an organic juice bar and a sandwich bar—select the ingredients for the perfect sandwich. 3 items for $4, 4 or more items $4.50. Open Mon.-Fri. 9:30am-5:30pm, Sat.-Sun. 10:30am-5:30pm.

WINERIES

Napa Valley is home to the wine country's heavyweights; vineyards include national names such as Inglenook, Christian Brothers, and Mondavi. The large vineyards are better for neophytes since tours are well-organized, and there's no pressure to say anything intelligent-sounding at the tastings. There are more than 250 wineries in Napa County, nearly two-thirds of which are in Napa Valley. Many wineries now charge for wine tastings, but free tours and tastings are still available. The fee is usually small ($3-6), and includes a tour with three or four tastes. (Sorry, no wineries offer all-you-can-drink tours.) The majority of smaller wineries require that visitors phone ahead to ensure that someone is around to pour the wine. (For general information on wines, see page 307.) The wineries listed below are among the valley's larger operations and have established tour programs that attract large numbers of visitors every day. To reach smaller places, pick up a list of vineyards from the Napa Chamber of Commerce or look for signs along the roadside. If you need a break from drinking, try soaking in some hot springs at Calistoga (page 313). Note that the vineyards below are *not* listed geographically. Instead they are listed, like most things in this book, in roughly preferential order with our favorites first. Visitors unfamiliar with U.S. drinking laws should be forewarned: you must be 21 or older to purchase or drink alcohol, which includes tastings at vineyards. And, yes, they do card. Vineyards in Napa often do not allow picnicking. All except the two noted have full wheelchair access.

Robert Mondavi Winery, 7801 St. Helena Hwy. (963-9611), 8 mi. north of Napa in Oakville. Spanish-style buildings, beautiful grounds. Spirited tour takes visitors through marvelous catacombs and past towering stacks of oak barrels filled with mellowing wine. The best free tour with tasting for the completely unknowledgeable, and the wine itself is decent. (Can you really tell the difference between a Château Lafitte-Rothschild and a Gallo when the label is covered?) Tours 10am-4pm on the hour. Reservations required. You can sign up when you arrive, but it's a good idea to call ahead; they book up fast, especially in the summer. Open daily 10:30am-5pm; Oct.-April 11am-4:30pm.

Domaine Chandon, 1 California Dr. (944-2280), in Yountville. One of the finest tours in the valley, can be given in French if prior arrangements are made. Owned by Moët Chandon of France (the people who make Dom Perignon), this is the place to learn the secrets of making sparkling wine—not champagne. 45-min. tours hourly 11am-5pm. Tastings by the glass ($3-5; includes bread and cheese) or by the bottle in the restaurant. Open daily 11am-6pm; Nov.-April Wed.-Sun. 11am-6pm.

Domaine Carneros, 1240 Duhig Rd. (257-0101). Go north on Rte. 29, then turn right on Rte. 121 and travel 2½ mi. Picturesque estate modeled after a French chateau. Sparkling wine $4 per glass. No free tastings, but the view of the valley is sweeping, and the tour and film are free. 30-min. tours at 11am, 1pm, 3pm. Open daily 10:30am-6pm; winter 11am-4pm.

Sterling Vineyards, 1111 Dunaweal Lane (942-3345), in Calistoga, 6 mi. north of St. Helena (go right on Dunaweal from Rte. 29N). Perhaps the most visually arresting of the valley's vineyards. Mounted on top of a small hill, surrounded by vines, with a view of the valley below. Aerial tram to vineyard, tour, and tasting $6. Limited wheelchair access. Open daily 10:30am-4:30pm.

Inglenook Vineyard, 1991 St. Helena Hwy. (967-3359), in South Rutherford (turn left at the big sign). One of the valley's mass-producers. Try the **John Daniels Cellar,** where you can buy a taste of vintage wines. Free tasting for other wines. Open daily 10am-5pm. J.D. Cellar open weekends in the summer with tasting on the hour from 11am-4pm. By appointment in the winter.

Beringer Vineyards, 2000 Main St. (963-7115), off Rte. 29 in St. Helena. One of the more popular vineyards. Free tours include Rhine House, a landmark mansion, and a tasting session. In summer, the tours are a mob scene. To avoid the crowds and taste Beringer's better wines, try the reserve room on the second floor of the Rhine House. Generous samples in the reserve room cost $2-3. Open daily 9:30am-6pm; winter 9:30am-5pm.

Beaulieu Vineyard, 1960 St. Helena Hwy. (963-2411), in Rutherford, 11 mi. from Napa. Tours of the wine-making area and cellars. Free tasting daily 10am-5pm. Tours 11:30am-3:30pm on the ½-hr.

Clos Du Val Wine Company, Ltd., 5330 Silverado Trail (252-6711), in Napa. Take Oak Knoll Rd. to Silverado Trail. An outdoor picnic area with whimsical drawings by Ronald Searle. Tasting room open all day, but call in advance to make sure there's room. $3 charge. Open daily 10am-5pm.

Stag's Leap Wine Cellars, 5766 Silverado Trail (944-2020), in Napa. The tiny vineyard that beat the Continent's best. Call at least a week in advance to arrange a tour and a superb tasting session ($3 for 5-6 wines). Open daily 10am-4pm.

Newlan, 5225 Solano Ave. (257-2399). A small premium winery, with the best in Pinot Noir and dessert wines. Free tastings daily 10am-4pm. Make an appointment for a tour. Limited wheelchair access. Open daily 11am-5pm.

Grgich Hills Cellar, 1829 St. Helena Hwy. (963-2784), in Rutherford, 12 mi. from Napa. Tours by prior arrangement only. Daily tastings free Mon.-Fri.; $2 Sat.-Sun. Some of the finest Zinfandels in the area. Open daily 9:30am-4:30pm.

Château Montelena, 1429 Tubbs Lane (942-5105). Take Rte. 29 past Calistoga, then right onto Tubbs Lane. An old castle houses this award-winning winery, which emphasizes estate-bottled reds. $5 charge for tasting, but feel free to stroll their beautiful grounds. Tours daily 11am, 2pm. Tasting room open daily 10am-4pm.

Vichon Winery, 1595 Oakville Grade (944-2811). Take a left off of Rte. 29 N. at the Carmelite Monastery sign. The gorgeous view of the valley merits the detour. Picnic tables available for wine-purchasers. Free tasting. Reservations requested for tours. Open daily 10am-4:30pm.

Hakusan Sake Gardens, 1 Executive Way (258-6160). Take Rte. 29S to the Rte. 12 intersection, turn left on Kelly, then left onto Executive Way. A pleasant self-guided tour through the Japanese gardens provides a delightful respite from the power-chugging at the vineyards. Generous, free pourings of *Hakusan Sake,* known as *Haki Sake* to locals. Open daily 9am-6pm, Nov.-March 9am-5pm.

SIGHTS

Despite impressions to the contrary, Napa does have non-alcoholic attractions. Ten mi. south of Napa is 160-acre **Marine World Africa USA** (643-6722), an enormous zoo-oceanarium-theme park (which is often mobbed on summer weekends). To get there, take Rte. 29S to Rte. 37W, and follow the signs. Bring a picnic and plan to spend the whole day, especially if bringing a child or two along. Although the park suffers from a mild case of Disney World artificiality, patrons are encouraged to interact with the animals. Trainers stroke the tigers as if they were domestic house cats and swim with dolphins and killer whales alike. Visitors can ride the elephants, and are allowed to pet many of the other animals at specific times. All proceeds benefit wildlife research and protection programs. (The park is accessible by BART Mon.-Sat.; call 415-788-2278 for more info. Open daily 9:30am-6:15pm. $25, seniors $21, ages 4-12 $17. Parking $4. Wheelchair and stroller access.)

Robert Louis Stevenson State Park (942-4575), on Rte. 29, 4 mi. north of St. Helena, centers around the abandoned bunkhouse where the Scottish writer, sick and penniless, spent a rejuvenating honeymoon in 1880. He gathered information for *Silverado Squatters* in the area, and eventually patterned Spyglass Hill in *Treasure Island* after looming Mt. St. Helena (park open daily 8am-sunset). The **Silverado Museum,** 1490 Library Lane (963-3757), in St. Helena, off Adams St., is a labor of love by a devoted collector of Stevensoniana. See manuscript notes from *Master of Ballantrae* and *Dr. Jekyll and Mr. Hyde* (open Tues.-Sun. noon-4pm; free).

Farther to the north, 2 mi. outside Calistoga, the **Old Faithful Geyser of California** (942-6463; not to be confused with its more famous namesake in Wyoming), on Tubbs Lane off Rte. 128, spurts boiling water 60 ft. into the air. The 3500°F jet appears on average every 50 minutes in summer and every 30 minutes in winter; the ticket vendor will tell you the estimated time of the next spurt. (Open daily 9am-6pm; winter 9am-5pm. $5, seniors $4, ages 6-12 $2. Bathrooms are not wheelchair accessible, but those in wheelchairs receive free admission.)

Calistoga is also known as the "Hot Springs of the West." Sam Brannan, who first developed the area, promised to make the hot springs the "Saratoga of California," but he misspoke and promised instead to make them "The Calistoga of Saratina." His cottage is now the base for the **Sharpsteen Museum,** 1311 Washington St. (942-5911), which traces the town's development (open daily 10am-4pm; in winter noon-4pm; free). If you have the time and money, try a hot mineral bath, steam bath, volcanic ash mud bath, and blanket sweat at **Nance's Hot Springs,** 1614 Lincoln Ave. (942-6211). Add a half-hour massage and the full treatment comes to around $58 (available 9am-3:30pm). **Indian Springs,** 1712 Lincoln Ave. (942-4913), has an exotic Olympic-sized pool complete with a fountain by the sculptor Hirshen. You can also chug the stuff bottled—Calistoga has a line of sparkling mineral waters and juices.

Four mi. along Rte. 128 (follow the signs from Calistoga), several giant **petrified redwoods** (942-6667) await picnickers. The 3.4-million-year-old trees are uninspiring, and the cheesy promotions fail to entice. The small grove is often mobbed by tour groups (open daily 10am-6pm, winter 10am-5pm; $3, seniors $2, children $1).

Farther north on Rte. 29, and then east, is the **McLaughlin Mine,** 26775 Morgan Valley Rd. (707-995-6070). California's largest working gold mine is—they claim— an excellent example of careful environmental management. Judge for yourself. (Tours May-Oct. on 2nd and 4th Fri.-Sat. of the month arranged through the Lakeport Information Center, 800-LAKESIDE, -52537433.)

The 110°F hot springs of Calistoga are not very refreshing during the hot days of summer. For a cool swim, head to **Lake Berryessa** (966-2111). Situated 20 mi. north of Napa (take Rte. 29N to Rte. 128E), the lake has cool water for swimming, sailing, and fishing, and 168 mi. of shoreline for sunbathing.

The annual **Napa Valley Wine Festival** (252-0872) takes place in November. **Napa Valley Fairgrounds** hosts a month-long summer fair in August, with wine-tasting, rock music, juggling, a rodeo, and rides. Music lovers can catch **Music-in-the-Park,** in the center of downtown Napa at the riverfront, for free jazz concerts in summer. Contact Napa Parks and Recreation Office (257-9529) for more information.

■■■ SONOMA VALLEY

The sprawling Sonoma Valley is a quieter (and less expensive) alternative to Napa. **Sonoma** (logically) is the largest town in the Sonoma Valley. Sonoma takes pride in its beautiful eight-acre town plaza. The expansive plaza is surrounded by delis, art galleries, hotels, novelty shops, and vintage clothing stores, yet—with a playground, plum trees, and a pond—it's the perfect place for a "rural" picnic. **Petaluma,** west of Sonoma, is distinguished by its odd mix of architecture, unflinchingly juxtaposing nearly every 20th-century genre.

PRACTICAL INFORMATION AND ORIENTATION

Visitors Information: Sonoma Valley Visitors Bureau, 453 E. 1st St. (996-1090), in Sonoma's central plaza. Open daily 10am-4pm. Also a **southern office** at 20890 S. Broadway (996-5793). Open daily 9am-7pm; Sept.-May daily 9am-5pm. Plenty of maps ($1.50-2.25), and a knowledgeable and friendly staff. Look around town for a copy of *The Review,* a free weekly with extensive winery listings. **Petaluma Visitors Center,** 799 Baywood Dr., Suite 1. Open June-Sept. Mon.-Fri. 9am-6pm, Sat.-Sun. 10am-6pm. Shorter hours in off-season.

ATM: 35 Napa St. and 1st, in Sonoma. 101 Western Ave. in Petaluma.

Bus: Sonoma County Transit (576-7433 or 800-345-7433) serves the entire county, including Santa Rosa in the north. Bus #30 runs between Sonoma and Santa Rosa (Mon.-Fri., 3 on Sat.; $1.90, students $1.55, over 60 and disabled 95¢, under 6 free). Within Sonoma, bus fare is 80¢, students 60¢, seniors and disabled 40¢. County buses stop when flagged down. Buses operate Mon.-Fri. 7am-6pm. 2 buses run daily between S.F. and Sonoma—call Golden Gate Transportation for more information (332-6600 from S.F., 544-1323 from Sonoma).

Volunteer Wheels: 800-992-1006. Door to door for people with disabilities.

Taxi: Sonoma Valley Cab (996-6733). 24-hr. service.

Bicycle Rental: Bicycle Factory, 110 Kentucky St., downtown Petaluma. Bikes $8 per hr., $22 per day. Must leave major ID or credit card as deposit. **Goodtime Bicycles,** 18503 Rte. 12 (938-0453), in Sonoma. Mountain bikes with helmet, basket, and map $5 per hr., $20 per day. Open Mon.-Sat. 9am-5pm, Sun. 10am-4pm.

Laundromat: Launder Land, 1221 Petaluma Blvd. Wash $1, dry 50¢.

Auto Safety/Road Conditions: 800-424-9393.

Crisis Lines: Sonoma Valley Crisis Line, 938-HELP, -4357. 24-hr. referrals. **Rape Crisis Hotline,** 545-7273. 24 hrs. **Poison Control,** 800-523-2222. **Disabled Crisis,** 800-426-4263. **Red Cross,** 577-7600.

Hospital: Sonoma Valley, 347 Andrieux St. (935-5000), in Sonoma. **Petaluma Valley,** 400 N. McDowell Blvd. (778-1111), in Petaluma.

Emergency: 911.

Police (non-emergency): **Sonoma,** 996-3602. **Petaluma,** 778-4372. **Sheriff,** 527-2121.

Post Office: Sonoma, 617 Broadway (996-2459), at Patten St. Open Mon.-Fri. 8:30am-5pm. **General Delivery ZIP Code:** 95476. **Petaluma,** 120 4th St. (769-5350). Open Mon.-Thurs. 8:30am-5pm, Fri. 8:30am-6pm, Sat. 10am-2pm. **General Delivery ZIP Code:** 95476.

Area Code: 707.

The Sonoma Valley runs between **Sonoma** in the south and **Glen Ellen** in the north, with **Rte. 12** traversing its length. The center of downtown Sonoma is Sonoma Plaza, a park which contains City Hall and the visitors center. **Broadway** dead-ends in front of City Hall at Napa St. The numbered streets run north-south and grow higher in number as they radiate out. **Petaluma** lies to the west and is connected to Sonoma by **Rte. 116** (follow the signs closely), which becomes Lakeville St. in Petaluma. Lakeville St. intersects **Washington St.,** the central downtown road. The valley is small enough to tour by bicycle. Keep your eyes peeled when using the roads; the local signposting is dreadful.

ACCOMMODATIONS AND CAMPING

Pickings are pretty slim for lodging in Sonoma Valley; if you can't find a vacancy in your price range, head west and try the cheaper motels along U.S. 101 in Santa Rosa or Petaluma. Campers with cars may want to check listings in the Russian River Valley (page 321).

Motel 6, 5135 Montero Way (664-9090), in Petaluma. From San Francisco, take the Old Redwood/Petaluma Blvd. exit off U.S. 101. Small pool, A/C, bed. Singles $30. $6 per additional person.

Motel 6, 1368 N. McDowell Blvd. (765-0333), in Petaluma. TV, "cooling system," and pool. Quiet, spacious, and almost tastefully decorated. Singles $30. $6 per additional person.

Sugarloaf Ridge State Park, 2605 Adobe Canyon Rd. (833-5712), near Kenwood. 50 sites. By far the most beautiful place to camp in Sonoma Valley. Pretty views and open field for frisbee. Drive carefully up the mountain road. Flush toilets, running water, no showers. Sites $14. Call MISTIX (800-444-7275) to reserve.

San Francisco North/Petaluma KOA, 20 Rainsville Road (763-1492 or 800-992-2267), in Petaluma. Take Penngrove exit, make a right turn onto Stony Pt. Rd. to Rainsville Rd. Campground has petting zoo, pool, and jacuzzi. RV and trailer park with cabins ($35). Some tent sites separated from trailers ($25 for 2 people; $4 per additional adult, $2 per child).

FOOD

Fresh produce is seasonal and available directly from the area farms or through roadside stands and farmers' markets. Obtain a free *Farm Trails* map from the Sonoma Valley Visitors Bureau, and inquire there about farmers' markets. Those in the area toward the end of the summer should ask about the ambrosial **Crane Melon,** grown nowhere else in the world but on the Crane Farm north of Petaluma. The **Sonoma Market,** 520 W. Napa St. (996-0563), in the Sonoma Valley Center, is an old-fashioned grocery store with deli sandwiches ($3-4.25) and very fresh produce. For fresh, inexpensive fruit (cantaloupe 59¢, apples 39-50¢ per lb.) head to the **Fruit Basket,** 18474 Sonoma Hwy. (996-7433). **Safeway,** 477 W. Napa (996-0633), is open 24 hrs.

Murphy's Irish Pub, 464 1st St. E. (935-0660), in Sonoma. Cozy place serving "pub grub." Irish stew is made from Sonoma county lamb with Sonoma French Bakery sourdough roll ($5.50). Popular fish and chips comes with cole slaw, salad, or peas ($6.50). 9 beers on tap (but none of them Bud). Open daily 11am-11pm.

Quinley's, 310 D St. at Petaluma Blvd. (778-6000). Newly remodeled burger counter first opened its doors in 1952. Listen to '50s tunes and enjoy your meal outdoors while sitting at the bar stools or picnic tables. Half-pound burger with all the fixins $2.75. Four-scoop shake or malt $1.75. Great standard food at great prices. Open daily 11am-9pm.

Sonoma Cheese Factory, 2 W. Spain St. (996-1931). A deli run wonderfully wild. Forget the *vino* for now—try Sonoma's other produce and go cheese-tasting (free). Dozens of cheeses, some varieties made in the back room. Take your toothpick and start sampling. Watch the process through a giant picture window. Sandwiches $3.50-6. Open Mon.-Fri. 8:30am-5:30pm, Sat.-Sun. 8:30am-6pm.

Sonoma French Bakery Inc., 470 E. 1st St. (996-2691). Fresh, delicious loaves (90¢-$2.50). Croissants and other flaky items around $1. Open Wed.-Sat. 8am-6pm, Sun. 7:30am-4pm.

The Chocolate Cow, Mercato Promenade (935-3564), across from the Visitors Bureau on 1st St. The air is thick with chocolate, the walls are crammed with bovinalia, the ice cream is (what else?) Ben and Jerry's, the cash cow of ice creams. They also have chocolate pasta (yum?). Open Sun.-Thurs. 10am-8pm, Fri.-Sat. 9:30am-10pm, Sun. 9:30am-9:30pm.

Happy Dog, 18962 Sonoma Hwy./Rte. 12 (935-6211), close to the Verano intersection on the outskirts of Petaluma. Competes with the nearby McDonald's and wins with the locals—the burgers (from $2.20) are bigger, made to order, and grilled over a flame while you watch. Open Mon.-Thurs. and Sat. 11am-8:30pm, Fri. 11am-9pm, Sun. 11am-8pm.

Taqueria Los Primos, 18375 Sonoma Hwy./Rte. 12 (935-3546), about 1 mi. north of Happy Dog. Freshly prepared, surprisingly light food. Huge portions and cheap prices—2-lb. vegetarian burrito with everything ($3.50). Patronized by a multilingual delegation of locals. A TV serves up your favorite Latino soap opera. Vegetarian-friendly. No wheelchair access. Open daily 9am-10:30pm.

The Cherry Tree, 2 locations: Rte. 121 and Rte. 12/121 (938-3480), south of Sonoma. A combination deli and fruit stand with superb black cherry cider (75¢ for 8 oz.). The main store, on Rte. 12, has an endless variety of gourmet picnic supplies. Open daily 7am-9pm.

La Famiglia, 220 Western Ave. at Liberty St. (778-8211), in Petaluma. A family-owned deli, with pasta salads ($5-5.85 per lb.) and sandwiches ($4-5.45). Open Mon.-Sat. 7:30am-7pm, Sun. 8:15am-4:30pm.

WINERIES

Sonoma Valley's wineries are less tourist-ridden and offer more free tasting than those in Napa. There are two main clusters, one near Sonoma and one near Kenwood. Near Sonoma, signs will point you to the different wineries; in Kenwood they are harder to find. If you a seek a slower pace, travel north to the **Russian River Valley,** where several vineyards cluster near Guerneville, Healdsburg, and Geyserville (page 321).

Sebastiani, 389 E. 4th St. (938-5532), a few blocks from the northwest corner of Sonoma's central plaza. This giant mass-producer draws 250,000 visitors per year, and is a perfect place to get an introduction to the noble drink. Interesting 20-min. tour of the ancient (looking) aging rooms. Free tasting and tours daily 10am-5pm.

Ravenswood, 18701 Gehricke Rd. (938-1960), off Lovall Valley Rd., in Sonoma. Produces some of the valley's best *vino,* strongly recommended by the locals. The picnic area and the view alone are worth the trip. Summer weekend BBQs ($4.75-8.75); free tasting and tours by appointment. Open daily 10am-4:30pm.

Glen Ellen Winery, 1843 London Ranch Rd. (935-3000), 1 mi. from Glen Ellen. Gorgeous grounds, complete with roaming peacocks. Picnic tables available. Free tours at 11am and 2pm. Open daily 10am-4:30pm.

Buena Vista, 18000 Old Winery Rd. (938-1266), off E. Napa St. Fine wines and an interesting self-guided tour of their famous old stone buildings, preserved as Mr. Haraszthy built them in 1857, when he allegedly founded the California wine industry. Beautiful grounds with trellises, berries, and great views. Shakespeare plays staged here Aug. and Sept. Picnic area and tasting room open 10:30am-5pm, Labor Day-July 4 10:30am-4:30pm. Free tasting downstairs; vintage wine and champagne tasting upstairs for small fee. The under-21 set can taste Johannisburg Riesling grape juice for free.

Château St. Jean, 8555 Rte. 12 (833-4134), in Kenwood. Brief self-guided tour of holding tanks. Expansive winery (250,000 cases) in a Mediterranean-villa setting. Whites are 85% of their production. Lookout tower with balcony. Tasting daily 10am-4:30pm. Tours daily 10:30am-4pm.

SIGHTS AND SEASONAL EVENTS

Local historical artifacts have been collected and preserved in the **Sonoma State Historic Park,** at E. Spain and 1st St., in the northeast corner of town. Within the park, an adobe church stands on the site of the **Sonoma Mission** (938-1519), northernmost and last of the Spanish missions. Built in 1826 when Mexico was already a republic, the mission houses a remnant of the original California Republic flag, the rest of which was burned in the 1906 earthquake/fire. (Open daily 10am-5pm. $2, seniors and ages 6-12 $1, under 6 free. Includes Vallejo's Home and the Petaluma Adobe, see below.)

General Vallejo's Home (938-1215), ¾ mi. west of Sonoma's Central Plaza on Spain St., is the Gothic-style home of the famed Mexican military and civil leader. As the political winds shifted, the general went on to serve as mayor of Sonoma and a California senator. The house still contains its original furnishings (no, they were not destroyed in the earthquake/fire of 1906). The grounds are garnished by a serene picnic area designed in part by Vallejo and his *esposa* (open daily 10am-5pm).

To find the **Jack London State Park** (938-5216) take Rte. 12 north of Sonoma about 4 mi. to Arnold Lane and turn left (follow the signs). At the turn of the century, the hard-drinking and adventurous Jack London (author of *Call of the Wild* and *White Fang)* bought 140 acres in Glen Ellen determined to create his dream home. Today, the land he purchased belongs to the State Park bearing his name. London's hopes for the property were never realized—the estate's main building, the Wolf House, was destroyed by arsonists in 1913. Only the chimney and fireplaces, made of volcanic stone, remain. London died three years after the fire and is buried in the park. The nearby House of Happy Walls, built by his widow, is now a two-story museum devoted to the writer. The park offers several vistas of the valley as well as the scenic Beauty Ranch Trail, which passes by the lake, winery ruins and silos, and several quaint cottages. (Park open daily 8am-sunset; museum open daily 10am-5pm. $3 per car.)

Back in Sonoma, the **Depot Museum** (938-1762) is a railroad depot reconstructed after the century-old original burned in 1976. Period clothing and furniture help reanimate 19th-century life. (Open Wed.-Sun. 1-4:30pm. 50¢, seniors and ages 10-18 25¢, under 10 with parents free.)

Just south of the city center, **Traintown** (938-3912) offers a steam engine tour through a 10-acre park, which includes a children's petting zoo. (Open June-Sept. daily 10:30am-5pm, Oct.-May Fri.-Sun. 10:30am-5pm. $3.50, children and seniors $2.50.) Farther south, just past the junction of Rtes. 37 and 121, lies **Sears Point International Raceway** (938-8448). The track revs up for auto and motorcycle racing year-round, including major international competitions. The pitside crowd and the dusty, car exhaust-filled atmosphere stand in sharp contrast to the wine tastings farther north. Call for a schedule of events. (Admission $8-45.)

Just past Glen Ellen on Rte. 12 lies the village of **Kenwood.** Kenwood has a surprising number of excellent but reasonably priced restaurants, including **The Vineyards Inn** at Rte. 12 and Adobe Canyon Rd. The town heats up on July 4, when runners gather to vie for bragging rights in the **Kenwood Footrace,** which features a tough 10-km course winding through the hills and vineyards. A chili cook-off and the **World Pillowfighting Championships** will help you pass the rest of the day. There's nothing like two people straddling a metal pipe over a mud pit and beating the hell out of each other with wet pillows to get the blood racing.

The town of **Petaluma** itself merits a visit, not simply for its cheap accommodations, but for its magnificent, old (i.e., over 85 years), and diverse buildings. The area was virtually untouched by the 1906 earthquake. Spanish churches, Bauhausian residences, Art Deco banks, and long apartment hotels with manual elevators stand side by side. Take it all in and then, in October, roll up your sleeves for the **World Wristwrestling Championships.**

■■■ SANTA ROSA

Luther Burbank once said, "I firmly believe, from what I have seen, that this is the chosen spot of all the earth, as far as nature is concerned." He told no lie. Little did he know, though, that developers would choose shopping malls and rows of suburban homes as the best way to make use of such stunning countryside. The commercial hub of Sonoma County, this bucolic city of 100,000 seems far smaller, and life moves at a pace more in tune with the surrounding countryside than the hustle and bustle associated with a city. Santa Rosa is surrounded by fields of grapevines and other crops, forests, and the occasional dairy pasture. The city enjoys fine weather year-round, with warm summers and mild winters, ideal weather for making wine and attracting tourists.

PRACTICAL INFORMATION AND ORIENTATION

Visitors Information: Greater Santa Rosa Conference and Visitors Bureau, 637 First St. (577-8674 or 800-404-ROSE, -7673). Friendly help, and brochures beyond the usual. Map $1. Open Mon.-Fri. 9am-5pm, Sat. 9am-2pm, Sun. 9am-1pm.

Sonoma County Wine and Visitors Center, 5000 Roberts Lake Rd. (586-3795), east of U.S. 101 at the Luther Burbank Center for the Arts. Maps of 105 member wineries and a tasting directory. Open daily 10am-5pm.

Greyhound: 586-9512 for Santa Rosa. There is a Greyhound pick-up and drop-off point at 3854 Santa Rosa Ave. To San Francisco daily 3am and 4pm; $9. Leaves San Francisco daily 12:20am and 12:40pm; $9. The closest full-scale station is in San Rafael (see Marin County listing, page 285).

Buses: Golden Gate Transit, 544-1323. Bus #80 runs between San Francisco's Transbay Terminal and Santa Rosa (4am-11pm; fare $4, seniors $2, ages 6-18 $3). Also runs commute-hour express buses from Santa Rosa to San Francisco. **Santa Rosa Transit** (576-7433) operates extensive local service. **Sonoma County Transit** putts to Petaluma and Sonoma. Everything runs from the transit mall at 2nd St. Plaza.

Taxi: Yellow Cab (544-4444). $2 initial fee, $2 per mi.

Car Rental: Bay Area Rental, 3264 Santa Rosa Ave. (575-1600). $28 per day with 150 mi. free. Must be at least 25, or over 21 with full coverage. Open Mon.-Fri. 7am-6pm., Sat. 8am-3pm, Sun. 9am-2pm.

Bicycle Rental: Rincon Cyclery, 4927 Sonoma Hwy. Suite H (538-0868), in Santa Rosa. Mountain bikes only—shop is near off-road trails. $7 per hr. with 2-hr. min., $25 per day, $100 per week. Open daily 10am-6pm.

Public Library: 3rd and E St. (545-0831). Open Mon. noon-9pm, Wed. 9:30am-9pm, Tues. and Thurs.-Sat. 9:30am-6pm, Sun. 2-6pm.

Laundromat: Wash Plus, 3401 Cleveland Ave. (544-5011). Wash $1.25; 20-min. dry 25¢. Open daily 7am-10pm. **Love's Coin Laundromat,** 926 W. College Ave. Wash $1.25; 20-min. dry 25¢. Open daily 7:30am-9:30pm.

Crisis: Poison Control, 800-523-2222. **Disabled Crisis Line,** 800-426-4263. **Red Cross,** 577-7600.

Hospital: Santa Rosa Memorial, 1165 Montgomery Dr. (546-3210).

Emergency: 911.

Police: 543-3559.

Post Office: 730 2nd St. (528-8763), between D and E St. Open Mon.-Fri. 8am-6pm, Sat. 10am-2pm. **General Delivery ZIP Code:** 95402.

Area Code: 707.

Santa Rosa rests at the intersection of **U.S. 101** and **Rte. 12,** 52 mi. from downtown San Francisco. **Cleveland Ave.** serves as a western boundary and contains many of the city's cheap motels. The town center is occupied by a mall, which interrupts A St. and 2nd through 5th St. **Mendocino Ave.** and **4th St.** define the downtown area. The town radiates out from there.

ACCOMMODATIONS AND CAMPING

Santa Rosa exudes average lodgings at above-average prices. Make reservations far in advance for summer.

Motel 6, 3 locations: 6145 Commerce Blvd. (585-8888). Second location at 2760 Cleveland Ave., 5 mi. north of downtown Santa Rosa (546-1500). Take the Steele Lane exit west off U.S. 101, then turn north onto Cleveland. Pool, A/C. Check-in after 4pm, check-out before noon. Third location at 3145 Cleveland Ave. (525-9010), in Santa Rosa, has large, nearly stylish rooms, and mid-sized pool. Wheelchair-accessible and non-smoking rooms. Check-out noon. All locations: Singles $30. $6 per additional adult. Reservations recommended during summer.

Sandman Motel, 3421 Cleveland Ave. (544-8570). Take Mendocino Ave. exit west off U.S. 101 and turn south onto Cleveland Ave. Cheerful rooms, jacuzzi, pool, and A/C. More comfy than its budget competitors. Singles $50. 2 beds $56. Reserve in summer and for weekends year-round.

Astro Motel, 323 Santa Rosa Ave. (545-8555), convenient downtown location. TV, A/C. A haven for late arrivals—they often have vacant rooms. Eclectic clientele and decoration scheme employing pink, orange, and red. Singles $32. Doubles $38.

Spring Lake County Park, 5585 Newanga Rd. (539-8092), off Summerfield Dr. It's hard to believe you're still in the city; Annadel State Park's miles of trails are easily accessible from the camping area. The nearby lake has a swimming lagoon with lifeguards. 30 sites, with water, toilets, and showers. Sites $14, dogs $1 extra with proof of vaccination. Vehicle entrance fee $4. 10 sites reserved for first-come, first-camped. Reservations not accepted for summer weekends.

FOOD

Although Santa Rosa is not exactly the gourmet capital of California, it offers an assortment of palatable restaurants. See Nightlife (page 320) for more food listings.

Annadeli, 2700 Yulupa Ave. (542-9050). Pack a picnic here before heading up to Annadel State Park. Merle puts together a sandwich just how you like it, $2-5. Open Mon.-Fri. 6am-6pm, Sat. 7am-4pm.

China Court, 590 Lewis Rd. (571-2086), near Mendocino Ave. Mandarin and Sze-chuan cuisine in the middle of suburbia. The sizzling chicken on a hot plate ($6.25) is especially good. Top it off with a candied apple and banana desert. Request the spicy string bean chicken ($6.75). Plenty of vegetarian dishes, $5-6. Open Mon.-Sat. 11:30am-9:30pm.

Copperfield's Bookstore and Café, 650 4th St. (576-7681), downtown. The sand-wiches are all named after authors in this vegetarian-friendly coffee and sandwich joint. Try the Kurt Vonnegut—a scrumptious veggie burger with lots o' toppings ($4.25). So it goes. Open Mon.-Fri. 7:30am-9pm, Sat. 9am-9pm, Sun. 9am-6pm.

Ting Hau, 717 4th St. (545-5204), downtown. The management here saves its time and effort for the food, not the decor. Despite dreary booths, this little Chinese eatery has a devoted and vocal following. Complete lunch for only $3.26 (served 11am-3:30pm). Open daily 11am-9pm.

East-West Café, 2323 Sonoma Ave. (546-6142), in Montgomery Village. This all-organic restaurant offers vegetarian and omnivorous fare, as well as heavenly baked goods. A sort of homemade, hippie Denny's. Monstrous Thai chicken salad, $7. Open Sun.-Mon. 8am-8pm ('til 8:30pm in summer), Tues.-Sat. 8am-9pm.

Organic Groceries, 2481 Guerneville Rd. (528-3663), near Fulton Rd. Every organic food you've ever heard of and then some—all in bulk quantities. Open Mon.-Sat. 10am-7pm, Sun. 11am-6pm.

SIGHTS AND SEASONAL EVENTS

The **Luther Burbank Home and Gardens** (524-5445), at Santa Rosa and Sonoma Ave., is a good place to sit and recharge. Luther Burbank had two of the most accomplished green thumbs in history. At the age of 26, the horticulturist moved to California from Lancaster, Massachusetts, to carry out his plant-breeding experiments. The gardens display several original Burbank hybrids, including the Shasta daisy, the spineless cactus, and the evil white *Agapanthus* (a short, frondy plant spiked with bell-shaped flowers, a favorite of California's gas station landscapers). Burbank, who resided in the house from 1886 to 1906, is buried under an ancient cedar in the garden. (Gardens open daily 8am-7pm. Free. Self-guided tour-map available in the gift shop or from the visitors bureau. House open April-Oct. Wed.-Sun. 10am-3:30pm. $2, under 13 free. Free tours on Memorial Day.)

Santa Rosa offers little else in the way of sights, unless you are interested in lots of suburban houses and San Quentin-esque shopping malls. The town does host several worthy annual events. August welcomes the **Dixieland Jazz Festival** (707-539-3494) with nonstop music and dancing. The **Sonoma County Fair** is concurrent with the jazz festival. Tartan enthusiasts will enjoy the **Scottish Gathering and Games,** a two-day athletic-genealogical frenzy over Labor Day weekend. This event, the largest gathering of Scots outside of the British Isles, features the bizarre and undeniably phallic caber toss, in which kilt-sporting brawny types throw trees (kilts help protect against splinters). In the autumn, Santa Rosa nourishes the countryside at both the **October Harvest Fair,** and the **World Championship Grape Stomp Contest.** (Call the Sonoma County Fairgrounds at 545-4200 for information.) Visit the **Thursday Night Market** (544-4980; June-mid-Dec. 5-8:30pm), when downtown 4th St. is closed to traffic, and crafts booths and food stands pack in the locals. You'll find a produce-oriented farmers' market Wednesday and Saturday mornings in front of the Veteran's Memorial Building near the fairgrounds (9am-noon) and at Montgomery Village on Sonoma Ave. and Rte. 12 (Feb.-Dec. 8:30-11am).

Santa Rosa residents are blessed with **Annadel State Park,** a huge patch of wilderness that hugs the residential neighborhoods to the southeast of town and stretches all the way to nearby Kenwood. Sixty mi. of trails perfect for running, hiking, and mountain biking traverse the hills and meadows of the park. Annadel offers views of the surrounding valleys and the city, as well as a fine swimming hole, **Lake Ilsanjo.** To avoid parking fees ($2), access the park via Parktrail Dr., off Summerfield Rd. Go up Parktrail Dr. until the road bends sharply up and to the right, and you'll see the trail leading up hill. You can also reach the park by hiking through Spring Lake County Park (see Accommodations and Camping, page 319).

If you are biking or driving, Sonoma County's backroads offer scenery that surpasses even Rte. 12's. **Bennett Valley Road** between Kenwood and Santa Rosa, **Petaluma Hill Road** between Petaluma and Santa Rosa, and **Grange/Crane Canyon Road,** connecting the two, afford excellent views of the countryside. Get a fairly small-scale map and ask people at bicycle shops to recommend scenic routes. If you are on a bike, remain conscious of drivers; the surroundings can distract you along the blind turns and hills. And drivers should be on the lookout for bicyclists.

NIGHTLIFE

Santa Rosa Brewing Company, 458 B St. (544-4677), at 7th, downtown. Yet another of California's trendy microbreweries. Wood furniture, sports monitors in every corner, and a CD jukebox showcasing the freshest in Led Zeppelin. Solid dinner fare; sandwiches or salads $6-7; nothing over $10. Hums on the weekend. All ages welcome. Open Mon.-Wed. 11:30am-midnight, Thurs.-Sun. 11:30am-2am.

Magnolia's, 107 4th St. (526-1006), in Railroad Sq. Hodge-podge of live music. Grown-ups in t-shirts and jeans. Cover varies up to $6. Open Mon.-Sat. 7pm-2am. Must be at least 21.

Acapulco, 505 Mendocino Ave. (544-8400). Rumored to be Santa Rosa's greatest margarita bar. (They sell for $4.) Cantina/bar open Mon.-Thurs. 11am-midnight, Fri.-Sat. 11am-1am, Sun. 11am-10:30pm. Karaoke Thurs. and Fri. at 9pm. Restaurant section is popular with families. Full Mexican dinners, $5.50-14. Get burritos by the foot to go (with rice, salad, chips, salsa, sauce, and sour cream). 3-footer serves 6-9 for $35. Open Sun.-Thurs. 11am-10pm, Fri.-Sat. 11am-11pm.

A'Roma Roasters and Coffee House, 95 5th St. (576-7765), in Railroad Sq. Santa Rosa's "flamboyant" hangout. Share an unfiltered cigarette with a green-haired friend and solve the world's problems over espresso ($1). Live music; call for schedule. Open Mon.-Thurs. 7am-11pm, Fri.-Sat. 7am-midnight, Sun. 9am-11pm.

John Barleycorn's Saloon and Eatery, 2700 Yulupa Ave. (526-3511). Kickin' music and locals keep it rocking nightly. And hey, if the scene is too much, you can always step out and watch America's future in the 7-Eleven ("Sev") parking lot next door. Live music every night. Never a cover. Open Mon.-Thurs. 5:30-10pm, Fri.-Sat. 10:30am-late, Sun. 3:30-9pm.

Magnolia's, 107 4th St. (526-1006), in Railroad Sq. Top-40 music. Casual crowd. Cover varies ($6 tops). Open Mon.-Sat. 7pm-2am. Must be at least 21.

■■■ RUSSIAN RIVER VALLEY

The Russian River Valley feels like a well-kept secret. Although many of the wineries here have been operating nearly as long as their counterparts to the southeast, they are not as well-known or as frequently visited. The area also encompasses a beautiful coastline, towering redwoods, and a scenic river to soothe the nerves of even the most frazzled traveler. The wineries offer tours and tastings, and encourage picnickers to enjoy their lovely grounds. If you've had your fill of wine and wineries, this serene area is also ideal for hiking, biking, and relaxed exploration.

PRACTICAL INFORMATION AND ORIENTATION

Visitors Information: Sebastopol Area Chamber of Commerce, 265 S. Main St. (823-3032). Open Mon.-Fri. 9am-5pm. **Healdsburg Chamber of Commerce,** 217 Healdsburg Ave. (433-6935). Open Mon.-Fri. 9am-noon and 1-5pm, Sat.-Sun. 10am-2pm. **Guerneville Visitors Center,** 14034 Armstrong Woods Rd. (800-253-8800 or 869-9212). Comprehensive collection of brochures on the Russian River area. Open Mon.-Thurs. 10am-5pm, Fri. 10am-6pm, Sun. 11am-3pm.

Public Transportation: Golden Gate Transit (544-1323). Provides transportation between the Russian River Valley and the Bay Area. Bus #78 heads north from 1st and Mission to Guerneville (Mon.-Fri. 4 per evening, 2hr., $4). **Sonoma County Transit** (800-345-7433 or 576-7433), has a county-wide route (#20) from Santa Rosa to the Russian River area. Leaves from 2nd St. and Santa Rosa Ave. Mon.-Fri. 8 per day, Sat.-Sun. 3 per day; $1.80.

Bicycle Rental: Bicycle Factory, 6940 McKinley St. (829-1880), in downtown Sebastopol. Mountain bikes $8 per hr., $22 per day (includes helmet, lock, and souvenir water bottle). Open Mon.-Fri. 10am-6:30pm, Sat. 9am-5pm, Sun. 9am-4pm. **Mike's Bike Rental,** 16442 Rte. 116 (869-1106), in Guerneville, across from the Safeway. Bikes $6 per hr., $27.50 per day. Open summer daily 9am-5pm. Call for winter hrs.

Emergency: 911.

Post Office: 290 S. Main St. in Sebastopol. Open Mon.-Fri. 8:30am-5pm.

The **Russian River** winds through western Sonoma County before emptying into the Pacific Ocean north of Bodega Bay. The river flows south, roughly following **U.S. 101** until **Healdsburg,** where it begins to veer west. A number of small towns, including **Guerneville** and **Monte Rio,** line this latter stretch of the river. (For information about the coastal towns of Jenner and Bodega Bay see the Northern Coast chapter, page 324.) **Sebastopol,** while not a river town itself, claims kinship to Healdsburg, Guerneville, and Monte Rio because of its location on **Rte. 116,** "the road to the Russian River." Traveling west on **Rte. 12** from Santa Rosa will bring you to Sebastopol. From Sebastopol, head north on Rte. 116 to reach Guerneville.

ACCOMMODATIONS AND CAMPING

Although the relative seclusion of the Russian River Valley is one of its most appealing characteristics, one consequence is a decided lack of budget motels. The tourist industry in The Russian River Valley caters to a well-heeled, elegant B&B-staying crowd. However, there are options for the budget traveler; multiple campgrounds and a few affordable lodge-resorts are also located in the area. Visitors with wheels should bear in mind that this area is remarkably compact. None of the towns are more than a 40 minute drive apart. The listings below appear in order of their geographical location along the river from Healdsburg to Monte Rio.

Oasis Cultural Center, 20889 Geyserville Ave. (857-3524), in Healdsburg. Self-described "center for evolution and transformation." Grounds are spotted with unusual people and animals, including ocelots, llamas, pygmy goats, and peacocks. Spend the night in a *yurt* (a tent with floors; $45 per night) or in a teepee ($30 per night). There's also a wine-cask room for "romantic couples." Hmmm.

Johnson's Beach Resort, 1st St. (869-2022), in Guerneville. Offers touristy camping in shady environs along the river, as well as clean but bare apartments with fully equipped kitchens. Sites $6, $2 per additional person. Apartments $30 for 2, $35 for 4. Reserve 1-2 months in advance.

Armstrong Woods State Reserve (869-2015), on Armstrong Woods Rd. off Rte. 116, 3 mi. north of Guerneville. 24 secluded, un-touristy tent sites along trails in a redwood grove ($10). 4 backpacker sites ($7). No reservations. Arrive early (before 11am), especially on summer weekends.

Ring Canyon Campground (869-2746), on Armstrong Woods Rd. 1½ mi. north of Armstrong Woods State Reserve, above. Privately operated campground offers sites with picnic tables and fire rings. Bathhouses have hot showers. 35 tent sites $17.44 per night for 2. 7 RV sites $17.44 per night for 2, $19.44 with hookup. Reservations recommended, especially on weekends.

Village Inn, 20822 River Blvd. (865-2304), in Monte Rio. Turn left at the Monte Rio stop sign and then turn left again across the bridge. 1906 New England-style country inn has antique-furnished rooms, a bar, and a restaurant with a dining terrace overlooking the river. Singles from $30 for 1-2 people. $10 higher on weekends.

Rio Villa Beach Resort, 20292 Rte. 116 (865-1143; fax 865-0115), in Monte Rio. Scenic location on the Russian River east of Guerneville. Varied options include several double occupancy rooms with private bathroom, TV, and refrigerator ($65, $75 weekends).

FOOD AND ENTERTAINMENT

While Sebastopol is lacking in convenient budget accommodations, this health-conscious community has contributed to the proliferation of good and good-for-you restaurants. For excellent baked goods, head north to **Healdsburg.** For musical entertainment, the **Ziggurat,** 16135 Main St. (869-1400), in Guerneville, north of Sebastopol, offers dancing and live music, including jazz and reggae. (Cover varies: $0-7. Doors open Thurs.-Sat. at 4pm, Sun. 2pm.)

Food for Thought, 6910 McKinley St. (829-9804), in Sebastopol. Large health food store with local organic produce, a terrific selection of breads, and an amazing deli that sells sandwiches ($2.50-4.50), salads, and pasta. Open Mon.-Sat. 9am-9pm, Sun. 10am-8pm.

East-West Café, 128 N. Main St. (829-2822), in Sebastopol. Perhaps the best vegetarian restaurant in Sonoma County. Free range chicken or tofu fajitas ($8). Open Mon., Tues., Thurs. 7am-9pm, Wed. and Sun. 8am-8pm, Sat. 8am-9pm.

Viva Mexico, 841 S. Gravenstein Hwy. (Rte. 116) (823-5555), in Sebastopol. Loved by locals. This window-counter take out serves giant burritos with rice, beans, and toppings ($4 vegetarian, $4.50 with meat). Combo plates are a great bargain. Open daily 11am-8:30pm.

Village Bakery, 7225 Healdsburg Ave. (829-8101), in Sebastopol. Taste Sebastopol sourdough bread (leavened with a culture from Gravenstein apples and Chardonnay grapes). Open Mon.-Sat. 7am-5:30pm.

Cousteaux French Bakery and Café, 417 Healdsburg Ave. (433-1913), in Healdsburg. Quite possibly the finest sourdough bread in the universe. Grab an award-winning loaf for less than $2. Come for "coffee, talk, and tunes" by local artists Thurs.-Sat. 7-11pm; winter Fri.-Sat. 7-11pm. Open Mon.-Sat. 6am-7pm, Sun. 6am-6pm; winter Mon.-Sat. 6am-6pm, Sun. 6am-5pm.

Downtown Bakery and Creamery, 308A Center St. (431-2719), in Healdsburg. Prides itself on using only the freshest, ripest ingredients. Try their delicious sherbets. Open Mon.-Fri. 6am-5:30pm, Sat.-Sun. 7am-5:30pm.

SIGHTS AND SEASONAL EVENTS

Most travelers approach the Russian River Valley from the south, often driving from San Francisco. Therefore, **Sebastopol,** the southernmost town in the area, is a natural starting point from which to explore. The understatedly hip Sebastopol is known locally for its Gravenstein apple orchards. Agricultural and hippie communities gracefully cohabitate within this peaceful and genuinely warm village. At night, don't miss the **Johnny Otis Cabaret,** 7231 Healdsburg Ave. (Rte. 116) (824-8822). Johnny Otis owns, decorates, and plays at this one-time deli turned jazz and blues hall. He performs every Friday at 9pm (first-come, first-served) and Saturday at 8 and 10pm (reservations required). There's live music by other artists Sunday through Thursday at 8pm. Cover varies from $3 to $8 (open 9am-late).

Sebastopol's **Apple Blossom Festival** at the end of April celebrates the arrival of new buds with entertainment, crafts, and food. The **Sebastopol Music Festival** also occurs at this time. The **Gravenstein Apple Fair** takes place in mid-August.

Traveling a few mi. northwest along Rte. 116 from Sebastopol brings visitors to **Forestville,** the site of the **Topolos at Russian River Winery,** 5700 Gravenstein Hwy. N. (887-1575). Fashioned after a barn, the winery offers free tasting and a posh restaurant with lunches ($6-10) and dinners ($9-16). (Open Feb.-Dec. Wed.-Mon. Restaurant open 11:30am-2:30pm and 5:30-9:30pm. Tasting room open 11am-5pm. Winter hours vary.)

Five mi. northwest of Forestville along Rte. 116 lies the largest hamlet in the valley and a genuine riverside town: quiet, woodsy **Guerneville** (GURN-vill). This old-time family resort center is known for its well-established gay community. **W.C. "Bob" Trowbridge Canoe Trips** (433-7247 or 800-640-1386) runs daytrips down the river from April to October (2-5hr., $34 per canoe). **Burke's Canoe Trips** (887-1222) offers similar daytrips for $28 per canoe, as well as multi-day trips. Call ahead for return service to your car.

Just outside town are the **Korbel Champagne Cellars,** 13250 River Rd. (887-2294), offering tours daily between 10am and 3:45pm. If you're wondering why Korbel dares to call its product "champagne," the guide will explain that usage of the term "champagne" is allowed only if it is preceded by "California" in letters of the same size. Tastings transpire from 9am to 5:30pm (until 4:30pm in winter). The **Russian River Jazz Festival** (869-3940) blasts trombone, trumpet, and piano melodies down the river the first weekend after Labor Day (tickets from $24).

Three mi. north of town, the **Armstrong Woods State Reserve** (see Accommodations, page 322), is a popular day-hiking destination. The park's 800 acres and the 5,000 acres of neighboring Austin Creek Park insure that there is more than enough room for all. The **Armstrong Woods Pack Station,** Box 970 (887-2939), offers horseback riding ($5 per day user fee for state parks; trail rides $40 per ½-day).

Healdsburg, 20 mi. to the northwest, lies on U.S. 101. A good half-dozen wineries litter the countryside hereabouts; information on all of them is available from the Healdsburg Chamber of Commerce (page 321). Healdsburg sponsors a summer series of **Sunday Concerts in the Park** (433-6935, 800-648-9922 in CA) at the Historic Plaza from 2 to 4 pm.

Northern Coast

When asked to describe California's Northern Coast, visitors and denizens alike are drawn irresistibly to superlatives. Phrases like "the most unspoiled beaches" or "the tallest trees in the world" frequently color descriptions of this varied region north of San Francisco. The powerful beauty of the Northern Coast's untamed nature calls out to travelers weary of the more urban sights and sounds of the lower state.

The Northern Coast begins in the San Francisco Bay Area and continues northward to the Oregon border. Road-trippers in the Northern Coast can take their pick of two scenic highway routes. Rte. 1 (see below) offers craggy coastal vistas on the shores of Marin, Sonoma, and Mendocino Counties. Near Rockport, Rte. 1 turns sharply inland and travels away from the coast for 90 mi., merging with U.S. 101 for the rest of the journey north. Prior to this union, U.S. 101 meanders through the heart of California's wine country and passes stopover town Ukiah. The shore the highways leave behind, which has come to be known as the Lost Coast, offers some of the wildest and most beautiful scenery in the state. The inland leg along U.S. 101 north of the Lost Coast brings travelers to Garberville and the Avenue of the Giants, where they can view the enormous redwoods the region is famous for. At Eureka and Arcata, U.S. 101 winds along the coast again and stately redwoods, protected by the long, thin strips of Redwood National Park, tower beside the route. Ocean mists, tall trees, cool air, and uncrowded scenic beaches characterize this memorable expanse of the coast.

Local transportation, such as it is, along much of the coast is provided by **Mendocino Transit Authority** (MTA; 462-1422), based in Ukiah, and **Humboldt Transit Authority** (HTA; 443-5826), based in Eureka. **Greyhound** runs on Rte. 101, only hitting the coast from Eureka north.

Staying in motels along the coast during the summer can be expensive; hostels and campgrounds are more reasonable alternatives. State Parks have excellent facilities. Between May and September, temperatures are cool at night. Place reservations by calling MISTIX (800-444-7275). In winter, after the masses have left, you'll find terrific bargains at the B&Bs and motels (rates usually $15-20 less than in summer), as well as increased intimacy with the land.

The **area code** for the Northern Coast is 707.

ROUTE 1: THE PACIFIC COAST HIGHWAY

Easy driving it is not, but Rte. 1 (the Pacific Coast Highway) north of San Francisco *is* one of the most breathtaking stretches of road in California. This famous highway snakes along rugged cliffs, pounding surf, and magnificent trees. Drivers and their passengers will appreciate the opportunities for recovery from the heartstopping journey available at the quaint, not-too-touristy burgs and hamlets that line the coast. For more on Rte. 1, please see Los Angeles (page 103), the Central Coast (page 192), and the San Francisco Bay Area (page 305).

North of Point Reyes National Seashore (see Marin, page 285), Rte. 1 takes a brief inland jaunt before making an ocean rendezvous at Bodega Bay and the Sonoma Coast. **Bodega Bay** is a small town that savors its seafaring roots. A budget traveler's best options in town are outdoors: camping, hiking, and beach-combing. For browsers, Bodega Bay is an antique store maven's haven. The **visitors center,** 850 Rte. 1 (875-2868), has information on the coast north to Oregon. Off Rte. 1, there are plenty of trails in the **Sonoma Coast State Park.** Campers can choose from 98 grassy, tree-studded sites at the **Bodega Dunes Campground** (875-3483; call MISTIX 800-365-2267 for reservations), ½ mi. north of the beach (tent sites $14; hike/bike sites on the dunes $3; hot showers). **Wright's Beach Campground** next door offers 30 sites ($19, seniors $17; no showers or hot water, but you can use the facilities at Bodega Dunes). **Bodega,** 7 mi. inland, was featured in Alfred Hitchcock's *The Birds.*

GRANT (G) PLAZA
H O T E L

465 GRANT AVENUE • SAN FRANCISCO • CA 94108

RECOMMENDED BY

Fodor's, Let's Go USA, Mobile Travel Guide, & Consumers Report Travel Letter

SAN FRANCISCO'S BEST LOCATION!
1-800-472-6899

Please present this coupon at
check-in and receive
$5.00 discount

HOTEL CALIFORNIAN
ATTN: Reservations
405 Taylor Street
San Francisco, CA 94102

Continuing north on Rte. 1, you'll find **Jenner,** which sits on the Pacific at the mouth of the Russian River. Jenner's beaches are popular with marine mammals in the summer. A few mi. up the coast from Jenner, **Fort Ross State Historic Park** (847-3286) features the only reconstructed Russian buildings in the continental U.S., relics of the czar's tenuous presence in 19th-century California. Those without the wheels (or stomach) to handle Rte. 1 can reach the park by bus; take **Mendocino Transit's** daily coast run from Point Arena on the way to Santa Rosa (see Sonoma Valley: Practical Information, page 314). A lonely wooden stockade perched on the edge of the Pacific cliffs above a small harbor, Fort Ross occupies a narrow strip of land hacked from the forest—the eastern limit of imperial Russia's grasp. The Russians departed in 1841 for lack of otter to exploit, and John Sutter (of mill fame) bought the fort for a song, primarily to acquire the redwood threshing table inside. The Russians lost the measly sum they'd pocketed when the convoy carrying Sutter's funds was ambushed. The fort now houses a limited but extremely interesting **Russian Museum,** featuring a model of the pulley system used to move cargo up and down the steep harbor cliffs (fort open daily 10am-4:30pm; $5). Twenty campsites (with flush toilets) are available in the park at **The Reef** ($10; first-come, first-served). The campground lies 1½ mi. south of the entrance to the fort.

North of Fort Ross, campgrounds seem to appear at every bend of the road (and there are many bends). A mere 4 mi. up Rte. 1, **Salt Point State Park** (847-3221; call MISTIX at 800-444-7275 for reservations) has 109 sites with toilets, showers, and fire pits among the redwoods (sites $14).

Farther north in Mendocino County (on Rte. 1 of course), **Point Arena** deserves a stop. The **lighthouse** and **museum** (882-2777) protrude from the incoming fog. The original building dates from 1869, but the 115-ft. lighthouse is of 1908 vintage, constructed after an earthquake demolished the first (open daily 11am-2:30pm; $2, children 50¢). The **MTA Coast Bus** (884-3723 or 462-1422) runs one loop daily from Point Arena to Santa Rosa ($2.50, students $1.75, seniors and disabled $1.25). Point Arena has 46 tent sites as well as hike/bike sites at **Manchester State Beach** (937-5804; sites $9, seniors $7). Head inland and step up 27 dramatic mi. to the east over Mountain View Rd. to **Boonville.** The main attraction here is Boontling, a strange local language. Look for the telephone sign ("Bucky Walter" in their lingo). A return to Rte. 1 and 30-mi. drive north will bring travelers to...

■■■ MENDOCINO

When the directors of the TV show *Murder, She Wrote* needed to simulate a town in rural Maine, they filmed in Mendocino. With weathered wood shingles and sloping roofs, Mendocino's clustered houses look out of place on California's Northern Coast. They are. The town was founded in 1852 by transplanted Easterners who thought the exposed location was a natural site for wind-powered milling operations. These entrepreneurs have been superseded, however, by artists and artisans, whose presence has ensured a healthy collection of galleries and craft shops. To a small sign reading "No RV parking on this street" someone has added "or anywhere else in this town"—Mendocino is small and aggressively protective of its isolation.

PRACTICAL INFORMATION AND ORIENTATION

Visitors Information: Ford House 735 Main St. (937-5397), the old home of the town's founder, Jerome Bursely Ford. Information on nearby camping and hiking and provides town maps. Open Mon.-Sat. 11am-4pm, Sun. noon-4pm. **Parks General Information** (937-5804 or 800-444-7275), Russian Gulch Park (east side of Rte. 1). Phone lines open daily 7am-10pm, office open daily 7am-6pm.

Mendocino Stage and Mendocino Transit Authority: The Stage routes 2 buses daily between Fort Bragg and Navarro. Pick up the MTA to get to Gualala with connecting service to Ukiah (Mon.-Fri.). For schedule information, contact the Stage at 964-0167 or MTA at 241 Plant Rd. (462-1422), in Ukiah. The nearest **Greyhound** is in Ukiah, 2 hrs. away. 2 buses per day to Ft. Bragg or Ukiah.

Bicycle Rental: Stafford Inn, 44850 Comptche-Ukiah Rd. (937-5615 or 800-439-5245), south of the Ford House. Bikes $10 per hr., $30 per day. Canoes $16 per hr., $44 per day.

Taxi: 964-8294. 24 hrs.

Dial-a-Ride: 964-1800, transportation for travelers with disabilities.

Laundromat: Lucy's Laundry, 124 S. Main St., Ft. Bragg (964-1713).

Crisis Lines: Rape, 964-4357. **Poison Control,** 800-523-2222. **Disabled Crisis,** 800-426-4263.

Pharmacy: Safeway, 660 Main St. (964-4058).

Hospital: Mendocino Coast District Hospital, 700 River Dr., Ft. Bragg (961-1234).

Emergency: 911.

Police: 961-2800 (station in Ft. Bragg). **Sheriff:** 964-6308.

Post Office: 10500 Ford St. (937-5282), 2 blocks west of Main St. Open Mon.-Fri. 7:30am-4:30pm. **General Delivery ZIP Code:** 95460.

Area Code: 707.

Mendocino sits on **Rte. 1** right on the Pacific Coast, 18 mi. East of Eden, 30 mi. west of U.S. 101, and 12 mi. south of Fort Bragg. The town is tiny; park your car and walk. Weather in the Mendocino area varies from 50°F to 70°F days. Travelers should come prepared for chilly weather caused by strong winds and occasional fog.

ACCOMMODATIONS AND CAMPING

Rooms are all expensive; reserve ahead to get a reasonable deal. Fortunately, there are hundreds of campsites nearby; make reservations through MISTIX (800-365-2267). Otherwise, look to Ukiah or Ft. Bragg for budget motels.

Jug Handle Creek Farm (964-4630 or 964-4615), in Caspar, 5 mi. north on Rte. 1. Part of the Jug Handle State Reserve. A beautiful 100-year-old house. Easy access to the beach and trails in Jug Handle State Park (see Sights, below). 20 covered foam mats (bring linen or sleeping bag). $18, students $12. Campground $6, children $3. Also 1 hr. of chores per night. Reserve in advance.

The Coast Motel, 18661 Rte. 1, Ft. Bragg (964-2852), ¼ mi. south of the intersection of Rte. 1 and Rte. 20. This simple budget motel is as close to Mendocino as you can get before paying the outrageous prices of the B&Bs in the town proper. A woodsy, rustic look. Singles $32, $42 in summer.

MacKerricher State Park (694-9112 or 937-5397). Excellent views of tide pool life, passing seals, sea lions, and migratory whales. View the ocean from the cliffs and contemplate the force of the waves breaking beneath you. This park is filled with things to discover and admire, from the smallest wild flowers to the migratory whales cavorting off shore. MacKerricher is the best park in the area. Campsites have drinkable water and bathrooms $14. Make reservations. Day use is free.

Van Damme State Park (937-5804), Rte. 1, 3 mi. south of town. 74 sites. Located near the intriguing pygmy forest (see Sights, below). Great trails run through fern-covered canyons. Showers and toilets. Sites $14, seniors $12. There are some primitive sites (no facilities) $9.

Russian Gulch State Park (937-0497), Rte. 1, 1 mi. north of town or 2-3 mi. north of Ft. Bragg on Rte. 1. 30 sites. Hot showers and flush toilets. No hookups. Simple, closely clustered sites in the woods. The park has access to a lovely sand beach. Sites $14, day use $5. Book through MISTIX up to 8 weeks in advance.

Hendy Woods State Park, (895-3141), Greenwood Ridge Rd. Just south of Rte. 128 near the town of Philo, about 35 mi. southeast of Mendocino in the redwoods. 92 sites. Hot showers and flush toilets, no hookups. Sites $14. A few mi. north is the **Dimmick State Wayside,** 30 sites without showers for $9.

FOOD

It goes almost without saying that all breads are fresh-baked, all vegetables locally grown, all wheat unmilled, all coffee cappuccino, and *almost everything* expensive. Consider a picnic.

The Mendocino Bakery and Café (937-0836) on Lansing St. serves up some tasty and pleasantly inexpensive eats. Delicious breakfast burrito $3.25, warm bowl of oatmeal $1.75, deli sandwich $3.75, and quiche $3. If you want coffee with that, bring your own mug or ask for one of theirs, just don't take one off the wall, those belong to regulars. Sit on the beautiful deck outside and enjoy the ocean breeze. Open Mon.-Fri. 8am-5pm, Sat.-Sun. 8am-9pm.

Mendo Burgers (937-1111) on Lansing St. behind the bakery. Caters to the greasy burger lover, although it also has veggie and turkey burgers. Refreshingly inexpensive and popular with the local crowd. Burgers $3.75. Outdoor seating. Open Mon.-Sat. 11am-7pm, Sun. noon-4pm.

Mendocino Ice Cream Co., 45090 Main St. (937-5884). Very much an ice cream parlor. Award-winning homemade flavors like Black Forest (with cherries and chocolate chips). Single scoop $1.75, on waffle cone $2. Also serves shakes, pies, and coffee. Open Mon.-Sat. 9am-10pm, Sun. 9am-9pm.

The Corners of the Mouth (937-5345), Old Red Church, Ukiah St. Housed in a lofty renovated pinkish-red church, this grocery has everything organic under the sun. Judy's long, hot, fresh-baked breadsticks are only 85¢. Open daily 9am-7pm.

Mendosa's Market, 1909 Lansing St. (937-5879). The closest thing to a real supermarket. A little pricey, but bearable. Open daily 8am-9pm.

Dick's Bar, 45070 Main St. Dark and filled with locals. Pinball and darts. Small, grungy, and popular with local hunting and fishing types. Inexpensive and offers an inside look at life in Northern California. Traditional bar fare (hot dogs, chili, nachos, etc.) for $1-2. Beer $1.25.

SIGHTS

The town of Mendocino resembles a quaint New England fishing village. The Yankee architecture and the wide assortment of shops make it a great place to browse. Prices are steep, but there is lots to see and the salespeople are usually friendly.

The greatest attribute of the town lies 300 yds. to its west, where the land screeches to a halt and falls off into the Pacific, forming the impressive coastline of the **Mendocino Headlands** (937-5397). Fingers of eroded rock jut into the pounding ocean surf below beautiful wildflower-laden meadows. Seals frolic near secluded archways and alcoves. The ocean wind whips the waves against the steep cliffs in an aquatic moshpit. For an unforgettable show, watch the sunset and enjoy the contrast between the sun's placid descent below the horizon and the chaos engineered by the wind and the water.

Poor drainage, thin soil, and the rigors of an oceanside existence have created an unusual *bonsai* garden just south of town, the **Pygmy Forest** at **Van Damme State Park.** This forest contains mature trees between two and three ft. tall. While the Pygmy Forest lacks the majesty of the towering Redwoods, it is intriguing. The stunted trunks reflect the difficulty of the life experienced by these tiny trees that cling to along the edge of a continent. The forest is located 3 mi. north on Little River Airport Rd., south of the park, and is wheelchair accessible ($5). For an alternate way to view the trees, (and to avoid the park's $5 fee) drive past the park on Rte. 1, turn left on Little River Airport Road, and drive about 3½ mi. until you see a parking lot and a sign for the pygmy forest. A less traversed (and less accessible) pygmy farm can be found in **Jug Handle State Park** (see Camping, above). Jug Handle's primary attraction, however, is its unique **ecological staircase.** A combination of erosion and tectonic uplift has created a terrace of five different ecosystems, each roughly 100,000 years older than the one below it.

Visitors to Mendocino in July can enjoy the **Mendocino Music Festival** (937-2044), a two-week orgy of classical music and opera (tickets $12-20).

■■■ UKIAH

Ukiah's heyday lasted until the late 19th century, when produce from all over the northern part of California passed through on the railroad. The architecture of the town heavily reflects this era. But the rail-station is closed now and Ukiah has lost its importance in the produce arena. Only beautiful Lake Mendocino distinguishes Ukiah from other motel-fast-food-strip-towns. Mundane Ukiah proper has all the conveniences a highway traveler needs, but it will take a journey up to the scintillating lake—surrounded by campgrounds—to entice the visitor to stay a little longer.

PRACTICAL INFORMATION AND ORIENTATION

Visitors Information: Greater Ukiah Chamber of Commerce, 200 S. School St. (462-4705). Open Mon.-Fri. 9am-5pm. Information on Ukiah and surrounding communities. **Pomo Visitor Center** (485-8685), on Marina Drive off Rte. 20 or Eastside Calpella Rd. Native American history and lake information. Open Wed.-Sun. 9am-5pm.

Army Corps of Engineers Park Office, 1160 Lake Mendocino Dr. (462-7581), next to Lake Mendocino. Camping information. Open Mon.-Fri. 7:30am-4:30pm.

Mendocino Transit Authority, 241 Plant Rd. (462-1422). Local service 60¢. Serves Ukiah, the Forks, and Mendocino College.

Greyhound: 1351 N. State St. (468-9354). Buses to Eureka (2 per day, $24.50) and San Francisco (2 per day, $18). Open Sun.-Thurs. noon-4:30pm, Fri.-Sat. 11am-4:30pm. The station is dirty and smells foul; spend as little time in it as you can.

Taxi: DIAL-A-RIDE, 468-5555. (Run by the MTA.)

Laundry: Wash and Dry, 112 Tolmage Rd. (off State St.). Wash $1.25, 10-min. dry 50¢. Open Mon.-Fri. 6am-11pm, Sat.-Sun. 10am-6pm.

Pharmacy: Payless, 680 S. State (462-6850), at Gobbi exit off U.S. 101.

Senior Information: Greater Ukiah Senior Citizens Center, 462-4343. Open Mon.-Fri. 9am-5pm.

Crisis Lines: Crisis Intervention, 463-4357. **Disabled Crisis Line,** 800-426-4263. **Rape and Abuse Crisis,** 463-4357. **Red Cross,** 463-0112. All 24 hrs.

Hospital: Community Hospital, 860 N. Bush St. (462-3111).

Emergency: 911.

Fire Department: 300 Seminary Ave. (463-6274).

Police (non-emergency): 463-6242; county 463-4411.

Post Office: 224 N. Oak St. (462-8814). Open Mon.-Fri. 8:30am-5pm. **General Delivery ZIP Code:** 95482.

Area Code: 707.

Ukiah (pop. 14,500) is located 110 mi. north of San Francisco on **U.S. 101.** The town sits steady in the heart of **Yokayo Valley,** where temperatures consistently reach the 90s in the summer, and range from the 40s to the 70s in winter. **State Street,** Ukiah's main drag and the location of many budget motels, runs roughly parallel and to the west of U.S. 101.

ACCOMMODATIONS AND CAMPING

Ukiah supports a multitude of inexpensive motels. A more scenic stay, however, can be found at one of the nearby campgrounds.

Holiday Lodge, 1050 S. State St. (800-300-2906). Clean, A/C, pool, cable TV; VCR rental plus unlimited movies ($7 extra). Non-smoking rooms available. Excellent (and complimentary) continental breakfast spread. Singles from $29. 2 people, 1 bed $31. Doubles $38. $3 discount for seniors and AAA.

Garden Court Motor Inn, 1175 S. State St. (462-5646). The nicest place to stay in Ukiah. A classic 1950s motel; carports, kitchenettes, picnic tables, and a flower garden. Enjoy the early evening air from one of the springy chairs outside. Singles from $28. Doubles from $35. Reservations essential.

National 9 Inn, 755 S. State St. (800-524-9999 or 462-8509). Cable TV, A/C, indoor pool, carports. Worn bathrooms in red, pink, and off-white. Non-smoking rooms. No wheelchair access. Check-in/out 11am. Singles $28. Doubles $35.

The Army Corps of Engineers maintains more than 300 sites at four **campgrounds** around Lake Mendocino. **Ky-en** ($12, lakeside spot $14) has beach sites, drinking water, restrooms, fire pits, and mobs of people on weekends. **Bu-Shay** ($12) has water, toilets, and hot showers—and it's much quieter than the other camp-grounds. Sites 1-30 have the most shade (important in summer). **Che-Ka-Ka** ($8) has water, toilets, fire pits, and easy access to a boat ramp. **Miti** is free, has only pit toilets, and is accessible only by boat or half-hour hike. All camps are first-come, first-served and are often crowded; arrive early. Call 462-7581 for more information.

Orr Hot Springs, 13201 Orr Springs Rd. (462-6277), is a rarely frequented but worthy alternative to Ukiah lodging. Take State St. north to Orr Springs Rd., then go 13½ mi. and look for signs. Walk-in tent sites ($25, Thurs.-Sun. $30) include full use of the grounds, kitchens, hot springs, and swimming pool (clothing optional). Call for directions and reservations. Available for day use, the hot springs are a pleasant break from the stress of the road ($15).

FOOD

Every Saturday (8:30am-noon) and Tuesday (4pm-6:30pm), the **Ukiah Farmer's Market** (743-1664) sets up shop at Perkins and Orchard Ave.

Bob & Judy's, 1250 Lake Mendocino Dr. (485-5323), justifies the trip to Ukiah. The plain wood building, ¼ mi. from the lakeshore, has an outdoor deck overlooking the valley's vineyards. You can enjoy scrumptious 4-egg omelettes served with potatoes and light, flaky biscuits for breakfast ($5.25-6.75). Or starve yourself all day to prepare for their MASSIVE finger-lickin' barbecued ribs dinner served with soup, salad, potatoes, veggies, bread, and dessert ($13). They actually get a kick out of giving people too much food. Lighter palates should try the "diet plate"—a 1/3-lb. hamburger, 1/3 lb. of cottage cheese, and fruit. Reservations recommended. Open Wed.-Sun. 7am-9pm.

Ron-De-Voo Restaurant, 1130 S. State St. (462-1152). Come to this diner for giant breakfasts. Pancakes, eggs, bacon, sausage, ham, and coffee for $5. Burger or sandwich and fries for $3.75. Dinners are good deals, too; steaks start at just $6. Open daily 6am-3pm and 5-9pm.

Ukiah Co-op, 308 E. Perkins (462-4778), across from the railway station. A natural foods grocery that also has prepared foods. In the mood for a braised tofu sandwich? Only $3. Open Mon.-Fri. 9am-7pm, Sat. 10am-6pm.

SIGHTS

Sparkling **Lake Mendocino** steals the sights show here. The 1822-acre lake has large-mouth, small-mouth, and striped bass, as well as bluegill and catfish to titillate anglers. (No permits needed.) **Water-skiing,** too, is oh-so-popular here. The lake's **marina** (485-1432), at Marina Ave. (off Rte. 120) on the water, rents paddle boats and ski boats.

The **Pomo Visitors Center** (485-8685), on Marina Dr. off Rte. 120, is an elegant redwood building modeled on a ceremonial Pomo dance house. Films and exhibits commemorate the virtually destroyed Pomo culture (open Wed.-Sun. 9am-5pm).

In town, the **Grace Hudson Museum and Sun House,** 431 S. Main St. (462-3370), at S. State St., is located in a lovely five-acre garden. Self-guided tours take you through the artist and her ethnologist husband's collection of Native American portraits. Also exhibits current work by local artists (open Wed.-Sat. 10am-4:30pm, Sun. noon-4:30pm). This is a great spot for a picnic if you can't make it to the lake.

■■■ AVENUE OF THE GIANTS

About 6 mi. north of **Garberville** off U.S. 101, the **Avenue of the Giants** winds its way through a 31-mi.-long canopy of the largest living creatures this side of sea level. The tops of the mammoth trees cannot be seen from inside a car—pull over and get out of your car to avoid straining your neck, wrecking your vehicle, and looking ridiculous. Interact with the redwoods; walk into the woods, find a small clearing in the middle of several tall trees, stare up at the blue sky above the tree tops, and spin around madly like a little kid. Our sources inform us that this activity (when not done in excess) results in an inexpensive, 100% natural, fat-free, and drug-free high.

Practical Information The **Garberville Chamber of Commerce,** 733 Redwood Dr. (923-2613; open daily 10am-6pm), will supply you with a free list of businesses on the Avenue, most of which you can safely dismiss as tourist traps. The **Eel River Redwoods Hostel** in Leggett (925-6425; see Accommodations, below) has a much better guide that lists hot local spots, six eco-tours, and ways to save money. The **Humboldt Redwoods State Park Visitors Center** (946-2263; open daily March-Oct. 9am-5pm, Nov.-March weekends only) has a free brochure that highlights the groves and facilities along the Avenue and suggests trails to the Avenue's most accessible attractions. **Greyhound** runs four buses out of Garberville (2 north and 2 south daily) to: Eureka ($12); Portland ($159); San Francisco ($33.50). Bus tickets are available at **Singing Salmon Music,** 432 Church St. (923-3259), one block east of Redwood Dr. (Open Mon.-Fri. 10:30am-5pm.) In an **emergency** call 911. The **post office** is located one block west of Redwood Dr. on Sprowel Creek Rd. (923-2652; open Mon.-Fri. 8:30am-5:30pm). The **General Delivery ZIP Code** is 95542.

Accommodations and Camping The **Eel River Redwoods Hostel,** 70400 U.S. 101 (925-6469)—16 mi. south on U.S. 101 in Leggett—is *the* place to hang your hat. This hosteling wonderland is located in an aromatic redwood grove right on the South Fork Eel River and provides access to a sauna, a jacuzzi, and a swimming hole (complete with inner tubes). The basics include laundry, loaner bicycles, and cabins for couples or families (reserve ahead for these). The center garden includes a teepee (hostelers may choose to sleep here), a Model-T Ford, two gazebos, a comfy hammock, and a burbling brook. Best of all, the hostel is open all day, and the extremely friendly owners will provide endless information on the area, and even give guided tours of the Avenue of the Giants if asked. The hostel also has a cozy British-style pub that serves a variety of beers including those from local microbreweries, and free spaghetti once a week. If you're traveling by bus, ask the driver to stop at the hostel or get off at **Standish Hickey State Park;** the hostel is a ½-mi. walk north from there. ($12, nonmembers $14.) If you absolutely *must* stay in a motel, try the **Redway Motel,** 3223 Redwood Dr. (923-2660), which offers clean, simple rooms (summer $26-60; winter $30-40).

In Humboldt State Park (946-2409), camping options are plentiful. **Albee Creek Campground** is located under the redwood canopy and has showers and flush toilets. (Sites $14.) Call MISTIX for reservations (800-444-7275). **Richardson Grove State Park** (247-3318) also offers breathtaking campsites with hot showers and bathrooms for the same price (8 mi. south of Garberville off U.S. 101).

Food Back in civilization, you will find a multitude of eating options in nearby Garberville. **Sentry Market** on Redwood Dr. is the largest supermarket for miles (open daily 7am-10pm). **D'Amato's,** 3460 Redwood Dr. (923-2174), just north of Garberville in Redway at 3460 Redwood Dr., is home to the area's best pizza (slices start at $1.50, large pizza $9.25, deli sandwiches $2.80). At the corner of Redwood and Sprowel Creek Road is **Nacho Mama's,** a take-out stand serving cheap Mexican food in satisfying quantities. Also in Redway is the **Mateel Café** (923-2030), the by-product of a Parisian chef and a Californian nutritionist who have since divorced. The nutritionist runs things now but never fear, the café still lures gourmets from as far away as San Francisco. The beautiful outdoor patio and live acoustic music compensate for a deliberately cheesy lounge area. Sandwiches and burgers run around $5 (open Mon. 2-9pm, Tues.-Fri. noon-9pm, Sat. 5-9pm).

Sights and Seasonal Events A slow meander through the forest is the best way to experience the redwoods' grandeur. The less crowded trails are found in the Northern Section of the park around **Rockefeller Forest,** which contains the largest grove of old-growth redwoods (200 years plus) in the world. Once inside the woods, if you're very, very quiet, you can sometimes hear the mighty trees creak. You should be sure to pay your respects to the **Dyerville Giant,** located in the red-wood graveyard at Founder's Grove, about midway through the Avenue of the Giants. It is difficult to appreciate the height of the trees while standing next to the upright trunk. However, because the Dyerville Giant rests on its side, over 60 human body-lengths long, it is possible to fully appreciate its size. Its root ball is three stories high. After surveying the tree from one end to the other, you might close your eyes and imagine what it would have been like to witness the Giant's fall.

Leggett, 16 mi. south of Garberville, is heralded as the home of the **Drive-Thru-Tree.** This 315-ft. redwood has a 21-ft. base which you can drive through ($3), like at a fast-food restaurant. Save your money. If you must pass through the bowels of a tree, there are plenty of walk-through trees nearby that cost nothing. Two mi. north, the **Standish Hickey Recreation Area** (925-6482), dubbed the "Gateway to the Tall Trees Country," has fishing, camping, and hiking—all under towering redwoods.

With its sizable population of artists, Garberville's art festivals are excellent and well-attended. **Jazz on the Lake** and the **Summer Arts Fair** begin in late June, fol-lowed by the dramatic outdoor theater of **Shakespeare at Benbow Lake,** in late July. Call the Chamber of Commerce (see Practical Information, page 328) for addi-tional information. The **Mateel Community Center** (923-3368), in Redway, spon-sors classes and local events. The highlight of local festivals comes in early August, when the Mateel Community Center presents **Reggae on the River.** This 12-hour reggae festival on the banks of the Eel River is considered the jammin'est in the U.S. Thousands crowd the Avenue to be splashed with the smooth vibes of the music. This celebration, complete with a volcano of food, drink, and other ingestible items, is celebrated as only Northern California can—the experience can be truly mind-expanding. Call the Reggae Hotline (923-3369) for information.

■■■ LOST COAST

Marketing seclusion and a modest, rural ambience continues to be a successful ven-ture for many of Northern California's seaside towns, although it's been quite some time since most of them were secluded or modest. Happily, a 90-mi. stretch of coast between Eureka and Rockport has been bypassed by this trend. Because this region's rugged terrain prevented cost-effective highway construction, Rte. 1 was moved inland and the "Lost Coast" was saved from the tourist crunch.

Characterizing the powerful beauty of the Lost Coast is difficult because the area is large, rural, and varied. Visitors are free to absorb the transcendent moments pro-vided by the stunning scenery at their own pace. Revel in the chaos of the crashing surf and the serenity of the setting sun—the Lost Coast offers a retreat from the hec-tic pace of life elsewhere.

Emergency services for the Lost Coast include the Garberville **sheriff** (923-2761), **ambulance** (923-3962), **fire and rescue** department (923-3475), and, of course, **911.** The **area code** is 707.

Right after Rte. 1 begins to turn inward, a small country road (number 431) turns north up a hill and out of sight into the foliage (a sign advises RVs and trailers to stay out). The 3-mi. road is dusty and precarious, but it leads to **Usal Beach,** one of the more secluded beaches on the Lost Coast. When you arrive here, you'll see a self-registration kiosk and camping areas (the state-maintained sites are unmarked and cost $3-9). About 100 yds. farther up the road, you'll find a short bridge and another road to the west which leads to sites closer to the beach and a parking area (camp-ing on the beach itself is permitted). The black sand is littered with bleached drift-wood, perfect for a bonfire. *There is no potable water here*; you must bring your own. Secure your tent carefully, or the strong winds may blow it away. Road 431 continues past the beach to a four-way intersection. The left and right forks lead to more campsites. Continue straight and through Timber Ridge only if you have a four-wheel-drive-vehicle and off-road experience; it is 22 mi. to the next decent dirt road, and you could comfortably bathe in some of the potholes found here.

Farther north along the coast is **Sinkyone Wilderness State Park** (take Rte. 1 to U.S. 101). Sinkyone has been heavily logged recently, however the coast remains beautiful. Get off in Redway and gas up; there are only a couple of gas stations in all of the Lost Coast. Head west out of town on the paved Redway Dr. After traveling 12 mi., you'll come upon Thorn Junction. Take the left fork (Briceland Thorne Rd.) through Whitethorn until it becomes a dirt road at the Mendocino County Line. If you are interested in pottery, the remote **Arcanum Ranch Pottery**, a residence and an award-winning pottery store, is worth the stop. All of the glazes are lead-free and highly original: mugs and bowls from $8. There are no set hours. Call ahead (986-7236) to make sure someone will be around (12500 Briceland Thorne Rd., look for the sign on the right-hand side as you travel south). Continuing along Briceland Thorne Rd., you'll come upon Four Corners Junction. Take the middle road. It is very narrow and will not allow two cars to pass side-by-side, so make sure to keep track of turnouts in case you have to back up. About 4 mi. up the road is the **Needle Rock Ranger Station** (986-7711), where information on the park is available and sites can be paid for. No reservations are accepted, there's no electricity, and the station is closed after 5pm. You can park here and hike to your campsite or drive all the way to **Bear Harbor**. The ranger station has a couple of rooms available ($14, call ahead). At Bear Harbor, be prepared to share the landscape with the **Roosevelt elk** who graze in the overlooking bluffs. Here, also, bring your own drinking water.

One candid local declared **Shelter Cove** "nothing but a big real estate scam." The town's one attraction is its overpriced gas station. Coming from Bear Harbor, take the left fork and turn left on Shelter Cove Rd. The gas station is on the left before you hit town (open weekdays 9am-5pm). When you leave, take Shelter Cove Rd. past Thorne Junction and turn left on Telegraph Ridge Rd. (also known as Wilder Ridge Rd.). This is safer than the more direct Kings Peak Rd., which is long, winding, and full of holes. Kings Peak Rd. is, however, the most direct way to **Kings Peak** (4086 ft.), the highest point on the shoreline of the continental U.S. Free primitive **campgrounds** (permits not required) punctuate the interior, while $5 car-accessible sites dot the roads leading through it. Pick up maps and camping information at the Bureau of Land Management, 1125 16th St., Arcata (822-7648; open Mon.-Fri. 9am-5pm), or at any chamber of commerce in nearby towns.

The next stop is **Honeydew**, at the intersection of Wilder Ridge Rd. (see above) and Mattole Rd. The main attraction here is the **general store** (open daily 9am-5pm with cash-only gas). This is the meeting spot for locals and, depending on the crowd, you may encounter some fascinating people.

Forty-five minutes north on Mattole Rd. is the intersection with Lighthouse Rd. (there's a sign right before a bridge for northbound traffic). At the end of Lighthouse (dirt) Rd. is the **Mattole Campground** (no permit required, no water, pit toilets), which is part of the **Kings Range Conservation Area.** Park anywhere that seems fit and pitch a tent. The wide, flat beach begins where the parking area ends. The beach is anchored by high cliffs on both sides. One hundred yds. before the campground, a dirt road leads up to the top of the hills, offering dizzying views of the beach. You can drive or hike up—a steep 1¼ mi. There is private property around, but it is well-marked; feel free to enter areas without signs.

About 2½ mi. south of the beach campsite is an abandoned lighthouse, accessible by foot, which also permits lodging on a first-come basis. Much of the beach can be hiked, but buy tide tables in Garberville or at the nearby Petrolia General Store (see below) to keep your hike dry and safe. Past Lighthouse Rd. on Mattole is **Petrolia**, which contains a general store (no gas) and a post office (open Mon.-Sat. 9am-5pm).

Ten mi. north of Petrolia, the road hugs the beach for several spectacular miles. Cattle from nearby ranches frequently wander onto the black sand, creating the spectacle of bovines contentedly chewing their cud on top of the ocean's brilliant blue. The beach here is private property, but public access paths show up on occasion, and camping is traditionally tolerated. Stop to do a little beach-combing—the sands of the Lost Coast often hide the sorts of goodies that get sucked up immediately at more traversed beaches.

Ferndale is the end of the line and the beginning of civilization. Ross Park and the two cemeteries on Ocean Ave. offer a last taste of the seclusion and scenery you have come to expect from the Lost Coast. The park's lush undergrowth makes for private picnicking (bring a blanket and bug repellent), while the amphitheater-like cemeteries allow you to stand far above Ferndale for a view of the quaint, Victorian town and the grazing dairy cattle. Those who need amenities can try the **Humboldt County Fairgrounds** (786-9511) on Arlington St., which offers campsites for $5 and RV hookups for $10. Showers, toilets, and water are all available. Except for exorbitantly priced B&Bs, accommodations are sparse. The **Eureka Baking Company,** 543 Main St. (786-4741), has fresh bread, muffins, pastries, sandwiches, and coffee (70¢, free refills) for reasonable prices (open Mon.-Fri. 6:30am-5:30pm, Sat. 7:30am-4pm, Sun. 9am-4pm). The **Ferndale Meat Co.,** 376 Main St. (786-4501), lays generous cheese and meat slabs on a choice of breads for $2.75 (open daily 8:30am-5pm). Down the block, the **Kinetic Sculpture Museum,** on Main St. in Ferndale, has inherited some of the entries from past Arcata Kinetic Sculpture Races (see Arcata, below), including the famous chicken-and-egg mobile and a "kinetic sculpture" constructed entirely from license plates (free).

■■■ EUREKA

When James Ryan stumbled upon this lost harbor in Humboldt Bay in 1850, he shouted *"Eureka!"* ("I found it") and named the town in the full ecstasy of his discovery. One hundred and forty years later, you may wonder what all the fuss was about. The number of attractive finds in Eureka today is small. Although some of the Victorian homes of the old town have been restored to their original glory, they are often sandwiched between seedy, boarded-up houses. Eureka is making a serious effort at reviving its image, but it has yet to discover the winning formula.

Practical Information and Orientation Tiny, but detailed maps are available at the **Visitors Bureau,** 1034 2nd St. (443-5097 or 800-338-7352 in CA, and 800-346-3482 from outside; open Mon.-Fri. 9am-5pm). The **Eureka Chamber of Commerce,** 2112 Broadway (442-3738 or 800-356-6381), has helpful information on restaurants and hotels. (Open Mon.-Fri. 9am-5pm.) **Greyhound,** 1603 4th St. (442-0370) at Q St., provides frequent service between Eureka and Arcata and zooms to San Francisco twice a day ($32). (Open Mon.-Fri. 6:30am-1pm and 4-10:20pm, Sat.-Sun. 6:30am-noon and 7-10:30pm.) **Dial-a-Ride** (443-9747) serves seniors and the disabled. For local transportation, the **Humboldt Transport Authority,** 133 V St. (443-0826), runs buses in the area between Scotia and Trinidad, including Arcata. Pick up most buses at 5th and D St. (Mon.-Fri. 6am-8pm; fare 40¢-$1.25). Call for bike transport information. **Eureka Transit,** 133 V St. (443-0826), offers bus service within Eureka. (Mon.-Fri. 6am-7pm, Sat. 10am-5pm; fare 60¢, seniors and disabled 40¢.) For equipment rental, contact **Adventure's Edge,** 408 F St. (445-3035). They rent tents for $8 per day, sleeping bags for $8.50 per day, and a cross-country ski package for $10 per day. (Open Mon.-Sat. 10am-6pm, Sun. noon-5pm.) The **laundromat** is located at Clark and Summer St. (Open daily 7am-9pm.) 24-hr. crisis lines are **disabled crisis** (800-426-4263) and **rape crisis** (445-2881). **Eureka General Hospital,** 2200 Harrison Ave. (445-5111), provides emergency service (822-3621). Contact the **police** at 441-4060, the **sheriff** at 445-7505, and the **fire department** at 441-4000. In an **emergency** call 911. The **post office** is at 337 W. Clark St. (442-1768; open Mon.-Fri. 8:30am-5pm, Sat. noon-3pm). The **General Delivery ZIP Code** is 95501. The **area code** is 707.

Eureka straddles **U.S. 101** 12 mi. south of Arcata, 280 mi. north of San Francisco. In town, U.S. 101 becomes **Main St.** and then **Broadway,** and runs north-south.

Accommodations and Camping Travelers will find an abundance of budget motels off U.S. 101, which bisects Eureka, but many are unappealing; be selective. Avoid walking alone at night. Even those dependent on public transportation may want to forego easier-to-find accommodations in Eureka for more comfortable, happier, hippier atmosphere of Arcata. **Motel 6,** 1934 Broadway (445-9631), in the southern end of town off U.S. 101 offers standard fare. (Rooms $30; non-smoking and wheelchair accessible.) **Patrick's Point State Park** (677-3570), 27 mi. north of Eureka has 123 sites with showers and flush toilets, terrific ocean views, and plush vegetation. Reservations through MISTIX (800-444-7275) are required two weeks in advance in summer. Hikers and bikers can almost always find space in overflow areas. (Sites $14 per vehicle, no hookups, hikers and cyclists $3, $5 for day use.) The point is also an excellent whale-watching location (see Redwood National Park, page 338). **Big Lagoon County Park** (445-7652), 20 mi. north of Eureka on U.S. 101 has sites with pit toilets and drinking water ($10). Arrive early.

Food Eureka Co-op (443-6027), 1st and E St. sells bulk grains, organic produce, and the rest. (Open Mon.-Sat. 10am-7pm, Sun. 10am-6pm.) There are also **two farmer's markets** that run from July to October. (Tues. 10am-1pm at the Old Town Gazebo, Thurs. 10am-1pm at the Eureka Mall). **The Humboldt Bay Coffee Co.,** 211 F St., Old Town Eureka (444-3969), is the place for local artisans, philosophers, and chess players to congregate and refuel. (Filling deli sandwich $4.75, muffins $1.10. Large coffee $1. Open Mon.-Thurs. 6:30am-9pm, Fri. 6:30am-11pm, Sat. 8am-11pm, Sun. 9am-7pm.) **Tomaso's Tomato Pies,** 216 E St., Old Town Eureka (445-0100) serves up generous servings of pizza. A $4 slice of "square" pizza can feed two. The salads are excellent (from $5) and sandwiches cost $6. (Open Mon.-Thurs. 11:30am-9pm, Fri.-Sat. 11:30am-9pm, Sun. 5-8:30pm.)

Sights Architecture buffs might appreciate the Chamber's drive-by tour of local Victorian homes. Don't walk; many homes in between are decidedly uninteresting. The **Wooden Garden of Romano Gabriel** is on permanent display at 325 2nd St. Gabriel has constructed a brilliantly colored "garden" of people, plants, and symbols, all from scrap wood. Some consider bizarre work primitive art on an epic scale; others call it a cluttered pile of wood. If you are nearby, stop and decide for yourself. Farther up the road past the Eureka exit, next to the gun club, is a **shore-bird wildlife sanctuary** where flocks can be seen during fall and spring migrations.

In **Samoa** (take Rte. 255 past the cookhouse) is the dunes recreation area—a peninsula with an impressive dune ecosystem that thrives. There's beach access and dune hiking (watch out for ATVs, All Terrain Vehicles).

The **Fort Humboldt State Historic Park** (445-6567), at Broadway and Highland St., southwest of Eureka, features a logging exhibit, a museum, and picnic areas.

■■■ ARCATA

Lying at the intersection of U.S. 101 and Rte. 299, Arcata (ar-KAY-ta) typifies the laid-back, stress-free existence attributed to the Northern Coast. Arcata's neighbor **Humboldt State University** (Earth First! was founded here) might seem overly liberal and directionless to some, but others will appreciate the relaxed life led by many students. Making friends is easy here; cheap and popular restaurants and college hangouts are a good place to start.

Practical Information Visitor information can be gathered at the **Arcata Chamber of Commerce,** 1062 G. St. (822-3619). In an **emergency,** call 911. The **area code** for Arcata is 707.

Accommodations and Camping For those with a car, camping is easy near Arcata, and a cluster of budget motels line the Giuntoli exit off U.S. 101 north of the city. **Clam Beach County Park** (445-7491), 7½ mi. north of Arcata on U.S. 101, provides basic facilities, water, pit toilets, dunes, and a terrific beach where you can dig clams seasonally. The park is very popular, so call ahead. (Sites $8.) Roughly 200 additional camping sites are available at **Big Lagoon County Park** and **Patrick's Point State Park,** both within 15 mi. of Arcata (see Eureka, page 334, for details).

There is, of course, always **Motel 6.** This clean, quiet motel lies at 4755 Valley West Blvd., (822-7061), at the Giuntoli exit off U.S. 101. As expected, they leave the light on. (Singles $31. Doubles $37.) The place to stay in the summer, however, is the **Arcata Hostel,** 1390 I St. (822-9995), at 14th St., about ½ mi. from the Grey-hound station. This private hostel is officially open from June 25 until the end of August, but sometimes there are rooms available during the year, and flopping on the couch can be negotiated. The permanent residents outnumber the hostelers here and may make you want to stay longer than you planned ($10 per night).

Food Try **Los Bageles,** 1061 I St. (822-3150), within walking distance of the hostel, for a Northern Californian leftist experience. Munch basic bagels, bread, and coffee while reading the extensive assortment of political flyers. (Open Mon. and Wed.-Fri. 7am-6pm, Sat. 7am-5pm, Sun. 8am-3pm. Most items under $1.) **Hey Juan!,** 1642½ G St. (822-8433), serves up tasty and dirt-cheap Cali-Mex fare: entree with beans and rice about $4. (Open Sun.-Thurs. 10:30am-11pm, Fri.-Sat. 10:30am-11:30pm.) **Humboldt Brewery,** 856 10th St. (826-BREW, -2739), a local microbrewery, has been so successful, it's spread next door into the cavernous imported beer garden. Enjoy the wonderful, atypical beer—try the Oatmeal Stout ($2.75 pint), the gold medalist in the '88 BeerFest, or the Red Nectar Ale, silver medalist in the '94 BeerFest—and relax to the excellent live music on weekends. This bar often hosts big names in country, folk, and blues (open Mon. and Wed. noon-10pm, Fri.-Sat. noon-12:30am, Sun. noon-9pm). **Crosswinds,** 860 10th St. (826-2133), is a vegan restaurant that serves food all can enjoy. The **Arcata Co-op** (822-5947), on 8th at I St., carries tofu, *tempeh, mochi,* and soy milk, and has a useful ride board (open Mon.-Sat. 9am-9pm, Sun. 9am-8pm). A **Farmers Market** (441-9699) invades town on Saturdays (9am-noon) in the Arcata Plaza, and Tuesdays (10am-1pm) in the Old Town Gazebo, from June to November. Pick up Arcata potatoes, a local favorite.

Sights Those who wish to tour the **Humboldt campus** should be sure to see the **whale skulls** by the biological labs and **Redwood Park,** which contains lots of nooks for picnicking among the Giants. Five minutes east of the city is the **Arcata Community Forest,** 566 acres of city-owned land. In 1979, an ecologically-minded citizens group began managing the park and developed a "sane, multiple-use management plan." Translated, that means wide-open picnic spaces. A former "sanitary" landfill, the 75-acre **Arcata Marsh and Wildlife Sanctuary** (822-6918) lies at the foot of I St. Wander the trails alone, or take a tour to see how this world-famous saltwater marsh/converted sewer system works with treated waste water (tours Sat. 8:30am).

The 14-year-old **Kinetic Sculpture Race,** held annually over Memorial Day weekend, qualifies as Humboldt County's oddest festival. A few dozen insane or intoxicated adventurers attempt to pilot unwieldy but endearing homemade vehicles on a grueling three-day 35-mi. trek from Arcata in the north across the bay to Eureka and then to Ferndale in the south via road, sand, and water. During the **summer,** the university students disperse and the town's population thins out considerably.

■■■ REDWOOD NATIONAL PARK

> *The Redwoods, once seen, leave a mark or create a vision that stays with you always. ...It's not only their unbelievable stature, nor the color which seems to shift and vary under your eyes, no, they are not like any trees we know, they are ambassadors from another time.*
>
> —John Steinbeck

Redwood National Park encompasses some of California's most impressive trees. A visitor cannot help but be awed by the towering giants and the astounding biodiversity they help to support. Elk and black bears roam the Prairie Creek area as whales swim by the coast (migrating southward Nov.-Jan. and returning March-May), and birds are everywhere. The park begins just south of the Oregon border and extends down the coast for almost 40 mi., encompassing three state parks while avoiding the tiny coastal towns which cling to Rte. 101. Many people drive through the park on Rte. 101, but few take the time to stop. Those who do will be amply rewarded—the craggy shore and the towering trees are incredible.

The region is famous for its fishing, and the variegated terrain is ideal for hikers and backpackers. The lack of public transportation within the park, however, requires extreme perseverance from those without cars. Beaches line the coastal trail which extends almost the length of the park. Day use of the state park costs $5 per car; hikers and bikers are also charged $5 each. Campsites are numerous and range from well-equipped (flush toilets and free hot showers; sites $14, hikers/bikers $3) to primitive (outhouses at best; free). Peak season coincides with the California school system's summer vacation, which begins in the third week of June and concludes in early September. The ideal time to visit is mid-April to mid-June or September to mid-October. The park is less crowded during these months and is free of summer fog. Call MISTIX (800-365-2267) for reservations, essential in the summer.

Crescent City, with park headquarters and a few basic services, stands at the park's northern end. The small town of Orick is situated at the southern limit and harbors an extremely helpful ranger station, a state park headquarters, and a handful of motels. Rte. 101 connects the two, traversing most of the park.

PRACTICAL INFORMATION AND ORIENTATION

Visitors Information: Redwood National Park Headquarters and Information Center, 1111 2nd St., Crescent City 95531 (464-6101). Open daily 8am-5pm. Headquarters of the entire national park, but the ranger stations are just as well-informed. Offers 1- to 3-day field seminars which range in topic from the ecology of the spotted owl to scenic photography ($10-75, advance registration essential). **Redwood Information Center** (488-3461), on U.S. 101, 1 mi. south of Orick. Shows free films about park and wildlife on request. Mountain bike trail info. Free map of the park and brochures on trails and campsites. Enthusiastic and extremely helpful rangers. **Crescent City Chamber of Commerce,** 1001 Front St., Crescent City (464-3174) provides plenty of information. Open Mon.-Fri. 8am-7pm, Sat.-Sun. 9am-5pm; Labor Day-Memorial Day Mon.-Fri. 9am-5pm. **Prairie Creek Ranger Station** (488-2171), on U.S. 101, in Prairie Creek Redwood State Park. Open June-Sept. daily 9am-6pm; Sept.-Nov. and March-June 8:45am-5:15pm. **Hiouchi Ranger Station** (458-3134), on U.S. 199, across from Jedediah Smith Redwoods State Park. Open daily 8am-7pm; Sept. 2-June 20 8am-5pm.

Park Fee: The national park is free, but Prairie Creek State Park costs $5 per car per day, hikers and bikers are charged as well.

Park Activity Information: 464-6101 (recorded information, 24 hrs.) Also tune in at **1610 AM** on your radio in Hiouchi and Orick areas.

Greyhound: 1125 Northcrest Dr. (464-2807), in Crescent City. 2 buses per day headed north and 2 going south. Buses can supposedly be flagged down at 3 places within the park: at the **Shoreline Deli** (488-5761), 1 mi. south of Orick on U.S. 101; at **Paul's Cannery** in Klamath on U.S. 101; and in front of the **Redwood Hostel**. Beware, however, of capricious bus drivers who may decide to ignore you. Call the Greyhound station directly preceding your stop, and ask the attendant to make the driver aware of your presence. Lockers available, $1 for 24 hrs. Open Mon.-Fri. 7-10am and 5-7pm, Sat. 7-10am and 6:30-7:30pm.

Local Bus: Dial-a-Ride (464-9314), operates in the immediate Crescent City vicinity. Rides are all the same price, regardless of distance. Open Mon.-Fri. 7am-11pm, Sat. 7am-7pm. $1, seniors and youths 75¢.

Road Conditions: 800-427-7623.

Highway Patrol: 464-3117.

AAA Emergency Road Service: Crescent City AAA, 1000 Northcrest Dr. (464-5626). Open Mon.-Fri. 8:30am-5pm.

Horseback Tours: Tall Trees Outfitters, 1000 Dryders Rd. In north Orick, turn east onto Dryders Rd. (488-5785). 2-hr. trail ride $30.

Laundromat: Econ-o-wash, 601 H St. Crescent City (464-9935). Open 7am-11pm. Wash 75¢-$2. Dry 25¢ for 10 min.
Rape Crisis: Del Norte County, 465-2851. 24 hrs.
Disabled Information: Access Brochure, available by mail or at the ranger's station. If notified in advance, rangers can help you make the most of your stay.
Hospital: Sutter Coast, 800 E. Washington Blvd. (464-8511; for **emergencies** ext. 8888), Crescent City. Ambulance service.
Emergency: 911.
Post Office: 751 2nd St. (464-2151), in **Crescent City.** Open Mon.-Fri. 8:30am-5pm, Sat. noon-3pm. **General Delivery ZIP Code:** 95531. Another office at 121147 U.S. 101 in **Orick.** Open Mon.-Fri. 8:30am-noon, 1-5pm. **General Delivery ZIP Code:** 95555. Free boxes available at **Orick Market** (see Orick Area, page 338).
Area Code: 707.

In the park, fruits and berries can be gathered for personal consumption; however, all other plants and animals are protected, even feathers dropped by birds of prey are off limits. **Fishing licenses** are required for fresh and saltwater fishing, and there are minimum-weight and maximum-catch requirements specific to both. One-day licenses range from $5-8. Call the ranger station or the License and Revenue Office at 916-739-3380. Three small towns, **Orick** in the south, **Klamath** in the middle, and **Crescent City** in the north provide basic services and are home to a few motels.

ACCOMMODATIONS

The most pleasant roost is the **Redwood Youth Hostel (HI/AYH),** 14480 U.S. 101, Klamath 95548 (482-8265), at Wilson Creek Rd. This hostel, housed in the historic Victorian DeMartin House, combines ultramodern facilities with a certain ruggedness. Its 30 beds and kitchen, dining room, and laundry facilities are all wheelchair accessible. There's a separate stove for vegetarians, a dozen recycling bins, two sundecks, staple foods for sale, and a laundry service ($1.25 per load, free for passing cyclists). Affording a spectacular view of the ocean and an ideal location, the hostel simply asks that you take your shoes off when you're inside the building and let the caretakers rest from 9:30am to 4:30 pm. (Check-in 4:30-9:30pm. Curfew 11pm. Closed 9:30am-4:30pm, so you'll have to be an early riser. $9, under 18 with parent $4.50. Linen $1.) Reservations are recommended, and must be made by mail three weeks in advance. See Sights, below, for information about park campgrounds.

SIGHTS

You can see Redwood National Park in just over an hour by car, but there's no reason to. Get out and stroll around or do not come at all—the redwoods should be experienced in person, not through tempered glass windows. The National Park Service conducts a symphony of organized activities for all ages. Pick up a detailed list of Junior Ranger programs and nature walks at any of the park's ranger stations (see Practical Information, page 336). From Memorial Day to Labor Day, the Jedediah Smith, Mill Creek, and Prairie Creek Campfire Centers all host nightly campfires and sing-alongs. Roving Rangers cruise the park's popular areas from 11am to 3pm in season to answer questions and tell stories. If you're lucky, you may bump into Jeff and Christie, two wonderfully helpful and entertaining rangers. Call the **Redwood Information Center** (488-3461) for details on park programs. Most activities are described in a seasonal newsletter, the *Redwood Visitor Guide,* available throughout the park. There's also an excellent booklet ($1.50) which details all trails in both the national and state parks, but the rangers can supply you with information about the trails most suited to your preferences free of charge. Hikers should take particular care to wear protective clothing—**ticks** and **poison oak** thrive in the park. After hiking, inspect your body, particularly your lower legs, your scalp, and any area covered by tightly-fitting garments (e.g. socks), for ticks. If you suspect that you have exposed yourself to poison oak, remove and wash your clothes and wash your skin immediately with **Fels Naphtha Soap** (call TeleNurse at 445-3121).

Orick Area

This region covers the southernmost section of the park. Its **visitors center** lies about 1 mi. south of Orick on U.S. 101 and ½ mi. south of the Shoreline Deli (the Greyhound bus stop). The main attraction is the **tall trees grove,** a 2½-mi. trail which begins 6 mi. from the ranger station. If you're driving, you'll need a permit; only 35 per day are issued on a first-come, first-served basis until 2pm. A minimum of three to four hours should be allowed for the trip. A **shuttle bus** ($7 donation per person) runs from the station to the tall trees trail (June 13-Sept. 7, 2 per day; May 23-June 12 and Sept. 8-20, 1 per day). From there, it's a 1.3-mi. hike down (about 30 min.) to the tallest redwoods in the park and, in fact, to the **tallest known tree in the world** (367.8 ft., one-third the height of the World Trade Center.) If you're hiking in and hoping for a motorized return trip, book the shuttle before you go. Backpackers may camp anywhere along the way after obtaining a permit at the ranger station. Be sure to consult a ranger before attempting the trek in winter, adverse weather conditions sometimes render the trail impassable. The coastal redwoods, which can live for over 2000 years (the oldest known specimen was not recognized until after it had been chopped down in the 1930s), grow in a 500-mi. belt from Monterey County into Oregon, up to 30 mi. inland. Many of the best specimens are in the park, protected from their nemesis—the chainsaw. Incidentally, the average time spent by visitors looking at the largest tree is one minute 40 seconds.

Orick itself (pop. 650) is a friendly town, overrun with souvenir stores selling "burl sculptures" (wood carvings pleasing to neither eye nor wallet). The rampant commercialism of the small town contrasts sharply with the surrounding natural beauty. Nevertheless, the town provides some useful amenities. Along U.S. 101 are a **post office,** the reasonably priced **Orick Market** (488-3225), and some motels. The market is open daily from 8am to 7pm and delivers groceries to Prairie Creek Campground at 7:30pm daily. Phone in your order before 6pm (minimum order $10; delivery free). The **Palm Café,** Rte. 101 in downtown Orick (488-3381), dishes out basic diner food to local dudes in rattlesnake cowboy hats (head and tail still attached), but visitors are also welcome. Burgers with fries are $4.25. Try the homemade cream pies for $1.45.

The **Park Woods Motel,** 121440 Rte. 101 (488-5175), has rooms for $35 for one or two people, and a two-bedroom unit with full kitchen is only $40. **Rolf's Prairie Creek Motel** (488-3841) offers smaller, somewhat worn rooms at lower prices; $28 for a single, $36 for a double. You can eat at Rolf's pricey restaurant ($12-16) or drive to Crescent City for the 39¢ Carls' Jr. burgers. Rolf's is located just after the turn-off to Davison Road. This dirt path runs through redwoods and then drops down to the ocean along Gold Bluffs Beach, passing the favorite grazing spots of some of the park's 500 **elk.** Watch for antlers sticking out of the grass, as the elk often snooze at mid-day. And don't be foolish enough to approach an elk on foot. When the elk decides you're too close, you might not have time to see him charge, but you'll certainly feel it.

In the second week of July, the **Orick Rodeo** (488-2525) brings bull riding, wild horse races, barrel races, and the crowning of a "rodeo queen."

Patrick's Point State Park lies about 15 mi. south of Orick along U.S. 101 and offers one of the most spectacular views on the California coast. Campers, boaters, and nature enthusiasts may want to spend a day or two at Patrick's Point before heading north to the redwoods. During **whale-watching** season (Oct.-Dec., March-May), the towering cliffs and ocean-jutting geography of the point provide the best seats in the house for observing the migration of these mammoth mammals.

Prairie Creek Area

The Prairie Creek Area, equipped with a **ranger station** and **state park campgrounds,** is perfect for hikers, who can experience 75 mi. of trails in the park's 14,000 acres. The **James Irvine Trail** (4.5 mi. one way) winds through magnificent redwoods, around clear and cold creeks, past numerous elk, through **Fern Canyon** (famed for its 50-ft. fern walls and crystalline creek), and by a stretch of the Pacific

Ocean (wear shoes that you don't mind getting wet). The trail starts at the Prairie Creek Visitors Center (see Practical Information, page 336). The less ambitious can elk-watch too, as elk love to graze on the meadow in front of the ranger station.

The **Elk Prairie Trail** (1.4 mi. one way) skirts the prairie and can be made into a loop by hooking up with the nature trail. (Elk may look peaceful, but they are best left unapproached.) **Revelation** and **Redwood Access Trails** were designed to accommodate people with disabilities. There are three campsites in Prairie Creek. **Elk Prairie** allows RVs and has hookups, hot showers, flush toilets, and drinking water. **Gold Bluffs Beach** does not allow RVs (cars are okay), but has all the same amenities except the showers are solar, making hot water conspicuously finite. Both sites are $14. **Butler Creek,** an isolated, primitive campground without amenities (sites $3), is a 2-mi. hike from Fern Canyon. Reservations are recommended for all three sites (MISTIX 800-365-2267).

Klamath Area

To the north, the Klamath Area comprises a thin stretch of park land connecting Prairie Creek with Del Norte State Park. The main attraction here is the rugged and beautiful coastline. The **Klamath Overlook,** where Requa Rd. meets the Coastal Trail, is another excellent **whale-watching site.**

The mouth of the **Klamath River** is a popular fishing spot (permit required; see Practical Information, page 337) during the fall and spring when salmon spawn, and during the winter when steelhead trout do the same. The town of Klamath has gone so far as to name itself the "Salmon and Steelhead Capital of the World." Sea lions in the spring and harbor seals in the summer congregate near the **Douglas Memorial Bridge,** or the part of it that survived a 1964 flood. Two golden bears guard each end of the bridge. A primitive campsite with 10 sites and no showers can be found at Flint Ridge, a ¼-mi. walk from the parking area. (Free. No permit required.)

Camp Marigold, 16101 U.S. 101 (482-3585 or 800-621-8513) has cabins with kitchenettes ($34) and is the best budget place in the area, after the Redwood Hostel (see Accommodations, page 337). The well-kept, woodsy cabins are a pleasant alternative to the mundane budget-motel look. There is no ranger station in the area.

Crescent City Area

Crescent City calls itself the city "where the Redwoods meet the Sea." In 1964, it met the sea for real, when a *tsunami* caused by oceanic quakes brought 500mph winds and leveled the city. Nine blocks into the town, the powerful wave was still two stories high. Today the rebuilt city offers an outstanding location from which to explore the National Park.

The **Crescent City Visitors Center,** in the Chamber of Commerce at 1001 Front St. (464-3174), has lots o' brochures (open Mon.-Fri. 8am-7pm, Sat.-Sun. 9am-5pm; Labor Day-Memorial Day Mon.-Fri. 9am-5pm).

Seven mi. south of the city lies the Del Norte Coast Redwoods State Park's **Mill Creek Campground** (464-9533), a state-level extension of the Redwood Forest. The park's magnificent ocean views—along with picnic areas, hiking trails, and nearby fishing—lure enough campers to fill the sites in summer. (Sites $14, hiker/biker $3, day use $5.) Food and lodgings in the city are depressingly overpriced. For the best deals, head to 9th St., the pre-*tsunami* location of U.S. 101. The surviving motels are cleaner and less expensive than those more centrally located. **El Patio,** 655 H St. (464-5114), offers decent rooms with an early '70s look for a modest price. Some rooms have kitchenettes; all have TVs. (Singles $24.20, doubles $30.80; $2 key deposit.) **Nickel Creek Camp** (take U.S. 101 to the end of Enderts Beach Rd.) has a walk-in, non-amenitized camp above the beach (5 sites; free). This isolated campground rests on the border of a jungle-like redwood forest and the beach. From here, it is a ½-mi. walk to the Enderts Beach Tidepool. Pick up a guide at a ranger station to help you identify some of the unusual life found here. **Crescent City Redwoods KOA,** 4241 U.S. 101 (464-5744), 5 mi. north of the city, is an extremely well-equipped, if overpriced, campground with showers, laundry facilities, mini-store, game room, and farm animals to feed and pet. (Tent sites $17.50, RVs with full hook-up $21.50.) Popular "Kamping Kabins" (from $32) have electricity and running water and offer a great place for groups to krash. Bring your own sleeping bag or bedding. Call for reservations.

The **Battery Point Lighthouse** (464-3089), on a causeway jutting out of Front St., houses a **museum** open only during low tide. Don't get caught once the sea starts coming in; find a dry spot, watch the waves break against the rocks, and listen for the eerie sound of the fog horn. (Open Wed.-Sun. 10am-4pm, tide permitting. $2, children 50¢.) **Demonstration Forest,** 4 mi. south of Crescent City on U.S. 101, provides a self-guided tour and lodge with exhibits. A video on planning and foresting is shown mid June to early September. From June through August, the National Park offers two-hour **tidepool walks** (1 mi.) at the end of Endert's Beach Rd. (turn off 4 mi. south of Crescent City). The fascinating walks will bring you close to starfish, sea urchins, sea anemone, and crabs in their natural setting. Call 464-6101 for details.

A lovely scenic drive from Crescent City along **Pebble Beach Drive** to **Pt. St. George** takes travelers past a stretch of coastline that looks transplanted from New England. Craggy cliffs, lush prairies, and an old lighthouse add to the atmosphere.

Crescent City is loaded with inexpensive restaurants. For a sit-down meal, **Los Compadres** (464-7871), awaits on U.S. 101 South, cooking up spicy Mexican food in *grande* portions. (Super burritos $4.55, chips and salsa $1; open daily 11am-9pm, in winter 11am-8pm.) **Alias Jones,** 983 3rd St. (465-6987), in the heart of downtown Crescent City, is known for serving hearty portions. For breakfast, try a cinnamon roll the size of a cake ($1.75) or a fruity muffin ($1.25). Lunches with taters on the side are $4-6. Your craving for buffalo meat can be satisfied at **Three Feathers Fry Bread,** 451 U.S. 101 (464-6003). These lean, tasty burgers will set you back $6, $4 for a regular cow burger. Forego the fries in favor of delicious, authentic fry bread $1.50. (Open daily 11am-7pm.) **Torero's,** 200 U.S. 101 (464-5712), dishes out filling, flavorful Mexican food lunch specials ($5, entrees $4-8). (Open Sun.-Thurs. 11am-8:30pm, Fri.-Sat. 11am-9:30pm). The **Safeway** in Jedediah Smith Sq., at 4th and M St., sells natural and not-so-natural munchies in bulk. (Open 24 hrs.)

Annual highlights in Crescent City include the **World Championship Crab Races** (800-343-8300) which feature races and crab feasts on the third Sunday in February. During **Easter in July** (487-8400), the lily completes its biennial bloom with a celebratory festival. The **Weekend in Bear Country** (464-7441), is a Beachfront Park festival held in mid-August.

Hiouchi Area

This inland region sits in the northern part of the park along Rte. 199 and contains several excellent hiking trails. The **Stout Grove Trail** can be found by traveling 2 mi. north of Jedediah State Park on U.S. 101, and then 3 mi. along South Fork Rd., which becomes Douglas Park Dr. It's an easy ½-mi. walk, passing the park's widest redwood, (18 ft. in diameter). The path is also accessible to people with disabilities; call 458-3310 for arrangements. Just 2 mi. south of the Jedediah State Park on U.S. 101 lies the **Simpson-Reed Trail.** A tour map (25¢ from the rangers station) will guide you on this pleasant trek. **Kayak** trips on the Smith River leave from the ranger station. The four-hour trip covers some challenging rapids. (2 trips daily Wed.-Sun. at 9am, approx. dates June 17-Aug. 2. Low water may force premature cancellation of the program. $6, ages under 10 not allowed.) Participants must weigh under 220 lbs. and be able to swim. Make reservations at the rangers station (see Practical Information, page 336). The **Howland Hill Road** skirts the Smith River as it travels through redwood groves. The scenic stretch of road (no RVs or trailers allowed) begins near the Redwood Forest information center and ends at Crescent City.

Six Rivers National Forest and the corresponding recreation area lie directly east of Hiouchi. The Smith River rushes through rocky gorges as it winds its way from the mountains to the coast. This last "wild and scenic" river in California is the state's only major undammed river. Consequently, its cool, clear water flows extraordinarily fast and provides excellent salmon, trout, and steelhead fishing.

Sacramento Valley and the Cascades

The Sacramento Valley is the California that few know. Instead of surfers, eight lane freeways, Hollywood, and the Golden Gate Bridge, this region is defined by farmlands and small towns. The pace of life is considerably slower than along the coast and tourists are scarce. The towns along I-5 are small, languid, and geared towards agriculture. Thus, except in Sacramento, residents wake up early and are quiet by nightfall. The state capital is worth a visit, if you're into early California history and state government. Chico, Red Bluff, and Redding are useful as bases for exploring the nearby marvels of the Lassen National Forest, Mt. Shasta, and the Lava Beds.

■■■ SACRAMENTO

Sacramento is the indistinctive capital of a highly distinctive state. Although it's the seventh largest city in California, Sacramento has a small-town USA feel. It is located near the center of the state, and therefore lacks the proximity to the Pacific that give Los Angeles and San Francisco so much of their character. Sacramento's status as the center of government for the U.S.'s most populous state is what keeps it on the map. Located in the middle of farm country, locals have dubbed it "Sac-of-tomatoes" or "Sacratomato" in honor of the ubiquitous red fruit. With its combination of wide tree-lined boulevards, Victorian homes, rising gang problems, and burgeoning growth, Sacramento is struggling to gain respect as a major metropolis without falling too deeply into large city woes.

PRACTICAL INFORMATION AND ORIENTATION

Visitors Information: Sacramento Convention and Visitors Bureau, 1421 K St. (264-7777), at the corner of 15th and K. Small and congenial, with a tidy stand of brochures. Open daily 9am-5pm. Also try the **Old Sacramento Visitors Center,** 1104 Front St. (442-7644), and **Old Sacramento Events Hotline** (558-3912). The **Beeline** (552-5252), gives recorded events information. The Fri. edition of the *Sacramento Bee* contains a supplement called *Ticket,* which gives a run-down of events, restaurants, and night spots. *News and Reviews* details weekly events, concerts, ticket prices, and cover charges for most clubs and bars.
Sacramento Metro Airport: 929-5411, 12 mi. north of downtown on I-5. Cabs are correspondingly expensive ($19-23 from the airport to downtown).
Amtrak: 800-872-7245 or 444-4280 for local info., on 5th at I St. Connections to: Reno ($52); L.A. ($67); Seattle ($114); San Francisco ($14). Terminal open daily 5:15am-midnight. Travelers should be careful in this area at night.
Greyhound: 715 L St. (800-231-2222), between 7th and 8th St. Relatively safe. Luggage lockers available for passengers. To: Reno (Gambler's Round-trip Special, 3-day min. stay, $17); L.A. ($39); San Francisco ($9). Open 24 hrs.
Sacramento Regional Transit Bus: 321-2877. Bus service in downtown Mon.-Fri. 5am-10pm. Express buses run Mon.-Fri. 6-9am and 3:30-6pm. Fare $1.25, seniors and ages 5-12 50¢; free transfer; day passes $3, seniors and children $1.25. Exact fare required. **Light rail** connects the business district with the eastern regions of the city. Trains run every 15 min. from 5am-midnight. Fare $1.25.
Yolo Bus Commuter Lines: 800-371-2877 or 371-2877. Connects downtown with Old Sacramento, West Sacramento, Davis, and Woodland. Open Mon.-Fri. 6am-10:30pm, Sat.-Sun. 8am-7pm. Fare $1, transfers 25¢.
Taxi: Old Checker Cab Company, 457-2222. 24 hrs.
Car Rental: Rent-A-Wreck, 4815 Franklin Blvd. (454-0912), between 12th and Fruitridge. $25 per day, $139 per week. 700 free mi.

AAA Emergency Road Service: 800-222-4357 or 331-9981, AAA members only. **Road Information:** 800-427-7623. 24 hrs.

Bicycle Rental: American River Bike Shop, 9203 Folsom Blvd. (363-6271), northeast of downtown. Bikes $4 per hr., $20 per day. Credit card or $100 cash deposit required. Open Mon.-Fri. 9am-7pm, Sat. 9am-6pm, Sun. 9am-5pm.

Weather: 646-2000. 24-hr. recording.

Traveler's Aid: 717 K St. (443-1719).

Gay Community Center: Lambda, 1931 L St. (442-0185). Open daily 9am-9pm.

U.C. Davis Medical Center: 2315 Stockton Blvd. (734-2011), at Broadway. **Emergency Services,** 734-2453; **Poison Center,** 734-3692, staffed 24 hrs.

Emergency: 911.

Police: 264-5471, at 6th and H St.

Post Office: Metro Station, 801 I St. (556-3400), at 8th. Open Mon.-Fri. 8am-5pm., Sat. 8am-noon. **General Delivery ZIP Code:** 95814.

Area Code: 916.

ORIENTATION

Sacramento (pop. 385,000) is located at the center of the Sacramento Valley. Five major highways converge on the city: **I-5** and **Rte. 99** run north-south, **I-80** runs east-west between San Francisco and Reno, and **U.S. 50** and **Rte. 16** bring traffic from the Gold Country into the capital. The capitol, a park, and endless state government buildings occupy the **downtown** area.

ACCOMMODATIONS

Sacramento's extraordinary supply of motel rooms may be jam-packed if a large convention is taking place; reserve a month in advance. A phenomenal number of cheap hotels line West Capitol Ave. in nearby West Sacramento. Some may be a bit seedy, however, so play it safe and be choosy.

Motel 6, 1415 30th St. (457-0777), at U.S. 50 and I-80. No surprises here. Recently renovated and refurbished. Pool. Singles $30, $6 per additional person.

Americana Lodge, 818 15th St. (444-3980). No Davy Crockett hats or old Coca-Cola signs, but has a small pool, an airport shuttle, A/C, and HBO. A fair trade. Check-out 11am. Singles from $36. Doubles $40. Confirm reservations with advance payment.

Mansion View Lodge, 711 16th St. (443-6631 or 800-446-6465 for reservations), between G and H St. Worth the trip if you're looking for a double and like pink. Most doubles are 2-room suites with daybeds. Singles $36. Doubles $40, $4 for an extra person. 10% AAA discount.

Capitol Park Hotel, 1125 9th St. (441-5361), at L St., 2 blocks from Greyhound. The only thing older than the hotel is its clientele. Well-worn rooms kept cool by large windows. An unbeatable location. Singles $28. Doubles $35. $5 key deposit.

Central Motel, 818 16th St. (446-6006), next to the Governor's Mansion. A/C and TV in standard rooms. Singles $30. Doubles $35. $5 for an extra person.

FOOD

Rubicon Brewing Company, 2004 Capitol Ave. (448-7032). Home of India Pale Ale, the winning brew at the 1989 and 1990 American Beer Festivals (pint $2.25). Cool, laid-back micro-brewery with high-quality food. Filling sandwiches served on fresh bread ($4-6). Also pours a good selection of "hand-crafted ales." Open Mon. 11am-11:30pm, Wed.-Thurs. 11:30am-11:30pm, Fri. 11am-12:30am, Sat. 9am-12:30am, Sun. 9am-10pm.

Freeport Bakery, 2966 Freeport Blvd. (442-4256). Regarded by many as the best bakery in Sacramento, this quaint little café is a terrific option for those craving something fresh out of the oven. Try a slice of cake ($1.95) or be adventurous and have a leek or bacon Lorraine ($3). Outdoor seating. Open Mon.-Fri. 7am-6:30pm, Sat. 7am-5:30pm, Sun. 8am-2pm.

Marlene's Vegetable Patch and Nutrition Center, 1119 8th St. (448-3327), between K and L, 1 block from Greyhound. Scrupulously vegetarian, right down to the "soy sour cream," but omnivores will hardly detect the difference. Filling lunch entrees ($5-7) and smoothies ($2). All-you-can-eat buffet and salad bar ($6). Open Mon.-Fri. 10:30am-2:30pm, and 9am-4pm for drinks and herbs.

Zelda's Original Gourmet Pizza, 1415 21st St. (447-1400). The best deep-dish pizza in Sacramento. A dark, cool retreat from Sacramento's heat, though a hike from the center of town. Medium cheese $8.50. Their Vegetarian Supreme ($12.50) is indeed both. Open Mon.-Thurs. 11:30am-2pm and 5-10pm, Fri. 11:30am-2pm and 5-11:30pm, Sat. 5-11:30pm, Sun. 5-9pm.

SIGHTS AND SEASONAL EVENTS

A sleazy neighborhood in the 1960s, **Old Sacramento** is now a full-fledged tourist attraction with ritzy shops filling the original building shells. Pick up a free self-guided walking tour map at the **Old Sacramento Visitors Center** (see Practical Information, above).

Try one or two of the excellent historical museums in Old Sacramento's northern end. The **California State Railroad Museum,** 111 I St. (552-5252, ext. 7245), at 2nd St., houses a fascinating collection of historical locomotives in its over 100,000 square feet of exhibition space. Start with the 13-minute film in the lobby, and you'll appreciate the museum much more. (Open daily 10am-5pm. $5, ages 6-12 $2, under 6 free.) The same ticket admits you to the **Central Pacific Depot and Passenger Station,** at 1st and J St., a reconstruction of a Golden Age station. The new **Discovery Museum** (264-7057), formerly the Sacramento History and Science Museum, is located next to the Railroad Museum. Visitors learn about Sacramento's past. (Open Wed.-Sun. 10am-5pm. $3.50, children $2.)

The gifts of Dearborn, Michigan to the world are on display at the **Towe Ford Museum of California,** 2200 Front St. (442-6802), south of V St. This museum has a collection of over 180 Ford cars and trucks. (Open daily 10am-6pm. $5, ages 14-18 $2.50, ages 5-14 $1, under 5 free.)

Art lovers should stop by the **Crocker Art Museum,** 216 O St. (264-5423), at 3rd St., which exhibits 19th-century European and American oil paintings, and also some photography and contemporary works by California artists. (Open Wed.-Sun. 10am-5pm, Thurs. 10am-9pm. $3.50, ages 7-17 $2, under 7 free. Tours available.)

The elegant **State Capitol** (324-0333), at 10th St. and Capitol Mall, in Capitol Park, was nearly replaced by twin modern towers in the 1970s. However, California tax payers spent over $68 million to restore the building and the result is a stately, impressive, and, dare we say, regal building. Tours last one hour; free tickets are distributed in room B27 on a first-come basis starting 20 minutes before tour time (tours daily 9am-4pm, on the hour). Colonnades of towering palm trees and grassy lawns make **Capitol Park** a welcome oasis in the middle of downtown's busy bureaucracy. The **Old Governor's Mansion** (324-0539), at 16th and H St., was built in 1877 and served as the residence of California's governor and his family until then-Governor Ronald Reagan requested more spacious accommodations. (Open daily 10am-4pm, 1-hr. tours on the hour. $2, ages 6-12 $1, under 6 free.)

Across town at 27th and L St., **Sutter's Fort** (445-4422) is a reconstruction of the 1839 military settlement that put Sacramento on the map. During the summer, Sutter's Fort offers an Interpretive Program in which workers reenact life during the Fort's heyday in the 1850s. Bake bread in adobe brick ovens, sew quilts, pack muskets, and spin yarn (and yarns). ($5, children $2.) The settlement also contains the informative and hands-on **State Indian Museum** (324-0471; both museums open daily 10am-5pm. Each $2, 6-12 $1, under 6 free.) All of these, plus the **Sacramento Children's Museum** (1322 O St., 447-5871), the **Leland Stanford Museum** (8th and N St., 324-0575), and the **Wells Fargo Museum** (1000 2nd St., 440-4263) are part of Sacramento's "Museum Mile."

The original **Tower Records** (444-3000) looms at the corner of 16th and Broadway. The spire of the Tower movie theater looks straight out of Gotham City ($6.75, matinees $3.75). One of the world's greatest record store chains began in 1941 when Russ Solomon started selling records in the back of his dad's drugstore.

Today, the Tower complex includes a movie theater, a café, and a video store. The complex is a popular hangout for younger Sacramentans (open 9am-midnight).

If you'd rather be outdoors, rent a four-person raft ($28) from **American River Raft Rentals,** 11257 S. Bridge St., Rancho Cordova (635-6400), 10 mi. east of downtown on U.S. 50 (open weekdays 9am-6pm, weekends 9am-8pm). The scenery isn't extraordinary and the water isn't white, but if the weather is nice, why should you let that stop you? The **American River Bike Trail** from downtown Sacramento to Folsom is another favorite of outdoors enthusiasts. Picnic areas and emergency phones are scattered along the way.

Sacramento hosts one of the world's largest Dixieland Jazz festivals, the **Dixieland Jazz Jubilee,** every Memorial Day weekend, with over 100 bands from around the world taking part (372-5277). Jazz lovers will find heaven in Old Sacramento during the festival; there seems to be a different quartet every 10 feet. Find a small bar and enjoy a festive performance. Local groups perform **Shakespeare in the Park** (558-2228; June-Aug.). The agriculturally oriented **California State Fair** (924-2000) takes place from mid-August to early September, and comes complete with a carnival. For weekend music and events, sift through the free weeklies: *Sacramento News and Reviews, Suttertown News,* and *Sac This Week.*

ENTERTAINMENT AND NIGHTLIFE

The Fox and Goose, 1001 R St. (443-8825), at 10th St. A "public house" with a 2-story ceiling serving only wine and beer (check out their selection of imported British labels) in a woody, relaxed setting. Live music nightly, generally acoustic during the week and electric on weekends. $2 cover. Check *News and Reviews* for band schedule and cover charges. Pints $2.85, wine $1.75-3.50. Open Mon.-Fri. 7am-closing, Sat. 9am-closing, Sun. 9am-1pm.

America Live, 645 Downtown Plaza (447-5483) is a conglomeration of seven different clubs that offer just about every evening activity imaginable. From comedy to sports to country to techno to an English-style pub, this place has it all. One cover charge ($0-5) lets you wander freely from room to room.

The Original Java City, 1800 Capitol Ave. is one of several neo-Bohemian coffeeshops that grace downtown. This popular joint caters to everyone; punks and college professors sip cappuccino ($1.65) on the same street corner.

Old Ironsides (443-9751) at 10th and S St., is a popular club with both the gay and heterosexual communities. Half of the space is devoted to live music (cover $3); the other half is a lively bar with cheap beer (drafts $1.50).

Faces, 2000 K St. (448-7798). The slickest of the many gay bars in the neighborhood, this expansive, sophisticated club offers 3 bar areas, a capacious dance floor, and an ice cream stand. Open daily 3pm-1:45am.

■■■ DAVIS

Davis is a quaint town with 45,000 bicycles, a branch of the University of California, wonderful public transportation—and not much else. On weekend nights during the UC Davis semester there's lots of action, but in summer, the students head home and the pace of life slows down considerably. In the midst of California's hustle and bustle, that may not be such a bad thing.

Practical Information And Orientation Visitor's information can be found at the **Chamber of Commerce and Visitors Center,** 228 B St. (756-5160; open Mon.-Fri. 8:30am-5pm). The **UC Davis Memorial Union Information Center** is in the Griffin Lounge on campus (752-2222, TDD 752-2228; campus events 752-2813; information 752-1011; open Mon.-Fri. 8am-5pm). The **Public Library** is at 315 E. 14th St. (757-5591). **Sutter Davis Hospital** is located at Rd. 99 and Covell Blvd. (756-6440; 24-hr. **emergency** 757-5111; TDD/TTY 756-6446). For **general emergencies,** call 911. The **post office** lies at 2020 5th St. (753-3496), at Poleline Rd. (Open Mon.-Fri. 8:30am-5:30pm, Sat. 10am-1pm. **General Delivery ZIP Code:** 95817.)

The **Amtrak** terminal is at 840 2nd St. (758-4220; one way to Sacramento $5, to San Francisco $14.) The **Greyhound** terminal sits at 826 2nd St. (753-2485). **Unitrans** (752-2877) buses connect downtown and the UCD campus (50¢, seniors and Davis students free). **Yolo Bus** (756-2877) services Davis, Woodland, and Sacramento (50¢-$1.50; daily and monthly passes available). **TAPS,** the UCD Intracampus Shuttle Service (752-MILE, -6453), offers free cross-campus service to faculty, students, and campus guests and an inter-campus Shuttle to Berkeley during school year (for a fee). With at least one bike shop on every block, Davis is the "bicycle capital of the world." **Ken's Bike and Ski,** 654 G St. (758-3223), rents bikes for $10 per day or $29 per week. At **Sport Life,** 514 3rd St. (758-6000), $11 gets you a day's use of in-line skates, knee pads, wrist guards, and a helmet.

Sights, Accommodations, and Food The **University of California at Davis** is the largest campus (in area) in the UC network, and also one of the nation's finest agricultural universities. The Campus Events and Information Office presents a variety of tours (752-2222 or 752-2813). The **Quail Ridge Wilderness Conservancy** is headquartered at 25344 County Rd. 95 (758-1387), ½ mi. north of County Rd. 31. The Conservancy itself is located away from the headquarters on the southern end of Lake Berryessa, but stop here first and they'll drive you out there. California oaks, bunchgrasses, and a variety of wildlife thrive in this wilderness area, presenting a view of what California looked like before asphalt and steel gave it a facelift of dubious value. Tours by appointment are available (758-1387). At the same address is an ecologically oriented **Research Farm.** For a donation of $2 per person ($30 minimum per group), you can get a new perspective on the world by sharing in a day of farm activities. Animals (both barnyard and exotic), aquatic plants, and hayrides make it a particularly enticing place. Call 758-1387 to arrange for a tour. The farm is a must-see for anyone interested in innovative horticultural procedures and ecologically sound farming. Frank Maurer, the coordinator behind the conservancy and the farm, is a fountain of knowledge.

Motels in Davis do not come cheap, and during university events, you'll be lucky to get a room. **Davis Motel,** 1111 Richards Blvd. (756-1910), at the I-80 and Davis exit just six blocks from campus, has attractive rooms with archways leading to the bathrooms. (Rooms for 1-2 people $44. Doubles from $48.) You'll find the basics at **Motel 6,** 4835 Chiles Rd. (753-3777). It is about 5 mi. from downtown, accessible by car or bus from the Amtrak terminal. (Singles $25. Doubles $31.) Even a bevy of RVs can't spoil the excellent location of the **West Sacramento KOA** (800-545-5267), at I-80 and W. Capitol Ave., which borders on Lake Washington. Pool, recreation room, laundry, 24-hr. showers. (RVs $28 per night. Tents $22.)

Davis holds a **farmer's market** on Wednesday evenings from 5:30 to 8:30pm and Saturday mornings 8am to noon, from June to August. Located next to Central Park on 2nd St. between C and E St., this gathering has just-picked produce, food vendors, and music (756-8763). Those looking to stock a picnic basket should also check out the **Davis Food Co-op,** 620 G St. (758-2667), which has fresh bread and organic produce (open daily 8:30am-10pm). **Murder Burger,** 978 Olive Dr. (756-2142), serves up half-lb. "burgers so good they're to die for" ($5). Creamy strawberry shakes made with fresh strawberries cost $2.35. (Open Mon.-Thurs. and Sat. 10am-8pm, Fri. and Sun. 10am-9pm.) **Caffé Italia,** 1121 Richards Blvd. (758-7200), draws crowds for large portions of pasta ($4 lunch, $7.50 dinner), pizza ($5 and up), and salads ($5.50 and up). (Open Mon.-Thurs. 6am-10pm, Fri.-Sat. 6am-11pm, Sun. 7-10pm.) Another popular student hangout is **The Graduate,** 805 Russell Blvd. (758-4723), in the University Mall (right next to campus, in a big barn-like structure). The Grad's cavernous dining area has eight large-screen TVs, video games, pool table, outdoor tables, and music and dancing Fri.-Sat. nights. Famous Gradburger 'n' fries will set you back $4.75. Lots of food and drink specials are offered throughout the week (99¢ burgers, 99¢ pitchers of beer). (Open daily 10:30am-1:30am.) Vegetarians may want to check out **Delta of Venus Coffee House,** 122 B. St. (753-8639). This alternative, neo-Bohemian restaurant serves espresso drinks, micro and imported beers, and light meals. (Whole wheat waffles $2.45. Organic, red, spicy beans and brown rice $3.)

■■■ CHICO

The merchants and residents of Chico have small-town America down to a science. Don't go out of your way to come here, but if you happen to stumble upon Chico, you'll find the pervasive sense of tranquility refreshing. However, beneath the quiet surface lurks Chico State, formerly the nation's foremost party school. If you are searching for the lively side of Chico, the university is located in the eastern section of town and fuels a dynamic party scene on weekends. In the words of more than one enlightened visitor, "the best thing about Chico is the cheap beer."

Practical Information The **Chamber of Commerce,** 500 W. 5th St. (891-5556), has wall-to-wall brochures about Chico. Check out the weekly *News and Review* for goings-on (open Mon.-Fri. 9am-5pm, Sat. 10am-3pm). The **State University Information Center** is at 898-6116 or 898-4636 (open Mon.-Sat. 10am-4pm). **Amtrak** (800-872-7245), has no ticket office, just a platform on 5th St. at Orange. Trains go to: Seattle (1 per day; $144); Sacramento (1 per day; $22); San Francisco ($36). Buses stop at **Greyhound,** 717 Wall (343-8266), one block from Main St., four times per day on north-south routes and go to: Sacramento ($12.50); Red Bluff ($7). (Open Mon.-Fri. 6am-7pm, Sat. 8:30am-1pm and 2-5pm; weekday evening service.) **Butte County Transit,** 893-4299 or 800-822-8145, links Chico with nearby towns. (Buses run Mon.-Fri. 6:30am-10pm, 1 per hr. Fare 70-90¢). **Chico Area Transit System (CATS)** (893-5252), runs five routes in Chico. (Buses run Mon.-Fri. 6:30am-6:30pm, Sat. 8:30am-6:30pm. 30-60¢.) **Enterprise,** 1600 Mangrove Ave. (899-1188), **rents cars** ($25 per day; must be 21 with major credit card). Wash at **Wascomat,** 254 E. 1st St., at Wall. (Wash 85¢; dry 25¢; detergent 50¢. Open Sun.-Thurs. 6:30am-10pm, Fri.-Sat. 6:30am-8:30pm.) **Rape Crisis** can be reached at 342-7273. **Chico Community Hospital** is at 560 Cohasset Rd. (896-5000). In an **emergency** call 911. **Police** are at 1460 Humboldt Rd. (895-4911). The **post office** lies at 550 Vallombrosa (343-5531; open Mon.-Fri. 7:30am-5:30pm, Sat. 9:30am-12:30pm). The **General Delivery ZIP Code** is 95926. The **area code** is 916.

Accommodations and Camping For outdoor sleeping, pick up a copy of the useful camping brochure available at the Chamber of Commerce. **Black Butte Lake Campgrounds** (865-4781) is well to the west of town, but worth the drive. Take Rte. 32 west and follow signs to Rd. 200. (RV and tent sites, with showers and flush toilets. Sites $12.) In town, **Chico Motor Lodge,** 725 Broadway (895-1877), downtown, is quiet and offers a pool, and spacious, spotless rooms, TV and A/C. (Singles $38.50. Doubles $41.50.) At the bright pink **Western Travel Inn,** 740 Broadway (343-3286), the cheap singles ($32) are immaculate. All rooms have phones, A/C. Some have small refrigerators. (Doubles $40.) **Motel 6,** 665 Manzanita Ct. (345-5500), is accessible only by car or a long walk. From Rte. 99, take the Cohasset Rd. exit. (Singles with A/C, TV $29. $6 per additional adult.)

Food There's a 24-hr. **Safeway** at 860 East Ave. A **farmers market** is held in the parking lot at 3rd and Broadway (July-Aug. Thurs. 5-8pm). **Café Sandino,** 817 Main St. (894-6515), is Chico's vegetarian stronghold. The café provides friendly service, Southwestern decor, and divine tamales ($4-5; open Mon.-Sat. 1:30-3pm, 5:30-9:30pm). **Woodstock Pizza,** 221 Nosmal Ave. (893-1500), features monthly and weekday specials guaranteed to keep your wallet a bit fatter. The large pizza special is filling (about $9). Woodstock's happy hour (2-6pm and 9-midnight daily) offers 32-oz. beers for $1.75 and pitchers for $2.75. (Open Sun.-Thurs. 11am-midnight, Fri.-Sat. 11am-1am.) Try **Oy-Vey's,** 146 W. 2nd. St. (891-6710). Coffee, bagels, sandwiches; they're mobbed during the term. Share the incredibly huge "Hungry man" breakfast (3 eggs, 4 sausages, 5 pancakes, ½-lb. home fries, and a bagel $5.75) with a friend. (Open daily 7am-3pm.)

Sights Chico is somewhat lean on sights, but parks, a pedestrian-friendly design, and an active civic effort to avoid malls all make Chico a charming place to browse. The **Phoenix Used Books and Records,** 132 Broadway St. (894-8463), offers excellent secondhand bargains, and is a fine place to start. (Open Mon.-Thurs. 10am-8pm, Fri.-Sat. 10am-10pm, Sun. noon-5pm.) Outdoors, there are Friday concerts in the Plaza (May-Sept. 7pm). **Bidwell Park,** (895-6144) at 2400 acres, is the nation's third-largest municipal park and extends 10 mi. from downtown. It has served as a set for several movies including *Gone With the Wind* and *The Adventures of Robin Hood.* (Tours offered daily 10am-4pm. $2, ages 7-12 $1.)

For a historic picnic, go 5 mi. east on Humbug/Honey Run Rd. to the **Honey Covered Bridge.** Built in 1894, it is the only three-level bridge in the U.S.

Although **Cal State Chico** isn't the most architecturally stimulating of campuses, it has distinguished itself as a perennial favorite in *Playboy's* list of the "Top Ten Party Schools." Chico's raucous bashes rage mostly during the term (Oct.-May), but a party school of this caliber doesn't shut down completely in the summer. **Rancho Chico Days** (formerly Pioneer Days, on the first weekend in May) are notoriously wild. The university **information center** (898-4428) offers tours daily at 11:30am.

■■■ LASSEN VOLCANIC NATIONAL PARK

In 1914, the earth radiated destruction as tremors, lava flows, black dust, and a series of enormous eruptions continued over several months, climaxing in 1915 when Lassen sneezed a 7-mi.-high cloud of ashes. Protected by Congress in 1916, Lassen's forests, lakes, peaks, and sulfurous springs forcefully demonstrate nature's processes—both destructive and recuperative. Lassen is less crowded than neighboring parks and is therefore an excellent destination for serious hikers seeking solitude amidst the forests and mountains.

PRACTICAL INFORMATION AND ORIENTATION

Visitors Information: Lassen Volcanic National Park Headquarters, in Mineral (595-4444). Wilderness permits. Superb rangers. Open daily 8am-4:30pm. **Manzanita Lake Visitors Center** (335-7575), at the northwest entrance. Open daily 9am-5pm. In after-hour **emergencies,** call 335-7373. **Hat Creek Ranger Station** (336-5521), off Rte. 299 in Fall River Mills. Open Mon.-Fri. 7:30am-5pm. **Almanor County Ranger Station** (258-2141), off Rte. 36 in Chester.

Mount Lassen Motor Transit: 529-2722. Transportation from Red Bluff to Mineral on a mail truck (Mon.-Sat. at 8am). Return trip leaves at 10:25am and 3:50pm ($6.90 one way). Greyhound buses leave from the Red Bluff station.

Road Conditions: 225-3028. **Weather Conditions:** 246-1311.

Emergency: 911.

Post Office: Rte. 36 in Mineral and Rte. 44 in Shingletown. Both open Mon.-Fri. 8am-4:30pm. **General Delivery ZIP Codes:** 96063 and 96088, respectively.

Area Code: 916.

Lassen Volcanic National Park is accessible by **Rte. 36** from Red Bluff to the south, and **Rte. 44** from Redding to the north. Both drives are about 50 mi. **Rte. 89,** running north-south, intersects both roads before they reach the park and carries travelers through the scenic park area. It is the park's only through-road. **Mineral,** along Rte. 36, and **Shingletown,** along Rte. 44, are the "gateway" towns along the park's western entrances and good places to buy supplies. From the southeast (Susanville and the Lake Almanor area), take Rte. 36 west to the intersection with Rte. 89. **Chester,** the nearest spot for gas and supplies on the north shore of Lake Almanor, is on the way to Warney Valley and Juniper Lake (located in the park's southeastern corner). To the northeast, the Butte Lake region is reached by a dirt road (there's a sign) off Rte. 44. (Admission to Lassen $5 per car, $3 per hiker or biker.)

Weather in the park is unpredictable. Some years, 20-ft. snowdrifts clog the main road until July 4; other years an early melt clears the road by April. Crazy as it may sound, it can snow any day of the year. Savvy travelers will call ahead and be prepared for a variety of temperatures.

CAMPING AND FOOD

Because of the chance of rockslides and lava flows, there are few permanent structures in the park, much less motels or cabins. The nearest indoor accommodations are 12 mi. north in **Old Station.** Less costly motels can be found in **Redding** and **Red Bluff,** to the west, and in **Chester,** to the east. Fortunately, camping in the park is beautiful and abundant. Unfortunately, you may experience near-freezing night temperatures, even in August. Check the snow situation before you leave; campgrounds may remain closed well into the summer because of the white stuff. The maximum stay is 14 days, except at Summit Lake, which limits visitors to one week. All sites are doled out on a first-come, first-camped basis; register on-site.

South Summit Lake Campground, in the middle of the park, 12 mi. south of the Manzanita Lake entrance. 48 sites. Very popular. Summit Lake's deep blue glitters through sparse stands of pine trees. Be sure to bring a sleeping pad; the soil is rocky. Drinking water, pit toilets, no showers. Sites $8.

North Summit Lake Campground, just north of South Summit Lake Campground. 46 sites. Identical views, identical facilities (except flush toilets here), identical crowding on weekends. Be on the lookout for deer. Sites $10.

Manzanita Lake Campground, just inside the park border, near the northwest entrance. 179 sites. Impressive views of Lassen Peak reflected in the placid Manzanita Lake. Always the first to fill. Drinking water, toilets, and showers. Sites $10.

Southwest Campground, near the entrance. A walk-in campground for those weary of waking to the sweet strains of their neighbor's muffler-less car. 21 sites and potable water. Those near the sulfur vents (phew!) are seldom crowded. Sites $8. RVs may park in the nearby chalet car park for $3.

Crags Campground, 45 sites used for overflow from Manzanita Lake (5 mi. away), but nicer than the Manzanita Lake Campground. Piped water and chemical toilets among the pine trees. Sites $6.

The following two campgrounds in the park are not accessible from Rte. 89.

Juniper Lake Campground, on the eastern shore of Juniper Lake, 13 mi. north up a dirt road from Chester. 18 sites. Pit toilets, fireplaces, lake water only (must be boiled or treated). Secluded and beautiful. Call for availability. Sites $6.

Warner Valley, 17 mi. up another dirt road from Chester. 18 sites with pit toilets, piped water, and fireplaces. Not recommended for RVs; very remote. Sites $8.

Backcountry camping is allowed at least 1 mi. from developed areas and roads, with a free wilderness permit available at any park ranger station (see Practical Information, above). Fires (including lighters and lanterns) are prohibited and the use of all soaps (including biodegradable ones) in the lakes is strictly forbidden. Nonetheless, those with sturdy boots, a reliable backpack, and a *warm* sleeping bag may find backcountry camping the best way to appreciate the beauty of Lassen.

Lassen National Forest surrounds the park, encompassing scores of developed campgrounds. A half-dozen, all with water and toilets but no showers, line Rte. 89 to the north for the first 10 mi. out of the national park. **Big Pine** is the closest (19 sites at $6). Of the remaining five, **Bridge** and **Cave** campgrounds ($8) have only trailer sites (but tents may be used if you don't mind bumpy ground). **Rocky** has eight free sites with limited parking that are suited for tent camping. Scenically, they are not too exciting. Two campgrounds sit on Rte. 36, a few mi. from the park entrance. To the west is **Battle Creek** ($10), to the east **Gurnsey Creek** ($9). These spots are prettier than the ones up north, but not as remote. Lassen is a major logging region; hundreds of dirt roads crisscross the forest. Choose one, pull off the road, and camp in a beautiful, isolated, and free location (fire permits required, available at Hat Creek Ranger Station). When camping, make allowances for the hungry **bears** that populate the area (see Essentials: Bear Necessities, page 53).

If you long for a bed and a hot shower, try **Rim Rock Ranch** (335-7114), in Old Station, on Rte. 44, 14 mi. off Rte. 89. Cabins come with linens, utensils, pots, and pans. (2-person cabin $35, larger cabins hold 4-12 people, $40 for 4, $5 per additional occupant. Open April-Nov.; one cabin open year-round, call for details.)

The cheapest way to sustain yourself is to buy groceries in one of the outlying towns and cook them yourself. If you can't cook, eat at the **Lassen Chalet** (595-3376), an inexpensive cafeteria-style restaurant near the Mineral entrance at the southwest corner of the park (open daily 9am-5pm). There is often a park volunteer at the Chalet to answer questions. At the park's opposite end, the **Manzanita Camper Service Store,** at the Manzanita Lake Campground (335-2943), sells pricey groceries, souvenirs, fishing licenses, guides, and maps (open daily 8am-8pm). There are hot **showers** next door (open 8am-9pm; 3 min. 25¢). A **laundromat** is in the same building (open daily 8am-9pm; $1.25 wash, 10-min. dry 25¢).

SIGHTS AND ACTIVITIES

Most sights in Lassen are accessible from Rte. 89. Drivers can pick up the *Lassen Road Guide,* a booklet keyed to roadside markers, at any park entrance ranger station ($3.25). The Park Service and the Forest Service also distribute a free newsletter that lists trails, campgrounds, conditions, and history. A comfortable drive through the park (including a few stops) should take about two hours.

If you start from the south along Rte. 89 you'll encounter **Sulfur Works,** where the Earth hisses its grievances against humanity. The guardrails may prevent you from getting burned, but the wind constantly changes direction—you're likely to get a faceful of pungent mist. The Sulfur Works boardwalk is easily accessible for handicapped visitors and the bubbling sites are truly bizarre. A bit farther north, **Emerald Lake** (marker #15), when partially thawed by summer sun, shimmers for a bright green, icy-cold 100 yds. around a snow-covered center. Swimming is fine for fish, but too cold (40°F) for the warm-blooded and thin-skinned.

Things heat up again about ½ mi. past Emerald Lake. The 1½-mi. hike to **Bumpass Hell** wanders through part of the park's largest hydrothermal area. Pick up a guide (35¢) at the trailhead. A moderate path ambles up a mountainside, providing views of Lassen and the lower peaks. (When covered in snow it's a strenuous climb.) Bumpass Hell is a massive cauldron of muddy, boiling, steaming water in which its discoverer lost his leg; to avoid any danger to your own life and limb, stay on the trail. Bumpass Hell is not the prettiest sight in the park, but is worth the journey because it *is* a perplexing and bizarre natural wonder. In spite of year-round snow, the water appears to ever-boil at **Cold Boiling Lake** (4 mi. farther north, closer to the Kings Creek trailhead also known as marker #32) due to its placement above a flatulent fissure.

Mt. Lassen itself is the world's largest plug-dome volcano. There is a good (and relatively short) trail to the 10,457-ft. summit. From marker #22, it's a steep 2½-mi. trek to the peak. Allow four to five hours to climb up and down the mountain. Even if it's sunny and 90°F at the trailhead, take along extra clothes (especially a windbreaker), sunblock, and water. Hiking in shorts and a t-shirt may be fine when you start, but the crest is cool and windy. Solid shoes are important too; 18 in. of snow can clog the upper 2 mi. of trail in mid-July. The view from the summit is striking— the sun shines on thousands of snow-covered acres and volcanic craters sweep down toward Emerald Lake. **Brokeoff Mountain,** nearby, has similar views. (Trail begins at #2). The round-trip here meets less traffic but still takes up to five hours.

The **Upper Meadow** by King's Creek and **Dersch Meadow** north of Summit Lake are good locations to spot grazing deer and circling birds of prey. The vast, ravaged area (#41, 44, and 50) on the northeast face, was formed the last time that Mt. Lassen erupted. Fallen trees and scarred trunks remain as silent testimony to the volcano's destructive powers. The mountain is slowly healing. Scientists conduct research here in the hope of aiding the recovery of the Mt. St. Helens' area.

Given the heavy year-round snow cover, much of Lassen is not suitable terrain for backpackers. Of the 150 mi. of trails (including a stretch of the **Pacific Crest Trail**), only the **Manzanita Creek Trail,** near Manzanita Lake Campground, and the **Horseshoe Lake** area east of Summit Lake are customarily free of snow by mid-June. Both make enjoyable overnight sojourns. Manzanita Creek Trail parallels a lovely creek which runs through rolling woodlands that bear scant resemblance to the boiling and sizzling cauldrons to the south. To the east, the Horseshoe Lake area is rich in ice-cold lakes and impressive pine forests where deer forage among a marvelous variety of mountain flowers and shrubs. A number of challenging day hikes cut through the eastern area, with parking available near most trailheads.

By mid-summer, the shallow waters of Lakes Manzanita and Summit usually warm to swimming temperatures. Several lakes in the park (including Summit) have native **rainbow trout.** Hat Creek is a renowned trout stream. A state license is required, and some areas may have additional rules (Manzanita, for example, has a "catch and release" policy). Be sure to check with the park rangers (see Practical Information, page 347).

■ NEAR LASSEN: WILDERNESS AREAS

The three nearby wilderness areas are even less traveled than Lassen. Pick up a **wilderness permit** (free) from the National Forest Service. **Caribou Wilderness** borders the park to the east; for the easiest border access, take Rte. 44 or Rte. 36 to the A-21 road for 14 mi., then take Silver Lake Rd. to the **Caribou Lake Trailhead.** This forested plateau is mostly shaded by lodgepole pines. Its multiple quiet, clean lakes support healthy water lilies and wildflowers in early summer.

Thousand Lakes Wilderness can be accessed from F.S. 16 off Rte. 89. Seven mi. from Rte. 89 the road forks; F.S. 16 continues to the left to **Magee Trailhead.** The strenuous trail leads to Magee Peak (8594 ft.) and then to deserted Magee Lake. Insect repellent is a must. **Subway Cave,** off Rte. 89 about ¼ mi. north of its junction with Rte. 44, invites exploration of its 600-yd.-long lava tubes. The cave is pitch black and cool, and the footing is uneven, so bring a friend, sturdy shoes, a sweater, and a lantern or a strong flashlight (with extra batteries).

Ishi Wilderness, which was named for the last survivor of a Yahi Yana tribe, is comprised of rugged terrain at a lower altitude, making it friendly to off-season exploration. Take Rte. 36 from Red Bluff approximately 15 mi. to Plum Creek Rd. and turn right on to Ponderosa Way. This road skirts the eastern edge of the wilderness, where most of the trailheads are located. Ishi is a series of river canyons, with dense islands of Ponderosa pine and sunburnt grasslands in the south (very hot in the summer). **Mill Creek Trailhead** runs along the 1000-ft. canyon, where gentle waters await swimmers. Keep an eye out for red-tailed hawks and golden eagles. The Tehana Deer Herd, the largest migratory herd in California, spends its winters in Ishi (no hunting allowed).

■■■ RED BLUFF

Midway between Chico and Redding, Red Bluff perches on a steep, brick-colored bank of the Sacramento River (hence its name). This is a good place to fuel and rest up for a jaunt into Lassen Volcanic National Park or on your way farther north. **I-5** skirts Red Bluff's eastern edge, while **Rte. 36** (running east to Lassen Volcanic Park) and **Rte. 99** (leading south into the Sacramento and San Joaquin Valleys) merge with the main streets of town.

Practical Information Get the usual brochures at the **Chamber of Commerce,** 100 N. Main St. (527-6220; open Mon. 8:30am-4pm, Tues.-Thurs. 8:30am-

5pm). There's an **ATM** at **Bank of America,** 905 Main St. (800-346-7693). **Greyhound,** 1425 Montgomery Rd. (527-0434), has frequent service to Redding ($5.50), Chico ($7), and Sacramento ($20). (Terminal open Mon.-Fri. 10am-5:30pm.) **Mt. Lassen Motor Transit** (529-2722) has county service. ($2, seniors and disabled $1.) The Mt. Lassen bus leaves weekdays at 8am and arrives in Mineral at 10am. The bus leaves Mineral at 3:30pm and arrives at Red Bluff after 5pm. (One-way fare $6.45.) **Vans Trans** (527-6610) will pick up passengers within the city limits. ($3, seniors and disabled $1.50. Mon.-Wed. 7:30am-6pm, Thurs.-Fri. 7:30am-9pm, Sat. 9am-4pm.) Wash at **Launderland,** in the K-Mart shopping center on Marin St. (Wash $1; dry 25¢; soap 50¢. Open daily 7am-10pm.) For **road conditions,** call 221-5613. A **24-hr. crisis helpline** is 246-2711. **St. Elizabeth Community Hospital** is on Sister Mary Columbia Drive (527-2112), at Main St. Call 527-0250 for an **ambulance.** In an **emergency** call 911. The **police** are at 555 Washington St. (527-3131). The **post office** is at 447 Walnut St. (527-2012), at Jefferson (open Mon.-Fri. 8:30am-5pm). The **General Delivery ZIP Code** is 96080. The **area code** is 916.

Accommodations **Crystal Motel,** 333 S. Main St. (527-1021), is a comfortable motel with nice rooms and nicer rates. (TV and A/C. Singles $22. Doubles $27. Some wheelchair-accessible rooms.) **Sky Terrace Motel,** 99 Main St. (527-4145), is not exactly the great wide open: small, spic 'n' span rooms, with TV, A/C, petite pool, and non-smoking rooms. (Singles $26. Doubles $32.) **Triangle Motel,** 1175 Montgomery Rd. (527-4542), a brief stroll out of town, is serene and immaculate, with phones, TV, A/C, and pool. (Singles $21. Doubles $30.) **Diversion Dam Reservation Area** (824-5196) offers camping 4 mi. southeast of town. Cross the river on Antelope Blvd. and walk east to Sale Lane. Go south on Sale Lane to the Dam area. Forest Service Campsites are at the mosquito-infested river's edge ($8, 10-day max.). With the greatly superior campsites of Lassen just an hour away, why stop?

Food Rte. 9 blossoms with orchards and roadside stands selling fresh produce: peaches, apricots, kiwi, cantaloupe, and plums in summer; pistachios, almonds, walnuts, and apples in fall. You can also pick up fresh produce at the **farmer's market** in the K-Mart parking lot on S. Main St. (527-6220; open June-Sept. Sat. 8am-until they run out of produce, about 10am.) To stock up for camping, try the **Food Connection** at 249 S. Main St. (527-9686; open 24 hrs.). If you're vegetarian, forget **Hal's Eat Em Up,** 158 Main St. (529-0173). Since most of the locals aren't, this place is a favorite for cheap, fast, and greasy food. (Big Hal Burger $2.80; open Mon.-Sat. 10am-9pm.) **The Feedbag,** 200 S. Main St. (527-3777), vends that budget-travel staple: big breakfasts. Rope in the Ranch-hand (2 eggs, large hash browns, 4 sausages, and 4 slices of toast) for $4.25. (Bottomless cup o' coffee 60¢; open Mon.-Sat. 6:30am-9pm, Sun. 7:30am-3pm.) **Egg Roll King,** 55 Antelope Blvd. (529-2888), is not exactly traditional, but the portions are satisfying and the prices great. (Dishes from $3; open daily 11am-9:30pm.) You can dine-and-dash or drive through.

Sights and Seasonal Events If the incessant hustle and bustle of gritty Red Bluff gets to you, and you need a rest stop on the freeway of life, try a self-guided car tour of **Victorian houses.** Start at the chamber of commerce on Main St. and roll by Red Bluff's most distinguished buildings. Follow the rusty blue signs. The **Kelly-Griggs House Museum,** 311 Washington St., built in the 1880s, "invites you to walk into a vanishing America" by following their guides through the renovated rooms of this Victorian mansion now peopled by authentically garbed mannequins that "live" among the beautiful antiques.

On Adobe Rd., a few mi. north of Red Bluff off Rte. 99, the **William B. Ide Adobe State Historic Park** honors the man who led the 1846 Bear Flag Rebellion. In a drunken fit, he "seized" the town of Sonoma from equally drunk Mexican officials and declared California's independence. The rebellion has since been immortalized with the phrase "beware the march of Ide." The home of California's first and only president has been restored with traditional adobe. (Open daily 8am-5pm. Free.)

In April, Red Bluff makes it into the record books with the **Red Bluff Roundup,** billed as the "the world's largest two-day rodeo." The four-day **Sun Country Fair** in mid-July includes carnival rides and games, live music, street dances, horseshoe tournaments, and a fiery chili cook-off.

■■■ MT. SHASTA

For centuries, residents of this part of the world have believed that Mt. Shasta (14,162 ft.) possesses mystical powers. The Shasta Indians worshiped a Great Spirit whom they believe created the snow-capped volcano as her own permanent residence. In 1987, thousands of New Age believers converged here to witness the great celestial event of Harmonic Convergence, which climaxed when a resident turned on her TV set and saw an angelic vision displayed on the screen.

However, spiritual questers are not likely to find a guru here: common advice to would-be disciples and climbers alike is to "go where the mountain calls you." If you are skeptical of the mountain's communicative abilities, sit a spell on Shasta's isolated, majestic, and snow-capped slopes—few travelers leave unconvinced.

PRACTICAL INFORMATION AND ORIENTATION

Visitors Information: Shasta-Trinity National Forest Service, 204 W. Alma St. (926-4511 or 926-4596, TDD 926-4512), 1½ blocks across the railroad tracks from the intersection of Mt. Shasta Blvd. and Alma St. Maps, information, fire permits, and knowledgeable help. Campers must pick up **wilderness permits** here. Outside, there's a trail register that climbers and solitary hikers should sign. Open daily 8am-4:30pm; Labor Day-Memorial Day Mon.-Fri. 8am-4:30pm. **Chamber of Commerce,** 300 Pine St. (926-4865), 1 block west from Shasta Blvd. Brochures covering Siskiyou County services. Open Mon.-Sat. 9am-5pm, Sun. 10am-3pm.

ATM: Bank of America, 100 Chestnut St. (926-8954).

Greyhound: No depot in town, but drivers may pick up and drop off passengers here if notified in advance. Depot in **Redding,** 1321 Butte St. at Pine (241-2531).

Amtrak: The nearest connection is at the unattended station in **Dunsmuir,** (about ten miles from Mt. Shasta), 5750 Sacramento Ave. (800-872-7245 for reservations). To: Portland (1 per day, \$84); Redding (1 per day, \$13); Sacramento (1 per day, \$13); the Bay Area (1 per day, \$61).

The Stage: 842-3531. Minibus transit between Weed, Mt. Shasta (from the Mt. Shasta Shopping Center), and Dunsmuir. Fare 90¢. Operates daily 6:30am-6pm.

Car Rental: California Compacts (926-2519), at Mott-Dunsmuir Airport, Mott Ave. from I-80. \$28 per day, \$170 per week. Must be 21 with major credit card. First 100 miles free, 21¢ per mile thereafter.

Equipment Rental: 5th Season, 300 Mt. Shasta Blvd. (926-3606). Sleeping bags \$15 for 3 days, \$5 per additional day; 2-person tent \$28 for 3 days. Cross-country ski rental in winter. Bike rentals \$3 per hour, \$24 first day, \$12 per additional day. Includes helmet and pump. Also rents mountain-climbing gear. Crampons and ice axe \$12 per day, \$15 for 2-3 days, \$4 per additional day. Open Mon.-Thurs. 9am-6pm, Fri. 9am-8pm, Sat. 8am-6pm, Sun. 10am-6pm.

Senior Info: Mt. Shasta Recreation Center, 926-2494.

Library: Mount Shasta Library, 515 E. Alma St. (926-2031). Open Mon.-Fri. 1-5pm.

Laundromat: Mt. Shasta Laundromat, 302 S. Mt. Shasta Blvd., across from the post office. \$1 wash, 25¢ dry. Open 24 hrs.

Weather and Climbing Conditions: 826-5555 (recording) 24 hrs. The Ranger Station offers a live report. **Missing Climber Notification:** County Sheriff's office, 842-4141.

AAA Road Service: 926-4760.

Crisis: Poison Control, 800-342-9293; **Red Cross,** 243-3021.

Hospital: Mercy Medical Center, 914 Pine St. (926-6111).

Emergency: 911.

Police: 926-2344.

Post Office: 301 S. Mt. Shasta Blvd. (926-3801). Open Mon.-Fri. 8:30am-5pm. **General Delivery ZIP Code:** 96067.
Area Code: 916.

Mt. Shasta is located 60 mi. north of Redding on **I-5** and about 50 mi. west of Lassen Volcanic National Park. If you're traveling by car, the town can be used as a base for exploring Lava Beds, Lassen, Burney Falls, and the Shasta Recreation Area. The city of Shasta is easy to find from any direction—just head toward the giant mountain.

ACCOMMODATIONS, CAMPING, AND FOOD

Alpenrose Youth Hostel, 204 Hinckley St. (926-6724). This beautiful chalet sits regally at the base of the mountain and is much nicer than any of the motels in town. An herb garden, sundecks, and a beautiful flower garden surround the dazzling interior. Very homey with wood-burning stove, open kitchen, and library. Magnificent manager. 12 beds. $13, $75 per week. Showers $2.

Shasta Lodge Motel, 724 Mt. Shasta Blvd. (926-2815), is a good alternative if the hostel is full. Close to the center of town with simple, clean rooms in a family atmosphere. Cable TV, A/C, phones. Singles and doubles $36.

Das Alpenhaus Motel, 504 S. Mt. Shasta Blvd. (926-4617), at High St. Although the pseudo-Swiss-chalet exterior is somewhat incongruous (you expect Julie Andrews and the Von Trapp brood to pour out the front door at any moment), the motel is nonetheless often full. TV, no phones. Some rooms with kitchenettes. Singles $32, winter $25.

Following Old McCloud Rd. (Rte. 89) south 1½ mi. from downtown up a moderate grade, you'll enter the national forest. With a permit (see Practical Information, above), you can **camp** anywhere (May-Sept.), but prepare for cold nights. The Forest Service can also give directions to water sources. Three mi. up Mt. Shasta on Everett Memorial Highway, you'll find **McBride Springs** campgrounds on the left, with drinking water and toilets but no showers (8 sites; $9).

Closer to town, the **KOA Trailer Park,** 900 N. Mt. Shasta Blvd. (926-4029), has tent sites amid the RVs (tents sites $15 for 2, with full utilities $21, $3 per additional adult, $2 per additional child). **Lake Siskiyou Campground** (926-2618), 4½ mi. southwest of town, has access to a beach, swimming, boat rental (paddleboats, motorboats, and canoes), and a coin-operated laundry (sites $13). Flee I-5 via the Lake St. exit, follow Hatchery Lane ¼ mi., then go south on Old Stage Rd. and W.A. Barr Rd. Beautiful **Castle Lake,** 9 mi. southwest of town, is primitive (pit toilets, no water or showers; 5 sites; free). Freestyle camping is permitted more than 200 ft. from the lake, ½ mi. beyond the campground. **Gumboot Lake,** 20 mi. west on South Fork Rd., is the most isolated camping area (4 sites). The drive is long and the sites are primitive, but the lake is utterly serene. Bug repellent is essential.

Shasta has a variety of grocery stores, although the only full-fledged supermarket is **Sentry,** 160 Morgan Way, in the Mt. Shasta Shopping Center off Lake St. (open daily 7am-10pm). In the summer, a produce stand across the street provides cheaper and fresher fruits and veggies. The **Mt. Shasta Supermarket,** at the corner of Chestnut and E. Alma St., is a source of produce and supplies for a picnic or hike (open Mon.-Fri. 8am-8pm, Sat. 8am-7pm, Sun. 8am-6pm). The **Bagel Bakery and Café,** 105 East Alma St. (926-2800), serves up espresso ($1). Soup and a few slices of their thick bread make a meal ($3.50). Friday evenings feature live music. (Open 6:30am-9pm daily.) **Willy's Bavarian Kitchen,** 107 Chestnut St. (926-3686), offers imported beers, vegetarian dishes, and the ever-favorite *gulasch mit nudeln* (goulash with noodles) for $8 (with soup or salad) out of an honest-to-goodness wood shack (open daily 11am-9pm). **Berryvale Natural Foods** caters to the health conscious with organic produce. (Open Mon.-Sat. 8:30am-7:30pm, Sun. 10am-6pm.)

SIGHTS AND SEASONAL EVENTS

In town, the **Mt. Shasta State Fish Hatchery,** 3 Old State Rd. (926-2215), ½ mi. west of I-5, monitors the production of more than five million baby trout every year in the state's oldest facility. You can pet the fish. (Open daily 7am-7pm; free.) The **town museum** (926-5508), with exhibits on the area's geology and the history of Native American and white settlement is nearby. Pick up trail maps here and check out the seismograph for the likelihood that Shasta will blow in the next hour.

Relatively easy ascents of Shasta, sometimes not requiring ice equipment, are possible during August from trailheads at the **Ski Bowl,** or **Horse Camp** (where there's a Sierra Club Lodge for $2 per night)—both off the Everitt Memorial Highway. Most climbers take two days, camping overnight and beginning their ascent around 3am. If you dare to climb, speak first with the amiable folks at the **ranger station** (see Practical Information, page 352). You must also sign the Forest Service register before departure (and sign out on your return). Even hikers following some of the more "modest" trails (**Black Butte** or **Castle Lake** to **Bradley Lookout**) should be sure to take extra clothing, since the weather is always unpredictable, and bring lots of drinking water, as stream water along the trails is uniformly non-potable.

The ranger station has information on many other hiking trails in the area. The 9-mi. **Sisson-Callahan National Recreation Trail** offers great scenery and follows a route taken by 19th-century trappers and prospectors. Take the Gazelle exit off I-5 north of Weed and then turn right onto Rte. 99. Follow this ½ mi. and turn left on Stewart Springs Rd. When you meet Forest Rd. turn right. Ten mi. later, you'll reach Parks Creek Summit, where you can join the **Pacific Crest Trail,** or go 2 mi. farther to **Deadfall Lakes** to start your hike. Walking from Parks Creek Summit to Lake Siskiyou is at least a day-long trip for the average hiker. Bring water and beware of unexpected weather. The trails to **Toad Lake** and **Porcupine Lake** are also worth a walk. All these trails offer incredible panoramic views.

Although **mountain bikes** are not allowed on hiking trails, the logging roads in the national forests make excellent backcountry biking trails. Those wishing to issue a summertime challenge to the mountain can take a chairlift to the top of Mt. Shasta (Mt. Shasta Ski Park, 926-8610) and then bike or coast (wheee!) down.

Rock-climbers will find plenty of opportunities to challenge gravity in the Mt. Shasta region. Enthusiasts of all skill levels may want to check out **Castle Crag State Park,** where the excellent granite climbing is sure to leave climbers exhausted, but smiling. For snowy days, the **Mt. Shasta Ski Park** (926-8610) has an artificial wall.

Nearby, **Lake Shasta** is a popular water-skiing surface and houseboat heaven for summertime water recreation. If Shasta is too crowded or the water level is low, try the artificially created **Lake Siskiyou.**

In winter, **cross-country skiing** is popular throughout the region; the ski season runs from mid-November to mid-April. The best cross-country skiing in the area may well be in the small town of McCloud, east of the mountain. The **Mt. Shasta Ski Park** (926-8686 or 926-8610), 10 mi. east of I-5, offers cross-country and downhill skiing. (Lift tickets $21, Super Tuesday $16. Night skiing Wed.-Thurs. 4-10pm offers 2 tickets for the price of 1. Ski rental $17 per day, seniors and children $14. Snowboard rental $22 per day.)

You can enjoy Shasta without breaking a sweat, if you let your car do the work. The **Everitt Memorial Highway** provides excellent views of the mountain as it winds its way 13 mi. from Mt. Shasta to the Ski Bowl trailhead. Nearby **Black Butte Mt.** is a far easier climb than Shasta, though still steep and rocky. Take the Truck Village exit off I-5, head east to the end of the block, then take a right and follow the road to the trail. The 2.6-mi. trail to an old fire lookout (only the foundation remains) winds up the tight curves of this volcanic dome (1-1½ hr. each way). Ten mi. east of Shasta, off Rte. 89 near McCloud, lies **Medicine Lake,** a volcanic cornucopia of lava flows, deposits, cones, faults, craters, and even an ice-cave.

If you prefer a more cerebral experience with the mountain, start at the **Golden Bough Bookstore,** 219 N. Mt. Shasta Blvd. (926-3228). Information about the latest New Age activities in the area is posted on the bulletin board out front. Step inside and peruse the spiritual book collection. The store's friendly owner can fill you in on almost every local going-on. (Open Mon.-Sat. 10am-6pm, Sun. 11am-2pm-ish.)

■ NEAR MT. SHASTA: REDDING

Woody Guthrie wrote "This Land Is Your Land" while in Redding in the 1930s. Anyone who spends any time in the dry, dusty town will understand why Guthrie was so anxious to share the land—or even give it away. However, Redding's position at the crossroads of I-5, Rte. 299, and Rte. 44 makes it a convenient supply stop before exploring nearby Shasta and Lassen Volcanic National Park.

Practical Information Get visitors information at the **Greater Redding Chamber of Commerce,** 777 Auditorium Dr. (225-4100), up Butte St. and over the freeway at the Convention Center interchange. (Open Mon.-Thurs. 8:30am-5pm, Fri. 8:30am-4:30pm.) Call the **Shasta Lake Ranger District,** 14225 Holiday Dr. (275-1589), for local conditions or camping restrictions (open Mon.-Fri. 8:30am-4pm). There is an unstaffed **Amtrak** station at 1620 Yuba St. (800-872-7245). Buy your ticket on the train or through a travel agent. Trains go to: Sacramento (1 per day, $32); San Francisco (1 per day, $46); Portland (1 per day, $91). **Greyhound,** 1321 Butte St. at Pine (241-2531), downtown, has a 24-hr. terminal. Buses go to: Sacramento (6 per day, $23); San Francisco (4 per day, $31); Portland (6 per day, $59). **Enterprise,** 361 Cypress (223-0700), rents cars for $24 per day with 150 free mi. (Must be 21.) **24-hr. helpline** is at 225-5252. A 24-hr. **rape crisis hotline** can be reached at 244-0117. **Redding Medical Center,** 1100 Butte (243-2341), downtown, offers 24-hr. emergency service. In an **emergency** call 911. The **police** are at 1313 California St. (225-4200). The **post office** is located at 2323 Churn Creek Rd. (223-7502; open Mon.-Fri. 7:30am-5:30pm, Sat. 9am-2pm). The **General Delivery ZIP Code** is 96049-9998. The **area code** is 916.

Accommodations and Camping Shasta Lodge, 1245 Pine St. (243-6133), has fresh, airy rooms (non-smoking), with HBO, TV, A/C, pool, and coffee. (Singles $26. Doubles $32.) **Stardust Motel,** 1200 Pine St. (241-6121), 3 blocks from Greyhound, has a pool, HBO, A/C, and a casino-like sign. (Singles $26. Doubles $29.) **Motel 6,** 2385 Bechelli Ln. (221-0562), adjacent to I-5, is more expensive, but safe and clean, with color TV and bathtubs. (Singles $34. Doubles $40.) **Oak Bottom Campground,** on Rte. 299 (241-6584), 13 mi. west of Redding on Whiskeytown Lake, has cold showers and no hookups. (105 sites. $14 for tents, $12 for RVs. Make reservations through MISTIX, 800-365-2267.) If it's too late to go on to a lake, **Salt Creek Campground,** just off I-5 on Salt Creek Rd. (238-8500), 20 mi. north of Redding, is a convenient commercial campground, with laundry, pool, showers, general store, and full hookups. (Sites $16.50 for 2 people, $2.50 per additional person.)

Food The **Safeway Market,** 1191 W. Cypress (241-4545), at Pine St., is a pragmatic place to pick up fruits and cold cuts. (Open 24 hrs.) At **Big Red's Bar-B-Q,** 2550 Bechelli Ln. (221-7427), tangy, tasty ribs are the specialty of the house. Rub elbows with the friendly locals as you savor the delicious food. (Half rack of ribs $7; sandwiches $4.25. Open daily 10:30am-7:30pm.) **Buz's Seafood,** 2159 East St. (243-2120), behind the Safeway, is a good seafood store and restaurant with the air of a market and the aroma of smoked fish. When local police officers eat here twice a day you know it's gotta be good. Fish and chips cost $2-5. Charbroiled snapper and swordfish are $5.50-8. Dungeness crab is in season from December to May. (Open Sun.-Thurs. 11am-9pm, Fri.-Sat. 11am-4pm.)

■■■ LAVA BEDS NATIONAL MONUMENT

You probably won't be impressed by your first glimpse of the Lava Beds National Monument. Driving in on a narrow access road, acres of flat, dry, and seemingly barren land stretch out in front of you, broken only by clumps of sagebrush. However, beneath this unpromising surface lies a complex network of lava-formed caves and tunnels unlike anything else on earth. Cool, quiet, and often eerie, caves created by the lava range from 18-in. crawl spaces to 80-ft. awe-inspiring cathedrals. Since the beds are located a significant distance from the highway and are not accessible by public transportation, the uncrowded trails, caves, and campsites afford plenty of time and space for exploring on your own. While Lava Beds' landscape lacks the drama of the Sierra Nevada or the Pacific coast, its unique formations have a special appeal. Explore a few caves, see the Indian drawings, and watch your opinion of Lava Beds grow to one of respect and awe.

The fertile regions around the monument were home to the Modoc Indians and their predecessors for hundreds of years before white settlers arrived in the 1850s. In 1872, the lava beds became the site of the Modoc War between U.S. troops and the Native Americans when the Modoc, who had no concept of land ownership, resisted efforts to move them from their home to reservations. Modoc chief "Captain Jack" and 52 of his warriors held their ground against up to 2500 U.S. soldiers for over five months by making use of the natural fortifications of the lava beds.

Today the seldom-visited Lava Beds monument offers historical sights, wildlife, and a fascinating natural environment of easily-accessible caves and lava beds. In spring and fall, nearby Tulelake provides a stopover for thousands of migratory birds, some of which have come from as far away as Siberia. The fall migration is particularly spectacular, with a million ducks and half a million geese literally darkening the sky. In winter, this is the best place in the lower 48 to sight a bald eagle.

Pick up free maps from the well-informed staff at **Lava Beds Visitors Center,** 30 mi. south of Tulelake on Rte. 139 (667-2282), and don't miss the exhibits on geology and history. (Open daily 9am-6pm; Labor Day-June 15 8am-5pm. $4 per vehicle.) The **area code** for the region is 916.

ORIENTATION

The park has two entrances, both located off Rte. 139 south of the farming community of **Tulelake** (TOO-lee-lake). The southeast entrance (25 mi. south of town) is closer to the visitors center. The center has exhibits on Modoc culture and a slide presentation on the war. The park staff also lends out heavy-duty **flashlights** (free; must be returned by 5:30pm, 4:30pm in winter) to cave explorers. The road to the northeast entrance leaves Rte. 139 about 5 mi. south of Tulelake. It winds through the wilder northern areas of the monument for 25 mi. and presents incredible vistas before reaching the visitors center. Although cold weather is possible at any time of the year, due to the altitude, summer weather tends to be quite moderate with minimal precipitation. You'll want to spend at least a half-day in the park (perhaps more, depending on your subterranean nerve), and you'll need a car or bike to see the northern areas. The visitors center is near a clustered of caves that are accessible by foot. The nearest spot to catch a bus, rent a car, or find a hospital is all the way across the Oregon border in **Klamath Falls,** 30 mi. north of Tulelake. Chico, Redding, and Red Bluff also offer these services. There is no public transportation to this remote area; hitchhiking is reportedly difficult and never recommended.

ACCOMMODATIONS AND FOOD

The only developed campground in Lava Beds is **Indian Wells Campground** (667-2282; no reservations accepted), opposite the visitors center. Drinking water and flush toilets are available from May to October, and there are ranger-led evening programs daily at 9pm (40 sites, $6). The monument encloses two **wilderness areas,** one on each side of the main north-south road. A wilderness permit is not required for areas within the park. Cooking is limited to stoves, and you must camp at least 100 ft. from trails. **Modoc National Forest** borders the monument on three sides. The most accessible campground in the forest is **Howard's Gulch,** 30 mi. south on Rte. 139. (11 quiet sites with water and pit toilets; free.) Off-road camping in the national forests is also free. Nearby are **Medicine Camp** and **Hemlock,** both of which have water and flush toilets ($5 each). More information on campsites is available at the **Modoc National Forest Doublehead Ranger Station** (667-2247) 1 mi. south of Tulelake on Rte. 39. (Open Mon.-Fri. 8:30am-4:30pm.)

Tulelake's **Ellis Motel** (667-5242), 1 mi. north on Rte. 139, has clean rooms and is rarely full. (Singles $27. Doubles $32.) Just south of town, also on Rte. 139, is the **Park Motel** (667-2913). (Singles $27. Doubles $33.) **Jock's,** at Modoc Ave. and Main St. (667-2612), is nearly a supermarket. (Open Mon.-Sat. 8am-8pm, Sun. 9am-6pm.) **Captain Jack's Stronghold Restaurant** (664-5566), 6 mi. south of Tulelake, 1 mi. past the turn-off to the Lava Beds, serves homemade soups and breads. (Open Mon. 5:30am-3pm, Tues.-Wed. 5:30am-8pm, Thurs.-Sat. 5:30am-9pm, Sun. 9am-8pm.)

SIGHTS

The series of underground caves that comprises Lava Beds National Monument was formed when superheated liquid mantle (over 1100°F) escaped to the earth's crust, cooled, and hardened in the shape of long tubes. If your subterranean experience has been limited to subways and parking garages, you should be warned that the footing in these caves is uneven and the ceilings may take a toll on your head. Sturdy shoes and helmets (available from the visitors center for $3.25) are essential, and if you bring your own light, have at least two sources on hand. No matter how hot it is outside, underground it's always cool and damp—take a sweatshirt or jacket.

The **Mushpot Cave,** located in the middle of the parking lot, has a short, well-lit, self-guided trail which will acquaint visitors with cave formations. On the 2¼-mi. **Cave Loop,** which starts and finishes at the visitors center, there are 13 caves with little more to guide you than an entrance stairway and sign. Lava caves are usually single rocky tubes, so confusing side passages are rare. The highlights of Cave Loop are **Golden Dome, Catacombs,** and **Labyrinth.** Less popular but more interesting are **Skull Ice Cave** (a few mi. north) and **Valentine's Cave** (a favorite of those who know the area, a few mi. south). You're allowed to explore caves alone, but you don't have to. For those wanting a friend in the dark, ranger-led cave tours leave daily at 2pm in summer. Otherwise, call to make a reservation.

Two mi. north of the visitors center is **Schonchin Butte.** The steep ¾-mi. ascent takes about 30 minutes and leads you to a working fire lookout that gives a broad view of the area. Farther toward the monument's northern entrance is **Captain Jack's Stronghold,** the natural lava fortress where Modoc warriors held back Colonel Wheaton's troops during the Modoc War. There's an excellent self-guided trail through the area (maps 25¢). Just outside the northern entrance is **Petroglyph Point,** site of one of the largest collections of carvings in California, some of which date back to the first century AD. The images in the ancient rock are astoundingly vivid. **Fern Cave** contains underground pictographs, cave paintings (on display Sat. 9am-2pm by appointment only; contact the Lava Beds visitors center). Gaze at these ancient, sacred pictographs on the walls of this even older cave and contemplate the transiency of life.

Klamath Basin National Wildlife Refuge, visible on the drive from Tulelake to Lava Beds, is a bird-watcher's paradise, teeming with waterfowl. For more information, contact the refuge manager in Tulelake (667-2231). The visitors center also sells books about local flora and fauna.

Since 1990, the middle of July has been reserved at the Lava Beds for a **Modoc Indian Gathering.** More than 25 tribes come together in this area, which is thought to have been one of the largest and oldest centers of Native American civilization. The public is welcome to attend this celebration of Modoc culture.

In Newell, 4 mi. south of the Lava Beds' northern entrance, visit the remains of a **Japanese Internment Camp,** where more than 18,000 Japanese-Americans were held by the U.S. government during World War II. The camp has been deserted since March 20, 1946 and is now mostly disassembled.

Gold Country

In 1848 California was a rural backwater of only 15,000 people. The same year, saw-mill operator James Marshall wrote in his diary: "This day some kind of met-tle...found in the tailrace...looks like goald." In the next four years some 90,000 '49ers from around the world headed for California and the 120 mi. of gold-rich seams called the Mother Lode. Despite the hype, few of the prospectors struck it rich. Miners, sustained by dreams of instant wealth, worked long and hard, yet most barely squeeze sustenance out of their fiercely guarded claims.

Many miners died of malnutrition. Mark Twain described the diet thus: "Beans and dishwater for breakfast, dishwater and beans for dinner. And both articles warmed over for supper." Poorly constructed mines and risky techniques killed many more. Still, the search continued with almost manic desperation. In Coloma during one miner's funeral, a mourner spotted "color" (gold) in the open grave. The coffin was quickly removed and all in attendance, including the preacher, took to the ground with pick and shovel.

Ultimately, California's gilded terrain proved most profitable to the merchants who outfitted the miners. Prices were astronomical; bread sold for $1 a slice ($2 but-tered). Five years after the big discovery, the panning gold was gone, and miners could survive only by digging deeper and deeper into the rock. In some instances, whole towns were destroyed in hopes of finding "color" underneath. All but a few mines were abandoned by the 1870s, along with most of the towns that had sprouted parasitically around them. Some of the towns were repopulated years later when new industries arose, or when it became possible to commute from homes in the hills to nearby cities with stronger economic foundations. A few of the old mines have since been reopened; sophisticated chemical processing techniques reclaim gold from the discarded ore of previous decades.

Although gold remains in "them thar hills," today the towns of Gold Country make their money mining the tourist traffic. Gussied up as "Gold Rush Towns," they solicit tourists traveling along the appropriately numbered Rte. 49, which runs through the foothills, connecting dozens of small Gold Country settlements. If you tire of Gold Country lore, don't despair. Vineyards, river rafting, and cave exploring are popular and don't involve the "g-word".

■■■ SOUTHERN GOLD COUNTRY

This region lives mesmerized by its own short past. The history of the area is lively and interesting, but be forewarned; the ramshackle condition of many historic sites belies their age. Today, Mark Twain's old cabin is a a dilapidated shack, almost indis-tinguishable from other old sheds some locals use to park their tractors in. In order to fully appreciate the Southern Gold Country, you have to use your imagination. The **area code** for Southern Gold Country is **209.**

CALAVERAS COUNTY

Unsuspecting Calaveras County turned out to be sitting on a literal gold mine—the richest part of the Mother Lode—when the big rush hit. Over 550,000 pounds of gold were pulled out of the county's earth. A journalist from Missouri by the name of Samuel Clemens (a.k.a. Mark Twain), a hapless miner but a gifted spinner of yarns, allegedly based "The Celebrated Jumping Frog of Calaveras County"—his first big hit—on a story he heard in the Hotel Angel's barroom. In the story, Jim Smiley proudly carries his champion leaper "Dan'l Webster" wherever he goes. When a stranger makes fun of him, Smiley offers to fetch the stranger a frog and bets on the success of Dan'l in a jumping contest. But he makes the mistake of leaving his cham-pion in the stranger's hands. The out-of-towner fills ol' Dan'l with heavy buckshot, weighing the poor frog down. The stranger wins the contest and rapidly rides away with his winnings. Life has since imitated (or in this case, capitalized on) art; Calaveras has held annual frog-jumping contests since 1928. Thousands of people gather on the third weekend of May to watch or to participate in the festive affair. The winning frog receives the invaluable prize of freedom.

Frogs can be found in large quantities all over Calaveras County, though most are of the inanimate, manufactured-for-tourists variety. Angels Camp even has goofy green frogs painted on its sidewalks at sporadic intervals. Ribbit.

Calaveras County hops with small towns. **Angels Camp,** at the juncture of Rtes. 49 and 4, is the county hub and population center, but it isn't very big. Scattered throughout the rest of the county are **Alteville, Copperopolis, Sheep Ranch, San Andreas,** and other small towns. Just south of Angels Camp is **Tuttletown,** Mark Twain's one-time home, now little more than an historic marker and a grocery store. **Mokelumne Hill,** 7 mi. north of San Andreas, is not a ghost town but rather a ghost story town—this town's modern claim to fame is an affinity for spooky tales. Spirited minstrels haunt the **Leger Bar** on Main St. along Rte. 49 (286-1401).

About 20 mi. due east of Angels Camp lies **Calaveras Big Trees State Park** (795-3840; open dawn-dusk; day use $5). Here the *Sequoiadendron giganteum* (Giant Sequoia) reigns over all. These magnificent trees aren't as huge as those on the coast, but they do reach heights of 325 ft. Two groves of the mighty creatures can be found in the park. The North Grove is a pleasant and easy hike. The trail here is wheelchair-accessible, short, and heavily trafficked by tourists. The South Grove is less traveled. Once you've inspected the giants to your satisfaction, you can have a swim in Beaver Creek and, if you choose, spend the night at the **campground** within the state park ($14 with hot showers; reservations can be made through MISTIX 800-444-7275). The snow comes early (sometimes Sept.) at Big Trees, so plan to visit in the summer or bring a hefty pair of snowshoes. Summertime visitors should be prepared for gnats and mosquitoes on warm days.

Calaveras County boasts gargantuan natural wonders below ground as well as above. There are three commercialized caves in the county: **California Caverns** at Cave City, **Mercer Caverns,** and **Moaning Cavern.** Some caves served as naturally air-conditioned bars during the Gold Rush. A shot of whiskey in a cool cave could be purchased with a pinch of gold dust. One of Cave City's caves housed town gatherings and church services. Known as the "Bishop's Palace," it came to be regarded as the largest building in town. Today, visitors can take walking tours ($6.25, $3 ages 6-12) and more extensive adventure-style tours ($45 and $64). Cave City (736-2708; open May-Oct.) is located on Cave City Rd. east of San Andreas, and Moaning Cavern (736-2708; open year-round) lies east of Angels Camp. The tours explore winding passages and spectacular formations; some caves contain deep underground lakes.

For nearly a century and a half, Calaveras County has produced fine wines. Vineyards stretch along Rte. 49. Free **wine tasting** is available at most family-owned wineries. The **Stevenot Winery,** 2690 San Domingo Rd. (728-3436; open 10am-5pm), is the county's largest facility. At the **Kautz Ironside Vineyards** (728-1251; open 11am-5pm) on Six Mile Rd., wine is stored in caverns hewn from solid rock.

SONORA AND COLUMBIA

The ravines and hillsides now known as Sonora were once the domain of the Miwok Indians, but the arrival of the '49ers changed this section of the Sierra foothills into a bustling mining camp. In its Gold Rush heyday, Sonora was a large and prosperous city that vied fiercely with nearby Columbia for the honor of being the richest city of the southern Mother Lode. Today, both Columbia and Sonora offer garden-variety gold country recreation. Sonora can make a good rest stop between Lake Tahoe and Yosemite. However, travelers faced with a choice between Calaveras County and Sonora-Columbia may want to opt for the former, because of its proximity to Stanislaus National Forest, caves, and wineries.

Practical Information and Orientation The visitors center in Sonora (800-446-1333 or 533-4420) has guides to Columbia State Park. In the spirit of authenticity, automobiles are banned, routed instead to large parking lots on the southern and western sides of town. The 24-hr. **Crisis Intervention Line** in Sonora is 800-444-9999. **Tuolomne General Hospital,** 101 Hospital Rd., Sonora (533-7100), offers 24-hr. emergency service. For **emergencies,** call 911. The local **police** can be reached at 532-8141. The Sonora **post office** is located at 781 S. Washington St. (532-4304; open Mon.-Fri. 8:30am-5pm, Sat. 10am-2pm). The **General Delivery ZIP Code** is 95370. The **area code** is 209.

Sonora's layout is complicated by the fact that two highways enter the town from three directions. **Washington St.** runs north-south through town, and at the north end becomes **Rte. 49.** At the south end, it branches, and the east fork (Mono Way) becomes **Rte. 108.** Halfway down Washington St., **Stockton St.** intersects it, and this is the other half of Rte. 49, heading south. Columbia lies 5 mi. north on Rte. 49.

Accommodations, Food, and Sights The oldest building in Sonora is the **Gunn House,** 286 S. Washington (532-3421)—the central adobe section dates to 1850. This hotel has terrific ambience and is furnished entirely with antiques. It'll make you dream of the glory days of prospecting. (1 bed $40-45, 2 beds $55-75). The **Rail Fence Motel,** 19950 Rte. 108 (532-9191), is an eight-room establishment located 5 mi. east of Sonora. With a pool, complimentary breakfast, and 10 mi. of hiking trails in back, this is a good deal—call for reservations. ($34.50 per person, $4 per additional person or a kitchen.) Also in Sonora is **Moccasin Point,** the closest **campground,** (852-2396), 6 mi. east of Chinese Camp off Rte. 120 in the Don Pedro Reservoir Area. (Water, toilets, and showers. Tent sites $13, RV hookup $17.)

Before you decide to dine out in Sonora, consider picnicking at **Coffill Park** on Washington St. You can stock up at the 24-hr. **Safeway,** 659 Washington St. (532-7015). Or for an indoor dining experience, scope **Wilma's Café,** 275 S. Washington St. (532-9957). Wilma is the wooden pig perched atop the pie case. In spite of the overwhelming pig motif, the pies, burgers, and pancakes at Wilma's are delicious. (Slice $2.15. Entrees $5-8. Open Sun.-Thurs. 6am-10pm, Fri.-Sat. 6am-midnight.) **The Diamondback Grill,** 110 S. Washington St. (532-6661), in the center of Sonora's old-town district, is a tiny restaurant that offers big portions and tasty specialty burgers, like the pesto-mozzarella burger ($5-6).

Columbia, the "Gem of the Southern Mines," now prospects for tourist dollars. Rich in Placer gold (loose gold found in rivers and dirt), Columbia once supported 4000 people and 150 saloons. There was so much gold for the taking that even after the town burned down twice in three years, people stayed, and after learning how to build with bricks, extracted $2.1 billion worth of the yellow stuff. What remains of the city today was purchased by the state in 1945 and designated a state park.

Columbia State Park (532-0150) dedicates itself to the whole-hearted practice of thinly veiled artifice. The "miners" here peel off their beards at night, the outhouse is nailed shut, and the horse and buggy carriage spend the nights in a nearby parking lot. Visitors to the park can pan for gold and peer into the town's numerous historical buildings as part of the "living history" environment. Entrance to the park and the mining museum (532-4301) within is free.

■■■ STANISLAUS NATIONAL FOREST

Well-maintained roads and campsites, craggy peaks, dozens of cool aquamarine lakes, forests of Ponderosa pines, and wildflower meadows make up the 900,000 acres of the Stanislaus National Forest. Here, peregrine falcons, bald eagles, mountain lions, and bears sometimes surprise the (un)lucky traveler. Yet, in spite of all its attractions, Stanislaus remains popular only as a place to camp when its better known cousin, Yosemite, is full.

Park headquarters are located in Sonora at 19777 Greenly Rd. (532-3671, 24-hr. recorded information; open summer 8am-5pm, call for winter hours). Camping does not require a permit unless you plan on pitching your tent in one of the wilderness areas or building a fire, and no campground in Stanislaus accepts reservations.

For a quick, scenic tour of the forest, locals recommend driving along curvy and narrow **Rte. 4** or **Rte. 108.** Drivers are rewarded by the views they encounter as they climb over Ebbett's Pass and Pacific Grade Summit. Be aware, however, that roads are often closed during the winter months and occasionally through much of the fall and spring.

The **Groveland District** covers the area adjacent to Yosemite's west side. The **ranger station** is nine miles past Groveland on Rte. 120 (962-7825; open Mon.-Fri. 7am-4:30pm, Sat. 7:30am-4:30pm). **Carlon** is the closest campsite to the entrance with pit toilets and potable water (free). **Little Nellio Falls** lies in the district's southeast corner and is usually deserted. The Groveland District is logged and littered with pockets of private property, as is the **Mi-Wok District**—the more interesting districts lie to the north.

The **Summit District,** the forest's most popular spot, has a **ranger station** off Rte. 108 at **Pinecrest Lake** (965-3434; open Mon.-Sat. 8am-5:30pm, Sun. and holidays 8am-4:30pm). Free **campsites** abound along Rte. 108. The **Trail of the Gargoyles,** north of the station off Rte. 108 on Herring Creek Rd., is lined with shapely geological formations. The trail skirts a canyon which documents nature's labor in lava flows, *lahar* (hardened mud), and ash. **Cherry Creek Canyon,** north of Cherry Lake, is a glaciated canyon with just enough walking space at its floor for hikers. A trailhead at **Eagle Meadow** leads down to **Coopers Meadow** and **Three Chimneys,** a brick-red volcanic formation.

Those seeking solitude might enjoy the **Carson-Iceberg Wilderness** in the northeast section of the forest. The absence of lakes and the steep terrain in this region eliminate it from most itineraries. Stanislaus Peak and Sonora Peak are accessible from the **Pacific Crest Trail** and reward persevering climbers with a humbling panorama of the Sierras. Walk along **Baster Creek** and you will find yourself surrounded by mountains.

The adjacent **Calaveras District,** with a **ranger station** on Rte. 4 at Hathaway Pines (795-1381; open Mon.-Sat. 8am-5pm), contains the **Dardanelles,** a series of cones and other volcanic by-products. There is a campground at the reservoir (8 mi. southwest of Rte. 4) with piped water, pit toilets, and wheelchair access ($9).

■■■ NORTHERN GOLD COUNTRY

Every gold miner's life was rough, but none had it rougher than those who worked the northern half of the Mother Lode. Here, granite peaks kept a rigid grip on the nuggets, while merciless winters punished persistent miners for their efforts. Today, the small towns of the Northern Gold Country are far removed from the less authentic "Main Street" scenes of the Southern Gold Country, and the natural beauty of this region handsomely rewards exploration. If you're lucky, you may catch a glimpse of a wiry prospector leading his donkey into the hills.

The **area code** for Northern Gold Country is **916.**

THE BUTTE MOUNTAINS

Six mi. north of **Sierra City** on Rte. 49 is the Bassetts turn-off (a store here dispenses gas, food, and other necessities). The **Butte** (BYOOT) **Mountains** lie further up the Bassetts turn-off road. Turn left at the Sardine Lake turnoff, pass Sardine Lake, and bear right—the trail that leads into the mountains begins about 1½ mi. past Packer Lake. The summit affords a spectacular view of undisturbed pine forests and jagged mountainsides dotted with evergreens and occasional patches of snow. This area is one of the most beautiful, least traveled spots in California.

Prepare for a stomach-dropping (road) and jaw-dropping (vistas) experience when you drive along **Rte. 49.** This twisting, undulating drive takes you down valleys, over mountains, and alongside the rushing Yuba River.

Traveling away from Rte. 49 along the Bassetts turn-off road leads to pristine **Gold Lake** at the four-way intersection. The adjacent **stables** (836-0040) offer guided rides around the area (from $17). Four mi. to the right from the intersection is **Frasier Falls,** a noisy, 600-ft. cascade with yet another fantastic view opposite. There are a half-dozen campgrounds in the area lining the route from the Bassetts turn-off to Frasier Falls, all of which are marked by signs on the main road. Sites are $8, lack showers, and are available on a first-come, first-camped basis.

South of Sierra City, Rte. 49 hugs the Yuba River and runs past several Forest Service **campgrounds** on the river's edge (running water, pit toilets; $8). These sites are typically busy on weekends, but space can often be found 12 mi. south of **Downieville** at **Loganville Campground,** which is ½ mi. from the river's edge.

Travelers should be careful of straying too far from Rte. 49 unless they have an off-road vehicle. If driving Rte. 49 seems adventurous to you, navigating the other "roads" in the area may be positively nerve-shattering.

Downieville, Sierra City, Forest City, and Alleghany

These miniature towns are remnants of the Northern Gold Country's past and do little to cater to tourists; depending on your point of view, they may be either appealingly or discouragingly rural. In friendly relaxed **Downieville,** the **Downieville Bakery** vends delicious breads and pastries. The basics are available at the **Downieville Grocery Store** (289-3596) on Main St. The **Downieville Motor Inn** (289-3243) and its kindly management provide simple, cozy accommodations. (Singles and doubles$36.)

The **Sierra Buttes Inn** (862-1300) is nestled within the tiny town of **Sierra City** 12 mi. south of Downieville on Rte. 49. This old, historic inn will take you back to the turn of the century. (Singles $15. Doubles $33.)

Twenty mi. south of Downieville on Ridge Rd. lie **Forest City** and **Alleghany.** For a really out-of-the-way place to stay, try the **Kenton Mine Lodge** (800-634-2002), about 5 mi. from Alleghany. If you are looking to banish everything urban from your life, this is a good place to start. (Singles from $27.50. Doubles from $45.) Bring your own food and definitely call for reservations and good directions. These two towns are even less commercialized than their neighbors. Rumor has it that with a good tailwind, you can spit the length of Alleghany.

MALAKOFF DIGGINS STATE PARK

Once the easy gold was gone, miners turned to more extreme means to unearth hidden "color." One of these was hydraulic mining, which involved forcing high-pressure water onto mountainsides and digging with relative ease through the resulting mud. This process washed away entire mountains, leaving behind strangely beautiful canyons such as those found at Malakoff Diggins. Runoff from the waterings silted the Yuba River and San Francisco Bay so heavily that navigation through these bodies was made all but impossible. But, as the saying went, "All for gold, and gold for all who stop at nothing."

Malakoff Diggins State Park is located off Tyler Foote Rd. about 26 mi. north of **Nevada City.** Stay at $10 campsites in the park (call MISTIX at 800-444-7275 for reservations) or in $20 primitive cabins without facilities close to the park's ghost town (call 265-2740 for more info). The fee for day use is $5 per car.

NEVADA CITY

Nevada City embodies commercialized restoration at its finest—the whole town seems to be in on creating the illusion of yesteryear. The effort makes Nevada City a leading candidate for the cleanest, most picturesque town in the Gold Country region. Nevada City is draped across a series of hills; the resulting steep, winding streets contribute significantly to its charm. Many buildings in the town are of historical interest, including the dozens of **Victorian homes,** the **National Hotel,** and the **Firehouse** (interior open daily 11am-4pm). A free walking tour map from the **Chamber of Commerce** (800-655-6569 or 265-2692; open Mon.-Fri. 9am-5pm, Sat. 11am-4pm) describes noteworthy structures. There is also a town **swimming pool** ($1; 265-8223;open Mon.-Sat. noon-6pm).

Nevada City's health-conscious congregate to refuel at **Earth Song,** 130 Argall St., a natural foods market and café (265-9392; open Mon.-Thurs. 7am-8pm, Fri.-Sat. 7am-9pm, Sun. 8am-8pm). Another popular hangout is the **Mekka Café** (237 Commercial, 478-1517; open Sun.-Thurs. 7am-11pm, Fri.-Sat. 7am-1:30pm). Stop by to admire its bordello/leopard skin/David Lynch-esque decoration, selection of books and chaises, and hip evening crowd. Thursdays feature music or poetry readings. Have an Italian soda ($1.25) or the house specialty, a fresh Café Mocha ($2.25).

A dose of history awaits you at the **Empire Mine State Historic Park** (273-8522; open daily 9am-6pm in summer, call for winter hours; take the Empire St. exit off Rte. 20 west of town). Peering down into the cool, dark air of the mine shaft, you can contemplate whether you'd go down there for a chance at the big money— $120,000,000 of gold was obtained from the mine. Enjoy the well-maintained, shaded grounds, admire the mansion and its gardens, or engage in conversation with the costumed actors who won't be satisfied until you believe you've gone back in time ($2, children $1). Living history tours are offered during summer weekends.

The Nevada City area contains trails for hikers and walkers of nearly every taste and ability. The **Bridgeport State Park** (take Rte. 20 to Penn Valley and turn right on Pleasant Valley Rd.) features an easy, relatively short 1¼-mi. hike over the largest covered bridge in the West, past fragrant spreads of wildflowers, and around the river canyon. Search for a free souvenir during the park's gold-panning demonstrations (Sat.-Sun. 11pm; bring your own pan).

COLOMA

Amidst the confusion of claims and counterclaims about the first, the richest, and the most important gold strike, one thing is indisputable, the 1848 Gold Rush began in Coloma at John Sutter's water-powered lumber mill, operated James Marshall. Today the **James Marshall Gold Discovery State Historic Park** (622-3470) in Coloma marks the spot. (Day-use fee $5, seniors $4. Display your pass prominently in your car window or you will be ticketed.) Near the site where Marshall discovered the precious metal, the water now flows quietly through the rushes, the tens of thousands of miners long since departed. A few hundred yards away is a replica of the original mill, constructed in 1968. Picnic grounds across the street surround the **Gold Discovery Museum,** 310 Back St. (622-3470), which gives a rather simplified version of the events triggered by the discovery. Dioramas and a film give visitors a feel for gold-rush days. The huge nuggets on display may inspire you to pan for gold (free with day use fee). For the record, neither Sutter nor Marshall made much from the discovery. (Open daily 10am-5pm. Winter hours may be shorter.)

The **Monroe Ridge Trail** provides an overlook of the town and passes by a statue of Marshall pointing at the incipient nugget. Camping is available at **Camp Lotus** (off Rte. 49, turn south across from Ponderosa Pines and follow the signs), right along the American River (showers, chemical toilets; sites $10). There is a **general store** at Camp Lotus which has the standard canned goods, candy, and soda for inflated prices. Anyone who camps here will be exposed to the rapids culture, composed of rafters and kayakers who challenge the river's Class III currents. The American River and its three forks are the most commercially traveled stretches of river in the West. There are a number of **rafting** outfitters in Coloma and neighboring Placerville. Contact **Three Forks White Water Tours** (800-257-7238 or 626-4718) or **Whitewater Connection** (800-336-7238) for more info. Farther north along Rte. 49, the river flows into a deep gorge perfect for hiking, swimming, and seclusion.

PLACERVILLE

Back in 1849, Placerville was known as "Hangtown." Even now, in these tamer times, a walk along Placerville's well-preserved streets should satisfy anyone's nostalgia for the 19th-century West. This small, friendly town has a nicely restored historic district full of little cafés, diners, bakeries, and antique shops.

Practical Information and Orientation For visitors information, go to the **Chamber of Commerce,** 542 Main St. (621-5885; open Mon.-Fri. 8am-5pm) offering free maps of the county. An **ATM** can be found at River City Bank, 348 Main St. **Greyhound,** 1750 Broadway (622-7200; open daily 8:30am-5:30pm), lies 3 mi. east of downtown. Buses head to: Tahoe (4 per day, $17); Reno (4 per day, $34); Sacramento (4 per day, $8.65). Rent a car at **Enterprise Rent-A-Car,** 583 Placerville (621-0866; cars from $24 per day). In an **emergency,** call 911. The **police** are at 730 Main St. (642-5210; ask for Stewart or Andy). The **post office** is at 3045 Sacramento St. (622-6443; open Mon.-Fri. 8:30am-5pm), south of U.S. 50. The **General Delivery ZIP Code** is 95667.

About one-third of the way from Sacramento to Lake Tahoe on **U.S. 50,** Placerville is strategically positioned to snare campers, boaters, and skiers. The town extends northwards to encompass **Hangtown Gold Bug Park** ($1, ages 5-16 50¢). Most streets, including Main St., parallel U.S. 50. **Rte. 49** also bisects the town, running north to Coloma (10 mi.) and Auburn, and south towards Calaveras County.

Accommodations, Food, and Sights As commercialized, but not as quirky or colorful as Nevada City, Placerville does have some of the conveniences of a city and at least one budget motel, the **Hangtown Motel,** 1676 Broadway (622-0637) with HBO and ordinary rooms. (Singles $30; doubles $34. Weekends $32; 36.) The motel's name comes from Placerville's infamous reputation for handing out justice speedily at the end of a rope.

Thirty mi. south of Placerville off Rte. 49 (get off slightly past Sutter Creek and head east) is **Indian Grinding Rocks State Park** (209-296-7488). The park contains an excellent museum (open Mon.-Fri. 11am-3pm, Sat.-Sun. 10am-4pm), a plant trail, and a restored village. (Park open from dawn to dusk; $5 per car.) There is also a campground with hot showers ($14; call MISTIX at 800-444-7275 for reservations).

Fresh food can be found at the **farmer's market** on Main St. (Thurs. 6-9pm and Sat. 8am-noon). For something meaty, follow the tantalizing scent of barbecued ribs wafting down the street, through the windowless metal door into the ever-full restaurant and circular bar of **Poor Red's,** Main St., El Dorado (622-2901), 5 mi. south of Placerville on Rte. 49. This dusty place is packed with locals from miles around; expect to wait up to two hours at peak eating times. Portions big enough to sate Fred Flintstone will reward your patience. (Barbecued ribs at dinner, $8. Lunch is cheaper and just as greasy: gigantic steak sandwich $6, barbecued pork lunch $3.25.) Watch out for the "Golden Cadillac," ($3.25) supposedly the strongest drink in the country. This two-glass liquor concoction packs a powerful punch. (Open Mon.-Fri. 11:30am-2pm and 5-11pm, Sat. 5-11pm, Sun. 2-11pm.)

The hills around Placerville are fruit country. Travelers with bicycle or car can tour the apple orchards and wineries off U.S. 50 on Carson Rd., North Canyon Rd., and Carson Dr. in the area known as **Apple Hill.** This association of farms is geared toward family recreation with picnicking, fishing, craft fairs, and pumpkin hunts. A complete listing/map of orchards is available from the Chamber of Commerce (above). Locals claim that **Denver Dan's,** 4344 Bumblebee Lane (644-2893), is the best orchard for consistently reasonable prices, while **Kid's,** 3245 N. Canyon Rd. (622-0841), has the best apple pie in the area. For free wine tasting, try **Lava Cap Winery,** at 2221 Fruitridge Rd. (621-0175; open daily 11am-5pm), or **Boeger Winery,** 1709 Carson Rd. (622-8094; open daily 10am-5pm). The best times to visit Apple Hill are spring (for flowers) and autumn (for apple harvest). **Gold Hill,** another local area similar to Apple Hill, focuses on peaches, plums, and citrus fruits.

Sierra Nevada

The Sierra Nevada is the highest, steepest, and most physically stunning mountain range in the contiguous United States. Thrust skyward 400 million years ago by plate tectonics and shaped by erosion, glaciers, and volcanoes, this enormous hunk of granite stretches 450 mi. north from the Mojave Desert to Lake Almanor. The heart-stopping sheerness of Yosemite's rock walls, the craggy alpine scenery of Kings Canyon and Sequoia National Parks, and the abrupt drop of the Eastern Slope into Owens Valley are unparalleled sights.

Appalled by the devastating logging that threatened the giant sequoia during the mid- and late-1800s, naturalist John Muir convinced Congress to establish Sequoia and Yosemite National Parks. Continuing environmental concern voiced by Californians resulted in the subsequent creation of other nationally protected areas in the Sierras, including Sequoia's sibling, Kings Canyon, in 1940.

The popularity of the Sierras is reflected in the wide variety of books, maps, and brochures on the mountains. National park and forest visitor centers generally have comprehensive selections, as do some bookstores and libraries. For more information on this region, Storer and Usinger's *Sierra Nevada Natural History* and Thomas Winnett's guide to the Pacific Crest Trail are well worth reading.

Temperatures in the Sierra Nevada are as diverse as the terrain. Even in the summer, overnight lows can dip into the 20s. Check local weather reports. Normally, only U.S. 50 and I-80 are kept open during the snow season. Exact dates vary from year to year, so check with a ranger station for local road conditions, especially from October through June. Come summer, protection from the high elevations' ultraviolet rays is necessary; always bring sunscreen, and a hat is a good idea. For additional outdoors advice, see Essentials: Camping and the Outdoors, page 47.

■■■ YOSEMITE NATIONAL PARK

In 1868 a young Scotsman named John Muir arrived by boat in San Francisco and asked for directions to "anywhere that's wild." He was pointed toward the Sierra Nevada. The natural wonders that awaited Muir inspired him to a lifetime of conservationism. In 1880 he succeeded in securing national park status for Yosemite. Today, few of the park's 3.5 million annual visitors know of his efforts, but most leave with an appreciation and love for Yosemite's natural treasures.

Hundreds of thousands of people make the pilgrimage to Yosemite each summer to gape at awe-inspiring granite cliffs, thunderous waterfalls, lush meadows, rock monoliths, and thick pine forests. The resulting pile-up makes for congestion more closely resembling an L.A. freeway than an Ansel Adams photograph.

Though the park seems safe from condos and resorts, a plethora of snack shops, souvenir stands, and gas stations has sunk the valley into commercial chaos. Even in the high country, purists complain of the park's crowds, but the ruling policy is that the splendors of this national park are for all to enjoy. Those in search of solitude should use the valley's facilities only to commence a journey into the wilderness beyond or visit one of Yosemite's less crowded neighbors.

The park covers 1189 sq. mi. of mountainous terrain. **El Capitán, Half Dome,** and **Yosemite Falls** lie in the Yosemite Valley, an area carved out by glaciers over thousands of years. Once you've seen these main attractions, though, head out to the other parts of the park. Little Yosemite Valley, accessible by hiking trails, offers two spectacular waterfalls: **Vernal** and **Nevada Falls. Tuolumne Meadows** (pronounced ta-WALL-um-ee) in the northeastern corner of the park is an Elysian expanse of alpine meadows surrounded by granite cliffs and rushing streams. **Mariposa Grove** is a forest of giant sequoia trees at the park's southern end.

Visitors to the Yosemite region are invariably delighted and inspired by their stay. The park has infinite offerings. Experience the drama of its beauty, and you'll understand why Muir remarked: "No description of heaven seems half so fine."

PRACTICAL INFORMATION

Visitors Information: A map of the park and a copy of the informative *Yosemite Guide* are available for free at visitors centers. Information folders and maps are available in French, German, Spanish, and Japanese. Wilderness **permits** are available at all visitors centers; it pays to write ahead and reserve in advance; call for information. All hours listed are valid **mid-May-mid-Sept.,** unless otherwise noted; call for off-season hours. **General Park Information,** 372-0265; 24-hr. recorded information 372-0200; TTY users 372-4726. Informed and friendly staff gives telephone advice about accommodations, activities, and weather conditions. Open Mon.-Fri. 9am-5pm. **Wilderness Office,** P.O. Box 577, Yosemite National Park 95839 (372-0308; 24-hr. recorded information 372-0307), next to Yosemite Valley Visitors Center. **Backcountry** and trail information. Open daily 7:30am-7:30pm. **Campground information:** 372-0200 (recorded).

Yosemite Valley Visitors Center, Yosemite Village (372-0229). Sign language interpreter available daily 2-5pm. Open daily 8am-8pm; winter 8am-5pm.

Tuolumne Meadows Visitors Center, Tioga Rd. (372-0263), 55 mi. from Yosemite Village. The headquarters of high-country activity, with trail information, maps, and special programs.

Big Oak Flat Information Station, Rte. 120 W. (379-2445), in the Crane Flat/Tuolumne Sequoia Grove Area. Open daily 8am-6pm.

Wawona Ranger Station, Rte. 141 (372-0398), at the southern entrance near the Mariposa Grove. Open daily 8am-5pm.

Park Admission: $3 if you enter on foot, bicycle, or bus. $5 for 7-day vehicle pass.

Delaware North Co. Room Reservations, 5410 E. Home, Fresno 93727 (252-4848, TTY users 255-8345).

Tour Information: Yosemite Lodge Tour Desk (372-1240), in Yosemite Lodge lobby. Open daily 7:30am-7pm, or contact any lodge in the park.

ATM: Bank of America Versateller, in Yosemite Village south of the Village Store. Open 6am-midnight.

Gas: available at **Chevron** stations in Yosemite Valley (7am-9pm), Wawona, Crane Flat, El Portal, and Tuolumne Meadows (all 8am-7pm). Fill up before you make the climb into the High Sierra—gas prices rise with the elevation.

Amtrak and Buses: see Orientation and Getting Around, below.

Auto Service, Towing, and Repair: Village Garage, 24-hr. towing (372-1221). Open 8am-5pm.

Equipment Rental: Yosemite Mountaineering School, Rte. 120 (372-1224), at Tuolumne Meadows. Sleeping bags $4 per day, backpacks $4 per day, snowshoes $6 per day. Climbing shoes rented to YMS students only. Driver's license or credit card required. Open daily 8:30am-5pm.

Bike Rentals: at **Yosemite Lodge** and **Curry Village** (372-1208 and 372-1200 respectively). $5 per hr., $16.25 per day. Both open daily 8am-7pm, weather permitting.

Stables: At Yosemite Valley, Kennel, Tuolumne Meadows, Waroona, and White Wolf. Guided rides start at $30. All open 7:30am-5pm; call 372-1248 for more information.

Camera Rental: Ansel Adams Gallery, in Yosemite Village next to the visitors center. Day rentals of tripods ($7) and both single-lens-reflex ($12) and compact 35mms ($7.50). Also offers a wonderful selection of prints and postcards. A great place to browse. Open daily 8:30am-6:30pm.

Laundromat: Housekeeping Camp, $1.25 per wash, 10-min. dry 25¢. Open 7am-10pm in summer. In winter, laundry facilities available at Camp 6, across the street from the Village Store. Open 7am-10pm.

Showers: Housekeeping Camp, $2 includes towel and soap, although in the mornings and evenings you'll have to wait in a long and dirty line. Open 7:30am-10pm. Also in Curry Village; open 24 hrs.

AAA Emergency Road Service: 372-1221.

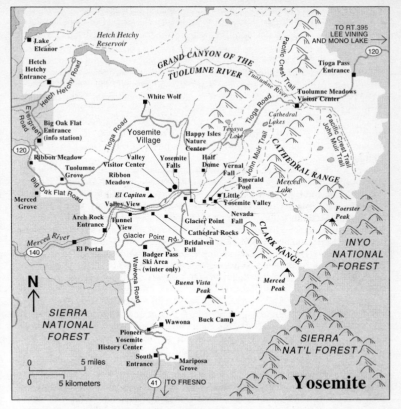

Weather and Road Conditions: 372-0209. 24 hrs.
Medical Services: Yosemite Medical Clinic, in Yosemite Village near the
Ahwanee Hotel (372-4637). 24-hr. emergency service and regular appointments.
Open Mon.-Fri. 8am-5pm, Sat. 9am-noon. **Dental Services,** next to the clinic
(372-4200). Mon.-Fri. 8am-4:30pm.
Emergency: 911; park rangers can be found throughout the park.
Post Offices: Yosemite Village, next to the visitors center. Open Mon.-Fri.
8:30am-5pm; Sept.-May Mon.-Fri. 8:30am-12:30pm and 1:30-5pm. **Curry Village,**
near Registration Office. Stamps available from machines year-round. Open June-
Sept. Mon.-Fri. 9am-3pm. **Yosemite Lodge,** open Mon.-Fri. 9am-4:30pm. **Gen-
eral Delivery ZIP Code:** 95389.
Area code: 209.

ORIENTATION AND GETTING AROUND

Yosemite lies 200 mi. due east of San Francisco and 320 mi. northeast of Los Angeles. It can be reached by taking **Rte. 140** from Merced, **Rte. 41** north from Fresno,
and **Rte. 120** east from Manteca or west from Lee Vining.

Yosemite runs public **buses** that connect the park with Merced, Fresno, and Lee
Vining. **Yosemite VIA,** 300 Grogan Ave., Merced 95340 (742-5211 or 800-VIA-
LINE, 842-5463), makes two round-trips per day from the Merced Amtrak station to
Yosemite ($15, round-trip $28; discount for seniors). **Yosemite Gray Line (YGL),**
P.O. Box 2472, Merced 95344 (383-1563), meets the morning train arriving in
Merced from San Francisco and takes passengers to Yosemite. The bus returns to
Merced in time to catch the return train to San Francisco. YGL also runs to and from

YOSEMITE NATIONAL PARK

Fresno ($22). From July through Labor Day, the **Yosemite Transportation System (YTS)** connects the park with Greyhound in Lee Vining (372-1240; one way $20.25). Reservations are required to buy a ticket. Greyhound does not sell tickets in Lee Vining, so be prepared to buy your ticket when you board the bus. You can also take **Amtrak** (800-USA-RAIL, -872-7245) from San Francisco to Merced ($29) and connect with the waiting YGL bus. Amtrak also provides transport via shuttle bus and train from L.A. to Fresno (one way $38) and Merced (one way $46).

The best bargain in Yosemite, aside from the price of admission, is the free **shuttle bus system.** Comfortable but often crowded, the buses have knowledgeable drivers and broad viewing windows. They run through the valley daily at 10-minute intervals from 7:30am to 10pm. **Hikers' buses** run daily to Glacier Point spring-autumn and to Tuolumne Meadows/Lee Vining July 1 to Labor Day. Call 372-1240 for information.

From any of the lodging facilities, you can purchase **tour tickets.** The basic **Valley Floor Tour** lasts two hours and points out sights such as Half Dome, El Capitán, Bridalveil Fall, and Happy Isles. The tour is conducted on open-air trams with amiable guides and costs $15 (ages 5-12 $7, under 5 free). The **Glacier Point Tour** lasts four hours and climbs to the point for a 3200-ft.-high view of the valley ($19.50, ages 5-12 $10, under 5 free; June 1-Thanksgiving). The **Mariposa Grove Tour** spends half a day visiting the big trees ($29, children $14), and the **Grand Tour** ($36, children $19, June 1-Thanksgiving) is a comprehensive, full day's outing. The two-hour **Moonlight Tour,** conducted on full and near-full moon nights, offers unique night-time views of the cliffs ($10). Call 372-1240 for reservations, departure times, and locations.

Although the inner valley is often congested with traffic, the best way to gain a rapid overview of Yosemite is by **car** or bus. Park at one of the lodging areas and ride the shuttle to see the valley sights, then hop back into your car to explore other places. Drivers intending to visit the high country in spring and fall should have snow tires (sometimes required in early and late summer). Of the five major approaches to the park, Rte. 120 to the Big Oak Flat entrance is most challenging to the stability of your stomach. The easiest route from the west is Rte. 140 into Yosemite Valley. The eastern entrance, Tioga Pass, is closed during snow season; the road to Mirror Lake and Happy Isles is closed to private auto traffic year-round, but is traversed by the free shuttle buses during the summer. (See Wintertime in Yosemite, page 373, for more information about winter driving.) While driving is convenient and fast, leave motorized transport behind for some wilderness exploration or you will miss the spirit of the park. **Bicycling** is also an excellent way to see Yosemite Valley; bike paths abound, and most sights are within a 4-mi. diameter across the Valley center. (See Practical Information for rental information.) You can also take guided **horseback trips** into Yosemite's backcountry. The park has four stables (see Practical Information), and reservations are needed to secure a spot.

ACCOMMODATIONS

Lodgings in Yosemite Valley are monopolized by the Delaware North Company and range from simple canvas tent cabins to the luxurious suites of the Ahwahnee Hotel, which start at over $200 in season. Rates are in constant flux, varying between mid-week and weekend, in-season and off-season. All lodgings have access to dining and laundry facilities, showers, and supplies. Reservations are necessary for all park lodgings, some as far as a year in advance. Call 252-4848 for information. Rates below are for summer weekends. If you are interested in staying outside the park, the flyer *Accommodations Outside Yosemite* may prove helpful. But remember, camping is the best (and cheapest) way to experience Yosemite.

Yosemite Lodge, in Yosemite Valley west of Yosemite Village. Small, spruce, sparsely furnished cabins under surveillance by deer. To catch cancellations, inquire before 4pm. Singles and doubles $48, with bath $63.

Curry Village, southeast of Yosemite Village. The flashing neon sign at the entrance heralds the crowded camp area. Back-to-back cabins are noisy but clean. Ice cream and pizza only a minute away. $48, with bath $63. Less private canvas-sided tent cabins $38.

Housekeeping Camp, west of Curry Village. Canvas and concrete units accommodate up to 4 people, and include double beds, chairs, and stoves. Bring insect repellent. $38 for 1-4 people.

Tuolumne Meadows Lodge, on Tioga Rd. in northeast corner of park. Canvas-sided tent cabins $38 for 2 people, $5 per additional adult ($2.50 for children).

White Wolf Lodge, west of Tuolumne Meadows on Tioga Rd. Cabins with bath $56. Canvas tent cabins $38 for 2, $6 per additional adult and $2.50 per child.

CAMPGROUNDS

Yosemite is camping country. Most of the valley's campgrounds are crowded, many choked with trailers and RVs. In Yosemite Valley's drive-in campgrounds, reservations are required from April to November and must be made through MISTIX (800-365-2267) up to eight weeks ahead. Or show up at the **Campground reservations office** in Curry Village at 9am or 4pm to catch a cancellation. With the exception of major holidays, you should be able to camp in one of the first-come, first-served campgrounds (**Wawona, Tamarack Flat, White Wolf,** and **Porcupine Flat**) if you arrive before noon. In summer, there is a 14-day limit for campers outside Yosemite Valley and a seven-day limit for those in the valley; some backpacker sites have a one- or two-day limit.

Most campgrounds are close to supply stores (see Food). No campgrounds provide RV hookups, but showers are available at **Curry Housekeeping** from spring through fall (open 24 hrs.; admission $2 including use of pool), and at **Tuolumne Meadows** and **White Wolf Lodges** in summer. At all campgrounds served by natural stream water (**Tamarack Flat and Porcupine Flat**), the *water must be boiled, filtered, or treated* to prevent *giardia,* a nasty intestinal disease.

Backpacker's Camp, 1½ mi. east of Yosemite Village across the river, behind North Pine Campground. Must have a wilderness permit and be a backpacker without a vehicle to camp here. Unadvertised. Low on facilities, high on camaraderie. Fishing is popular. Running water, toilets, and showers nearby. 2-night max. stay. $3 per person. Open May-Oct.

Sunnyside, at the west end of Yosemite Valley past the Yosemite Lodge Chevron station. A walk to the climber's camp, called **Camp 4** by regulars, will immerse the innocent in the spooky climbing subculture, in which seasoned adventurers swap stories of exploits on vertical rock faces. Water, toilets, and tables. $3 per person. Often fills up early with visitors without reservations.

Lower and **Upper River,** 1 mi. east of Yosemite Village along the Merced River. Reserved sites, more secluded than the Pines campgrounds at the eastern end of the valley. No RVs at Upper River. No pets anywhere. Water, toilets, tables, and showers. Sites $14. Both open April-Oct.

Tamarack Flat, 23 mi. northeast of Yosemite Valley. Take Rte. 120 east. Drive-in sites (no RVs). Fills up later than other campgrounds. Toilets and tables, but no drinking water or showers. Pets allowed. Sites $6. Open June-Oct.

Tuolumne Meadows, 55 mi. east on Rte. 120. Half of the 314 sites can be reserved through MISTIX; other sites are for same-day reservations. Drive into the sprawling campground, or escape the RVs by ambling to the 25 walk-in sites. Great scenery and nearby trailheads. Pets allowed in the Western Section sites. Water, toilets, showers, and tables. 1-night max. stay. Drive-in sites $12, backpacker sites (i.e. no vehicle and with permit) $2 per person. Open June-Sept.

Wawona, Rte. 41 in the southern end of the park. 100 sites beautified by tables, toilets, and water. No showers. Pets. Sites $10.

White Wolf, off Rte. 120 E. Water, toilets, tables, fire pits. Pets allowed. 87 sites. $10 per site. Open June-mid-Sept.

Porcupine Flat, off Rte. 120 E. RV access to front section only. Pit toilets, potable stream water. 52 sites. $6 per site. Open June-Oct.

Hodgdon Meadow, on Rte. 120 near Big Oak Flat entrance. Suitable for winter camping or for finding solitude year-round. Water, tables, and toilets. Sites $12.

Lower Pines, in the busy eastern end of Yosemite Valley. Slick, commercial, and crowded, the campground has toilets, water, showers, and tables. Sites $14. This is the designated **winter camping** spot.

For information on **backcountry camping,** see Beyond Yosemite Valley, page 372.

FOOD

Restaurants in Yosemite are expensive and dreary, dishing out bland American fare. Bring your own food for a campfire feast. Overpriced groceries are available from the **Yosemite Lodge, Wawona,** or the **Village Stores** (open daily 8am-10pm; Oct.-May 8am-9pm).

The Loft, in the Yosemite Village complex, above Degnan's Deli. Lunch sandwiches are $5.50-6.70, dinner entrees $8-14, burgers on French bread $7.50. Pricey, "relaxed dining." Open May-Oct. daily 11:45am-2pm and 5:30-10pm.

Yosemite Lodge Cafeteria, in the Lodge complex. Provides schoolbox-type lunches for a picnic (2 sandwiches, a hard-boiled egg, fruit, and dessert $5). Order the day before you go. Open daily 6:30am-8pm; Oct.-May 8am-7pm.

Village Grill, in Yosemite Village. A snack bar with low prices: hamburgers $2.65-3.50, breakfast (2 eggs, sausage, biscuit, hash browns) $2.50. Open daily 7:30am-8pm.

Degnan's Delicatessen, in Yosemite Village. Sandwiches ($3-4.25), drinks, and an adjacent ice cream parlor. Part of a larger convenience market; there are tables outside. Prepare for insects in the evening. Open daily 7am-10pm.

SIGHTS AND THE OUTDOORS

By Car or Bike

You can see a large part of Yosemite from the bucket seat, but the view is better if you get out of the car. The *Yosemite Road Guide* ($3.25 at every visitors center) is keyed to the roadside markers, and outlines a superb tour of the park—it's almost like having a ranger tied to the hood. The drive along **Tioga Road** (Rte. 120 E) presents one panorama after another. The road through Tioga Pass is the highest highway strip in the country; exiting the eastern side of the park, it winds down into the lunar landscape near Mono Lake. Driving west from the Pass brings you to **Tuolumne Meadows** and its open, alpine spaces, shimmering **Tenaya Lake,** and innumerable scenic views of granite slopes and canyons. The approach from the south passes through **Wawona Tunnel.** Dominating the spectacle on the other side of the tunnel are 7569-ft. **El Capitán** (the largest granite monolith in the world), misty **Bridalveil Falls,** and the **Three Brothers** (three adjacent granite peaks). A drive into the heart of the valley leads to thunderous 2425-ft. **Yosemite Falls** (the highest in North America), **Sentinel Rock,** and **Half Dome** within view.

For a different perspective on the valley, drive to **Glacier Point,** off Glacier Point Rd. Hovering 3214 ft. above the valley floor, this gripping overlook is guaranteed to impress the most jaded of travelers. Half Dome rests majestically across the valley, and the sight and sound of **Vernal Falls** and **Nevada Falls** punctuate the silence.

Walk among the giant sequoias at **Mariposa Grove,** off Rte. 41. The short hiking trail begins at the **Fallen Monarch,** a massive trunk lying on its side, and continues to the 209-ft., 2700-year-old **Grizzly Giant,** and the fallen **Wawona Tunnel Tree.** Ancient Athens was in its glory when many of these trees were saplings.

Bicyclists can pick up a brochure which indicates the safest roads at the visitors center. Roads are fairly flat near the villages, more demanding farther afield. Those near **Mirror Lake,** open only to hikers and bikers, guarantee a particularly good ride, and the valley roads, filled with traffic, are easily circumvented by the bike paths. For further information on bike routes, contact the bike rental stands at Yosemite Lodge (372-1208) or Curry Village (372-1200).

Day Hiking in the Valley

To experience Yosemite the way it was meant to be, you need to escape the Valley's motor-bound tourists and travel the outer trails on foot. A wealth of opportunities rewards anyone willing to lace up a pair of hiking boots, even if just for a daytrip.

Day-use trails are usually fairly busy, sometimes positively crowded, and occasionally (i.e. July 4th weekend) the site of human traffic jams. A colorful trail map with difficulty ratings and average hiking times is available at the visitors center for 50¢ (see Practical Information). Misty **Bridalveil Falls** is an easy ¼-mi. walk from the shuttle bus stop. The **Mirror Lake Loop** is a level, 3-mi. walk to the glassy lake, which is slowly silting up to become a meadow. These two trails, as well as pretty **Lower Yosemite Falls,** are wheelchair accessible.

Upper Yosemite Falls Trail, a back-breaking 1-mi. trek to a windy summit, rewards the intrepid with an overview of the 2425-ft. drop. Leaving the marked trail is not a wise idea—tragic accidents do happen.

One of the most popular trails in Yosemite begins at **Happy Isles.** From this point, you can trek 211-mi. and reach Mt. Whitney via the John Muir Trail, but you might prefer the 1½-mi. **Mist Trail** past Vernal Falls to the top of Nevada Falls, a steep and strenuous climb up hundreds of tiny stairs. The views of the falls from the trail are outstanding, and the proximity to the water shrouds the trail in a continuous drizzle that is welcome during the hot summer months. Take the **free shuttle** from the valley campgrounds to Happy Isles; there is no parking available. The Mist Trail continues to the base of **Half Dome,** a monolithic testament to the power of glaciation. Expert climbers tackle the Dome's sheer front; halfway up, a yard-wide ledge serves as a luxury resort on the otherwise smooth vertical wall. Look closely from below; the profile of an Ahwahnee princess is supposedly stained into the rock. For those uninitiated to the world of rock-climbing, there is a challenging hike up the back side which requires the aid of climbing cables (open summer only). You'll need all day to make it here and back in time for the last shuttle—this 17-mi. round-trip is considered the most difficult hike in the valley. Skip the climb if it looks stormy; lightning has been known to strike the wet summit of Half Dome and run down along the metal cables.

The wildflower-laden **Pohon Trail** starts from Glacier Point, crossing Sentinel River (spectacular Sentinel Falls, the park's second largest cascade, lies to the north) on its way to Taft Point and other secluded lookouts. For a taste of "real" rock-climbing without requisite equipment and training, Yosemite day hikers scramble up **Lembert Dome** above Tuolumne Meadows. This gentle (by rock-climbing standards) incline riddled with foot and hand holds is nonetheless a solid granite face. Vertigo sufferers beware and all proceed with caution. The 4-mi. approach to **Cathedral Lakes** from the west end of the meadows is another worthwhile hike.

Activities

Park rangers lead a variety of informative hikes and other activities for visitors of all ages. **Junior ranger** (ages 7-9) and **senior ranger** (ages 10-12) activities allow children to hike, raft, and investigate aquatic and terrestrial life. These three-hour summer programs, usually held mid-week, require reservations at least a day in advance through the **Valley Visitor Center** and cost $2 (open 8am-8pm). Rangers also guide adult visitors along a number of free walks. **A First Look at Yosemite** leaves daily at 9am from the Valley Visitor Center. The tour, accessible to people with disabilities, is an informative introduction to local history, legends, and scenery. The three-hour, somewhat strenuous **Vernal Falls hike** explores the Merced River Canyon twice per week in summer (for reservations, call 372-0299). Other free, park-sponsored adventures include morning photographic hikes, art classes in the Art Activity Center, Indian cultural events in the Miwok-Paiute Village, and spectacular stargazing from Glacier Point. Check for other events and times in the free *Yosemite Guide* (available at all visitors centers).

John Muir gave Teddy Roosevelt a personal tour of the valley in 1903, and Muir continues to guide visitors in more than just spirit. During warm weather months, dramatist Lee Stetson leads free, one-hour hikes in which he assumes the role of the man who was instrumental in the preservation of Yosemite. (Meet at the visitors center. Check the *Yosemite Guide* for times.) Stetson also hosts *An Evening with John Muir,* a 90-minute one-man show, and *Conversation with a Tramp* on alternate evenings Tuesday to Friday, 8pm. (Tickets $4, under 12 $2, infants not admitted. Buy tickets at the door or from the visitors center. Check the *Yosemite Guide*.)

The world's greatest climbers come to Yosemite to test themselves at angles past vertical. If you've got the courage (and the cash), you can join the stellar Yosemite rock climbers by taking a lesson with the **Yosemite Mountaineering School.** The basic **rock-climbing classes,** offered daily in summer (usually mid-April to Sept.), teach you the basics on the ground, then take you 80 ft. up a cliff and introduce you to bouldering and rappelling ($48 plus $6 for rock shoes rental). Intermediate lessons on weekends and alternating weekdays are $50-60. Advanced classes are also offered. You'll need to buy a lunch and beverage for the day of the climb. You must be at least 14 and in "reasonably good condition" to take the group lessons. Private lessons for younger children are also available. Reservations are useful and require advance payment, though drop-ins are accepted if space allows. For information contact Yosemite Mountaineering School, Yosemite 95389 (372-1335; Sept.-May 372-1244; open 8:30am-5pm).

If you have a license you may **fish** year-round in any of Yosemite's lakes, streams, or rivers, but don't expect to catch anything unless you're an expert (or lucky). Each year a few of the lakes are selected to be stocked with trout, but the names of these lakes are not made public. Anglers may obtain a **fishing license** from grocery stores in Yosemite Valley, Wawona, Tuolumne, and White Wolf. (Resident license $19.50, non-resident $46.50, 10-day non-resident $20.50. 14 and under fish free.) **Rafting** is permitted on the Merced River from 10am to 6pm. No motorized crafts are allowed. Verify restrictions with rangers. **Swimming** is allowed throughout the park except where posted. The **public pools** at Curry Village and Yosemite Lodge charge $1.50 admission for those who are not guests of the hotel. **Bird-watchers** should pick up a field checklist at the visitors center. And those interested in giving a little something back to the park can join a group of **ecotourists** who restore damaged park assets and work to maintain the natural habitats of the park's many animals (call 372-0265 for more information).

BEYOND YOSEMITE VALLEY: BACKCOUNTRY

Some folks never leave the valley, but a wilder, lonelier Yosemite awaits those who do. The visitors center has day-hike fliers for areas outside Yosemite Valley, but there are many more trails than shown on the map. The mountain shop at Tuolumne rents and sells equipment (see Practical Information, page 366), but you'll save money and have a better selection if you plan ahead and buy at a backpacking store in a major city. Preparation is key before an backcountry adventure. For advice on keeping yourself and the wilderness intact, see Essentials: Wilderness Concerns, page 53. Obtain a **topographical map** of the region you plan to explore, (learn to read it) and plan your route. **Wilderness Press** (see Camping and the Outdoors: Useful Publications, page 48) offers detailed, high-quality topographical maps and hiking guides suited for backcountry trips.

Backcountry camping is prohibited in the valley (you'll get slapped with a stiff fine if caught), but it's generally permitted along the high-country trails with a free **wilderness permit** (call 372-0310 for general information). Each trailhead limits the number of permits available. Reserve by mail between March 1 and May 31 (write Wilderness Office, P.O. Box 577, Yosemite National Park 95389), or take your chances with the 50% quota held on 24-hr. notice at the Yosemite Valley Visitors Center, the Wawona Ranger Station, and Big Oak Flat Station. Popular trails like **Little Yosemite Valley, Clouds Rest,** and **Half Dome** fill their quotas regularly. To receive a permit, you must show a planned itinerary, although you needn't follow it exactly. Many hikers stay at the undeveloped mountain campgrounds in the high country for the company and for the **bear lockers,** used for storing food. Hikers can also store food in hanging bear bags or in rentable plastic **canisters** from the Yosemite Valley Sports Shop ($3 per day). Canisters may be mandatory on more popular hiking routes in 1995. Check with rangers. Keeping bears away from human food is important—bears who forage for human food are frequently shot. If you protect your food, the bears won't develop the habit and will therefore avoid premature death. Some of the mountain campgrounds have chemical toilets. There are also five High Sierra walk-in campsites; contact the Wilderness Office for details.

A free shuttle bus to **Tuolumne Meadows** will deposit you at the heads of several trails. **Lembert Dome** has a trail to its peak that is ideal for inexperienced hikers eager to test their skills. The **Pacific Crest Trail** follows a series of awe-inspiring canyons. South Yosemite is home to the **Giant Sequoia and Mariposa Grove,** the park's largest. Several trails of varying lengths wind through this stretch of mammoth trees, some of which began life over 3000 years ago. Some of these trails connect to other national park or forest trails that continue as far as Washington State.

WINTERTIME IN YOSEMITE

Icy waterfalls and meadows masked with soft snow transform Yosemite's landscape dramatically in its quietest season. November snows harden into a deep freeze by late December. Access to the park is affected—Tioga and Glacier Point Roads and Rtes. 120 and 41 may be closed, but Rte. 140 from Merced is usually open and clear. Always phone ahead to verify road conditions (372-0209), carry tire chains, and drive with extreme caution.

Winter camping in **Lower Pines, Sunnyside (Camp 4), Hodgden Meadows,** and **Wawona** is possible, and most indoor accommodations offer reduced off-season rates. While the high Sierras close down entirely when the snow falls, the main park facilities in the Valley (such as the visitors center) remain open. The Merced and Fresno **buses** continue to operate (see Orientation) and park tours move "indoors" to heated buses.

Cross-country skiing on your own is free, and several well-marked trails cut into the backcountry of the valley's South Rim at **Badger Pass** and **Crane Flat.** Both areas have blazes on the trees so that the trails can be followed even when there's several feet of fresh snow. Skiing season usually runs from late November to early April. Guided cross-country ski tours are offered by the Yosemite Cross-Country Ski School (372-1244; overnight trips including cabin and meals run about $110). **Yosemite Park & Curry Co.** (372-1338) offers ski rentals starting from $14. Winter transforms many summer hiking trails into increasingly popular **snowshoe trails.** Rent snowshoes from the **Tuolumne Mountaineering Shop** (372-1244; $6). Rangers host a free snowshoe walk or you can explore the peaceful forest on your own.

The state's oldest ski resort, **Badger Pass Ski Area,** south of Yosemite Valley on Glacier Point Road (372-1338), is the only downhill ski area in the Park. The family atmosphere encourages learning and restraint (no snowboards). Free shuttles connect Badger with the Yosemite Valley lodges. The Curry Co. offers downhill lessons. (Lessons $16 for 2 hrs., private lessons from $35. Rental package $15.50 per day. Lift tickets Sat.-Sun. $28 per day, Mon.-Fri. $23. Over 60 free. Open 9am-4:30pm.) Discount ski packages (accommodation and rentals) are available through Yosemite Lodge for weekdays. Inquire at Curry Co. (372-1338).

Ice Skating at Curry Village costs $5 ($4.50 children) for a day's admission and $1.75 for skate rental. (Open mid-Nov. to early March Mon.-Fri. 2-10pm, Sat.-Sun. 8am-10pm.) **Sledding** and **tobogganing** are permitted at Crane Flat off Rte. 120.

■■■ MONO LAKE

As fresh water from streams and springs drains into the "inland sea" of Mono Lake (MOE-no) it evaporates, leaving behind a mineral-rich,13-mi. wide expanse that Mark Twain called "the Dead Sea of the West." Although Mono supports no fish, brine flies and shrimp provide a buffet for migratory birds. The lake derives its moon-like appearance from remarkable towers of calcium carbonate called *tufa*, which form when calcium-rich freshwater springs well up in the carbonate-filled salt water. At over 700,000 years old, this extraordinary lake remains the Western Hemisphere's oldest enclosed body of water.

Tourists and ecologists love Mono for its unique rock formations and varied bird population, but thirsty Los Angeles loves it for its water. The steady diversion of water to the dry south has lowered the lake's level nearly 50 ft. since 1941, endangering the delicate *tufa* and the birthplace of over 90% of California's shore gulls. The increased salinity has devastated the trout stock of adjacent streams, and newly exposed dust is polluting local air. Locals and lake lovers continue to fight for increased water flow to the lake, while Southern California's population continues to grow and bathe at Northern California's expense. The grassroots movement to protect the area has gained momentum; drivers continue to plaster their vehicles with "Save Mono Lake" bumper stickers.

The town of **Lee Vining** provides the best access to Mono Lake and the ghost town of **Bodie**. Lee Vining is located 70 mi. north of **Bishop** on U.S. 395 and 10 mi. west of the Tioga Pass entrance to **Yosemite**.

PRACTICAL INFORMATION AND ORIENTATION

Visitors Information: Mono Lake Visitors Center and Lee Vining Chamber of Commerce, (647-6595 or 647-6629) on Main St. in Lee Vining, in the large orange and blue building. Incredibly friendly staff, all of whom are part of the crusade to save Mono Lake from the clutches of the L.A. Dept. of Water and Power. Examine the exhibits, articles, books, and free slide-show on the endangerment of the lake and obtain maps, brochures, and books covering all of Mono County. Walking tours and canoe tours are also available. (See Sights, below.) Open daily 9am-9pm; Labor Day-Memorial Day 9am-5pm.

Mono Basin Scenic Area Visitors Center: (647-3044), ½ mi. north of Lee Vining off U.S. 395. This center provides information on Mono County's wilderness areas and excellent interpretive tours (free). They also sell topographical maps and issue **wilderness permits.** Open summer daily 9am-7pm; call for winter hours.

U.S. Forest Service, Lee Vining Ranger Station: (647-6525), 2 mi. west of U.S. 395 on Rte. 120. Large ranger station with camping information. Obtain **backcountry permits** here (free). Permits distributed daily on a first-come, first-served basis, or reserve March-May. Open summer daily 8am-4:30pm.

Greyhound, in the Lee Vining Market (647-6301; 800-231-2222 for fares and routes). To: L.A. (11am, 1 per day); Reno (at 1:50am, 1 per day). Buy your ticket at the next stop, because they don't sell them here. Open daily 8am-9pm.

Canoe Rental: Sierra Country Rentals (920-0024), at U.S. 395 and 2nd St. Canoes for $27 per day, $57 for 3 days.

AAA Emergency Road Service: 647-6444.

Laundromat: Main St. next to Lee Vining Market. Wash $1, dry 25¢, soap 50¢. Open daily 7am-9pm. No phone; inquire at Nicely's next door.

Emergency: 911.

Post Office: (647-6371), on 4th St., behind the blue house in Lee Vining. Open Mon.-Fri. 8:45am-2pm and 3-5:15pm. **General Delivery ZIP Code:** 93541.

Area Code: 619.

Store owners don't bother with addresses or phone numbers—Lee Vining is only two blocks long. U.S. 395 runs through, making a cameo appearance as Main St.

ACCOMMODATIONS AND FOOD

It can be difficult to find affordable lodging and meals in Lee Vining. Explore camping and picnics as alternatives to the jaw-dropping rates at hotels and restaurants.

Blue Skies Motel (647-6440), at U.S. 395 and 2nd St. Cozy singles $45, doubles $55. Closed in winter.

El Mono Motel (647-6310), on Main St. Contemplate the tufa and birds of Mono Lake from the porch swing in front. Doubles $42, with private bath $55.

The King's Inn (647-6300), 2 blocks west of Main St. on 2nd St. Rooms with TVs, showers, in-room coffee/tea, and magazines. A few kitchen units available. Pets allowed. Rooms for 1-2 people from $45. Wheelchair access.

Gateway Motel (647-6467), on Main St. Trim rooms with color TV are relatively affordable in winter (singles $35). In summer rates climb to $69.

Murphey's RV Park (647-6358), 1 block west of Main St., behind Murphey's Motel. Full hookups ($12) and tent sites ($4 per person). Showers $2. Only a few overnight spaces available; on weekends and holidays arrive before 10am.

Lee Vining's location makes it an ideal stopover on the way from Reno or Death Valley to Yosemite. As a result, accommodations are often scarce on Friday afternoons and holidays. Go early, and reserve rooms and campsites in advance. There are six Inyo National Forest **campgrounds** ($0-8) within 15 miles of town. Head west from town on Rte. 120. There are also two campgrounds less than 6 mi. north of town. **Sawmill Campground** (free) and **Tioga Lake Campground** ($8) are 9000 ft. up, at the edge of Yosemite. **Ellery Lake Campground** has sites next to a bubbling creek ($8 with drinking water and chemical toilets; call 647-6525 for information). Dispersed camping is permitted in the scenic area above the shoreline (free permit required in Inyo National Forest; see Practical Information). Make reservations for these campgrounds well in advance with the Lee Vining District Ranger.

The **Lee Vining Market** is the town's closest thing to a grocery store (647-6301, next to the laundromat on Main St.; open daily 8am-9pm). **Nicely's** is packed with local color. Try a chili dog with cheese and onions or a veggie sandwich with salad for about $5. (647-6477, on Main St. north of the visitors center. Open daily 6am-10pm, closed Wed. in winter.) **Mono Cone** is a local landmark, and its opening signals the beginning of summer. Corn dogs ($1.65), floats ($2.25), and frosty cones ($1) are the best parking lot munching in town (open summer daily 11am-8pm.)

SIGHTS

In 1984, Congress set aside 57,000 acres of land surrounding Mono Lake and called it the **Mono Basin National Forest Scenic Area** (647-6525). **South Tufa Grove,** 10 mi. from Lee Vining, harbors an awe-inspiring collection of calcium carbonate formations. (Take U.S. 395 south to Rte. 120, then go 4 mi. east and take the Mono Lake Tufa Reserve turn-off 1 mi. south of Tufa Grove.) The *tufa* towers, which resemble giant drip sandcastles, startlingly poke through the smooth surface of what Twain called the "solemn, silent, sailless sea." Four mi. north of Lee Vining on U.S. 395 is **Mono Lake County Park,** a public playground with bathrooms, picnic tables, swings, wheelchair access to the lake, and a smaller *tufa* forest.

The **Mono Lake Foundation** offers excellent guided canoe tours of the lake on weekends that include a crash course on Mono Lake's natural history, ecology, and conservation. Tours are scheduled for 8, 9:30, and 11am on Saturday and Sunday; earlier tours are better for sighting birds and avoiding gusty winds. Arrange tours through the visitors center ($12, ages 4-12 $6). Also check the visitors center for free guided **walking tours** of the lake, beginning daily at 6pm from the South Tufa parking lot. **Navy Beach,** ½ mi. from the South Tufa Grove, is one of the saltiest swimming holes in America. The Reserve Rangers at **Panum Crater,** an extinct volcano located 4 mi. east of town on Rte. 120, offer interesting interpretive nature walks and evening presentations. Inquire at the Mono Lake Ranger Station for details; see Practical Information (activities daily June 22-Sept. 2).

June Lake, a canyon carved by glaciers and now filled with water, is 10 mi. south of Lee Vining on U.S. 395. If you have time, take the scenic loop along Rte. 158. The sparkling lake and its surrounding ring of mountains are prized by visitors as a wayward slice of the Alps. During the summer, June Lake is an angler's heaven, with brook, golden, rainbow, and brown trout stocked weekly. Day hikes, wilderness backpacking, swimming, and boating are all within easy distance of the June Lake loop, and **campsites** in the area are plentiful (sites $8-10; few have showers). The **Oh! Ridge Campground** has water and flush toilets(!). (Sites $10, Open April-Nov.)

If you've seen Columbia, Placerville, Coloma, and Sonora, you're probably thinking you'll never find an authentic, unexploited old ghost town. But wait—tucked away in the high, forsaken desert, **Bodie** is the real McCoy, even if it does charge admission ($5; self-guide booklet $1). Described as "a sea of sin, lashed by the tempests of lust and passion," in 1880 the town was home to 10,000 people, 65 saloons, and one homicide per day. Today the streets and buildings are strewn with abandoned furniture, automobiles, wagons, and train engines, well-preserved by the dry climate and by the state of California. Bodie is accessible by a paved road off U.S. 395, 15 mi. north of Lee Vining (the last 10 mi. are a dusty delight), and by a dirt road all the way from Rte. 167 out of Mono Inn. (Ghost town open daily 9am-7pm; Labor Day-Memorial Day 9am-4pm. For information call Bodie State Historic Park at 647-6445 or write to P.O. Box 515, Bridgeport, CA 93517.)

■■■ SEQUOIA AND KINGS CANYON NATIONAL PARKS

Though they may not attract the throngs of visitors that the "Big Three"—Yellowstone, Yosemite, and the Grand Canyon—do each summer, the twin parks of Kings Canyon and Sequoia can go sight-for-sight with any park in the U. S. The relatively uncrowded roadways and campsites of these parks are another substantial perk.

Kings Canyon and Sequoia, home to cool waters, glacially chiseled rock, snowy mountains, and blooming meadows, offer a wide range of wilderness experiences. Developed areas like Grant Grove and Giant Forest offer informative trails, lodging amenities, and paved vehicle access, while the backcountry at Road's End in Kings Canyon and along the High Sierra Trail through Sequoia offers only wilderness and the occasional echo of fast-fading footsteps.

Summer season in these parts lasts from Memorial Day through Labor Day, snow season from November to March (although backcountry trails may have snow as late as mid-June). The road into Kings Canyon is typically closed from the first week of November until the last week of April due to winter storms and the threat of rockfalls. Travelers should also note that August is the parks' most crowded month.

PRACTICAL INFORMATION

Kings Canyon and Sequoia Main Line: 565-3341. Offers 24-hr. direct contact with a park ranger in addition to dispatch service to any office within the parks. Recommended by many visitors centers over dialing direct.

Parks General Information Line: 565-3134.

National Park Service Headquarters: Superintendent, Ash Mountain, Three Rivers, CA 93271 (565-3456), 1 mi. beyond the Three Rivers entrance, on Rte. 198 out of Visalia. Information on both parks provided. Books, maps, wilderness permits, and free brochures about the sequoia in German, French, Spanish, and Japanese. Open daily 8am-5pm; Nov.-May 8am-4:30pm.

Park Shuttle: Buses operate out of Giant Forest in Sequoia National Park and take visitors to and from Lodgepole, Moro Rock, Sherman Tree, and Crescent Meadow from 8am-5:30pm. Single ride $1, $3 per family. Day pass $3, $6 per family.

Park Admission: 7-day vehicle pass valid in both parks $5; 1-yr. pass valid in all national parks and monuments $25.

Recorded Road, Weather, and Campground Information: 565-3351. 24 hrs. Updated daily around 9am.

Backcountry Information: 565-3708, Mon.-Fri. 8am-4:30pm. Backcountry permits are free. Reserve 15 days in advance by mail or fax; one-third of the permits for any given trail are held on a first-come, first-served basis at the trailhead or at the nearest ranger station. Call for more information on how to reserve.

Hospitals: Fresno Community Hospital, Fresno (442-6000); **Kaweah Delta Hospital,** Visalia (625-2211).

California Highway Patrol: 488-4321 or 488-4322.

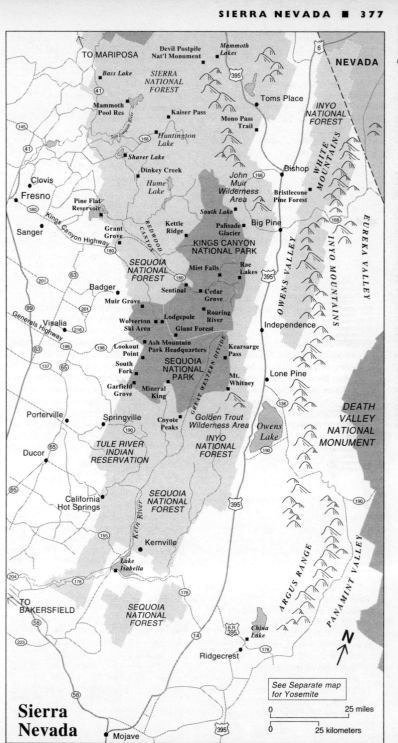

Emergency: 911.
Sheriff: Fresno County, Fresno (488-3111); Tulare County, Visalia (733-6211).
Area Code: 209.

Sequoia National Park

Take advantage of Three Rivers's services before entering the parks. The road from town to Giant Forest is too tedious to justify repeated travel in the middle of the day.

Foothills Visitors Center: Three Rivers 93271 (565-3134), at the park headquarters 1 mi. beyond the Three Rivers entrance, on Rte. 198 out of Visalia. Information on both parks. Books, maps, and wilderness permits available. Open daily 8am-5pm; Nov.-April 8am-4pm.

Lodgepole Visitors Center: 565-3782, ext. 782. On Generals Hwy. 4 mi. east of the Giant Forest. In the heart of Sequoia National Park, near the big trees and gaping tourists. Open daily 8am-5pm; Oct.-April 9am-5pm. **Children's Nature Center** open July-Labor Day daily 10am-5pm. Campground reservations daily 9am-7pm. Wilderness permits daily 7am-4pm.

Giant Forest Village Information Booth: In Giant Forest Village. Information and park maps. Open daily summer 9:30am-3:30pm.

Mineral King Ranger Station: 565-3768, ext. 812, 1 mi. before the end of Mineral King Rd. The headquarters for the remote Mineral King region in southern Sequoia National Park (inaccessible in snow season). Maps, hiking information, books, first aid, and wilderness permits. Open summer daily 7am-5pm.

Cross-Country Ski and Snowshoe Rental: Sequoia Ski Touring Center, Sequoia National Park 93262 (565-3435 or 565-3381). Open Mon.-Fri. 9am-5pm, Sat.-Sun. and holidays 8am-6pm.

Food and Supplies: Lodgepole's Market is well stocked. Open daily 8am-9pm. The smaller **Giant Forest Market** keeps the same hours. 2 stores in nearby **Three Rivers, Village Market** (Mon.-Fri. 8am-7pm, Sat.-Sun. 9am-5pm) and **Three Rivers Market** (daily 7:45am-7pm) offer better selection and prices.

Gas: Chevron, Lodgepole Village, on Generals Hwy.; open daily 8am-8pm; winter 8am-5pm. Road emergencies call 565-3381 or 565-3341. As in Kings Canyon, gas here is 60¢ more per gallon than outside the park. Fill up in **Three Rivers.**

AAA Emergency Road Service: 565-3381 or 1-800-400-4AAA, -4222.

Showers and Laundromat: Across from the Visitors Center in Lodgepole. 2-min. shower 25¢. 75¢ wash, 10-min. dry 25¢. Showers available 7am-1pm and 3-9:30pm. Laundry opens at 7am, last load at 8:30pm.

Post Office: At Lodgepole. Open Mon.-Fri. 8am-1pm and 1:30-4pm. **General Delivery Zip Code:** 93262. The lobby, open 24 hrs., has a stamp machine.

Kings Canyon National Park

Grant Grove Visitors Center (335-2856), Grant Grove Village, 2 mi. east of the Big Stump Entrance by Rte. 180. Books, maps, and exhibits. Nightly campfire programs and daily hikes. Open daily 8am-6pm, winter 9am-5pm.

Cedar Grove Ranger Station (565-3793), 30 mi. farther down Rte. 180 by the Kings River. Near the trailheads for hikes into the Kings Canyon high country. Books, maps, first aid, and wilderness permits (required for hikes and trips into a wilderness area). Open summer daily 9am-5pm. The **Road's End** kiosk located 6 mi. east of Cedar Grove Village issues wilderness permits summer daily 7am-3pm, after which they are available until 4:30pm at the ranger station. Roads usually close during the snow season.

Food and Supplies: The **Cedar Grove Market** in Cedar Grove Village carries a selection of supplies (including camping basics) and groceries. Open summer daily 8am-9pm.

Gas: Chevron stations are located in Grant Grove and Cedar Grove. Open summer Mon.-Fri. 8am-7pm, Sat.-Sun. 8am-8pm; winter Grant Grove only 8am-5pm. Fill up before you enter the parks—prices are 60-70¢ (!!) per gallon higher inside. No towing service, but attendants at Grant Grove can handle minor repairs and lockouts. In emergencies, call 335-9071; 335-2314 after hours. Those in need of major repairs or service outside the Grant Grove area are advised to call **Michael's** in Reedley (638-4101) or **Judd's** in Squaw Valley (638-6874).

AAA Emergency Road Service: 800-400-4AAA, -4222.

Showers: at **Grant Grove Lodge** (open 11am-4pm) and the **Cedar Grove Chevron station** (open summer 8am-8pm). Both locations $2, child $1.

Laundromat: at **Cedar Grove Chevron station** (open in summer 8am-8pm). Wash 75¢, 10-min. dry 25¢. Last load 6:30pm.

Post Office: In Grant Grove Village across from the Visitors Center. Open June-Sept. Mon.-Fri. 8:30am-1:30pm and 2:30-4:30pm, Sat. 8:30am-1:30pm. (A stamp machine and mailbox are available next to the Visitors' Center year-round.) **General Delivery ZIP Code:** 93633.

ORIENTATION

The two parks are accessible to vehicles from the west only. From Fresno follow **Rte. 180** east into the foothills; it's about 60 mi. to the entrance of the detached **Grant Grove** section of Kings Canyon. Rte. 180 ends 30 mi. later in **Cedar Grove.** The road into this region is closed in winter. From **Visalia,** take **Rte. 198** to Sequoia National Park. This road, which passes Lake Kaweah and runs alongside the Kaweah River, is punctuated with scenic views and turnouts. **Generals Highway** (Rte. 198) connects the Ash Mountain entrance to the **Giant Forest** in Sequoia, and continues to Grant Grove in Kings Canyon. Snow more than 15 ft. deep covers the road in winter, and it is usually open only from mid-May to October. The road twists through 130 curves and 12 major switchbacks as it ascends 2000 ft.; allow two hours for the drive from Ash Mountain to Grant Grove. If you desire, avoid the exhausting drive and stick to Rte. 180. From the east, trails lead into the parks from the John Muir Wilderness and Inyo National Forest, both accessible from spur roads off **U.S. 395.**

In summer, the treacherous road to **Mineral King** opens up the southern parts of Sequoia. From Visalia, take **Rte. 198;** the turnoff to Mineral King is 3 mi. past Three Rivers. From the turn off, allow two hours for the stunning drive.

Public transportation to the parks is nonexistent, but the limited **shuttle** service can free you from your car once you are inside Sequoia Park (see Practical Information, page 366). **Sequoia-Kings Canyon Guest Services** (565-3381), operates three daily bus tours around Giant Forest and one through Kings Canyon, but they are pricey and leave little time to explore. (2-hr. Giant Forest tour $10, children $5. 8-hr. Kings Canyon tour $12-22, depending on where you board, children $6-11. Inquire at visitors centers in either park.)

Seasonal changes are dramatic in this area of the Sierras. Dogwood, aspen, and oaks provide brilliant color in October and November. Winter snowfalls leave all trails and many roads impassable to those without skis or snowshoes. Spring here is unpredictable, bringing late storms (snow is not uncommon in June), low fogs, and flooding meltwater. Summer is the high season, and visitors flock to the park. Be prepared for nighttime temperature drops, particularly in the higher elevations.

ACCOMMODATIONS

Sequoia Guest Services, Inc. (S.G.S.), P.O. Box 789, Three Rivers, CA 93271 (561-3314), monopolizes indoor accommodations and food in the parks. **Giant Forest** and **Grant Grove** offer "rustic sleeping cabins" with canvas tops during the summer season (May-Oct.) for $32; add $6.50 for a wooden roof. These *Little House on the Prairie*-esque abodes feature wood stoves and lamps in lieu of electricity, and occupants use a communal bath. The wood-roofed cabins are offered at Grant Grove during the low months (Oct.-April) for $27.50. Giant Forest has motel accommodations in the winter starting at $58.50. Cedar Grove and Stony Creek offer commodious motel lodgings during the summer ($77.50). Guest Services also operates a "tent hotel" at the **Bearpaw Meadow Backcountry Camp,** 11 mi. along the High Sierra Trail from Grant Forest. Call for rates.

Two other options are available just outside of the park boundaries (Kings Canyon Lodge and the Montecito-Sequoia Lodge), but both will place an unnecessarily large dent in your budget. If you are desperate for electricity, the Best Western and Sierra Lodge in Three Rivers have rooms starting at about $50.

CAMPING

While campgrounds in these parks occasionally fill to the brim, you should be able to drive up late and snatch a spot somewhere on a non-holiday weekend. Only Lodgepole, in Sequoia, fills regularly, partly on account of its proximity to the Giant Forest and partly because it's the only campground in the parks that accepts summer reservations (through MISTIX, 800-365-2267). Most campgrounds are open from mid-May to October (2-week max. stay during the summer, 1 month otherwise). There are no RV hookups in the parks, but dump stations are available at campsites where noted. Contact a ranger station for more information, or call 565-3351 for a 24-hr. recording.

Backcountry camping is free, but be sure to acquire a permit (see Practical Information, above). For the best campsites, leave your car behind, and hit the trail with your pack, bedroll, and tent on your back.

Sequoia National Park

Lodgepole, 4 mi. northeast of Giant Forest Village in the heart of Sequoia National Park by Kaweah River. Full of RVs (no hookups). Phone, store. The center of the park's ranger-led activities, including nature walks and in winter, snowshoeing. Unless you are showing up late on a busy weekend and need to make a reservation, there's no good reason to pay the extra $2 to stay here—sites are crowded and offer limited shade. Sites $12 during peak summer season; free once snow accumulates, $10 otherwise. Reserve sites through MISTIX (800-365-2267) mid-May-mid-Sept.

Buckeye Flat, past park headquarters, a few mi. into the park from the Ash Mountain entrance on Rte. 198. Buckeye affords a truly unique camping experience, with sites near a fabulous waterfall. Buckeye prohibits trailers and RVs owing to the long and twisting road leading to it. RVs are welcome at **Potishwa,** a full-service campground nearby with 44 sites. Both are good choices for cold nights because of their lower elevation. Both $10.

Dorst, 12 mi. north of Giant Forest. This huge campground (218 sites) provides convenient access to Sequoia attractions, but affords far greater privacy than its even larger counterpart (Lodgepole) down the road. Flush toilets. Sites $10.

South Fork, on South Fork Rd. 12 mi. off Rte. 198. Near ranger station and some backcountry roads. Pit toilets; not recommended for trailers or RVs. Sites $5.

Atwell Mill and **Cold Springs,** 20 mi. along Mineral King Rd., in the Mineral King area. Secluded and primitive (pit toilets), but has piped water and picnic tables. Steep, winding roads and prohibition on trailers keep RVs away. Super trailheads and scenery. Store, restaurant, phone, and unleaded gas (from an antique pump, not always available) are 3 mi. away in Silver City. 60 tent sites, $6.

Kings Canyon National Park

Sunset, Azalea, and **Crystal Springs** are within a stone's throw of Grant Grove Village but are still relatively quiet. Azalea has a trailer dump station and Sunset features flat tenting spots, brilliant views of the San Joaquin Valley, and an amphitheater with daily programs. Crystal Springs is the smallest and the quietest. All have restrooms and water. Sites $10. Azalea is open year-round; free in winter.

Sheep Creek, Sentinel, Canyon View, and **Moraine,** at the Kings River near Cedar Grove. Store, food, laundry, and showers nearby. Within a few mi. of Roads End and Kings Canyon trailheads. Sheep Creek has a dump station. Sentinel is near the Cedar Grove Amphitheater. By far the nicest tent sites at both Sheep Creek and Sentinel are in the back; those at Sentinel tend to be flatter. Moraine, with remarkable vistas of Kings River Canyon, serves primarily as overflow and is open only on the busiest weekends. All have restrooms and water; sites $10. Canyon View accepts reservations from organized groups only. Very full on weekends. Access roads and campgrounds closed mid-Oct.-mid-May.

Sequoia National Forest

Princess (800-283-CAMP, -2267 for reservations). Perched next to a beautiful meadow, this campground lies just a few mi. outside of Kings Canyon on the road from Grants Grove to Cedar Grove. Evidence of the area's logging history is visible (gigantic stumps dot the grounds). Unfortunately, areas near the camp are also occasional targets for current operations. Sites $8.

FOOD

Park food, like lodging, is monopolized by Sequoia Guest Services. It might be time Guest Services encountered a little capitalist competition; none of their current offerings are very appetizing. Bring a stove and fuel or rent a cabin with a kitchen and cook for yourself (see Accommodations, page 368). A park-operated market sits next door to each of the park eateries. Supplies purchased here may produce a more affordable meal if you're cooking for a group. Outside the parks' culinary vacuum lie a number of tempting alternatives, particularly in nearby Three Rivers.

Lodgepole Deli, on General's Hwy. Passable deli sandwiches are made-to-order for $5. Breakfast (7-11am) runs $3-5. 2 scoops ice cream $2. Open daily 7am-9pm.
Giant Forest Lodge Cafeteria, located next to the Giant Forest Market. Dinner entrees $4-5; a full meal $8. Open daily 6:30am-9pm.
Grant Grove Restaurant, in Grant Grove Village. Coffee-shop atmosphere. Breakfast $4-6, lunch $5-6, dinner $8-12. Open daily 7am-9pm.

Outside the Park

Noisy Water Cafe (561-4517), along Rte. 180 in Three Rivers. "The Home of the Hummingbirds"—named for the frequent visitors to the feeders that hang outside the back window—is the overwhelming favorite among the townfolk. Unique, tasty sandwiches ($4.50-6); liberal *chimichanga* ($7.25). Breakfasts ($4-7) and dinners ($7-12). Open daily 6am-10pm.
Heart's Delight (561-0905), Rte. 198 in Three Rivers. Inexpensive, filling sandwiches ($3-4). Hefty, homemade bean burritos ($1.85). Open daily 7:15am-9pm, Labor Day-Memorial Day 7:15am-8pm.

SIGHTS

The sights of this region, like lodging and food, are organized around four primary areas: Giant Forest and Mineral King in Sequoia National Park, and Grant Grove and Cedar Grove in Kings Canyon National Park. Predictably, the two greatest attractions correspond to the names of the parks; most of the visitors are here to see the sequoia trees and breathtaking Kings River Canyon.

The northern two-thirds of Kings Canyon and the eastern two-thirds of Sequoia are unblemished by roads so the backpacker and packhorse have free rein. Stables located at Wolverton Pack Station, Grant Grove, and Cedar Grove are open in the summer for **horse rentals and guided tours.** Call 565-3341 for information. **Bicycles** are not permitted on hiking trails or in the backcountry, and cyclists may find the mountain roads tortuous. The ranger station or visitors center has more information.

Sequoia

Giant Forest is the center of activities in Sequoia and host to one of the world's greatest concentrations of giant sequoia trees. The grove was named by John Muir, who explored the area and fought for its preservation. The contrast between the common pine and fir trees and the majestic sequoias is startling. The tallest marvel is **General Sherman,** discovered and named in 1879 and believed to be the world's largest living thing. (Unless you get picky and count the giant underground fungus recently discovered in Michigan. Either way, this is far more impressive than a fungus.) The tree stands 275 ft. tall and measures 102 ft. around at its base; its trunk is estimated to weigh 1385 tons. This 2700-year-old creature is at last mature, and, while still growing, gains only a millimeter in height each year. Don't gripe about the protective fence, sequoias have shallow root systems and compaction of the soil can be deadly. Lying flat on your back affords the most dramatic view of the tree—ignore the funny looks you might receive. The 2-mi. **Congress Trail,** the park's most popular (and crowded) trail, boomerangs around General Sherman. A pamphlet (50¢) sold at the trailhead provides a quick lesson in sequoia forest ecology. Other trails wind through the Giant Forest, allowing you to see dozens of giants as well as younger trees. Pick up a trail guide to the Giant Forest area at the Lodgepole Visitors Center (see Practical Information, page 366).

Perhaps the most spectacular sight in the Giant Forest area is the view from atop **Moro Rock,** 1½ mi. from the village. A rock staircase winds ¼ mi. up this granite monolith to the top, which offers a stunning 360° view of the southern Sierras. If the arduous climb up the stairs doesn't take your breath away, the view certainly will; the Great Western Divide lies to the east and pine-covered foothills receding into the San Joaquin Valley recline to the south and west. At sunset the bare rock tops of the Western Divide turn an otherworldly shade of orange. For a more personal panorama, try scrambling around on the rocks just to the right of the daunting staircase. To behold the majesty of Moro Rock itself, stop 200 yds. before it at **Hanging Rock. Sunnet Rock** is another exposed granite formation, accessible via an easy 1-mi. trail from the village. Lodgepole Campground is the trailhead for the **Tokopah Falls Trail,** an easy 2-mi. hike to a glaciated gorge and a series of cascades.

Nine mi. from Giant Forest Village on Rte. 198 is **Crystal Cave,** one of the few caves on the western side of Sequoia open to the public. Reached by a ½-mi. hike, the cave is lined with smooth stalagmites and stalactites moistened by a dark underground stream. The largest chamber is **Marble Hall,** 141 ft. long and over 40 ft. high. The temperature inside remains a constant 50°F, so wear warm clothing. (Naturalists lead tours late June to Labor Day daily on the hr. and ½-hr.; May-June and Sept. Fri.-Mon. on the hour. Cave open 10am-3pm. $4, ages 6-12 $2. Tickets must be purchased in advance at Lodgepole.)

The **Mineral King** area was acquired by the park system in 1978 after lawsuits prevented the Walt Disney Corporation from building a ski resort on the site. Disney probably would have built a better road, but some of the best scenery in the park has been preserved for those willing to brave the winding drive to get to it (complete with blind-corners and steep dropoffs)—don't take the Winnebago on this one. The valley is 7500 ft. deep, with steep trails leading up to mountain lakes and meadows. Some of the surrounding peaks stand over 12,000 ft. tall. A bonanza mining area in the 1800s, the region now offers magnificent day and backcountry hiking and climbing. For an easy, rewarding day hike, try the walk to **Aspen Flat** from Mineral King Pack Station. The trail is flanked by soda springs and wildflowers.

Short day hikes with less harrowing access roads include **Garfield Grove,** 5 mi. up the Kaweah River from South Fork campground, at the extreme southern boundary of Sequoia National Park. The **Muir Grove,** just west of the Dorst campground, is less pristine but more accessible. From Quail Flat, 4 mi. along Generals Hwy. from the turnoff to Grant Grove, you can hike down **Redwood Canyon.** This small valley, a tributary of the Kaweah River's North Fork, contains the world's largest grove of redwood trees. The trail forms two loops, allowing you to explore the whole grove.

Kings Canyon

The most developed portion of Kings Canyon National Park is **Grant Grove.** The **General Grant Tree,** the third-largest of the sequoias, gives the region its name. At 267.4 ft. tall, it is perhaps the most aesthetically pleasing, displaying "classic" sequoia form. It has been designated the "Nation's Christmas Tree," and serves as a living shrine for the American war (especially Civil War) dead. Just north of the park entrance on Rte. 180 lies the **Big Stump Basin Trail,** a self-guided walk through an old logging camp. Here remain scars left by early loggers who erroneously viewed the enormous sequoia as a timber gold mine. They abandoned their efforts after assailing the unyielding trees with dynamite and hatchets.

Hidden in the visitors center parking lot behind the post office is the steep, switchback-riddled road to **Panoramic Point.** In addition to affording fantastic views of the nearby mountains, the point serves as the trailhead for **Park Ridge Trail,** one of the prettiest in the park. One of the more secluded regions of the two parks is the **Cedar Grove** area, which rests inside the towering granite walls of Kings Canyon. The drive on Rte. 180 is scenic and mountainous. (Be sure to stop at roadside turnoffs to peer down at the riverbed below.) Sheer rock walls dominate the view for much of the drive, and at the bottom of the canyon the Kings River glistens. The final approach to the grove passes **Boyden Cavern** (736-2708). Tours of the 5-mi. cavern are offered ($5.50, seniors $5, children $2.75). Boyden crawls with massive stalagmites and stalactites, and sandcastle-like marble formations. (45-min. tours leave on the hour June-Sept. daily 10am-5pm; May and Oct. 11am-4pm.)

Once within the budding grove, you can explore the Kings River's banks and marvel at the depth of the canyon (8000 ft. in some spots, surpassing even the Grand Canyon). This region is spectacular in the hours just before dusk, when the setting sun dances brilliantly off gilded cliffs. As an added bonus, most trails and roads are virtually deserted by this time. **Zumwalt Meadows,** accessible via a 1½-mi. trail, is the more secluded and beautiful of the two Parks' meadows and the choice among white-tailed deer. **Roaring River Falls** and **Mist Falls** are at their best in late spring and early summer, when the streams are swollen and swift. Roaring River Falls is easily reached by road, but seeing Mist Falls requires a tough 3-hour hike.

Road's End is exactly that, a naturally U-shaped glacial valley with parking for those entering the backcountry. The most popular backcountry foray from Road's End is the **Rae Lakes Loop,** which traverses a sampling of the Sierra's best: glaciated canyons, gentle meadows, violent rapids, and inspiring lake vistas. Most hikers take a clockwise route to avoid a daunting uphill grade. Well-spaced camping grounds pace the four- to five-day trek at about 7-mi. intervals. Obtain backcountry permits at the Cedar Grove Ranger Station or the Road's End Kiosk (see Practical Information, page 366).

In the summer, rangers organize a variety of activities including nature walks, children's campfires, day hikes, and films. Reservations are recommended (for Lodgepole area walks 565-3782; for Grant Grove 335-2856). Scheduling of other activities depends on demand, climate, and Smokey the Bear. Contact a ranger station or look in the *Sequoia Bark,* the free park newspaper for a calendar of events.

■■■ SEQUOIA NATIONAL FOREST

The Sierras continue their march southward for 60 mi. below Kings Canyon and Sequoia National Parks before petering out in the low ranges of the Mojave Desert. The Sequoia National Forest covers this southern tip of the Sierras, encompassing the region bounded on the north by the Kings River and on the west and east by two valleys, the San Joaquin and the Owens. The Kern River slices through the middle of the forest.

The **forest headquarters** in Porterville, 900 W. Grand Ave. (209-784-1500), 15 mi. east of Rte. 99 midway between Fresno and Bakersfield, sells a detailed map of the forest for $2.50 (open Mon.-Fri. 8am-4:30pm). The Sequoia National Forest features five designated "wilderness areas." If you enjoy being on your own, and want a real backwoods experience, pick up a **wilderness permit** at a district ranger's office. Check with the appropriate ranger station on your way into the forest to ascertain weather and fire conditions and purify all water taken from rivers or streams.

The northern section of Sequoia National Forest surrounds Kings Canyon Hwy., the road which connects the Grant Grove and Cedar Grove areas of Kings Canyon National Park. The **Hume Lake District** contains the **Boole tree,** an impressively ugly sequoia, and most of the **Monarch Wilderness Area.** Experienced hikers can take the **Deer Cove Creek Trail** to remarkable **Grand Dike** rock outcropping and wildflowers. Look for the trailhead 1 mi. before Rte. 180 re-enters Kings Canyon National Park near Cedar Grove. The **Hume Lake Ranger District Office,** 35860 E. Kings Canyon Rd. (Rte. 180), Dunlap 93621 (338-2251; recorded info. after-hours), east of Fresno near the forest entrance, provides camping information. (Open Mon.-Sat. 8am-4:30pm; winter Mon.-Fri. 8am-4pm.)

The simplest way to explore the **southern districts** of the forest is to admire the sweeping panoramas from the **Western Divide Hwy.** (open April-Oct.). Among the sights along the Western Divide is **Dome Rock,** a massive granite monolith, about midway between Porterville and Kernville. A 1-mi.-long drive on an unpaved road and a short walk up the side of the dome reward you with a 360° view. This section of the Sequoia Forest is managed out of the **Tule River Ranger District Office,** 32588 Rte. 190, Springville 93265 (209-539-2607), between Lake Success and the forest boundary, and the **Hot Springs Ranger District Office,** 43474 Mt. Rd. 50, Rte. 4, Box 548, California Hot Springs 93207 (805-548-6503). (Both offices open mid-May-mid-Sept., daily 8am-4:30pm; winter Mon.-Fri. 8am-4:30pm.)

Approaching the forest from the south, the road coils north along the Kern River from **Cannell Meadow Ranger District Office,** P.O. Box 6, Kernville 93238 (619-376-3781), at the northern tip of Lake Isabella (open daily 8am-5pm; in winter Mon.-Fri. 8am-4:30pm). The **Greenhorn Ranger District Office,** 15701 Rte. 178, Bakersfield (mailing address: P.O. Box 1629, Bakersfield 93386-1629) (805-871-2223), has the scoop on the forest surrounding Lake Isabella. (Open Mon.-Sat. 8am-4:30pm; winter Mon.-Fri. 8am-4:30pm; call 871-2642 after hours for a recording.)

■■■ SIERRA NATIONAL FOREST

Covering 1.3 million acres, the Sierra National Forest fills the gap between Yosemite National Park and Sequoia and Kings Canyon National Parks. The terrain is diverse: rolling, oak-covered foothills on the edge of the San Joaquin Valley to the alpine peaks of the Sierra Nevada crest. Recreation centers around the region's rivers and lakes, including the always crowded Huntington Lake and Shaver Lake.

The forest is organized into four ranger districts. The main **information office** (209-297-0706) is at the Sierra National Forest's Supervisor's Office, located along Rte. 168 just outside of downtown Clovis (mailing address: 1600 Tollhouse Rd., Clovis 93612). A great map of the forest costs $3.25. Buy it. Road signs can be rare and large-scale maps are often inadequate, if not inaccurate. (Open Mon.-Fri. 8am-4:30pm.)

Designated wilderness areas comprise 46% of the forest. A **backcountry** permit is required and can be acquired at any of the ranger stations (free). Trailhead quotas are in effect from July through Labor Day in the Ansel Adams, John Muir, Dinkey Lakes, and Kaiser Wildernesses; those who arrive without reservations are often disappointed (reservations $3 per person). Even those who plan to stick to car camping are advised to plan ahead. For campground reservations call 800-280-2267.

Information on the northwestern **Mariposa District** can be obtained by calling or writing the **Batterson Office,** 43060 Rte. 41, Oakhurst 93644 (209-683-4665; open Mon.-Fri. 8am-4:30pm). **Bass Lake** is thronged in summer by parched San Joaquin Valley residents; fishing, boating, and water-skiing head the list of popular activities. Next to Nelder Grove Campground is the **Shadow of the Giants Trail,** a 1-mi.-long path extending through the grove's 106 sequoias. A separate trail leads to the largest tree in the grove, the 246-ft. **Bull Buck Tree.** You can also meander along the **Way of the Mono Trail.** (Take Rte. 41 to the Bass Lake turn-off and follow Rd. 222 about 4 mi. to the parking lot at the trailhead.)

Bordered by the San Joaquin River, the **Minarets District** surrounds **Mammoth Pool Reservoir,** created by a hydroelectric dam. The mountains around the pool are 2000 ft. above the shore, forming a steep, narrow valley dotted with oak and Ponderosa pine. Boating, fishing, hiking, and swimming are available when the road to Mammoth Pool campground is open (usually June-Oct.). For more information, contact the **Minarets Ranger District Office,** 57003 Rd. 225, North Fork 93643 (877-2218; open daily 8am-4:30pm), off Rte. 41 south of Bass Lake.

The far reaches of the **Kings River District** rise as high as 13,000 ft. at the Sierra Crest. Most of the region's activity centers around the **Dinkey Creek** area and the **Pine Flat Reservoir** (those in search of a scenic "Sunday drive" will find the paved road beyond the reservoir very rewarding). At the reservoir, **Kings River Ranger District Office,** 34849 Maxon Rd., Sanger 93657 (855-8321; open Mon.-Fri. 8am-4:30pm), 1 mi. off Trimmer Rte., dispenses advice and permits. Dinkey Creek, reached from Shaver Lake on Rte. 168, now offers a ranger station (841-3404; open daily 8am-4:30pm, except for holidays). **Whitewater rafting** on the Kings River is popular, especially in late spring; contact the ranger for recommendations on rafting outfits. Trailbikes, ATVs, and four-wheel-drive-vehicles raise dust on the five off-highway routes providing access to camping and fishing.

Easily accessible from Rte. 168, the **Pineridge District** is the most popular region of the national forest and the **Pineridge Ranger District Office,** P.O. Box 300, Shaver Lake, 93664 (841-3311), is one of the forest's busiest information centers (open daily 8am-4:30pm). The **Shaver Lake Chamber of Commerce** also provides information (P.O. Box 58, Shaver Lake 93664; 841-3350; open Mon.-Tues. and Fri. 9am-5pm). **Huntington Lake** lies farther east along Rte. 168, and its shimmering waters see a lot of use. Sailboat regattas occur throughout the summer. In winter **cross-country skiing** and snowmobile routes, as well as frolicsome "snowplay" areas, are maintained along Rte. 168. Beyond Kaiser Pass, the road becomes narrow and slightly treacherous—honk your horn on the sharp blind turns. The terrain at the upper end of this road is definitively High Sierra—alpine lakes, flowers, and craggy summits.

■■■ EASTERN SLOPE

The magnificent eastern slope of the Sierra Crest is more of a wall than a "slope." While the western side of the sierras descends slowly over a number of miles, the eastern side drops off precipitously, its jagged rock faces forming a startling silhouette. Although barely visible from the San Joaquin Valley, the peaks of the High Sierra tower fearsomely over the towns of the Owens Valley. To the south, the copper-brown sand dunes of the vast California desert strike a dramatic contrast with their snow-capped neighbors.

This contrast between east and west is a result of the lifting and faulting processes that shaped the Sierra ridge some 10 million years ago. The eastern slope traces the fault line where years ago the Owens Valley collapsed to expose 14,000-ft. slabs of rock to glaciation. The western slope, watered by cooling ocean air rising to its crest, is carpeted by dense forests at middle elevations. The clouds dissipate before they can cross the mountains, leaving the eastern side remarkably arid.

Tioga Road in Yosemite traverses the Sierras and shows this pattern remarkably well. From the flower-speckled Tuolumne meadows on the gently rising western slope, the road climbs the 9941-ft. Fort Tioga Pass and plummets 3500 ft. to desolate Mono Lake in just 6½ mi. A hike through **Kearsarge Pass** is another excellent way to appreciate the area's rapid climate change. This backcountry route departs from Onion Valley near Independence and winds its way across the Sierras before ending at Road's End in Kings Canyon National Park, 16 mi. away. Access to the trail on both ends is conveniently paved, ideal for easy drop off and pick up. The Kearsarge Pass trail is one of the most popular range-crossing routes. (Information and maps available at any Inyo Ranger Station.)

The tiny towns that stretch from Mt. Whitney to Yosemite National Park are linked by U.S. 395, the access route to the Sierras' eastern face. Small as they are, these towns eagerly support the crowds of campers, climbers, and camera-carriers who congregate in their valley each summer.

■ LONE PINE AND INYO NATIONAL FOREST

The Inyo National Forest is comprised of a scattered collection of land parcels, many of which don't contain a single tree. The definition of "forest" was evidently stretched by the water-hungry in order to protect this important Sierra watershed from development. "Inyo" means "dwelling place of the great spirits" in the language of the Native Americans who once inhabited this area. The strikingly desolate and powerful landscape of Inyo gives credence to its name.

The town nearest the forest is Lone Pine, named for the solitary pine tree which grew by its creek. Much has changed since Lone Pine was an active supply town for the mining industry during the 1870s; the tree is long gone, the mines closed, and the town totally rebuilt following an earthquake which leveled all structures and created nearby Diaz Lake. Since the 1920s, Lone Pine's hills and deserts have been the setting for many Western movie classics, including *Rawhide*, the Lone Ranger series, and more recently, *Maverick*. Follow the boot treads of Gene Autry, Hopalong Cassidy, and Susan Hayward along dusty Movie Road west of town.

PRACTICAL INFORMATION AND ORIENTATION

Visitors Information: Interagency Visitors Center (876-6222), at U.S. 395 and Rte. 136 about 1 mi. south of town, in the shadow of Mt. Whitney. Excellent selection of maps and guidebooks, plus small exhibits. Knowledgeable federal, state, and county staffs. Open daily 8am-4:50pm.

Chamber of Commerce: 126 S. Main St. (876-4444), in Lone Pine. Same services and information as the visitors center, but at a more convenient location. Somewhat lacking in the brochures but the delightful employees (all 2 of them) will provide you with needed information. Open Mon.-Fri. 9am-5pm.

Mt. Whitney/Inyo National Forest Ranger Station: 640 S. Main St. (876-6200), in downtown Lone Pine. Naturalists sponsor interpretive programs on the region's wildlife and history. Pick up **wilderness permits** (required in the backcountry) here. They also sell topographical and trail maps if you plan on camping at a non-established site. Open May 22-Oct. 15 daily 7am-11:30am and 12:30-3:30pm; winter Mon.-Fri. 8am-4:30pm. June-Sept. 15 quotas for some popular trails within the forest. (Mt. Whitney trail quotas in effect slightly longer). Half the permits are available daily on a first-come, first-served basis; the other half can be obtained by mail March 1-May 31. **Get permits for Mt. Whitney right away.** Write to P.O. Box 8, Lone Pine 93545 to get the necessary reservation request forms.

ATM: Bank of America, 400 N. Main in Lone Pine Center (876-5513).

Greyhound: 107 N. Main St. (876-5300), at La Florista Flowers. 1 bus per day to Reno ($50) and L.A. ($28). Open Mon.-Fri. 7am-7pm, Sat. 7am-3:25pm and 6-7pm.

Car Rental: Lindsay Automotive, 316 S. Washington St. (876-4789). Rates from $35 per day. 150 free mi. Must be 21 with credit card. Open 8am-5pm.

Car Repair: Unocal 76, 238 S. Main, 876-5902. RV dump, gasoline, and propane gas available. Free public restrooms. Open daily 6am-10pm.

AAA Emergency Road Service: 876-4600.

Bicycle Rental: Bent's Bikes, 132 N. Main (876-4547) in Lone Pine. Mountain bikes $7 per hr., $25 per day. Limited number available, so call ahead. Open Tues.-Sat. 10am-6pm.

Pack Trips: Mt. Whitney Pack Trams, on Whitney Portal Rd. 935-4493 in summer, 872-8331 in winter. Hours vary.

Fishing Licenses: Slater's Sporting Goods: 130 S. Main (876-5020). Local fishing info, license ($7.50 per day), supplies. Open daily 7am-9pm; winter 7am-4pm.

Laundromat: Coin Op Laundromat, 105 Post St., at Main behind the High Sierra Inn. Wash $1, 12-min. dry 25¢. Soap 50¢. Open daily 8am-7pm.

Showers: Kirk's Barber Shop, 104 N. Main (876-5700; 876-4354 if Kirk's gone).

Hospital: Southern Inyo, 501 E. Locust (876-5501).

Emergency: 911.

Inyo County Sheriff: Lone Pine Substation (876-5606); Headquarters (878-2441).

Post Office: 121 Bush St. (876-5681), between Main and Jackson. Open Mon.-Fri. 9am-5pm. **General Delivery ZIP Code:** 93545.
Area Code: 619.

Lone Pine straddles **U.S. 395** and is the first Sierra town you hit when traveling northeast on Rte. 136 from **Death Valley.** Independence, the county seat, lies 14 mi. to the north. LA is 212 mi. along U.S. 395 and Rte. 14 to the southwest.

ACCOMMODATIONS AND CAMPING

Motels abound but prices can be high. Timing is key if you want the best deals (weekdays are cheaper). Make reservations at least two weeks in advance for weekends and holidays, and at least a day ahead for weekdays. Rates fluctuate; call ahead to find out which prices are in effect. Camping is inexpensive and conveniently located; again, be sure to arrive early on weekends and holidays.

Alabama Hills Inn, 1920 S. Main (876-8700), 1 mi. south of Lone Pine. Named for the frequently filmed geological faults nearby, this new motel is close to Peter's Pumpkin, Wounded Knight, and other natural rock sculptures. Weekday singles $38, doubles $42. $3 more on weekends. Inquire about discounted winter rates.

Mt. Whitney Motel, 305 N. Main (876-4207). The rooms combine the worst decor from 3 different decades, but this fashion *faux pas* is diluted by the beckoning pool. Singles $36 weekdays, $49 weekends; $33 in winter.

Trails Motel, 633 S. Main St. (876-5555). It'll cost you a little extra, but pleasant surroundings, microwaves, fridges, and a pool provide compensation. Rooms for 1-2 people, June -Oct. $46. Winter rates plummet as low as $28.

Diaz Lake Campground (876-5656), U.S. 395, 2 mi. south of Lone Pine. 200 sites at an 86-acre lake with swimming, fishing, boating, and water-skiing. Flush toilets, showers, tables, grills, well water, and concessions. Sites $7, max. 2-week stay.

Tuttle Creek Campground, follow Whitney Portal Rd. 4 mi. west of Lone Pine, turn south onto Horseshoe Meadows Rd. 82 sites (no fee, donations accepted). This excellent base camp for day hikers provides restrooms and water.

Portagee Joe Campground, head west on Whitney Portal Rd. ½ mi. to Tuttle Creek Rd.; turn south 200 yds. to campground. 15 sites, $6 each. Pit toilets, tables, grills, piped water, and a merry stream. Open year round.

There are 11 public campgrounds in the Lone Pine area of Inyo National Forest. Those at higher elevations—including **Whitney Portal**—are surrounded by cool evergreens and provide phenomenal views of the valley below. (Sites $10. 7-night max. stay.) Contact the Mt. Whitney Ranger (876-6200) or call 800-280-2267 for more information and reservations. (Individual sites $5-10; group sites $25.) Hot showers ($2) for campers are available at Kirk's Barber Shop (see Practical Information, page 386) or on the mountain at the Whitney Portal store ($2.50). (See Sights and Activities, below, for more on camping.)

FOOD

Lone Pine has its share of coffee shops and 24-hr. mini-marts, but not much else. The eateries in town are nondescript. If you're camping, grab groceries in town at **Joseph's Bi-Rite Market,** 119 S. Main at Mountain View (876-4378; open Mon.-Sat. 8:30am-9pm, Sun. 8:30am-8pm).

PJ's Bake and Broil, 446 Main (876-5796). Down-to-earth and so are their prices. Their chicken-fried steak ($7) is mammoth and an excellent post-climb treat. If you have any room left, the pie (freshly made every morning at 4am) *a la mode* ($2.50) is fabulous. Only restaurant around open 24 hrs.

Ernie's Tin Roof (876-4574), on U.S. 395, 2 mi. south of Lone Pine. Peaceful setting on Diaz Lake. Substantial Sun. brunch. Spanish omelette with crisp vegetables $5. Scrumptious seafood dishes, most a little steep, but you can get a shrimp boat with fries for $5.25. Open Feb. 2-Dec. 24 Tues.-Wed. 11am-5pm, Thurs.-Sat. 11am-10pm, Sun. 8am-10pm.

Sierra Cantina, N. Main St. (876-5740). All-you-can-eat Mexican lunch ($7) or dinner ($11). Offers some eclectic original recipes. Open Thurs.-Mon. 11:30am-8pm.
Mt. Whitney Restaurant, 2275 Main (876-5751). Serves the self-proclaimed "best burgers in town" from $3. Open daily 6am-10pm.

SIGHTS AND ACTIVITIES

With the cragged edges of **Mount Whitney** as the star of the show, the parts of Inyo National Forest bordering Kings Canyon and Sequoia National Parks make up a suitable supporting cast. All of the Sierra's tallest peaks are here (all but one is member of the 14,000 ft.+ club), generally within 10 to 15 mi. of U.S. 395. These regions can be explored by day hikes and overnight trips, using cheap national forest campgrounds as your base. All campsites have water and are about $6 per site. Beware of the high altitude, and allow extra time for hikes.

The **Whitney Trailhead** (876-6200) is 13 mi. west of Lone Pine. Turn west on Whitney Portal Rd. at the town's only traffic light. The canyon entrance at **Whitney Portal** provides fantastic camping with piped water and supplies (sites $10). The 11-mi. trek to the top of the lower 48 states' highest peak usually takes between two and three days. On March 1, the Forest Service begins to accept reservations for wilderness permits, and quotas are filled rapidly even though the deadline is May 22. Unclaimed permits are released at 8am on the doorstep; the line begins forming as early as 3pm the previous day. Write or phone the Mt. Whitney Ranger District office (see Practical Information, page 386) for more permit and climbing information. While more a strenuous hike than a climb, you may nonetheless need an ice axe and crampons during the spring and early summer. For rock-climbers, the East Face of Mt. Whitney is a year-round challenge.

Multitudes of less strenuous day hikes access stunning Eastern Sierra scenery. The **Cottonwood Lakes Trail** (10,000 ft. at the trailhead) squeezes between the forests that edge the John Muir Wilderness and Sequoia National Park. Follow Whitney Portal Rd. for 4 mi. from Lone Pine and take Horseshoe Meadow Rd. 20 mi. to the trailhead. Sites with water cost $3. Those who make the hour-long hike along **Horseshoe Meadow Trail** to **Golden Trout Wilderness** will pass several dozen high mountain lakes that mirror the Inyo Mountains. Camping and equestrian facilities are offered at Horseshoe Meadow (sites $10).

Although natural features are the area's greatest draw, the Eastern Sierra harbors at least one cultural attraction of significance. The **Lone Pine Film Festival** (876-4314), held in Lone Pine on Columbus Day, marks a yearly tribute to the Alabama Hill's glamorous career as a movie backdrop. These tortured crags authenticated over 250 Western classics, including *How the West was Won*. Roy Rogers, Natalie Wood, and Errol Flynn paraded past these hills.

North of Lone Pine along U.S. 395 lies **Manzanar Relocation Camp,** recently named a national historic site. The camp was the first of ten **internment centers** established to contain Japanese Americans following Japan's 1941 attack on Pearl Harbor. Perceived as enemy sympathizers and security risks, 11,000 Japanese Americans were held here from March 1942 through 1945. Visitors can walk through the remaining structures and grounds for no charge. Little remains to be seen. The **Eastern California Museum,** 155 N. Grant St. (878-2411), in Independence, has an absorbing and highly specialized collection featuring handicrafts from the area's native Paiute and Shoshone Indians, exhibits on early miners and ranchers, and a display on Manzanar. The museum's reconstruction of a pioneer village is authentic down to the smallest details (open Wed.-Mon. 10am-4pm; donation $1).

If you enjoy pain and bicycling, the annual **Death Valley to Mt. Whitney Bicycle Road Race** (over Mother's Day weekend) was designed with you in mind. Perennially ranked as one of the most masochistic organized activities in the United States, the two-day race starts at Stovepipe Wells (elevation 5 ft.) and ends at the Mt. Whitney trailhead some 100 mi. and 8355 ft. later. In spite of its status as an official United States Cycling Federation event, non-members are welcome to join in the fun. Call the Chamber (see Practical Information, page 386) for an entry form. If running's more your style, Lone Pine also hosts a **marathon** the previous weekend. The course climbs as high as 6200 ft. and is among the nation's hardest.

■■■ BISHOP AND OWENS VALLEY

In 1861, Samuel Bishop brought 600 cattle and his boots from Fort Tejon to settle at what is now Bishop Creek. Grazing herds are still plentiful; you are sure to spot them along Rte. 395 on the way into town. Most visitors are drawn to Bishop to rest, stock-up and refuel before venturing into the surrounding wilderness areas.

PRACTICAL INFORMATION

Visitors Information: Bishop Chamber of Commerce, 690 N. Main St. (873-8405), at the City Park. Maps and information on the Owens Valley area. Get a free copy of the Bishop Visitors Guide for up-to-date listings of special events. Open Mon.-Fri. 9am-5pm, Sat.-Sun. 10am-4pm. Park open 24 hrs.

White Mountain Ranger Station: 798 N. Main St. (873-2500). Excellent lists of campgrounds and nearby trails. Weather report and a message board. To camp in the wilds, you must first obtain a **wilderness permit.** These permits are limited, even if you reserve by mail. Write to the White Mountain Ranger District March 1-May 31. Some permits first-come, first-served, but be ready for fierce competition. Ranger Station programs include Sat. evening campfire talks. Open late June to Sept. 15 daily 7am-4:30pm; winter Mon.-Fri. 8am-4:30pm.

ATM: several are located along Main St.

Fishing Licenses: Permits and regulations are available at **K-mart** and most **sporting goods stores.** Maps are at the ranger station. The Fish & Game Office does **not** sell permits. Call Chamber of Commerce for fishing report.

Greyhound: 201 S. Warren St. (872-2721), behind the city parking lot. One bus per day to L.A. ($35.75) and Reno ($54.75). Open daily 1pm-2pm.

Car Rental: Ford Rent-A-Car, 1440 N. Sierra Hwy. (873-4291), $36 per day, 150 free mi., 18¢ per additional mi. Must be 25 with driver's license and major credit card. Open Mon.-Sat. 8am-5pm. **Luther Motors,** 380 S. Main St. (873-4234), $40 per day, 150 free mi., 20¢ per additional mi. Must be 21.

AAA Emergency Road Service: 873-8221.

Dial-A-Ride: 872-1901 or 800-922-1930. Fare 50¢ round-trip within Bishop city limits, 75¢ to areas just outside of the city. Will drop you and your companions at a trailhead for $30 per hour. Also runs shuttles to Mammoth Lakes ($2.50) and Crowley Lake ($1.75). Call the day before to check on specific times and make reservations (limited number of seats and vehicles). Open Mon.-Fri. 8:30am-4pm, Sat. 10am-3pm.

Bicycle Rental: Bikes of Bishop, 651 N. Main (872-3829). Maps of area tours. Mountain bikes $25 per day.

Swimming: Community pool is directly behind the visitors center. Showers and changing rooms. Open Mon.-Sat. 6am-9pm; winter limited. $2, under 17 $1.50.

Laundromat: Sierra Suds (873-8338), at Church and Warren, behind Joseph's Bi-Rite. Wash $1.25, 10-min. dry 25¢. Open daily 7am-10pm. A far more enjoyable washing experience available down the street at the **Wash-Tub** (873-6627), with pool tables and video games galore.

Showers: Yet another excuse to visit the fun-filled folks at the Wash-Tub (see above). Hot showers for $2, soap and towel for 50¢ more.

Weather and Road Information: 873-6366; weather only, 873-3213.

Senior Information: Senior Center, 873-6364.

Hospital: Northern Inyo, 150 Pioneer Lane (873-5811). 24-hr. emergency service.

Emergency: 911.

Police: 207 W. Line, 873-5866 or 873-5823; **Sheriff:** 873-2441.

Post Office: 595 W. Line St. (873-3526). Open Mon.-Fri. 8:15am-4:45pm, Sat. 10am-2pm. **General Delivery ZIP Code:** 93514.

Area Code: 619.

ACCOMMODATIONS AND CAMPING

You're best off camping in Bishop. Hotels aren't scarce; it's just that the cheap ones are hiding. Most motels listed offer fish cleaning and storage facilities; what would you guess is one of the valley's most popular pastimes?

Elms Motel, 233 E. Elm (873-8118 or 1-800-848-9226). A refreshing change from the traditional L-shaped strip motel. A number of small "cottages" house 2 rooms apiece. These bright rooms are tucked away in a quiet area. TV and coffee-makers. Singles $35. Doubles $38.

El Rancho Motel, 274 Lagoon St. (872-9251), 1 block west of Main St. near Greyhound. Mints by the bed are just one of the classy touches here. TV, A/C, in-room coffee. Rooms for 1-2 from $35.

Mountain View Motel, 730 W. Line St. (873-4242). On the opposite side of town, in a quiet and pleasant location. While none of the rooms actually afford the implied vistas, they do offer handy refrigerators and remarkably tasteful decor for the money. Singles $38. Doubles $45.

Sierra Foothills Motel, 535 S. Main St. (872-1386). Amenities include heated pool, sauna, *and* indoor whirlpool—a welcome retreat from a hard day of hiking. A pleasant room awaits your steamed body. Singles $35. Doubles $38.

Brown's Town (873-8522), 1 mi. south of town on U.S. 395. Turn west on Schrober Lane. Picnic area available for day use. Also on the premises: a daily video show and **Brown's Museum,** with antiques and original buildings of Bishop (free). RV sites $13, tent sites $10, 7-min. showers 50¢ (for campers only).

Creekside RV Park (873-4483), South Gate Rd. 16 mi. southwest of Bishop on the south fork of Bishop Creek. As close to fishing as can be, with its own stocked pond and stream too. Water and hot showers. Tent sites $10. Full hookups $15.

Mill Pond Recreation Area (873-5342), 6½ mi. northwest of Bishop on U.S. 395, ¼ mi. south on Ed Powers Rd., 0.8 mi. west on Sawmill Rd. Next to Mill Pond Riding Stables. Piped and stream water, pond for swimming and sailing, tennis courts, archery, horseshoe pits, and flush toilets. Sites $8, hookups $10.

There are over 20 **Inyo National Forest** campgrounds in the Bishop Ranger District. **First Falls** at Big Pine, **Grandview** in the Bristlecone Forest, and **Willow** (closest to Bishop) at Bishop Creek are all free. Willow is typically open only as overflow, leaving the creatively named Intake 2 as the closest site to town. Grandview has no water; the other two have only stream water, which must be treated before drinking. **Bishop Creek Canyon** rests conveniently on the road to North Lake, a hot spot for trout fishing (restrooms, water; $11 per night). Creekside camping is available at **Horton Creek** 9 mi. northwest of Bishop (restrooms, fishing; no fee). Other sites are $8-10 and have piped water. Group units are $20-40; call MISTIX (800-280-2267) for reservations.

If you're traveling in a group, a cabin may be your best option. **Bishop Creek Lodge** (873-4484), South Lake Rd. offers 2-person rustic cabins, with gas stoves, barbecue, linens, dishes, and shared bathroom facilities ($55 per night; 2-day min. stay). With a general store, lodge, restaurant, and cocktail bar, the Bishop Creek Lodge has been popular for over 60 years. Take Rte. 168 14 mi. west from Bishop, then follow the signs toward South Lake Recreation Area.

The **Bishop Creek Cardinal Village** (873-4789) lies 16 mi. west of Bishop on Rte. 168. Canyon cabins (from $65) sleep 2-16 people. Facilities for volleyball and horseshoes pale against the area's three lakes and fishing streams. The lodge serves meals.

FOOD

Whiskey Creek, 524 N. Main St. (873-7174). Not the cheapest place in the world, but locals swear it's worth every penny. Particularly popular for breakfast, when the prices are more manageable. Their list of dinner "favorites," which includes burritos and a rib basket, require a shorter stack of cents ($6.25-$8.95) than most of their specialties, which climb as high as $18.95. Open 7am-circa 10pm.

Bar-B-Q Bill's, 187 S. Main St. (872-5535). A plastic heifer on the roof outside heralds wagon-wheel decor (alas, no wagon-wheel coffee tables) and cattle-train service within, but the food redeems all. You can grab a prime rib sandwich *a la carte* for about $5.50, or order a satisfying BBQ combo starting at $6.75. Soup and salad bar $4.50. Open Mon.-Thurs. 11am-9pm, Fri.-Sat. 11am-10pm. During winter, the cows head home around 8pm.

La Casita, 175 S. Main (873-4828). The struggle for bragging rights as the town's best Mexican restaurant is surprisingly intense. Yet while both **El Charro** (which incidentally, offers the only thing resembling a **nightlife** in town: dancing Thurs.-Sat.) and the newer **Amigos** both have significant supporting factions, the bulk of the locals would vote La Casita. A primarily traditional menu with entrees hovering around the $6 mark. Open daily 11:30am-9pm.

The Bishop Grill, 281 N. Main (873-3911). A downtown diner popular at knight. Dinners $5.50. Onion rings fit for a king ($2). Packed with locals, especially at breakfast. The waitstaff here won't treat you like a queen, but the service is no-nonsense and the food is diner-greasy good. Prices a pawn can afford. Open daily 6am-8pm.

Erick Schat's Bakkery, 763 N. Main St. (873-7156). While Erick's spelling may be a little lacking, his bakking prowess more than compensates. No trip to the valley is complete without a loaf of Erick's original sheepherder's bread ($2.25). Unbelievable cookies. Open Mon.-Thurs. and Sat. 6:30am-6pm, Fri. 6:30am-10pm, Sun. 6am-8pm.

Pyrenees Soup and Sandwiches, 150 N. Main St. (873-7275). Light lunches $3-5. Half a world away from its namesake, but well-frequented by locals for the delicious homemade soups and hearty sandwiches. Open Mon.-Sat. 10am-3pm.

ACTIVITIES

The Owens Valley is a backpacker's Eden. East of Bishop, the **White Mountains** raise themselves to heights rivalling the Sierras. If you want to tackle the strenuous 15-mi. climb to the top of White Mountain itself (14,246 ft.), park your car on White Mountain Rd., 22 mi. from Rte. 168. Camp for free at **Grandview Campground,** on White Mountain Rd., where you can use the pit toilets, tables, and grills. Carry your own water, as none is available on this trail or at the campground. Serious hikers may want to connect here with the Inyo Segment (11,000 ft.) of the **Pacific Crest Trail.** Rangers at Inyo National Forest, 873 N. Main St. (873-2400), in Bishop, can provide permits and guidance to this unearthly sweep along the Kern River.

Scattered across the face of the White Mountains are California's **bristlecone pines,** the oldest living things on the planet. Gnarled, twisted, and warped into fantastic shapes, the trees may grow only one inch every 100 years. The slow growth at extreme altitudes (up to 12,000 ft.) has allowed the **"Methuselah"** specimen in **Schulman Group** to survive 4700 years to date (to preserve the tree, they don't tell you which one it is). Many of the pines in the **Ancient Bristlecone Pine Forest** are over 4000 years old. Follow Rte. 168 off U.S. 395 at Big Pine for 23 mi. At the top of the pass turn left at the sign to the Bristlecone Pine Forest and the White Mountains Research Station. The paved road takes you to Schulman Grove, where there are two short and interesting hikes as well as a recently completed **visitors center** (873-2500; open daily 9am-5pm, Labor Day-Memorial Day Sat.-Sun. 9am-5pm) with interpretive displays and programs. The 12-mi. drive on unpaved roads to **Patriarch Grove** is treacherous; four-wheel-drive is recommended. Along the way, there are several impressive viewpoints to keep your spirits up.

Over the Inyos from Deep Springs lies the uninhabited **Eureka Valley.** The valley's magnificent and haunting **sand dunes** are the largest land-locked dunes in the world. If the sand is cool, flip off your shoes, climb to the top of the dunes, and roll down. The friction between the sand you disturb and the nearly 700 ft. of grains beneath makes a bizarre, loud, unfathomably deep sound. These desolate dunes were once a favorite haunt of Charles Manson. Eureka Valley is also the home of madly reproducing **wild horses,** bane to ranchers and ecologists, but a delight to travelers. Seeing the horses is a matter of luck, but early morning is your best bet. Getting to Eureka Valley and the dunes is tricky. Roads lead into the valley from the Owens Valley near Big Pine and from various points on the Nevada side, but none is reliable and not even the proverbial wild horses could drag you through when the road is washed out or snowed in. Check with the Department of Transportation, next to the post office in Bishop, or with the rangers, for specifics. See Desert Survival, page 169, for tips on desert travel.

Seven mi. south of Big Pine on U.S. 395 is a wildlife viewpoint, where you can get a great view of the valley and, sometimes (try early morning or evening), **elk herds.** Elk also congregate on the mowed alfalfa fields, just south of Big Pine on 395.

The Owens Valley cradles wilderness areas that will sate any explorer or adventurer. **Big Pine Canyon** guides Big Pine Creek over daring changes in altitude and through thick groves of Jeffrey Pines. Follow Glacier Lodge Rd. for 10 mi. Hikers will find the backcountry trailhead to the **Palisade Glacier,** the Sierra's largest, a satisfying trek and a popular destination for rock- and ice-climbers. West of Bishop rises **Bishop Creek Canyon,** which was carved by an intimidating creek. Follow Line St. from Bishop for 18 mi. to **Sabrina Basin** or the South lakes. **Sabrina Basin Trailhead** offers secluded hiking and fishing opportunities. Steeper switchbacks off the main trail lead to the less populated **George Lake.** Continue another 5 mi. along Rte. 168 to **South Lake Trailhead,** where leisurely trails lead to Green, Treasure, and Chocolate Lakes. Both trailheads have overnight parking and camping facilities. Sites with piped water near Sabrina and South Lakes cost $8. Together, Sabrina, North, and South Lakes provide spectacular high country **fishing** for seekers of brown and rainbow trout. The official angling season spans April 30 through October. Contact the chamber (873-8405) for tournament and general fishing information.

The recreation areas along **Rock Creek Canyon** are well used year-round. Hair-raising precipices, plunging canyons, and velvet wildflowers mesmerize earnest photographers and casual gawkers. From U.S. 395, turn at Tom's Place and continue up Rock Creek Canyon to the end of the road (park at Mosquito Flat). **Little Lakes Valley** is surrounded by 13,000-ft. peaks, and many of the lakes in its basin beckon those seeking brook, rainbow, and brown trout. In 1864, William Brewer and his party were the first white men lucky enough to cross **Mono Pass Trail** and set eyes on beautiful **Ruby Lake** and its staggering sheer granite walls. There are numerous campgrounds on the way to **Mosquito Flat** and plenty of day parking at each of the five trailheads. Campsites are $6-8 and include toilets. **Mosquito Flat Trailhead** is a free walk-in site with stream water only. The campgrounds are closed during the winter months, though the trails remain open for phenomenal cross-country skiing.

Those who prefer traveling on four legs may be interested in **Pine Creek Saddle and Pack Trains** (387-2797; call either before 9am or after 4pm), which provides guided tours of the area on gentle horses and mules. ($15 for 4 hrs.; $35 for 5 hrs.; $55 per day, including lunch.) Hang gliding and paragliding are also popular here. Owens Valley has favored its soaring visitors with unequaled world distance and altitude records. Novices can obtain instruction at **Vertical World Systems** (873-8367) at Bishop Airport off 703 Airport Rd. If flight is not for you, keep your feet on the area's solid granite crags—a draw for climbers from across the globe. Route specifics and equipment are available from **Wilson's Eastside Sports,** 206 N. Main (873-7520).

For those who can resist outdoor adventure, Owens Valley preserves its history at the **Paiute Shoshone Indian Cultural Center,** 2300 W. Line St. (873-4478). Exhibits here illustrate the history and culture of some of the seven local tribes (open Mon.-Fri. 9am-5pm, Sat.-Sun. 10am-4pm). The **Laws Railroad Museum** (873-5950) is a monument to the Carson & Colorado railroad that grunted through the Owens Valley for almost 80 years. The restored depot, post office, and passenger cars can be toured (daily 10am-4pm; free). Follow Rte. 6 from Bishop to Silver Canyon Rd.

In **winter**, the evergreen forests, the lake basins, and the peaceful "range of light" (as Muir described the Eastern Sierra) make for spectacular **cross-country skiing.** Bishop Creek and Rock Creek drainages are reportedly the best areas to explore. **Bishop Creek Lodge** offers 14 mi. of groomed trails and a ski school (873-3015 or 873-4484; open Fri.-Sun.). The Forest Service occasionally grooms 3km of trails through the **Four Jeffrey Campground** area. Call the ranger station for details (see

Practical Information). Rock Creek Lodge (935-4464) offers access to other terrain considered excellent by locals.

Bishop hosts a range of annual events. The City Park (behind the visitors center) has hosted free **Monday evening concerts** for 40 consecutive summers (in the gazebo; June-Aug. 8-9pm). A massive **rodeo** and **fair** is held in town every Labor Day weekend, and you can park your RV at the fairgrounds for $7 per night (873-8405). Each night during the rodeo and fair, after the cowboys and cowgirls finish taming the wild broncos, they settle down with some herbal tea and recite some of their favorite verse at the **Cowboy Poetry Festival.** Bishop's **Mule Days** are a Memorial Day weekend tradition. An auction, parade, racing, and other raucous celebrations launch the packing season. Bishop's annual **Fly-in,** a celebration of aerial sports, draws balloons and planes from the valley in a neck-craning display on the third weekend of September.

■■■ MAMMOTH LAKES

Home to one of the most popular ski resorts in the United States, the town of Mammoth Lakes is rapidly transforming itself into a giant, year-round playground. Mountain biking, rock-climbing, and hiking now complement the traditional snow-bound pursuits. Mammoth is an outdoorsperson's fantasy—spectacular peaks overlook a community in which every establishment seems to exist solely for the excursionist's benefit. Yet for all its glitz, the town's residents keep it friendly. The nightlife on weekends is lively, as the young and athletic locals mingle with the constant stream of visitors who come to this mountain paradise for "extreme" sports and a good time.

PRACTICAL INFORMATION AND ORIENTATION

Visitors Information: Visitors Center and Chamber of Commerce (934-2712 or 800-367-6572), on Main St. inside Village Center Mall West, across from the post office. Pick up a free copy of the *Mammoth Times.* Open Sat.-Thurs. 8am-6pm, Fri. 8am-8pm; winter daily 8am-6pm.

Inyo National Forest Visitors Center (924-5500), east off U.S. 395 north of town. Nature exhibits, nature walks, restrooms, pay phone. Information on which campgrounds, roads and sights are open. *Mammoth Trails Hiking Guide* ($2) provides excellent descriptions of area day and overnight hikes in the area. Open daily 6am-5pm; Oct.-June Mon.-Sat. 8am-4:30pm.

Greyhound: The bus stops in the parking lot behind McDonald's on Main St. One bus daily to Reno (at 1:05am) and to L.A. (at 12:30pm). Board here and buy your ticket at the next station. Information at Bishop or call 213-620-1200.

Inyo-Mono Dial-A-Ride: 800-922-1930. Bus provides service to Bishop, Bridgeport, Lee Vining, June Lake, and Crowley Lake. Leaves from Mammoth McDonald's at 9:30am and leaves from Bishop at 2pm. Round-trip $2.50. Call 1 day ahead for reservations and door-to-door pickup (if needed).

Mammoth Area Shuttle (MAS): 934-0687. The red line services the main lodge and town (free). During ski season, shuttles start at 7-7:30am, and run every 15 min. until 5:30pm. Other lines connect to various base chairlifts. Pick up brochure at visitors center. Sat. service to Tamarack for cross-country skiing (call 934-2442). In summer, shuttle services Devil's Post Pile.

Mammoth Adventure Connection: 800-228-4947. Year-round van pickup/dropoff for up to 30 mi. round-trip ($7.50 one way).

Mammoth Shuttle System: 934-3030. Provides year-round on-call service (7am-11pm in summer, 7am-5:30pm in winter). Transit within town goes for $3; it will cost you $8 to get to the lodge. Still a good deal compared to **Mammoth Cab** (934-3346) at $1.95 per mi.

Car Rentals: U-SAVE Auto Rental (800-272-USAV, -8728). Rents compacts from $215 per week with 700 free mi. Four-wheel-drives start at $275 weekly. Rentals also available at the **Chevron** (934-8111) next to the post office. $40 per day, 50 free mi., 18¢ per additional mi.

AAA Service: 934-3385.
Eastern Sierra Road Report: 873-6366.
Equipment Rental: Sandy's Ski Sport, Main St. (934-7518). Mountain bikes $7 per hr., $18 per ½-day, $25 per day. Tents $12 for 1 day, $5 each additional day. Snow ski rentals from $12 per day, ski packages from $16 per day. Backpacks, fishing poles, sleeping bags, and in-line skates also available. Open Mon.-Sat. 8am-8pm, Sun. 8am-8pm. **Sierra Sports,** 3704 Main St. (924-2834), supplies fishing information and gear. Rent rods from $6 and buy nightcrawlers for $1 a pack.
Laundromat: (934-2237) on Laurel Mountain Rd., behind the 76 station. Wash $1.25, 10-min. dry 25¢. Open daily 8:30am-6:30pm, last load at 5pm. Can also handle sleeping bags and larger items.
Local Weather: 934-7669.
Mammoth Mountain Snow Conditions: 934-6166. **Mammoth Mountain Ski Area:** 932-2571. **June Mountain Ski Area:** 648-7733.
Hospital: Centinela Mammoth, 85 Sierra Park Rd. (934-3311). Open 24 hrs. **Alpine Fracture and Medical Clinic** (934-2553), is also available.
Emergency: 911.
Post Office (934-2205), on Main St. across from the visitors center. Open Mon.-Fri. 8:30am-5pm. **General Delivery ZIP Code:** 93546.
Area Code: 619.

Mammoth Lakes is located on **U.S. 395** about 160 mi. south of Reno and 40 mi. southeast of the eastern entrance to Yosemite National Park. **Rte. 203** runs through the town as **Main St.,** and then veers off to the right as **Minaret Summit Rd.** In the winter, the roads in from Southern California are jammed with weekend skiers making the six-hour journey up to the slopes. Once in town, navigation is generally easy, particularly with a free map from the visitors center.

ACCOMMODATIONS AND CAMPING

As with most ski resorts, lodging is much more expensive in the winter. However there are a surprising number of bargains available to the bargain shopper. The best deals generally go to those traveling in big groups and on weekdays. If you're traveling with three or more people, look for condominium rentals and enjoy all the comforts of home—including a kitchen and a garage—for as low as $45 per night (total) in summer. (Check with **Mammoth Reservation Bureau** at 1-800-527-6273.) If you are on your own, winter lodging is cheapest at the dormitory-style motels. Make reservations for these as far in advance as possible; they go fast. Good deals abound in the summer.

There are nearly 20 Inyo Forest public campgrounds in the area, at **Mammoth Lakes, Mammoth Village, Convict Lake,** and **Reds Meadow.** All sites have piped water. Call the Mammoth Ranger District (924-5500) for more information. Reservations taken for all group sites ($20-$35), as well at nearby Sherwin Creek, through MISTIX (800-283-CAMP, -2267).

Hilton Creek International Hostel (HI-AYH) (935-4989), on the outskirts of Lake Crowley, about 10 mi. south of town; take 395 south, get off at first Lake Crowley Dr. exit (there are 3) and continue another 2-3 mi. to the hostel. Mailing address: Rte. 1, P.O. Box 1128, Crowley Lake 93546. Converted park station with 22 beds including a family room (by reservation). In a supreme location, complete with aspen grove, babbling brook, and mountain view. Skiing, backpacking, inner-tubing, biking, multilingual conversations, and local music. $10, nonmembers $13. Under 18 with parents and seniors half-price. Add $2 in winter.
ULLR Lodge (934-2454), turn left from Main St. onto Minaret Rd. Ski-chalet style, with sauna and shared kitchen. A wide variety of rooms and prices. Dorm style rooms with a hall bathroom and rooms with television and private bath. Prices go up on weekends and in the winter. Rooms range from $15-58. Call for more info.
Kitzbuhel Lodge (934-2352). Turn right off Main to Minaret, then right on Berner. Bring your friends, bring your relatives, bring your dog if necessary—get enough people together and you can have an entire floor, including rec room, kitchen,

and balcony, to yourselves for $10 per person during the summer. Minimum group size depends on the time of the year, so call ahead. Lodge also offers ideal arrangements for lone travelers during the winter: dorm-style beds go for $20. Other amenities include jacuzzi, cable TV, and ski-storage. Reserve early.

Asgard Chalet, 19 Davison Rd. (962-6773 or 924-2188). Excellent for groups. Dormitory and 7-18 person lodging units available. Single beds in dorm space go for $19.50. Small room sleeps 1-3. $12-15 per person; winter $18.50. Perched on the hill, Asgard houses one of the best views in town.

Budget Inn, 54 Sierra Blvd. (934-8892), right off Main St. Vies with the neighboring **Motel 6** for cheapest "traditional" motel. Budget wins by a nose during the summer ($35 versus $40 for a room with 1 queen bed), and its relatively spacious rooms—half complete with balconies, the other with access to the roof—make it a solid contender year-round ($50 for 2 in winter). Jacuzzi too.

New Shady Rest Campground, on Rte. 203 across from McDonald's, a 2-min. walk from town. This convenience doubles as a detraction—camping just isn't the same when you can see the Golden Arches through the trees. $9 per night. Piped water, flush toilets, no RV hookups. 14-day max. stay. 95 sites, half available for walk-in tenting year-round; half available late May to mid-Sept.

Mammoth Mountain RV Park (934-3822), across from the USFS Visitors Center. Free ski shuttle, hot showers, spa, and indoor pool. Hookups $26 in winter, $21 in summer. Dogs $1 extra.

Camp Hi Sierra (934-2368), ¼ mi. west of New Shady Rest on Lake Mary Rd. Run by the L.A. Dept. of Recreation, this camp also has a helpful office stocked with information, a recreational lodge, wooded sites with mountain vistas, and free hot showers. Tent sites $12, cabins $22. Open June-Sept. 15.

FOOD AND NIGHTLIFE

The usual fast-food franchises (including one of the classiest looking McDonald's you will ever see) exert seemingly hegemonic control over cheap meals, but those looking for a more creative bite to eat need not despair.

Angel's (934-7427), at Main St. and Sierra. An almost unanimous recommendation among the locals. A tad expensive (dinner entrees $6-13), but after a day on the slopes, you can convince yourself that you earned it. Angel's specializes in BBQ, but you can get a deliciously huge beef burrito for $7. The bar features over 70 beers from 19 different countries and serves up drafts in pewter mugs. Open Mon.-Fri. 11:30am-10pm, Sat.-Sun. 5pm-10pm.

The Stove (934-2821), on Old Mammoth Rd., 4 blocks from Main St. In the minds of most locals, The Stove = big breakfasts. Visitors will flip over the huge stack of pancakes ($3.65). Down-home dinner entrees $8-10. Open daily 8am-9pm.

Giovanni's (934-7563), on the corner of Old Mammoth Rd. and Meridian in Minaret Village. Mix and match sauces, crusts, and toppings for a perfect pizza (larges start at $12). Pasta from $5.25. Open Sun.-Thurs. 11am-9pm, Fri.-Sat. 11am-10pm.

Susie's Subs (934-7033), Old Mammoth Rd. just before Chateau. Pack a sub for a portable slope-side lunch. Most subs $3.50-4.50. Open Mon.-Fri. 10am-6pm, Sat.-Sun. 8am-6pm.

Paul Schat's Bakery & Cafe (934-6055), Main St., next to Sandy's Ski & Sport. This mouth-watering bakery draws daunting brunch crowds on weekends. Meals (breakfast, lunch) from $4. Open 6am-6pm;winter 6:30am-6pm.

After hours, revelers can be found at **Grumpy's** on 37 Old Main St. (934-8587), shooting pool until 1am on weekdays, 2am on weekends. **Whiskey Creek** (934-2555), at Main and Minaret, is open (and usually lively) until 1:30am every night.

SIGHTS

There's plenty to see in Mammoth Lakes, but unfortunately most of it is accessible only by car. If you lack wheels, try the **MAS** (see Practical Information, page 393) in winter or **Mammoth Adventure Connection** (800-228-4947) year-round. They offer van pickup/drop-off for up to 30 mi. round trip ($7.50 one way). **Devil's Post-**

pile National Monument, an intriguing geological oddity, was formed when lava flows oozed through Mammoth Pass thousands of years ago and then cooled to form columns 40 to 60 ft. high. The column's cross-sections range from geometrically precise equilateral triangles to strange heptagons. Ancient glaciers exposed and polished the basalt posts to create the mammoth jewels that glitter today. A pleasant 3-mi. walk away from the center of the monument is **Rainbow Falls,** where the middle fork of the San Joaquin River drops 140 ft. past dark cliffs into a glistening green pool. From U.S. 395, the monument and its nearby bubbling **hot springs** can be reached by a 15-mi. drive past Minaret Summit on paved Rte. 203. The road is operational only in summer and may be closed as late as July 4 in years with heavy snows. The campground near the ranger station has sites for $10. To save the monument area from being completely trampled, rangers have introduced a shuttle service between a parking area and the monument center, which all visitors—drivers and hikers alike—must use between 7:30am and 5:30pm (drivers have free access 5:30pm-7:30am). (Shuttle 30 min. Round-trip $7, ages 5-12 $4.)

Although there are over 100 lakes near town (60 of them within a 5-mi. radius), not one actually goes by the name of "Mammoth Lake." The most mammoth lake in the basin, the 1-mi.-long **Lake Mary,** is popular for boating, fishing, and sailing. **Twin Lakes** is the closest lake to the village, only 3 mi. down Rte. 203. **Lake Mamie** has a picturesque picnic area, and many short hikes lead out to **Lake George,** where exposed granite sheets attract climbers. **Horseshoe Lake,** is popular for swimming and is also the trailhead for the impressive Mammoth Pass Trail. **Lake Crowley,** 12 mi. south of town, is popular with anglers, yielding over 80 tons of rainbow trout between May and October. Here, motorboats can be rented for $42 per day; parking is $3 per day, campsites $7. Anglers converge on the area during **Flyfishing Days** in mid-July, for some of the best trout in the contiguous U.S. The backcountry waters in particular are squirming with trout. Ask the visitor center about permits and sport shops. Fishing without a license carries a $690 fine. Pick up a booklet with other regulations when you dutifully purchase your permit.

You can ride the **Mammoth Mountain Gondola** (934-2571) during the summer for a spectacular view of the area. (Open daily 11am-3pm. Round-trip $10, children $5.) **Obsidian Dome** lies 14 mi. north of Mammoth Junction and 1 mi. west of U.S. 395 on Glass Flow Rd. (follow the sign to "Lava Flow"). The dark, glassy volcanic rock is a wobbly climb, so take sturdy shoes. **Mammoth Sporting Goods** (934-3239) can equip you with gear and information for more challenging climbs up the area's ragged sheets and boulders.

Summers in Mammoth are packed with small festivals celebrating everything from chili cooking to motorcross racing. A new event, the **Mammoth Lakes Jazz Jubilee** (934-2478) in mid-July has already become a local favorite. The **National Mountain Biking Championships** (934-0651) in early July (which attracts nearly 10,000), and the **Mammoth Motorcross Race** (934-2571), the weekend before, is one of the most popular of the area's many athletic competitions.

Hot-air balloons, climbing walls, mountain bike paths, and even dogsled trails attract visitors to Mammoth. You can evaluate your options at the **Mammoth Adventure Connection** (800-228-4947), in the Mammoth Mountain Inn. Courageous cyclists can take the gondola to the top of **Mammoth Mountain Bike Park,** where trails start from 11,053 ft. and head straight *down* the thawed winter-time ski trails, bared to expose many, many, sharp rocks. Helmets are required. Get tickets and information at the **Mammoth Mountain Bike Center** at the base of the mountain (934-0606; $5 per day for helmet rentals, bike rental $25 for 4 hrs., $35 per 8-hr. day; open daily 9:30am-6pm). The gondola runs daily 10am-5:30pm ($18 per day for gondola ticket and trail use). A **rope course** ($30-40) and **climbing wall** ($10 per hr.) are the latest attractions at Mammoth (open July 1-Labor Day; call 924-5638 for reservations). **High Sierra Ballooning** (934-7188) can put you in flight for $125. Those in search of an equestrian experience can contact **Sierra Meadows Ranch** (934-6161), for horseback riding ($25 per hr., $75 per day). The Park has more than 50 mi. of trails, most of them significantly easier than the famed Kamikaze run, as well as an obstacle arena and timed slalom racecourse. Drop by the Mammoth Ranger Station (924-5500) for a map of bike trail networks on Forest Service land. Grumpy's hosts free volleyball tournaments during the summer.

SKIING AND WINTER RECREATION

With 132 downhill runs, over 26 lifts (plus 2 gondolas), and miles of nordic skiing trails, Mammoth is one of the country's premier winter resorts. The season extends from mid-November to June; in a good year, downhill skiing can last through the 4th of July. To keep costs low, visit during a slow time (avoid weekends and especially, any time near or on a major holiday), and be prepared to cook your own meals. Economical multi-day lift tickets are available (regular price $40 per day; $175 for a 5-day pass). Rent skis either at home or in town; resort-run shops usually charge 10-20% more. Mammoth Mountain lift tickets can be purchased at the **Main Lodge** at the base of the mountain on Minaret Rd. (934-2571; open Mon.-Fri. 8am-3pm, Sat.-Sun. 7:30am-3pm), at **Stormriders** at Minaret Rd. and Canyon Blvd. (open 8am-9pm daily), or at **Warming Hut II** at the end of Canyon and Lakeview Blvds. (934-0787; open Mon.-Fri. 8am-3pm, Sat.-Sun. and holidays 7:30am-3pm). A free shuttle bus (MAS) transports skiers between lifts, town, and the Main Lodge (see Practical Information). The Forest Service can provide information on the area's cross country trails.

Mammoth has miles of trails and open areas for snowmobiles. The **Mammoth Lake Snowmobile Association** (934-6157) maps out open and restricted areas. Visitors over 16 can rent snowmobiles at **Center Street Polan's** (934-4020). For those seeking an alternative winter adventure, the Mammoth area is pioneering public bobsledding. Though runs are tamed to speeds appropriate for non-Olympians, the turns and straightaways are exhilarating. Runs are lighted for night racing. Call **Bobsleds International** (934-7533) on Minaret Rd. for more information.

June Mountain Ski Area (648-7733), located 20 mi. north of Mammoth Lakes at Lake U.S. 395 north and Rte. 158 west has less stellar skiing than Mammoth. Lift tickets ($35 per day) are available in the Tram Haus next to the parking lot.

Lake Tahoe

Lake Tahoe is neither one big casino nor an untamed paradise; careful planning here has balanced the natural and civilized worlds. The budget traveler's best bet is to eat cheap in **Stateline,** sleep cheap in **South Lake Tahoe**, and head to **North Lake Tahoe** to enjoy the splendor of the waves or woods. Activity in North Lake Tahoe centers around **Tahoe City,** where Western families come season after season, year after year, to enjoy the lake's extraordinary recreational and natural resources. The area has a warm, familiar atmosphere; everyone is happy to have escaped the chaos and pollution of urban civilization. Tahoe City is not the most economical place to find a motel in Lake Tahoe, but it is rich with campsites and excellent trails. An active club and bar scene in Tahoe City offers an alternative to casino nightlife, with an energetic younger crowd and plenty of local entertainment.

It would be impossible to list all the attractions and activities that await the budget traveler in Tahoe. Explore on your own, chat with the friendly locals, and discover the beauty of this area for yourself.

PRACTICAL INFORMATION AND ORIENTATION

Visitors Information: South Lake Tahoe Visitors Center, 3066 U.S. 50 (541-5255), at Lion's Ave. Tons of helpful brochures and maps. A local map, coupons, and a lengthy directory can be found in *101 Things to Do in Lake Tahoe* (free). The *Handbook for the Handicapped* is an extensive directory of facilities and information. Open Mon.-Fri. 8:30am-5pm, Sat. 9am-4pm. **Lake Tahoe Visitor Center,** "the A-frame" 4018 Lake Tahoe Blvd. (544-3133), 1 block from Stateline. **Visitors Bureau,** 950 North Lake Blvd. (581-6900), in Tahoe City.

U.S. Forest Service, 870 Emerald Bay Rd., S. Lake Tahoe (573-2600). Supervises campgrounds and publishes *Lake of the Sky Journal* (loaded with recreational coupons) and *Lake Tahoe Summer* (with local bus schedules). Winter recreation information. Free, but mandatory **wilderness permits** for backcountry hiking are available here. Taylor Creek (Rte. 8), open daily during the summer (after June 18th Mon.-Fri. 8am-4:30pm, Sat.-Sun. 8am-5:30pm), weekends only off-season.

Buses: Greyhound, 1098 U.S. 50 in Harrah's Hotel Casino (588-9645), by Raley's in S. Lake Tahoe. To San Francisco (5 per day, $20) and Sacramento (5 per day, $18). All rates subject to seasonal price changes. No lockers. Open daily 8am-5pm. **Tahoe Casino Express** (800-446-6128) provides shuttle service between Reno airport and casinos (8am-midnight; $15).

Tahoe Area Regional Transport (TART): 581-6365. Connects the western and northern shores from Tahoma to Incline Village. 12 buses daily 7am-6pm. Fare $1.

South Tahoe Area Ground Express (STAGE): 573-2080. 24-hr. bus service around town, service to the beach (every hr.). Connects Stateline and Emerald Bay Rd. Fare $1.25; 10-ride pass $10. Most casinos operate free shuttle service along U.S. 50 to CA ski resorts and motels. A summer beach bus program connects **STAGE** and **TART** at Meeks Bay to service the entire lake area.

Taxi: Sierra Taxi, 577-8888. Open 24 hrs.

Car Rental: Tahoe Rent-a-Car (544-4500), U.S. 50 at Tahoe Keys Blvd. in S. Lake Tahoe. 100 free mi. Cars from $29 per day. Must be 24.

Moped Rental: Country Moped, 800 Emerald Bay Rd. at Rte. 89 S and 10th St. (544-3500). Mopeds $10 per hr., $38 per day; scooters $15 per hr., $48 per day; in-line skates including protective gear $5 per hr., $20 per day. Open daily 10am-7pm.

Bicycle Rental: Anderson's Bicycle Rental, 645 Emerald Bay Rd. (541-0500), convenient to the well-maintained west shore bike trail. Mountain bikes $6 per hr., ½-day $18, full day $22. Deposit (usually an ID) required. Open daily 8am-6:30pm, Sept.-May 9am-6:30pm. **Tahoe Cyclery,** 355 Lake Tahoe Blvd. (542-2390), caters to the alternative biking crowd. Grungy but friendly shop offers a diverse assortment of rentals: mountain bikes $5 per hr., full day $20; in-line

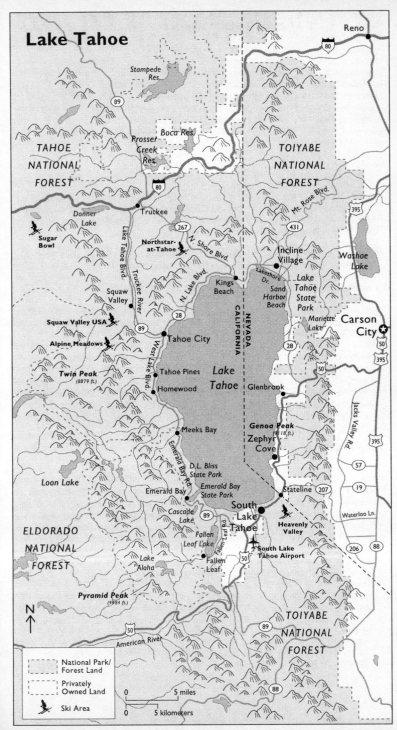

Lake Tahoe

skates $5 per hr., full day $20; winter snowboards $25 per day for boots and boards; skis $10 for a day package; snowshoes $15 per day. Extremely helpful staff. Open daily summer and winter 9am-7pm, spring and fall 10am-6pm. Bike rentals shops abound and prices are generally the same.

Library: 1000 Rufus Allen, S. Lake Tahoe (573-3185). Open Tues.-Wed. noon-8pm, Thurs.-Sat. 10am-5pm. The Tahoe Douglas County Library in Zephyr Cove sells cheap paperbacks and allows travelers to check out books.

Laundromat: South Y Coin-op (541-4745), at the intersection of Rte. 89 and U.S. 50. Open Mon.-Sat. 7am-7pm, Sun. 10am-4pm. **Carnelian Bay Launderland,** 5075 N. Lake Blvd. (581-4497). Open daily 7am-10pm.

Public Pool and Recreation Center: 1180 Rufus Allen Blvd. (542-6056), across from Campground by the Lake. Adults $2.75, children $1.50, seniors and disabled $1.75. Use of weight room same price as pool. Open Mon.-Sat. 8am-8pm, Sun. 11:30am-5:30pm.

Road Conditions: in CA, 800-427-7623; **Lake Tahoe Hotline,** 542-4636 (weather, entertainment, recreation, and restaurants).

24-Hr. Hotlines: Rape Crisis, 544-4444. **Mental Health,** 573-3251. **Gamblers Anonymous,** 800-287-8670. **Poison Control Center,** 800-342-9293. **Alcoholics Anonymous,** 546-1126 in North Tahoe, 541-1243 in South Tahoe.

Lake Tahoe AIDS Task Force: 542-0131.

Emergency: 911.

Clinic: Stateline Medical Center, 176 U.S. 50 at Kahle Dr. (588-3561). Open daily 8am-8pm. **Sierra Recovery Center,** 972-B Tallac Ave. (541-5190). Solutions for substance abuse.

Post Office: Stateline Station, 1085 Park Ave. (544-6162), next to Greyhound. Open Mon.-Fri. 8:30am-5pm. **General Delivery ZIP Code:** 95729. **Tahoe City,** 950 N. Lake Blvd., Suite 12 in the Lighthouse Shopping Center (583-3936). Open Mon.-Fri. 8:30am-5pm, Sat. noon-2pm. **General Delivery ZIP Code:** 96145.

Area Code: 916 in CA, 702 in NV.

Lake Tahoe is located 118 mi. northeast of Sacramento and 35 mi. southwest of Reno. **U.S. 50, Rte. 89,** and **Rte. 28** overlap to form a ring of asphalt around the lake. The versatile Rte. 89 is also known as Lake Tahoe Blvd., W. Lake Blvd., and Emerald Bay Rd. Rte. 28 masquerades as N. Lake Blvd. and Lakeshore Dr. The most-traveled roads to the lake are **U.S. 395** from Carson City and the Owens Valley area and **I-80** from San Francisco or Reno. In winter, tire chains are required and four-wheel-drive is highly recommended.

ACCOMMODATIONS

The strip off U.S. 50 on the California side of the border supports the bulk of Tahoe's 200 motels. Others line Park Avenue and Pioneer Trail off U.S. 50, which is quieter. Be wary of fluctuating room prices, a $20 room on Tuesday may jump to $80 on Friday. Also note that rates within Tahoe City are higher. Lately, many of the smaller budget motels have been replaced by luxury high-rise—and high-price— hotels. The remaining inexpensive hotels are booked solid on weekends year-round. Look for discount coupons (as much as $10 off weekday rates) in news- papers. The cheapest deals are clustered near Stateline on U.S. 50 and may display their prices. Rates will often increase $5-10 in summer and winter. (The nearby campgrounds are a good option in the warmer months.)

Edwards Lodge, in Tahoma along Rte. 89 (525-7207). 11 cabins for let during the summer, 7 during the winter. Large cabins with 2 stories, several beds, a kitchen, a big wooden deck, and a TV are nestled in a forest of pines. A good option for a group of 4-6. Convenient to many ski areas. Pool. Cash only. Cabins $70-85.

El Nido, 2215 Lake Tahoe Blvd. (541-2711). Pleasant, with some newly refurbished rooms. TV, VCR (rent movies from the front desk for $3.50), hot tub, and casino shuttle to Stateline. Singles $35, summer and winter $45 (includes a continental breakfast).

Lake Shore Lodge, 3496 Lake Tahoe Blvd. (544-2834). Cheap during the week but beware of seasonal and weekend rate increases. TV, pool. Mon.-Thurs.: singles $20; doubles $25. Fri.-Sat.: $25; $30.

Family Tree Restaurant and Motel, 551 N. Lake Blvd. (583-0287), at the Big Tree in downtown Tahoe City. Good location, good showers, and low prices. Off-season singles and doubles $29, winter and summer $50 and $55. (Calling ahead may save you money.)

Motel 6, 2375 Lake Tahoe Blvd., 95731 (542-1400). Standard-issue but very popular, especially on weekends. Pool and TV. Singles $28, $4 per additional adult. Reservations recommended.

CAMPING

The Forest Service at the visitors bureau provides up-to-date information on camping (see Practical Information, page 398). The helpful rangers supply excellent leaflets on the surrounding trails and wilderness areas. **Bayview** is the only free campground for miles (544-5994; 2-night max.; open June-Sept.). Advance reservations for all sites are essential (MISTIX at 800-365-2267 for state campgrounds).

Nevada Beach (573-2600), 1 mi. from Stateline on U.S. 50. Flush toilets and drinking water; no showers. Popular with families. Sites are 100 yds. from the shore.

D.L. Bliss State Park, Rte. 89 (525-7277), a few mi. west of Emerald Bay. Hot showers, blissful beach. 14-day max. 168 sites; $14, near-beach sites $19. Open June to Labor Day. Crowded and popular day-use beach. Use is restricted by the number of parking spaces. Arrive by 10am to stake your claim. The 9-mi. **Rubicon trail** (see Hiking, page 403), leads to Emerald Bay, Vikingsholm, and Eagle Falls.

Emerald Bay State Park, Rte. 89 (541-3030), 10 mi. west of town. Less shade and more rocks than D.L. Bliss. 14-day max. stay. 5-min. hot showers 50¢. Sites $14. Day use $5, seniors $4. Open June-Labor Day. See Beaches, page 402.

Sugar Pine Point: General Creek (525-7982), on the West Shore south of Tahoma. 50¢ hot showers, BBQ pits, flush toilets. Ideal for groups (up to 40 adults $60, 40 youths $30). Single sites $14, over 61 $13. Day use $5, seniors $4. Located in a pine grove, cross Rte. 89 to reach the lake.

FOOD

The casinos offer perpetual low-priced buffets, but there are restaurants along the lakeshore with reasonable prices, similar large portions, and much better food. Groceries are cheaper on the California side of Tahoe. Try **Raley's Supermarket,** 4018 U.S. 50 (544-3418; open 24 hrs.), or **Grass Roots Natural Foods,** 2040 Dunlap, one block east of the intersection of Rte. 89 and U.S. 50 (541-8059, open daily 9:30am-7pm).

The Bridgetender, 30 West Lake Blvd. (583-3342), in Tahoe City. The specialty is a ½-lb. burger ($4-6), and there is no lack of burger variety—try a Cajun bacon cheeseburger ($5.45). Enjoy your burger on the outdoor patio and watch the Truckee River roll by. A pool table, wide range of beers on tap, festive atmosphere, and late hours make the bar a hopping night spot. Open daily 11am-10pm. Bar open until 2am.

Red Hut Waffles, 2749 U.S. 50 (541-9024). Two thumbs and two fingers up. Don't let the exterior scare you away, inside it's quaint and homey. Delicious home-style cooking. Frequented by a young local crowd. Friendly staff. Plate-size waffle with fruit, whipped cream ($3.50). Boasts a 4-egg monster omelette for $5. (Finish it if you dare!) Bottomless cup of coffee 50¢. Open daily 6am-2pm.

Cantina Los Tres Hombres, Rte. 89 at 10th St. (544-1233) and Rte. 28 in Kings Beach (546-4052). $7.75 margarita pitchers (the standard flavors plus some exotic ones, kiwi, passionfruit, raspberry, etc.), free chips and salsa during happy hour (4-6pm). Dinners from $7. Lunch specials $6. Offers a variety of vegetarian dishes including large and yummy vegetable burritos. Healthy, athletic, outdoorsy crowd. Open 11am-10:30pm; bar open until 1am.

Firesign, 1785 W. Lake Blvd. (583-0871). The stone hearth, wood tables, and homey country-style feeling make this a popular restaurant. Out-of-the-ordinary cooking and outdoor seating. Dill and artichoke omelette, with home fries, toast, and muffin $6.50. Sandwiches $4.25. Open daily 7am-3pm.

The Siam Restaurant, 2180 U.S. 50 (544-0370). Thai restaurant with large portions at low prices ($5). Spicy dishes are a fire hazard. Open Mon.-Tues. and Thurs.-Sun. 11am-10pm.

Za's, 395 N. Lake Blvd. (583-1812), in Tahoe City behind Pete and Peter's Bar. Gourmet pizzas. Pizza by the slice $2.00. Pasta from $4. Available for take-out. Open daily 4:30-10pm.

SUMMER SIGHTS AND RECREATION

Beaches

Lake Tahoe supports numerous beaches perfect for a day of sunning and people-watching. On the south shore, **Pope Beach,** off Rte. 89, is wide and shaded by pines (less traffic on the east end). **Nevada Beach** is close to the casinos off U.S. 50, offering a quiet place to reflect on your losses. Campsites are available. Farther along Rte. 28, you will likely see cars parked on the shoulder away from beach access roads. It's a popular custom with locals to hike down the steep, wooded hill to the secluded shores below, often leaving their clothes behind. **Zephyr Cove Beach** is a favorite spot for the younger college crowd. Sand volleyball, beer, and bikinis make it the closest thing to Southern California in Lake Tahoe. **Hidden Beach** (just south of Incline Village) and **Kings Beach** (just across the California border from Hidden Beach) come complete with wave boards and the occasional bodybuilder. The nude beach near Hidden is a local gay and lesbian hangout. Kings has nets and a basketball court for pickup games. **Chambers Beach,** between Homewood and Tahoma, draws a sociable younger crowd eager to utilize the volleyball nets on the public side and the pool, bathrooms, and bar on the private side. **Meeks Bay,** 10 mi. south of Tahoe City, is quieter and has a sandy beach. In the summer, the Tahoe City and South Tahoe Bus connect here.

Magnificent **Emerald Bay** in the lake's southwest corner contains Tahoe's only island, **Fannette** (the most photographed sight in the area). No trip to Tahoe is complete without a visit to Emerald Bay. The park offers **hiking** and **biking trails** of varying difficulty, **camping,** (both open and designated), and terrain for **rock-climbing.** The alpine lakes behind the bay and breathtaking **Eagle Falls** make this a paradise of condensed natural beauty. Outdoor enthusiasts should note that the Emerald Bay State Park connects with the Desolation Wilderness. Those interested in Tahoe's history might enjoy the **Vikingsholm** tour and exhibit. See the best example of Scandinavian architecture in the U.S. and learn why there is a tea room nestled on top of Fannette's rocky exterior. (541-3030; open for tours mid-June-Labor Day 10am-4pm. $2, under 18 $1.)

Biking

Would-be cyclists without wheels become genuine cyclists in the Tahoe-Truckee area. The region supports numerous bike rental shops (usually lined up used-car-lot-style along the major roads). Sharing roads with automobiles can be dangerous, especially at the west shore and around Emerald Bay, where visiting drivers gawk at the dizzying heights and tend to swerve. The forest service office at Taylor Creek (see Practical Information, page 398) and bike rental places can give advice on safer and often more scenic routes. Rental rates run about $5 per hour, $20 per full day.

South Lake Tahoe boasts a variety of scenic trails for bikers of all abilities. **Angora Ridge** (4 mi.) is a moderate trail accessible from Rte. 89 that meanders past Fallen Leaf Lake to the Angora Lakes. **Fallen Leaf Lake** is a spectacular destination (by bike or by car) but watch out for vehicles towing boats and trailers on narrow roads. The steep mountain peaks that surround the lake are breathtaking when viewed from beside Fallen Leaf's chilly blue waters. For serious mountain bikers, **Mr. Toad's Wild Ride** (3 mi.) is a strenuous, winding trail that climbs to 9000 ft. It can be reached from U.S. 50 or Rte. 89, with parking located off the major roads. **The Flume Trail,** another advanced ride, completes a 23-mi. loop or can be enjoyed as a one-way 5-mi. trip to Marlette Lake. The trail can be accessed from Tunnel Creek Rd. near Incline Village.

Squaw Valley, northwest of the lake on Lake Tahoe Blvd., opens its slope to hikers and mountain bikers during the summer. The cable car (full-day pass $24) transports bikers and their wheels 2000 vertical ft. You find your own way down.

For those seeking less strenuous adventures, several paved bike trails encircle the lake. The **Pope-Baldwin Bike Path** (3.4 mi.) runs parallel to Rte. 89 along the South Shore while the **South Lake Tahoe Bike Path** runs from El Dorado Beach over the Upper Truckee River. Parking is available at the Truckee River Trailhead (Rte. 89, south of Tahoe City), Kaspian Campground (Skyland), and General Creek Campground at Sugar Pine Point State Park (south of Homewood).

No bicycle riding is allowed in Desolation Wilderness areas.

Hiking

Hiking is one of the best ways to explore the beautiful Tahoe Basin. Detailed information, including trail maps for all types of hikes, is available at the visitors center.

Those who want a leisurely excursion will enjoy the **nature trails** that explore the area around the center. The **Lake of the Sky Trail** (0.6 mi. round-trip) leads to the **Tallac Historic Site,** which features a look at turn-of-the-century Tahoe life. The Tallac Trail is disabled-accessible.

More experienced hikers may want to test their mettle on the moderate to strenuous trails on the West and the South Shores. Backcountry users must obtain a (free) **Wilderness Permit** for any hike into the Desolation Wilderness (see Practical Information, page 398). Due to sudden weather changes in the Sierra mountains, hikers should always bring a jacket and drinking water.

The nearly complete 150-mi. **Rim Trail** (577-0676) circles the lake and skirts the upper elevations of the basin. The **Rubicon Trail,** which runs 7.2 mi. along the south shore with trailheads at **D.L. Bliss State Park** and **Vikingsholm,** is a popular choice. (Vikingsholm is a Scandinavian-style castle built in the 1920s. See Emerald Bay, above.) The **Eagle Falls Trail,** accessible from the castle's parking lot, climbs through the Sierra high country to the Desolation Wilderness and to Eagle Lake. **Mt. Tallac** (trailhead across from Baldwin Beach on Rte. 89) rewards day hikers with stunning views of Fallen Leaf Lake and Lake Tahoe as it ascends the front face of the mountain. **Mt. Rose** (trailhead on Rte. 431 off Rte. 28 north of Incline Village) is another challenging day hike into the wilderness area. Along the West Shore, the **Meeks Bay Trail** (trailhead at Meeks Bay Resort off Rte. 89) offers a moderate hike past a chain of alpine lakes to Phipps Pass.

Echo Lake, off U.S. 50 south of Tahoe, is a condensed version of Tahoe; the gray stone and pine trees tower around the lake, providing an unmatched feeling of seclusion. There's a **chalet** (659-7207) on one side that sells snacks and boat service to the other side of the lake ($6.50 one way, 8am-6:30pm). Trailheads near Echo Lake lead into Desolation Wilderness areas (permit required). Another 2 mi. along U.S. 50, just before **Twin Bridges,** is the **Horsetail Falls Trailhead.** The waterfalls here make those at Eagle Lake look like a leaky faucet. To really appreciate them, you'll have to make the short (1.3 mi.) but tough hike through the canyon; the trail becomes slippery and steeper as it ascends. Inexperienced hikers should beware— every year, the Forest Service has to helicopter-rescue people.

Northwest of Lake Tahoe, the well-traveled **Pacific Crest Trail** crosses I-80 near Donner Lake, a few mi. west of Truckee; the small town is an ideal place to pick up the trail going north.

Rock-Climbing

Invaluable climbing information is available from **Alpine Skills International (ASI)** (426-9108) and most sporting goods stores. ASI offers all levels of classes ($75-400). The **Alpenglow Sport Shop,** 415 North Lake Blvd., Tahoe City (583-6917), provides free rock- and ice-climbing literature. **The Sports Exchange,** 10095 W. River St., Truckee (582-4510), rents climbing shoes ($3-7 per day) and also houses Gym Works, a challenging indoor climbing gym with over 2,500 square feet of climbing space and bouldering ($7 per day, $35 per month).

A host of popular climbing spots are scattered through the South and West Shores and the Donner Summit area. The **90-ft. wall** at Emerald Bay, **Twin Crags** at Tahoe City, and **Big Chief** near Squaw Valley are some of the more famous climbs in the area. The climbing at **Donner Summit** is world-renowned.

Climbing can be deadly and should never be undertaken without the proper knowledge, safety precautions, and equipment. Those unprepared for more dangerous climbs can enjoy terrific bouldering at D.L. Bliss State Park and at Split Rock in Donner Memorial State Park.

Water Sports

River rafting is an exciting and refreshing way to appreciate the Tahoe scenery. Unfortunately, the quality (and existence) of rafting on the American and the Truckee Rivers depends on the amount of snowfall during the preceding winter. Consequently, late spring and early summer are the best times to hit the rapids. If water levels are high, keep a look out for raft rental places along the Truckee. (Call 800-466-RAFT, -7238 for more information.) If California droughts continue to make conventional rafting scarce, all need not be lost. Floating around in an **inner tube** is popular with many would-be rafters. Make sure inner tubes are permitted on the body of water you select, don't go alone, and always know what lies downstream before you shove off.

In the summer, **Windsurf Tahoe** will rent you a board ($14 for first hr., $10 per additional hr.) and a wetsuit ($10 per day). You'll want to rent a wetsuit, since the average temperature of the lake remains a chilly 39°F year-round (though in the shallows it can warm up to 70°F). Most drowned bodies are never recovered, one tourist leaflet cheerfully reveals, because the cold prevents the decomposition that usually makes corpses float to the surface. In fact, the Native Americans who used to live around Lake Tahoe "buried" their dead in the lake; changes in water temperature and current movements have on occasion brought these perfectly preserved bodies to the surface.

Wildlife enthusiasts should visit the Profile Chamber near the Taylor Creek Visitors Center (see Practical Information, page 398), especially in late September and October. The creek literally turns red with tens of thousands of **salmon** swimming upstream. The chamber lets you get face-to-face with the fish as they prepare to spawn and die in the creek where they were born.

Several marinas rent out **fishing boats** and **paddle boats**. Stop by the Visitor Center for the latest information on fishing regulations. Licenses are available at local sporting good stores. Tahoe is a difficult lake to fish, be prepared to walk away empty-handed. If you feel the need for speed, get a group of people together and rent a **motorboat** and **water-skis** ($54 per hour) or a **jet-ski** ($45 per hour) at **Zephyr Cove** on U.S. 50 (702-588-3833). Zephyr Cove also rents out fishing boats and paddle boats. Incidentally, you're more likely to run into friendly monster "Tahoe Tessie" in gift shops than in the water.

Other Activities: Horseback Riding, Ballooning, and Bungee Jumping

Horseback riding is both popular and plentiful in the Tahoe area. Trails are often accessible to horses as well as hikers, ask the Forest Service for specifics. **Cascade Stables,** off Rte. 89 on Cascade Rd. in South Lake Tahoe ($15 per hr.; 541-2055), rents horses. **Camp Richardson Corral,** Rte. 89 (541-3113) in South Lake Tahoe provides trail rides for $16. **Horsefeathers,** a horseback riding outfit located at the **Tahoe Donner Equestrian Center** in Truckee (587-9470), gives breakfast tours on horseback ($24) and one-hour trail rides ($17).

Hot air ballooning is also available in the Tahoe Area. **Lake Tahoe Balloons** (544-1221) takes customers up 12,000 ft. for an incredible view of the region. Budget travelers beware, the prices, like the balloons, are high. A 30-min. no-frills ride is $95, for $20 more you can have a 45-min. ride, a champagne breakfast, and transportation to and from your lodgings. For the brave or insane, some companies offer **bungee jumping** from hot air balloons. Call **Adrenaline Adventures** (882-5867) for more information. Budget travelers shouldn't despair; there is more than enough beautiful scenery to be seen from the ground.

WINTER SIGHTS AND RECREATION

Downhill Skiing

When the snow falls, skiers in Tahoe have many options. There are approximately twenty ski resorts in the Tahoe area. Check the visitors center for prices and maps. Pick up a copy of *Ski Tahoe* (free) for valuable coupons and more information. All the major resorts offer lessons and rent equipment. Look for multi-day packages that offer significant discounts over single-day rates. Some may even include accommodations, meals, and equipment rental. Lifts at most resorts operate from 9am-4pm. (Arrive early for the best skiing and the shortest lines.)

Alpine Meadows (583-4232 or 800-824-6348) off Rte. 89 north of Tahoe City, is an excellent, accessible family vacation spot with more than 2,000 skiable acres. Alpine Meadows usually has the longest season of any resort in Tahoe. Conditions permitting and with the aid of snowmaking, Alpine Meadows stays open from October to May. Snowboards not allowed. Full-day lift ticket $41, ages 65-69 $29, 70 and over free, ages 6-12 $16. Basic ski rental $19, ages 6-12 $14, under 7 $8.

Squaw Valley (583-6985) off Rte. 89 just north of Alpine Meadows, was the site of the 1960 Olympic Winter Games. Squaw boasts 32 ski lifts and 4000 acres of terrain. The resort also offers night skiing, cross-country skiing and ice skating in the Olympic Ice Pavilion. Full-day lift ticket $41, seniors and children under 13 $5. Ski rental $20, under 13 $12. Snowboard rental $25.

Northstar (587-0257), on Rte. 267 and North Star Dr. in Truckee, 6 mi. northwest of Tahoe City. Skiable terrain extends for 1800 acres. Full-day lift ticket $40, ages 60-69 $20, 70 and over $5, ages 5-12 $18.

Heavenly (702-586-7000) on Ski Run Blvd. off Hwy. 50 is one of the largest and most popular resorts in the area with 23 lifts and 4,800 skiable acres. Reaching over 10,000 ft., it is also Tahoe's highest ski resort. Full-day lift ticket $40, 65 and over and under 13 $19. Ski rental $18.

Ski Homewood (525-2992) on the West Shore is a relatively inexpensive ski area. Catering primarily to locals, it offers excellent skiing at more affordable prices by avoiding the expensive frills of other resorts. Weekends and holidays: full-day lift ticket $29; 60 and over and ages 9-13 $10. Weekdays: $25; 60 and over and ages 9-13 $8. Ski rental $18, under 13 $12. Snowboard rental $25.

Sugarbowl (426-3651) on the backside of Donner Pass west of Truckee is another less expensive resort. Full-day lift ticket $35, 60 and over $15, children $8.

Mt. Rose (702-849-0747), 11 mi. from Incline Village on Rte. 431, and **Boreal Ridge** (426-3663), 10 mi. west of Truckee on I-80, both charge $31 for lift tickets.

Cross-country Skiing and Other Snow Activities

For cross-country skiing, head to **Royal Gorge** (426-3871) on Old Hwy. 40 just below Donner Summit, the nation's largest cross-country ski resort, with 70 trails totalling 300km in length. **Tahoe Donner** (587-9484), has 33 trails covering 70km of terrain. (All-day track pass $14, ages 13-17 and 60-69 $12, under 13 $9.) **Incline** (702-832-1150), in North Lake Tahoe, and **Spooner Lake** (702-749-5349), in Nevada where Rte. 28 and U.S. 50 meet, offer 35km and 25km of trails respectively.

The **Zephyr Cove Snowmobile Center** (882-0788) in the Zephyr Cove area of Lake Tahoe offers 2-hr. guided tours through the Sierra Nevada. (Single rider $68, double rider $95.) Some might prefer the slower pace (and quiet) afforded by **snowshoeing**. Rentals are available at many sporting goods stores for about $15 per day.

■■■ TRUCKEE

Truckee got its name from a classic tale of miscommunication. When a Paiute Indian greeted the Stephen-Townsend-Murphy party in 1844 with the word "Tro-kay" ("peace"), they thought it was his name and gave it to a local river, and in turn, to a lumber camp at the foot of the Sierras. Two years later, the ill-fated excursion led by George and Jacob Donner arrived from Illinois and stubbornly ignored the tribe's advice not to attempt to cross the Sierras in winter. That year snowstorms hit a month early, dumping 22 ft. by December 10. The 90 men, women, and children turned to cannibalism. Only half of the party survived.

With improved roads and cellular phones, wilderness exploration has become safer and Truckee has responded by becoming a rest stop for Weekend Warriors—skiers in winter, and hikers, river rafters, rock climbers, and mountain bikers in summer. Truckee's proximity to Lake Tahoe and numerous ski resorts makes it a good base camp for excursions throughout the Tahoe Area. If you are in Truckee, be sure and read through the Tahoe sections on Recreational Activities (page 402 and page 405).

PRACTICAL INFORMATION AND ORIENTATION

Visitors Information: Truckee-Donner Chamber of Commerce, 12036 Donner Pass Rd. (587-2757 or 800-548-8388), across the street from the factory outlet mall. Excellent brochures, maps, and photocopied handouts. Open Mon.-Fri. 10am-4pm, Sat.-Sun. 10am-3pm. Call for winter hours.

U.S. Forest Service Office: 587-3558, at the intersection of Rte. 89 and I-80. Info on Forest Service campsites. Open daily 8am-5pm.

Amtrak: 800-872-7245, in the visitors center. No lockers. To: Reno (1 per day, $12); Salt Lake City (1 per day, $111); Sacramento (1 per day, $41); San Francisco (1 per day, $49). Station is not staffed; order tickets in advance.

Greyhound: 587-3822, also in the visitors center. To: Reno (4 per day on the Gambler's Special—purchase a $15 ticket and the Reno Nugget will reimburse you $10 when you arrive); San Francisco (6 per day, $30); Sacramento (6 per day, $16). Open Mon.-Sat. 9am-5:30pm.

Bicycle Rental: Paco's Bicycles, 11200 Donner Pass Rd. (587-5561). Bikes $5 per hr., $22 per day. Weekly special (Mon.-Thurs.) mountain bikes for $12 per day. Open Mon.-Sat. 10am-6pm, Sun. 10am-4pm.

Equipment Rental: Sierra Mountaineer (587-2025), at the corner of Bridge and Jibbom (1 block off Donner Pass Rd. in downtown Truckee). Backpack ($8 per day), sleeping bag ($7.50 per day), 3-man tent ($21.50 per day), camping stove ($6 per day). Open 10am-6pm.

Laundromat: Launderland on Rte. 89, in the mall with Pizza Junction. Wash $1.25. Dry 50¢. Open daily 7am-10pm.

AAA Emergency Road Service: 583-6967; **Highway Patrol:** 587-3518, 24 hrs.

Road Conditions: 800-427-7623 or 530AM. **Weather:** 546-7251.

Rape Hotline: 544-4444. 24 hrs.

Hospital: Tahoe Forest (587-6011), at Pine Ave. and Donner Pass Rd.

Emergency: 911.

Post Office: Rte. 267 (587-3442), 1 block north of Commercial Row. Open Mon.-Fri. 8:30am-5pm, Sat. 11am-2pm. **General Delivery ZIP Code:** 96161.

Area Code: 916.

Truckee lies just off **I-80** in the woodsy Sierra Nevadas, 100 mi. northeast of Sacramento, 33 mi. west of Reno, and 15 mi. north of Lake Tahoe. Officially known as **Donner Pass Rd.** (and also part of Rte. 89 and Old Hwy. 80), **Commercial Row,** which parallels the railroad tracks, is the main drag.

CAMPING, ACCOMMODATIONS, AND FOOD

Accommodations are more numerous and often less expensive in the Tahoe area and especially in South Lake Tahoe, but Truckee has a few finds for the budget traveler. Twelve campgrounds lie within 10 mi. of Truckee, and range in price from free to $14. **U.S. Forest Service** sites (587-3558) are clustered northward along Rte. 89 at **Prosser Reservoir, Boca Reservoir,** and **Stampede Reservoir.** Prosser and Stampede charge $8, and Boca is free. South on Rte. 89 lie **Granite Flat** (3 mi.; free) and **Silver Creek** (9 mi.; $9). Three mi. west along I-80, **Donner Memorial** (582-7894) charges $14 ($7 for seniors) for popular, fully equipped sites. Donner Lake and Donner Summit make this the most scenic of the campsites. Reservations at all campsites are always a good idea, especially on weekends. Call MISTIX (800-444-7275) for reservations.

> **Star Hotel (and Hostel),** 10015 W. River St. (587-3007), 1 block south of the railroad tracks on Bridge St. Clean, rustic rooms with a *Little House on the Prairie* look. Kitchen privileges and a communal lounge. No smoking. Continental breakfast for hotel guests. Hostel beds ($11). Bring a sleeping bag or rent linen for $1. Private rooms with shared bath are available at the hotel ($35-66). Always full during the ski season; make reservations early.
>
> **Donner Spitz Hütte ASI Lodge.** At the end of Hwy. 40 (426-9108), in Norden. Only accessible by car. Swiss-style ski lodge on top of the historic Donner Pass, offers sleeping bag bunks and breakfast for $22. Open only in the summer and winter. Most guests are enrolled in the skiing and climbing programs offered by the lodge. Optional $12 family-style dinner. Call first and make a reservation.

Take your pick of touristy delis and greasy coffee shops, or else forage for yourself at the **Safeway** supermarket on Rte. 89, about 1 mi. west of downtown (open 24 hrs.). **Squeeze-In,** on Commercial Row, across from the Fire Station, offers 57 varieties of omelettes ($6-7) all squeezed into one little restaurant (open daily 7am-2pm). **Taco Station,** 10130 W. River St. (587-8226), designed to look like an old train depot, this restaurant serves up tasty and reasonably priced Mexican food (chicken taco $2.30; chicken, beef, or vegetable burrito $3; open daily 10:30am-9pm).

SIGHTS AND SEASONAL EVENTS

The local historical society has produced a short town trail (maps at the chamber of commerce) and maintains part of the **Old Truckee Jail** on Jibboom St. as a small museum (open Fri.-Mon. 11am-4pm; free).

The Donner Party is remembered in the **Donner Memorial State Park** (582-7892), 3 mi. west of Truckee. Take I-80 to the Donner Lake exit, then go west on old U.S. 40 until you reach the park entrance. The park includes the **Emigrant Trail Museum,** which documents the infamous incident, which began when 90 Midwesterners (led by the Donner family), headed for the comfort of California in April 1846. The ill-fated group took a "short-cut" advocated by the daredevil adventurer, Lansford Hastings. What Hastings didn't mention was that he'd never traveled the route. The party hacked through the wilderness, losing cattle and abandoning wagons as they went. The onset of an early winter at Truckee (later Donner) Lake in December devastated the group. Only 48 survived. (Museum open daily 10am-5pm. $2, under 12 $1.) There is another monument at the **Graves Cabin Site** on old U.S. 40, east of the I-80 interchange. Camping at the park is $12 per night.

March brings the **Snowfest** winter carnival (583-7625). Celebrations color the sky with the **Truckee Air Show** (587-4119) at the end of June. And the second week in August brings a **Rodeo** (587-2757). On **Christmas Eve,** sky-divers plummet to Earth in Old St. Nick's garb—watching it is a psychedelic experience even without chemical influence.

San Joaquin Valley

California, the land of trend setters, movie makers, and cutting-edge pop culture, has a way of attracting the spotlight. Yet, there is another side of California, embodied in the San Joaquin Valley, that quietly minds its own agribusiness. Lifestyles here are conservative, unadorned, and far from the spotlight that scrutinizes the Valley's western neighbors. The San Joaquin is known to most travelers as the "middle-of-nowhere" that separates Los Angeles and San Francisco. One of the most vital agricultural regions in the country, the valley stretches from the Tehachapi Range south of Bakersfield to just north of Stockton, ending where the Sacramento Valley begins. It is bounded on the east by the Coastal Ranges and on the west by the Sierra Nevada. The land is flat, the air is oven-hot, and the endless onion fields and rows of fruit trees are broken only by the razor-straight slashes of I-5 and Rte. 99. Although the valley's livelihood is the bread and butter of California's economy, nowhere else in the state does one feel quite so removed from things typically Californian.

A bit of advice: don't underestimate the **heat.** Temperatures reach three digits in early summer and sit there for week (even months). It's a dry heat, so it's bearable, but the sun will blister and dehydrate the unwary. Drink lots of water and fruit juices so you don't dry out. Winters can get very cold—especially at night—although snow on the valley floor is rare.

The valley is the only route to the national parks and forests of the Sierras, but the coast is practically inaccessible from here. Some of the larger towns such as Bakersfield and Visalia are peaceful places to live, but tourists intent on enjoying the best of California should stock up on supplies, rest well for the night, and move on.

■■■ BAKERSFIELD

Bakersfield may seem a bit surreal when approached from the freeway at night as motel signs light up the surrounding farmland. Most visitors to the town are truckers and stopover drivers.

Practical Information and Orientation The **Greater Bakersfield Chamber of Commerce,** 1033 Truxtun Ave. (327-4421) has a friendly, eager-to-please staff (open Mon.-Fri. 9am-5pm). The **Amtrak** station (395-3175 or 800-872-7245), sits on the corner of 15th and F St. six blocks west of downtown. Daily service is provided to LA ($20) and Yosemite ($44). (Open 4:30am-8pm and 9pm-midnight daily.) The **Greyhound** station at 1820 18th St. (800-231-2222), has buses to LA ($14) and Yosemite ($34). Public transportation is provided by **Golden Empire Transit** (327-7686; call Mon.-Fri. 8am-5pm for schedule and fare information). **Get-A-Lift** (327-4114) operates a shuttle service for disabled and elderly passengers. The **Bakersfield Checker Cab Co.** (327-8853), provides cabs at $1.80 per mi. Get a car of your own at **Rent-A-Wreck,** 1130 24th St. (322-6100), on the corner of 24th and M. For laundry needs, check out the **Stockdale Coin Laundry,** 3524 Stine Rd. (832-9585), in the Stockdale Shopping Center (open daily 7:30am-10pm). The **Bakersfield Memorial Hospital,** 420 34th St. (327-1792), on the corner of 34th and Q St. provides 24-hr. emergency care. In an **emergency,** call 911. The **police** can be found at 1601 Truxtun Ave. (327-7111). The **post office** is at 1730 18th St. (861-4346; open Mon.-Fri. 9am-5pm). The **General Delivery ZIP Code** is 93301. The **area code** is 805.

Bakersfield surrounds a section of **Rte. 99,** which bisects the city from north to south. **Rte. 178** leads out of town to the northeast by Kern River County Park, Lake Isabella, and Sequoia National Forest. From San Diego and Los Angeles, Bakersfield is an easy detour off **I-5** onto Rte. 99. It can be reached via **Rte. 58** from the Mojave Desert and Barstow to the east.

Accommodations and Food The ubiquitous **Motel 6,** 5241 Olive Tree Court (392-9700), has four locations in Bakersfield. The Olive Tree Ct. site has the cheapest rates (singles $24, doubles $28). The **Downtowner Inn,** 1301 Chester Ave. (327-7122), is convenient to bus and train stations (singles $33, doubles $43).

Come to **Maitia's Basque Restaurant,** 3535 N. Union Ave. (324-4711), to enjoy heaping lunch specials for $6. Weekend diners remain rooted to their seats long after eating to share in the lively conversation. (Lunch served Mon.-Fri. 11am-2pm. Dinner served Sun.-Thurs. 5:30-10pm, Fri.-Sat. 5:30-10:30pm.) For lighter fare, visit the **House of Marina** at 101 Union St. (633-5322). This vegetarian health food restaurant serves vegi-burgers, soups, and greens and doubles as a Christian-themed gift shop. (Open Mon.-Thurs. 9am-6pm, Fri. 9am-3pm.) Fans of Mexican food may want to check out **El Adobe Mexican Restaurant,** 2620 Ming Ave. (397-1932). Create a tasty two-item combo with rice and beans for $5 (open daily 11am-9pm). **The Chips Are Down,** 4166 California Ave. (324-3400), is a coffee shop that proves that even Bakersfield has a funky side (open Sun.-Thurs. 8am-9pm, Fri.-Sat. 8am-10pm).

■■■ FRESNO

What California's eighth-largest city lacks in exuberance it makes up for in efficiency; this is, after all, the banking center for the San Joaquin Valley. The trains run on time, the streets are freshly paved, and there are no lines at the post office. The new order has settled gracefully around the old, rather than barreling in and knocking it down. Fresno has art museums, a philharmonic orchestra, outstanding parks, and a rich history. This is also William Saroyan country, and Ansel Adams survived here for many years. However, Fresno is not Partytown, USA—you probably won't want to spend more than a day or two here. Nonetheless, this centrally located city makes for a convenient rest stop en route to or from the Sierras.

PRACTICAL INFORMATION

Convention and Visitors Bureau: 808 M St. 93721 (233-0836 or 800-788-0836). Professional staff divulges information on city and county businesses, events, and attractions. Not used to budget travelers looking for a place to crash, but they'll try their best. Open Mon.-Fri. 8am-5pm. **Fresno County and City Chamber of Commerce:** 2331 Fresno St.(233-4651). Open Mon.-Fri. 9am-5pm.

Airport: Fresno Air Terminal, (498-4095) Clinton Way, northeast of downtown (bus #26).

Amtrak: 2650 Tulare at Santa Fe Ave. (486-7651; for ticket info call 800-872-7245). 4 trains per day to San Francisco ($39) and Los Angeles ($38).

Greyhound: 1033 Broadway (800-231-2222). To: San Francisco (9 per day, $21) and Los Angeles (20 per day, $24). Luggage lockers for ticketed passengers only.

Fresno Area Express (FAX): 498-1122. 15 routes run north-south or crosstown, most begin at the courthouse (Fresno and Van Ness), or 2 blocks west at Fresno and Broadway. Fare 75¢, seniors and disabled 35¢, under 6 free. Transfers free. Service every ½ hr. on most routes Mon.-Sat. 6:30am-6:30pm, Sun. 10:30am-5:45pm. Route map is available at the main office in City Hall, 2223 G St.

Taxi: Yellow Cab, 275-1234. 24 hrs.

Car Rental: Action Rent-a-Car, 2100 Willow Ave. (291-1982). The cheapest wheels in town; $17 per day with 50 free mi. per day and 15¢ per additional mi. Must be 21 with a credit card.

AAA Emergency Road Service: 435-8680. 24 hrs. Members only.

Road Conditions (CalTrans): 800-427-ROAD, -7623. 24-hr. recording.

Weather Conditions: 442-1212 (recording). **Ski Report:** 443-6111 (recording).

Events: Beeline, 443-2400.

Public Library: 2420 Mariposa (488-3195), at N St. Open Mon.-Thurs. 10am-8pm, Fri. 10am-6pm, Sat. 10am-5pm.

Laundromat: Plaza, 3097 Tulare (266-1107), at U St. Wash 75¢, dry 25¢, soap 50¢. Open 24 hrs.

Herb Bauer's Sporting Goods, 6264 N. Blackstone (435-8600). Good equipment selections. Open Mon.-Fri. 9am-9pm, Sat. 9am-6pm, Sun. 10am-5pm. Fresno is a smart place to stock up on camping supplies before heading into the Sierras.
Gay Community Information Referral Number: 268-3541. Open Mon.-Fri. 9am-6pm. There is no Gay Community Center in Fresno.
HIV Nightline: 800-273-AIDS, -2437.
Rape Crisis: 222-RAPE, -7873. 24 hrs.
Poison Control Center: 445-1222. 24 hrs.
Medical Emergency: Fresno Community Hospital and Medical Center, (442-6000), Fresno at R St. Open 24 hrs.
Police, Fire, Paramedics: 498-1414.
Emergency: 911
Post Office: 1900 E St. at El Dorado Street (487-7700). Clean and efficient. Open Mon.-Fri. 8:30am-5pm. **General Delivery ZIP Code:** 93706.
Area Code: 209.

ORIENTATION

Fresno sits in the center of the San Joaquin Valley. Greyhound and Amtrak both link Fresno with San Francisco 185 mi. to the northwest and Los Angeles 217 mi. to the southwest. If driving, it is far simpler to drive into Fresno along Rte. 99 which runs north-south through the Valley than along any of the state or country routes that cross the Valley east-west.

Fresno is an ideal base for preparing a foray into the cool mountains of the Sierra Nevada. **Rte. 41** slices due north out of Fresno bound for Yosemite National Park, **Rte. 168** winds its way northeast past Huntington Lake and Shaver Lake through the peaks of the Sierra National Forest, and **Rte. 180** traverses the eastern portion of the valley before climbing into Sequoia National Forest and Kings Canyon National Park.

Rte. 99 cuts northwest-to-southeast across metropolitan Fresno; **Rte. 180** runs due east-west, and **Rte. 41,** north-south. The confluence of these roads marks Fresno's **downtown.** Before entering Fresno, arm yourself with a detailed map. The irregular road layout and one-way streets make downtown navigation bewildering. Streets parallel to Rte. 99 are imaginatively named after famous letters of the alphabet. **Broadway,** where you'll find the bus station, is where I St. ought to be; **Fulton St.** runs in J St.'s place; and **Van Ness Avenue** stands in for K St. Six blocks of Fulton Street are closed to traffic—this is **Fulton Mall,** a good reference point. **Tulare Avenue** is the main drag crossing the alphabetized streets.

Fresno has a high rate of violent crimes, even for California; as always, exercise **caution,** especially in the area around Broadway.

ACCOMMODATIONS AND CAMPING

An alternative place to stay, if you are on your way north, is **Merced,** an hour north of Fresno. Two HI-AYH hostels in Merced are the **Merced Home Hostel** and the **Yosemite Gateway Home Hostel** (both at 725-0407; $10, nonmembers $13). The hostels can also give you information about bus service from Merced to Yosemite. If Merced (pronounced mur-SED) isn't your bag, these are some reasonable places to stay in downtown Fresno. **Campgrounds** in the area serve the purpose—but it's not far to Yosemite, Kings Canyon, or Sierra National Parks...why stick around?

Travelers Inn, 2655 E. Shaw (294-0224). A cut above Motel 6; suitably decorated, spacious rooms. Color TV, A/C, pool, spa. Reserve as far as a month in advance for summer weekends. Singles $35. Doubles $42.
Motel 6, 933 N. Parkway Dr. (233-3913), off Rte. 99 at Olive St. exit; also 4080 N. Blackstone Ave. (222-2431), Rte. 99 at Rte. 41. A/C, pool, clean rooms. Security guard and 24-hr. desk attendant. Singles $24. Doubles $30.
Motel 7, 888 Broadway (485-7550), near the bus station. Don't wander alone in the neighborhood and use your room's door and window locks. Tastefully furnished. Singles $28. Doubles $34.

Fresno Downtown Motel, 2127 Inyo (268-0621), 3 blocks from Greyhound station; 5 blocks from Amtrak. Near convention center; neighborhood patrolled regularly by police. Pool, phones, HBO. Singles $32. Doubles $42.

Island Park Recreation Area, Army Corps of Engineers campground at Pine Flat Lake (787-2589), 17 mi. east of Fresno. Take Rte. 180 to Sanger, then northeast about 14 mi. to Trimmer Springs. Showers, but no hookups. 52 developed sites. 2-week max. stay. April-Sept. Sites $12.

Millerton Lake State Recreation Area (822-2225), in Friant, 20 mi. northeast of Fresno on the western shore of Millerton Lake. Accessible by Friant Rd. from Rte. 41. Fishing, hot showers and flush toilets. Arrive early or reserve through MISTIX (800-444-7275). Sites $14.

FOOD AND ENTERTAINMENT

Thanks to the county's rich harvests—and its Armenian, Mexican-American, Japanese, and Southeast Asian communities—good food abounds in Fresno. Ethnic restaurants cluster north and west of downtown. The old **Chinatown** west of the railroad tracks at Kern St. and G, F, and E St. has many Asian (mostly Japanese) and Mexican restaurants and stores; however, caution is advised after dark. American restaurants, clubs, and bars line N. Blackstone and Shaw, two main drags in the more affluent parts of Fresno frequented by CSUF students. The **Tower District,** bordered by Olive and Wishon 1 mi. outside of downtown, is the center of Fresno's nightlife.

The **farmer's market** (441-1009), at Divisadero and Tulare, downtown, is a misleadingly named indoor expanse of international shops and restaurants (open Mon.-Sat. 8am-9m). At the **outdoor produce market,** at Merced and N St. (open Tues., Thurs., and Sat. 7am-3pm), vendors drive pickup trucks into a parking lot, hang scales from their awnings, and sell, sell, sell.

Old Fresno Hofbrau, 2820 Tulare (264-4014), at R St. is the kind of place where bankers and ranchers (yes, ranchers) eat lunch. Dark and cool, even in the heat of the day. Turkey, ham, roast beef, or pastrami sandwiches ($5, with salad). Top it all off with a slice of apple pie ($1.75). The bar serves cold drafts ($1.50). Open Mon.-Sat. 11am-10pm, bar open Mon.-Sat. 7pm-2am.

Central Fish Market, 1535 Kern (237-2049), at G St., a few blocks from Greyhound. Both a full grocery store and a Japanese restaurant with clean, fresh, fish and produce. The small restaurant serves tasty Japanese meals (shrimp or chicken, veggies, rice, and salad) for $3-4. Market open Mon.-Sat. 8am-8pm, Sun. 8am-7pm; restaurant open Mon.-Sat. 11am-6:30pm, Sun. 11am-5:30pm.

Santa Fe Hotel, 935 Santa Fe Ave. (266-2170), at Tulare. Family-style Basque food served at long tables. The decor might not be much, but they make up for it in quality and quantity of food. Enormous lunches $7, dinner $8-12, under 12 half-price. Open Tues.-Sun. 11:30am-2pm and 5-9pm.

George's, 2405 Capital Ave. (264-9433), is an Armenian grill, with shish kebab sandwiches ($6.40) and daily lunch specials ($5-7) as well as cheap breakfasts. Open daily 6am-10pm; also has Galleria location open daily 6am-3pm.

Silver Dollar Hofbrau, 333 E. Shaw (227-6000). Sports bar: satellites, big TVs. Sandwich and salad $4.75. Open Sun.-Thurs. 11am-11pm, Fri.-Sat. 11am-11:30pm.

SIGHTS

Fresno's major museum is the **Fresno Metropolitan Museum of Art, History and Science,** 1555 Van Ness (441-1444), at Calaveras. The museum shows both regional and traveling exhibits and strives to incorporate video and interactive displays. It features a permanent exhibit on the life of acclaimed writer and Fresno native William Saroyan. (Open Thurs.-Sun. 11am-5pm. $4, seniors, students, and children $3. Wed. 11am-7pm free. Wheelchair access. Take bus #28.) The **Fresno Art Museum,** 2233 North First St. (485-4810), houses changing contemporary exhibits on Mexican and American Art ($2, students and seniors $1, under 16 free; open Tues.-Fri. 10am-5pm, Sat.-Sun. noon-5pm).

The largest of Fresno's many neighborhood parks is **Roeding Park,** West Belmont Ave., at Rte. 99 (take any northbound bus and transfer at Belmont). Pick up a free map at the city parks office (488-1551), near the Belmont Ave. entrance. Roeding's 157 acres enclose the **Chaffee Zoological Gardens** (498-4692), which contains the intriguing Winged Wonders Bird Show (open daily 9am-5pm; winter 10am-6:30pm; $4, seniors $3, ages 2-11 $2, under 2 free), the **Homer C. Wilson Camellia Garden** (open upon request; free), and a surprisingly varied topography. Eat in the grove of your choice: pine, ash, or eucalyptus.

California State University at Fresno, at Cedar and Shaw Ave., is the cultural heart of the city. Buses #28, 34, 38, and 39 all pass the university campus. The university supports serious theater, lectures, and entertainment (278-2078 for information center; open 9am-3pm). If you're in town during the second weekend in March, don't miss the **Rodeo** on the campus grounds.

Fresno takes pride in being the birthplace and long-time home of **William Saroyan,** the Pulitzer Prize-winning novelist and playwright. The convention center theater is named after him, and every May the city holds the **Saroyan Festival,** which includes writing contests and Armenian folk music.

If you're in the Fresno area with a car during the first two weeks of March, inquire about the **Blossom Trail** at the Visitors Bureau. It's a 67-mi.-long self-guided driving tour that highlights the wonders of the agricultural centerpiece of California.

The Squaw Valley Herb Gardens double as the studio of renowned Californian artists Nachtigall and Friesen. The **California Herbfest** (in April) and the **Raindance Festival** (in October) take place here. Reservations are a must (332-2909).

■■■ STOCKTON

Stockton lies off I-5 in the fertile farmland that surrounds the Sacramento River Delta. However, the city's agrarian roots have been greatly overshadowed by urban influences and the accompanying inner-city ills. Stockton's location makes it a convenient rest stop for some journeys, but be warned, Stockton has little to offer tourists and some sections feel decidedly unsafe. Our advice: keep right on driving or make it a quick stop.

Practical Information The **Stockton/San Joaquin Convention and Visitor's Bureau,** 46 W. Fremont St. (800-350-1987 or 943-1987; open Mon.-Fri. 8am-5pm), provides information on the entire region, maps, and brochures. **Amtrak** is at 735 S. San Joaquin Dr. (946-0517). Trains go to San Francisco-Oakland (4 per day, $16) and Los Angeles (3 per day, $58). **Greyhound** is located at 121 S. Center St. (466-3568), 4 blocks south of downtown. Buses leave for San Francisco (2 per day, $10); Los Angeles (10 per day, $38); San Diego (10 per day, $55). The train and bus stations can be frightening places to spend time, get in and out as quickly as possible, especially at night, and travel with a friend. The local bus system is **Stockton Metropolitan Transit District (SMART).** (943-1111; runs 5:30am-10pm on the half-hour; fare 75¢, ages 12-17 60¢, seniors 30¢.) For **American Express** go to 2321 W. March St. (952-6606; open Mon.-Fri. 8:30am-5:30pm). **Dameron Hospital** is located at 525 W. Acacia St. (944-5550). In an **emergency,** call 911. **Police** can be reached at 937-8877. The **post office** is at 4245 West Lane (open Mon.-Fri. 7:30am-5pm). The **General Delivery ZIP Code** is 95208. The **area code** is 209.

Accommodations Motels north of town on I-5, at the March Lane exit are nicer and feel safer than places in the city center.

Inn Cal Travelodge, I-5 and March Lane (477-5576), has peaceful rooms with A/C and cable TV (singles $39, doubles $47). **Motel 6,** I-5 at the Hammer Lane exit (931-9511), offers standard singles with A/C, cable TV for $28, $6 per additional person. To stay at the **University of the Pacific,** you must be a "guest of the university" and know an enrolled student. Contact the UOP Housing Office, 2nd floor, Bannister Hall (946-2331). Doubles with private bath cost $15, with kitchen facilities $15-20.

Food Stockton's diverse population has spawned a variety of good, inexpensive eateries. Fresh produce can be had at the **Farmers Market** on the corner of Pacific Ave. and March Lane (open Sun. 9am-1pm).

The **Cancun Restaurant,** 248 N. El Dorado St. (465-6810; open daily 11am-10:30pm), serves up good food in a family atmosphere. Lunch specials ($3) include your choice of burrito, enchilada, tacos or quesadilla with beans, rice, salad, and tortillas. For terrific burritos and tacos, visit the **Arroyos Cafe,** 324 S. Center (462-1661; open daily 9am-midnight). **Lekim's,** 631 N. Center St. (943-0308; open Mon.-Sat. 9am-10pm), dishes out authentic Vietnamese cuisine at reasonable prices. A seven-page menu gives you plenty of options, including sauteed chicken with coconut and curry, $5. (Open Mon.-Sat. 9am-10pm.) One of the classier restaurants in town, the **Alder Market,** 151 W. Alder St. (943-1921), is a refuge for gourmets. (Quiche of the day $6. Free basket of *foccacia* with your meal.) On some nights you can purchase a ticket for dinner theater at the Alder Market—$35 buys a hearty dinner and a two-hour show. The **Blackwater Café,** 912 N. Yosemite (943-9638), serves as a rendezvous for the young and hip of Stockton. It features a wide selection of espresso drinks ($1-3), cappuccino ($1.75), snacks, and imported and microbrewed beers. There's live acoustic music on some weekends and every Wednesday is chess night. (Open Mon.-Fri. 7am-midnight; Sat.-Sun. 10am-midnight.)

Recreation There are a few activities in Stockton to help stranded travelers wile away the time. Swimming, fishing, boating, and water-skiing are popular activities on the delta surrounding Stockton. For more information, contact the **California Delta Chambers,** 49 Main St., Isleton 95641 (916-777-5007). Those who are tired of traditional daytime fishing may want to grab a line, a pole, and a lantern and hit the water come nightfall. Nightfishin' is mighty big in the Delta.

Baseball fans can watch Stockton's own minor league farm team, the **Stockton Ports** (they don't go on strike). The Ports (944-5943), play at Billy Hebert Field, located at the corner of Alpine and Sutter Streets. The Philly Phanatic and other big-timers occasionally drop by for a visit. The **Stockton Asparagus Festival** is held every April. For more information call 943-1987.

NEVADA

Nevada once walked the straight and narrow path. Explored by Spanish missionaries and settled by Mormons, the Nevada Territory's arid land and searing climate seemed a perfect place for ascetics to strive for moral uplift. But the discovery of gold in 1850 and silver in 1859 won the state over permanently to the worship of filthy lucre. When the precious metal ran out, Nevadans responded by shirking the last vestiges of virtue—gambling and the quick 'n easy marriage and divorce became the state industries. In a final break with the rest of the country, Silver Staters legalized prostitution on a county by county basis and began paying Wayne Newton enormous amounts of cash for his concerts.

■■■ LAS VEGAS

The American dream—pioneers on the plain searching for a better life—has been stripped of spirituality, tubed in neon, and manifested in the raw promise of every pull of the slot machine. Even the most jaded traveler will be impressed by Los Vegas, if only by contemplating the electric bills generated by a town which runs non-stop 24 hours a day, 365 days a year. Since Bugsy Segal built his dream of a then-extravagant casino-hotel, the Flamingo Hilton, in the middle of the desert, Las Vegas has continued to exploit the American dream. But what this means for the budget traveler is, in some ways, a dream come true: all-you-can-eat buffets, luxurious hotel rooms for unbelievable prices, and free entertainment, as each casino is a self-contained amusement park with its own theme—circus, medieval castle, Roman Empire. For an education in tacky American culture, Las Vegas is crash course 101. If you aren't in Las Vegas to gamble you will quickly feel you have worn out your welcome and if you are in Las Vegas to gamble, odds are, you will quickly wear out your wallet. If the need to escape hits, take I-15 west toward the greener pastures of the California coast.

PRACTICAL INFORMATION

Visitors Information: Las Vegas Convention and Visitors Authority, 3150 Paradise Rd. (892-7575 or 892-0711), at the gigantic Convention Center, 4 blocks from the Strip, by the Hilton. Up-to-date information on hotel bargains and buffets. Open Mon.-Fri. 8am-6pm, Sat.-Sun. 8am-5pm.

Tours: Gambler's specials number among the cheapest and most popular ways to reach Las Vegas. These bus tours leave early in the morning and return at night or the next day; ask in L.A., San Francisco, or San Diego tourist offices. You can also call casinos for info. Prices include everything except meals and gambling.

Gray Line, 1550 S. Industrial Rd. (384-1234). Bus tours: Hoover Dam/Lake Mead Express (2 per day at 8am and noon, 5 hr., $18); the South Rim of the Grand Canyon (2 days, one night lodging and park admission included; bus leaves Mon., Wed., Fri. at 7am; singles $147, doubles $111 per person, triples or quads $99 per person; March-Oct.; reservations required). Mini City Tours (1 per day, $17.50).

Airport: McCarran International (798-5410), at the southeast end of the Strip. Main terminal on Paradise Rd. Within walking distance of the University of Nevada campus and the southern casinos. Taxi to downtown $23. Vans to hotels on the Strip and downtown ($5-7).

Amtrak: 1 N. Main St. (386-6896), in Union Plaza Hotel. Ticket office open daily 6am-7:30pm.

Greyhound: 200 S. Main St. (304-4561 or 800-752-4841), at Carson Ave. downtown. Ticket office open daily 6am-1am; terminal open 24 hrs.

Public Transportation: CAT, 228-7433. Route 301 serves downtown and the Strip 24 hrs. Route 302 serves the airport. Both are $1.50, seniors and under 17 50¢. All other routes $1, seniors and under 17 50¢; daily 5:30am-1:30am.

Car Rental: Rebel Rent-a-Car, 5466 Paradise Rd. (597-0427 or 800-372-1981). $20 per day; unlimited mi. within Clark County. Must be 21 with major credit card. $7 daily surcharge for under 25. $100 deposit.

Taxi: Yellow and **Checker Taxis** (873-2000). $2.20 flat, $1.50 per mi.

Help Lines: Rape Crisis Center Hotline, 366-1640. **Gamblers Anonymous,** 385-7732. 24 hrs. **Suicide Prevention,** 731-2990. **Gay and Lesbian Community Center,** 912 E. Sahara Ave. (733-9800).

Emergency: 911.

Post Office: 301 E. Stewart (385-8944). Open Mon.-Fri. 9am-5pm, Sat. 9am-1pm. General delivery open Mon.-Fri. 10am-3pm. **General Delivery ZIP Code:** 89114.

Area Code: 702.

Getting to Vegas from L.A. is a straight, 300-mi. shot on **I-15.** Las Vegas has two major casino areas. The **downtown** area, around **Fremont** and **2nd St.,** is foot-friendly; casinos cluster close together, and some sidewalks are even carpeted. The other main area, known as the **Strip,** is a collection of mammoth casinos on both sides of intimidatingly busy **Las Vegas Boulevard South.** Other casinos lie on **Paradise Blvd.,** parallel to Las Vegas Blvd. Many areas of Las Vegas are unsafe. Always stay on brightly lit paths and do not wander too far from the major casinos and hotels. The neighborhoods just north and west of downtown are especially dangerous.

Gay and lesbian travelers should know that it is illegal for homosexual couples to display public affection in Nevada and the law is strictly enforced with summonses and even arrests.

ACCOMMODATIONS AND CAMPING

Room rates at most hotels in Vegas fluctuate widely. A room that costs $20 during a special promotion can cost hundreds during a convention. To avoid unpleasant surprises, check local publications and *make reservations as far in advance as possible.* The earlier you reserve, the more chances you'll have of snagging a special rate. Coming to town on Friday or Saturday night without reservations is flirting with disaster. If you do get stuck, call the **Room Reservations Hotline** (800-332-5333 or 892-0777). Hotels use two rate ranges—one for Sunday to Thursday nights, a higher one for Friday and Saturday nights.

Hostels and Downtown Hotels

These meat and potatoes joints lack the creativity of Las Vegas's fantasy hotel world. However, the guaranteed low rates make up for the absence of neon.

Las Vegas Hostel, 1208 Las Vegas Blvd. S. (385-9955). Spartan, airy rooms. Free breakfast; ride board in kitchen. Tours to Zion, Bryce, and the Grand Canyon ($125). Check-out 7-10am. Office open daily 7am-11pm. Shared room and bath $9, private room with shared bath $20. Winter rates lower. Key deposit $3.

Las Vegas International Hostel (735-4050 or 735-2911). Call for address (unavailable at press time), free pickup and reservation. Common room, pool table, TV, kitchen. Free BBQ several times weekly. Free breakfast. Tours to Death Valley, Grand Canyon, Bryce and Zion ($49-$85). Dorm rooms with A/C and private bath $14, winter $10, $75 per week. Private rooms with TV and A/C $28, doubles $35.

Gold Spike, 400 E. Ogden Ave. (384-8444), in the downtown area a few blocks from Fremont. 109 rooms and 422 slot machines. Fixed rate $22.

Jackie Gaughan's Plaza, 1 Main St. (386-2110 or 800-634-6575). Towers over downtown with 1037 rooms and 1700 slots. Amtrak station in hotel lobby. Rooms Sun.-Thurs. $25-40, Fri.-Sat. $50. Prices can soar to $120, however.

The Strip and the Larger Hotel-Casinos

The strip is where the action is. Many of the hotels and casinos are within walking distance of each other. Remember to reserve a room as far in advance as possible. Fremont Street is great for walking but beware of hooligans.

Circus Circus, 2880 Las Vegas Blvd. S. (734-0410 or 800-634-3450). Major casino with 2800 rooms and some of the best prices. Rooms with TV for 1-4 people Sun.-Thurs. $21-42, Fri.-Sat. $55-75; holidays $65-85. Roll-away bed $7.

▶ **Frontier,** 3120 Las Vegas Blvd. S. Hotel-casino with nearly 1000 rooms and among the best rates on the Strip. Rooms Sun.-Thurs. $35, Fri.-Sat. $55.

▶ **Excalibur,** 3850 Las Vegas Blvd. (597-7777 or 800-937-7777). Giant white castle complete with over 4000 rooms. When paged, guests are referred to as "Lady" or "Lord." They beat this medieval theme into the ground. Rooms Sun.-Thurs. $39-60, Fri.-Sat. $79-90.

Binton's Horseshoe, 128 E. Fremont St. (382-1600 or 800-237-6537). Smaller, more intimate, loungey atmosphere. Jewish deli on the casino floor. Rooms Sun.-Thurs. $30-40, Fri.-Sat. $45-60.

▶ **Stardust,** 300 Las Vegas Blvd. S. (732-6111 or 800-824-6033). Titanic hotel with 2300 rooms and 1680 slots. Sun.-Thurs. $36-150, Fri.-Sat. $60-150.

Sam's Town, 5111 Boulder Hwy. (456-7777 or 800-634-6371). 5 mi. from the Strip. This self-sufficient gamblerama has 650 rooms and 3000 slots. Rooms Sun.-Thurs. $32-36, Fri.-Sat. $35-39.

Camping

Lake Mead National Recreation Area (293-8906), 25 mi. south of town on U.S. 93/95. Sites $8. (See Near Las Vegas: Lake Mead, page 418.)

KOA Las Vegas (451-5527). Take U.S. 93/95 south to the Boulder exit and turn left. Free casino shuttle. Pool, laundry, slots, and video poker. Sites $22, RV spots $25. A/C $3 extra.

Circusland RV Park, 500 Circus Circus Dr. (734-0410), part of the Circus Circus hotel on the Strip. Laundry, shower, pool, jacuzzi, and convenience store. Sun.-Thurs. $13, Fri.-Sat. $17.

BUFFET BONANZA

The hungry budget traveler is in luck in Las Vegas. In terms of sheer bulk for your buck casino-land is hard to beat. Almost every hotel-casino in Vegas courts tourists with cheap, all-you-can-eat buffets. In most cafeterias, buffet food is served non-stop 11am-10pm. The food is usually standard, heavy, greasy American, but always plentiful. Alcoholic drinks in most casinos cost 75¢-$1, but are free to those who look like they're gamblin'.

Caesars Palace, 3570 Las Vegas Blvd. S. (731-7110), Anything at Caesars is a step up from the competition. Even if you can't afford a room you can enjoy the "Platinum Buffet;" breakfast $7 (Mon.-Fri. 7:30-11am), lunch $8.50 (Mon.-Fri. 11:30am-2:30pm), dinner $12.75 (daily 4:30-10pm).

Circus Circus, 2800 Las Vegas Blvd. (734-0410), has the cheapest buffet in town; daily breakfast $3 (6-11:30am), brunch $4 (noon-4pm), dinner $5 (4:30-11pm).

Excalibur, 3850 Las Vegas Blvd. S. (597-7777), has the Round Table Buffet; daily breakfast $3.50 (7-11am), lunch $5 (11am-4pm), dinner $7 (4-10pm).

Luxor, 3900 Las Vegas Blvd. S. (262-4000), is a bit classier. Manhattan Buffet; daily breakfast $4 (7:30-11am), lunch $5 (11am-4pm), dinner $7 (4-11pm).

Treasure Island, 3300 Las Vegas Blvd. S. (894-7111), a couple bucks more of elegance with a choice of American, Italian, and Chinese; daily breakfast $5 (7-10:45am), lunch $7 (11am-3:45pm), dinner $9 (4-11pm).

CA$INO-HOPPING AND NIGHTLIFE

Gambling is illegal for those under 21. Casinos, nightclubs, and wedding chapels in Las Vegas stay open 24 hrs. Hotels and most casinos give "funbooks," with alluring gambling coupons that can stretch your puny $5 into $50 worth of wagering. But remember: in the long run, *odds are you will lose money.* (That is why the casinos try so hard to convince you to stick around.) Do not wager more money than you can afford to part with. Keep your wallet in your front pocket, and beware of the thieves who prowl casinos to nab big winnings from unwary jubilants. Some casinos (Circus Circus and Caesars) offer free gambling lessons; more patient dealers at slow tables may offer a tip or two (in exchange for one from you).

Caesars Palace, 3570 Las Vegas Blvd. (731-7110), is by far the most enjoyable casino in town. Marble statues grace hallways and lobby. Actors dressed in Roman garb wander through the hotel all day and night posing for pictures and uttering proclamations. A giant moving walkway sucks people into the palace from Las Vegas Blvd. The Forum Shops is an upscale mall inside the hotel with a "sky" which changes color to mimic the outside day. During the **Festival Fountain show,** statues stand, move, talk, battle, and shout amidst a fantastic laser-light show—ah, all the trappings and decorum of old Rome (shows every ½-hr. 10am-11pm). Next door, the **Mirage,** 3400 Las Vegas Blvd. S. (791-7111), includes among its many attractions: Siegfried and Roy with their tigers, a dolphin habitat, an indoor tropical rain forest, and a "volcano" that erupts in fountains and flames every half-hour from 8pm to 1am, barring bad weather. The new **Treasure Island,** 3300 Las Vegas Blvd. S. (894-7111), features pirate battles with cannons staged on giant wooden ships in a "bay" on the street. (Daily every 1½ hrs. from 4:30pm-midnight. Free.) The **Luxor,** 3900 Las Vegas Blvd. S. (262-4000), has boat rides through the Nile River and the hotel lobby (daily every 20 min. 9am-12:30am; $3). Or head to the **King Tut Tomb and Museum** which houses replicas of the artifacts uncovered at the pharaoh's grave (open Sun.-Thurs. 9am-11pm, Fri.-Sat. 9am-11:30pm; $3). The three 3-D **holographic films,** *Search of the Obelisk, Luxor Live,* and *The Theater of Time* have dazzling special effects. The **MGM Grand,** 3799 Las Vegas Blvd. S. (891-1111), has themes centered on Hollywood, especially the *Wizard of Oz.* **MGM Grand Adventures** has Disney-esque attractions that will convince you that you're not in Kansas (open daily 10am-10pm; $15, seniors $9, ages 4-12 $10). **Circus Circus,** 2880 Las Vegas Blvd. S. (734-0410), attempts to cultivate a (dysfunctional) family atmosphere; While parents run to the slot machines and card tables to wager the big bucks, their children can spend 50¢ tokens upstairs on the souped-up carnival midway and enjoy the titanic video game arcade. Two stories above the casino floor, tightrope-walkers, fire-eaters, and rather impressive acrobats perform from 1pm to midnight. Within the hotel complex is the **Grand Slam Canyon,** a Grand Canyon theme park with roller coasters and other rides—all enclosed in a glass shell. (Open Sun.-Thurs. 10am-10pm, Fri.-Sat. 10am-midnight; $15, under 12 $12.) **Excalibur,** 3850 Las Vegas Blvd. S. (800-937-7777), has a medieval England theme that may make you nostalgic for the Black Plague. The list goes on and on in a gaudy assemblage of theme casinos, each vying with the others to entice prospective gamblers.

Extra bucks will buy you a seat at a made-in-the-U.S.A. phenomenon—the **Vegas Spectacular.** The overdone but stunning twice-nightly casino-sponsored productions feature marvels such as waterfalls, explosions, fireworks, and casts of thousands (including animals). You can also see Broadway plays and musicals, ice revues, and individual entertainers in concert. Some "production shows" are topless; most are tasteless. To see a show by the musical stars who haunt the city, such as Diana Ross or Frank Sinatra, you may have to fork over $35 or more. (You'll have to liquidate your assets for a ticket if Barbra Streisand decides to tour again.) Far more reasonable are the many "revues" featuring imitations of (generally deceased) performers. In Vegas you can't turn around without bumping into an aspiring Elvis clone, or perhaps the real Elvis, pursuing anonymity in the brilliant disguise of an Elvis impersonator. A cheaper alternative might be a more intimate lounge act, some charging only a drink minimum. All large hotels have city-wide ticket booths in their lobbies.

Nightlife in Vegas gets rolling around midnight and keeps going until everyone passes out or runs out of money. The casino lounge at the **Las Vegas Hilton,** 3000 Paradise Rd. (732-5111), has a disco every night (no cover, 2-drink min.). At Caesars Palace (731-7110) you can rock the boat at **Cleopatra's Barge,** a huge ship-disco (open Tues.-Sun. 10pm-4am; free). The **Hard Rock Café,** 4475 Paradise Rd. (733-8400), features its trademark Cadillac awning and rock-and-roll memorabilia. (Meals served Mon.-Fri. 11:30am-11:30pm, Sat.-Sun. 7am-midnight; bar open as long as humanity continues to drink.) The **Fremont Street Blues and Reggae Club** (594-7111) on Fremont and 4th, rocks the casbah with live music every night (open Sun.-Thurs. 7pm-3am, Fri.-Sat. 7pm-5am). A popular disco, **Gipsy,** 4605 Paradise Rd. (731-1919), southeast of the Strip, may look deserted at 11pm, but by 1am the medium-sized dance floor packs in a **gay, lesbian,** and straight crowd. **Carrow's,** 1290 E. Flamingo Rd. (796-1314), has three outdoor patios, plus plenty of people and plants. During happy hour (4-7pm), the filling hors d'oeuvres are free.

Laughter may be the best medicine for a painful losing streak. The **Comedy Stop at the Trop,** in the Tropicana, 3101 Las Vegas Blvd. S. (739-2714 or 800-634-4000), offers three comedians for $16 (includes 2 drinks); two shows every night (8 and 10:30pm).

Fans of klassical music and kitsch will be delighted by the **Liberace Museum,** 1775 E. Tropicana Ave. (798-5595), devoted to the flamboyant late "Mr. Showmanship." There's fur, velvet, and rhinestone in combinations that boggle the rational mind and out strip the Strip. (Open Mon.-Sat. 10am-5pm, Sun. 1-5pm. $6.50, seniors $4.50, ages 6-12 $2.) The **Guinness World Records Museum,** 2870 Las Vegas Blvd. S. (792-3766), showcases freaky stuff from the most tattooed lady to the world's largest pizza (open daily 9am-9pm; $4.45, seniors, military, and students $4). Join the flying Elvises at the **Las Vegas Skydiving Center** (877-1010) which will take you on a free-fall almost 2 mi. down at 120mph (call for more info.).

■ NEAR LAS VEGAS: LAKE MEAD

Hoover Dam, the Western Hemisphere's highest concrete dam and the brainchild of President Herbert Hoover, straddles Nevada and Arizona. The 4.4 million cubic yards of concrete hold back the Colorado River, creating artificial **Lake Mead.** Built in the 1930s, the dam stretches 226 ft. high and 1,244 ft. across the Black Canyon. U.S. 93/95 runs right over the Hoover Dam. There is no public transportation to the dam. **Gray Line** buses and **Ray and Ross Tours** offers service from Las Vegas (see Las Vegas Practical Information, page 414). **Guided tours** through the powerplant in the bowels of the dam are offered continuously throughout the day. (45 min. tours given in the summer 8am-6:45pm; rest of the year 9am-4:15pm. $3, kids under 11 free.) Bring water in the summer—it can get up to 110°F. *Let's Go* does not recommend taking a piece of the dam home with you.

The **visitors center** (293-8367) lies on the Nevada half of the dam (open daily 8am-7pm in the summer; 9am-4:30pm rest of the year). A new center is being built and may be open in late 1995. There are several parking lots (free) at intervals along U.S. 93/95. Shuttle bus service is available from the more remote lots. Numerous National Park Service **campgrounds** lie within the recreation area. All cost $8 per night and are first-come, first-served. None have showers. The sites fill quickly on holiday weekends, so get there early. Backcountry camping is permitted and free in most areas. The most popular campground is **Boulder Beach** (293-8906), accessible by Lakeshore Road, located to the right of the visitors center off U.S. 93/95.

■■■ RENO

Reno, the "biggest little city in the world," feels like an outlet branch of Las Vegas. It has the same artificial, non-stop environment (the casinos are immune to the rhythm of the sun). Gambling is the city's staple. However, Reno has an ace that Las Vegas can only covet: its proximity to the Lake Tahoe and California. When dazzled by the innumerable flashing lights of Reno, it may be difficult to believe that the scenery and relative tranquility of the Tahoe area are only a short drive away. But they are.

Reno became famous in the early 1920s when several renowned public figures, including "America's Sweetheart" Mary Pickford, dropped by to utilize the state's lenient divorce laws. Reno's nouveau fame attracted the broke as well as the wealthy, stories of easy money spread and all types of people flocked to Nevada's casinos to test their luck. Today with only 40% of its workforce linked to the gaming industry, Reno is not yet one big casino. There are several notable cultural attractions in town and many intriguing destinations nearby.

PRACTICAL INFORMATION AND ORIENTATION

Visitors Information: Reno-Sparks Convention and Visitors Center, 4590 Virginia St. at Kitsky (800-367-RENO, -7366). Open Mon.-Sat. 7am-8pm, Sun. 9am-6pm. There is also an information booth downtown next to **Fitzgerald's,** 255 N. Virginia St.

Drinkin' an' Gamblin' Age: 21.

Cannon International Airport: 2001 E. Plumb Lane at Terminal Way (328-6400), on I-395, 3 mi. southeast of downtown. Services major airlines as well as Southwest Airlines, a no-frills, discount West Coast airline. Most major hotels have free shuttles for their guests; otherwise, take bus #24 from the visitors center (see above). Taxi fare to downtown from hotel taxi stands runs around $8-9.

Amtrak: 135 E. Commercial Row and Lake St. (329-8638 or 800-872-7245). Ticket office open 8-11:30am and 1-4:30pm. Arrive at least 30 min. in advance to purchase ticket. To: San Francisco (1 per day, $58); Sacramento (1 per day, $52); Salt Lake City (1 per day, $111); Chicago (1 per day, $217).

Greyhound: 155 Stevenson St. (322-2970), ½ block from W. 2nd St. Open 24 hr. To: San Francisco (14 per day, $34); Salt Lake City (3 per day, $49); L.A. (10 per day, $39). The station has lockers (0-6 hours $2; 6-24 hours $4), a minimart, and a restaurant. **Arrow Trans** (786-2376) and **Reno-Tahoe Connection** (825-3900) both offer bus service to S. Lake Tahoe ($18 per person, 4-person min., or $72 base fare).

Reno Citifare: Local bus system at 4th and Center St. (348-7433). Services the Reno and Sparks areas. Most routes operate 5am-7pm, though those in the city center operate 24 hrs. Fare $1, seniors and disabled 50¢, ages 6-18 75¢. Buses stop approximately every 2 blocks.

Car Rental: Apple Rent-a-Car, 550 W. 4th St. (329-2438). $18.50 per day, $140 per week. Driver's license required; no minimum age. **Lloyd's International Rent-a-Car,** 2515 Mill St. (800-654-7037 or 348-4777). Driver's license and major credit card required. $25 per day, $140 per week; 150 free mi. per day.

Laundromat: Reliable Cleaners, 727 W. 5th St. (323-6001). Wash $1.25, 10 min. dry 25¢. Open Mon.-Fri. 7am-6pm, Sat. 8am-5pm.

Road Conditions: Nevada (793-1313).

AAA Emergency Road Service: 826-5322 or 1-800-222-4357. 24 hr.

Northern Nevada Language Bank, 323-0500. 24-hr. help in 15 languages. **Crisis Lines: Rape Crisis,** 323-6111 or 800-992-5757; **Poison Control,** 328-4129; **Red Cross,** 322-3416. All lines are open 24 hrs.

Pharmacy: Cerveri Drug Store, 190 E. First St., at 1st and Lake St. (322-6122). Open Mon.-Fri. 7:30am-6pm, Sat. 9am-5pm.

Hospital: St. Mary's, 235 W. 6th St. (323-2041), near Arlington. **Emergency Medical Care:** 789-3188. 24 hrs.

Weddings: You can pick up a marriage license at the **Courthouse,** 117 S. Virginia St. (328-3274; daily 8am-midnight, including holidays), for $35. There are numerous chapels in Reno eager to help you tie the knot. **Adventure Inn,** 3575 S. Virginia St. (828-9000 or 800-937-1436), offers customers a free stretch limo service with marriage. In addition to a marriage chapel, Adventure Inn has 45 unique rooms and suites, all complete with spa or pool. The Super Space Suite features an 18-ft. pool, strobe lights, and fog dispenser. Marriage packages include a services in the Waterfall chapel complete with minister, music, photos, flowers, and a two night stay in one of the theme rooms. Prices for the full package start between $425 and $495. For those on a strict budget, the bare-bones service is available at the **Starlite Chapel,** 80 Court St. (786-4949) for $29. Free parking during ceremony is an added incentive.

Divorce: To obtain a divorce permit, you must be a resident of Nevada for at least 6 weeks and pay a $140 service fee. Permits are available at the courthouse divorce office Mon.-Fri. 8am-5pm. For the ceremony, there's **Divorce Made Easy** (323-3359) offering "While You Wait" service.

Post Office: 50 S. Virginia St. at Mill (786-5523). Two blocks south of city center. Open Mon.-Fri. 9am-5pm, Sat. 10am-2pm. **General Delivery ZIP Code:** 89501. General Delivery office open Mon.-Sat. 10am-5pm.

Area Code: 702.

Only 14 mi. from the California border and 443 mi. north of Las Vegas, Reno sits at the intersection of **I-80** and **U.S. 395,** which runs along the eastern slope of the Sierra Mountains. Scan West Coast big-city newspapers for **gambler's specials** on bus and plane fare excursion tickets. Some include casino credits.

Although the city sprawls for miles, most of the major casinos are clustered downtown along Virginia and Sierra Streets, between 2nd and 4th St. The adjacent city of **Sparks** also has several casinos along I-80. Many of the buses stop at the major casinos. The *Reno/Tahoe Travel Planner,* available at the Visitor's Bureau (see above) contains a local map and is an excellent guide to the city. The weekly *Showtime* lists current events and performers and is a prime place to look for gambling coupons. *Best Bets* provides listings of discounted local events and shows. *Sierra Outdoors* is a great guide for outdoor enthusiasts. These free papers are available in most hotels and casinos. Also check the local *Reno-Gazette Journal.*

ACCOMMODATIONS AND CAMPING

Downtown Reno is compact, and its wide and well-lit streets are heavily patrolled in the summer. But be streetwise and avoid walking near the northeast corner alone after dark. Reno has a battery of inner-city hotels, though most are unsavory. Head towards southwestern downtown for the cheapest accommodations. The prices below don't include Reno's 9% hotel tax but your bill will.

El Cortez, 239 W. 2nd St. (322-9161), 2 blocks east of Greyhound station. Pleasant management and terrific bargains. Rarely are city block hotels so clean and quiet. TV. City center is a 5-min. walk away. Check-out 11am. $27, off-season $20. Add $3 on weekends and holidays.

Windsor Hotel, 214 West St. (323-6171), 1½ blocks from Greyhound Station toward Virginia St. The hall showers and rooms are wonderfully clean. Fans turn lazily overhead in compensation for the lack of A/C. Laundry, amicable folk. 24-hr. desk buzz-in. Singles $22, with bath $24. Doubles $28. Fri.-Sat. add $4 to all prices.

Motel 6, 5 locations in the Reno area, each about 1½ mi. from the downtown casinos: 866 N. Wells Ave. and 666 N. Wells Ave. (786-9852 and 329-8681), north of I-80 off Wells Ave. exit; 1901 S. Virginia St. (827-0255), 1½ mi. down Virginia St. to Plumb Lane, near Virginia Lake; 1400 Stardust St. (747-7390), north of I-80 off Keystone Ave. exit, then west on Stardust St.; 240 S. Victorian Ave., Sparks (358-1380). Off-season (winter): Singles $28, per additional adult $7. Summer: Singles $30, doubles $36, triples, $39, quads $42. The place to stay if you're traveling with children; guests under 18 free when accompanied by parents. Make summer weekend reservations at least 2 weeks in advance, 1 month on holiday weekends.

Some of the best deals in town can be found in the major casinos, where all sorts of hidden discounts exist on rooms which ordinarily run $100 plus per night. Be nosy and ask enough questions (and pretend that you plan to do your fair share of gambling) and you just may find yourself paying $35 for a room on the 20th floor of the Hilton. Rates at **Fitzgerald's,** 255 N. Virginia St. (785-3300) can plunge to $18 in winter, $38 on summer weeknights. Thursday night specials abound. Usually there is a welcome center in the casino which can give advice on discounts and specials.

You can park your RV overnight at the **Reno Hilton,** 2500 E. 2nd St. (789-2000), full hookup $18.53. But, the **Toiyabe National Forest** begins only a few mi. southwest of Reno and has a much better view. If you're equipped to camp, you might make the drive to the woodland sites of **Davis Creek Park** (849-0684), 17 mi. south on U.S. 395 then ½ mi. west (follow the signs). Here you'll find yourself surrounded by pines and sage at the base of the Sierra Nevada's Mt. Rose. There is full service, including showers, but no hookups. (63 sites available first-come first-serve for $8 per site per vehicle, $1 per pet. Picnic area open 8am-9pm.) The nearby 14-mile Offer Creek Trail leads to Rock and Price Lakes and interlocks with the Tahoe Rim Trail. Camping and fishing on the trail are free but require permits (available at grocery and sporting goods stores).

FOOD

Eating in Reno is amazingly cheap. To entice gamblers in, and to prevent them from wandering out in search of food, casinos offer a range of all-you-can-eat cuisine. Bargain cuts of prime rib, all-you-can-eat buffets, and 99¢ breakfasts offer huge quantities of food at low prices, but buffet fare is often greasy, overcooked and tasteless. For better food, look past the casinos and try one of Reno's other inexpensive eateries. The large Basque population, which originally came from the Pyrenees to herd sheep in Nevada, brought with them a spicy and hearty cuisine locals recommend.

Louis' Basque Corner, 301 E. 4th St. (323-7203), at Evans Ave., 3 blocks east of Virginia, is a local institution. The friendly bar, family-style dining (everyone eats the same meal at one sitting), and hearty full-course dinner with wine make the price ($14, under 10 $6.50) happily bearable. Specialties include paella, beef tongue, and lamb. Open Mon.-Sat. 10am-2:30pm and 5:30-10pm, Sun. 4:30-9:30pm.

The Blue Heron, 1091 S. Virginia St. (786-4110), at Vassar St. For those seeking a change of pace from casino food and willing to travel about half a mile from the center of town, this all-vegetarian restaurant offers satisfying portions of healthy cuisine and tasty daily specials. Fantastic veggie burger on multigrain bun, $5.50. Filling entrees ($9) include soup or salad and delicious freshly baked bread. Also has a small enviro-market with appropriate vegetarian goods and a few microbeers. Open Mon.-Fri. 11am-9pm, Sat.-Sun. noon-8pm.

Santa Fe Motel, 235 Lake St. (323-1891), offers Basque dinners in a classic dining room with green and white checked tablecloths. Wood bar, ancient slots, and jukebox take you back to the '50s. Hefty portions, served family-style. A local favorite for good food and friendly atmosphere. Dinner $12; discounts for under 10. Open daily noon-2pm and 6-9pm.

Bamboo Garden, 231 W. 2nd St. (323-6333), next to the El Cortez (see Accommodations, above). This jungle-green spot concocts spicy Thai and Chinese lunches for $4-5 (Mon.-Fri. 11:30am-2:30pm). Entrees $6-10. Open daily 10:30am-10pm.

Fitzgeralds, 255 N. Virginia St. (786-3663). The 3rd floor feels a bit like the bridge of the *U.S.S. Enterprise* with its domed roof, but the setting is pleasant, the service good, and the American-style buffet greasy, cheap, and tasty. Breakfast (7-11am, $3), lunch (noon-4pm, $4.50), and dinner (4-10pm, $4.90). Beverages included.

Cal Neva, 38 E. 2nd St. (323-1046). 2-egg breakfast with ham, toast, and jelly (99¢),1-lb. prime rib dinner served 4-10pm ($7), includes rolls, all-you-can-eat salad bar, vegetable, and potato. Midnight sirloin steak special starts at 10:30pm, ($1.99). Seafood lovers will appreciate the lobster dinner (3 tails $9.60).

Latino Market, 895 S. Virginia St. (324-0933). Sells authentic Latin spices, flavorings, and food (*frijoles, chilates*) at reasonable prices. Watch for specials. Open Mon.-Sat. 10am-10pm, Sun 10am-6pm.

SIGHTS AND ENTERTAINMENT

Those new to the gambling scene might try the **Behind the Scenes Gaming Tour,** which takes you to the other side of the one-way mirrors, and instructs you in the rudiments of the games. Learn how the casinos take your money. The two-hour tours show the surveillance at CalNeva, go behind the scenes at four major casinos, and give tourists a chance to play a few practice games. ($6; tours leave from Ticket Station daily 12:30pm; 100 N. Sierra, 333-2858). Don't forget: gambling is illegal for persons under 21 years of age; if you win the jackpot at age 20, it'll be the casino's lucky day and not yours. (Compulsive Gambling Center Hotline 800-332-0402; 24 hrs.) Many casinos offer free gaming lessons and minimum bets vary between establishments—the best gamblers shop around before plunking down. Beer is usually free if you look as if you're gambling. Most casinos charge heftily for admission to their live shows, but **Circus Circus,** 500 N. Sierra (329-0711), has free 10- to 15-minute "big-top" performances (daily 11:15am-4:45pm and 6:10-11:40pm every ½ hr.) The carnival atmosphere makes it a popular destination for families.

Public displays of affection by homosexual couples are illegal in Nevada. Members of the same sex sharing a hotel room may be required to book a room containing two twin beds. However, Reno has a fairly large homosexual community and several gay bars. The **Chute No. 1,** 1099 S. Virginia St. (323-7825), is a popular gay bar for dancing (open 24 hrs.).

The **Fleischmann Planetarium,** at the University of Nevada, Virginia St. and N. McCarran Blvd. (784-4812), screens a neck-straining, 360° ceiling show. (Open summer Mon.-Fri. 8am-10pm, Sat.-Sun. 11am-10pm; spring Mon.-Thurs. 8am-5pm and 7/9pm, Fri. 8am-10pm, Sat. 11:30am-10pm, Sun. 11am-5pm and 7-9pm. Movie admission $5, seniors and under 13 $3.50.)

The local Basque influence is reflected in Reno's annual **Basque Festival** (785-3350), held in early August. This weekend of frenetic celebration features traditional contests, dancing, live music, and more food than the Circus Circus buffet. Classic car lovers may enjoy **Hot August Nights** (829-1955). This event in the first week of August celebrates America's love affair with the cars and the rock and roll of the '50s and '60s. The annual **Reno Rodeo** (323-0924), one of the biggest in the West, spreads over eight days at the end of June. Fans of free concerts will enjoy the **summer band concerts** in Wingfield Park at 1st and Arlington, sponsored by the Chamber of Commerce (June-Aug. Mon.-Fri. noon-1pm; free). Call 334-2260 for information. The **Hot Air Balloon Race** (826-1181, in Rancho San Rafael) and the **National Air Races** (972-6663, at the Stead Airport) draw an international group of contestants and spectators. In September, nearby **Virginia City** hosts **Camel Races** (847-0311), where camels and ostriches race through town. Take U.S. 395 south, then Rte. 341 about 25 mi.

Pyramid Lake

Thirty mi. north of Reno off Pyramid Way on the Paiute Indian Reservation lies emerald green Pyramid Lake. Named for the pyramidal rock island in its midst, the lake is open for day use and camping. **Camping** is allowed anywhere on the lakeshore, but only designated areas have toilet facilities. A $5 **permit** is required for use of the park and the area is carefully patrolled by the Paiute tribe. Permits are available at the **Ranger Station** (476-1155; open Mon.-Sat. 9am-5pm) and at **Long's Drugs** (590 E. Prater Way; 900 E. Plumb Ln.; 2300 Odie Blvd.; 5019 S. McCurran Blvd.) in Reno/Sparks. Surrounded by sagebrush-covered hills, this remnant of an ancient sea is a local escape from city life. It contains a hot spring and a series of rocks on the north shore which beg to be climbed. Those looking for solitude should try the south and east shores; the areas north of the ranger station are clogged with RVs.

■ NEAR RENO: CARSON CITY

It's not entirely clear why visitors still persist in coming here: there is only one big casino left in town; the Forest Service shrugs its shoulders when pressed for natural sights within a short drive; and the historical sights aren't that compelling. With over half the population linked to the government—the state legislature meets every two years whether it needs to or not—Carson City is perhaps the most balanced industrial and residential community in Nevada. Though the casino is always open, much of the town goes to bed early; residents are happy to leave it that way. For information on Carson City, contact the **Chamber of Commerce,** 1900 S. Carson St. (882-7474; open Mon.-Fri. 8am-5pm, Sat.-Sun. 10am-3pm). Carson City lies 30 mi. south of Reno on U.S. 395 and 14 mi. east of Lake Tahoe on U.S. 50.

GRAND CANYON

One of the greatest natural wonders in the United States, if not the world, the Grand Canyon is a sight that must be seen to be believed. The statistics are impressive, the canyon is 277 mi. long, 10 mi. wide, and more than a mile deep, yet the numbers mean nothing compared to the reality of standing on the brink of the plummeting cliffs. It is difficult to believe that the Colorado River which trickles along the canyon floor could have created the looming walls of limestone, sandstone, and shale, even over millions of years. Don't just peer over the edge—hike down into the canyon and observe the region's wildlife. The area is home to mountain lions, eagles, deer, and falcons. Most importantly, exploring the canyon will give you a true sense of the immensity and beauty of this natural phenomenon.

The **Grand Canyon National Park** consists of three areas: **South Rim,** including Grand Canyon Village; **North Rim;** and the canyon gorge itself. The slightly lower, slightly more accessible South Rim draws 10 times more visitors than higher, more heavily forested North Rim.

The 13-mi. trail that traverses the canyon floor makes a two-day adventure for sturdy hikers, while the 214 mi. of perimeter road prove a good five-hour drive for those who would rather explore from above. Despite commercial exploitation, the Grand Canyon is still untamed; every year several careless hikers take what locals morbidly refer to as "the 12-second tour." Please remember to observe all safety precautions and the rules of common sense.

■■■ SOUTH RIM

In summer, everything and everyone, on two legs or four wheels, converges around this side of the Grand Canyon. If you plan to visit during this mobfest, make reservations for lodging or campsites, and mules if you want them well in advance—and be prepared to battle crowds. During the winter there are fewer tourists, but the weather is brisk and many of the canyon's hotels and facilities are closed.

PRACTICAL INFORMATION AND ORIENTATION

Visitor Information: The **visitors center** (638-7888) is 6 mi. north of the south entrance station. Open daily 7:30am-7:30pm. Info. on road conditions surrounding the park and programs 24 hrs. Also information on tours, taxis, trips, etc. Ask for their *Trip Planner.* For written info. ahead of time, write the Superintendent, Grand Canyon National Park, P.O. Box 129, Grand Canyon, AZ 86023.

Lodging Reservations: For booking ahead of time write, call, or fax Reservations Dept., Grand Canyon National Park Lodges, Grand Canyon AZ 86023 (638-2401, fax 638-9247). For same-day reservations, it's best to call 638-2631 and ask to be connected with the proper lodge.

Nava-Hopi Bus Lines: 800-892-8687. Leaves Flagstaff Amtrak station for Grand Canyon daily at 5:45am, 8:05am, and 3:45pm; departs from Bright Angel Lodge at Grand Canyon for Flagstaff daily at 10:10am, 5:15pm, and 6:45pm. $12.50 each way, under 15 $6.50; $2 entrance fee for Canyon not included. Times vary by season, so call ahead.

Grand Canyon Railway: 800-THE-TRAIN, -843-87246. Offers historic steam train rides from Williams. The 2¼-hr. ride each way includes food, strolling musicians, and voice-over explanations of the scenery. ($47; teens $23.50, under 12 $14.50.)

Accessibility: 638-2631. **Free wheelchairs,** *The Grand Canyon National Park Accessibility Guide,* and free permit for automobile access to the West Rim Drive (summer only). Wheelchair-accessible tours are offered by prior arrangement.

Transportation Information Desk: In **Bright Angel Lodge** (638-2631). Reservations for mule rides, bus tours, Phantom Ranch, taxi, even helicopter rides. Open daily 6am-7pm. A **free shuttle bus** system operates along the West Rim Loop (daily 7:30am-sunset) and the Village Loop (daily 6:30am-10:30pm). A $3 hiker's shuttle offers transport between Grand Canyon village and the South Kaibab Trailhead near Yalci Point (leaves Bright Angel daily at 6:30am, 8:30am, 11:30am).

Equipment Rental: Babbit's General Store, in Mather Center Grand Canyon Village (638-2262 or 638-2234), near Yavapai Lodge. Rents comfortable hiking boots ($8 for the first day, $5 each additional day), sleeping bags ($7-9, $5 per additional day), tents ($15-16, $9 per additional day), and other camping gear. Hefty deposit required on all items. Open daily 8am-8pm.

Auto Repair: Grand Canyon Garage (638-2631), east of the visitors center on the park's main road (near Maswik Lodge), provides 24-hr. emergency service.

Road Conditions: Call 638-2631 or 779-2711 for recorded message.

Pets: They are allowed in the park, provided they are on a leash. Pets may not go below the rim. There is a **kennel** on the South Rim; call 638-2631, ext. 6039.

Medical Care: Grand Canyon Clinic (638-2551 or 638-2469), several mi. south on Center Rd. Open Mon.-Fri. 8am-5:30pm, Sat. 9am-noon. After-hours emergency care available.

Emergency: 911.

Post Office: (638-2512) next to Babbit's. Open daily 7:30am-5pm. Lobby open Mon.-Sat. 5am-10pm. **ZIP code:** 86023.

Area Code: 602.

There are two entrances to the park: the main **south entrance** lies on **U.S. 180N,** the eastern **Desert View** entrance lies on **I-40W.** To get to the Grand Canyon from points in California, drive through Barstow, at the junction of CA Rte. 58, I-15, and U.S. 40. From Barstow, the fastest route to the Canyon is I-40E, and then Rte. 64N. From Las Vegas, the fastest route to the Canyon is U.S. 93S to I-40E, and then Rte. 64N. The **entrance fee** to the Grand Canyon is $10 per car and $4 for travelers using other modes of transportation—even bus passengers must pay. Upon arriving in the South Rim, grab a copy of the small but comprehensive *The Guide,* available at the entrance gate and the visitors center (free).

ACCOMMODATIONS AND CAMPING

Compared with the six million years it took the Colorado River to cut the Grand Canyon, the six months it takes to get a room on the South Rim is a blink of an eye. Since the youth hostel closed in 1990, it is nearly impossible to sleep indoors anywhere near the South Rim without reservations or a wad of cash; if you arrive unprepared you can try the visitor's center, but the chance of finding a vacancy is slim. (see Practical Information, above). Most accommodations on the South Rim other than those listed below are very expensive. The campsites listed frequently fill by 10am in summer. Campground overflow usually winds up in the **Kaibab National Forest,** adjacent to the park along the southern border. Here you can pull off a dirt road and camp for free. No camping is allowed within ¼ mi. of Rte. 64. Sleeping in cars is *not* permitted within the park, but is allowed in the Kaibab Forest. For more information, contact the Tusayan Ranger District, Kaibab National Forest, P.O. Box 3088, Grand Canyon, AZ 86023 (683-2443). Backcountry campsites within the park require a free Backcountry Use Permit which is available at the Backcountry Reservations Office (638-7884), ¼ mi. south of the visitors center. You must reserve permits and campsites well in advance. Once reserved the permit must be picked up *no later than 9am* the day you plan to camp, or it will be cancelled. The Nava-Hopi bus pauses at Bright Angel Lodge, where you can check your luggage for 50¢ per day. Reservations for **Bright Angel Lodge, Maswik Lodge, Trailer Village,** and **Phantom Ranch** can be made through Grand Canyon National Park Lodges, P.O. Box 699, Grand Canyon 86023 (638-2631). All rooms should be reserved 6 months in advance for the summer, 6 weeks for the winter.

Lodging

Bright Angel Lodge, Grand Canyon Village. Rustic cabins with plumbing but no heat. Very convenient to Bright Angel Trail and both shuttle buses. Singles and doubles from $37, depending on how much plumbing you want. $7 per additional person. Historic cabins for 1 or 2 people are $61, $7 per additional person.

Maswik Lodge, Grand Canyon Village. Small, clean cabins with shower $48 (singles and doubles). $7 per additional person. Reservations required.

Phantom Ranch, on the canyon floor, a 4-hr. hike down the Kaibab Trail. Reservations required 6 months in advance for April-Oct., but check at the Bright Angel Transportation Desk (see Bright Angel Lodge) for last-minute cancellations. Don't show up without reservations made—they'll send you back up the trail, and it's a steep hike. Dorm beds $21. Cabins for 1 or 2 people $55, $11 per additional person.

Camping

Camper Village, 7 mi. south of the visitors center in Tusayan, offers both RV and tent sites from $15-22 per night. Call 638-2887 for reservations.

Cottonwood Campground, 16.6 mi. from the Bright Angel trailhead on the North Kaibab trail. 14 free sites; closed Nov.-April.

Indian Garden, 4.6 mi. from the South Rim Bright Angel trailhead, lies 3100 ft. below the rim and offers 15 sites, toilets, and water; open year-round; free.

Mather Campground, Grand Canyon Village, 1 mi. south from the visitors center. 320 shady, relatively isolated sites without hookups $10; 7-day max. stay. Make reservations for March-Nov. (call MISTIX at 800-365-2267 up to 8 weeks in advance). The rest of the year sites go on a first-come, first-served basis.

Trailer Village, next to Mather Campground. Clearly designed with the RV in mind. Campsites resemble driveways and lack seclusion. Showers and laundry nearby. Open year-round. 84 sites with hookup $17 for 2 people. $1.50 per additional person; 7-day max. stay.

Desert View Campsite, 26 mi. east of Grand Canyon Village. No hookups. 50 sites $8. Open mid-May-Oct. No reservations; nearby restrooms and phone; arrive early.

Ten-X Campground, in the Kaibab National Forest (638-2443), 10 mi. south of Grand Canyon Village on Rte. 64. Open May-Sept. on a first-come, first-served basis. Toilets, water, no hookups, $10. Group sites for up to 100 people available through reservations.

FOOD

Food on the South Rim is generally good and often inexpensive. **Babbit's General Store** (638-2262), in Maswik Lodge, is more than just a restaurant—it's a supermarket. Stock up on trail mix, water, and gear. (Open daily 8am-8pm; deli open 8am-7pm.) The **Maswik Cafeteria,** also in Maswik Lodge, has a variety of inexpensive options grilled and served in a delightful cafeteria atmosphere. (Open daily 6am-10pm.) **Bright Angel Dining Room** (638-2631), in Bright Angel Lodge, has hot sandwiches ($4-6; open daily 6:30am-10pm). The soda fountain at Bright Angel Lodge offers 16 flavors of ice cream (1 scoop $1) to hikers emerging from the Bright Angel Trail (open daily 11am-9pm).

SIGHTS AND ACTIVITIES

At your first glimpse of the canyon, you will realize that the best way to see it is to hike down into it, an enterprise that is much harder than it looks. Even the young at heart must remember that an easy hike downhill can become a nightmarish 89° incline on the return journey. Heat exhaustion, the second greatest threat after slipping, is signaled by a monstrous headache and termination of sweating. You *must* take two quarts of water along; it's absolutely necessary. A list of hiking safety tips can be found in the *Grand Canyon Guide,* available at the entrance gate and the visitors center. Overestimating your limits is a common mistake. Parents should also think twice about bringing children more than a mile down the trails—kids have good memories and might exact revenge when they get bigger.

The two most accessible trails into the Canyon are the **Bright Angel Trail,** which begins at the Bright Angel Lodge, and **South Kaibab Trail,** originating at Yaki Point. Bright Angel is outfitted for the average tourist, with rest houses stationed strategically 1½ mi. and 3 mi. from the rim. **Indian Gardens,** 4½ mi. down, offers the tired hiker restrooms, picnic tables, and blessed shade; all three rest stops usually have water in the summer. Kaibab is trickier, steeper, and lacks both shade and water, but it rewards the intrepid with a better view of the canyon. Remember that hiking back up is much, *much* more arduous and takes *twice as long* as the hike down.

If you've made arrangements to spend the night on the canyon floor, the best route is the **Kaibab Trail** (3-4 hrs., depending on conditions) and back up the Bright Angel (7-8hrs.) the following day. The hikes down Bright Angel Trail to Indian Gardens and **Plateau Point,** 6 mi. out, where you can look down 1360 ft. to the river, make excellent daytrips. But start early (around 7am) to avoid the worst heat.

If you're not up to descending into the canyon, follow the **Rim Trail** east to Grandeur Point and the **Yavapai Geological Museum,** or west to **Hermit's Rest,** using the shuttles as desired. Watch your footing. The Eastern Rim Trail swarms at dusk with sunset-watchers, and the Yavapai Museum at the end of the trail has a sweeping view of the canyon during the day from a glassed-in observation deck. The Western Rim Trail leads to several vistas, notably **Hopi Point,** a favorite for sunsets, and the **Abyss,** where the canyon wall drops almost vertically to the Tonto Plateau 3000 ft. below. To watch a sunset, show up at your chosen spot 45 minutes beforehand and watch the earth-tones and pastels melt into darkness.

The park service rangers present a variety of free informative talks and hikes. Listings of events are available at the visitors center daily. A free presentation at 8:30pm (7:30pm in winter) in **Mather Amphitheater,** behind the visitors center, highlights the canyon.

■■■ NORTH RIM

If you are coming from Utah or Nevada, or if you simply want a more solitary Grand Canyon experience, consider the North Rim. Here the canyon is a bit wilder, a bit cooler, and much more serene—and the view is just as inspiring as that from the South Rim. Unfortunately, because it is less frequented, it's tough to get to the North Rim by public transportation.

PRACTICAL INFORMATION AND ORIENTATION

Visitors Information: National Park Service Information Desk (638-2611; open 8am-5pm), in the lobby of Grand Canyon Lodge.

Health Services: North Rim Clinic (638-2611 ext. 222), located in cabin #7 at Grand Canyon Lodge. Walk in or make an appointment. Open Mon., Fri., and Sun. 9am-noon and 3-6pm, Tues. 9am-noon, Thurs. 3-6pm.

Public Transportation: Transcanyon, P.O. Box 348, Grand Canyon, AZ 86023 (638-2820), late May to Oct. Buses depart South Rim at 1:30pm, arrive North Rim at 6pm, and depart North Rim at 7am, arriving at South Rim at 11:30am ($60, round-trip $100). Call for reservations.

Accessibility: Many North Rim viewpoints, facilities, and some trails are wheelchair accessible. Inquire at the Information Desk (638-2611) for more details.

Emergency: 911.

Post Office: Located with everything else in the Grand Canyon Lodge (638-2611; open Mon.-Fri. 8-11am and 11:30am-4pm, Sat. 8am-2pm). **ZIP Code:** 86023.

Area Code: 602.

The **entrance fee** for the North Rim is $10 for cars, $4 for those on foot, bike, bus, or holy pilgrimage. From the South Rim, the North Rim is a 200-plus-mi., stunningly scenic drive. Take Rte. 64 east to U.S. 89 north, which runs into Alt. 89; off Alt. 89 take Rte. 67 south to the edge. Between the first snows (at the end of October) and May 15, Rte. 67 is closed to traffic. Then, only a snowmobile can get you to the North Rim. Park visitor facilities are **closed in winter.**

ACCOMMODATIONS, CAMPING, AND FOOD

Since camping within the confines of the Grand Canyon National Park is limited to designated campgrounds, only a lucky minority of North Rim visitors get to spend the night "right there." If you can't get in-park lodgings, visit the **Kaibab National Forest,** which runs from north of Jacob Lake to the park entrance. Camp in an established site, or pull off the main road onto any forest road and camp for free. Campsite reservations can be made through MISTIX (800-365-2267). If you don't have reservations, mark your territory by 10am.

Canyonlands International Youth Hostel (HI-AYH), 143 E. 100 South, Kanab, UT 84741 (801-644-5554), 1 hr. north of the Grand Canyon on U.S. 89, an equal distance south of Bryce, Zion, and Lake Powell. Dormitory-style rooms and buffet breakfast, all for the amazingly low price of $9. Reservations recommended.

Premium Motel, 94 S. 100 E. (801-644-9281), right around the corner from the hostel; head here if the hostel is full. A/C, phone, color TV. Singles $22. Doubles $26. Triples $30.

Grand Canyon Lodge (638-2611), on the edge of the rim. Call TW Recreational Services (801-586-7686). The pioneer cabins are the best deal at $59 for 4 people, $64 for 5. Frontier cabins are $49 for singles or doubles, $54 for triples. Front desk open 24 hrs. Western cabins and motel rooms are available at higher rates. Open daily 8am-7pm; late Oct. to mid-May Mon.-Fri. 8am-5pm.

Jacob Lake Inn (643-7232), 44 mi. north of the North Rim at Jacob Lake. Dining room, coffee shop. Cabins $57-64 for 2, $67-69 for 3, $72-74 for 4, $77 for 5, $82 for 6. Pricier motel units. Also offers 50 campsites (May-Oct. 15) at $10 per vehicle. Half the sites available first-come, first-served; others can be reserved through MISTIX (800-283-2267; $7 fee) or by calling Jacob Lake RV Park (643-7804).

North Rim Campground, the only campground in the park, has 82 sites on Rte. 67 near the rim. You can't see into the canyon from the pine-covered site, but you know it's there. Near food store; has laundry facilities, recreation room, and showers. Sites $10. Reserve by calling MISTIX (800-365-2267). Closes Oct. 21. Max. stay 7 days.

DeMotte Park Campground, 5 mi. north of the park entrance in Kaibab National Forest. 25 sites $8. First-come, first-served. Open camping also permitted in the National Forest surrounding the Grand Canyon; you must be ½ mi. from official campgrounds and ½ mi. from the road.

Both eating options on the North Rim are strategically placed at the **Grand Canyon Lodge** (638-2611; dining room open 6:30am-9:30pm). The restaurant slaps together dinners for $4.50-12 and breakfasts for $3.50. A skimpy sandwich at the "buffeteria" extorts $2.50. North Rim-ers are better off eating in **Kanab** or stopping at the **Jacob Lake Inn** for snacks and great shakes (meal about $5; open daily 6:30am-9pm).

SIGHTS AND ACTIVITIES

A ½-mi. paved trail takes you from the Grand Canyon Lodge to **Bright Angel Point,** which commands a seraphic view of the Canyon. **Point Imperial,** an 11-mi. drive from the lodge, overlooks Marble Canyon and the Painted Desert.

The North Rim offers nature walks and evening programs, both at the North Rim Campground and at Grand Canyon Lodge (see Accommodations, above). Check at the info. desk or campground bulletin boards for schedules. Half-day **mule trips** descend into the canyon from Grand Canyon Lodge ($35; 638-2292; open daily 7am-8pm). For river rafting info., pick up a *Grand Canyon River Trip Operators* brochure and select among the 20 companies which offer trips. These trips often last several days and usually need to be scheduled well in advance.

On warm evenings, the Grand Canyon Lodge fills with an eclectic group of international travelers, U.S. families, and rugged adventurers. A young crowd frequents the **Lodge Saloon** (638-2611) for drinks and a jukebox disco. (Open daily until 10:30pm, last call 10:15.) Others look to the warm air rising from the canyon, a full moon, and the occasional shooting stars for their intoxication at day's end.

BAJA CALIFORNIA

Peeled away from the mainland geological ages ago by earthquakes, Baja California is a 40,000 square mile desert peninsula between the Sea of Cortés on the east and the Pacific Ocean on the west. A solid stream of tourists flows from California into Baja to surf, fish, and drink to their hearts' content.

The completion of the Transpeninsular Hwy. has made it quicker to travel the peninsula by **car,** but be prepared to be cruising along at 60mph and suddenly careen into a rutted curve that can only be taken at 30mph. Remember that extra gas (unleaded) may be in short supply; don't pass a PEMEX station without filling your tank. If you will be driving in Baja for more than 72 hours, you need to get a free permit by showing vehicle title and proof of registration.

All major towns in Baja are served by **bus.** If you plan to navigate the peninsula by bus, be forewarned that you have to leave at inconvenient times, fight to procure a ticket, and then probably stand the whole way. A much better idea is to buy a reserved seat in Tijuana or Ensenada and traverse the peninsula in one shot while seated. Anyway you cut it, Baja beaches and other points of interest off the main highway are often inaccessible on public transportation; buses don't stop at coastal spots between Tijuana and San Quintín.

If your travels in Mexico will be limited to Tijuana and Ensenada you will probably not need to exchange your dollars for pesos; the vast majority of shops and res-turants in these cities are more than willing to take greenbacks. If you plan to travel farther into Baja prices will be quoted in pesos and some establishments will not accept U.S. dollars or if they do, will give you a bad exchange rate. The proper exchange rate is about 3.385 pesos per U.S. dollar. For extended forays into Mexico we recommend *Let's Go: Mexico.*

■■■ TIJUANA

Tijuana's skanky charm, cheap beer, and sprawling, unapologetic hedonism attracts tourists like flies. The city's banners boldly proclaim Avenida Revolución the "Most Visited Street in the World," and when you see the crowds, you'll believe it. If you crave a black-velvet portrait of Elvis, a fluorescent sarape, or other *objets d'art,* Tijuana is your promised land. Nightlife is as raunchy as it gets: every weekend, swarms of Californians and U.S. Marines drown themselves in drink and dancing at flashy discos.

Tijuana is good at being bad—it's been U.S. citizens' number one cheap party spot ever since Prohibition cramped the '20s. Today's Tijuana is the fourth-largest city in Mexico, and boasts the fastest growth rate (13.6%) of the world's major cities. As was said (affectionately, we believe) of Lord Byron, Tijuana is "mad, bad, and dangerous to know."

ORIENTATION AND PRACTICAL INFORMATION

Getting to Tijuana from San Diego is easy: take the red **Mexicoach** bus (800-628-3745) from its miniterminal beside the border (every ½-hr., $1.25). It will drop you off beside the Frontón Palacio on Revolución between 7th and 8th St. Long customs inspection lines when returning can be a hassle on busy days, but usually U.S. citizens buzz right through. Bring proper ID to re-enter the U.S. A passport will insure the speediest passage, but a U.S. driver's license will also do the trick. Driving across the border may seem appealing at first, but the hassles of obtaining Mexican insur-ance, not to mention the limited parking and rampant car theft, make this a *bad* idea. You must buy insurance—or face the possibility of having your car confiscated in the event of an accident. Save yourself a headache; leave your car in a parking lot on the U.S. side and join the throngs of people walking across the border. Parking rates start at US$3 per day and increase closer to the international line.

If you arrive at the central **bus station,** avoid the taxis' high rates and head for the public bus (1.20 pesos). When you exit the terminal turn to your left, walk to the end of the building, and hop onto a bus marked "Centro Linea." After a half-hour ride, it will let you off on **Calle 3** and any of the central Avenidas, most notably **Revolución.** Calles run east-west in numerical order; avenidas run north-south.

Tourist Office: Av. Revolución y Calle 1 (tel. 88-05-55). English-speaking staff offers maps and advice. Open Mon.-Sat. 9am-7pm, Sun. 10am-5pm. A booth on Revolución between Calles 3 and 4 has maps and may be less crowded.

State Attorney for the Protection of the Tourist: Staff takes seriously any problems tourists may encounter. Don't hesitate. Same address and phone number as tourist office (above). Answering machine operates after hours.

Customs Office: At the border (tel. 83-13-90). Open Mon.-Fri. 8am-3pm.

U.S. Consulate, Tapachula Sur 96 (tel. 81-74-00), in Col. Hipódromo, adjacent to the Agua Caliente racetrack southeast of town. In an emergency, call 619-585-2000. Open Mon.-Fri. 8am-4:30pm.

Currency Exchange: Banks along Constitución change at the same rate. *Casas de cambio* abound and offer better rates. Nearly every establishment will gladly accept US$, so changing money may not be necessary.

Post Office: Negrete at Calle 11 (tel. 84-79-50). *Lista de Correos.* Open Mon.-Fri. 8am-7pm, Sat.-Sun. 9am-1pm. **Postal code:** 22000.

Bus Station: tel. 26-29-82. Tijuana is a major transportation hub; buses leave frequently from the huge terminal. **Auto Transportes de Baja California** to Ensenada (15 pesos). **Greyhound** to San Diego (US$4).

Car Insurance: If you'll be driving in Mexico, spend US$5 per day to get insurance. There are several drive-through insurance vendors just before the border at Sycamore and Primero. They also distribute a free maps and travel tips.

Red Cross: In an emergency dial 132. Some English spoken. Open 24 hrs.

Pharmacy: Farmacia Botica "Sherr," Constitución 700 (tel. 85-18-20), at Calle 3. Some English spoken. Open 24 hrs.

Hospital: Hospital General, Av. Padre Kino, Zona Río (tel. 84-09-22). No English.

Police: Constitución at Calle 8. In case of **emergency** dial 134. For other matters, dial 38-51-60. There's always a bilingual officer at the station. If the police can't or won't help, try the tourist office and/or the consulate.

ACCOMMODATIONS

Tijuana's budget hotels cluster on Calle 1 between Revolución and Mutualismo. The busy area is relatively safe during the day. Come nightfall, however, the neighborhood becomes something of a red-light district. If possible, avoid walking here at night. When returning to your hotel, Calles 2 or 3 are usually safer than other routes.

Hotel Las Palmas, Calle 1 #1637 (tel. 85-13-48), between Mutualismo and Martínez. Rooms with sinks face a quiet courtyard. Communal bathrooms have at best tepid water. Happily roach-less. Check-out noon. Key deposit 5 pesos. Singles 30 pesos (about US$9). Doubles 60 pesos (US$18).

Hotel El Jalisciense, Calle 1 #1715 (tel. 85-34-91), between Niños Héroes and Martínez. Has all the necessities for a romantic evening: soft couches in the hall, large wood paddles on the keys, and *agua purificada* for post-workout refreshment. Bedrooms with private bath. Singles and doubles 60 pesos (US$18).

Motel Díaz, Revolución 650 (tel. 85-71-48), at Calle 1 next to Hotel Plaza del Oro. Playful pastel color scheme. Rooms feature 2 night tables, phone, and bathroom fans. Check-out 1pm. Singles and doubles 75 pesos (US$22).

Hotel San Jorge, Constitución 506 (tel. 85-85-40), between Calles 1 and 2. Bunker-sized rooms. Check-out 12:15pm. Singles 55 pesos. Doubles 75 pesos (US$22).

Hotel Perla de Occidente, Mutualismo 758 (tel. 85-13-58), between Calles 1 and 2. Distance from the center of the action makes this a quiet haven. Large beds,

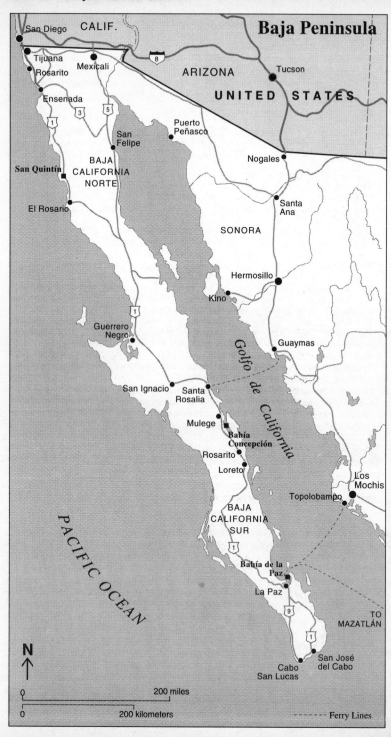

roomy bathrooms. Check-out 1pm. Singles 50 pesos (US$15). Doubles 70 pesos (US$20).

FOOD

Inexpensive *típico* restaurants line Constitución and streets leading from Revolución to Constitución. Even less expensive are the closet-size Mom-and-Pop mini-restaurants—most are probably safe. The best indicator is the overall cleanliness of the establishment. Do not drink tap water.

Los Panchos Taco Shop (tel. 85-72-77), Revolución at Calle 3. Orange plastic booths are packed with hungry locals eating cheap Mexican favorites. Tortillas freshly rolled on the premises. Breakfast served too. *Quesadillas* US$1.50, turkey omelette US$2.60. Open Mon.-Fri. 8am-midnight, Sat. 8am-3am, Sun. 8am-2am.

El Pipirin Antojitos (tel. 88-16-02), Constitución between Calles 2 and 3. Load up your tacos with a counterful of condiments. Seating under the orange arches. *Super quesadilla* 12 pesos (US$3.50). Open daily 9am-9:30pm.

Tía Juana Tilly's, at Revolución and Calle 7, buttressing the Jai Alai Palace. Still vaguely legendary. The bar—which now includes a restaurant, dance floor, and outside patio—has been generating high-action, high-price atmosphere since 1947. All national drinks US$3, beer US$1.75. Beef taco, chicken burrito, or cheese enchilada US$4.75. Open Mon.-Thurs. 11am-midnight, Fri.-Sat. 11am-3am.

Chico Pollo, Niños Héroes and Calle 1. Open-air restaurant specializing in roasted chicken. Whole bird with rice, beans, salad, and tortillas 24 pesos. ¼ chicken with all the above 5 pesos. Open daily 10am-8pm.

SIGHTS AND ENTERTAINMENT

Fun in TJ revolves around clubs and money and their concomitant vices—shopping, drinking, and gambling. Would-be shoppers should be aware that bargaining is expected at most streetside stands. If the price you are quoted seems high, offer what you would be willing to pay; odds are the vendors will accept. If they don't, someone else probably will; keep walking. Watch veterans (if you can spot any) for hints on what to do. **Teniente Guerrero Park,** Avenidas F and G, off Díaz Mirón, is one of the more pleasant parts of Tijuana and only a few blocks from Revolución. The much larger **Morelos State Park,** Blvd. de los Insurgentes 26000 (tel. 25-24-70), features an exotic bird exhibit and a picnic area. (Open Tues.-Sun. 9am-5pm. 3 pesos, children 1 peso.) The **Museo de Cera** (tel. 88-24-788), on Calle 1 between Revolución and Madero, is home to a motley crew of wax figures, including the Ayatollah Khomeini, Mikhail Gorbachev, and Tom Cruise. (Open Mon.-Fri. 10am-7pm. US$3.) The nearby **Mexitlan** (tel. 38-41-01), Calle 2 and Ocampo, provides a nutshell tour of Mexican historical, religious, and cultural monuments. (Open Wed.-Fri. 10am-6pm, Sat.-Sun. 9am-9pm. US$3.25.)

The cultish game of **jai-alai** is played every night at 8pm in the **Frontón Palacio,** Revolución at Calle 7. With the ball traveling at speeds reaching 180mph, jai-alai is reputedly the world's fastest game. The gambling is carried out in greenbacks. Seating costs US$3-15. (13 games Thurs.-Tues. 8pm-1:30am.)

Betting on greyhound and horse racing occurs at **Agua Caliente Racetrack** (tel. 81-78-11), also called the **Hipódromo.** (Races daily 7:45pm, Sat.-Sun. also at 2pm.) The enclosed Turf Club (tel. 81-78-11, ext. 681), has comfortable seating and a restaurant; grandstand admission is free. (Open daily 6-11pm.) To reach the track, hop on a red communal taxi on Revolución and Calle 3 (1.50 pesos).

Tijuana has two bullrings, **El Toreo de Tijuana,** downtown, and **Plaza Monumental,** 3km east on Agua Caliente. The former presents *corridas* (bullfights) on chosen Sundays at 4pm from early May to July; the latter is more modern, employs famous *matadores* and hosts fights from early August to mid-September. Tickets to both rings are sold at the gate and sometimes at a booth on Revolución between Calles 3 and 4 (tel. 85-22-10). Admission ranges from US$8-40. The same taxis that service the racetrack (above) will bring you to the rings. The Plaza Monumental may also be reached via the blue and white buses that wait on Calle 3 near Constitución.

The **Tijuana Centro Cultural,** on Paseo de los Héroes at Mina (tel. 84-11-11), awaits as "your window to all of Mexico." The center's **Space Theater** shows a film on Mexican culture and history (Mon.-Fri. hourly 3-9pm, Sat.-Sun. hourly 11am-9pm; 14 pesos). Also look for the impressive exhibit on Mexican history and geography. (Open daily 11am-7pm. US$1, free with movie admission.) A performance center (**Sala de Espectáculos**) and theater (**Caracol al Aire Libre**) host visiting cultural attractions, including the **Ballet Folklórico,** *mariachis,* and theater.

All of this is fine and dandy, but if you're here to party, a brief stroll down Revolución at dusk will get you bombarded by thumping music and abrasive club promoters hawking two-for-one margaritas.

NIGHTLIFE

Clubs may check ID (the drinking age is 18). Criteria for what's acceptable varies. Many places body-search entering patrons for firearms.

People's Sports 'N' Rock (tel. 85-45-71), Revolución and Calle 2. Teeming masses of half-naked people writhe on the dance floor, while mellower crowd enjoys margaritas (US$3.75). No cover. Open Sun.-Thurs. 9am-2am, Fri.-Sat. 9am-4am.

Tecate Joe's (tel. 85-38-72), Revolución and Calle 2, across the street from People's Sports 'N' Rock. Chaos. Waiters blow away on shrill soccer whistles while pummeling their way through an older crowd sweating missiles on the tiny dance floor. No cover. Open Mon.-Fri. 11am-2am, Sat.-Sun. 11am-4am.

Tilly's 5th Avenue (tel. 88-29-93), Revolución and Calle 5. Wooden dance floor in the center resembles a boxing ring. Beer US$1, margaritas US$3. Cover Fri.-Sat. US$5. Open Mon.-Thurs. 11am-2am, Fri.-Sun. 11am-4am.

Magic O (tel. 88-29-93), Revolución and Calle 5. More whistling waiters. Wear your sunglasses lest you spin away from the hallucinogenic color scheme and checkered floors. No cover. Open Sun.-Thurs. 5pm-3am, Fri.-Sat. 5pm-5am.

Caves (tel. 88-05-09), Revolución and Calle 5. Flintstone-like entrance leads to a dark but airy bar and disco. Smiling management stalks with tequila, searching for the next customer. No cover. Open Sun.-Thurs. 11am-2am, Fri.-Sat. 11am-4am.

■■■ ENSENADA

The secret is out—beachless port city Ensenada is fast becoming a weekend hot spot. The masses of Californians that arrive every Friday night have *gringo*-ized Ensenada to an extreme degree; everyone speaks English and the store clerks need calculators if you try to buy something with pesos. Still, Ensenada is less brash than Tijuana, and pleasant when the *gringos* go home and the cool sea breeze kicks in.

Orientation and Practical Information Ensenada is 108km south of Tijuana on Route 1. **Buses** from Tijuana arrive at the main terminal (tel. 8-67-70), at Calle 11 and Riveroll. **ABC Autotransportes** runs buses every hour on the half-hour to Tijuana (6:30am-8:30pm, 1¼hr., 18 pesos). **Transportes Aragon** (tel. 4-07-17), on Riveroll between Octava and Novena, also has buses to Tijuana (hourly 6am-9pm; 15 pesos, students and seniors half-price). Turn right as you come out the door of the main terminal and travel 10 blocks to **Mateos** (also called First), the main tourist drag. Five blocks to the left along Mateos you'll find inexpensive motels. The **tourist office,** at Blvds. Castero and Gatelum (tel. 8-24-11), dispenses brochures from expensive hotels, some town maps, and Baja travel material. (Open Mon.-Fri. 9am-7pm, Sat.-Sun. 9am-3pm.) The **Chamber of Commerce,** Mateos 693 (tel. 8-37-70), at Macheros, is closer to the center of town, with brochures and city maps. (Open Mon.-Fri. 8:30am-2pm and 4-6:30pm.) Banks offering **currency exchange** clump along Av. Juárez, but few will exchange traveler's checks. **Bancomer,** on Juárez at Ruíz (tel. 8-11-08), is the best choice. All open Mon.-Fri. 9am-1:30pm. **Señor Barquet Jaime Ozuna Rental Agency,** Alvarado 143b (tel. 8-32-75), rents cars for 140 pesos per day, including insurance (mileage extra). For medical care, contact the **Red Cross,** on Blvd. de Jesús Clark at Flores (tel. 4-45-85). **Farmacia Del**

Sol, Cortés at Reforma (tel. 6-37-75), in the Limón shopping center, is open 24 hrs. **Hospital General,** Transpeninsular Hwy. km111 (tel. 6-78-00), is also open 24 hrs. In an **emergency,** dial 132. **Police** are available at Calle 9 at Espinoza (tel. 6-24-21). The **post office** is on Mateos at Club Rotario 93 (tel. 6-10-88), 1 block past the *arroyo*. (*Lista de Correos*. Open Mon.-Fri. 8am-7pm, Sat.-Sun. 9am-1pm. **Postal code: 22800.**) The **telephone code** is 617.

Accommodations and Food Most rooms lie about a 20-minute hike from the beaches and a good 10 minutes from the club scene. Owners usually accept both greenbacks and pesos. **Motel Pancho** (tel. 8-16-25), on Alvarado at Calle 2, one block off Mateos, has big rooms and clean bathrooms. It's also close to popular bars. (Check-out noon. Singles US$17. Doubles US$25.) **Hotel Colonial,** Miramar 120 (tel. 8-16-15), at Mateos, outfits rooms with large dressers and mirrors. (Singles US$15. Doubles US$18. Traveler's checks accepted.) The rooms at **Hotel Rosita** (tel. 8-16-25), on Gastelum between Calles 3 and 4, are dark, but the beds hold people and the toilets flush. (Singles for 1 or 2 people 20 pesos (US$6), with private bath 30 pesos (US$9). Doubles for 2 to 3 with bath 35 pesos (US$10).

The cheapest restaurants are along Juárez and Espinoza; those on Mateos and near the water jazz up the surroundings and prices for *los turistas*. Fresh fruit stands abound, but the best bargains are at the large supermarkets on Gastelum. The tastiest grilled tacos in Baja California are available at **Asadero Chispa,** on Mateos at Guadalupe. Scrumptious burritos made with whole beans and beef strips on 1-ft.-wide tortillas are 10 pesos. Tacos are 3.50 pesos. (Open Tues.-Sun. 11am-11pm.) **Cafetería Monique Colonial** (tel. 6-40-41), Calle 9 and Espinoza, offers cheap, middle-brow food. (Breaded steak with salad and fries 19.50 pesos. Open Mon.-Sat. 6am-10pm, Sun. 6am-3pm.) Rustic **Restaurante El Charro,** Mateos 475 (tel. 8-38-81), between Bastelum and Ruíz, excites the palate with half-chickens served with fries and steaming tortillas for 18 pesos. (Open daily 11am-2am.) Chefs at **Las Parillas** (tel. 6-17-28), Espinoza at Calle 7, grill up fresh meat cutlets on the flaming pit. (*Super hamburguesa* 9 pesos. Open daily noon-11:45pm.)

Sights Seeing Ensenada requires more than a quick cruise down Mateos. To see the entire city, climb the **Chapultepec Hills.** The steep road leading to the top begins at the foot of Calle 2. Less taxing is a stroll down **Blvd. Castero,** where herds of curio shops make for hours of mindless shopping fun. **Sulivan Unidad Deportiva** (tel. 6-44-45), on Del Mar and Mateos, is a simply massive sports complex (1 peso). Nearby roller-skating rink **Roller Ensenada** (tel. 6-01-59), is frequented by gyrating teens whirling to late-80s pop hits. (Open Tues.-Sun. 10am-11pm.) **Cine Ensenada** (tel. 8-30-40), shows Mexican and American feature films daily from 4pm to 8:30pm. (Thurs.-Tues. 7 pesos, Wed. 3.50 pesos.)

To find good sand, beachgoers must travel outside the city. About 11km north of town is **Playa San Miguel,** accessible by buses marked "San Miguel" departing from Gastelum and Costero. Clean but crowded **Playa Estero,** 8km south of Ensenada, can be reached by buses departing from the Plaza Civica.

Entertainment Most popular hangouts along Mateos are members of that common hybrid species, the restaurant/bar/disco. After 8pm, the hybrids metamorphisize to full-fledged dance club monsters. Better known than Ensenada itself is **Hussong's Cantina,** on Ruíz between Mateos and Calle 2 (tel. 8-32-10). It's the prototypical Mexican watering hole. **Papas and Beer** (tel. 4-01-45), across the street, is a high-tech music emporium where the twentysomething crowd swills margaritas (US$4). There's plenty of dancing here after 10pm on Thursday theme nights. Ladies' night on Fridays includes Chippendale-style dancers. (Cover US$5 Thurs.-Sat. after 8pm. Open daily noon-3am.)

HAWAII

No alien land in all the world has any deep, strong charm for me but that one, no other land could so longingly and beseechingly haunt me, sleeping and waking, through half a lifetime, as that one has done. Other things leave me, but it abides; other things change, but it remains the same.... In my nostrils still lives the breath of flowers that perished twenty years ago.

—Mark Twain

Hawaii, 2400 mi. off mainland America, is both physically and psychologically set apart from the rest of the United States. Here, as nowhere else, you will find lush vegetation, expansive beaches, towering surf, and sultry breezes that keep the weather wonderful year-round. Acres of untainted tropical forest border luxurious resort areas and bustling urban enclaves. Meanwhile, active volcanoes crag the horizon and release billows of grey into the air. If it sounds Elysian, that's because it *is*.

The state's cultural geography is as varied as that of the land. Hawaii is one of the most ethnically diverse regions in the world; as a community with no clear racial majority, the state serves as a bridge between East and West as well as North and South, and as a melting pot for a multitude of cultures. This diverse cultural heritage expresses itself in the arts, literature, and cuisine of Hawaii's residents.

132 islands comprise the Hawaiian chain, though only seven are inhabited. Honolulu, the cosmopolitan capital, resides on the island of Oahu, as do most of the state's residents and tourists. The Big Island (officially called Hawaii) is famed for its Kona coffee, macadamia nuts, volcanoes, and black sand beaches. Maui boasts the historic whaling village of Lahaina, fantastic surfing, and the dormant volcanic crater of Haleakala. The green isle of Kauai, at the northwestern end of the inhabited islands, ranks first for sheer beauty. Molokai, once stigmatized because of its leper colony, now crawls with imported African wildlife, while on tiny Lanai exclusive resorts have replaced pineapples as the primary commodity. The seventh populated isle, Niihau, is closed to most visitors, supporting just a few hundred plantation families who still converse in the Hawaiian language. Together, the islands present, in the words of Twain, "the loveliest fleet of islands that lies anchored in any ocean."

When in Hawaii, enjoy the weather and the islands' natural environs. With a little effort you can escape the touristy commercialism and get a true taste of Hawaii's unique flavor.

■■■ PRACTICAL INFORMATION

Visitors Information: Hawaii Visitors Bureau, 2270 Kalakaua Ave., 7th floor, Honolulu 96815 (923-1811). Open Mon.-Fri. 8am-4:30pm. The ultimate source. The other islands staff offices at major towns, as listed in the appropriate sections.

Camping and Parks: Department of Land and Natural Resources, 1151 Punchbowl St., Room 310, Honolulu 96813 (587-0301). Open Mon.-Fri. 8am-4pm. Information and permits for camping in state parks, and trail maps. **National Park Service,** Prince Kuhio Federal Bldg., #6305, 300 Ala Moana Blvd., Honolulu 96850 (541-2693). Permits are given at individual park headquarters. Open Mon.-Fri. 7:30am-4pm.

Embassies: Australian Consulate, 1000 Bishop St., Honolulu (524-5050). Open Mon.-Fri. 8am-4pm.

Phones: Local calls within each island 25¢. Inter-island calls vary depending on time of day. Most hostels and numerous establishments along Kuhio Ave. carry Phone Line USA vending machines, which dispense cards with enough money on them to make international phone calls at reduced charges. Call 800-831-1666.

PRACTICAL INFORMATION

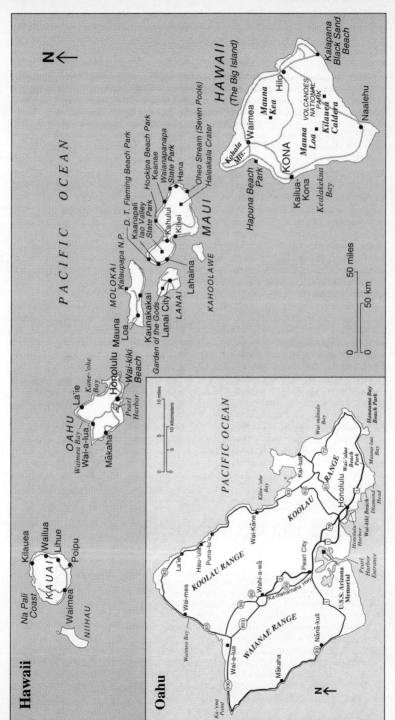

Car Rental: Alamo, Hertz, Dollar, Avis, and **Budget** all have outlets on the islands. Alamo and Dollar rent to those 21 and over with a major credit card for a $15 daily surcharge. All other major carriers rent only to those 25 and older. Phone first, since each agency offers occasional special rates.

Public Libraries: Anyone with an identification card and an address can obtain a library card, even a non-resident. Borrowed books can be returned to any branch.

Travelers with Disabilities: Write to Accessibility Planning and Consulting, 1154 Fort St. Mall, Suite 206, Honolulu, HI 96813 (800-953-7267 inter-island, 800-556-1141 from mainland). *The Accommodation Guide* and *The Restaurant Guide* also assess wheelchair accessibility.

AIDS/STD Hotline, 922-1313 in Oahu, 800-321-1555 from other islands.

Postal Abbreviation: HI.

Area Code: 808.

Capital: Honolulu.

Time Zone: Hawaii (3 hr. behind Pacific in spring and summer; 2 hr. otherwise). 11-13 hrs. of daylight year-round.

Drinking Age: 21.

Sales Tax: 4.167%; hotel rooms 10.167%. **Road Tax:** $2 per day for rented cars.

Major Newspapers: the *Advertiser* and the *Honolulu Star-Bulletin.* On Maui, *The Maui News.*

Motto: *Ua mau ke ea o ka aina i ka pono.* (The life of the land is perpetuated in righteousness.)

State Bird: *Nene,* a rare clawed goose.

State Marine Mammal: Humpback Whale.

State Flower: Hibiscus.

■■■ GETTING THERE

Reaching paradise isn't as expensive as you might think. While prices increase in winter (Feb.-April), reasonable fares can be found even then. Investigate the *L.A. Times* or the *New York Times* "Sunday Travel" section for discount packages, which usually include airfare from major mainland cities, accommodations, and a bevy of fringe benefits such as car rental. Be sure to learn the nitty-gritty details; tour packages often list sights without including admission fees, and rates listed are almost always a per person rate based on double occupancy. An individual traveling alone usually winds up paying more.

If all you want is a plane ticket, look for special advance purchase fares or bulk rates from cut-rate travel agencies. From Los Angeles and San Francisco, tickets on many major carriers start at $300 round-trip and go up from there. **Cheap Tickets** (947-3717 in Hawaii; 800-234-4522 on the mainland) in Honolulu, for instance, offers fares substantially below APEX rates. (See also Essentials: Getting There and Getting Around, page 30.)

■■■ GETTING AROUND

■ ISLAND HOPPING

When weighing which islands to visit, think carefully about what you like to do. Each offers its own atmosphere and range of activities. **Oahu** is heavily populated and revolves around tourism, making it the most accessible island in the chain, but as a consequence, there are few unexplored and unexploited places. The Big Island (**Hawaii**) has lots of open space and the added attraction of Volcanoes National Park. **Kauai,** the Garden Island, at the northwestern end of the chain, has lush green cliffs and dramatic waterfalls surrounded by cherished surfing waters. **Maui's** strong winds have made it one of the premier windsurfing destinations in the world, and with the windsurfers comes a hopping nightlife. **Molokai** is for the solitude-seeking traveler. With 6,000 inhabitants, the "Friendly Isle" still moves to the slow, quiet rhythms of the Pacific. **Lanai,** the most remote island of all, is for the off-road adventurer who enjoys hiking and diving. Regular **ferry** service exists only between Maui, Molokai, and Lanai. **Cruise ships** and private fishing boats will carry passengers to the other islands, but their prices are often exorbitant. **Airlines** are faster, more convenient, cheaper, and often offer special deals on car rentals. The major inter-island carriers, **Hawaiian** and **Aloha Airlines,** can jet you quickly (about 40min.) from Honolulu to any of the islands. Travel agents, such as **Pali Tour and Travel, Inc.** 1300 Pali Hwy. Suite 1004, Honolulu, 96813 (533-3608), sell Hawaiian Air inter-island coupon books that are extremely convenient for island-hopping (6 flights for $312). Hawaiian Airlines also sells 5-, 8-, 10-, and 15-day **passes** offering unlimited inter-island flights for $169, $189, $229, and $269 respectively. The **Hotel Exchange,** 1946 Ala Moana Blvd., Hawaiian Colony (942-8544) sells Aloha Airlines tickets for $103 each, good for any inter-island round-trip flight except for those which depart and arrive at Princeville Airport, Kauai. Check the miscellaneous section of the classified ads in the *Star-Bulletin* or *Advertiser* for individuals selling these coupons at cut-rate prices. Most carriers offer the same fare to each island they serve as well as AAA discounts. Inter-island flights are often extremely scenic, particularly in the early morning or late afternoon. For the best views, sit on the right side heading north and on the left flying south.

Hawaiian Airlines (838-1555) on Oahu, (800-367-5320) from mainland. One way $74. Open 5:30am-9pm.
Aloha Airlines (484-1111) on Oahu, (800-367-5250) from mainland. One way $74. Flies to every island except Lanai and Molokai. Open daily 5:30am-9:30pm.
Island Air (484-2222) on Oahu, (800-323-3345) from mainland. Owned by Aloha Airlines. Smaller planes to major resorts and rural airports. Also fills in service to Molokai for Aloha. $74. Open daily 5:30am-9:30pm.

Surfboards cost an extra $20 each way. Get to the ticket counter early, if you wish to fly through the air with the greatest of ease.

■ PACKAGE TOURS

Aloha and Hawaiian Airlines often coordinate with resorts and/or car rental agencies to create economical packages. Ask a local travel or reservations agent about deals best suited to your needs, and keep a sharp eye out for ads in pamphlets and newspapers.

Many companies offer one-day **airplane** and **helicopter cruises** of the islands (kind of like on *Magnum, P.I.*). Consult a travel agent about current deals and specials or look in the Sunday paper travel section.

■ ON THE ISLANDS

To get around in Hawaii, do as the Hawaiians do. Drive. While the **bus** system is fairly reliable and extensive on Oahu, it is patchy on the Big Island and Kauai, and local transit is nonexistent on the other islands (see individual island listings). You will probably want to rent your own set of wheels for a sojourn on any island other than Oahu.

Car rental agencies fill major island airports and tourist areas in towns. If you have not booked a rental through an airline or other package deal, check local weekly and monthly travel guides for specials and ask about weekly rates. Because car rental agencies are not state-regulated, use of an automatic, air-conditioned compact car can range from $12 to $40 a day. Hawaii is a no-fault insurance state, so insurance coverage is *optional,* but most companies will not honor your individual coverage, even if you already own a car. Many car companies will insist that you sign for a collision damage waiver (CDW) anyway, threatening to hold the driver responsible to the company itself should an accident occur. Some major credit cards, including American Express, will provide a CDW for your rented car, provided that it is neither "exotic" nor a four-wheel-drive. Waiting to start your car rental search until arrival at an airport is a sure way to be stuck with the most expensive rates. Whenever possible, do research before you get there and make reservations in advance.

Bicycle and **moped rentals,** available in most tourist centers, are an enjoyable way to see Hawaii in an easygoing, close-up manner without the hassle of parking.

If you want to know the ropes for cycling in Hawaii, pick up a free copy of *The Rights and Responsibilities for Oahu's Bicyclists* from the **Hawaii Bicycling League,** P.O. Box 4403, Honolulu, HI 96812 (735-5756). The League also sponsors weekly bike rides, free for all to join. Call the League or look in the *Honolulu Weekly* for a schedule. Inter-island airlines charge about $20 to bring your bike with you on the flight. Mainland airlines charge about $45.

■■■ ACCOMMODATIONS AND CAMPING

Despite rumors to the contrary, reasonable room rates do exist on the islands. In general, the closer hotels are to the major tourist attractions and the better the view, the more they charge. Rates at larger resorts also vary frequently with seasons and special events. If you come to town for a canoe race, a golf tournament, or a Triathlon, expect prices to skyrocket. In general, high tourist season runs from mid-December to late April. Look for special deals that often include rental car and air transportation. **Sands and Seaside Hotels,** (800-451-6754 from the islands, 800-367-7000 from the mainland), manages some of the cheapest resort hotels ($70 per night) and is the only locally owned chain of hotels on the islands.

Hostels and the **YMCA** provide cheap shelter on most islands. Another alternative is the ever-growing number of **bed and breakfast organizations** which offer rooms in private homes. **B&B Hawaii,** P.O. Box 449, Kapaa 96746 (822-7771 on Kauai; 800-733-1632 on the other islands), **B&B Honolulu (Statewide),** 3242 Kaohinani Dr., Honolulu 96817 (595-7533; fax 595-2030), and **All Islands B&B,** 823 Kainua Dr., Kailua, HI 96734 (800-542-0344 or 263-2342), operate throughout the state. Prices start from about $50 for a double room with breakfast. Suites, cottages, apartments, small inns, and condos are also available. All locations are personally inspected by the service. Some B&Bs (especially those on the Big Island) will give you a better rate if you call them directly on the island.

Camping can kill two birds with one sleeping bag—it'll save you money and bring you closer to the natural beauty you came to see. Make sure to always check for facilities before you go to camp—not all sites have potable water. Parks on the islands are regulated through the **state, county,** and **national park** systems. The national campgrounds on Maui and The Big Island require no permit, but they do enforce a 3-day maximum stay. State parks are popular and rigidly regulated. Free **camping permits** are required (applicants must be at least 18 years old; available from the Dept. of State Parks in Honolulu). Camping is limited to five nights per 30 days. Sites are open Friday through Wednesday on Oahu, daily on the other islands.

Some state parks on Maui and the Big Island have **cabins,** which are single rooms with wooden sleeping platforms, cooking facilities, bathroom, and shower facilities ($30 per night, 6-person max.). Though these are usually booked at least a month in advance, people often cancel, and many are available on a walk-in basis. For more information, write or visit one of the **State Parks Division** offices (also called the **Department of Land and Natural Resources;** all open Mon.-Fri. 8am-4pm).

The **county parks** on each island are generally geared toward locals, with softball fields and the like. Camping at one of these usually requires a $3 per day permit. Though illegal, free camping outside of designated parks is widely practiced throughout the state by locals, although visitors might be harassed by the police (or locals) if they are too obvious or too permanent (especially on Oahu and Maui). Nevertheless, with some discretion and enough sense to avoid four-wheel-drive tire tracks and empty beer cans, many consider picking their own quiet beach. However, illegal camping is better avoided.

■■■ LIFE AND TIMES

■ HISTORY

Between 25 and 40 million years ago, molten rock welled up from the depths of the earth and burst through the ocean floor at the bottom of the Pacific Ocean. Over millennia, as the Pacific Plate shifted to the northeast, the 1600-mi. archipelago known as the Hawaiian Islands was formed. The oldest islands in the northwest have been worn away to tiny coral atolls by the erosion of the sea, while at the other end of the chain fiery eruptions still pull new land from the ocean's depths.

Long before plate tectonics had gained wide scientific currency, the ancient Hawaiians grasped the idea of how the volcanic mechanism worked. Their legends told of the fire goddess Pele, who fled from island to island, moving southeast down the chain to escape the watery intrusions of her older sister, the ocean. Their journey to the islands was no less remarkable—traveling across thousands of miles of ocean as early as the 6th century AD, the first inhabitants carried with them roots, seeds, dogs, chickens, and a pig or two in their double-hulled canoes. From these meager beginnings, the Polynesian settlers built a culture. They formed several skirmishing kingdoms, worshiped a host of gods, and considered themselves *keiki o ka aina* ("children of the land"). By the time Captain Cook arrived in 1778, a rigidly hierarchical society and advanced irrigation techniques supported a population estimated at 800,000. The *kapu* system of laws and customs maintained order, allowing the ancient Hawaiians to develop skills in agriculture, medicine, the arts and dance, and, of course, surfing.

But the imperial story played out in other colonized nations took its course in Hawaii; Cook's inadvertent stop propelled Hawaii into the modern world. King Kamehameha I of the Big Island—today revered as the leader who united the islands and created modern Hawaii—exploited the introduction of Western arms and conquered all of the other islands except Kauai within 20 years of Cook's arrival. However, the European trade ships brought more than just weapons. Western influences slowly eroded Hawaiian culture, and Western diseases, primarily syphilis and tuberculosis, decimated the Hawaiian population; one hundred years after Cook's arrival, only 50,000 native Hawaiians remained.

Following the arrival of Calvinist missionaries from Boston in 1820, the *haole* (HOW-lee, meaning "Caucasian") presence in island life became entrenched. By 1853, 30% of Hawaiians belonged to Christian churches. An expanding sugar (and later pineapple) industry supplanted the original whaling and sandalwood trade. American plantation owners brought in Chinese, Japanese, and Filipino workers to supplement the Hawaiian work pool, depleted by exploitation and disease. American sugar magnates, leery of a strong monarchy and seeking to ensure a market for their product, overthrew King Kalakaua in 1893 and asked that the U.S. annex the islands. In 1898, in the midst of swatting Spain in the "splendid little war," the U.S. heeded their request.

Hawaiian commerce developed uneventfully until the Japanese attack on Pearl Harbor dramatically summoned the U.S. into World War II. In the heat of the panic, *nisei* (first generation Japanese-Americans) were denied, at first, the right to serve in the U.S. armed forces. The government's eventual relaxation of their unjust ruling and the valiant service of the *nisei* in combat were factors in mitigating racial prejudice. In 1959, Hawaii became the 50th state.

Of the 132 volcanic islands which still stand above the highest tide, only seven are inhabited (one, Niihau, is privately owned). In Hawaii there is no clear ethnic majority. Yet, in spite of the population's heterogeneity, there is surprisingly little racial tension. Instead, Hawaii's residents have merged parts of each ethnic heritage into a "local" society. Today, natives and other citizens are pushing for greater emphasis on a unique Hawaiian culture.

■ LITERATURE

Many foreign and indigenous writers have chronicled the Hawaiian spirit in their novels, stories, and poems. Mary K. Pukui's anthologies translate selected Hawaiian verses spanning ancient through missionary times. Three renowned authors, Mark Twain, James Michener, and Jack London, captured their impressions of the islands in stories or essays; Michener's mammoth text *Hawaii* takes the reader all the way from the island's volcanic formation through statehood.

For an overview of the Hawaiian literati, page through one of these books: Martha Beckwith, *Hawaiian Mythology;* Jack London, *Stories from Hawaii;* James A. Michener, *Hawaii;* Mary Kawena Pukui and Alfons L. Korn, *The Echo of Our Song: Chants and Poems of the Hawaiians;* Gordon Morse, *My Owyhee* and *My Moloka'i;* Mary Kawena Pukui, *Olelo No'eau: Hawaiian Proverbs and Poetical Sayings;* Marjorie Sinclair, *Kona;* Genevieve Taggard, *Origin: Hawaii;* Mark Twain, *Letters from Hawaii;* W.D. Westervelt, *Myths and Legends of Hawaii.*

■ ART AND ARCHITECTURE

Visitors of an artistic bent will find in Hawaii a rich heritage of native crafts, and a smattering of famous Western imports. Perhaps the islanders' most celebrated handicraft is the production of *leis.* Although commercial vendors have bastardized the original craft with synthetic materials, you can still find the traditional garlands of leaves, flowers, nuts, and shells in local shops. **Niihau shell leis,** perhaps the ultimate status symbols of the islands, are still painstakingly made by hand from seashells found on that tiny island. Ornate **woodcarvings** and baskets, slippers, and table mats woven out of *lauhala* (the leaf of the pandanus tree) are crafted by native artisans throughout the islands. **Scrimshaw** first came to Hawaii when mainland sailors idled away their free time on the island by carving images onto whales' bones and teeth; the craft was later refined and practiced by residents. Today, because so many species of whales are endangered, most of the "scrimshaw" you will see is synthetic. Steer clear of authentic whale bone scrimshaw.

European fine arts landed on the islands with Captain Cook. Since then, several artists have grown to worldwide prominence. Most renowned of these is Madge Tennent, "Hawaii's Gauguin," who painted dramatic oils of Hawaiian women, which are on exclusive display at the Tennent Art Foundation Gallery in Honolulu. Engravers Huc M. Luquiens and John M. Kelly are renowned for their etchings of island landscapes and individuals, respectively. First celebrated for his Mexican murals, Jean Chalet came to Hawaii in 1949 and took the indigenous culture as his subject, becoming a leader in the Hawaiian artistic community until his death in 1979. In the 90s, many Hawaiian artists have depicted Hawaii's natural beauty in giving their work a conservationist slant. Robert Lyn Nelson's underwater landscapes feature a colorful range of sealife. Others find inspiration in ancient and modern Hawaiian culture.

The ethnographic Bishop Museum in Honolulu houses the world's best collection of Polynesiana and Hawaiiana, with extensive galleries, archives and demonstrations of Hawaiian crafts. The Honolulu Academy of Art has a wide collection of Western works, while the Contemporary Museum of Art hosts exhibitions on present-day artistic themes. Hawaii's most impressive collection of Asian art is housed at the East-West Center Learning Institute (at the University of Hawaii). Several **art marts** throughout the islands display the works of contemporary Hawaiian artists; a good show is held every weekend outside the Honolulu Zoo (see Honolulu Sights, page 451).

Hawaii's cities are an amalgamation of contrasting architectural styles. Oriental temples, Hawaiian huts and Western structures coexist, but there has been no recognizable cohesion into an architectural style particular to the islands (although the

State Capital, built in 1969, is a remarkable attempt). Landscape design, rather than architecture, is the forte of Hawaiian designers, as a stroll through the island's sculpted parks and gardens will attest.

■ FOOD AND DRINK

Hawaii offers the most unusual array of foods in the U.S. Although imported meat and dairy products are expensive, a profusion of restaurants and take-out vendors make eating out affordable. The Big Island is the macadamia nut capital of the world and home to premium Royal Kona, the only coffee commercially grown in the U.S. Kauai has cookies and sugarcane ice cream; Maui, potato chips; and Oahu, international restaurants.

For a taste of Hawaii as pleasing to the wallet as the palate, go to one of the local take-out establishments. Plate lunches, a long-standing island tradition, are served at lunchwagons and take-out stands everywhere for about $3. A typical plate includes rice, macaroni salad, *kim chee* (pickled cabbage), and an entree such as chicken *katsu* (a breaded cutlet) or teriyaki beef. Wash it all down with a tropical fruit juice. Many plate lunch specials feature such Hawaiian staples as *kalua* pig, *lau lau* (pork or chicken wrapped in *ti* and *taro* leaves), *lomi lomi* salmon (a mixture of tomatoes, onions, and salmon), *haupia* (coconut pudding), and two-finger *poi* (a taro root pudding thick enough to be eaten with two fingers. Construct an interesting meal out of a potpourri of island *pupus*, or appetizers. You can get all of these items at a commercial *luau* with Polynesian entertainment at many restaurants, like **Germaine's,** 1451 S. King, Honolulu (941-3338; $44.50 per person).

On the whole, the islands' Chinese restaurants offer some of the most economical meals, including varieties of *mein* (noodles), *manapua* (pork-filled dough), *won ton* and *dim sum* (various dumplings and small dishes). Japanese fare is usually a bit more expensive with delicate, delicious servings. *Sashimi*—fresh raw fish-—is a favorite delicacy, usually served with *soyu* (soy sauce), fresh ginger and hot horseradish. Japanese fast foods, such as *saimin* (*ramen* noodles, served even in Hawaiian McDonald's), and *bento* (box lunches), are the most affordable varieties. Other local favorites that reflect Hawaii's multicultural history include Korean *kalbi* ribs and *kim chee*, Portuguese *pao duce* (sweet bread) or *malasadas* (fried dough), and shave ice. Shave ice is a popular treat—the ice is finely shaved and then topped with flavored syrup. It's what a snow cone was meant to be!

Since it's in a sub-tropical zone, Hawaii is blessed with a variety of produce. Fresh pineapple, sugar cane, and papaya are all cheap and plentiful in the islands. More exotic are lychee, guava, and the round breadfruit. Pomegranates and star fruit are also worth trying, as is the *lilikoi* (passion fruit). For a visually confounding taste sensation, try the yellow watermelon grown on the Big Island in summer. It's much sweeter than its pink cousin; unfortunately, its yellow skin is so thin that it can't even be shipped, not even to Oahu, so you'll have to go to the Big Island to indulge.

■ RECREATION

The Hawaiian Islands are scattered with hidden treasures: rare birds, tropical fish, botanical delights, and sandy beaches with beckoning waves. Hiking, snorkeling, swimming, bird- and whale-watching, and fishing number among the outdoor activities visitors can enjoy at little or no expense. Surfing was invented in Hawaii during the islands' nativity and has since burgeoned into an worldwide activity. Diehard surfer dudes from California and beyond traverse the globe to hang ten on the 20-footers breaking off Oahu's North Shore. The hybrid sport of windsurfing dominates the beaches of Maui, while between the islands the seafaring paddle traditional outrigger canoes or sail catamarans. Boogie-boarding is an easier and less expensive option.

The less aquatically inclined should explore the islands' singular geographical features. The beauty of the islands is consciously preserved in twenty state and two national parks. The Inland valleys of Maui, the Big Island, Kauai, and Oahu—prime

RECREATION

spots for illegal marijuana cultivation—can put hikers in danger of trespassing; stay on defined trails. Robert Smith has authored some excellent guides to island hiking on sale at local bookstores. Brooks Brothers naturalists will find no dearth of fine golf courses.

The variety of island spectator sports is relatively limited. Polo tournaments and surfing competitions are the more exotic events, but college and pro-football players arrive for the Aloha, Hula, and Pro Bowls during the winter months.

The Hawaii Visitors Bureau has planted "warrior" markers along the highway to point out historical landmarks. Consult the following organizations for maps. Whatever you do, don't pick up tiki idols lying around construction sites.

Hawaiian Trail and Mountain Club, P.O. Box 2238, Honolulu 96804. Watch for listings of free hikes in the weekly "Pulse of Paradise" column of the *Honolulu Star-Bulletin.*

State Forestry Division, 1151 Punchbowl St. #325, Honolulu 96813 (587-0166). Provides free maps for its 24 trails. Include a 9 in. x 12 in. self-addressed, stamped envelope to receive maps. Open Mon.-Fri. 7:45am-4:30pm.

■ WEATHER

The eight major islands and the more than 100 smaller islands that comprise Hawaii exhibit 21 of the earth's 22 climatic zones. Within each island one finds incredible diversity; Kauai contains the wettest spot on earth, but it is only 15 mi. from sunny, dry Poipu. Seasons are virtually nonexistent, although local weather around any given island fluctuates constantly. Coastal areas are usually drier; the leeward side of a mountain is usually calmer as well as hotter than the windward side. From April to October, temperatures range 73-88°F; November to March, it's slightly cooler (65-83°F) and wetter. The Big Island's Hilo is a tropical rain forest—over a hundred inches of precipitation fall each year—while the land to the south at Kau is a sun-scorched desert. The mountain areas catch a cool breeze, especially at night and early morning, so pack a sweater. On any island, be prepared for mountain showers and "liquid sunshine," a cool mixture of rain sprinkles, sunshine, and rainbows.

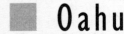 Oahu

At the time of Captain Cook's landing, Oahu was something of a backwater. Oahu's real importance came with the creation of Honolulu harbor. The harbor established it as a regular stopover for vessels plying the China trade, prompting many *haoles* (Caucasians) to settle in Honolulu. By the time the first missionaries arrived in 1820, the city had become the economic and cultural center of Hawaii, and the migrating royal court was obliged to spend more time there. Oahu's preeminence increased in ensuing decades as Honolulu's commercial traffic expanded and the U.S. Navy acquired exclusive rights to the inlet at Pearl Harbor. The dredging of Pearl Harbor's mouthway in 1900 allowed Oahu to develop almost overnight into the headquarters of the U.S. Pacific Fleet. The bombing of the harbor by Imperial Japan on December 7, 1941 signaled the entrance of the U.S. into World War II; 20 years later, the arrival of American jets took Hawaii's tourism to a higher plane. Today, bases for all branches of the U.S. military claim vast portions of Oahu's land.

Honolulu itself is a vibrant multi-ethnic city, inhabited by a mixture of native Hawaiians, Caucasians, Japanese, Chinese, Samoans, Koreans, and Filipinos. Despite the discrimination many of these groups have faced in the past, relations among them are now remarkably friendly; nearly half of all island marriages are interracial.

Oahu can be roughly divided into four sections. **Honolulu** and its suburbs constitute the metropolitan heart of the island. The **North Shore,** from Kahuku to Kaena

RECREATION

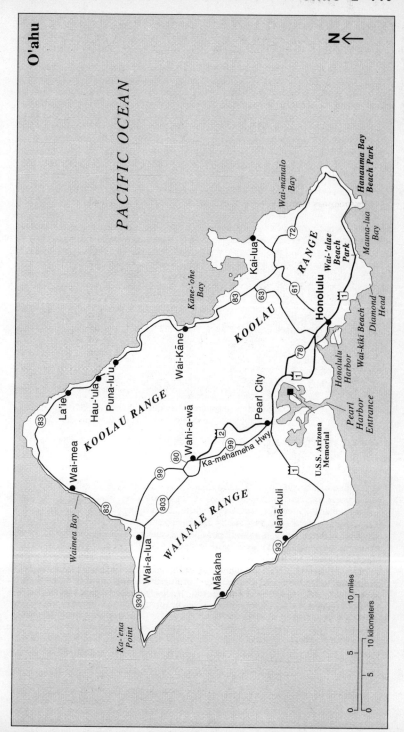

O'ahu

N ←

PACIFIC OCEAN

Wai-mānalo
Bay

Hanauma Bay
Beach Park

Kai-lua

72

RANGE

Wai-'alae
Beach Park

Honolulu

Mauna-lua
Bay

61

Kāne-'ohe
Bay

63

1

83

Diamond
Head

Wai-kiki Beach

KOOLAU

78

Wai-Kāne

Honolulu
Harbor

Puna-lu'u

Pearl City

Hau-'ula

1

La'ie

KOOLAU RANGE

Wahi-a-wā

Pearl
Harbor
Entrance

Wai-mea

2

99

80

Ka-mehameha Hwy

U.S.S. Arizona
Memorial

99

83

803

1

Waimea Bay

WAIANAE RANGE

Nānā-kuli

Wai-a-lua

93

Mākaha

930

Ka-'ena
Point

0   5   10 miles

0   5   10 kilometers

Point, is the home of the winter swells that surfers around the world dream of. The **Windward Coast** (on the east), especially around Hanauma Bay, is rife with tropical fish and coral reefs. The **Leeward Coast** (on the west) is raw and rocky.

The slopes of two now-extinct volcanic mountain ridges, **Waianae** in the west and **Koolau** in the east, run parallel from northwest to southeast and make up the bulk of Oahu's 600 square mi. The narrow inlets of **Pearl Harbor** push in from the sea at the southern end of the valley between the two ridges. Honolulu spreads along six mi. of oceanfront southeast of Pearl Harbor, hemmed in by the Koolau Range in the northeast. Three mi. east of downtown, **Waikiki Beach** extends outward toward the volcanic crater of **Diamond Head,** the island's southernmost extremity. The Honolulu district continues around Diamond Head to Koko Head in **Hawaii-kai.** Skipping only the Leeward Coast and Kaena Point, well-maintained highways circle the island and navigate the central valley. White sand beaches drape Oahu's shores and hiking trails ramble through the inland mountains and vales.

■■■ HONOLULU

Honolulu is the cultural, commercial, and political locus of Hawaii. Its industrial-strength harbor and concrete-and-glass business district attest to its status as a capital city (pop. 370,000) and major Pacific seaport. At the same time, acres of white sand beaches make it one of the world's premier tropical vacation getaways. Waikiki, the quintessential tourist haven, boasts an abundance of glitzy restaurants and night-clubs interspersed among 70,000 hotel rooms. Most visitors confine themselves to the downtown area, rarely venturing into uptown Honolulu, where ambitious housing projects (made possible by the lavish tourism tax revenues) house thousands of Hawaiians unable to bear the staggering increase in the cost of living. Honolulu's temperate island setting influences the lifestyle of its residents. Motorists in rush hour retain an amazingly friendly disposition toward their fellow road warriors. In the office, informal dress is the rule, especially on "Aloha Friday."

Yet, Honolulu is considered by many to be too busy and fast-paced. A traveler who does not leave this section of the island of Oahu will see only a small segment of what Hawaii has to offer. Other areas are less crowded, less developed and more peaceful. However, at the expense of solitude, Honolulu offers a varied nightlife and bargains are available from establishments competing fiercely for your dollar.

PRACTICAL INFORMATION AND ORIENTATION

Visitors Information: Hawaii Visitors Bureau, 2270 Kalakaua Ave., 7th Floor, Honolulu 96815 (923-1811). Information on Oahu and the rest of the state. Pick up the *Accommodation Guide, Restaurant Guide,* a map of points of interest, and a walking tour of downtown Honolulu. Most brochures contain information for the disabled traveler. All are free. Open Mon.-Fri. 8am-4:30pm; closed holidays. Information centers located in both the overseas and inter-island air terminals and at the Ala Moana Shopping Center.

Chamber of Commerce: Hawaiian Main, 522-8800.

Outdoor Information: Department of State Parks, 1151 Punchbowl St. #310, Honolulu 96813 (587-0300), at S. Beretania St. (building with relief art at top). Information, trail maps, and while-you-wait permits for camping in state parks. Open Mon.-Fri. 8am-4pm. **Department of Parks and Recreation,** 650 S. King, Honolulu 96817 (523-4525). Information and permits for Oahu's county parks. Open Mon.-Fri. 7:45am-4pm. Permits available no more than 2 weeks in advance.

Bank of America, 321 Seaside Ave. (922-1611). Open Mon.-Thurs. 8:30am-3:30pm, Fri. 8:30am-6pm, Sat. 9am-noon. Many other branches on Oahu.

American Express: Hyatt Regency Waikiki, reception area, 2424 Kalakaua Ave. (926-5441). Open daily 8am-4pm, although some travel services are offered until 9pm. The only office that accepts client mail.

Bus: 848-5555. Covers the entire island, but different lines start and stop running at different times. Call to avoid getting stuck somewhere remote. Also, backpackers beware: they won't let you carry on big packs or luggage. Fare 85¢. Bus passes

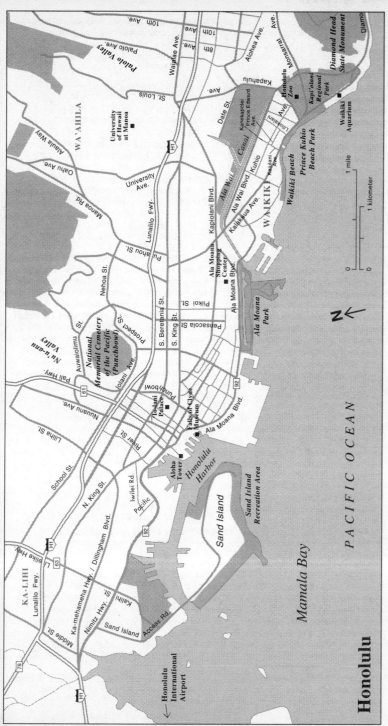

HONOLULU

Honolulu

valid for 1 month are available for $20 at satellite city halls, at Foodland grocery store, Bank of Hawaii branches, and 7-Elevens. Free Honolulu/Waikiki route maps available at tourist pamphlet stands throughout Waikiki. The *Bus Guide* ($3), in ABC stores, provides comprehensive information about touring Oahu by bus.

Transit for Travelers with Disabilities: Handi-Van (841-4322): curb-to-curb transport if reservations are made at least a day in advance. Service Mon.-Fri. 8am-4pm. Travelers with disabilities can also obtain a **Handicapped Bus Pass.** For either service, write City Department of Transportation Services, Attn. Handi-Van or Handicapped Bus Pass, 725 Kapiolani Blvd., Honolulu, HI 96813. **Handi-Cabs of the Pacific,** P.O. Box 22428 (524-3866). $35 for airport-to-Waikiki service. 24-hr. advance notice required.

Taxi: Sida, 439 Kalewa St. (836-0011). All cabs charge 25¢ per 1/7 mi. Flag rates are about $2. Airport to Waikiki $20. Also try **Charley's** (622-4177). All taxis charge 35¢ per large bag.

Car Rental: Discover Rent-a-Car 1920 Ala Moana Blvd. (949-4767). $25 per day for drivers 21 and older. Or, if you are 25 or older, **VIP Rentals,** 234 Beachwalk (923-9824). $22 per day, 3-day min. **Paradise Adventures,** 355 Royal Hawaiian Ave. (946-7777), rents cars and jeeps to those 18 and above. Ages 18-20 $40 per day, 21-24 $35 per day. Credit card or $500 deposit required. 2-day min. **Hertz** (800-654-3131) has facilities at airports on Kauai, Maui, Oahu, and the Big Island and offers special inter-island rates and AAA discounts.

Moped and Bicycle Rental: Mopeds, though not as safe as cars, are a great way to get around Honolulu, especially on Kalanianaole Hwy., the route to Hanauma Bay. They can cover about 40 mi. on $1 worth of gas. Most rental agencies require credit cards and a min. age of 18. **Aloha Funway Rentals,** 1778 Ala Moana (942-9696) and 3165 N. Nimitz Hwy. (831-2277), near the airport. Mopeds $20 per day, $80 per week; bikes $20 per day. Open daily 8am-5pm. **Moped Connection,** 750A Kapahulu Ave. (732-3366). Mopeds $16 per day, $75 per week. Credit card or $100 cash deposit required. Open Mon.-Fri. 9am-6pm, Sat.-Sun. 9am-3pm.

Camping Equipment: The Bike Shop, 2nd floor, 1149 S. King St. (596-0588), from Waikiki, take Ala Wai Blvd. to McCully Ave., go left at Beretania St. onto Pensacola Ave., then turn left after 2 blocks to King St. High quality equipment for sale and a little bit of everything. Staff has suggestions on trails and trips. Open Mon.-Fri. 9am-7pm, Sat. 9am-5pm, Sun. 10am-5pm.

Water Equipment Rental: Many rental outfits are located on beaches and look like lemonade stands. Quality boards, along with helpful lessons, can be found at **Star Beachboys,** Kuhio Beach, to the left of the Kuhio Beach park pavilion. Canoe rides ($7), private surfing lessons ($25 per hr.), boogie-boards ($5 per hr.). **Snorkel Bob's,** 702 Kapahulu Ave. (735-7944), is *the* place for snorkel equipment rentals, even underwater cameras. Equipment is $9 per day, $15 per week and $14 per day gets you higher quality equipment. A fish map and a copy of the legend of Snorkel Bob are included. Inter-island returns $3 extra.

Bookstore: Honolulu Book Shops, Ala Moana Shopping Center (941-2274).

Library: Hawaii State Library, 478 S. King St. (586-3500). Open Mon., Wed., and Fri.-Sat. 9am-5pm; Tues. and Thurs. 9am-8pm. Next to Iolani Palace. Extensive Hawaii and Pacific collection. **Waikiki Public Library,** 400 Kapahulu Ave. (732-2777). Open Tues. and Thurs.-Sat. 10am-5pm; Mon. and Wed. 10am-8pm.

Laundromat: Most hostels have laundromats on the premises. For others, **Waikiki Laundromats** (923-2057) has several locations open daily 7am-10pm, including one across from the **International Market Place,** and one in the **Outrigger West Hotel,** 2330 Kuhio Ave. Wash $1, dry $1.

Swimming Pool: Manoa Recreation Center, 2721 Kaaipu Ave. (988-6868). Bus #5 from Ala Moana Center. Open Mon.-Sat. 11am-5pm, Sun. 1-5pm. Free.

Weather Report: Normally sunny and 60-80°F. If in doubt, call the National Weather Service at 836-2102 for confirmation. **Surf Report:** 836-1952, 24 hrs.

Crisis Lines: Information and Referral Service, ASK-2000, 275-2000. **Coast Guard Search/Rescue,** 800-552-6458. **AIDS Hotline,** 922-1313. **Interpreter Service,** 526-9727.

TDD: 643-8TDD, -8833 for hearing-impaired users. **643-TALK,** -8255 for hearing users.

Gay and Lesbian Information: Gay and Lesbian Community Center, 1820
University Ave., 2nd floor (951-7000). Offers general information about the gay
and lesbian community. Open Mon.-Fri. 9am-5pm.

Pharmacy: The Pillbox, 1133 11th Ave., Kaimuki (737-1177). 24-hr. emergency
service. Open daily 10am-11pm. **Kuhio Pharmacy,** 2330 Kuhio Ave. (923-4466).
Open Mon.-Fri. 9am-4:30pm and Sat. 8:30am-1:30pm.

Health Centers: Queen's Medical Center, 1301 Punchbowl St. (538-9011). 24-
hr. emergency room, 547-4311. **Waikiki Health Center,** 277 Ohua St., Waikiki
(922-4787).

Emergency: 911.

Post Office: Main Office, 3600 Aolele Ave. (423-3990). Near the airport. The only
one that accepts General Delivery. Open Mon.-Fri. 8am-7:30pm, Sat. 8am-2:30pm.
General Delivery ZIP Code: 96813. **Waikiki Branch,** Royal Hawaiian Shopping Center, 3rd floor, Bldg. C. Open Mon.-Fri. 9am-4:30pm.

Area Code: 808.

Honolulu International Airport is 20 minutes west of downtown, off the Lunalilo
Freeway (H-1). If Waikiki is your destination, take the Honolulu exit, then move
immediately into the left lane to get the interchange onto the freeway into town.
Although 15 minutes longer, the **Nimitz Hwy.** (Rte. 92) will take you all the way to
Waikiki. Buses #19 and #20, among others, go the 9 mi. to Waikiki, but you won't
be able to bring your luggage unless it can fit on your lap. **Airport Motorcoach**
(839-0911) offers continuous service from the airport to Waikiki and hotels ($6). 24-
hr. advance return reservations are required (call 6:30am-10:30pm). **EM Tours and
Transportation** (836-0210) will pick up at any time ($7).

The **H-1 Freeway** stretches the length of Honolulu, as does the Nimitz. One-way
and no-U-turn signs abound in the downtown area, so make sure to get a good street
map before you drive through, and plan your route in advance. If all else fails, locals
are generally helpful with directions. Besides *mauka* (inland) and *makai* (seaward), you are also likely to hear such directions as *ewa* (west; pronounced EHVA)
and Diamond Head (east). Downtown Honolulu is about six blocks long and four
blocks wide; its main drags are **Kapiolani Blvd., King St.** (running east only), and
Beretania St. (running west only). In Waikiki, **Ala Wai Blvd., Kuhio Ave.,** and
Kalakaua Ave. run parallel to the ocean and are the main routes of transit.

Honolulu and the surrounding environs contain a plethora of places for **biking**
and **running. Ala Moana Beach Park,** near Waikiki, has a scenic running path. Jog
over to **The Running Room,** 768 Kapahulu Ave. (737-2422), for information about
running events and pick up a copy of *The Runner's Guide to Oahu* for a list of good
running trails. (Open Mon.-Fri. 10am-7pm, Sat.-Sun. 9am-5pm. Also call the Honolulu Marathon Association at 734-7200.) Bike paths are found mostly in Manoa and
near the University of Hawaii. **Hitchhiking** is illegal on Oahu and inadvisable in general. *Let's Go* does not recommend hitchhiking.

Parking is a nuisance all over Honolulu, especially in Waikiki. At Waikiki's west
end, free parking can be found along the Ala Wai Canal; on the east end, free parking is available on Monsarrat Ave., just south of the **zoo.** The zoo parking lot's
meters charge an unbeatable $1 for four hours. Downtown, the **Prince Kuhio Fed-
eral Building** (300 Ala Moana Blvd.) offers the only free parking for miles around.

ACCOMMODATIONS

Honolulu, and especially Waikiki, cater to an affluent tourist crowd, but there *are*
bargains for those willing to search and do without the grass-skirted frills. Because
Hawaii is a stop on many round-the-world tickets, hostels are great places to meet
travelers bound for the West Coast, Australia, or Europe. They fill up quickly.
Reserve early by telephone or by mail. Check for housing specials in the *Honolulu
Advertiser,* available on street corners for 50¢. The number of Bed and Breakfast
establishments on the island is constantly growing and B&Bs are becoming a more
convenient and affordable housing option. **B&B Pacific Hawaii,** 19 Kai Nani Place
(262-6026), will book bed and breakfast rooms all over the island from $45 per cou-

ple. (See Hawaii: Accommodations, page 438, for more B&B agencies.) As for hostels, AYH hostels are generally quiet and clean; elsewhere you take your chances. In almost all youth hostels in Hawaii, there is a strong pick-up scene, so be prepared.

Hostels

Interclub Waikiki, 2413 Kuhio Ave. (924-2636). To prevent vagrancy, guests must show an airline ticket to stay. Primarily international clientele. Manager Mr. Lim runs a clean, friendly hostel with excellent security. Female or mixed dorms. Laundry, refrigerators, and outdoor grill. Lounge and pool table. Garden and fish pond. Safe/lockers. Smoking and drinking allowed. No curfew; reception open 24 hrs. Check-out 10am. Bunks $15. Doubles $45. $10 key deposit.

Honolulu International (HI/AYH), 2323A Seaview Ave. (946-0591). 1½ mi. north of Waikiki, near University of Hawaii at Manoa. By car, take University Ave. exit off H-1. By bus, take #6 from Ala Moana Shopping Center to Metcalf and University Ave. (near Burger King). Small and peaceful, though somewhat remote. Kitchen, locker, and clean single-sex facilities. Rec. room with TV and movies. Windows are netting; watch your belongings. Beds guaranteed for 3 nights; if you want to stay longer, the management can usually arrange to move you to the Hale Aloha hostel. Reception open 7:30-10am and 5pm-midnight. Check-out 10am. Lights out 11pm; rooms locked noon-4:30pm; kitchen and TV room stay open. $12, nonmembers $15. Sheet sack $1. Reservations recommended.

Hale Aloha (HI/AYH), 2417 Prince Edward St. (926-8313), in Waikiki, 2 blocks from the beach. Take Waikiki #8 bus to Kuhio and Uluniu, walk beachward 1 block, turn right. Single-sex rooms. TV room, free use of snorkeling gear. Beds guaranteed 3 nights although you might be allowed to stay longer. 24-hr. check-in. Check-out 11am. No lockout or curfew; quiet hours 11pm. Dorm bunks $15 per night; doubles $35. Sleep sack rental $1. Key deposit $5. Make reservations.

Hawaiian Seaside Hostel, 419 Seaside Ave. (924-3306), two blocks from the beach. For the backpacker ready to party. Overseas airline ticket or foreign passport required. No keys issued; rooms always unlocked. Co-ed bunks of 6-10 people per room. Kitchen in each room. Laundry and TV room. Safes and lockers. Open 24 hrs. Check-out noon. $9.75 first night, $13 thereafter. $5.25 check-in deposit.

YMCA, 401 Atkinson Dr. (941-3344), downtown, across from Ala Moana Shopping Center. Lots of semipermanent residents. Women must take rooms with private baths. Check in or out at noon. Singles $30, with bath $36.50. Doubles $43.50, with bath $55. $10 key deposit.

YMCA, 1810 University Ave. (946-0253). Usually a dormitory for University of Hawaii students, the Atherton YMCA lets available rooms to visitors during the summer. Linen provided. TV lounge and laundry room, but no kitchen facilities. Check-in Mon.-Fri. noon-4pm, Sat. 9-11:30am. Rooms $20 per night. $150 damage deposit (cash) and $25 application fee also required.

Polynesian Hostel, 174 Kapahulu Ave., in Waikiki Grand Hotel, Room #615 (922-1340). The well-maintained Polynesian Hotel has sold some rooms to the hostel. Terrific location. Older patrons. TV, kitchenette. 6-7 people per converted hotel room. Access to pool. No curfew. Bunks $15, $95 per week. $10 key deposit.

Hotels

Hale Pua Nui Hotel, 228 Beachwalk Ave. (923-9693), 1 block from the beach. Clean and comfortable. 22 units, each with cable TV, kitchenette, and two beds. Dec.-Mar. and June-Sept. $55 per day, $325 per week; otherwise $44 per day, $267 per week. Room key deposit $50 (refundable). Call ahead for reservations.

Outrigger Hotels (800-462-6262) runs a few lower-priced, large hotels in Waikiki which offer economical package deals, including breakfast. Pools, TV, A/C. Discounts on car rentals and reduced rates for AAA and AARP members.

Royal Grove Hotel, 151 Uluniu Ave. (923-7691). Small rooms close to Waikiki Beach. Economy rooms have a stirring view of Vivian's Bar-B-Q. Elderly clientele. Single or double room with bath, TV, and fridge, $38. With kitchenette, $42.50.

CAMPING

Permits for camping are available for **free** (at the Dept. of State Parks and Dept. of Parks and Recreation; see Practical Information, page 444); be sure to have one, or the police and rangers who patrol the campgrounds will send you packing. Four **state parks** (Sand Island, Keaiwa Heiau, Kahana Bay, and Malaekahana) allow camping. Numerous **county parks** do as well, but the safety of these parks is dubious. In particular, the leeward (western) side of the island is notorious for assaults and robberies. State and county parks enforce a five-day limit and are closed Wednesday 8am until Friday 8am. When camping, pack rain gear—showers are common.

Malaekahana State Recreation Area (293-1736), north of Laie. Take the Kamehameha Hwy. up the windward coast and watch carefully for the sign. The queen of Oahu's state parks, Malaekahana is ranger-patrolled for safety. Showers, toilets, picnic tables, and BBQ pits. Cabin for up to 10 people $50. Cabin for 6 $40. Make reservations 6 months in advance.

Bellows Field State Park (523-4525), just north of Waimanalo Bay. Take Tinker Rd. at the sign for Bellows Air Force Station. Facilities are a little rough-hewn, but the beach is beautiful and good for swimming or windsurfing. Showers, restrooms, picnic area. Open weekends only.

Keaiwa Heiau State Park, from Waikiki, follow H-1 to Moanalua Hwy. (Rte. 78). Take Aiea turnoff to second traffic light; turn right and follow Aiea Heights Dr. until it ends. Remains of a *heiau* (a healing temple) and an herb garden. Camping area #4 is grassy and sheltered from winds. 4½-mi. trail leads around the park past the wreckage of a cargo plane. Restrooms, cold showers, tables, and BBQ pits.

Kahana Beach State Park, by car, take Kamehameha Hwy. By bus, take #55 (Kaneohe/Circle Island). This park is a 30-yd. strip of land between the Kamehameha Hwy. and the ocean. The bay is calm, a rarity on the windward side of the island, and safe for swimming. Highway traffic can be loud. Restrooms, picnic tables, outdoor showers, and BBQ pits.

Sand Island State Park, take Nimitz Hwy. (Rte. 92) to Sand Island access road. Near Honolulu harbor; don't expect sand and be prepared for airplane noise. Restrooms, showers.

FOOD

Eating in Honolulu is an international dining experience that combines American fast food and Asian cuisine. Look for breakfast specials at many hotel coffee shops and scan the "Dining Out" sections in the Sunday papers for specials throughout Oahu. Otherwise, many restaurants are overpriced and unexciting. If you have access to a kitchen or are planning a picnic, you may want to stock up at the **Food Pantry,** 2370 Kuhio Ave. (923-9831; open 24 hrs.) or **Star Market,** 2470 S. King (973-1666; take University Ave. from Waikiki and turn left on S. King; open daily 6am-1am). Both stores have a wide selection and excellent produce.

For truly local flavor, take a trip to the **farmers' market** across from Kewalo Basin, just west of Ala Moana Park. They have wonderfully **fresh seafood** and the delicate Hawaiian *lau lau*—a taro leaf stuffed with fish. Go early in the morning and bargain for the day's catch. The best Hawaiian **shave** (not crushed) **ice** can be found at **Island Snow** in the Royal Hawaiian Shopping Center (Bldg. C; open 8am-10pm).

The neighborhoods surrounding Waikiki support many inexpensive restaurants that avoid the corny tourist ambience. The **Kapahulu, Kaimuki, Moiliili,** and **downtown** districts are all within 10 minutes of Waikiki by bus, and with a good map, you can walk from one district to the next quite easily. Small Chinese and other Asian food counters serve excellent, authentic, and affordable lunches and *dim sum* all over Chinatown, especially on **Hotel Street.** A variety of ethnic restaurants, including Hawaiian, Japanese, Thai, and French, are located between the 500 and 1000 blocks of **Kapahulu Avenue** and in the surrounding area. Catch bus #2 going *mauka* (inland) up Kapahulu Ave. from the Diamond Head area of Waikiki.

Finally, travelers to Waikiki will be deluged with ads and flyers recommending luaus. These feasts with Polynesian dancing are expensive ($30-50) and touristy, but some can be entertaining and belly-filling.

Perry's Smorgy, 2380 Kuhio Ave. (926-0184). All-you-can-eat smorgasbord. Dine on mahimahi, roast beef, pasta, desserts, fresh fruit, and endless Kona coffee in the indoor/outdoor garden (beautiful after dark). Open daily: Breakfast 7-11am, $5. Lunch 11:30am-2:30pm, $6. Dinner 5-9pm, $8.

Rainbow Drive-in, 3308 Kanaina Ave. (737-0177), at Kapahulu. Don't let the modest exterior fool you, probably the best plate lunches around are right here. Plate lunches come with rice and macaroni salad. Try the mixed plate of Hawaiian-style BBQ pork, boneless chicken, and mahimahi for $5.20. Open daily 8am-9pm.

Leonard's Bakery, 933 Kapahulu Ave. (737-5591). Virtually a landmark, this Hawaiian institution has served perfect, hot *malasadas* (a Portuguese dessert of sugared fried dough) for years (45¢). Open daily 6am-10pm.

Down to Earth Natural Foods, 2525 S. King St. (947-7678), adjacent to Star Market. Excellent vegetarian dishes (chili and rice $2.25) to take out or eat in. Wide variety of health food, bulk grains, cereals, and produce. Open daily 8am-10pm. Deli open daily 10am-9pm.

Ruffage Natural Foods, 2443 Kuhio Ave. (922-2042). More a store than a restaurant; the dolphin-safe tuna with organic sprouts and tomato sandwich goes light on your stomach and conscience. Open Mon.-Sat. 8:30am-7pm, Sun. 10am-6pm. Sushi bar open daily 5:30-10pm.

Auntie Pasto's, 1099 S. Beretania St., at Pensacola (523-8855). Cozy red-brick *ristorante* conjures up exceptional Italian meals and the ambience of the old country. Stuffed calamari $7. Pasta $5.25 and up. Parking is difficult to find; consider taking the bus. Open Mon.-Thurs. 11am-10:30pm, Fri. 11am-11pm, Sat. 4-11pm, Sun. 4-10:30pm.

Sizzler, 1945 Kalakaua (955-4069), several blocks from the main beach area. Large, quiet, and popular with families. Jamboree breakfast with eggs, bacon, and all-you-can-eat pancakes, $3.60. Some traditional island dishes. Open 24 hrs.

Patti's Kitchen, Makai Market, Ala Moana Shopping Center (946-5002), also in the Windward Mall in Kaneohe. Build your own buffet-style Chinese plate lunches ($4.45-6). Two entrees with rice and noodles $4.30. Egg roll $1. Also has a counter selling *dim sum*. Open Mon.-Sat. 9am-9pm, Sun. 10am-6pm.

Tsuruya Noodle Shop, Makai Market, Ala Moana Shopping Center (946-7214). Enormous cauldrons of *soba* and *udon* (noodles with soup) for $3.50-6. Popular with Japanese tourists. Open Mon.-Sat. 9am-9pm, Sun. 10am-6pm.

KC Drive-in, 1029 Kapahulu Ave. (737-5581). Coffee shop atmosphere contrasts with mildly exotic menu. Teriyaki, curry, noodles, and a peanut butter milkshake $2.60. Entrees $4-7. Open Sun.-Thurs. 6am-11:30pm, Fri.-Sat. 6am-1:30am.

Zippy's, 1725 S. King St. and throughout the islands. 4am + $5 in your pocket = Zippy's. Standard American entrees $2-5. Open 24 hrs.

SIGHTS AND ACTIVITIES

Honolulu is littered with tokens of excessive commercialization. The prevalence of plastic grass skirts, Kon-Tiki idol replicas, and clamshell wind chimes—not to mention billions of yards of plastic leis—makes it difficult to proclaim Honolulu cosmopolitan. However, the city, which proudly claims no ethnic majority, is increasingly being regarded as a model for America's pending multiculturalism.

To avoid the hassle of parking and getting lost; let someone else do the driving. The one-hour loop on the #14 bus cuts across a sampling of Honolulu's wide and varied neighborhoods. Waikiki is, of course, centered around Waikiki Beach; Kaimuki and Kahala are small, close-knit communities; Moiliili's lifeblood is the university; downtown and Chinatown are the shipping and business districts.

The **Waikiki Trolley** (591-2561) stops at major sites and museums in Waikiki and downtown Honolulu. You can listen to the two-hour narrated tour or get off and on at your leisure. Stops include Chinatown, the Capitol, Bishop Museum, Aquarium, Academy of Arts, and Iolani Palace. A trolley leaves the Royal Hawaiian Shopping

Center every 15 minutes from 8am to 4:30pm. (Day pass $15, under 11 $5; 5-day pass $25, under 11 $10.)

Waikiki

Originally a marshy swampland and hideaway for Hawaiian royalty, Waikiki's wetlands were drained into the Ala Canal to launch the island's tourist industry. In the 1950s, the image of a ¾-mi. crescent of white sand beach set against the profile of **Diamond Head** lured platoons of vacationers and honeymooners to Waikiki. Hotels sprouted everywhere, with each high-rise built to maximize the highly coveted ocean view from the *lanai* (porch). Today, visitors of all ages flock to Waikiki for rest, relaxation, sun, surf, nightlife, tacky souvenirs, random sex, and romance.

Waikiki Beach, actually comprised of several smaller beaches, is lined with shops and hotels of all varieties. Farthest to the east is the **Sans Souci Beach,** in front of the Kaimona Otani Hotel. Site of an old natatorium (an outdoor swimming pool by the sea with impressive stone bleachers) built as a war memorial, Sans Souci has shower facilities but no public restrooms. Hippies and hip yuppies intermingle there in a carefree way (it's a lifestyle choice). The **Queen's Surf Beach,** closer to downtown, attracts swimmers, skaters, and an increasing number of rollerbladers. The beach area to the left of the snack bar is a popular tanning spot for gays. Between the Hawaiian Regent and the Hyatt Regency, breakers shelter **Kuhio Beach Park** from the heavy surf. Enjoy the calm waters while watching the surfers venture beyond the breakers for the big waves.

Next to the Waikiki Beach Center (across from the Hyatt Regency) are four *kahuna stones,* which are supposed to possess healing powers. For a taste of an earlier age in Hawaiian tourism, wander through the lobbies of the newly renovated turn-of-the-century Moana Hotel, which surrounds a phenomenal banyan tree on Waikiki Beach, or visit the historic **Royal Hawaiian Hotel**, whose pink grandeur was unveiled in 1927. At the far west end of the beach, **Fort de Russy Beach Park** features the liveliest games of beach volleyball this side of Southern California.

If you seek more secluded beaches, but want to stay in the vicinity, go east on Diamond Head Rd. (a moped will do) until you hit Kahala Ave. **Kahala Beach** is blocked by houses and private property, but since all Hawaiian beaches are public, public access paths lead onto the beach. Try the path in the 4600s of Kahala Ave. You will lose amenities (no food, public bathrooms, or showers), security (no lifeguard), sand (short shore), and swimmability, but you will gain peace and solitude (in the company of other placid *Let's Go* readers). Bring your snorkeling gear.

If you want a break from sun and surf, hike the 1 mi. into the **Diamond Head Crater.** To get there, take bus #58 from Waikiki. Bring a flashlight to guide you through a pitch-dark section of the tunnel. The view of Waikiki is spectacular, and if you go on the right day, you might catch a rainbow arching over the U.S. military base in the center of the crater. The magnificent estates on the slopes of Diamond Head belong to scions of Hawaii's original missionary families. It has been said that the missionaries came to Diamond Head to do good, and did very well indeed.

The **Damien Museum,** 130 Ohua St. (923-2690), behind the St. Augustine Church offers a lesson in Hawaiian history. Through original documents and a one-hour video, the museum displays the history of Father Damien's Molokai leper colony (open Mon.-Fri. 9am-3pm, Sat. 9am-noon; free). The **Honolulu Zoo,** 151 Kapahulu Ave. (871-7175), across from Kapiolani Park on the east end of Waikiki, is the best zoo on the islands. Daily activities for children include shows and animal demonstrations. The new Africa Savannah section covers nine acres and hosts such wildlife as cheetahs, giraffes, and white and black rhinos. Call for a recorded schedule of events. (Open Thurs.-Tues. 8:30am-4pm, Wed. 8:30am-7pm. $4, under 13 free.) Outside the zoo local painters exhibit their work in the **Art Mart** (Wed. and Sat.-Sun. 10am-4pm). For a close encounter with marine life, the **Kahala Hilton Hotel** has free dolphin feedings every day at 11am, 2pm, and 4pm.

No longer the exclusive domain of children, kite flying has become a competitive sport. Contact the **Kite Fantasy,** 2863 Kalakaua Ave. (922-5483). They'll teach you to fly some of their stunt kites for free, with the option to buy (open daily 9am-5pm). Another aerial spectacle is provided by the Hilton Hawaiian Hotel's **fireworks display,** which happens every Friday at 7:30pm; Kuhio Beach affords a magnificent view.

Across from the kite shop is the **Waikiki Shell,** home to many concerts as well as the **Kodak Hula Show** (833-1661). See Waikiki at its photogenic tackiest. This production packages hula dancing and palm tree climbing into bite-size tourist portions. It is tacky and touristy to say the least, but also very entertaining. Watch your fellow tourists interact with the game-show-style host; you'll find it very hard not to laugh. Say you're on your honeymoon and get "leid" in front of everyone (1-hr. shows Tues.-Thurs. at 10am; free). For more authentic dance performances, contact the **Hawaii Visitors Bureau** (923-1811) and ask about any upcoming performances or competitions among the *hula halau* (schools). Major competitions are usually held in the spring. The **Queen Kapiolani Rose Garden,** at Monsarrat and Paki Ave., is always a welcoming and fragrant retreat. Look, but don't touch; the roses are protected by magic *kahuna stones* (open 24 hrs.; free). You can also view fish (and 2 dolphins) at the **Waikiki Aquarium,** 2777 Kalakaua Ave. (923-9741). The aquarium has recently added a wave machine and an exhibit on mahimahi (dolphin fish; open daily 9am-5pm; $3, under 16 free).

Downtown

Several cultural and historical attractions are found around the downtown area. **Chinatown,** found at the intersection of Nuuanu Ave. and Hotel St., is worth seeing, but you may want to leave your valuables behind in a hostel safe. The **Chinese Chamber of Commerce,** 42 N. King St. (533-3181), has information on the Chinese community and sponsors tours of Chinatown for $5. (Chamber open Mon.-Fri. 8am-4pm, Sat. 8:30am-noon; tours run Tues. 9:30am-noon.) For a transcendent olfactory experience, stop and smell the beautiful strands of ginger leis ($3 each) at the lei shops on Maunakea St. Different kinds of leis have specific symbolic meaning, but they are best known as signs of welcome. Before the advent of jet planes, locals would celebrate "Boat Day" by purchasing leis at these stalls to garland arriving friends at the pier. Today most visitors make do with a gift of honey roasted peanuts on the plane; treat yourself to a garland of flowers.

The **Maritime Museum,** Pier 7, 1st floor, has displays on the history of surfing and the 19th-century whaling industry. It also has a collection of old ships from the Honolulu Harbor (open daily 9am-5pm; $7, ages 6-17 $3). The **Falls of Clyde,** a unique four-masted ship built in 1878 and once used as an oil tanker, is dry-docked in the harbor.

The **Iolani Palace** (538-1471), at King and Richard St., the only royal residence ever built in America, was first the home of King Kalakaua and his sister Queen Liliuokalani. The deposed Liliuokalani spent nine months here as a prisoner. Now millions of dollars back the museum's search for the original palace furniture. In the interim, the palace displays sumptuously carved *koa* furniture and elegant European decor. You can tour the grounds on your own, but the official tour inside the building gives interesting historical facts. (45-min. tours begin every 15 min. Wed.-Sat. 9am-2:15pm; $4, ages 5-12 $1, under 5 not admitted.) Call 522-0832 for reservations or go to the barracks or the palace grounds at least a half hour beforehand to reserve tickets. The palace grounds include the **Coronation Pavilion,** where the Royal Hawaiian Band gives free concerts on Fridays at noon.

Across King St. stands the warrior-like **Kamehameha I statue,** erected in 1883 in honor of the Hawaiian ruler who unified the islands in 1791. In commemoration of his rule, his statue is draped with leis on June 11, when *palau* (horseback) riders parade through Waikiki. At the corner of Beretania and Richard St. stands Hawaii's postmodern **State Capitol,** an architectural mosaic of Hawaii's landscape. The pillars represent palm trees, while the inverted dome of the house chambers rises like a volcano, and reflecting pools call to mind the blue Pacific nearby. Outside stands a sculpture of Father Damien (open Mon.-Fri. 9am-4pm; free). South of the State Capitol at Punchbowl and King St. is **Kawaiahao Church.** The church, built from coral rocks, was completed in 1842. Services are held in Hawaiian at 8am and 10:30am on Sundays. The church is sometimes called "the Westminster Abbey of Hawaii" because it was used for coronations and funerals of Hawaiian kings and queens. The graves of early missionaries lie on the grounds between the church and the **Honolulu Mission House Museum,** 553 S. King St. (531-0481). Museum guides give a 45-minute tour of missionary period rooms. (Open Tues.-Sat. 9am-4pm, Sun. noon-4pm. $3.50, under 15 $1, under 5 free.) The museum also offers walking tours of the historic district, including a tour of the mission house (3-hr. tours Mon.-Fri., 9:30am). For a complete guide to this district, pick up the **Capital District Walking Tour** from the Hawaii Visitor's Bureau.

Nearby, the **Honolulu Academy of Arts,** 900 S. Beretania St. (532-8701), houses one of the finest collections of Asian art in the U.S. The 35 galleries and six garden courts also display 17th-century samurai armor, African art, and temporary exhibits. (Open Tues.-Sat. 10am-4:30pm, Sun. 1-5pm. Tours Tues.-Sat. 11am, Sun. 1pm. Suggested donation $4, students and seniors $2.) The **Bishop Museum,** 1525 Bernice St. 847-3511), in Kalihi, houses an eclectic and well-respected if somewhat disorganized collection of artifacts from the Indo-Pacific region. It is the best Hawaiiana museum in the world, and deserves a good portion of your day. The museum's planetarium features a show on the history of Polynesian celestial navigation (Sun.-Thurs. 11am and 2pm, Fri.-Sat. 11am, 2pm, and 7pm; reservations required). The museum's Hawaiian Hall offers lei-making and hula demonstrations daily from 9am to 3pm. (Call 848-4106 for further information. Open daily 9am-5pm. $8, ages 6-17 $7.) Take bus #2 (School St.) from Waikiki.

On December 7, 1941 a stunned nation listened to the reports of the Japanese bombing of the U.S. Pacific Fleet in **Pearl Harbor.** Today, the **U.S.S. Arizona National Memorial** (422-2771) commemorates that event. The memorial is an austere, three-part structure built over the sunken battleship in which over a thousand sailors perished. The memorial's unique sagging center represents the demoralizing defeat of the *Arizona;* the higher ends of the structure symbolize the U.S.'s military victory when Japan surrendered in 1945. The Navy offers free tours of the memorial from 8am to 3pm, including a 30-minute film, and sends launches out to the hull every 15 minutes. No children under six years of age or under 45" tall are admitted on the launch. Dress is casual, but swimsuits and flip-flops are prohibited in order to preserve the somber and respectful mood. Veterans often throw leis into the viewing well over the hull. The **visitors center** is open Monday through Sunday 7:30am to 5pm with the last program starting at 3pm. Take the #20 bus from Waikiki, the #50, 51, or 52 bus from Ala Moana, or the $2 shuttle from the major Waikiki hotels (839-0911). Tickets to the memorial are free, but two-hour-plus waits are not unusual. (Bring a book.) While waiting for your number to be called, you can visit the **U.S.S. Bowfin Submarine Museum and Park** (423-1341) next door. Navy buffs will be kept occupied with genuine torpedoes and a generous dose of naval history. Tours of the submarine and the museum take 20 minutes each. (Open daily 8am-5pm. $8, military (active or veterans) $5, ages 4-12 $3.) If you are at Pearl Harbor on the first Saturday of the month, consider stopping by the Nimitz Gate at noon for a free four-hour tour of the **Navy Visit Ship** at the Pearl Harbor Navy Base (471-0281).

Wake up early on Wednesday, Saturday, or Sunday morning and pop over to the "swap meet" held from 7am to 3pm in Aloha Stadium. It's a great chance to people-watch or buy a gift. Rows of vendors sell everything from t-shirts to fruits and vegetables (admission $1 per car).

Mauka (Inland)

Mauka from downtown is the lush **Nuuanu Valley;** the next valley to the east is the **Manoa Valley.** At the mouth of the Manoa Valley lies the **University of Hawaii,** where lecture attendance drops as the surf rises. The campus bulletin boards are a great place to find out about apartments for rent, tickets for sale, and upcoming film, theater, and music events.

One of the best day hikes on the island begins at the end of Manoa Rd. and trails through one mi. of lush tropical greenery to **Manoa Falls.** Once there, you can take a cool freshwater dip in the pool under the falls. Trail conditions are determined by the weather; visit after a dry spell and the falls are less impressive but after a heavy rain you'll be mud-sliding and torrent-watching at the same time. Take bus #5 from Ala Moana to the end of Manoa Rd. The falls and Lyon Arboretum (see next paragraph) are close together and make for a beautiful day of hiking. Another good hike winds through tree-lined **Waahila Park.** The undemanding trail appears underused. Take the #14 St. Louis Heights bus, or, by car, turn up St. Louis Dr. from about the 3000 block of Kapiolani Blvd. Go uphill until you see the Waahila Ridge sign.

The **Lyon Arboretum,** 3860 Manoa Rd. (988-3177), at the end of Manoa Valley four mi. from Waikiki, maintains a superb collection of tropical plants, shrubs, and trees. Free tours (1½ hr.) are offered on the first Friday, third Wednesday (both at 1pm), and third Saturday (at 10am) of every month (open Mon.-Fri. 9am-3pm, Sat. 9am-noon; $1). The visitors center has a map with suggestions for different 20- to 30-min.-hikes in this peaceful bit of paradise.

The ridge just *ewa* (west) of Manoa with its expansive views is the perfect place to watch the sunset. Go up Makiki St. to Round Top Dr. and follow this switchback road to romantic **Puuualakaa Park,** where you can see Honolulu light up for the night. If you are driving, be aware that the park gates close at 7:45pm. Hawaii's biggest attraction (over 6 million visitors each year) is the **National Memorial Cemetery of the Pacific,** 2177 Puowaina Dr. (546-3190). This memorial, also known as the **"Punchbowl Cemetery,"** because of its location in the Puowaina Crater, contains the graves of 22,000 soldiers who died in the Spanish-American War, both World Wars, Korea, and Vietnam.

The **Contemporary Museum,** 2411 Makiki Heights Dr. on the outside slope of Punchbowl (526-1322), displays impressive works by David Hockney and other internationally renowned artists. (Open Tues.-Sat. 10am-4pm, Sun. noon-4pm. $5.)

Parallel to the Manoa Valley, the **Pali Hwy.** (Rte. 61) winds its way through Nuuanu Valley and over into Kailua, on the windward side of the island. On the way, stop at **Hanaiakamalama (Queen Emma's Summer Palace),** 2913 Pali Hwy. (595-3167), formerly a posh summer retreat for the Kamaaina elite. A nonprofit organization provides tours. (Open daily 9am-4pm. $4, seniors $3, ages 12-18 $1, under 12 50¢.) Take bus #4 (Waikiki) or any bus that begins with "Kailua"or "Kaneohe" from Ala Moana Shopping Center; the ride is about one hour. If you are driving, pull into the **Pali Lookout** as you near the top of Pali. Although this observation point is always packed with tourists, the view overlooking the windward side is undoubtedly one of the finest in all the islands. But hang onto your hat—the wind blusters. According to legend, Kamehameha the Great consolidated his kingdom when the wind blew Oahu's soldiers over this dramatic cliff.

ENTERTAINMENT AND NIGHTLIFE

Bars, restaurants, and theaters abound in Waikiki, making nightlife as wild as your feet and liver will allow. Indoor cinemas allow the less rambunctious to escape the city's bright lights. The University of Hawaii's **Hemenway Theatre** (956-6468), in the Physical Sciences Building, shows second-run films for $3.50. The **Honolulu Academy of Arts,** 900 S. Beretania St. (532-8768), features foreign films. There is a full season of symphony and opera at the **Niel Blaisdell Center** (521-2711). Year-round theater (musical and dramatic) is staged at the **Manoa Valley Theater** (988-6131). Don't miss the **Honolulu Zoo's** "wildest show in town" summer series of Wednesday night concerts (971-7171). Admission is free, concerts start at 6pm. Different musicians are featured every week; call to find out who's performing.

Hawaii IMAX Theatre, 325 Seaside Ave. (923-4629), will give you an inside look at Hawaii's volcanoes, literally. The enormous screen and surround sound are enough to make you pick up your feet in fright as the lava flows vividly before you.

Films are shown on the hour. The regular feature, **"Hidden Hawaii,"** alternates with a different film. (Open noon-9pm. $7.50, ages 3-11 $3.)

Also peruse the *Honolulu Weekly,* distributed free of charge on Tuesdays, for information on shows, movies, and events, as well as witty restaurant reviews.

Bars and Clubs

The Wave, 1877 Kalakaua Ave. (941-0424), on the edge of Waikiki. Fine locale. Loud music and dancing. Mixed crowd. Open daily 9pm-4am. Cover for live bands.

Pink Cadillac, 478 Ena (942-5282). One of the few dancing options for the 18-21 set. Neo-rave and neon lights. Hip-hop and progressive. Predictably young crowd. Open 9pm-1:45am. Cover: under 21 $10; 21 and over $5, Fri.-Sat. $3.

Anna Bananas, 2440 S. Beretania (946-5190), near the university. The crowd is generally local bikers and surfers with a liberal sprinkling of college students. Steinlager on draft $2.25. Open 11:30am-2am.

Rose and Crown, 131 Kaiulani Ave. (923-5833). A stately British public house smack in the middle of Waikiki. Popular with Australians. Single draft $1.50, 34 oz. Bud $4. Open 11am-2am.

Moose McGillycuddy's, 310 Lewers St. (923-0751). A bar that opens at 8am and a long happy hour (11am-8pm) attract a serious party crowd from the surrounding hostels. Lively pick-up scene. Dancing to live music daily 9pm-1:30am.

Seagull Bar and Restaurant, 2463 Kuhio Ave. (924-7911), Kuhio Village Resort in Waikiki. Dark bar with an international crowd. A lot of young hostelers hang out here for the low drink prices. Slam a beer for a mere $1.50. Open daily 1pm-2am.

Hula's Bar and Leis, 2103 Kuhio Ave. (923-0669). Popular gay bar; dark, intimate, and laid-back. Popcorn maker in back. No cover. Open daily 10am-2am

■■■ SEASONAL EVENTS

A variety of events in Oahu testify to Hawaii's ethnic diversity, reflect on its colorful history, and celebrate its outdoor spirit. The Hawaii Visitors Bureau publishes a *Calendar of Events,* which gives a complete listing. Also check the "What's-On" listings in the Friday paper.

Narcissus Festival (553-3181), mid-Jan. Celebrate the Chinese New Year with fireworks and a raucous lion dance in Chinatown.

Buffalo's Annual Big Board Surfing Classic, late Feb. On Makaha Beach, Leeward Oahu. A surfing competition with entertainment and food.

Cherry Blossom Festival (949-2255), late Feb.-March. The Japanese community puts on tea ceremonies, cooking demonstrations, fashion shows, and more all over the island. Also, look for *bon* dances most weekends in summer.

Oahu Kite Festival, late March. Kite flying competitions and demonstrations. Call Kite Fantasy, 922-5483 (see Waikiki, page 451).

Annual Hawaiian Festival of Music (637-6566), mid-April. Waikiki Shell, Honolulu. Hawaiian and mainland groups compete for awards in a festival of symphonic strings, choirs, madrigal-crooning monks, swing groups, and bands.

Lei Day (266-7654), May 1, in Kapiolani Park. Lei-making contests, and pageants. Local schools celebrate by singing Hawaiian songs, dancing, and stringing leis.

King Kamehameha Day (536-6540), June 11. A parade through downtown and Waikiki follows lei-draping ceremony at the Kamehameha statue on King St.

King Kamehameha Annual Hula and Chant Competition (536-6540), late June. Neil Blaisdell Center, Honolulu. Modern and ancient hula and chant competition. *Halaus* compete amidst cheers from a boisterous crowd.

Aloha Week Festivities (944-8857), mid-Sept. The highlight of week-long events is the elaborate parade with *pau* riders on horseback.

Triple Crown of Surfing (377-5850), Dec. 1-9, contingent upon weather and surfing conditions. The finals are held at Banzai Pipeline and aired on national TV.

THE OTHER SIDE OF THE ISLAND

Everything on Oahu outside Honolulu is considered "the other side." In general, the farther from the city you scoot, the fewer tourists you will encounter. Concrete and glass quickly fade into pineapple and sugarcane fields sprinkled with small outlying communities. **H-2** going north traverses a fertile plateau before descending the sugar-and-surfer town of Haleiwa on the North Shore. Well-maintained highways lead east from Haleiwa and the scenic windward coast. To the west you can only travel as far as Kaena Point, where the paved road ends and a rough, rocky trail begins. You can see the Leeward Coast by traveling west on **H-1** from Honolulu until it becomes **Farrington Highway (Rte. 93).**

A drive around the perimeter of the island can be done in five hours, but it's best to give yourself at least a full day. Start on the Windward Coast and work your way around the perimeter. To reach the southern Windward Coast, take bus #55 from Ala Moana. To see the North Shore, hop on bus #52 at Ala Moana. Both buses run every hour daily from 7am until 6pm. The **Kamehameha Hwy. (Rte. 83)** skirts most of the Windward Coast and North Shore. The drive is absolutely spectacular; if it's sunny, consider renting a convertible.

ACCOMMODATIONS AND CAMPING

There is a smaller pool of accommodations in these less densely populated areas. Call for information on nearby bed and breakfasts places (see Honolulu: Accommodations, page 447). Many of the main grocery stores, such as Foodland, have bulletin boards outside listing daily to long-term accommodations available from private homeowners. If you find a town you can't bear to leave, checking the board could provide an alternative to distant hostels or returning to the touristy clutches of Honolulu.

Backpacker's Vacation Inn and Plantation Villas, 59-788 Kamehameha Hwy. (638-7838), ¼-mi. north of Waimea Bay. Adjacent to placid Three Table Bay and neighboring Shark's Cove. International crowd of travelers and water sport enthusiasts. Plantation Village consists of cottages with bunks, bathroom, shared kitchen and laundry facilities, and color TV. Comfortable, rambunctious, youthful atmosphere. Honolulu Airport pick-up twice daily. Weekend BBQs. Co-ed bunks and rooms. Free use of boogie-boards and snorkeling equipment. 50% discounts on some nearby sights. Bunks $16. Doubles $35-45. Summer rates $96 per week. Key deposit $20.

Thomsen's Bed and Breakfast, 59-420 Kamehameha Hwy. (638-7947; fax 638-7694), is located in a comfortable 2-story home near Sunset Beach. Studio apartment above garage has cable TV, phone, kitchenette, and private bath. $65 per night for 2 people, $350 per week. Call for reservations.

You may see signs for hostels, other than Backpackers, along the Kamehameha Hwy., but be wary, they may not be licensed. **Camping** can be beautiful along the coast, but unfortunately, there have been reports of violence against tourists at some campgrounds in recent years. It's not always easy to pick a safe place by sight, but piles of empty beer cans and trash are signs that someone else may consider a place their territory; it's best to steer clear and pick another spot. Remember that rangers patrol the beach to roust illegal campers. Don't risk it; get a permit.

■■■ WINDWARD OAHU AND HANAUMA BAY

Miles of beaches and rural towns span the 40-mi. coast, running from Laie in the north to Mokapu Point in the south; the result is the most scenic drive on the island. The Koolau Range rises out of the ocean and the highway slices through the mountains, skirting the cliffs along the sea. Farther south, Kalanianaole Hwy. wraps around a rugged 2-mi. stretch to Koko Head, the eastern boundary of Honolulu.

FOOD

Fruit vendors, plate lunches, and shave ice are plentiful on the Windward Coast.

Bueno Nalo, 41-865 Kalanianaole Hwy. (259-7186), in Waimanalo. The best restaurant for miles. Delicious Mexican meals ($6-8). Try the absolutely incredible cheese enchiladas. Open daily 11:30am-9pm.

Frankie's Drive-Inn, 41-1610 Kalanianaole Hwy. (259-7819), Waimanalo. Frankie has been serving up cheeseburgers (95¢) at this take-out since 1953. Yummy ice cream shakes. Take-out only. Open Mon.-Sat. 9:30am-4:30pm.

Waimanalo BBQ, 41-857 Kalanianaole Hwy. (259-8700), is a great place to stop after a day at the beach. Delicious ice cream ($1.50) and all flavors of shave ice. Plate lunches and island food $4-6. Open "from the time I get here 'til the time I go home," but 9am-4:30pm is pretty definite.

Kaaawa Country Kitchen and Grocery, 51-480 Kamehameha Hwy. (237-8484), Kaaawa. Across from Swanz Beach Park. This Mom-and-Pop country drive-in has kept the locals of Kaaawa satisfied for more than 30 years. The teri-beef ($4.50) is tasty. Open Mon.-Fri. 6:30am-2:30pm, Sat.-Sun. 6:30am-3:30pm.

SIGHTS

From Waikiki, take **Kalanianaole Hwy.** (Rte. 72) east to **Koko Head Crater.** Some of the friendliest and most colorful fish in the Pacific reside in **Hanauma Bay,** formed where the ocean has washed away the crater's eastern wall. These federally protected waters are the spot supreme for snorkeling in Oahu. For the clearest underwater trip, come early in the morning (before 10am). The tourists flock here in droves; park officials stop letting cars into the parking lot when things get too crowded. A 10-minute walk to the left of the bay brings you to the less well-known **Toilet Bowl.** Locals climb in when it's full and get flushed up and down as waves fill and empty the chamber through natural lava plumbing. When the surf's high, swimmers should be cautious; the sides are rocky and the ocean is always unpredictable.

One mi. farther on Kalanianaole Hwy., a similar mechanism drives the **Halona Blow Hole** to release its spray. The dramatic effect is dependent upon tidal conditions and can vary from a weak squirt to a full-blown Moby Dick spout. From here, the island of Molokai, 20 mi. away, can be viewed, and on a clear day, as many as four of the neighboring islands may be sighted. **Secret Beach,** to the right of Halona Blow Hole, was the site of Burt Lancaster and Deborah Kerr's famous kiss in the sand in *From Here to Eternity.* The lone traveler may find consolation in watching the sea turtles that sometimes visit around the bay (although they probably won't be up for a passionate smooch).

Sandy Beach, 25 minutes from Waikiki just beyond Halona, is a top spot for bodysurfing, boogie-boarding, people-watching, and serves as the center of the Hawaiian summer surf circuit. The beach is expansive and pleasantly sandy, but the summer swells burst onto the shore with spine-crashing force, making swimming unattractive to the weak at heart.

The highway continues toward Mokapu Point, providing a succession of postcard-worthy views. **Manana (Rabbit) Island** (so named because it was thought to resembles a swimming hare with flattened ears) and smaller **Kaohikaipu (Turtle) Island** are offshore. **Makapuu Beach,** 41-095 Kalanianaole Hwy., is a prime place to bodysurf. Before swimming, check the flags hoisted by the lifeguards, red flags mean danger, no swimming. Across from Makapuu lies **Sea Life Park** (259-7933), a minor-league Sea World, with performing penguins and the world's only "wholphin," a whale-dolphin hybrid. ($20, seniors and ages 6-12 $9, ages 4-5 $4. Open Sat.-Thurs. 9:30am-5pm, Fri. 9:30am-10pm.)

Kaiona Beach Park is located just past Makai Pier. The next beach you'll come to is **Waimanalo Beach Park,** which offers a shady tree area, clean facilities, and a cooling onshore breeze. The best bodysurfing for novices can be found at **Sher-**

woods and, on weekends, at **Bellows Air Force Base.** Both are on Kalanianaole off the road to Kailua; neither park provides lifeguards.

Kailua Town and the nearby **Kailua Beach Park** are *the* places to go for prime beach area unadulterated by large hotels. Kalanianaole ends by intersecting **Kailua Road.** Follow this road toward Kailua Town and Kailua Beach Park (450 Kawailoa Rd.). This is excellent **windsurfing** territory, as the enthusiastic beach locals will attest. The sandy beach and strong, steady onshore winds are perfect for windsurfers of all abilities. If you left your rig at home, two nearby companies rent equipment. **Windsurfing Hawaii** (261-6067) rents beginner boards for $30 per day (harness $5 extra) and shortboards for $40 per day. They also have boogie-boards ($10 per day), wave skis ($25 per day), and two-person kayaks ($35 per day). Sailboarding lessons are $35 per person for a three-hour group clinic. Look for the van in the beach parking lot Monday through Saturday. **Kailua Sailboard Company,** 130 Kailua Rd. (two blocks from the park, 262-2555), rents "standard" longboards for $27 per day (harness $5 extra) and Bic Ace tech shortboards for $30 per day (open 8:30am-5pm). They also offer three-hour beginner lessons for $39 at 10:30am and 2pm daily. When the winds are blowing, those left on shore may cringe as they are pelted with powdery sand (particularly perilous to contact lens wearers). If you can bear the grit, this is a great place to swim.

White sand and emerald green waters make nearby **Lanikai Beach** (Mokulua Dr. east of Kailua) the best place on Oahu to savor the sunrise. (Kailua Rd. in the other direction takes you to **Kaneohe** via Kamehameha Hwy.) Grab your snorkel gear and swim or wade out into the bay; better yet, use an inner tube and float around effortlessly. If you enjoy tropical flowers, visit the free **Haiku Gardens,** 46-316 Haiku Rd. (247-6671), where many weddings are held (open daily sunrise to sunset). The **Ulupo Heiau temple,** 1200 Kailua Rd., next to the YMCA was supposedly built by the legendary *menebunes,* a mischievous little people. The temple still stands as a platform of black lava rock overlooking the Kawainui marsh. Smooth stones lead across the jagged lava of the *heiau* and down the far side to the roots of a great banyan tree, where a natural spring wells up.

Look for the **Valley of the Temples,** 47-200 Kahekili Hwy., a burial ground where the serene **Byodo-In Temple** can also be found. A replica of a temple in Uji, Japan, it was built in 1968 to commemorate the 100th anniversary of Japanese immigrants' first arrival in Hawaii. Stroll through the tropical gardens and by the running stream filled with 10,000 brightly colored Japanese carp (but watch out for the resident peacock with attack-dog tendencies). Ring the three-ton brass bell to bring happiness and the blessings of the Buddha. (Open daily sunrise to sunset. $2.)

Approaching the North Shore on the Kamehameha Hwy., you will reach **Kualoa Regional Park** and **Chinaman's Hat,** an island named for its conical shape. Much of *Karate Kid II* was filmed on the island. North of here, **Swanzy Beach State Park, Kaaawa Beach Park,** and **Kahana Bay Park** are good places to picnic or swim. Right around the bend from **Punaluu** is the entrance to **Sacred Falls Park,** legendary birthplace of the pig god. The falls are a 2-mi. walk from the parking lot. The trail crosses a stream twice and takes about an hour each way. The falls and the cool, refreshing pool underneath make the hike worthwhile.

Past **Laie** the land gives way to abandoned sugar plantations. **Amorient Aquafarms** (293-5311) runs a 175-acre shrimp and fish farm near Kahuku. Stop at their roadside stall to sample fresh catfish or Black Tiger shrimp. Rounding the island's northern tip at Kahuku, you will also see strange two-armed windmills gyrating on the hillside—another experimental energy project. The **Polynesian Cultural Center,** staffed by Mormon students from adjacent Brigham Young University (not the one in Utah), puts on a show that combines entertainment with tradition in presenting some of the oral histories that play an important part in Polynesian cultures. The show is way overpriced (admission $25; with buffet $42).

■■■ NORTH SHORE AND CENTRAL OAHU

Home to sugar cane fields and surfers, it is hard to believe that the North Shore is on the same island as Honolulu. You'll find a plethora of people who, like Odysseus, have turned quick stops into six- or eight-year sojourns. Once there, you may understand why. Many Oahu locals who work in Honolulu come home to the North Shore and its more traditionally Hawaiian way of life. The pace is slow and peaceful in the summer—you can spend a day counting the different blues of the sky and ocean. Things heat up in the winter when the surfer crowd descends to shred the waves along **Sunset Beach** and the **Banzai Pipeline,** inundating the North Shore with surfing competitions and bikini contests. The best things to see here are those you stumble across on your own—secluded bays free from footprints, coral reefs full of brightly colored fish, or if you're lucky, the perfect wave.

FOOD

Kua Aina Sandwich, 66-214 Kamehameha Hwy., in Haleiwa (637-6067). Crowds line up at lunch time for delicious giant burgers on kaiser rolls ($4.60). Don't miss the homemade crispy french fries $1.10. Open daily 11am-8pm.

Pizza Bob's (637-5095), in the back of the Haleiwa Shopping Center. Happy hour (Mon.-Fri. 3-5pm) includes 99¢ draft beers. On weekdays try the lunch special of soup or salad and two slices of pizza with Maui potato chips and soda, $5.50. Large pizza $12. Open Mon.-Fri. 11am-10pm, Sat.-Sun. 11am-4pm.

Meg's Country Drive-in, 66-200 Kamehameha Hwy. (637-9122), next door to Kua Aina. Twenty varieties of plate lunches ($3-5) and *shaka min.* Also sells scrumptious smoothies. Open 7am-6pm, breakfast served 'til 11:30am.

Coffee Gallery, 66-250 Kamehameha Hwy. (637-5571). They did away with the backyard compost mulcher after nearby businesses complained about the smell, but they're still die-hard environmentalists. Daily vegan soup with fresh baked bread for $3. Open Mon.-Thurs. 6am-9pm, Fri. 6am-11pm, Sat.-Sun. 7am-11pm.

The Sugar Bar, 67-069 Kealohanui (637-6989), in Waialua, is a true dive, with an interesting mix of bikers, surfers, and locals. Area bands play on Fri. and Sat. to an enthusiastic crowd. No cover. Open 11am-2am.

SIGHTS

Even if you left your supply of Mr. Zog's Sex Wax (and your surfboard) at home, you will still have ample opportunity to frolic in the untamed waters. The action on the North Shore centers around **Haleiwa;** once a plantation town, Haleiwa is now enlivened by surf shops and art galleries. **Surf-n-Sea,** 62-595 Kamehameha Hwy. (637-9887), rents snorkeling gear ($9.50 per day), windsurfing equipment ($12 first hr.; $3.50 per additional hr.), surfboards ($5; $3.50), and boogie-boards ($3; $2) and gives surfing and sailboarding lessons. To the north of Haleiwa is **Waimea Beach Park,** where locals jump off a high rock formation into the sea. This beach shares its name with **Waimea Valley** (638-8511), an 1800-acre nature preserve with tropical gardens and a 45-ft. waterfall extravaganza. Performers dive off the cliffs daily at 11am, 12:30, 2, 2:45, and 3:30pm (also 5pm in the summer). Admission to the Falls Park is $20, ages 6-12 $9, ages 4-5 $4, free for people in wheelchairs and their pushers. Ask about free nighttime strolls offered the day before and the day of the full moon. For free round-trip shuttle service from Waikiki call 988-8276. About ¼ mi. north of Waimea on Pupukea Rd. lies **Puu O Mahuka Heiau,** the largest temple of its kind on the island—it was used for human sacrifices until 1794. Today, when visitors leave offerings they stick to fruits and flowers. Turn right off Kamehameha onto Pupukea Rd. at the Foodland and follow the signs that say "State Monument."

Back on Kamehameha Hwy., another few minutes drive will bring you to breathtaking **Sunset Beach** and the **Banzai Pipeline,** infamous winter wavelands of the world. The beaches are big enough to stay sprinkled rather than packed with people. For a bird's eye view, you can fly (or fall 10,000 ft.) with **Skydive Hawaii,** Rte. 930, Dillingham Airfield. (Tandem jumping $225, accelerated free fall $300. Call

521-4404 or 637-9700 for reservations.) Or if you prefer, head to secluded, beautiful, and windy **Makuleia Beach**.

Rte. 82 leads you through Wahiawa, another plantation town and home to tattoo parlors and the **Sacred Healing Stones,** which became so popular in the first part of this century that they had to be enclosed in a concrete, cubical "temple" for their protection. On the way, take a poke around the unapologetically commercial **Dole Pineapple Pavilion,** 64-1550 Kamehameha Hwy. (621-8468). Displays offer the visitor a crash course on the ins and outs of the pineapple business. Inside you can buy pineapple memorabilia, from t-shirts to the puzzling, non-dairy Dole Whip. Be sure to drink some of the delicious free pineapple juice flowing from the plastic pineapple towering in the corner of the store. If your stomach churns at the thought of supporting corporate America, then eat next door at the **Helemano Plantation,** 64-1510 Kamehameha Hwy. (622-3929), a non-profit organization that provides residences and jobs for the mentally retarded (Chinese buffet $8.25).

Honolulu is less than an hour away along Rte. 99 and H-2. As you drive back, you'll notice the suburban sprawl of Mililani extending Honolulu's tentacles farther into the countryside.

Maui

Fun-loving Maui is appropriately named for the demigod of mischief. According to legend, the sun once moved too quickly across the sky, leaving behind unripened fruits, too little daylight for farmers and fishermen to do their work, and not enough heat for women to dry their cloth. Hina asked her son, Maui, for help. From the top of Haleakala ("House of the Sun") Maui captured the sun with 16 ropes. The sun begged to be freed, promising to move more slowly. Maui released the sun, but left behind a few ropes, now bleached white, to remind the sun of their agreement.

Maui certainly captured the sun, as well as the sand, the waves, and more than 2 million visitors a year. The island's resort areas are crowded and the beaches and waters are filled with families on vacation. But with a little effort (and a car), one can find unspoiled stretches of sand. A large, semi-permanent population of windsurfers provide a more youthful, laid-back alternative to the plentiful supply of short-stay tourists.

Maui is like several islands in one. The West Maui Mountains slope down to an arid coastline of drowsy little towns (including Kaanapali, the resort haven). A land bridge between two ancient volcanoes supports the Wailuku-Kahului sprawl (pop. 63,000), as well as acres of wind-blown sugarcane. Home of the mystifying Haleakala volcano, the East Mountains contain an imperiled native ecosystem, while Paia's aggressively '60s feel foreshadows the laid-back lushness of the Hana coast. For the water-weary, the western side of the island is dry and mountainous, with grazing cattle and farmlands. The east is a rainforest enveloped by the famous Hana Highway.

PRACTICAL INFORMATION AND ORIENTATION

Visitors Information: Visitor Information Kiosk (877-3894), at the Kahului Airport terminal. Helpful orientation with free map. Open daily 6am-9pm. **Maui Visitors Bureau,** 1727 Wili Pa Loop, (244-3530). Going toward Kahului on Mill St., take a left onto Imi Kala St. Friendly assistance with itinerary planning, activities, and accommodations, but they will not make reservations. Information on Molokai. Open Mon.-Fri. 8am-4:30pm.

Outdoors Information: Haleakala National Park, P.O. Box 369, Makawao 96768 (572-7749), provides recorded information on weather conditions, daily ranger-guided hikes, and special activities. For information on camping and cab-

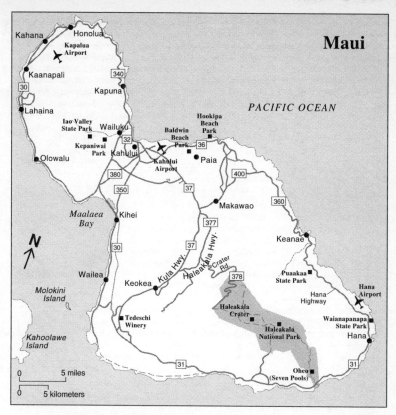

Maui

Kahana
Honolua
Kapalua Airport
Kaanapali
340
Kapuna
30
Lahaina
Iao Valley State Park
Wailuku
32
Kepaniwai Park
Kahului
Olowalu
Kahului Airport
380
350
37
Maalaea Bay
Kihei
30
Wailea
37
Keokea
Molokini Island
Kahoolawe Island
0   5 miles
0   5 kilometers

PACIFIC OCEAN

Hookipa Beach Park
Baldwin Beach Park
36
Paia
400
Makawao
377
Kula Hwy.
Haleakala Hwy.
Crater Rd.
378
Haleakala Crater
Tedeschi Winery
Haleakala National Park
31
Keanae
Puaakaa State Park
Hana Highway
Hana Airport
Waianapanapa State Park
Hana
31
Oheo (Seven Pools)

ins call 572-9177. Park Headquarters (572-9306) is open daily 7:30am-4pm. **Department of Parks and Recreation,** War Memorial Gym, 1580 Kaahumanu Ave. (243-7389), between Kahului and Wailuku. Information and permits ($3) for county parks. Open Mon.-Fri. 8am-4pm. You may have to knock on the window. **Division of State Parks,** 54 High St. (244-5354), at Main St. in Wailuku. Maui and Molokai state parks information. Go downstairs by the parking area. Open Mon.-Fri. 8-11am, noon-4pm.

Bus: Trans Hawaiian (877-7308) offers hourly service between Kahului Airport and the major Lahaina-Kaanapali $13; reservation is necessary only for return. Runs daily 7am-7pm on the hr. The **Lahaina Express** also provides free transport between the Kaanapali Resorts and Lahaina. Schedules in the *Lahaina Historical Guide* (available at the tourist stands in Lahaina).

Boats: Ferries are an ideal mode of transport from Maui to Molokai and Lanai. Going by boat is more exciting and cheaper than flying. The **Maui Princess** (661-8397) runs daily from Lahaina to Kaunakakai (Molokai) at 7am and from Molokai, to Lahaina at 3:55pm. Crossing takes about 1¾ hr. and costs $25 one way. **Expeditions** (661-3756) runs daily between Lahaina and Manele, Lanai, $25 one way.

Tours: GrayLine Maui (877-5507, 834-1033 in Honolulu, 800-367-2420 from the mainland) offers frequent tours. To: Iao Valley/Lahaina ($25); Hana (10-hr. extravaganza including lunch; $75.) Call Honolulu office for info. and reservations.

Taxi: Resort Taxi (661-5285). $9 ride into Kahului or Wailuku from the airport.

Car Rental: A capital idea on this island. Make reservations in advance to save money. Under 21-derlings will find renting anything with 4 wheels exceedingly problematic. Try teaming up with older travelers at hostels. **VIP,** Haleakala Hwy. (877-2054), near Kahului Airport. $25 per day. Call hostels to see if they can get you better rates. Used vehicles at **Word of Mouth** (877-2436 or 800-533-5929), on Dairy Rd., near Kahului Airport. $19 per day, $23 per day with A/C. 3-day min. Must be 25. The **national chains** have desks or courtesy phones at the airport.

Bicycle Rental: Bicycle touring on West Maui, with its flat roads, is highly rewarding. On the other hand, the twisting and crowded Hana Hwy. is deadly. **The Island Biker,** Kahului Shopping Center (877-7744), rents quality 21-speed mountain bikes for $18 per day, $60 per week. 5% discount with student ID. Open Mon.-Fri. 9am-5pm, Sat. 9am-3pm. **A&B Rentals,** 3481 Lower Honoapiilani Rd. (669-0027), near Kaanapali. $10 per day for typical bikes, or $50 per week. Open daily 9am-5pm.

Moped and Scooter Rental: A&B Moped and Scooter Rentals, 3481 Lower Honoapiilani Rd. (669-0027). Scooters $23 for 8 hr., $28 for 24 hr. Ask about weekly rates. Must be 18 with a major credit card. Open daily 9am-5pm. **Wheels R Us** (667-7751), Lahainalua Rd., Lahaina. New mopeds $29 for 24 hrs. Open daily 8am-5pm.

Water Equipment Rental: If you are planning an extended stay on the island, consider buying your equipment. Several places offer used boogie-boards at sale prices. The **Maui Windsurf Company,** 520 Keolani Pl. (877-4816 or 800-872-0999), near the Kahului Airport. Fanatic Angulo and other sailboards $45 per day, $250 per week. Roof rack and harness included. 2½-hr. beginner lessons (equipment included) $59. Open daily 8:30am-6pm. **Maui Dive Shop,** Azeka Pl., Kihei (879-3388), also at Wakea Ave., Kahului (661-5388), and 626 Front St. (667-0722), in Lahaina. Mask $3, snorkel $1.50, boogie-board $5, wetsuit $5. Open Mon.-Fri. 8am-5pm, Sat. 8am-6pm. **Hawaiian Reef Divers,** 129 Lahainalua Rd. (667-7647 or 667-6002), Lahaina. Good deals, friendly advice, and an excellent beach map. Snorkel set $2, boogie-boards $3 per day. Boat trips with snorkeling or scuba diving offered. Open daily 8am-6pm.

Library: 254 High St., Wailuku. Open Mon., Thurs. 9am-8pm, Tues.-Wed., Fri. 9am-5pm.

Laundromat: Happy Valley Wash 'n' Wear, 340 N. Market St., Wailuku. Wash 75¢, dry 25¢. Detergent vending machine. Open 24 hrs. **Cabanilla Kwik 'n' Kleen,** Lahaina Shopping Center, Lahaina. Open 24 hrs.

Weather: Land, 877-5111. Marine, 877-3477.

Whale Report Center: 661-8527. Information on humpback whale-watching.

Gay and Bisexual Information: 572-1884 (serves Maui, Molokai, Lanai). 24 hrs. **Out in Maui Hotline,** 872-6061, provides info. on gay and lesbian events.

Help Lines: Sexual Assault Crisis Center, 242-4357. 24 hrs. **Coast Guard Rescue,** 800-331-6176.

Travelers with Disabilities: Hawaii Care Van (669-2300) provides shuttle and tour service for a fee. **Wheelers** has one accessible van for rent. Call their main office (800-456-1371) for more info.

Hospital: Maui Memorial, 221 Mahalani St. (244-9056), Wailuku. 24-hr. **emergency room,** 242-2343.

Emergency: 911.

Post Office: Lahaina, Baldwin Ave. Open Mon.-Fri. 8am-5pm, Sat. 10am-2pm. **General Delivery ZIP Code:** 96761. **Paia,** Baldwin Ave. Open Mon.-Fri. 8am-4:30pm, Sat. 10:30am-12:30pm. **General Delivery ZIP Code:** 96779. **Wailuku,** 250 Imi Kala St., across from The Mill Yard. Open Mon.-Fri. 8:30am-4:30pm, Sat. 9-11am. **General Delivery ZIP Code:** 96793. **Kihei,** 1254 S. Kihei Rd., in Azeka Market Place. Open Mon.-Fri. 9am-4:30pm, Sat. 9-11am. **General Delivery ZIP Code:** 96753.

Kahului is the major **airport,** landing regular flights from the mainland and other islands. Planes also fly into **Kaanapali** and **Hana.** The **visitors information** booth in front of the Kahului terminal's entrance provides free maps, information, and directions. A taxi runs to hotels ($8-10), but the wise traveler will rent a car upon arrival; it's the only way to travel around the island efficiently.

Maui consists of two mountains joined at an isthmus. The highways follow the shape of the island in a broken figure-eight pattern. The **Kahului Airport** sits on the northern coast of the isthmus. To the west lie **Kahului** and **Wailuku. Rte. 30** leads to hot and dry **Lahaina** and **Kaanapali**, the major resort area. **Rte. 34** leads counter-clockwise around the same loop from the isthmus to where the paved road ends at **Kapuna.** Circling the slopes of Haleakala southbound along the eastern loop, **Rte. 31** runs past **Kihei** and **Wailea. Rte. 36** winds through rainy terrain, over 54 one-lane bridges and 600 hairpin curves, to **Hana. Rte. 40** or **Rte. 37** will lead you to **Rte. 377,** and then **Rte. 378,** which heads up 10,023-ft. **Haleakala.** Most roads are well-marked. Heed the four-wheel-drive warnings—most rental car contracts stipulate that dirt road driving is at the driver's own risk.

The **Upcountry** includes the area along the west slope of Haleakala and is home to a blend of artists and agriculturalists. The **Hana Coast** technically spans from the Keanae Peninsula to Kaupo, but the locals feel that anything beyond Paia and Ulu-palakua is on the "other side." **Central Maui,** wedged between two of the wettest spots on earth, averages only 30 in. of rain per year, yet through a miracle of engineering it supports acres upon acres of sugar canes. On the north shore, the influx of surfers and windsurfers has brought some resentment from the locals. Wailuku and Kahului lost much of their plantation-town charm as shopping malls and gas stations moved in. Finally, **West Maui** remains a mystery, since the mountains are privately owned and jealously guarded. Along the southwest coast, however, long beaches are home to the resort centers of Kaanapali and Lahaina.

Hitchhiking is illegal, but that doesn't stop some. The usual method is to stand roadside without the thumb signal, arms crossed. Local drivers, cognizant of the lack of public transport, are pretty well-disposed to giving lifts. But not the tourists, nor the police. Despite our sympathy for the car-less, we do not recommend hitch-hiking or picking up hitchhikers (no matter how terrific they look). Although most areas feel friendly, there have been recent reports of assaults on women in Maui.

ACCOMMODATIONS AND CAMPING

One of the fringe benefits of increasing tourism on Maui is the competitive pricing of vacation rentals. Some go for as little as $20 per night. Check the classified section of the *Maui News* and the bulletin boards throughout the island. **Mana Food,** 49 Baldwin Ave. (579-8078), in Paia, has a good board to check.

Package deals are another way for budget travelers to save. **Maui International Connection,** 520 Keolani Pl., Kahului (877-4999 or 800-963-6284), is a reliable source for hotel-car-windsurfing gear packages that cost about $500 for one week (open Mon.-Fri. 9am-5pm).

Campsites and hostels provide economic alternatives to Maui's resort hotels. The Wailuku hostels cater to windsurfers and others aquatically inclined. You can often find people with whom to share a car at hostels. During the winter, and especially around windsurfing events, hostels are packed—so book a month in advance.

Renting a car and camping on the island may be the best and cheapest way to enjoy Maui's natural magnificence. East Maui, with its safe and well-organized campgrounds, is perhaps the surest option. The opening of **Camp Pecosa** gives West Maui its first organized campsite. If you choose to camp, be selective: avoid areas that may be local hangouts, and stay away from the road. Police ask campers who are not in official camping sites to leave when they come across them, but rarely get sand in their shoes by actively searching for them. Some campers park their cars at a public park, and then walk down the road or beach for some distance. Early morning rain showers (especially along the Hana Coast) and ferocious mosquitoes make a light tent a sound investment. Long pants, sweaters, and blankets are a must, as the nights get cold.

Three **national park sites** on Maui allow walk-in free camping with a three-day maximum stay. Two state parks, **Waianapanapa** and **Polipoli,** allow camping, though the latter requires a four-wheel-drive-vehicle for access. State parks are **free** for a five-day maximum stay; required permits are available at any state Department of Parks (see Practical Information, page 444). County parks cost $3 per day (permits available at county parks office—see Practical Information, page 444).

Central Maui

Banana Bungalow Hotel and International Hostel, 310 N. Market St., Wailuku (244-5090 or 800-846-7835). Basic hostel supercharged with youthful energy from lively clientele. Windsurfers and international guests will plug you into the local tourist subculture. More activities than 1 person could do: daytrips, night trips to clubs, athletic games, dart tournaments. TV room with A/C, VCR. Laundry. Bulletin board with housing and windsurfing equipment info. Kitchen. Airport pick-up. Bunks $15. Singles with double bed $32. Doubles $39. $5 key deposit.

Northshore Inn, 2080 Vineyard St. (242-8999), Wailuku. No organized activities, but secure, friendly, and clean. Katie Moore, the owner, runs a tight ship. Comfy common room with TV. Fan and fridge in each room. Full kitchen. Laundry. Occasional barbecues. Airport pick-up. Many European and Australian tourists and windsurfers. Hostel bunks in spacious rooms $10. Singles $26. Doubles $35. $10 key deposit. Sheet rental $1. Towel rental 50¢.

Akahi Farms, 915 Kaupakulua Rd., Haiku (572-8792). A spiritual retreat for large groups, this beautiful 55-acre garden estate welcomes eco-tourists on a space-available basis. Simple rooms with futons and shared solar-heated showers. A 10-minute drive to Paia. Shared rooms $30 (includes tax). The farm also runs **Bamboo Mountain Sanctuary,** 911 Kaupakalua Rd., Haiku (572-5106). This B&B is in a former Zen monastery. Doubles with breakfast and shared bath $75.

Maui Palms Hotel, 170 Kaahumanu Ave. (877-0071), Kahului. Tired hotel by the ocean. The outside must have been decorated by the Partridge family. Clientele seems semi-permanent. TV, no A/C. Singles $45. Doubles $50. Triples $65.

H.A. Baldwin Beach Park, Rte. 36, ½ mi. west of Paia, a popular family beach. One of the 2 county parks. Summer home of friendly migrant surfers following the good waves. Outdoor shower, port-a-johns, and drinking water. Close to town and major (loud) highway. No shelter or shade in tent area. Tent and permit required. $3 per person, under 18 50¢. For permit information contact the County Dept. of Parks and Recreation (see Practical Information, page 460).

Rainbow Beach Park, Rte. 39, between Paia and Makawao. From Paia take Rte. 39 (Baldwin Ave.) toward Makawao. Park is on the right just past Makawao Union Church. Unreachable without a car, and a bit close to the road. Despite the name, not near the beach. Set on a pretty, grassy field. Covered eating pavilion, drinking water, and portable toilets. $3 per person, under 18 50¢. Permit required from the County Dep't of Parks and Recreation (see Practical Information, page 460).

West Maui and the Resort Area

Tony's Place, 13 Kauaula Rd., Lahaina (661-8040), off Front St. before town. Tony offers 3 bedrooms in his clean, quiet home. Just 5 min. from Lahaina's Old Town. Cable TV, kitchen. Two rooms with twin beds and shared bath, $60. One room with queen bed, $50. Summer and weekly discounts.

Nani Kai Hale, 73 N. Kihei Rd., Kihei (875-0630 or 800-822-4409, from U.S. 800-367-0630). Condominium on Sugar Beach, a 6-mi. sandy, shallow beach with no waves. Cable TV, fans. Wheelchair accessible. Laundry facilities. Cramped doubles with bath $40; Dec. 15-April 15 $45. One bedroom with kitchenette and deck $65, high-season $95. 4-day min. stay. Reserve ahead by phone.

Wailana Sands, 25 Wailana (879-2026 or 800-882-8550), off the 500 block of S. Kihei Rd. in Kihei. In a quiet cul-de-sac, this small resort is surrounded by much ritzier condos. Full kitchen, small pool, no view. Motel atmosphere. 4-day min. stay. 1-bedroom studio $45, Dec. 16-April 15 $65. Reserve a month in advance.

Windmills Park, between Honolua and Honokohau. White sand beach with some rocks—no facilities, but near Honolua Bay, a prime snorkeling spot. Campground operated by the Maui Land and Pineapple Company (669-6201). Free permit required, available at their Honolua office: 4900 Honoapiilani Hwy (Rte. 30).

Camp Pecusa, 800 Olowalu Village (661-4303), on Rte. 30, ¼ mi. north of the 14 mi. marker. Privately owned by an Episcopalian Church. Lots of loose, dry dirt and some centipedes. But you'll get a chance to see humpback whales cavorting in season (Nov.-May). Outdoor shower (sun-heated), wash basin, portable toilets, and tables. $5 per person on a walk-in basis (8am-6pm).

Hana Coast

Waianapanapa State Wayside, Hana Hwy., on the Paia-side of Hana, offers the best state camping facilities on the island. Near a black sand beach, blow holes, a *heiau*, and Waianapanapa Cave, as well as abundant coconut, papaya, and mango trees. The cabins (with linen, towels, kitchen, refrigerator, stove) require reservations up to a year in advance, but ask anyway. All sites include restrooms, picnic tables, barbecue grills, and outdoor showers. Take advantage of the hiking trail to reach Hana. Apply for a permit with the Dept. of State Parks. Camping is free; cabins sleep 6: $10 for 1 person, $14 for 2, $30 for 6.

Oheo, at mile marker 42 on Rte. 31, near Kipahulu. A flat, grassy campground sporting 2 portable toilets but no drinking water or firewood. Set up some catch-basins for the rain that always seems to be falling. Popular and busy, great hikes, including one to the 7 sacred pools, and another through a tropical rainforest. No permit required, but a 3-day max. stay.

Joe's Place, 4850 Ua Kea Rd. (248-7033), in Hana. From the Hana Hwy. going south, take left fork at police station. Hotel on right. Clean, comfortable rooms— like a hostel, but nicer. Kitchen (but buy food outside, it's cheaper). Singles and doubles $45, with bath more. Check-out 3pm; reservations hold until 6pm.

YMCA Camp Keanae (242-9007), Hana Hwy., Keanae, halfway between Paia and Hana, has a few hostel beds available for travelers, when it hasn't been booked by church groups. Primitive facilities, thin mattresses, flimsy springs, old kitchen (2 burners don't work), but a beautiful area overlooking the Keanae Peninsula. Check-in 4-6pm. Checkout 9am. Bunk $8. Call to reserve.

Upcountry

Hosmer Grove, Rte. 378, 7000 ft. up Haleakala's slope. Small campground with drinking water, toilet, grills, firewood, and covered tables. Excellent self-guided nature trail (pick up pamphlet at start of trail) attracts a constant stream of visitors. At this elevation, it can get a bit chilly and wet, so bring a sleeping bag. Part of Haleakala National Park, no permit required, but max. stay is 3 nights.

Polipoli State Park, Waipoli Rd., off Rte. 377. Plenty of hiking and a great view at 6200 ft. Good to cool off in the summer, but cold at night. It's well-nigh impossible to get to without 4WD (a dirt road up switchbacks for your last 2 mi.). No showers or electricity, but there is one 10-person cabin with gas lanterns ($10 for 1 person, $14 for 2). Get a permit at the Dept. of State Parks (see Practical Information, page 460). Camping free. Reservations taken 1 yr. in advance for cabin.

Haleakala Crater Campground, P.O. Box 369, Makawao 96768 (572-9306), 4 mi. from Halemauu parking lot. Camping and cabins within the crater itself. The cabins at **Kapalaoa, Paliku,** and **Holua** are each equipped with 12 bunks, wood-burning stove, and cooking utensils. They lie 6 mi., 10 mi., and 4 mi. from the parking lot, respectively. The park allocates cabins by a highly competitive lottery. You must apply before the last day of the month 3 months prior to your visit. Holua and Paliku areas also serve as campgrounds. Free camping permits issued at park headquarters (1 mi. up from park entrance) on the day of your hike. Max. stay 2 nights in cabins, 3 in campgrounds.

For unequipped campers, **Maui Expedition,** 87 S. Puunene Ave., Puunene (871-8787), rents and sells camping gear (open Mon.-Thurs. 9am-6pm, Sat. 8am-5pm). **Maui Sporting Goods,** 92 Market St. (244-0011), in Wailuku, sells tents, backpacks, sleeping bags, ground pads, beef jerky, and more (open Mon.-Fri. 8am-6pm, Sat. 8am-5pm, Sun. 10am-3pm).

FOOD

Locals claim it is possible to live on Maui without spending a penny on food. The waters around the coast teem with fish, and the trees drip breadfruit, mango, coconut, pine nuts, papaya, and guava. The ground also bears its share of delicacies, including pineapple and the sweet Kula onion, world-famous and sold for up to $6 per pound at the local market. For the less resourceful and the law abiding (picking fruit is trespassing), Maui also has supermarkets which stock thick, crispy, kettle-cooked Maui chips (not "Maui-style" potato chips, which are different: commercialized and not as tasty), with or without chocolate coating. *Guri guri*, a locally made pineapple or strawberry sherbet, has lured generations of islanders to its main supply source at **Tasaka Guri Guri,** in Kahului's Maui Mall (871-4512; open Mon.-Thurs. 9am-6pm, Fri. 9am-9pm, Sat. 9am-5pm, Sun. 10am-3pm).

The cheapest places to eat are away from the resorts. **Wailuku** and **Paia** support the largest concentration of inexpensive restaurants. **Down to Earth Natural Foods,** 1160 Makawao Ave., Makawao (572-1488), and 1910 Vineyard St., Wailuku (242-6821), are health food stores with small salad bars. (Open Mon.-Fri. 8am-7pm, Sat. 8am-6pm, Sun. 10am-5pm.) To dine in style, however, visit the hotels' attractive restaurants. Try the **Gazebo Bar** in the Napili Shores Hotel in Kaanapali for breakfast ($3.50 and up, open daily 7:30am-noon).

Several restaurants on the island are also popular nighttime destinations. Check listings for places that are open late.

Central Maui

Mushroom, 2080 Vineyard St. (244-7117), below the Northshore Inn, is a bright, friendly, family-run restaurant that serves excellent fried rice with vegetables ($3) and entrees with rice, salad, and soup for $5.50. Open daily 10am-2:30pm. Discount available for Northshore Inn guests.

Charlie P. Woofer's Saloon and Restaurant, 142 Hana Hwy. (579-9453), Paia. Charlie's is packed with surfers. Giant breakfasts. Fresh flowers adorn wooden tables. The pancakes come ¼-in. thick ($4.75). Hearty Italian and Mexican dinners, burgers, and pizza ($5-11). Open daily 7am-2pm and 5-10pm.

Tasty Crust, 1770 Mill St., Wailuku (244-0845). A bare-bones backpacker diner. Giant hotcakes ($2.20, served all day). Open Mon. 5:30am-1:15pm, Tues.-Sun. 5:30am-1:15pm and 5-9pm.

Tin Ying Chinese Restaurant, 1088 Lower Main St., Wailuku (242-4371). Mellow atmosphere. An extensive menu of Chinese favorites starting from $5-8. The mu shu pork is superb—could it be the local-grown ginger? Many vegetarian options. Silverware on request. Open daily 10am-9pm.

Restaurant Matsu, Maui Mall Shopping Ctr. (871-0822). Japanese-style fast food. Chicken curry $5. Monster bowl of plain *udon* $4.20. Mon.-Thurs. 9am-5pm, Fri. 9am-8pm, Sat. 9am-4pm, Sun. 10am-3pm.

Pic-Nics, 30 Baldwin Ave., Paia (579-8021). The island avocado and Swiss ($4.75) is delicious. Newspaper menu also serves as a guide to Hana—it includes translations of the names of all 54 bridges of the Hana Drive. Open daily 7:30am-7pm.

West Maui and the Resort Area

Margarita's Beach Cantina, 101 N. Kihei Rd. in Kealia Beach Plaza (879-5275). Good Mexican food in generous portions and fair prices. Restaurant overlooks the ocean (free whale-watching in season). Most dishes with choice of beef, chicken, or tofu. Entrees $5-14. Happy hour (daily 2:30-5:30pm) features 96¢ margaritas. Open daily 11:30am-10pm. Bar open 'til midnight.

Scarole's Village Pizzeria, 505 Front St., Lahaina (661-8112). Their brochure says "the New York side of Lahaina," and the place is run by a friendly, retired ex-New Jerseyite. Grab a quick Sicilian slice ($2.75) to tide you over. Sit down or take out. Full bar, excellent lunch and dinner specials. Open daily 11am-11pm.

Hana Coast

The tourist crowd keeps the prices of the few restaurants and stores in this area high. It is best to stock up on groceries in Kahului. If in town, you can stop by the **Hana Ranch,** off Hana Hwy. This snack bar has teri-sandwiches with fries ($5), clean restrooms, and shady picnic tables. (Open daily 7:30am-8pm.)

Upcountry

Casanova's Italian Restaurant and Deli, 1188 Makawao Ave. (572-0220), in Makawao. In addition to serving moderately priced Italian cuisine, Casanova's is a popular night spot, with a *lanai* convenient for drinking and chatting. A "beautiful people" hangout with lots of surfers and beachgoers. Deli open Mon.-Sat. 8am-6:30pm, Sun. 8:30am-6:30pm. Restaurant open Mon.-Sat. 5:30-9:30pm. Doubles as a bar, dance club. Dancing nightly; occasional live bands on Fri. and Sat. ($5 cover). Bar/club open Mon.-Tues. until 12:30am, Wed.-Sat. until 1am.

Kitada's KauKau Korner, 3617 Baldwin Ave. (572-7241), in Makawao. A mom-and-pop place, more like a store with tables, established in the 1940s. Mrs. Kitada serves sandwiches and burgers for $1.50-2.75, plate lunches for $3.50-4. The beef teriyaki is as good as it gets. Open Mon.-Sat. 6am-1:30pm.

NIGHTLIFE

West Maui hosts the island's hottest dance scene but there are a few other nighttime hangouts elsewhere on the island.

Moose McGillicuddy's, 844 Front St., Lahaina (667-7758). Celebrate a very happy happy hour (daily 3-6pm). Drafts ($1) and margaritas ($2) attract a young tourist crowd seeking that special someone to spend the rest of their night with. Dancing after 9pm.

Blue Tropix, 990 Front St., Lahaina (667-5309). High-energy dance action. Cover $5 after 9pm, but worth it; things don't move until after 10pm. Open until 2am.

Old Lahaina Café, 505 Front St., Lahaina (661-3303). Pleasant spot with a beautiful ocean view. Breezy, open-air café hosts daily happy hour noon-6pm. Open 7:30am-10pm. You may want to leave before the nightly luau crowd arrives.

Hamburger Mary's, 2020 Main St., Wailuku (244-7776), is the best bet for dancing in Central Maui. Open daily 10am-2am; dancing nightly.

Wunderbar, 89 Hana Hwy., Paia (579-8808), in Central Maui, is a relaxed place to hang out and discuss the day's surf. Open daily 7:30am-2am.

Polli's, 1201 Makawao Ave., (572-7808), in Makawao. Laid-back watering hole. Open Sun.-Fri. 11:30am-10:30pm, Fri.-Sat. 11:30am-11pm.

SIGHTS AND ACTIVITIES

Maui's cultural and historical sights focus on the missionaries, the diverse ethnic background of the sugar workers, and the natural history of Maui itself. Mark Twain, who spent his final years here and is buried on the island, is another of the island's other claims to fame. The free *Maui Beach Press* has listings of both local and tourist resort events, and the free *This Week Maui* occasionally lists some free activities amidst its glossy ads. (You may be pleased to know that Captain James Cook never set foot on Maui.)

Central Maui

While near the saddle of the island, be sure to step into the unspoiled **Iao Valley,** on the southern slope of Puu Kukui. Mark Twain called Iao "the Yosemite of the Pacific." The valley is especially beautiful in the moonlight, but beware—it's a popular spot for UFO sightings. (Perhaps the aliens read *Let's Go* too.) West on Rte. 32, toward the valley, lies calm **Kepaniwai Park.** In 1790, Kamehameha I slaughtered the Maui army here, filling the brook with the dead in what is called the *kepaniwai* (meaning "the damming of the waters"). Their blood reputedly ran all the way down to the Wailuku ("bloody") River. Today, the park is home to pavilions dedicated to some of the peoples who have populated Maui: Japanese, Filipino, Chinese, Hawaiian, Native Americans, and Portuguese. The **Iao Valley State Park** (open daily 7am-7pm), at the end of Rte. 32, includes the **Iao Needle,** a 1200-ft. basalt spire covered with vegetation and a valley floor blooming with wild orchids. Some say the name is onomatopoeic—the cry of an unfortunate god who sat on this pointed peak. A more likely legend names the valley after Iao, Maui's daughter. When one of Iao's suitors was untrue, Maui petrified him. The park has a few hiking trails that will take you away from the tourist onslaught. Just before the park's parking lot is the **John F. Kennedy Profile,** a cliff that bears a likeness of the former president. Did the extraterrestrials have anything to do with it? Tour buses arrive by 10am, and clouds by 2pm; both leave by 6pm.

In the 19th century, the Baileys, a New England missionary family, sailed around Cape Horn to reach Maui's pagan paradise. Decked in period decor, the Baileys' home serves as the small **Maui Historical Society Museum,** on Rte. 32 between Wailuku and Iao Valley (open daily 10am-4:30pm; $3, ages 6-12 $1, under 6 free).

On a nearby hill, you can visit a relic of the ancient religion that the Baileys came to stifle. The **Hale Kii** (House of Images) served as a place of worship throughout the 18th century until it was destroyed by natural erosion in 1819. Reconstructed in 1958, the *heiau* is now a temple of love, as local high school sweethearts will confirm. Follow Main St. (Rte. 32) to the traffic light at Rte. 330. Make a left, pass the macadamia nut grove, and turn right on Rte. 340. Continue to Kuhio Place, and follow the nerve-wracking route to the right.

You probably couldn't spend 30 minutes in the **Sugar Museum,** 3957 Hansen Rd., in Puunene, if you tried. It explains the history of the cane industry in Maui (open daily 9:30am-4:30pm. $3, ages 6-17 $1.50, under 6 free). For more produce facts, go to the **Tropical Plantation**, Rte. 30, between Wailuku and Lahaina, and browse the display rooms about Maui fruit production (open daily 9am-5pm).

Swimmers should head east from Wailuku on the Hana Hwy. (Rte. 36) to **Baldwin Beach Park.** It has lifeguards, showers, and restrooms. To the left (west) of the beach is **Baby Beach,** a cove cradled by a high reef which prevents almost all waves. Windsurfers and surfers flock to **Spreckelsville** for the wind and waves. Beginner and intermediate windsurfers staying in Wailuku will be pleased to find that **Kanaha Bay** has reliable wind. To reach the **Kanaha Beach Park**, take Hana Hwy. to Rte. 32A, on Amala St., turn right and continue to the parking lot. The park has showers and restrooms. Windsurfing nirvana can be attained (by experts only) at the world-famous **Hookipa Beach Park.** Hookipa (on Hana Hwy. east of Baldwin Beach) is worth a visit just to be awed by the hot-dog wave riders. Sunbathers should prepare to be sandblasted on many of Maui's beaches after noon as the same wind which keeps windsurfers coming back keeps swimmers and suntanners away.

Paia is an old plantation town now transformed into windsurfer heaven. The creative clothing stores are a combination of tie dyes and European chic. Most of the windsurfers are eager to get a good start on the next day's waves—nightlife suffers and entertainment choices are limited.

West Maui

Between the Kaanapali Airport and Lahaina stretches the 4-mi. **Kaanapali Beach,** a resort area from which you can often see the neighboring islands of Molokai, Lanai, and Oahu. **Launiupoko State Wayside Park** is a swimming beach with picnic tables, restrooms, outdoor showers, and barbecue grills. At the **14 mi. marker,** near Olowalu, you can enjoy coral reefs, tropical fish, and calm waters at one of the most spectacular snorkeling spots in Hawaii. **Honolua Bay,** north of Kapalua, is another excellent snorkeling spot. Do not attempt to use Rte. 34, as a short cut back to Kahului—the winding, narrow road is endless and remote. Near Lahaina, **Fleming Beach Park** is another favorite for both snorkeling and bodysurfing.

Lahaina

Kamehameha the Great relocated the capital of his dynasty from the Big Island to Lahaina in 1810, commemorating his unification of the entire Hawaiian chain. Lahaina eventually grew to be the favored port of whaler ships but, Honolulu eclipsed it in other commercial markets. In 1845, Hawaii's capital moved to Honolulu, leaving behind a rough, dusty town where brothels stood next door to churches and grog was the drink of choice. Today, Lahaina is a tidy tourist town that entices visitors with tales of its whaling past and whale-watching.

Lahaina is the tourist center of Maui, with a Planet Hollywood and numerous t-shirt shops. It also provides most of the nightlife on the otherwise "early to bed, early to rise" island. If you visit during the day, leave your car behind; traffic on one-lane Front St. is dead-locked by noon. Come at evening and catch the happy hours of the restaurants and bars lining the waterfront. Then dance the night away with the young vacationers—just follow the blaring music. Lahaina also infects visitors with its calm. When Mark Twain visited, he planned to stay one week and work; instead he stayed a month and never lifted a pen.

The **Cannery** in Lahaina and **Whaler's Village** in Kaanapali are two made-for-tourists shopping malls. In the middle of Whaler's Village on the second floor, a one-room museum exhibits an extensive collection of scrimshaw, the art of etching on whale bones (open daily 9:20am-1pm and 1:30-10pm). Whale-watching is a popular activity along the coast in the spring and fall. The enormous tree in Lahaina's town square is an East Indian **banyan tree,** rivaling Kauai's for the title of the islands' largest. The tree was eight feet tall when it was brought from India in 1873. Today, with 12 main trunks surrounding a core of central trunks, it shades 2/3 of an acre.

Lahaina is home to many art galleries—some quite good, most with friendly staff. Friday night is **art night,** and the galleries stay open late; mingle with the local intelligentsia and pick up free wine and hors d'oeuvres.

The sugar mill at the end of Lahainaluna Rd. still operates, as does the island's only remaining steam locomotive. However, today the locomotive carries tourists, not sugar, between Lahaina and Kaanapali (one way $5; round-trip $8; under 12 half-price). For a free ride don't forget about the hotel shuttles (see Practical Information, page 460). An **OMNI theater,** 824 Front St. (661-8314), in Lahaina, presents Hawaii's history on the big, BIG screen, with the breathtaking *Hawaii: Island of the Gods!* shown daily on the hour from 10am to 10pm. ($7, under 12 $4. $1 discount coupons available at tourist centers.)

Maui's multi-ethnic heritage is apparent at the **Jodo Mission** at 12 Ala Moana, off the north end of Front St., which was built to commemorate the arrival of Japanese immigrants in 1868. The largest **Buddha** outside of Japan sits with his back to the West Maui Mountains. Another possibility is the **Wo Hing** museum, 858 Front St. (661-5553), which continuously screens Thomas Edison's 1898 and 1903 films of Hawaiian daily life. The museum is located in a hall built in 1912 as a social center for Chinese residents (open daily 9am-4pm; free).

For a daytrip from Lahaina, take the boat to **Club Lanai** (871-1144). This privately owned club is like a country club and a national park rolled into one; it sponsors diving trips, swimming, snorkeling, glass-bottomed boat rides, and nature walks. These activities, lunch, open bar, and use of water equipment are yours for a mere $79.

East Maui and the Kihei Resort Area

Kihei, in East Maui, is the other resort area. Its tourists are squirreled away in condominiums and less elaborate hotels than Kaanapali's (except in Wailea). **Kamaole Beach** is a perennial favorite for families and sun worshipers. (Its facilities include showers and toilets.) Off Kihei lies the half-crater of **Molokini.** Once a naval bombing target, it now teems with fish. Check *This Week Maui* for half- or full-day snorkeling tours—$39 for an afternoon tour seems to be the going rate. The underwater experience may be disappointing; the snorkelers seem to outnumber the fish. **Makena** beaches are private, quiet, and quite swimsuit-free. Oneloa, or Big Beach, stretches 3000 ft. long and 100 ft. wide. Next to it, on the other side of a cinder cone, is the more secluded Puuolai, Little Beach, a great site for spotting giant humpback whales. These beaches are ideal for sunbathing, but strong currents make swimming dangerous. Farther south, **Ahihi Bay** and **La Perouse,** two of Maui's marine reserves, are excellent snorkeling spots (no facilities).

Hana Coast

The Hana Coast was once the center of Hawaiian culture. In the '70s, there was talk of making the area a national park, but Hawaiians resisted, wanting to preserve their fishing grounds and private lands. Land is a precious commodity here, but luckily the Hawaiian families have, for the most part, left the coast in its natural state.

The **Hana Highway** may be the world's most beautiful stretch of road; carved from cliff faces and valley floors, its alternate vistas of smooth sea and lush terrain are made only somewhat less enjoyable by its tortuous curves. The road to Hana is not a means to an end; most sights lie along the way, not in the small and simple town of Hana itself. Be prepared to spend an entire day on the trip. Pull over and savor the sights along the way—you may need them just to steel your resolve for the rest of the twisted drive. Wild ginger plants and fruit trees laden with mangos, guavas, and bananas perfume the air. Locals claim to have kept the best sights hidden, but they seem happy to tell enthusiastic hikers about many of them. **Keanae,** situated on a small peninsula, is an age-old producer of taro. Take a look around **Puohokamoa Falls,** in **Puaakaa State Park** (home of two waterfalls, several natural pools, and clean restrooms) and **Waianapanapa State Park** (120 acres, surfing, camping, showers). The hikes accessed on the Hana Coast range from short jaunts to waterfalls and pools to balmy oceanside walks near rocky cliffs to trails through the dense jungle, hidden lava tube caves, and the vestiges of early Hawaiian civilization. The **Hana-Waianapanapa Coastal Trail,** the ancient Hawaiian "King's Highway," from the campground on Pailoa Bay to Kainalimu Bay, is beautiful; a few of the stepping stones placed long ago along the jagged lava remain, though most have eroded (2 mi. one way). Between Kuaiwa Point and Paina Point, the trail passes an ancient Hawaiian *heiau,* about ½ mi. from the Waianapanapa campground. North of the campground, about ½ mi. past Hana Airport, are the **Waianapanapa** and **Waiomao Caves.** Bring a flashlight and swim in the underground lava tubes, now filled with fresh water. According to legend, a Hawaiian princess once hid from her cruel husband in these caves. But the prince caught sight of the feather *kahili* the princess's servant was using to fan her mistress and murdered his wife. Every spring, red shrimp turn the cave waters crimson, a living reminder of the slain princess.

Blue Pond, a small pool at the edge of the ocean, deserves its name as its water is pure azure. The water—half fresh, half salt—looks inviting and feels even better. To find the pond, follow the Hana Hwy. from Paia, take a left on Ulaino Rd., just before the Airport Rd. and follow signs to the Kahanu Botanical Gardens. Once you get there, either park and walk, or ford the stream with your car. At the end of the road, you can park and walk across the river mouth at the beach. Go left on the stone beach and walk about 100 yds. to reach more streams.

The burg of **Hana** on the eastern slope of Haleakala is a one-horse town, immortalized in song for its **Hasegawa General Store** (248-8231; open Mon.-Sat. 8am-5:30pm, Sun. 9am-3:30pm). The original store burned down in 1990, but they have relocated to a nearby warehouse. The store is worth a look, but you may want to follow Hana residents' lead and purchase your food for less in Kahului. Two mi. past Hana, turn seaward on Haneoo Rd. to get to sandy **Koki Beach,** the only bodysurfing beach for miles. Travel for another ½ mi. and leave your footprints on red sand at **Hamoa Beach** (restrooms and shower facilities). **Red Sand Beach** or Kaihalulu Beach is a small cove favored by nude suntanners. To reach the beach, follow the path at the end of Uakea Rd. for 10 minutes, beginning at the Hana Community Center. The sand is coarse, but the beach is beautiful and surrounded by cliffs. Farther south from Hana along Rte. 31 is the **Kipahulu District,** part of Haleakala National Park. Over 20 pools exist in the 1 mi. of the **Oheo** stream immediately above the ocean. *Oheo* ("the gathering of pools") is also known to tourists as "the Seven Sacred Pools." From the pools there is a lovely path (400 ft.) up Oheo Gulch to Waimoku Falls. The trail, in the Haleakala National Park, is rough, but the beauty of the undisturbed waterfalls, pools, and bamboo groves more than compensates for the effort. **Charles Lindbergh's grave** lies in the Kipahulu Hawaiian Church's idyllic graveyard, about 2 mi. down the road from the Pools. The aviator spent his last years here and helped to restore the church.

Upcountry

Haleakala Crater, the "House of the Sun," dominates the eastern end of the island from its perch 10,000 ft. above the sea. The famous peak, the largest dormant volcano in the world (that's dormant, not extinct—Haleakala last erupted in 1790, and could erupt again), presents a moonscape of volcanic cinder cones. Haleakala "Crater" is not technically a crater, but a deep valley, formed by wind and water erosion.

Haleakala National Park is open 24 hrs.; daily admission is $4 per car for a seven-day pass. (If you arrive during odd hours—say 3am—you'll be greeted by a sign that says "Closed—Drive Through," sparing you the $4.) If you drive the 36 mi. from Kahului Airport up the mountain (via Rte. 37, to Rte. 377, to Rte. 378), the sunrise, views, chilly weather, and number of people who had the same bright idea will astound you. Morning temperatures are generally in the low 40s. Arrive at least one hour before sunrise, bring coffee and blankets, and watch the sky gradually brighten. Clouds usually roll in about 10am, but as the weather is often fickle in the mountain, call for information first (572-7749 for a weather report). It's a long trip up the mountain and you'd be surprised how fast you can get fogged in. On the way back down, use a low gear to save your brakes and avoid squashing cyclists—long trains of them, tailed by large bike-trailer trucks, effectively enforce a 15mph speed limit. Several companies will haul bikers all the way up the mountain just so they can coast down. Stop off at lower elevations to check out the rare silversword plant and Hawaiian *nene* geese.

The **Park Headquarters** (572-9300), open daily 7:30am-4pm, about 1 mi. up from the entrance, provides camping **permits,** displays on Haleakala wildlife, and funky postcards. **Haleakala Visitors Center** (572-9172), near the summit, has a few exhibits on the region's geology, archaeology, and ecology, as well as one of the best views of the crater. The **Puuulaula Center,** at Haleakala's summit, is where you'll probably end up if you forget a sweater or jacket (open 24 hrs.). Free natural history talks are given at 9:30, 10:30, and 11:30am (open daily sunrise-3pm). From April to June, the park sponsors a variety of free events. The rangers also give three-hour guided hikes starting at Hosmer Grove Shelter (Mon. and Thurs. at 9am), and lead a crater hike (meet at Sliding Sands Trailhead, Tues. and Fri. at 10am). Although the hikes are completed by visitors of all ages, the uphill hike from the bottom of the crater is especially difficult due to the high elevation.

Sliding Sands Trailhead is located at the Visitors Center and leads down a steep 4 mi. to the bottom of the crater. If you can spare the time (and the energy), **Hale-manu Trailhead** will eventually bring you out of the crater. The hike is 11½ mi. long and takes about seven hours to complete at a steady pace. The experience is other-worldly—the vast, dry landscape resembles the surface of the moon so much that NASA trained astronauts here for their lunar landing. (Don't worry, the laws of gravity still apply.) The silence is as vast as the crater itself as the path cuts through barren slopes of red and black, speckled with the glittering silversword plant. You can park your car at the Halemanu parking lot. (Some travelers try to hitch a ride to the summit.) Try to start before 11am, and bring sturdy walking shoes, water, sunscreen, and rain gear. The Sliding Sands Trail connects with the trail to **Kaluuokaoo Pit,** the closest major cinder cone. Early Hawaiians threw the umbilical cords of their newborns into the pit to safeguard them from the valley's evil rodents. (See Camping, page 463, for information on **campgrounds** in Haleakala National Park.)

Farther south on Rte. 37 is the **Tedeschi Winery** (878-6058), which offers minute, but free tastes of their "Maui Blanc" pineapple wine (free tours are given 9:30am-2:30pm; open daily 9am-5pm). Although it won't help you sober up, sip Maui's home-grown Kona coffee at **Grandma's Coffee House,** Rte. 37, in Keokea (open Mon.-Sat. 6am-5pm, Sun. 7am-3pm). **Makawao** is a growing community which typifies Upcountry. **Viewpoints Gallery,** 3620 Baldwin Ave. (572-5979), an artists' cooperative, houses beautiful works by local artists. Look out for renditions of the Maui Spirit (open daily 10am-6pm). Top off your day by dancing at **Casanova's** (see Food: Upcountry, page 465) or drink up at the more relaxed **Polli's** (See Nightlife, page 467).

SEASONAL EVENTS

O'Neill Invitational (572-4883), first week in April at Hookipa Beach Park, Paia. International windsurfing tournament. Hostels and hotels are booked. Watch the big boys and big girls come out to play.

Na Mele O Maui Music Festival, early April.

Hula Pakahi, May 1. A solo hula competition held at the Intercontinental Maui Hotel. This is **Lei Day,** too—be prepared.

King Kamehameha Canoe Regatta, mid-June, Kahului Harbor. Free viewing from nearby beaches. The season's inaugural event.

Hi-Tech Pro Am, early Sept. at Hookipa Beach Park, Paia. International windsurfing tournament. Speed competition at the Molokai Channel Crossing. Call Paul Enman (579-9765).

Maui Grand Prix, mid-Oct. at Hookipa Beach Park, Paia. No, not a car race, but a major surfing event. Surfers from 12 countries compete.

Aloha Citizen's Classic, late Oct. at Hookipa Beach, Paia. One of the biggest windsurfing events at Hookipa and the final event of the pro World Tour. Contact Paul Enman (579-9765).

Halloween (667-7411), Oct. 31. This is a big event in Lahaina. Trick, treat, and party.

The Run to the Sun, a 36-mile jog from the beach to Haleakala's summit. Call the Valley Isle Road Runners (871-6441) for details.

The Big Island of Hawaii

Pele, Polynesian goddess of the volcanoes, is believed to reside on Hawaii, the southeastern-most island in the Hawaiian chain. She generates the hot, dry weather of the Kona (leeward) side, while her lover, Kamapua'a, is responsible for the rain and wet of the Hilo (windward) side. Their frequent meetings mix things up a bit, creating the eleven climatic zones found on the Big Island, the desert-like North Kona coast, the snow-covered peaks of Mauna Kea, and the rainforests, valleys, and waterfalls of the Hamakua Coast.

The Big Island emerged from the confluence of five major volcanoes on top of a hot spot in the Pacific Plate. Two are still active: "Long Mountain," **Mauna Loa** (13,677 ft.), and **Kilauea** (4000 ft.), home of **Halemaumau Crater.** Kilauea is currently in its 51st phase of eruption without showing any signs of exhaustion, and crowds flock daily to the island to tread on newly created earth. Although the eruptions are powerful, the volcanoes do not emit dangerous ash clouds, and the lava flow is quick only near the summit and in underground lava tubes. Currently the lava is flowing into the sea, emitting a long cloud of smoke. When the lava finds an open vent, visitors are thrilled with a small burst of fiery rock.

The Big Island is twice the size of all the other islands combined, but is home to only 130,000 people—scarcely a tenth of the state's population. Its vast and varied agricultural production supports Hawaii's post-sugar economy. The towns of **Hilo** and **Kailua-Kona,** on opposite sides of the island, are the main tourist gates. The rest of the island is considered "country" by residents. The northwestern corner is the **Kohala Peninsula,** former sugar land and the northern border of the island's gigantic cattle range. The southern portion of the island is **Kau,** where the first Polynesian immigrants settled. You'll need a car to enjoy the countryside, but keep a careful eye on the fuel gauge, as distances between gas stations can be great. If you decide to rent a car in Kailua and drop it off in Hilo (or vice versa), ask about the drop-off charge—it can be steep (about $60). The Big Island has a rudimentary bus system, but a car is necessary to see most sights. The trip from Hilo to Kailua-Kona by car via **Rte. 19** takes 2¼ hrs.; via **Rte. 11** budget 3¼ hrs. Despite its appearance on a map, **Saddle Road** is no faster than Rte. 19. Hawaiian and Aloha Airlines fly

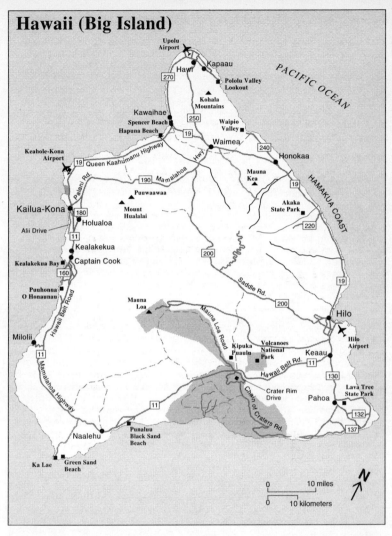

Hawaii (Big Island)

between the two city airports (one way $25). Keep in mind that there is no public transportation from the airports to the towns.

■■■ HILO

After Honolulu, Hilo is the largest city in the state—a more relaxed, less tourist-ridden, and economically depressed version of its big cousin. Moist tradewinds have made Hilo the center of the Hawaiian orchid and anthurium industry. A primarily residential city, Hilo works well as a base from which to visit the island's other attractions: the rugged **Hamakua** (½ hr. north), the green **Waipio Valley** north of Hamakua, the *paniolo* (cowboy) country above that, and, of course, **Volcanoes National Park** (45 min. southwest).

PRACTICAL INFORMATION AND ORIENTATION

Visitors Information: Destination Hilo (935-5294; call before noon) is your best bet for friendly information on sights and itinerary planning, but lacks walk-in office. You can also try the **Hawaii Visitors Bureau**, 250 Keawe St. (961-5797). Open Mon.-Fri. 9am-4pm. The **Visitor Information Kiosk,** across the parking lot at 300 Kamehameha Ave., is a good source for bus schedules, maps, brochures, and a self-guided walking tour of historic downtown Hilo. **Wailoa Center,** P.O. Box 936, Hilo 96720 (933-4360), on the *makai* (seawards) side of the State Building. Helpful in planning itineraries. Maps, displays. Open Mon.-Fri. 8am-4:30pm. **State Visitor Information Center,** Hilo Airport (935-1018). **Big Island Center for Independent Living,** 1190 Waianuenue (935-3777), in Hilo, has assistance for visitors with disabilities. **Basically Books,** 46 Waianuenue Ave. (961-0144), has a tempting selection of maps and Hawaii specific titles and collectibles. Open Mon.-Fri. 9am-5pm, Sat. 10am-4pm.

Outdoors Information: For information on County Parks, contact the **Parks and Recreation Office,** 25 Aupuni St., #210, Hilo 96720 (961-8311). From the Kamehameha Hwy. turn left onto Pauahi St.; past Wailua Park, turn left on Aupuni St. **Permits** are available for $1 per person per night. Open Mon.-Fri. 7:45am-4:30pm. Information on State Parks is available at the **Dept. of Land and Natural Resources,** 75 Aupuni St. #204, Hilo 96720 (933-4200). Free permits with a 5-day max. stay. Open Mon.-Fri. 7:45am-4pm. **Volcanoes National Park Visitor Center,** Volcano, Hawaii 96785 (967-7311), on Rte. 11, 13 mi. from Hilo. Offers trail maps, free ranger-guided hikes and important safety information. Open daily 8am-5pm. **Division of Forestry and Wildlife,** Dept. of Enforcement, P.O. Box 936, Hilo 96720 (933-4291), next to the State Parks Office. Information on hunting, fishing, hiking, and forest regulations. Open Mon.-Fri. 7:45am-4:30pm.

Buses: Hele-on-Bus, 25 Aupuni St. (935-8241). Information on bus schedules. Operates Mon.-Sat. 6:30am-6pm. Luggage and backpacks $1 extra per piece. Runs between Kona and Hilo once per day, making a convenient circuit of the island ($5.25). Travelers with disabilities can be accommodated with curb-to-curb service; call 1 day in advance: 961-3418 in Hilo, 323-2085 in Kona. Bus leaves Hilo from the Mooheau bus terminal at 1:30pm and arrives at Lunahai Ctr. in Kona (last stop) at 4:25pm. The reverse trip leaves Kona at 6:45am and arrives in Hilo at 9:45am. Downtown Hilo, 308 Kamehameha Ave. (935-8850), sells bus tickets for $5. Otherwise, have exact change. Open Mon.-Fri. 8:30am-5:30pm.

Taxi: Ace Taxi, 935-8303. The trip from the airport into the city runs about $10.

Car Rental: All national and state chains are located at Hilo airport. Make reservations several days in advance or take advantage of fly/drive deals for cheaper rates. **Budget,** 935-7293, rents economy cars for $33-36 per day. **Harper Car & Truck Rentals,** 1690 Kamehameha Ave. (969-1478), offers a rate of $33 per day. Drivers must be at least 25 with a major credit card. Rental cars are not permitted on Saddle Rd.

Water Equipment Rental: Nautilus Dive Center, 382 Kamehameha Ave. (935-6939). Mask or snorkel $3 per day, fins $3. Also offers beginner and certified dive charters, $55. Open Mon.-Sat. 9am-4pm.

Library: 300 Waianuenue Ave. (933-4650). Open Mon. and Wed. 9am-8pm, Tues. and Thurs.-Sat. 9am-5pm.

Local Attractions and Cultural Events: 935-1666, ext. 1800.

Senior Citizens Events: 935-1666, ext. 1801.

Laundromat: King's Laundromat, 58 Mamo St. Open daily 6am-9pm. No phone.

Coast Guard: 935-6370 or 800-522-6458.

Weather: 935-1666, ext. 1520; marine ext. 1522; surf ext. 1521. Hilo can be wet; Kona is generally sunny. **Eruptions Bulletin:** 967-7977. 24-hr. recording.

Crisis/Help Line: 969-9111.

Hospital: Hilo, 1190 Waianuenue St. (969-4111), by Rainbow Falls. 24-hr. emergency service.

Emergency: 911 or 961-6022.

Police: 961-2211, emergencies 935-3311.

Post Office: Airport Access Rd. (935-6685), by the airport. Open Mon.-Thurs. 8:15am-4:45pm, Fri. 8:15am-5:30pm, Sat. 8:15am-12:30pm. **General Delivery ZIP Code:** 96720.
Area Code: 808.

Hilo rests at the mouth of the Wailuku River. Its airport, **General Lyman Field,** is accessed by inter-island service and flights from the mainland. Stop by the airport's visitor information booth; their maps and information are great for directions.

ACCOMMODATIONS AND CAMPING

With the exception of Kona, tourism on the Big Island has never been as expensive or as popular as on Oahu and Maui. In Hilo rooms become scarce only during spectacular events like volcanic eruptions. Booking rooms locally, rather than from the mainland, can save you $5-10 per day. You can pick up a listing of the Big Island's B&Bs at an airport information kiosk or obtain one in advance by writing the Hawaiian Island Bed and Breakfast Association, P.O. Box 726, Volcano, HI 96788.

Arnott's Lodge, 98 Apapane Rd., Keokea. (969-7097; from Hawaii 800-953-7973; from mainland 800-368-8752). By car, from Airport Rd., turn right at first traffic light. Turn right again at the next light (next to Dairy Queen) onto Kalanianaole St. Go 1½ mi. and make a left onto Keokea. Apapane Rd. is on the right about 50 yds. down. Small lava-rock beach 1-min. walk away. This hostel is a backpacker's mecca in tropical Hilo. Clean, brightly painted, spacious accommodations serviced by friendly staff. Laundry machines, TV/VCR, kitchens. Nightly BBQ $2 or bring food with you (no grocery stores nearby). Spectacular and affordable ($15-30) **daytrips** to lava flow, Mauna Kea, snorkeling, Waipio Valley, and others are worthwhile even if you're not a lodge guest. Bunk $15. Singles $26. Doubles $36, group discounts (in advance). ISIC holders and VIPs of Backpackers, Australia/ New Zealand get a 20% discount. Stay 6 nights and the 7th is free.

Hilo Hotel, P.O. Box 726, Hilo 96720 (961-3733), at 142 Kinoole St. downtown, across from Kalakaua Park. Located in the heart of downtown Hilo near shops and restaurants. Clean, with a touch of old-time elegance. A/C, refrigerators, free coffee, and an occasional sweet roll in the morning. Restaurant Fuji serves cocktails and free *pupus* (appetizers) Tues.-Fri. 4-6pm. Singles and doubles $39-45.

Dolphin Bay Hotel, 333 Iliahi St., Hilo 96720 (935-1466), in the Puueo section of town, four blocks from downtown, across the river. 18 units. Cool, tropical gardens. Amiable managers can help plan your excursions. Fans, TV, kitchens. Singles from $42. Doubles from $52. $10 per additional person. Prepayment required; make deposit 10 days prior to stay to confirm reservations.

Wild Ginger Inn Bed & Breakfast, 100 Puueo St. (800-882-1887 from mainland, 800-935-5556 from HI), 1 block from downtown. Bright rooms with baths in a friendly, charming setting. Abundant breakfasts served on porch overlooking the garden. Singles and doubles $39. Deluxe room with cable TV $59. Non-smoking.

Country Club Hotel, 121 Banyan Dr. (935-7171). Somewhat tired resort hotel with a largely residential clientele. Simple rooms with A/C, TV, and lanai. Singles and doubles $45. Room on oceanfront $55. $7 per additional person.

MacKenzie State Park (961-8311), off Rte. 137 in the Puna district, 32 mi. from Hilo. Tent or trailer camping near good shore fishing and an old Hawaiian trail along the wild volcanic coastline. Secluded; avoid camping alone. No drinking water. Max. stay 5 days. Free permit required (see Practical Information, above).

Onekahakaha Beach Park and **Kealoha Beach Park** (both 961-8311) are within 3 mi. of Hilo, but visitors should be aware that these parks often have a large number of territorial residents with nowhere else to go. Tent camping, bathrooms, and shower facilities. $1 permit required (see Practical Information).

FOOD AND ENTERTAINMENT

Throughout the island you'll find macadamia nut bread, cookies, cakes and pies to accompany steaming cups of locally grown Kona coffee. Free samples of macadamia nuts are given out at the **Hawaiian Holiday Macadamia Nut Company** in

Haina, off Rte. 19 near Honokaa. The only downtown supermarket is **KTA,** 321 Keawe St. (935-3751). A 24-hr. **Safeway,** located behind Prince Kuhio Plaza on Rte. 11, has a better selection and more palatable prices.

Downtown Hilo is loaded with small, inexpensive ethnic restaurants with excellent lunch plates, sushi counters, and *okazu-ya.* Follow the locals.

> **Bear Coffee,** 106 Keawe St. (935-0708), in old Hilo. Cappuccino, coffee blends, and delicious pastries. Probably the only yuppie hangout in Hilo. Serves pizza, burritos, and sandwiches for $4-5. Open Mon.-Fri. 7am-4pm, Sat. 7am-3pm.
>
> **Reuben's Mexican Food,** 336 Kamehameha Hwy. (961-2552). Authentic Mexican food. Choose from 34 entrees for $7-9. Good beers and margaritas. Open Mon.-Fri. 11am-9pm, Sat. noon-9pm. Also at 75-5719 Alii Dr., Kailua (329-7031).
>
> **Ken's Pancake House,** 1730 Kamehameha Ave. (935-8711). A Hawaiian IHOP. Breakfast all day, as well as burgers, sandwiches, etc. ($3.50-$5). Macadamia nut, coconut, or fresh banana pancakes $4.25. Variety of syrups (coconut, maple, and fruit flavors). Irene and company will brighten your rainy morning. Open 24 hrs.
>
> **Mun Cheong Lau,** 172 Kilauea Ave. (935-3040). A dark restaurant that serves Cantonese cuisine in gigantic portions for under $6. Try the crispy chicken in pineapple sauce with rice ($4.80). Take-out available. Open Wed.-Mon. 11am-11pm.
>
> **Hilo Homemade Ice Cream,** 1477 Kalanianaole (959-6859), down the road from Arnott's. Delicious vegetable curry rice with chicken or beef $4. Shave ice and fabulous ice cream; try their *lilikoi* sherbet or Kona coffee ($1.20 for a small cup or cone). Open daily 10am-5pm.
>
> **Abundant Life Natural Foods,** 292 Kamehameha Hwy (935-7411) sells organic produce, vitamins and bulk foods. The take-out deli (open Mon.-Fri. 8:30am-2pm) offers daily vegetarian specials and fruit smoothies ($2.25). Open Mon.-Fri. 8:30 - 6pm, Sat. 8am-5pm and Sun. 11am-3pm.
>
> **Suisan's Retail Fish Market,** at Lihiwai and Banyan (935-9349). Buy some just-caught *ahi* (tuna) steaks here ($4 per lb.), take them back to Arnott's and broil them lightly ($1 BBQ fee). Also sells whole fish, oysters, and ogo seaweed. Be adventurous and sample *poke* (marinated raw fish). Open Mon.-Sat. 8am-3:45pm.

The Kona resort area (see page 480), is the best spot on the island for nightlife. The pace in Hilo is slower and tourists may feel unwelcome in some of the downtown bars. However, **Lehua's Bay City Bar & Grill,** 90 Kamehameha Ave. (935-8055), is a fun spot with live rock music and dancing Fri.-Sat. after 9pm. **Harrington's,** 135 Kalanianaole St. (961-4966), is a good place for a drink. This relaxed bar has a lounge area overlooking a small bay. Live jazz and Hawaiian music are played nightly.

SIGHTS AND ACTIVITIES

Hilo receives 300 in. of rain per year and the windward coast receives 50-100 in. This wet climate has created a setting of true tropical splendor. The area surrounding Hilo is carpeted with lush mountain greenery and sprinkled with plunging waterfalls, a testament to the Big Island's stunning beauty. If things get too wet for you, just head for the sunny Kona-Kohala coast (about a 2-hr. drive away).

A morning stroll around **Liliuokalani Garden** (an elaborate Japanese-style garden named after one of the royal princesses) is a nice way to start the day. The garden is linked by a little footbridge to palm-covered **Coconut Island.** You'll get a great view of Mauna Kea before the clouds roll in. Early birds get the fruit at the **Farmers Market** on Saturday morning (open sunrise- noon). You can sample coconut milk from the nut itself. (The market is located in front of the bus stop, where Mamo St. intersects Kamehameha Ave.) Fifty different vendors of coffee, flowers, produce, local crafts, and jewelry set up shop at the **Hilo Open Market** (961-2659) at Banyan Dr. and Rte. 11. (Open Mon.-Sat. 9am-5pm, Fri 9am-8pm, Sun. 10am-4pm.)

Yet another morning possibility is the lovely **Rainbow Falls,** up Waianuenue Ave. As the sun begins to peek over the trees, rainbows appear everywhere, formed by the mist of the plunging falls. On the way to Rainbow Falls, turn left to see Boiling Pots, where bowl-shaped depressions "boil" with the high tide. (No swimming—as if you need to be told.) Fortunately for all those who sleep late, **Akaka,** the tallest waterfall in Hawaii (420 ft.), is impressive at any time of day. (From Hilo go north on Rte. 19, take a left on Rte. 220 to Akaka State Park at the end of the road. Free.)

To see historic Hilo, get a walking tour pamphlet at the visitors bureau. The tour takes you past older Hilo buildings, now either empty or filled with shops. Learn about the lives of early Hawaiian missionaries in the **Lyman House Museum,** 276 Haili St. (7 25-min. tours daily. Open Mon.-Sat. 9am-5pm, Sun. 1pm-4pm. $4.50, children $2.50.)

Hilo is the orchid capital of the world. Enough botanical gardens and nurseries have sprung up around the city to supply every senior prom in the country. Many of the nurseries charge a tour fee or request donations, so your cheapest option is to simply view the spectacular front-yard flora along any residential street, or take the 4-mi. scenic drive off Rte. 19 north of Hilo. The **Hilo Tropical Gardens,** 1477 Kalanianaole Ave. (935-4957 or 935-1146), is a botanical delight that deserves a visit. (Open daily 9am-4pm. $3, ages 13-17 $1.50, under 13 free. Includes Kona coffee and an orchid "for the ladies.") **Orchids of Hawaii,** 2801 Kilauea Ave. (959-3581), is a flower shop with beautiful leis and an exotic variety of orchids and anthuriums (open Mon.-Fri. 7:30am-4:30pm). If traveling south of Hilo along Rte. 11, you won't be able to miss the **Mauna Loa Macadamia Nut Visitor Center**. A majestic drive through a grove of macadamia nut trees brings you to a factory and a study in corporate promotionalism. With a gift store selling ice cream, cookies, and more, this is the perfect place to find that present for the die-hard macadamia nut fan. (Open daily 8:30am-5pm.) The **Panaewa Zoo Rainforest** (959-7224), tucked away in the Panaewa forest reserve (halfway between Hilo and Volcanoes National Park on Rte. 11), is a small but entertaining zoo with a wide variety of inhabitants. The pygmy hippo is the show-stealer among performing tigers, monkeys, and tropical birds. (Open daily 9am-4pm. Feedings at 9:15am and 3pm. Free.)

■ NEAR HILO

Recent lava flows have covered the once glistening shores of Kaimu Black Sand Beach and various parts of the highway as well, making Rte. 11 the only way to round South Point from Hilo. **Lava Tree State Park,** with eerie lava casts of trees engulfed during the 1790 eruption, is still accessible. From Hilo, take Rte. 11 south to Keaau, turn onto Rte. 130 to Pahoa, and then take Pahoa-Pohoiki Rd. (Rte. 132). Continue around the loop on Rte. 132 past the **Kapoho Lighthouse** and the gardens nearby. Here a 1960 lava flow covered Kapoho Village; only trees and the lighthouse remain. Visitors can also see lava trees near the volcano itself; if your time is limited you may want to head straight to Volcanoes National Park.

■■■ THE VOLCANO AREA

The volcanoes of the Big Island are unique in their size, frequency of eruption, and accessibility. Resting above the geological hot spot that fashioned each of the Hawaiian islands in turn, the two mountains in **Volcanoes National Park** continue to spout and grow, adding acres of new land each year. **Kilauea Caldera,** with its steaming vents, sulfur fumes, and periodic "drive-in" eruptions, is the star of the park, although the less active **Mauna Loa** and its dormant northern neighbor, **Mauna Kea,** are in some respects more amazing. Each towers nearly 14,000 ft. above sea level and drops some 16,000 ft. to the ocean floor. Mauna Loa is the largest volcano in the world, while Mauna Kea, if measured from its ocean floor base, would be the tallest mountain on earth. (Park entrance $5 per car, valid for 7 days.)

At the **visitors center** in **Kilauea,** Crater Rim Rd. (967-7311; open daily 7:45am-5pm), visitors can see 25-minute films shown every hour from 9am to 4pm and receive bulletins of the latest volcanic activity. Trails of varying difficulty lead around Kilauea and to the summit of Mauna Loa; speak to a ranger before setting out.

Offerings left in the volcanoes themselves include *leis*, fruit or sweets, and rocks wrapped in *ti* leaves. You will see stacks of rocks a few feet high dotting the strange landscape of the lava flows. If you truly want to appease Pele and protect yourself from her wrath, take a bottle of gin with you and pour it into one of the lava lakes; Pele will then smile on your adventure.

ACCOMMODATIONS AND CAMPING

Staying in the volcano area is expensive because of the limited number of hotels.

Holo Holo Inn, 19-4036 Kalani Holua Rd., Volcano Village 96784 (967-7950). From Hilo, take Rte. 11 almost to the National Park, turn right at Haunani Rd. in Volcano Village, then left on Kalani Holua Rd. Perfect locale just 2 mi. from the visitors center. Several large, clean rooms with beds and dressers. Huge family-style eat-in kitchen makes this place feel like home. Howard the Feisty Territorial Goose is now in a cage. Worth at least 1 day on any itinerary. Bunk $15. Call after 4:30pm and reserve in advance.

My Island Volcano B&B (967-7216), in Volcano Village. Beautiful rooms in a historic missionary-style home. Large common area has TV and collection of Hawaiiana and volcano info. Delicious all-you-can-eat breakfast. Knowledgeable and thoughtful owners. Singles $35, with bath $45. Doubles $55, with bath $65. The owners rent other apartments and houses on the island. Call, or write P.O. Box 100, Volcano, 96785 for additional accommodations information.

Volcano House, P.O. Box 53, Hawaii Volcanoes National Park 96718 (967-7321). A bit expensive, but affords the opportunity to eat and sleep on the rim of an active volcano. The 1220-ft. vantage point is certainly a unique perspective. Rooms without a crater view start at $79. The hotel also runs the **Namakani Paio** cabins, located 3 mi. behind the Volcano House in an *ohia* forest. Check-in after 3pm. Singles or doubles $32 with $6 per additional person. Linen and blankets provided. Each cabin has a picnic table and outdoor grill. $10 key deposit.

Volcanoes National Park, 967-7311. Free campsites at **Kipuka Nene, Namakani Paio** (near Kilauea Crater), and **Kamoamoa** (on the coast)—each with shelters and fireplaces, but no wood. 7-day max. No reservations.

Mauna Kea State Park, on the slopes of Mauna Kea off Saddle Rd. (Rte. 200), is the largest state park and offers views of both Mauna Kea and Mauna Loa. 7 cabins available (permit required). Camping is officially prohibited. Nights at the 6500 ft. elevation call for a sweater. You might see *nene* geese in the wild. Saddle Rd. is off-limits to rental cars.

Kalopa State Recreation Area, at the end of Kalopa Rd., 3 mi. *mauka* (inland) from Mamalahoa Rte. 19. Camping, group lodging, picnicking, nature trails. Sites surrounded by a wonderful *ohia* forest.

Two patrol cabins on the Mauna Loa summit trail may be used for free by hikers en route to the summit. One is at **Red Hill,** bordering Puuulaula Caldera, 7½ mi. from the end of Mauna Loa Strip Rd. (10,000 ft.). The other is 9½ mi. farther, at **Mauna Loa Summit,** next to Mokuaweoweo Caldera (13,250 ft.). Bunks, mattresses, and blankets are sometimes provided; bring your own sleeping bag, stove, and fuel. The ascent usually takes three days. No reservations are necessary, but register at the Kilauea visitors center.

FOOD

Since the best time to view the lava is after dark, you may want to pack a dinner and spend the late hours in the park. The **Kilauea General Store** (967-7555) in Volcano Village has groceries, homemade banana bread, and custom sandwiches ($3.50) to go (open daily 6:30am-7:30pm). The **Volcano Golf & Country Club** (967-8228) is located in the park beyond the visitors center toward Kona. Breakfast (7-10am) and lunch (10:30am-8pm) are served daily. Dinner is served on Saturday and Sunday (5:30-8pm). The portions are generous and the prices reasonable, with soup and sandwich for $7. Don't forget your plaid pants. The **Volcano Winery** (967-7479) at the end of Volcano Golf Course Rd. is worth a trip (and a sip) if only to taste wine from the southernmost winery in the U.S. They sell some exotic varieties of wine made from passion fruit, yellow guava, and honey ($8-9 per bottle; tasting is free). Buy a bottle and bring it to the late-night lava show.

SIGHTS

Because of the unpredictability of volcanic activity, the sights of **Volcanoes National Park** are constantly changing. Many rangers patrol the area, especially around the lava flow, but they cannot prevent some visitors from getting too close to the edge. Certain dangers are obvious—the lava flows destroy everything in their path—but also be wary of dangerous sulfur fumes and unstable footing. Keep a safe distance.

Although most tourists hope to witness the eruption in action, the park contains other worthwhile sights. It is a good idea to stop in at the **Kilauea Visitors Center,** where you can learn about the history of the area and the location of current volcanic activity. Even if you are not a guest, Arnott's Lodge has excellent weekly trips to the park ($25) where you can catch the flows "prime time." The **Chain of Craters Road** before the visitors center will take you past lava fields and down to a recent addition to the park: a new black sand beach.

The 11-mi. scenic drive around the Kilauea Caldera on **Crater Rim Drive** is a good way to see the volcano by car. The road is accessible via Rte. 11 from the east and west or via the Chain of Craters Rd. from the south. Well-marked trails and lookouts dot the way, so stop frequently to explore. You might also take the easy hike along the vista-filled **Crater Rim Trail,** which traverses *ohia* and giant fern forests, *aa* (rough) and *pahoehoe* (smooth) lava flows, and smoldering steam and sulfur vents. *Pilau!* ("It stinks!") Walk through the **Thurston Lava Tube,** formed by lava that cooled around a hot core which continued to move, leaving the inside of the flow hollow. **Devastation Trail** is a mile-long psychedelic trip though landscape out of Dali's imagination. The cinder cones and dead *ohia* trees were blasted by Kilauea Iki ("little Kilauea," west of "big" Kilauea Crater) in 1959. You can stop by the sauna-like **steam vents** and warm yourself on a chilly day, or take the five-minute hike to the **Halema Zumau Overlook,** and look down into the dormant **Halemaumau crater,** the goddess Pele's official residence.

The **Hawaiian Volcano Observatory** is closed to the public, but the free **Jaggar Museum** next door explains the geological background with a pictorial history of the volcano. Other displays focus on Hawaiian legends. (Open daily 8:30am-5pm.) The 4-mi. **Kilauea Iki Trail** starts at the Kilauea Iki overlook on Crater Rim Rd. This excellent two-hour hike is an absolute must for those who want to explore the park in more detail. It leads around the north rim of Kilauea Iki, through a forest of tree ferns, down the wall of the little crater, past the vent of the '59 eruption, over steaming lava, and back to Crater Rim Rd. (Whew!) On the way you'll pass *ohelo* bushes laden with red berries. Legend has it that you must offer some berries to Pele before eating any or you'll incur her wrath. The 3½-mi. **Mauna Iki Trail** begins 9 mi. southwest of park headquarters on Rte. 11. It leads to ashen footprints left in 1790. From here you can hike down into the coastal area.

Kipuka Puaulu (Bird Park), north off Mauna Loa Rd., is a patch of green land that eons of lava flows have miraculously missed. An easy 1-mi. loop trail leads through Kipuka Puaulu from the parking lot, 1 mi. up Mauna Loa Rd. from Rte. 11. Keep an eye out for native Hawaiian birds such as the bright red, black-winged *apapane*. The drops and strands of lava along the way bear names such as "Pele's Tears" and "Pele's Hair." Heed the rangers' advice, however, and leave these excretions with Pele lest she bring you bad luck. Many tourists spirit them away, only to regret the thievery and mail the rocks back. The park keeps a collection of the lava fragments tourists have sent back along with the apologetic letters accompanying them on display at the Kilauea Visitors Center.

Moving from the terrestrial to the celestial, **Mauna Kea,** to the north, has long served as an international center for visual astronomy. An unpaved road, navigable by four-wheel drive only, leads to the summit from Saddle Rd. (Rte. 200). Due to the

K
O
N
A

sensitivity of the observatory, cars are prohibited from going up in the night without a special red headlight filter. Resembling Maui's Haleakala, the terrain is stark and the views unearthly. The possibility of altitude sickness at 13,796 ft. is deterring.

■■■ KONA

Occupying the western side of Hawaii, Kona claims a disproportionate share of the Big Island's white sand beaches, resorts, and realtors. It is also home to the town of **Kailua** (officially **Kailua-Kona**) a resort center with shops, nightlife, and perfect weather. The white sand beaches at **Hapuna** and **Kawaihae** and the resort coves are perfect for tanning. The calm deep waters along this coast of the Big Island offer splendid snorkeling, scuba diving, and big game fishing. Upland, the fertile slopes of Mauna Kea and Hualalai yield the nation's only domestic coffee harvest.

Look in the *Coffee Times* (available free at most supermarkets) for great coupons and current local activities. This alternative paper has information on cafés and performances, even though it emphasizes coffee, not tourism.

Kailua-Kona itself is small enough to see in a short walk, and a number of historic sites are right in the heart of the city. Take time to visit King Kalakaua's summer home or the national historic park at Puuhonua O Honaunau. Many resorts feature petroglyphs or *heiaus* on their grounds. **Kealakekua Bay** is the site of another event in Hawaiian history; Captain Cook, the islands' first recorded Western visitor, dropped anchor and later met his death in this idyllic cove.

PRACTICAL INFORMATION AND ORIENTATION

Visitors Information: Hawaii Visitors Bureau, 75-5719 W. Alii Dr. (329-7787), across from the Kona Inn Shopping Center. Very helpful. Bus schedules, brochures, maps, and accommodations information. Open Mon.-Fri. 8am-noon and 1-4pm. See also Hilo Practical Information, page 474.

Outdoors Information: Department of Parks and Recreation, Yano Memorial Hall, Captain Cook (323-3060), by the police station. Information on county parks, camping, and permits. Open Mon.-Fri. noon-2pm. See also Hilo Practical Information, page 474.

Bus: Hele-on-Bus, 935-8241. Traverses the West Coast out of Kona, Mon.-Sat. 1 per day. To Hilo: $5.25 at 6:45am in front of Waldenbooks in Lanihau Center. Arrives 9:45am. Exact change required. Infrequent runs make it an impractical way to get around Kona.

Car Rental: Major car rentals at Kona airport. **V/N Car Rentals,** 75-5799 Alii Dr. (329-7328 or 326-9466). Bare-bones cars from $12.50 per day, although you're more likely to find one with A/C for $25 per day. 3-day min. 21 or older with major credit card or $300 cash deposit. Open Mon.-Fri. 7am-4pm, Sat. 7am-1pm.

Bikes and Mopeds: DJ's, 75-5663A Palani Rd. (329-1700), across from the King Kamehameha Hotel. Mopeds $30 for 24 hrs., 2-person scooters $50 for 24 hrs. Cash or credit card deposit. Open daily 7:30am-6pm. All moped rentals require valid driver's license. **Hawaiian Pedals,** Kona Inn Shopping Village. 21-speed mountain bikes $20 per day, $63 per week. Open daily 9am-5pm.

Water Equipment Rentals: Sandwich Island Divers, Kona Market Place (329-9188), all the way in the back. Masks, fins, and snorkels $6 per day, prescription masks $8.50, boogie-boards $8.50 per day. Charters, introductory dives, and scuba rentals are also available at affordable rates. Open daily 8am-8pm. **Jimbo's Kayaks** (328-8404) rents kayaks for $20 for 5 hrs. They deliver the gear to you.

Library: 75-138 Hualalai Rd. Open Mon., Wed., and Sat. 10am-5pm, Tues. and Thurs. 10am-8pm, Fri. noon-5pm.

Laundromat: Tyke's Laundromat, 74-5583A Pawai Pl. (326-1515). Wash $1, 7-min. dry 25¢. Open Mon.-Sat. 7am-9pm, Sun. 7am-6pm.

Coast Guard: 935-6370 or 800-331-6176.

Crisis/Help Line: 969-9111.

Kailua-Kona Medical Clinic: 75-137 Hualalai Rd. (329-1346). Open Mon.-Fri. 8:30am-5pm, Sat. 8:30am-noon.

Hospital: Kona (322-9311), off Rte. 11 south of Kailua-Kona. Follow well-marked signs on road.
Police: 911 or 329-8181.
Emergency: 911 or 323-2645.
Post Office: (329-1927) Palani Rd., in the Lanihau Ctr. behind the bank of Hawaii in Kailua-Kona. Open Mon.-Fri. 8:30am-4:30pm, Sat. 9am-noon. **General Delivery ZIP Code**: 96740.
Area Code: 808.

Kailua-Kona is served by **Keahole Airport,** 9 mi. north of town. A taxi into town is about $16, plus 30¢ per bag. The city is split by two streets running parallel to the ocean: Alii Drive, nearest the ocean, and Kuakini Hwy., one block *mauka* (inland) Kealakekua Bay and the town of Captain Cook are another 9 mi. south on Rte. 11.

ACCOMMODATIONS

Staying overnight in Kailua-Kona can be expensive, since its hotels cater to the affluent traveler. It's cheaper and more fun to stay away from the resort area, and daytrip into Kailua to use the hotels' beaches (all of which can be reached via public access paths). Some dress up and use the hotels' pools and lounges—if the hotel figures out you're not a guest they will ask you to leave, but it's not likely—those who act rich will fit right in. For the nearest **camping,** see Kohala.

Manago Hotel, P.O. Box 145, Captain Cook, 96704 (323-2642), on Rte. 11 between mile markers 109 and 110. This family-run hotel is dark but clean and comfortable. Generally older clientele. Inexpensive Japanese-American restaurant is a lunchtime favorite for guests and townies alike (open Tues.-Sun. 7-9am and 11am-2pm; dinner Tues.-Thurs. 5-7:30pm, Fri.-Sun. 5-7pm). Office open 6:30am-8:30pm. Austere singles $22. Doubles $25. Spacious and elegant rooms with bath from $35, doubles $38.

Kona Hotel (324-1155), in Holualoa on Rte. 180, southeast of Kona. Rooms are antique, high-ceilinged, and with a musty odor. Some with ocean view. Each has two beds, a dresser, and a latch (no lock) for the door. Communal bathrooms. Singles $20. Doubles $26.

Kona Seaside, 75-5646 Palani Rd., Kailua-Kona 96740, (922-5333 in Honolulu; from the outer islands 800-451-6754; from the mainland 800-367-7000). What this place lacks in character, it makes up in comfort, price, and location (right in the resort area). Check-out noon. Pool, A/C, TV. Singles and doubles $54.

Hale Maluhia (House of Peace) **B&B,** 76-770 Hualalai Rd., Kailua-Kona 800-559-6627 or 329-5773). 3 mi. from the center of town, this lovely B&B serves large, complimentary buffet breakfasts and offers free beach equipment. Common area has pool table, VCR, and TV. Outdoor hot tub. Singles with shared bath $50, with private bath and TV $65. Add $5 for doubles.

FOOD

Kailua-Kona has a range of tourist-oriented restaurants. You can find atypical home-style establishments or dive right into the early-bird specials (5-6pm) at most hotels. **Sack 'n' Save** in the Lanihau Center is open 24 hrs. and has a bakery and deli as well as a large selection of value-priced groceries. **Kona Healthways** (329-2296), in the Kona Coast Shopping Center on Palani Rd. sells the obligatory selection of bulk health foods. (Open Mon.-Fri. 8:30am-6pm, Sat. 8am-5pm, Sun. 11am-3pm.)

If you're interested in **Kona coffee,** you can taste the real thing for free at the **Mauna Loa Coffee Roastery,** 160 Napoopoo Road, Na Poopoo (328-2511; open daily 9am-5pm). Informative displays describe the history and mechanics of Kona coffee making. For a special roast (such as espresso), swagger down to the **Bad Ass Coffee Company** 75-5699D Alii Dr. or on Rte. 11 in Keauhou—but prepare to pay more. The donkey-decorated bathrooms are a must-see. Avoid "Kona-blended" coffee: coffee with beans from other parts of the world to dilute the power of Kona.

Buns in the Sun (326-2774), in the Lanihau Center adjacent to Longs Drugs. A great value—assorted homemade muffins (85¢), croissants ($1), and a variety of sandwiches on freshly baked bread with the works ($4.25). There are a few tables inside and outside. Open Mon.-Sat. 5am-4pm, Sun. 6am-2pm.

Stan's, 75-5646 Palani Rd. (329-2455), in the Kona Seaside. Breakfast specials include all-you-can-eat hotcakes for $4.25. Complete dinners from $7.50. Harbor view and ocean breezes. Open daily 7-9:30am and 5:30-8pm.

Ocean View Inn, 75-5683 Alii Dr. (329-9998), across from the boat dock. Popular establishment serves seafood, American, Chinese, and Hawaiian fare in a '50s diner setting. Breakfast $4, lunch $3-7, dinner $7-10. Try *laulau* and *poi* for $3. Vegetarian dishes around $4. Portions tend to be small. You may have trouble finding a smoke-free section. Open Tues.-Sun. 6:30am-2:45pm and 5:15-9pm.

Betty's Chinese Kitchen, Palani Rd., in the KTA Shopping Center. Large portions and a daily buffet. Sweet and sour pork is a popular choice. Daily plate for $4-5. Open Mon.-Sat. 10am-8:30pm.

Aloha Café Theater (322-3383), off Rte. 11 in Kealakekua. Sip an espresso ($1.25) at film revivals and live productions: plays, concerts, and dance performances grace this theater. Bring your beret and shades and look artistic. During the day enjoy the quiet *lanai* overlooking a park and the ocean. Healthy meals ($7) and fresh-baked muffins daily ($1.25). Open Mon.-Sat. 8am-8pm, Sun. 9am-2pm. Theater schedule confirmed a day before showtime.

Quinn's, 75-5655A Palani Rd. (329-3822). A local institution, Quinn's offers excellent food for medium money. Bar and terrace. Monte Cristo or club sandwich with fries for an army, $7. Open Mon.-Sat. 11am-1am, Sun. 11am-11pm.

SIGHTS AND ACTIVITIES

In Kona about the only things that break up the sparkling sands are fast-food restaurants, hyperkinetic nightclubs, and history. **Magic Sands** (also called "Disappearing Sands" because the sands get washed away for a couple of weeks every winter and then mysteriously return) at the **Kona Magic Sands Hotel,** 77-6452 Alii Dr. (329-9177), is a good place to park your towel and wade. It's a very popular place for snorkeling, bodysurfing, and boogie-boarding (restrooms and showers too). This small beach is often crowded. **Honokohau Beach** is 500 yds. north of the Honokohau Small Boat Harbor off Kaahumanu Hwy. Although this beach may have more sand than Magic Sands, it has fewer clothes—it's Kailua's only nude beach. Besides people-watching, there is good surfing to be found here. **Hulihee Palace,** 75-5718 Alii Dr. (329-1877), King Kalakaua's former pad (built in 1838), has been beautifully restored—much more completely than Queen Emma's summer cottage on Oahu. (Open daily 9am-4pm. Admission $4, ages 12-18 $1, under 12 50¢.) Across from the palace is **Mokuaikaua,** the first Christian church in Hawaii (1836). Also called the Church of the Chimes, the building has been lovingly cared for and is still used for sermons and as a museum. The chimes sound daily at 4pm (open daily sunrise-sunset). The church maintains an extensive collection of information on the first missionaries to arrive in "Owyhee," including copies of original documents.

A must-see is the **Hilton Hotel** in Waikoloa Village. This study in ostentation has boats and tramcars to shuttle the guests around the complex via its man-made lagoon. Despite its location next to the beach, the hotel has constructed its own beach. It even captured a couple of dolphins to create the **Dolphin Quest,** an extremely popular attraction in which the public can swim with the aquatic mammals for $68 per person. Drop a card in the lobby to enter the lottery to win a spot.

Up Hualalai Rd. on Rte. 180, **Holualoa** offers a different life-style from the resort-swamped coast. This tiny coffee town features a number of arts and crafts vendors as well as a new vantage point for the bay below. The **Kona Arts Center** in Holualoa sits in an abandoned coffee mill. The center offers craft workshops and serves as a gallery for local artists (open Tues.-Sat. 10am-4pm).

Despite other attractions, the beaches remain the main draw in Kona. White, sandy stretches line the coast through Kailua and up Rte. 19 to very beautiful and very crowded **Hapuna Beach** and **Spencer Beach Parks,** 35 mi. north. Hapuna

Beach Park's wide swath of sand and blue water make it especially appealing. Both parks are wheelchair accessible and have shade, snack bars, restrooms, and excellent snorkeling. There are also hotel-owned coves where you can rent sailboards.

Farther south on Rte. 11 is **Kealakekua Bay,** a marine reserve with superb snorkeling. From Rte. 11 turn right onto Napoopoo Dr.; this winding road leads down to the historic bay (about 15 min.) where in 1778 Captain Cook tried to restock his ship during the *Makahiki,* a holy season honoring the god Lono. The Hawaiians thought Cook's white sails and masts heralded the return of Lono, and they proclaimed Cook a god at the **Hikiau Heiau** on the bay. A year later Cook was killed on the far side of the bay when he tried to stop a fight between his crew and the islanders. A white monument marks the site.

ENTERTAINMENT

Kona's weekday nightlife centers around resort activities. On the weekends, the nightclubs and discos fill with locals and visitors.

Merry Wahine Bar (885-8805) in the **Big Island Steak House** at the King's Shops, Waikoloa Beach Resort. Popular weekend spot for young surfers and vacationers. DJ spins dance music nightly from 10:30pm. Domestic beer $2.75.

Jolly Roger Restaurant, 75-5776 Alii Dr. (329-1344). Full bar and live music nightly 9:30pm-1:30am. Happy hour 11am-7pm. Mai tai $2. Daily drink special. Fri.-Sat. $2 cover.

Eclipse, 75-5711 Kuakini Hwy. (329-4686). A small restaurant/disco with a young resort crowd dancing to top 40 music Fri.-Sun. nights. Wed. is country-western. Cover $2.

Bombadil's Food and Drink, 75-5864 Walua Rd. (329-1292), across from Hilton's tennis courts. Sports bar and matching crowd. Pricey. Open daily 11am-10pm.

Kona Surf, 78-128 Ehukai St. (322-3411). The place to catch real headliner acts. Illustrious Jerry Garcia has played here. Call for information on current acts.

■ SOUTHEAST OF KONA: KAU

Driving south from Kaiwi toward Ka Lae (South Point), you come to **Puuhonua O Honaunau,** often referred to as the City of Refuge (take Rte. 160 off Rte. 11). This was a last-ditch sanctuary for Hawaiians fleeing from battle or escaping punishment for breaking the *kapu* (the sacred laws that ruled Hawaiian life). Having reached the *puuhonua* and received absolution at the hands of the *kahuna pule* (priest), the ritually purified offender could safely resume life at home. King Kamehameha II destroyed all other such sanctuaries when he abolished the *kapu* in 1819, but saved this one because it contained the bones of his ancestors. Stop by the **visitors center** for a map (328-2288; open daily 7:30am-5:30pm; orientation talks 10am-3:30pm; craft demonstrations 9am-4:30pm; $2). Picnicking and sunbathing are forbidden, and swimming in solemn Keoneeleele Cove is highly inappropriate. Despite the onslaught of tour buses, this unique site maintains a sense of dignity and sacredness that other attractions have lost. The shady beach and view of the water may lead you to a feeling of serenity similar to that experienced by the ancient Hawaiians. The authentically built **Koa** wood canoe and Hawaiian hut are probably the last of their kind in the world.

Two detours on the road to Puuhonua O Honaunau are worth investigating. Though officially called **St. Benedict's Catholic Church,** this small Gothic church has been dubbed "Painted Church," because of the murals and frescoes on its side panels and ceiling. The church was built in the 1900s by a Belgian priest and painted to look like the Cathedral of Burgos in Spain (open daily sunrise-sunset). The other noteworthy stop is the endearing **Wakefield Botanical Gardens and Restaurant,** 1 Rodeo Rd. (328-9930), a relatively unknown tropical garden along the yellow coconut trail. The garden restaurant's Mexican entrees aren't as exciting as their desserts; try the blueberry cheesecake or the macadamia nut pie ($2.95). (Open daily 11am-3pm.) The café offers free tours of the garden, where a petrified tree stump is proudly displayed.

Farther south, you can camp at the county park in **Milolii,** a traditional fishing village (i.e. no electricity). In the friendly town of **Waiohinu,** you can see the southernmost hotel in the U.S., **Shirikawa's Hotel and Motel,** P.O. Box 467, Naalehu 96772 (929-7462), 58 mi. southeast of Kailua-Kona on Rte. 11. It's near a monkeypod tree planted by Mark Twain in 1866.

From the town of Waiohinu, you can drive 12 mi. down a rough, one-lane road to South Point (off-limits to some rental cars), the southernmost point in the U.S. Get out where the cars are parked and hike the 2½-mi. trail to **Green Sands,** where a high copper content has turned the beach—you guessed it—pure natural green.

Around Naalehu and heading north back toward Volcanoes National Park and Hilo, camp at **Punaluu Black Sand Beach.** A county park, Punaluu has wheelchair-accessible bathrooms, pavilions, outdoor showers, fire pits, public phones, and an unsurpassed view of the rising sun.

■■■ KOHALA AND THE HAMAKUA COAST

The drive along the northwestern coast takes you into the rural heartland of Hawaii. (Kohala without a car or moped means hitchhiking—it is inaccessible by bus. *Let's Go* does not recommend hitching in any situation.) It's too far for most bicyclists: 55 mi. from Hilo to Kamuela/Waimea, 39 mi. from Kona. Once home to several sugar mills, much of the area deteriorated into ghost towns with the death of the sugar economy. The Kona side of Kohala offers camping near beaches, and the flat, wide-shouldered roads are ideal for cycling; the center is *paniolo* (cowboy) country; and the Hilo side, known as the Hamakua Coast, guards the emerald Waipio Valley. Despite its physical beauty, magnificent Kohala is remarkably empty of tourists.

ACCOMMODATIONS

All parks require a $1 camping **permit,** available at the county parks office (see Hilo Practical Information, page 474) except for Hapuna Beach State Park, where the permit is free. Mahukona and Kapaa Beach Parks have restroom facilities and allow camping, but neither is on a beach. Instead, they are perched on rocky coastlines.

Hapuna Beach State Park (882-7995), off Rte. 19, 3 mi. south of Kawaihae. Wide, white, sandy beach for swimming, volleyball, and sunning. Lots of shaded picnic tables. A-frame shelters $7 (4-person max.); no tent camping. Reserve in advance.

Spencer Beach Park, off Rte. 27 near Kawaihae. Ranger patrolled and crowded. Wheelchair-accessible facilities. Calm waters and white beach. Not quite as exciting as Hapuna, but good for tent camping.

Keokea Beach Park, off Rte. 27, 6 mi. past Hawi. Beautiful spot, rarely crowded. Good fishing, showers, restrooms, electricity. Obscure location, but near several grocery stores.

Tom's Place (775-0368 in Waipio, 935-7466 in Hilo—call often, and wait a while), in Waipio Valley. Requires 4-wheel-drive or a 1-hr. hike from the Waipio Lookout for access. Tom's 'bout 83 years old, and his memory of the valley goes back a long way. A perfectly enchanting place. No electricity, but gas lamps, cold showers, and communal kitchens (bring your own food). Singles $15. Doubles $15.

SIGHTS

Going north up Rte. 19, tropical paradise gives way to desolate lava fields, left intact since 1859. You may notice the environmentally friendly "graffiti". White stones set against the black rock spell out politically correct messages. The **Waikoloan complex** to the left of the road is home to **petroglyphs** sandwiched between holes six and seven on the golf course. If the juxtaposition of resort culture and ancient Hawaii seems too incongruous, travel down the road to **Puukohola Heiau** (at the intersection of Rte. 19 and Rte. 270). Stop at the **visitors center** (882-7218) for a brief introduction and a guide (open 7:30am-4pm) to the last major religious structure of the old culture, **Puukohola Heiau.** Kamehameha the Great built this *heiau* about 200 years ago in honor of Ku Kailimoku, before his conquest of the Big Island. In 1791, a prophet told him that constructing the temple would enable him to conquer the entire chain of Hawaiian islands. About four years and many human sacrifices later, the prophecy was realized.

Rte. 270 will lead you out of the desert and around the Kohala Mountains to the tropical plantation town of **Hawi.** The birthplace of King Kamehameha is marked by the cast of a statue that stands in Honolulu. Rte. 270 ends at the **Pololu Valley Lookout.** A half-hour hike leads down from here to a broad, black sand beach. On the way to the lookout, swing by **Don's Deli,** Rte. 270 in Kapaau (889-5822) for a quick meal. Try a deli sandwich ($4.25) or bagels and lox ($5). Don also serves ice cream and smoothies. (Open Mon.-Fri. 8am-6pm, Sat.-Sun. 10am-5pm.)

From the Kona Coast beyond Hapuna Beach, head up the mountain on Rte. 250. On a clear day, you'll feast on the stunning view of Mauna Kea with Mauna Loa to her right. Rte. 250 ends in **Waimea,** the heart of ranch country. The **Parker Ranch,** a.k.a. the "Texas of the Tropics," is the largest cattle ranch in the United States, spanning some 250,000 acres. About three-quarters the size of Oahu and home to 50,000 head of Hereford cattle, the ranch annually produces enough beef for 40 million quarter-pounders. Stop by the **Parker Ranch Visitors Center and Museum** (885-7655), for audio-visual presentations on the fascinating history, operations, and lifestyles of Parker Ranch and its *paniolos,* Hawaiian cowboys. (Open daily 9am-5pm. $5, ages 4-11 $3.75.) Mr. Richard Smart, present owner of the Parker Ranch, has recently opened his private home, **Puuopelu** (855-5666), to the masses. Also open is **Mana House,** the original residence built by John Palmer Parker in 1847. From the visitors center, turn left onto Rte. 19. The gates appear shortly after a green Quonset hut on your right. (Open Tues. and Sat. 9am-5pm for self-guided tours. Admission to visitors center and historic homes $10, ages 4-11 $7.50.)

The **Kamuela Museum** (885-4724) houses the largest collection of artifacts of the Hawaiian monarchy, including a royal shark hook which used human flesh as bait. The Solomons, owners of the museum, have amassed a wonderfully eclectic collection of Hawaiiana, Americana, and Sinophernalia. The Chinese roses are marvelous. (Open daily 8am-5pm. $5, under 12 $2.)

A 30-minute drive on Rte. 19 from Kamuela to **Honokaa** will take you through cattle country strewn with misty, rolling hills. Looking at the cattle, horses, and landscape, it's hard to believe that the desert-like Kohala coast is just 45 minutes away. If it's mid-May, you might happen on the **Honokaa Rodeo.** Otherwise, hop along 8 mi. down Rte. 24 to the edge of the lush **Waipio Valley** for one of the most striking panoramas anywhere in the islands. This 2000-ft. gorge is the crowning point of a series of breathtaking canyons between Waipio and Pololu. Bountiful flora and fauna made Waipio (the islands' largest gorge) the center of ancient Hawaiian civilization. In 1780, Kamehameha was chosen here by reigning chiefs to be the future ruler. For a wonderful reprieve from the artificiality of the resorts, hike through this natural wonder. The steep jaunt down into the valley takes one hour. The way up is along a paved road. Many trails lead back into the valley and along the beach.

Paradise Safari's four-wheel drive wagons will take you star-gazing on Mauna Kea (322-2366). An evening trip costs $95. The **Waipio Valley Shuttle** (775-7121) takes visitors on a 90-minute drive to 1200-ft. waterfalls, lotus ponds, taro patches, and other scintillating and historic sights. Catch the Jeep shuttle at the top of the valley. Purchase tickets and check in at the **Waipio Woodworks Art Gallery** (775-0958), ½ mi. from the Waipio Valley lookout. Reservations are highly recommended. (Tour $30, under 11 $15. Open Mon.-Sat. 8am-4pm. Write P.O. Box 5128, Kukuihaele, HI 96727 for more information.) The adventurous should consider the 9-mi., five-hour hike between the Waipio Valley Lookout and Waimanu Bay. Waimanu Valley holds ancient Hawaiian ruins, and the scenery is sublime.

■■■ SEASONAL EVENTS

Kona Stampede, 2nd weekend in March at Honaunau Arena. Call Dr. William Bergin (885-7941).

Merrie Monarch Festival, in late March-early April. Hula contests, local music, and festivities. Call Dorothy Thompson (935-9168).

Parker Ranch Rodeo and Horse Races, July 4 in Waimea (Parker Ranch Arena). Wild West entertainment. Yee-haw! Call Robby Hind (689-6798).

Annual Naalehu Carnival and Rodeo, July 4-6 in Naalehu. Rodeo events, farm fairs, games, contestants, beer garden, and Hawaiian entertainment.

Kona Ahi Marlin Jackpot Fishing Tournament, July in Kailua-Kona. Call George Molholm (322-3832).

Gatorade Ironman World Triathlon Championship, mid-Oct. in Kailua-Kona. The original and ultimate endurance test: a 2.4-mi. swim, 112-mi. cycle, and 26.2-mi. run. If you are not up to the challenge, pick up a T-shirt and pretend.

Kona Coffee Festival, Nov. in Kona. High-strung morning people converge to pay homage to the caffeine god.

The Hawaii County Band performs free monthly concerts at the Liliuokalani Gardens. Call Destination Hilo (see Hilo Practical Information, page 474).

Kauai

Kauai literally means "place around the neck," where the favored child in a Hawaiian family traditionally rides. It's easy to believe that Hawaii-loa, mythical creator of the Hawaiian islands, loved the Garden Island better than its brethren; still largely unspoiled by tourist development, Kauai's natural beauty surpasses that of all the other large islands. Lacking the nightlife of Maui and Oahu, the island is largely frequented by honeymooners and older couples. The island has also served as a backdrop for moviemakers seeking a prototype of paradise; portions of *King Kong, Blue Hawaii, Raiders of the Lost Ark,* and *Jurassic Park* were filmed in Kauai.

Kauai, known as "The Garden Isle," boasts a variety of ecosystems from the lush vegetation of Hanalei Valley to the dry cliffs of the Waimea Canyon. The steady cascade of water down Kauai's Mt. Waialeale, the wettest spot on earth, carved the amphitheater valleys of Kalalau and the 3000-ft. deep Waimea Canyon out of rock. The sugar industry protects much of the land from large-scale building and provides travelers with views of the expansive cane fields and their rich red soil.

PRACTICAL INFORMATION AND ORIENTATION

Visitors Information: Hawaii Visitors Bureau, Lihue Plaza Bldg., 3016 Umi St. #207, Lihue (245-3971), at Rice St. Stop by to pick up the fun and informative Kauai Illustrated Pocket Map. Write for their vacation planner, a directory of services, events, and coupons: P.O. Box 507, Lihue 96766. Open Mon.-Fri. 8am-4pm. **Kauai County Parks Office,** 4193 Hardy St., Lihue (245-8821). The office is located behind the convention center in a long building by the parking lot. Information and permits for camping in county parks. Open Mon.-Fri. 7:45am-4:30pm. After-hours permits available until 8pm at the Police Dept., 3060 Umi St., Lihue. **Division of State Parks,** 3060 Eiwa St. #306, Lihue 96766 (241-3444), at Hardy St., in the State Office Bldg. Information on camping in state parks. Permits issued Mon.-Fri. 8am-4pm. **Kauai Chamber of Commerce,** 2979 Kele #201 (P.O. Box 1969), Lihue 96766 (245-7363).

Local Attractions and Cultural Events: 246-4441, ext. 1800.

Taxis: An expensive last resort. **Hanamaulu Taxi** (245-3727), 25¢ per ¼-mi. 24-hr. service. **North Shore Cab** (826-6189) offers end-of-the-road specials for hikers. Open daily 5am-9pm.

Car Rental: The best deals come as part of hotel-car or air-car packages. Make reservations. **Alamo Rent-a-Car,** Lihue Airport (800-327-9633 or 245-0646). **Budget Rent-a-Car,** Lihue Airport (800-527-0700 or 245-9031). Open daily 6am-9pm. Also see Accommodations: Kauai International Hostel, page 488.

Public Transportation: Kauai has next to no public transportation. Even the locals express frustration. Rent a car if you can or try to make do with a bicycle

Bicycle Rental: Kauai's main roads leave little room for slow 2-wheelers, so think twice before renting and plan your journey carefully. **Pedal 'n' Paddle,** P.O. Box 1413, Ching Young Village, Hanalei 96714 (826-9069). Mountain bikes $20 per day, $80 per week. Another location at Kauai Village, Kapaa is open daily 8am-7pm (822-2005). Inter-store drop-offs permitted.

Camping and Water Equipment Rental: Pedal 'n' Paddle (see Bicycle Rental, above) Snorkeling equipment $7 per day, $20 per week. Bodyboards $7 per day, $20 per week. 2-person kayaks $45 per day. Dome tent $8 per day, $30 per week. Backpacks, blankets, and trail stoves also available. **Kauai Sea Sports** (800-685-5889 or 742-9303) on Poipu Rd. in Koloa on the South Shore rents snorkeling equipment and boogie boards for $4 per day, $15 per week. Full scuba gear $37 per day. Open daily 9am-5pm.

Laundromat: Kapaa Laundry Center, Kapaa Shopping Center, Kuhio Hwy. (822-3113). Drop off and self-service, Mon.-Sat. 7am-9pm.

Coast Guard: 245-4521 or 245-8111.

Library: Lihue Public Library, 4344 Hardy St., Lihue. Open Mon. and Thurs.-Sat. 9am-5pm, Tues. and Wed. 10am-8pm.

Weather: 245-6001. **Marine Conditions:** 245-3564.

Help Lines: Crisis, 245-7838. 24 hrs. **Kauai Helpline,** 245-3411. 24 hrs.

Hospitals: Wilcox, O.N. Memorial Hospital and Health Center, 3420 Rte. 56, Lihue (245-1010). **Kauai Veterans** (338-9431), in Waimea. Both open 24 hrs.

Emergency: 911.

Police: 3060 Umi St., Lihue (245-9311).

Post Office: 4441 Rice St., Lihue (245-4994). Open Mon.-Fri. 7:30am-5pm, Sat. 9am-1pm. **General Delivery ZIP Code:** 96766.

Area Code: 808.

Kauai is the farthest northwest of the large islands in the Hawaii chain. Roughly circular, the island falls away from **Mt. Waialeale** (the wettest spot on earth) at its center to a coastline ringed by one two-lane highway. The island is divided into five districts: the **Lihue** district, the commercial center; the **Koloa** district to the south, home to many resorts as well as some good surfing; the **Kawaihau** district to the north of Lihue, centered at Kapaa; the **Hanalei** district, on the north shore; and the **Waimea** district of the west, home to the rugged, inaccessible mountains and canyon of the same name. The northern areas experience frequent showers, but the south and the west are fairly dry.

Driving in Kauai is both heaven and hell—the island boasts some of the straightest highways this side of paradise, and some of the slowest drivers. ("Dude, the waves aren't going anywhere.") Lunch and closing times see the highways fill up and slow to a crawl, especially between Lihue and Kapaa. Highways connect Lihue and the Lihue Airport with the major towns: **Wailua** is 7 mi., **Kapaa** 10 mi., **Hanalei** 35 mi., and **Haena** 41 mi. counterclockwise on **Rte. 56.** Clockwise on **Rte. 50, Poipu** lies 14 mi. and **Waimea** 25 mi. from Lihue. The Rte. 50/56 circuit leaves a wide, roadless gap on the remote northwestern **Na Pali Coast** of Kauai. Thirty mi. from Lihue, **Waimea Canyon Rd.** branches off Rte. 50 and heads up Waimea Canyon to Kokee. Always wear your seatbelt—the police keep busy by handing out $25 fines.

Lihue Airport, a 26-minute flight from Honolulu, is Kauai's major airfield. **Princeville Airport** serves mainly the Princeville resort area and is serviced only by **Island Air** (800-652-6541; flights to all islands from $69).

ACCOMMODATIONS

Most of Kauai's accommodations lie in the Lihue-Kapaa area on the east coast, conveniently located between the North and South Shores. Kapaa is located only minutes from Lihue and has a pleasant, quaint atmosphere. Lihue is the more industrial of the towns. The Kokee Lodge offers furnished cabins in a state park setting (see Camping, below, for more information).

Kauai International Hostel, 4532 Lehua St., Kapaa (800-858-2295 or 823-6142, in Kauai). Co-ed dorms, laundry facilities, and outside kitchen. Max. stay 7 nights. Open 24 hrs. No curfew. Free linen and wonderfully thick mattresses. Car rental deal with Hertz includes subcompact for $25 per day, $125 per week. Terrific location, but can be noisy. Bunk $15 per night. Private room $40 per night.

Kay Barker's B&B, P.O. Box 740, Kapaa 96746 (822-3073; from the mainland 800-835-2845), in the lush Wailua homesteads off Rte. 580 past the Opaekaa falls. A car is necessary to reach this gracious country home offering spacious rooms with private bath. Continental breakfast included. Singles $35-60. Doubles $45-70. Call early for reservations.

Mokihana Timeshare, 796 Kuhio Hwy., Kapaa (822-3971, 206-676-1434 for reservations). An excellent choice for groups of 2 or 3. Common TV room, pool, tennis court. Desk open 7:30am-9pm. Check-out noon. Studio with kitchenette and beach view $55. 2-bedroom unit $65. 25% non-refundable deposit required.

Tip Top Motel, 3173 Akahi St., Lihue (245-2333) is a new, clean, and spartan, with A/C. Coffee shop and lounge. Ask for a room with TV. Singles and doubles $50.

Garden Island Inn, 3445 Wilcox Rd., Nawiliwili 96766 (800-648-0154 or 245-7227), about 3 mi. ($9 taxi) from Lihue airport. Across from Kalapaki Beach, this inn offers comfortable rooms in a garden setting, complete with goldfish-stocked pools, cable TV, fridge, daily maid service, phone, coffee maker, and microwaves. Car/room packages also available. Located right on the highway, which can be noisy. Near the Westin Kauai Lagoons Hotel. Singles and doubles $55-85.

Hale Lihue Motel, 2931 Kalena St., Lihue (245-2751 or 245-3151). Rock-bottom prices, and facilities to match. Cramped, dark, concrete cubicles are stuffy at night. Light sleepers beware: you'll have to open the window, and the other residents can be noisy. Check out 11am. If nobody answers the phone, keep trying—the manager is in and out. Singles $23. Doubles $26. Weekly and monthly rates.

CAMPING

Camping is an economical way to enjoy Kauai's beauty. Three state parks and six county parks officially allow camping. Of the state parks, Kokee is inland, Polihale is on a beach, and the Na Pali Coast State Park is only accessible by boat. **State permits** are available from the Division of State Parks (see Practical Information, above) and are **free,** with a five-night maximum stay. County parks worth checking out are Haena and Hanalei Beach Parks and Salt Pond Beach Park. Although they can't compare with the previous parks in terms of scenic beauty, Niumalu, Hanamaulu, and Lucy Wright Beach Parks also allow camping. **County permits** are available for $3 per person per day for a maximum of seven days per park and 60 total days per year from the County Parks Office. Permits can also be obtained from the police station on weekends or from rangers on the spot, but permits cost $5 per person per day. The park offices have lots of information on hiking and trails.

While camping, look out for your safety. Pick your site carefully. Also, heed posted warnings about local water conditions—some apparently calm areas are definitely not safe for swimming. And bear in mind that fresh water on Kauai may contain harmful bacteria. Always treat (with iodine, a filter, or by boiling) any water from mountain streams before drinking it. At the risk of sounding motherly, we suggest that you also bring warm clothes—the nights are cold at higher elevations.

Polihale State Park, Rte. 50, about 37 mi. northwest of Lihue at the end of 5 mi. of dirt road. The haul cane road (right turn at the yellow "road narrows" sign) gets you into the park proper, but is rough and sandy. Plan on staying for a couple of days; your vehicle won't want to make this journey twice in one day. Gorgeous beach park beneath the looming splendor of the Na Pali coast. Swimming not recommended except at Queen's Pond (left at the great tree in the road) but shore-fishing is good. Picnicking and tent facilities. Restrooms, showers, BBQ pits.

Kokee State Park, at the end of Rte. 550, 16 mi. north of Kekaha. Tent and trailer camping near extensive trails, picnic facilities, scenic forests, and canyon. Plum picking, pig hunting, and trout fishing in season. More information at the visitors center. Restrooms, showers, BBQ pits.

Kokee Lodge Cabins, P.O. Box 819, Waimea 96796 (335-6061), offers cabins for 3-7 people, with refrigerators, stoves, showers, utensils, and linens. Be fore-warned that the resident roosters crow all day long. 5-day max. stay. Check-in 2pm. Check-out 11am. Office open 9am-4pm daily. Simple cabin $35, fragrant cedar cabin $45. Full deposit required, refundable on 1-week cancellation notice. Book early for summer.

Kahili Mountain Park, P.O. Box 298, Koloa 96756 (742-9921), off Rte. 50, between mile markers 7 and 8. 215 acres with a small lake and a few hiking trails. Located in woods 7 mi. from Poipu Beach. Quiet and peaceful in the summer but located near a school. Run by the Adventist Church. 2-day min. stay. Check-in noon. Check-out 10am. Cabins for 4 with private bath, shower, and kitchen $40. New cabin $50. Prices listed are for doubles; add $6.60 for each extra person. Laundry room. Linen, dishes, and detergent provided.

YMCA, Camp Naue (246-9090), on the North Shore beach near Kalalau trail, in Haena. Close to some prime snorkeling spots and Haena Beach Park. Fall asleep to the sound of waves lapping against the shore. Space for 40 people in 2 bunk-houses. Individual shower stalls. Tent sites available. Bunks $12. Thin mattresses; bring your own linen. Sites with tents $10, plus $7 per each additional person.

FOOD

Kauai is a culinary as well as visual feast. Consider satisfying two senses simulta-neously: pack a picnic. For groceries, check out the **Big Saves** in Lihue at Hardy St. and Rte. 56 and in Waimea at 9861 Rte. 56 (both open daily 7am-9pm), and **Old Koloa** at 5510 Rte. 530 (open daily 6am-11pm). There's a 24-hr. **Safeway** at 831 Kuhio Hwy in Kapaa; it has a **pharmacy** (open Mon.-Fri. 8:30am-7:30pm, Sat.-Sun. 8:30am-5pm). **Papaya's Natural Foods,** Kauai Village in Kapaa (823-0190; open Mon.-Sat. 10am-8pm), has organic produce and bulk-bins.

Hamura's Saimin Stand, 2956 Kress St. (245-3271), in Lihue. Doesn't look like much, but locals line up for the excellent *saimin* noodles, invented by original owner Aiko Hamura ($2.25-3) and sit down at the interesting zig-zag counter. Open Mon.-Thurs. 10am-11pm, Fri.-Sat. 10am-1:30am, Sun. 10am-9:30pm.

Bubba's, 1384 Kuhio Hwy., Kapaa and at Hanalei Center, Hanalei (823-0069). With posted slogans like "We cheat tourists, drunks, and attorneys" and "If you don't want onions say so" you might hesitate to ask for an extra napkin. The Bubba Burger comes with mustard, relish and onions ($2.25). The official motto is "Try it our way." In Kapaa, open Sun.-Thurs. 10:30am-10pm, Fri.-Sat. 10:30am-2am. In Hanalei, open daily 10:30am-6pm.

Korean BBQ Restaurant, 4-356 Kuhio Hwy. (Rte. 56), Kapaa (823-6744). Across from **Sizzler** (which, by the way, has all-you-can-eat hotcakes for $3, 10am-10pm). Grilled or BBQ meats (beef, spareribs, chicken, and *mandoo*) and a pleth-ora of noodle and soup dishes ($4-6). No vegetarian dishes. Open Sun.-Mon. and Wed.-Sat. 10am-9pm.

Village Snack and Bakery Shop, Ching Young Village (826-6841), off Rte. 56 in Hanalei. Lunch special includes soda, salad, and overstuffed sandwich for $6. Take it to the beach. Those not planning on wearing a bikini may want to indulge in the Belgian waffles with macadamia nuts, fruit, and whipped cream $7. Owned by a sweet couple who make the sweetest coconut pudding cake ($2.65). Open Mon.-Sat. 6am-7pm, Sun. 6am-2pm.

Mikal's (926-4564) on Kuhio Hwy., Hanalei at the entrance to Ching Yang Village fuels the flower power set with its vegetarian Yowza Burger ($5.25) and tropical fruit smoothies ($2.75). This take-out stand with a few tables is popular with hip-pies and dred-locked surfers. Open Mon.-Fri. 11am-3pm and 5-9pm, Sat.-Sun. 11am-6pm. Herbivores and carnivores can fight it out at the **Shave-Ice Lady** stand across the street (next to Bubba's).

K A U A I

SIGHTS AND ACTIVITIES

Explore Kauai from the two coastal highways (Rte. 50 going south and Rte. 56 going north) that embrace the island from Lihue Airport. Kauai has some of the best surf spots on the islands, and the classic Hawaiian Reef diving beckons to the nautically inclined. Beach potatoes, white sand and calm waters abound. Kauai also sustains a myriad of unique flora and fauna. All this creates some of the most inexpressibly gorgeous scenery in the United States. An excellent way to view this is via a **helicopter** tour. Though expensive, an aerial tour of Kauai ranks with life's more exhilarating experiences. Make sure your tour includes the Kalalau Valley and Na Pali Coast, and bring a camera. A reputable company is **Papillon Hawaiian Helicopters.** (In Kauai, call 826-6591; to reserve, 800-367-7096, 6am-3pm. Tours from $89 for 45 min.)

Fortunately for the budget traveler, most of Kauai's points of interest are free. Picturesque views exist above and below the water; many visitors are satisfied just watching the expert surfers tackle the waves. Those with a voyeuristic streak can follow the bickering honeymooners ("Honey, I *know* how to work the damn video-camera!") as they tour the island.

Lihue

The **Kauai Museum,** 4428 Rice St. (245-6931), is a small museum with a remarkable collection of Hawaiian artifacts as well as presentations on the geological and cultural history of Kauai. While there, don't miss the 40-minute video of the island as filmed from a helicopter and by underwater scuba divers. Large exhibits feature crafts made from koa wood and native Hawaiian quilt-making. Other exhibits describe plantation life, island ecology, and the history of missionaries on Kauai. (Open Mon.-Fri. 9am-4:30pm, Sat. 9am-1pm. $3, under 18 free. Free to families Sat. 9-11am. Free tours Thurs. 9:30am.) Hurricane Iniki may have put the **Westin Kauai** hotel (245-5050) in Nawiliwili Harbor temporarily "out of business," but that hasn't stopped it from capitalizing on its man-made "paradise." You can see kangaroos, monkeys, and flamingos on the 45-minute wildlife tour of the man-made **lagoon.** Visitors may even catch a glimpse of an indigenous bird. Kauai has much natural beauty accessible for free, so save your money. (Open daily 10am-4pm. $19, ages 6-13 $10).

Kilohana Plantation, 3-2087 Rte. 50 (245-5608), 1.7 mi. south of Lihue, was the plantation estate of Gaylord Park Wilcox. Those who wish to see what life was like on an old Hawaiian plantation may take a carriage ride throughout the grounds. (20-min. ride Tues.-Sat. 11am-6:30pm, Mon.-Sun. 11am-5pm. Adults $7, under 12 $4.) There is no charge for roaming around the plantation itself, although most of the rooms are now occupied by shops. The original furnishings in the dining and living rooms, however, provide a singular glimpse of Old Hawaii.

Heading north on Rte. 56, turn *mauka* (inland) on Rte. 583 to reach **Wailua Falls,** likely the most spectacular of Kauai's several hundred cascades. Steep and unimproved trails lead down to the top of the falls from the end of the road. Watch the falls cascade 400 ft. into a blue-green pool. Turn right after the Wailua Golf Course on Rte. 56 North to get to **Lydgate State Park.** Park at the far end of the lot. The path along the shore will lead you to the "city of Refuge," part of an ancient *heiau* located just past the white sand beach and sheltered wading pool.

At **Wailua Marina State Park,** 7 mi. from Lihue before the Wailua River Bridge, you can take a boat up the Wailua River to the **Fern Grotto** ($10, under 12 $5). **Smith's Tropical Paradise** (822-4654 or 822-9599) and **Waialeale Boats** (822-4908) run boats that leave every half hour from 9am to 4pm (round trip 1 hr. and 20 min.) The cheesy island music and mandatory hula dancing fun on the boat ride may steer you to rent a kayak instead (see Pedal 'n' Paddle), but be prepared to compete with the tour boats and water-skiers for space. In spite of the crowds, Smith's Tropical Paradise in Kapaa is a stunning 30 acres of gardens and lagoons. Get marooned here for at least a half-day (open 8:30am-4pm; admission $5, under 12 $2.50).

Near Lihue: Princeville, Hanalei, and Haena

Traveling east on Rte. 56, watch buildings gradually give way to lush, unspoiled beaches and other natural wonders. The best sights in eastern Kauai lie along Rte. 56. On the drive, stop at **Kilauea Point National Wildlife Refuge** (828-1413), 709 ft. above sea level on a bluff near Kilauea Bay, off Kuhio Ave. To get here, follow the signs from the highway. Share the magnificent vista with thousands of seabirds and an occasional dolphin or seal. (Open Mon.-Fri. 10am-4pm. Free until renovations are completed.) When you have sufficiently savored the view, drive a bit farther down Rte. 56, take a right onto Kalihiwai Rd. and another right on the first dirt road, and park at the end to take the steep public access path to the crystalline water of **Secret Beach** (shh!). This breathtaking beach is no longer a secret, but you can still sun, camp, or swim in relative seclusion. Don't try the beach in winter—the surf shrinks it considerably. After returning to Rte. 56 and crossing the bridge, you will re-encounter Kalihiwai Rd. Follow it until Anini Rd. and take Anini to the **Anini Beach,** an ideal and sometimes deserted swimming area. To find a secluded spot you can follow the road in either direction. In August, you may be able to watch celebrities (including Sylvester Stallone) at the polo club across the street. The **Hanalei Valley Lookout,** off the left side of the road, spans a valley of *taro* patches and rice paddies. Stop at **Pooku Stable,** P.O. Box 888 (826-6777, 826-7473, evenings 826-6484), to ride horseback to the waterfalls for a picnic ($95).

The town of Princeville sparkles with the glitz of tourism. The **Princeville Hotel-Sheraton** is a super-charged multimillion-dollar resort establishment. The town contains a Foodland, a gas station, and a few shops.

The land of **Hanalei** was made famous in by Peter, Paul, and Mary in their song "Puff the Magic Dragon." (Some locals have their own interpretation of the title and "little Jackie Paper"—sources report that *pokalolo,* some of the best marijuana in the world, is grown in the middle of various cane fields.) Hanalei Bay is an excellent destination for surfers of different levels. Beginners should stay inside the reef near the Hanalei Pier on the east side of the bay. **Lumahai Beach** is probably on the postcard you'll send home. After visiting it, you'll see that pictures can't do it justice. For the best view of the beach, park off Kuhio Hwy. and walk down the trail next to the "Danger: No Lifeguard" sign. Parking is also available next to the beach itself. For terrific snorkeling, head to **"Tunnels,"** a protected reef area with colorful fish. Somewhat distant, but legal parking is available at Haena Beach Park down the road.

On the drive to **Haena,** notice the enormous **Maniniholo Dry Cave,** named after the head fisherman of the *menehunes,* a legendary diminutive people said to have inhabited the island. Farther along, in **Haena State Park,** you can spelunk in **Waikapalae Cave,** or to experience the cooler side of paradise, dip into the lagoon at the **Waikanaloa Cave** (it may be dry during times of drought). Park your car in the visitors parking lot to your right. Waikapalae Cave is a short walk on the path directly across the road. Between the two caves and to your left you will see an old path with cracked pavement. A short walk up this road will take you to the entrance of a much more secluded section of the **Blue Room** cave. The water here is usually a deeper blue because it is hidden from the onslaught of silt-churning tourists. It's also deep; if you plan on swimming, bring a boogie-board or be prepared to tread water.

At the end of Kuhio Hwy. (Rte. 56) you'll find two popular beaches: **Haena Bay** and **Kee Beach.** Both are excellent snorkeling and swimming spots in the summer. Kee is noted particularly for its sunsets, and was the site of passionate beach love scenes in *The Thorn Birds.* The trailhead for the **Kalalau Valley Trail,** which follows an ancient Hawaiian path 11½ mi. down spectacular Na Pali Coast, begins at the Kee Beach parking lot. Along with Waimea Canyon, the **Na Pali Coast,** with its rugged cliffs plunging into white sand beaches and aquamarine ocean, is a must-see destination on Kauai. Be sure to allow at least two hours for a hike to **Hanakapiai Beach,** and two or more hours to clamber into the valley to see the falls. Hikes into the valley or to **Kalalau Beach** can range from several hours to three days in length (see Camping, page 488 for accommodations options). The wilderness coastal areas beyond Haena are accessible only by hiking or by boat. Hikers planning on going the full distance to the beach may want to have Captain Zodiac (826-9371), in Hanalei, drop off their extra gear off Kalalau Beach ($30). The Cap'n may take people to the beach too ($60 one way; May-Sept. only). Rip currents from September through April make swimming at Kalalau perilous.

Near Lihue: Poipu, Waimea, and Kokee

On Rte. 50 west from Lihue, detour on to Rte. 520. You'll pass through the **Tree Tunnel** of eucalyptus trees to the restored **Old Koloa Town,** Hawaii's first sugar mill town, now gentrified by boutiques. A right off Rte. 520 at Kapili Rd. leads to **Kiahuna Plantation** (742-6411), Hector Moir's lavish gardens filled with 3000 varieties of plant life (open daily 9am-6pm; free). At the end of Rte. 520 is a fork in the road at the "Welcome to Poipu Beach" sign. A right turn takes you past **Prince Kuhio's birthplace** and the **Spouting Horn,** where waves force water to spout through lava tubes. Beyond the Spouting Horn, the adventurous will find secluded beaches among steep cliffs. Going left at the fork, spacious but crowded beaches line the coast from the resort area on Poipu Rd. To escape the hordes, continue along the dirt road at the end of Poipu Beach Rd. Make a right at the stop sign and sign in at the guard booth (open 7:30am-6:30pm). You have reached **Mahaulepu Beach.** Follow the dirt path along the stream at the far right side of the beach and it will take you to two very cool caves (climb through the first one to reach the next). Two other nearby beaches are more accessible: **Brennecke's** (known for bodysurfing) and **Acid Drops** (for board surfing).

Thirty mi. west of Lihue, Rte. 50 meets Rte. 550 at tiny **Waimea,** site of Captain Cook's first landing in 1778. Waimea is little more than a village—stock up on groceries before you get this far out. One mi. east of Waimea is **Infinities,** the best "left" (a beach where the waves break left instead of right) in all of Hawaii. Park by the road (there will be cars there if the surf is pumping). People hike through the bull pasture to reach the shore. Try not to intrude upon the locals or the regular surfers; they can be hostile to outsiders. At any rate, the shallow water and reef bottom make Infinities surfing territory for experts only. Beginners can enjoy watching the masters work their magic. Off the highway, 1½ mi. down Menehune Rd., a marker points to the interlocking stones of **Kikiaola** (or Menehune) **Ditch.** Very little remains of this ancient man-made aqueduct.

Turning inland, Rte. 550 begins an ascent past the dramatic **Waimea Canyon Lookout.** With stunning colors streaking across the dark red walls of the canyon and hardy green plants clinging to its crevices, this is serious Kodak Moment material. Farther up Rte. 550, **Kokee Lodge** offers a place to eat, pitch a tent, or just visit the small but free museum (open daily 10am-4pm). Kokee Lodge is part of **Kokee State Park,** and a permit is required for camping (see Camping, page 488 for information on permits and the lodge). The park has an abundance of trails, including some that venture into **Alakai Swamp**—ask at the museum for trail maps and advice on routes. A cheap, if thorny, summer breakfast option is hunting for wild blackberries along the road or trails. The hike gets you away from the late-morning crowds of Nikon-toting tourists.

Near the end of Rte. 550 is the consummate **Kalalau Valley Lookout.** Still farther up the road rests the entrance to the muddy **Pihea Trail.** Take some time to hike along the ridge overlooking the lush Kalalau Valley before turning inland down into the Alakai swamp. On the way back down the mountain to the coast, thrill-seeking drivers will enjoy the twisted majesty of **Waimea Canyon Drive,** to the left of Rte. 550.

For years, tourists have taken Rte. 50 west to hear the sands speak at **Barking Sands Beach.** Walking across the sand supposedly causes the particles to make a "woofing" sound. Join the locals and be entertained by the futile attempt of your fellow tourists to produce the effect. These days the sand seldom barks, woofs, or even yips. Drive to the end of Rte. 50 and then along 5 mi. of dirt road to **Polihale Beach Park.** This secluded park and surf spot, equipped with showers, shelters, tables, grills, and ever-popular toilets, is bordered by the **Na Pali Cliffs** and a swimming beach. It is also your best bet for guaranteed sunshine on Kauai. Camping is free, but a state permit is required (see Camping, page 488). **Salt Pond Beach Park,** Lolokai Rd., Hanapepe. Take Rte. 50 from Lihue and turn left on Lele Rd. in Hanapepe. Then turn right on Lolokai. This county park has an excellent, protected swimming beach and is immaculate, thanks to Uncle Louie, the "mayor" of Salt Pond Beach. (Lit pavilions, showers, and restrooms, but no camping.)

ENTERTAINMENT

Visitors to Kauai will discover that nightclubs aren't the only places to go for an exciting evening, which is fortunate because the island has few clubs and bars. If you happen to be on the Garden Isle at the right time, you might catch some celebrating, local-style. Take in Sheraton-sponsored native music, at the **Sheraton Coconut Beach Hotel,** P.O. Box 830, Coconut Plantation, Kapaa (822-3455, ext. 651 for reservations), daily at 7:45pm with no cover.

    Charlie's Place, 4-1421 Kuhio Hwy., Kapaa (822-3955), is a favorite local club that offers live music every night from 9pm to midnight. Try to catch the Saturday night Jazz Jam—bring your sax. For a night on the town with the more touristy set, head to **Gilligan's** at the **Outrigger Hotel** off Kuhio Hwy. in Kapaa. You just may meet the '90s equivalents of Gilligan, the Skipper, the Movie Star, Mary Ann, etc. (No cover. Disco nightly 9:30pm. Comedy show Thurs. 8:30pm-10:15pm, followed by dancing. 21 and up.) You won't find any castaways at the **Hyatt Regency** on Poipu Rd. near the 1500 block. Only Mr. Howell could afford **Kuhio's Nightclub,** a dance bar with a dress code (collars required, and leave your Tevas at home: no open-toed shoes permitted). You might meet the Professor at **Stevenson's Library,** also in the hotel, a more casual but still pricey pick-up joint.

SEASONAL EVENTS

    Waimea Tan Festival, usually in late Feb., in Waimea. Canoe races and festivities. Call Calvin Shirai (338-1316)
    Prince Kuhio Festival, March 26, in Lihue. Pageantry, song, and dance from the era of Prince Kuhio. Call the visitors bureau (245-3971) for more information.
    King Kamehameha Day, June 11, in Lihue. *Hoolaulea* ("festive gathering").
    Kauai County Fair, early Sept., at the Kauai Memorial Convention Hall, Lihue. Exhibits, entertainment, games, and food booths.

 # Molokai

A few years ago, a would-be developer called a town meeting to propose a high-rise resort on Molokai. Of the island's 6800 residents, 6000 were on hand to hear the plan. As the developer began to speak, a woman in the audience stood and said, "You haven't yet called this meeting to order with prayer." After the prayer, the residents sat through the proposal, and then voted it down almost unanimously.

    This is the essence of Molokai: a small, devoutly religious, tightly knit community with clearly defined, common ends. The sentiment is not anti-tourist—the locals seem to love people too much for that—but it *is* anti-development. Because of this, Molokai has refused to become an overdeveloped advertisement for itself or a mere depository for the tourist dollar. Agriculture, fishing, and cattle-raising manage to support the small population.

    Molokai's history has been somewhat intimidating to visitors; in ancient times, the island was restricted to the *khans,* or high priests, who trained at the three *heiaus* (temples). King Kamehameha's 1865 designation of the isolated Kalaupapa peninsula as a prison for those afflicted with Hansen's disease (leprosy) only lends

MOLOKAI

increased credibility to the island's nickname, "the forbidden isle." Visitors to the island have always been few, and the native population (Molokai is unique in that it is the only island with a Hawaiian majority) retains much of its original lifestyle and the spirit of Aloha. Molokai is difficult to explore without a car, and cars are expensive. However, the Father Damien tour of Kalaupapa makes a trip worth your while.

PRACTICAL INFORMATION AND ORIENTATION

Visitors Information: Molokai Chamber of Commerce, P.O. Box 515, Kaunakakai 96748. They sponsor an information booth at the airport. Free maps and cheerful advice. Open Mon.-Fri. 8am-4pm. You can also obtain a map from the Hawaii Visitors Bureau on Oahu or Maui. Call **Destinations Molokai** (553-3876)—a non-profit organization dedicated to introducing visitors to the island—for accommodations and car rental information. **Molokai Visitors Association,** P.O. Box 960 on Kamehameha Hwy. at the 0-mi. marker (800-553-0404 or 800-800-6367), offers travel tips and suggestions. Pick up a helpful map of Kaunakakai town and the sights of the island. The knowledgeable staff is happy to talk. Open Mon.-Fri. 8am-4pm. Two free local newspapers, *Dispatch* and the *Molokai Advertiser-News,* list weekly events and news along with occasional classified ads for house and car rentals.

Parks Information: Molokai Division of Parks, P.O. Box 1055, Kaunakakai 96748 (553-3204), at the east end of Kaunakakai, behind the baseball field and fire station in the Mitchell Pauole Center. Information on camping and county parks on Molokai. Open Mon.-Fri. 8am-4:15pm. Issues camping permits ($3). Free permits for Palaau State Park issued at the **Division of Water and Land,** near the post office in Hoolehua, 1 mi. from the airport. Open Mon.-Fri. 8am-4pm. Write or visit the **Department of Parks and Recreation,** Maui County, Wailuku, Maui 96793 (243-7389), for maps of Molokai and camping permits for county parks on Molokai and Maui. Open Mon.-Fri. 7:45am-4:30pm. The **Division of State Parks,** P.O. Box 1049, Wailuku, Maui 96793 (243-5354), also has information on state parks on Molokai and Maui. It also provides a Palaau State Park Permit. Open Mon.-Fri. 8am-11am, noon-4:15pm.

ATM: Bank of Hawaii, corner of Ala Malama and Kamehameha V Hwy.

Airlines: Hawaiian Air (567-6510) and **Island Air** (836-1111) run frequent flights to Molokai. **Air Molokai** (553-3636) has the cheapest flights—$42.50-48 one way, $85-96 round-trip. If you're traveling between Molokai and Maui, it's cheaper to take the Maui Princess. ($25 one way; see page 461.)

Tour Services: Molokai Off-road Tours and Taxi, P.O. Box 747 Kaunakakai 96748 (553-3369). Tours of the island for $40 per person.

Car Rental: Budget (567-6877 on Molokai; otherwise 800-527-0700). **Dollar** (567-6156 on Molokai; otherwise 800-367-7006). $43 per day. $5 per day surcharge if under 25. Credit card required. Highest rate in summer months. All agencies are at the airport and are open daily 6:30am-6:30pm. Reserve up to 8 months in advance for major holidays.

Taxi: Kukui Tours (553-5133) offers a 24-hr. taxi service. Call for reservations. Prices are steep: airport to west end $22. Also **TEEM Cab** (553-3633).

Equipment Rental: Molokai Fish and Dive Shop, Ala Malama Blvd., Kaunakakai 96748 (553-5926). The only place to rent masks, snorkels, fins, and diving gear. Masks $3, snorkels $1.50, fins $4, complete set $8. Boogie-boards $7, ice chest and ice $4, friendly info. free. The staff has the inside scoop on the best snorkeling and fishing spots. Open Mon.-Sat. 9am-6pm, Sun. 8am-2pm. **Fun Hogs Hawaii** (567-9292), Kaluakoi Hotel Beach Activities Center, rents mountain bikes ($6 per hr., $20 for 24 hrs.) and kayaks ($30 per day). A guided 2½-hr. coastline kayak tour is $35. Also rents tents for $20 per day. Open daily 9am-5pm.

Library: Ala Malama St., Kaunakakai (553-5483). Open Wed. noon-8pm; Mon.-Tues. and Thurs.-Fri. 8am-5pm.

Laundromat: Kaunakakai Launderette, Makaena Pl. behind the outpost's store. Cold wash 75¢, hot wash $1. Open daily 7am-9pm.

Crisis Lines: Sexual Assault Crisis Center, call collect to Maui 242-4357.

Pharmacy: Molokai Drugs, 301 Ala Malama Blvd. (553-5790). Open Mon.-Sat. 8:45am-5:45pm

Hospitals: Molokai General (553-5331), in Kaunakakai. **Molokai Family Health Center** (553-3276), Ala Malama, in Kaunakakai.
Emergency: 911.
Police: 553-5355. Located in the Mitchell Pauole Center at the eastern end of Ala Malama St., Kaunakakai.
Post Office: Ala Malama at Kamoi St. (553-5845), in Kaunakakai. Open Mon.-Fri. 9am-4:30pm, Sat. 9-11am. **General Delivery ZIP Code:** 96748.
Area Code: 808.

Molokai, situated between Maui and Oahu in the middle of the Hawaiian chain, is 10 mi. wide and 38 mi. long. **Kamehameha V Hwy.** (Rte. 450) snakes along the southeastern coast and between the island's two dormant volcanoes, low Puu Nana and forested Kamakou. The highway forks into two roads: **Maunaloa Hwy.** (Rte. 460), which travels to Maunaloa on the western side of the island, and **Kalae Hwy.** (Rte. 470), which goes north toward Kalaupapa. **Hoolehua Airport,** a 55-mi. (22-min.) flight from Honolulu, lies between the mountains in the island's center, and is accessed by all major roads. **Kaunakakai,** Molokai's principal town, sits 8 mi. south on the southern shore.

ACCOMMODATIONS AND CAMPING

Molokai's rooms tend to be simple and priced in the $40-60 range, outside of the token posh resort, **Colony's Kaluakoi Hotel and Golf Club** (552-2555; room with TV, VCR $90), in Maunaloa near Papohaku Beach. To get there, turn right off Maunaloa Hwy. onto Kaluakoi Rd. and continue to the end. The even pricier **Ke Nani Kai** condominiums, also on Kaluakoi Rd., may have vacancies. Call the different B&B associations for possibilities in Molokai (listings can be obtained in advance by writing the Hawaiian Island Bed and Breakfast Association, P.O. Box 726, Volcano 96788; also see Accommodations and Camping, page 438). If you are planning on staying in a hotel, consider a money-saving room and car package. **Destination Molokai,** P.O. Box 960, Kaunakakai 96748 (800-800-6367), offers room and car packages from $80 a day.

Campsites on Molokai are easily accessible, uncrowded, and tremendously beautiful. Free camping is possible along the far end of Kamehameha V Hwy. and in **Halawa Valley.** Because of the dearth of people on Molokai, you're likely to have the parks to yourself. Contact the Department of Parks and Recreation (see Practical Information, page 494) before you set off to hike or camp and be careful where you pitch your tent—much of the island wilderness is private land. Don't forget to stock up on insect repellent to ward off the island's unofficial bird, the mosquito.

Pau Hana Inn, P.O. Box 860, Kaunakakai 96748 (553-5342, 800-423-6656 from the mainland), turn seaward off Rte. 450 at the modern, white church across from the school. Easily the most reasonable deal on the island. Popular with *kamaainas* (locals). Rooms are diminutive and spare, but clean. Swimming pool and oceanfront garden complete with banyan trees. Inexpensive restaurant features entertainment Fri. and Sat. nights. Ceiling fans, no room phones. Singles and doubles from $45, all ground-floor. Office open 6am-7pm.

Hotel Molokai, P.O. Box 546, Kaunakakai 96748 (553-5347, 800-423-6656 from the mainland), about 1½ mi. east of Kaunakakai. On Kamehameha V Hwy. (Rte. 450). One unit equipped for people with disabilities. Located on the beach, clean pool, authentic Polynesian architecture, and the best restaurant around. Rooms with bath, ceiling fans, and *lanai*. Office open 8am-6pm. Check-out noon. Singles and doubles from $55. Family units $115.

Papohaku County Beach, near Kaluakoi resort on the west end. A beautifully maintained secluded spot with restrooms and Molokai's most breathtaking beach (with strong surf). Strong candidate for "best campground in Hawaii." Shaded, grassy camping area with restrooms, water, BBQ pits. Tents are helpful and "officially" required. 3-day max. stay. Permits available from the Molokai Division of Parks ($3; see Practical Information, page 494).

Palaau State Park, about 9 mi. northwest of the airport off Rte. 470. An isolated state campground with restrooms, picnic tables, BBQ grills, and a view of the Kalaupapa Settlement nearby. For the camper who prefers woods to beaches. But be careful: wandering off the well-groomed hiking trails might send you over the 1500-ft. sea cliffs. Purify the water here before drinking. 5-day max. stay. Free. Contact the Division of State Parks for permit (see Practical Information, page 494).

One Alii County Beach Park, on the south shore just east of Kaunakakai on Rte. 450 at the baseball field. The most complete camping park on the island, but not in an attractive setting. The park is flanked by the highway and is a popular hangout for late-night teenage revelers. Convenient location to town, but the Papohaku County Beach (see above) is just as well-equipped and much more secluded and picturesque. 3-day max. stay. Sites $3 per person, under 18 50¢. Permits required from the Molokai Division of Parks (see Practical Information, page 494).

FOOD

The few restaurants on the island are clustered in Kaunakakai. They tend to be local diners with low prices and simple dishes. Not much attention is paid to ambience—go to the hotels for that.

Kanemitsu Bakery, 79 Ala Malama St. in Kaunakakai (553-5855). Kanemitsu's fresh bread is justifiably famous throughout the islands—french onion, wheat, raisin, and a number of fruity flavors, including peach, coconut, and pineapple. Restaurant serves a breakfast of coffee, sausage, 2 eggs, and toast ($4.25), and lunch plates ($4.50). Open Wed.-Mon. 5:30am-8pm.

Molokai Pizza Café (553-3288) at Wharf St. and Kamehameha V Hwy. The newest restaurant in town. Tasty food and clean, bright decor. Pizzas: small $7, medium $9, large $11. $1.85 per slice. Also serves pasta, sandwiches, and sundaes. Open Sun.-Thurs. 11am-10pm, Fri.-Sat. 11am-11pm. Eat in or take out.

Holo Holo Kai (553-5347), in the Hotel Molokai 2 mi. east of Kaunakakai. Grilled mahimahi (fish) and *huli huli* (chicken teriyaki) for $12 at lunch, with a splendid ocean view of Lanai. At night the prices go up and the view is, well, Lanai at night. Sizable box lunches and juice $7. Sandwiches served poolside 1:30-6pm. Breakfast is the vest value. Papaya pancakes $4.25. Open daily 7am-2pm and 6-9pm. The hotel features local entertainers Fri.-Sat. nights.

Kualapuu Cook House (567-6185), on Farrington Ave. (Rte. 480), just off Rte. 470 in Kualapuu. A little more expensive than the restaurants in Kaunakakai, but well worth it. Wooden interior complements hearty food. 2 pancakes, eggs, and bacon $5.75. Try the Paniolo Burger (oozes with BBQ sauce and cheese; $3.50) or the chocolate macadamia nut pie ($3). Open Mon.-Fri. 7am-8pm, Sat. 7am-4pm.

Molokai Drive-Inn, Kamoi Ave. at Kamehameha V Hwy., in Kaunakakai, near the Pau Hana Inn. American and island take-outs include cheeseburgers, shave ice, and mounds of fries. Open daily 6am-10pm, sometimes 11:30pm on weekends.

Outposts Natural Foods (553-3377), Makaena Pl. off Ala Malama St. Small health food store sells the basics. Cereals, homemade sandwiches and salads, as well as tropical fruit smoothies ($2.75). Open Mon.-Fri. 9am-6pm, Sun. 9am-5pm. Juice bar/lunch counter where the burrito with beans, cheese, and sprouts is a full meal for $4.50. Open Mon.-Fri. 10am-3pm. Take-out only.

SIGHTS AND ACTIVITIES

Central Molokai and Kalaupapa

To reach **Palaau State Park** from Hoolehua Airport take Maunaloa Hwy. (Rte. 460) west and take a left onto Rte. 470. A short trail leads to the new **Kalaupapa Overlook,** where you can view the site where lepers were forced to settle and the spectacular Makanalua Peninsula, 1500 ft. below. The overlook has an informative display about the Kalaupapa settlement that includes photographs of the patients.

Another short trail, well-marked and well-trodden, leads to **petroglyphs** carved on the bottom face of a suspended stone and to five-ft. **Kauleo Nanahoa,** nicknamed the Phallic Rock. (The effect has been enhanced with carving.) According to legend, when a childless woman spends the night under its moonlit shadows (presumably alone), she becomes pregnant.

Just outside Palaau Park walk left down a chained-off dirt road toward the original Kalaupapa Overlook. The road is closed to traffic, but you can walk down. This same road is the start of the 3-mi. trail that leads down into the **Kalaupapa Settlement**. In 1866, the Hawaiian government decided that all lepers would be sent to Kalaupapa. At that time, there was no cure for the disease; nor was there much understanding of how it was spread. To a large extent, the unfortunate lepers were left to their own devices at the crude settlement. Father Damien, Brother Joseph Dutton, and a group of Franciscan sisters from New York were able to bring a measure of human compassion to the lepers while calling attention to their plight. Today, Kalaupapa is a dignified community for patient-residents. Only escorted people of age 16 or above are allowed by state law to enter. In other words, if you don't buy a ticket in town you'll have to settle for the view from the lookout. Buy your ticket and head down the 27 switchbacks of the trail to Kalaupapa. All the island's other attractions aside, the **Father Damien Tour** (567-6171) alone is worth a trip to Molokai. Richard Marks, a tour guide and caustic patient of Kalaupapa, will make you laugh. (Father Damien Tours offered daily at $25 for a ½-day tour. Bring your own lunch. Tours start at 10:30am at the trail end and finish around 2:30pm. Call Damien tours between 7-9am, preferably the day before, and leave a message that you're coming; this is your "permit" to enter the site.) Allow two hours for the hike down, be ready for slippery rocks, and be aware that your knees will take a pounding. Wear comfortable walking shoes. If you do not want to walk the trail, alternative transportation options are the **Molokai Mule Ride** (includes a tour and lunch) or flying in by plane (call Island Air or Air Molokai, in Practical Information, page 494).

The development of sulfone drugs in the 1940s ensured that leprosy would no longer be a dreaded malady. Although the number of residents at Kalaupapa has steadily decreased over the years, many people have chosen to remain here. Now, most residents are in their 70s and 80s and come and go as they please. Residents of Kalaupapa appreciate any sincere interest in their history and in Father Damien, the "Martyr of Molokai"—he contracted leprosy and died in 1889 from the disease after serving the colony off and on for 15 years. But unless you explore aggressively, you will come in contact only with sales personnel and state employees.

Kaunakakai and East from Kaunakakai

Take Kamehameha V Hwy. (Rte. 450) east from Kalae Hwy. (Rte. 470) to tiny Kaunakakai. Before reaching town, glance at Father Damien's century-old **Kapuaiwa Grove** of coconut trees. Near the canoe shack on Ala Malama, you will come across a stone foundation—all that remains of Kamehameha V's summer home.

Continuing east on Kamehameha V Hwy. (Rte. 450) past Kaunakakai, are the first in a series of **Hawaiian fishponds** built by hand between 1300 and 1700. These coral and basalt pools, essential to the livelihood of ancient Hawaiian warriors, were used to raise saltwater fish. Some fishponds were up to 2000 ft. long, and although overgrown, their outlines are still visible. A little past the mile 10 marker is **St. Joseph Church,** built by Father Damien in 1876, a tiny, picturesque church with a small graveyard. Go right in, even if the door is shut. Farther down the road, you'll see the red steeple of **Our Lady of Sorrows Church,** built by Damien in 1874.

The remains of the 13th-century **Iliiliopae Heiau**, one of the largest temples on the islands, can be found between mile markers 15 and 16 on Rte. 450. Just after a small bridge, walk *mauka* (inland) up the path marked with a mailbox labeled "234". After 10 minutes, there will be a house on your right. On your left is a sign: "Wailau trail, 12 hr. minimum." Follow the trail for two minutes. All that remains of the *heiau* is an assembly of rocks, 100 yds. long by 30 yds. wide. By one estimate, it contains 200,000 rocks, transported via human chains along the Wailau trail from

MOLOKAI

the northwestern end of the island. According to legend, ancient *Kahunas,* or magical priests, trained here and sacrificed many victims to the gods.

Molokai Wagon & Horse Ride (558-8380) offers daily tours of the *heiau* and a giant mango grove, as well as a chance to see Hawaiian crafts in a refreshingly noncommercial atmosphere. (Mon.-Sat. 10:30am, lunch at the Hotel Molokai. Reservations required. $37 with lunch, $30 without.) Alongside the road toward Halawa Valley are the ruins of the **Moanui Sugar Mill,** which operated from 1870 to 1900.

The water near the mile 20 marker on Kamehameha V Hwy. has the best **snorkeling** on Molokai. The shallow reefs and calm, clear waters are ideal for beginners. For good sunbathing, head to the west end of the beach.

The highway ends a bit farther along with a spectacular descent into **Halawa Valley** and a small gray sand beach. This nerve-shattering drive is long—go only if you are planning to do the two-hour trek from the valley to **Moaula Falls.** Enjoy a refreshing swim at the falls after your arduous journey. Watch out, however, for the falls' fabled sea-monster: an enormous *moo* (lizard). The valley's lone snack bar offers parking and directions for the hike up to the falls (open daily 6:30am-5:30pm, but you may have to wait with the hungry cats for the owner). If you have energy left after the first hike, take the 2-mi. trail to the falls' lower pool (take the left branch at the fork). The slippery stepping-stones make the wide stream difficult to cross, and impossible if it has rained recently. Think twice about bringing along your camera unless it can swim. From the lower pool, clamber over to Hipuapua Falls by following Halawa Stream.

The Halawa Valley was devastated by a *tsunami* in 1946, and the salt water left the area unfit for agriculture. Only a handful of inhabitants returned to the ruins.

West from Kaunakakai: Papohaku and Maunaloa

Traveling west on Mauna Loa Hwy. (Rte. 460), you'll drive over **Puu Nana** (Viewing Hill), past the Kaluakoi turnoff for Papohaku and Kepuhi beaches, and into the excruciatingly quiet plantation town of **Maunaloa.** Once a thriving pineapple plantation community, rows of brown company cottages now stand barren among overgrown roads. Dole shut down its operations in 1976, but recently residents have been attempting to turn Maunaloa into a cultural cornucopia. A great rest-stop is **Jojo's Café** (552-2803) on Maunaloa Hwy. The entrees are expensive, but the Portuguese bean soup with rice ($3.50) is satisfying. Sample a delicious piece of homemade apple or pecan pie ($2.50). (Open Mon.-Sat. noon-2pm, 5-7:45pm.)

To reach Molokai's most scenic beaches (lots o' sand, but rough surf), take a right off Rte. 460 back at the Kaluakoi turnoff. **Kepuhi** is a long white sand cove, where the **Kaluakoi Resort** now stands. The resort consumes much of the island's limited water supply, causing resentment among Molokai's farmers. Beyond the hotel's golf course and to the right, dirt tracks lead to several secluded white sand coves with protected waters and spectacular snorkeling. The deep water and offshore currents, however, make this area suitable only for the more experienced snorkeler.

A right off Rte. 460 leads to **Papohaku,** Hawaii's longest white sand beach (2 mi.) and the site of excellent camping facilities (see Accommodations and Camping). Come here to watch the sun set over the choppy waves of the Pacific. At the end of the road is the entrance to the **Molokai Ranch Wildlife Park,** a 1000-acre refuge for African endangered species. Barbary sheep, Rhea axis deer, zebras, antelopes, and technicolor pheasants roam incongruously in the tropical shade of this Pacific isle, safe from their natural predators. Miles of dry land surround the green acres, protecting the transplanted beasts in a re-creation of the Serengeti desert. Take the fascinating **Molokai Wildlife Safari** (552-2681 or 800-254-8871) to have giraffes eat off your chest. (1½ to 2-hr. tours depart Fri.-Mon. at 10:30am and 2pm; Wed. at 2pm. $35; ages 6-18 $25; under 6 $10.) The tour includes a short oral presentation about the animals, a bus tour around the 350-acre park, and refreshments at the Giraffe Pen. The animals are more lively during the earlier tours. The park also offers horseback trail rides through a cattle ranch (Wed.-Fri. and Sun. at 8:30 and 11am; $35). Daily mountain bike rides cost $15 for four hours, $25 for eight hours.

SEASONAL EVENTS

Molokai Makahiki (553-3688 or 538-0367), in January, is a "time of peace" celebrated with sporting events, games, and food. **Molokai Ka Hula Piko** (553-3876), the third Saturday in May, commemorates the birth of the hula on Molokai with hula and cultural demonstrations and visits to sacred sites. On September 27, canoes powered by women race from Molokai to Oahu (22 mi.) in the **Bankoh Na Wahine O Ke Kai.** The finish line is at Duke Kahanamoku Beach in Honolulu. October brings **Aloha Week,** with street dances, *luaus,* athletic events, and parades. Later in the month, there's the **Bankoh Molokai Hoe,** the male version of the *Na Wahine O Ke Kai.*

 # Lanai

More than 1000 years after the Polynesians had inhabited the other Hawaiian islands, Lanai (la-NAH-ee—say la-NYE, and you'll have booked a trip out to the "porch" instead) remained empty. Empty of people, that is—it was believed that evil spirits dwelled on the island until it was opened for settlement by Kaululaau, the exiled nephew of a Maui king. Banished to Lanai, he eradicated the spirits so that a human population could move in.

Lanai's recent history is recorded in the annals of corporate mythology. In the mid-19th century, Walter Gibson came to the island in order to start a Mormon colony. He was excommunicated, and his colony failed, but Gibson answered his true calling as a rancher and landowner, amassing 90% of the island by his death. In 1922, young entrepreneur James Dole bought 98% of the island to grow pineapples. Pineapples proved to be the perfect crop for Lanai's reddish, volcanic soil, and the island soon received the title "Pineapple Isle."

Castle and Cooke Company, of which Dole is a subsidiary, still owns 98% of the island, but Lanai's new main crop is destined to be the same as that of other islands: tourism. Now labeled the "Private Island," it caters almost exclusively to the rich and famous. Two of the three hotels on the island are luxury resorts. There is no equipment available for rental on Lanai—most visitors can afford to bring their own. Lanai is a paradise for scuba divers, boasting 12 of the 15 best diving sites in Hawaii, and for those who bask in back-road solitude. Only 30 mi. of paved roads touch the island; the rest must be explored by foot or jarring Jeep rides. The opening of a modern airport in June, 1994 has made Lanai more accessible to tourists—hurry and enjoy its natural beauty before the invasion comes.

PRACTICAL INFORMATION

Visitors Information: Destination Lanai, P.O. Box 700, Lanai City, HI, 96763 (565-7600). Member of the Hawaii Visitors Bureau. Has maps, information, and friendly advice. Open Mon.-Fri. 8am-4pm.

Camping Permits: Lanai Company, P.O. Box L, Lanai City, HI 96793 (565-8232). 7-day max. stay. Write or call in advance; only 6 sites available.

Pay Phones: Located in Dole Park across from Richards Shopping Center, in the airport, and in the hotels.

Taxi: Lanai City Services, 1036 Lanai Ave. (565-7227). Airport to Lanai City $8. Open Mon.-Fri. 7am-6pm, Sat.-Sun. 8am-6pm.

Car Rentals: Lanai City Services, 1036 Lanai Ave. (565-7227, from Maui 244-9538, from Oahu 533-3666). Cars $60 per day; Jeeps $109. Open Mon.-Fri. 7am-6pm, Sat.-Sun. 8am-6pm. A car is absolutely necessary on this island. Jeeps are better: worthwhile sights and beaches are on unpaved roads, forbidden to "non-Jeeps."

Public Transportation: Although there is no mass transit on the island, the resort hotels provide a shuttle service on which a nice, polite traveler may be able to catch a ride, depending on the kindness of the driver. Shuttles depart from the Lodge to the Manele Bay Hotel on the hour and return on the half-hour. They can also be hailed at the flagpole across from the post office (conveniently close to the camping permit office). Moreover, if you're really nice, you may be able to finagle a ride to and from the airport and harbor.

Library: at Fraser and 6th. Open Mon.-Fri. 8am-5pm.

Laundromat: Launderette Lanai, 7th St., near Blue Ginger Cafe.

Hospital: Lanai, 628 7th St. (565-6411). 24-hr. emergency room. Day clinic, 10am-8pm (565-6423).

Police: 565-6525.

Emergency: 911.

Post Office: (565-6517) on Lanai Ave. in Lanai City, on the other side of Dole Park from Hotel Lanai. Open Mon.-Thurs. 9am-4:30pm, Fri. 9am-3pm, Sat. 10am-noon. **General Delivery ZIP Code**: 96763.

Area Code: 808.

Hawaiian Airlines, Island Air, and **Air Molokai** (565-7219) will take you to **Lanai Airport,** near the southern end of the island. (See Getting Around.) **Expeditions** (661-3756) runs daily to Manele harbor for $25. You can also cruise to Lanai on a day-long boat trip from Maui. Most cruises include breakfast or lunch and island tours. **Tom Barefoot's Cashback Tours,** 834 Front St. (661-8889), in Lahaina, Maui, will sail tourists to Lanai for $79. Round-trip travel time is four hours, and the tour spends the day at **Club Lanai** (871-1144; includes breakfast, lunch, bar). Contact the Maui branch of the Hawaii Visitors Bureau for information on one-day tours to the island (see Practical Information for Maui, page 460).

ACCOMMODATIONS, CAMPING, AND FOOD

Make reservations early if you plan to stay on a weekend, especially between January and May (hunting season for quail, deer, and turkey). There is only one legal campground on Lanai at Hoopoe Beach (see below); the Lanai Co. allows residents to camp at will on the islands, but gives no such leeway to tourists.

The **Hotel Lanai,** 828 Lanai Ave. (565-7211 or 800-624-8849), in Lanai City, was built in 1927 as a home for Dole supervisors and guests. Renovations have restored the rooms' original 1920s style. There are 10 simple but bright rooms, so book at least 2 months in advance. Singles and doubles cost $95. The hotel's cheery restaurant serves inexpensive meals all day long in a comfortably furnished, wood-paneled dining room. Try the raisin bread French toast for breakfast ($4). Sandwiches and burgers run $6-9. (Open Mon.-Sat. 7:30am-10am, 11:30am-1:30pm, and 5:30-9pm, Sun. 7:30am-noon and 6:30-9pm.) **B&Bs** provide reasonable lodging alternatives. **Lucille Graham** (565-6378) offers two rooms in her house (singles $50, doubles $65). **Dreams Come True** (565-6961) has rooms (singles $55, doubles $75) and self-contained houses (3 BR/2 bath $190). The two posh resorts on Lanai: The Lodge at Koele and the Manele Bay Hotel are elegant and tasteful, but far beyond most *Let's Go* budgets (double $250-400). The only **camping** sites available are at **Hulopoe Beach,** one of the island's best swimming and fishing beaches, 20 min. from the city. With only 10 in. of rain per year, you can forego your rain fly, but beware the Manele Bay Hotel's overeager efforts to maintain their gardens; sprinkler run-off can nearly flood your campsite. The six sites are in a well-maintained grassy area with picnic tables set slightly apart from the beach area. Restroom facilities and outdoor showers are available. ($5 per person per day, with a $5 yearly registration fee. 7-day max. stay.) Contact the Lanai Company for reservations at 565-8232.

Provisions can be procured at **Richard's Shopping Center,** 434 8th St. (565-6047), or at **Pine Isle Market,** 356 8th St. (565-6488), next to the Fish and Game Dept. The island still runs on plantation time—stores close daily for lunch (noon-1:30pm) and may close at the whim of the owner. The **Blue Ginger Cafe** (565-6363), on 6th St., serves cheap greasy fare (open daily 7am-2pm and 5:30-9pm). The best spot for a meal is definitely the Hotel Lanai (see above).

SIGHTS

A Jeep and patience will get you around the island—new dirt roads are forged by farmers and tourists every year. Maps are almost useless because so few of the roads are included. But don't worry too much about losing your way on Lanai; the island's routes are either short and circular or dead ends. Make mental note of your path and significant landmarks, stay calm, and you'll eventually end up where you started.

Lanai rewards the adventurous; others will be confined to a few dynamic views. If you're exploring, watch your gas tank—there is only one station on the island (Lanai City Services, on Lanai Ave.). Be sure to wear bright colors; the island is popular year-round with hunters. One minute on the Lanai and you're guaranteed to be covered in red dust—leave the nice duds at home.

Lanai's most celebrated sights lie along the **Munro Trail,** a loop through the rainforest where naturalist George C. Munro planted specimens of plant-life from his native New Zealand about 80 years ago. Head north on Rte. 440 out of Lanai City, and turn right onto this well-beaten dirt road at Koele cemetery. You can hike (or if you have four-wheel-drive and off-road experience, drive) along this hot, dry, but rewarding route. The washed-out roads and gargantuan potholes make driving difficult. After two steep miles, you'll see **Hookio Ridge,** where Lanai warriors unsuccessfully tried to defend their home against invaders from the Big Island in 1778.

The road becomes exceedingly treacherous to vehicles after climbing the **Lanaihale Overlook.** At this point, Alewi Rd. snakes back down toward Rte. 441, 4 mi. south of Lanai City. On a clear day, head all the way up to the 3370-ft.-high overlook for a view of as many as five other islands: Oahu far to the northwest, Molokai and Maui close by to the north and northeast, Hawaii on the southeastern horizon, and little Kahoolawe (which has become a Navy bombing range) between Lanai and Hawaii. Keomuku Hwy. (Rte. 440) runs northeast to **Shipwreck Beach.** After 6 mi. the paved road ends. Take the dirt road to the left. The narrow, sandy beach is ideal for exploring. Littered with wind-blown refuse, including shells and glass balls that float ashore from as far away as Japan. (The glass balls are used to float fishing nets.) These waters were used as a dumping ground for old ships—an imposing wreck lies 250 yds. from the beach. It is a favorite spot for divers (and sharks). At the end of the dirt road a short path leads to well-preserved **petroglyphs.**

If you take the right-hand dirt road at the end of the highway and travel south along the shoreline you will reach **Keomuku,** a sugar-producing settlement that became a ghost town in 1901. Some of the old buildings are inhabited; respect the "No Trespassing" signs.

Northwest of Lanai City, volcanoes, wind and water have come together to form the **Garden of the Gods.** (From Koele Lodge, take a left onto the road before the tennis courts and then follow the dirt Polihua Rd. 7 mi.) Here, rock formations "grow" in the rich, red soil. Some towers and shrines were built by human visitors. The name perhaps promises more than it delivers, but the formations are magnificent at sunset. Continuing along the difficult dirt road will bring you to **Kaena Point,** the northernmost tip of the island. Turtles nest at nearby **Polihua Beach.** Strong currents make the beach suitable only for turtle-watching.

The best beach on Lanai is **Hulopoe Beach Park,** more commonly called **White Manele Beach,** at the southern end of Manele Rd. (Rte. 441), 9 mi. from Lanai City. This is the perfect spot for all sports, with a fully developed park, superb surf, and a partially protected beach for swimming (showers and restrooms available, but no lifeguards). Skin diving or snorkeling here is rewarding, but leave your spearfishing gun at home—it's a protected park. Next to Hulopoe Bay is **Manele Bay,** a black sand beach with the Expedition's harbor. Both bays are favorite haunts for **spinner dolphins.** Although they frequent these protected coves most often during the winter (Dec.-May), you may catch sight of their acrobatics early in the morning.

To reach the **Luahiwa Petroglyphs** travel south from Lanai City on Rte. 440 toward Manele Bay. Turn left on the first dirt road and continue along the base of the ridge just beyond the black water tank. The petroglyphs of humans, canoes, and animals are etched on the large black rocks beyond the tank.

LANAI

At the southernmost tip of the island visit **Kaunolu,** an ancient Hawaiian village housing the **Halulu Heiau,** one of the island's best-preserved temples. Kamehameha had a home on the nearby bluffs. Look for **Kahekili's Jump,** the tallest cliff on Lanai, from which the king's warriors dived into the sea to prove their bravery. Those who survived were honored as great soldiers.

Index

★ FREE T-SHIRT ★

JUST ANSWER THE QUESTIONS ON THE FOLLOWING PAGES AND MAIL TO:

Let's Go Survey
Macmillan Ltd.
18-21 Cavaye Place
London SW10 9PG

WE'LL SEND THE FIRST 1,500 RESPONDENTS A LET'S GO T-SHIRT!

(Make sure we can read your address.)

■ LET'S GO 1995 READER ■ QUESTIONNAIRE

1) Name _____

2) Address _____

3) Are you: female   male

4) How old are you?   under 17   17-23   24-30   31-40   41-55   over 55

5) Are you (circle all that apply):   at school   at college or university
                                       employed   unemployed   retired

6) What is your annual income?
£10,000- £15,000   £15,000 - £25,000   £25,000 - £40,000   Over £40,000

7) Have you used *Let's Go* before?

   Yes   No

8) How did you hear about *Let's Go* guides?

   Friend or fellow traveller
   Recommended by bookshop
   Display in bookstore
   Advertising in newspaper/magazine
   Review or article in newspaper/ magazine

9) Why did you choose *Let's Go*?

   Updated every year
   Reputation
   Prominent in-store display
   Price
   Content and approach of books
   Reliability

10) Is *Let's Go* the best guidebook?

   Yes
   No (which is?) _____
   Haven't used other guides

11) When did you buy this book?

   Jan   Feb   Mar   Apr   May   Jun
   Jul   Aug   Sep   Oct   Nov   Dec

12) When did you travel with this book? (Circle all that apply)

   Jan   Feb   Mar   Apr   May   Jun
   Jul   Aug   Sep   Oct   Nov   Dec

13) Roughly how much did you spend per day on the road?

   Under £10   £45- £75
   £10- £25   £75- £100
   £25- £40   Over £100

14) What were the main attractions of your trip?
(Circle top three)

   Sightseeing
   New culture
   Learning language
   Sports/Recreation
   Nightlife/Entertainment
   Local cuisine
   Shopping
   Meeting other travellers
   Adventure/Getting off the beaten path

15) How reliable/useful are the following features of *Let's Go*?

   v = very, u = usually, s = sometimes
   n = never, ? = didn't use

Accommodations	v u s n ?
Camping	v u s n ?
Food	v u s n ?
Entertainment	v u s n ?
Sights	v u s n ?
Maps	v u s n ?
Practical Info	v u s n ?
Directions	v u s n ?
"Essentials"	v u s n ?
Cultural Intros	v u s n ?

16) Would you use *Let's Go* again?

Yes
No (why not?) _____

_____

_____

17) Which of the following destinations are you planning to visit as a tourist in the next five years?
(Circle all that apply)

Australasia
Australia
New Zealand
Indonesia
Japan
China
Hong Kong
Vietnam
Malaysia
Singapore
India
Nepal

Europe And Middle East
Middle East
Israel
Egypt
Africa
Turkey
Greece
Scandinavia
Portugal
Spain
Switzerland
Austria
Berlin
Russia
Poland
Czech/Slovak Republic
Hungary
Baltic States

The Americas
Caribbean
Central America
Costa Rica
South America
Ecuador
Brazil
Venezuela
Colombia
Canada
British Columbia
Montreal/Quebec
MaritimeProvinces

18) What **major** destinations (countries, regions, etc.) covered in this book did you visit on your trip?

_____

_____

_____

_____

_____

_____

_____

_____

_____

_____

_____

_____

19) What other countries did you visit on your trip?

_____

_____

_____

_____

_____

20) How did you get around on your trip?

Car	Train	Plane
Bus	Ferry	Hitching
Bicycle	Motorcycle	

Mail this to:

Let's Go Survey

Macmillan Ltd.
18-21 Cavaye Place
London SW10 9PG

Many Thanks For Your Help!